THAILAND
HANDBOOK

THAILAND
HANDBOOK

CARL PARKES

MOON
PUBLICATIONS INC.

THAILAND HANDBOOK

Published by
  Moon Publications
  722 Wall Street
  Chico, California 95928, U.S.A.

Printed by
  Colorcraft Ltd.

Please send all comments,
corrections, additions,
amendments, and critiques to:

CARL PARKES
C/o MOON PUBLICATIONS
722 WALL STREET
CHICO, CA 95928, U.S.A.

Printing History
1st edition—December 1992

Library of Congress Cataloging-in-Publication Data
Parkes, Carl
  Thailand Handbook / Carl Parkes
    p.   cm.
  Includes bibliographical references and index.
  ISBN 0-918373-82-4 : $16.95
  1. Thailand—Guidebooks. I. Title.
DS563.P37 1992
915.9304'44—dc20   92-13301
                                    CIP

Editors: Mark Morris, Beth Rhudy
Copy editors: Asha Johnson, Mark Arends
Design and production: David Hurst
Maps: Bob Race, Brian Bardwell, Anne Hikido
Index: Mark Arends

Cover photo of Golden Chedi at Wat Pra Keo, Bangkok, by David Hurst

ISBN 0-918373-82-4

Printed in Hong Kong

Dedicated to the people of Thailand
and their heroic struggle for democratic freedoms.

CONTENTS

ABBREVIATIONS

a/c — air-conditioned   OW — one way

B — *baht*   pp — per person

km — kilometers   RT — roundtrip

MAPS

MAP SYMBOLS

- NUMBERED HIGHWAY
- MOUNTAIN
- WATER
- TOWN / VILLAGE

- AIRPORT
- HOTEL / LODGING
- POINT OF INTEREST
- ATTRACTION

- RAILROAD
- BRIDGE
- FERRY

- INTERNATIONAL BORDER
- MAIN ROAD
- OTHER ROAD / PATH

ACCOMMODATION CHARTS

ACKNOWLEDGEMENTS

Writers write alone, but survive only with generous doses of help and encouragement. Top marks at Moon Publications go to editor Mark Morris, managing editor Beth Rhudy, copy editors Asha Johnson and Mark Arends, and art director Dave Hurst, all of whom labored well beyond the call of duty. The superb maps are credited to Bob Race, Brian Bardwell, and Annie Hikido. Gratitude is also given to sales director Donna Galassi, senior editor Taran March, Bill Dalton, and other Moonbeams who helped realize the book.

Support has also been provided by the Tourist Authority of Thailand (TAT) offices, though special thanks must be awarded to Santichai Euachongprasit (Los Angeles TAT) and Sumonta Nakornthab (Bangkok TAT).

I am also indebted to the people of Thailand who took me into their homes and left me with memories to last a lifetime.

Contributions From Readers
In addition to the Moon staff, tourist authorities, and people of Thailand, I would also like to thank the many readers who wrote to me about their travel adventures:

America: Susan Brown (NY), Burl Blackburn (VA), Frank Cotter (MN), Rhys Evans (CA), Leigh Fox (GM), Steve Gilman (GA), Celeste Holmes (CA), Martin Offenberger (CA), Dan Moody (CA), Jan Morris (KY), Micheal Newman (LA), Claudia Siegel (NJ), Jefferson Swycaffer (CA).

Canada: Bob Cadloff (Quebec), Bruce Moore (British Columbia), Lenny Morgan (British Columbia).

Europe: Maarten Camps and Claantie van der Grinten (Netherlands), Alan Cummings (Scotland), Rick Dubbeldam (Netherlands), Mark Gregory (England), David Host (England), John Maidment (England), Anthony Maude (England), A.P. Moorhouse (England), Tim Prentice (England), Nick Slade (England), David Veale (England), Erik van Velzen (Netherlands), Herbert Walland (Austria), Ralf Neugebauer (Germany).

Australia: Martin Ellison (Darlinghurst), Cas Liber (Elizabeth Bay), Kevin Mulrain (Sydney), Catherine Spence (Mona Vale).

Asia: Philip Drury (China), Bruce Swenson (Japan).

Many other people have helped whom I do not list; some have been mentioned in the text, while others I cannot name for fear of compromising their positions.

A Personal Note
Finally, I would like to extend my deepest gratitude to all my friends in San Francisco and throughout the world who have supported me with their friendship and love: Terra Muzick, David (Norton) Ashby, Wayne (Riceman) Avila, Trixie Unger, Terri Gomes, John Kaeuper, Jerome Deltour, Jim (Jimbo) Pire, Amy Pieh, Dean (Wolfman) Bowden, Linda and Nerd, Ellen and Dave, Cathy Doerr, never-forgotten Lee and Pam Winick, Deke!, Rita and Eric, Scott and Lynn, Dara and Significant Other, Helena (Bo-Leee-Ness) Havelock, Ed and Pat Samarin, Steve Levin and Samba 86, Stephanie, Harry, Mark and Christine Hardeman, Chris Burt and Toby T., Mark T. (Dick Butkus) Larsen, Bill Bodewes in Amsterdam, Gary Flynn Down Under, Gail Davis, Joel Halpern, Party Marty, Hugh Linton, Donna (Nip) Nakashima, Samba Annie, Bob Nilsen, Richard and Fran Reynolds, Suzie, Rachael, Hazel, Vince, Joe Z. and Nancy, my beautiful sister Claudia, and my loving parents.

IS THIS BOOK OUT OF DATE?

Travel books are a collaboration between author and reader. Every effort has been made to keep this book accurate and timely, but conditions change quickly in a region as dynamic as Thailand. Please let us know about price hikes, new guesthouses, closed restaurants, transportation tips, map errors, and anything else that may prove useful to the next traveler. A questionnaire in the back of this book will help us find out who you are, and what improvements might help the next edition of this book.

Nothing is as useful as accurate maps to the towns and regions of Thailand. A photocopied *Thailand Handbook* map can be neatly folded into your shirt pocket for quick reference and to

help with updating the next edition of my book. While sightseeing, cross off guesthouses and restaurants which have closed down, and carefully mark the exact location of new guesthouses and other travel facilities that you would recommend to fellow travelers. Pick up a business card from the guesthouse, note the prices and conditions, and mail it along with the corrected maps to:

Carl Parkes
c/o Moon Publications
722 Wall Street
Chico, CA 95928
U.S.A.

NOTE ON TRANSLITERATION

The question of transliteration of Thai into Roman script is a vexing proposition since several divergent systems are used thoughout the country. The Thais themselves are as inconsistent as travel writers, often spelling a single destination in a half-dozen different forms. For example, a small town south of

Bangkok can be spelled Phetchburi, Petchaburi, or Petchburi, while the old capital north of Bangkok can be spelled Ayudaya, Ayutthaya, or Ayuthaya. Place names in this book follow the most common and/or shortened usage, though alternative spellings are often included for reference.

THE EVENTS OF 1992

In the early hours of 18 May 1992, a senior Thai military officer received instructions from the Supreme Command headquarters under Prime Minister Suchinda Kraprayoon to open fire on thousands of protesters gathered near Democracy Monument in Bangkok. During the next four days of violence, the Thai army sprayed bullets on unarmed demonstrators in a shocking Tiananmen-style barrage that took scores of lives, severely shook the Thai people, military, and monarchy, and forever altered the world's perception of Thailand.

The seeds of the turmoil can be traced back to February 1991 when military leaders overthrew in a bloodless coup an elected civilian government led by Prime Minister Chatichai Choonhavan. Corruption was the stated reason for the coup; the real motivation was the army's fear of civilian control and an independent prime minister. General Suchinda, leader of the coup, promised to return Thailand to democracy with fresh elections and constitutional reforms.

Instead, Suchinda imposed a constitution that appointed him prime minister. Suchinda compounded his mistakes by appointing a powerful senate full of military personnel. His move prompted a hunger strike on 4 May 1992 by Chamlong Srimuang, the charismatic former governor of Bangkok, and demonstrations that brought over 200,000 protesters into the streets.

On the evening of Sunday, 17 May 1992, police and military units set up barbed wire and roadblocks at Phanfa Bridge near Democracy Monument in Banglampoo. At 0400 the following morning, army paratroopers arrested Chamlong Srimuang and attacked the demonstrators with machine guns and armored vehicles. Dozens of unarmed protesters were mowed down or picked off by sharpshooters firing down from rooftops. The military stormed the Royal Hotel the next day with guns blazing, beating and then hauling away over 1,000 demonstrators in full view of the international press. After another day of violent protests and deaths, Thailand's revered monarch, King Bhumibol Adulyadej, summoned Suchinda and Chamlong to Chitralada Palace and demanded an end to the violence. Suchinda resigned on 24 May 1992 and constitutional amendments were quickly passed, but it wasn't until 11 June that King Adulyadej appointed a respected former prime minister, Anand Panyarachun, to take up the post as prime minister until fall elections.

Anand, a former ambassador to Washington, had been previously installed as an interim prime minister in February 1991 following the military coup led by Suchinda. Anand served only 13 months, but earned a great deal of praise by presiding over an administration widely regarded as the cleanest and most efficient in decades. After the elections of March 1992, the military-backed coalition first chose legislator and millionaire businessman Narong Wongwan as prime minister. This embarrassing appointment was canceled soon after U.S. authorities revealed that Narong had been denied a visa because of alleged involvement in heroin trafficking. Suchinda was then appointed prime minister.

In mid-June 1992, Prime Minister Anand Panyarachun announced a 26-member cabinet made up of businessmen and civil servants. Among the new ministers were Arsa Sarasin, a career diplomat who once served as ambassador to the U.S., U.S.-educated Panas Simasathien as finance minister, and Defense Minister Banchob Bunnag, who unlike many of his predecessors is not a politicized soldier. Elections are expected to return civilian control to the government and, to some extent, curtail the political influence of the Thai military.

INTRODUCTION

Bangkok and the Golden Triangle, Chiang Mai and Kanchanaburi, opium warlords and the king of Siam—these are images to fire the imagination. In a world gone increasingly dull, Thailand remains a land of magic and mystery, adventure and romance, far-flung destinations still strange and exciting in a Westernized world.

Thailand's dreamscape derives from writers and adventurers who recorded their early journeys of discovery and inner exploration. Marco Polo's records on Asia were followed by the verses of Conrad, Verne, Hesse, Maugham, Gurdjieff, Malraux, Fleming, Ginsberg, and Watts. Today a new generation of writers such as Theroux, Iyer, and Krich continues to explore and examine the Brave New World of modern Thailand.

Thailand's image as an Eastern paradise also derives from the *The King And I* and sobriquets bestowed by creative copywriters and the national tourist office—Land of Smiles, Land of the Free, The Most Exotic Country in Asia. While the hyperbole is somewhat excessive, Thailand unquestionably deserves its accolade as one of the world's premier vacation destinations.

And what a strange, surprising place it is.

Both exotic and contemporary, Thailand is no place for sentimental colonialism or quaint desires that unspoiled paradises will remain forever lost. Today, cities in Thailand are some of the most highly developed and technologized in the world, and most Thais prefer Hollywood and holograms to meditation and mantras. The collision of East and West is modern reality, but also, at times, just as fascinating and revealing as the relics of empire and history.

In the last decades annual tourist arrivals have exploded—for excellent reasons: superb archaeological sites, glittering temples, lively nightlife, outstanding shopping, superlative culture, exuberant festivals, people ranging from the rulers of international banking empires to remote hilltribes just moving into the 20th century, culinary treasures to delight even the most demanding gourmet, and a society where Western influence has not yet triumphed over local custom.

Thailand is also blessed with an incredibly varied range of natural attractions: expansive national parks, fertile plains, remote jungles, pristine beaches washed by turquoise waters, and tropical islands bathed in endless sunshine.

BURMA (MYANMAR)

MAE SAI

FANG

CHIANG SAEN
CHIANG RAI

LAOS

VIETNAM

SOUTH CHINA SEA

MAE HONG SON

PAI

CHIANG MAI

NAN

VIENTIANE

LAMPHUN

LAMPANG

MAE SARIANG

LOEI

NONG KHAI

SI SATCHANALAI

UDON THANI

SAKHON NAKHON

SUKOTHAI

PHITSANULOK

MAE SOT

KAMPHANG PHET

KHON KAEN

NAKHON SAWAN

THAILAND

THREE PAGODAS PASS

KORAT (NAKHON RATCHASIMA)

PHIMAI

LOPBURI

UBON RATCHATHANI

AYUTHAYA

SURIN

KANCHANABURI

NAKHON PATHOM

BANGKOK

PETCHBURI

CHA AM

PATTAYA

CAMBODIA

HUA HIN

KO SAMET

CHANTABURI

TRAT

PRACHAP KHIRI KHAN

KO CHANG

0   100 mi

0   100 km

CHUMPHON

RANONG

KO TAO

KO PHANGAN

KO SAMUI

SURAT THANI

GULF OF THAILAND

PHANGNGA

KRABI

NAKHON SI THAMMARAT

PHUKET

KO LANTA

TRANG

HAT YAI

SONGKLA

ANDAMAN SEA

LANGKAWI I.

ALOR STAR

SUNGAI GOLOK

SUNGAI PETANI

KOTA BARU

MALAYSIA

© MOON PUBLICATIONS, INC.

All this is perfectly complemented by the Thai people, who have graciously preserved the traditions of a unique culture while embracing the conveniences of modern living. Perhaps because of their religion and belief in *chai yen* ("cool heart") and *sanuk* ("life is a pleasure!"), Thais display an extraordinary sense of serenity, courtesy, humor, and well-being. More than anything else, it is the people that make Thailand such a wonderful place to visit.

To see the real Thailand—the Thailand that lies just underneath the Western veneer—you must travel with wide eyes and an open mind to find those magical moments: sunrise on a mountain peak above a sea of swirling clouds, saffron-robed monks slowly encircling a gold-encrusted pagoda, old women burning incense and finding their fortunes in a smoky temple, sinewy fishermen setting sail from blazing white beaches, hilltribe peoples who don't believe that man has walked on the moon, and river journeys through the Golden Triangle.

Avoid spending money just to isolate yourself against what appears to be an alien culture. Treat the residents and other travelers as you would have them treat you. Don't measure people by Western standards or your own cultural values. Keep a cool heart but an optimistic attitude. Remain open to chance encounters with travelers, shopkeepers, students, and monks.

The success of your journey ultimately lies in your hands. Have a great adventure.

HIGHLIGHTS OF THAILAND

Where to go and what to see are often difficult decisions for Westerners since few are familiar with the history, geography, or tourist attractions of Thailand. Sadly, few people contemplating a vacation in the region could even name the major destinations in this exotic corner of the world. Despite the amazing number of possibilities, travel destinations familiar to the general public are largely limited to Bangkok, Chiang Mai, Pattaya, Phuket, and Ko Samui. A fine beginning, but there's more—far, far more—to Thailand than just this short list.

But to really make an intelligent decision on where to go and what to see, you'll need to diligently study maps to become familiar with the geography and conduct an organized reading campaign of travel guidebooks, background histories, and armchair travelogues to fire up your imagination.

Most visitors begin their tour in the capital city of Bangkok. Despite its stifling heat and unbearable traffic, Bangkok ranks as the most fascinating city in Southeast Asia. To properly explore the temples, museums, shopping centers, and restaurants would take months, if not years.

SIGHTSEEING HIGHLIGHTS

Bangkok

Thailand's rich and kaleidoscopic tapestry of tourist attractions is enough to keep most visitors busy for years, though a single region could be explored well in several weeks or a month. Visitors generally arrive by air at Bangkok, a chaotic and unnerving metropolis of immense traffic jams and modern high-rises. Appalled by the problems, many travelers make the mistake of pausing only long enough to buy a plane ticket and then moving out as quickly as possible.

While Bangkok is certainly an urban planner's nightmare, it is also home to dozens of dazzling Buddhist temples, outstanding restaurants, superb shopping, and one of the liveliest nightlife scenes in the world. You will also be surprised at the vitality and friendliness of many of its eight million residents . . . if you survive the heat and congestion.

South of Bangkok: Damnern Saduak is Thailand's most authentic floating market, two hours south of Bangkok, and is much less commercialized than the capital's artificial floating bazaar. Take a tour or, better yet, explore it yourself with an early start.

East Coast

Enough historical monuments, beaches, and natural wonders are located within a 200-km radius of Bangkok to keep most visitors busy for their entire vacation.

Pattaya: Thailand's eastern seaboard boasts several highly developed beach resorts, of which Pattaya is the most famous. One of the largest beach resorts in Asia, this low-powered Riviera of the East annually attracts over a million pleasure-seekers to

(continued)

its breathtaking range of water sports, restaurants, and legendary nightlife. Lively, chaotic, exciting, polluted, highly commercialized, and tacky, Pattaya in the past catered almost exclusively to military personnel or single businessmen who filled the bars and nightclubs. Today the resort appeals primarily to families, with attractions such as zoos, botanical gardens, and water parks for the kiddies. Although the beaches are inferior to those of Phuket or Samui, the proximity to Bangkok makes it convenient for visitors with limited time.

Ko Samet: To escape the high-rise development of Pattaya, many travelers continue eastward to this *kris*-shaped island south of Rayong. The beaches here are fairly good (though they can't compare with those in the deep south) and facilities are limited to simple bungalows and midlevel hotels.

Ko Chang: On the border of Cambodia lies the newest island resort in Thailand, with excellent beaches, magnificent topography, plus dozens of other untouched islands nearby. Ko Chang is rapidly developing into another Ko Samui; go now before the hotels arrive.

West Of Bangkok
A quick and relaxing journey into the Thai countryside can be made west of Bangkok.

Nakhon Pathom: Often visited on a day-trip from Bangkok or as a brief stop en route to Kanchanaburi, this small town one hour west of Bangkok is home to the world's tallest Buddhist monument.

Kanchanaburi: This beautiful and relaxing region, three hours west of Bangkok, offers inexpensive floating guesthouses, refreshing waterfalls, hiking, national parks, and cool caves filled with Buddhas. Highly recommended for history buffs (the Bridge on the River Kwai is located here), nature lovers, and anyone annoyed with Bangkok's traffic jams.

Three Pagodas Pass: The only legal land connection with Burma is subject to political skirmishes but offers some historical connections and lovely landscapes.

North Of Bangkok
Historical sites north of Bangkok are often visited on day-trips, but the vast number of monuments and lengthy travel times demand a tour of several days.

Ayuthaya: For over 400 years the riverine island town of Ayuthaya, two hours north of Bangkok, served as the second royal capital of Thailand. Though largely destroyed by the Burmese in 1767, many of the restored architectural ruins provide eloquent testimony to the splendor of Thailand's most powerful empire. Ayuthaya and Sukothai are Thailand's largest and most impressive archaeological sites.

Lopburi: Although nothing special, Lopburi offers some modest Khmer ruins, an old summer capital for Ayuthayan kings, and makes a convenient stopover en route to the Northeast.

Central Thailand
Thai history started in the flat plains of central Thailand which now provide the broadest spectrum of historic architecture in the country.

Sukothai: In 1238 the Thai people proclaimed their independence from Khmer suzerainty and founded Sukothai, the first truly independent Thai capital. For over a century Sukothai ruled the region and created a Golden Age of Thai Arts which left behind a treasure trove of outstanding temples, stupas, and elegant Buddhas. Most of the ruins have been restored and surrounded by manicured gardens and refreshing pools. A brief visit to *both* Ayuthaya and Sukothai is highly recommended for visitors interested in Thai architecture or history.

Si Satchanalai: A satellite town of Sukothai with architecture dating from the 13th and 14th centuries. Easily visited on a side trip from Sukothai.

Mae Sot: This small but intriguing town located on the Burmese border offers visitors an ethnic flavor in an untouched region; highly recommended for independent travelers.

Northern Thailand
An entire vacation could be spent enjoying the amazing variety of sights in northern Thailand.

Chiang Mai: With its wealth of cultural and historical attractions, superb shopping, great food, friendly people, and delightful weather, Chiang Mai deservedly ranks as one of Thailand's leading tourist destinations. Unlike many Asian cities, which have lost their charm and character through unmanaged growth, this city has graciously preserved some of its lovely teak homes and tree-shaded roads. Chiang Mai also serves as a convenient base for trekking into the countryside, touring the infamous Golden Triangle area, and visiting the historic towns of Lamphun and Lampang.

Hilltribes: Living in the remote highlands near the Thai-Burma-Laos borders are shifting agriculturalists who cling to ancient life-styles despite encroaching Westernization and assimilation efforts by the Thai government. An organized trek of 5–10 days is a unique and memorable experience.

Mae Hong Son: The Shangri-La atmosphere of this small village near the Burmese border attracts travelers who want to get slightly off the beaten track. Mae Hong Son, unfortunately, has recently exploded with new hotel developments and lost some of its charm to mass tourism.

Pai: A beautiful village with all the charms but none of the problems of Chiang Mai and Mae Hong Son. Excellent trekking and river rafting. Highly recommended.

Golden Triangle: For over 20 years a steady stream of travelers has bused from Chiang Mai to Thaton, floated down the Kok River to Chiang Rai, and then continued up to Chiang Saen—the real heart of the Golden Triangle. Today, opium production has largely shifted to Laos and Burma, and tour buses are more common than drug warlords—don't expect a Wild West atmosphere.

Chiang Saen: Historic center on the banks of the Mekong River, Chiang Saen is a sleepy town rich in atmosphere. Highlights include doing absolutely nothing and journeys on the Mekong River.

Northeastern Thailand

The sprawling plateau bordered by Laos and Cambodia is Thailand's forgotten destination. Known locally as the Issan, the dry and rugged northeast is home to a boisterous people with a distinctive culture, a dozen impressive Khmer temples, and several worthwhile national parks. The best attractions are located near Korat and Nong Khai.

Khao Yai National Park: Thailand's most popular park, four hours northeast of Bangkok, boasts a dozen hiking trails, refreshing waterfalls, and protected wildlife such as elephants and hornbills. A popular stop en route to the Khmer monuments of the northeast.

Korat: Nakhon Ratchasima is an undistinguished city which serves as the gateway to the Khmer temples and national parks of the northeast.

Khmer Monuments: Once under the suzerainty of the Khmers, the northeast today offers several impressive stone castles erected by the Cambodians to honor their gods and kings. Two of the most impressive are at Phimai and Phanom Rung near Korat, a convenient base for visitors with limited time. Several other impressive monuments are farther east near Buriram and Surin.

Ban Chiang: This important archaeological site, where the world's first Bronze Age civilization flourished some 6,000 years ago, is primarily of interest to archaeologists.

Nong Khai: Situated on the Mekong River and only 20 km from Vientiane, Nong Khai is the finest town in northeastern Thailand. Nong Khai remains sleepy, though the opening of Laos and the imminent completion of the bridge will dramatically increase tourism.

West of Nong Khai: Some of the most beautiful scenery in Thailand is located west of Nong Khai on the banks of the Mekong River. Several towns have inexpensive guesthouses and acceptable cafes. A great journey for motorcyclists.

Phu Kradung National Park: A forested plateau situated between 1,200 and 1,500 meters; mysterious, moody, and icy cold at nights. Use Loei as your base.

Ubon Ratchathani: Famous for its Candle Festival, which marks the beginning of Buddhist Lent. Festivals are a major attraction in the northeast—more information below. Ubon also features boat rides down the Mekong and meditation temples popular with Western students.

Surin: Visitors from around the world arrive each November to attend the enormously popular Elephant Roundup. Surin and nearby Buriram are also good bases from which to explore the numerous Khmer monuments.

Southern Thailand

The tropical beaches of southern Thailand are, together with those of the Philippines and Indonesia, the finest in Southeast Asia. All are in various stages of development and appeal to different classes of travelers.

Hua Hin: The first major beach resort south of Bangkok appeals to European families seeking a middle-priced sun-and-fun destination without the tawdriness of Pattaya. Safe, clean, and easy to reach, though overdevelopment has destroyed much of its old charm.

Prachap Khiri Khan: A wonderful little seaside town almost completely untouched by mass tourism. Nothing to do but wander around and smile at the locals.

Ko Samui: This Penang-sized island, with its superb beaches and lovely coconut palms, was first opened in the 1970s by hippie travelers who quietly whispered about the tranquil, virgin hideaway. By the mid-1980s, commercial developers were constructing international-standard hotels, restaurants, nightclubs, and a small airport to receive daily flights from Bangkok. Despite these disturbing trends, much of Ko Samui remains a destination of great beauty and tranquility.

Ko Phangan: Budget travelers have largely abandoned Ko Samui for the large island a few hours north. Beaches are small and unimpressive, but are compensated by the mellow atmosphere and sense of isolation.

Phuket: Blessed with magnificent coves and powdery white beaches, Phuket has developed into Southeast Asia's largest and most popular seaside resort—the Waikiki of the East. Although far more commercialized than Ko Samui, the island offers the upscale visitor an outstanding array of luxurious hotels, superb restaurants, water sports, and

(continued)

nightclubs that go full tilt until sunrise. A wild place for those with enough money to keep the game going. Travelers torn between choosing lively Phuket or idyllic Ko Samui and Ko Phangan should visit all three islands.

Ko Phi Phi: This exquisite little island located midway between Phuket and Krabi is the first of an archipelago that stretches all the way to Malaysia. Ko Phi Phi is stunning, small, and packed to capacity during the winter tourist season. Travelers are already discovering the more remote, untouched islands to the south.

Krabi: A very busy town which serves the tourist traffic during the heavy winter months. Overrun with *farangs* (Westerners), but a good base for reaching the nearby beaches and tropical islands.

Pranang: Superb topography on a tiny peninsula near Krabi. Popular for over a decade and now fully developed with upscale resorts and a handful of simple guesthouses.

Ko Lanta: Ko Lanta will almost certainly be the next big island resort in the deep south. Beaches are fairly good, but facilites are primitive and the island is very difficult to reach. Best sand is at the southern perimeter.

Trang: Well off the beaten track, Trang has some good beaches and upcoming resorts with dive facilities.

Hat Yai: The largest town in Southern Thailand is great for shopping, food, and nightlife, plus excursions to the nearby beach resort of Songkhla.

Narathiwat: A small and sleepy fishing village blessed with charm, character, and a complete absence of tourists. Nothing of great interest, though a fine escape from the tourist trail.

Ko Tarutao: Several islands west of Satun have been designated a national park by the Thai government. Beaches, jungle, and fishing villages are the main attractions.

Within a 200-km radius of Bangkok are several well-developed beach resorts, the world's tallest Buddhist monument, the Bridge on the River Kwai, and the splendid ruins of Ayuthaya. Central Thailand has several historic cities which once served as ancient capitals. Chiang Mai in the north serves as both the cultural and artistic center of Thailand, as well as a convenient base for trekking into the mountains and touring the infamous Golden Triangle. Northeastern Thailand offers outstanding Khmer monuments, plus the rare opportunity to get somewhat off the beaten track. South Thailand is a wonderland of pristine beaches and well-developed resort islands such as Ko Samui and Phuket.

The thumbnail sketches on pages 3-6 will provide a quick glimpse of the major attractions found in this book. Further descriptions are provided at the beginning of each chapter under "Sightseeing Highlights."

I would rather be ashes than dust—
I would rather my spark should burn out
*   in a brilliant blaze*
Than it should be stifled in dry rot.
I would rather be a superb meteor,
Every atom of me in magnificent glow,
Than a sleepy and permanent planet.
Man's chief purpose is to live, not to exist:
I shall not waste my days trying to prolong them.
I shall use my time.

—Jack London

THE LAND

Stretching over 1,800 km from north to south, Thailand's 513,115-square-km territory (about the same size as France) has been compared in shape to an elephant dangling its trunk toward Malaysia. Thailand is located east of Burma (Myanmar), south of China and Laos, north of Malaysia, and west of Indochina. It's formed of 74 provinces *(changwats)* composed of hundreds of districts *(amphoes)* which are subdivided into thousands of precincts *(tambons)*, large towns *(muangs)*, and small villages *(bans)*.

The four physiographic regions—central, north, northeast, and south—include everything from tropical rainforests and limestone mountains to hot, dry plains and sandy beaches. Most people live in the central plains, an immensely fertile region annually flooded by the Chao Praya River into a vast hydroponic basin. To the north are towering mountains which have long kept Thailand isolated from northern Asia. Dominated by the massive Korat Plateau and lying in the rain shadow of the Indochina Cordillera, the hot and dry northeast is a region plagued by poor soils and droughts worsened by deforestation. Finally, the south is a heterogeneous topography of tropical jungle, mangrove swamps, and sandy beaches.

With a tropical climate covering four topographic zones, Thailand should be a wonderland for the naturalist and lover of forests. Unfortunately, this isn't the case. Government-licensed logging consortiums, often controlled by upper-level ministers and members of parliament, have almost completely stripped the country of tropical rainforests. As recently as 40 years ago, 70% of Thailand was covered by forest; today the official figure is 18% and some claim it may be as low as 12%. Conservationist Dr. Boonsong Lekagul, who for three decades has publicly campaigned for preservation of the remaining forests, agrees with international estimates that by the end of the century Thailand's remaining ground cover may be almost completely destroyed.

The consequences of all this are enormous. Because even the national parks—created to be the last refuge for endangered species—have been devastated by legalized logging and illegal poaching, little remains of Thai wildlife: *banteng, gaur,* and over 90% of the nation's bird population are gone. Exacerbating the problem is Thailand's refusal to sign the Convention on International Trade in Endangered Species, a move which would help curtail the international market for Thailand's threatened fauna. Worse yet, massive logging has brought droughts in the northeast and floods in the south, including the November 1988 disaster which killed over 400 people. This catastrophe led to the 1989 banning of commercial logging by Prime Minister Chatichai Choonhavan. Although late in the game, it appears that the Thai environmental movement is gaining the support of the Thai population.

CLIMATE

Thailand has a humid, tropical climate with three seasons: hot from Nov. to March, extra hot from March to June, and hot and wet from June to November.

Heat and rain can raise hell with your vacation plans. Temperatures perpetually hover between hot and excruciatingly hot, depending on whether it's the so-called cool winter season from Nov. to March or the hot summer months from March to June. Winter can be surprisingly cold in the northern regions when icy winds sweep down from China. High temperatures and a humidity factor of almost 100% can be quite a shock for Westerners accustomed to more moderate climes, but there's little you can really do about it except stay out of the midday sun and escape into an air-conditioned hotel or restaurant.

Aside from the east coast beach resorts, the best time to visit Thailand is during the winter months from Nov. to March. This, however, is the peak of the tourist season when hotels, beaches, and monuments are crowded with visitors. To escape the hordes, consider visiting during the hot season months (March to June) or immediately after the monsoons end in early November.

THAILAND'S CLIMATE

	JAN.	FEB.	MAR.	APRIL	MAY	JUNE	JULY	AUG.	SEPT.	OCT.	NOV.	DEC.
BANGKOK												
Maximum °C	32	32	34	35	34	33	32	32	32	31	31	31
Maximum °F	90	90	94	95	94	92	90	90	90	88	88	88
Rainy Days	2	1	3	4	18	19	19	19	17	14	4	1
CHIANG MAI												
Maximum °C	29	31	34	36	35	34	31	31	31	31	31	31
Maximum °F	84	88	94	96	95	94	88	88	88	88	88	88
Rainy Days	2	2	3	5	15	17	18	18	21	23	17	10
PHUKET												
Maximum °C	32	33	34	34	34	33	33	34	34	34	33	32
Maximum °F	90	92	94	94	94	92	92	94	94	94	92	92
Rainy Days	5	3	5	12	23	20	20	23	18	10	5	2
KO SAMUI												
Maximum °C	29	29	30	32	33	32	32	32	31	31	30	30
Maximum °F	84	84	81	90	92	90	90	90	88	88	81	81
Rainy Days	10	5	4	7	14	16	18	20	22	17	6	2

Monsoons, not temperature, are the most important weather factor in Thailand. Derived from the Arabic word *mansim* (seasonal winds), monsoons are created by the differences in annual temperature trends over land and water. The climatic dividing line is formed by the equator. Summer monsoons begin with the warm, humid air masses that flow northeastward from the Indian Ocean and end in the fall when the winds reverse direction with the dry southwesterlies. Rainfall varies with topography: the northeast receives the least, while the southwest coast is deluged during the late-summer months.

Fortunately for the traveler, Thailand's monsoon season isn't as imposing as in other Asian countries—you can still enjoy Thailand in the rainy season. Monsoons flood streets and ruin holidays on the beach, but they're no cause for real alarm. For many seasoned travelers, the violent but brief rains of summer bring the real drama of Asia, providing an opportunity to witness nature in all her uncontrolled fury.

FLORA AND FAUNA

Despite a ban on logging in 1989, Thailand's rainforests continue to disappear at an alarming rate. Unless the destruction is stopped, most will be gone or seriously damaged by the year 2000. Saving the rainforests is an immensely complicated task, but you can help by supporting the following organizations and refusing to buy tropical hardwood products such as teak, rosewood, and mahogany furniture. You can also help by joining the worldwide outcry against the destruction of indigenous tribal homelands and writing directly to the governments involved. Finally, tell the World Bank to stop funding rainforest-killing development projects and write to your congressional representatives, corporate executives, and the editor of your local newspaper. Most importantly, remain concerned while you travel through Thailand and Southeast Asia; tourism is the world's biggest industry and the discriminating traveler thus has powerful leverage against the despoliation of the environment.

Wildlife has been another casualty of the destruction of the Thai rainforests. Rainforests are home to 90% of the world's primates, 80% of the world's insects, and half of the world's plants. Thailand's endangered species include famous animals such as the eastern sarus crane, giant sea turtles, and the Asian elephant, plus less-well-known animals such as Ridley's leaf-nosed bat, the flat-headed cat, and the violin beetle; an international study lists over 100 endangered species in Thailand. The end of the rainforests will bring wildlife destruction only comparable to the mass extinction that wiped out the dinosaurs 65 million years ago.

Spreading the message has largely been the work of the environmental groups listed below, plus the efforts of the World Wildlife Fund and Friends of the Earth. But you, as a traveler, can also help by refusing to purchase animal goods made from protected or endangered species. The United States is the world's largest consumer of wildlife! Travelers often don't realize that seemingly innocuous products made from hides, shells, and feathers—on sale in public markets throughout Thailand—are often illegal and species-threatening souvenirs. Regulations are complex, but prohibited products include sea turtle items, crocodile hides, pangolin (anteater) leather, most wild bird feathers, and all ivory products. Just as destructive is the purchase of coral items, since coral collection is directly responsible for the near-complete destruction of sea beds in many Southeast Asian countries. Prohibited items will be seized by customs officials and you risk a substantial fine. When in doubt, don't buy.

Environment Organizations

Rainforest Action Network: RAN and the World Rainforest Movement are a worldwide network of concerned citizens who hope to crystallize concern and devise campaigns to stem the destruction of the tropical rainforests. Membership includes a monthly newsletter which covers battles to protect the forests and a quarterly report drawn from its worldwide affiliates. Membership costs US$25/year. 450 Sansome St., Suite 700, San Francisco, CA 94111, tel. (415) 398-4404.

Nature Conservancy: An international agency which protects habitats through acquisition and purchase of rainforest land, a "debt-for-nature" swap which raises money for local environmental organizations. 1815 North Lynn Street, Arlington, VA 22209, tel. (703) 841-5300.

Rainforest Alliance: A small nonprofit organization dedicated to saving the forests with public-awareness programs, research into the timber industry, and publication of a quarterly newsletter. Membership costs US$20/year. 295 Madison Ave., Suite 1804, New York, NY 10017, tel. (212) 599-5060.

Wildlife Fund Thailand: Under the royal patronage of the queen and an associate office of the World Wildlife Fund, WFT is a highly respected nonprofit organization dedicated to wildlife conservation and the wise use of natural resources. 255 Soi Asoke Sukumvit 21, Bangkok 10110, tel. (02) 258-9134, fax (662) 258-9403.

> *The use of traveling is to regulate imagination by reality, and instead of thinking how things may be, to see them as they are.*
>
> —Samuel Johnson

HISTORY

Thailand's earliest recorded inhabitants were Buddhist Mons who formed the loosely knit Dvaravati kingdom in the Chao Praya basin from the 6th to 11th centuries. From the 8th to 12th centuries, Hindu Khmers expanded westward from Cambodia and absorbed the Mons into their powerful empire. Mons today have largely disappeared in Thailand, although a sizable Mon community still exists in Burma.

The Thai (Tai) people probably arrived later; two theories speculate as to their origins. Most believe they migrated from southern China during the 11th and 12th centuries and settled among the Khmers and Mons already residing in the central plains. Others argue that Neolithic cave settlements near Kanchanaburi and discoveries of a 6,000-year-old bronze culture at Ban Chiang prove that the Thais preceded the Mons and Khmers.

EARLY PERIODS

Sukothai Period, 1220-1378

The brief but brilliant kingdom of Sukothai marks the true beginning of the Thai nation and remains to this day a source of great pride. While Sukothai's preeminence lasted less than 200 years, it gave rise to uniquely personified forms of architecture, sculpture, and even political structure. Under the leadership of King Ramkamheng (1278-1318), revered today as the father of Thailand, Sukothai fused Khmer and Mon traditions into a dynamic kingdom which ruled Southeast Asia from Laos to Malaysia. Military power and economic prosperity allowed the development of highly refined artistic achievements, including the world-renowned Sawankalok celadon and Buddha styles of great creativity and sensitivity. Ramkamheng's successors were less ambitious; by the late 14th century Sukothai had become a vassal state of upsurgent Ayuthaya.

Ayuthaya Period, 1378-1767

Sukothai's gradual decline was followed by the rise of Ayuthaya. Within a century of its founding by an ambitious Thai prince from U Thong, this riverine capital had become a major military power and the grandest city in Southeast Asia. Western visitors who arrived during the 16th and 17th centuries described Ayuthaya as a splendid metropolis with a population larger than London's. Among the *farangs* (foreigners) was Constantine Phaulkon, a Greek adventurer who rose to great power in the court of King Narai. After he attempted but failed to convert the king to Christianity, a palace rebellion broke out in which Phaulkon was executed and all Westerners expelled.

It was during this period of self-imposed isolation that Ayuthaya created its own golden age of arts and architecture. This came to an end after the Burmese became jealous of their wealth and mounted a series of military campaigns against the city. In 1763 the Burmese attacked and, after two years of resistance, slaughtered most of the population and burned the city to the ground. Not only did they destroy the artistic and literary heritage of Ayuthaya, they also pulled down many of the magnificent Buddhist temples and reliquaries—a horrific act which still profoundly shocks the Thais.

Bangkok (Rattanakosin) Period, 1767-Present

The destruction of Ayuthaya was a devastating setback. But with typical Thai resilience, an ambitious half-Chinese soldier named Taksin rallied the nation and established a new capital in Thonburi, a sleepy fishing village just across the river from modern Bangkok. Within 10 years Taksin drove the Burmese from Thailand and expanded Siamese sovereignty from Chiang Mai to the deep south. As the son of a Chinese tax collector, Taksin repopulated the country with Teochew Chinese trade merchants, whose taxes provided significant revenue for the fledgling state. But the strain of long years of warfare took its toll, and Taksin apparently went insane with delusions of grandeur and paranoia. After imagining himself an incarnate Buddha, Taksin was executed in the manner prescribed for royalty: placed in a velvet sack and beaten to death with a sandalwood club.

General Chakri, a popular Thai military leader on expedition in Cambodia, was called back to Thonburi and crowned King Rama I, first ruler of the dynasty which continues to the present day. Fearful of attack by Burmese forces, Rama I transferred his capital across the river to present-day Bangkok and attempted to re-create the former magnificence of Ayuthaya with the construction of royal temples and palaces. The city continued to be called Bangkok by Western mapmakers, but Rama I renamed it a multi-syllabled Sanskrit moniker abbreviated as Krung Thep ("City of Angels"). Rama II (ruled 1809-1824), an outstanding poet, is chiefly remembered as the author of the Thai Ramayana. The British defeat of the Burmese during the reign of Rama III (1824-1851) allowed the Thais to expand their national boundaries to Malaysia, Laos, and Vietnam.

A MODERN NATION

The King And I

Thailand's modern phase began with King Mongkut (Rama IV, 1851-1868), better known to the Western world as the autocratic despot in *The King and I*. Mongkut was actually an enlightened ruler whose imaginative diplomacy kept Thailand free from the European colonial expansionism that swallowed Burma, Malaysia, and French Indochina. During his 25 years of monkhood prior to being crowned Rama IV, Mongkut learned a dozen languages, studied astronomy and modern history, and, perhaps most importantly, established the Thammayut sect of Buddhism which purified the religion and made it less vulnerable to Western ideology.

His search for knowledge convinced him that Thailand's only hope for political independence lay through European-style reforms such as those proposed by his children's English governess, Anna Leonowens, who eventually penned her fanciful memoirs, *The English Governess at the Siamese Court*. Anna was apparently an unhappy and homesick widow who plagiarized old books on Burma and stitched it all together in her book, which portrayed Mongkut as Rousseau's Noble Savage and Anna as the prim Victorian Christian who single-handedly modernized the backward nation. Anna's gruesome tales of Eastern harem life supported her after she left Bangkok (and certainly made a

great deal of money for Yul Brynner), but no race of people enjoy having foreigners laugh at one of their great men—both the book and film are banned in Thailand. Still, several years ago the present queen took an entourage of 45 people to see Yul Brynner star in the New York stage production!

King Chulalongkorn

Mongkut's son, Chulalongkorn, continued Mongkut's policies of transforming Thailand from a medieval kingdom into a modern and progressive nation. Chulalongkorn outlawed slavery, developed educational opportunities, and balanced the territorial ambitions of the British and French with modest concessions to both countries. During his 42-year reign (1868-1910)—second longest in the country's history—Chulalongkorn completely reorganized Thailand's administrative system and abandoned several ancient royal customs, including ceremonial prostration. He nevertheless clung to some autocratic customs such as polygamy on a grand scale, keeping a grand total of 92 wives who bore him some 77 children. Chulalongkorn also continued to appoint men of royal descent to high administrative posts, a practice which offended the European-educated elite. Despite his reluctance to grant full democratic rights to his people, his long list of achievements has made him the most honored of all past kings.

Modern Times

Chulalongkorn's bold reforms also created a new bourgeois intelligentsia unhappy with their lack of power within the royalist government. The pressure cooker finally blew in 1932 when a bloodless coup d'etat instigated by French-educated Thai intellectuals supported by the military toppled the absolute monarchy. A constitutional government headed by an army general was formed and Siam was renamed Thailand.

The Thai government declared war on the Western allies in 1941 after the Japanese invaded, a face-saving formality which allowed them to recover territories lost to the French and British. With the defeat of the Japanese, a group of Free Thai politicians seized power and placed King Rama VII on the throne. This experiment with democracy ended when the young king was mysteriously murdered in his bed and a military dictatorship seized power. Except for a three-year hiatus of democratic rule in the mid-1970s, Thailand has since been ruled by an alliance of military and civilian politicians.

GOVERNMENT

Thailand is a constitutional monarchy with a bicameral legislature consisting of the Senate appointed by the king and the National Assembly elected by the people. The National Assembly is composed primarily of several liberal-leaning parties who often form coalitions to work with the military. Both chambers elect the prime minister, who chooses a cabinet of 20 ministers.

Thailand's leading political figure of the early 1980s was smiling Prem Tinsulanonda, a handsome enigma who confounded the critics by holding the job of prime minister for almost eight years—an amazing accomplishment when you consider that Thailand since 1932 has suffered through 17 coups and 13 constitutions. Nineteen eighty-eight proved to be a watershed in Thai politics after public pressure for an elected leader brought the arrival of Chatichai Choonhavan, a business-minded politician who favors democracy over military rule.

Democratic rule ended with a military coup on 23 Feb. 1991 and the establishment of the military National Peacekeeping Council (NPC). Led by armed forces commander and political critic General Sunthorn Kongsompong, the bloodless seizure of power culminated a long period of animosity between civilian leaders and the military hierarchy, whose traditional strength had been eroding during the democratic rule of Chatichai Choonhavan.

Thailand today has a compromise government elected by the public, staffed by civilians, but dominated by the military. Former army leaders such as retired General Chaovalit Yongchaiyut—among the most powerful political figures in Thailand—have openly committed themselves to a purer parliamentary system, though civilians must acknowledge the supreme power of the Thai military. Chaovalit now heads the New Aspiration Party (NAP), which competes with NPC-backed Samakkhi Than and junta leader General Suchinda Kraprayoon for national leadership. The emerging hierarchy seems to be elected democratic leaders and influential military personnel, a large government bureaucracy, and powerful Chinese businessmen who control the economy.

THE MONARCHY

Another stabilizing factor is the overwhelming prestige of the royal family. Although the monarchy was shorn of its powers half a century ago, the Thais continue to view their king as a near-divine being who carries the real force of governmental power.

The present king, Bhumibol Adulyadej, was born in 1927 in Cambridge, Massachusetts, where his father was studying medicine at Harvard University. Adulyadej received his education in Switzerland before claiming the throne as Rama IX in 1949. Not only amiable and intelligent, he is also a gifted painter and talented jazz saxophonist who has led all-star jam sessions with such luminaries as bandleader Les Brown and singer Patti Page! His jazz compositions include "Hungry Man's Blues" (Can you imagine Queen Elizabeth writing a jazz ballad?) and the three-movement "Manora Ballet," previewed in Vienna during a royal visit. Despite an automobile accident which took an eye, his deft handling of a sailboat won him the gold medal at an international yachting competition. In what is now the longest reign of any Thai king, Adulyadej has earned immense popularity as the working monarch who guides and unifies the nation as head of state and protector of national traditions.

Based on Thailand's laws of succession, Crown Prince Maha Vajiralongkorn, the king's only son, will succeed his father to the throne, although his sister, Princess Maha Chakri Sirindorn, enjoys great popularity among the Thai people.

Portraits of the king, queen, and royal family are seen everywhere in Thailand. All foreign visitors are expected to behave respectfully toward the royal family, an acceptable caveat since there is little doubt that the Thai monarchy has *earned* this honor.

ECONOMY

Thailand's relatively stable political situation and prudent economic policies have catapulted it into the ranks of Asia's powerhouse economies. Together with South Korea, Taiwan, and Japan, almost everything seems to be going right in Thailand (Inc.). Economic growth of over 10% exceeds the performance and prospects of almost every other Southeast Asian country. The country enjoys a balance-of-payments surplus estimated at over US$1 billion from increased exports of traditional agricultural commodities and manufactured goods such as textiles, integrated circuits, and gemstones. Thailand's emergence as an industrialized economy is evident in the fact that electronics have surpassed once-dominant textiles and basic commodities to become the nation's leading export in 1992. The Thai Monetary Authority has held annual price inflation to under six percent for 20 years while using a prudent debt-management program that keeps official borrowing in check. While much of the private-sector economy from banking to manufacturing is controlled by the Sino-Thai business community, a spillover effect has raised average annual personal income to a respectable US$1050.

In a country as pleasurable as Thailand it is perhaps not surprising that tourism is the leading foreign-exchange earner. Total arrivals have soared from one million in 1976 to almost six million last year, and Thailand now nudges Hong Kong as the region's leading convention destination.

But the astounding success of its "Visit Thailand 1987" campaign brought problems such as room shortages, skyrocketing hotel tariffs (room rates increased 25% in 1989), polluted resorts (Pattaya beaches were closed the same year), and transportation bottlenecks. The current hotel-building frenzy has dramatically increased the number of hotel rooms and kept rate increases to a minimum, though visitors should prepare themselves for high prices and transportation delays.

THE PEOPLE

THE THAIS

Thailand is one of the most racially homogeneous countries in Southeast Asia: about 82% of the country's 60 million inhabitants are Thai. This Mongoloid race largely speaks a common language, shares a unified script, and follows the same Buddhist faith. As a racially tolerant people they have assimilated large numbers of Mons, Khmers, Chinese, and other smaller groups to a degree which precludes any typical Thai physiognomy or physique.

Thais generally speak one of four dialects which are mutually intelligible with some degree of difficulty. Central Thai, the official dialect of government and business, has come to dominate over the northern dialect spoken in Chiang Mai and the northeastern dialect laced with Khmer loanwords. A southern dialect is spoken near the Malay border.

Thais on the whole are a delightful people who believe that life is to be enjoyed so long as no one impinges on another's rights. Many decline to be fanatical about productivity or deadlines. Foreign visitors are often perplexed with their stubborn resistance to the Westerner's fast-paced, ulcer-prone life. This attitude is epitomized by the phrase *mai pen rai* (never mind).

Thais have personal first names such as Porn ("Blessings"), Boon ("Good Deeds"), Sri or Siri ("Glory"), Som ("Fulfillment"), or Arun ("Dawn"). Since Thais are normally addressed by their first name rather than their family name, don't be surprised if they call you "Mr. John" or "Miss Judy." The prefix Khun is the ubiquitous title which substitutes for Mr. or Mrs. Affectionate nicknames such as Frog, Rat, Pig, Fat, or Shrimp are more popular than first names!

Perhaps because of their Buddhist upbringing, Thais detest any form of conflict and will go to great pains to avoid confrontation and preserve harmony. This attitude—*jai yen* ("cool heart")—is strongly favored over *jai rohn* ("hot heart").

LANGUAGE

Far too many travel books have called Thai an impossible language. The truth is that the vocabulary and syntax are not difficult to grasp. With a few weeks of diligent practice and a basic dictionary almost anyone can communicate the essentials. And like everywhere else, even a few rudimentary phrases will help make friends and save money.

Thai is a monosyllabic and tonal language with 44 consonants, 24 vowels, and five tones. Script is written from left to right without separation between words. There are no prefixes or suffixes, genders, articles, plurals, or verb conjugations. If this makes Thai appear to be a simple language, consider the following.

Thai is a tonal language in which each word can be pronounced with five different tones: low, middle, high, rising, or falling. Each tone completely changes the meaning of the word. *Suay* with a rising tone means "beautiful" but with a falling tone means "bad fortune." Obviously, most Thai words should be double-checked with a native speaker for correct pronunciation.

The transliteration of Thai script into Romanized script is an inexact science and there is no accepted standardization of spelling. Each word can be spelled several different ways—such as the avenue in Bangkok variously rendered as Rajadamnern, Ratchadamnoen, and Rajdamnoen. A town south of Bangkok can be spelled either Petchburi, Petchaburi, or Phetchaburi. The simplest possible spelling has been used in this book, but it's no more correct than anybody else's.

Thai has several unique sounds that cannot properly be expressed with Roman letters. For example, there are sounds midway between D and T and others midway between B and P. Fortunately, Thai pronunciation is much more logical and consistent than English. Pity the poor Thai student studying English when confronted with cough, rough, though, thought, and through!

Common Expressions

Mai Pen Rai: Roughly translates to "Never mind" or "It doesn't matter," suggesting a state of mind similar to the Buddhist philosophy of disregarding the unimportant events of life since what happens is inevitable and it doesn't help to get uptight. This rather happy-go-lucky attitude is an essential element of the Thai spirit, although it sometimes irritates the rigid Westerner. Learning to say *mai pen rai* in the event of a delayed train or lost luggage will help keep your sanity while on the road!

Sanuk: "Pleasure" or "fun." Thais believe life is meaningless without fun! Everything is judged as either pleasurable or not pleasurable. Food, drink, sex, sports, festivals, and fairs are all great fun. Even a poorly paid job is acceptable if pleasurable. *Tuk tuk* drivers roar around corners on two wheels for the sake of *sanuk.*

Pai Tio: To wander aimlessly, hang out, or just waste time. Going *pai tio* is definitely *sanuk.* Strolling aimlessly on a warm evening is the ultimate in *pai tio.* When a Thai asks you where you are going, just respond with a friendly *pai tio.* Here are some other useful words and expressions.

Conversation

hello (used by males)	*sawadee krap*
hello (used by females)	*sawadee ka*
please/thank you	*kaw roo nah/krap kun*
excuse me	*kaw toots*
yes	*mi*
no	*mai*
How are you?	*Sabai dee rue?*
fine	*sabai dee*
What is your name?	*Khun cheu arai?*
My name is —.	*Phom cheu —.*
Where do you live?	*Yoo tee nai?*
Do you understand?	*Khao jai mai?*
I don't understand.	*Mai khao jai.*
I cannot speak Thai.	*Phut Thai mai dai.*
never mind	*mai pen rai*

Getting Around

Where is —?	*— yoo tee nai?*
when?	*meua rai?*

today	*wan nee*
tomorrow	*meua wan nee*
How many kilometers?	*Gi kilo pai?*
bus station	*sathan rod meh*
train station	*sathan rod tai*
police	*sathan tamruat*
gas station	*pam namman*
embassy	*sathan toot*
post office	*prai sani*
restaurant	*raan ahan*
hospital	*rong payaban*
airport	*sanam bin*
market	*talaat*
telephone	*tora sap*
bathroom	*hang nam*
hotel	*rongrem*
city	*nakhon*
district	*amphoe*
town	*muang*
village	*ban*

street	thanon	Something cheaper?	Me tuk gwa ti mai?
lane	soi	Do you have a cheaper room?	Me hawng tuk gwa ti mai?
bridge	saphan		
river	mae nam	Ten baht okay?	Sip baht dai mai?
canal	klong	Okay, I'll take it	Toklang
island	ko		
beach	hat	**Numbers**	
bay	ao	1, 2, 3	nung, song, sam
mountain	doi	4, 5, 6	si, ha, hok
hill	khao	7, 8, 9, 10	chet, pat, kow, sip
		11, 12	sip-et, sip-song
Bargaining		20, 25	yi-sip, yi-sip-ha
Do you have —?	— mi mai?	30, 40	sam-sip, si-sip
How much?	Thao rai? (ki baht?)	100, 1000	nung roi, nung pan
Too expensive!	Fang pai!		
You must be joking!	Kun pot len!		

One form of action you *must* avoid is face-to-face criticism. Unlike Westerners, who criticize friends without ruining relationships, Thais see criticism as a highly personal attack which often leads to grave consequences. To make friends and enjoy yourself in Thailand, keep a *jai yen*.

Thais are also obsessed with social ranking. Correct social conduct only happens after superior-inferior roles have been determined through direct questions such as "How much do you earn?" and "How old are you?" Westerners should consider such inquiries as friendliness or a form of flattery rather than an invasion of privacy. Social ranking is also reflected in the Thai language, including dozens of ways to say "I" depending on the speaker's so-

cial status. The top of the structure is fairly obvious: the king, his family, and the Buddhist priesthood. Below that are the variables of age, social connections, lineal descent, earnings, and education.

THE CHINESE

Thailand's largest and most important minority group are the Chinese. Early immigrants included the Hokkiens, who arrived during the late 18th century (Rattanakosin Period) to serve as compradores and tax collectors for the Thai royalty, and the near-destitute Teochews, who became the leading merchants in early Bangkok. Later arrivals included thousands of economic

Chinese calligrapher

refugees fleeing massive crop failures and widespread starvation in 20th-century China.

As elsewhere in Southeast Asia, Chinese immigrants worked hard, educated their children, and today completely dominate the trade and finance sectors of the local economy. It has been estimated that 60% of Thailand's largest companies are controlled by Sino-Thais (Thai nationals of Chinese descent), and almost 100% of Thai banks are controlled by a handful of extremely wealthy Sino-Thai families.

But unlike other countries in Southeast Asia, the massive concentration of wealth in Chinese hands has not brought widespread racial conflicts or discriminatory legislation. Thailand's racial harmony is perhaps the result of widespread intermarriage. According to legend, King Mongkut (himself of Chinese lineage) encouraged Chinese immigration and intermarriage with Thai women, social intercourse which he hoped would give future generations the traditional Chinese qualities of industry and thrift. As a result, it is now difficult if not impossible to distinguish ethnic Thais from Sino-Thais; perhaps 50% of Bangkok's population is ethnically Chinese. Sino-Thais have taken on Thai surnames and speak Thai rather than Chinese. Consequently, the Thai government has rarely been motivated to pass discriminatory laws but has let the Chinese help build the economic miracle of modern Thailand.

HILLTRIBES

Inhabiting the hills near Chiang Mai are some half-million seminomadic tribespeople who migrated down from southern China over the last few centuries. The 20 distinct tribes range from sophisticated groups like the Meos to primitive peoples like the Phi Tong Luang. All were relatively isolated from the outside world until commercialized trekking and government assimilation programs began in the 1970s. More information under "Chiang Mai."

RELIGION

BUDDHISM

Theravada Buddhism, the state religion of Thailand, is practiced by 90% of the population. Buddhism began in southern Nepal with the teachings of its founder, Siddhartha Gautama (563-483 B.C.), a wealthy aristocrat who rejected his princely upbringing after four alarming encounters with an aged man, a sick man, a corpse, and finally an ascetic. Shocked and disillusioned, Siddhartha renounced his royal life and began a 45-year quest for truth. After self-mortification and temptation failed, he solved the riddle of existence while meditating beneath the sacred bodhi tree at Bodgaya, India. The Buddha then set in motion the Wheel of Life (his teachings) and organized his *sangha* (monastic community), comprised of *bhikkus* (monks). These pilgrims codified existing Buddhist doctrine and dialogues onto palm leaf to form a three-part compendium of works called the Tripitaka ("Three Baskets of Wisdom").

Buddha's great achievement was to reform a calcifying Hinduism by reinterpreting traditional Hindu doctrines such as karma, reincarnation, and nirvana into a dynamic movement which promised salvation through personal effort rather than Brahmanic magic. He envisioned a middle path lying between the extremes of ascetic self-denial and worldly self-indulgence as the most practical way to achieve freedom from the endless cycle of death and rebirth.

After his death, some 500 disciples gathered to recite his teachings and form the Theravada branch of Buddhism to help maintain the purity of original traditions. The early Christian era saw the rise of Mahayana Buddhism, a school which promised a tangible paradise through the worship of supernatural intermediaries called bodhisattvas. Buddhism spread rapidly throughout India and was carried to Southeast Asia by the missionaries of In-

amulet

BOB RACE

CONTEMPORARY BUDDHISM

Modern worldwide Buddhism is divided into the Theravada school adopted in Sri Lanka, Thailand, and Burma, and the Mahayana version favored in China and Japan. Thais further subdivide Theravada into the less rigorous Mahanikaya order, the majority cult, and the stricter Thammayut order followed by less than 10% of the Buddist population. Thailand's Buddhist *sangha* (monastic community) is currently headed by Somdej Pra Yanasangworm, the same monk who supervised the young King Bhumipol during his 15-day residency at Wat Bowornives in Bangkok. As one of the most powerful individuals in the country, Somdej faces several thorny challenges: the declining interest in Buddhism among the young, the corrupting influence of *phi* propitiation (see below), and widespread decadence within the Buddhist *sangha*. Today in Thailand, it's not uncommon for monks to predict lottery outcomes, practice faith healing, distribute phallic symbols, sell magical charms, and charge hefty fees for ceremonial services. The country's monastic image was further damaged after it was revealed that several monasteries were selling bogus royal decorations.

Rebellion against conventional Buddhism is symbolized by Pra Bodhirak, an unorthodox but immensely popular and charismatic rebel who preaches his iconoclastic viewpoints from the Santi Asoke ("Peace, No Sorrow") headquarters on the eastern outskirts of Bangkok. Defrocked and under heavy legal pressures from the government, Bodhirak insists that Thai Buddhism has been badly corrupted by the decadent practices and superstitious beliefs mentioned above. His message of nonmaterialism and religious purity has hit home: popularity has soared and even the current governor of Bangkok supports Bodhirak's platforms of religious reform.

Spirit Propitiation

Buddhism might be Thailand's dominant faith but it has never completely replaced older religious traditions such as Hinduism and spiritualism. Hindu ceremonies still play an important role in Thai society, largely because ceremonies for life passages such as births, deaths, and marriages were never prescribed by the Buddha. Brahmanic astrologers also prepare the national calendar and preside over annual rice-planting ceremonies.

But more important are the powers of astrology, the occult, and wandering supernatural spirits called *phis,* homeless and unhappy apparitions who can cause great harm to the living unless appeased with frequent offerings. *Phis* are propitiated (not worshipped) for dozens of reasons: to influence the future, grant wishes, guarantee the success of a financial venture, pass a school exam, restore health to a sick family member, or win the biweekly lottery. Believed to exist in all shapes and sizes, some *phis*

(continued)

enjoy a permanent existence unbounded by the law of karma while others are reincarnations of dead human beings who have returned to haunt the living. People who died violently or whose funeral rites were improperly performed are especially dangerous since witches can force them to consume the internal organs of the living. Others can make you remove your clothes in public! Although these practices are not in accordance with the teachings of the Buddha (karma teaches individual responsibility; spirit propitiation places responsibility on outside forces), *phi* homage doesn't necessarily conflict with the reverence that Thais feel for Buddhist philosophy. The average Thai is a Buddhist who was married according to Hindu rituals but makes frequent offerings to placate animist spirits.

Spirit Houses

Some of the most powerful forms of *phis* are the guardian spirits called *chao phi*, of which the guardian spirit of the house *(chao thi* or *pra phum* in Khmer) is the most important. Thais believe that every plot of land harbors a spirit who must be provided with a small doll-like house. This curious spirit home, located on the exterior lawn where no shadow will ever fall, is furnished with a replica of the residing spirit holding a double-edged sword and a big book which lists deeds of the occupants. Other figurines include slaves, elephants, and sensuous dancing girls . . . to keep the ghost happy! After proper installation by a Brahman priest at the auspicious

Brahma

place and time, human occupants continue to make daily offerings of flowers, joss sticks, and food to placate the touchy spirit.

Thais also honor eight other household spirits, including one troublesome fellow who resides in the door threshold. That's why it is proper behavior to step *over* rather than *on* the threshold. In recent years it has become popular to erect extremely elaborate shrines dedicated to the four-faced Hindu god, Lord Brahma. Thailand's most famous Brahmanic image is displayed at the Hyatt Grand Erawan Hotel shrine in Bangkok, although in the strictest sense this is not a spirit house but in a category all its own.

Monkhood

To gain heavenly merit, improve their karma through correct living, and bring honor to their parents, many young Thai men elect to become monks for periods from a few days to several months. Initiates take vows of poverty and are allowed few possessions: three yellow robes, an alms bowl, and a strainer to filter any living creature from the water. Final daily meals are eaten before noon, while the remainder of the day is spent meditating and studying Buddhist scriptures. Although instructed to remain unemotional and detached about worldly concerns, many are surprisingly friendly to Westerners and quite anxious to practice their English. The Golden Mount in Bangkok is an excellent place to meet the monks.

dian King Asoka (272-232 B.C.). The final irony is that Buddhism, as a major force, eventually died out in the country of its origin.

MUSLIMS

Nearly one million Malay Muslims live in the southern provinces bordering Malaysia. Many are fishermen or rubber tappers who sometimes view public education and religious strictures mandated by the Thai government as an attack on their cultural autonomy. Muslim separatist movements such as the United Pattani Freedom Movement have largely been suppressed by the Thai government.

THEMES FOR TRAVEL

A sensible approach to travel is to specifically seek out those destinations or activities that carry the strongest appeal. Far too many visitors find themselves wandering around Thailand, unsure of where to go or what to see. Remember that travel can be a craft done well or badly, conscientiously or with a general disregard for detail, but like most things, it is much more satisfying if you do it properly. Imagine Thailand as a colossal gallery that can only be sensibly explored selectively. Mash too many experiences together and you end up with an unsatisfying mess. Find a few themes and follow them. It doesn't really matter what they are—just don't spread yourself too thin.

A well-thought-out itinerary begins with a logical travel plan followed with flexibility and a sense of spontaneity. What kind of a traveler are you and what are your interests—history, art, culture, dance, people, beaches, sports, nightlife? If you enjoy history and museums, you should focus on those places such as Bangkok, Chiang Mai, Ayuthaya, Sukothai, and the northeast, where museums and archaeology are the major attractions. Most importantly, do your background reading *before* you go. Music, dance, and performing-arts aficionados should concentrate on places where traditional theater and festivals still survive. Top choices are Bangkok, Chiang Mai, and the northeast. Shopping—always one of the top attractions—is best conducted in the handful of towns which specialize in local crafts such as Chiang Mai and silk-weaving villages in the northeast. Or would

MEDITATION IN THAILAND

Increasing numbers of travelers are investigating Buddhism and *vipassana* (insight) meditation during their visit to Thailand. Students of Buddhism cite several reasons to study in Thailand. Many feel that Thai centers offer a superior atmosphere and purer level of instruction than Western locales. Fees are another issue. Month-long meditation retreats in the U.S. and Europe can be prohibitively expensive, but instruction in Thailand is free except for small donations to cover basic costs. Finally, Thai meditation centers provide the opportunity to break the bonds of Western conditioning and completely enter the spiritual realm of Southeast Asia.

The best resource on meditation *wats* is the 105-page *Guide to Meditation Temples of Thailand* published by Wayfarer Books, P.O. Box 5927-B, Concord, CA 94596, U.S.A. Authored by a distinguished travel writer and dedicated student of *vipassana*, this comprehensive US$10 guide also includes information on visas, travel, health, language, and ordination procedures.

Meditation courses are available in several forms. Some of the most popular are the weekly lectures at Wat Mahathat in Bangkok and two-week retreats sponsored at Wat Suan Mok in Southern Thailand. Travelers on two-month visitor's visas can easily spend several weeks at other Thai temples which welcome Westerners. Long-term students should obtain a three- or six-month nonimmigrant visa from a Thai consulate.

Perhaps the most surprising aspect is that several temples are supervised by Western monks who teach meditation practices in English. Other temples use Thai language as the medium of instruction, but have Western monks who conduct additional classes in English. Only temples with English-language instruction, or a sizable community of Western monks, are listed below.

Note that most temples have limited residential space and prefer that prospective students write in advance regarding meditation retreats.

Bangkok

Bangkok is an excellent spot to begin your research.

Wat Mahathat: The International Buddhist Meditation Centre in the Dhamma Vicaya Hall to the rear of Wat Mahathat is an excellent information source on Buddhism and meditation retreats. Founded by a Thai monk and his English wife, along with scholars from adjacent Mahachulalongkorn Buddhist University, the center sponsors weekly lectures on Thai Buddhism and weekend meditation retreats to nearby temples. Their weekend at Buddha Monton in Nakhon Pathom costs 500B for food, accommodations, and transportation from Wat Mahathat. Upcoming English-language lectures are listed in the *Bangkok Post*. The center (tel. 511-0439 or 511-3549) also intends to publish a list of meditation *wats* that welcome Westerners.

(continued)

World Fellowship of Buddhists: English-language meditation classes for Western visitors are held on the first Sunday of every month 2000-2100 in the center on Sukumvit Road. Their small bookstore sells English literature on Buddhism and a badly outdated guide to meditation temples in Thailand. WFB occasionally sponsors 10-day *vipassana* retreats at Wat Jewel Mountain and other monasteries near Bangkok. 33 Sukumvit Road between Soi 1 and Soi 3, tel. 251-1188.

Wat Phleng Vipassana: English-language instruction on *abhidhamma* (Theravada psychology), *samathai* (inner tranquility), *metta* (loving kindness), and *vipassana* are given by the vice abbot. Many Westerners have studied meditation here. The mailing address is Soi Ying Amnuay, Charan Santiwong Road, Bangkok Noi, Thonburi.

Northern Thailand

Two monasteries near Chiang Mai are open to Westerners.

Wat Ram Poeng: One-month *vipassana* courses are given by Thai monks with English interpretation provided by Westerners or bilingual Thais. A good place for beginners who want to stay in Chiang Mai while slowly investigating Buddhism. Wat Ram Poeng (tel. 211620)—also called Wat Tapotaram—is located just outside Chiang Mai, south of Wat Umong on Canal Road. Wat Ram Poeng, Suthep, Amphoe Muang, Chiang Mai Province.

Wat U Mong: *Vipassana* meditation techniques and *dharma* talks are given by a German monk on Sunday afternoons from 1500 to 1700. A few foreign monks live in the *kutis* (monks' huts) near the lake in the rear of the grounds. Wat U Mong, Suthep, Amphoe Muang, Chiang Mai Province.

Northeastern Thailand

Near Ubon Ratchathani (Ubon for short) are two *wats* that welcome Western students. Wat Pa Nanachat is one of the most popular temples in Thailand for Western students of *vipassana* meditation.

Wat Nong Pa Pong: Wat Nong Pa Pong is the principal residence of a meditation master named Achaan Cha, a disciple of the famous Achaan Man

(1870-1949) who is credited as the inspiration for over 40 forest monasteries located throughout the northeast.

A book by Jack Kornfield titled *A Still Forest Pool* provides a useful introduction to the meditation theories of Achaan Cha. Kornfield once studied at Wat Nong Pa Pong, but now conducts meditation retreats in northern California at Spirit Rock Meditation Center (tel. 415-488-0164).

Wat Nong Pa Pong is 15 km southwest of Ubon Ratchathani. Wat Nong Pa Pong, Amphoe Warin, Ubon Ratchathani Province. Westerners generally have better luck at Wat Pa Nanachat.

Wat Pa Nanachat: Westerners interested in Buddhism and *vipassana* meditation are advised to visit the forest monastery located across the road from Wat Nong Pa Pong. Wat Pa Nanachat, "Temple of the International Forest," is a Western-oriented temple with a Canadian abbot, a Japanese vice-abbot, and several dozen European and American monks who speak English. Laypeople are welcome to stay as guests and conduct a brief study of Buddhism and insight meditation.

Wat Pa Nanachat is 15 km southwest of Ubon and noted by an English-language sign on the right side of the road. Wat Pa Nanachat, Amphoe Warin, Ubon Ratchathani Province.

South Thailand

Probably the most popular temple for short-term visitors is the monastery located just north of Surat Thani, very close to Ko Samui.

Wat Suan Mok: Wat Suan Mok is the home of Pra Achaan Buddhadasa (Phutthathat), a progressive and eclectic teacher who ranks among the most famous and controversial monks in Thailand. Buddhadasa's teachings and 16-stage meditation system combine traditional Buddhist beliefs with influences from Islamic Sufi and Japanese Zen.

Westerners can attend 10-day meditation intensives beginning on the first day of each month. Visitors should register several days in advance. Fees are US$2 per day. Several Westerners ordained as monks at Suan Mok help with public lectures and personal instruction. Wat Suan Mokkhabalaram, Chaiya, Surat Thani Province.

---

you prefer a total escape at a beach resort? The list is almost endless—educational tours, study programs, cultural minorities, adventure travel, restaurants, nightlife—but research and planning are essential for a successful and rewarding journey.

The following section is designed to help you

ferret out those attractions and activities worth special consideration. I've included a short list of personal favorites but suggestions for future editions of this book will be highly appreciated. Send your list of top tens to *Thailand Handbook*, Moon Publications, 722 Wall Street, Chico, CA 95928, U.S.A., and I'll publish the results.

ARTS AND CRAFTS

History And Architecture

While an endless procession of decaying old temples or ruined cities may not appeal to everyone, most visitors enjoy visiting a limited cross section of the more impressive monuments and historical sites. Each country in Southeast Asia offers a selection of architectural gems, but Thailand is especially rich when measured by antiquity and artistic merit. Quick walking tours are given for most historical neighborhoods, but visitors with limited time should concentrate on Bangkok, Ayuthaya, Sukothai, Si Satchanalai, Chiang Mai, and the Khmer monuments in the northeast.

Performing Arts

Travelers who enjoy dance and drama will be thrilled with Thailand's extraordinarily rich bounty of performing arts: traditional dance and theater at the National Theater in Bangkok, street shows at modest shrines and Buddhist memorials, hilltribe shows in the north, roving theater companies in the northeast, and Muslim dances in the south.

Local theater and dance-dramas are recommended as both great entertainment and a window of insight into the histories, cultures, and value systems of the people. Performances can be either tourist-oriented or authentic spectacles intended for the local population. Though tourist performances are sometimes dismissed as mere contrived rip-offs, they're well advertised, reasonably priced, and often employ the finest dancers, musicians, and actors from the local community.

However, anyone who would like to really understand Thai theater must also search out local performances. Here you'll experience the real Thailand, complete with sweating crowds, old women cracking peanuts, kids running up and down the center aisle, and a dozen other distractions that make the experience so memorable.

The major drawback to authentic theater is that performances are often difficult to find. Outside a handful of towns which have developed strong theatrical traditions, you'll need to conduct an organized search by scanning English-language newspapers such as the *Bangkok Post* and magazines, inquiring at local tourist offices, and asking everyone from taxi drivers to waitresses. Your best chances are on temple grounds during religious festivals. Even in such sacred settings, highbrow classical theater is often wedged between blasting rock 'n' roll bands, reruns of old Hollywood films, and slapstick comedies heavy with sexual innuendo.

Shopping

While shopping might seem to be a somewhat artificial theme for travel, visitors who understand the markets and enjoy bargaining will find Thailand one of the world's great emporiums. Thailand, in the opinion of this author, is a superior shopping destination to Hong Kong or

Singapore, despite the widespread reputation of those two cities.

Each region of Thailand produces unique arts and crafts. The trick is to know what to buy and where to buy it. Unlike Western countries where distribution networks efficiently spread products across dozens of markets, the best-quality handicrafts at the lowest prices tend to be sold primarily near their points of origin. Of course, products from Chiang Mai are available in Bangkok, but villages where the handicrafts are originally produced generally offer the best selection.

Shopping directly from the producer has several advantages. You'll be able to watch the craftsman in action and gain a greater appreciation for the work. You can also request custom jobs and negotiate prices. Perhaps most important is that money spent goes directly into the artist's pocket rather than to the middlemen.

SPORTS AND RECREATION

Almost 30 years ago a small English company began organizing truck journeys from London to Nepal, spawning an industry now encompassing over 100 companies which specialize in off-the-beaten-track destinations. Most of the trips still revolve around the big favorites such as trekking in Nepal and animal safaris in Africa, but a growing number are now directed toward Thailand and Southeast Asia. All emphasize small groups, experienced guides, and the importance of low-impact travel. Costs average US$100-200 daily, exclusive of airfare.

Some expeditions are rather mundane and can be easily accomplished by the independent traveler at far lower cost. Others, such as isolated river journeys, are virtually impossible without professional assistance.

Trekking

The forests and tribal areas of Thailand often surprise hikers expecting the crowds and commercialization of Nepal. Despite increasing numbers of trekkers, Thailand still offers new territory for hikers determined to escape the well-trodden paths.

Trekking comes in all forms. Easy one-day hikes across rolling hills are plentiful in almost all the national parks and wildlife preserves. Mod-

erately difficult hikes lasting several days are popular in the tribal areas of Northern Thailand near Chiang Mai. Extremely challenging treks lasting several weeks or months are unknown in Thailand, but are plentiful in other Southeast Asian areas such as Borneo and Indonesia.

In most cases, guides can be hired in local villages and from national park headquarters. Longer journeys through remote regions require professional assistance from trekking organizations in Chiang Mai and other northern towns.

River Journeys

What could be more romantic than slowly drifting down a muddy river, past simple villages and golden temples, pretending to be Conrad or Kipling? Such fantasies are still possible in Thailand, though you should also be prepared for noisy boats called longtails and a great deal of Westernization.

Beaches

History, culture, and the performing arts may be rewarding themes for travel, but relaxing on a Thai beach is unquestionably a far more popular pastime. And what a great place for escape . . . stunning sands, crystal-clear waters, water sports, and glorious sunsets.

Beach resorts are plentiful in all price ranges, from luxurious developments with first-class facilities to isolated beaches where the cost of lodging and food hardly breaks US$10 per day. Twenty dollars a day often guarantees a clean and comfortable bungalow with a private veranda, barbecued fish dinners, and perfect sunsets. Even short-term visitors who generally limit their vacations to Hawaii or Mexico should consider a holiday in Thailand since higher airfares are largely balanced by the lower costs of food and accommodations.

Selecting a beach without some background research can be a difficult task since Thailand offers scores of resorts in varying states of development. One key to finding the perfect hideaway with the proper mix of primitivism and comfort is to consider the evolutionary cycle of Thai beach resorts. Virtually all of today's leading resorts—Phuket, Ko Samui, and Pattaya—began as deserted beaches favored by independent travelers who lived in simple grass shacks and survived on fish and rice. Discovering the financial incentives of tourism, local villagers soon constructed guesthouses and cafes. Increasing numbers of travelers quietly tiptoed down, hoping that nobody else would discover their secret paradises. But word leaked out and soon the trickle became a rush as planeloads of land speculators and hotel operators joined the deluge. Within a decade what was once an idyllic stretch of sand had become an international clone of Waikiki or Mazatlan.

Although this sounds discouraging—and it is hard to deny that the hippie trails of the '60s have surrendered to mass tourism of the '90s— all is not lost. Even today, all over Thailand, a small number of adventurous backpackers are sitting on deserted tropical beaches, being welcomed into the homes of villagers, and exchanging smiles with friendly children.

What's the perfect resort? Opinions differ, but for this author it begins with a long and wide stretch of thick, clean, powder-white sand. Water should be warm, clear, and aquamarine blue. The ocean floor should be flat and sandy. The wind should blow with enough velocity for windsurfing and sailing but not so hard as to ruin sunbathing. Behind the beach should stand a forest of palm trees interspersed with hiking trails and isolated villages. Beaches fitting this description are relatively plentiful in Thailand.

However, facilities that harmonize with the environment are often lacking. Imagine a major resort being developed without any sort of zoning, government controls, or centralized planning. Tragically, many of Thailand's most promising beach resorts have not transformed themselves into tropical paradises but travelers' ghettos of dilapidated guesthouses or touristy nightmares of faceless high-rises and noisy bars. Perfect resorts are neither backpackers' slums nor Asian Waikikis. They are locally developed, owned, and operated so that profits return to the people rather than the New York Stock Exchange. Guesthouses are clean, spacious, and constructed from natural materials such as bamboo or palm fronds. Restaurants serve local fare, such as fish and vegetables, rather than pseudo-French or American fast food. Nightlife should include traditional entertainment and folk music along with the inevitable discos and video bars. Traffic and noise is minimized by limiting local traffic to service vehicles only. Cars and motorcycles are kept well away from the beach and residential areas. Best of all, some still use

lanterns and candles rather than electricity—a radical idea still fashionable at several remote islands.

Scuba Diving

The world's fastest-growing sport is quickly gaining popularity in Thailand, where tropical waters host outstanding coral reefs and colorful marinelife. Experienced divers can explore underwater wrecks and coral canyons, while beginners can obtain PADI and NAUI certification from dozens of accredited dive schools.

Dive Areas: Diving in Thailand revolves around Pattaya near Bangkok, Phuket, and the Similan Islands some four hours north of Phuket. Diving is also popular near Ko Samui on the east coast of Southern Thailand. The newest diving region is in the far south near the town of Trang, where Western operators are now opening some of the last untouched waters in the region.

Dive Companies: Dives can be arranged with dive shops and hotels in Bangkok, Pattaya, Ko Samet, Trat, Ko Samui, Phuket, and Trang. Organized tours are arranged by the following operators. More dive groups are listed in *Skin Diver* magazine.

See and Sea Travel Service: America's largest and most respected dive operator leads groups to the Philippines, Indonesia, and Thailand. The owner, Carl Roessler, strongly urges all divers to try his live-aboard dive cruises rather than the typical land-based dive. 50 Francisco St., Suite 205, San Francisco, CA 94133, tel.

(415) 434-3400, (800) 348-9778.

Tropical Adventures: A dive wholesaler representing over 35 fully outfitted live-aboard boats located throughout the world, including the 147-foot *Island Explorer* in Indonesia and the 51-foot *Wanderlust* in Thailand. 111 Second St. N, Seattle, WA 98109, tel. (206) 441-3483, (800) 247-3483, fax (206) 441-5431.

DIVE OPERATORS

OPERATOR	ADDRESS	PHONE
Pattaya		
Dave's Divers Den	Beach Rd. Soi 6	(038) 423286
Max's Dive Shop	Nipa Lodge Hotel	(038) 428195
Mermaid Sports	Mermaid Inn, Jomtien Beach	(038) 231907
Pattaya Dive Center	Siam Bayview Hotel	(038) 428728
Reef Dive Shop	Ocean View Hotel	(038) 428084
Seafari Sports	Royal Garden Hotel	(038) 428126
Steve's Dive Shop	Beach Rd. Soi 4	(038) 428392
Ko Samet		
Delfimarin Diwa	Box 6 Ban Phe	no phone
Ko Chang		
Laem Ngop	Guesthouse 16 Moo 1 Laem Ngop	(039) 512634
Ko Samui		
Ko Samui Divers	Malibu Club, Chaweng Beach	(077) 421465
Lamai Dive Center	Nice Resort, Lamai Beach	(077) 421435
Phuket		
Andaman Divers	Patong Beach	(076) 321155
Fantasea Divers	Box 20, Patong Beach	(076) 321309
Holiday Dive Club	Patong Beach	(076) 212901
Marina Sports	Marina Cottages, Kata-Karon	(076) 381625
Ocean Divers	Patong Beach Hotel	(076) 321166
Phuket Aquatics	62 Rasada Rd., Phuket Town	(076) 216562
Phuket Divers	7 Phunphon Rd., Phuket Town	(076) 215738
Phuket Dive Center	Coral Beach Hotel	(076) 321106
Poseidon Club	Phuket Island Resort	(076) 381010
Reef Explorers	Chalong Bay	(076) 381957
Santana	Patong Beach	(076) 321360
Siam Diving Centre	Box 244, Kata Karon Beach	(076) 381608
South East Asia	Patong Beach	(076) 321292
Trang		
Rainbow Divers	63 Soi 2 Wisekun Rd.	(075) 218820

SCUBA DIVING IN THAILAND

DIVE SITE	DIVE SEASON	DEPTHS	VISIBILITY	ATTRACTIONS
DIVE LOCATIONS				
Pattaya	all year	18-30 m	6-10 m	Ko Lan, Ko Pai, Ko Rin
Ko Samet	Nov.-June	18-30 m	10-20 m	corals and shipwrecks
Ko Chang	Nov.-June	18-30 m	10-25 m	Ko Wai, Ko Kradat
Ko Samui	March-Oct.	15-40 m	10-25 m	Ko Tao, Ko Angthong
Phuket	Nov.-April	30-45 m	10-25 m	Ko Racha, Shark Point
Similans	Dec.-April	25-90 m	35-40 m	Ko Huyong, Elephant Rock
Surin Islands	Dec.-April	25-70 m	20-40 m	corals and sharks
Ko Phi Phi	Jan.-March	25-40 m	15-30 m	Phi Phi Lae
Trang	Jan.-May	20-45 m	20-40 m	Emerald Cave and wrecks
Ko Tarutao	Dec.-May	15-35 m	15-35 m	Ko Khai, Ko Ngam

Golfing In The Kingdom

Golf—not scuba, trekking, or *takraw*—is the fastest-growing sport in Thailand. Once the preserve of the rich and famous, golf is now played by almost a half-million Thais and by thousands of overseas visitors who arrive for the sole purpose of playing the game. Thailand has over 50 golf courses, with at least another 50 in the planning stages. Many of the courses are of international standards and, except on weekends, almost empty. Fairways are well maintained and the greens neatly manicured. Perhaps more of a surprise is that most of the caddies are females who have given up work in the ricefields to help Western and Japanese tourists enjoy the finest golf in Southeast Asia. The best news is that golf is still very affordable; Japanese find it cheaper to fly to Thailand for the weekend than to pay the greens fees back home! Fees currently run about US$12-18 for 18 holes, plus a few more dollars for caddy and club rentals.

The variety of courses is almost endless: sculpted greens overlooking the seas, fairways surrounded by green paddy fields, mountains towering over the roughs. Thailand's amazing selection has brought international tournaments and professional golfers such as Johnny Miller and Steve Ballesteros. And, not surprisingly, large numbers of expatriates have retired in Thailand and established informal golfing associations that welcome foreign visitors.

The largest concentration of courses is located near Bangkok, along the eastern seaboard near Pattaya, and on Phuket Island which now has four international courses. A selection of the more popular courses is described in a small pamphlet called *Golfing* published and distributed by the Tourism Authority of Thailand. Further details can be found in the guide *Golfing in the Kingdom* published by Pacific Rim Press and available in Bangkok bookstores.

One of Thailand's largest multinational playing groups, the Bangkok Wanderers, whose unstated objective is to play as many Thai courses as possible, recently named their 20 favorite venues. Among the top choices were the Navatanee, Rose Garden, Royal Thai Army, Royal Gems, Pinehurst, Muang Ake, Krung Thep Kreetha, and Lard Ped (all near Bangkok); the Bangphra and Panya Resort (near Pattaya); Royal Hua Hin (Hua Hin), Lanna and Chiang Mai Green Valley (Chiang Mai); and Blue Canyon North and Phuket Golf & Country Club (Phuket).

ADVENTURE TRAVEL

American Companies

Over 20 companies throughout the world organize adventure tours to Thailand and other regions in Southeast Asia. Adventure travel companies fall into three categories: wholesalers who organize *and* promote their exclusive journeys, retailers who market a wide variety of wholesalers, and mixed vendors who sell both in-house expeditions and third-party trips. Contact the following companies for thick catalogs and detailed trip dossiers.

Mountain Travel-Sobek: The largest adventure travel operator on the West Coast offers over 140 different worldwide trips, including a nine-day bicycle tour in northern Thailand, a nine-day sea-kayaking trip near Phuket, hilltribe trekking, and a 14-day combination tour from north to south. Their 90-page catalog includes descriptions, photos, and day-by-day itineraries. 6420 Fairmount Ave., El Cerrito, CA 94530, tel. (510) 527-8100, (800) 227-2384, fax (510) 525-7710.

Adventure Center: One-stop source for American companies and English adventure travel operators such as Explore, Encounter Overland, and Dragoman. Experienced and dependable. 1311 63rd St., Suite 200, Emeryville, CA 94608, tel. (510) 654-1879, (800) 227-8747, (800) 228-8747 in California.

Overseas Adventure Travel: The largest adventure travel company on the East Coast specializes in cultural and natural journeys throughout Asia, including a two-week excursion to Thailand. Guide credentials are very impressive. 349 Broadway, Cambridge, MA 02139, tel. (617) 876-0533, (800) 221-0814, fax (617) 876-0455.

Wilderness Travel: Owner Bill Abbott states that almost 80% of his customers are repeat business or referrals from past clients, a great record which speaks highly of this California-based operation. Southeast Asian tours include a cultural tour of Indonesia, expeditions to Borneo and New Guinea, and a 22-day journey from Thailand to Nepal. 801 Allston Way, Berkeley, CA 94710, tel. (800) 368-2794, (510) 548-0420, fax (510) 548-0347.

InnerAsia: *Very* first-class organization with unique treks in Nepal, Bhutan, India, and Indonesia. Recent additions include extremely rare visits to Laos, Vietnam, and the Arakan region of Burma, plus side trips to Thailand. 2627 Lombard St., San Francisco, CA 94123, tel. (415) 922-0448, (800) 777-8183.

Geo Expeditions: A 20-day cultural excursion to the historic capitals of Thailand and Burma. Box 3656, Sonora, CA 95370, tel. (800) 351-5041, fax (209) 532-1979.

Backroads Bicycle Touring: Bicycle journeys in Northern Thailand from Chiang Mai to the Golden Triangle. 1516 Fifth St., Berkeley, CA 94710, tel. (510) 527-1555, (800) 245-3874, fax (510) 527-1444.

Off The Deep End Travels: Bicycle trip and festival tour through the Golden Triangle region of Northern Thailand. Tours range from 12 to 18 days. Box 7511, Jackson, WY 83001, tel. (307) 733-8707.

Asian Pacific Adventures: Standard vacations and an unusual biking tour on Phuket in Southern Thailand. 826 South Sierra Bonita Ave., Los Angeles, CA 90036, tel. (213) 935-3156, (800) 825-1680 outside California.

All Adventure Travel: This retailer sells adventure travel tours from all the leading operators such as Bolder Adventures, Journeys, and Asian Pacific Adventures. Box 4307, Boulder, CO 80306, tel. (800) 537-4025.

Creative Adventure Club: Alternative travel adventures to Southeast Asia, including jeep safaris in Northern Thailand and the Asian Express from Singapore to Bangkok. Request a sample copy of their *Adventures Magazine* from this small but highly original tour group. Box 1918, Costa Mesa, CA 92626, tel. (714) 545-5888, (800) 544-5088.

European Companies

Explore: Traditional tours and adventure travel programs including Thailand trekking, the Malay Peninsula, and an unusual schooner voyage through Indonesia's Nusa Tenggara. 7 High St., Aldershot, Hants, England, GU11 1BH, tel. (0252) 319448.

Encounter Overland: Europe's most experienced adventure travel operator offers the classic 11-week overlander from London to Kathmandu and a 30-day journey from Bali to Bangkok. 267 Brompton Rd., London SW5 9JA.

Exodus: English adventure operator with a 24-day volcano-climbing expedition in Indonesia and several treks through Borneo. 9 Weir Rd., London SW12 OLT, tel. (01) 675-5550.

Dragoman: Small company with overland expeditions across Africa, Asia, and South America plus a three-week Southeast Asian extension. 10 Riverside, Framlingham, Suffolk IP13 9AG, England, tel. (0728) 724184.

Australian Companies

World Expeditions: Australia's largest adventure travel company sponsors three Thai excursions, including a tropical sail from Pattaya to Ko Samet. Third floor, 377 Sussex St., Sydney, NSW 200, tel. (02) 264-3366.

Intrepid Travel: Southeast Asian adventures including river rafting, trekking in Khao Sok National Park, and research expeditions to investigate new regions. 801 Nicholson St., North Carlton 3054, Victoria, tel. (03) 387-3484, fax (03) 387-9460.

Specialized Operators

Some of the best tours are arranged through American agencies which specialize in Thailand rather than the entire world.

Adventures in Paradise: Ken Fish and Sandy Ferguson, in conjunction with a Thai-based company, operate an amazing range of personalized tours to some of the most remote and untouched regions in Thailand, Laos, Cambodia, and Vietnam. Recent excursions include an Issan and Laotian Explorer, trekking in Northern Thailand, and the world's first Kosher tour of Thailand, with kosher meals and synagogue visits! 155 West 68th St., Suite 525, New York, NY 10023, tel. (800) 736-8187, fax (212) 595-9672.

Adventures in Paradise can also be contacted at their head office at 426/1 Soi 10, Paholyothin Rd., Bangkok 10400, tel. (662) 271-3905, fax (662) 271-3818.

Bolder Adventures: Rusty and Marilyn Staff are first-person experts who organize tours to both familiar and remote destinations in Thailand. With the help of local contacts and experienced professionals, Rusty and Marilyn take you to national parks and ancient capitals. Box 1279, Boulder, CO 80306, tel. (800) 397-5917, fax (303) 443-7078.

Himalayan Travel: Sales agent for one of Thailand's largest alternative tour operators, with trekking and rafting in the Golden Triangle, elephant safaris near Mae Hong Son, and bicycle tours in the north. 112 Prospect St., Stamford, CT 06901, tel. (800) 225-2380, fax (203) 359-3669.

Thailand Travel Adventures: Kasma Lohaunchit Clark, a native of Thailand but now a resident of the San Francisco Bay region, leads four annual tours with special emphasis on remote islands in Southern Thailand. 4119 Howe St., Oakland, CA 94611, tel. (510) 655-8900.

TOUR COMPANIES

American Tour Operators

Organized tours sometimes make sense since they allow you to see the highlights of Asia without the hassles of language difficulties, transportation delays, and the time wasted finding suitable accommodations. Often there is no cheaper way to get airfare and hotels, since large tour operators buy in bulk and can pick up sizable discounts. Don't dismiss tours for fear of simply being shepherded around—the If-it's-Tuesday-this-must-be-Bangkok syndrome. Simple packages often include only transportation and hotels, leaving you free to independently wander around in each town. The more expensive tours include bus tours, dining, and entertainment, but you're never under any obligation to follow the crowd. Finally, tours often bring about a feeling of togetherness and sharing.

Dozens of packagers and tour operators such as American Express, Thomas Cook, and Olson Travelworld sell tours to Southeast Asia, but you should carefully read the fine print and check on what's included in the price. Probably the most important factor is the experience of the guides and the general emphasis of the package. Rather than trying to see all of Southeast Asia at breakneck speed, it's better to limit yourself to a few highlights or perhaps just a single destination. Ask your agent about the quality and location of the hotels, what kinds of meals are included, how large the group will be, and cost of insurance and penalties for cancellation.

If none of these package tours seem appealing, investigate the specialized tour operators and adventure packages described above. Call the following companies to request a brochure: Abercrombie and Kent, tel. (800) 323-7308; Olson Travelworld, tel. (800) 421-2255; Pacific Delights, tel. (800) 221-7179; Globus Gateway, tel. (800) 221-0090; Maupintour, tel. (800) 255-4266; Odyssey Tours, tel. (800) 456-7436; or Travcoa, tel. (800) 992-2004.

Tour Companies In Thailand

Several major tour operators in Bangkok offer package tours to Thailand, Indochina, and elsewhere in Southeast Asia. These companies can be contacted in advance or after arrival in Bangkok.

Deithelm Travel: A Swiss-based tour company with first-class tours to every nook and cranny of Thailand, including biking in Northern Thailand and sea canoe excursions near Phuket. Deithelm is also famous for their tours to Vietnam, Cambodia, and Laos. 140/1 Wireless Rd., Kian Gwan II Building 14th floor, Bangkok 10330, tel. (02) 255-9150, fax (662) 256-0248.

World Travel Service: Thailand's oldest and largest travel agency has 44 branches throughout the country. Complete descriptions of the tours are listed in their brochure, *Bangkok Informer*. 1053 Charoen Krung Rd., Bangkok 10500, tel. (02) 233-5900, fax (662) 236-7169.

Arlymear Travel: Glenn Stallard (Gant Satiradej) runs a smaller operation than World or Deithelm. CCT Building 6th floor, 109 Surawong Rd., Bangkok 10500, tel. (02) 236-9317, fax (662) 236-2929.

For information on other tours, overseas study, or exchange, see p. 44.

LUXURY CRUISES AND PRIVATE YACHTS

Luxury Cruise Ships

Perhaps 80% of the world's luxury cruises do the popular tourist routes through the Caribbean, Mexico, Alaska, and Hawaii, but a growing number of companies offer deluxe cruises through Asia and Southeast Asia with stops in Bangkok and southern Thai islands.

The following companies will send colorful brochures, but bookings must be made through independent travel agents. Large nationwide agencies include Travel of America (800-358-2838 nationwide, 800-228-8843 in California).

Royal Viking Line: Their "Captain's Pacific Journey" tour sails from San Francisco through the South Pacific to Australia, Africa, India, Phuket, Singapore, Bangkok, Hong Kong, and Tokyo. 95 Merrick Way, Coral Gables, FL 33134, tel. (800) 422-8000.

Pearl Cruises: Sponsors a variety of tours including a 20-day "Great Cities of Asia" from Bangkok to Hong Kong via Singapore, Brunei, and the Philippines. 1510 S.E. 17th St., Fort Lauderdale, FL 33316, tel (800) 556-8850.

Renaissance Cruises: Sponsors three super-luxury cruises from Singapore to Bali (20 days from US$7000), Nusa Tenggara (14 days from US$5000), and Singapore to Hong Kong (22 days from US$7000). 1800 Eller Dr. Box 35307, Fort Lauderdale, FL 33335, tel. (800) 525-2450.

Cunard Lines: Cunard sails through Southeast Asia on their *Sea Goddess II, Sagafjord,* and *Vistfjord* from autumn to spring. 555 Fifth Ave., New York, NY 10017, tel. (800) 221-4770.

Princess Cruises: Fall departures on their *Island Princess* and *Pacific Princess.* 10100 Santa Monica Blvd., Los Angeles, CA 90067, tel. (800) 421-0522.

Salen Lindblad: Salen Lindblad organizes Indonesian and Southeast Asian tours aboard their *Frontier Spirit.* 133 E. 55th St., New York, NY 10022, tel. (800) 223-5688.

Thailand-based Cruise Lines

Luxury cruises can also be booked through two private companies based in Thailand.

Siam Cruises: *Andaman Princess,* the finest luxury cruise ship in Thailand, conducts three- to five-day sails in the Gulf of Thailand from May through September, and five-day excursions through the Andaman Sea from Phuket from Oct. to April. Onboard facilities include several entertainment lounges, saunas, and a fitness room. 33/10 Chaiyod Arcade Sukumvit Soi 11, Bangkok 10110, tel. (02) 255-8950, fax (662) 255-8961.

Seatran Travel: A Thai company with two luxurious ocean liners. All departures are from Phuket. Excursions on the older *Seatran Queen* include east of Phuket (three days, US$175-300), Similan Islands (four days, US$200-325), and Phuket to Hat Yai (three days, US$200-325). Excursions on the more luxurious *Seatran Princess* include Phuket-Similan-Ranong (four days, US$225-300), Phuket-Ko Phi Phi-Tarutao (four days, US$250-375), and Phuket-Sumatra-Penang (six days, US$700-800). Seatran Travel, 1091/157 Metro Trade Center, New Petchburi Rd., Bangkok 10400, tel. (02) 251-8467, fax (662) 254-3187.

Cruise Discounts

Luxury cruises cost US$200-500 daily including roundtrip airfare. Too expensive? Discounts of 20-35% are available from most of the "last-minute" discount clubs listed above, and from Cruise Line at (800) 327-3021 and Cruises Inc. at (800) 854-0500.

Yacht Charters

Private yachts can be chartered through American- and European-based companies, and from several private firms in Thailand.

Ocean Voyages: Ocean Voyages, a very special organization, arranges charters for individuals and groups on every type of vessel from sleek yachts to superb classic sailing ships. Possibilities include high-performance yachting onboard the *Omni,* excursions with a husband-wife writer team on the *Endymion,* and luxury cruises on the famous 72-foot *Storm Vogel.* All yachts are captained by professionals who have spent years sailing and studying anchorages, local histories, anthropology, and marine ecology. Mary Crowley can also help with scuba diving, racing events such as the King's Regatta in Phuket, and charters in the South Pacific, the Caribbean, and the Mediterranean. 1709 Bridgeway, Sausalito, CA 94965, tel. (415) 332-4681.

Asia Voyages Pansea: Private yachts for cruising, scuba diving, and big-game fishing, plus escorted tours and beach resorts, can be arranged from Asia Voyages Pansea offices in Thailand, Hong Kong, Singapore, Denpasar (Bali), and Europe. Their yachts sail from Phuket Nov.-April and from Ko Samui July-October. Asia Voyages, Charn Issara Tower, 942 Rama IV Rd., Bangkok 10500, tel. (02) 235-4100, fax 236-8094. Other offices are located in Chiang Mai (tel. 053-235655), Phuket (tel. 216137), Hong Kong (tel. 521-1314), Singapore (tel. 65-732-7222), Bali (tel. 361-25850), Paris (tel. 1-43261035), Brussels (tel. 2-217-9898), and London (tel. 1-491-1547).

South East Asia Yacht Charter: Owner Dave Owens in Phuket manages five yachts, including the 45-foot *Tonga Queen,* 48-foot sloop *Buccabu,* French-skippered *Celestius,* Aussie-skippered *Wanderlust,* and American-sailed *Quilter II.* 89-71 Thaweewong Rd., Phuket 83121, or Box 199, Patong Beach, Phuket, tel. (076) 321292.

Sea Canoes: An excellent way to see the remarkable limestone formations and deserted beaches near Phuket is onboard clean and quiet inflatable sea canoes. Trips range from overnight excursions in Phangnga Bay to week-long expeditions from Phangnga to Krabi. Reservations can be made with Diethelm Travel, or at Sea Canoes offices in Phuket and Chaweng Beach Hotel on Ko Samui.

> *Of the gladdest moments in human life, methinks, is the departure upon a distant journey into unknown lands. Shaking off with one mighty effort the fetters of Habit, the leaden weight of Routine, the cloak of many Cares and the slavery of Home, man feels once more happy.*
>
> —Richard Burton,
> *Journal*

EVENTS AND ENTERTAINMENT

Nightlife

Each country in Southeast Asia offers something of interest for night owls, but Bangkok is generally considered the entertainment capital of Southeast Asia. Many of the nightclubs and pubs popular with Westerners are owned and operated by Westerners, though Thai entrepreneurs are successfully competing in Bangkok and beach resorts such as Phuket. Discos are plentiful in luxury hotels but most should be avoided since they're expensive, pretentious, and almost identical in atmosphere to their Western counterparts. Much better are those clubs that offer live entertainment, usu-

ally by talented Thai musicians who compete with the famous entertainers of the Philippines. Nightclub owls will soon discover that Filipinos are the premier musicians in Southeast Asia and that the best clubs hire Filipino bands.

Thailand is known throughout the Western world for its go-go bars and massage parlors where thousands of call girls sell their services to both Thai nationals and visiting Westerners. Bangkok nightlife centers such as Patpong and Soi Cowboy are worth investigating and welcome both single males and couples, though the devastation of AIDS makes casual sex an almost suicidal proposition in Thailand.

FESTIVALS IN THAILAND

A highly recommended travel theme is the religious, ethnic, and national celebrations of Thailand. No matter their size or importance, festivals generally guarantee a colorful parade filled with floats, exotically costumed participants, the exhibition of valuable religious icons, traditional dance and drama, foodstalls, charlatans, hucksters, and rare opportunities to photograph without the risk of offending somebody's sense of privacy. Religious celebrations predominate. Those listed below are worth planning into your itinerary even if it involves additional time and expenses. Festivals are described in greater detail in each chapter.

Approximate dates are indicated despite festival dating being an inexact science in Thailand. National celebrations, such as independence days, are dated by Western calendars and fall on the same annual date. However, most Thai festivals are connected with Buddhism or agricultural cycles and dated by lunar calendars. These festivals change year to year and consequently float around the calendar. Exact dates should be checked with the Tourist Authority of Thailand (TAT). Current listings of upcoming events are also given in the *Bangkok Post*.

January

Don Chedi Memorial Fair: The decisive battle of King Naresuan and the Burmese is reenacted each year January 24-30. Don Chedi is west of Bangkok and north of Kanchanaburi.

Borsang Umbrella Festival: A colorful little festival to honor the town's main handicraft is held just outside Chiang Mai.

Pra Nakhon Khiri Fair: Petchburi, a small town south of Bangkok, sponsors a light-and-sound presentation that illuminates its outstanding monuments.

February

Chinese New Year: Chinese comprise a large segment of the Thai population, though their celebration tends to be a private event shared between family members.

Maha Puja: Buddha's revelations to his 1,250 disciples at Bodhgaya is marked with merit-making ceremonies such as releasing of caged birds, burning of incense, and a lovely procession of flickering candles around the temple. Held on the full moon of the third lunar month.

Prathat Phanom Chedi Fair: This important festival held in Nakhon Phanom, northeastern Thailand, honors a holy relic of the Buddha.

Chiang Mai Flower Festival: An elaborate procession of floral floats, marching bands, and the pride of Chiang Mai: beautiful women. Be prepared for enormous crowds.

Red Cross Fair: A commercialized, crowded, and somewhat disappointing festival in Bangkok with nightly dance performances, music, and exciting *takraw* competition.

March

Pra Buddhabat: Buddhist devotees gather at the

shrine of the holy footprint near Saraburi for religious rites and a bazaar.

Thao Suranari Fair: This festival honors the national heroine who rallied local people to repel invaders from Vientiane. An homage-paying ceremony and victory procession are held at her memorial in Korat (Nakhon Ratchasima), northeastern Thailand.

April

Pattaya Festival: Thailand's major beach resort hosts a week-long festival of beauty queens, floral floats, fireworks, cultural dancing, kite flying, and motorcar races. One of the biggest beach celebrations in Thailand.

Chakri Day: This national holiday, held on 6 April to commemorate the reign of Rama I (founder of the Chakri Dynasty), is the only day of the year when Bangkok's Pantheon at Wat Pra Keo is opened to the public.

Songkran: Thailand's New Year is celebrated nationwide as the sun moves into Aries. Buddha images are purified with holy water, young people honor their parents by pouring perfumed water over their hands, and traditional sand pagodas are built in the temples. Fun-loving Thais have cleverly turned this religious ritual into a wild and crazy water-throwing festival during which everyone is smeared with white powder and drenched with buckets of ice-cold water. Unsuspecting tourists are a prime target—leave the camera at your hotel!

Pra Pradang Songkran Festival: The Mon community in Samut Prakan south of Bangkok sponsors a Mon festival with parades, Mon beauty queens, and continual deluges of water throwing. Organized tours of this unusual festival can be booked through the Siam Society in Bangkok.

May

Coronation Day: King Bhumibol's coronation is celebrated on 5 May with a private ceremony in the royal chapel.

Royal Ploughing Ceremony: This elaborate Hindu ritual marks the beginning of the rice-planting season. A richly decorated plough is pulled by garlanded buffaloes across the Sanam Luang in Bangkok while Brahman priests solemnly plant sacred rice seeds and predict the success of the coming harvest.

Visaka Puja: This most sacred of all Buddhist holidays commemorates the birth, death, and enlightenment of Buddha. Merit-making ceremonies are identical to the Maha Puja.

Rocket Festival: People of the dry northeast hold this festival to ensure plentiful rains. Bamboo rockets are launched into the sky before the night's activities of music, dancing, and drinking. Held on the second weekend in May throughout the Issan. The town of Yasothon hosts the most famous of all rocket festivals, complete with beauty queens and an elaborate parade.

July

Asaha Puja: Commemorates Buddha's first sermon to his five disciples and marks the beginning of the annual three-month rains retreat. Also called Khao Phansa or Buddhist Lent and a popular time for young Thai males to temporarily enter the Buddhist priesthood. Held on the full moon of the eighth lunar month.

Candle Festival: Ubon Ratchathani celebrates the beginning of Buddhist Lent with a gigantic procession of floats carrying huge candles designed to burn for its duration.

August

Longan Fair: Lamphun celebrates the popular fruit with a Miss Longan Beauty Contest, agricultural displays, and a small parade.

Queen's Birthday: Municipal buildings are illuminated with colored lights during this national holiday held on 12 August.

September

Phuket Vegetarian Festival: Islanders of Chinese ancestry follow a strict vegetarian diet for nine days. The festival begins with a parade of white-clothed devotees who walk across fire and drive spears through their cheeks—the Chinese version of Hindu Thaipusam.

October

Tod Kathin: The end of Buddhist Lent and the rainy season is celebrated with elaborate boat races in Nan, Surat Thani, Nakhon Phanom, and Samut Prakan. Highlighted by a procession of royal barges down the Chao Praya to Wat Arun, where the king presents new robes to the monks.

Wax Candle Festival: The end of the Buddhist rains retreat is celebrated in Sakhon Nakhon with a parade of beautifully embellished beeswax floats in the form of miniature Buddhist temples.

Chonburi Buffalo Races: Local farmers near Bangkok sponsor races and a beauty contest for decorated buffaloes.

Chulalongkorn Day: Thailand's beloved king is honored with a national holiday on 23 October. Wreaths are laid at his equestrian statue in Bangkok's Royal Plaza.

Pra Chedi Klang Nam Festival: The riverside *chedi* in Samut Prakan, some 30 km south of Bangkok, hosts a popular festival with colorful processions and boat races.

(continued)

November

Loy Kratong: Thailand's most famous and charming festival honors both the Buddha and ancient water spirits. Banana-leaf boats carrying a single candle are floated on the rivers and lakes—a wonderful and delicate illusion. Loy Kratong is celebrated in both Sukothai and Chiang Mai, although Sukothai is a better venue because of the smaller crowds. It's sometimes possible to see both festivals since Sukothai's is often held the previous night.

Golden Mount Fair: Bangkok's most spectacular temple fair features folk drama, barkers, freak shows, countless foodstalls, and a lovely candlelight procession around the temple.

Ayuthaya Boat Races: An international event which attracts both local and foreign crews.

Deepavali: The Hindu Festival of Lights is celebrated at a small, ornate Indian temple on Silom Road in Bangkok. Religious zealots perform amazing feats of self-mutilation.

Surin Elephant Roundup: Over 100 elephants engage in staged hunts, comical rodeo and elephant polo, and a tug-of-war between a lone elephant and 100 men. Visitors can ride the pachyderms around town. Held in Surin on the third Saturday in November.

Pra Pathom Fair: Folk dramas, beauty pageants, and a parade take place in Nakhon Pathom at Pra Pathom Chedi, world's tallest Buddhist monument.

River Kwai Bridge Week: A nightly *son et lumiére* relates the grim history of this world-famous bridge. Visitors can ride World War II-vintage steam engines across the bridge.

December

King's Birthday: Bhumibol's birthday on the 5th of December is celebrated with a grand parade and citywide decorations of flags, portraits of the king, and brilliantly colored lights.

CONDUCT AND CUSTOMS

Theft

Losing your passport, air ticket, traveler's checks, or cash can be a devastating experience, but with a certain amount of caution you shouldn't have any problem.

First, bring as few valuables as possible. Leave the jewelry, flashy camera bags, and other signs of wealth at home. To speed up the replacement of valuable documents, keep duplicate copies of all valuable papers separate from the papers themselves. Immediately report any theft to the local police and obtain a written report including traveler's check serial numbers. Check the security of your hotel room and ask for a room with lockable windows and a private lock. Valuables should be checked in the hotel safe and an accurate receipt obtained. Be cautious about fellow travelers, especially in dormitories. Keep your gear in full sight whenever possible. Be cautious about pickpockets in crowds, on buses, during festivals, and at boat harbors.

Theft in Thailand is usually by stealth rather than by force, and armed robbery is rare except in isolated situations. A common problem is razorblade artists on public buses in Bangkok; carry your bag directly in front of you and be extra alert whenever somebody presses against you.

Hotel fraud is a problem in some hotels and guesthouses, where dishonest clerks sometimes remove credit cards from stored luggage and run up large bills with the cooperation of unscrupulous merchants. Credit cards should be sealed to discourage unauthorized charges, and a complete receipt of stored goods including the serial numbers of traveler's checks should be obtained from the desk clerk. American Express reports that Thailand has the highest ratio of fraudulent-to-legitimate cards of all its markets, second highest in monetary value only to the United States!

Knockout drugs are another problem. Numbers of Western visitors are robbed each year by professional con artists who often spend hours (even days!) gaining your confidence before administering a sleeping drug. Never accept food or drinks from a stranger, and be wary of strangers who offer tours of the city or private boat cruises in Bangkok.

Finally, try to maintain a balance between suspicion and trust. Most Thais are honest, so don't get paranoid about everybody who wants to show you around or practice their English. Meeting the people will almost certainly be your most cherished moments while on the road.

ETIQUETTE

Thai value systems regarding dress, social behavior, religion, authority figures, and sexuality are much more conservative than those of the average Westerner. Although the Thais are an extremely tolerant and forgiving race of people blessed with a gentle religion and an easygoing approach to life, visitors would do well to observe proper social customs to avoid embarrassment and misunderstandings.

Royalty

Thais hold their royal family in great reverence. All visitors are expected to show respect to all royal images, including national anthems preceding movies and royal portraits on Thai currency. While many Thais will tactfully criticize their national and local governments, Thai royalty is never openly reproached.

Buddha Images

Thais are a deeply religious people who considered all Buddhist images extremely sacred—no matter their age or condition. This is no joke! Sacrilegious acts are punishable by imprisonment—even when committed by foreign visitors. Several years ago, two Mormon missionaries posed for photographs on top of a Buddha image in Sukothai. The developing lab in Bangkok turned the negatives over to a Bangkok newspaper, which published the offending photographs on the front page. Public outrage was so strong that the foreigners were arrested and put in jail. More recently *Sports Illustrated* was refused permission to use religious shrines as backdrops for its swimsuit issue, and a *Vogue* model was arrested the following year for posing beside a religious monument in Phuket.

Monks

Buddhist monks must also be treated with respect. Monks cannot touch or be touched by females, or accept anything from the hand of a woman. Rear seats in buses are reserved for monks; other passengers should vacate these seats when necessary. Never stand over a seated monk since they should always remain at the highest elevations.

Temple Dress Codes

All Buddhist temples in Thailand have very strict dress codes, similar to Christian churches in the West. *Shorts are not acceptable attire in Buddhist temples—men should wear long pants and a clean short-sleeved shirt.* Women are best covered in either pants or a long skirt, and shoulders should not be exposed. Leather sandals are better than shoes since footwear must be constantly removed. Rubber flip-flops are considered proper only in the bathroom, not religious shrines. Buddhist temples are *extremely* sacred places; please dress appropriately.

Modest Dress

A clean and conservative appearance is absolutely necessary when dealing with border officials, customs clerks, local police, and bureaucrats. A great deal of ill feeling has been generated by travelers who dress immodestly. When in doubt, look at the locals and dress as they do.

Shorts are considered improper and low-class attire in Thailand, only acceptable for schoolchildren, street beggars, and common laborers . . . not wealthy tourists! Except at beach resorts, you should never wear skimpy shorts, halter tops, low-cut blouses, or anything else that will offend the locals. Long slacks and a collared shirt are recommended for men in urban environments. Women should keep well covered. Swimwear is only acceptable on the beach.

If you're really an outrageous and flamboyant type of individual, go ahead and be yourself since Thais accept eccentric behavior from town crazies and oddball Westerners. Otherwise, dress conservatively and try to blend into local society.

Emotions

Face is very important in Thailand. Candor and emotional honesty—qualities highly prized in Western society—are considered embarrassing and counterproductive in the East. Never lose your temper or raise your voice no matter how frustrating or desperate the situation. Only patience, humor, and *jai yen* bring results in Thailand.

Personal Space

Thai anatomy has its own special considerations. Thais believe that the head—the most sacred part of the body—is inhabited by the *kwan*, the spiritual force of life. Never pat a Thai on the head even in the friendliest of circumstances. Standing over someone—especially someone older, wiser, or more enlightened than yourself—is also considered rude behavior since it implies social superiority. As a sign of courtesy, lower your head as you pass a group of people. When in doubt, watch the Thais.

Conversely, the foot is considered the lowest and dirtiest part of the body. The worst possible insult to a Thai is to point your unholy foot at his sacred head. Keep your feet under control; fold them underneath when sitting down, don't point them to-

(continued)

ward another person, and never place your feet on a coffee table.

The left hand is also unclean and should not be used to eat, receive gifts, or shake hands. Aggressive stances such as crossed arms or waving your arms are also considered boorish.

A Graceful Welcome

Thailand's traditional form of greeting is the *wai*, a lovely prayer-like gesture accompanied with a little head nodding. Social status is indicated by the height of your *wai* and depth of your bow: inferiors initiate the *wai*, while superiors return the *wai* with just a smile. Under no circumstances should you *wai* waitresses, children, or clerks—this only makes you look ridiculous! Save your respect for royalty, monks, and immigration officials.

AIDS Alert

Love and lust in Thailand have taken an ugly turn since authorities first detected AIDS in 1984. According to a government survey released in 1991, Thailand has over 300,000 HIV-positive cases, while several thousand people had developed AIDS-Related Complex. The World Health Organization reckons that AIDS could infect over five million Thais by the year 2000, with more than a million dead by then. Thailand almost certainly has the worst AIDS problem in the world. See also "AIDS," below.

Drugs

Unless you care to spend the next 20 years of your life in prison, don't mess with drugs in Thailand. Local law enforcement officials make little distinction between grass and heroin. Penalties are harsh: over 700 foreigners are now incarcerated in the Bangkok and Chiang Mai prisons on drug charges—not pleasant places to spend a large portion of your life. Raids conducted at popular travelers' hotels in Bangkok and Chiang Mai often involve drugs planted by overzealous police officers. Taxi drivers sell drugs to travelers and turn them in for the reward and return of the drug. Arrested, booked, and fingerprinted, the frightened Westerner spends a night in jail before posting a sizable bail and passport as collateral. Even the smallest quantities bring mandatory jail sentences; life imprisonment is common for sizable seizures. The obvious message with drugs in Thailand is *don't*.

Asian Bureaucracy

Dealing with immigration officials, ticket clerks, and tourist officers is much smoother if you dress properly and keep your emotions under control. You must never lose your cool no matter how slow, mismanaged, or disorganized the situation. Yelling and table pounding will only screw things up for you—in fact, Thai paper pushers *enjoy* slowing things up for the obnoxious foreigner. Smile, be polite, try some humor, and then firmly ask for their help and suggestions. Stubborn bureaucrats can suddenly become extraordinarily helpful to the tourist who keeps his cool and knows how to play the game.

Women Travelers

Should women travel alone in Thailand? I have talked to dozens of solo women travelers and the general agreement is that Thailand is a great place for female travelers. Crime rates are lower than in the West, plus the Buddhist society of Thailand has always placed great emphasis on respect for females.

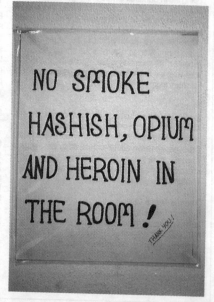

NO SMOKE HASHISH, OPIUM AND HEROIN IN THE ROOM! THANK YOU!

ACCOMMODATIONS AND FOOD

STAYING IN THAILAND

While transportation costs are rather fixed, eating and sleeping expenses can be carefully controlled. Hotels are available in all price ranges, depending on what level of comfort you demand. Thailand has everything possible from expensive hotels that cater to wealthy tourists to good-quality guesthouses and inexpensive hotels designed for Thai tourists and Western travelers.

Guesthouses

Shoestring travelers who don't mind simple rooms with common bath and minimal furniture can sleep for under US$5 in most towns. Some of these places are bare-bones Chinese hotels located near the train or bus terminals, but others are clean and friendly guesthouses filled with Western backpackers. Thailand's informal network of guesthouses are a vast improvement over the sterility of large international hotels and are the ideal solution for long-term travelers since they're great spots to relax, meet other people, and exchange travel information. Many have dormitories for under US$2.

Hotels

An excellent compromise between low-end guesthouses and luxury resorts are hotels which cater to Thai tourists and Thai businessmen. Almost every town in Thailand has a good selection of these hotels. Prices are very low and standards are perfectly adequate for most Westerners. Rooms with a fan, decent furniture, and private bath with shower cost just US$4-6 per day. Rooms with air-conditioning only cost US$10-15. While not a necessity at breezy beach resorts or in the hills, a/c becomes almost a necessity in hot and smoggy cities such as Bangkok.

Moderate Hotels: Hotels in the US$25-40 range usually include hotel restaurants, lounge, TV, room service, and other standard amenities. Except for a few places such as Bangkok and Chiang Mai, midpriced hotels are far less common than guesthouses or luxury hotels.

Luxury Hotels: Thailand's top-end hotels are considered some of the finest in the world. Although recommended for an occasional splurge, it must be said that the cheaper the hotel, the more intriguing the people you'll meet and the more memorable the travel experience. Among the 10 "Great Hotels of the World" described in *Travel & Leisure* and recommended by the readers of *Condé Nast Traveler* are the Oriental, Shangri La, and Regent in Bangkok. New properties in Phuket, Ko Samui, and northern Thailand will probably make the lists in future years.

EATING IN THAILAND

Finding good food at bargain prices is the same as anywhere else in the world. Avoid those places signposted "We Speak English" or displaying credit card stickers. Instead, search out cafes filled with local customers, not groups of tourists. Don't be shy about road stalls and simple cafes; these often provide the tastiest food at rock-bottom prices. By carefully patronizing a selection of local cafes and quality street stalls, it's surprisingly easy to enjoy three outstanding meals for less than US$10 a day.

Restaurants

Your journey through Thailand could also follow a gastronomic theme. Though Thai food seems vaguely Chinese to most Westerners, a surprising amount of individuality is found in Thai cuisine, a spicy and pungent mixture of curries, coconut creams, and tiny chilies that should be cautiously removed from each dish.

Dining choices in Thailand range from five-star hotel restaurants to simple foodstalls on the side of the road. First-time visitors sometimes dismiss hawker food as unclean and assume that any meal served on a rickety aluminum table must be inferior to a first-class restaurant. Nothing could be further from the truth. If a steady queue of Mercedeses waiting for noodle soup is any indication, hawker food provides stiff competition for many of Thailand's finer restaurants.

In fact, street food should be your first choice for several reasons. Large congregations of foodstalls in a single location ensure a greater array of food than in any single restaurant. Secondly, since there is virtually no overhead, prices are kept low—a filling and delicious meal can be served for less than US$2. But perhaps most importantly, foodstall dining is a great way to meet people, make friends, and gain some insight into Thai lifestyles.

Although restaurants and streetstalls are found throughout Thailand, certain towns have developed reputations as international food meccas. The best selection is found in Bangkok, where hundreds of hawkers prepare superb dishes at rock-bottom prices. Certainly the most exciting food venue is the night market in Chiang Mai.

PASSPORTS, VISAS, AND CERTIFICATES

Passports
Essential travel documents include a valid passport and the necessary visa. American passports are issued by the U.S. State Department at offices in most major cities and through state courts and certain post offices. Europeans and Australians can obtain passports from their respective governments. Allow plenty of time for processing, especially during the busy spring and summer months.

Visas
Visas are stamps placed in your passport by foreign governments that permit you to visit that country for a limited time and for a specified purpose, such as tourism or business. Visas are issued by embassies and consulates located both at home and in most large Asian cities. Several different types of visas are available.

Fifteen-day Visa: Visitors who intend to stay 15 days or less, and have sufficient funds and proof of onward passage, may enter the country without a visa. Immigration officers at the airport simply stamp your passport on arrival. The biggest problem with this option is that visa-free entry is difficult to extend, and visitors who overstay their allotted 15-day period are fined 100B per day by immigration officers at the airport. Travelers who intend to stay longer than 15 days should avoid the aggravation and obtain a visa in advance from a Thai diplomatic mission.

Thirty-day Transit Visa: One-month nonextendable transit visas cost US$10, but few visitors bother with this type of visa.

Sixty-Day Tourist Visa: The most popular option is the 60-day tourist visa, which costs US$15 and requires a valid passport and three passport photos. This visa must be utilized within 90 days from the date of issuance; do not apply for a visa earlier than three months before your arrival in Thailand. Tourist visas can be extended once for an additional 30 days.

Ninety-day Nonimmigrant Visa: A 90-day visa costs US$20 and is available to businessmen and visitors with valid reasons such as formal research or language studies. An official letter from your business or school in Thailand is usually necessary to obtain this visa. Employment is forbidden unless a work permit is obtained.

VISA OPTIONS

No Visa	15 days
Transit Visa	30 days
Tourist Visa	60 days
Nonimmigrant Visa	90 days

Multiple-entry Visas
Visitors intending to make several entries and exits from Thailand—and who want to avoid time-consuming delays at Thai immigration offices—can obtain multiple-entry visas from any Thai embassy or consulate. A double-entry tourist visa good for a total of four months in the kingdom costs US$30, twice the cost of a single tourist visa. A double-entry nonimmigrant visa is valid for 180 days, but visitors must leave the country after the first 90 days.

Travelers going to Burma can avoid some problems by obtaining a reentry visa for 500B at the Immigration Division on Soi Suan Plu in Bangkok.

THAI DIPLOMATIC OFFICES

Australia	111 Empire Circuit, Canberra 2600.	731149
	Exchange Bldg., 56 Pitt St., Sydney	
	464 Saint Kilda Rd., Melbourne	
Canada	85 Range Rd., #704, Ottawa, Ontario, K1N 8J6	(613) 237-0476
	250 University Ave., 7th floor, Toronto 110	
	1155 Dorchester Blvd., #1005, Montreal 102	
	700 W. George St., 26th floor, Vancouver	
Denmark	Norgesmindevej 1B, 2900 Hellerup, Copenhagen	01-62-50-10
France	8 Rue Greuze, Paris 75116.	4704-3222
England	30 Queens Gate, London SW7 5JB.	(01) 589-2834
Germany	Ubierstrasse 65, 5300 Bonn 2.	(0228) 3550-6568
Hong Kong	8 Cotton Tree Dr. 8th floor, Central.	521-6481
Italy	Via Nomentana 132, 00162 Rome.	832-0729
Japan	14-6 Kami Osaki 3-Chome, Shinagawa-ku, Tokyo.	441-1386
Malaysia	206 Jalan Ampang 504505, Kuala Lumpur	477222
	1 Jalan Tunkoabdul Rahman, Penang.	23352
	4426 Jalan Pengkalan Chepa, Kota Baru	(09) 782545
Netherlands	Buitenrustweg 1, 2517 Den Hague	070-452088
New Zealand	2 Cook St., Box 17-226, Wellington	735385
Philippines	107 Rada St., Makati, Manila.	815-4219
Singapore	370 Orchard Rd., Singapore 9	737-2158
Switzerland	Eigerstrasse 60, 3007 Bern	(031) 462281
U.S.A.	2300 Kalorma Rd. NW, Washington, D.C. 20008	(202) 667-1446
	801 N. Labrae Ave., Los Angeles, CA 90010	(213) 937-1894
	53 Park Place #505, New York, NY 10007	(212) 732-8166

Visa Extensions

Thailand is such a popular destination that large numbers of visitors decide to extend their visas. The 15-day entry permit and 30-day transit visa cannot be extended. Tourist visas can be extended once for 30 days for a fee of 500B, but only at the discretion of Thai immigration. Dress well or run the risk of having your extension denied!

Bring along three passport photographs and copies of the passport pages which show your personal data, visa, and entry stamps. Applications for extensions should be made two or three days in advance at regional offices located throughout the country, or at the Thai Immigration Division (tel. 286-7013) on Soi Suan Plu off Sathorn Rd. in Bangkok. Passport photo services and photocopy machines are located across the street.

Tax-clearance Certificate

Visitors who stay in Thailand over 90 days in a calendar year must, whether they have received any income or not, obtain a tax-clearance certificate by posting a 20,000B refundable bank guarantee or obtaining a personal guarantee from a landowning Thai citizen. The bank guarantee is unsuitable for aliens who don't intend to return to Thailand. The second type of guarantee is often given by the independent brokers and tax officers at the immigration office as a means to supplement their income.

Tax-clearance certificates must also be obtained by visitors with a nonimmigrant visa code B (business visa) and all permanent alien residents in Thailand.

International Health Certificates

Under the International Health Regulations adopted by the World Health Organization (WHO), a country, under certain conditions, may require from travelers an International Certificate of Vaccination against yellow fever. However, the WHO has recently eliminated the special page for cholera vaccinations. This international certificate is no longer required for entry into Thailand.

International Student Identity Card

The green-and-white ISIC card can help qualify you for discounts on airlines and some hotels in Thailand. Eligible students can obtain cards from STA and Council Travel offices worldwide.

Fake cards are sold at discount agencies in Bangkok on Khao San Rd. and near the Malaysia Hotel.

International Driver's License

International Driver's Licenses are available from local automobile associations such as AAA. Major car rental agencies such as Avis and Hertz may require this license, but I've never been asked to show a driver's license at any motorcycle rental agency.

International Youth Hostel Card

Though invaluable in Europe and expensive in Asian countries such as Japan, the IYHF card is of very limited use in Thailand, which only has a handful of hostels. Youth hostel offices throughout the world sell membership cards and their *International Youth Hostel Handbook* to Africa, America, Asia, and Australasia.

COMMUNICATIONS, MONEY, AND MEASUREMENTS

Mail

Mail can be received at large post offices via *poste restante,* a French term for general delivery. Instruct your friends to capitalize *and* underline your last name to prevent your mail being misfiled under your first name. You must show your passport and pay a small fee to pick up your mail. Letters are held for several months before being returned to sender. Mail should not be sent to embassies or American Express.

Mailing packages home is best done from major towns and tourist centers where post offices sometimes provide packing services. Packages are limited to 10 kilos; above that and you'll need to use private shipping firms. Use registered mail for important documents and keep all receipts to help trace missing parcels.

Telephone

Thailand has one of the best phone systems in Southeast Asia. Direct international calls can be made from Overseas Telephone and Telegraph centers by dialing 001, country code, area code, and local number. These centers are located near central post offices and are open 24

hours a day. Minimum charge is for three minutes, with person-to-person connections costing US$13 for the first three minutes and station-to-station calls for US$10.

Phone calls from hotels can be very expensive, since hotels routinely tack on stiff surcharges of up to 50% per call. From hotels, it's best to make a short call and have your friends call you back.

Local city calls from public phones with red hoods cost one *baht* (1B) for the first three minutes, with additional 1B coins needed after hearing multiple beeps. Long-distance calls within Thailand are made from silver phones with blue roofs.

International calls to Thailand can be made by dialing 011, country code (66), area code for the particular city, and local number. Area codes listed in this book include a zero at the front; Bangkok is 02 and Chiang Mai is 053. This 0 at the beginning of the area code is dropped when telephoning or faxing Thailand from overseas. For example, to reach Bangkok dial 011-66-2 plus the local number.

Electricity

Electric current is 200 volts at 50 cycles. A transformer and adapter are needed to operate 110-volt electric shavers and hair dryers.

Time

Thai time is seven hours ahead of GMT (London). Noon in Bangkok is 2100 the previous day in San Francisco and Los Angeles, 2300 in Chicago and New Orleans, and midnight in New York. Elsewhere, noon in Bangkok is 1700 in Auckland, 1500 in Sydney, 1300 in Perth, 0500 in London, and 0600 in Paris and Rome.

INTERNATIONAL CLOCK FOR THAILAND

San Francisco	-15
New York	-12
London	-7
Paris	-6
Sydney	+3

National Currency

Thailand's basic unit of currency, the *baht* (B), is pegged to a basket of currencies heavily weighted toward the dollar. Exchange rates are approximately 25 *baht* to the dollar. Rates fluctuate little against the dollar but swing somewhat against European currencies depending on their rates of exchange with the dollar.

Each *baht* is divided into 100 *stang*, although *stang* coins are rarely seen in circulation. Coins come in one *baht*, two *baht*, five *baht*, and 10 *baht*. Thai coinage is very confusing to Westerners since it's labeled in Thai script and identical coins have been minted in different sizes. For example, the 5B coin has progressively shrunk from a monstrous nickel-and-copper heavyweight down to the size of an American quarter, with various incarnations in the middle.

Bank notes are easy to distinguish since their values are printed in Arabic numerals and each note is of a different color. *Baht* notes come in denominations of 10B (brown), 20B (green), 100B (red), and 500B (purple).

There is no currency black market in Thailand.

Traveler's Checks

Smart travelers bring a combination of cash, traveler's checks, and a credit card. Each has its own advantages and disadvantages depending on the circumstances. Cash is useful in emergencies, so stash a few U.S. twenties in your pack. Most of your currency should be in the form of traveler's checks. Traveler's checks bring slightly better exchange rates at banks than cash, plus they can be quickly refunded if lost or stolen. To speed the refund process you must keep an accurate list of serial numbers and a record of when and where you cashed each check.

Traveler's checks are safe and convenient but certainly not free. Banks and companies that issue traveler's checks make their profit by charging a one percent fee when you purchase the checks and a hefty amount on the float. This double whammy can be minimized by purchasing traveler's checks from institutions that sell checks without the standard service charge. The float can be minimized by leaving most of your funds in your home bank and making periodic withdrawals or money transfers through a large international bank.

Large-denomination checks such as hundreds are easier to carry and cash than a massive pile of tens and twenties. Exchange rates are much better at banks than hotels. Banks are located in every town and village in Thailand and open Mon. to Fri. from 0900 to 1530. Exchange rates are almost identical at all banks—including airport banks— so searching out the best rate is a waste of time.

Credit Cards

Smart travelers also bring credit cards for several reasons. First, they're invaluable for major purchases such as airline tickets and electronic equipment. Many of the cards now include an insurance policy on plane tickets and purchases—an important benefit in case of disputes over fraudulent or nondelivered merchandise. Credit cards save money by letting you enjoy an interest-free one-month loan until the bill arrives.

Major credit cards also allow you to obtain cash advances from almost any bank in Thailand, an economical proposition since cash advances are normally converted into dollars at the more-favorable "interbank foreign exchange rate," the wholesale rate used by international banks. Obtaining cash with your credit card is extremely easy. You can, for example, walk into any branch of Thai Farmers Bank (the nation's largest bank with branches *everywhere*), present your credit card, fill out a short form, and have your money in less than 10 minutes. Remember that cash advances are generally regarded as loans with interest accruing from the moment of the loan. Have a friend back home pay your monthly Visa or MasterCard bill.

Bank Transfers

Most major banks in Thailand have international money-transfer operations which will wire money from your home account to their Asian representative. Before leaving on your vacation, open an account at an institution such as Bank of America, Citicorp, or American Express, and request a list of their representatives in Thailand. Funds can be transferred by telex or mail. Telex transfers are fast and convenient but expensive because of service charges (US$20 per transaction), the telex charge (US$20 each way), one percent commission on traveler's checks, and the currency spread. As an example, American Express offers check-cashing privileges and cash advances in Bangkok, but they charge a stiff US$80 transfer fee from the U.S. for the first US$2000, hardly a sensible way to receive funds from home.

Mail transfers take two or three weeks but they avoid telex charges. Another option is to open a managed account at a large stock brokerage firm such as Merrill Lynch and use their services. The secret to travel money management: keep your money working in a money market account, search for the lowest fees for transfers of funds, demand commission-free

traveler's checks, and open a bank account in Thailand.

Thai Bank Accounts And ATM Cards

Visitors who intend to stay in Thailand over a month should consider opening a savings account at a large Thai bank such as Thai Farmers or Bangkok Bank. Both have offices in every town in Thailand. Accounts can be opened in minutes by depositing your traveler's checks and providing a permanent address such as an apartment room number or the address of a Thai or expatriate friend. Room numbers from guesthouses or hotels are not considered permanent addresses.

The advantages are amazing: interest paid on your account is usually higher than back home; you will get a savings account card and bank book; money can be withdrawn from any branch in Thailand. You should also pick up an ATM card which can be used in most larger towns in Thailand for quick withdrawals. With a Thai bank account, you'll be making interest on your travelers checks, you don't need to carry travelers checks or much cash, and you can make withdrawals almost anywhere in Thailand. The sign of an informed traveler in Thailand is their Thai banking account and local ATM card.

Cash can also be obtained from ATMs with bank cards issued from an American bank. Virtually all U.S. banks belong to an ATM network that dispenses cash 24 hours a day. To find out the location of these outlets, call Cirrus (800-424-7787) or the Plus System (800-843-7587). Cirrus has 160 outlets in Thailand, including the airport, major hotels in Bangkok, and Siam Commercial Banks throughout the country.

HEALTH

Thailand is a surprisingly healthy place and it's very unlikely that you will lose even a single day to sickness. Immunizations and inoculations are no longer required for a visit to Thailand, though you should contact a doctor who specializes in travel medicine for a general checkup. Current recommendations can be checked by calling the Center for Disease Control (CDC) in Atlanta at (404) 639-2572 for general information and (404) 639-1610 for malaria tips. Another source of information is *Health Information for Interna-*

tional Travel, published annually by the CDC and sold by the U.S. Government Printing Office (202-783-3238). More up-to-date facts are published by the CDC in their biweekly "Blue Sheets."

Vaccinations

Your doctor will provide you with necessary shots, malaria pills, and perhaps the International Certificate of Vaccination, a small yellow booklet which records your immunizations. This card is occasionally demanded by immigration officials from visitors arriving from an area infected with yellow fever. Cholera and smallpox vaccination requirements for Thailand have been dropped, though vaccination records for tetanus/diphtheria, typhoid, measles, and polio shots should be checked by your doctor and boosted if necessary.

Malaria

After a general checkup and necessary immunizations, discuss the issue of malaria with your doctor. Malaria is a common problem in the jungle areas along the Cambodian and Burmese border, though most visitors have little to worry about. Travelers who plan to get well off the beaten track and explore remote jungles should take malaria pills, remain well covered, wear dark clothing, use mosquito nets, purchase insect repellents which contain deet (diethylmetatoluamide), and faithfully follow the recommended regimen of antimalarial pills.

The CDC recommends a weekly dosage of Mefloquine, sold in the U.S. under the trade name of Lariam. Mefloquine is a new antimalarial which has proven highly effective against both chloroquine- and Fansidar-resistant *P. falciparum* infections. Chloroquine, once the most popular weekly malarial pill, is no longer recommended since it is ineffective against chloroquine-resistant *P. falciparum*. Fansidar (pyrimethamine/sufadoxine) should also be avoided.

AIDS

Unlike the situation in the Western world, heterosexual intercourse is the most common cause of AIDS in Thailand. Former Population and Community Development Association (PDA) head Mechai Viravaidhya estimates that 50% of the prostitutes in Thailand carry the virus, and that up to 10% of the male population are infected. The epidemic is most advanced in the provinces of Northwestern Thailand, where government surveys estimate that over 75% of the prostitutes carry the AIDS virus, and up to 20% of the young men aged 20 to 24 are HIV positive.

The eerie quality of the raging epidemic is its invisibility. Most of those infected with AIDS have not yet developed symptoms and continue to engage in gay and heterosexual prostitution, unwittingly infecting their customers. Thailand's roaring sex-for-money trade will probably continue growing into the 1990s. And so will AIDS. Sexually active Westerners and Thais alike would do well to practice safe sex: complete abstinence.

Medical Insurance

The final two steps for predeparture planning are to pack a small medical kit and consider purchasing medical insurance. Keep your kit to the minimum since most inexpensive medical supplies are sold throughout Thailand. Short-term travel-insurance policies covering medical emergencies, trip cancellations, and flight insurance are sold by STA, other student travel groups, and private companies such as Cigna Travel Guard (800-826-1300), Access America (800-284-8300), and International SOS Assistance (800-523-8930). Before buying one of these short-term policies, read the fine print for exclusions and check your personal insurance plan to see if overseas medical treatment and evacuation are covered. No need to pay twice for the same services.

> *If the doors of perception were cleansed every thing would appear to man as it is, infinite.*
>
> —William Blake

SERVICES AND INFORMATION

TOURIST INFORMATION

The Tourist Authority of Thailand (TAT) can help with general travel information. Brochures and festival schedules can be requested from overseas TAT offices or picked up at the branches in Thailand.

Maps

Visitors are advised to purchase the Nelles Verlag map of Thailand, the two maps produced by Nancy Chandler, and the appropriate maps from Prannok Witthaya and Bangkok Guides. Maps are widely available in luxury hotels and at Asia and D.K. bookstores.

Nelles Verlag Thailand: The best map of Thailand can be purchased at bookstores throughout the country at lower prices than in the U.S. or Europe. Maps published by Shell and Esso are poor.

Latest Tours Guide to Bangkok and Thailand: Lists major bus routes in Bangkok—an absolute necessity for bus riders.

Map of Bangkok and *Map of Chiang Mai:* Both of these immensely useful and highly recommended maps are the personalized creations of artist Nancy Chandler, a former resident who offers her trustworthy advice on public markets, restaurants, and tourist attractions. Nancy now lives in the San Francisco Bay Area but makes annual research trips to update her maps.

Bangkok Guides: Thai mapmakers came of age in the early 1990s with the release of the

THAI TOURIST OFFICES

OVERSEAS

Australia	56 Pitt St., 12/F, Sydney 2000.	(02) 277549
England	49 Albemarle St., London WIX3FE	(01) 499-7670
France	90 Champs Elysees, Paris 75008	4562-8656
Germany	58 Bethmannstrasse, D-6000, Frankfurt.	(069) 295704
Hong Kong	Fairmont House #401, Central.	868-0732
Japan	Hibiya Mitsui Bldg., Yurakucho, Tokyo	(03) 580-6776
Malaysia	206 Jalan Ampang, Kuala Lumpur.	248-0958
Singapore	370 Orchard Rd..	235-7901
U.S.A.	5 World Trade Center #2449, New York, NY 10048	(212) 432-0433
	3400 Wilshire Blvd. #1101, Los Angeles, CA 90010	(213) 382-2353

DOMESTIC

Bangkok	4 Rajadamnern Nok Ave., 10100	(662) 282-1143
Chiang Mai	135 Chiang Mai-Lamphun Rd., 50000	(053) 248604
	Hat Yai Soi 2, Niphat Uthit 3 Rd., 90110	(074) 243747
Kanchanaburi	Saengchuto Rd., 71000	(034) 511200
Korat	2102 Mittraphab Rd., 30000	(044) 243427
Pattaya	382 Chai Hat Rd., 20260.	(038) 428750
Phitsanulok	209 Boromtrilokanat Rd., 65000	(055) 252742
Phuket	73 Phuket Rd., 83000	(076) 212213
Surat Thani	5 Talat Mai Rd., 84000.	(077) 282828

highly detailed *Guide Map of Chiang Rai,* a godsend for motorcyclists exploring Northern Thailand. Bangkok Guides also produces the useful *Guide Map of Southern Thailand, Guide Map of Krabi,* and *Guide Map of Ko Samui.* Contact Bangkok Guides at 40/6 Moo 8, Soi Onnuch, Suan Luang, Phrakhanong, Bangkok 10250, tel. (02) 311-1439.

Prannok Witthaya Maps: Maps from Prannok Witthaya are somewhat confusing but cover regions missed by Bangkok Guides. Their *Map of Chiang Mai & Around* is an important resource for motorcycle touring west of Chiang Mai. Better efforts include their well-researched maps to Pattaya, Ko Samui, Phuket, and Krabi. Prannok Witthaya, 823/32 Prannok Rd., Bangkok 10700, tel. (02) 411-2954.

National Highways Department Maps: Four sectional maps of Thailand are published by the Highways Department of the Thai government. These are helpful for finding highway numbers but of limited use for most visitors since smaller towns are only marked in Thai script. Available from the TAT office in Bangkok.

United States Geological Survey Maps: Topographic maps originally produced by the U.S. government are available in D.K. bookstores throughout Thailand. Although somewhat useful for independent trekkers, superior locally produced maps are available from Prannok Witthaya and Bangkok Guides.

Association of Siamese Architects Maps: These four stylish maps *(Bangkok, Grand Palace, Canals of Thonburi, Ayuthaya)* are well drawn, but overpriced and useless except for the guide to Thonburi temples.

Travel Costs

The basic rule for estimating costs is that time and money are inversely related. Short-term travelers must spend substantially more for guaranteed hotel reservations and air connections. Long-term travelers willing to use local transportation, budget hotels, and street stalls can travel more cheaply in Thailand than almost anywhere else in the world. Expenses vary widely, but many budget travelers report that land costs average about US$20-25 per day or US$500-800 per month. Total costs can be divided into four main categories: airfare, local transportation, accommodations, and food.

Airfare: Airfare takes a big chunk of every-body's budget, but you'll be surprised at how many kilometers can be covered per dollar with some planning and careful shopping. Roundtrip airfare from the United States or Europe should average around US$800. Except for a few short flights, there is little need for internal air flights.

Remember that independent travelers should buy a one-way ticket to Bangkok and onward tickets from travel agencies along the way. Discount agencies in Thailand offer some of the world's lowest prices because of fierce competition, and an unwillingness of local agents to follow fares suggested by international consortiums.

Local Transportation: Trains, buses, taxis, and other forms of internal transportation are ridiculously cheap by Western standards. For example, a 36-hour train ride from Hat Yai to Bangkok costs under US$20 in second-class, an overnight bus from Bangkok to Chiang Mai costs US$12, a taxi from the Bangkok airport to most hotels costs US$8.

Useful Telephone Numbers

Useful phone numbers of U.S. government agencies include the Citizens Emergency Center (202-647-5226) for the latest travel advisories and emergency assistance, Bureau of Public Affairs (202-647-6575) for government travel publications and telephone numbers of overseas embassies, and Desk Officers (202-647-4000) for specific information on Thailand. Travel agents experienced with Thailand are a godsend but as rare as whale's teeth; student travel agencies are your best hope. Best of all, seek out and talk with other travelers who have been to Thailand.

Travel Newsletters, Magazines, And Clubs

Great Expeditions: Detailed, concise articles on off-the-beaten-track destinations. Geared to the young and adventurous traveler. Highly recommended. US$18/six issues. Free sample. P.O. Box 18036, Raleigh, NC 27609, tel. (800) 743-3639.

International Travel News: Big, opinionated, and highly informative monthly magazine with dozens of honest travel articles. Recent stories have covered ceremonies of Indonesia, adventure in New Zealand, and trekking in Thailand, plus columns on cruises, readers' tips, and seniors abroad. An excellent deal. US$14/12 issues. 2120 28th St., Sacramento, CA 95818, tel. (916) 457-3643.

Condé Nast Traveler: Outstanding writing, photography, and graphics plus hard-hitting commentary and authoritative advice make this the finest travel magazine on the market. Europe, America, and Africa but not much on Thailand or Southeast Asia. US$15/12 issues. Box 52469, Boulder, CO 80321, tel. (800) 777-0700.

Globetrotters Club: England's leading club for independent-budget-world travelers. Membership includes a handbook, six annual newsletters, and a list of over 1,200 members who occasionally accept homestays. Monthly travel club meetings are held in New York, southern California, and in London at 52 St. Martins Lane. Volunteers are encouraged to organize monthly travel slide shows in their communities. US$14/year, US$5 initiation fee. BCM/Roving, London WC1N 3XX, England.

Consumer Reports Travel Letter: A 12-page monthly newsletter with dependable advice on airline and hotel discounts, auto rentals, coupon books, rail travel, and a limited number of destinations. Overpriced but very professional. US$37/12 issues. Subscription Department, Box 51366, Boulder, CO 80321.

Travel Bookstores

Bookstores located in major cities carry a mind-boggling selection of travel guides, maps, accessories, and literature. For rare, out-of-print editions contact Cellar Books (313-861-1776), Oriental Book Company (1713 East Colorado Blvd., Pasadena, CA 91106, tel. 818-577-2413), and Oxus Books (121 Astonville Street, London SW18 5AQ, tel. 01-870-3854). The following bookstores offer catalogs: Book Passage, tel. (800) 321-9785; Easy Going, tel. (800) 233-3533; Phileas Fogg's, tel. (800) 233-FOGG; Compleat Traveller, tel. (212) 685-9007; Back Door Press, tel. (206) 771-8308; Travel Books Unlimited, tel. (301) 951-8533; Globe Corner, tel. (800) 358-6013; Forsyth Travel, tel. (800) 367-7984; and the Literate Traveler, tel. (310) 398-8781.

Book Catalogs

A small number of publishers specialize in books on Thailand and Southeast Asia.

American Publishers: Contact the following private companies for their latest catalog:

Hippocrene (171 Madison Ave., New York, NY 10016, fax 718-454-1391), Humanities Press (800-221-3845), Globe Pequot Press (800-243-0495), Third World Resources (Data Center: 415-835-4692), Intercultural Press (207-846-5168), Lawyers Committee for Human Rights (212-629-6170), Greenwood Press (203-226-3571), Waveland Press (312-634-0091), Schenkman (802-767-3702), and Anima (717-267-0087).

University Presses: University presses which offer books on Asia include Yale (203-432-0940), Cornell (800-666-2211), Columbia (914-591-9111), University of California (800-822-6657), and the University of Hawaii (2840 Kolowalu Street, Honolulu, HI 96822).

Asian Publishers: Many of the best books on Asia and Southeast Asia are published overseas and rarely distributed in the West. Contact Oxford Press (18th floor, Warwick House, Taikoo Trading Estate, 28 Tong Chong St., Quarry Bay, Hong Kong), Times Editions (Times Centre, 1 New Industrial Rd., Singapore 1953), Graham Brash (36 C Prinsep St., Singapore 0718), R. Ian Lloyd Productions (18A Tanjong Pagar Rd., Singapore 0208), Select Books (19 Tanglin Rd. #03-15, Tanglin Shopping Center, Singapore 1024), and the Institute of Southeast Asian Studies (Heng Mui Keng Terrace, Pasir Panjang, Singapore 0511).

Thai Publishers: The best selection of books on Thailand is published in Thailand and rarely reaches the U.S. or Europe. Contact Asia Books (5 Sukumvit Rd. Soi 61, Bangkok 10112), D.K. Books (90/21-25 Rajaprarob, Makkasan, GPO 2916, Bangkok 10400), and White Lotus Press (GPO Box 1141, Bangkok 10501).

TOURS, STUDY, AND EXCHANGE

University Research Expeditions Program: The University of California invites volunteers to participate in a variety of research projects and assist field researchers with studies on marine biology, zoology, anthropology, and archaeology in both the U.S. and abroad. UREP, University of California, Berkeley, CA 94720, tel. (510) 642-6586.

San Jose State University: Educational programs led by professors and local experts. Recent tours include a visit to "stress-free" Thailand

. . . 10 days on Ko Samui! SJSU Travel Program, Office of Continuing Education, San Jose, CA 95192, tel. (408) 924-2680.

Smithsonian Associates Travel Program: Field expeditions and art tours led by university professors. Smithsonian Institution, 1100 Jefferson Dr. SW, Washington, D.C. 20560, tel. (202) 357-4700.

Interhostel: Designed for adults over 50 years of age, Interhostel sponsors educational programs in cooperation with overseas universities such as in Chiang Mai and Bangkok. University of New Hampshire Interhostel Program, 6 Garrison Ave., Durham, NH 03824, tel. (800) 733-9753.

International Research Expeditions: This nonprofit organization matches public volunteers with field research scientists throughout the world. Recent excavations include the prehistoric archaeology of Southern Thailand. 140 University Dr., Menlo Park, CA 94025, tel. (415) 323-4228.

Distant Horizons: Cultural and educational tours led by art historians and museum curators whose specialized knowledge provides a deeper understanding. 679 Tremont St., Boston, MA 02118, tel. (800) 333-1240.

Joel Greene Tours: Special-interest tours that emphasize art history, anthropology, archaeology, scuba, and conchology. Conchology? In Sumatra? Joel personally leads all the tours. Box 99331, San Francisco, CA 94109, tel. (415) 776-7199.

Environmental Tours

Earthwatch: This nonprofit institution sponsors scholarly field research aimed at preserving the world's endangered habitats and species. Projects cost US$800-2500. 680 Mount Auburn St., Box 403N, Watertown, MA 02272, tel. (617) 926-8200, fax (617) 926-8532.

International Expeditions: Nature travel which promotes the philosophy of environmental awareness and conservation through tourism. Closely involved with rainforest preservation in the Amazon; few tours to Southeast Asia. One Environs Park, Helena, AL 35080, tel. (800) 633-4734, fax (205) 428-1714.

Journeys: Explorations which focus on local cultures and natural environments. Asian expeditions concentrate on Nepal and India, with two short excursions in Thailand. 4011 Jackson Rd., Ann Arbor, MI 48103, tel. (800) 255-8735, fax (313) 665-2945.

Voyagers International: Voyagers organizes worldwide natural-history tours for leading nonprofit conservation organizations, plus individual programs led by naturalists and professional photographers. Box 915, Ithaca, NY 14851, tel. (800) 633-0299, fax (607) 257-3699.

Questers Nature Tours: Nature tours to the national parks of Costa Rica, Hawaii, Mexico, Trinidad, Indonesia, Malaysia, and Thailand. 257 Park Ave. S, New York, NY 10010, tel. (800) 468-8668, fax (212) 473-0178.

Geostar Travel Tours: Small outfit with a limited number of nature expeditions to Central America, Africa, and Malaysia. 1240 Berglund Court, Santa Rosa, CA 95403, tel. (707) 579-2420, (800) 624-6633, fax (707) 579-2704.

RESPONSIBLE TOURING

Before selecting a tour company, you might want to consider the following guidelines suggested by the Center for Responsible Tourism. If your prospective tour group or travel agent fails the test, investigate the Adventure Travel groups described on pages 25-27.

1. Does the tour organizer demonstrate a cultural and environmental sensitivity? How are local people and culture portrayed in advertising brochures?

2. Who benefits financially from your trip? What percentage of your dollar stays in the country you visit rather than ending up with an international hotel chain, airline, or travel agency?

3. Is a realistic picture of your host country presented, or a sanitized version packaged for tourists?

4. Will you use local accommodations and transportation or be assigned to tourist facilities that prevent a real understanding of the environment?

5. Does your travel itinerary allow adequate time for meeting with local people? If it doesn't, don't go!

6. Has the tour operator or travel agent mentioned anything beyond what's listed in the glossy advertisements? Ask about the social, economic, and political realities of Southeast Asia.

Select Tours: Inexpensive short-stay visits to Bangkok, Chiang Mai, and Phuket. A small company with unique offerings. P.O. Box 210, Redondo Beach, CA 90277, tel. (310) 343-0880, (800) 356-6680, fax (310) 318-2325.

Special Interest Tours

Close Up Expeditions: Small group photographic travel adventures designed to meet the needs of shutterbugs. Tours are led by professionals to Thailand and Burma. Lyon Travel Services, 1031 Ardmore Ave., Oakland, CA 94610, tel. (510) 465-8955, fax (510) 465-1237.

Trains Unlimited: Railroad enthusiast tours to South America, Europe, South Africa, and possibly the steam locomotives in the Philippines. 235 W. Pueblo Ave., Reno, NV 89509, tel. (800) 359-4870.

Archaeological Tours: Specialized tours led by distinguished scholars such as the director of Burmese studies at Northern Illinois University. 30 E. 42nd St., #1202, New York, NY 10017, tel. (212) 986-3054, fax (212) 370-1561.

Valour Tours: Military tours for veterans to the battlefields of Europe and the Pacific theater. Southeast Asia programs include Bataan day in Manila and the Leyte landing. Box 1617, Schoonmaker Building, Sausalito, CA 94965, tel. (415) 332-7850.

Reality Tours

Augsburg College: The Center for Global Education coordinates global education and foreign policy seminars which examine the problems of international development from the perspective of the poor and disenfranchised. Travel groups have studied health care in Nicaragua, women of color in El Salvador, and land reform in the Philippines. 731 21st Ave. S, Minneapolis, MN 55454, tel. (612) 330-1159.

Global Exchanges: People-to-people political tours to learn firsthand about pressing issues confronting third-world nations. Meetings are arranged with labor organizers, peace activists, farmers, environmentalists, and government leaders concerned with land reform. 2141 Mission #202, San Francisco, CA 94110, tel. (415) 255-7296.

Food First: Reality tours which offer firsthand experience of the economic and political realties of the poor in the U.S. and abroad. Past groups have visited Haiti, Nicaragua, El Salvador, and Kerala, India. 145 Ninth St., San Francisco, CA 94103, tel. (415) 864-8555.

Study Abroad

Council on International Educational Exchange: America's foremost organization concerned with international education and student travel, CIEE and their travel subsidiary, Council Travel, are an excellent source of information. Ask for *Work, Study, Travel Abroad* for US$13, *Volunteer* for US$9, and the free booklet, *Basic Facts on Study Abroad*. Undergraduate programs on Thai history and culture are given at Khon Kaen University. 205 E. 42nd St., New York, NY 10017, tel. (212) 661-1414.

Institute for International Education: The largest educational-exchange agency in America works closely with the U.S. government, World Bank, universities, private foundations, and corporations to promote international development. Their reference books are expensive but extremely comprehensive. 809 United Nations Plaza, New York, NY 10017, tel. (212) 883-8200.

Experiment in International Living: The oldest organization of its kind in the world, the Experiment promotes world understanding through homestays, language training, and graduate study programs. Semester abroad programs are given in Bali and Chiang Mai. College Semester Abroad, School for International Training, Kipling Rd., Brattleboro, VT 05302, tel. (800) 451-4465.

Universities in Thailand: Applications can also be made directly to universities although the response rate is rather dismal. Try Dr. Mathana Santiwat, Academic Affairs, Bangkok University, 40/4 Rama IV Rd., Bangkok 10110; International Students Program, Mahidol University, Nakhon Pathom 73170; International Studies Program, Khon Kaen University, Khon Kaen. Further suggestions are appreciated.

Working Abroad

Teaching English: One of the few opportunities for working in Thailand is teaching English in Bangkok, Chiang Mai, or other large towns. Pay is very low (US$3-8 per hour) when compared to Japan or Korea (US$10-25 per hour), but you'll have an opportunity to study the culture, attempt to learn the language, and develop friendships with the people.

Teaching opportunities are limited to universities and teachers' colleges, private English-language schools, and fly-by-night operations run from somebody's house. Universities throughout the country pay about US$400 per month plus a small housing allowance. Private English-language schools such as the American University (AUA) and YMCA pay well but the competition is keen. Fly-by-night language schools which advertise in the guesthouses on Khao San Rd. are the lowest-paying jobs.

WorldTeach: WorldTeach is a nonprofit social-service program which places volunteer teachers in countries such as China, Costa Rica, Kenya, and Thailand where over 40 teachers work together with the Population and Community Development Association and Thai Ministry of Education. Programs require a bachelor's degree but previous teaching experience and Thai language skills are not required. Harvard Institute for International Development, One Eliot St., Cambridge, MA 02138, tel. (617) 495-5527, fax (617) 495-1239.

Homestay Programs

Servas: The world's largest homestay program is designed for thoughtful travelers who wish to build world peace and international understanding through person-to-person contacts. Travelers' fees are US$45 annually while hosts contribute US$15 per year. Servas has thousands of host families in Europe and America but only a handful in Asia. 11 John St., Room 706, New York, NY 10038, tel. (212) 267-0252.

Hospitality Exchange: A small but spirited homestay group useful in America and western Europe. Hosts tend to be college-educated professionals in their mid-forties perhaps acting on cooperative values fostered in the sixties. Membership is only US$15, but you must be willing to be both a host and a traveler. 116 Coleridge St., San Francisco, CA 94110, tel. (415) 826-8248.

WHAT TO TAKE

Luggage

Overpacking is perhaps the most serious mistake made by first-time travelers. Experienced vagabonders know that heavy and bulky luggage absolutely guarantees a hellish vacation. Travel light and you'll be *free* to choose your style of travel. With a single carry-on pack weighing less than 10 kilos you can board the plane assured that your bags won't be pilfered, damaged, or lost by baggage handlers. You're first off the plane and cheerfully skip the long wait at the baggage carousel. You grab the first bus and get the best room at the hotel. Porters with their smiling faces and greased palms become somebody else's problem.

First consideration should be given to your bag. The modern solution to world travel is a convertible backpack/shoulder bag with zip-away shoulder straps. Huge suitcases that withstand gorilla attacks and truck collisions are best left to group tours and immigrant families moving to a new country. Serious trekking packs with outside frames are only suitable for the genuine backpackers they were designed for. Your bag should have an internal-frame, single-cell, lockable compartment without outside pockets to tempt thieves. A light, soft, and functional bag should fit under an airplane seat and measure no more than 18 by 21 by 13 inches. Impossible, you say? It's done every day by thousands of smart and experienced travelers who know they are the most liberated people on the road.

Packing

Second consideration is what to pack. The rule of thumb is that total weight should never exceed 10 kilos (22 pounds). Avoid vagabondage by laying out everything you *think* you need and then cut the pile in half. To truly appreciate the importance of traveling light, pack up and take a practice stroll around your neighborhood on the hottest day of the year.

Take the absolute minimum and do your shopping on the road. The reasons are obvious: Asia is a giant shopping bazaar filled with everything from toothpaste to light cotton clothing, prices are much lower than back home, and local products are perfectly suited for the weather.

Half of your pack will be filled with clothing. Minimize by bringing only two sets of garments:

wash one, wear one. A spartan wardrobe means freedom and flexibility, plus it's great fun to purchase a new wardrobe when the old clothing no longer comes clean. Give some serious thought to what you *don't* need. Sleeping bags, parkas, bedding, and foul-weather gear are completely unnecessary in Thailand. Experienced travelers buy their umbrellas when it rains and sweaters when it gets chilly.

Then pack everything into individual plastic bags. Put underwear and socks in one bag, shirts in another, medical and sewing supplies into a third. Place the larger bags with pants

and shirts at the bottom of your pack and smaller packages with books and socks at the top. Plastic compartmentalization keeps your bag neat and organized, and possibly even dry when the longtail boat capsizes in Northern Thailand! Here's a handy list of suggested items: two pairs of long pants—one casual, one formal; one stylish pair of shorts; two short-sleeved shirts with pockets; two pairs of underwear and socks; a modest bathing suit; one pair of comfortable walking shoes; sandals or rubber thongs; a mini towel; a medical kit; a sewing kit; two small padlocks; and a Swiss Army knife.

GETTING THERE

PLANNING YOUR TRIP

The basic overland route runs between Southern Thailand and Bangkok, with excursions to the east coast, northeastern Thailand, and the north. Tramped since the hippie days of the '60s, today it's a busy path firmly networked with hotels, restaurants, and other facilities for value-minded overlanders.

To add to those remote and exotic destinations in Thailand, many travelers make side trips to Burma (Myanmar), Hong Kong, Malaysia, the Philippines, and Indonesia. Burma can be reached on an inexpensive roundtrip ticket from Bangkok, or visited as a stop en route to India. The Philippines can be easily reached on roundtrip tickets from Bangkok, although more adventurous travelers might consider entering or exiting Manila from Kota Kinabalu. Because Indonesia's outer islands such as Kalimantan and Sulawesi are so time-consuming to properly explore, these are often considered separate journeys starting from Singapore.

After touring Thailand and Southeast Asia, you'll want to continue your Asian odyssey through the Indian subcontinent, north to Japan, or eastward through the South Pacific. Two popular options from Bangkok include a flight to India or Nepal via Burma, or a flight to Japan via Hong Kong. Options from Bali include a direct flight to Australia, an overland journey across Nusa Tenggara followed by the short flight from Timor to Darwin, or a return flight to Singapore with stops in Sulawesi or Kalimantan. No matter

what route, it's a grand adventure through one of the world's great regions.

Routes From America

Planning your route begins with your point of origin. Thailand is an important link in any round-the-world journey, whether beginning from the United States, Australia, or Europe.

Northern Loop: The northern Pacific loop includes stops in Japan, Korea, Taiwan, and Hong Kong before continuing into China or down to Bangkok. This one-way ticket—often on an airline such as Korean Air or China Air—costs under US$700 from budget travel agencies in San Francisco and Los Angeles.

South Pacific Loop: The southern Pacific loop includes stops in the South Pacific, New Zealand, and Australia before arriving in Bali and continuing up to Thailand. This ticket—often standby on UTA—costs under US$900 to Bali from the same agencies.

Roundtrip: A popular and relatively inexpensive itinerary begins with the northern Pacific loop, travels through Thailand and Southeast Asia, and is followed by a journey across the South Pacific back to the States. This outstanding trip covers Japan and Northeast Asia, Southeast Asia, Australia, New Zealand, and the South Pacific for under US$2000 in total airfares.

Routes From Australia

Travelers from Australia heading to Thailand often fly direct to Bali or Singapore, although dozens of routes are far more intriguing. Timor is an inexpensive and adventurous gateway from Darwin. From Timor, you can island-hop by plane or public bus across Nusa Tenggara to Bali. Another possibility is the short flight from Cairns to Port Moresby in Papua New Guinea, followed by flights to Jayapura on Irian Jaya, the Moluccas, Sulawesi, and finally Bali.

Bali to Bangkok generally involves overland transportation to Jakarta, from where several airlines fly to Singapore. Southern Thailand and Bangkok can be easily reached by train, bus, or plane from Singapore.

Routes From Europe

Europeans have the choices of overlanding, direct flights to Bangkok, or inexpensive charters which include stops in the Middle East or India. Budget agencies listed below can advise on exact routings and current prices.

In addition to the large international carriers, chartered flights are available on smaller airlines. Condor Airlines of Germany flies from Frankfurt to Chiang Mai and Surat Thani, the closest major airport to Ko Samui. Spain's Air Europa flies from Barcelona and Madrid to Bangkok via Bahrain, France's Corsair International flies from Paris to Bangkok, Switzerland's Balair flies from Zurich to Phuket, Finland's Finnair flies from Helsinki to Bangkok, and Finland's Martinair flies from Amsterdam to Bangkok and Phuket.

Travel Time And Itineraries

Allow as much time as possible. With only two or three weeks, it's much better to visit a single place such as Northern Thailand than attempt the if-it's-Tuesday-it-must-be-Phuket tour.

Travelers with an open schedule will find that Southeast Asia divides itself into convenient boxes which correspond to the length of visa. For example, Thailand, the Philippines, and Indonesia grant most nationalities a two-month stay—just about an ideal amount of time to spend in each country. Burma grants two weeks, while most visitors spend about a week in Singapore and Hong Kong.

Thailand is a big place that needs at least a month to be properly explored. Visitors on shorter schedules should consider an organized tour or limit themselves to a few destinations such as Bangkok, Chiang Mai, and an island of their choice.

BY PLANE

Thailand is centrally located in the heart of Southeast Asia and served by over 50 international airlines from all major world capitals. Most international airlines fly to Bangkok's Don Muang International Airport, though direct flights are also available to Penang, Hat Yai, and Chiang Mai.

Travelers on a very short holiday (under three weeks) should purchase roundtrip tickets from their homeland to ensure reserved seats. Consider a package tour, which often includes discounted hotels and internal flights to popular destinations.

Travelers with over a month should skip roundtrip tickets and purchase one-way tickets to Bangkok. All future travel arrangements should be made in Thailand, an option which adds flexibility and saves money since Thai travel agents sell some of the world's cheapest airline tickets.

Air From North America

Thai Airways International: Asian carriers are considered some of the finest in the world in terms of safety records, service, and food, as shown by readers polls in *Condé Nast Traveler* which consistently place Thai International in the world's top 10. Thai International (tel. 800-426-5204) flies daily from Seattle and Toronto via Tokyo (four times weekly) or Taipei (three times weekly). Roundtrip fare from Seattle is US$1124 during the low season and US$1231 high season. Thai also provides direct service from Los Angeles to Bangkok via Seoul three times weekly, the fastest route to Thailand.

Thai International fares are somewhat higher than discounted fares from consolidators, but they have fewer restrictions and cancellation penalties. Thai International also runs promotional fares, however, that often match, or beat, fares from discounters. For example, roundtrip promotion fares during the winter months from Dec. to March cost just US$840, a great deal on a first-class airline.

The merger of Thai International and Thai Airways Company (the domestic airline) benefits the traveler, who can now purchase international and domestic air tickets from a single source. Thai International also offers reasonably priced package tours that include transportation, accommodations, and sightseeing.

United Airlines: United Airlines (tel. 800-538-2929) flies daily to Bangkok from Canada (Toronto and Vancouver) and major U.S. cities via Tokyo, Taipei, or Seoul. Roundtrip fares are US$1124 from the West Coast and US$1440 from New York. United also offers low-priced promotional fares during the winter. United (tel. 800-328-6877) sells organized tours.

Northwest Airlines: Northwest Airlines (tel. 800-447-4747) flies daily from Los Angeles or San Francisco, and New York via Tokyo, to Bangkok. Daily service from Toronto via Detroit or Los Angeles costs US$1566. Fares are identical to those of Thai International and United.

Canadian Airlines International: Canadian (tel. 800-426-7000) flies daily from Toronto and Montreal via Vancouver to Bangkok. Promotional fares are available during the winter months, the best time to visit Thailand.

Other Airlines: Korean Air, China Air, and other Asian-based airlines offer super-APEX flights from West Coast cities to Bangkok for US$900-1100. Discounted flights for US$750-850 are available from budget agencies and wholesalers which advertise in major metropolitan newspapers. These flights are often fully booked in advance, so book several months in advance of your departure date. Budget agencies such as student services and consolidators are described below.

Air From Europe

Thai International, British Airways, Philippine Airlines, and Qantas offer direct flights from London to Bangkok for about US$1800. Other major

European airlines fly direct to Bangkok at similar prices.

Discounted fares are available from smaller airlines such as Kuwait Airlines, Gulf Air, Royal Jordanian, and Aeroflot. These flights require a time-consuming change of planes in their home airports.

Budget tickets are available from discount agencies such as Trailfinders (tel. 01-603-1515), Hann Overland (tel. 01-834-7367), and other wholesalers listed in *Time Out* and *TNT* magazines.

Air From Australia

Regular one-way economy tickets cost A$1700 from Sydney and Melbourne and A$1400 from Perth. Advance-purchase one-way tickets cost A$950 from Sydney and Melbourne and A$650 from Perth. These tickets must be booked and purchased at least 21 days in advance.

Cheap-flights specialists include Student Travel Australia, Travel Specialists (tel. 02-267-9122), and Sydney Flight Centre (tel. 02-221-2666).

Air From Southeast Asia

Flights are also available from nearby Asian destinations. Two of the most useful flights are from Sumatra to Phuket via Penang, and from Penang to Phuket. These flights are quick, reasonably priced, and save a full day of land travel.

Current estimated fares to Bangkok from the following cities:

Calcutta-Bangkok	US$180
Hong Kong-Bangkok	US$200
Jakarta-Bangkok	US$260
Kathmandu-Bangkok	US$240
Kuala Lumpur-Bangkok	US$160
Manila-Bangkok	US$280
Singapore-Bangkok	US$180
Taipei-Bangkok	US$280
Tokyo-Bangkok	US$440

Air Around Southeast Asia

Airfare around Southeast Asia need not be any more expensive per kilometer than airfare in the West. Discount tickets are sold in almost every major city from student and budget travel agencies. Check prices, do some comparison shopping, and carefully examine tickets and restrictions before handing over your money. En-

---

AIRLINE 800 NUMBERS

Cathy Pacific	(800) 233-2742
Garuda	(800) 332-2223
Malaysian	(800) 421-8641
Northwest	(800) 225-2525
Philippines	(800) 435-9725
Singapore	(800) 742-3333
Thai	(800) 426-5204
United	(800) 241-6522

sure that you have a confirmed ticket and not just standby. Confirmed tickets have an OK sign next to the destination; RQ means request and refers to a standby.

Don't believe agents who claim they have the lowest prices in all of Southeast Asia. Tickets are cheapest in the city of origin, so buy your tickets from Bangkok in Bangkok and your tickets from Singapore in Singapore.

ASEAN Promotional Fares are discounted roundtrip tickets that may help plan your Asian vacation. Sample fares include Bangkok-Manila-Jakarta-Bangkok for US$550, Bangkok-Singapore-Manila-Bangkok for US$460, and Bangkok-Bali-Jakarta-Bangkok for US$550.

Departure Tax

Bangkok airport departure tax is 200B for international flights and 20B for domestic. Passengers in transit must also pay these taxes.

OTHER MODES

Trains From Malaysia

The *International Express (IE)* departs Singapore every morning and arrives in Kuala Lumpur by nightfall. Visitors may overnight in the Malaysian capital or continue north by night train to Butterworth, the terminus for Penang. The *IE* departs Butterworth the following day around 1300, crosses the Thai border, and arrives in Hat Yai about three hours later. The *IE* departs Hat Yai at 1700 and arrives in Bangkok early the following morning. Schedules change frequently and should be double-checked with the stationmasters in Singapore or Malaysia.

The *IE* is limited to first- and second-class and is somewhat expensive because of supplemental charges for a/c, superior classes, and sleeping berths. The Singapore to Bangkok train costs US$100 in first-class coach with sleeper and takes 41 hours, including a 10-hour layover in Kuala Lumpur.

While the 1,860-km *International Express* from Singapore to Bangkok has romantic appeal and is probably the most luxurious train in Southeast Asia, it's a long and exhausting journey best experienced in shorter segments.

Ordinary trains no longer run between Malaysia and Thailand. Diesels from Butterworth terminate at the border town of Padang Besar, from where travelers can walk across to Thailand and wait for public transport. This transfer is very time-consuming; most travelers prefer a private bus or shared taxi from Butterworth or Kota Baru.

Bus From Malaysia

Crossing the Thai border by public bus on the west coast can be tricky. Most buses terminate at Changlun, a small and isolated Malaysian town some 20 km from the border. From Changlun, you must hitchhike the distance to Sadao in Southern Thailand—not an easy task. Private buses are faster and more convenient. Buses direct from Penang to Hat Yai, Ko Samui, and Phuket can be booked through travel agents in Penang.

Public transport on the east coast of Peninsular Malaysia is fairly straightforward. Ordinary buses from Kota Baru terminate at the Thai border, a one-km walk along the train tracks to Sungai Golok in Thailand. Both trains and public buses leave Sungai Golok for Hat Yai and Bangkok.

Taxi From Malaysia

Shared taxis are fast, comfortable, and well priced. This option avoids getting stranded at the border waiting for a bus or train. Share taxis—usually lumbering old Mercedeses or Chevys—can be found in Penang at the waterfront taxi stand and in Georgetown downstairs from the bus terminal. Budget hotels in Penang can arrange pick-up directly from your hotel.

Share taxis also leave from the central taxi stand in Kota Baru. These terminate at the border from where you go through immigration and catch a *tuk tuk* to the train or bus station in Sungai Golok.

Sea From Malaysia

Looking for something unusual? Longtailed boats depart several times daily from Kuala Perlis in Malaysia for Satun in Southern Thailand, a useful service for visitors coming from Langkawi. Be sure to have your passport stamped by immigration officials in Satun.

Buses continue up to Hat Yai and points north. Asia Voyages Pansea (described below) sails from Sumatra and Penang to Phuket. Private services from Langkawi to Phuket are also available on a monthly basis.

Freighters

Freighters are working cargo ships which accept a limited number of passengers on their long journeys. The biggest drawback is the scarcity of passenger freighters which travel to and from Southeast Asia. Presently, only Chilean Lines (65-70 days, US$5500-6000), Lykes, and Pace Lines offer service from the U.S. West Coast to the Orient.

Contact Freighter World Cruises (tel. 818-449-3106) or TravLtips (tel. 800-872-8584) for information and reservations. Both publish freighter newsletters, as does the Freighter Travel Club of America, Box 12693, Salem, OR 97309. Another excellent resource is *Ford's Freighter Travel Guide*, available from Ronald Howard, 19448 Londelius Street, Northridge, CA 91324, tel. (818) 701-7414.

TICKET TIPS
AND TRAVEL ALTERNATIVES

Thailand can be reached on dozens of airlines at all possible prices. Airline tariffs vary widely and substantial savings can be made by using legal loopholes and the services of a well-trained travel agent.

First, read the local newspapers and then call airline, cruise, student, and discount-travel agencies for ticket and tour information. Contact all the national tourist offices for more information. Serious travelers can plan their itinerary and discover obscure air routes by studying the *Official Airline Guide* at the library. Let a travel agent do the booking.

Another consideration is that some countries require incoming travelers to show a ticket out of the country. This could be an onward plane ticket or a miscellaneous charge order (MCO). The best option is to purchase the cheapest ticket and get a refund later on. To save time and hassles, buy your onward ticket with cash or traveler's checks from a major carrier with offices in major cities.

Immigration officials at Bangkok International Airport rarely check on the outward-bound ticket requirement.

First-class, Business, Economy, And APEX Tickets

Ticket prices vary enormously depending on dozens of factors, including the type of ticket, season, choice of airline, your flexibility, and experience of the travel agent. It's confusing, but since airfare comprises a major portion of total travel expenses, no amount of time getting it right is wasted. The rule of thumb is that price and restrictions are inversely related; the cheaper the ticket the more hassles such as penalties, odd departure hours, layovers, and risk of last-minute cancellations.

First-class and Business Tickets: These are designed for travelers who need maximum flexibility and comfort, and are willing to pay the price.

Economy Tickets: Economy is cheaper than business and avoids advance-purchase requirements and cancellation charges.

APEX Tickets: Advance-purchase excursion (APEX)—the airlines' main method for deep discounts—are about 25% less than economy, but they're loaded with restrictions concerning advance payment, length of stay, and cancellation penalties. Read the fine print, *very* carefully.

Super-APEX is similar to APEX but even cheaper. Quantities are limited and sell out quickly; buy them early. APEX and super-APEX tickets are recommended for visitors with limited time who need guaranteed air reservations.

Mileage Tickets

Mileage tickets permit the traveler to pay the fare from A to B and make unlimited stops en route. For example, the ticket from San Francisco to Bangkok costs US$1361 and permits 9,559 miles. One possible routing is San Francisco-Tokyo-Seoul-Taipei-Hong Kong-Manila-Bangkok.

Tickets are generally good for one year and a mileage surcharge is tacked on for travel beyond the allotted distance. Though mileage tickets are practical for certain routes, significantly less expensive tickets covering similar stops are sold by student and discount travel agencies.

Circle-Pacific Tickets

Circle-Pacific fares are another tempting piece in the puzzle of international airfares. Scheduled on major international airlines, these tickets allow you to circle the North Pacific, Southeast Asia, and the South Pacific for about US$2400 in economy class. Restrictions are a problem, however, since they're limited to four stopovers, cost US$50 per extra stop, demand 14 days advance purchase, carry cancellation penalties, have a six-month expiration, and charge US$50 for each reissuance. Worse yet, only those cities served by the principal carrier and partner are possible stopovers. This eliminates most of the smaller but vitally important connections such as Singapore-Jakarta.

Circle-Pacific fares are sold in North America by United (800-JET-AWAY), Northwest (800-447-4747), and Canadian (800-426-7000).

Budget and student travel agencies also put together Circle-Pacific tickets, often at much lower prices than the airlines. Sample routings and prices from budget agencies are listed below.

Round-the-world Tickets

Another variation of APEX are the RTW tickets sold by several international carriers. RTW tickets cost US$2984 in economy class and allow unlimited stopovers on a combination of carriers. Tickets are good for one year but stops are limited to major cities served by the airlines. Contact the above airlines for further information. You should also contact student and discount agencies regarding their cheaper and less-restrictive RTW tickets.

Bargain Tickets

The cheapest tickets to Asia are sold by wholesalers who take advantage of special rates for group tours by purchasing large blocks of unsold seats. Once an airline concludes it can't sell all of its seats, consolidators are offered a whopping 20-40% commission to do the job. They then hand most of the commission back to the clients in the form of reduced ticket prices.

Tickets obtained from consolidators are legal and, in most cases, completely trustworthy. The advantages are obvious: cheap tickets (prices average 25-40% less than economy fares), plenty of choice, and guaranteed reservations on first-class airlines. The drawbacks: buckets rarely provide travel counseling, they keep you guessing about which airline you'll fly, tickets often carry penalties (see below), and routings can be slow and byzantine. Try to get the cheapest ticket, on the best airline, with the fewest unnecessary stops.

Where do you purchase these cheap tickets? Consolidators don't deal with the public, but rather sell their tickets through student bureaus, independent travel agents, and travel clubs. In fact, you can buy consolidator tickets from almost everyone except the consolidators themselves and the airlines.

Roundtrip prices currently average US$500 from the U.S. West Coast to Tokyo, US$550/650 low season/high season to Hong Kong, and US$750-850 to Bangkok, Singapore, and Manila. Roundtrip surcharges for East Coast departures are US$150-200. Current fares are advertised in the Sunday travel sections of major newspapers such as the *New York Times, Los Angeles Times,* and *San Francisco Examiner.* Advance planning is essential since the best deals often sell out months in advance.

Make a note of the following penalties and restrictions. Peak fares are in effect from June to August (add US$50-100) and tickets purchased less than 90 days in advance are subject to an additional US$50-150 surcharge. Flight cancellations or changes before the ticket issue usually cost US$50, but cancel your flight within 30 days of departure or any time after the ticket has been issued and you'll forfeit up to 25% of the fare.

Student Travel Agencies

Some of the best advice on ticketing can be found at agencies which specialize in the youth and student markets.

Student Travel Australia: STA serves not only students and youths, but also nonstudents and tour groups. In the United States call an office direct or dial (800) 777-0112.

International Youth Hostel Federation: This group and their associated American Youth Hostels (AYH) also provide budget travel information and discounted tickets.

Council Travel: This excellent travel organization, a division of the Council on International Educational Exchange, has 37 offices in the U.S. and representatives in Europe and Australia. Prices are low and service reliable since they deal only with reputable airlines to minimize travel problems. Best of all, Council Travel sales agents are experienced travelers who often have firsthand knowledge of Southeast Asia. Council Travel also sells the Youth Hostel Association Card, International Student Identity

Card (ISIC), the Youth International Educational Exchange Card (for nonstudents under 26), plus travel and health insurance. Their larger offices: San Francisco, tel. (415) 421-3473; Los Angeles, tel. (213) 208-3551; Seattle, tel. (206) 632-2448; Chicago, tel. (312) 951-0585; Boston, tel. (617) 266-1926; New York, tel. (212) 661-1450.

Budget Agencies In Europe

Trailfinders: Travelers in England should contact the nation's largest budget travel agency at 194 Kensington High St., London W8 7RG, tel. 01-938-3939.

Council Travel: Council travel has 10 offices in Europe including: London (tel. 071-437-7767), Paris (tel. 1-45631987), Lyons (tel. 78370956), and Dusseldorf (tel. 211-329088). Same services as listed above.

Globetrotter Travel: Swiss and German travelers can try Okista, SSR, Asta, Ontej, Unitra, Artu, Alternativ Tours, Asien-Reisen, or Globetrotter Travel Service. Globetrotter, the largest student travel agency in Germany, also distributes a very useful travel magazine entitled *Travel Info*. A few Globetrotter addresses: Rennweg 35, 8001 Zurich, tel. 01-211-7780; Neuengasse 23, 3001 Bern, tel. 031-211121; Falknerstrasse 1, 4001 Basel, tel. 061-257766; Rutligasse 2, 6003 Luzern, tel. 041-221025; Merkurstrasse 4, 9001 Gallen, tel. 071-228222; Stadthausstrasse 65, 8401 Winterthur, tel. 052-221426.

Couriers

Aside from working as a travel agent or hijacking a plane, the cheapest way to reach Southeast Asia is by carrying urgent mail for one of the following courier companies. Roundtrip tickets from the West Coast average US$250 to Taipei, US$350 to Tokyo and Hong Kong, US$400 to Singapore, and US$450 to Sydney. Courier flights are also available to Bangkok, but rarely go to Manila or Indonesia. Standby couriers can save an additional US$100-150.

Anyone can do this, and it's perfectly legal (no drugs or guns are carried, just stock certificates and registered mail), but there are several restrictions: you're limited to carry-on luggage and length of stay averages only two to four weeks. Departures are available from both Los Angeles and San Francisco.

In northern California, call:

TNT Skypack	(415) 692-9600
MicomAmerica	(415) 872-0845
Jupiter Air	(415) 872-0845
UTL Travel	(415) 583-5074
Crossroads	(408) 434-6446

In Los Angeles, call:

TNT Skypack	(310) 410-1419
MicomAmerica	(310) 670-5123
DIF Travel	(310) 851-2572
Crossroads	(310) 643-8600
UTL Travel	(310) 645-4301
Way To Go	(213) 466-1126
Polo Express	(310) 410-6822

In New York, call:

Now Voyager	(212) 431-1616
Discount	(212) 655-5151
Courier	(800) 922-2359

Last-minute Travel Clubs

Travel clubs are clearinghouses which sell leftover space on airlines, cruises, and tours at a 15-50% discount. Most specialize in cruise discounts and charge an annual membership fee of US$20-50. *Warning:* Most are honest, but some travel clubs are fraudulent scams operated by the same people who sell time-share condos and commodity futures. Proceed with caution. Contact: Worldwide Discount, tel. (305) 534-2082; Discount Travel, tel. (215) 668-2182; Moment's Notice, tel. (212) 486-0503; Stand Buys, tel. (800) 255-0200; Vacations to Go, tel. (800) 338-4962.

GETTING AROUND

Air

Domestic flights are provided by Bangkok Airways and Thai Airways which merged with Thai International several years ago. The consolidation greatly benefits international travelers, who can now purchase all necessary tickets in one package, thus ensuring a worry-free trip with guaranteed connections and seats. Major destinations are served by Airbuses and Boeing 737s, while smaller towns are reached with Shorts 330 aircraft.

Internal flights are fairly expensive when compared to rail travel, but highly recommended on those routes not served by train or luxury buses. For example, the flight from Chiang Mai to Mae Hong Song takes only 30 minutes and costs 310B while the bone-crushing bus ride takes a full 12 hours and costs 120B.

Bangkok Airways, Thailand's only domestic airline, flies six times daily from Bangkok to Ko Samui, and several times daily between Samui, Phuket, and Hat Yai. Bangkok Airways also flies from Bangkok to Phnom Penh in Cambodia.

Train

Trains are the best form of transportation in Thailand. Not only are they comfortable, punctual, and inexpensive, they're much safer than buses and an excellent way to meet people. The drawbacks? Trains are slow: they don't go everywhere (but you'd be amazed the places they do go!), and they're often fully booked during holidays. Trains from Bangkok to Chiang Mai in the north or to Hat Yai in the south should be booked well in advance.

Types and Classes: Thai trains come in four types. Diesel railcars and ordinary trains stop at every single town and are very, very slow—avoid these except on short journeys. Rapid trains are almost twice as fast as ordinary trains and have a modest 20B supplemental charge. Express trains have a 30B supplemental charge and are slightly faster than the rapid trains.

Trains are also divided into three classes. Third-class is the cheapest but the seats are hard and sleeping facilities are limited to floor space, usually littered with peanuts, children, and grandmothers. However, third-class is quite adequate on all but the longest journeys. Second-class offers padded seats and more leg room, costs double the price of third-class (about the same price as an a/c bus), and can be reserved with sleeping berths. First-class's private two-person compartments are double the price of second-class. Put this all together and the fastest/cheapest train ticket is third-class on rapid or express trains. Best choice for overnight travel is second-class with lower sleeping berth.

Charges: Supplementary charges are placed on all trains except for diesels and ordinary services. Rapid trains are 20B extra; express costs 30B more, second-class a/c is an extra 50B. Sleeping berths also carry supplemental

THAILAND AIR ROUTES

MAE HONG SON
CHIANG RAI
NAN
CHIANG MAI
LAMPANG
PHRAE
LOEI
UDON THANI
PHITSANULOK
SAKHON NAKHON
KHON KAEN
UBON RATCHATHANI
KORAT (NAKHON RATCHASIMA)
BANGKOK
0   100mi
0   100km
KO SAMUI
SURAT THANI
NAKHON SI THAMMARAT
PHUKET
TRANG
HAT YAI
PATTANI
NARATHIWAT
PENANG

© MOON PUBLICATIONS, INC.

charges. Second-class, non a/c is 70B in the upper and 100B in the lower berth. Second-class a/c is 170B lower and 200B upper berth. First-class with a/c is 250B double cabin and 350B single cabin. To compute the final cost, you must know the type of train (ordinary, rapid, express), the class (first, second, third), and whether you want a/c or a sleeping berth.

Timetables: Train schedules, available free of charge from the Rail Travel Aids counter in Bangkok's Hualampong Station, are among the most important pieces of travel information in Thailand. Purple brochures list condensed timetables for the southern train line; blue brochures list the north, northeastern, and east-

ern lines. Other information on exact fares, refunds, breaks in journeys, ticket alterations, and validity of return tickets is also described. Complete timetables for each trunk line are sold at the same counter.

Thailand Rail Pass: Blue 20-day rail passes which cost 1500B include unlimited second- and third-class travel, supplemental charges not included. Red passes for first-class travel cost 3000B, all supplemental charges included.

Bus

Bus transport in Thailand is fast, clean, and reasonably comfortable on shorter journeys. Most buses provide reclining airline-style seats and video movies (Chinese soap operas and kung fu are popular) plus smiling hostesses who crank up the air-conditioning and serve icy drinks. Seats are often reserved—a great relief from the disorganized condition of most Asian buses.

Bor Kor Sor: The least-expensive bus option is the ordinary coach operated by the government bus company, Bor Kor Sor (pronounced Baw Kaw Saw). Ordinary buses connect all towns, while a/c coaches called *rot thua* run between major cities. Bor Kor Sor terminals are located in every town in Thailand, though often on the edge of town and somewhat difficult to reach with public transportation. Bor Kor Sor buses are cheaper than private buses.

Private Buses: Over a dozen private bus companies in Thailand provide a/c services between most major tourist destinations. Fares are 30-70% more expensive than government buses, but complimentary meals and transportation from your hotel to their bus terminal are often included.

Buses are convenient despite some serious drawbacks. Coaches constructed for Thai body sizes are ridiculously cramped for long-legged Westerners. The latest craze is VIP and Super-VIP buses, which have fewer seats and allow almost a full reclining position, well worth the additional cost on longer journeys.

Safety is another concern. Far too many bus drivers behave like suicidal maniacs hell bent on destruction. Sensible precautions include never sitting in the front row or riding with drivers who plaster Rambo photographs all over the front window. Also beware of confidence artists on buses who use knockout drugs. As elsewhere in

THAILAND TRAIN ROUTES

CHIANG MAI
LAMPANG
NONG KHAI
KHON KAEN
PHITSANULOK
NAKHON SAWAN
UBON RATCHATHANI
LOPBURI
KORAT (NAKHON RATCHASIMA)
NAM TOK
AYUTHAYA
NAKHON PATHOM
BANGKOK
ARANYAPRATHET

KO SAMUI
NAKHON SI THAMMARAT
PHUKET
HAT YAI
KOTA BARU
GEORGETOWN
MALAYSIA

NOT TO SCALE

© MOON PUBLICATIONS, INC.

Southeast Asia, *never accept food or drink from strangers.*

Car Rentals

Thailand is an outstanding country to tour with a rented car. Contrary to popular belief, traffic is moderate and manageable throughout the country, with the notable exception of Bangkok. Highways are in good condition and most directional signs are labeled in English.

Familiar agencies such as Avis (tel. 255-5300 in Bangkok, 800-331-1212 in the U.S.) and Hertz (tel. 253-6251 in Bangkok, 800-654-3131 in the U.S.) maintain offices in all the larger towns and beach resorts. Rental fees are comparable to American rates and often include a driver, insurance, and unlimited mileage.

Smaller local agencies are less expensive, but check the car's condition before handing over your money. Most offer reduced monthly rates which include insurance and unlimited mileage. Split by four people, this can be an economical and flexible way to tour Thailand.

An International Driver's License is required and insurance is mandatory. Licenses can be picked up by both members and nonmembers from any AAA office.

Motorcycle Rentals

Motorcycle touring is one of the fastest-growing segments of independent tourism in Thailand. Motorcycles are the *perfect* way to get off the beaten track to reach the isolated mountain lodges and small villages where authentic Thai life-styles remain unaffected by mass tourism. While problems with rough roads and the irrational driving habits of the Thais may seem daunting, an amazing number of Western tourists are now touring Thailand by motorcycle.

A few sensible suggestions for a safe journey: Most importantly, drive *very* defensively at a safe local speed, and always give way to larger vehicles. A helmet with a visor will help protect against windburn, dirt, and insects in the evening hours. Always wear a helmet, long shirt, long trousers, and hard shoes to help survive minor

mishaps. Be extra cautious on dirt roads and remember to use your rear brake rather than the front; this is the most common mistake made by beginning motorcyclists. As a rule of thumb, you should never ride at night, and avoid riding near sunset.

Bikes can be rented near the Malaysia Hotel in Bangkok, Pattaya, Kanchanaburi, Sukothai, Chiang Mai, Mae Hong Son, Chiang Rai, Mae Sai, Nong Khai, Korat, Hua Hin, Ko Samui, Phuket, Krabi, and Hat Yai—almost everywhere possible in Thailand.

Motorcycles are cheap to rent. Small 100cc scooters which cost 100-150B daily are perfectly adequate for local touring and visiting attractions within a few days' journey. Larger bikes such as 125-175cc Honda trail bikes cost 150-200B daily and provide enough power to climb the steepest of roads in Thailand. Big bikes over 500cc are available in Pattaya and to a lesser degree in Chiang Mai.

Carefully inspect the bike for damage and make note of any problems such as dangling rearview mirrors and loose chains. You'll be required to leave your passport as deposit, so exchange enough money to finance your motorcycle tour. Motorcycles in the best condition are rented in the early morning, so shop early for vehicles with the lowest mileage. Oil levels should be checked daily and bikes should be locked inside the compound of your guesthouse each night.

Road conditions are excellent and traffic is very light except in larger cities such as Bangkok and Chiang Mai. Gasoline stations are relatively plentiful and bike mechanics can be found in almost every village. The Thai government has put up English-language signs throughout the country and, with a good map, it's almost impossible to get lost. Avoid the major highways since the finest rides are on small roads which wind through the hills and along the remote rivers. Northern Thailand is the mecca for motorcyclists, with incredible winding roads and terrific scenery.

DAVID HURST

BANGKOK

Thailand's sprawling, dynamic, and frustrating capital offers more variety, sights, and wonders than any other destination in Asia. Far too many visitors, hearing of the horrendous traffic jams and searing pollution, stop only long enough to glimpse a few temples and pick up a cheap air ticket before departing for more idyllic environs. To some degree this is understandable. Packed into the sweltering plains of the lower Chao Praya are some 10 million residents, 80% of the country's automobiles, and most of the nation's commercial headquarters—a city strangled by uncontrolled development. Without any semblance of a city center or urban planning, traffic grinds to a standstill during rush hours and dissolves into a swamp after summer monsoons. Worse yet is the monotonous sprawl of Chinese shophouses and faceless concrete towers that more closely resemble a Western labyrinth than anything remotely Eastern. It's an unnerving place.

To appreciate the charms and fascinations of Bangkok you must focus instead on the positive: dozens of magnificent temples that form one of Asia's great spectacles, countless restaurants with superb yet inexpensive food, legendary nightlife to satisfy all possible tastes, excellent shopping, and some of the friendliest people in the world. Nobody enjoys the heat, humidity, or traffic jams, but with patience and a sense of *mai pen rai*, Bangkok will cast an irresistible spell.

History

Unless a Thai is condescending to foreign ignorance, he will never call his capital city Bangkok ("City of Wild Plums") but rather Krung Thep, "City of Angels." Krung Thep actually begins the string of honorariums which comprise the official name, a mammoth tongue twister which, according to Guinness, forms the longest place name in the world.

Bangkok sprung from a small village or *bang* filled with wild olive and plum trees called *kok*. At first little more than a trading suburb to Thonburi (Money Town), Bangkok rose to prominence after Burmese forces destroyed Ayuthaya in 1767 and General Taksin moved his armies

> *I did not know why, the insipid Eastern food sickened me. The heat of Bangkok was overwhelming. The wats oppressed me by their garish magnificence, making my head ache, and their fantastic ornaments filled me with malaise. I felt very unwell.*
>
> —Somerset Maugham,
> *The Gentleman in the Parlour*

south. Taksin soon went insane (claiming to be the final Buddha) and was dispatched to Buddhist nirvana in time-honored fashion—a sharp blow to the back of the neck.

With General Taksin out of the way, Rama I, Taksin's chief military commander, was recalled from Cambodia to found the dynasty which rules to the present day. Fearing further Burmese attacks, Rama I moved the city across the river and relocated the Chinese merchants south to Sampeng, today's Chinatown. Bangkok was formally established on 21 April 1782, with the consecration of the city's foundation pillar at Lak Muang. Rama I constructed his capital to rival once-glorious Ayuthaya: palaces were

erected with brick salvaged from Ayuthaya, temples were filled with Ayuthayan Buddhas, and concentric canals were dug to emulate the watery kingdom. The city was then renamed Krung Thep, a title rather ignominiously ignored by Western cartographers, who continued to call it Bangkok.

Bangkok was first centered at the Royal Palace and Wat Pra Keo, a royal chapel constructed in 1785 to enshrine the statue of the Emerald Buddha. Modernization was slow until the coronation of King Mongkut (Rama IV) in 1851. Mongkut expanded the city limits, entered into treaties with the U.S. and several European powers, and, in 1862, ordered the construction of the first road (New Road) over an old elephant trail which connected the Royal Palace with Chinatown. In the same year, Anna Leonowens arrived in Bangkok to become the governess of Mongkut's children and would later misrepresent them in her published reminiscences, *The English Governess at the Siamese Court.* This misleading yarn eventually inspired the stage and film musical, *The King and I.*

Chulalongkorn (King Rama V) ascended the throne in 1868 to introduce far-reaching reforms and Westernization. By 1908 Bangkok had a grand total of just 300 automobiles. After the

REQUIEM FOR A CITY

Once known as the Venice of the East, modern Bangkok is now a City in Crisis. Economic boomtimes have tranformed the once-charming town into an environmental horror show where street-level pollution has long since passed international danger levels, waterways not filled with concrete are clogged with garbage, and rush-hour traffic grinds to a complete standstill. One out of five residents lives in illegal slums with no piped water or electricity. Residential pollution, the unregulated dumping of dangerous chemicals and fertilizers, and a complete lack of oxygen have killed the Chao Praya River. Each day, Bangkok produces 5,400 tons of garbage but only 4,200 tons are collected; the remainder is dumped on street corners or in the waterways. Construction of artesian wells and high-rise buildings on soft soil is sinking the low-lying city under sea level, a horrifying prospect that may become reality within a single generation.

But it is the horrendous traffic that typifies what is most frightening in the City of Angels. Bangkok's traffic crisis—almost certainly the worst in the world—

is the result of government inaction and unwillingness to make tough decisions. The problem is that most cities throughout the world use 20-25% of their surface area for streets, but in Bangkok it's only six percent. The city's 1.5 million cars will double in number in just seven years, but road surface is expected to increase by only 10 percent. The gridwork of roads found in *all* major international cities has *never* been constructed in Bangkok. Instead, city authorities have allowed Bangkok to grow without any form of urban planning, depending on the self-interest of private investors rather than the controlling force of government policy.

The result is world-class traffic jams. According to the Traffic Committee, the average speed during rush hours has dropped to under four kilometers per hour; people *walk* at five km per hour. The remainder of the day, traffic moves at just seven km per hour. When Dr. Sumet Jumsai, the nation's foremost authority on architecture and urban planning, was asked about Bangkok, he said, "It's irreversible destruction. The city is dying."

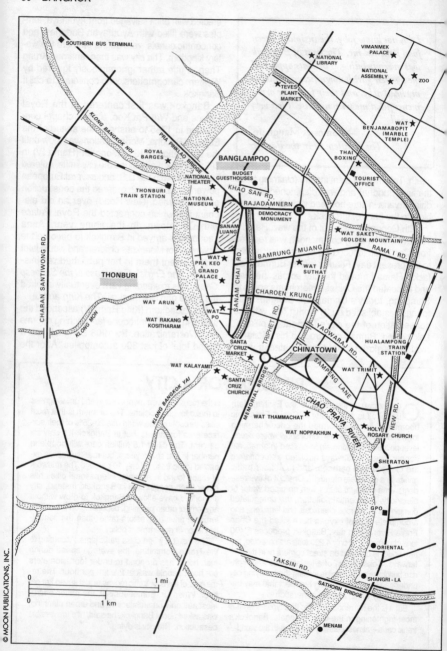

SOUTHERN BUS TERMINAL

NATIONAL LIBRARY

VIMANMEK PALACE

NATIONAL ASSEMBLY

ZOO

TEVES PLANT MARKET

WAT BENJAMABOPIT (MARBLE TEMPLE)

KLONG BANGKOK NOI

PRA PINKLAO BRIDGE

ROYAL BARGES

THONBURI TRAIN STATION

BANGLAMPOO

BUDGET GUESTHOUSES

KHAO SAN RD.

THAI BOXING

TOURIST OFFICE

NATIONAL THEATER

RAJADAMNERN

NATIONAL MUSEUM

DEMOCRACY MONUMENT

WAT SAKET (GOLDEN MOUNTAIN)

CHARAN SANTIWONG RD.

SANAM LUANG

BAMRUNG MUANG

RAMA I RD.

THONBURI

WAT PRA KEO GRAND PALACE

SANAM CHAI RD.

WAT SUTHAT

WAT ARUN

CHAROEN KRUNG

KLONG MON

WAT RAKANG KOSITHARAM

WAT PO

TRIPHET RD.

YAOWARAJ RD.

HUALAMPONG TRAIN STATION

SANTA CRUZ MARKET

CHINATOWN

WAT KALAYAMIT

MEMORIAL BRIDGE

SAMPENG LANE

WAT TRIMIT

NEW RD.

SANTA CRUZ CHURCH

KLONG BANGKOK YAI

CHAO PRAYA RIVER

WAT THAMMACHAT

WAT NOPPAKHUN

HOLY ROSARY CHURCH

SHERATON

TAKSIN RD.

GPO

ORIENTAL

SHANGRI-LA

SATHORN BRIDGE

MENAM

0   1 mi

0   1 km

© MOON PUBLICATIONS, INC.

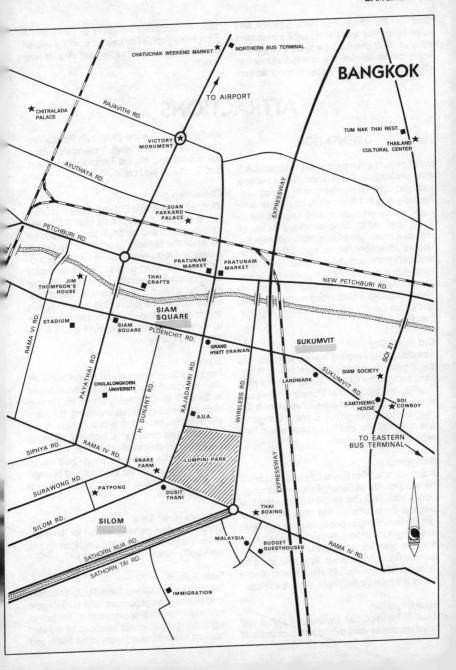

death of Chulalongkorn in 1910, Bangkok was ruled by several more kings until a bloodless coup in 1932 changed the system of government from an absolute to a constitutional monarchy. A series of 18 military coups occurred from 1932 to the latest takeover in 1990, while Bangkok's population soared from 1.5 million in 1960 to a present settlement of over nine million.

ATTRACTIONS

ORIENTATION

Bangkok isn't a compact or easily understandable city such as San Francisco, but rather a vast and octopus-like metropolis spread haphazardly across 1,500 square kilometers. Similar in many respects to Los Angeles (heat, smog, and traffic), Bangkok should be visualized as a multiplicity of neighborhoods with distinctive attractions, ethnic populations, variations of nightlife, and styles of hotels and restaurants that appeal to different types of travelers. The quickest way to orient yourself is to study Nancy Chandler's outstanding map of Bangkok, and divide the city into the following neighborhoods.

Old Royal City
The old royal city around the Grand Palace has the largest concentration of sightseeing attractions such as the Grand Palace, Wat Pra Keo, Wat Po, and the National Museum. Hotels and noteworthy restaurants are relatively rare in this neighborhood, though this is one of Bangkok's few precincts that can be recommended for a walking tour (see below).

Banglampoo
Adjacent to the Old Royal City and the central parade grounds of Sanam Luang is Banglampoo, a traditional Thai neighborhood which has become Bangkok's leading stopover for budget travelers. Banglampoo lacks great nightlife or shopping but compensates with a superb location near great temples and the immensely convenient Chao Praya River. Anyone looking for guesthouses under US$5 should head directly for its principal thoroughfare, Khao San Road.

New Royal City
Most of the important government offices and royal residences were moved here prior to World War II. Top draws are Chitralada Palace (the home of the present king), Vimanmek Palace, the outstanding Marble Temple, Parliament, and Dusit Zoo. No hotels.

Chinatown
Wedged between the Old Royal City and Silom Rd. is one of Southeast Asia's great Chinese neighborhoods and the single finest place to experience the sensory overload of the Orient. A map and suggested walking tour are provided in the following pages. Chinatown hotels cater primarily to wealthy Chinese businessmen, but a handful of inexpensive guesthouses are located in adjacent Little India. Travelers searching for a strong and completely authentic encounter might consider staying here rather than in Banglampoo.

Silom
Bangkok's financial center and original tourist enclave is located along a major boulevard known as Silom Road. Sightseeing attractions are minimal and the congestion is unnerving, but Silom offers dozens of moderate to super-luxury hotels, exclusive restaurants, high-end shopping boutiques, great sidewalk shopping, and the infamous nightlife area of Patpong Road. Riverside hotels such as the Oriental and Shangri La are world famous for their extremely high levels of service.

Malaysia Hotel Area
Once the budget travelers' center for Bangkok, hotels and guesthouses along Soi Ngam Duphli have sadly declined in recent years.

Siam Square
Bangkok's alternative to Silom Rd. is a relatively low-density neighborhood with ultraelegant hotels and modern shopping centers. The lack of sightseeing attractions is balanced by the vast gardens which surround many of the hotels and

the enormous shopping complexes which guarantee some of the best shopping in all of Asia. Hotels are generally expensive, although a few clean guesthouses are located near the house of Jim Thompson.

Sukumvit Road

Once considered on the outer fringes of Bangkok, Sukumvit has recently developed into the leading area for moderate-budget tourists. The biggest disadvantage is the enormous distance from Sukumvit to important temples and government services such as the General Post Office and the tourist office. However, Sukumvit has a great selection of hotels in the US$25-50 price range, many of the finest Thai restaurants in the country, wonderful sidewalk shopping and countless boutiques, and the mind-boggling nightlife of Nana Complex and Soi Cowboy. Despite the relatively remote location and problems with noise and pollution, Sukumvit is highly recommended for middle-level travelers and anyone intrigued by the nightlife possibilities.

SUGGESTED WALKING TOURS

Finding your way around Bangkok can be difficult since street names are rarely marked and the numbering system for addresses is often baffling. Bear in mind that the larger thoroughfares *(thanon)* are intersected by smaller streets *(sois)* that often end in cul-de-sacs. Public transportation—whether in an ordinary bus or an a/c taxi—can be extremely time-consuming, especially during morning and evening rush hours when traffic grinds to a dead stop.

Faced with such obstacles, visitors often think that Bangkok is best experienced on an organized tour rather than a self-guided walking tour. Not true! While organized tours are convenient and relatively inexpensive, reasons to avoid them are plentiful: tour buses get stuck in traffic, visits to major monuments are frustratingly brief, shopping traps designed to extract kickbacks are commonplace, and only the most common (and hence touristy) sights are included in your tour. Worse yet, tours rarely allow an opportunity to freely wander around an ordinary Thai neighborhood and experience the charm and friendliness of the local residents.

Bangkok actually has several compact neighborhoods that can be easily enjoyed on self-guided walking tours by almost anybody with a good map and sense of adventure. A few tips: always get an early start to avoid the midday heat, bring along Nancy Chandler's map of Bangkok, and whenever possible use riverboats to reach your starting point.

The following tours are arranged in order of interest: the Old Royal City should be your first tour, followed by Chinatown, and then either Sukumvit or the New Royal City. Break up your walking expeditions with boat trips, cold drinks, and long visits to air-conditioned shopping centers!

First Day—Old Royal City

Temples within the Old Royal City and near the Royal Palace can be toured on foot in a single day. Only a slightly crazed tourist would attempt a single-day walking tour of *all* the temples within the Old Royal City; a leisurely two-day walking tour is needed for the remaining sights such as Wat Suthat and the Golden Mountain.

Visitors staying in Banglampoo can easily walk over to the Grand Palace or National Museum to begin the tour. Visitors staying near Silom Rd. should take a public riverboat to the Tha Chang boat stop. From Sukumvit Rd. or Siam Square, take a taxi or public bus to the Grand Palace.

Begin your tour promptly at 0830 with the Grand Palace or enjoy a guided tour of the National Museum Tues.-Thurs. at 0930. Afterward, wander around the Sanam Luang, visit the amulet market near Wat Mahathat, enjoy some dancing at Lak Muang, and then tour Wat Po to see the Reclining Buddha. Finally, take a river shuttle across the Chao Praya River to Wat Arun. This concentration of temples will probably suffice for most visitors with only a casual interest in Thai religious architecture.

Second Day—Old Royal City

Your walking tour on the second day begins at the Royal Palace and heads away from the river toward Democracy Monument. A short visit can be made at Wat Rajapradit and the more impressive Wat Rajabopit before arriving at Wat Suthat, one of the most majestic temples in the old city. Adjacent to Wat Suthat stands the Giant Swing and a small but intriguing Brahman temple. Nearby sights include a wonderful Chinese temple on Tanao Road and shops selling religious supplies and immense bronze Buddhas on Bamrung Muang Road. The tour ends with a visit to the amulet market at Wat Rajananda and the curious Lohaprasat before climbing up to the summit of the Golden Mountain. Fast walkers can accomplish this tour in about 4 hours.

Third Day—Chinatown

Rather than touring the limited attractions in the New Royal City, spend your third day walking around Chinatown, Little India, and the adjoining riverside markets. The famous Golden Buddha is also located in this neighborhood. Best of all, strolling through Chinatown provides a welcome relief from the endless procession of temples, plus gives you an opportunity discover Chinese culture and enjoy some people watching. An early start is essential to avoid the midday heat.

Fourth Day—New Royal City

Begin your day with a river trip on the Chao Praya from the Tha Orienten (Oriental Hotel boat stop) in the south to Tha Pra Arthit (Banglampoo) boat dock in the north. First, walk through the backpackers' enclave along Khao San Road and briefly visit Wat Bowonivet before heading up Rajadamnern Avenue to the tourist office and the magnificent Marble Temple. Farther on are the Vimanmek Palace and the Dusit Zoo—a long hike best aided with public transportation.

Fifth Day—Sukumvit To Siam Square

The best remaining walking tour is from Sukumvit Rd. to Siam Square, an easy-to-follow excursion which includes conventional tourist attractions such as Kamthieng and Jim Thompson's House, great sidewalk shopping along Sukumvit Rd., comfortable a/c shopping inside the Central and Zen centers, and plenty of great little restaurants and pubs for cold drinks. And not a temple in sight!

Begin your tour from Sukumvit Soi 21 (Siam Society and Soi Cowboy), and walk west past bookstores, local markets, sidewalk shops, tailors, and cafes to the expressway overpass where Sukumvit changes name to Ploenchit Road. Continue west to Central Department Store, the fascinating Erawan Shrine, newish Zen Shopping Center (Zen shopping?), and

Siam Square Shopping Center where Ploenchit—logically enough—becomes Rama I Road. Farther on is the immense Tokyu Shopping Center and finally, Jim Thompson's House, tucked away on a quiet side street.

Alternatively, hire a taxi to quickly visit the remaining tourist sights scattered around Bangkok. Highlights include the Siam Society and Kamthieng House on Sukumvit Rd., Jim Thompson's House near Siam Square, Snake Farm, and a visit to Suan Pakkard Palace.

Sixth Day—River Journeys

A full day can be enjoyed on the Chao Praya River and canals which circumscribe the city. Suggested itineraries are described on pages 99-103.

ADMISSION FEES

The Grand Palace/Wat Pra Keo complex will probably be your first experience with the notorious two-tier fee system for selected temples, museums, and historical sites in Thailand. In late 1985 the Fine Arts Department began charging foreigners significantly higher admission fees than Thais. For example, entrance to the Grand Palace is 100B for foreigners but free for Thais. Major monuments in Ayuthaya and Sukothai now charge Westerners 20B admission to each temple but only 5B for Thais. Although rarely noticed by tourists (lower entrance fees for locals are posted only in Thai script), this double standard has proven contentious for Western travelers, who resent the gouge-the-rich-tourist mentality.

Tragically, this mercenary attitude—as propagated and approved by the Fine Arts Department and Thai government—has spread throughout Thailand. Although basically an honest people, many Thais now consider tourists fair game for overcharging on everything from ice cream cones to antique Buddhas. There is absolutely no reason to play along with this little game; allowing yourself to be overcharged makes you the fool and encourages merchants to overcharge future travelers. Although there is little one can do about temple admissions, travelers who wish to avoid being ripped off on other purchases should learn the correct prices and refuse to pay any type of surcharge. Complaints about the double-pricing standard should be di-

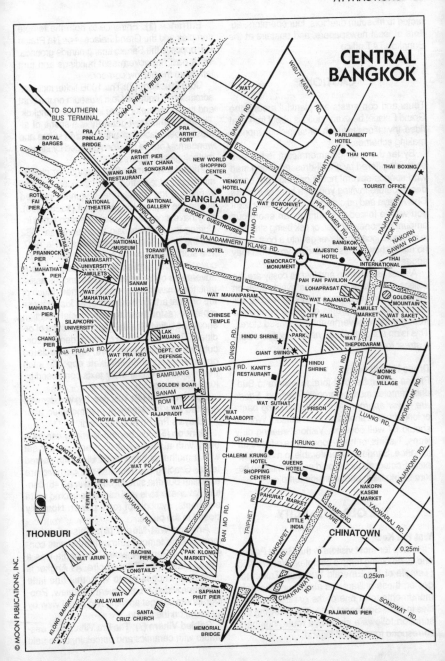

CENTRAL BANGKOK

CHAO PRAYA RIVER

TO SOUTHERN
BUS TERMINAL

ROYAL
BARGES

PRA PINKLAO
BRIDGE

PRA ARTHIT PIER

PRA
ARTHIT
FORT

WISUT KASAT RD.

WAT

PARLIAMENT
HOTEL

PRACHATHI RD.

SAMSEN RD.

THAI HOTEL

THAI BOXING

WANG NAR
RESTAURANT

WAT CHANA
SONGKRAM

NEW WORLD
SHOPPING
CENTER

VIENGTAI
HOTEL

TANAO RD.

PRA SUMEN RD.

TOURIST OFFICE

KLONG
BANGKOK NOI

PINKLAO RD.

PRA ARTHIT

NATIONAL
THEATER

NATIONAL
GALLERY

BANGLAMPOO

WAT BOWONIVET

RAJADAMNERN
NOK AVE.

ROT
FAI PIER

BUDGET GUESTHOUSES

NAKORN
SAWAN RD.

LONGTAILS

RAJADAMNERN KLANG RD.

BANGKOK
BANK

PRANNOCK
PIER

MAHATHAT
PIER

NATIONAL
MUSEUM

TORANI
STATUE

ROYAL HOTEL

DEMOCRACY
MONUMENT

MAJESTIC
HOTEL

THAI
INTERNATIONAL

THAMMASART
UNIVERSITY
AMULETS

SANAM
LUANG

WAT MAHANPARAM

PAH FAH PAVILION

LOHAPRASAT

GOLDEN
MOUNTAIN

MAHARAJ
PIER

WAT
MAHATHAT

WAT RAJANADA

AMULET
MARKET

WAT SAKET

SILAPKORN
UNIVERSITY

CHINESE
TEMPLE

CITY HALL

CHANG
PIER

NA PRALAN RD.

LAK
MUANG

HINDU SHRINE

PARK

WAT
THEPDIDARAM

WAT PRA KEO

DEPT. OF
DEFENSE

GIANT SWING

HINDU
SHRINE

MAHACHAI RD.

WORACHAK RD.

MONKS
BOWL
VILLAGE

BAMRUANG

MUANG   RD.

KANIT'S
RESTAURANT

GOLDEN BOAR
SANAM
ROM

WAT
RAJAPRADIT

DINSO RD.

WAT SUTHAT

PRISON

LUANG RD.

ROYAL PALACE

CHAROEN

KRUNG

RD.

WAT PO

CHALERM KRUNG
HOTEL

SHOPPING
CENTER

QUEENS
HOTEL

RAJAWONG RD.

NAKORN
KASEM
MARKET

MAHARAJ RD.

TIEN PIER

FERRY

BAN MO RD.

TRIPHET RD.

PAHURAT MARKET

LITTLE
INDIA

SAMPENG
LANE

YAOWARAJ RD.

CHINATOWN

THONBURI

WAT ARUN

RACHINI PIER

LONGTAILS

PAK
KLONG
MARKET

CHAKRAPET RD.

0   0.25mi

0   0.25km

KLONG BANGKOK YAI

WAT
KALAYAMIT

SAPHAN
PHUT PIER

SANTA
CRUZ CHURCH

CHAKRAWAT RD.

SONGWAT RD.

RAJAWONG PIER

MEMORIAL
BRIDGE

© MOON PUBLICATIONS, INC.

rected to museum directors, tour operators, editors of local newspapers, and upstairs at the Bangkok TAT office.

CAUTIONS

Touts and con artists are plentiful around the Grand Palace; be extra cautious about free boat rides, invitations to lunch, or suspicious money-making schemes.

By far the most common scam is the free boat ride offered by a well-dressed young man who spends several hours gaining your confidence before inviting you on a boat tour of the Chao Praya and adjoining canals. At some point you will be forced to contribute an enormous amount of money for fuel, or risk being stranded in a remote location. Never get into a boat alone, no matter how honest or sincere your host may appear.

Almost as common and just as costly are the college students who offer unbelievable deals on Thai gems. These smooth-talking fellows will promise fabulous profits on gems purchased from reputable government-supervised stores. This is an absolute fraud: *never buy gems from a street tout.*

Dress Regulations

Please remember that foreign visitors to Buddhist temples must be properly dressed. *Shorts are never appropriate in temples.* Long pants or long dresses should be worn instead. Women should be well covered. Visitors wearing dirty jeans, T-shirts, or halter tops will be refused admittance. Sandals are preferable to rubber slippers. Photographers should ask permission before taking flash photos inside temples.

THE OLD ROYAL CITY

Wat Pra Keo

First stop for most visitors is the Grand Palace and its adjoining temple complex, Wat Pra Keo (Temple of the Emerald Buddha). Taken together, these brilliant and almost unbelievable monuments form one of the greatest spectacles in all of Southeast Asia. The following description follows a clockwise route; numbers correspond to map and legend.

Entrance (1): Entrance to both the temple complex and the Grand Palace is on Na Pralan Rd. opposite the Sanam Luang parade grounds. Walk past the government buildings and turn left down the narrow corridor.

Coin Museum (2): The 100B ticket includes admission to both the Coin Museum on the right and the Vimanmek Palace in northern Bangkok. Through the narrow gateway is a scene of almost unbelievable brilliance: golden spires and wonderfully ornate pavilions guarded by strange mythological creatures.

Ramakien Murals (3): The interior cloister murals depict tales from the Ramakien, the Thai version of the Ramayana. Originally painted during the reign of King Mongkut (1825-1850), they have since been restored seven times including the Rattanakosin bicentennial in 1982 and the king's 60th birthday celebration in 1987. The story begins by the north gate with the discovery of Sita, and advances through various adventures of her consort Rama and his assistant, the white monkey-god Hanuman. Much of the original artistic merit has been lost to these repeated restorations, though special attention should be paid to the delightful depictions of ordinary Thai life: laughing children, demure concubines, grinning gamblers, and emaciated opium smokers. Marble tablets opposite each fresco provide explanatory texts composed by King Chulalongkorn.

Golden Chedi (4): This dazzling wonder was erected by King Mongkut and modeled after Ayuthaya's Pra Sri Ratana Chedi.

Mondop (5): Just beyond is a richly carved library with a solid-silver floor and interior set with a mother-of-pearl chest filled with sacred texts. Gracing the four interior corners are exquisite Buddha statues carved in a 14th-century Javanese style and miniature sacred white elephants, symbols of royal power. Normally closed to the public.

Angkor Wat Model (6): This miniature model of the famous Khmer temple was constructed by Rama IV when Cambodia was a vassal state of the Thai empire. As Angkor is difficult or impossible to visit, this fine little model provides a convenient overview. Photographers can get an intriguing aerial view by standing on the railing.

Gabled Viharn (7): The Pra Viharn Yot, decorated with ceramics and porcelain, once held

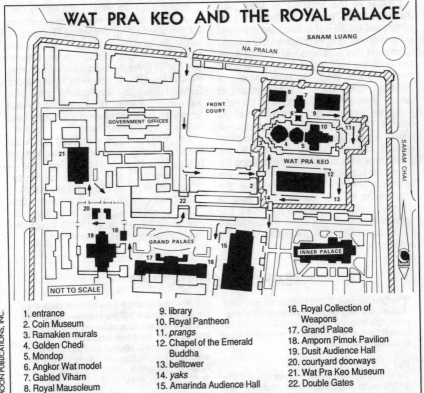

WAT PRA KEO AND THE ROYAL PALACE

1. entrance
2. Coin Museum
3. Ramakien murals
4. Golden Chedi
5. Mondop
6. Angkor Wat model
7. Gabled Viharn
8. Royal Mausoleum
9. library
10. Royal Pantheon
11. *prangs*
12. Chapel of the Emerald Buddha
13. belltower
14. *yaks*
15. Amarinda Audience Hall
16. Royal Collection of Weapons
17. Grand Palace
18. Amporn Pimok Pavilion
19. Dusit Audience Hall
20. courtyard doorways
21. Wat Pra Keo Museum
22. Double Gates

the historic Manangasila stone, which served as the throne for King Ramkamheng of Sukothai. Discovered by King Mongkut in the ruins of Sukothai during his monkhood, the stone has since been brought here.

Royal Mausoleum (8): The Pra Naga in the northwest corner of the complex holds urns containing the ashes of royal family members. Closed to the public.

Library (9): The west facade of the Montien Dharma, second library of the temple complex, is considered the finest of its kind in Thailand. As with other temple libraries, this building was constructed to protect sacred texts and copies of the Tripitaka, the holy Buddhist scripture.

Royal Pantheon (10): Ground plan of Prasat Pra Thepbidon is a Greek cross capped by a yellow *prang*. Standing inside are life-size stat-

ues of the first seven kings of the Chakri Dynasty. Open annually on 6 April.

Mythological Animals: Surrounding the magnificent Royal Pantheon are bizarre mythological animals such as the *kinaree*, a half-human, half-bird creature of Himalayan origins, and glaring guardian lions known as *norasinghs*. Flanking the main entrance are slender *chedis* supported by a frieze of mythical *garuda* birds—important since the *garuda* is Vishnu's animal and Rama is the reincarnation of Vishnu.

***Prangs* (11):** Covered with glazed ceramic tiles, these eight Khmer spires were erected by Rama I as symbols of the eight planets. Each color corresponds to a different celestial body. Two are located inside the palace walls; another six stand outside the grounds along the east gallery.

Chapel of the Emerald Buddha (12): Bangkok's Royal Temple is Thailand's most important and sacred *wat.* Constructed at the end of the 18th century by King Rama I, this splendid example of Thai aesthetics and religious architecture houses the Emerald Buddha, Thailand's most venerated image. So small and distant that it can hardly be seen, the green jaspar (*not* jade or emerald) image symbolizes the independence, strength, and good fortune of the country. Thais believe this religious talisman holds the magical power of the king, who thrice annually changes the holy garments from a golden tunic studded with diamonds during the hot season to a gilded monk's robe for the rainy season. A solid gold robe is placed over the image during the cool season. Shoes must be removed and photography is prohibited. Extreme respect should be shown in this chapel: it's the equivalent of St. Peter's for Catholics and Mecca's Kaaba for Muslims.

Interior walls are painted with superb frescoes. A few moments studying these murals will prove rewarding, since most Thai temples follow similar conventions as to mural placement. For example, murals between the window frames generally depict *Jataka* scenes from the life of Buddha. The universe is portrayed in Buddhist astrological representation on the back wall behind the altar. The wall fronting the altar (above the entrance) relates the temptation and victory of Buddha over Mara.

Two points of interest are located outside the chapel. Guarding the entrance are two mythical bronze lions, considered by art historians as masterpieces of Khmer art. Also note the unusually ornate *bai sema* or boundary stones.

Belltower (13): An elaborate belltower stands in the opposite corner. Belltowers typically summon monks for sermons and meals, though Wat Pra Keo no longer has resident monks.

TEMPLE ARCHITECTURE

Thailand has over 30,000 Buddhist temples which share, to a large degree, common types of structures. The following descriptions will help you sort through the dazzling yet bewildering buildings found throughout the country.

Wat

The entire religious complex is known as a *wat.* This term does not properly translate to "temple," since temple implies a singular place dedicated to the worship of a god while *wats* are multiple buildings dedicated to the veneration—not worship—of the Buddha. *Wats* serve as religious institutions, schools, community meeting halls, hospitals, entertainment venues, and as homes for the aged and abandoned. Some even serve as drug-rehabilitation centers.

Wat titles often explain much about their history and function. Some are named after the kings who constructed them, such as Ayuthaya's Wat Pra Ram, named for King Ramatibodhi. Others use the word Rat, Raja, or Racha to indicate that Thai royalty either constructed or restored the building. Others are named for their Buddha images, such as Wat Pra Keo in Bangkok, which holds the Keo or Emerald Bud-

dha. Pra (also spelled Phra)—the term which often precedes important Buddha images—means "honorable." Thailand's most important *wats* are called Wat Mahathat, a term which indicates that they hold a great *(maha)* relic *(that)* of the Buddha. Wat Mahathats are found in Bangkok, Chiang Rai, Sukothai, Ayuthaya, Phitsanulok, Petchburi, Nakhon Si Thammarat, Yasothon, and Chai Nat.

Bot

Bots, the most important and sacred structures in the religious compound, are assembly halls where monks meet to perform ceremonies and ordinations, meditate, give sermons to lay people, and recite the *patimokkha* (disciplinary rules) every fortnight.

The Exterior: Ground plans vary from quadrilateral *cellas* with single doors to elaborate cruciform designs with multiple entrances. All are identified by *bai sema,* eight boundary stones which define the consecrated ground and help ward off evil spirits. *Bai semas* are often protected by small tabernacles richly decorated with spires and runic symbols. *Bot* window shutters and doors are often carved and decorated with gold leaf and mir-

religious prasat

BOB RACE

Yaks (14): Exit from the Wat Pra Keo compound is made past towering manlike creatures called *yaks,* sharp-fanged mythological creatures dressed in Thai costumes and wielding huge clubs. *Kinarees* and *garudas* brandishing *nagas* complete the amazing scene.

Royal Palace

Bangkok's former royal palace, an intriguing blend of Italian Renaissance architecture and classical Thai roofing, was begun in 1783 by King Rama I and improved upon by subsequent rulers. If Wat Pra Keo evokes the Orient, then the Grand Palace will remind you of Europe.

Amarinda Audience Hall (15): Originally the private residence of Rama I and Hall of Justice, Vinchai Hall today serves as a royal venue for coronations and ceremonial state events. An antique boat-shaped throne on which early kings received homage stands behind; the present king uses the Western throne in the front.

Royal Collection of Weapons (16): A brief look at the history of Thai weaponry. Left of the weapon museum is a gateway leading to the Inner Palace, once the residence of the king's children and concubines. Closed to the public, though the king celebrates his birthday here with friends and the local diplomatic corps.

Grand Palace Audience Hall (17): Eccentric, half-Western and half-Oriental, the Chakri Maha Prasat was constructed in 1882 by King Chulalongkorn to commemorate the centenary of the Chakri Dynasty. Designed by a British architect, this Italian Renaissance palace was incongruously superimposed with a Thai *prasat* roof at the king's request—a strangely successful fusion of disparate styles. The Grand Palace served as the royal residence until King Ananda was shot in bed under mysterious circumstances in 1946. His brother, the current King Rama IX, subsequently moved out to the more spacious Chitralada Palace. Visitors are al-

---

rored tiles, or engraved with mother-of-pearl designs. But the most arresting sights are the multitier roofs covered with brilliant glazed tiles. Roof extremities end with *chofas,* graceful curls which represent *nagas* or mythological *garudas.* Wriggling down the edges of the bargeboards are more *nagas* which act as heavenly staircases between earthly existence and Buddhist nirvana. Some of the best artwork is found in the triangular pediments: images of Vishnu riding Garuda or Indra riding elephant-headed Erawan.

The Interior: Stunning interior murals often follow identical arrangements. Paintings behind the primary Buddha image depict scenes from the *Traiphum,* the Buddhist cosmological order of heaven, earth, and hell. Have a close look at the punishments of the damned—they might remind you of Hieronymus Bosch's painting of Dante's Inferno (devils dancing around, people being speared or boiled alive, etc.). Less interesting side walls are decorated with incidents from the life or earlier incarnations of the Buddha. The most spectacular murals, always located on the front wall above the main entrance, depict the Buddha's enlightenment or his temptation by Mara. Shoes must be removed before before entering all *bots* in Thailand.

Viharn

Secondary assembly halls where lay people pay homage to the principal Buddha image. *Viharns* are architecturally identical to *bots* except for the lack of consecrated boundary stones. Larger *viharns* are surrounded by magnificently decorated cloisters filled with rows of gilded Buddha images.

Chedi

Chedi is the Thai term for the Indian stupa. In ancient times, these dome-shaped monuments held relics of the Buddha such as pieces of bone or hairs. Later prototypes were erected over the remains of kings or saints, and today anybody with sufficient *baht* can have one constructed for his or her ashes. *Chedis* consist of a three-tiered base representing heaven, hell, and earth, and a bulbous stupa placed on top. The small pavilion (*harmika*) near the summit symbolizes the Buddha's seat of meditation. Above this is a multitiered and highly stylized umbrella ringed with moldings representing the 33 Buddhist heavens. Pinnacles are often capped with crystals and precious jewels. The world's largest *chedi* is in Nakhon Pathom, one hour west of Bangkok.

(continued)

chedi

BOB RACE

lowed inside the state reception room decorated with European furnishings.

Amporn Pimok Pavilion (18): At one time, Rama IV would alight from his elevated palanquin, present himself to the crowd below, enter this delicate little pavilion, remove his ceremonial hat and gown, and then proceed into the throne hall. So quintessentially Thai is the architecture that Rama V reproduced it at his Bang Pa In summer retreat, and a replica was exhibited at the World's Fair in Brussels.

Dusit Audience Hall (19): Mounted on a marble platform in the shape of a Latin cross, this magnificent building is widely considered Thailand's finest example of royal architecture. Once used for outdoor receptions, today the building serves for the ceremonial lying-in-state of deceased kings. Note the interior paintings, throne built by King Mongkut, and four guardian figures donated by wealthy Chinese businessmen.

Courtyard Doorways (20): Exit the Grand Palace through these wooden doors delightfully carved and painted with colorful sentries.

Wat Pra Keo Museum (21): Features inside this fine little museum include a scale model of the Royal Palace and Wat Pra Keo complex—useful to sort out the confusing labyrinths. Javanese Buddhas and the famous Manangasila Throne are displayed upstairs. Best of all (this is important), it's air-conditioned!

Double Gates (22): Final exit to the front courtyard and Na Pralan Road.

Lak Muang

Across the road from the Royal Palace stands a newly renovated marble pavilion housing a *lingam*-shaped monument covered with gold leaf and adorned with flowers. This foundation stone, from which all distances in Thailand are measured, was placed here by King Rama I to provide a home for the unseen landlord-spirits of

Prang

These towering spires, among Thailand's most distinctive and exciting monumental structures, trace their architectural heritage back to the corner towers of Cambodian temples. Although these phallic-shaped structures are set on a square base like the

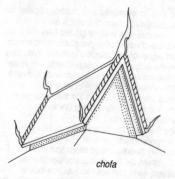

chofa

chedi, many have achieved a more elegant and slender outline than Cambodian prototypes. Lower tiers are often ringed by a frieze of demons who appear to be—depending on your perspective—either dancing or supporting the tower. Summits are typically crowned by the Hindu thunderbolt, symbol of Shiva and a religious holdover from ancient traditions. Thailand's most famous *prang* is Wat Arun, just across the river from the Grand Palace.

Mondop

These square, pyramidal-roofed structures enshrine highly venerated objects such as palm-leaf Tripitakas (Buddhist bibles) or footprints of the Buddha. Thailand's most famous example is the *mondop* of the Temple of the Buddha's Footprint at Saraburi.

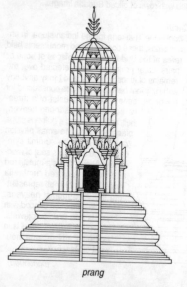

prang

the city. Thais believe these magical spirits possess the power to grant wishes, win lotteries, guarantee healthy children, and protect the fate of the city.

Thai classical dance performances sponsored in the rear pavilion by satisfied suppliants include Ramakien routines, the most popular version being an Eastern *Swan Lake* called the Manora. Sponsors pay the dancers 100B for a short *ram tawai* (thanksgiving dance) while wealthy patrons ante up 1000B for a longer drama. Early morning and late afternoon are the busiest and best times to watch the dancing; extra busy two or three days before a lottery.

National Museum

This museum—the largest and most comprehensive in Southeast Asia—serves as an excellent introduction to the arts of Thailand and the religious iconography of Buddhism.

Collections are open Wed.-Sun. 0900-1600.

Admission is 20B. Tickets can be purchased and bags checked at the front entrance. Photography is prohibited. The bulletin board adjacent to the ticket counter often has notices on upcoming cultural and festival tours sponsored by the National Museum and the Siam Society—excellent tours at extremely good prices. Detailed information on the extensive holdings is provided in the *Guide to the National Museum Bangkok* sold at the front desk.

Orientation: The National Museum is comprised of a half-dozen buildings. The Sivamokhapiman Hall holds the ticket office and Thai History rooms. Scattered on the outside grounds are the Royal Chariot Pavilion, Wat Buddhaisawan, and the Red Pavilion, three excellent examples of traditional 18th-century architecture. To the rear is the Central Wing. Once used by the king's brother, these old royal structures have been subdivided into almost 20 rooms filled with everything from stuffed ele-

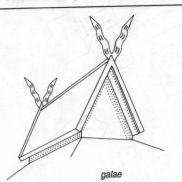

galae

Prasat

Elegant little buildings with ground plans in the form of a Greek cross, *prasats* may either serve religious or royal functions. Those designed for secular or royal purposes are capped with familiar multiple rooflines; religious *prasats* are crowned with *prangs*. Thailand's most famous *prasat* is at Bang Pa In, one hour north of Bangkok.

Other Structures

Sala: Open-walled structures used by pilgrims to escape the heat and by monks as casual dining rooms. *Salas* also serve as overnight shelters for pilgrims during temple festivals.

Ho Rakang: Bell or drum towers that summon monks to services and meals.

Ho Trai: Elevated, graceful libraries which house Buddhist canonical texts. *Ho trai* are built on stilts to prevent rats and white ants from devouring the precious manuscripts.

Kuti: Monk's quarters, often the simplest yet most attractive buildings in the *wat* complex. Older *kutis* are frequently on the verge of collapse; those in Petchburi are most evocative.

Kanbarien Hall: Religious instruction halls.

sema

phants to golden amulets. The two-storied South Wing, constructed in 1967, features early Thai statuary and artifacts from the Srivijaya, Dvaravati, and Lopburi periods. The North Wing includes later artwork from the Sukothai, Ayuthaya, and Bangkok periods.

The following highlights take three or four hours to cover. Visitors with limited time will probably best enjoy Wat Buddhaisawan, funeral chariots in the hall to the right, the Lopburi sculpture in the South Wing to the left, and the Sukothai Buddhas on the second floor of the North Wing.

Free Tours: To quickly sort through the artifacts, which range from Neolithic discoveries of Ban Chiang to contemporary Bangkok pieces,

museum volunteers conduct free guided tours starting at 0930 from the ticket desk. *These tours are highly recommended!* Without a tour, the bewildering collections often confuse and frustrate Western visitors who lack any formal background in the basics of Oriental art. English-language tours are given Tues.-Thurs. mornings. French tours are given on Wednesdays, German on Thursdays, and Japanese on Tuesdays. Special tours in Chinese and Spanish can also be arranged. Tours change frequently; call 224-1333 for further information.

Sivamohapiman Hall (2-4)
The ticket office and bookstore are located in the front, public restrooms to the rear.

NATIONAL MUSEUM

NORTH WING (GROUND FLOOR)

NORTH WING (UPPER FLOOR)

CENTRAL WING

PINKLAO RESIDENCE

SOUTH WING (GROUND FLOOR)

SOUTH WING (UPPER FLOOR)

WAT BUDDHAISAWAN

RED PAVILION

SIVA MOKHAPIMAN HALL

NOT TO SCALE

© MOON PUBLICATIONS, INC.

Gallery of Thai History (3): Galleries to the rear of the admission counter are somewhat gloomy and confusing, but nevertheless help sort through Thai epochs from Sukothai to the modern era. The prize exhibit is the famous Sukothai stele of King Ramkamheng, a stone slab which has generated a great deal of controversy regarding its authenticity. Also of interest are exhibits on possible origins of the Thai peoples, and dioramas of important events in Thai history.

Gallery of Pre-Thai History (4): Highlights include Paleolithic artifacts from Ban Kao near Kanchanaburi, and world-famous pottery and bronze ornaments from Ban Chiang in Udon Thani Province.

Wat Buddhaisawan (6)

Finest among the assorted historic buildings on the museum grounds is this superb chapel, widely considered one of the best surviving examples of early Bangkok monastic architecture. Wat Buddhaisawan was constructed in 1787 to house a greatly revered Buddha image (Pra Buddha Sing), which, according to legend, was fashioned in Sri Lanka. However, two identical images are also found in Chiang Mai and Nakhon Si Thammarat, and, as you might expect, residents in those communities are convinced that they possess the original Buddha. For the average Western visitor, it is the soaring interior roofline, shiny wooden floors, light streaming in through the open windows, and magnificent murals that remain the great attraction.

Chariot Hall (9)

Stored inside this large shed are immense ceremonial carriages still used for royal open-air cremations in nearby Sanam Luang. The largest prototype weighs over 20 tons and requires the physical manpower of several hundred men outfitted in traditional palace uniforms. Also displayed is a replica of the royal cremation pavilion used by the late King Rama VI.

Red Pavilion (10)

Once the home of Rama I's sister, the Tamnak Daeng (Red House) provides a quick look at the atmosphere and furnishings of a royal residence, circa 1782-1809. The Tamnak Daeng is constructed of prefabricated walls which allowed it to be moved several times before being placed on the museum grounds.

Central Wing (12-29)

Audience Hall (12): Formerly the hall of the surrogate monarch (a deputy ruler appointed to succeed the ruling king), the Issaravinitchai Hall now houses special exhibits such as recent archaeological discoveries and shows that have returned from international tours.

NATIONAL MUSEUM

1. entrance
2. ticket office and bookstore
3. Gallery of Thai History
4. Gallery of Pre-Thai History
5. King Vijiravudh Pavilion
6. Wat Buddhaisawan
7. Heir to the Throne Pavilion
8. Sala
9. Chariot Hall
10. Red Pavilion
11. King Rama IV Pavilion
12. Audience Hall
13. treasure room
14. palanquins
15. shadow puppets
16. royal gifts
17. ceramics
18. models
19. stamps and coins
20. ivory

21. antique weaponry
22. royal regalia
23. woodcarvings
24. steles
25. model boats
26. curiosities
27. costumes and textiles
28. flags
29. musical instruments

SOUTH WING-GROUND FLOOR

30. Asian art
31. museum office
32. Khmer and Lopburi
33. Hindu sculpture
34. Lopburi

SOUTH WING-UPPER FLOOR

30. Dvaravati
31. Dvaravati

32. Dvaravati
33. Javanese images
34. Srivijaya

NORTH WING-GROUND FLOOR

35. coin gallery
36. Buddha images
37. textiles
38. decorative arts
39. Bangkok
40. photographs

NORTH WING-UPPER FLOOR

35. Lanna and Chiang Saen
36. Sukothai
37. Sukothai
38. Ayuthaya
39. Ayuthaya
40. Bangkok

THAI ART STYLES

Thai Art Periods

Dvaravati	6th-11th centuries
Srivijaya	8th-13th centuries
Khmer (Lopburi)	11th-14th centuries
Chiang Saen	12th-14th centuries
Sukothai	13th-15th centuries
Ayuthaya	14th-18th centuries
Bangkok (Rattanakosin)	18th-20th centuries

Mon (Dvaravati) Style, 6th-11th Centuries

Thailand's earliest sculptural and architectural records were left by the Mons, a mysterious race of people who formed the loosely knit Dvaravati kingdoms of lower Thailand and Burma. Archaeologists surmise that Nakhon Pathom served as the Mon capital until the westward push of the Khmers in the 8th century drove them north to Haripunchai (modern-day Lamphun). Mon power dominated northern Thailand until the arrival of the Thais in the 13th century.

Architecture: Except for the early temples of Pagan—heavy structures built by the Burmese but based on Mon designs—little Mon architecture has survived the ravages of time, weather, and heavy-handed renovation. Thailand's premier Mon monument is Wat Kukut in Lamphun.

Sculpture: Mon Buddhist sculpture, often characterized as immobile and excessively solid, was perhaps influenced by Hindu Gupta art and the Ajanta cave temples. Mon Buddha images were cast of bronze using the lost-wax method, or carved of limestone in either a standing position or sitting on a throne in the so-called European manner. Whether cast or carved, all are quite remarkable in their depiction of Mon physiognomy: strong square jaws, flat noses, and thick lips. Outstanding Mon sculpture can be seen in the museums of Bangkok, Ayuthaya, and at Nakhon Pathom, where a hall adjacent to the golden chedi houses an immense seated Buddha.

Khmer (Lopburi) Style, 11th-14th Centuries

Between the fall of the Mon empire and the rise of Sukothai, much of central and eastern Thailand was ruled from Khmer military outposts at Pimai, Lopburi, Sukothai, and Kanchanaburi. Khmer art—sometimes called the Lopburi style after the town where much of the best art was produced—stands in sharp contrast to other Thai styles since it was inspired by Hinduism rather than Buddhism, and was funded by Khmer kings who considered themselves warrior gods and reincarnations of Shiva rather than benign Buddhist rulers. Cambodian art exudes energy and power, the mysterious and militaristic counterpart to gentle Thai art.

Architecture: By translating into stone the great myths of Hindu cosmology, Khmer architecture also created new motifs such as the prang, a bulbous tower of phallic proportions which symbolizes the Hindu-Buddhist paradise of Mount Meru. Well-preserved Khmer architecture can be seen in Sukothai, Lopburi, and Kanchanaburi, but the finest examples are scattered across the northeastern plains near Korat.

Sculpture: Khmer sculpture is typified by a seated, meditating Buddha who smiles enigmatically beneath the protective hood of the seven-headed naga. Other popular icons, either carved in stone or cast in bronze, include Hindu gods, bodhisattvas, and mythical garudas. The Lopburi style—by far the most famous of the various Khmer schools—developed a unique variation by fusing older Buddhist and Mon styles with Cambodian stylizations: thick upturned lips, elaborate headdresses, and enigmatic faces set with puzzling expressions of serenity and mystery.

Northern Styles, 10th-16th Centuries

Northern styles are often divided into several overlapping and somewhat bewildering movements centered at Haripunchai, Chiang Saen, and Chiang Mai, the final capital of the Lanna Kingdom.

Haripunchai: Located in the sleepy town of Lamphun just south of Chiang Mai, the kingdom of Haripunchai (10th-13th century) served as the last bastion of Mon (Dvaravati) power until conquered by King Mengrai in 1292. Reconstruction and remodeling have erased the distinctive Mon characteristics of most Dvaravati temples, with the notable exception of the square chedi of Wat Kukut in Lamphun. Haripunchai Buddhas with Mon triple-curve eyebrows and thick lips are displayed in the Bangkok and Lamphun museums.

Chiang Saen: Situated on the western banks of the Mekong just across from Laos, this small and practically deserted town served as the first capital of the Lanna Kingdom. Chiang Saen architecture is chiefly known for the 7th-century Wat Pra That Chom Kitti and Wat Pasak constructed by King Mengrai's grandson (1325-1335). Early Chiang Saen Buddha images with large hair curls and prominent eyes were influenced by the Pala school of northern India. Later Chiang Saen sculptures display a distinctive Thai style firmly rooted in the Sukothai tradition.

Chiang Mai or Lanna: Both the Haripunchai and Chiang Saen schools are sometimes lumped together with art of the powerful Lanna Kingdom, which flourished in northern Thailand between the 13th and 16th centuries. Lanna was established by King Mengrai, an ambitious Thai who conquered Chiang Saen and

Haripunchai before establishing a series of new capitals at Fang, Chiang Rai, and finally, Chiang Mai. Mengrai's successor, King Tiloka (1442-1488), proved himself an energetic patron of religion and the arts.

Chiang Mai continued to produce robust art until the Burmese conquered northern Thailand in the 16th century. As was the custom with devout Buddhists, most temples in Chiang Mai have been extensively restored and little of the original flavor has survived. Two important exceptions are Chedi Chet Yot, built in 1455 to celebrate Buddha's 2,000th anniversary, and Chedi Si Liem, built around 1300 by King Mengrai; both are considered masterpieces of Lanna architecture. Lanna sculpture can be seen in the museums at Bangkok and Chiang Mai.

Sukothai Style, 13th-15th Centuries

Reasons for the migration of the Thai (Tai) people into Siam are somewhat hazy. Some historians hold that the Mongol invasion of Kublai Khan forced them south from Yunnan into the fertile rice-growing plains of central Thailand. More likely, they slowly wandered down over the centuries or possibly had lived in the region since the early Bronze Age. The Thais remained an unorganized but subjugated race until the 13th century, when a pair of Thai princes revolted against Khmer rule and established the kingdom of Sukothai in central Thailand. This brief but brilliant period is now considered the Golden Age of Thai Art.

Architecture: Sukothai architecture, initially little more than pre-existing Khmer buildings embellished by Thai artists, matured during the reign of King Ramkamheng (1278-1318) into a dazzling array of architectural styles: octagonal-based Mon monuments, Sri Lankan *chedis* supported by stucco elephants, bulbous Khmer *prangs* surmounted by Hindu symbols, and soaring temples capped with distinctive lotus-bud finials. One hundred years of inspired construction left behind one of Southeast Asia's architectural gold mines, surpassed only by Pagan and Angkor Wat in Cambodia. Other impressive monuments in the same style can be seen in nearby Si Satchanalai and Kampang Phet.

Sculpture: Although the architecture of central Thailand is justifiably famous, Sukothai's creative genius is best epitomized by bronze statuary of enigmatic walking Buddhas—unquestionably some of the finest sculpture ever created in Southeast Asia. Conceived with an asexual and highly stylized body, hand raised in the gesture of teaching, arms like the trunk of an elephant, and hair like the stingers of scorpions, this walking Buddha somehow transcends religious anthropomorphism to capture the transcendent state of Buddhist nirvana. Sukothai sculptors also devised a Buddha footprint with 108 auspicious signs, and were the first artists to portray Buddha in the four positions of standing, walking, sitting, and reclining.

Ayuthaya Style, 1350-1767

Central Thailand, from the decline of Sukothai to the rise of Bangkok, was ruled by a powerful empire in Ayuthaya. Founded in 1350 by a U Thong prince who recognized the military importance of its location on the oxbow Lopburi River, Ayuthaya prospered from its enlightened trade policies, financed endless military campaigns, and by the 18th century boasted a population of over one million. European visitors of the age described it as one of the world's most impressive cities.

Architecture: If Sukothai was the Golden Age of Thai Sculpture, then Ayuthaya was the Golden Age of Thai Architecture. It was a period of great constructions; King Ramatibodhi alone erected over 400 monuments based on Khmer and Sri Lankan prototypes. Important architectural developments included towering *chedis* crowned by slim spires, the evolution of Khmer-influenced *prangs,* and overlapping roofs which characterize much of modern Thai architecture. Although Ayuthaya was almost completely destroyed by the Burmese in 1767, much of its former grandeur has been reconstructed by the Fine Arts Department.

Sculpture: Ayuthayan sculpture, on the other hand, became stereotypical and lost the spirituality which characterized the sculpture of Sukothai. Although often dismissed as indelicate, monotonous, and overly preoccupied with intricate detail, many Westerners appreciate the uncompromising expressions and remote authority of Ayuthayan bronzes. The Bangkok National Museum has several outstanding pieces.

Painting: Ayuthayan classical painting developed a relatively high level of expertise despite its two-dimensionality and lack of Western perspective. Very little has survived—most was tragically destroyed by the Burmese or lost to inferior application techniques which left the murals vulnerable to Thailand's wet climate. For this reason, the finest examples are found outside Ayuthaya in Petchburi, Uttaradit, and Bangkok.

Bangkok (Rattanakosin) Style, 1767-Present

After Ayuthaya was destroyed in 1767, the Thais moved downriver and restarted their capital at Thonburi, a small customs port directly across from the present city of Bangkok. The seat of government was moved to modern Bangkok for reasons of military defense.

Architecture: A building program, designed to recreate as far as possible the brilliance of Ayuthaya, was soon set in motion by the Chakri kings. Early monasteries and palaces, constructed by Rama I

(continued)

and modeled on earlier prototypes, featured typical Ayuthayan structures such as *chedis, prangs,* and *viharns.* (Thai architectural features are described above.) Temples constructed during the reign of Rama III were often embellished with Chinese touches, while Rama V fused Thai features such as multi-leveled roofs with Western neoclassical styles then popular in Europe. While this particular marriage wasn't successful, Bangkok-Period architecture is often a delightful combination of grand proportions, rich decorations, and blinding colors—all the elements that Westerners associate with the exotic East.

Sculpture: While Bangkok Period architecture was a major triumph, sculpture of the period was generally uninspired, lifeless, and slavishly obedient to Ayuthaya models. Creative traditions withered after Rama I shipped more than 1,200 bronze images from Ayuthaya to Bangkok. When Bangkok sculptors finally returned to the task of casting images, both competency and creativity had been lost. Rattanakosin sculpture in the National Museum in Bangkok graphically demonstrates its dismal state.

Painting: Sculpture may have sharply declined in creativity and sensitivity during the Bangkok period, but classical Thai painting enjoyed its own Golden Age. Scenes taken from the Ramakien, Jataka Tales, and Traiphum which decorate the inner walls of temples and royal residences often follow a standard arrangement: panels between the windows depict scenes of the Buddha's life; walls behind the Buddha altar relate the punishments of hell (surprisingly similar to the demonic paintings of Hieronymus Bosch); walls above the main entrance often portray Buddha in battle with the evil goddess Mara.

Treasure Room (13): Includes golden jewelry and precious gems from U Thong, Nakhon Pathom, and a stunning collection of objects discovered at Wat Rajaburana in Ayuthaya.

Palanquins (14): Funeral palanquins and elephant howdahs used in royal processions are displayed in the Phimuk Monthain gallery. Finest piece is the exquisite ivory howdah presented to King Chulalongkorn by a Chiang Mai prince.

Shadow Puppets (15): Stage properties, *khon* masks worn by dignitaries of the court of Rama VI, Chinese marionettes, Siamese polo sticks, and a rare collection of giant shadow puppets make this one of the more intriguing rooms in the central museum.

Ceramics (17): Highlights include 19th-century Bencharong ware, Sawankalok pottery, and Japanese and Chinese porcelains. Beautifully crafted mother-of-pearl screens are exhibited in the upstairs room.

Ivory (20): The sacred role of white elephants is noted with carved ivory tusks and sculpted elephant armor incised with religious talismans.

Antique Weaponry (21): A life-sized elephant mounted by a Thai warrior and covered with battle regalia dominates a room filled with antique firearms and 18th-century swords.

Royal Regalia (22): The central room offers thrones, a small royal pavilion, coronation regalia, and examples of the five traditional emblems of Thai royalty: *chatras* (tiered umbrellas), crowns, golden swords, fly whisks, and small golden shoes.

Woodcarvings (23): Extravagant teakwood carvings include circular monastery pulpits, Khmer *prangs,* mythological creatures such as *kinarees,* and a pair of doors salvaged from the Wat Suthat fire of 1959.

Steles (24): Resembling an ancient graveyard, this room displays teetering stones inscribed in Sanskrit, Pali, Khmer, and Thai.

Costumes and Textiles (27): A rare collection of Cambodian *ikats,* Indian brocades, Chinese silks, painted *phanung* garments, and Thai weavings executed with great skill. The upstairs room is devoted to religious artifacts and a monk's sole possessions: begging bowl, three orange robes, razor, a water sieve to filter out living creatures, sash, and a small sewing pouch.

Musical Instruments (29): Thai and other Southeast Asian instruments (Javanese *gamelans,* etc.) are displayed on an elevated veranda. Note the Thai *phipat* orchestra, comprised of xylophones, metallophones, gongs, cymbals, and flutes.

South Wing—Ground Floor (30-34)

Asian Art (30): This room demonstrates the overwhelming power and influence of Indian culture on early Thai art. Indian merchants, philosophers, and holy men reached Thailand shortly after the beginning of the Christian era, bringing with them Indian languages (Pali and Sanskrit), art, and religions which still influence modern Thai society. Among the highlights are 5th-century Sarnath Buddhas, 7th-century Gupta Buddhas, and 10th-century Pali-style steles.

Also displayed are images from Sri Lanka, Burma, Tibet, China, and Japan.

Khmer and Lopburi (32 and 34): Khmer culture and political power extended across Thailand from the 8th to 13th centuries, reaching an apex in the northeast and at the small ad-ministrative outpost of Lopburi. This room, and the room beyond the director's office, illustrate both pure Khmer styles (Kompong Prae, Baphuon, and Bayon) and Khmer/Thai fusions called Lopburi, named after the town where the two styles were successfully blended.

ICONOGRAPHY OF THE BUDDHA IMAGE

Visitors to the National Museum and temples of Thailand are often confused by the variety of Buddhas they find. The following description will help sort out the basic symbolism and describe the delicate balancing act between religious symbolism and the artist's urge to create new forms.

First-time visitors often consider Buddhist images monotonous lookalikes created with little imagination or originality, a not unfair judgment since Buddhist sculptors have traditionally been copyists who depicted Buddha images exactly as described in Pali religious texts. Creativity was also stifled by the sculptor's desire to exactly reproduce earlier images which had demonstrated magical powers. According to legend, an authorized Buddha image carved during Sakyamuni's lifetime absorbed his magical potency; sculptors believed that exact likenesses of the original would share these magical powers and provide the pious with supernatural protection.

The image's comprehensible and undisturbing symbolism is conveyed in dozens of ways: feet must be engraved with 108 auspicious signs; toes and fingers should be of equal length; hands should resemble the opening of lotus buds; arms should extend all the way to the knees; the magical spot between the eyes and protuberance from the forehead must represent enlightenment.

Despite these religious straitjackets, Thai artists successfully created a half-dozen unique styles which stand today as some of Asia's most refined art. Important characteristics which typify Dvaravati (6th-11th centuries), Khmer (11th-14th centuries), Northern (10th-16th centuries), Sukothai (13th-15th cen-

calling the earth to witness

turies), Ayuthaya (1350-1767), and Bangkok styles (1767-present) are described on pages 74-76.

Mudras Of The Buddha

Buddhist images throughout Thailand share common body positions (seated, standing, walking, and reclining) and hand gestures *(mudras)* which symbolically represent important events in the life of Buddha. Standing images depict Sakyamuni taming evil forces and bestowing blessings. Walking figures illustrate the Buddha returning to earth after preaching to his mother and deities in heaven. Reclining images embody the Buddha at the exact moment of nirvana—not sleeping, as visitors often assume! Sitting Buddhas relate various stories: meditating,

(continued)

reclining

witnessing divinity, or setting in motion the Wheel of the Law. Understanding the following *mudras* will prove invaluable when examining Buddha images throughout Southeast Asia.

Calling the Earth to Witness *Mudra*: Seated in either a full- or half-lotus position, the Buddha reaches forward to touch the ground with his right hand, an immensely popular *mudra* which symbolizes the Buddha's victory over the demons of Mara and testifies to his enlightenment.

Dispelling Fear *Mudra*: Either the left, right, or both hands are held at shoulder level with the palms turned outward. Used by both walking and standing Buddhas, this *mudra* evolved from a legend in which the Buddha raised his hand to subdue a rampaging elephant intent on his destruction. Also called the "Triumph over Evil" or "Giving of Protection" *mudra*.

meditation

Meditation *Mudra*: With one hand resting on the other and both legs crossed in a lotus position, this classic attitude represents the final meditation and enlightenment under the bodhi tree. Eyes are closed and breath is held to concentrate on the truth.

Adoration *Mudra*: Generally performed by bodhisattvas or lesser angels giving homage to the Buddha, this hand gesture is formed by joining both hands together vertically at the level of the breast—exactly like the Buddhist *wai*.

Dispensing Favors *Mudra*: Almost identical to the position of Dispelling Fear except that the palm is completely exposed, open, and empty, this *mudra* symbolizes the Buddha's vows of assistance and gifts of truth.

Turning the Wheel of the Law *Mudra*: Both hands are held before the chest with the thumb and forefinger of the right hand forming a circle. Representing the position that set in motion the wheel of the Buddhist law, this indestructible wheel also symbolizes karma, samsara, and the reality of nirvana.

dispelling fear

turning the wheel of law

TERRA MUZICK/3

Hindu Sculpture (33): Brahmanical devotional objects dating from the 3rd to 5th centuries have been discovered at two major sites in Thailand: Si Thep in Petchabun and the southern peninsula near Chaiya and Surat Thani. This room features a 7th-century stone Vishnu image found in Southern Thailand near Takua Pa, considered the most impressive Hindu sculpture uncovered in Thailand.

South Wing—Upper Floor (30-34)

Dvaravati (30-32): The pre-Thai artistic period was dominated by Mon culture (6th-11th centuries), a racial group which created empires at Nakhon Pathom near Bangkok and Haripunchai (modern-day Lamphun) in the north. Influenced by Indian post-Gupta styles and Amaravati traditions from South India and Sri Lanka, Mon art chiefly excelled in magnificent Buddhist sculpture with distinctive facial modelings. Displayed in these rooms are terra-cotta images in bas relief, stone Wheels of the Law which retell Buddha's first sermon at Sarnath, and extremely delicate busts which convey the inner calm of the enlightened Buddha.

Java (33): This small but worthwhile collection of images from Central Java (Borobudur and Prambanan) and East Java (Singosari and Malang) was donated by the Dutch colonialists to King Chulalongkorn during a state visit in 1896. The more important pieces were returned in the 1920s.

Srivijaya (34): The kingdom of Srivijaya, with its center either in Sumatra or at Chaiya in peninsular Thailand, dominated much of Southeast Asia during its heyday from the 7th to 9th centuries. As an entrepot for trade between India, Indonesia, and China, the resulting art style blends various schools such as Mon, Indian, Indo-Javanese, Khmer, and Chinese. Bodhisattvas and eight-armed goddesses surround a marvelously sinuous Bodhisattva Avalokitesvara from Chaiya.

North Wing—Ground Floor (35-40)

Coin Gallery (35): Numismatists will enjoy the collection of Chinese porcelain counters, 17th-century Cambodian coinage, bullet coins from the Sukothai era, and blocks of beaten metal which served as currency until the 19th century.

Buddha Images (36): Rather than a unified period room, this collection includes statues from various epochs. Dominating the enclosure is a colossal quartzite Buddha carved in Dvaravati style and seated in the so-called European fashion.

Textiles (37): Brocades, embroideries, cotton prints, and silks from the Bangkok Period.

Decorative Arts (38): Minor arts of the 19th and 20th centuries, such as lacquerware, ceramics, nielloware, silverwork, mother-of-pearl inlay, and illustrated manuscripts made of palm leaves and paper.

Bangkok (39): The Bangkok Period, also known as Rattanakosin, includes Thai art created since the founding of Bangkok in 1782. Early images imitated the styles of Ayuthaya with richly ornamented headdresses and impassive faces.

North Wing—Upper Floor (35-40)

Lanna (35): Lanna and Chiang Saen were art styles which flourished in Northern Thailand from the 13th to 16th centuries. Buddha images tend to be small but carefully cast with great attention.

Sukothai (36-37): The following two rooms contain the supreme art of Thailand, and one of the great movements of Southeast Asian art. Sukothai was an enlightened empire which ruled much of Thailand from the 13th to 15th centuries. Highlights of the first room include a pair of magnificent bronze statues: a four-armed Vishnu with a strangely flaired robe, and an eight-armed Harihara with hands formed in various *mudras*. The following room features more Buddhas, including a black bronze walking Buddha cast in an androgynous style. Although the long hike through the museum has exhausted you, this room deserves a close and careful inspection.

Ayuthaya (38-39): Ayuthaya served as the Thai capital between the fall of Sukothai and the establishment of Bangkok. Buddhas created during this period continued the traditions of Sukothai with a gradual embellishment of the headpieces and robes. Bejeweled Buddhas in a pose of subduing Mara are particularly fine.

Bangkok (40): Final stop covers modern Thai Buddhas and the minor arts from the Bangkok (Rattanakosin) Period. The collection seems rather lifeless and formalized after the exquisite pieces in the Sukothai and Ayuthaya rooms.

Wat Mahathat

The "Temple of the Great Relic" was constructed during the reign of King Rama I and houses Mahachulalongkorn University, one of the two highest seats of Buddhist learning in the country. It also serves as national headquarters for the Mahanikaya sect practiced by over 90% of the Buddhist population.

Wat Mahathat has little of great architectural value, but it functions as an important center for the study of Vipassana (insight) meditation. Westerners can obtain information on introductory seminars (given weekly in English, usually on Friday afternoons) and monthly meditation retreats from the International Buddhist Meditation Center (Dhamma Vicaya Hall, tel. 511-0439) in the rear center of the *wat* complex. Weekly lectures are often listed in the *Bangkok Post*.

Weekends and *wan pra* (Buddhist holy days) are an excellent time to visit the lively outdoor market which runs right through the temple grounds. With such great religious importance, it is hardly surprising that the temple serves as a major market for Buddhist amulets. Sales booths are found on Prachan Road near the Sanam Luang, and in a small *soi* (alley) which crosses Maharat Road and opens onto the riverside plaza. Located here are numerous shops filled with amulets, freshly cast Buddha images, and monk accessories such as begging bowls and orange robes.

National Art Gallery

The modern art museum opposite the National Theater exhibits traditional and contemporary works by both Thai and Western artists. Current shows are listed in the *Bangkok Post*. The gallery is open daily except Mondays and Fridays 0900-1600. Admission is 10B.

Earth Goddess Statue

Just opposite the Royal Hotel stands a small white pavilion and female statue erected by King Chulalongkorn as a public water fountain. This small monument merits a careful study since it illustrates one of the most beloved tales of Buddhist folklore, a story retold endlessly in murals and statues throughout Thailand.

According to legend, Buddha in the throes of meditation was repeatedly tempted by the evil goddess Mara and her sensual dancing ladies. Rather than submitting to temptation, the Buddha continued his meditation under the watchful gaze of the Earth Goddess Torani. So

SPORTS AT SANAM LUANG

Although the huge public ground in front of the Grand Palace is used for royal cremations and the annual plowing ceremony, you'll more likely to come across traditional Thai sports such as kite flying and *takraw*.

Kite Fighting: Thailand is one of the few countries in the world where a children's sport has developed into a form of combat. Kite fighting began after an Ayuthayan governor quelled a local rebellion by flying massive kites over the besieged city and using jars of explosives to bomb it into submission. Less violent competitions, such as the coveted King's Cup in April, are held today between two different types of kites with gender-inspired characteristics. Male kites *(chulas)* are sturdy, three-meter star-shaped fighting vessels fixed with bamboo barbs on reinforced strings. Female kites *(pakpao)*, on the other hand, are diminutive one-meter kites set with long tails and loops of string. The male kite attempts to snag the female and drag her into his territory, while the female uses her superior speed and maneuverability to avoid the male and force him to the ground.

Takraw: One of Thailand's most popular sports, *takraw* comes in several versions. Circle *takraw* involves bouncing a light ball made of braided rattan, the object being to keep the ball in motion as long as possible without using the hands. Points are awarded for employing the least-accessible body parts such as knees, hips, and shoulders. Basket *takraw* players attempt to kick the rattan ball through a ring elevated 6-10 meters above the ground. Net *takraw*—unquestionably the most exciting version— is played almost exactly like volleyball without hands. Overhead serves and foot spikes in this variation require an amazing degree of dexterity and acrobatic skill!

Fish Fighting: Though formally banned by the Thai government, pairs of male Siamese fighting fish *(Betta splendens regan)* still do combat in the side streets for the benefit of gamblers. Captured in swamps and raised in freshwater tanks, when placed in common tanks these pugnacious fish transform themselves into vividly colored fighting creatures complete with quivering gills and flashing tails. Also popular is insect fighting, which pitches enormous horned male beetles against each other for the charms of a female attendant. The battle ends when the weaker beetle dies on its back.

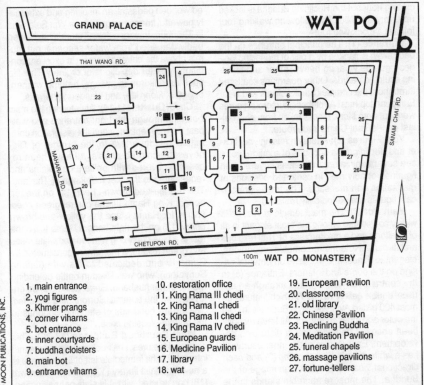

WAT PO

GRAND PALACE

THAI WANG RD.

MAHARAJ RD.

SANAM CHAI RD.

CHETUPON RD.

0   100m   **WAT PO MONASTERY**

1. main entrance
2. yogi figures
3. Khmer prangs
4. corner viharns
5. bot entrance
6. inner courtyards
7. buddha cloisters
8. main bot
9. entrance viharns
10. restoration office
11. King Rama III chedi
12. King Rama I chedi
13. King Rama II chedi
14. King Rama IV chedi
15. European guards
16. Medicine Pavilion
17. library
18. wat
19. European Pavilion
20. classrooms
21. old library
22. Chinese Pavilion
23. Reclining Buddha
24. Meditation Pavilion
25. funeral chapels
26. massage pavilions
27. fortune-tellers

© MOON PUBLICATIONS, INC.

impressed was Torani with his courage, compassion, and moral willpower, that she wrings her long hair, setting loose a tidal wave which sweeps away Mara and her evil armies.

Wat Po

Bangkok's oldest and largest temple complex was founded in the 16th century, when Ayuthaya was the capital, and radically remodeled between 1781 and 1801 by Rama I, who renamed the complex Wat Pra Chetupon. The area was extended in the 1830s by Rama III in his quest to establish an open-air university for his Thai subjects. This educational wonderland included inscriptions on traditional sciences, extracts from the *Jatakas,* marble tablets that taught the rules of traditional Thai massage, litanies of the reincarnations of Vishnu, treatises on astrology and palmistry, illustrations on world geography, and

rishi figures contorted to demonstrate control over the physical body. In 1832 Rama III constructed an immense chapel to house the statue of the Reclining Buddha; Wat Po is often called the "Temple of the Reclining Buddha."

Wat Po today is one of the more fascinating temple complexes in Bangkok, because of both its curiosity value and artistic achievement. Crammed into the courtyards are a bewildering number of chapels, rock gardens, bizarre statuary, educational tablets, belltowers, and dozens of small *chedis.* The complex has two major highlights: the superb *bot* to the right of the entrance, and the gigantic reclining Buddha in the rear courtyard. Guides are available at the front entrance on Soi Chetupon, though their services are hardly necessary.

Wat Po is open daily 0800-1700. Admission is 10B. Visitors can wander around the yards past closing hour but the Reclining Buddha is locked up firmly at 1700. The following walking tour follows a clockwise route.

Entrance (1): The principal entrance (in the back alley) is flanked by a pair of menacing Chinese guards wearing heavy armor and sporting sculpted beards. Other guardians scattered throughout the complex smoke cigars and wear European top hats! All of these humorous figures were cut from stone blocks taken from ship ballast on the Thai-China trade route.

Yogi Figures (2): After purchasing your ticket and declining the services of a guide, you'll see several miniature mountains covered with figurines of holy men in contorted positions of meditation and massage. The fragile plaster-cast figures are periodically replaced.

Main Bot (8): The main temple at Wat Po is widely considered among the most elegant in all of Thailand and a masterpiece of Thai religious architecture. Note the remarkable proportions, elegant rooflines, and exquisite ornamental design on the doors and interiors. Entrance (5) to the central courtyard is made through an unusual double gallery (6 and 7) which features almost 400 gilded Ayuthaya-style Buddhas in both the outer and inner chambers. All have recently been encased behind glass, a disturbing development. Each corner of the inner courtyard has a white-marble Khmer *prang* (3) and each directional *viharn* (9) features an image of the Buddha. The most remarkable stands in the east *viharn* where the Buddha Lakanard dispenses blessings to the faithful.

Before entering the main *bot,* note the 16 fine bronze lions which guard the eight stairways, and the famous bas reliefs which surround the base. These tablets relate the story of the Ramakien, the Thai version of the Hindu Ramayana. Rubbings of woodcut copies (not the original stones) can be purchased at the souvenir shop. Also see the Chinese landscapes, *farangs* on horseback, and black-faced Moorish traders on the exquisite mother-of-pearl doorways.

The main doorway to the *bot* is located to the east, away from the river. The interior features a high nave flanked by twin rows of thick square columns painted with floral patterns and hung with drawings of old Bangkok. Note the loudspeaker system! Directly ahead is a well-illuminated Buddha magnificently elevated on a gild-ed wooden pedestal, an inspiring and extremely powerful image removed from Wat Sala Sina in Thonburi. Interior sidewall murals have been badly damaged from water seepage, but murals above the entrance remain in excellent condition; look for depictions of ordinary Thai life such as children in swings, bathing women, beggars, *klong* life, and wandering hermits.

Chedi Quartet (11-14): After touring the main *bot,* exit through the front entrance and walk past the main entrance and the restoration committee headquarters to the quartet of Disneyesque-colored *chedis*. All have been recently recovered with brilliant porcelains and rededicated to the first four kings of Thailand. The orange-and-brown *chedi* (11) on the left honors King Rama III, the central green *chedi* (12) is for Rama I, and the yellow-and-brown *chedi* (13) on the right honors Rama II. To the rear is a blue *chedi* (14) with red and white roses and green foliage, a monument constructed by Rama IV and dedicated to his wife (Queen Suriyothai), who was killed in battle defending the life of her husband. Great views can be enjoyed from the summit. Surrounding the *chedi* cloister are hundreds of standing Buddhas in the double-blessing pose.

West Courtyard Buildings (17-22): This courtyard features a half-dozen halls of marginal interest. To the immediate left of the entrance is a new Buddhist library (17) and a modern *wat* (18) constructed with little style or imagination. The so-called European Pavilion (19)—more Chinese than Western—fronts a small pond flanked with monkey statues and a model of the *chedi* at Nakhon Pathom; a good place to relax and mix with the resident monks. Other buildings include classrooms (20), a display of traditional Thai musical instruments, an old library (21) restored with decorative flowers, green tiles, and small *nagas* at each corner, and the Chinese Pavilion (22) with its centerpiece tree.

Reclining Buddha (23): Certainly the most famous sight at Wat Po is the gigantic Reclining Buddha housed under a claustrophobic shed in the western courtyard. The 46- by 15-meter image, constructed of plaster over a brick core, represents the Buddha passing into nirvana. Thailand's largest reclining Buddha is difficult to appreciate in such tight settings, but special attention should be paid to the intricate mother-of-pearl designs on the footsoles which depict the 108 signs of the true Lord Buddha.

Massage Pavilion (26): As intriguing as the giant image is the College of Traditional Medicine in the eastern courtyard. This royal-sponsored mini-university of massage, herbal medicine, and Chinese acupuncture offers inexpensive, traditional Thai rubs: 80B for 30 minutes, 150B for one hour. Thirty hours of professional instruction spread over 10 days (three hours daily) or 15 days (two hours daily) costs 3000B. Fortune-tellers (27) ply their trade in the adjacent courtyard.

SEEING MORE OF THE OLD ROYAL CITY

A walking tour of the Old Royal City continues on the second day with a look at the temples and monuments east of the river. Time permitting, continue down Rajadamnern Avenue to Banglampoo and the Pra Arthit boat stop, or take a taxi to the Marble Temple in the New Royal City.

Wat Rajapradit

Constructed in 1864 by King Mongkut to complete the holy triumvirate of Ayuthayan temples, this picturesque but minor *wat* is noted for its widely diverse collection of architectural styles. The Thai-style *bot* is raised on a stone platform and surrounded by gray marble columns incised in an unusual checkerboard design. Interior murals offer clear views of Bangkok during the 1860s and royal ceremonies held during the 12 months of the year. Resident monks can unlock the door. To the left is an Ayuthayan-style *prang* superbly carved with images of four-faced Brahma, while a Bayon-style *prang* stands to the right. To the rear of the *bot* is a Sinhalese-style *stupa* wedged between construction clutter and sleeping attendants.

Wat Rajapradit is open daily 0800-1900 and can be easily visited on the walk from the Grand Palace to Wat Suthat. No admission charge.

Your walking tour then passes a strange bronze pig near the canal, a funny little monument which commemorates the birth year of Queen Saowapha, a consort of King Chulalongkorn.

Wat Rajabopit

One of the more unusual temples in Bangkok, Wat Rajabopit was constructed in 1863 by King Chulalongkorn on the plan of the famous *stupa* at Nakhon Pathom. Entrance is made through doorways carved and painted with whimsical figures of European guards. Surrounding the *chedi* is a circular cloister decorated with ceramic tiles and interrupted at cardinal points by three *viharns* and the principal *bot* on the north. The *bot* displays familiar Thai rooflines on the exterior, but surprises you with its interior: a miniature Italian-Gothic chapel inspired by Western models. Special note should be made of the Chinese Bencharong tiles which cover the exterior walls and blend beautifully with the darker golds and blues of the glazed roof tiles. Another glory of Wat Rajabopit is the symmetrical mother-of-pearl inlays in the 10 doors and 28 windows, some of the finest inlay work in all of Thailand.

To the west of the *chedi* courtyard is a royal cemetery constructed by Rama V to honor his parents and relatives. Tombs have been styled after Indian *chedis*, Cambodian *prangs*, and miniature Gothic cathedrals. The garden even includes a walkway reconstructed in Cambodian fashion with dancing *asparas* and roofline *nagas*.

Wat Rajabopit is open daily 0800-1700. No admission charge.

Wat Suthat

The massive *viharn* and *bot* of Wat Suthat form one of the most powerful and elegant monuments in Bangkok. The complex was initiated by Rama I in the early 19th century and completed by his two successors over the next three decades.

Wat Suthat is open daily 0800-1700. No admission charge. For best effect, enter from Bamruang Road (opposite the Giant Swing) rather than from the side doors on Triphet Road.

Courtyard: The spacious and well-proportioned courtyard serves as an open museum filled with stone figurines, outstanding bronzework, and Buddha images in various poses. Surrounding the *viharn* balustrade are 28 hexagonal Chinese pagodas and eight genuine masterpieces: absolutely superb bronze horses that flank the four corners of the *viharn*. All have assumed a sheen of fine green patina; several retain their original red eyes. Chinese statuary of

American sailors and Chinese warlords strategically stand near connecting doorways.

Viharn: The magnificent *viharn* of Wat Suthat—noted for its exceptional height and powerful proportions—exudes a monumental effect rarely witnessed in Thai religious architecture. The entire sanctuary is elevated on two ascending platforms and bordered by four Chinese stone pagodas which house Buddhas in various poses. Entrance to the central chapel is made through a grandiose portico which frames three massive wooden doors, carved under the direction of Rama III to depict the mythical forest of Himavada. Shoes must be checked outside.

The immense gathering hall houses an eight-meter 14th-century bronze Sakyamuni Buddha previously resident in Sukothai's Wat Mahathat. Widely considered one of the great masterpieces of Thai sculpture, the Pra Sakyamuni Buddha richly deserves the veneration accorded by pilgrims and the sumptuous setting created for it by Rama I and II. Other interior elements include partially restored frescoes that illustrate the lives of various bodhisattvas, eight square marble pillars which support the soaring roof, and an enormous carved wooden pedestal which buttresses the central image. A room with great power.

Bot: Looming beyond the wall which separates the anterior and posterior courtyards is an enormous whitewashed *bot* constructed between 1839 and 1843 by King Rama III. The surrounding courtyard features elaborate *bai sema* boundary stones protected inside stone chambers, and various oddities such as stone European soldiers and sculpted trees. Entrance into the *bot* can be extremely tricky to find; try all possible gateways, including the small gate at the southwest corner.

Dominating the interior is a life-size black Buddha figure donated by Rama III and a school of 80 kneeling disciples who listen to the master with backs turned to the entrance. But it is the interior murals—regarded as among the finest in Thailand—that are the chief attraction in the *bot.* Dating from the reign of King Rama II (1809-1824) and painted in flat tints, these murals employ primitive perspectives which predate Western techniques. The 24 window panels retell the *Jataka* tales of previous incarnations of the Buddha, shutters illustrate the celestial city of Indra, and the front wall shows Buddha overcoming the evil temptations of Mara.

A restoration committee headed by the Fine Arts Department has been charged with returning the badly damaged murals to original condition. After the remaining stucco has been resealed against the wall, the missing sections are sketched in and painted anew with special watercolors. Distinctive brush techniques are used to differentiate restorations from the original artwork.

Giant Swing

Opposite Wat Suthat tower a pair of red teak pillars once used for the Brahmanic "Ceremony of the Swing," an annual festival which honored the earthly return of the Hindu god Shiva. Until being halted in 1935, teams of young Hindu priests would swing a full arch of 180 degrees and attempt to snatch a bag of gold coins between their teeth. Some bit the gold, others bit the dust.

Hindu Shrine

Though Brahmanism has been an integral part of Thai royal life since the 14th century, few

red-eyed beauty

temples in Bangkok exclusively honor the Hindu triumvirate of Brahma, Shiva, and Vishnu. These three small chapels, situated near the Giant Swing, pay homage with displays of an Ayuthayan-style Vishnu, dancing Nataraja Shivas, and four-headed Brahmas. A replica of the giant swing complete with golden chariot and mythical *kinaree* bird stands in front. Side chapels used for Brahmanic wedding ceremonies display other exquisite Hindu images. The rear alley serves as a production center for enormous bronze Buddhas.

A small Brahmanic Vishnu shrine is located on Mahachai Road adjacent to Wat Suthat.

Religious Supplies

Streets adjoining Wat Suthat specialize in religious paraphernalia such as bright orange robes, image stands, alms bowls, fans, and attractive umbrellas. Dozens of shops sell monstrous bronze images that eventually grace many of the temples in Thailand.

Baan Baht—the so-called "Monks Bowl Village"—is a tiny corner of Bangkok where the forging of alms bowls clings tenuously to the old traditions. Much of this traditional craft has been lost to modern manufacturing methods.

Chinese Temple

Two blocks west of City Hall is a lively Chinese temple called San Chao Pah Sua. Rather than a sedate Buddhist *wat,* Chinese temples are a continual beehive of activity as worshipers arrive to burn incense and have their fortunes told with sticks and kidney-shaped blocks of wood. Caged birds at the front can be purchased and set free to improve your karma.

Wat Rajanada And The Amulet Market

Erected in 1846 by Rama III, the main sanctuary features remarkable wall paintings of paradise and hell above the entrance, and side walls decorated with angels and celestial symbols. Entrance is made from a gate on the right side. The small *viharn* on the left is noted for its unusual design and the Rattanakosin-style Buddhas displayed on the central altar.

Wat Rajanada is chiefly noted for its popular amulet market at the far left end of the courtyard. Much of the informal street trade in amulets once conducted at Wat Mahathat has been moved into more permanent stalls on these

MAGICAL MEDALLIONS

Thais believe that protection against malevolent spirits, reckless *phis,* and black magic can be guaranteed with amulets—small talismanic icons worn around the neck or waist. Extraordinarily powerful amulets derive their magic from having been blessed by Buddhist monks or issued by powerful organizations such as the military or monarchy. For example, those recognized by the king and distributed to policemen have acquired considerable renown for their protective powers. Small votive tablets found buried inside the relic chambers of ancient stupas are also deemed extra powerful. Amulet collection is big business here in Thailand; over a dozen publications are devoted exclusively to their histories and personal accounts of their powers.

Each profession favors a certain style: taxi drivers wear amulets to protect against accidents, thieves to protect against the police; American soldiers during the Vietnam War became fascinated with their miraculous powers. Color is also important: white amulets arouse feelings of love, green protects against ghosts and wild animals, yellow promotes successful business deals, red offers protection against criminals. But black is the most powerful color—it provides *complete* invincibility.

Among the more bizarre amulets are those fashioned after the phallus *(palad khik)* and realistically carved from rare woods, ivory, or horn. Related to Hindu lingam worship, *palad khik* are attached to cords and worn around the waist. A great way for Westerners to make friends and influence people is to proudly wear an amulet of the king or queen.

grounds. Buddhist amulets make great gifts and, unlike Buddha images, may be legally taken out of the country without an official permit.

Lohaprasat

To the rear of Wat Rajanada stands a curious pink building which resembles, more than anything else, an ornate wedding cake festooned with 37 candle-spires. Lohaprasat was designed to resemble ancient temples in Sri Lanka and India which, according to legend, served as mansions for the Buddha and his disciples. The first thousand-room structure was erected in India by a rich lady disciple named Visakha, the second in Anaradapura by a Sri Lankan king who decorated the roof with precious stones and ivory. Both prototypes have long since disappeared, leaving Bangkok's structure the world's only surviving example of this unique style. Lohaprasat is now closed and no longer an active *wat*, but local groundskeepers can provide a key.

Pah Fah Pavilion

In a rare case of civic improvement, the recent destruction of the Chalerm Thai movie theater on Rajadamnern Avenue—and the subsequent erection of the Pan Fah Pavilion—has created an attractive tableau of royal *salas*, Wat Rajanada, and the Lohaprasat.

Golden Mountain

One of the few places from which to peer (smog permitting) over sprawling Bangkok is high atop the 78-meter artificial mountain just outside the ancient capital walls. Modeled after a similar hill in Ayuthaya, the hilltop is surmounted by a modest *chedi* which enshrines Buddha relics donated to King Chulalongkorn by Lord Curzon, Viceroy of India. Visitors climbing the 320 steps are often approached by young monks anxious to practice their English and older, cynical monks more interested in rock music than nirvana. The walkway winds past graves fixed with photos of the deceased, Buddhist shrines, and miniature mountains. Summit views sweep across the Royal Palace, Wat Arun in Thonburi, and modern edifices such as the multi-hued Baiyoke Towers.

Wat Saket, at the foot of the mount, sponsors Bangkok's liveliest temple festival each November. Once used as a dumping ground for victims of plague, the *wat* is undistinguished aside from its late-Ayuthayan lacquered windows and the International Central Library of Buddhist Literature on the right of the main walkway.

THE NEW ROYAL CITY

The following sights are located in northern Bangkok, a modern administrative center blessed with traditional temples, an old royal palace, and pleasant neighborhoods almost completely untouched by mass tourism. Also known as the Dusit or New Royal City, this region was established around the turn of the century by King Chulalongkorn to escape the

cramped conditions in his riverside Royal Palace.

Various walking tours are possible depending on your time and interest. One option is to begin with a boat ride to the Pra Arthit pier in Banglampoo, followed by a quick look at Pra Arthit Fort and a stroll through the backpackers' center of Khao San Road. Wat Bowonivet and shopping in the New World Center are also recommended. The famous Marble Temple (Wat Benjamabopit) can be reached by taxi, or with a long hike along Rajadamnern Nok Avenue or through the neighborhoods which flank the Chao Praya River. Vimanmek Palace and the Dusit Zoo complete the tour. Visitors short on time should go directly to the Marble Palace.

Pra Arthit Fort

Also known as Pra Sumane, this octagonal fort was constructed by King Rama I to defend the northern extremity of his young capital against Burmese and Cambodian invasion. The present reconstruction dates from 1982 and is based on old drawings and photographs.

Khao San Road

A walk through the neighborhood of Banglampoo is highly recommended for both budget backpackers searching for inexpensive guesthouses and tourists exploring the back streets of Bangkok. Khao San Road is not only one of the liveliest travelers scenes between Kuta and Kathmandu, but also an excellent place for cheap air tickets, inexpensive clothing, and delicious fruit smoothies. Shopping opportunities include several used bookstores with hard-to-find travel guides, sidewalk cassette emporiums, and a great selection of Thai handicrafts. Travel agents on Khao San Road sell the cheapest airline tickets in town, plus the most economical tours of Bangkok and outlying districts. Also worth checking out are the local notice boards with information on upcoming Buddhist retreats and employment opportunities teaching English, plus local merchants who pay cash for used Levis, Walkmans, and wives.

A few blocks north is a popular shopping district dominated by the New World Shopping Center; daily bargains on the main floor and better-quality merchandise on the upper seven floors. Adjacent streets are filled with inexpensive clothing and foodstalls.

Wat Bowonivet

Wat Bowonivet is an architecturally modest but spiritually important temple where many of Thailand's kings and princes have traditionally served their monkhood. The temple was constructed in the early 19th century by King Rama III, but gained great fame when Prince Mongkut (of *The King and I* fame) founded the Thammayut sect of Thai Buddhism and served as chief abbot during a portion of his 27-year monkhood. Today, the complex serves as home to the Supreme Patriarch and the national headquarters of the Thammayut monastic sect, an order which follows a stricter discipline than that of the traditional Mahanikaya. Because of its royal origin and highly disciplined form of Buddhism, Wat Bowonivet enjoys an elevated reputation among the Thai people.

Courtyard: Several small but noteworthy images are displayed in the courtyard off Prasumen Road. The overall plan revolves around a central gilded *chedi* with two symmetrical chapels to the north and south. To the right of the central *bot* is a Buddha's footprint, a walking Buddha in the Sukothai style, two small Buddhas in the Lopburi style, and, on a raised niche, a Javanese Buddha perhaps imported from Borobudur. To the left is a Dvaravati Buddha. A beautiful reclining Buddha is located at the rear wall.

Bot: Though the *wat* lacks many of the graceful attributes so characteristic of other leading monasteries, a few special features make this temple worth a brief visit. The building is constructed in an unusual T-shape with its head facing north. Of special merit inside the *bot* is a bronze Sukothai Buddha, cast in 1257 to commemorate the country's liberation from Khmer rule and considered one of the finest of the period. Another Buddha image, finely bathed in diffused half-light, sits to the rear. Flanking these two Buddhas are standing images which represent Buddha's chief disciples, Mokkanlana and Saributr. The top tier of the gorgeously decorated gilt altar features a small image known as Pra Nirantaraj, one of 18 statues distributed among the monasteries of the Thammayut sect by King Mongkut.

The walls are blanketed with extraordinary murals. Far removed from the traditional concept of Thai art, these dark and mysterious frescoes are the highly personalized work of a Thai artist named Kru Ing Khong, who revolutionized classic Thai artwork with his original use of three-dimensional perspective, moody shading, and fascinating use of Western subjects: Englishmen at the horse races, American ships arriving with missionaries, Colonial buildings, and Dutch windmills.

Murals between the windows depict scenes of various religious ceremonies, while high above the windows are 16 tableaux symbolic of the Buddhist Trinity: the Buddha, his Dharma, and the Sangha. Column murals relate the spiritual transformation of man, progressing from the dark and gloomy colors on the bottom to the lighter and more exalted hues near the ceiling. As a unified ensemble, the murals are unique in the history of Thai painting.

Chedi: Centerpiece of Wat Bowonivet is the great golden *chedi* which enshrines sacred relics and ashes of Thai royalty.

Viharns: Behind the *bot* and *chedi* are two *viharns*, normally closed to the public. The larger structure contains two famous statues brought from Sukothai and Phitsanulok; the smaller hall offers wall paintings depicting episodes from the famous Chinese story of Sam Kok.

Along with Wat Mahathat near the Grand Palace, Wat Bowonivet is a popular temple for meditation instruction. English-speaking visitors can inquire at the international section.

Wat Indraram

A short taxi ride or long hike through traditional neighborhoods is required from Banglampoo to the Marble Temple in the New Royal City. The most direct route is down Rajadamnern Avenue, past Democracy Monument and the Tourist Office. A more relaxing option is across the canal from the New World Shopping Center and then north through the winding alleys that skirt the Chao Praya River. A brief diversion can be made to the 33-meter Buddha image at Wat Indraram. Constructed in 1830 of brick and plaster, this absolutely hideous Buddha redeems itself with great views from the tower to the rear of his head.

Benjamabopit (Marble Temple)

The most famous attraction in the Dusit area, and one of the finest examples of modern Thai architecture, is on Sri Ayuthaya Road near the Chitralada Palace.

Wat Benjamabopit was erected by Rama V at the turn of the century to replace an older temple torn down to expand the Dusit Palace. Designed by the half-brother of the king, the elegant complex is largely constructed of white Carrara marble imported from Italy, hence the popular nickname "Marble Temple."

Wat Benjamabopit is open daily from sunrise until 1700. Admission is 10B. The *wat* is best visited in the early morning hours when resident monks gather to collect alms and chant in the chapel. Services are also held in the late afternoon.

Bot: Beyond the unusual ornamental railing which encircles the complex is a central hall with overlapping multiple roofs, and two small pavilions containing a bronze Buddha seated under a *naga* and a white alabaster image imported from Burma. The four directional gables are elaborately carved with Vishnu riding a *garuda* (east), the three-headed elephant Erawan (north), a *unalom* which represents the curl of the Buddha's forehair (west), and a Wheel of the Law (south). Guarding the *bot* are two mythical marble lions seated in the Burmese position. Considered as a unified emsemble, Wat Benjamabopit is a masterpiece of superb harmony and pleasing symmetry.

Dominating the interior is a large gold statue of Pra Buddha Chinarat, an excellent copy of the highly venerated image in Phitsanulok. An urn under the altar holds ashes of King Chulalongkorn, while wall niches around the central image, transept, and nave contain murals of famous *prangs* and *chedis* from Sawankalok, Ayuthaya, Nakhon Pathom, Nakhon Si Thammarat, Lamphun, Nakhon Phanom, and Lopburi. Also note the vibrant and distinctive stained-glass windows designed by Siamese artists but crafted in Florence, Italy.

Gallery Statues: Perhaps the most famous sight at the Marble Temple is the outstanding collection of 53 Buddha statues displayed in the rear cloisters. To present a complete iconography to his subjects, King Chulalongkorn gathered together in one spot the finest examples—both originals and copies—of bronze Buddhas in the world. Taken together, they provide an amazing opportunity to study the artistic development and range of styles from Thailand, India, Sri Lanka, China, and Japan. Each has been carefully labeled as to the country of origin and

period . . . better than art school! Notable masterpieces include a "Starving Buddha" cast from an original in Lahore, two standing Buddhas of the Sukothai Period, Burmese images from Pagan, copies of Japanese and Chinese Buddhas, plus rare stone Dvaravati images protected against theft by iron grilles.

Vimanmek Palace

Vimanmek is a beautiful and gracious L-shaped palace believed to be one of the world's largest golden teakwood structures. The palace was designed by a German architect named Sandreczki and constructed in 1893 by King Rama V on Si Chang Island in the Gulf of Siam. Chulalongkorn's fascination with Western architecture was reflected in the Victorian style and gingerbread fretwork which allowed the sun to make lacy patterns on the walls. In 1901 the king ordered the unfinished palace disassembled and moved to his new royal enclave of Suan Dusit in Bangkok. Vimanmek ("Castle in the Clouds") served as a royal residence for Rama V and his family (92 wives and 77 children!) until abandoned for larger quarters in 1908. The palace fell into disrepair until being completely renovated by Queen Sirikit and Princess Sirindorn in 1982, the year of the Bangkok Bicentennial.

Vimanmek today is a three-story, 81-room museum displaying a rich collection of royal regalia and the eclectic assemblage of King Chulalongkorn: period furniture, the country's first shower whose hidden water tank was manually filled by royal pages, and a photograph of Thomas Edison inscribed "to the King and Queen of Siam."

The palace is open daily 0930-1630. Admission is 50B at the door, but free with your ticket stub from the Grand Palace. Complimentary guided tours are given hourly until 1500.

Dusit Zoo

Opposite Chitralada Palace, Thailand's largest zoo offers a modest collection of Asian animals such as elephants, rhinos, and monkeys. Also situated within the grounds is an artificial lake where pedalboats and rowboats can be rented. Though hardly spectacular, the zoo provides a welcome escape from the heat and congestion of Bangkok. Dusit Zoo is open daily 0800-1800. Admission is 10B.

CHINATOWN

Chinatown is one of the most exotic and stimulating ethnic enclaves in Southeast Asia, the extraordinary showcase of Old Bangkok. Bounded by the Chao Praya River on the west and Charoen Krung Rd. on the east, this seething, frenetic, and jam-packed neighborhood offers visitors a chance to escape the temple rut and experience the old East of Maugham and Conrad. Although the main boulevards have now assumed the monotonous veneer of modernity, behind the facade lies the *real* Chinatown: smoky temples filled with robed Taoist monks, pharmacies selling antelope horn and cobra venom, rattan vendors, innumerable shops where Chinese merchants demonstrate their legendary commercial talents, jewelry emporiums piled high with gold chains and necklaces, and countless street peddlers who add to the perpetual spectacle.

Chinatown was founded in the late 18th century after King Rama I asked Chinese merchants to vacate the land intended for his Grand Palace. Early Teochew (Chiu Chow) entrepreneurs built their thriving businesses along Sampeng Lane, a narrow and claustrophobic alley which served as a commercial center by day, but which became an untamed district of brothels, gambling dens, and opium parlors at night. By the early 20th century, Soi Sampeng had been dubbed the "Green Light District," since local brothels hung green rather than red lanterns over their doorways. Today, Chinatown has traded its notorious reputation for the complacency of commerce, but enough exotic culture remains to make this one of the best walking tours in Bangkok.

Walking Tour: The scattered attractions and kaleidoscopic sense of disorder make an organized walking tour of Chinatown rather difficult. The following tour is simply meant to steer you in the right direction and help you find the more fascinating side streets and shopping districts. Visitors short on time should concentrate on Sampeng Lane, Wat Leng Nee Yee, the shopping alley of Soi 16, and the Pahurat Cloth Market.

Rajawong Pier

Begin your tour with a boat ride from Silom Rd. or Banglampoo to Tha Rajawong (Rajawongse Pier) and walk up Rajawong (Ratchawong) Road past several banks and a lovely green trading firm constructed in a Moorish-German style. Turn left on Anuwong Rd. and then right on Krai Alley to your first attraction.

Boonsamakan Vegetarian Hall

Bangkok's finest Chinese woodcarvings are displayed in this lovely, yellow century-old vegetarian hall nestled away in a quiet back alley. Exterior details along the front porch include Chinese dragons and mythical phoenixes, miniature wooden tableaux of Chinese opera scenes protected behind glass cases, plus three-dimensional painted tilework of Chinese legends. All have been carved with great care by master craftsmen. Inside are three elaborately carved altars adorned with gilded masterpieces and eight-sided doors which lead into anterior chambers.

Chinese vegetarian halls are only crowded during the annual Vegetarian Festival, which honors the nine deities enshrined here on the main altar. Otherwise, this beautiful hall remains quiet and peaceful, unlike most Chinese shrines and temples, which typically teem with worshipers. Just opposite is a stage used for Chinese opera troupes which perform during the Vegetarian Festival, held in the ninth month of the Chinese calendar.

Sampeng Lane

Soi Sampeng, or Soi Wainit 1, epitomizes what is most alluring and memorable about Chinatown. Much too narrow for cars, this canvas-roofed lane is crammed with shopkeepers, porters hauling heavy loads, clothing merchants (both wholesale and retail), and rare examples of prewar architecture. Walk *extremely* slowly to enjoy the extraordinary scene. Sensory overload at its finest! A few shops are worth special attention.

Gold Shop: At the intersection of Soi Mangkorn is Tang Toh Gang, a remarkable seven-storied yellow building with an imposing tier of balconies designed by a Dutch architect. Tang Toh Gang once served as the central Gold Exchange for Chinatown.

Guan U Shrine: Left on Soi Issaranuparp is a small temple with a large wooden horse; feed him some oats and then ring the bell around his neck.

Talaad Kao: Chinese visit this medieval mar-

CHINATOWN

PAK KLONG MARKET

SAPHAN PHUT PIER

ARTS & CRAFTS SCHOOL

TRIPHET RD.

CHALERM KRUNG THEATER

BURAPA RD.

PAHURAT CLOTH MARKET

SHOPPING CENTER

WAT

SIKH TEMPLE

CHINESE TEMPLE

INDIAN RESTS.

CENTRAL DEPT. STORE

CHAKRAPET RD.

LITTLE INDIA

RIVERSIDE RESTAURANT

CHAKRAWAT RD.

NAKHON KASEM "THIEVES MARKET"

CHAO PRAYA RIVER

WAT CHAKRAWAT RACHAWAS

SAMPENG LANE

WAT CHAICHANA SONGKRAM

LUANG RD.

BOONSAMAKAN HALL

KRAI ALLEY

ANAWONG RD.

YAOWARAJ RD.

LAI KEE DIM SUM

RAJAWONG PIER

RAJAWONG RD.

MAHACHAK RD.

THONBURI

MANGKORN RD.

WAT KANMATUYARAM

WAT KUSAN SAMAKORN

SUAPA RD.

SOI ISSARANUPARP

GOLD SHOP

GUAN U SHRINE

SOI 16

WAT LENG NEE YEE

WAT KANIKAPHON

PEI YING SCHOOL

LANTERNS

TALAAD KAO

RELIGIOUS GOODS

LANG BOYA TEMPLE

LI THI MIEW TEMPLE

YAOWAPANICH RD.

LUANG KOCHA MOSQUE

PLAENG NAM RD.

CHINESE WEDDING SHOPS

BROADWAY HOTEL

WAT SAMPHA TAWONG

CHINATOWN HOTEL

SONGWAT RD.

NEW EMPIRE HOTEL

MR. CHEWS REST.

CHAROEN KRUNG RD.

WAT THEPSIRIN

PATHOM KONGKA MONASTERY

WAT PATHOM KONGKA

GOLDEN BUDDHA

KRUNG KASEM RD.

RIVER CITY PIER

ROYAL ORCHID SHERATON HOTEL

CHAROEN KRUNG RD.

HUALAMPONG TRAIN STATION

0   100m

BANGKOK CENTRE HOTEL

RAMA IV ROAD

© MOON PUBLICATIONS, INC.

FLOATING SLEEVES AND PAINTED FACES

Chinese opera, a sometimes bewildering combination of high-pitched singing, clashing music, and stunning costumes, is an artistic expression with no real counterpart in the West. That alone makes it worth watching at least once. To compensate for the stark simplicity of the staging, costumes are brilliant and unbelievably elaborate—heavy embroidered gowns, superb makeup, and amazing sleeves that float expressively without support.

Although the dissonant music irritates most Westerners, it can at times be ravishingly melodic and completely haunting. Stories taken from ancient Chinese folklore are told with symbolic gestures but few props. Role identification is linked to makeup, which ranges from the heavy paint worn in Peking-style opera (derived from older masked drama) to the lighter shades favored by the Cantonese. The more complicated a character the more complex the makeup: a red face indicates courageous character, black a warrior's face, blue is cruelty, white face is an evil personality, purple for barbarian warlords, yellow for emperors.

Costumes and movement are also highly stylized. The more important characters wear larger headdresses and express themselves with over 50 different hand and face movements. Cantonese opera is the most common genre, followed by highly refined Peking opera, considered the classic version. Soochow Opera, with its lovely and soft melodies, is rarely performed.

Chinese opera is a dying art performed only in the lone theater in Bangkok's Chinatown.

Chinese opera star

ket in the early morning hours to purchase fresh seafood as well as poultry and vegetables. Talaad Kao (Old Market) winds down around 1000, but an amazing amount of commercial activity continues through the day on Soi Issaranuparp.

Make a U-turn and walk past the Guan U Shrine and across Soi Sampeng to the next attraction.

Chinese Lanterns: Turn right on Soi Issaranuparp and look for the tiny shops where the ancient art of lantern making still survives. Continue down the alley to the next attraction.

Pei Ying School

Hidden behind Lao Peng Tao Chinese Shrine on Songwad Rd. is an imposing old European-style building once considered the most prestigious private primary school in Bangkok. Pei Ying

was founded in 1916 by Teochew merchants to encourage the study of the Chinese language and customs. King Rama VII visited the school in 1927 and lectured the audience about his Chinese bloodline. However, since World War II the Thai government has limited the role of Chinese schools; today only five hours per week can be used for the study of Chinese at Pei Ying School.

Return to Soi Sampeng, walk south past the wholesale clothing outlets, and turn right on Yaowapanich Road. Note the historic old mercantile buildings on Songwad Rd. with their fine doorway plasterwork of durians, mangosteens, and mangos.

Luang Kocha Mosque

Few people realize that Chinatown encompasses a sizable Indian and Muslim community. Luang Kocha Mosque (Masjid Luang Kocha or Masjid Wat Koh) is a European-style building that more closely resembles a private English mansion than the center of worship for Chinatown Muslims. Deserted during the week, the mosque is packed on Friday afternoons; men worship upstairs while women discreetly pray behind curtains on the ground floor. The derelict graveyard to the rear has ancient tombstones of Yunnanese Muslim soldiers of the 93rd Division of the Chinese Nationalist Army.

Wat Sampha Tawong

Wat Sampha Tawong, also known as Wat Koh, is chiefly noted for its grand and imposing three-story *bot,* a highly unusual if not altogether beautiful structure. Around the perimeter stand lovely wooden monks' quarters and other auxiliary buildings.

The imposing *wat* has an unpleasant history. To pave the way for the construction of this lavish building some three decades ago, an ancient 18th-century *bot* decorated with murals dating from the reign of King Rama VI (1881-1925) was ordered demolished. Art lovers and historians vehemently protested, but their efforts failed to prevent the destruction of one of Thailand's great art treasures.

Wat Pathom Kongka

This unassuming temple, once known as Wat Sampeng, was constructed during the Ayuthaya Period and so predates the founding of Bangkok by nearly a century. One of the oldest *wats* in Bangkok, Wat Pathom Kongka formerly served as an execution ground for nobles convicted of state crimes. Today, you're more likely to find traditional Chinese funerals in the open pavilions outside the cloistered courtyard.

The temple compound is split by Songwad Road. The main chapel with its *bai sema* stones enclosed in Cambodian-style huts and *viharn* surrounded by cement *stupas* lie close to the Chao Praya River. The monks' quarters and religious schools are in the other section.

Golden Buddha

Wat Traimit, better known as the "Temple of the Golden Buddha," is one of Bangkok's most popular attractions and home of the world's largest golden Buddha. The gleaming Buddha deserves a brief look, but be forewarned: the image itself has little (if any) artistic value, and the entire complex has sadly disintegrated into a tawdry tourist trap, filled with pleading touts and barking escorts who herd around bus loads of camera-toting tourists.

However, the history of the Buddha is worth recounting. According to local accounts, the three-meter statue once sat neglected and unloved in Wat Chotinaram, a disused temple in the business quarter of Bangkok. No one realized its true value since the Sukothai-era image had long been sealed in stucco to disguise its nature from Burmese invaders. In 1953 the East Asiatic Company purchased the land and took over the premises. The Buddha was first moved to a temporary building, and later transferred in 1955 to Wat Traimit. During the process, workmen dropped it from a crane and cracked its plaster skin. A heavy rainstorm that night further weakened the covering. The following morning, a resident abbot noticed a metallic glow emanating from the crack and ordered the protective shell peeled back. Underneath the stucco facade lay a 5½-ton golden image.

Local abbots claim the Buddha is 75% pure gold, though scientific measurements have never been made. To the left of the statue is a piece of original stucco covering.

Wat Traimit is open daily 0830-1700. Admission is 10B.

Yaowaraj Road

This is the main boulevard which cuts through Chinatown. Walk slowly to appreciate the spectacle: dazzling gold stores with mirrored interiors and richly carved wooden chairs, traditional calligraphers working on the sidewalk, herbal stores filled with antler horn and strange roots, cacophonous restaurants, and deafening noise from the people and traffic—sensory overload to rival anything in Asia.

A Cold Drink: Completely exhausted, you need to relax and enjoy a cold drink. Several good restaurants are located on Yaowaraj Road. Mr. Chew's Shark Fin Restaurant is a popular stop for—what else—shark's-fin soup and other expensive delicacies made from birds' nests and rhino horn. More luxurious settings are found in the a/c Waikiki Cafe, located on the ground level of the Chinatown Hotel.

Gold Shops: Chinese love gold, and

nowhere else in Bangkok will you find so many gold shops packed together. Filled with every possible form of gold, the shops are themselves artistic creations with their glass facades, up-swept ceilings, vermilion lacquer counters, gaudy red walls, glowing neon lights, carved wooden chairs, and legions of anxious salespeople.

Foreigners should note, however, that the unit weight used nationwide is the *baht* system, not the international metric system. One *baht* (no reference to the monetary unit) of orna-mental gold equals 15.16 grams, while one *baht* of bullion gold is equal to 15.244 grams. Orna-mental gold is only 96.7% pure, no matter what the salesman claims.

Chinese Opera: Chalermrat Theater and its resident Tai Dong Chinese Opera Troupe are the last of five opera houses which existed be-fore the onslaught of Chinese cinemas and home videos. Today, the opera company must alternate seasons with movies, but lucky visi-tors might stop in to experience the last of a dying breed. Performances are given Sunday af-ternoons and daily except Mondays at 1900; admission is 100B-400B.

Wedding Shops

From Yaowaraj Rd., walk east along Plaeng Nam Rd. and then left on Charoen Krung Rd., formerly New Rd. after King Rama V estab-lished the first formal road in Bangkok. To the left are small shops specializing in items for Chi-nese weddings, such as elaborately embroi-dered pink pillows, wedding invitations, delicate tea sets, and pink mattresses to help with the first night. Calligraphers on the street paint gold letters over a red background, auspicious colors for any occasion.

Soi 16 Market

This narrow covered alley, also known as Soi Is-saranuparp, is a shorter version of Soi Sampeng with emphasis on food products rather than clothing and plastics. Ignore the filthy floor and enjoy the displays of Chinese snacks, fresh chickens, and exotic fruits. On the left is Lang Boya, a small Chinese temple marked with a sign proclaiming "Tourists Are Welcome To Visit And Take Photographs Inside The Temple." Unlike many other groups in Asia, Chinese wel-come discreet photographers inside their tem-ples; a small donation is appropriate.

Wat Leng Nee Yee

Also called Wat Leng Noi Yi and Wat Mangkon Malawat, this "Dragon Flower Temple" is the most spectacular temple in Chinatown. It was founded in 1871 and has since become one of the most venerated sites for the Chinese of Thailand.

Above the imposing gateway is a nine-story tower which serves as a Museum of Religious Artifacts, not yet open to the public. Inside the spacious courtyard stands an old vegetarian hall and a traditional medicine shop where cures are prescribed by the Chinese god of medicine.

The central complex is divided into several *viharns*. The dominating hall features three gild-ed Buddhas draped with saffron robes and flanked by gilded statues of the 18 *arahats*. Also located in the central chamber is a fat Maitreya Buddha (the final Buddha before the destruction of the world), six Dharmapala figures found in every large Chinese temple, and the Four Heav-enly Kings, Hindu deities converted to Bud-dhism. To the right is another hall with images of Taoist Star Deities who heal all illnesses; to the left are statues of Taoist patriarchs and the founder-abbot of the temple. The extreme left has a small but beautiful garden and vegetarian hall filled with elaborately carved furniture.

Services are held daily at 1600.

Alley Of Religious Goods

Immediately to the south of Wat Leng Nee Yee is a narrow alley crammed with red and gold religious items: incense sticks, paper offerings shaped like gold bars, elaborate shrines for gods of the earth, and brilliantly colored attire for Chinese deities.

Wat Kanikaphon

The lane continues up to a bright orange *wat* constructed by a former brothel madam to atone for her sins. Kanikaphon means "Women who sold women"! Attached to the temple is a Chi-nese *sanjao* (shrine) where devotees perform the *kong tek,* a ceremony in which paper goods fashioned after automobiles and yachts are burned to send to departed relatives. Never has it been so easy to please dead ancestors and ensure that they don't haunt the living.

Wat Kanmatuyaram

Tucked away in a small alley opposite Cathay

Department Store is a small Buddhist temple built in 1864. Duck through the small iron doorway to see a striking, whitewashed, Sri Lankan-style *chedi* and a small *bot* graced with some of Thailand's most important murals. Executed in the reign of King Rama IV, these unretouched murals illustrate the lives of Bangkokians in the mid-18th century, and the various incarnations of the Buddha. Admittance is by official authorization only.

Wat Kusan Samakorn

This quaint Vietnamese temple features a seven-tiered Chinese pagoda on the left, and a small central chapel with a large robed Buddha. The original temple was built in 1854 by two Vietnamese monks, but reconstructed after a fire in 1913. Chinese paintings on the wall recount popular stories of 24 children who demonstrated gratitude toward their parents, an important trait in Chinese culture.

Wat Chaichana Songkram

Wat Chaichana Songkram ("Having Won the War") was constructed in the mid-18th century on land donated by a victorious army leader who served under King Rama III. Much of the complex is modern, but to the rear stand a pair of old bell-shaped *chedis*, a Khmer *prang*, and a two-story library filled with religious artifacts.

Nakon Kasem Market

Once Bangkok's antique center, most of the dealers in the so-called "Thieves Market" have since moved to shopping centers near the tourist centers. A few dusty stores hold on, surrounded by hardware shops and copper merchants. Merchandise runs the gamut from imitation antiques to vintage clocks and Chinese porcelains.

Wat Chakrawat Rachawas

Though not a temple of great architectural merit, this sprawling complex merits a visit for its curiosity factor and to witness the Chinese funerals which are held on a near-daily basis. The principal oddities are the crocodiles which sleep in the small pond off the central courtyard. The original croc was a one-eyed monster named Ai Bord; he now sits stuffed after losing a fight with a younger pondmate.

The *mondop* situated on the artificial hill which overlooks the pond houses a replica of a Buddha's footprint. To the rear is a grotto with a supernatural Buddha shadow and a fat disciple who stuffed himself into obesity to end his sexual passions. Inside the nearby *bot* and *viharn,* both now under reconstruction, are excellent murals that feature life-sized angels and *Jataka* murals from the reign of King Rama V. All have been totally retouched.

Pahurat Cloth Market

Sampeng Lane terminates at the old cloth market where Sikh and Chinese merchants peddle Indian saris, Malaysian batiks, and Thai silks from enormous open-air tables. Also of interest are the Hindu wedding stores and shops selling paraphernalia for Thai classical dancers.

Little India

Your walking tour now enters a claustrophobic neighborhood sometimes referred to as Little India.

Sikh Temple: Up a narrow alley towers a seven-story white temple dedicated to the Sikh community of Thailand. A health clinic and maternity ward are located on the upper floors.

Indian Restaurants: Adjoining alleys are filled with travel agencies which serve the Indian trade and inexpensive *marsala dosa* restaurants. A comfortable if somewhat expensive choice is the Royal India Restaurant, where you can dine in a/c surroundings. Less expensive cafes include the Moon Restaurant located in the rear alley adjacent to the canal, and the popular Cha Cha Restaurant on Chakrapet Road. All offer good food in earthy surroundings.

Pak Klong Market

Pak Klong Talaad, at the foot of the Memorial Bridge, is the city's largest wholesale fruit and vegetable market. The action begins at dawn as boats laden with foods arrive to unload their wares. By early afternoon the merchants have packed up and swept the aisles, though this fascinating market is worth visiting at any hour to experience the overpowering sense of medieval commerce.

River taxis back to Silom Rd. and Banglampoo leave from Saphan Phut landing at the terminus of Triphet Rd., and from Rachini Pier just across the canal from Pak Klong.

THONBURI

Thonburi, on the west bank of the Chao Praya, briefly served as the capital of Thailand after the fall of Ayuthaya until Rama I moved his court to the opposite shore. Temples located near the river can be toured on foot by wandering through the narrow lanes; interior *wats* can be reached by public boat.

Wat Arun

This monumental 86-meter Khmer-style *prang*, one of Thailand's largest religious monuments, towers above the Chao Praya to form Bangkok's most impressive and famous landmark. Wat Arun was constructed by Rama II on the site of a former royal temple which once held the precious Emerald Buddha. Despite problems of erecting such a massive structure on the city's swampy soil, Rama III finally completed the complex in 1842. Rama IV added the final touch: thousands of multiglazed Chinese porcelains donated by Buddhist devotees. The present king donates new robes to the resident monks on the occasion of the Tod Kathin Festival, a merit-making ceremony formerly made downriver from the Grand Palace in royal barges.

Better known as the Temple of the Dawn, Wat Arun symbolically represents the Buddhist universe, with its trident-capped central tower indicating Mount Meru and the four smaller towers depicting the four worldly oceans. The central *prang* is intersected by four door niches with the god Indra riding his three-headed white elephant. Other figures include the moon god on his white horse and illustrations of the four most important episodes from the life of Buddha: birth, meditation under a protective *naga*, sermon to the five ascetics, and entry into nirvana. Visitors can make the steep climb up to the midway point for views over the Chao Praya and Thonburi.

Located on the grounds are several other worthwhile buildings. The *bot* in the northwest corner features four unusual *chedis* and interior murals which depict the life of Buddha. A restored *mondop* between the *bot* and *viharn* contains a Buddha footprint and twin towers used as belfries. The *viharn* behind the prima-

ry *chedi* contains a silver and gold Sukothai image brought back from Vientiane by Rama II.

Wat Arun is accessible by shuttle boat from the Tha Tien Pier behind Wat Po. Open daily 0800-1700. Admission is 10B.

Wat Kalayamit

Located near the entrance to Klong Bangkok Yai, this immense temple has dimensions dictated by the huge Buddha image it enshrines. Interior walls of the main *bot* and adjacent chapel are decorated with mural paintings dating from the reign of Rama III. The spacious courtyard is decorated with Chinese gateways and statues, and a bronze bell reputed to be the largest in Thailand. Thais of Chinese origin favor this temple and giant image, which they call Sam Po Gong.

Wat Prayoon

Also constructed during the reign of Rama III, Wat Prayoon consists of two chapels with mother-of-pearl decorations, an artificial hill decorated with *chedis*, frangipani trees, and a pool filled with turtles. According to legend, the hill was modeled after a mound of melted wax formed by a candle of Rama III.

Wat Suwannaram

This extremely well-proportioned and finely decorated *bot* illustrates the transitional architecture of the Ayuthaya and Bangkok periods. Interior frescoes are attributed to two famous painters from the court of Rama II. Lower murals display scenes from the last 10 *Jataka* tales of the previous lives of the Buddha, while the entrance wall features the victory of the Buddha over Mara. These 19th-century murals, remarkable for their sensitivity and originality of composition, are considered among the finest in Bangkok.

Wat Dusitaram

Though the primary *bot* is of little architectural interest, Wat Dusitaram also features interior murals of great interest. A traditional arrangement is followed. Side walls between the windows show episodes from the life of Buddha, the front fresco masterly renders the Buddhist victory over Mara, while the Buddhist cosmology is depicted on the back wall.

Royal Barges Museum

More than 50 longboats, all carefully restored for Bangkok's 1982 Rattanakosin bicentennial, are dry-docked inside the shed near Klong Bangkok Noi. Crafted in the early part of this century, and only waterborne for very special royal events, these barges are designed after mythical creatures featured in the *Ramayana*. The principal barge, *Sri Suphannahongse,* is named after the mythical swan which graces the prow. Perhaps the largest dugout in the world, this gilded 45-meter glider weighs over 15 tons and requires the efforts of 54 oarsmen and a rhythm keeper who bangs the beat in time with the chanting of ancient boat poems. Equally impressive is the 44-meter *Anantana-garaj*, with its carved figurehead of a seven-headed *naga*.

The museum is open daily from 0800 to 1700. Admission is 10B.

Bangkok Floating Market

Thonburi's floating market epitomizes what is most crass and callous in the tourist trade. Once an authentic and colorful scene, the market completely died out in the '60s as modernization forced boat vendors to move into modern shopping centers. Threatened with the loss of revenue, tour operators came up with a rather awful solution: hire a few Thai ladies to paddle around and *pretend* to be shopping. Disneyland feels genuine when compared to this outrage, perhaps the most contrived rip-off in the East.

MODERN BANGKOK

Jim Thompson's House

Jim Thompson was the legendary American architect-entrepreneur who settled in Thailand after WW II and almost single-handedly revived the moribund silk industry. No trace was found of Thompson after he disappeared in 1967 while hiking near Cameron Highlands. Jim's maze of seven Thai-style teak houses has since been converted into a small private museum filled with his priceless collection of Asian antiques, pottery, and curiosities. A small gift shop sells fine reproductions of Vessantara *Jataka* and Brahma Jati horoscopes.

Thompson's house is open Mon.-Sat. 0900-1600. Admission is an unreasonable 130B. A more comprehensive collection of Thai art is found in the National Museum and the modest layout here disappoints many visitors. Traditional Thai homes, functioning as residences rather than museums, are plentiful in Chiang Mai and smaller towns such as Tak and Sukothai.

Those seriously interested in Thai arts might also visit the private collection at the Prasat Museum, in the Bangkok suburb of Hua Mak. Phone (02) 253-9772 for more information.

Phallic Shrine

Dedicated to Chao Tuptim (the pomegranate goddess), a female animist spirit, this tangled mini-jungle shrine is noted for its hundreds of stylized and realistic phalluses contributed by childbearing devotees. Rather than simply a fertility symbol, the curious memorial also ensures prosperity since the lingam traditionally symbolizes both regeneration and good fortune. Devotees of both sexes arrive daily to burn incense and donate brightly painted phalluses in all possible shapes and sizes.

Bangkok's strangest shrine is located on the grounds of the Hilton Hotel at the end of Soi Som Si next to Klong Saen. No admission charge.

Siam Society

Thailand's premier research group publishes the scholarly *Journal of the Siam Society*, restores deteriorating murals, and maintains a 10,000-volume library of rare and valuable editions. Research facilities are open to members only; write to the Executive Secretary, 131 Soi Asoke (21), Bangkok 10110, Thailand.

Of special interest to foreign visitors is the Society Travel Club (tel. 02-258-3491), which sponsors professionally led excursions to important temples, archaeological digs, and noteworthy festivals. These tours, unquestionably some of the best available in Thailand, are reasonably priced and open to the public. Upcoming tours are listed in the *Bangkok Post*.

Kamthieng House: To the left of the Siam Society headquarters is a restored century-old residence, formerly the home of a prominent family in Chiang Mai until being dismantled and reconstructed on the present site. Kamthieng is chiefly noted for its ethnological artifacts and collection of hilltribe costumes, plus exterior details such as teak lintels which serve as magical talismans that hold ancestral spirits and guarantee the virility of the inhabitants.

Kamthieng House is on Soi 21 just off Sukumvit Road. Open Tues.-Sat. 0900-1200 and 1300-1700. Admission is 30B.

Suan Pakkard Palace

Bangkok can be a city of anachronisms. Hidden between the high-rises and construction sites are several charming homes surrounded by large, peaceful gardens. Suan Pakkard is an old Thai residence complex which was disassembled and brought down from Chiang Mai by Princess Chumbhot, one of Thailand's leading art collectors. The royal residence was converted into a public museum after the passing of Prince Chumbhot and his wife.

Suan Pakkard is composed of five traditional houses arranged around small lotus ponds and meticulously trimmed lawns. All are filled with an eclectic range of Thai artifacts, from Ban Chiang pottery to Khmer sculpture. House I contains a Gandhara Buddha from Pakistan, an 8th-century Khmer goddess, and valuable celadon from Sawankalok. House II once served as the royal bedroom. House III, the reception area, features a gilded throne and a Chinese cabinet graced with five-colored Bencharong ceramics. House IV is a dining room constructed with leg wells for long-legged Western guests.

Suan Pakkard's most impressive structure is the 450-year-old Lacquer Palace located to the rear of the gardens. Transferred from Ayuthaya in the face of Burmese invasion, the gold and black lacquer interior panels show the early influences of Westernization on traditional Thai art and chronicle everyday life in 16th-century Ayuthaya.

The semiprivate gardens which surround the home provide a welcome relief from the dirt and noise of Bangkok.

Suan Pakkard is open Mon.-Sat. 0900-1600. Admission is 60B.

Snake Farm

Also known as the Pasteur or Saowapha Institute, the world's second-oldest snake-research facility was established in 1923 to develop antivenins and vaccines for poisonous snakebites.

ROMAN-ROBOT FANTASIES

From Hong Kong to Singapore, economic success has dramatically transformed Asian skylines from low-rise colonial to high-tech Houston. But Bangkok's boom has unleashed a wave of innovative architecture unrivaled anywhere else in the region. Refusing to clone Western prototypes, the architects of Bangkok have invented some amazing fantasies: corporate headquarters that resemble Roman palaces, condo complexes that fuse art-deco facades with Thai rooflines, fast-food emporiums buried inside rocket ships, Mediterranean stucco homes, Bavarian half-timbered cottages—Hollywood holograms in the City of Angels.

This new and exciting movement is led by an iconoclastic architect named Sumet Jumsai and an innovative design firm called Plan Architect. Sumet's Bank of Asia robot building near Silom Road—a humorous mixture of an external skeleton fitted with giant nuts and bolts—illustrates the marriage of high-tech themes with cartoon consciousness. The postmodern McDonald's on Ploenchit Road combines gleaming glass walls with Roman columns. Suburban developments include English castles complete with moats, and the new headquarters for the *Nation* newspaper, an 11-story sculpture inspired by the whimsical designs of cubist painter Georges Braque. Bangkok is now more than just Thai temples and nocturnal delights, it's home to some of the most creative modern architecture in the world.

The serpentarium now houses over 1,000 snakes for both educational and medical purposes. Cholera, smallpox, typhoid inoculations, and rabies treatments are available.

The main draw at the institute is the fascinating snake show. The demonstration begins with a 20-minute slide show on the work of the institute and dangers of Thailand's poisonous snakes. Afterward, the crowd gathers in the central pit to watch Siamese king cobras milked for their venom. Snake handlers gleefully squeeze the creatures only inches from your camera lens, close enough to watch the milky venom ooze from the fangs! The adjacent museum holds indigenous species such as green pit vipers, banded kraits, and other nonpoisonous snakes.

The Pasteur Institute is open daily 0830-1600. Snake shows are conducted weekdays at 1030 and 1330, weekends at 1030 only. Admission is 50B.

Erawan Shrine

Thailand's devotion to animist spirits and Hindu deities is best appreciated in the famous shrine on the grounds of the Erawan Grand Hyatt. The memorial was erected after hotel construction was halted by a series of seemingly random disasters: marble destined for the lobby disappeared at sea, workmen died under mysterious circumstances, and cost overruns threatened to crush the hotel project. Spirit doctors, desperately summoned for advice, commanded the hotel owners to erect a shrine to Brahma. The mishaps ended and word of the miracle spread throughout Thailand.

Today, the Erawan Shrine is a continual circus of devotees bearing incense, flowers, and images of the elephant-god Erawan, the three-headed mount of Brahma. Supplicants whose prayers have been fulfilled often sponsor performances of Thai dance. Western visitors are encouraged to make their own offerings; prices for goods are posted at the front entrance. This crazy and magical place is made even more sensational by its bizarre location at a major Bangkok intersection.

Lumpini Park

Bangkok's oldest park serves as one of the few green lungs for the congested city. Daytime heat empties the park, but early morning hours are an excellent time to watch the two categories of Lumpini fitness fanatics: the traditionalists and the modernists. The former, mostly older Thai folk, arrive at sunrise to practice the Chinese art of *tai chi*. Designed to work the muscles in a slow-motion *kung fu*, the ancient dance is now accompanied by portable stereos playing Chinese dirges or modern disco. Competing with the traditionalists are the joggers who pound the pavement on a 2½-km circuit. Kite flyers, soccer players, and bodybuilders fill the park during the afternoon.

Wat Thamma Mongkol

Completed in 1985 as Bangkok's most modern temple, this 14-story 95-meter-high blockhouse is capped with a traditional *chedi* which en-

shrines relics of the Buddha. Combining traditional religion with high-tech conveniences, an elevator whisks visitors to the top for spectacular views. Bangkok's tallest *chedi* is located on Sukumvit Rd. at Soi 101.

A RIVERSIDE WALK AND THE ORIENTAL HOTEL

Bangkok's *farang* community once made their commercial and diplomatic headquarters on the banks of the Chao Praya, near New Road (now called Charoen Krung) and the venerable Oriental Hotel. A short walking tour of the area can be combined with some shopping, an Indian lunch, and mail pick-up from the General Post Office.

Oriental Hotel

Start your tour at the historic hotel, which consistently ranks as one of the world's finest. Wander into the nostalgic Authors Lounge and perhaps enjoy a cocktail on the riverside veranda. Fine antiques and designer silks are sold in the adjacent Oriental Plaza Shopping Center.

East Asiatic Company

Just opposite the Oriental Hotel is a handsome white building constructed in 1901 to house one of Bangkok's original trading firms. The East Asiatic Company was founded by Dutch investors in 1897, and today ranks as one of the world's principal trading conglomerates. A Dutch flag still flies over the central cupola.

Assumption Cathedral

Slightly up Oriental Lane and on the right stands Bangkok's principal Catholic church. Constructed in 1910, the interior features a marble altar imported from France and a soaring roofline splashed with technicolor hues.

French Embassy

Built in the mid-19th century, this lovely European-style residence still evokes the atmosphere of old Bangkok with its louvered shutters and spacious verandas.

Old Customs House

Formerly the head office of the Thai Customs Department, this sadly neglected 19th-century building is one of the finest remaining European structures in Bangkok. Fortunately, the future looks promising. The Treasury Department has registered the building as a historic site with the Fine Arts Department, and private investors intend to renovate and convert the building into a Thai cultural hall.

Haroon Mosque And Muslim Cemetery

Bangkok's community of Muslims worship in the small mosque nestled in a narrow alley behind the Old Customs House. Continue walking away from the river toward the GPO.

An Indian Lunch

This neighborhood is home to a large community of Indians and Pakistanis who patronize local cafes. Highly recommended is the Sallim Restaurant located in the alley beyond the GPO and past the Woodlands Hotel. Excellent food at rock-bottom prices.

Portuguese Embassy

The first Europeans to initiate trade with Siam were the Portuguese from their maritime empire at Malacca. In 1820 they erected the first embassy in Thailand. Much has been reconstructed though original portions are still visible from the river and over the tall protective wall.

River City Shopping Complex

Final stop on your short walking tour is the four-story air-conditioned shopping complex adjoining the Sheraton Royal Orchid Hotel. Special art exhibits are often featured on the ground floor, while the third and fourth floors are entirely devoted to Asian antiques. An auction is held each month; exact dates are listed in the *Bangkok Post.*

CHAO PRAYA RIVER CRUISE

A boat cruise along the Chao Praya River is one of the highlights of any visit to Bangkok. River travel offers a rare opportunity to enjoy Bangkok without the hassles of congestion and pollution, plus it opens up fresh vistas impossible to experience from a public bus or taxi. Passengers seem ready to smile, plus there's that exhilarating sense of speed and wonderful breeze on your face.

First, you'll need to recognize the three principal types of boats that operate on the Chao Praya. Longtail boats *(hang yao)* are narrow high-powered racers that serve the outlying canals. This mode of travel is discussed below under "Do-It-Yourself Canal Tours." Shuttle boats are squarish and very slow boats which make short hauls across the river; useful for quickly crossing to Thonburi and visiting important temples such as Wat Arun. Express boats *(rua duan)* are long white boats with red stripes operated by the Chao Phya Express Boat Company. These boats run daily 0600-1800 every 20 minutes from the Krung Thep Bridge in south Bangkok to Nonthaburi, a suburb 18 km north. Note that *express boat service ends at 1800.* The one-way journey includes a total of 36 stops (26 on the Bangkok side and 10 on the Thonburi side) and takes approximately 75 minutes. Government-controlled fares range 3-10 *baht* depending on the distance. Rather than lingering on the crowded rear landing, walk to the front of the boat where seats are more plentiful.

The following boat tour includes only the central section from Tha Orienten (*tha* means pier) in the south to Na Pra Arthit (Pra Arthit Pier) in Banglampoo.

Oriental Pier

Public boats leave from the pier down the alley from the Oriental Hotel. Private tours cost 200-300B per hour, so unless you're looking for an expensive tour, ignore the touts who haunt the pier. Buildings around the Oriental Hotel are described above.

Holy Rosary Church

This recently restored church was constructed in 1787 by Portuguese Catholics who moved from Thonburi after the destruction of Ayuthaya by Burmese invaders.

Wat Thong Noppakhun And Wat Thammachat

Both little-known temples on the Thonburi side are noted for fine proportions in Ayuthaya style and their lovely murals dating from the reigns of Rama III and IV.

Memorial Bridge And Tha Saphan Phut

The boat landing just beyond the iron-green bridge, opened by King Rama VII in 1932, leads

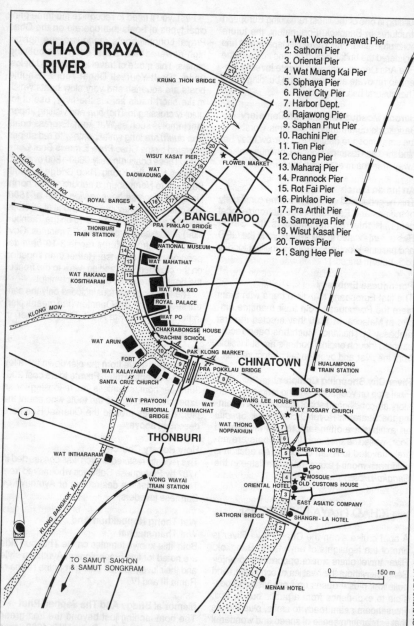

CHAO PRAYA RIVER

KRUNG THON BRIDGE

1. Wat Vorachanyawat Pier
2. Sathorn Pier
3. Oriental Pier
4. Wat Muang Kai Pier
5. Siphaya Pier
6. River City Pier
7. Harbor Dept.
8. Rajawong Pier
9. Saphan Phut Pier
10. Rachini Pier
11. Tien Pier
12. Chang Pier
13. Maharaj Pier
14. Prannock Pier
15. Rot Fai Pier
16. Pinklao Pier
17. Pra Arthit Pier
18. Sampraya Pier
19. Wisut Kasat Pier
20. Tewes Pier
21. Sang Hee Pier

KLONG BANGKOK NOI

WISUT KASAT PIER

FLOWER MARKET

WAT DAOWADUNG

ROYAL BARGES

THONBURI TRAIN STATION

PRA PINKLAO BRIDGE

BANGLAMPOO

PRA PINKLAO BRIDGE

NATIONAL MUSEUM

WAT MAHATHAT

WAT RAKANG KOSITHARAM

KLONG MON

WAT PRA KEO

ROYAL PALACE

WAT PO

WAT ARUN

CHAKRABONGSE HOUSE
RACHINI SCHOOL

FORT

PAK KLONG MARKET

WAT KALAYAMIT
SANTA CRUZ CHURCH

PRA POKKLAU BRIDGE

CHINATOWN

HUALAMPONG TRAIN STATION

WAT PRAYOON
MEMORIAL BRIDGE

WAT THAMMACHAT

GOLDEN BUDDHA

WANG LEE HOUSE

HOLY ROSARY CHURCH

WAT THONG NOPPAKHUN

THONBURI

WAT INTHARARAM

SHERATON HOTEL

WONG WIAYAI TRAIN STATION

GPO
MOSQUE
OLD CUSTOMS HOUSE

ORIENTAL HOTEL

EAST ASIATIC COMPANY

KLONG BANGKOK YAI

SATHORN BRIDGE

SHANGRI - LA HOTEL

TO SAMUT SAKHON
& SAMUT SONGKRAM

0   150 m

MENAM HOTEL

© MOON PUBLICATIONS, INC.

to the colorful Pak Klong Market and the Little India neighborhood. Public longtails from this landing stage make inexpensive runs up Thonburi canals.

Wat Prayoon

Constructed during the reign of King Rama III, this temple is noted for its mother-of-pearl door decorations and artificial hill decorated with miniature *chedis* and frangipani trees.

Santa Cruz Church

This unmistakable church, originally constructed by Portuguese Catholics after the fall of Ayuthaya, was reconstructed in 1913 with its distinctive narrow profile and towering cupola.

Rachini School

Behind a low white wall stands a beautiful European-style building bearing the insignia of "Royal Seminary." Rachini was the first school devoted to the education of Thai women and it is still regarded as the finest in Thailand.

Wat Kalayamit

An immense temple which shelters an equally gigantic Buddha. Also noted for its interior mural dating from the reign of King Rama III.

Tha Rachini

This useful boat stop, adjacent to Pak Klong Market, is where shuttle boats cross to the Thonburi attractions of Wat Kalayamit and Santa Cruz Church. Adventurous visitors will enjoy a short walk through the winding alleys of the old Portuguese quarter.

Chakrabongse House

Hidden behind the thick foliage is one of the few remaining royal residences which once graced the riverbanks. Tha Tien Palace was constructed in 1909 by an Italian architect for the son of King Rama V.

Tha Tien

This landing stage provides access to Wat Po, a public ferry across to Wat Arun, and public longtails which serve the canals of Thonburi.

Wat Rakang Kositharam

One of the most original temples left from the Rattanakosin Period, this rarely visited monument is noted for its decorated roof supports of unusual size and elegance, retouched interior frescoes, and beautiful three-sectioned library restored several years ago by the Association of Siamese Architects. The opposite shore is dominated by Wat Po, the Grand Palace, and Wat Pra Keo.

Tha Maharaj And Thammasart University

This distinctive red pier leads to Wat Mahathat, the National Museum, and Thammasart University. Long the hotbed of liberal politics, Thammasart earned worldwide attention in 1973 when a student-led revolution succeeded in overthrowing the military government. In 1976 the university was attacked and hundreds of students murdered after right-wing forces reseized power from the democratically elected government.

Tha Pra Arthit And Banglampoo

After a quick stop at Tha Rot Fai (terminus for the Thonburi Railway Station), the express boat pulls into Pra Arthit Pier and the backpackers' enclave of Banglampoo.

DO-IT-YOURSELF CANAL TOURS

Bangkok's waterways offer exceptional sightseeing opportunities and reveal what is most attractive about the city. Three major canals lead off the river: Klong Bangkok Yai in the south, Klong Mon in the center, and Klong Bangkok Noi in the north. All three arteries are intersected by dozens of smaller canals that wind through dense jungle and vine-choked foliage, all flanked with stilted houses and small temples rarely visited by Westerners. Best of all are the children who smile and wave as they cannonball into the murky waters. Miraculously, the pollution and congestion of modern Bangkok seem light years away.

Private chartered longtail boats are somewhat expensive at 200-300B per hour, but hurried visitors who don't mind the Rich Tourist image may find them worth the cost.

Less pricey and more authentic are ordinary longtails which race up and down the smaller canals, picking up and dropping off Thai passengers until they finally turn around and return to their starting point. These longtails depart frequently from five piers in central Bangkok: Mahathat, Chang, Tien, Rachini, and Saphan Phut. Which pier to choose hardly matters since the scenery is similar throughout the canal network. Ignore the private operators and instead wait patiently for the next ordinary longtail, which will cost 10B in each direction or 20B return.

You have two options: stay on the boat for the roundtrip or disembark at one end, walk through the plantations to another canal, and catch an ordinary longtail back to the starting point. Boatmen rarely speak English, but it's almost impossible to get lost. Just sit down, smile, and enjoy the ride.

Canal enthusiasts can purchase *50 Trips Through Siam's Canals* by George Veran or the recently published but rather sketchy *Bangkok's Waterways* by William Warren. The *Thonburi Canal* map by the Association of Architects is also useful.

Warning: Beware of slick professionals who offer free guided tours and then blackmail you for a 1000B gasoline fare in the middle of the river. Never get into a longtail boat alone.

Klong Bangkok Noi

Ordinary longtails that travel up the northern canal of Klong Bangkok Noi depart from three different piers: Tha Tien landing stage near Wat Po, Tha Chang near Wat Pra Keo, and Tha Maharaj behind Wat Mahathat. Four different *hang yao* routes are possible, but most roar up Klong Bangkok Noi before exploring the smaller and more fascinating canals of Bang Sai, Bang Ramat, Bang Phrom, and Bang Yai. Attractions along these canals include the Royal Barge Museum, Wat Suwannaram, and Wat Suwankhiri. Make a roundtrip journey, or hop off to explore these Thonburi temples.

Klong Mon

Longtails up the central canal of Klong Mon leave from both the left side of Tha Chang and Tha Tien behind Wat Po. If you choose the more convenient pier at Tha Tien, you want the smaller landing to the right. Some longtails race up Klong Mon and then continue up the smaller canal of Bang Chuak Nang. For a longer and more colorful journey, ask for a boat heading for Bang Noi (not Bangkok Noi). The journey passes temples, orchid farms, and coconut trees which lean over the narrow canals. Get off at the end when

the driver makes his U-turn, wander 45 minutes south through traditional neighborhoods to Wat Chim on Klong Bang Waek, and then flag down a longtail back to the Memorial Bridge. Getting lost is half the fun on this trip.

Klong Bangkok Yai

Longtails up this southern canal depart from Tha Rachini, a few blocks south of Wat Po. After following the river for some distance, the longtail veers off and follows either the narrow *klongs* of Bang Dan, Phasi Charoen, or Sanam Chai. Perhaps the most colorful route in Thonburi, stops can be made at Wat Sang Krachai, Wat Werurachin, Wat Intararam, Wat Pak Nam, and a snake farm on Klong Sanam Chai.

Klong Tan

This unusual journey originates under the New Petchburi Road Bridge (near Pratunam Market) and passes through beautiful residential neighborhoods to Klong Tan. Some boats go left to Bangkapi, while others turn right down Klong Tan to Sukothai Road Bridge at Soi 73. Buses return back to the center of town.

ORGANIZED RIVER TOURS

Several tour companies offer formal cruises along the Chao Praya and intersecting canals. Tickets can be purchased at the point of departure and from most travel agencies.

Budget Cruise: Each Saturday and Sunday at 0800 a sleek boat leaves Maharaj Pier behind Thammasart University, stops briefly at the Thai Folk Arts and Crafts Center in Bang Sai, and reaches the Royal Summer Palace at Bang Pa In at noon. The return journey visits the fascinating Wat Pailom Stork Sanctuary before arriving back in Bangkok around sunset. This all-day river cruise costs just 150B. A relaxing day except for the obnoxious loudspeaker. Contact Chao Praya Express Boat Company at (02) 222-5330 or (02) 411-0305.

Chao Phya Express Company: Three-hour Bangkok Noi canal tours leave the Sheraton Royal Orchid Hotel daily at 1500 and cost 150B. Call (02) 465-3836 or (02) 466-4505 for further information.

Crystal Tour: Three-hour rice-barge tours to Klong Mon, Taling Chan, and Bangkok Noi leave from the Sheraton Royal Orchid Hotel daily at 1500. The 250B fee includes refreshments and soft drinks. Call (02) 251-3758.

World Travel Service: Four-hour longtail and rice-barge tours run up the Chao Praya River to Rama VI Bridge. Tours cost 320B, leave daily at 1400, and include a short visit to the Boonrawd Brewery. Call (02) 233-5900.

Asia Voyages: A teakwood rice-barge makes an overnight cruise from Bangkok to Ayuthaya via Bang Pa In. The 3000B fare includes on-board accommodation, tour guides, and all meals. Asia Voyages (tel. 02-235-4110) is the largest operator of private yachts in Thailand.

Oriental Queen: An air-conditioned cruiser leaves the Oriental Hotel daily at 0800 and returns around 1800. The 800B cruise includes a buffet lunch, a visit to Bang Pa In, a guided tour around the historic ruins of Ayuthaya, and splendid sunsets on the return voyage. Call World Travel Service for more information.

CHEAP FUN IN BANGKOK

Bangkok no longer ranks as the bargain center of the East, but visitors with limited funds can still enjoy themselves for a handful of *baht*. The secret is to find activities popular with Thais rather than wealthy *farangs* on a two-week holiday. Here are a few suggestions:

Chao Praya Express River Cruise: For less than one U.S. dollar, anyone can enjoy one of the finest river trips in Asia. A 75-minute journey from the Oriental Hotel up to Nonthaburi in the north costs just 10 *baht*. Such a deal.

Wat Po Massage: Bangkok is filled with expensive emporiums offering both straight and sexual massages for over 300B per hour. For an authentic rub in a safe environment, try the Wat Po Massage School where an hour's rub costs 150B.

Free Thai Dance: Colorful if somewhat amateurish Thai dance can be enjoyed at both the Lak Muang Shrine near the Grand Palace and the Erawan Shrine at the Erawan Grand Hyatt Hotel. Better performances, at the same reasonable price, can be seen on Sunday afternoons on the grassy courtyard at the National Theater.

Weekend Market: Bangkok's largest and most colorful market is held on weekends in Chatuchak Park. Operated largely by the Issan peoples of the northeast, Chatuchak has everything imaginable at rock-bottom prices.

Blind Musicians: Have a close look next time you pass a group of middle-aged musicians wearing sunglasses. Most likely they are blind musicians playing a discordant mixture of Thai ballads, folk songs, and Tin Pan Alley.

Meditation Classes: Free meditation instruction is given weekly at the International Buddhist Center at Sukumvit Soi 3, and inside the international hall at Wat Mahathat. Upcoming lectures are listed in the *Bangkok Post*.

Motorcycle Mania: Enjoy death-defying motorcycle stunts? Thanks to the ingenuity of Thai teenagers, you can now hire motorcycle taxis that weave through traffic with wild abandon. Hold on to your seat.

Tai Chi in the Park: Get up early and watch the old men go through their slow-motion paces in Lumpini Park. Then jog along the par course, feed the ducks, and paddle a boat around the small pond.

National Museum Tour: Whether you're a backpacker or a billionaire, best bets for a culture fix are the free 0930 tours given at the National Museum.

Golden Sunsets: Sunsets are best enjoyed on top of the Golden Mountain near Wat Saket, and from the luxurious Tiara Restaurant of the Dusit Thani Hotel. Somewhat different crowd, but the same great sunset.

Bus It: A cheap way to explore Bangkok is by public bus from city center to the end of the line. Stay on the bus and you'll return without fuss. Avoid all buses during rush-hour traffic.

Go Fly a Kite: From February to April, kite aficionados gather for aerial warfare at Sanam Luang. Watch the action, then buy a kite and try your luck.

Street Dining: Foodstalls provide a wonderful opportunity to rest your aching feet while burning the roof of your mouth. Watch for Issan specialties: fried crickets and roasted grasshoppers.

Thai Movies: Whether *kung fu* from Hong Kong, sappy love stories with supernatural overtones, or slapstick comedy, Thai cinema is worth the experience. Tickets are cheap and most theaters are air-conditioned.

Impress Your Girlfriend: Thai orchids are among the cheapest in the world. So hang the expense and lavish your lady with bouquets for under 30B.

Patpong Bars: If your curiosity gets the best of you, and you just want to look (not touch), head for the Patpong bars during happy hour for the bump-and-grind show.

Get High: Legal highs can be enjoyed at the top of rainbow-colored Baiyoke Towers, Bangkok's tallest building. Ride the elevator to the fourth floor and transfer to the express lift up to the Sky Lounge on the 43rd floor. If the smog god has smiled on you, enjoy the panoramic views and soft drink.

OUTSKIRTS OF BANGKOK

Wat Thamakai

Located just a few kilometers north of Bangkok Airport in Pathum Thani Province, this rural center was founded 20 years ago to offer instruction in Thamathayard meditation. The central *bot* is a marvel of modern Thai architecture which, unlike most Siamese temples, is characterized by pure, simple lines rather than highly ornate decoration. The theme of simplicity continues in the interior, where a black marble floor and plain white walls accent the presiding Buddha image illuminated with a single spotlight.

Wat Thamakai honors the legendary meditation techniques of a Bangkok monk named Pra Mongkol Thepmooni. As taught by the monk from Wat Paknam, meditation involves initial concentration on an imaginary crystal ball, then transferring that focal point to the center of the student's mind. There, the sphere expands to incorporate the universe and ultimately induces Thamakai, the visible Buddha.

Young Thai males come here to enter the monkhood during two-month retreats, held during the summer vacation months from March to May. After a month of preparation, the students are ordained at a mass ceremony at the Marble Temple and then return to further their knowledge of Buddhism. Visitors will often find the initiates silently meditating under umbrellas arranged around the pond.

Public Thai-language lectures on meditation and the life of Buddha are given every Sunday from 0930 to 1530. Visitors are requested to dress in white.

Prasart Museum

Notable private collections of Thai art can be viewed at Jim Thompson's House and Suan Pakkard Palace in Bangkok, the Ancient City, and in the museum of Khun Prasart Vongsakul. Once a successful real estate developer, Prasart has spent the last decade constructing reduced-scale reproductions of historic Thai buildings and filling them with his priceless collection of Sukothai Buddhas, Bencharong porcelains, and paintings in the Thai classical style.

Prasart Museum is in the Bangkok suburb of Hua Mak. For further information, contact the Prasart Collection, Peninsula Plaza, 153 Rajadamri Rd., Bangkok 10500, tel. (02) 253-9772.

Safari World

Southeast Asia's largest wildlife park includes a wildlife section toured by coaches, a bird park, with walk-in aviary, Macaw Island, restaurants, and an amusement park. A friendly American lady from the San Francisco Bay Area oversees animal care and acquisitions.

Safari World is in Minburi District at Kilometer 9 on Ramintra Road. Take bus 26 from Victory Monument to Minburi, then a direct minibus. Open daily 1000-1800; tel. (02) 518-1000. Admission is 250B.

Siam Water Park

Also in the Bangkok suburb of Minburi, the park is popular with families and children who plunge down the longest water slides in Thailand. A small open zoo and botanical gardens are located on the grounds. Take bus 26 or 27 from Victory Monument. Open daily 1000-1800; tel. (02) 517-0075. Admission is 200B.

Nonthaburi

A pleasant day-trip can be made by express riverboat to Nonthaburi, a small town 20 km north of Bangkok. Disembark at the pier near the clocktower and walk left up to the Nonthaburi Prison. The Correctional Staff Training compound on the left has a small museum with displays of torture used to execute prisoners during the Ayuthaya and modern periods. Foreign prisoners convicted of drug crimes can occasionally be visited. Central Nonthaburi has a floating restaurant and an old wooden provincial hall restored by the Fine Arts Department and converted into a museum of anthropology. Also worth visiting is a modern mosque, several Ayuthaya Period *wats,* and the Singha Brewery, where Thailands' most popular beer is brewed. A ferry from the Nonthaburi dock leads across the river to Wat Salak Dtai and Wat Chalern Pra Kiet, a beautiful temple renowned for its architecture and idyllic location amid breadfruit trees and abandoned buildings.

Organized tours of nearby gardens are organized each weekend by the Suan Tan Noi Tour Company, tel. (02) 583-9279 or (02) 583-7853.

OUTSIDE BANGKOK

Damnern Saduak Floating Market

The floating markets of Thailand are unique wonders. Amid the lowland canals and winding rivers, women in straw hats continue to paddle *sampans* piled high with vegetables, fruits, and flowers—a vanishing look at Thai life from a century ago. Despite the popularity of fast-food outlets and concrete shopping centers, authentic floating markets still serve several communities near Bangkok.

Don't bother visiting the completely artificial Wat Sai Floating Market in Bangkok, one of the worst examples of mercenary tourism in the world. Instead, make the journey to the small town of Damnern Saduak, located 109 km southwest of Bangkok, midway between Nakhon Pathom and Samut Sakhon. Though firmly on the tourist route, it remains an almost completely authentic experience . . . but only before the bus loads of tourists begin arriving at 0930. Visitors who arrive before 0900 will have the spectacle to themselves, but arrivals after 0930 will be deluged with thousands of tourists. Either be here early, or skip Damnern Saduak.

Damnern Saduak has three floating markets. The principal market at Ton Kem is formed by a narrow canal flanked with foodstalls and souvenir shops. Handicraft bazaars in the rear should be avoided since the merchandise is overpriced and the salesgirls can be very aggressive. Farther south are the rarely visited markets at Her Kui and Khun Pitak. Photographers at Ton Kem will get their best shots from the bridge which crosses over the canal, and from the produce shed on the right. Chartered *sampans* cost 50-80B for a short 20-minute look and 250-300B for a one-hour tour, though everything of interest can be seen from the bridge and adjacent walkways.

Transportation: Because of the distances involved, most visitors take an organized tour which includes a brief stop at the Nakhon Pathom *chedi* and an afternoon visit to the Rose Garden. Independent travelers can reach Damnern Saduak by public bus 78, leaving every 20 minutes from the Southern Bus Terminal in Thonburi. To beat the tour buses, catch an early morning bus between 0500 and 0700. The bus ride takes two hours and terminates in downtown Damnern Saduak. The floating market, located two km up the adjacent canal, can be reached by walking on the path to the right of the canal or by taking a public *sampan* for 10B at the bridge. You can also take a minibus from downtown or hike along the road south of the bridge just past the information booth.

Transportation alternatives include a bus or rented motorcycle from Kanchanaburi, or an overnight stay in a Damnern Saduak hotel. From Kanchanaburi, take yellow bus 461 to Bang Pae and then bus 78 to Damnern Saduak. Allow two

floating market

hours for the journey. Further details are available from Kanchanaburi guesthouses.

Motorcyclists will enjoy the cool, dark ride from Kanchanaburi to the Ratchaburi turnoff, then follow the large English-language signs which point the way to Damnern Saduak. South of Bang Pae are a snake farm and several beautiful *wats,* including a new complex which resembles a Japanese Zen temple.

Accommodations: An inexpensive hotel with an English sign is located up the alley off the main road in Damnern Saduak. A cheaper option is the Floating Market Guesthouse (tel. 032-25110), located on the road which parallels the canal, 200 meters before the market. Look for the coconut factory on the right. Bamboo bungalows in poor condition cost 50-80B. They also claim to have bikes, motorcycles, and boats for rent, though the place is usually deserted.

Restaurants: Damnern Saduak has plenty of restaurants, but most visitors will opt for the cafes which overhang the market. The coffee shop near the bridge is run by a friendly lady who can't understand why anyone would want Thai noodles for breakfast.

Ancient City

Ancient City, also called Muang Boran, is a 200-acre outdoor park and architectural museum filled with full-sized and reduced-scale replicas of Thailand's 65 most important monuments and temples. Constructed by an art-loving philanthropist and Bangkok's largest Mercedes-Benz dealer, Muang Boran provides an excellent introduction to the country's architecture, including reproductions of buildings which no longer exist, such as the Grand Palace of Ayuthaya. The complex is laid out in the shape of Thailand with monument locations mirroring the actual geography of Thailand.

Best suited for the visitor with a serious interest in architecture, the vast park is enormous, somewhat neglected, rarely visited, and murderously hot in the summer.

Muang Boran is 33 km south of Bangkok along the old Sukumvit Highway. Muang Boran group tours (tel. 02-222-8145) can be booked from travel agents or directly from their office at 78 Rajadamnern Avenue near Democracy Monument. Muang Boran also publishes a detailed guidebook to their park and a lavish bilingual periodical devoted to Thai art and architecture; old editions are heavily discounted. Independent travelers can take a/c bus 8 or 11 from Sukumvit Rd. to the clocktower in Samut Prakan (also called Paknam), then minibus 38 to the front gate. The Crocodile Farm can be included on the same tour.

Muang Boran is open daily 0830-1700. Admission is 60B.

Crocodile Farm

The world's largest reptile farm was founded in 1950 by a former hotel pageboy to save crocodiles from extinction and, parenthetically, turn their hides into wallets, briefcases, and shoes. Today, over 30,000 crocodiles patiently lounge around murky swimming pools waiting for their hourly wrestling matches and frenzied feedings at 1700. After their moment of glory, the beasts are skinned into trendy suitcases and exotic dishes for Chinese restaurants. Also included is a small zoo blessed with oddities such as smoking chimpanzees and dancing elephants. Touristy and weird.

The Crocodile Farm is 25 km south of Bangkok in Samut Prakan, six km before Ancient City. Air-conditioned buses 8 and 11 from Sukumvit Road go directly to the entrance. Open daily 0800-1800. Admission is 100B.

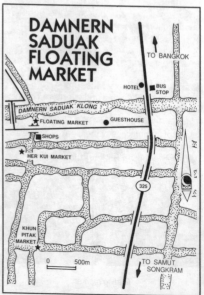

DAMNERN SADUAK FLOATING MARKET

TO BANGKOK

HOTEL

BUS STOP

DAMNERN SADUAK KLONG

FLOATING MARKET

GUESTHOUSE

SHOPS

HER KUI MARKET

325

KHUN PITAK MARKET

0   500m

TO SAMUT SONGKRAM

© MOON PUBLICATIONS, INC.

Rose Garden

Located on the banks of the Nakorn Chaisri River and set amid lovely landscaped gardens, this country resort features an eight-acre lake, aviaries with over 300 exotic birds, orchid and rose nurseries, championship 18-hole golf course, and replica of a Thai village where cottage industries such as silk weaving and umbrella painting are demonstrated. Overnight facilities include a resort hotel with 80 first-class rooms overlooking the river. Reservations can be made through travel agencies or by contacting the resort at (02) 253-2276 or (02) 253-0295.

The one-hour cultural show, given daily at 1500, is widely considered the finest in Thailand. No matter how contrived or touristy, this show consistently thrills with its nonstop performances of Thai dance, martial arts, a traditional wedding, Buddhist monkhood ordinations, *takraw,* and a demonstration of working elephants.

Rose Garden is 32 km west of Bangkok, on the road to Nakhon Pathom. Most travelers visit the park on a package tour which includes the floating market at Damnern Saduak and the *chedi* at Nakhon Pathom. Luxury hotels in Bangkok provide daily connections, as does Bangkok Sightseeing Travel Agency which charges 220B for a daily roundtrip bus ride at 1300 from the Indra Hotel. The resort can also be reached by public bus from the Southern Bus Terminal in Thonburi.

The Rose Garden is open daily 0800-1800. The 200B fee includes admission to the gardens and cultural show.

Thai Human Imagery Museum

Prominent personalities and events in Thai history are examined in a small museum opened near the Rose Garden in 1987. Exhibits include figures of former kings of the Chakri Dynasty, 15 great Buddhist monks with descriptions of their achievements, an upstairs hall dedicated to Confucius, and a demonstration room where the fiberglass figures were created. Artists fashioned the forty figures from fiberglass rather than wax after considering the possible effects of Thailand's intense heat.

The museum is 31 km west of Bangkok. Open daily 0900-1800. Admission is 150B.

Samphran Elephant Park

This 22-acre farm sponsors daily demonstrations of crocodile wrestling, magic shows, an elephant tug-of-war, roundup, and re-creation of the famous elephant battle between King Naresuan the Great and a Burmese prince.

The park is 31 km west of Bangkok, on the left side of the road just one km before the Rose Garden. Open daily 0900-1800. Admission is 150B.

Wat Pailom Bird Sanctuary

Wat Pailom, near Pathum Thani on the Chao Praya River 32 km north of Bangkok, is one of the world's last sanctuaries for rare Indian openbilled storks *(Anastomus oscitans),* which migrate from Bangladesh each December through June. Once a burial ground for execution victims, the bizarre landscape lies covered with denuded trees piled with over 10,000 enormous nests.

Tragically, Wat Pailom, one of the more remarkable nature reserves in Thailand, now seems doomed. Recently constructed upriver dams have choked off the water supply for the dipterocarpus trees, and modern fertilizers have poisoned the apple snail, the storks' primary source of food. The Wildlife Fund of Thailand is now attempting to relocate the storks to more suitable colonies at Suphanburi and Ayuthaya.

Wat Pailom is best visited on the weekend river cruises leaving in the mornings from the Maharaj Pier. Contact the Chao Praya Express Boat Company at tel. (02) 222-5330 or (02) 411-0305.

> *As Calcutta smells of death and Bombay of money, Bangkok smells of sex, but this sexual aroma is mingled with the sharper whiffs of death and money.*
> —Paul Theroux,
> *The Great Railway Bazaar*

ACCOMMODATIONS

Bangkok offers a wide range of hotels and guesthouses in all categories and possible price ranges. Budget homestays for 100-300B are plentiful in the Banglampoo District, while some of the finest hotels in the world are found near Siam Square and hugging the banks of the Chao Praya River. Where to stay depends on your finances, and whether you want to be near the river, sightseeing attractions, nightlife centers, or shopping districts. The following summary may help you decide.

HOTELS

Districts

For quick orientation in Bangkok, think of the city as individual neighborhoods with distinct personalities, hotel price ranges, and styles of restaurants and nightclubs. The city has four major hotel districts (Banglampoo, Silom Road, Siam Square, and Sukumvit Road) and several less-frequented areas such as Chinatown and around the Malaysia Hotel.

Old Royal City: The old royal city around the Grand Palace has the largest concentration of sightseeing attractions but very few hotels or restaurants. Banglampoo is the best choice if you want to stay near the temples in the old royal city.

Banglampoo: Over the last decade, Banglampoo has become the backpackers' headquarters with dozens of budget guesthouses and inexpensive cafes. Banglampoo lacks great nightlife or shopping, but compensates with a superb location near great temples and the immensely convenient Chao Praya River. Anyone looking for guesthouses under US$10 should head directly for its principal thoroughfare, Khao San Road.

Chinatown and Little India: Chinatown hotels cater primarily to wealthy Chinese businessmen, but a handful of inexpensive guesthouses are located in adjacent Little India. Travelers searching for a strong and completely authentic encounter with Indian culture might consider staying here rather than in Banglampoo.

Silom Road: Bangkok's original tourist enclave is located near the Chao Praya River and along a major boulevard known as Silom Road. Sightseeing attractions are minimal and the congestion is unnerving, but Silom offers dozens of moderate to superluxury hotels, exclusive restaurants, high-end shopping boutiques, great sidewalk shopping, and the infamous nightlife area of Patpong Road. Riverside hotels such as the Oriental and Shangri La are world famous for their extremely high levels of service. Budget accommodations are limited to some older properties and a few grungy Indian hotels near the GPO.

Malaysia Hotel Area: Once the budget travelers' center for Bangkok, hotels and guesthouses along Soi Ngam Duphli have sadly declined in recent years. Although the neighborhood can no longer be recommended, the nearby YMCA represents good value in the lower price range.

Siam Square: Bangkok's most luxurious hotel district is a relatively low-density neighborhood with ultraelegant hotels and modern shopping centers. The lack of sightseeing attractions is balanced by the vast gardens that surround many of the hotels, and the enormous shopping complexes that guarantee some of the best shopping in all of Asia. Hotels are expensive, but several low-priced and very clean guesthouses are located near Jim Thompson's house.

Sukumvit Road: Once considered on the outer fringes of Bangkok, Sukumvit has recently developed into the leading area for moderate-budget tourists. The only drawback is the enormous distance to important temples and government services, but Sukumvit has the best selection of hotels in the US$25-50 price range. Other positive notes include many of the finest Thai restaurants in the country, wonderful sidewalk shopping, countless boutiques, and racy nightlife in Nana Complex and Soi Cowboy. Despite the remote location and problems with noise and pollution, Sukumvit is highly recommended for middle-level travelers and anyone motivated by nightlife and shopping.

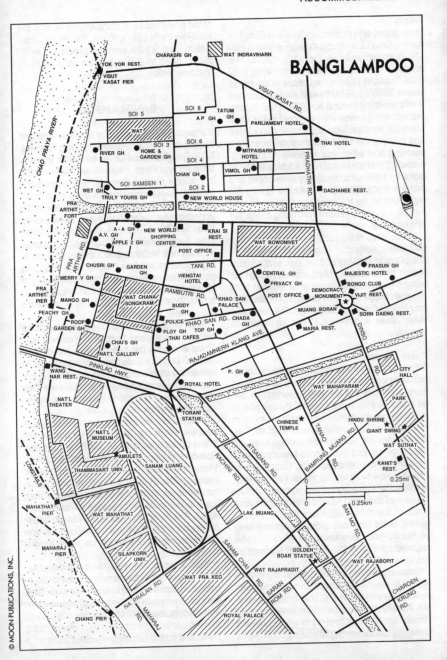

BANGLAMPOO

Prices

Hotel prices and occupancy levels in Bangkok have followed a wild roller-coaster ride of boom-and-bust cycles since the early 1980s. The country's incredible surge in tourism after 1987 (Visit Thailand Year) forced prices at top hotels above 3000B (US$120) and kept occupancy levels hovering around 85-95%. This, in turn, brought a huge expansion in recent years. Over 20 major hotel projects have been announced and many of the major international hotels are planning new wings and extensions. The estimated 12,000 additional rooms which will be in place by 1995 will dramatically ease prices and make it much easier to find a room during the high season from November to March. Also helping are condominiums now being converted into high-rise hotels.

Prices cited in the hotel charts are published rack rates, subject to negotiation during periods of low occupancy and the slow season from March to November. Most rooms, except for budget guesthouses, carry an additional 10% service charge and 11% government tax. Discounts are often given at the front desk for longer stays (three or more days) and for corporate accounts.

Reservations

Advance reservations for moderate to luxury hotels are essential during the peak season from December to February. Reservations can be made by mail and by phone, though phone reservations are problematic since reservation clerks often have difficulty with English. Fax reservations are *highly* recommended since the hard-copy printout guarantees fewer mistakes than written or phone requests. Most hotels in Thailand now have fax machines. Fax numbers are listed with most hotel descriptions. The international code for Thailand is 66, and the area code for Bangkok is 02. Since the 0 at the beginning of the area code is dropped when dialing or faxing from overseas, Bangkok can be reached by dialing 662 (not 6602) followed by the seven-digit phone number.

Travelers arriving at the Bangkok airport without reservations can check on vacancies and make reservations at the Thai Hotel Association Reservation Counter in the arrival lounge. Hotels are listed according to price, with the cheapest rooms starting at around 500B. None of the guesthouses in Banglampoo or near the Malaysia Hotel belong to the Thai Hotel Association. Phone calls from the airport to the following guesthouses *might* turn up a vacancy and reservation.

BANGLAMPOO

Bangkok's headquarters for backpackers and budget travelers is centered around this friendly little neighborhood just a few blocks from the temples and Chao Praya River. Named after the village *(bang)* where *lampoo* trees once thrived, Banglampoo now serves as a freak street for world travelers who hang out in the guesthouses, cafes, and travel agencies on Khao San Road. There's a great deal of interest here. Early-morning risers can enjoy an espresso from one of the sidewalk cafes, while late-night strollers will love the sidewalk shopping and general sense of mayhem. People watching in Banglampoo is excellent and prices on air tickets, local tours, clothing, and other souvenirs are some of the best in town.

Best of all, Banglampoo is a friendly place with excellent vibes from both travelers and Thais who work the guesthouses and restaurants. Though it's undeniably a travelers' ghetto with all the standard trappings, much of the adjacent neighborhood exudes an authentic Thai atmosphere rarely found in the other tourist areas in Bangkok.

At last count, Banglampoo had over 60 guesthouses, which charge 40-60B for dorms, 60-100B for singles, and 80-200B for doubles. Rooms with private baths cost another 50-80B. Many of the guesthouses also have small a/c rooms in the 200-350B price range. Guesthouses constructed in the last few years often have larger rooms with private baths for 200-400B. The trend appears to be toward better facilities at a slightly higher fee, though low-end rooms still vastly outnumber the more expensive ones.

Banglampoo does have some drawbacks. Rooms are often extraordinarily small and claustrophobic, furnished with only a single bed. Theft can be a problem because of plywood walls and inadequate locks. Motorcycles which race around late at night can ruin your sleep; find a clean and comfortable room tucked away on a

RAJADAMNERN AVENUE BUSES

39, 59	Airport
3AC, 39AC	Airport
70	Boxing Stadium
12AC	New Petchburi
39AC	Northern Bus Terminal
45	Rama IV
15, 121	Silom
2, 11AC	Sukumvit, Eastern Bus Terminal

CHAKRABONGSE ROAD BUSES

3	Weekend Market, Airport

PRA SUMEN ROAD BUSES

53	Chinatown, Train Station

side street rather than directly on Khao San Road. Finally, Banglampoo is an artificial and trendy scene (banana pancakes, hippie clothes, etc.) that some travelers find unappealing.

But the worst problem is that most guesthouses in Banglampoo are perpetually filled from morning until night. Finding a room is time-consuming since reservation lists are rarely honored and rooms fill *immediately* after checkout. Room searches are best conducted in the early morning 0700-1100 when travelers depart for the airport and bus stations. Take the first available room, and transfer to another room the following day if noise is a problem. Travelers arriving from the airport in the late afternoon or evening should expect a long—but ultimately successful—search. Take a taxi from the airport to Khao San Rd., then leave your traveling partner and bags in a sidewalk cafe while you search for an available room. And keep smiling . . . Bangkok is a great place once you find a room!

Budget Accommodations

Most Banglampoo guesthouses are identical in cleanliness and size. There isn't much sense in recommending specific guesthouses, since all will be fully booked simply from word-of-mouth reputation. A small selection of slightly better choices is shown on the map and briefly described here. Most guesthouses are located near Khao San Rd. Travelers who would like to distance themselves from the scene should

check ones near the river, or across the bridge to the north.

Buddy Guesthouse: Located in the middle of Khao San Rd., Buddy Guesthouse is a good place to begin your room search. Though perpetually filled, you can drop your bags and enjoy a quick meal in the comfortable cafe located in the rear. A less-packed restaurant is located upstairs. Buddy Guesthouse, like most other guesthouses in Banglampoo, has a variety of rooms from basic cubicles to small a/c rooms with private bath. 137 Khao San Rd., tel. (02) 282-4351, 60-250B.

Hello Guesthouse: A 30-room guesthouse with a popular streetside cafe. 63 Khao San Rd., tel. (02) 281-8579, 60-150B fan, 180-250B a/c.

Ploy Guesthouse: A big place with very large rooms with private bath. Entrance is around the corner from Khao San Road. The lobby on the second floor includes a small cafe and the coldest soft drinks in Bangkok. Recommended. 2 Khao San Rd., tel. (02) 282-1025, 60-200B.

Chart Guesthouse: An easy-to-find 20-room guesthouse with a great cafe. All rooms have fans; no a/c. 61 Khao San Rd., tel. (02) 281-0803, 60-140B.

C.H. Guesthouse: Big and popular place with 27 rooms and a packed video cafe on the ground floor. Recommended. 216 Khao San Rd., tel. (02) 282-2023, 60-150B fan, 200-220B a/c.

Lek Guesthouse: One of the original guesthouses in Banglampoo. Always filled, but worth checking with Mr. Lek Saranukul. 125 Khao San Rd., tel. (02) 281-2775, 80-140B.

Central and Privacy Guesthouses: Both Central and Privacy guesthouses to the east of Tanao Rd. are quiet and somewhat run-down but exude a homey Thai feeling. Alleys branching off Khao San have several more peaceful guesthouses. 69 Tanao Rd., tel. (02) 282-7028, 60-120B.

Bangkok Youth Hostel: Bangkok's hostel, near Khao San Rd., is poorly organized and rather unfriendly. All rooms come with common bath. 105 Chakrabongse Rd., tel. (02) 282-7454, 60B dorm, 160-220B.

Apple 2 Guesthouse: For a slightly Fellini-esque experience, walk past the grazing cows and horses of Wat Chana Songkram (an animal refuge in the middle of Bangkok!) to the alleys and guesthouses which surround the temple. Apple 2 is a long-running favorite located in a quiet back alley. The big rambling teak house with songbirds and upstairs rooms is also called "Mama's." 11 Trok Kai Chae, tel. (02) 281-1219, 70-120B.

Peachy Guesthouse: Slightly more expensive than Khao San cubicles, but the rooms are clean, spacious, and furnished with writing tables and standing closets. Air-conditioning is available. Perpetually filled, but sign the waiting list. Avoid rooms facing Pra Arthit Rd. or adjacent to the TV room. 10 Pra Arthit, tel. (02) 281-6471, 100-160B.

Merry V Guesthouse: One of the best guesthouses behind Wat Chana Songkram has clean rooms and a very comfortable restaurant. 35 Soi Chana Songkram, tel. (02) 282-9267, 60-160B.

Truly Yours Guesthouse: Some of Banglampoo's quietest guesthouses are located across the bridge north of Khao San Road. All provide an opportunity to experience Thai homestays in a traditional neighborhood. Samsen 1 Rd. has Truly Yours and Villa Guesthouse, while Samsen 3 Rd. has the River, Clean and Calm, and Home and Garden guesthouses. Worth the walk. All charge 60-120B.

Samsen 6 Guesthouses: North of Khao San Rd. are several small homestays and guesthouses far removed from the hype of Banglampoo. Located near the midpriced Vorapong Guesthouse (250B fan, 300B a/c) are the inexpensive AP, Tatum, and Vimol guesthouses. Not a tourist in sight.

Tavee Guest House: To really escape the travelers' scene in Banglampoo, walk north up Chakrabongse Rd. and turn left on Sri Ayuthaya Rd. at the National Library. Near the river are three idyllic guesthouses including the Shanti, Sawatdee, and Tavee. The latter is at 83 Sri Ayuthaya, tel. (02) 282-5349, 60-120B.

Moderate Accommodations

Banglampoo isn't exclusively for budget travelers. Bridging the gap between the inexpensive guesthouses and the upscale hotels are several midpriced hotels and guesthouses that offer both fan and a/c rooms. During the fiery summer months from March to June even the tightest of travelers will pay extra for air-conditioning.

Khao San Palace Hotel: The dark and small rooms, probably the cheapest a/c rooms in Bangkok, come equipped with private baths, warm water, and horizontal mirrors geared to short-time business. 139 Khao San Rd., tel. (02) 282-0578, 280-340B fan, 360-420B a/c.

Nith Charoen Hotel: Another good midpriced hotel located in the heart of Banglampoo. Comfortable lounge with a useful bulletin board. 183 Khao San Rd., tel. (02) 281-9872, 300-340B fan, 420-460B a/c.

A-A Guesthouse: One of Banglampoo's best-value guesthouses has five floors of rooms ranging from common-bath cheapies on the fourth and fifth floors, to private-bath a/c on the lower floors. Quietly tucked away in a small alley. 84 Pra Sumeru Rd., tel. (02) 282-9631, 120-160B common bath, 200-240B private bath with fan, 300-380B private bath with a/c. Highly recommended.

New World House: A large, modern apartment complex with luxury features at a bargain price. All rooms are a/c, with private bath, telephone, laundry service, and views over Banglampoo. Recommended for anyone who intends to stay a week or longer. Located just across the river. 2 Samsen Rd., tel. (02) 281-5596, 300-350B daily, 1800-2000B weekly, 7000-8000B monthly.

Luxury Accommodations

Luxury is a relative term in Banglampoo. None of the following hotels compare with the Oriental or Shangri La, but all provide adequate facilities for travelers who want the location with a touch of luxury. In other guidebooks, the following hotels would be classified as "moderate."

Royal Hotel: This well-priced hotel is within easy walking distance of Bangkok's attractions—an excellent place in a great location. Reservations can be made from the hotel counter at the airport. Budget travelers and overheated travel writers often spend their mornings in the a/c coffee shop reading the *Bangkok Post.* 2 Rajadamnern, tel. (02) 222-9111, fax (02) 224-2083, 1400-1800B.

Viengtai Hotel: Banglampoo's longtime favorite has sharply raised prices and failed to make any improvements; not recommended. 42 Tanao, tel. (02) 282-8672, fax (02) 281-8153, 1200-1500B single or double.

(previous page) Wat Arun sunset;
(this page, top) Phitsanulok monks; (bottom) hilltribe costumes (all photos by Carl Parkes)

Majestic Hotel: The finest hotel in Banglampoo is somewhat overpriced but compensates with a good restaurant and great location near the temples and tourist office. 97 Rajadamnern, tel. (02) 281-5610, fax (02) 280-0965, 1800-3200B.

Thai: Here, singles run 800-1200B, doubles 1000-1500B. 78 Prajatipati, tel. (02) 282-2831.

Getting To Banglampoo Hotels

From the airport, the easiest way to reach Banglampoo is either the minibus for 100B or an ordinary taxi for 200B. The minibus leaves to the left of the blue limo sign inside the arrival lounge. Taxis leave from the stand outside. Public buses pass along the highway directly in front of the airport. Ordinary buses 3, 17, 44, 56, and 59 all go to Banglampoo, as do a/c buses 3AC and 11AC. The tourist office in the arrival lounge has the latest information on public transportation into Bangkok.

MALAYSIA HOTEL AREA

Surrounding the Malaysia Hotel are about 20 budget guesthouses and several midpriced hotels which comprise Bangkok's original travelers' center. From the late 1960s to the early 1980s this neighborhood—also known as Soi Ngam Duphli after the main boulevard—was a hotbed of budget guesthouses, discount travel agencies, and banana-pancake cafes. Travelers on the Kathmandu-to-Bali trail made their home at the Malaysia, a near-legendary hotel that offered comfortable rooms at rock-bottom prices.

Unfortunately, the Malaysia Hotel sharply raised its room rates in the 1980s and added such novelties as girlie lounges and pinball machines. Discouraged by the changes, travelers quickly abandoned Soi Ngam Duphli and moved over to Banglampoo to enjoy the far superior

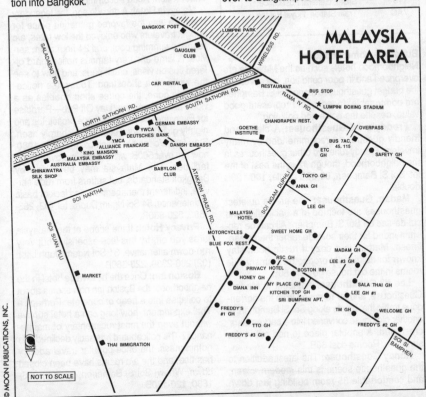

atmosphere and location of Khao San Road.

Soi Ngam Duphli today continues to offer some of the same kinds of services (guesthouses, budget travel agencies, etc.), but suffers from being noisier, more polluted, and far seedier than Banglampoo. Hard drugs and prostitutes are now commonplace. The neighborhood survives with first-time visitors who haven't heard about Banglampoo, and males who want inexpensive accommodations centrally located between the nightlife areas of Silom Rd. (Patpong) and Sukumvit (Nana Complex and Soi Cowboy).

From the airport take a direct minibus for 100B, a share taxi for 200B, or a/c bus 4AC from the highway.

RAMA IV ROAD BUSES	
5	Siam Square, Banglampoo
115	Silom, General Post Office
7AC	Train Station, Royal Palace

Budget Accommodations

Neighborhood hotels such as the Malaysia are overpriced and in poor condition, but several of the budget guesthouses along Soi Si Bamphen are comfortable, friendly, and represent good value, despite the noise and pollution.

Freddy's #2 Guesthouse: A clean and friendly guesthouse recommended by many travelers. Freddy runs two other guesthouses in the neighborhood, though #2 is the best of the lot. Soi Si Bamphen, 60-80B single, 100-120B double.

Madam Guesthouse: The area's quietest guesthouses are located in a back alley and cul-de-sac off Soi Si Bamphen. All can be recommended for their solitude rather than cleanliness. Madam is a cozy if rustic homestay known for its friendly proprietor. Ramshackle rooms in the old house go from 60B.

Lee #3 Guesthouse: Adjacent to Madam Guesthouse, and far removed from the horrendous traffic that blasts along Soi Si Samphen, is another old house converted into a backpackers' crash pad. A popular place to nod out in the sunshine. Rooms cost 60B.

Honey Guesthouse: The latest addition to the guesthouse scene is this modern, clean, and comfortable 35-room building just down

from the Malaysia Hotel. Rooms are available with common or private bath, with fan or a/c. Hefty discounts are given for monthly residents. The adjacent Diana Inn (Greco-Roman style) is also recommended. 35 Soi Ngam Duphli, tel. (02) 286-3460, 120-160B inside rooms, 180-200B with balcony.

K Guesthouse: Also on Soi Si Bamphen, stays here are 90B single or double.

L.A. Guesthouse: Near the Lee, rooms run 120-150B single, 140-180B double. 27 Soi Ngam Duphli, tel. (02) 286-8556.

Moderate Accommodations

Midpriced hotels in this neighborhood have sadly declined in recent years, but the nearby YMCA and King's Mansion are excellent value. These two hotels are located midway between the Malaysia Hotel and Silom Road and described under "Silom Road Accommodations."

Malaysia Hotel: A decade ago, the legendary Malaysia was the favored gathering place for budget travelers who enjoyed the low rates, a/c rooms, swimming pool, and 24-hour room service. A large and very famous noticeboard offered tips on visas, crash pads, and how to see the world on a shoestring. Today, the noticeboard is gone, the coffee shop doubles as a video arcade, and the "Day Off Pub—Paradise for Everyone" features freelance prostitutes and nightly girlie shows. Rates have sharply risen. Standard a/c rooms, which cost 120B in 1980, now run over 500B, without any improvement in facilities. The Malaysia may be cheap by Bangkok standards, but suffers from rude service, indifferent management, and lack of basic maintenance. 54 Soi Ngam Duphli, tel. (02) 286-3582, 520-800B.

Privacy Hotel: If the scene at the Malaysia turns you off, try this less-expensive but very run-down alternative. 31 Soi Ngam Duphli, tel. (02) 286-2339, 220-360B.

Boston Inn: Once the best-value hotel in the neighborhood, the Boston Inn now seems about to collapse into a heap of concrete. Perhaps a Thai experiment: how long can a hotel survive without even the most rudimentary of maintenance? The noticeboard has sadly declined into nothingness, the once-popular travel agency has fled, and the a/c rooms have been closed down. Whew! Soi Si Bamphen, tel. (02) 286-1680, 120-180B.

CHINATOWN

Few travelers stay in Chinatown, but the chaotic neighborhood offers a chance to escape the standard tourist enclaves and experience real ethnic intensity. Most hotels are on the main boulevards of Chakrapet, Yaowaraj, and Rajawong. Larger properties are signposted in English, while the smaller places, marked only with Chinese signs, are sometimes reluctant to take Westerners.

Chao Phaya Guesthouse: Beautifully situated on the banks of the Chao Praya (Phaya) River, this aging place is easily spotted from the river taxis that cruise between the Old Royal City and Silom Road. Bangkok needs more waterfront guesthouses like this one. 1128 Songwad Rd. (two blocks south of Rajawong Rd.), tel. (02) 222-6344, 500-800B.

Riverview Guesthouse: Another riverside choice located north of the Royal Orchid Sheraton. The eight-floor hotel has both fan and a/c rooms and a view restaurant on the top floor. Somewhat funky but a great location. Reservations are absolutely necessary; use their fax number. 768 Soi Panurangsri, Songwad Rd., tel. (02) 234-5429, fax (02) 236-6199, 600-900B.

New Empire Hotel: Located near Wat Traimit, the New Empire is noisy and somewhat decrepit, but compensates with large rooms and a decent swimming pool. 572 Yaowaraj Rd., tel. (02) 234-6990, 220-300B fan, 300-400B a/c.

Chinatown Hotel: The largest and finest hotel in Chinatown is often filled with Chinese businessmen and tour groups. All rooms come with private bath, color TV, telephone, and minibars. 526 Yaowaraj Rd., tel. (02) 226-1267, fax 226-1295, 1200-1500B.

LITTLE INDIA

Over a dozen inexpensive Indian-owned hotels in the 100-200B price range are located in the alleys behind Pahurat Market. The clientele is almost exclusively Indian or Pakistani, and room conditions are extremely basic, but nobody cares how many people you pack into the cubicles. On the other hand, this neighborhood has excellent Indian cafes and enough atmosphere to transport you back to Mother India. Best of all, not a tourist in sight.

Champ Guesthouse: Located in the heart of Little India and slightly better than most of the adjacent dives. The Chaidee Guesthouse just opposite has rooms from 100B. Several tasty and very inexpensive Indian cafes are nearby. Chakrapet Road, 150-200B fan, 250B a/c.

Asia Guesthouse: Another option to consider is this small guesthouse tucked away in a quiet alley. Chakrapet Rd., 120-180 fan, 200-250B a/c.

Sunny Guesthouse: Just beyond the popular Cha Cha Restaurant is another fairly clean guesthouse that cheerfully accepts Westerners. Formerly called the Rani Guesthouse. Chakrapet Road, 100-150B.

Golden Bangkok Guesthouse: Probably the best hotel in Little India, but only recommended for the hardened traveler. Chakrapet Road, 300-400B a/c.

SILOM ROAD

Silom Road, from the Chao Praya River to Rama IV Road, is Bangkok's financial district and the original tourist enclave in Bangkok. Once a luxurious residential neighborhood for wealthy merchants, today some of the city's finest luxury hotels and a large number of mid-priced properties are located here. The area also offers leading department stores, antique and jewelry shops, and the sleazy nightlife that thrives along notorious Patpong Road. Silom is exciting and vibrant, but also noisy and crowded with high rises. An inner-city experience.

Budget Accommodations

Silom accommodations are mostly in the mid to upper price range, though a few inexpensive guesthouses and hotels priced under 600B are found in the side streets. Most of the low-end hotels are operated by Indians and Pakistanis.

Naaz Guesthouse: Indians patronize several of the small and very inexpensive guesthouses on New Rd. near the GPO. Conditions are extremely rough, but if you want a cheap crash pad and don't mind the Calcutta atmosphere, then the Naaz might be adequate. Other similar spots are around the corner on Soi Puttaosod and to the rear on Nares Road. Several

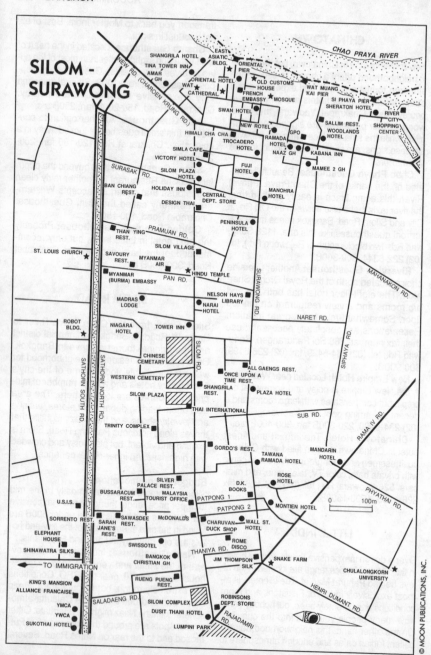

SILOM - SURAWONG

CHAO PRAYA RIVER

NEW RD. (CHAROEN KRUNG RD.)

SHANGRILA HOTEL
EAST ASIATIC BLDG.
TINA TOWER INN
AMAR GH
ORIENTAL PIER
ORIENTAL HOTEL
WAT CATHEDRAL
OLD CUSTOMS HOUSE
FRENCH EMBASSY
MOSQUE
WAT MUANG KAI PIER
SI PHAYA PIER
SHERATON HOTEL
RIVER CITY SHOPPING CENTER
SWAN HOTEL
NEW HOTEL
SALLIM REST.
WOODLANDS HOTEL
GPO
HIMALI CHA CHA
RAMADA HOTEL
TROCADERO HOTEL
SIMLA CAFE
NAAZ GH
KABANA INN
VICTORY HOTEL
FUJI HOTEL
MAMEE 2 GH
SILOM PLAZA HOTEL
BAN CHIANG REST.
HOLIDAY INN
CENTRAL DEPT. STORE
MANOHRA HOTEL
DESIGN THAI
PENINSULA HOTEL
SURASAK RD.
PRAMUAN RD.
THAN YING REST.
SILOM VILLAGE
ST. LOUIS CHURCH
SAVOURY REST.
MYANMAR AIR
HINDU TEMPLE
MYANMAR (BURMA) EMBASSY
PAN RD.
NELSON HAYS LIBRARY
MADRAS LODGE
NARAI HOTEL
SURAWONG RD.
NARET RD.
MAHANAKON RD.
ROBOT BLDG.
NIAGARA HOTEL
TOWER INN
SILOM RD.
CHINESE CEMETERY
ALL GAENGS REST.
WESTERN CEMETERY
ONCE UPON A TIME REST.
SHANGRILA REST.
PLAZA HOTEL
SILOM PLAZA
THAI INTERNATIONAL
SUB RD.
RAMA IV RD.
SIPHAYA RD.
TRINITY COMPLEX
SATHORN NORTH RD.
SATHORN SOUTH RD.
GORDO'S REST.
TAWANA RAMADA HOTEL
MANDARIN HOTEL
U.S.I.S.
BUSSARACUM REST.
SILVER PALACE REST.
MALAYSIA TOURIST OFFICE
D.K. BOOKS
ROSE HOTEL
PATPONG 1
PHYATHAI RD.
SORRENTO REST.
SAWASDEE REST.
PATPONG 2
MONTIEN HOTEL
SARAH JANE'S REST.
McDONALD'S
CHARUVAN DUCK SHOP
WALL ST. HOTEL
ELEPHANT HOUSE
SWISSOTEL
ROME DISCO
SHINAWATRA SILKS
BANGKOK CHRISTIAN GH
THANIYA RD.
JIM THOMPSON SILK
SNAKE FARM
TO IMMIGRATION
RUENG PUENG REST.
CHULALONGKORN UNIVERSITY
KING'S MANSION
ALLIANCE FRANCAISE
YMCA
YWCA
SILOM COMPLEX
ROBINSONS DEPT. STORE
RAJADAMRI RD.
SUKOTHAI HOTEL
SALADAENG RD.
DUSIT THANI HOTEL
LUMPINI PARK
HENRI DUMANT RD.

0   100m

© MOON PUBLICATIONS, INC.

good Indian restaurants are nearby. 1159 New Rd., tel. (02) 235-9718, 100-150B.

Madras Lodge: Better hotels which cater to the Indian community are on alleys off Silom Road. Madras Lodge and Cafe is a newish three-story hotel located about 200 meters down Vaithi Lane, two blocks east of the Hindu Temple. An exceptionally quiet location. Silom Rd. Trok 13, tel. (02) 235-6761, 180-300B fan, 400-600B a/c.

Bangkok Christian Guesthouse: Clean, safe, and comfortable but probably too strait-laced for most visitors: geared to "Christian travelers visiting the work of the Church in Thailand." On the other hand, it's blessed with a pleasant garden and home-like atmosphere; a quiet refuge within easy walking distance of Silom and Patpong. 123 Sala Daeng, Soi 2, tel. (02) 233-6303, 400-500B fan, 600-800B a/c.

Swan Hotel: This inexpensive little hotel is ideally located within walking distance of the GPO, inexpensive Indian restaurants, and river taxis behind the Oriental. All rooms include private bath and telephone, plus there's a small pool and adequate coffee shop. The Swan needs some obvious improvement, but it remains excellent value for budget travelers. Reservations are accepted for a/c rooms only,

and flight number and arrival time are required. Credit cards and traveler's checks are not accepted. 31 Soi Charoen Krung (Former Customs House Lane), tel. (02) 234-8594, 400-550B fan, 650-800B a/c.

Kabana Inn: Opposite the GPO and river taxis, the Kabana is another Indian-operated hotel with relatively clean rooms at bargain rates. All rooms are a/c with telephone and hot showers. 114 New Rd., tel. (02) 233-4652, 1200-1500B.

King's Mansion: Though constantly filled with long-term residents, this aging property is one of the better bargains in the Silom Rd. area. King's Mansion is located near many embassies, Thai Immigration, and only 10 minutes from Silom and Patpong. Air-conditioned rooms with private bath cost under 5000B per month. 31 South Sathorn Rd., tel. (02) 286-0940, 400-450B fan, 500-600B a/c, 650-750B a/c with refrigerator and TV.

Moderate Accommodations

YMCA Collins House: This modern, spotless, and comfortable hotel is one of the better hotel bargains in Bangkok. All rooms are a/c with private bath and mini refrigerator. There's also a

ADDITIONAL SILOM ROAD ACCOMMODATIONS

HOTEL	SINGLE	DOUBLE	ADDRESS	PHONE (02)
Christian Guesthouse	600B	800B	123 Sala Daeng Soi 2	233-6303
Dusit Thani	3000-4800	3300-5000	946 Rama IV	236-0450
Mandarin	1800-2400	2100-2700	662 Rama IV	233-4980
Manohra	1700	1900	412 Surawong	234-5070
Narai	2200	2400	222 Silom	233-3350
New Fuji	900-1000	1000-1100	299 Surawong	234-5364
New Peninsula	900-1200	1000-1300	295 Surawong	234-3910
New Trocadero	900-1200	1000-1300	343 Surawong	234-8920
Niagara	360	400	26 Soi Suksavithaya	233-5783
Plaza	1500	1700	178 Surawong	235-1760
Rose	600	800	118 Surawong	233-7695
Royal Plaza	700-900	700-900	30 Naret	234-3789
Sheraton Tawana	2900-3200	3100-3400	80 Surawong	236-0361
Silom Plaza	1600-2200	1800-2400	320 Silom	236-8441
Swiss Guesthouse	400	500	3 Convent	234-3729
Victory	800	900	322 Silom	233-9060

pool and health club. Reservations require one night's deposit. 27 South Sathorn, tel. (02) 287-1900, fax (02) 287-1996, 1100-1600B.

YWCA: The McFarland wing is less luxurious but also less expensive than the newer YMCA Collins House. Unfortunately, the swimming pool is perpetually filled with screaming kids. 13 South Sathorn, tel. (02) 286-1936, 500-700B.

New Rotel: A new hotel with modern a/c rooms furnished with color TV, small refrigerator, and telephone. American breakfast is included. A fine little place with friendly management. 1216 New Rd., tel. (02) 233-1406, fax (02) 237-1102, 800-1200B.

Swissotel: Formerly the Swiss Guesthouse under the direction of Andy Ponnaz, this recently renovated and reconstructed Swiss-managed hotel has 57 a/c rooms with all the amenities. Good location, with swimming pool and restaurant. 3 Convent Rd., tel. (02) 233-5345, fax (02) 236-9425, 3200-3800B.

Luxury Accommodations

Luxury hotels are the strong suit of this neighborhood. First choice are the fabulous hotels which face the Chao Praya River. Several new properties are now being constructed across the river in Thonburi.

Oriental Hotel: Since it first opened in 1876, this award-winning hotel on the banks of the Chao Praya has remained the undisputed grande dame of Bangkok. Much of the Oriental's fame comes from the authors who have stayed here: Somerset Maugham, Graham Greene, Noël Coward, and even (gasp) Barbara Cartland. Even if you can't afford to stay, have a look at the Writers' Bar, try the Siamese buffet lunch, or enjoy an evening cocktail on the terrace. The Oriental has recently opened a 100-million-*baht* health spa and Thai herbal-treatment center. Some of the old charm has given way to modernization, but the Oriental remains among the best hotels in the world. 48 Oriental Ave., tel. (02) 236-0400, fax (02) 236-1939, 5200-6800B. Or try the Oriental Suite at 45,000B per night!

Shangri La Hotel: This US$100 million hotel boasts 650 beautiful rooms facing the river and overlooking a stunning swimming pool. Facilities include a health club, business center, and a spectacular glass-enclosed lobby with seven-

meter-high windows. A 15-story New Wing was opened in early 1992. Many consider the Shangri La more impressive than the Oriental. 89 Soi Wat Suan Plu, tel. (02) 236-7777, fax (02) 236-8579, 4400-5800B.

Royal Orchid Sheraton Hotel: This new hotel upriver from the Oriental has 700 rooms with uninterrupted views of the river. The adjacent River City Shopping Complex features two floors devoted to antiques. 2 Captain Bus Lane, tel. (02) 234-5599, fax (02) 236-8320, 4600-5500B.

Montien Hotel: This locally owned and operated hotel with a strong French flair is considerably less pretentious than most other luxury hotels in Bangkok. 54 Surawong, tel. (02) 234-8060, 2500-3800B.

The Sukothai: Thailand's first capital serves as the inspiration for one of the newer luxury hotels in the Silom district. A good location away from the traffic and surrounded by greenery. 13 South Sathorn Rd., tel. (02) 287-0222, fax (02) 287-4980, 4400-5800B.

SIAM SQUARE

Named after the Siam Square Shopping Center on Rama I, this centrally located neighborhood is the city's premier shopping district and home to many of Bangkok's most exclusive hotels. Shopping opportunities include numerous air-conditioned complexes (Central, Zen, Tokyu, and Narayana Phand for Thai handicrafts), plus the colorful flea market known as Pratunam. Siam is also an entertainment center with dozens of cinemas and coffee shops patronized by trendy Thais. Finally, the Siam/Pratunam neighborhood is conveniently situated between the nightlife centers of Sukumvit and the cultural attractions in the Old Royal City.

Budget Accommodations

Though mainly known as an upscale hotel district, several good-value guesthouses and hotels with rooms under 600B have recently opened opposite the National Stadium on Rama I Road. The following hotels are bunched together on Soi Kasemsan 1 and can be quickly inspected.

National Scout Hostel: Few Westerners stay here, but inexpensive dorms are located on the fourth floor. Rama I Rd. adjacent to the

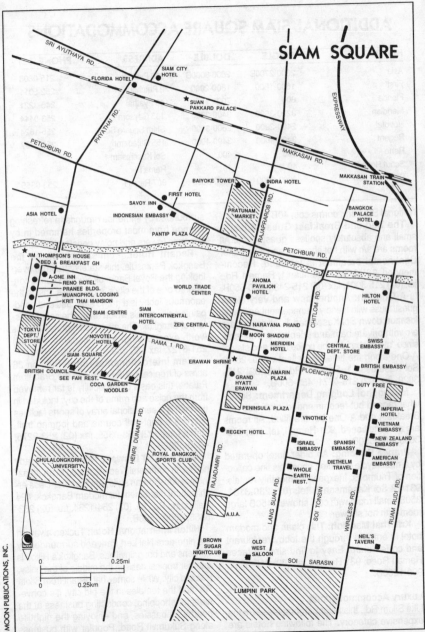

SIAM SQUARE

SRI AYUTHAYA RD.

SIAM CITY HOTEL

FLORIDA HOTEL

EXPRESSWAY

SUAN PAKKARD PALACE

PHYATHAI RD.

PETCHBURI RD.

MAKKASAN RD.

MAKKASAN TRAIN STATION

BAIYOKE TOWER

INDRA HOTEL

RAJAPRAROB RD.

FIRST HOTEL

BANGKOK PALACE HOTEL

SAVOY INN

PRATUNAM MARKET

ASIA HOTEL

INDONESIAN EMBASSY

PANTIP PLAZA

PETCHBURI RD.

JIM THOMPSON'S HOUSE

BED & BREAKFAST GH

A-ONE INN

RENO HOTEL

PRANEE BLDG.

MUANGPHOL LODGING

KRIT THAI MANSION

WORLD TRADE CENTER

ANOMA PAVILION HOTEL

CHITLOM RD.

HILTON HOTEL

SIAM CENTRE

SIAM INTERCONTINENTAL HOTEL

ZEN CENTRAL

NARAYANA PHAND

TOKYU DEPT. STORE

NOVOTEL HOTEL

MOON SHADOW

MERIDIEN HOTEL

CENTRAL DEPT. STORE

SWISS EMBASSY

SIAM SQUARE

RAMA 1 RD.

PLOENCHIT RD.

BRITISH EMBASSY

BRITISH COUNCIL

SEE FAH REST.

ERAWAN SHRINE

AMARIN PLAZA

DUTY FREE

COCA GARDEN NOODLES

GRAND HYATT ERAWAN

IMPERIAL HOTEL

PENINSULA PLAZA

HENRI DUNANT RD.

VINOTHEK

VIETNAM EMBASSY

NEW ZEALAND EMBASSY

CHULALONGKORN UNIVERSITY

ROYAL BANGKOK SPORTS CLUB

REGENT HOTEL

ISRAEL EMBASSY

SPANISH EMBASSY

AMERICAN EMBASSY

RAJADAMRI RD.

DIETHELM TRAVEL

WHOLE EARTH REST.

WIRELESS RD.

RUAM RUDI RD.

LANG SUAN RD.

SOI TONSIN

A.U.A.

NEIL'S TAVERN

BROWN SUGAR NIGHTCLUB

OLD WEST SALOON

SOI SARASIN

LUMPINI PARK

0   0.25mi

0   0.25km

© MOON PUBLICATIONS, INC.

ADDITIONAL SIAM SQUARE ACCOMMODATIONS

HOTEL	SINGLE	DOUBLE	ADDRESS	PHONE (02)
Asia	2500-2700B	2800-3000B	296 Pyathai	215-0808
First	1600-1800	1800-2000	2 Petchburi	252-5011
Florida	600	700	43 Pyathai	245-3221
Meridien	3200-3600	3400-3800	135 Gaysorn	253-0444
Novotel	2400-2900	2600-3200	Siam Square Soi 6	255-1824
Regent	3400-4000	3400-4000	155 Rajadamri	251-6127
Reno	350	400	Soi Kasemsam 1	
Scout Hostel	40	40	Rama I	
Siam Intercon	3200-3600	3400-3800	967 Rama I	253-0355

National Stadium, dorms cost 40B; men only.

The Bed and Breakfast Guesthouse: A small and absolutely spotless guesthouse. All rooms are a/c with hot showers and telephone. Continental breakfast is included. Recommended. 36/42 Soi Kasemsan 1, Rama 1 Rd., tel. (02) 215-3004, fax (02) 215-2493, 400-550B.

A-One Inn: Another new and very clean guesthouse with friendly management and quiet location down Soi Kasemsan 1. All rooms are a/c with private bath and telephone. Very safe since "my husband is the police man and stay at A-One along the time." Excellent value. 25/13 Soi Kasemsan 1, Rama 1 Rd., tel. (02) 215-3029, fax (02) 216-4771, 450-600B.

Muangphol Lodging Department: Somewhat ragged but recommended if the Bed and Breakfast and A-One Inn are filled. All rooms are air-conditioned. 931 Rama I, tel. (02) 215-3056, 450-550B.

Pranee Building: An older hotel operated by a motorcycle collector; check his fine collection of Triumphs. Inexpensive monthly rentals. 931/12 Soi Kasemsan 1, tel. (02) 280-3181, 350B small room with cold shower, 450B large room with hot shower.

Krit Thai Mansion: This clean and modern hotel is entered through the lobby restaurant and coffee shop. Easy to find since it faces Rama I Road. 931 Rama I, tel. (02) 215-3042, 900-1200B.

Luxury Accommodations

Like Silom Rd., this neighborhood excels in the expensive category. The following hotels are surrounded by immense grounds, a refreshing change from most properties hemmed in by concrete towers and noisy construction zones.

Regent Hotel: Formerly known as the Bangkok Peninsula, this stately structure overlooking the Royal Bangkok Sports Club is considered one of the city's finest hotels. Inside the enormous lobby is a grand staircase and hand-painted silk murals which relate the colorful history of Bangkok. The afternoon high-tea ritual is worth experiencing. 155 Rajadamri, tel. (02) 251-6127, fax (02) 253-9195, 4400-5500B.

Siam Intercontinental Hotel: Built on 26 acres of tropical gardens next to the Srapatum Palace, this oasis of tranquillity is far removed from the noise and grime of the city. Included in the tariff is a sensational array of sports facilities such as a mini-golf course and jogging trail. Rama I, tel. (02) 253-0355, fax (02) 253-2275, 4600-5800B.

Grand Hyatt Erawan: The venerable lady has been completely reconstructed in an amazing pseudo-Roman style; another first-class architectural monument for modern Bangkok. 494 Rajadamri Rd., tel. (02) 254-1234, fax (02) 253-5856, 4000-8500B.

Hilton International Hotel: Tucked away on the nine-acre Nai Lert Park and surrounded by gardens and bougainvilleas, Bangkok's Hilton is another tropical oasis in the middle of the noisy, polluted city. While somewhat distant from Silom Rd. and the temples in the old city, it's convenient for shopping, conducting business at the nearby embassies, and enjoying the nightlife along Sukumvit Road. Popular with business travelers. 2 Wireless Rd., tel. (02) 253-0123, fax (02) 253-6509, 4400-7000B.

SUKUMVIT ROAD

Thailand's longest road (it stretches all the way to Cambodia!) serves as the midpriced tourist center of Bangkok. Though very distant from the temples, Sukumvit offers dozens of good-value hotels in the middle-price range, great sidewalk shopping, popular yet inexpensive restaurants, cozy English pubs, great book-stores, numerous tailor and shoe shops, and discount travel agencies. The racy nightlife scene at Nana Complex and Soi Cowboy is second only to Patpong.

Hotels are available in all prices, but the neighborhood's claim to fame is the middle-priced lodgings (600-1200B) that flank Sukumvit from Soi 1 and Soi 63. These are truly excep-tional values with comfortable a/c rooms, swim-ming pools, travel services, taxis at the front door, and fine restaurants. Deluxe hotels above 1500B are starting to appear, though it will be years before the neighborhood can compete with the five-star wonders on Silom Road and around Siam Square.

Visitors looking for long-term rentals and sub-lets should check the Villa Market bulletin board at Soi 33. Also listed are ads for used cars and motorcycles, plus furniture and miscellaneous goods being sold by departing expatriates.

Budget Accommodations

Budget accommodations include a dozen-plus hotels with rooms for 400-600B. Many were constructed in the 1960s in Motel 6-style to serve the American military trade from Vietnam. Though extremely basic and in need of im-provement, rooms are air-conditioned, plus a small pool and restaurant are often included. Also described below are simple guesthouses constructed in the last few years; these won't have pools but the rooms will be cleaner. Budget travelers who spend more time sight-seeing than lounging in their room will probably find all the following places suitable for a short stay.

Miami Hotel: An old hotel with dozens of de-cent rooms overlooking the courtyard swimming pool. Fan rooms are very basic, but all a/c rooms include TV, private bath, and maid service. One of the most popular cheapies on Sukumvit Road. Reservations can be made from the hotel counter at the Bangkok airport. Soi 13, tel. (02) 253-0369, fax (02) 253-1266, 200-250 fan, 550-650B a/c.

Crown Hotel: Another old hotel constructed for the American GI trade in the 1960s. Very funky, but the small pool provides a refreshing dip in the hot afternoon. All rooms are air-con-ditioned; a longtime favorite with many visitors. Soi 29, tel. (02) 258-4438, 450-650B.

Uncle Rey's Guesthouse: A clean but cramped high-rise with fully furnished, small a/c rooms with private bath and hot showers. Tucked away in an alley opposite the Nana Hotel. No pool, no yard. Soi 4, tel. (02) 252-5565, 400-550B.

Happy Inn: A small and very simple hotel with clean rooms and a good location near the nightlife and shopping centers. Soi 4, tel. (02) 252-6508, 500-600B.

Sookswasdi Guesthouse: An older but very quiet motel with large rooms equipped with kitchen facilities. Somewhat rustic but fairly clean; popular with long-term visitors. Located on a back alley off Soi 11, tel. (02) 253-3425, 250-450B.

Atlanta Hotel: An old travelers' favorite that hangs on with a minimum of maintenance. The dreary lobby is compensated with fairly clean rooms, a cheery little cafe, and a surprisingly good pool in the backyard. Proprietor Dr. Charles Henn, son of the German immigrant who founded the Atlanta in 1952, is now reno-vating the property with attention to the in-creasingly rare '50s decor. The cheapest hotel in the Sukumvit neighborhood. Soi 2, tel. (02) 252-1650, 150-250B fan with common bath, 200-300B fan with private bath, 400-500B a/c with private bath.

Moderate Accommodations

Mermaid's Rest: Beautiful, small, Scandina-vian-run guesthouse with fan and a/c rooms, outdoor barbecue with European buffet, and small swimming pool around a pleasant gar-den. Highly recommended. Soi 8, tel. (02) 253-2400, fax (02) 253-3648, 350-400B fan, 600-700B a/c, 700-900B a/c in the new wing.

White Inn: A beautiful and unique lodge dec-orated in an olde English-Tudor style with a/c rooms, swimming pool, and sun terrace. Highly

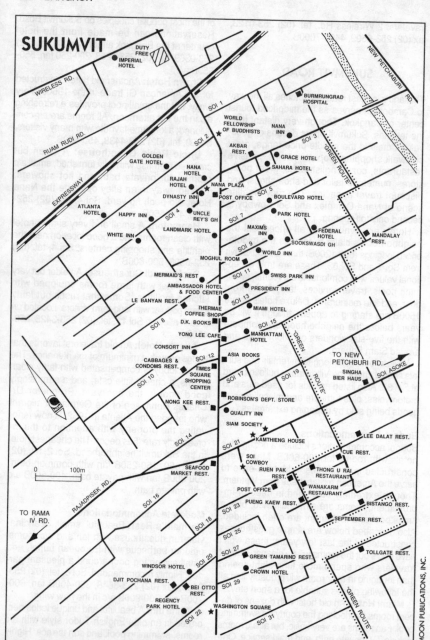

SUKUMVIT

- DUTY FREE
- IMPERIAL HOTEL
- WIRELESS RD.
- NEW PETCHABURI RD.
- SOI 1
- BURMRUNGRAD HOSPITAL
- WORLD FELLOWSHIP OF BUDDHISTS
- SOI 2
- NANA INN
- AKBAR REST.
- SOI 3
- GRACE HOTEL
- GREEN ROUTE
- GOLDEN GATE HOTEL
- NANA HOTEL
- SAHARA HOTEL
- RUAM RUDI RD.
- RAJAH HOTEL
- NANA PLAZA
- SOI 5
- BOULEVARD HOTEL
- DYNASTY INN
- POST OFFICE
- EXPRESSWAY
- ATLANTA HOTEL
- HAPPY INN
- SOI 4
- UNCLE REY'S GH
- SOI 7
- PARK HOTEL
- LANDMARK HOTEL
- MAXIM'S INN
- FEDERAL HOTEL
- SOOKSWASDI GH
- MANDALAY REST.
- WHITE INN
- SOI 9
- WORLD INN
- MOGHUL ROOM
- SOI 11
- MERMAID'S REST.
- SWISS PARK INN
- AMBASSADOR HOTEL & FOOD CENTER
- PRESIDENT INN
- LE BANYAN REST.
- SOI 13
- MIAMI HOTEL
- THERMAE COFFEE SHOP
- SOI 8
- D.K. BOOKS
- SOI 15
- YONG LEE CAFE
- MANHATTAN HOTEL
- CONSORT INN
- GREEN ROUTE
- ASIA BOOKS
- TO NEW PETCHBURI RD.
- CABBAGES & CONDOMS REST.
- SOI 12
- SOI 10
- TIMES SQUARE SHOPPING CENTER
- SOI 17
- SOI 19
- SINGHA BIER HAUS
- SOI ASOKE
- NONG KEE REST.
- ROBINSON'S DEPT. STORE
- QUALITY INN
- SIAM SOCIETY
- LEE DALAT REST.
- SOI 14
- KAMTHIENG HOUSE
- SOI 21
- CUE REST.
- SEAFOOD MARKET REST.
- SOI COWBOY
- RUEN PAK REST.
- THONG U RAI RESTAURANT
- WANAKARM RESTAURANT
- POST OFFICE
- RAJADPISEK RD.
- SOI 16
- PUENG KAEW REST.
- SOI 23
- BISTANGO REST.
- TO RAMA IV RD.
- SEPTEMBER REST.
- SOI 18
- SOI 25
- SOI 27
- TOLLGATE REST.
- WINDSOR HOTEL
- SOI 20
- GREEN TAMARIND REST.
- DJIT POCHANA REST.
- BEI OTTO REST.
- SOI 29
- CROWN HOTEL
- REGENCY PARK HOTEL
- SOI 22
- WASHINGTON SQUARE
- SOI 31
- GREEN ROUTE

0   100m

© MOON PUBLICATIONS, INC.

recommended. Soi 4, tel. (02) 252-7090, 650-900B.

Dynasty Inn: Fine little place with comfy cocktail lounge, CNN on the cable TV, and very clean a/c rooms. Excellent location just opposite the Nana Hotel; often filled by noontime. Soi 4, tel. (02) 250-1397, fax (02) 252-9930, 800-900B.

Nana Hotel: A big hotel with all the standard facilities such as nightclubs and restaurants. Recently refurbished a/c rooms include private bath, TV, and refrigerator. The Nana is conveniently located within easy walking distance of the nightlife and shopping districts; one of the better middle-priced spreads on Sukumvit. Recommended for visitors who want a big hotel at a decent price. Soi 4, tel. (02) 252-0121, 850-1000B.

Golden Gate Hotel: A basic but clean hotel with a/c rooms, TV, massage parlor, and 24-hour coffee shop. Soi 2, tel. (02) 251-5354, 800-900B.

Maxim's Inn: Sukumvit in recent years has added a dozen small hotels in the *sois* near the Ambassador Hotel, especially between *sois* 9 and 13. All are clean and comfortable, but Maxim's is more luxurious and has a better location at the end of a short alley. If filled, check

---

SUKUMVIT ROAD BUSES

1AC	Chinatown, Wat Po
2	Banglampoo
11AC	Banglampoo, National Museum
13AC	Northern Bus Terminal, Airport
8AC	Siam Square, Grand Palace

---

the adjacent World Inn; same price range. Soi 9, tel. (02) 252-9911, fax (02) 253-5329, 900-1200B.

President Inn: Several new, small inns are located in the short alleys near Soi 11. Most were constructed in the early 1990s, so the rooms and lobbies remain in good condition. Choices include the President Inn, Business Inn, Bangkok Inn (German management), Comfort Inn, and Swiss Park Inn. All charge 800-1200B for clean a/c rooms furnished with color TV, telephone, and mini refrigerator. President Inn, Soi 11, tel. (02) 255-4230, fax (02) 255-4235, 800B-1200B.

Luxury Accommodations

Ambassador Hotel: An enormous hotel and convention complex with 1,000 rooms, 14

ADDITIONAL SUKUMVIT ROAD ACCOMMODATIONS

HOTEL	SINGLE	DOUBLE	ADDRESS	PHONE (02)
Federal	500-600B	600-700B	Sukumvit Soi 11	253-0175
Fortuna	600-700	700-800	Sukumvit Soi 5	251-5121
Grace	800-1000	800-1000	Sukumvit Soi 3	253-0651
Grand Tower Apts.	500-600	700-900	Sukumvit Soi 55	259-0380
Impala	2000-2200	2300-2500	Sukumvit Soi 24	259-0053
Manhattan	1200-1400	1400-1600	Sukumvit Soi 15	252-7141
Narai Guesthouse	300-400	450-550	Sukumvit Soi 53	258-7173
Park	600-800	700-900	Sukumvit Soi 7	252-5110
Quality Inn	550-650	650-750	Sukumvit Soi 19	253-5393
Raja	1000-1200	1200-1400	Sukumvit Soi 4	251-8563
Rex	450-500	650-750	Sukumvit Soi 32	391-0100
Ruamchitt	250-350	350-450	Sukumvit Soi 15	251-6441
Sri Guesthouse	280	350	Sukumvit Soi 38	381-1662
Sukumvit Crown	350	350	Sukumvit Soi 6	253-5673
Sunisa Guesthouse	250	280	Sukumvit Soi 4	252-5565
Wattana Flats	400	450	Sukumvit Soi 19	252-9694
Windsor	1800-2200	2100-2500	Sukumvit Soi 20	258-0160

restaurants, health center, tennis courts, and jumbo swimming pool (easily crashed). Soi 11, tel. (02) 251-0404, fax (02) 253-4123, 2600-3800B.

Landmark Hotel: Sukumvit's largest and most luxurious hotel. Superb location near shops, restaurants, and nightclubs. Carefully aimed toward the business traveler, each of the 415 rooms is equipped with a computerized videotext that provides airline schedules, stock market data, and important business contacts . . . including the names and phone numbers of top executives. Other pluses include rooftop restaurants on the 31st floor, a swimming pool,

health club, convention facilities, and a friendly staff. Soi 6, tel. (02) 254-0404, 3800-5000B.

Tara Hotel: Another recently constructed hotel in the four-star range. Spacious lobby with teakwood carvings, garden swimming pool on the eighth floor, and a skyview cocktail lounge on the 22nd floor. Soi 24, tel. (02) 259-0053, fax (02) 259-2896, 3600-4200B.

Swiss Park Hotel: A centrally located 108-room hotel opened in early 1991. Features a rooftop swimming pool, cafe on the seventh floor, and business center. Soi 11, tel. (02) 254-0228, fax (02) 254-0378, 3000-3600B.

ADDITIONAL SUKUMVIT ROAD ACCOMMODATIONS

RESTAURANTS

Bangkok richly deserves its reputation as one of the world's great culinary destinations. Spread across the city are some 30,000 registered restaurants and countless street-side stalls that produce some of the tastiest food in the East. Whether heart-pounding curries or aromatically smooth soups, it's almost impossible to go wrong in the City of Angels.

Gourmets with a serious interest in the restaurants of Thailand will find further information and a discount dining program in *The Restaurant Guide of Thailand* published annually by The Siam Dinner Club. *Bangkok Restaurant Guide* published in 1988 (the first and last edition) by Asia Books is dated, but still recommended for the neighborhood maps and detailed descriptions of restaurant specialties. Gault Millau's *The Best of Thailand* attempts to "distinguish the truly superlative from the merely overrated" restaurants in Bangkok. Also check the restaurant listings in the *Bangkok Post* and local tourist magazines.

Most of the following summaries describe popular restaurants which have been in business for an extended period, or newer cafes that show great potential. The listings range from cheap sidewalk cafes (where you'll find some of the best food in Bangkok) to expensive Thai restaurants that specialize in regional and royal cuisines. Most of the restaurants are shown on the maps in the "Accommodations" section.

Specific restaurant recommendations are difficult for several reasons. Many establishments tend to change ownership and location with the seasons. Leading chefs often move to other restaurants, or open their own operations to exploit their culinary reputation. And, as elsewhere in the world, successful restaurants often rest on their laurels and eventually go into decline, raising prices and letting food quality suffer. For these reasons, suggestions from readers and residents in Bangkok are highly valued.

FOOD AND DRINK

Whether enjoyed in a first-class restaurant or a simple street-side stall, the cuisine of Thailand is unquestionably one of the great culinary treats of the East. Thai food—a hot and spicy spectrum of exotic flavors—takes its roots from the best of neighboring countries: smooth coconut creams from Malaysia, rich peanut sauces from Indonesia, fiery curries from India, sweet-and-sour sauces from China. Thai cuisine derives its essential character from local ingredients such as coconut milk, lemongrass, tamarind, ginger, coriander, basil, and peanuts blended together with the ubiquitous and intimidating chili. Adorning nearly all dishes to some degree, Thai chilies vary in pungency in inverse proportion to their size. The tiny ones called *prik kee noo* (ratshit peppers) are treated with respect *even* by the Thais. On the other hand, the large green and yellow *Capsicum annum* are noticeably less aggressive. To survive the heat, remember that even the hottest of chilies lose much of their fierce flavor when safely cocooned in a mouthful of rice. When in doubt, do as the Thais do—eat more rice.

Ordering a meal outside a tourist venue can, at times, be difficult since few restaurants offer English-scripted menus or have English-speaking waiters. The best solution is to indicate a dish being served to other Thai patrons, or wander in the kitchen, peer in the pots, and point to whatever looks promising. Westerners who find chopsticks the major challenge of Eastern dining will happily note that Thais—being an immensely practical people—eat with forks and spoons, the spoon being the main implement rather than the fork. Tables are generally set with a variety of condiments: fermented fish sauce made from anchovies or shrimp paste called *nam pla*, a hot, pungent sauce known as *nam prik*, and a vinegar-green chili extract called *nam som*. Tamarind sauces and cucumbers fried in coconut oil are other popular accompaniments.

The perfect complement to a Thai dinner is an ice-cold bottle of either Singha or Kloster, light, smooth, and tasty beers brewed according to German recipes. Two spirits to approach with extreme caution are Mekong and Kwang Tong, 70-proof molasses-based spirits that pack an abnormal, almost psychotropic wallop—the tequila of Thailand. Moon-

(continued)

shine whiskey is popular since distillers can easily undercut by five times the price of heavily taxed legal whiskey. It's said that only two households in each village don't make moonshine: the government's excise office and the Buddhist *wat*.

A THAI MENU
Meat, Chicken, And Fish
gai: chicken
mu: pork
nua: beef
pet: duck
kung: prawns
pla: fish

Cooking Methods, Condiments, And Sauces
pat: fried
yang: barbecued or roasted
nam pla: fish sauce
nam prik: red spicy sauce
nam som: vinegar with chili sauce
nam buay wan: sweet plum sauce
nam yam hai: oyster sauce
nam king: ginger sauce
nam preo wan: sweet and sour sauce

Soups
tom kha kai: Rich chicken and coconut-milk soup flavored with lemongrass, lime leaves, galangal, and shallots. Thailand's greatest soup is served throughout the country.

tom yam: Hot-and-sour broth prepared with lemongrass, lime leaves, and chili. Called *tom yam kung* with shrimp and *tom yam kai* with chicken. Almost as good as *tom kha kai.*
kow tom: thick rice soup
kow tom pla: thick rice soup served with fish
kow tom mu: thick rice soup served with pork
kow tom kung: thick rice soup served with prawns
kang chut: a mild-flavored soup with vegetables and pork
kang liang: a spicy soup with shrimp, vegetables, basil, and pepper

Rice Dishes
kow pat: fried rice
kow pat kai: fried rice with chicken
kow pat mu: fried rice with pork
kow pat kung: fried rice with shrimp
kow na: steamed rice
kow na kai: steamed rice with sliced chicken
kow na pet: steamed rice with roast duck

Noodle Dishes
kuay teow: wide rice noodles
kuay teow ratna: rice noodles in a meat gravy
kuay teow hang: rice noodles with meat and vegetable served without the meat gravy
kuay teow pat thai: rice noodles fried Thai style
bah mee: wide yellow wheat-and-egg noodles
bah mee ratna: wheat noodles in meat gravy

BANGLAMPOO

Alfresco dining along Khao San Rd. is a pleasant way to meet other travelers and exchange information, though none of the cafes will win any awards for great cuisine or elaborate atmosphere. Banglampoo's other problem, besides the mediocre food, is the noisy video cafes that ruin good conversation and turn otherwise colorful people into boob-tube junkies. A pleasant escape, but hardly a reason to visit Asia; patronize those restaurants that are video-free.

Inexpensive
Buddy Cafe: One of the more elegant cafes on Khao San Rd. is tucked away behind the Buddy Guesthouse. The Thai food is bland but safe, a good introduction for first-time visitors fearful of chilies. The upstairs restaurant provides a pleasant escape from the mayhem of Khao San Road.

Thai Cafes: Several unpretentious cafes around the corner from Khao San on Chakrabongse Rd. offer a good selection of unusual dishes. Best in the morning when the food is freshest; very inexpensive.

Night Foodstalls: Authentic Thai food is found nightly in the foodstalls at the west end of Khao San Rd. and a few blocks north toward the New World Shopping Center.

New World Shopping Center: Nearly every shopping center in Thailand has a food complex located on the top floor. Prices are rock bottom, the quality is generally good, and the service is instantaneous since most are self-service foodstalls.

Moderate
Krai Si: Small, clean, and very chilly restaurant with Japanese sushi, sashimi, tempura, and

bah-mee hang: wheat noodles with meat and vegetable served without the meat gravy

Curry Dishes

kang pet: spicy curry made from sweet coconut milk flavored with lemongrass, chilies, and shrimp paste. Served with either pork, chicken, beef, fish, or prawns. Perhaps the most popular dish in Thailand.

kang matsaman: milder version of Muslim curry laced with beef, potato, onion, coconut milk, and peanut

kang wan: green curry thickened with coconut milk, eggplant, sweet basil, and lime leaves. Be careful with this one.

kang kari: yellow curry with tumeric; a mild version of an Indian curry

kang baa: Thailand's hottest curry—for veteran fire-eaters only

Salads

yam: salad

yam nua: beef salad with mint, basil, spring onion, garlic, and chili

yam het: mushroom salad

yam mamuang: green mango salad

yam tang kwa: cucumber salad

yam hoi: cockle salad

Drinks

nam plao: plain water

nam tom: boiled water

nam cha: tea

nam manao: iced lime juice

nam som khan: fresh orange juice

nom: milk

coffee ron: hot coffee with milk

coffee yen: iced coffee with milk

o liang: iced black coffee with sugar

Mekong: Thai whiskey distilled from grains and molasses

sang som: rum liquor made from sugar cane

lao kao: rice liquor, locally produced

Sidewalk Snacks And Desserts

satay: barbecued skewers of meat served with peanut sauce and cucumbers in vinegar and sugar

sang kaya: custard made from coconut milk, sugar, and eggs

chow kway: black-grass pudding shredded and mixed with a sugar syrup over ice

boh bok: green-grass drink made from crushed vines and sugar water. Bitter.

roti sai mai: small flat pancakes with strands of green or pink spun sugar wrapped inside

kanom buang: miniature tacos made from batter poured on a hot griddle, and then folded over and filled with shredded coconut, egg yolk, and green onions

tong krob: golden yellow balls made from egg yolks and rice flour, then dusted with sugar

kao glab pat maw: thin crepe filled with fried shrimp, pork, peanuts, sugar, coconut, and even fish sauce. Delicious.

Western specialties. Look for the sidewalk sushi man.

Royal Hotel Coffee Shop: Travelers in Banglampoo will find this the closest restaurant to escape the searing heat. An excellent place to relax in the morning, enjoy a good cup of coffee, and read the *Bangkok Post.*

Wang Nar: Located underneath the Thonburi Bridge, this riverside restaurant is an outstanding spot for authentic, reasonably priced Thai food. Patrons can sit outdoors on the deck or inside the a/c restaurant to the rear. Sample prices: chicken curry 50-80B, catfish 60-80B, ring ring fish 70B, urgent beef pork liver 60B. Super atmosphere. Highly recommended. 17 Chao Fa Road.

Yok Yor: Also located on the banks of the Chao Praya, Yok Yor serves Thai, Chinese, and Japanese dishes in a rather wild atmosphere: waitresses are dressed in sailor outfits and passengers disembarking from the river taxi saunter right through the restaurant! Try *hoh mok,* duck curry, and *noi na* ice cream for dessert. Yok Yor is on Wisut Kaset Rd., down from the National Bank, a very pleasant 30-minute walk through back alleys which skirt the river.

Maria Restaurant: Rajadamnern Ave. serves as an administrative center during the day, and as restaurant row in the evening. Scattered along the broad avenue are a half-dozen moderately priced restaurants popular with Thai civil servants and businesspeople. Maria's is a large a/c place with both Chinese and Thai specialties. Rajadamnern Avenue.

Vijit's: Several old favorites are also located around Democracy Monument on Rajadamnern Avenue. All are patronized by Thais who seek a semiluxurious yet casual restaurant. Vijit's resembles an old American diner from the 1950s, and serves both Asian and Western dishes. Both indoor and patio dining. **Sorn**

FRUITS OF THAILAND

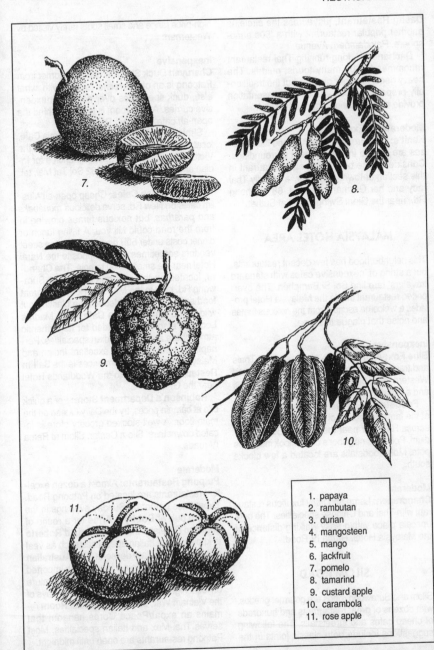

1. papaya
2. rambutan
3. durian
4. mangosteen
5. mango
6. jackfruit
7. pomelo
8. tamarind
9. custard apple
10. carambola
11. rose apple

Daeng Restaurant, just across the circle, is another popular restaurant with a '50s atmosphere. Rajadamnern Avenue.

Dachanee: A long-running Thai restaurant recommended by many tourist guides. The heavy decor is rather gloomy, but the traditionally prepared dishes and skillful presentation provide compensation. Prachathi Road.

Moderate To Expensive

Kanit's: Both French specialties and Italian pizzas are served in very elegant surroundings. Considered the best European restaurant in this section of town. Owned by a friendly Thai lady and her German husband. 68 Ti Thong Rd., near the Giant Swing and Wat Suthat.

MALAYSIA HOTEL AREA

This neighborhood has few decent restaurants, but a string of inexpensive cafes with standard travelers' fare line Soi Si Bamphen. The overpriced restaurant inside the Malaysia Hotel provides a welcome escape from the noxious fumes and noise that plague this area.

Inexpensive

Blue Fox: A crazy scene of slightly bent Thais and travelers escaping the searing heat. Good Western food, bland-monotonous Thai dishes, and a rather notorious nightclub in the evening.

Foodstalls: Get tasty, authentic Thai food at the large collection of foodstalls located just across Rama IV near the Lumpini Boxing Stadium. Point to a neighbor's dish or look inside the pots. More foodstalls are located a few blocks south.

Moderate

Chandrapen: Large and fairly luxurious restaurant with Thai and Chinese specialties. The only upscale place within easy walking distance of the Malaysia Hotel. Rama IV Road.

SILOM ROAD

Silom and Surawong roads are gourmet ghettos, with dozens of great restaurants and hundreds of cheap cafes and streetstalls. The following suggestions include both classic joints in the

high-price range and small spots rarely visited by Westerners.

Inexpensive

Charuvan Duck Shop: Around the corner from Patpong is an old travelers' favorite with, what else, duck specialties over rice and inexpensive curries. An a/c room is located behind the open-air cafe. 70 Silom Road.

Simla Cafe: The less-expensive Simla Cafe, located off Silom Rd. in a small alley behind the Victory Hotel, is another popular choice for Indian and Pakistani dishes. 382 Soi Tat Mai, tel. (02) 234-6225.

Budget Indian Cafes: Cheap open-air Muslim cafes on New Rd. serve delicious *murtabaks* and *parathas,* but noxious fumes blowing in from the road could kill you. A filling lunch or dinner costs under 50B per person. Indian street vendors sometimes gather opposite the Narai Hotel near the small Hindu temple. **The Chandni**, located on the second floor at 422 Surawong Rd. next to the Manohra Hotel, has great food served under a video screen blasting out wild Hindu films. **Madras Cafe** in the Madras Lodge is also recommended for its authentic atmosphere and South Indian specialties. Perhaps the best choice for excellent Indian and Malay food at rock-bottom prices is the **Sallim Restaurant**, adjacent to the Woodlands Hotel near the GPO.

Robinson's Department Store: For a quick bite at bargain prices, try the Dairy Queen on the main floor. A well-stocked grocery store is located downstairs. Silom Center, Silom at Rama IV roads.

Moderate

Patpong Restaurants: Almost a dozen excellent restaurants are located on Patpong Road. Expatriates gather on Sunday evenings in the English pub at **Bobby's Arms** for a round of draft and Dixieland music. **Trattoria d'Roberto** is known for its Italian specialties such as veal dishes and chocolate desserts. **The Australian Club** is a comfortable a/c lounge with imported beers from Down Under, plus helpful literature on local nightlife spots. Dating from the days of the Vietnam War, the venerable **Thai Room** remains an expat/Peace Corps hangout that serves Thai-Mex and Italian specialties. Most Patpong restaurants are open until midnight.

Himali Cha Cha: The long-running Himali Cha Cha, located up a small alley off New Rd. near the GPO, is known for its tasty curries, *kormas,* fruit-flavored *lassis,* tandoori-baked breads, and North Indian specialties served in an informal setting. Cha Cha, owner and head chef at Himali, was once Nehru's private chef. 1229 New Rd., tel. (02) 235-1569.

Once Upon A Time: A wonderful romantic restaurant with outdoor dining under little twinkling lights. Nicely located in a quiet back alley, but within walking distance of most hotels. Decho Road, Soi 1; moderate to expensive.

All Gaengs: Unlike most Thai restaurants, All Gaengs has been stylishly decorated with art deco touches and a shiny baby grand piano. Along with the jazz, enjoy shrimp curry, *yam* dishes, and *nuea daed dio,* a beef dish served with a spicy dipping sauce. Surawong Road.

Expensive

Riverside Restaurants: Alfresco dining on the banks of the Chao Praya is a memorable if expensive experience. **Sala Rim Nam** is a touristy but beautiful restaurant with excellent Thai salads and traditional dance; use the free boat service from the Oriental Hotel. **Salathip Restaurant** at the Shangri La Hotel does an excellent Sunday brunch on the veranda overlooking the river. **River City Barbecue,** on the rooftop of the River City Shopping Center, is a self-service Mongolian barbecue cafe with excellent views from the tables at the edge of the roof. **Normandie Grill** is a world-famous French restaurant located in pseudo-dining cars on the roof of the Oriental Hotel.

Bussaracum: Restaurants found in luxury hotels generally cater to the foreign palate and temper the degree of garlic and chilies used in their dishes. For something more authentic, try this elegant dining establishment for pungent dishes whose recipes stem from the royal palace. *Saengwa* (grilled prawns), *phat benjarong* (vegetables with meats), and *gang kari gai hang* (chicken curry) are recommended. Chef Boonchho has been selected one of the top ten chefs in the world. 35 Soi Phipat 2, tel. (02) 235-5160. Bussaracum 2, a newer and more modern extension, is wedged inside the Trinity Complex. 425 Soi Phipat 2, tel. (02) 234-2600; very expensive.

Than Ying: Many of the finest restaurants in the Silom neighborhood are tucked away in the neighborhood alleys between Silom and Sathorn Tai roads. Than Ying is an old favorite known for its authentic royal-style Thai cuisine. 10 Soi Pramuan.

Rueng Pueng: Traditional Thai dishes from all regions of the country plus outstanding salads are served in a converted Thai house, a common sight in Bangkok these days. 37 Soi 2, Saladeng Road, down from the Christian Guesthouse.

Panoramic View Restaurants: Wonderful views of Bangkok can be enjoyed from the revolving La Rotonde Grill on top of Narai Hotel and in the Tiara Restaurant on the 22nd floor of the Dusit Thani.

SIAM SQUARE

Many of the best restaurants in this neighborhood are located in luxury hotels, while inexpensive cafes and foodstalls are found in the a/c shopping complexes.

Tokyu Food Centre: Shopping centers are your best bets for quick, inexpensive Thai and Western dishes. Tokyu Food Centre, at the intersection of Rama I and Phyathai roads, features a roomy, a/c, sixth-floor dining emporium with dozens of great foodstalls.

Inexpensive

Old West Saloon: A mini nightlife and restaurant scene has sprung up in recent years along Soi Sarasin, south of Siam Shopping Center near Lumpini Park. Old West, one of the oldest Western clubs in Bangkok, features Thai-cowboy grub and live country music behind the swinging saloon doors. 231 Soi Sarasin, tel. (02) 252-9510.

Moderate

Coca Garden Noodles: A colossal, noisy restaurant packed with Chinese families and groups of hungry teenagers. Serves a wide variety of inexpensive noodle dishes, along with chicken, fish, and seafood specialties. Self-cook Mongolian barbecues and sukiyakis are the most popular dishes. 461 Henri Dunant Rd. at the southeast corner of Siam Square Shopping Center, tel. (02) 251-6337.

Blue Moon and Moon Shadow: Located in the short alley adjacent to the Meridien Hotel are two small cafe-clubs modeled after American Western saloons. The Blue Moon bar features some of the best jazz and R&B combos in Thailand, while the downstairs Western cafe specializes in seafood entrees. Try the *pla krai* in green-chili curry. 145 Gaysorn Rd., tel. (02) 253-7552.

Siam Intercontinental: This hotel's all-you-can-eat luncheon buffet is one of Bangkok's least-expensive splurges. The Indra Regent also has a moderate-priced buffet. Diners must be well attired; no shorts or sandals.

Whole Earth Restaurant: Outstanding if slightly expensive vegetarian and Thai specialties accompanied by classical guitar or folk music. 933 Soi Languan, Ploenchit Road.

Amarin Plaza: Upscale Japanese and Thai restaurants are located on the lower floor. Note the wild Greco-Roman-Thai architecture of the adjacent McDonald's.

SUKUMVIT ROAD

Sukumvit Road and adjacent side roads offer the best selection of restaurants in Bangkok. Inexpensive street stalls and medium-priced restaurants are most plentiful along Sukumvit between the freeway and Soi Asoke. High-end restaurants are concentrated on the back streets which run parallel and north of Sukumvit. Three excellent neighborhoods to explore include Soi 23, the Green Route, and Soi 55. Specific restaurants in these popular enclaves are described below.

Inexpensive

Ambassador Food Center: Over 50 fast-food stalls serve up Thai, Japanese, and Western dishes at reasonable prices. This is a great place to look and learn about Thai dishes, and begin your food crawl in the Sukumvit neighborhood. Most dishes cost under 30B, and you pay by coupon. The street-side **Bangkapi Terrace** is a good place to escape the midday heat and enjoy a very cheap luncheon buffet. Soi 11.

Yong Lee Restaurant: A very funky cafe popular with budget travelers and local *farangs* who rave about the Thai and Chinese specialties. Soi 15.

Thong Lee Restaurant: A very popular and simple shophouse with good food at low prices. Try the *muu phad kapi* (spicy pork in shrimp paste), and the *yam hed sot* (fiery mushroom salad). Soi 20.

Night Foodstalls: Some of the best food in Bangkok is found in the foodstalls along Sukumvit Road. Many of the dishes are pre-cooked and displayed in covered pots. Also try *som tam*, a spicy salad made from shredded raw papaya and palm sugar, fried chicken with sticky rice, and *pad thai*, sautéed bean sprouts with chicken and peanuts. Delicious! Foodstalls are located near the Grace Hotel, the infamously seedy Thermae Coffee Shop, both ends of Soi Cowboy, Washington Square nightlife center, and on Sukumvit at Soi 38. Wonderful food and a great way to mix with the locals.

Moderate

Cabbages and Condoms: Owned and operated by Mechai Viravaidhya, "Condom King" and former director of the national birth control center (next door), this curiously named place offers excellent food in a/c comfort plus some truly strange items at the front desk . . . condom keychains and T-shirts you won't find back home! Highly recommended. Soi 12, tel. (02) 252-7349.

Lemongrass Restaurant: Embellished with antiques in both the interior dining room and exterior courtyard, Lemongrass offers atmosphere and regional dishes from all parts of Thailand. Try the hot fish curry, barbecued chicken, *larb pla duk yang* (smoked catfish in northeastern style), and *nam takrai*, a cool and sweetish drink brewed from lemongrass. Soi 24 near the Calypso Cabaret, tel. (02) 258-8637.

Singha Bier Haus: An imitation German chalet owned and operated by the Singha Beer Company. German and international dishes are served with musical entertainment ranging from polkas to Barbara Streisand imitators. 179 Soi Asoke (Soi 21), tel. (02) 258-3951.

Djit Pochana: One of the most successful restaurant chains in Thailand has three outlets in Bangkok that serve authentic Thai dishes without compromise to Western palates. Try their excellent-value luncheon buffet. Soi 20, tel. (02) 258-1605.

Robinson's Department Store: Cheap eats in this pricey emporium include McDonald's on the main floor, and a downstairs Food Court with several self-service cafes that serve Thai and Japanese dishes. Sukumvit Soi 19.

Tum Nak Thai: According to the *Guiness Book of World Records,* Tum Nak Thai is the world's largest restaurant: 10 acres of land, a capacity of 3,000 seats, over 100 professional chefs, and 1,000 servers decked out in national costumes. Some waiters use roller skates to speed up service! A classical dance show is given nightly at 2000. Take a taxi from your hotel. 131 Ratchadapisek Rd., tel. (02) 277-8833.

Moderate To Expensive

Indian Restaurants: Akbar's on Soi 3 and the **Moghul Room** on Soi 11 are top-quality restaurants offering a wide choice of dishes from both North and South India. The Navrattan curry, chicken *korma,* mutton marsala, and *dahls* are recommended.

Soi 23 Restaurants: Almost a dozen popular restaurants are located down Soi 23, a few blocks off Sukumvit Road. **Ruen Pak** is an excellent-value cafe located in a renovated wooden house. **Thong U Rai** has traditional Thai dishes served in a pub atmosphere with live music. **Cue** is a relatively expensive Swiss Inn that serves French and European cuisine. Also located in a private, intimate house is the famous **Le Dalat,** a classy Vietnamese restaurant known for its *naem neuang,* a tasty version of Vietnamese eggrolls. For over two decades, **Wanakarm Restaurant** has been serving Thais and *farangs* traditional dishes in a/c dining rooms and in the romantic garden. **Pueng Kaew** is a newer place with experimental Thai-Western dishes listed on both the Thai and English-language menus. **September** serves European cuisine in an art deco 1930s atmosphere. **Bistango** is a Western-style steakhouse with meat, chicken, and seafood specialties. And finally, the **Black Scene** is a trendy

place with live jazz nightly at 2100. All these restaurants are easily reached from Sukumvit hotels; an excellent place to wander and snack in the late evening.

Seafood Market Restaurant: This *very* expensive seafood restaurant is worth a look even if the prices cause heart failure. Don't miss the enormous Phuket lobsters and giant prawns. Soi 16 at Soi Asoke, tel. (02) 258-0218; expensive.

Bankeo Ruenkwan: This old and partially renovated house serves up top-quality seafood in a/c comfort. Soi 12, tel. (02) 251-8229; expensive.

Green Route Restaurants: Many of Bangkok's finest restaurants are located on the so-called "Green Route," a street which runs between Sois 39 and 63, midway between Sukumvit and New Petchburi roads. **Gourmet Gallery** at Soi 49 provides an elegant setting with creative cuisine and classical music. **The Library** at Soi 49 is an upscale restaurant owned by a Thai singer who invites in local celebrities and jazz-fusion musicians. **Laicram** at Soi 49 is a well-known Thai restaurant with royal dishes, while the **Piman** on Soi 49 features nightly performances of Thai classical dance. All of these restaurants provide an expensive but elegant dining experience.

Soi 55 Restaurants: Another concentration of fine restaurants is on Soi 55 (Soi Thonglor) between Sukumvit and the Green Route. The **Art House** is a first-class Chinese restaurant set in a lovely country house surrounded by formal gardens and a pleasant pond. **Barley House** is a funky bohemian cafe that features nightly jazz and country bands. Bangkok's finest French restaurant might be **L'Hexagone,** with its pastel interiors and wildly decorated bathrooms. Much less formal is **Sanuk Nuek,** a simple cafe with live folk music. Victorian decor and English pub grub are found at the **Witch's Tavern.**

ENTERTAINMENT

Mention entertainment in Bangkok and most visitors will immediately think of the brothels and massage parlors that have made Thai nightlife a world-famous phenomenon, but the city also offers a limited range of classical entertainment, from traditional dance to elaborate dramas. Culture vultures should take advantage of the opportunities in Bangkok, since Thai performing arts are almost exclusively found in Bangkok and, to a lesser degree, in Chiang Mai.

The three basic venues for cultural entertainment include free Thai dance at various locations, high-end spectacles at the National Theater and the Thailand Cultural Centre, and the familiar dinner-dance shows sponsored nightly by a dozen restaurants in Bangkok.

CULTURAL PERFORMANCES

Free Thai Dance

While professional performances of Thai dance-drama are both infrequent and pricey, travelers can easily enjoy the following free shows.

Lak Muang Shrine: Amateurish but authentic *likay* is sponsored around the clock by various donors in the pavilion to the rear of the City Pillar shrine, near the Grand Palace. Have a quick look, but don't expect a masterful performance from the young girls and tired grandmothers who slowly go through the paces.

Erawan Hotel Shrine: The famous monument in the courtyard of the Erawan Grand Hyatt Hotel is among the more intriguing scenes in Bangkok. No matter the hour, a steady stream of devotees arrives to offer flowers and wooden elephants, burn an unbelievable amount of incense, and hire the somewhat unenthusiastic dancers as gratitude for granted wishes. Visitors are welcome to photograph the dancers and improve their karma by making offerings to four-faced Brahma, the Hindu deity associated with the shrine. Prices for incense and the small wooden elephants are posted at the entrance. Another sign gives prices to hire the dancers: four girls for 15 minutes costs 360B. Erawan Shrine, an amazing place, is most active in the early evening hours and just before the weekly lottery. Erawan Grand Hyatt Hotel, Ploenchit at Rajadamri roads.

Bangkok Bank Show: Outstanding performances of Thai dance, drama, and traditional music are given each Friday at 1700 on the fourth floor of the Bangkok Bank, Parn Fah Branch, just off Rajadamnern Ave. in the Banglampoo District. The room is modern and dull, but the performances are quite good, so good in fact that shows are always packed; arrive an hour early or expect to stand in the back. Upcoming shows are listed on the noticeboard in the TAT office. This venue is within easy walking distance of the guesthouses in Banglampoo. 101 Rajadamnern Klang Ave., tel. (02) 282-7487.

Classical Dance And Drama

Considering the size and economic dominance of Bangkok, one would expect to find an overwhelming selection of dance, drama, music, art, and other cultural activities. Surprisingly, cultural events are limited to infrequent performances at the National Theater, smaller cultural centers, diplomatic centers, and local universities. A fairly complete listing of upcoming events is found in the *Bangkok Post* and in the Cultural Activities Programme published bimonthly by the Thailand Cultural Centre, available from the TAT office.

National Theater: Full-length *khon* performances are sponsored by the Fine Arts Department several times yearly in the National Theater. Though a somewhat expensive experience, these majestic pageants should not be missed if you are fortunate enough to be in Bangkok on the lucky weekend.

The National Theater also sponsors less elaborate cultural events on Saturdays and Sundays at 1000 and 1400. Performances range from Thai variety shows to presentations of the *manora*. Special presentations are given on the last Friday of each month at 1730. Shows cost 30-80B and include a Thai-language commentary. Call (02) 221-5861 or (02) 224-1342 for further information.

THAI PERFORMING ARTS

Khon

The glory of Thai classic theater is the *khon,* a stunning spectacle of warriors, demons, and monkeys who perform acrobatics and highly stylized movements while wrapped in brilliant costumes. *Khon* has its roots in court-sponsored ballets which thrived under royal patronage until the military revolution of 1932 ended Thailand's absolute monarchy.

Accompanied by the surrealistic sounds of the Thai *pipat* orchestra, the *khon* typically takes its storyline from either the Javanese Inao legend or the Indian Ramayana, called the Ramakien ("Glory of Rama") in Thailand. Actors and actresses never speak but rather mime narration provided by professional troubadours and choruses. Originally a masked drama, modern *khon* has unmasked heroes and celestial beings, though demons and monkeys continue to wear bizarre head coverings. *Khon* is also an endangered artform, the only remaining venue in Thailand being Bangkoks' National Theater. Performances are sponsored several times yearly—an superb theatrical experience not to be missed.

Lakhon

While *khon* is male-oriented and relies on virtuosity in strength and muscular exertion, the courtly *lakhon* impresses its audience with feminine grace and elegant fluidity. *Lakhon* presents episodes from the Ramakien, Manora folktales of southern Thailand, and Lakhon Jatri, itinerant folk dances used to exorcise evil spirits. *Lakhon* is traditionally accompanied by a chorus and lead singers instead of *khon*-style recitation, though these distinctions are no longer strictly followed.

The costumes of elaborately embroidered cloth and glittering ornaments surpass the brilliance of even the *khon.* Unlike the *khon,* actresses are unencumbered by masks, allowing them to combine singing and dialog with their dance postures. Highly refined body gestures display a complex encyclopedia of movements while emotion is conveyed by the demure dartings of the eyes and highly stylized, very specific movements of the hands. The dance itself lacks the dramatic leaps and whirling pirouettes of Western ballet—the feet are kept firmly planted on the stage—but a great deal of dramatic tension and sensuality are achieved by the movement of the upper torso. *Khon* and *lakhon* are often combined into grand shows for the benefit of both visitors and Thais.

Likay

If *khon* and *lakhon* are classical art, then *likay* is slapstick comedy performed for the masses. The

obvious lack of deep artistic talent is made up for with unabashed exuberance and a strong sense of earthiness. As a form of people's theater performed at most provincial fairs, *likay* relies heavily on predictable plots, outrageous double entendres, and lowball comedy. Performers interact directly with the audience, which responds with raucous laughter at their political sarcasms and sexual innuendo. Costumes worn by the untalented but enthusiastic actors run from gaudy jewelry to heavy makeup. It is ironic that television, the universal destroyer of traditional theater, has helped keep *likay* alive with daily performances of soap-opera sophistication.

Thai Puppetry

A third type of court drama was the *nang,* or shadow play, which enjoyed great popularity during the reign of King Mongkut. Thai puppetry is occasionally performed in three versions at dinner-dance shows.

Nang Yai: This form of puppetry uses larger-than-life-sized leather puppets painted with vegetable dyes for daytime performances and left translucent for nighttime shows. Oxhide figures are manipulated in front of the screen by puppeteers and illuminated by candles which cast eerie colored shadows. Exam-

(continued)

ples of this vanished art are displayed in the *wayang* room of the National Museum.

Nang Talung: This variation, closely related to the *wayang kulit* of Indonesia, uses smaller and more maneuverable puppets. Still popular in southern Thailand where performances are occasionally given during temple festivals.

Hun Krabok: This version, a vanished art, uses rod puppets similar to Chinese stick puppets. Puppets are still created by the famous Thai painter, Chakrabhand Posayahrit.

Popular Dance

Fawn Lep: Ladies from the north of Thailand perform classical movements while wearing long artificial fingernails.

Ram Wong: A slow and graceful dance which cleverly fuses traditional *lakhon* hand movements with Western dance steps. Performed at most informal gatherings and *very* popular after a few shots of Mekong whiskey! Westerners who try the *ram wong* always appear incredibly clumsy, although their comical efforts are appreciated by the gracious Thais.

Sword Fighting—*Krabi Krabong*

Originally devised by warriors to practice combat techniques, sword fighting is only performed today in conjunction with a dinner-dance show. A complete cycle begins with sharpened swords and then moves through combat with poles, knives, and finally hand-to-hand combat. Real swords give the fighters deadly potential in this skillful and exciting sport.

Traditional Music

Backing up the *khon, lakhon,* and *likay* is the music of the *pipat,* Thailand's strange but captivating orchestra. Most Westerners find the surrealistic flavor of Thai music difficult to appreciate as it seems to lack harmony or melody. Traditional Thai music is based on a five-tone diatonic scale with neither major nor minor keys—more closely related to medieval Christian music or the abstract compositions of Ravel than conventional Western compositions.

Similar to Javanese and Balinese *gamelan,* the Thai percussive orchestra is composed of five to 15 instruments such as drums, xylophones, gongs, metallophones, woodwinds, strings, and flutes. Musical passages indicate specific actions and emotions (marching, weeping, anger) which are immediately recognized by the dancers. Thai music is abstract, highly syncopated, and emotionally charged but delightfully moving with repeated hearings.

Perhaps the best option is the free student shows given Sunday afternoons on the front lawn. Schedules are sometimes listed in the *Bangkok Post,* but it's more dependable to simply wander by the National Theater on a Sunday morning and see if a crowd is gathering. Stageside spots can be reserved by leaving a blanket on the lawn. Local food vendors sell inexpensive snacks from the adjacent stalls.

Thailand Cultural Centre: Many of Bangkok's finest cultural performances take place in the newish cultural center located on Ratchadphisek Rd., a few blocks north of New Petchburi Rd. en route to the airport. Opened by the king in 1987, the cultural center features a 200-seat main auditorium graced with outstanding Ramayana murals, a smaller 500-seat performance hall, and a library where fine-art exhibitions are held. Recent shows have included Thai classical music, folk puppet theater, demonstrations of *khon* drama, chamber orchestras, German vocal music, piano recitals, and opportunities to meet leading Thai artists. Pick up a complete schedule at the tourist office, or call 247-0028 for more information.

Dinner Dance Shows

First-time visitors who wish to sample an overview of Thai dance can attend performances in almost a dozen air-conditioned Thai restaurants listed in the accompanying chart. While these highly abbreviated performances are somewhat artificial and resented by visitors who dislike the "instant culture" mentality, the performances are usually of a high standard, plus the glittering costumes and elegant dance styles are always impressive.

Dinner dance shows follow a standard arrangement. A northern Thai *khon toke*-style dinner is followed by brief demonstrations of *khon, lakhon,* and *likay* folk dancing, Thai martial arts, puppetry, and sword fighting. Dinner is usually served around 1900, and the show begins 60-90 minutes later. Photographers should arrive early and request a seat near the stage.

Prices for the dinner with show range from 300B to 500B; some restaurants offer the show without meal for 200-300B. Transportation from the hotel to restaurant is often included with the ticket. Performance times and prices can be double-checked by calling the restaurant or inquiring with the TAT.

Dinner dance shows can be seen at several luxury hotels, and at private restaurants located in renovated homes. Tickets can be purchased from most travel agents, but prices are lowest from the bucket shops in Banglampoo and near the Malaysia Hotel.

Baan Thai: Like most Thai restaurants with dance performances, Baan Thai recreates a traditional Thai house with polished teakwood floors, elegant furnishings, and tropical gardens. Nightly shows from 1900. 7 Sukumvit Soi 32, tel. (02) 258-5403.

Piman: One of Bangkok's more elegant and expensive shows takes place inside this beautiful reproduction of a Sukothai-era house. Admission 500B. 46 Sukumvit Soi 49, tel. (02) 258-7866.

Chao Phraya Restaurant: Travelers staying in the guesthouses of Banglampoo often attend the cultural show across the Pinklau Bridge in Thonburi. Packages sold by travel agents include transportation, dinner, show, and possibly a cocktail in the adjacent Paradise Music Hall.

Hotel Shows: Dance performances are also given in the Sala Rim Nam Restaurant located across the river from the Oriental Hotel (free boat service), and the Sala Thai Restaurant on the rooftop of the Indra Regent.

NIGHTLIFE

Bangkok's nightlife is perhaps the most notorious in the world. Bars, brothels, live sex shows, massage parlors, gay nightclubs, roving transvestites, sex cabarets, all-night coffee shops thick with call girls, child prostitutes, and barber shops that provide more than just haircuts—the range of sexual services is simply amazing. Bangkok alone has an estimated 100,000 prostitutes, and it's said that almost one-fifth of all visitors to Thailand come for sex. Despite the devastating effect of AIDS, local opposition, and the conservative moral attitudes of the Thai people (the vast majority are incredibly puritanical), Thailand's roaring sex industry seems destined to remain a major attraction well into the 1990s.

The sex circus begins at the Bangkok Airport, where male visitors are sometimes propositioned by transvestites who boldly drag their unsuspecting prey into terminal bathrooms. Airport taxi drivers negotiate the fare, then offer up girls in all ages and prices. Many Bangkok hotels—from low-end to prestigious—also serve as "knock-knock" emporiums, where spare girls are sold by the employees or sent uninvited up to rooms at night. Hotels have 24-hour coffee shops, barber shops with private rooms in the rear, and massage parlors filled with young girls sold by the hour or night.

The scene continues throughout the city. Over on Patpong, street touts thrust out Polaroids of young virgins and well-worn scraps of cardboard that list their sexual talents. Teams of transvestites cruise the tourist enclaves, looking to drag fresh-faced tourists off to drive-in motels that serve as short-time brothels. Local publications such as *This Week in Bangkok* advertise escort services ("more than 50 Thai fashion model girls at your service"), marriage agencies ("view our video of 250 young girls selected for their good looks"), gay nightclubs ("students who come to enjoy"), barber shops ("pretty lady barbers will attend to all your needs"), and go-go bars ("over 50 charming hostesses and dancers") wedged between brief descriptions of temples and upcoming Rotary Club functions. Wherever you wander in Bangkok, you'll come across countless short-time motels where attendants quickly whisk curtains behind arriving cars, girlie bars with upstairs shows, and three-story massage parlors as luxurious as Las Vegas casinos. Never has sex been marketed with such originality.

First-time visitors often assume that prostitution in Thailand is a hangover from the Vietnam War era when American servicemen took their R&R in Bangkok and Pattaya. Actually, Thai society has long been tolerant of prostitution; brothels were commonplace in Chinatown and in the Pratunam *klongs* long before the arrival of mass tourism. Today, even the smallest of Thai towns have long-established houses frequented exclusively by local men; *farangs* are often refused admittance in the mistaken belief that AIDS is a foreign disease.

Visitors also wonder about the women themselves. Although a small percentage have been sold into sexual slavery by their parents to middlemen who resell them to the brothels, a vast majority are freelancers who enter the business on their own free will. The motivation, of course, is money, since it's said that the most beautiful

RESTAURANTS WITH THAI CLASSICAL DANCE

RESTAURANT	ADDRESS	AREA	PHONE (02)
Baan Thai	Sukumvit Soi 32	Sukumvit	258-5403
Maneeya's Lotus Room	Ploenchit Rd.	Siam Square	252-6312
Chao Phraya	451 Arun Amrin Rd.	Thonburi	424-2389
Oriental Hotel	Charoen Krung Rd.	Silom	437-9417
Piman	Sukumvit Soi 49	Sukumvit	258-7866
Ruen Thep	Silom Village	Silom	233-9447
Indra Regent Hotel	Rajaprarop Rd.	Siam Square	251-1111
Sawasdee	66 Soi Phipat	Silom	237-6310
Siam Intercontinental	Rama I Rd.	Siam Square	253-0355
Suwanahong	Sri Ayuthaya Rd.	Siam Square	245-4448
Tun Nak Thai	131 Rajadapisek	Sukumvit	277-3828

women can earn considerably more than the prime minister. Most are poorly educated farm girls who use their income to support their parents and offspring in impoverished regions such as the northeast.

Rather than the hardened prostitutes of New York or Germany, Thai working girls tend to be demure and compliant ladies who choose their dates on the basis of good looks and a good heart rather than simply monetary rewards. Often the temporary liaison becomes a more permanent bond as they travel and live together during the following weeks. She shows him the country, bargains for him in the local market, cooks him local dishes, and teaches him some of her language. The foreigner provides her with a degree of sophistication and possibility of marriage, while she becomes the attentive and loving paridigm of Eastern femininity.

Visitors are also surprised to learn that prostitution is illegal in Thailand. For that matter, even topless dancing is prohibited, not to mention the other services available in the massage parlors and darkened nightclubs. Proposals have been made to legalize prostitution to control AIDS, but most Thais prefer to keep the business as private as possible. Police periodically raid brothels and go-go bars, but this formality is done more to ensure a steady stream of payoffs than to stop the flesh trade.

The Bangkok Scene

Nightclubs and girlie bars that cater to foreigners are concentrated in several neighborhoods. By far the most notorious area is Patpong Rd. between Silom and Surawong roads. Visitors who want to briefly experience the mayhem should spend a few hours wandering through the clubs, and skip the more hardened enclaves located elsewhere. The second-largest number of clubs is located on Soi Cowboy, a short street near the intersection of Sukumvit Rd. and Soi 21. Nana Complex at Soi 4 and Washington Square near Soi 22 are other nightlife centers in the Sukumvit neighborhood. Diehards who want to explore the underbelly of Bangkok might check the Grace Hotel and the Thermae Lounge, both located in Sukumvit.

Tidbits and gossip about the bar scene in Bangkok can be culled from Bernard Trink's column in the Saturday *Bangkok Post*. Trink does a good job describing what's happening, plus offers dependable tips on weekly discounts and special events in the nightclubs.

Patpong

Bangkok's most notorious red-light district is located on Patpong 1 and 2 between Silom and Surawong roads. Once owned by the Patpong family and made popular by American soldiers on leave from Vietnam, this infamous collection of go-go bars, cocktail lounges, live shows, street vendors, pushy touts, and preteen hustlers forms a scene straight from Dante's *Inferno*.

During the day Patpong is almost deserted except for a pair of excellent bookstores and several cozy pubs which screen the latest videos in air-conditioned comfort. Between 1800 and 2000 the bars spring to life with smaller crowds and happy-hour prices—an excellent time to look around without draining your wallet. A lively and highly recommended night market now takes place along Patpong 1 and on the sidewalks of Silom and Surawong roads. From 2000 until around 0100, some 30-50 go-go bars and live-show nightclubs operate at full tilt, packed with both overseas visitors and Thais who generally accept rather than condemn the sex trade.

Single males, Western females, and even families are welcome to enter a club, watch a show, and perhaps attempt a conversation with the unexpectedly friendly ladies. Surprisingly, farang women are often the center of attention and soon become the conversation centerpiece for the entire bar. Moral questions aside, the whole scene is much less depressing or intimidating than red-light areas in the West.

Conversations usually begin with a "What hotel you stay?" and "Where you come from?" to help the girl gauge the customer's wealth. Jokes and general silliness are more welcome than philosophical discussions or inquiries into their personal lives. After some chitchat, most girls will request a cola drink (they get 15B for every 50B lady's drink) to keep the mamasan (female manager) happy. Visitors who decline will usually be left alone to enjoy the show, but even the briefest of glances will bring another lady to your side. To minimize the hassle, it's best to sit at the bar rather than offer yourself as a permanent target in a rear-side banquette. Drink prices are posted at the bar, and running tabs are kept in individual containers at your table. Rip-offs and overcharging are very rare in Patpong, so relax and enjoy yourself.

Girls may be taken from the bars by paying a bar fine of 200-400B, though this charge can be avoided by meeting the girl out front after closing hours. Services for the night run 300-1000B depending on the popularity of the girl, the hour of the night (prices drop toward closing hour), and how wealthy she considers her client. Most girls cannot be trusted; valuables should be checked in the hotel safe and bar girls should sign in at the hotel register. First-class hotels often prohibit entrance to hookers for security reasons.

Patpong 1: The best strategy for selecting a club is to walk the entire street and quickly peek inside the flashier establishments. Better clubs on Patpong 1 include **King's Castle**, **Queen's Castle**, and the **Mississippi Club**, where scenes from The Deer Hunter were filmed. Patpong also served as Saigon's Tu Do Street for Robin Williams's Good Morning Vietnam. The **Kangaroo Club** on the north end is an Australian-run pub that provides an air-conditioned escape for males, females, and harried couples. **Napoleon Lounge** is an old favorite that serves as a daytime restaurant and nighttime jazz club.

Patpong 2: This narrow alley provides an easy alternative to the madness on Patpong 1. **Bobby's Arms** has a Sunday evening music fest of straight-ahead mainstream jazz performed by both Western and Thai artists. The open-air beer bars (also called bar beers!) on Patpong 2 are less threatening options where you can relax and watch the passing crowd. Ladies in the north-end watering holes are friendly and under less pressure to push drinks than their counterparts on Patpong 1. **Sugar Shack** is a go-go bar that allows visitors to go-go dance with the girls.

Live Sex Shows: The most irritating sidelight to Patpong is the hordes of overly aggressive barkers who accost Westerners with offers of private shows featuring young girls whose special talents are explicitly listed on calling cards. After performing their bizarre biological feats, the girls are joined by a young Thai male who tests his endurance, perhaps knocking over your drink in the process. Very few visitors enjoy these shows, but if you must, be sure to establish the total cover charge and price for drinks before going upstairs for the show—misunderstandings are common. Tourists who are presented extortionate bills should pay up and then contact the tourist police on the Surawong Rd. end of Patpong 1, or the larger police station at the intersection of Silom and Rama IV roads. The tourist police will collect your refund and correct the situation for the next visitor.

Patpong 3: This dead-end alley off Silom Rd. is home to several gay clubs that feature transvestites (gatoeis) in hilarious follies revues. Solo women and mixed couples are welcome to have a drink and enjoy the show. Also on Patpong 3 are several small restaurants such as the

Telephone Cafe and the wildly popular **Rome Club** disco, where trendy gays and visiting *farangs* come to enjoy the superb sound and lighting system.

Soi Taniya: Japan comes to Bangkok. Taniya Rd., three short blocks east of Patpong, more closely resembles a nightlife district in Tokyo than Bangkok. Just for an odd experience, walk past the private gate (the Japanese have apparently purchased the entire street) and pseudo-art-deco Thaniya Plaza building to glance at the Japanese nightclubs, laser karaoke bars, and sushi joints all marked with Japanese script. Most are private clubs which bar admittance to Westerners unless accompanied by a member. It's said that the most beautiful women in Thailand work here on "Soi Ginza," making an astronomical 5000B per night.

Soi Cowboy

Bangkok's second-most-active bar area is off Sukumvit Road between Sois 21 and 23. The area gets its name from a black American nicknamed "Cowboy" who owned one of the first bars on the street. Soi Cowboy is a refreshing change from the hype and hustle of Patpong, more relaxed and low-key with less pressure to spend or buy the girls a drink. Crowds tend to be smaller and made up of Western expatriates rather than locals and tourists. For this reason, many of the girls speak more English than the girls of Patpong, and expect less money since they lack the sophistication and aggressiveness of their Patpong counterparts. Drinks run around 40-50B, buyout fees 150-300B. Soi Cowboy is also a good place to meet Western residents, and pick up inside tips and anecdotes about the nightlife scene in Bangkok. Set with terrific foodstalls and friendly pubs, Soi Cowboy is the slow and sleazy counterpoint to the flash and glitter of Patpong.

Bars tend to change name and ownership with the seasons, but the current favorites include **Midnight** (Calypso transvestite revue at midnight), a country-western pub called **Annie's Lounge**, brightly illuminated **Tilac**, and the very popular **Butterfly Nightclub** on the corner of Soi 21. Many of the newer, surprisingly sophisticated clubs have been enlarged by knocking down the walls between two smaller bars. Adjacent Soi 23 offers several good British pubs that serve bangers and mash along with the latest videos. Top choices include **Mike O-Henry's Old Dutch Cafe, BH German Beer House, George & Dragon British Pub**, and the **Rong Phuk Restaurant**.

Nana Plaza

Bangkok's newest go-go bar scene features three floors of clubs, cafes, and rock 'n' roll cabarets with outstanding sound systems. Ground floor of the U-shaped complex has a few open-air beer bars for drinks without hassles. The better clubs are all located on the second floor. **Asian Intrigue** sponsors rather campy music revues nightly at 2000 and 2300 that run the gamut from Thai classical dancers to simulated love scenes; a fun place popular with single males and mixed couples. **Woodstock** is a dark and smoky lounge that features disco tunes, girls, and some of the better rock bands in Bangkok. Other bars on the second floor include the **Farang Connection, Blackout, Hog's Breath Saloon** ("better than no breath at all"), **Sexy Night**, and **Three Roses**. Also on the second floor is the acceptable **Nana Guesthouse** where rooms cost 200B for two hours, or 350-450B all night. A snooker hall and another short-time hotel are upstairs.

Nana Entertainment Complex is on Soi 4, directly across from the Nana Hotel.

Washington Square

Another low-key nightlife scene is located on Sukumvit Rd. between Sois 22 and 24. Behind the Washington Cinema, which dominates the square, you'll find a small cluster of cheap food-stalls and nightclubs that evoke an American atmosphere. Darts, snooker, videos, and Sunday afternoon barbecues are the main attractions rather than go-go girls and sex shows.

The liveliest spot is the popular **Bourbon Street** which features cajun creole cuisine and live Dixieland and other jazz on weekends by the Bourbon Street Ramblers. Other American West saloons include the **Texas Lone Star Saloon** with "Food, Wimmin & Likker", the well-named **No Probl'm Cocktail Lounge**, and the **Silver Dollar Bar** ("No Weapons Allowed").

Coffee Shops

Moving sharply downscale several notches are a handful of coffee shops which allow freelance prostitutes to ply their trade. Most are rather deserted until about midnight when the bars on Patpong and Soi Cowboy close their doors. Bar girls who haven't found a date then grab a *tuk tuk* to the Grace or Thermae and hang out until sunrise. Mixed couples and female travelers will find these coffee shops very seedy.

Grace Hotel: Thailand's sleaziest sex scene takes place inside the 24-hour coffee shop located on the ground floor of the Grace Hotel. Like some sort of Oriental bazaar, the noisy dive is always jammed with Patpong rejects and freelancers too wild or independent to be employed by any self-respecting bar or nightclub. Three jukeboxes at opposite corners play three different tunes simultaneously . . . just too weird.

Massage Parlors

Countless massage parlors, Turkish baths, and steam baths are found throughout Bangkok. Large numbers have cropped up in the last few years on lower Sukumvit and along New Petchburi Road, north of Sukumvit. Massage parlors come in two varieties: legitimate places which offer traditional "Ancient Massage" for 150-200B per hour, and sex houses filled with numbered ladies patiently waiting in viewing rooms. Absolutely guaranteed to infuriate Western women, these giant pleasure palaces are equipped with one-way mirrors through which customers watch up to 250 masseuses file their nails and zone out on TV while waiting for a customer.

It's a flesh market of the most curious type. Customers make their selection by picking a girl and giving her number to the parlor manager. The girl is called out, the style of massage is chosen, and the bill is paid at the cashier's counter. The couple then retires to an upstairs room furnished with a bed and bathtub, often decorated with colored lights and strategically placed mirrors. After a hot bubble bath, the customer lies down on an inflated rubber mattress to be covered with all types of body oils and liquid soaps. The masseuse then uses her entire body, also liberally covered with oils and soaps, to "make massage."

All sorts of services are available and subject to negotiation with the girl. Regular massages without sex cost from 250B (plus tip) per hour. A one-hour full-body massage with sex (called a B-course massage) costs 500-1000B. Special services include fantasy rooms with steamy videos, infamous "Tora Tora" massages,

and soapy sandwiches performed by two ladies from 1200B. Additional sexual favors can be negotiated in the room, but it's best to avoid an ugly scene and pay the entire charge before going upstairs. Other permutations and combinations can be explained by the manager.

Escort Agencies

Escort agencies and "guide services" advertise their services in local newspapers. Selections can be personally made at the office from photo albums and videotapes, or ordered sight un-

---

THAI KICK BOXING

Thai boxing is the street-fighter's dream of Western boxing mixed with karate and a bit of tae kwon do. Barefoot pugilists prior to World War II wrapped their hands in hemp mixed with ground glass and the fight went on for as long as anyone could stand . . . or had any blood left. Today the boxers wear lightly padded gloves and a few rules have been introduced to control the carnage.

An interesting ritual takes place before the match begins. Wailing music from a small orchestra of Javanese pipe, two drums, and cymbal sets the mood. Often fixed with colored cords and protective amulets, the two contestants enter the ring, kneel and pray to the spirits for victory, and then begin a surrealistic slow-motion dance designed to show off their talents while emulating their teachers' movements. Spectators make their bets as the boxers pound and kick each other with ever-increasing frenzy. The drama is heightened by the cacophonous musical accompaniment. At the end of five three-minute rounds or the merciful intervention of the referee, the fight ends and a winner is declared.

Thai kick boxing can be experienced at the Lumpini Stadium on Rama IV Road (near the Malaysia Hotel) every Tuesday and Friday at 1800, and Saturdays at 1800 and 1330. Superior boxers meet at Rajadamnern Stadium (near the TAT office) every Monday, Wednesday, and Thursday at 1800, and on Sundays at 1700 and 2000. Admission is 50-200B. This spectacle is best watched from ringside rather than with the rabble up in the circular gallery. Thai boxing goes center stage on TV every Sunday afternoon.

male Monroes

seen with a phone call. The service charges will far exceed the bar fines collected from go-go nightclubs.

Transvestite Revues

"Boys Will Be Girls" is a familiar theme here in the Land of Smiles. For several decades, female-impersonator revues have been a popular form of entertainment in the seaside resort of Pattaya. Recently, these spectacles have taken root in Bangkok and on Patong Beach in Phuket. Small gay clubs in Bangkok sponsor cozy revues in intimate surroundings, but tourists generally favor the elaborate and very professional shows in the 600-seat Calypso Theater. The two-hour performance includes dancing sailoresses, comedy skits with audience participation, leather queens, Thai and Chinese dancers in stunning costumes, and above all, a delightful sense of humor and good cheer. Photographers are welcome. Sukumvit Rd. at Soi 24. Shows nightly at 2000; admission is 300B.

DISCOS, NIGHTCLUBS, AND BARS

Discos

Discotheques in Bangkok are absolutely astounding, rivaled in the East only by the clubs of Manila. Discos in the luxury hotels are okay, but none can compare with local Thai nightclubs that rage on from 0900 to 0200. Cover charges run 60-100B during the week, and 120-200B on weekends; a complimentary drink or two (or three) is usually included. Some discos provide traditional entertainment with a DJ spinning records, while others are videotheques where music is backed by laser rock videos.

Rome Club: A relatively small but exceedingly hot videotheque frequented by fashionably dressed gays, trendy art-club types, and *gatoeis* who hang out in the upstairs annex. The older and more sophisticated clientele peaks around midnight during the highly recommended transvestite revue. Solo males seeking companionship should carefully inspect the hands and Adam's apple of all prospective dates . . . unless seeking a wild war story for the boys back home. Rome Club is conveniently located in the gay nightlife district of Patpong 3.

Freakout: Trendy young Thais favor the heterosexual discos and pubs centered on either side of Silom Plaza. Dining tables in the plaza provide good people-watching, while adjacent discos such as Virgin and Freakout Supertheque pack in the young crowds. Unlike most discos in Bangkok, some of the Thai ladies will socialize and dance with Western men. Silom Plaza on Silom Road, near Thai International Airlines.

Woodstock Nightclub: Entertainment in this funky club alternates between live rock 'n' roll bands on weekends and recorded music during the week. The Woodstock is almost exclusively oriented toward solo males and disappointing as a disco, but an outstanding place for live music.

LIVE THAI ROCK 'N' ROLL

Unlike Manila, most of the clubs in Bangkok feature recorded music rather than live entertainment. The scene, however, has improved with the arrival of *dontree pher chee-vit*, a fresh musical force which breaks away from the traditional love themes to raise issues of social injustice.

Early efforts at political consciousness by a group named Caravan proved too radical for public airing, but Carabao in the late '80s caused a major sensation with their song "Made in Thailand." The hit both ridiculed Thai obsession with foreign-made goods and inadvertently promoted the government's Buy-Thai program! Other Carabao songs have described the plight of Bangkok's prostitutes and poor rural farmers. Instead of simply plagiarizing Western pop melodies to back up Thai lyrics, Carabao has successfully fused American country rock with traditional Thai music. Remember the 1986 disco hit "One Night in Bangkok"? Banned in Thailand.

Nana Entertainment Complex, Sukumvit Soi 4, just opposite the Nana Hotel.

NASA Spacedrome: Bangkok's flashiest disco is a multimillion-dollar dance emporium that packs in over 2,000 sweating bodies every weekend. At midnight, a spaceship descends to the floor amid smoke, flashing lights, and the theme song from *2001: A Space Odyssey*. For sheer spectacle, nothing else compares in Thailand. NASA Spacedrome is located on Ramkamheng Rd., 100 meters north of New Petchburi Rd. in the Bangkapi neighborhood. A taxi from Sukumvit should cost about 100B.

The Palace: Perhaps the trendiest of all Bangkok discos, the Palace is frequented by young Thais who hail from the wealthiest families in Thailand. 379 Vipavadee Rangsit Hwy., on the road to the airport.

Paradise Music Hall: Another gigantic dance emporium with the standard amenities of flashing lights, laser videos, and booming disco music. A very wild place on weekends. The Paradise is on Arun Amarin Rd. in Thonburi, just across the bridge from Banglampoo; a good choice for travelers staying on Khao San Road. Taxis from Khao San cost 50-80B.

Bars

Bangkok has few bars in the traditional sense, largely because any ordinary restaurant, including the smallest street-side noodle shop, can legally sell beer and other spirits. Also, Thais prefer to socialize with friends at home or in restaurants than sit quietly and drink in a cocktail lounge. However, a new breed of nightery has emerged in the early 1990s that caters to foreigners and English-speaking Thais who appreciate tavern ambience. Bars on Patpong, Soi Cowboy, and Nana Complex are described above. A few other bar areas are detailed below.

Soi Sarasin: A very welcome addition to Bangkok's night scene are the intimate nightclubs and cozy restaurants located on Soi Sarasin, just off Rajadamnern Rd. and immediately north of Lumpini Park. Modeled after European bistros with clean decor and sidewalk tables, these clubs appeal to young Westerners and professional Thais rather than the go-go crowd. Best bets include the **Brown Sugar**, with good jazz, and the **Old West Saloon**, which recreates an American Wild West atmosphere.

Soi Lang Suan: Around the corner from Soi Sarasin is another street with a good selection of pubs favored by expats and yuppie Thais. Among the most popular are **Round Midnight** for jazzophiles, and the trendy European-run **Vinothek** with its extensive wine cellar.

Soi Gaysorn: Located in the short alley adjacent to the Meridien Hotel (Siam Square area) are two small cafe-clubs modeled after American Western saloons. The **Blue Moon** bar features some of the best jazz and R&B combos in Thailand, while the downstairs Western-style **Moon Shadow Cafe** specializes in seafood entrees.

Sukumvit Soi 33: Cozy clubs curiously named after European painters are tucked away in a quiet *soi* off Sukumvit Road. All offer happy hour drink specials and are popular with Western expatriates who live nearby. Try the **Vincent Van Gogh** or **Renoir Club**.

(top) Ko Samui;
(bottom) palms at sunset, Ko Samui (photos by Carl Parkes)

(top) Get it while it's hot (Songkhla);
(bottom) drying fish at market, Songkhla (photos by Carl Parkes)

SHOPPING

Bangkok enjoys a well-deserved reputation as the Shopping Capital of Southeast Asia. Popular products include Thai silks, gemstones, tailor-made suits and dresses, inexpensive shoes, bronzeware, and traditional handicrafts. Imported items such as electronics, watches, and cameras are much cheaper in the duty-free ports of Hong Kong or Singapore; otherwise, it's impossible to beat the deals in Bangkok.

Prices are fairly uniform across town, but selection varies slightly between neighborhoods: Chinatown is best for gold chains and photography equipment, Silom Rd. for silks and antiques, Sukumvit for leather goods and tailors, Siam Square for high fashion and cheap clothing, Banglampoo for handicrafts and tribal artifacts.

Serious shoppers should purchase Nancy Chandler's outstanding *Market Map of Bangkok* and *Shopping in Exotic Thailand,* published by Impact Publications.

TIPS

The Tourist Authority of Thailand strongly suggests that all visitors to Thailand shop with great care. Far too many tourists are being overcharged and sold fraudulent merchandise with worthless guarantees.

Bargaining

Bargaining is absolutely necessary except in the large department stores. It's challenging and fun—*if* you keep your sense of humor. Haggle with a smile; let the shopkeeper laugh at your ridiculous offer while smiling back at his absurd asking price. Bargaining is a game, not a life-or-death struggle. Expect a discount of 20-30%, not the 50% reduction given in other Southeast Asian countries such as Indonesia. As elsewhere in Asia, knowing a few numbers and key phrases will send prices plunging.

Refunds, Receipts, and Guarantees

As a general rule, goods once purchased cannot be exchanged or returned. Deposits are also nonrefundable. Carefully examine all merchandise since receipts and guarantees issued by local retailers are of dubious value after you have returned home.

Touts

Touts are paid commissions for rounding up customers. All expenses, including taxi rides and lunches, are added to your bill. Avoid them.

Fakes

Thailand also enjoys a reputation as the Counterfeit Capital of Asia. Most fakes, such as ersatz Lacoste shirts and Cartier watches, are advertised and sold as fakes. More dangerous to your pocketbook is colored glass being peddled as rubies, and newly manufactured Buddhas sold as genuine antiques. Experts at Bangkok's National Museum estimate that 90% of the items sold at the city's antique stores are counterfeit! Unless you are an expert, or prepared to gamble large sums of money, a sound policy is to shun expensive jewelry and pricey antiques.

What To Buy

The following sections describe some of the more popular items for sale in Bangkok, and offer a few suggestions on where to shop.

Silk: Thai silk is world famous for both its high quality and beautiful designs. Be cautious, however, of silk fabric being sold at extraordinarily good prices. Cheap silk is often just rayon or rough silk cleverly interwoven with synthetics. A yard of high-quality silk, handwoven and dyed with modern, colorfast German dyes, should sell for about 500-800B per meter. Check for variations in the size of the silk thread, which gives Thai silk its distinctive uneven texture. Or burn a small piece: synthetics turn to ash but real silk forms little sweat-like beads and does not disintegrate.

Precious Stones: In the last decade Bangkok has become one of the world's major centers for gemstone cutting and jewelry design. An estimated 250,000 stonecutters work in the capital, surpassing the numbers in even Amsterdam and Hong Kong. There are a few caveats. Thailand, once one of the world's primary sources of precious stones, has now almost completely exhausted its domestic supply. Last year Thailand was forced to import over 80% of the gemstones cut in the country, including a worthless milk-white rock called a geuda (corundum) which is found in great quantities in Sri Lanka. When heated to temperatures between 2,912 and 3,272 degrees this nondescript stone becomes a "sapphire," a scientific process which helps explain the flood of inexpensive sapphires in Bangkok! That's not all. Several years ago it was revealed that Miss Thailand wore a tiara made from artificial stones and letters in the *Bangkok Post* regularly complain about stones being sold at five times their fair value from *government-backed* lapidaries. Little help is offered by the TAT.

The jewelry racket in Bangkok is pushed by friendly, clean-cut students and *tuk tuk* drivers who take you anywhere for just ten *baht*. All are crooks and should be avoided.

The bottom line is that anyone intending to make a sizable purchase of precious stones in Thailand should ask the jeweler to accompany him to a facility for an independent appraisal. The Tourist Police are completely helpless. The Asian Institute of Gemological Sciences on Silom Rd. can determine the nature of the stone, but will not offer a monetary valuation. Gem receipts should always be marked "Subject to identification and appraisal by a registered gemologist." Some shops will offer 50% refunds to unhappy customers, but require you to sign a declaration that removes them from all further legal prosecution. Alternatively, pay with a credit card and cancel payments after you have been defrauded.

Antiques: As mentioned before, most Thai wooden antiques are actually clever fakes produced by "instant antique" factories where hundreds of wooden images are carved, treated with special chemicals, and aged under the sun. All antiques, regardless of type or age, can only be exported with written permission from the Antique Art Business Division (tel. 02-224-1370) of the Fine Arts Department. Obtain registration and permission by taking the piece to the Fine Arts Department on Na Prathat Rd. across from Sanam Luang, together with two six- by nine-centimeter photographs of the object. An export fee of 50-300B is charged depending on the piece. This permit must be obtained at least five days in advance of departure. Store owners can often obtain this permit for a nominal fee. Confirm that the shop can handle this process; once the sale has been completed, some shops find little motivation to follow through with the procedure.

Fake antiques do not require export permits. However, since Airport Customs officials are not antique experts, they often confuse fake with authentic antiques and block export as you try to get on the plane.

Buddha Images: Thai laws prohibit the export of *all* Buddha images and images of other deities dating from before the 18th century. The only exceptions to this rule are Buddhist amulets. The problem has apparently been misguided tourists who have converted their Buddha images into lamps and doorstops, a sacrilegious act that infuriates the Thais. Buddha images can be exported for reasons of religious homage, educational purposes, and cultural exchange programs. Letters of certification issued by your organization must be submitted to the Fine Arts Department.

As a result of government pressure, most Buddhas sold in Bangkok (whether real or fake) are exclusively Burmese images which are exempt from the law. Rather than worrying about exporting a Buddha, many shoppers opt for images of kneeling monks and female deities.

Hilltribe Handicrafts: Thai hilltribes are well known for their elaborate jewelry, colorful textiles, and esoteric items such as opium pipes and bamboo flutes. All are best purchased in Chiang Mai rather than Bangkok. Consider purchases carefully; hilltribe souvenirs which seem exotic in Thailand quickly lose their charm back home. Practical items such as wearable clothing and high-quality handicrafts generally make more sense than a trunkload of cheap and junky oddities.

Other Goods: Bronzeware cutlery sets siliconized to prevent tarnishing are excellent buys in Thailand. Another popular gift is nielloware, a special type of silver inlaid with black enamel designs and crafted into lighters, ashtrays, and bracelets. Celadon pottery, a cottage industry centered in Chiang Mai, attempts to reproduce the sublime glazes of Sawankalok prototypes. Thai lacquerware, similar to Burmese models, is also produced in Chiang Mai.

WHERE TO SHOP

Merchants recommended by the Tourism Authority of Thailand are listed in the TAT publication, the *Official Shopping Guide,* and denoted on the shop's front window by a decal of a female vendor seated with a pair of baskets. Unfortunately, this regulation means very little in Bangkok, so conduct your shopping with extreme caution.

Silk

Thailand's two most famous silk shops are Jim Thompson Thai Silk at 9 Surawong Rd. near Patpong, and Shinawatra Silk at Sukumvit Rd. Soi 23. Shinawatra has another outlet on Sathorn South Road. Kanitha on Silom Rd. has been producing world-famous designer fashions for over 20 years. Design Thai at 304 Silom is another quality shop with decades of experience. Quality silks at somewhat lower prices are available in many of the major department stores.

Antiques

Bangkok's best selection of antiques is inside the Art and Antique Center on the third and fourth floors of the River City Shopping Complex. A major antique auction is held here on the first Saturday of each month. Silom Road and the riverside shops on New Road are other good sources of antiques. Also near Silom is the famous Elephant House on a small side street off Sathorn South Road. They specialize in Burmese antiques, teak furniture, and decorative artwork.

Several good antique shops are located on Sukumvit Road. Krishna's Antiques at Soi 6 has four floors of exquisite crafts and rare collectibles. L'Arcadia on Soi 23 is a small shop that specializes in Burmese antiques and reproductions; ask to see their upstairs showcase. Nearby Rasi Sayam at 32 Soi 23 is an excellent shop operated by Honathan Hayssen, a Stanford MBA graduate who pays producers for quality not quantity.

Handicrafts

Most handicrafts are best purchased in Chiang Mai, on the highway that runs between Chiang Mai and Sankamphang. Not only will you find the finest merchandise at the lowest prices, you can also watch the craftsmen in action.

However, for a quick overview, visit the wonderful Narayana Phand Handicraft Store on Rajadamri near Ploenchit Road. Supported by the Thai government, this sprawling store has every possible handicraft at fixed prices. Also worth visiting is Queen Sirikit's Chitralada Shop on the fourth floor of the Oriental Hotel, and their outlets at the Chitralada Palace and at the Vimanmek Palace. Doll collectors should visit Bangkok Dolls in the Peninsula Hotel or their main outlet at 85 Soi Rajatapan near Makkasan Road.

Department Stores And Shopping Centers

Service and selection are unrivaled at the immense shopping complexes located throughout Bangkok. Most of the better department stores are located in the Siam Square-Ploenchit Road area.

Central: Thailand's original department store chain has branches on Silom Rd. (the smallest and least useful outlet), a much better store on Ploenchit Rd., a new addition in the Zen Complex, and an immense emporium in the Lard Prao neighborhood. All stores have an upstairs handicraft market and a mind-boggling selection of quality clothes at reasonable prices.

Duty-free Shop: Much to the dismay of local merchants, the Tourism Authority of Thailand has opened a duty-free shop on Ploenchit Road. The liquor and tobacco sections offer great bargains but better prices on other goods are available elsewhere.

Mah Boonkrong Center: Bangkok's largest indoor shopping mall includes endless arcades full of trinkets, restaurants, cinemas, a concert hall, and the upscale Japanese-owned Tokyu Department Store. Don't miss the wonderful food emporium.

Amarin Plaza and Sogo: Prices are atmospheric but some of the highest-quality goods are sold in the Romanesque complex on Ploenchit Road. Sogo has expanded into the adjacent Erawan Grand Hyatt Hotel.

Peninsula Plaza: Over 70 small boutiques and a comprehensive branch of Asia Books are located in the dazzling shopping center on Rajadamri Rd. near the Regent Hotel.

Zen Central: Adjacent to the new World Trade Center is Bangkok's most prestigious shopping complex, with dozens of boutiques and a large Central Department Store.

Street Markets

Shopping in Bangkok can be roughly divided into air-conditioned shopping malls and traditional markets where Thai housewives pick up their vegetables. The following local venues are great for photographs and a glimpse of old Bangkok, a slice of life that is rapidly disappearing from modern Thailand. Your best choices are the Weekend Market for general shopping, Pratunam for clothing, and Pak Klong for authentic atmosphere.

Weekend Market: The granddaddy of all Thai flea markets is Chatuchak's monstrous affair out near the airport on Paholyothin Road. Once located on the Sanam Luang near the Royal Palace, Chatuchak now sprawls over 35 acres with hundreds of booths selling everything imaginable at rock-bottom prices. An attempt has been made to sectionalize areas selling one kind of product (see Nancy Chandler's map), but most visitors are content to simply wander around and see what they discover. Items for sale include used books and magazines (including back issues of *Sawasdee*), real and fake antiques, textiles and hilltribe artifacts, used Levis 501s, fruit, Siamese fighting fish, and an animal market with endangered birds and other prohibited species. Afterwards, eat at the famous Djit Pochana Restaurant down Paholyothin Rd. toward the airport; their inexpensive luncheon buffet is highly recommended.

Take a bus and watch for the large carnival tent on the left. Open weekends 0900-1800.

Pratunam Market: A sprawling rabbit warren of hygienic foodstalls, vegetable wholesalers, and shoe merchants is located at the intersection of Petchburi and Rajaprarop roads, slightly north of Siam Square. Pratunam is famous as the best place in Bangkok to shop for inexpensive clothing. Open 24 hours; don't get lost!

Pak Klong Market: Thailand's most colorful and smelly vegetable/fruit market hangs over the riverbanks near the Memorial Bridge. Bangkok's answer to London's Covent Garden is a fascinating experience, a hive of ceaseless activity where porters wheel about stacks of crates while old ladies peddle enormous piles of fragrant orchids. Bring your camera and nose plugs.

Banglampoo Market: Conveniently located near the budget guesthouses on Khao San Rd. are several alleys packed with inexpensive clothing and backpackers' supplies. The adjacent New World Department Store has great bargains on the main floor and an inexpensive self-serve cafeteria on top.

Teves Flower Market: A permanent sidewalk market with plants and (occasionally) flowers flanks a canal one km north of Banglampoo, near the National Library.

Thieves' Market: Touted in many tourist books as an antique shopping district, the only antiques and thieves located here are the shopkeepers. Best buys include brassware, imitation antiques, old furniture, Chinese porcelains, and industrial supplies. Located near Chinatown and correctly called Nakhon Kasem, most of the better merchants have abandoned the area and moved into posher digs along Silom and Sukumvit roads. Bargaining is *de rigueur*.

It seems to me that the reader of a good travel book is entitled not only to an exterior voyage, to descriptions of scenery and so forth, but to an interior, a sentimental or tempermental voyage, which takes place side by side with the outer one.

—Henry Douglas

INFORMATION AND SERVICES

TRAVEL FORMALITIES

Tourist Information

The national headquarters of the Tourist Authority of Thailand (TAT) (tel. 02-282-1143, fax 02-280-1744) is at 4 Rajadamnern Ave. near Democracy Monument and Banglampoo. The office is well organized and very helpful, but you need to request their photocopied sheets on specific destinations. A bulletin board lists upcoming festivals, dance performances, and warnings about safety and rip-offs. Useful publications available from the TAT and luxury hotels include *Thailand This Week, Out & About, Angel City,* and *Look.* The TAT publications department across the hall sells large-scale highway maps and souvenir slides. The Bangkok Airport TAT office (tel. 02-523-8972) is a convenient place to pick up information before heading into town. All TAT offices in Thailand are open daily 0830-1630.

Complaints about unfair business practices can be directed to the tourist police (tel. 02-221-6206) located next door to the TAT office; open daily 0800-2400.

Visas

Bangkok is a popular place to pick up visas for onward travel. Most nations maintain diplomatic relations with Thailand and have embassies in Bangkok. Embassies are generally open Mon.-Fri., but accept visa applications only from 0900 to 1200. Some issue visas within two hours, while others require your passport be left overnight. Embassies are spread out all over town and can be *extremely* time-consuming to reach with public transportation. It's much easier to let a travel agency obtain your visa for a nominal fee. Addresses, phone numbers, and operating hours of diplomatic missions are listed in most tourist magazines and booklets.

For most Western tourists, visas are unnecessary for travel to Malaysia (up to 30 days), Singapore (two weeks), Hong Kong (one month), the Philippines (21 days), and Indonesia (two months). These enlightened governments stamp an entry permit in your passport on arrival

at immigration. Don't you wish that everybody did this?

Visas *are* necessary for most Western visitors to Burma (Myanmar), Vietnam, Laos, Cambodia, Nepal, and India. Nepalese visas are issued on the spot and must be used within 30 days. Philippine visas should be obtained before arriving to avoid the byzantine procedures at Manila's immigration department. The Indian Embassy is a disorganized mess with hordes of impatient people getting their first taste of Indian bureaucracy. Visas for Burma, Vietnam, Laos, and Cambodia are generally obtained by travel agents in conjunction with group tours, and rarely given to individual travelers.

Maps

Sprawling and confusing Bangkok is a city that requires a good map. The two essential guides are Nancy Chandler's *Map of Bangkok,* and *Latest Tour's Guide* for bus routes. Buy both to quickly understand the layout of Bangkok. Maps can be purchased at most bookstores and from many guesthouses and hotels.

Nancy Chandler: Nancy's *Map of Bangkok* has been the best tourist map of Bangkok for over a decade. Sensibly drawn with color codes and sectional details, Nancy does a great job pointing out good restaurants and obscure shopping districts. Somewhat expensive at 80B, but highly recommended for all visitors to Bangkok.

Bus Maps: Most of the bus routes in Bangkok are shown on *Latest Tour's Guide to Bangkok and Thailand* and *Tour N Guide Map* published by Thaveephol Charoen. Both cost 40B and include tidbits on markets, guesthouses, bookshops, river and canal tours, embassies, and airline offices. Further details on bus routes are shown in the *Bus Guide,* a small booklet published by Bangkok Guides.

Association of Siamese Architects: A series of four colorful hand-drawn cultural maps with details on Bangkok and the canals of Thonburi. The map of Thonburi is somewhat useful, but the other maps are too vague and sketchy.

Bookstores

Bangkok's bookstores are among the finest in

Southeast Asia. Thailands' book industry is dominated by two large publishers and book distributors, **Asia Books** and **Duang Kamol (D.K. Books)**. Book selection varies between the two book chains because of exclusive distribution systems. D.K. Books is a major distributor with outlets in Bangkok, Chiang Mai, Pattaya, Phuket, and Hat Yai. Asia Books is limited to Bangkok outlets located on Sukumvit Road Soi 15, Sukumvit Soi 3, Landmark Plaza, and in the Galerie Lafayette on Rajadamri Road. D.K. Books has outlets in Siam Square, Sukumvit Rd. opposite the Ambassador Hotel, and on Surawong Rd. near Patpong. Prices vary dramatically, so it pays to check around.

Independent Bookstores: A handful of smaller bookstores are also located in Bangkok. **The Bookseller** on Patpong Rd. has a great selection of English-language books and foreign magazines. Other independent outlets are located in Siam Square and on Patpong Road.

Used Books: Used English-language books are difficult to find in Bangkok, but a few stores carry a reasonable selection. **Chalermnit Books** on Ploenchit near the Grand Hyatt Erawan is worth a try, as is the small bookstore on Soi 24 near the Impala Hotel. **Elite Used Books** on Sukumvit Soi 33 has a wide choice of guides and background reading obtained from Western expats living in the neighborhood. A small bookstore on New Rd. near the Oriental Hotel has used books in the rear room. For new and rare books on Asia, plus old maps and prints, check the excellent **White Lotus Bookstore** (tel. 02-286-1100) at 26 Soi Attakarn Prasit Rd., off Sathorn South near the Malaysia Hotel.

Libraries

The National Library located north of Banglampoo, and Chulalongkorn University Library near Siam Square, have a limited selection of English-language books and magazines. The A.U.A. (tel. 02-252-8953) at 179 Rajadamri Rd. has a decent library sponsored by the U.S. Information Service with background reading on Thai history and foreign magazines. A photocopy service is provided at nominal cost. Scholars should head directly to the Siam Society (tel. 02-258-3491) library on Sukumvit Soi 21. Siam Society has the largest research facilities in Thailand, but it's open to members only. Other possibilities include the British Council (tel. 02-252-6136) in Siam Square and the Neilson Hayes Library (tel. 02-233-1731) at 195 Surawong Road.

Travel Agents

Bangkok has a wide choice of travel agencies dealing in everything from nightclub tours to jungle safaris. Local sightseeing tours can be arranged through agencies located in all major hotels. Prices vary sharply: one-day tours of the floating market cost 700B from Silom travel agents, but only 300B from discount shops in Banglampoo.

Major Tour Operators: Major tour packages to overseas destinations such as Vietnam are best purchased from **Diethelm Travel** (tel. 02-252-4041) at 544 Ploenchit Rd., or **World Travel** (tel. 02-233-5900) at 1053 Charoen Krung Road.

Discount Travel Agencies: Bucket shops near the guesthouses on Khao San Rd. and the Malaysia Hotel are excellent sources for cheap flights, visas, and discount bus and train tickets. All offer similar prices and services, but a degree of caution should be exercised. Don't be lulled into complacency by a large office or well-established location. Take precautions! Never hand over your money until you have carefully examined your ticket for price, expiration dates, and endorsements.

Student Travel Australia: STA, the world's largest student travel organization, is more expensive than other bucket shops, but you won't need to worry about fraudulent activities. STA has several offices in Bangkok. The office adjacent to the Viengtai Hotel is very slow and hopelessly crowded. Faster STA service is found in their office near the Thai Hotel (tel. 02-281-5314) in Banglampoo, and from the STA head office (tel. 02-233-2582) at 33 Surawong Rd., near Patpong Rd. in the Silom District.

Railway Tickets: A limited number of travel agents in Bangkok are authorized to sell reserved train tickets: **Viang Travel** (tel. 02-280-1385) in the Viengtai Hotel in Banglampoo, **Airland Travel** (tel. 02-251-9495) at 866 Ploenchit Rd., **SEA Tours** (tel. 02-251-4862) on the fourth floor of Siam Center on Rama I Rd., and **Songserm Travel** (tel. 02-250-0768) at 121 Soi Chalermia, Phyathai Road. Most will deliver tickets to your hotel for a nominal charge.

Guides: Personal and group-tour guides can be hired from the Professional Guide Association (tel. 02/250-0453), 420/9 Siam Square Soi 1, Rama 1 Road, Bangkok 10500. A full-day tour costs 1200-1500B.

Medical Care

Excellent medical facilities and English-speaking doctors are available at several hospitals in Bangkok. All boast modern equipment and doctors trained in overseas medical universities. Locals recommend the **Bumrungrad Hospital** on Sukumvit Soi 3, and the **Samitivej Hospital** (tel. 02-392-0011) on Sukumvit Soi 49. In the Silom neighborhood, try the **Bangkok Christian Hospital** (tel. 02-233-6981) at 124 Silom Rd. (near Patpong), and the **Bangkok Nursing Home** (tel. 02-233-2610) on Convent Road. A complete list of hospitals and clinics is found in the Yellow Pages of the English-language edition of the Bangkok Telephone Directory.

Language Instruction

Several language schools in Bangkok offer courses for foreigners. Tuition fees average about 300B per hour, and most courses last two to six weeks. The following schools also teach English, and sometimes hire foreigners with TOEFL certification.

American University Alumni: AUA offers comprehensive group lessons in both Thai and English, sells language tapes and books, has a cheap cafeteria open to the public, and operates a large library filled with Western books and magazines. AUA is the largest English-language school in Thailand. Another AUA branch is located in Chiang Mai. 179 Rajadamri Rd., tel. (02) 252-8170.

Union Language School: A small but highly respected school in the Silom area offers the most rigorous Thai-language course in Bangkok. The emphasis is on practical communication rather than theoretical studies. 109 Surawong Rd., tel. (02) 233-4482.

YMCA: The Y's Siri Pattana Thai Language School teaches Thai in an informal setting, and prepares foreigners for the more advanced *Baw Hok* Grade-6 examination, a requirement for all *farangs* seeking educational jobs in Thailand. 13 Sathorn Tai Rd., tel. (02) 286-1936.

Nisa Thai Language School: Nisa offers both introductory Thai and preparation for the *Baw Hok.* 27 Sathorn Tai Rd., tel. (02) 286-9323.

Inlingua: Professional training from a member of a Swiss-based global network of 200 international language schools. Central Chidlom Tower, 7th floor, Ploenchit Rd., Bangkok 10330, tel. (02) 254-7028, fax (02) 254-7098.

Private Instruction: Most of the formal language schools can also arrange private instruction in your home or hotel. Private instructors also advertise in the *Bangkok Post.*

Educational Courses

Increasing numbers of visitors seek opportunities for in-depth study of Thai history and culture.

Chulalongkorn University: Thailand's most prestigious university offers a four-week "Perspectives on Thailand" course in Thai language, culture, and history on their campus in Bangkok. The program is given twice yearly (January and July), meets six days a week 0900-1600, and costs US$1000. Write to Perspectives on Thailand, 7th floor, Sasin Graduate Institute of Business Administration, Chulalongkorn University, Bangkok.

Oriental Hotel Cultural Programs: Bangkok's finest hotel offers short courses on the history and culture of Thailand. Lectures conducted by leading authorities cost 1800B daily or 9000 weekly, and are presented in the afternoons Mon. to Fri. in their annex across the river from the hotel. Choices include Thai Ways (Mondays), Thai Beliefs (Tuesdays), Performing Arts (Wednesdays), Contemporary Thailand (Thursdays), and Architecture (Fridays). Additional classes are also offered on Thai silk painting, gemology, mask dance, music, flower arrangements, meditation, and private tours of the Grand Palace and National Museum. Call (02) 236-0400, ext. 5, for information.

Educational Tours

Travel agents sell the standard assortment of Thailand tours, but many visitors prefer the educational tours sponsored by public and private organizations in Bangkok. Led by archaeologists, art historians, and other experts in their fields, these well-priced tours are highly recommended for all visitors.

Siam Society: Bangkok's leading private cultural organization sponsors monthly group tours to important historical and archaeological sites in

Thailand. They also take groups to major festivals and conduct environmental surveys in national parks through their Natural History Section. Upcoming tours in Thailand and to Burma, Angkor, and China are listed in the *Bangkok Post*. For further information, call their office in Bangkok or write and request a copy of their monthly newsletter which lists upcoming lectures and group tours. Yearly membership at 1500B includes access to their 20,000-volume library, subscriptions to the *Siam Society Newsletter* and *Journal of the Siam Society,* free admission to most lectures, and discounts on Society books and study trips. Siam Society, 131 Sukumvit 21, Soi Asoke (Soi 21), Bangkok 10110, tel. (02) 258-3491 and (02) 258-3494.

National Museum: The National Museum occasionally sponsors tours similar to the Siam Society's. Upcoming tours are listed on their bulletin board in the museum ticket office.

Volunteer Guide Group: Unique and personalized tours of Bangkok temples, plus overnight visits to nearby villagers, can be arranged through a small student-run group in Bangkok. Each visitor is accompanied by a student guide who will explain local customs and traditions. Public transportation is used and the tour is free except for a membership fee of 100B and travel expenses for your guide. Volunteer Guide Group, Box 24-1013, Ramkamheng Rd., Bangkok 10241.

Thai Cooking Schools

Professionally taught courses on the finer points of Thai cooking are now offered by several hotels and private organizations in Thailand.

Oriental Hotel Cooking School: Long recognized for its outstanding restaurants, the Oriental sponsors weekly cooking courses taught by some of the country's most knowledgeable chefs. Classes are held Mon.-Fri. 0900-1200 and cost 2500B per day or 11,000B per week.

Buddhist Meditation

Increasing numbers of travelers are investigating Buddhism and *vipassana* (insight) meditation during their visit to Thailand. Westerners can choose from several countryside temples that offer accommodations and English-language *vipassana* instruction. Meditation courses last two to six weeks and are free except for a small donation. A selection of meditation temples is described in the "Introduction."

The best resource on meditation *wats* is the 105-page *Guide to Meditation Temples of Thailand* published by Wayfarer Books, P.O. Box 5927-B, Concord, CA, USA 94596. This comprehensive US$10 guide also includes information on visas, travel, health, language, and ordination procedures.

Information on meditation temples can be obtained in Bangkok at the following centers.

Wat Mahathat: The International Buddhist Meditation Centre in the Dhamma Vicaya Hall to the rear of Wat Mahathat is Bangkok's best resource for information on Buddhism and meditation retreats. Founded by a Thai monk and his English wife along with scholars from adjacent Mahachulalongkorn Buddhist University, the center provides information on retreats and weekly lectures on Thai Buddhism and its significance to Thai culture. Weekend retreats at Buddha Monton in Nakhon Pathom cost 500B for food, accommodations, and transportation from Wat Mahathat. Upcoming English-language lectures are listed in the *Bangkok Post.* The center intends to publish a list of meditation *wats* that welcome Westerners. Call (02) 511-0439 or (02) 511-3549 for more information.

World Fellowship of Buddhists: English-language meditation classes for Western visitors are held on the first Sunday of every month 2000-2100. Their small bookstore offers some English literature on Buddhism, and a badly outdated guide to meditation temples in Thailand. The fellowship occasionally sponsors 10-day *vipassana* retreats at Wat Jewel Mountain and other monasteries near Bangkok. Sukumvit Rd. between Soi 1 and Soi 3.

Telephone

International telephone calls can be made from all hotels in Bangkok, and 24 hours a day, seven days a week from the telecommunications annex next to the General Post Office. Calls to North America and Europe from the telecommunications annex cost about US$10 for the first three minutes. Be sure to ask the fees before dialing from any hotel; outrageous charges are commonplace.

Local phone calls cost 1B at red phones and 3B from private phones in stores and restaurants. Most phones only accept the small 1B coin. The connection is cut after three minutes if

BANGKOK PHONE NUMBERS

airport	523-6201
eastern bus terminal	391-2504
General Post Office	233-1050
immigration	286-9176
international calls	100
Northern Bus Terminal	279-4484
phone information	13
Southern Bus Terminal	411-0511
tourist assistance	281-0372
tourist office	282-1143
tourist police	221-6209
train station	223-7010

a new coin is not inserted after the sound of a signal. (Thai area codes are listed in the "Introduction.")

Mail

The General Post Office on New Road is open Mon.-Fri. 0800-1630 and 0900-1200 on weekends and holidays. The poste restante charges 1B for each letter, and requires a passport to shuffle through the piles. A packing service with boxes in various sizes and wrapping paper is located on the right side of the lobby, an immensely useful service unavailable elsewhere in Asia. The maximum weight limit for each parcel is 10 kilos (22 lbs).

Branches of the post office are located in Banglampoo (two outlets), Siam Square, and in the Sukumvit neighborhood at Soi 23. Letters can also be mailed from any hotel.

Newspapers

Thailand's two major English-language papers are the *Bangkok Post* and the *Nation*. Both are invaluable sources of information on events, festivals, local gossip, international news, and sports back home.

Bangkok Post: The best English-language newspaper in Southeast Asia has several good features. The "Society" page provides daily announcements of upcoming cultural events, festivals, workshops, seminars, art exhibitions, and tours sponsored by the Siam Society. Letters to the editor in the "Postbag" often uncover what's best and worst about Thailand from the *farang* point of view. Editorial has an opinion column, "Dateline Bangkok," which reports on Thai-language newspapers, and "Around the World," with brief extracts from international newspapers. "Horizons," a Thursday supplement which focuses on travel in Thailand, is mindless hype peppered with an occasional piece worth clipping. The Saturday edition has several worthwhile columnists: "The Trink Page" (an iconoclastic and highly opinionated blurb on the nightlife scene), Ung Aang Talay (restaurant critic), and "Bangkok Bylines" (shopping advice). Also read the "Juke Page" on Friday (music reviews from classical to rock), and "Book Reviews" and "Maew Mong" (Thai political commentary with humor) on Thursdays.

The Nation: The Friday morning edition includes a useful tourist supplement called Saen Sanuk. The *Nation* employs fewer local columnists than the *Post*, but has a very independent voice regarding local politics: front-page editorials on military coups are more critical here than in the *Bangkok Post*.

> *Not all those who wander are lost.*
> —J.R.R. Tolkein, *Lord of the Rings*

TRANSPORTATION

AIRPORT ARRIVAL

Bangkok International Airport

Bangkok's Don Muang International Airport, 25 km north of the city, is a busy, modern place with all the standard facilities. After arrival, you first pass through immigration control to have your visa stamped, or to obtain a 15-day Permit to Stay, which is stamped on your immigration card, not in your passport. Custom formalities is fastest through the green lanes marked "Nothing to Declare." Passengers connecting directly to domestic flights to Chiang Mai, Phuket, and Hat Yai can take the enclosed walkway to the domestic terminal.

After immigration and customs, you will enter the arrival lounge filled with irritating taxi touts who direct you toward expensive private coaches and limousines; give these guys a miss unless you want to pay double the ordinary rate. The arrival lounge has a post office, left-luggage facilities that charge 20B per day per item, an emergency medical clinic staffed 24 hours a day, and international and local phones. Two restaurants, including an inexpensive self-service cafe and a deluxe joint, are located on the fourth floor. Baggage trolleys are free.

Tourist Office: First stop should be the Tourism Authority of Thailand counter for maps, weekly magazines, and other free information. Correct prices for transportation into town are posted here.

Thai Hotel Association: Hotel reservations at member hotels can be made at the adjacent THA counter. They will also call on room vacancies, and the cheapest listing (the Miami Hotel) starts at 500B per night.

Airport Bank: Unlike some airports in Asia, exchange rates are very good here at the Thai Military Bank inside the arrival lounge.

Transportation Into Bangkok

Bangkok's hotels are 30-90 minutes from city center depending on traffic. A variety of transportation is available, but ordinary taxis and minibuses are the most popular choices.

Taxi: Taxis are the best option for groups of travelers and solo travelers who want to quickly reach their hotel. Taxis are regulated by the airport authorities and cost a fixed fee. Coupons must first be purchased from the Thai Airways transportation counter to the left and then presented to the taxi driver. Two different types of services are available: ordinary taxis at 200B per carload, and airport taxis at 300B. Both types hold three or four people (depending on the quantity of luggage), and deliver you direct to your hotel.

Incoming city taxis can also be hailed in the upstairs departure area and from the highway out front. Taxis are unmetered, but a sharp bargainer can ride into town for about 160-180B. To avoid problems with the local taxi mafia, take the registered taxis with yellow-and-black license plates and avoid the unregistered models with black-and-white plates.

Minibus: Solo travelers on a budget will find air-conditioned minibuses the best choice in terms of convenience and price. Minibuses cost 120B per person, leave every 30 minutes from the front door, and deliver you direct to your hotel. Purchase tickets at the transportation counter at the left side of the arrival hall. Though somewhat slow because of traffic and the drop queue, minibuses are a fun way to meet other travelers and exchange quick stories and travel tips.

Limousine: Thai Airways operates air-conditioned limos direct to your hotel for 300B. These aren't limousines in the traditional sense, but only overpriced taxis with a fancy name.

Thai Airways Bus: A shuttle bus operates from the airport to the Thai Airways terminal at the Asia Hotel on Phyathai Road every 30 minutes 0700-2200. The shuttle costs just 60B, but onward taxis or buses largely negate any possible savings.

Public Bus: Ordinary non-air-conditioned buses—crowded and slow but very cheap—can be flagged down on the highway. Air-conditioned buses listed in the chart are less frequent but more comfortable and usually have empty seats. Ordinary bus 59 and a/c bus 3AC go to the budget accommodation district of Banglampoo. Service is sporadic for all buses; expect a wait of 20-30 minutes.

TRANSPORT FROM THE AIRPORT TO BANGKOK

TRANSPORT	DEPARTURE & DESTINATION	FARE	LAST SERVICE
Limousine	Tickets from airport counter	300B	Midnight
Taxi	From airport departure lounge	200	All night
Taxi	From highway out front	150-180	All night
Minibus	From airport counter direct to any hotel	120	2100
Bus3AC	Banglampoo	10	2000
Bus4AC	Siam Square, Silom, Malaysia Hotel	10-15	1900
Bus 10AC	Thonburi, Southern Bus Terminal	10	2000
Bus 13AC	Siam Square, Sukumvit	10-15	2000
Bus 29AC	Siam Square, Train Station	10	2200
Bus 29	Siam Square, Train Station	10	2200
Bus 59	Banglampoo	2	2200

Train: Commuter trains leave from the small Don Muang Railway Station every hour for Hualampong Station in central Bangkok. The 40-minute journey in third-class coach costs 5B, but 25-35B in rapid and express trains. To reach the train terminal, turn right in the arrival lounge and follow the signs. You must walk across the highway via a pedestrian bridge, turn left, and continue 100 meters toward the Airport Hotel.

A special a/c diesel commuter train leaves from the Don Muang station at 0850, 1140, 1435, 1655, 1940, and 2205. Tickets purchased from the limousine counter cost 100B and include transportation from the airport to the train station and a ride from Hualampong station to your hotel.

Pattaya: Buses for Pattaya cost 200B and leave at 0700, 1200, and 1900. Tickets can be purchased at the limo counter.

Airport Accommodations

The nearby Airport Hotel has first-class rooms in the US$50-100 range, and a special three-hour rate at 400-500B. 333 Chet Wudtakas Rd., Don Muang, tel. (02) 566-1020.

GETTING AROUND BANGKOK

Bangkok is a hot, bewildering metropolis without any recognizable city center—a place where only the certified insane attempt to walk any great distance. Aside from roaming the neigh-borhood near your hotel, a taxi, *tuk tuk,* or bus will be necessary. The good news is that public transportation is very cheap; the bad news is that traffic and air pollution are among the world's worst. Avoid rush hours, 0800-1000 and 1500-1800, when the entire city comes to a complete standstill.

Taxis

Taxis in Bangkok are plentiful, air-conditioned, and equipped with meters that drivers refuse to use, regarding them instead as decorative ornaments for snuffing out cigarettes and hanging flowers. Bangkok is probably the last major metropolis in the world with unmetered taxis, a sad commentary on the government's inability to restore order in the chaotic capital.

This state of affairs means that all fares must be negotiated in advance with the driver. Fares vary according to the distance, time of the day and amount of traffic (higher during rush hour), rain, and the number of one-way streets the driver must negotiate. The rule of thumb: offer half the fare the driver proposes, then agree to pay three-quarters. Fares have risen sharply in recent years due to higher petroleum prices and horrendous traffic jams that turn 20-minute jaunts into 60-minute ordeals. Medium-length journeys (e.g., Sukumvit to Silom) should cost 50-80B while longer trips (outer Sukumvit to the Grand Palace) average 80-120B. Never pay more than 150B to go *anywhere,* and ignore those absurd fares (often double or triple) posted in the luxury hotels. So much for the old saw about asking hotel employees for correct taxi prices!

Tuk Tuks

Affectionately named after their obnoxious sounds that resemble chainsaws on acid, these motorized *samlors* are noisy three-wheelers that race around at terrifying speeds, take corners on two wheels, and scream through seemingly impossible gaps. *Tuk tuks* are the cheapest form of private transportation in Bangkok and generally cost 20-40% less than taxis. However, you must bargain hard and settle all fares in advance. Few drivers speak English or understand maps, so be sure to have your destination written down in Thai or know how to pronounce it properly.

Negotiation is usually done by raising a few fingers to indicate your offer: two for 20B, three for 30. Smile and grin during price negotiation. If the driver won't come down to a reasonable price then do the taxi ballet . . . walk away shaking your head until he pulls up and waves you inside. Then hold on to your seat.

Ordinary Buses

Non-air-conditioned buses are slow and crowded, but they cover a comprehensive network and cost only two or three *baht*. The oddly named *Latest Tour's Guide to Bangkok and Thailand* shows the more popular bus routes used by visitors. Signs at bus stands also help. Buses are extra useful during rush hours when they speed along specially marked bus lanes. Service is sporadic in the evening and ends around midnight. Visitors unfamiliar with the bus system will find taxis more convenient at night. Study your bus map and write down several different numbers, unless you care to wait 45 minutes to an hour. *Beware of thieves using razor blades,* especially on crowded buses.

Air-conditioned Buses

Blue-and-white a/c buses are *much* more comfortable and less crowded than ordinary buses. Empty seats are plentiful except during rush hours. Fares range 5-15B depending on the distance. Some buses show their destinations in English on the exterior. Service ends nightly at 2000.

Riverboats

The Chao Phya Express Boat is hands-down the *best* way to move between any location on the river—especially useful between Banglampoo and the General Post Office. These open-air boats are fast, cheap, exciting, and a refreshing escape from the horrors of land transportation. Boats operate daily from 0600 to 1800 and charge 3-10B depending on the distance.

Two other types of boats work the Chao Praya River. Short and stubby ferries called *reua kham fak* shuttle across the river. These cross-river barges charge 1B per crossing.

The latest addition to the water transportation scene are noisy longtail boats called *hang yaos,* which roar along several canals in central Bangkok and charge 5-10B depending on their final destination. The longtail service on Pratunam Canal from Pratunam Market to Democracy Monument is quite useful.

LEAVING BANGKOK

By Bus

Provinces throughout Thailand can easily be reached with public and private buses. Bangkok has three public bus terminals which serve different sections of the country. Each station has different departments for ordinary and air-conditioned buses. All are well organized and have English-language signs over most ticket windows. Visitors are often approached by employees who direct them to the appropriate bus. Departures are frequent for most destinations throughout Thailand; the most difficult task is reaching the terminal!

Northern/Northeastern Bus Terminal: Destinations in the north and northeast are served by two sprawling, adjacent terminals on Paholyothin Road, on the highway toward the airport near Chatuchak Market. Take any bus going toward the airport and look for the modern complex on the right side of the highway. The Northern Terminal is divided into two wings. The first section on the right is for air-conditioned coaches (tel. 02-279-4484), the second for ordinary buses (tel. 02-279-6222).

Southern Bus Terminal: All buses to southern Thailand depart from the new terminal on Nakhon Chaisri Rd. in Thonburi. Tickets are sold from the windows near the main road. Call

A/C BUS SERVICE FROM BANGKOK

DESTINATION	TERMINAL	KMS	HRS	FARE	DEPARTURES
Ayuthaya	Northern	74	1½	35B	every 10 minutes
Ban Phe (Samet)	Eastern	223	3	80	0700, 0800, 0900, 1600
Bang Pa In	Northern	63	1	30	every 20 minutes
Chiang Mai	Northern	713	9	280	0900-1000 (4 x), 2000-2145 (8 x)
Chiang Rai	Northern	844	13	300	1930, 1945, 1950, 2000
Hat Yai	Southern	1031	14	380	every 15 minutes 1730-2015
Hua Hin	Southern	201	3	90	hourly
Kanchanaburi	Southern	129	2	60	hourly
Kampang Phet	Northern	358	5	150	1200, 2230
Korat	Northern	256	4	100	every 15 minutes
Krabi	Southern	867	14	300	1900, 2000
Lampang	Northern	668	8	220	0930, 1100, 2030, 2130, 2200
Lopburi	Northern	153	3	80	every 20 minutes
Nakhon Pathom	Southern	56	1	30	every 30 minutes
Pattaya	Eastern	132	2	60	every 40 minutes
Petchburi	Southern	135	2	60	hourly
Phitsanulok	Northern	498	5	90	hourly
Phuket	Southern	891	14	300	0800, 1830, 1900, 1930, 2000, 2030
Rayong	Eastern	182	3	80	hourly
Sukothai	Northern	440	5	160	1040, 2220, 2240
Samui Island	Southern	779	16	290	2000
Surat Thani	Southern	668	12	230	2020, 2040
Surin	Northern	451	6	170	1100, 2130, 2200, 2210
Tak	Northern	420	5	150	1300, 2210, 2230
Trat	Eastern	315	7	120	hourly 0600-1000, 2000-2400

(02) 435-1200 or (02) 435-1199 (a/c) and (02) 434-5557 (ordinary) for further information.

Eastern Bus Terminal: The Eastern Bus Terminal on Sukumvit Rd. near Soi 63 serves east coast resorts such as Pattaya, Rayong, Ko Samet, and Ko Chang. Take any bus going down Sukumvit and watch for the small terminal on the right. Call 391-9829 or 392-9227 for information on a/c services, and 392-2391 for regular buses.

Private Buses: In addition to these three government terminals, a dozen-plus small, independent bus companies operate from private terminals located throughout the city. Private buses are 30-50% more expensive than government buses, but complimentary meals and hotel pick-up are often provided, an important consideration in Bangkok. Private buses can be booked through travel agents, but compare prices carefully as they vary enormously.

By Train

Bangkok has two train stations. Hualampong Station (tel. 02-233-7010, 02-223-7020 for current schedules) near Chinatown handles trains to the north, northeast, and *some* services to the south. The Bangkok Noi Station in Thonburi handles *most* trains to the south. Travelers going south must carefully check on the correct station.

Trains from Bangkok should be booked well in advance, especially for popular destinations such as Chiang Mai, Surat Thani (junction for Ko Samui), and Hat Yai. Seat reservations can be made from select travel agents. Tickets are also sold directly at Hualampong Station in the Advance Booking Office to the *right* of the entrance; customers in the long lines to the left are purchasing same-day tickets. Be sure to pick up condensed timetables, extraordinarily useful pieces of paper.

By Air

Taxis to the airport cost 180-200B and take 30-90 minutes depending on traffic. Excess *baht* can be re-exchanged into foreign currency at the Thai Military Bank, and last-minute international phone calls can be made from the phone booth in the arrival lounge. The fourth floor has an inexpensive food mall and a semiluxurious restaurant operated by Thai International.

Airport departure tax is 200B for international and 20B for domestic flights.

PHOTOGRAPHY IN THAILAND

Dragging heavy camera equipment around Thailand has a series of drawbacks: it adds weight and bulk to your pack, the paranoia factor rises, film is often expensive, you become a target for thieves, and you will inevitably offend a few people by taking their photo. On the other hand, there are several good reasons to bring your camera: photography can be an exciting and creative hobby, your visual senses are sharpened while searching for photos, and more than anything else, your travel memories are forever saved to be shared with friends and family. Finely crafted slide shows are an excellent way to recapture that once-in-a-lifetime Asian odyssey.

Those travelers who are ambivalent about photography or want to avoid a full-sized camera outfit can opt for a small but high-quality auto-focus camera such as those made by Canon or Minolta. These lightweight cameras cost about US$100 and take excellent photos, but they lack interchangeable lenses and offer little creative control. A good choice is the compact auto-focus from Olympus which includes a handy wide-angle-to-telephoto zoom.

Serious photographers should consider a high-quality 35mm camera with three interchangeable lenses, at a cost of US$600-1200. An excellent choice would be an Olympus OM2, Nikon 8008, or Minolta Maxxam 7000, which offer all the features found on the cheaper models (auto-focus, auto-wind, etc.) together with interchangeable lenses.

Three lenses are recommended. The standard 50mm lens seems necessary, but it's really the least useful or interesting option. A 24mm or 28mm wide-angle lens is highly recommended for landscapes, architecture, and groups of people. This small, lightweight, and very inexpensive lens is the single most useful of the three. One good option is a wide-angle zoom lens such as a 20-35mm. Your third lens should be a zoom telephoto such as a 75-150mm or 90-250mm—absolutely invaluable for candid people photos and dramatic compression shots.

Because of their deep color saturations, the slide films of choice for most professional photographers are Kodachrome 64 or Fuji Velvia 100. If you're an average photographer who carries a camera every day but shoots judiciously, figure on using two or three rolls of film per week. A sensible plan is to bring enough rolls for the first few weeks, and purchase additional film in Thailand. Film prices are comparable to the U.S. Print film and all slide transparencies can be processed in one-hour photo stalls located throughout Thailand. (Kodachrome requires at least three weeks since the nearest lab is in Australia.) You'll also need a small flash, extra batteries, and a few filters.

EAST COAST

With over 2,600 km of coastline along the Gulf of Thailand and Andaman Sea, Thailand offers a wide selection of beaches and resorts with everything from first-class resorts to perfect tranquillity on unspoiled islands. While most of the better beaches and island resorts are located down south, the east coast between Bangkok and Cambodia is blessed with good beaches and pristine islands that can be reached in less than a day from Bangkok with public transportation.

But the east coast is more than just beaches and offshore islands, it is an area rich in natural resources where the future of Thailand has been laid. Government officials and economic planners have chosen the eastern seaboard as the new economic growth zone for the 21st century. Discoveries of immense deposits of natural gas and the urgent need for an alternative deep-water port to Bangkok has brought massive development on an unparalleled scale. City planners envision a megalopolis of cities stretching from Bangkok to Rayong, forming a gigantic economic engine which would rival the eastern seaboard of the United States and the Tokyo-Osaka region. Pattaya—the original beach resort in Thailand—is now flanked by the deep-water port at Laem Chabang to the north and massive oil refineries to the south. Entire cities, soon to be home to over a million Thai citizens, are under construction at breakneck speed. More than any other region, the east coast represents the future of Thailand.

Sight-seeing Highlights

The twin attributes of beach resorts and economic development have given the east coast a schizoid personality that combines pleasure with business. The end result of all this development is that the best tourist destinations are being pushed farther east toward Cambodia as travelers seek out the more idyllic beaches and islands. Visitors with sufficient time may enjoy a leisurely journey which stops at each of the following destinations, but hurried travelers should head directly to the beach or island that has the strongest appeal. Distances from Bangkok are shown after each destination.

Bang Saen (103 km): Although rarely visited by Western visitors, Bang Saen is a pleasant beach with an authentic Thai flavor where locals come to picnic and relax on beach chairs.

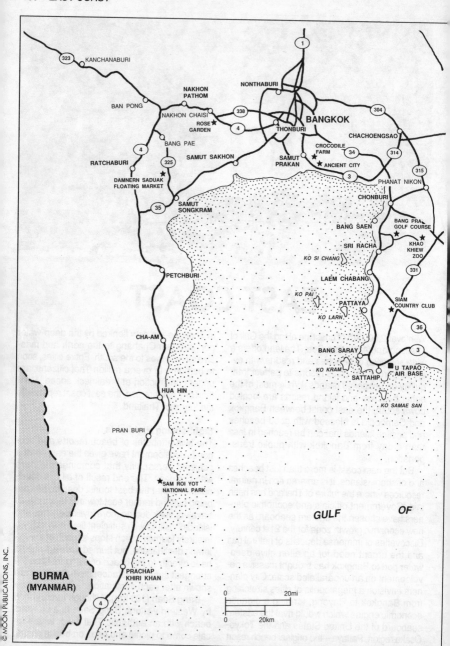

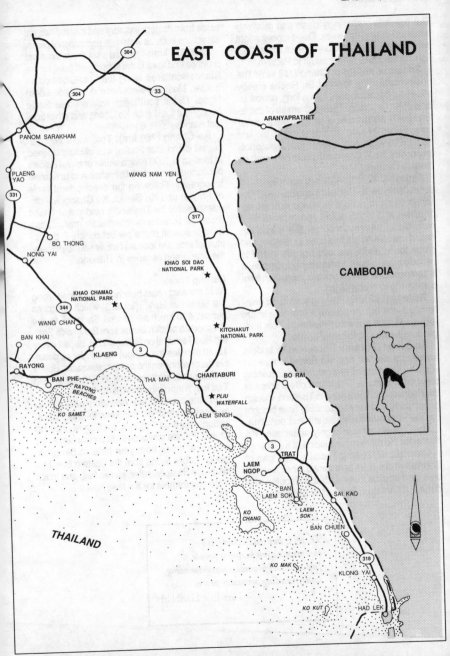

EAST COAST OF THAILAND

304
304
33
ARANYAPRATHET
PANOM SARAKHAM
PLAENG YAO
331
WANG NAM YEN
BO THONG
317
NONG YAI
KHAO SOI DAO NATIONAL PARK
CAMBODIA
KHAO CHAMAO NATIONAL PARK
344
KITCHAKUT NATIONAL PARK
WANG CHAN
BAN KHAI
KLAENG
3
RAYONG
BAN PHE
THA MAI
CHANTABURI
BO RAI
RAYONG BEACHES
PLIU WATERFALL
KO SAMET
LAEM SINGH
3
TRAT
LAEM NGOP
BAN LAEM SOK
SAI KAO
KO CHANG
LAEM SOK
BAN CHUEN
THAILAND
KO MAK
318
KLONG YAI
KO KUT
HAD LEK

The beach is surprisingly clean and relatively deserted during the week. Day-trippers might consider a quick visit to Bang Saen rather than fighting the traffic farther south to Pattaya.

Sri Racha and Ko Si Chang (118 km): The busy little fishing town of Sri Racha chiefly serves as departure point for the long, narrow island of Ko Si Chang. The southern tip of the island holds the remains of an old royal summer palace used by King Chulalongkorn in the late 19th century. Though a very modest historical monument, Ko Si Chang can easily be visited en route to Pattaya.

Pattaya (137 km): After two decades of uncontrolled growth, Thailand's original beach resort is trying to restore its image with an aggressive and highly publicized improvement campaign. The resort's personality is split between upscale hotels that cater to families and group tours, and a raucous nightlife suited to bachelors and sailors. Pattaya's mediocre beach is compensated with all types of recreation from parasailing to scuba diving.

Rayong (185 km): Rayong town is an uninspiring place but the southern coastline offers fairly good sand and accommodations from budget bungalows to mid-range hotels.

Ko Samet (210 km): Discovered by budget travelers a decade ago, Ko Samet is now favored by Thai families and group tourists rushing down from Pattaya. The island offers some of the cleanest and finest sand in Thailand, though its popularity and easy accessibility have brought problems of overdevelopment and pollution. Budget travelers have largely abandoned Ko Samet for the more remote island of Ko Chang.

Chantaburi (320 km): The fairly large town of Chantaburi lies in an area famed for rubber, rubies, and tropical fruits such as rambutan and durian. Chantaburi is a rather ordinary town aside from its gem industry and nearby natural attractions such as waterfalls and national parks.

Trat (315 km): Thailand's southeasternmost province and town is the jumping-off point for the islands scattered along the Thai-Cambodian border. Most travelers head directly to Laem Ngop, 15 km southeast, where boats leave throughout the day for Ko Chang and other tropical islands.

Ko Chang (360 km): Thailand's second-largest island after Phuket was officially opened to tourism in 1990 after a series of travel articles publicized its wonderful beaches and unspoiled topography. Following the development cycle of Phuket and Ko Samui, Ko Chang will unquestionably be Thailand's next major island resort as sun-lovers relentlessly march eastward in search of the perfect beach. A dozen-plus islands are located farther south, perhaps the final island escapes in Thailand.

Getting There

All of the east coast beaches are located along the Sukumvit Hwy. (Route 3) which stretches almost 400 km from central Bangkok to the Cambodian border. Buses from Bangkok's Eastern Bus Terminal on Sukumvit Rd. depart every 15-30 minutes throughout the day for all possible destinations on the eastern seaboard. Buses to distant destinations such as Chantaburi and Trat leave mornings only 0600-1200.

Private bus and tour operators offer similar services in small a/c minivans to major destinations such as Pattaya, Ko Samet, and Ko Chang. Private minibuses are convenient since pick-up is made from your hotel in Bangkok, though public buses from the Eastern Bus Terminal are cheaper, safer, just as fast, and much more comfortable for the long haul.

> *Travel is not really trade; it's communication between people. Just as travel promotes understanding, understanding promotes peace.*
>
> —Lars-Eric Lindblad

BANGKOK TO PATTAYA

BANG SAEN

Proceeding southeast from Bangkok, six km past the commercial city of Chonburi, lies the beach resort of Bang Saen. Once the premier weekend escape for Bangkokians, Bang Saen was replaced by Pattaya after the arrival of better highways and faster buses. Today it caters to economy-minded Thai families and groups of teenagers who sit under umbrellas or stroll along the two-km-long beach lined with coconut palms and casuarina trees.

Buses from Bangkok stop just beyond the Bang Saen intersection. Minitrucks continue four km down the road to the beach.

Attractions

Bang Saen is only average as a beach resort, though the lack of high-powered development gives it a degree of charm and a refreshingly laid-back atmosphere. A small information office is located adjacent to Ocean World.

The Beach: The beach itself is clean and relatively uncrowded on weekdays, but solidly packed on weekends and holidays. The water varies from a nice marine blue to muddy shallows at low tide. Beachside vendors rent multi-colored umbrellas, chairs, inner tubes, and sell snacks and beverages. Being a novelty at the Bang Saen beach, Westerners often find themselves invited to join locals for food and endless rounds of Mekong.

Ocean World: Popular with Thai parents and their children, this water amusement park has several swimming pools, slides, and a small roller coaster. Open daily 0930-1800.

University Aquarium: The medium-sized aquarium, on the road between the highway and the beach, was presented in 1982 to Srinakharinwirot University by the Japanese government. Tropical marinelife from the Gulf of Thailand is featured.

Monkey Cliff: A community of wild monkeys inhabits the hill and Chinese shrine at the north end of Bang Saen beach. The small temple honors the goddess spirit of a wife whose fisherman husband never returned from a fishing expedition. Chinese ascribe magical powers to the site and come to fly kites to honor the faithful wife.

Khao Khiew Open Zoo: Tour groups often visit this open-air zoo located 18 km from Bang Saen up a side road off Sukumvit Highway. The zoo was opened in 1973 to provide overflow for the cramped Dusit Zoo in Bangkok.

Bang Pra Golf Course: Located midway up the road to the zoo, this 18-hole, 7,249-yard (longest in Thailand) course has a 54-room motel, lodge, and swimming pool. Tambon Bang Pra, Bangkok reservation tel. (02) 240-9170, 1500-2300B.

Accommodations

Bang Saen Villa Resort: The only hotel situated directly on the beach has a swimming pool, airy restaurant, and a small banquet room. 140-16 Mu 14 Tambon Saensuk, Chonburi 20130, tel. (038) 381772, fax (038) 383221, 680-980B.

Bang Saen Beach Resort: A 40-acre landscaped resort with swimming pool, "gathering terrace," and accommodations in the 29-room hotel complex and 102 individual bungalows.

The resort is operated by the TAT as a training site for their nearby College of Tourism. 55-150 Tambon Saensuk, Chonburi 20130, Bangkok tel. (02) 253-3956, local tel. (038) 376675, 550-750B fan bungalows, 800-1200B a/c.

Guesthouses: Several inexpensive guesthouses in the 300-500B range are located on the beachfront road near Ocean World. Try the Seaside Palace, Seaview Bungalows, Picnic, and Sansabai Bungalows.

SRI RACHA

The next place of interest on the Sukumvit Highway is the busy fishing village of Sri Racha, best known as the production center for a pungent-sweet fish sauce called *nam prik si racha*. Sri Racha is a tidy little place which has won awards as the cleanest town in the kingdom. Facilities include several banks which exchange traveler's checks, postal center, and immigration office.

Attractions

Temples: Surasak 2 Singha Rd. has the small Wat Sri Maha Racha on the north side, and a larger Chinese temple in a back alley to the

south. The market is worth a wander, as are the stilted houses flanking the nearby pier.

Ko Loi: For a quick ride, ask the *samlor* driver to take you to a famous offshore island linked to the mainland by a 1½-km bridge. The temple features a *chedi, viharn,* and lifelike wax statue of a monk known for his miraculous healing powers. In 1959 the monk disappeared for good (allegedly with all the donations) but superstitious Thais continue to visit his shrine. The causeway is flanked with colorful fishing boats laden with arrow-shaped fish traps constructed from *nipa* palm. Fare is 10B each direction.

Accommodations

Few visitors spend the night in Sri Racha, though several inexpensive hotels are located along the waterfront and on the roads which connect the highway with the seashore. All have breezy open-air restaurants where you can enjoy the local seafood specialties.

Samchai Hotel: Located on the rickety pier across from Surasak 1 Rd., the Samchai has simple fan-cooled rooms from 120B, and a/c rooms from 250B. 3 Chomchonpon Rd., tel. (038) 311134.

Siri Wattana Hotel: Another seaside hotel with rooms with bath for 80-120B, plus views over the ocean. 35 Chomchonpon Rd., tel. (038) 311307.

Grand Bungalows: Better rooms are found in the hotel on the southern pier. 9 Chomchonpon Rd., tel. (038) 312537, 400-1000B.

Restaurants

Seafood Restaurants: Lining the seafront are several seafood restaurants serving local specialties such as sautéed oysters and shellfish. Another popular restaurant is located at the end of the pier past the stilted houses. Few have English-language menus or list prices, so check carefully before ordering.

Central Market: The most economical spot for meals is the market near the clock tower and opposite city hall.

Home & Garden Restaurant: On Jermjonpol Rd. near the Sukumvit Hwy. is a more luxurious if less atmospheric restaurant.

Transportation

Buses from Bangkok's Eastern Bus Terminal take about 90 minutes to reach Sri Racha, from

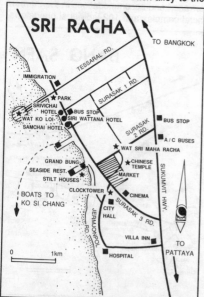

SRI RACHA

TO BANGKOK

TESSARAL RD.

IMMIGRATION

PARK

SRIVICHAI HOTEL

WAT KO LOI

SAMCHAI HOTEL

SIRI WATTANA HOTEL

BUS STOP

SURASAK 1 RD.

SURASAK 2 RD.

BUS STOP

A/C BUSES

WAT SRI MAHA RACHA

GRAND BUNG.

SEASIDE REST.

STILT HOUSES

CHINESE TEMPLE

MARKET

CLOCKTOWER

CINEMA

BOATS TO KO SI CHANG

JERMJONPOL RD.

SURASAK 3 RD.

CITY HALL

SUKUMVIT HWY.

VILLA INN

HOSPITAL

TO PATTAYA

0   1km

© MOON PUBLICATIONS, INC.

WEIRD WHEELS

The most amazing sidelight to Sri Racha is its bizarre but strangely elegant *samlors,* three-wheeled motorbike-rickshaws elongated to outrageous lengths and fitted with huge car or smaller motorcycle engines. Originally constructed from Harley Davidsons, these contraptions roamed the streets of Bangkok before being banished to Sri Racha since they were not equipped with reverse gears. All are marked on the side with painted numbers which serve as license plates. Local drivers include Thongkam Sonri, who parks his tricycle near the Savings Bank, Somsak Parnsomboon, who hails from Lopburi, and Urai Chantawat, one of the few female drivers in Sri Racha. All can provide sightseeing tours at about 60B per hour.

Unfortunately, their days are numbered since new licenses are no longer issued. The original 499 vehicles now number under 100, and the remaining permits command up to 10,000 *baht* each. Motorcycle enthusiasts will love these contraptions!

where you can walk or hire a *samlor* down to the waterfront and departure pier for Ko Si Chang. Buses from Sri Racha to Bangkok and Pattaya can be hailed on the highway or taken on Chomchonpon Rd. just past the Srivichai Hotel.

KO SI CHANG

Ko Si Chang, about 12 km off the coast from Sri Racha, once served as Thailand's custom port and was listed among the country's most popular weekend destinations. Today it's a sleepy place chiefly visited for the decaying palace of King Chulalongkorn and its highly revered Chinese temple. The long and narrow island has a small fishing village with several guesthouses and an arid climate suitable for prickly pear cactus and other desert plants.

Attractions
Ko Si Chang's two principal sights can be seen as you approach on the boat ride from Sri Racha: a Chinese temple standing prominently to the right, and the ruins of the old royal palace to the left. Si Chang is very compact and both places are within walking distance from the ar-

rival pier. Alternatively, hire a *samlor* for a three-hour, 80B tour that includes the Chinese temple, the old royal place, a tiny beach on the north coast, mango plantations, and a Buddhist cave in the center of the island.

Chinese Temple: It's a hot climb up to San Chao Por Khao Yai, but you're rewarded with outstanding marbled floors inside the shrine, a cool natural grotto with Buddha images, plus a Buddha's footprint and excellent views from the 268-meter summit. This temple is much revered by the Chinese who visit the shrine in great numbers at Chinese New Year.

Chulalongkorn's Summer Palace: The ruins of King Rama V's old summer retreat are one km left of town at the end of a roadway too narrow for cars. Construction began in 1889 after Rama's physician recommended Si Chang as a place for rest and recuperation for his royal consort and her son. Among the early buildings were the two-story Wattana Palace, the octagonal-shaped Phongsri on a nearby hill, and the Aphirom with front and rear porches. A well was dug to supply water, a lighthouse erected to provide safe passage for passing ships, and 26 roads were constructed to link the scattered residences.

In 1892 the king erected a royal compound with four throne halls, 14 royal domiciles, and a royal hillside *chedi* to honor the birth of his new son. Constructed entirely of teakwood, one of the four throne halls was later disassembled and transferred to Bangkok, where it was restored and reopened as the Vimanmek Palace. The final visit of King Chulalongkorn in 1893 was cut short when French gunships, in a territorial dispute, attacked the Thai Navy and occupied Ko Si Chang from 1893 until 1907.

The remaining buildings were deserted and largely disassembled for firewood until 1978 when Chulalongkorn University established a marine science research center on the island. In 1991 the Thai government in conjunction with the Fine Arts Department announced an ambitious restoration project.

The surviving foundations, crumbling staircases, beautiful flowering trees, and eerie reservoir blanketed with dead leaves form a pleasant if somewhat unspectacular sight. The Bell Rock near the top of the hill rings nicely when struck with a stick. It's hard to locate: look for the Thai script with yellow paint. The Asdangnimitr Temple, farther up the hill, once served as the king's meditation chambers but is now locked to protect Rama's portrait and a Buddha image cursed with ungainly large ears.

Accommodations

The solitary fishing village on Ko Si Chang has three simple guesthouses located to the left of the pier. Two guesthouses, signposted in Thai script only, have small rooms from 100B. The English-signposted Tiewpai Guesthouse has private rooms for 120B, a dormitory for 40B, and a/c rooms for 250B. The proprietor offers half-day boat trips around the island that stop at Hin Klom (Round Stone Beach) and small Tawang Beach for swimming and snorkeling. Scuba divers can explore the underwater wrecks during the dive season from November to February.

Transportation

Ko Si Chang can be reached with small fishing boats which depart hourly from the Sri Racha pier on Soi 14, between the seafood restaurants. The shuttle sputters past Russian ocean-liners, a large naval station, and cargo ships before docking at the island's nondescript Chinese fishing village. The last boat back to Sri Racha departs at 1500.

PATTAYA

Once a "sleepy fishing village" popular with harried Bangkokians and American GIs on R&R, Pattaya has since mushroomed into a major beach resort covered with high-rise hotels, roaring discos, fine restaurants, throbbing go-go bars, and lively nightclubs that comprise Thailand's original beach resort. Those seeking peace and solitude on a deserted beach should forget Pattaya and head south or east to the less commercialized beaches. Visitors who seek out nonstop entertainment and a honky-tonk environment will love Pattaya, one of the most convoluted and schizophrenic destinations in the world.

Today, this low-powered Riviera of Southeast Asia is undergoing an image crisis as it transforms itself from a bachelor's paradise to a sophisticated retreat catering to middle-aged couples and families. Pattaya's image problem stems from inadequate sewage facilities, flooding, uncontrolled commercial sprawl, drugs, prostitution, a mysterious series of murders, and water pollution so severe that tourist officials strongly discourage swimming anywhere along South Pattaya Beach. The *Far Eastern Economic Review* recently cited Pattaya's problems as a classic lesson for other Asian countries of the dangers of unplanned tourism development.

Criticism from travel agents, tour operators, and local hotel owners has finally pushed local authorities into action. Several new water-treatment plants are under construction, and South Pattaya will soon be renovated with a landfill project with a new beachfront road, pedestrian promenade, piers for excursion boats, parks, and a concert hall. Both despised and loved, Pattaya may yet prove itself the first Asian resort destroyed by tourism but saved by government intervention.

Although it's still fashionable to condemn Pattaya as superficial, overbuilt, unplanned, congested, polluted, tawdry, and having nothing to do with the *real* Thailand (all true), most of the three million annual visitors seem to come away satisfied with its wide range of hedonistic offerings.

ATTRACTIONS

Named after the southwestern monsoon wind which sweeps the east coast during the summer months, Pattaya is a beach resort dedicated to the pursuit of pleasure and love of *sanuk*. The range of activities is nothing short of amazing—sunbathing, parasailing, skin diving, golf, game-fishing, zoos, night markets, and the world-famous nightlife. Traditional culture is not much in evidence, but perhaps just to remind visitors that Pattaya is located in exotic Thailand rather than Miami Beach or Waikiki, outlying attractions include an elephant camp, Buddhist temples, and an orchid farm with Thai dancers.

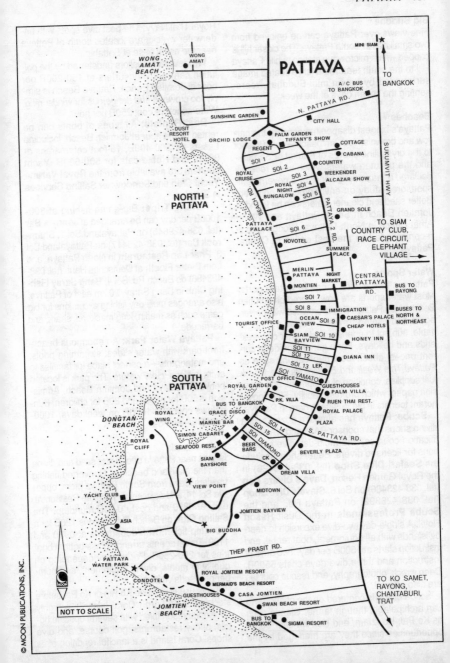

© MOON PUBLICATIONS, INC.

NOT TO SCALE

PATTAYA

TO BANGKOK

MINI SIAM

WONG AMAT BEACH

WONG AMAT

A/C BUS TO BANGKOK

SUNSHINE GARDEN

N. PATTAYA RD.

CITY HALL

SUKHUMVIT HWY.

DUSIT RESORT HOTEL

ORCHID LODGE

PALM GARDEN

TIFFANY'S SHOW

COTTAGE

CABANA

REGENT

SOI 1

COUNTRY

SOI 2

WEEKENDER

ROYAL CRUISE

SOI 3

ALCAZAR SHOW

ROYAL NIGHT BUNGALOW

SOI 4

SOI 5

GRAND SOLE

NORTH PATTAYA

BEACH RD.

PATTAYA PALACE

SOI 6

PATTAYA 2 RD.

NOVOTEL

SUMMER PLACE

TO SIAM COUNTRY CLUB, RACE CIRCUIT, ELEPHANT VILLAGE

MERLIN PATTAYA

NIGHT MARKET

CENTRAL PATTAYA RD.

BUS TO RAYONG

MONTIEN

SOI 7

SOI 8

IMMIGRATION

BUSES TO NORTH & NORTHEAST

OCEAN VIEW

SOI 9

CAESAR'S PALACE

TOURIST OFFICE

SIAM BAYVIEW

SOI 10

CHEAP HOTELS

HONEY INN

SOI 11

SOI 12

DIANA INN

SOUTH PATTAYA

SOI 13 LEK

SOI YAMATO

POST OFFICE

ROYAL GARDEN

GUESTHOUSES

PALM VILLA

BUS TO BANGKOK

P.K. VILLA

RUEN THAI REST.

ROYAL PALACE

ROYAL WING

GRACE DISCO

MARINE BAR

PLAZA

DONGTAN BEACH

SIMON CABARET

SOI 14

S. PATTAYA RD.

ROYAL CLIFF

SEAFOOD REST.

SOI 15

SOI DIAMOND

BEER BARS

BEVERLY PLAZA

SIAM BAYSHORE

CK

DREAM VILLA

YACHT CLUB

VIEW POINT

MIDTOWN

JOMTIEN BAYVIEW

ASIA

BIG BUDDHA

THEP PRASIT RD.

PATTAYA WATER PARK

ROYAL JOMTIEM RESORT

TO KO SAMET, RAYONG, CHANTABURI, TRAT

CONDOTEL

MERMAID'S BEACH RESORT

CASA JOMTIEN

GUESTHOUSES

JOMTIEN BEACH

SWAN BEACH RESORT

BUS TO BANGKOK

SIGMA RESORT

Big Buddha

Fine views over Pattaya can be enjoyed from two small hills in South Pattaya. The closer hill is capped with a microwave station, while Pattaya Hill to the south features a large seated image surrounded by seven mini-Buddhas, representing the seven days of the week.

Beaches

Pattaya's biggest disappointments are the narrow and brownish four-km beach—vastly inferior to the crystalline shores of Phuket or Samui—and the polluted waters which were recently declared a "hazardous zone" by a government-sponsored study on environmental pollution. Better sand and cleaner waters can be found at Jomtien Beach in South Pattaya and Wong Amat Beach in North Pattaya. Wong Amat is recommended as the best option to Central Pattaya.

Water Sports

Pattaya offers a wide range of water sports. Most water sports are now offered on Jomtien Beach since Pattaya Bay is crowded with powerboats and fishing trawlers. Prices are negotiable, subject to change, and higher on weekends and holidays. For a general guide to current prices, check local publications such as *Pattaya This Week* and *Explore Pattaya*. Check fuel supplies, condition of equipment, and never sign papers which promise liability. Fleecing ignorant tourists is big business here in Pattaya.

Scuba: Pattaya has almost a dozen scuba diving shops that sponsor PADI and NAUI certification courses, and multi-day dive expeditions for licensed divers. Better shops include the **Seafari Dive Shop** (tel. 038-428126) in the Royal Garden Resort, **Dave's Divers Den** (tel. 038-423486) on Soi 6, **Steve's Dive Shop** (tel. 038-428392) on Pattaya Rd., and the **Scuba Professionals** in the Dusit Resort Hotel. A single-day two-dive excursion to nearby islands with all equipment, boat rental, and instruction starts at 1500B per day. Two days of instruction and three dive days costs 5500B. Deep wreck, photography, and rescue courses are also offered.

Scuba diving is centered on the offshore Ko Lan archipelago, though farther islands such as Ko Pai, Ko Luam, and Ko Rim offer better opportunities since they are managed by the Royal Thai Navy. The best dive spots with underwater wrecks are located south of Pattaya near the naval base at Sattahip.

Windsurfers: Visitors undeterred by the pollution can rent windsurfers at 150-200B per hour at Jomtien Beach. Pattaya Beach is simply too crowded and dangerous for windsurfing. Waterscooters cost 250B per hour.

Boat Rentals: All types of boats can be rented by the hour at Jomtien Beach, including Lasers for 300-400B, 16-foot catamarans at 300B, and Hobie cats for 500-600B. Yacht charters are available from the **Royal Varuna Yacht Club** and **Sundowner Sailing Services** in Sattahip.

Fishing Trips: Big-game fishing at 800-1000B per day can be arranged at **Jenny's Bar** (tel. 038-429645) on Pattayaland Soi 1, **Shamrock Bar** (tel. 038-425417) on Pattayaland Soi 3, **Phar Lap Restaurant** in North Pattaya, and from **Dieter Floeth** at Deutsches Haus (tel. 038-423486) on Beach Rd. Soi 4. **Bang Saray Fishing Club** in Bang Saray, 20 km east of Pattaya, also arranges multi-day fishing excursions for big game such as marlin, king mackerel, shark, and barracuda.

Pattaya Water Park: An enormous beachfront park with water slides, swimming pools, and restaurants—a perfect place for families to swim in clean, clear waters. The park is located between Pattaya and Jomtien Beach. Admission is 50B for adults and 30B for children. Bungalows cost 800-1000B on weekdays, 1000-1400B weekends.

Outer Islands

Islands near Pattaya offer better sand and diving than the mainland beaches. Converted fishing trawlers leave from South Pattaya piers, opposite Soi 14, and adjacent to Tangkae Restaurant, daily at 0830 and cost 40-50B roundtrip. **The Sailing Club** on Beach Rd. charges 120B for a roundtrip ticket, with departures at 0930 and 1100. Travel agents arrange glass-bottom boat trips for 200-250B. Prices vary depending on quality of meals, diving equipment, and number of islands visited.

Tours usually include Ko Rin or Ko Pai before stopping at Ko Larn ("Coral Island"), a highly developed resort fixed with several upscale hotels, pricey restaurants, golf course, and dive shops. Coral Island is a fanciful rendition of its rather prosaic name (true translation: Bald Island). Pack food and drinks if you're counting *baht*.

Golf

Pattaya is one of the golfing centers of Thailand. Golf tours are organized through several clubs, including the **Sugar Shack** on Pattaya Beach Rd. (note the bags of clubs piled behind the pool table), **Caesar's Bar** near the police station, and the **Red Lion Pub** in South Pattaya. **Pattaya Sports Club** holds Thursday tournaments at various courses around Pattaya.

Siam Country Club: Thailand's finest course is located 20 minutes from downtown Pattaya. The 7,016-yard course charges 750B plus caddy fees for 18 holes. Call (038) 428002 for reservations.

Panya Golf Course: Pattaya's newest 27-hole course is located 40 minutes from Pattaya on the road to Bangkok. Also see "Bang Pra Golf Course," described above under "Bang Saen."

Royal Thai Navy Course: Phu Ta Luang Course (tel. 038-428422), 35 minutes distant near the naval town of Sattahip, charges just 200B plus caddy fees.

Mini Siam

Over 100 miniature reproductions of Siamese temples and palaces are located on Sukumvit Rd., about three km northeast from Central Pattaya. Recent additions include the Eiffel Tower, Big Ben, and a Thai cultural show given at 1600. Open daily 0900-2000. Admission is a ridiculous 200B, though it's easy to bargain with the admission office.

Attractions Outside Pattaya

Many of the most popular attractions are located in the countryside outside Pattaya. All can be reached with rented car or motorcycle, though travel agents sell tickets which include free roundtrip transportation from your hotel.

Nong Nooch Village: A 600-acre tourist resort with landscaped gardens, minizoo, orchid garden, and cultural shows daily at 1000 and 1500. Tickets from travel agents and from the head office (tel. 038-422958) opposite the Nipa Lodge include transportation and cost 250-300B.

Pattaya Elephant Village: Pachyderms haul logs and play soccer at the elephant *kraal* located five km from town on the road to the Siam Country Club. Elephants now lead the unemployed list after teak logging was banned in Thailand several years ago. Reservations can be booked from most travel agents. Admission is 200B; shows are given daily 1430-1630.

Bira Circuit: Named after Prince Bira, one of Thailand's best known racing enthusiasts, this 2.4-km racetrack has international events and a popular race school managed by Pacemakers AG, a European-based company involved in the racing-tire business. Rentals cost 500-800B per hour and include go-carts, Formula 3 models, and Ford 2000s.

Wat Yarna Sangvararam: Seven architecturally unique pavilions and temples in Thai, Chinese, Japanese, Indian, and Western styles are located in a 360-rai park 15 km south of Pattaya. Meditation courses are offered for visitors and the grounds are open daily 0600-1800.

Bang Saray: A small, relatively undisturbed fishing village known for game fishing and seafood restaurants lies some 20 km south of Pattaya. Fisherman's Lodge, headquarters for the Thailand Game Fishing Association, sponsors fishing trips and has a/c rooms from 600B. Fishermen's Lodge has a swimming pool, marina, and 16 standard rooms from 600B.

ACCOMMODATIONS

Pattaya divides itself into several districts. North Pattaya and Wong Amat Beach have swankier deluxe hotels, fine restaurants, and low-key nightlife suitable for families with children. Wong Amat Beach is a highly recommended area with several luxurious hotels tucked away in a semirural setting on the best beach in the area. South Pattaya has moderately priced hotels and restaurants, plus notorious nightlife that ranges from go-go bars to transvestite cabarets that rage until dawn. Jomtien Beach to the south is a family resort region with luxurious hotels, soaring condo complexes, and the best selection of water sports in the region.

Some 266 hotels are estimated to be operating in and around Pattaya. Further construction of 55 condominiums and 10 new hotels will boost Pattaya's estimated 18,000 rooms to over 25,000 by 1995. Tariffs vary according to day and season. Weekdays are cheaper than weekends, and rates are cut about 40% during the slow season from May to October. Business has been poor in recent years (occupancy rates are now under 50%), so bargain for discounts at the front desk.

Budget Accommodations

Contrary to popular belief, Pattaya has a good selection of fan-cooled hotels in the 200-250B price range and a/c rooms in the 300-400B range. Most are basic cubicles but come equipped with adequate furniture, private bath, and are perfectly acceptable for short stays. Pattaya's cheapest hotels are located on Soi Post Office, Soi Yamato, and Pattaya 2 Rd. opposite Soi 11.

Soi Post Office: Post Office Alley has several good travel agencies, the well-stocked D.K. Books, and almost a dozen small hotels with decent fan rooms for 200-250B and a/c rooms for just 300-350B. **Sureena** has both fan and a/c rooms while **Sun & Sand** has 10 a/c rooms. **Thips Guesthouse** is very cheap at just 200-250B. **Post Stuben Guest Haus** and the French-owned **Riviera Beach Hotel** have a/c rooms from 350B. **Hasse Erickson** is a Swedish favorite with both fan and a/c rooms. **Malibu** at the end of the road has similar rooms plus a free, rankly amateurish nightclub show with transvestites and Thai dancers.

Soi Yamato: Named after a Japanese restaurant located on the left, this alley has eight hotels in the 200-350B price range. **Porn Guesthouse** has a/c rooms from 300B and several fan rooms for just 150B. German-operated **Eiger Bar** has fan rooms from 180-220B. **Hotel Norge** is, as you might imagine, a Norwegian haunt with a/c rooms from 200B plus an electricity fee. **Texxan Inn** is owned by a retired USAF officer who serves enormous breakfasts and has nightly CNN broadcasts 1900-2000. **Meridian Hotel** on Pattaya Beach Rd. is a big place with a/c rooms from 500B. **PS, Siam,** and **Nipa** guesthouses are other low-priced choices.

Pattaya 2 Road Guesthouses: Ten inexpensive hotels are located back on Pattaya 2 Rd. just opposite Soi 11. Small rooms cost 150-200B with fans and 200-250B with a/c. Bargain for discounts; some places let rooms for just 100B.

ADDITIONAL PATTAYA ACCOMMODATIONS

HOTEL	SINGLE	DOUBLE	ADDRESS	PHONE (038)
Bayview	2200-2600B	2200-2600B	Central Pattaya Soi 10	428728
Eiger Bar	200-250	200-250	39-40 Soi Yamato	
Grand Palace	2000-2400	2000-2400	North Pattaya	428541
Hasse Ericksson	250-350	250-350	183/78 Soi Post Office	428208
Malibu Travel	300-350	300-350	183/82 Soi Post Office	426229
Mermaid's Beach	1200	1200-1400	Jomtien Beach	231907
Montien Pattaya	1800	2000-2800	Central Pattaya	428155
Nipa House	300-350	300-350	219/33 Soi Yamato	425851
Norge Hotel	250-350	250-350	219/17 Soi Yamato	424129
Ocean View	1400	1400	Central Pattaya	428084
Orchid Lodge	1500	1700	North Pattaya	428161
Pattaya Palace	1800	1800	North Pattaya	428487
Post Stuben	350-400	350-400	183/55 Soi Post Office	426049
Siam Bayshore	1800	1800	South Pattaya	428678
Siam Merlin Pattaya	1800	2400	Central Pattaya	428755
Sun & Sand 1	300-350	300-350	Soi Post Office	421713
Sureena B&B	200-350	300-400	183/11 Soi Post Office	429526
Texxan Inn	300-350	300-350	219/22 Soi Yamato	421383

Summer Place: Pattaya's cheapest hotel has basic rooms with fan from 150B and metered a/c rooms for an additional 50-100B per night. Summer Place is quiet and friendly, but a long walk from the nightlife and restaurant districts. 379 Soi Suk Rudee, tel. (038) 428659, 150-350B.

Sea & Sun Inn: Overlooking the beach is a small but clean hotel with fan rooms from 300B and a/c rooms from 400B. Good location and friendly management. 325 South Pattaya Rd., tel. (038) 422945.

Diana Inn: Simple rooms and a good pool make this a popular spot for budget travelers who want basic frills at low cost. Pattaya 2 Rd., Soi 11, tel. (038) 429675, 350-600B.

Palm Villa: Pattaya's best budget hotel has all a/c rooms, an attractive swimming pool, and is within easy walking distance of the bars. Pattaya Rd. 2, Soi 13, tel. (038) 429099, 400-600B.

Royal Night Bungalows: An old and slightly seedy hotel centrally located on a quiet alley. The Motel 6 of Pattaya. Soi 5, tel. (038) 428038, 400-600B.

Moderate Accommodations

Most Pattaya hotels priced in the 600-1000B price range include a/c rooms with private bath, a restaurant, and a small swimming pool. Some charge an additional 20% for tax and service.

Honey Inn: A clean, quiet, and well-located hotel with a spacious swimming pool and discounts for long-term visitors. 529 Soi 10 Pattaya 2 Rd., tel. (038) 421543, fax (038) 421946, 550-700B standard, 700-800B deluxe doubles.

P.K. Villa: Superbly located right on the beach, Pattaya's largest villa has a good pool, breezy restaurant, and friendly atmosphere. 595 Beach Rd., South Pattaya, tel. (038) 428462, fax (038) 429777, 500-800B low season, 600-900B high season.

Lek House: A new hotel with large swimming pool, billiards hall, and rooftop terrace. All rooms furnished with TV, refrigerator, and hot showers. Pattaya 2 Rd. Soi 13, tel. (038) 425550, 800-1000B.

Caesar Palace Hotel: Las Vegas comes to Pattaya in this pseudo-Romanesque 200-room hotel. The compound includes a large pool and tennis courts. Pattaya 2 Rd. Soi 10, tel. (038) 428607, fax (038) 422140, 900-1200B.

Luxury Accommodations

Luxury hotels are concentrated in North Pattaya and on Jomtien Beach to the south.

Royal Wing Cliff Hotel: Pattaya's most expensive and exclusive hotel offers 86 executive suites in their Royal Wing, private butlers, a beautiful pool, and elevators down to the private beach. Cliff Rd., tel. (038) 421421, fax (038) 428511, 4500-8000B.

Dusit Resort Hotel: Situated on 15 acres of lovely gardens with great views, two swimming pools, three tennis courts, sauna, billiards, and a health club. Best hotel in North Pattaya. 240 Pattaya Beach Rd., North Pattaya, tel. (038) 425611, fax (038) 428239, 2600-4500B.

Wong Amat: Far from the madding crowd, this low-rise bungalow is nicely set on the best beach in Pattaya. Popular with discriminating Europeans; highly recommended. Wong Amat Beach, tel. (038) 418118, 1500-2000B single, 1600-2200B double.

Jomtien Beach

Mermaid's Beach Resort: European escape with 100 well-designed rooms, private dive boats, and swimming pool just 100 meters from the sandy beach. Jomtien Beach, tel. (038) 231907, fax (038) 231908, 850-1400B double.

Ambassador Jomtien: Thailand's largest hotel has international restaurants, an amoeba-shaped swimming pool, and 5,000 rooms with views over the Gulf of Thailand. Monstrous in conception. Jomtien Beach, tel. (038) 231501, 1200-3000B.

RESTAURANTS

Pattaya's dining choices include everything from Arabic and French to Scottish and Japanese—a place where Thai food is an endangered species. Seafood is the emphasis due to the town's location on the Gulf of Thailand. Many of the best Thai restaurants are not located on Beach Rd., but rather on the side roads leading up to Sukumvit Highway.

Inexpensive

Soi Diamond Street Stalls: Good cheap alfresco dining, popular with hookers, transvestites, and sailors. Cheap street stalls are also located on Soi Post Office, Soi Yamato, and Soi Pattayaland 1 and 2. Look for the stalls that sell Thai herbal wines at 10B per shot.

Moderate

Central Pattaya Road: Several popular restaurants with low prices and wide selections are located just east of Pattaya 2 Road. The marketplace is also worth investigating.

PIC Kitchen: Classical Thai cooking in a lovely setting accompanied by jazz musicians and traditional Thai dancers on Wednesday evenings. Great atmosphere. Soi 4.

Ruen Thai: Open-air restaurant with traditional Thai dancing nightly at 1930. Pattaya 2 Rd. opposite Royal Garden Hotel in South Pattaya.

Wee Andy's: A Scottish cafe chiefly known for its misspelled menu of "flied lice, sirloin stakes," and "gurrys." 19 Pattaya Beach Road.

More Thai Restaurants: Other Thai restaurants worth hunting out include **Nai Klae** near the Alcazar, **Som Sak** on Soi 1, **Dee Prom** on Central Pattaya Rd., and **Klua Suthep** on Soi 4. All are moderately priced.

Expensive

Food Fair: Seafood restaurants at the south end of Beach Rd. let you personally select your entrée, cooking styles, and accompanying sauce, but it's advisable to avoid well-dressed touts and to double-check cooking charges before ordering. Nearby **Nang Nual** and the **Lobster Pot** on Beach Rd. opposite Soi 14 are similar options.

Dolf Riks: Indonesian dishes and Thai specialties are prepared by an Indonesian-born food critic and artist in Nakorn Center, North Pattaya. Expensive.

NIGHTLIFE

South Pattaya between Soi 13 and Soi 16 is a nonstop barrage of heady go-go bars, seedy nightclubs, high-tech discos, and outrageous live shows that cater to every possible sexual persuasion. No matter how you feel about flesh for sale, it's an amazing experience to wander down Pattaya Beach Rd. past mud wrestlers, Thai kick boxers, open-air cinemas, touts, transvestite clubs, and whatever new gimmick sweeps the night scene. Much of the action revolves around open-air beer bars in South Pattaya, where friendly ladies hail customers from the street.

Soi Diamond: A good place to start is on Soi Diamond, a small and totally crazy lane opposite the huge Grace Disco. Lively ladies working the street drag reluctant customers up to the bar stools and push them into the better bars such as **Caligula** (live shows), **Blackout** (better furnishings), **Baby A Go-Go** (best club on Soi Diamond), and **Limmatquai** (inexpensive drinks). After a few drinks, ride the circular **Chiquita Bar** that revolves like a carousel; Hunter S. Thompson on acid would love this place.

Transvestite and gay bars are wedged in the back alley. Free-lancers from open-air bars are plentiful; fees from private clubs include a 300-500B bar fine, 200-400B hotel "guest charge," and 400-800B for the girl. The **No Hands Bar** on Soi Post Office has rather unusual services upstairs. Despite all the sex and sin, Pattaya nightlife is lighthearted and good-natured, lacking the depressing pathos of Western red-light districts.

Transvestite Shows: South Pattaya's best entertainment options are the hilarious transvestite shows that take place nightly in the **Simon Cabaret** (50-100B depending on where you sit) and the monstrous **Marine Bar**, which caters to "girls, guys, and in-betweens." If you haven't noticed by now, transvestites *(gatoeis)* are plentiful here in Pattaya. Since most Westerners have a difficult time distinguishing between girls and *gatoeis,* proceed with caution unless you seek a wild war story.

Professional shows of world-class caliber are given at **Tiffany's** and **Alcazar Cabaret**, both located in North Pattaya. Alcazar features a troupe of 60 *gatoeis* who perform three times nightly in their 800-seat theater . . . the largest transvestite show troupe on earth! Tiffany's is an 850-seat theater with 50 performers who pose for photo sessions after the three nightly shows. Both places charge 300-350B depending on where you buy your ticket.

Gay Clubs: Pattaya has over a dozen gay clubs that offer boys, near-boys, and nightly cabaret shows. The largest concentration of gay clubs is on Soi Pattayaland 1, 2 and 3 where the **Cock Pit**, **Le Cafe Royal**, **Rainbow Bar and Gym**, **Rendezvous**, and **Boys, Boys, Boys** are located. Other places include the **Nautilus** in North Pattaya next to Dolf Riks and **Adam & Eve** on Soi 2.

Discos: Pattaya has several large discos filled with Thai teenagers, cruising call girls, and Western tourists. **Disco Duck** in the Pattaya Resort Hotel on Central Pattaya Rd. is your best bet for flashing lights and extremely loud rock music. **Marine Disco** upstairs from the Marine Bar is a funky place filled with hookers and sailors. **Pattaya Palladium** on Pattaya 2 Rd. Soi 1 bills itself as the largest disco in Thailand; recorded music on weekdays and live bands on weekends. All charge 80-120B for admission plus a free drink.

INFORMATION AND SERVICES

Tourist Office: The TAT office (tel. 038-428750) at 382 Beach Rd. has maps, hotel lists, and can help with upcoming festivals and sporting events. They also have information on other east coast destinations such as Rayong, Chantaburi, and Ko Chang. The Tourist Police office (tel. 038-429371) is located next door.

Maps: The TAT has a very good, free map available from their office. The *Pattaya/Eastern Part* map published by Prannok Witthaya has a larger-scale version of Pattaya plus an excellent map of the entire eastern seaboard.

transvestite follies

Tourist Magazines: The latest word on hotels, restaurants, and nightlife can be culled from free magazines such as *Explore Pattaya* and *Pattaya This Week*. Trink's gossipy column in the *Bangkok Post* is also worth checking for bar and restaurant promotions. English-language local newspapers cover real estate investments and advertise bankrupt nightclubs for sale.

Books: Duang Kamol Bookstore (D.K. Books) on Soi Post Office has the best selection of travel guides in Pattaya. As of this writing, there are no current and/or comprehensive guides to Pattaya and the east coast of Thailand.

Visas: Visas may be quickly extended at the Chonburi Immigration office on Soi 8. Visa photos and the necessary Xeroxes can be made at the small office just outside their front gate. Thirty-day extensions cost 500B.

Telephone: International calls can be made 24 hours daily from all major hotels, the exchange service in South Pattaya, and from . . . Simon Cabaret! The telephone area code for Pattaya is (038).

Post Office: The Pattaya Post Office (tel. 038-429341) is located, sensibly enough, on Soi Post Office between Sois 13 and 14.

Travel Agents: Budget travel agencies are most plentiful on Soi Post Office (Tai Pan, Lee Tours) and on Soi Yamato. Day tours offered include Ko Samet (600B), Chonburi Temples and Museums (600B), Chantaburi Gem Mines (900B), Bangkok (1200B), Damnern Saduak Floating Market (1200), Ayuthaya (1200B), and River Kwai (2200B). The Chonburi and Chantaburi tours are worthwhile, but the other excursions are far too time-consuming as single-day options. Prices for tours and international travel vary widely, so shop around before signing those traveler's checks.

Cautions: Pattaya police urge visitors to not carry too much money, never accept drinks or food from strangers (knockout drugs are common), keep off motorcycles unless an experienced driver, and check prices before buying *anything*.

TRANSPORTATION

Transportation To Pattaya

Pattaya is 147 km southeast of Bangkok.

Train: The State Railways of Thailand has daily service at 1053 and 1738 from Hualamphong Station. The three-hour journey passes through attractive scenery and is a wonderful alternative to the buses.

Bus: Ordinary and a/c buses depart every 30 minutes between 0630 and 2100 from Bangkok's Eastern Bus Terminal on Sukumvit Rd. Soi 63. These government-franchised buses cost 50B a/c and take about three hours to reach the small, very poorly marked *bor kor sor* (government) bus station located on North Pattaya Rd. near the Sukumvit Highway. The beach is about four km down the road; hire a private *songtao* to your hotel for about 40B, or flag down a public *songtao* and pay just 5B.

Private bus companies such as Diamond Coach and Erawan operate daily a/c buses from major Bangkok hotels direct to your hotel in Pattaya. These buses cost double the a/c government buses but avoid the hassle of getting to the government bus station on Sukumvit Road.

Hydrofoil: Thai Intertransport has hydrofoil service from the Menam Hotel in Bangkok to Pattaya and Hua Hin for about 1000B.

From Bangkok Airport: Buses depart from Bangkok Airport every two hours from 0900 to 2000. Tickets cost 100B and are sold at the Thai Limousine desk.

Getting Around

Pattaya is a relatively small town that can be easily explored on foot or with public transportation.

Minitrucks: Compact Pattaya is served by *songtaos* which cruise the main roads and, within the city limits, charge a flat fee of 5B. Chartered *songtaos* outside the city limits cost 10B to Nakula Beach and 40B to Jomtien Beach.

Motorcycles: An excellent way to avoid obnoxious mini-truck drivers and reach outlying attractions is with a rented motorcycle. All bikes should be checked carefully for damage before depositing your passport with the rental agency and taking off. International Drivers Licenses are rarely checked. Small bikes under 150cc cost 150-200B per day and are perfectly adequate for local rides. Larger bikes fitted with an amazing variety of illegal modifications are available from vendors on Pattaya Beach Road. All of these monster bikes are imported as disassembled parts from Japan and reconstructed by local motorcycle enthusiasts. Most are for sale at very low prices (50,000B for a late-model Ninja 750), but few are legally registered with the Thai government.

No matter what size you select, be very careful riding around town; a frightening number of tourists end their vacations on the streets of Pattaya.

Cars and Jeeps: Both self-drive and chauffeur-driven cars can be hired from **Avis** at the Dusit Resort in North Pattaya, the Royal Garden Hotel in Central Pattaya, and the Royal Cliff Hotel towards Jomtien Beach. **Hertz** is based at the Montien Hotel. Jeeps can be rented from vendors on Beach Rd. but be advised that insurance is rarely available and visitors are held responsible for any damage or injury caused in an accident.

Leaving Pattaya

To Bangkok: Ordinary and a/c government buses depart every 30 minutes between 0600 and 2100 from the government bus terminal on North Pattaya Rd. near the Sukumvit Highway. These buses terminate in Bangkok at the Eastern Bus Terminal on Sukumvit Rd. Soi 63, from where city buses continue into town. Ordinary service costs 35B; a/c coaches are 55B.

An easier option are the orange buses which travel down Beach Rd. every 30 minutes, stopping for passengers at the intersection of Beach and South Pattaya roads. Wave frantically at the bus driver as he dodges the weaving cars and motorcycles. Tickets to Bangkok cost 35B.

Private bus companies such as Diamond Coach and Erawan provide pickup at Pattaya hotels and drop-off at major hotels in Bangkok. **Diamond Coach** buses (tel. 038-428195) leave from the Nipa Lodge Hotel at 0830, 1230, and 1700. **Erawan Coach** buses (tel. 038-423871) leave from the Siam Bay View Hotel at 0900, 1300, and 1700. These buses cost 120B one way and take about three hours to reach Bangkok. A very popular service; tickets should be purchased several days in advance.

To Northern Bus Terminal: Visitors heading from Pattaya north to Chiang Mai should take a

bus direct from Pattaya's bus terminal on North Pattaya Rd. to Bangkok's Northern Bus Terminal. This connection saves precious hours and avoids the traffic snarls that plague Bangkok.

To Bangkok Airport: Buses from the terminal on North Pattaya Rd. to Bangkok Airport cost 100B and depart every two hours from 0700 to 1700. Thai International offers a private bus service for 200B from the Royal Cliff Beach Resort. All take almost three hours to reach the airport.

To North and Northeast Thailand: Destinations in the north such as Chiang Mai and Mae Sai, and northeastern towns such as Korat and Ubon can be reached directly by buses departing from a private bus terminal located on Sukumvit Hwy. near Central Pattaya Road. Buses to Chiang Mai depart at 1330 and 1645, to Korat and Khon Kaen every 15 minutes from 2100 to 2330.

To Rayong and Ko Samet: Orange public buses to Rayong can be hailed on the main highway. Minibuses continue from Rayong down to Ban Phe, the departure point for boats to Ko Samet. Private minibus service is available from Pattaya to Ban Phe, though you'll pay three times the ordinary rate for the convenience factor.

> *The sole cause of man's unhappiness is that he does not know how to stay quietly in his own room.*
>
> —Blaise Pascal, *Pensées*

RAYONG TO CAMBODIA

RAYONG TOWN

The town of Rayong is a rather nondescript provincial capital, 220 km on the old Sukumvit Highway (Route 3) or 185 km on the newer Route 36 from Bangkok. Rayong Province is a fruit-growing center, famous for its durian, pineapple, fish sauce *(nam pla)*, and fish paste

(kapi). Rayong chiefly serves as a transit point for excursions to Ko Samet via the nearby port town of Ban Phe, though miles of unspoilt beaches are located to the east between Ban Phe and Laem Mae Phim.

Attractions
Sights in Rayong are limited to a few temples and historical shrines that commemorate the lib-

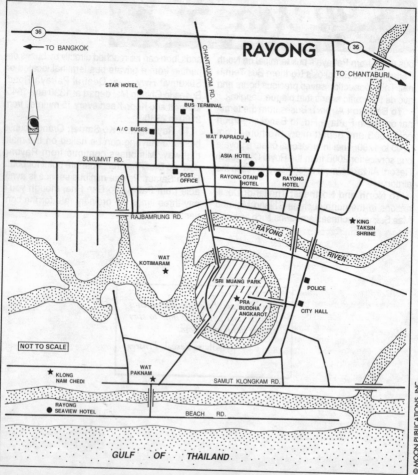

eration of Thailand from Burmese occupation.

Wat Papradu: Located in the center of town a few blocks east of the bus terminal, this Ayuthaya Period temple enshrines a large 12-meter reclining Buddha that lies on its left rather than traditional right side. The entrance alleyway is adjacent to the Asia Hotel.

King Taksin Shrine: Two blocks south of Sukumvit Hwy., on the grounds of Wat Lum Mahachai Chumphon, is a shrine which honors the early Siamese king who rallied his army and freed the country from Burmese forces.

Pra Buddha Angkarot: The principal Buddhist image in Rayong is located in Sri Muang Park near City Hall. The 70-rai park provides a welcome escape from the concrete blandness of Rayong.

Klong Nam Chedi: A 10-meter white *chedi* of indeterminate age lies on an islet at the mouth of the Rayong River, about two km southwest of town. An annual festival with boat races and folk plays is held here in November.

Fish Sauce: Rayong and Ban Phe are famous for their production of pungent sauces and thick pastes made from small silver fish which are allowed to decompose in the open air for about seven months, crushed, filtered, and bottled on the spot.

Accommodations

Hotels in Rayong are found along Sukumvit Hwy. and around the bus terminal.

Budget: The **Rayong Hotel** at 65 Sukumvit Rd. and **Rayong Otani** have fan rooms from 100B and a/c from 250B. Both are located on the south side of the road, four blocks east of the bus terminal. The **Asia Hotel** on the north side of the road has a/c rooms for 250-400B.

Star Hotel: Top-end choice is the new 240-room Star Hotel located behind the bus terminal. Facilities include a swimming pool, Japanese restaurant, sauna, and nightclub. 109 Rayong Trade Centre Rd., tel. (038) 614901, fax (038) 614608, 750-850B.

RAYONG BEACH

Most visitors travel directly from Bangkok or Pattaya to Ko Samet, skipping the long and clean beach which stretches almost 15 km southwest from Ban Phe to the craggy cape at Laem Mae Phim. Much of the region lies within the Ban Phe Forest Preserve and has escaped the crass commercialism of Pattaya and Ko Samet. The narrow, casuarina-lined beach is rather ordinary near Ban Phe, but quite white and clean farther south toward Laem Mae Phim. The Thai government has designated the Rayong coastline as a tourist development area to divert travelers away from congested Bangkok.

Accommodations

The entire beach is dotted with over 30 mid-priced bungalows and a few upscale hotels and resorts which cater to wealthy Bangkokians and Chinese who arrive during the summer months to enjoy the famous fruits. A good map of the beach with accurate locations of bungalows can be obtained from the TAT office in Pattaya.

Most places charge 400-600B for individual bungalows and 800-1000B for a/c chalets. **Rayong Resort** (Bangkok tel. 02-258-4461) has 45 deluxe rooms from 1200B nicely set on Laem Tarn Cape, three km northwest of Ban Phe. **Rung Napa Lodge** (Bangkok tel. 02-277-0288), 14 km southeast of Ban Phe, has 13 lodges priced from 600B. **Wang Kaew Resort** (Bangkok tel. 02-252-5053), 17 km southwest of Ban Phe, has camping tents and cozy bungalows from 800B. **Palmeraire Beach Hotel** (Bangkok tel. 02-213-1162), three km past Wang Kaew Resort, is a luxurious hotel with swimming pool, tennis courts, Chinese restaurant, and 60 rooms priced from 800B. Beaches near the Palmeraire and beyond are almost completely deserted.

BAN PHE

The small fishing town of Ban Phe, 15 km from Rayong, is the jumping-off point for Ko Samet. The town has some fine old wooden architecture and a colorful fish market at the pier. Located just south of the pier is the Sobha Gardens, a small botanical enclave with three classical Thai houses furnished with traditional fixtures.

Accommodations

Most visitors go directly to Ko Samet, but inexpensive guesthouses and hotels are available if you miss the last boat at around 1700. **T.N. House,** two blocks north, is a new and very clean guesthouse with rooms from 120B. **Nu-annapa Hotel**, two blocks back from the pier, is an older property with fan rooms from 150B and a/c rooms from 250B. Top-end choice is the **Pine Beach Hotel**, 300 meters south of town, where a/c rooms go from 400B.

Transportation

Ban Phe can be reached directly with ordinary and a/c buses from Bangkok's Eastern Bus Terminal on Sukumvit Road. Malibu Travel in Pattaya has direct minibus service. The Pattaya TAT can help with public buses from Pattaya. From Rayong, take a minibus from the bus terminal to Ban Phe.

Malibu Travel, located in the alley opposite the pier, has hourly minibuses to Pattaya for 120B. Nearby **SK Travel** has similar services. **DD Tours** on the waterfront sells ordinary (40B) and a/c (70B) bus tickets to Bangkok. Ordinary *bor kor sor* buses for Pattaya and Bangkok depart hourly just south of the pier. The cheapest way to Chantaburi and Trat is with motorcycle taxi to the main highway for 15B, from where you can flag down ordinary buses heading east.

KO SAMET

This hot and dry island, lying 6½ km offshore from Bang Phe, is blessed with extremely fine white beaches and clear blue waters sandwiched between craggy headlands. Thais know Samet as the island where Sunthorn Phu, Thailand's greatest poet, based his most famous work, *Pra Apaimanee*. Ko Samet's great appeal is its easy accessibility to Bangkok and crystalline sands that remain among the purest and finest in all of Thailand.

The island was first discovered in the mid-1970s by young Thai weekenders seeking a quick escape from Bangkok. In October 1981 the island was declared a national park and put under the administration of the Forestry Department to prevent overdevelopment and avoid the curses of high-rise hotels, noisy discos, traffic jams, prostitutes, and other problems common to Pattaya and Phuket.

But developers continued to build without permits and local officials did nothing to stop the encroachment. By the late 1980s the island was overrun with bungalows that dumped raw sewage into the ocean and suffered from a complete lack of sanitation and basic infrastructure. Ko Samet became the latest environmental disaster in Thailand.

On 23 May 1990, a special task force of Thai police launched a blitzkrieg, closing down dozens of bungalows and rounding up unlicensed operators. The island was declared off-limits for 48 hours and tourists were restricted to day visits. The crackdown quickly failed after intense political and economic pressure was applied from corrupt forestry officials and influential businessmen. The significance of the Samet crackdown lay more in its symbolism than substance, though it helped raise a national outcry about overdevelopment of once-unspoiled paradises.

What will happen to Ko Samet? The government is caught in a quandary about separating encroachers who hold back-dated titles and those who hold genuine land titles issued before the island was declared a national park. Park rangers are always there to collect the 5B national park admission fee, yet decent roads and an adequate sewage system still seem years away. Ten years ago there was virtually nothing on the island, but today there are dozens of hotels that push windsurfing, Jet Skis, motorboats, motorbikes, and videos during the evening meal. Trash piles up on the beach while offshore coral reefs suffer from overfishing and pollution.

Though the squeaky sand is about the finest in Thailand and the beautifully shaped coves remain inviting, Samet desperately needs attention before it will begin to approach the comfort and attractiveness of Ko Samui or Phuket. Unless the Thai government takes immediate action, the future of Samet—along with other islands such as Ko Phi Phi and Ko Chang— seems extremely bleak.

Accommodations And Beaches

Samet's eastern coastline is partitioned into a series of beaches and coves filled with bungalows in all possible price ranges. Those on the northern and central beaches are the most developed and expensive. Southern beaches offer less-expensive bungalows and primitive bamboo huts badly overpriced at 80-120B per person. Prices rise sharply during weekends and holidays when Thai teenagers, hippies, gays, and folk musicians pack the island.

Ko Samet is, technically speaking, a national park where camping is legal and free anywhere on the island despite signs to the contrary posted by unscrupulous bungalow operators. Bring a tent to improve your life-style.

Ko Samet is extremely dry except for a short rainy season from May to July. The island is parched like Death Valley during the high season from November to February, when water shortages might bring additional charges for showers and drinking water.

Beaches below are described starting from Hat Sai Kao at the northern end to Ao Kiu at the southern tip.

Hat Sai Kao

"Diamond Sand," Ko Samet's longest and most impressive beach, is popular with families with children and tourists down from Pattaya. Located 10 minutes by foot from Na Dan ferry landing, Sai Kao Beach offers over a dozen moderately priced bungalows with restaurants and watersport facilities that face the broad beach. As with nearly all places on Ko Samet, most bungalow operations have old huts constructed a decade ago and new bungalows erected just last month. All charge 150-300B for simple huts with common bath, and 300-600B for individual bungalows with fan and private bath.

Water sports include windsurfing (100B per hour), boat trips around the island (150B), and snorkeling expeditions to nearby islands (500B per day). A concrete mermaid and phallic shrine have been erected at the southern end of the beach. Magnificent sunsets can be enjoyed from the promontory above the white Buddha.

The following is a sampling of moderately priced bungalows:

Diamond	150-500B
Ploy Talay	200-500B
Sai Kaew Villa	300-800B
Seaview	100-250B
Toy	150-300B
VK Villa	150-300B
White Sand	200-500B

Pai Beach

Paradise Beach (also called Phai Beach) is a small cove with several bungalows, travel offices such as Citizen Travel, and a small post office with post restante facilities.

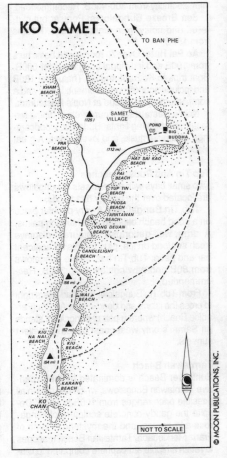

KO SAMET

TO BAN PHE

KHAM BEACH

SAMET VILLAGE

POND

BIG BUDDHA

(125 l)

(112 m)

PRA BEACH

HAT SAI KAO BEACH

PAI BEACH

TUP TIN BEACH

PUDSA BEACH

TARNTAWAN BEACH

VONG DEUAN BEACH

CANDLELIGHT BEACH

(56 m)

WAI BEACH

KIU NA NAI BEACH

(62 m)

KIU BEACH

(54 m)

KARANG BEACH

KO CHAN

NOT TO SCALE

© MOON PUBLICATIONS, INC.

Naga's Bungalows: Justifiably one of the most popular gathering spots on Samet, Naga's serves freshly baked goods and decent fish specialties, plus keeps a sprawling library of yellowing paperbacks. Try the lemon meringue pie, fudge brownies, and piña colada sundae. Snorkeling equipment, surfboards, and sailboats can be rented here and at nearby **Odd's Little Huts** (formerly Nui's Bungalows). Glass-bottom boat tours of the nearby coral beds cost 150B. Rooms at Naga's and Odd's cost 100-300B.

Samed Villa: Good restaurant with bamboo furniture, plus varnished bamboo bungalows with electricity from 300-400B. Recommended.

Sea Breeze Bungalows: Popular but cluttered and noisy from nightly videos. Rooms from 150B.

Ao Pai Huts: Over 70 rooms with basic huts from 100B and individual bungalows for 600B. Boat trips to Ko Kudi and Ko Thalu cost 180B and include snorkeling equipment, lunch, and a complimentary barbecue at Nop's Restaurant.

Nop's Restaurant: Four levels of dining terraces with blinking lights, Buddhas, woodcarvings, Balinese music, and lovely views. A great place to dine.

Tup Tin And Pudsa Beaches

Two small bays with several sets of bungalows are located over the craggy headlands.

Tub Tin Bungalows: A very popular place on a good beach blessed with hanging palms. A large, well-decorated restaurant displays fresh seafood on ice, plus there's an adjacent bar and patio. Tub Tin has simple bungalows from 80B and new chalets from 300B. Recommended.

From Tub Tin Bungalow, the road veers right to cross the island and dead-end at Ao Pra (Paradise Beach) where a pair of bungalows stands on Samet's only west coast beach. Excellent sunsets.

Tarntawan Beach

Sunflower Beach is dominated by the expansive Tarntawan Bungalows, which has huts in all possible price ranges from 100B to 600B. Despite the gaudy concrete sculpture of kangaroos and horses, and the mysterious tomb of Franz Merklebach, Tarntawan Beach manages to retain a hippie atmosphere compared to Diamond and Wong Duan beaches.

Vong Deuan Beach

Ko Samet's second most popular beach (after Hat Sai Kao) is located on a beautifully arched bay bisected by a rickety pier. After the island seizure of 1990, local park officials erected a sign which stated "no overnight stay on visit to Samed Island. Accommodations have been seized as legal evidence for forest encroachment."

Vong Deuan (Wong Deurn or Deuan) is a yuppie destination filled with tourists from Pattaya and Europeans on package holidays. **Sea**

Horse Travel, in the middle of the beach, changes traveler's checks, has a mobile telephone, and sells tickets to Ko Chang and Bangkok. Swiss-managed **Delfimarin Diwa Diving Center** arranges scuba dives to nearby coral beds, shipwrecks, and longer multi-day journeys to islands near Ko Chang.

Vong Deuan can be reached directly from the Ban Phe Pier, but you'll need to inquire about the correct boat. Boats back to Ban Phe depart daily at 1130, 1530, and 1830. The beach has five midpriced to expensive bungalows.

Tents: Tents can be rented from the shop at the north end of the beach from a beautiful lady named Pia; 50B for small tents and 150B for large ten-man tents.

Malibu Garden Resort: All-white A-frame huts with private bath and electricity for 400-750B. Tel. (01) 321-0345.

Sea Horse: The cheapest place on Vong Deuan Beach has simple bamboo huts for 150B, midsized wooden huts facing the water for 250B, and larger huts to the rear for 350B. All are overpriced when compared to Ko Samui or Ko Chang.

Vong Deuan Resort: A relatively luxurious place with standard bungalows from 600B and seaview chalets from 900B. Bangkok tel. (02) 250-0424.

Vong Deuan Villa: Located at the southern end of the beach, Vong Deuan Villa has a miniature golf course, billiards tables, and charges 600B for small fan-cooled bungalows, 1500B for a/c rooms, and 2500B for VIP chalets. Although an incredible rip-off, the restaurant has good food with great views from the terrace. Tel. (01) 321-0789.

Candlelight Beach

Also called Ao Thian, this long and rocky beach has two sets of primitive bungalows that offer an escape from the commercialism of other beaches.

Candlelight Bungalows: A variety of bamboo and brick huts for 100-350B. The office is located in the octagonal building above the open-air restaurant.

Lung Dam Bungalows: Adjacent to the collapsing pier are bungalows priced from 80B.

Wai Beach

A fairly nice beach dominated by the upscale Samet Ville Resort. Fan-cooled rooms cost 600B per person and include three meals, drinks, and the boat ride from Ban Phe. Call DD Tours in Bangkok at (02) 392-9277.

Kiu Beach

Ko Samet's most attractive beach is clean, quiet, and graced with a beautiful row of swaying palm trees. Sunsets can be enjoyed from the western beach and from the hillside viewpoint.

Kiu Coral Beach Bungalows: Old bamboo bungalows with common bath cost 80B, 150B with private bath, and 300-500B in better chalets. Their restaurant has a 13-page menu with seafood and Wild Boar Curry. Ao Kiu is a very long walk from Hat Sai Kao Beach, but well worth the trouble if you're looking for peace and solitude. The *Thep Chomlatee* boat departs daily from Ban Phe at 0830.

Transportation

Air-conditioned buses leave every hour for Ban Phe from the Eastern Bus Terminal in Bangkok. Alternatively, hourly buses go to Rayong from where minibuses continue to Ban Phe.

Travel agencies on Khao San Rd. in Bangkok arrange direct minibuses to Ban Phe including boat trip to Ko Samet for about 220B, an expensive if convenient alternative to public transportation.

Boats to Ko Samet leave regularly from Ban Phe from 0800 to around 1700. Be careful climbing onto these converted fishing boats—mishaps are common. Boats go to Na Dan (Samet Village) at the north end, Hat Sai Kao, Vong Deuan, and other beaches. Unless you enjoy long and dusty hikes, ask around and take a boat direct to a specific beach.

Minibuses return from Ban Phe back to Rayong until sunset. Don't believe taxi driver scare stories, "Last bus already go." See "Ban Phe" for more information.

CHANTABURI

Chantaburi, a busy commercial city 330 km from Bangkok, is famous for its gem industry, durian plantations, and Vietnamese-Christian population which fled religious persecution in the late 19th century. Because of its proximity to Cambodia, Chantaburi (City of the Moon) has figured prominently in Thai history as the site of border skirmishes between the Thais and the French who occupied the city from 1893 to 1904.

Contemporary Chantaburi shows strong Chinese influence in its temples, shrines, restaurants, script, and surprising number of beautiful Thai-Chinese women. The downtown section is a hopeless, confusing network of streets, but the riverside area and adjacent parks are relaxing places to wander and watch the local people.

Attractions

Chantaburi has few Western visitors, though the town has enough charm and attractions to merit a quick visit. The following half-day walking tour covers the highlights.

Riverside Walk: Begin your walk on Sukapiban Rd. (also called Rim Nam Rd.) at the bridge behind the Kasem Sarn I Hotel. This narrow road features old-style houses with intricate woodcarvings and elaborate wooden altars that evoke a timeless atmosphere. Watch for religious-supply stores, Chinese funeral shops selling paper cars and cardboard yachts, 19th-century Chinese medicine halls, and old buildings fixed with French-colonial shutters and filigree plasterwork.

Church of the Immaculate Conception: Chantaburi's great historic structure was constructed in French style between 1906 and 1909 by Vietnamese-Chinese Catholics persecuted by Emperor Gia Long. Inside the Gothic interior are 26 Moorish-style arches and pediments painted pale green, wooden pews, stained-glass windows imported from Europe, and a semicircular teak roof with three shellwork chandeliers.

Gem Dealers: Much of the jewelry sold in Thailand contains gemstones dug from the open-pit mines near Chantaburi. Chinese gem dealers operate from sidewalk stalls and in elaborate Greco-Roman showrooms just off Sukapiban Rd. near the bridge. Business is liveliest on weekends; only recognized customers are allowed into the larger gem shops.

King Taksin Park: A large public park with an artificial lake and statue of King Taksin provides an escape from the traffic. The nearby food-stalls and Versailles Coffee Pub are great places to eat and mingle in the evening.

Central Market: Wedged between a confusing network of streets and alleys is the lively market filled with local fruits and handicraft specialties, such as famous reed mats from the nearby village of San Hin.

Attractions Outside Chantaburi

Chantaburi travel agents can arrange tours to the following sights. Local buses leave from the terminal on Saritdet Road.

Wat Bot: Sited on a promontory overlooking the river, Wat Bot offers some chipping murals dating from the reign of King Rama IV that depict the 10 previous lives of the Buddha.

Gem Mines: Over 70% of Thai gemstones come from the region near Chantaburi, Trat, and Sisaket on the Cambodian border. Tours to nearby mines such as Khao Ploi Wan (Sapphire Ring Mountain), 11 km southwest of Chantaburi, can be arranged through local agencies. A Sri Lankan-style *chedi* constructed during the reign of King Mongkut caps the small hill. Blue sapphires, garnets, zircons, and highly prized Siamese rubies are also mined east of Chantaburi near Ban Nong Bon and Bo Rai.

Laem Singh: The struggle between Thai and French forces is commemorated by two buildings constructed by the French in 1893 on Singh Cape, 31 km south of town. Tuk Daeng ("Red House") once served an officers' mess hall and administrative headquarters, while the leaning

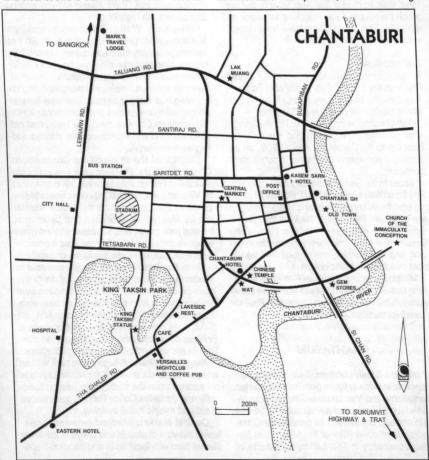

CHANTABURI

TO BANGKOK

MARK'S TRAVEL LODGE

TALUANG RD.

LAK MUANG

SUKAPIBAN RD.

LEBNARN RD.

SANTIRAJ RD.

BUS STATION

SARITDET RD.

KASEM SARN 1 HOTEL

CHANTARA GH

OLD TOWN

CITY HALL

STADIUM

CENTRAL MARKET

POST OFFICE

CHURCH OF THE IMMACULATE CONCEPTION

TETSABARN RD.

CHANTABURI HOTEL

CHINESE TEMPLE

WAT

GEM STORES

RIVER

KING TAKSIN PARK

KING TAKSIN STATUE

LAKESIDE REST.

CHANTABURI

HOSPITAL

CAFÉ

SI CHAN RD.

VERSAILLES NIGHTCLUB AND COFFEE PUB

0   200m

EASTERN HOTEL

THA CHALEP RD.

TO SUKUMVIT HIGHWAY & TRAT

© MOON PUBLICATIONS, INC.

brick Khok Khi Kai ("Chicken Shit Prison") held prisoners below the chicken coop.

Pliu Waterfall: A small waterfall is located in Khao Sabap National Park, 17 km southeast of Chantaburi. Facing the falls is a stone pyramid dedicated to a consort of King Rama V who tragically drowned at Bang Pa In while her attendants watched; to touch royalty meant a mandatory death sentence.

Krating Waterfall: A 50-meter waterfall and several caves are located in Kitchakut National Park, 28 km north of town past orchards of rambutan and durian.

Khao Soi Dao National Park: Nature lovers can overnight in the government bungalows located in this national park, 70 km north of Chantaburi.

Accommodations

Inexpensive and quiet hotels are located down near the river, a 20-minute walk from the bus station. Hotels in the middle of town are very noisy but convenient for gem dealers.

Kasem Sarn I Hotel: An excellent hotel with very large and clean rooms, all with private bath and decent furniture, plus towels and maid service. A simple cafe is located outside to the right. This hotel is located outside the main traffic circles and therefore very quiet. From the bus terminal, turn left and walk down Saritdet Rd. toward the Chantaburi River. 98/1 Benchama Rachutit Rd., tel. (039) 312340, 120-140B fan, 220-250B a/c.

Chantara Guesthouse: Less expensive rooms are located on the riverfront road just behind the Kasem Sarn I Hotel. The Chantara is marked only in Thai script; look for a green two-story building with balconies. 248 Sukapiban Rd., tel. (039) 312310, 60B common bath, 120B private bath. Request a room with a view.

Chantaburi Hotel: A busy and noisy place centrally located near the markets and King Taksin Park. 42/6 Tachalab Rd., tel. (039) 311300, 120-140B fan, 220-250B a/c.

Mark's Travel Lodge: Top-end choice is the curiously named hotel on the western edge of town. This 220-room hotel is popular with business types and gem dealers. 14 Raksak Chamun Rd., tel. (039) 311531, 300-600B a/c.

Restaurants

Chantaburi is known for its fresh seafood and thick rice noodles, exported throughout the world. As described by a local tourist publication, the noodles are famous for their "toothsomeness."

Lakeside Restaurants: Best place for dinner are the foodstalls and outdoor cafes which surround the north side of King Taksin Park. A very large place on Tha Chalep Rd. displays almost 20 sample dishes, including clams sautéed in black bean sauce and crunchy sweet-and-sour fish. Highly recommended.

Central Market: Dozens of streetstalls serve Thai and Chinese dishes every night at the market on Ampawa Road.

Versailles Coffee Pub: Trendy Thai teenagers enjoy the Romanesque bar and restaurant on Tha Chalep Rd. near King Taksin Park. Versailles Nightclub is next door.

TRAT

Trat, 312 km from Bangkok, is the provincial capital and leading commercial center of southeastern Thailand. After the fall of Ayuthaya in 1767, Trat served as the launching point for King Taksin's counterattack against the Burmese invaders. Trat and nearby islands were ceded to France in 1894 for Chantaburi, but returned to Thai control in 1906 in exchange for French control over western Cambodia.

As the last major town before the Cambodian border, Trat remained almost completely off the tourist trail until the discovery of Ko Chang in the early 1990s. Trat now chiefly serves as a transit point for visitors heading to Ko Chang and other islands in the southeast. Trat is an ordinary town with an extraordinary future; you can almost feel the heady air of prosperity.

Attractions

Trat Province is just starting to attract visitors to its gem-mining towns, remote beaches, and modest historical sights.

Wat Bupparam: Located two km southwest of town, Wat Pai Klong is an old temple constructed in 1652 during the reign of King Thong of Ayuthaya. The temple consists of a *bot* surrounded by small *chedis* and three *mondops* which contain footprints of the Buddha.

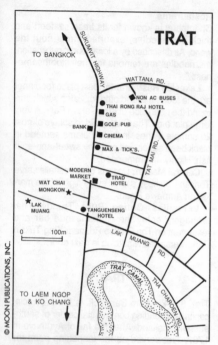

TRAT

TO BANGKOK

SUKUMVIT HIGHWAY

WATTANA RD.

NON AC BUSES

THAI RONG RAJ HOTEL

GAS

BANK

GOLF PUB

CINEMA

MAX & TICK'S.

TAT MAI RD.

MODERN MARKET

TRAD HOTEL

WAT CHAI MONGKON

LAK MUANG

TANGUENSENG HOTEL

0   100m

LAK   MUANG   RD.

TRAT CANAL

THA CHAROEN RD.

TO LAEM NGOP & KO CHANG

© MOON PUBLICATIONS, INC.

Accommodations

Max & Tick's Guesthouse: The backpackers' center in Trat is a clean and friendly place with current information on Ko Chang and other nearby islands. Check the bulletin board. Mad Max once operated a guesthouse in Krabi, moved here to join operations with Tick, but has returned to his brothers' K.R. Mansion in Krabi. Look for the sign marked D.C. Guesthouse. 58-60 Sukumvit Rd., tel. (039) 511449, 60-120B.

Trad Hotel: A decent hotel with small coffee shop is located up the alley opposite the morning market. Tel. (039) 511091, 140-250B fan, 240-750B a/c.

Tanguenseng (TNS) Hotel: A clean and relatively new hotel in the center of town. 66-77 Sukumvit Rd., tel. (039) 511028, 100-200B.

Restaurants

Modern Market: The new market on Sukumvit Rd. is the best place for cheap eats in a clean environment, plus shopping for basic supplies. Check the impressive fish market in the rear. Inexpensive foodstalls are located on the ground floor. Top Star Cafe on the third floor is a semi-luxurious option.

Golf Pub & Coffee Shop: Western decor, records mounted on the walls, live music in the evening, and a good selection of Thai and Western dishes make this a popular *farang* hangout. The Thai owner once lived in the States. Sukumvit Rd. past the cinema. Inexpensive.

Transportation

Ordinary buses from Bangkok's Eastern Bus Terminal on Sukumvit Rd. depart in the mornings until 0900, cost 65B, and take about eight hours to reach Trat. Air-conditioned buses cost 120B, but do the journey in six hours.

LAEM NGOP

Laem Ngop, 17 km south of Trat, is the departure point for boats to Ko Chang and other remote islands. *Laem* means cape; *ngop* is the traditional Khmer rice farmer's hat. Most of the activity is centered around the pier where dozens of backpackers wait for the next boat to Ko Chang. Exchange services are available from the Bangkok Bank minitruck parked in the adjacent lot. Traveler's checks can be cashed at several resorts on Ko Chang, but only at very poor rates. Extra food supplies and drinking water should be picked up from the nearby shops and restaurants. A large sign behind the parking lot commemorates a sea battle between the Thai and French navies in 1941.

Accommodations

Laem Ngop has several small guesthouses that cater to backpackers and travelers who miss the last boat to Ko Chang in the late afternoon.

Laem Ngop Guesthouse: Laem Ngop's best guesthouse is located 200 meters up the highway away from the pier. The owner, Captain Daniel Frudaker, is an American marine consultant who has been involved with local tourism for almost a decade. Daniel is a gold mine of information on transportation, accommodations, and new islands south of Ko Chang, plus he sponsors diving excursions, sportfishing, and extended cruises. 46 Moo 1, tel. (039) 512634, 40-60B.

Other Guesthouses: Overflow from Daniel's place is handled by **Chut Kaew Guesthouse**

and **Laem Ngop Inn** farther up on the right side of the road. Both have rooms for 100-150B. **Swampy Bungalow**, 10 km from Laem Ngop, has been recommended as a more luxurious alternative with a great restaurant.

Transportation

Travel agencies on Khao San Rd. in Bangkok have small minibuses direct to Laem Ngop. Services are provided by both Sea Horse and S.T. Travel. Minibuses are convenient, but the air-conditioning rarely works and they travel at frightening speeds. Both services will attempt to put you on private boats that take you to remote beaches where you are a captive audience. Skip this scam and take another boat to the beach of your choice.

Public buses from Bangkok's Eastern Bus Terminal to Trat are both safer and more comfortable for the full-day journey. Minibuses from the main road in Trat continue 17 km south to Laem Ngop and charge just 10B per passenger.

Ordinary and a/c buses depart throughout the day for Pattaya and Bangkok. The Sea Horse minibus departs daily for Bangkok at 1145.

KO CHANG

Ko Chang ("Elephant Island") is, after Phuket, Thailand's second-largest island, some 30 km in length and eight km broad at its widest point. Covered with dense jungle and bisected by a steep wall of mountains, Chang remained almost completely untouched until an article published in 1989 by *Absenteuer & Reisen* (a German travel magazine) proclaimed the island as the next paradise in Thailand. Guidebook coverage the following year by Lonely Planet and several German companies brought worldwide attention to the entire archipelago.

By early 1990 the island had achieved fame as Thailand's next major resort destination. Speculators and land developers quickly arrived to construct bungalows and hotels to take advantage of the expected tourism boom. Land prices soared to astronomical heights as local residents hopelessly fought to retain control of their island. Fishermen abandoned their traditional occupations and converted their trawlers into shuttle ferries.

Local authorities soon jumped on the tourism

RUBY FEVER IN BO RAI

As in Chantaburi, gem mining is an important industry where thousands of miners risk malaria and land mines in the gem-rich war zones near guerrilla-controlled Cambodia. An estimated 50,000 miners a month cross the Ban Thad Mountains into the mineral-rich and malaria-infested Cambodian jungles to seek their fortune. Reminiscent of the gold-rush days in America's Wild West, a few lucky prospectors make incredible discoveries of vast deposits of rubies and sapphires. Others return with little more than deadly cerebral malaria or limbs lost to land mines. Despite all the political brouhaha over upcoming peace agreements, the Khmer Rouge continues to oversee a sophisticated mining operation that brings in an enormous amount of cash desperately needed to finance their war against the government in Phnom Penh. Authorities estimate that the Khmer Rouge earn upwards of US$5 million a month from renting out land to foreign miners and mining companies.

Bo Rai, 40 km north of Trat on Highway 3389, is the center of Thailand's wild gem trade, a town firmly in the clutches of ruby fever. Here, along dusty narrow streets, hundreds of miners bargain over thousands of rubies piled high on sidewalk card tables. District officials estimate that over 100 million *baht* changes hands each day; some stones are worth over 25 million *baht* each. Experts claim that perhaps 70-80% of the world's rubies come through this border area, where young men with sunglasses and pistols sit in sidewalk bars, drinking beer in the early morning haze. Bo Rai is a frontier town where strangers are eyed with suspicion. Proceed with caution.

Accommodations in Bo Rai include the Honey Inn near the market where fan rooms go from 120B and a/c rooms at double the price. Paradise Hotel near the post office has better fan-cooled rooms with private bath from 200B and upscale a/c rooms from 300B.

Mini-trucks to Bo Rai leave from the front of the main shopping complex in Trat.

bandwagon. The Thai government constructed a large pier on the east side of Ko Chang and then began blasting a concrete road which will soon encircle the entire island. Ko Chang now resembles the early stages of Ko Samui: a tropical island firmly mesmerized by the promise of mass tourism.

Despite all the construction and development, Ko Chang remains one of the most beautiful islands in Thailand. Most accommodations remain simple bamboo bungalows rather than concrete hotels filled with package tourists, and a majority of Chang's 5,000 residents still make their living from fishing rather than tourism. Few locals speak much English and most seem relatively uninterested in catering to foreigners. When I last visited Ko Chang, the island had only one Land Rover and three bicycles for rent (one was broken). Discos, nightly videos, noisy motorcycles, and beer bars are still several years away. Ko Chang is a wonderfully refreshing change from the hustle of Samui and Phuket. The time to visit Ko Chang is *now*.

East Coast Attractions

Most visitors are content to simply relax on one of the west coast beaches. Ko Chang, however, is a spectacular island blessed with thick tropical jungle, small waterfalls, and narrow trails which follow the deep interior valleys.

Dan Mai: The only sizable village on the east coast has a small market, fishing pier, and a surprisingly large villa owned by the local mayor. Mayom Pier, four km to the south, will probably become an important embarkartion point upon completion of the road to the west coast. The largest town on Ko Chang is Salak Pet, a somnolent fishing village located in a protected cove on the south coast.

Visitor Center: Local authorities have erected a small visitor center near Mayom Waterfall on the east coast. Inside the deserted structure is a three-dimensional model of Ko Chang with English labels, a map of Thailand's national parks, and aerial photos of local beaches marked in Thai script. Adjacent concrete bungalows with private bathrooms cost 300-500B per night and can be hired from local park officials.

Mayom Waterfall: Located a few km south of Dan Mai is a six-level waterfall and swimming pond 500 meters off the primitive road. The falls have been visited by several Thai kings including Chulalongkorn, who carved his initials on several rocks. English-language signs point the way. Tham Mayom Huts, about 50 meters north, has five simple bungalows priced from 100B.

Don Keo Waterfall: An unmarked path just north of the broken wooden bridge leads through rubber plantations to these modest falls. On the east coast, about 10 minutes south of Saithong Guesthouse.

West Coast Beaches

Ko Chang's best beaches are all on the west coast. Most accommodations are simple bamboo bungalows with a mattress on the floor and illuminated by oil lamps. Open-air showers and common bathrooms are located to the rear. Restaurants are funky places with good food but rudimentary service; you'll probably be ignored to the point of starvation until you approach the front counter.

Construction of new bungalows is going on at a furious pace as professionals from Bangkok arrive to milk the tourist boom, so expect major changes from the following descriptions. In general, you should take a ferry to the beach of your choice and then wander around to inspect a few places. Most bungalows are filled during the high season from October to March, but tents can be rented while waiting for vacancies. Ko Chang is, technically speaking, a national park where camping is legal anywhere.

The following beaches on the west coast are described from north to south. Beaches on the south, north, and east coast are described below.

White Sand Beach

Hat Sai Khao, the longest and most popular beach on Ko Chang, is the original escape on the island. The concrete road which skirts the back side of the beach goes south to Klong Prao Beach and cuts through the mountains at the northern end to Klong Son Beach. Alternatively, a narrow trail heads north over the ridgetop and brings you to Klong Son in one hour. White Sand Beach is a good place to enjoy the sand and meet other travelers.

Over a dozen bungalows are spread along the beach. All charge 60-100B for bamboo huts with mattresses on the floor and common bathrooms located back toward the road. Bungalows are almost identical, but restaurants vary from primitive to almost sophisticated. Bungalows are described starting from the northern end.

White Sand Beach Resort has 10 rooms tucked under the trailhead to Klong Son Beach. The beach here is relatively deserted due to its

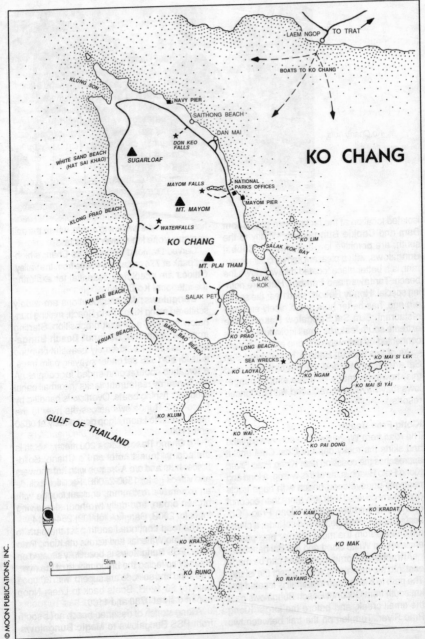

GULF OF THAILAND

© MOON PUBLICATIONS, INC.

0   5km

Ko Chang huts

isolated location at the far northern end. **Boom Dam** and **Cookie Bungalows**, slightly to the south, are primitive low-end choices. **Sabbai Bungalows**, with a pleasant semicircular restaurant, is a better place located midway down the beach. **Tantawan** and **Bamboo Huts** are nothing special. **Honey Resort**, sited near the southern end, has better huts and a nicely elevated restaurant. **Sun Sai Bungalow Resort** at the extreme south features small individual houses connected by pathways fronting a rocky beach.

As of this writing, Sabbai, Honey, and Sun Sai are recommended. By the time you read this, however, many of these simple bungalows may have been replaced with midpriced resorts.

Klong Prao Beach
The road from White Sand Beach veers inland and skirts the rocky cape at Chai Chet until it approaches the coastline near Klong Prao River. Klong Prao Beach is, as of this writing, a long and relatively undeveloped beach with huge tracts of property covered with little more than coconut groves and wild vegetation. Klong Prao ("Coconut Canal") offers peace and solitude; a pleasant change from the more popular backpacker enclaves on White Sand and Kai Bai beaches.

Attractions: Some great hikes can be made east into the mountains which bisect the island. The path to Klong Prao Waterfall is located two km south from Coconut Beach Bungalows past the small creek, and before the larger Klong Prao River. Turn left on the trail between two houses and hike two km to a cafe, where the trail continues one km upriver to the falls.

Carved Diamond Mountain, Ko Chang's highest peak at 774 meters, is visible from the valley. Guides are absolutely essential for exploring the interior of Ko Chang.

Bungalows: Accommodations are widely scattered along Klong Prao Beach, making bungalow hopping a difficult proposition. Starting from the north end, **Coconut Beach Bungalows** features 12 extremely beautiful bamboo huts for 60-160B set under swaying palm trees, a romantic spot recommended for couples. A lovely nearby restaurant flanks the small canal filled with fishing boats. Overflow is handled by Coconut 2 Bungalows across the river to the north. Boats to Laem Ngop depart daily at 0830 and 1100.

Ko Chang Resort some 200 meters south is the original tourist hotel on Ko Chang. Solid-timber huts and a/c A-frames with hot showers and videos go for 1500-2500B. Facilities include an expensive restaurant, cocktail lounge with broken organ, and daily two-hour skin diving tours for 200B. Bangkok tel. (02) 254-2614.

The road continues south past the path to Klong Prao Waterfall and across the Klong Prao River. **PSS Bungalows** is beautifully situated on a sandy tip facing the broad mouth of the river. The sand and solitude are superb, with 20 good huts for 80-120B. Boats back to Laem Ngop depart daily at 0730 and 1100.

A long stretch of deserted beach goes south from PSS Bungalows to **Magic Bungalows**, one of the best-value places on Klong Prao Beach. Magic has over 30 huts, great sand, and a popular restaurant stilted over the clear waters. Highly recommended. Adjacent **Good Luck Bungalows** (Chok Dee) faces a rocky beach and is not good value.

Kai Bae Beach

The last major beach on the west coast has a narrow strip of sand crowded with over a dozen bungalows. **Coral Bungalows** on the rocky promontory has 30 primitive huts, but wonderful views from the open-air restaurant. **Nang Naun 2** faces a rocky beach, with huts crowded together except for several bungalows situated on the rear-side lagoon. **Kae Bae** and **Kae Bae Beach Bungalows** are similar, but the beach improves to the south. **Porn Guesthouse**, a much better choice, has over 20 huts imaginatively arranged between the hillside and the narrow white-sand beach. **Nang Nuan 1** is the last bungalow on Kai Bae Beach.

Snorkeling is fairly good at the offshore islands. Local charters cost 100B per hour for 10-man vessels to 200-250B for fishing boats.

Kruat Beach

Beyond the rocky promontory are several bays that will soon be developed with beachside and hillside bungalows. Until the completion of the road, a narrow path wanders through the jungle and over the mountains to the southern beach at Bang Bao.

South Coast Beaches

The south coast of Ko Chang has several beaches marked for major development during the 1990s. Boats from Laem Ngop go direct to both Bang Bao and Long beaches, plus several of the nearby islands such as Ko Prao, Ko Laoya, Ko Wai, and Ko Ngam.

Bang Bao Beach: A beautiful bay and private pier are located on the primary beach on the south coast of Ko Chang. Most of the beach is dominated by Bang Bao Resort and Sunset Bungalows, private developments that receive complaints about overcrowding, inadequate water supplies, and decrepit bungalows. Sea Horse Travel often sends their passengers here; resist their generous offer and find a boat heading to White Sand or Klong Prao beaches.

Long Beach: Perhaps the most spectacular beach and finest waters on Ko Chang are located near the southeastern tip. Captain Daniel's Bungalows mysteriously burned down several years ago, but new operations will probably be running by the time you arrive. The water here is crystal clear and shallow enough for safe swimming. Long Beach is a short boat ride away from the beautiful islands of Ko Prao, Ko Laoya, Ko Ngam, and Ko Wai.

East Coast Beaches

The east coast of Ko Chang is rarely visited because of its brownish sand and mangrove swamps. One exception is the lovely bungalows at Hat Saithong, operated by two friendly Thais named Lo and Kanon. **Saithong Bungalows** has 24 superior huts with common bath at 100-120B and 10 almost-luxurious huts with private bath from 200B. Lo can arrange motorcycle rentals, full-day fishing and skin-diving excursions, and local guides to explore the nearby mountains. Daniel and Lo often wait for customers at the Laem Ngop Pier. A very peaceful and relaxing scene.

North Coast Beaches

Mention should also be made of Klong Son, an almost completely untouched fishing village in a well-protected harbor on the north coast. **Klongson Bungalows** in the village has five bamboo huts facing the bay and a series of connected rooms facing courtyard planks. **Chi Minh Place**, 300 meters behind town in the jungle, has several homestay bungalows with meals included. Klong Son has a small mosque, supply shop, and several seafood restaurants on a rickety fishing pier. Motorcycle taxis reach Klong Son from Saithong Guesthouse, or hike one hour over the mountains from White Sand Beach.

Transportation

Fishing trawlers converted into ferry boats leave from Laem Ngop daily from 0900 to late afternoon. Prices are fixed at rather unreasonable levels: 20-40B to Saithong and Dan Mai on the east coast, Klong Son for 50B, 60-80B to White Sand Beach and Kai Bae, 80-100B to Bang Bao and Long Beach. Ko Laoya, Ko Prao Resort, and Ko Wai also cost 100B. These tariffs are outrageous: bargain directly with the captain. Tickets should be purchased from the boat owner rather than the middleman who operates a counter at the pier.

Boats from Ko Chang back to Laem Ngop leave twice in the mornings around 0830 and 1100. Exact departures are posted at most guesthouses. Guesthouse owners will flag down the boat and provide shuttle services out to the ferry.

Completion of the concrete road around most of the island by 1995 will probably completely change the transportation scene. Ferries from Laem Ngop might drop you at the Dan Mai Pier on the east coast, from where *songtaos* will continue to the beaches on the west coast. As with Ko Samui, drivers will call out "White Beach, White Beach, White Beach" or "Bang Bao, Bang Bao, Bang Bao."

ISLANDS SOUTH OF KO CHANG

The rapid development of Ko Chang has inspired many travelers to explore the islands farther south toward Cambodia. Though most of the islands lie within the boundaries of Ko Chang National Park and should be open to public camping and small-scale bungalow development, many are controlled by private developers, powerful politicians, rich movie stars, Thai royalty, and military officers who have erected expensive resort complexes.

Ko Prao
The small island just offshore from Salakpet has 25 luxurious a/c chalets that charge over 1000B per night.

Ko Ngam
Ko Ngam is a very pretty island bisected by a narrow spit of sand. **Ko Ngam Resort** charges 800-1200B per night.

Ko Laoya
Owned by a Trat politician, this lovely little island has a beautiful beach, teak bungalows from 900B, and a seafood restaurant popular with Thai group tours from Bangkok. Trat tel. (039) 512552.

Ko Wai
Ko Wai Resort has several small huts situated on a small and brownish beach. Local divers

recommend the offshore coral beds, but I found the diving rather mediocre.

Ko Mak
Ko Mak Resort (Bangkok tel. 02-579-5507), owned by a Thai movie star, has 10 rooms priced 900-1200B that cater to Thais rather than *farang*. Boats leave from Ao Cho and cost 300B per person.

Ko Kradat
Owned by a Thai princess, Ko Kradat ("Paper Island") features a seven-km beach and fairly good diving. **Ko Kradat Resort** has 36 bungalows from 1400B.

Ko Kut
The second-largest island in the Ko Chang archipelago remains a place where backpackers can get off the beaten track without spending a small fortune. Most of the bungalows are located on the west and northwest coasts. Several rivers with waterfalls run from the central mountain ridge down to the west coast.

A half-dozen inexpensive bungalows have recently opened, including Lazy Days Resort owned by Tao and Josh, two Israelis who have joined operations with Mad Max. Rooms with elevated beds and common bath cost from 100B, plus the restaurant serves surprisingly good food. Contact Max in Trat or Josh at the harbor for travel arrangements.

Ko Kut is a three-hour boat ride from Laem Ngop. Several boats make the trip each day despite dire warnings from other operators that "last boat already go." Boats with enough passengers occasionally leave from Klong Yai to Ko Kut.

THE ROAD TO CAMBODIA

Highway 318 continues southeast from Trat down to the Cambodian border. Most of the region is a military security zone with dozens of checkpoints, though several small towns with excellent beaches seem ripe for discovery. When the conflict in Cambodia is finally resolved, it may become possible to continue east to Kampong Son, Phnom Penh, and finally, Angkor Wat.

monks on Ko Chang beach

Towns And Accommodations

Ban Chuen and Klong Yai are the two largest towns on Route 318 from Trat to Cambodia. The road ends at Ban Hat Lek, but Western visitors are rarely allowed to travel past Klong Yai.

Ban Chuen: Ban Chuen, 60 km from Trat and 14 km before Klong Yai, has the best beach in the region. Most of the area is used by the Thai military as an R&R escape for their border patrols. Mini-trucks from Trat will drop you at the highway turnoff, from where motorcycle taxis charge 15B for the five-km journey down to the beach. Accommodations in local bungalows cost 150-180B.

Klong Yai: The last major town in southeast Thailand is where smuggling operations between Thailand and Cambodia bring in over 10 million *baht* per day. Klong Yai has several bungalows and hotels including Bang Inn Villa, Pavinee, and Suksamaran Hotel. Boats occasionally leave from Klong Yai to Ko Kut.

Transportation

Trucks to Ban Chuen and Klong Yai leave behind the modern shopping complex on Tai Mai Road. Taxis can also be hired for a quick daytrip. The latest information on transportation, hotels, and recommended beaches can be obtained from Mad Max in Trat and Captain Daniel in Laem Ngop.

> *One who has hotel reservations and speaks no French is a tourist.*
> —Paul Fussell, *Abroad*

VICINITY OF BANGKOK

WEST OF BANGKOK

West of Bangkok lie the three provinces of Nakhon Pathom, Ratchaburi, and Kanchanaburi. Nakhon Pathom and Ratchaburi provinces are alluvial lowlands once almost entirely covered with ricefields and coconut palms. Today, both are peppered with towns that have transformed themselves from tiny hamlets into thriving industrial estates in less than a generation. Kanchanaburi Province is chiefly known for its bridge, and natural wonders such as lakes, waterfalls, and national parks.

Sightseeing Highlights

The region between Bangkok and the Burmese border offers an outstanding range of attractions, from Buddhist *stupas* and war monuments to Khmer temples and stunning landscapes. Urban sprawl now connects Bangkok with Nakhon Pathom and Kanchanaburi is firmly on the tourist trail, but the remainder of the region remains largely untouched by mass tourism.

Nakhon Pathom: The world's tallest Buddhist monument is located in this nondescript town about one hour (54 km) west of Bangkok.

Nakhon Pathom is generally visited on a day-tour from Bangkok, or as an afternoon pause en route to Kanchanaburi.

Ratchaburi: Almost 50 km southwest of Nakhon Pathom is a busy commercial town known for several historic *wats* and the production of huge water jars used in households throughout Thailand. Bamboo reed pipes are still handcrafted in the nearby village of Ban Ko Bua.

Kanchanaburi: This town, 122 km west of Bangkok, is one of Thailand's upcoming centers for both domestic and international tourism. Westerners generally visit the famous bridge and cemeteries which commemorate the events of World War II, while domestic tourists use Kanchanaburi as a weekend escape from the horrors of Bangkok. The medium-sized town is beautifully situated on the River Kwai and within easy day-trips to nearby waterfalls and national parks, a combination which often inspires Western visitors to extend their stay from days to weeks.

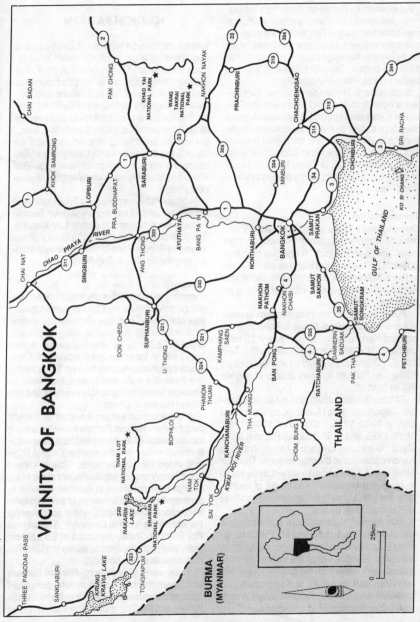

VICINITY OF BANGKOK

© MOON PUBLICATIONS, INC.

Kanchanaburi Province: Aside from the historic monuments of Kanchanaburi town, the chief attraction west of Bangkok is the magnificent array of rivers, lakes, and waterfalls located between Kanchanaburi town and the Burmese border. Travelers can also visit the border post at Three Pagodas Pass.

Suphanburi: The modern town of Suphanburi is occasionally visited as a short stop between Kanchanaburi and Ayuthaya. A quick three-hour *samlor* tour visits the colossal seated Buddha at Wat Palelai and the ruined *prang* of Wat Mahathat. Southwest of Suphanburi is the Don Chedi Memorial, U Thong National Museum, and weird Buddhist theme park at Wat Wai Pong Rua.

Transportation

One-day tours to the *chedi* at Nakhon Pathom and Kanchanaburi can be booked from travel agents in Bangkok. A one-day train tour is described below under Kanchanaburi. Quickie tours, however, are not recommended in a region so immensely rich with sightseeing attractions.

Public transportation from Bangkok is plentiful and well organized. Buses to Nakhon Pathom and Kanchanaburi depart every 15 minutes for 0700-2300 from the Southern Bus Terminal in Thonburi. Discount travel agencies on Khao San Rd. sell minibus tickets at slightly higher cost.

All trains heading south stop in Nakhon Pathom. Departures from Hualampong Station are daily at 0900, 1235, 1400, 1515, 1600, 1730, 1830, 1920, and 2155. Nakhon Pathom takes about 90 minutes to reach by train. Trains to Kanchanaburi leave the train station in Thonburi at 0800 and 1350 and take almost three hours to reach Kanchanaburi. You could, of course, take the train to Nakhon Pathom and continue to Kanchanaburi by bus.

The town of Kanchanaburi is the principal transportation hub in the region. Public buses from Kanchanaburi reach most outlying attractions. Remote sights are served by minitrucks which leave from the smaller towns. Motorcycles can be rented in Kanchanaburi; a sensible and immensely convenient way to visit the widely scattered attractions.

NAKHON PATHOM

Nakhon Pathom, 54 km west of Bangkok, is a busy commercial center chiefly visited for its famous *chedi* located in the center of town near the train station. The city is regarded as one of the oldest municipalities in Thailand and perhaps the country's first center of Buddhist studies. The surrounding countryside is renowned for its delicious pomelos, fragrant white rice, beautiful women, and thriving wine industry. Here's a tip: skip the sweetish, almost sickening whites and try the elegant yet unpretentious reds. Thai wines and brandies have vastly improved in recent years.

Nakhon Pathom sponsors a Fruit Festival in September and an immensely popular Temple Festival each November during Loy Kratong. The final claim to fame is that Nakhon Pathom served as Phnom Penh in the Academy Award-winning movie, *The Killing Fields*.

History

According to tradition, the city was founded several centuries before the Christian era as a seaside port for the mythical kingdom of Suwannaphum. During this period, King Asoka the Great (272-232 B.C.) sent two senior monks from India to introduce the principals of Theravada Buddhism. Passing through Three Pagodas Pass, the main land conduit from India to Thailand, Buddhism probably made its first impact at Nakhon Pathom.

Archaeological evidence begins in the 6th century when Nakhon Pathom flourished under the patronage of the Mon people, a Dvaravati-Buddhist empire which thrived in Central Thailand in the 6th-10th centuries. Little is known of the history or geographical extent of the Mon, though their presence at Nakhon Pathom is confirmed by local discoveries of several stone inscriptions, small *stupas*, and a coin bearing the inscription "Lord of Dvaravati." The original Pra Pathom Chedi, a pagoda of Sri Lankan style, was probably erected during the Mon Period in the late 10th century.

In the early 11th century, Nakhon Pathom and Western Thailand fell to King Suryavarman, who incorporated Siam into his militaristic Khmer empire. The original Pra Pathom Chedi

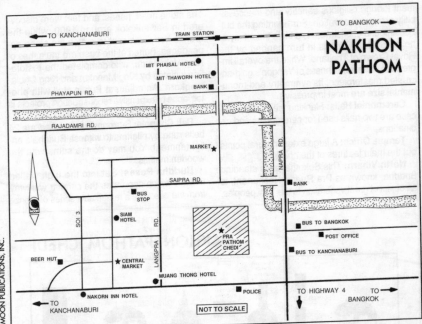

NAKHON PATHOM

TO KANCHANABURI ← ----- TRAIN STATION ----- TO BANGKOK →

MIT PHAISAL HOTEL
MIT THAWORN HOTEL
BANK

PHAYAPUN RD.

RAJADAMRI RD.

NAPRA RD.

MARKET ★

SAIPRA RD.

BANK

BUS STOP

SIAM HOTEL

SOI 3

LANGPRA RD.

★ PRA PATHOM CHEDI

BUS TO BANGKOK

POST OFFICE

BUS TO KANCHANABURI

BEER HUT

★ CENTRAL MARKET

MUANG THONG HOTEL

NAKORN INN HOTEL

POLICE

TO KANCHANABURI ←

NOT TO SCALE

TO HIGHWAY 4 ↓   TO BANGKOK →

© MOON PUBLICATIONS, INC.

(a Buddhist structure) was pulled down and re-built in the form of a Hindu/Brahman *prang* some 40 meters high. The Khmers held the city until 1057 when it fell to King Anawratha of Pagan. Recognizing the cultural advances of the Mon, the Burmese king soon imported the artistic and religious traditions of the Mon to his powerful capital in central Burma.

Nakhon Pathom was abandoned in the 11th century, but re-established in the 17th century by King Mahachakraphet as a defensive position against Burmese invasion. In 1860, King Mong-kut ordered the restoration of the decaying *chedi*, an ancient Indian-style pagoda which he first spotted during his early years as a monk in the region.

Nakhon Pathom Chedi

Your first glimpse of the massive *chedi* at Nakhon Pathom is staggering. Soaring over 120 meters into the hot blue skies, this is the most sacred Buddhist monument in Thailand and the world's largest *chedi*, surpassing even the gilded wonder in Yangon. Although the dome-shaped reliquary lacks the staggering de-

tail of Yangon's Shwedagon, its fairyland of aux-iliary *bots*, Buddha images, and curious sub-structures makes for a fascinating afternoon of exploration. For best impact, approach the *chedi* from the north side facing the train station.

The history of the main *chedi* began with a simple Sri Lankan-style *stupa* constructed by the Mons in the 10th century, followed by a Hindu-Brahman *prang* erected by the Khmers in the early 11th century, and the present enor-mous cupola begun in 1860 and completed in the early 20th century during the reign of King Chulalongkorn.

Before climbing into the temple complex, note the dozens of amulet booths, palmists, and food-stalls to the left of the main entrance which serve iced coffee and bamboo staffs filled with sticky rice laced with coconut milk.

Chedi: The bell-shaped *stupa*, covered with glazed orange tiles imported from China, is be-lieved to contain a Buddha relic of great reli-gious importance. It encases an older *stupa* of hemispherical form with a *prang* superimposed; a replica can be seen nearby. The innermost *stupa* may hold the original Dvaravati monument though religious sanctity and inaccessibility prevent excavation. Surmounting the bulbous mound of brickwork is a triple trident (symbol of Shiva) which is in turn capped by the Royal Crown of Thailand. While the overall impression lacks the richness of Yangon's gold-encrusted masterpiece, its symmetry and monumental size are most impressive.

Ceremonial Halls: Flanking the Grand Staircase are two halls used for ceremonies and ordinations.

Temple Office: A large exterior mural points out the main features of the *chedi*.

North Viharn: This Sukothai-style standing Buddha, known as Pra Ruang Rochanarit, is an object of great veneration to the Thai peoples.

The stone head, hands, and feet were discovered in Sawankalok around 1900, while the bronze body was cast to match the stone appendages. Buried at the base are the ashes of King Vajiravudh, who completed the restoration initiated by King Mongkut and King Chulalongkorn. An adjacent Public Hall with photographs of expensive reconstruction projects is also used for ordinations of monks.

Bell Chapels: Surrounding the *chedi* are 24 bells rung by pilgrims to witness Buddha's enlightenment. You may do the same with the wooden mallets.

Buddha Poses: Set into the high-walled cloister which separates the circular walkway from the *chedi* are a remarkable series of bronze

NAKHON PATHOM CHEDI

NUN'S HOUSES
ORIGINAL CHEDI REPLICA
SEATED BUDDHA
NAKHON SI THAMMASART REPLICA
HOLY TREES
MEDITATION CHAMBERS
MINIATURE MOUNTAIN
DVARAVATI SEATED BUDDHA
SOUTH VIHARN
PREACHING BUDDHA
CHINESE TEMPLE
SEATED BUDDHA
EAST VIHARN
RECLINING BUDDHA
WEST VIHARN
SALA
BUDDHA STATUES
CHEDI
NORTH VIHARN (PRA RUANG ROCHANARIT)
NOT TO SCALE
MINIATURE MOUNTAIN
MUSEUM
BELL CHAPELS
PUBLIC HALL
TEMPLE OFFICES
CHAOPO PRASATONG
GRAND STAIRCASES
CHEUN RUTHAI GARDEN
PRAKAN PAKKLOD
CEREMONIAL HALLS

naga

BOB RACE

Buddhas cast in every possible position of meditation, and labeled in English with indescribable translations: "The Buddha look back over one's shoulder." Note the round Chinese-style moon windows with wooden shutters.

Museum: This disorganized museum on the lower platform boasts art treasures such as Dvaravati statuary and Wheels of the Law, plus a great deal of kitsch oddities such as old money and stuffed fish. The Chinese Temple and the Sala Soprong beyond the stairway are used by resting pilgrims.

Dvaravati Seated Buddha: Carved from a piece of white quartzite, this monumental stone image is widely considered one of Thailand's great artistic masterpieces. The solemn, magnificent figure is seated in the so-called Western Style, an unusual pose favored by the Mons who apparently borrowed the arrangement from Greco-Roman models. Robe contours and Western expression might remind you of Alexander the Great, the world conqueror who led his armies to the edge of Pakistan and whose artistic styles filtered east across India to the Mons of early Thailand. Do not miss this image.

Northeast Courtyard: Down below the circular platform stands the House of Chaopo Prasatong, Prakan Pakklod, and one of many holy trees connected with the life of Buddha.

East Viharn: Inside the eastern chapel sits an enlightened Buddha under a bodhi tree painted by an artist of King Rama VI, and an important mural which traces the *chedi's* architectural evolution from a white, 11th-century Mon *stupa* to a Khmer *prang* erected after Suryavarman's triumph. Both were covered by the present *chedi* erected in 1860 by King Mongkut. The side walls display portraits of 48 ancient kings and heroic warriors.

Miniature Mountain: Nakhon Pathom's great *chedi* has plenty of oddities designed to impress, edify, and confuse the visitor. Depending on whom you talk to, this artificial grotto represents either monks' meditation chambers, a low-end Disneyland, or Mt. Meru, Buddhist abode of the gods.

South Viharn: The central antechamber holds an earth-touching Buddha surrounded by five disciples, and a Khmer Buddha meditating beneath a hooded *naga*. In front are two decorative chimneys used by Chinese worshipers to burn incense and gold paper. The southeast courtyard is filled with decrepit nuns' quarters and sacred bodhi trees.

Southern Courtyard: At the bottom of the staircase is another Buddha seated in the European position; not as impressive as the earlier example, but better for photographs. To the left is a replica of the original *chedi;* to the right a replica of the famous *chedi* at Nakhon Si Thammarat.

West Viharn: A much-venerated nine-meter Buddha cast in the reign of Rama IV reclines in the outer chamber, while a smaller image with adoring pilgrims reclines in the interior chamber. Note the hilarious sign, "Please take off your shoes and keep them in this chapel before they are invisible." Truly, the Buddha can work wonders. Impressive old wooden buildings used as monks' retreats are located inside the southwest courtyard.

Cheun Ruthai Gardens: The northeast garden has yellow bodhisattvas and circulating alms bowls used as surrealistic coin tosses.

Sanam Chand Palace

Another attraction in town is the summer residence built by King Vajiravudh (Rama VI) in an eccentric melange of Thai and English Tudor architectural styles. Some of the buildings are used for private government offices and closed to the public. Most curious is the statue of Yalay, King Vajiravudh's beloved pet dog killed "by some envious people."

Thap Charoen Hall was constructed in 1911 as the residence for the king's entourage. The beautiful gardens and hall were opened to the public in 1990 after several years of restoration by the Fine Arts Department. Today, the lovely white wooden building serves as the Institute of Western Regional Culture under the supervision of Silpakorn University. The culture of western Thailand is recounted with displays of paintings by Petchburi artists, puppets from Samut Songkram, and basketry from the Thai Song tribe.

Sanam Chand Palace is located two km west of the Pra Pathom Chedi. Open Tues.-Sat. 0900-1700.

Accommodations

Although usually just a stopover en route to Kanchanaburi, good hotels in all price ranges are available.

A few budget lodgings include: **Mit Phaisal**, 100-160B single or double. 120 Phayapan, tel. 242422; **Siam Hotel**, 140-300B single or double. 2 Rajadamnern, tel. 241754; and **Muang Thong**, 100-200B single or double. 1 Rajwithi, tel. 242618.

Mit Thaworn: Two cheap hotels are located near the train station. The Mit Thaworn (Mittaowan) and adjacent Mit Phaisal (Mitphaisan or Mitfaisal) have rooms acceptable for a short stay. Both are located up a short alley off the busy street market. 305 Rot Fai Rd., tel. (034) 243115, 100-160B.

Nakorn Inn: Best upscale choice in town is the Nakorn Inn off the main road. This hotel has a coffee shop, convention room, and 70 a/c rooms. 55 Rajwithi Rd., tel. (034) 251152, fax (034) 254998, 500-800B.

Restaurants

Finding a good restaurant in Nakhon Pathom is somewhat difficult. For a quick snack, try the fruit market on the road between the railway station and the Pra Pathom Chedi, or the foodstalls on the grounds of the monument. Another option is the central market on Rajavithi Road. Nakhon Pathom is known for its version of *kao lam,* sticky rice and coconut steamed in a bamboo joint.

More formal settings are located in the a/c **Beer Hut,** and the **Nakorn Inn** which features live music in the evenings.

Transportation

Ordinary buses from Bangkok's Southern Bus Terminal in Thonburi depart every 15 minutes and take an hour to reach Nakhon Pathom. Trains depart nine times daily from Bangkok's Hualampong Station and twice daily from the train station in Thonburi. Trains from the south also stop in Nakhon Pathom.

To return to Bangkok or continue to Kanchanaburi, take bus 81 from the east side of the *chedi,* next to the canal. The floating market at Damnern Saduak can be reached in one hour with bus 78 from the southeast corner of the *chedi.*

KANCHANABURI

Kanchanaburi, 130 km west of Bangkok, is known for the bridge made famous by Pierre Boulle's celebrated novel of World War II, *The Bridge on the River Kwai,* and the subsequent Academy Award-winning motion picture directed by David Lean. The bridge is rather ordinary, but Kanchanaburi's relaxed atmosphere, historic sights, and nearby waterfalls, caves, and river trips make this one of the *most* enjoyable destinations in Thailand.

Allow plenty of time to explore the town and province. A minimum of three days is needed to visit the sights around town and perhaps take a one-day river journey up the River Kwai. Several more days are needed to visit the nearby national parks, caves, forests, waterfalls, and to make an excursion to the Thai/Burmese border at Three Pagodas Pass. Kanchanaburi is an excellent place to discover Thai countryside without having to travel all the way to the far north or extreme south.

Topography is somewhat confusing around the region. Two River Kwais are found in the province: Kwai Yai (Big Kwai) flows from Sri Nakarin Lake, while Kwai Noi (Little Kwai) starts at Krung Kravia Lake near the Burmese border. Both rivers merge near Kanchanaburi to form the Mae Klong River which flows into the Gulf of Thailand.

History

Located along the road to the strategic Three Pagodas Pass, Kanchanaburi and more importantly, Kwai Yai Valley, have long been one of the pivotal trade routes and military garri-

KANCHANABURI

NOT TO SCALE

son centers of Thailand. The valley was first inhabited by Neolithic tribals who fashioned pottery and crude utensils over 3,000 years ago. Archaeological evidence of early human habitation is displayed at the Ban Kao Neolithic Museum, some 40 km west of Kanchanaburi. The region was captured in the 13th century by Khmer commanders who established a military citadel and religious complex at the village of Muang Sing. The ruins were restored and reopened to the public in 1987. After the fall of the Khmers, Ayuthayan rulers constructed a garrison town 20 km west of Kanchanaburi, but, in 1548, the Burmese successfully marched several hundred thousand warriors through the Three Pagodas Pass to wage warfare on Ayuthaya. After the fall of Ayuthaya to the Burmese two centuries later, King Rama I founded contemporary Kanchanaburi as a military camp to monitor Burmese aggression. The town, valley, and jungle pass also played a pivotal role in World War II.

Kanchanaburi recently received worldwide attention around proposals to construct a massive dam near the Burmese border. Outcries from environmentalists and Britain's Prince Charles, plus a general disenchantment over massive dam projects, led to the cancellation of the proposal several years ago. Nam Choan Dam was also scrapped to save several species of endangered wildlife and prevent widespread soil erosion. Environmental causes have gained widespread public support in recent times.

JEATH War Museum

First stop should be the JEATH War Museum, named after a moniker which abbreviates the primary nations which participated in local action: Japan, England, America/Australia, Thailand, Holland. Modeled after POW camps of the period, the simple bamboo structures contain war memorabilia, photographs of emaciated prisoners, personal recollections, and graphic descriptions of tortures committed by the Japanese. The museum is managed by a Thai monk, Maha Tomson Thongproh, who lives in the adjacent Wat Chaichumphon. More than just a museum, JEATH is a simple yet immensely moving memorial to the 16,000 Allied POWs and 50,000-100,000 Asians who died from lack of medical attention, starvation, and torture during construction of the 400-km Death Railway.

The museum is open daily 0830-1630 and admission is 20B.

The Bridge

Kanchanaburi's most famous sight is the simple bridge constructed in just over 16 months by some 60,000 Allied prisoners and 250,000 Asian slave-laborers. The present structure is physically uninspiring—just eight gray, riveted spans on moss-stained concrete pylons—though the historical and emotional elements are fascinating. Best time to visit is at 1030, 1430, and 1630 when the Nam Tok train slowly crosses the bridge. The remainder of the day the structure serves as a footbridge across the river to cool picnic grounds on the other bank. Be careful walking across the bridge and watch out for sprinting motorcycles. A popular light-and-sound show is held at the bridge during River Kwai Week in late November or early December.

Misconceptions about the bridge are commonplace, since most visitors only know the movie *The Bridge on the River Kwai*. The iron bridge in Kanchanaburi isn't the original wooden bridge which played a pivotal role in the movie. The old wooden bridge, which once crossed the river about three km south, was abandoned by the Japanese in favor of the sturdier iron structure disassembled and hauled up from Java. Author Boulle's character, Colonel Nicholson (portrayed by Alec Guinness), was a fictionalized commander who never existed during the construction of the bridge. Colonel Nicholson and other British engineers were portrayed in the movie as instrumental in the design of the bridge; in reality, the Japanese were solely responsible for the project. The movie also overlooked the thousands of Asians who worked on the bridge and died in appalling numbers during construction of the railway. A final point is that the film portrays Commander Shear's (played by William Holden) escape from camp to reach Allied hands in Sri Lanka and his love affair with a beautiful nurse. Shear then returns to Kanchanaburi to blow up the bridge. In fact, nobody ever escaped from Kanchanaburi and lived to tell his story.

The bridge is five km north of town and too far to walk; hire a bike, motorcycle, or take a minibus from Chao Kunen Road.

Around The Bridge

Surrounding the bridge are several other stops worth a brief visit, plus a messy assortment of tourist shops and riverside restaurants. **Solos Restaurant** has good views from the patio terrace, plus offers an escape from the tour buses and schoolchildren.

Train Museum: Just opposite the bridge is a steam engine and an ingenious Japanese supply truck that operated on both road and rails.

Art Gallery: Some 30 meters south of the bridge is a big garish building which features some of the finest modern murals in Thailand.

Paintings on the second floor relate ancient battles between the Thais and Burmese, while third-floor murals tell Thai history and provide portraits of prime ministers and other important political figures. This private museum also features Khmer-style woodcarvings, a pair of elaborate Burmese Buddhas, and excellent paintings of Chinese deities.

Japanese War Memorial: Also located slightly south of the bridge is a simple monument erected by the Japanese and dedicated to those who "died through illness during the course of the construction"—a pleasant-enough euphemism.

A LIFE FOR EVERY SLEEPER

One of the most famous stories of World War II was the construction of the railway between Kanchanaburi in Thailand and Thanbyuzayat in Burma. Construction began on 16 September 1942 after Japanese sea routes were effectively blocked by Allied aircraft and submarine operations near Singapore and in the Straits of Malacca. To provide supplies to their bases in Burma, the Japanese conscripted over 50,000 Allied prisoners and 250,000 Asian laborers from Japanese-held countries in Southeast Asia. Initial estimates by engineers that completion of the 415-km railway would take five years were overruled by the Japanese High Command, who ordered the project finished in an incredibly short span of just 12 months.

As progress on the Death Railway fell behind schedule, the Japanese demanded more men who, under the most primitive conditions, worked around the clock and died in frightening numbers from malaria, dysentery, beri-beri, cholera, and starvation—described on death certificates as "Post Dysenteric Inanition." The cost was a "life for every sleeper" (railroad tie) laid over its most difficult sections.

The flimsy wooden bridge which first crossed the River Kwai was abandoned in favor of a stronger iron structure imported from Java. On 16 October 1943 the line was joined at Konkoita as Japanese film crews recorded the event for propaganda purposes. Although an estimated 50,000-100,000 lives were sacrificed, the project was not a success; the bridge was only used *once* before American B-24 bombers from Sri Lanka destroyed the fourth, fifth, and sixth spans in February 1945. The Allies controlled the bridge after the war, but sold the structure for US$2 million to the Thai goverment a few years later. As war reparations, the Japanese replaced the missing curved girders with two incongruously square beams ironically stamped "Made in Japan."

a life for every sleeper

Kanchanaburi War Cemetery

With its neatly arranged tombstones and poignant messages, this final resting place for 6,982 Allied war prisoners forms one of the most moving tableaux in Southeast Asia. A private foundation in London keeps the cemetery supplied with fresh flowers and supports the Thai gardeners who maintain the lovely grounds. The dead are eulogized by a brass plaque at the entrance, yet not a single grave marker commemorates the estimated 50,000 Asians who perished during construction of the bridge. Among the gravestone messages:

"We think of him still as the same and say: He is not dead, he is just away."

"At the going down of the sun and in the morning, we will remember them."

"Your duty nobly done, my son, sleep on. Mother."

"We shall always remember you smiling, sleep on beloved."

Chinese Cemetery

The adjacent Chinese Cemetery is a study in contrasts. Pauper tombs are hidden away against the walls, while tombstones of the wealthy are elevated like Chinese pagodas. Burial sites are arranged according to the principals of *fung shui,* a Taoist belief in divine geomancy which attempts to balance the ancient principals of yin and yang.

Other Sights

Several other modest attractions are scattered around Kanchanaburi.

Lak Muang: Kanchi's town pillar encloses a Hindu phallic symbol at the original town center, not far from an old town gate and several historic buildings now used as municipal offices. Palmists and fortune-tellers do business across the street from the pillar.

Smashed Car: A curious monument to bad driving sits on Sangchuto Rd. near the a/c bus terminal. Well worth a photograph.

Old Town: Unlike many of the newer towns in Thailand, Kanchanaburi retains vestiges of its past on several small streets such as Pak Praek Rd. and near the vegetable market on Chao Kunen Road.

River Trips

What would a visit to Kanchanaburi be without a boat trip? Most guesthouses can arrange short evening cruises or full-day expeditions to nearby attractions. Three-hour sunset cruises in longtail boats from Nita's Raft House cost 100B to visit the bridge and Chung Kai War Cemetery. Expensive full-day raft trips can also be arranged through better hotels and conventional travel offices such as DT Tours. River trips with "Thai Water Skiing" and "starring Master Entertainer and Dare Devil Sunya" leave on demand from Sunya Rux's Discotheque Raft.

River trips can also be made at upriver locations. Luxury raft hotels sponsor extended river trips from September to March, but not during the dry season when the river is low or during the dangerous rainy season. Alternatively, eight-man longtails can be chartered at Pak Sang Pier (near Nam Tok some 60 km upriver from Kanchi) to visit upriver caves and waterfalls. Prices from Pak Sang Pier are posted at the train station: to Lawa Caves 300B, Sai Yok Yai Falls 500B, Daow Dung Cave 700B. More details below. Be prepared to bargain with the boatman.

Tours And Trekking

A wide variety of tours can be arranged through most guesthouses and hotels. Sample tours from Nita's Guesthouse: Tham Than Lot National Park, Erawan Waterfall, and sapphire mines (120B), Erawan Falls and the bridge (80B), and Prathat Caves, Erawan Falls, and the bridge (100B). Mr. Pirom Angkudie, civil servant, historian, and amateur archaeologist, can be recommended for his three-hour sunset tours of nearby historical and cultural attractions.

Trekking near Sangklaburi and the Burmese border is another possibility. Travelers Trekking in the V.N. Guesthouse charges 2000B for a four-day trek that includes visits to Karen villages, an elephant ride, bamboo river trip, bat cave, and swimming under waterfalls. Best Tours on Khao San Rd. in Bangkok can help with reservations.

Budget Accommodations

Local accommodations can be divided between floating guesthouses on the Kwai Yai River and a variety of conventional hotels located on Sangchuto Road. River-based guesthouses in the center of town are pleasant during the week but incredibly noisy on weekends when Bangkokians flood the region. To escape the all-night parties and blasting disco boats, try the guesthouses north of the park toward the bridge.

The following guesthouses are described starting from central Kanchanaburi and moving toward the bridge.

Nita Guest House: Kanchi's best land-based guesthouse features quiet rooms, communal dining facilities, and a comfortable living room. Owned and operated by warm and wonderful Nita Mrigalakshana, who speaks her English with a broad Texas accent and now works at the new Sheraton Hotel. 3 Visuthararangsi, tel. (034) 511130, 50-80B single, 100-150B double.

Nita Raft House: Several floating crash pads are located along the banks near the city park. Nita's is a popular choice, but store your valuables at her guesthouse for safety reasons. Ask for Supachai and Miss Seangthip. 27 Pakprak Rd., tel. (034) 514521, communal floorspace is 40B, 80B doubles.

Sam's Place: One of the better riverside choices in central Kanchanaburi features a beautiful foyer and cozy restaurant (with a *farang* menu), wooden reclining chairs facing a pond filled with ducks, and several detached bamboo bungalows with small porches. American-educated Sam and his staff can help with river trips, motorcycle rentals, and advice on local transportation. Songkwai Rd., tel. (034) 513971, 60-80B common bath, 150-200B private bath, 250-300B large bungalow with private bath.

Nitaya Guesthouse: Located at the north end of the riverside park is an old favorite with over a dozen rickety bamboo bungalows, disco boat, and river tours at 1300 daily. Songkwai Rd., tel. (034) 513341, 60-80B common bath, 150-180B private bath.

ADDITIONAL KANCHANABURI ACCOMMODATIONS

HOTEL	SINGLE	DOUBLE	ADDRESS	PHONE (034)
Jolly Frog	50-100B	80-150B	28 Maenamwae	514579
Luxury	100-150	150-200	284 Sangchuto	511168
Prasobsuk	150-200	200-250	277 Sangchuto	511777
P.S. Guesthouse	50-80	120-150	54 Rongheeboi	
Suniya Raft House	40	80	River Kwai	
Thai Seree	100	150	142 Sangchuto	511128

River Guesthouse: Several new guest-houses have recently opened on Soi 2 to the north of central Kanchanaburi. All are somewhat distant from the discos and fairly quiet. River GH is a simple place run by Mr. Ek, who also sponsors boat tours. 42 Rongheeboi Rd. Soi 2, tel. (034) 512491, 50-100B s or d.

Rick's Lodge: A friendly place run by a German-speaking Thai from Bangkok. Rick's has several floating bungalows and 12 bi-level rooms senselessly crammed together back from the river. River views are blocked by trees. Try the homemade Farmhouse Bread in the Salad House across the street. 48/5 Rongheeboi Rd. Soi 2, tel. (034) 514831, 140-200B.

P.S. Guesthouse: Excellent views and a cozy restaurant make this a good choice. 54 Rongheeboi Rd. Soi 2, tel. (034) 513039, 50-80B common, 120-150B private bath.

Jolly Frog Guesthouse: The largest guesthouse in Kanchanaburi has over 50 rooms facing a central courtyard filled with palms and grass. Rooms inside the two-story thatched buildings are small and ordinary with mattresses placed on the floor. Services include motorcycle rentals, a spacious circular dining hall, German management, and minibuses to Bangkok daily at 1100 and 1430. 28 Maenamwae Rd., tel. (034) 514579, 50-80B common, 120-150B private bath.

U.T. Guesthouse: A genuine homestay in a light blue, modern, two-story house located about 100 meters back from the river. Peaceful, friendly, and cozy with just three double rooms plus dormitory. 275 River Kwai Rd., tel. (034) 513539, 60B per person.

Bamboo Guesthouse: The most idyllic guesthouse in Kanchanaburi is located at the end of a dirt road about 300 meters before the bridge. Big lawn with a small pond; often filled but otherwise highly recommended. Call first to check on vacancies. 3-5 Soi Vietnam, tel. (034) 512532, 60-120B bamboo bungalows, 250-500B upstairs rooms in a red brick building.

V.L. Guesthouse: The only other land-based budget guesthouse worth recommending (besides Nita's) is this modern place opposite the River Kwai Hotel. Rooms are very clean, well furnished, and include a private bath; an excellent deal for anyone who dislikes riverside accommodation. 18/11 Sangchuto Rd., tel. (034) 513546, 120-160B fan, 250-300B a/c.

Moderate Accommodations

Most mid-priced rooms in the 400-800B range are located outside of town and described below under "River Kwai Raft Resorts." Located within the city limits are a few moderate places, chiefly patronized on weekends by Thais from Bangkok.

Duck Raft House: For better facilities in the 550-650B price range (s or d), check the offices of this floating hotel near Nita Raft House.

Kasem Island Resort: Kanchanaburi's first upscale raft hotel features seven bamboo cottages and 20 houseboats with private baths, patios overlooking the river, and an excellent floating restaurant. Facilities are only adequate but managers are making improvements. Ka-sem Island head office is located at Chukadon Wharf, 27 Chaichumpol Rd., tel. (034) 511603, Bangkok reservation tel. (02) 391-6672, fax (02) 391-5085, 650-750B.

River Kwai Family Camp: This land-based resort seven km north of town offers horseback riding (250B per hour), canoe rentals (100B), and two-day wildlife safaris organized by Mrs. Lee Rhodes. Popular with expatriate families from Bangkok. Box 2, tel. (034) 512733, 450-700B.

Luxury Accommodations

The tourist boom of the recent years has finally brought the big boys to Kanchanaburi. Proper-ties opening in the early '90s include a Sheraton, Imperial, and a hotel operated by the Siam City chain.

Rama River Kwai Hotel: Kanchi's oldest up-scale hotel is popular with businessmen, tour groups, and Japanese visitors. All rooms are a/c and come with private bath, TV, and video. . . . but why stay here when you can float on a raft? 284 Sangchuto, tel. (034) 511269, 600-1000B.

Sheraton River Kwai: A joint Thai/Ameri-can property opened recently near the famous bridge. Facilities include two pools, tennis courts, and five restaurants. Tambon Ta Makam, tel. (034) 234-5599, fax (034) 236-8320, 2200-3600B.

River Kwai Raft Resorts

Kanchanaburi province currently lists over 50 registered raft hotels located on the upper reach-es of the Kwai Yai (near Nam Tok and Sai Yok Falls), at Sri Nakarin Lake, and on Krung Kravia Lake near the Burmese border. The daily per-person charge of 500-800B often includes three meals and boat transportation. Some are quite simple and operate without electricity; others have swimming pools and a/c rooms with hot water.

Those most popular with Westerners are de-scribed below. Travel agents in Bangkok make reservations, though these are only necessary on weekends. Most of the following properties provide transportation from downtown Kan-chanaburi to the raft hotel. The local tourist office and travel agents near the bus stop can also help with details and phone calls.

Jungle Rafts: Operated by Frenchman Jacques Bes and his Mon employees, Jungle Rafts is probably the most popular river resort in the Kanchanaburi region. Bungalows include running water and private bath but lack elec-tricity, phones, TVs, and other signs of civiliza-tion. Thai-French evening meals are followed by Mon dances accompanied by Burmese gongs and cymbals. Jungle Rafts is located on the Kwai Noi River, 60 km from Kanchanaburi. Reservations can be made from travel agents in Bangkok or directly from River Kwai Floatel Company. Upper Kwai Noi River near Pak Sang Pier, Bangkok tel. (02) 245-3069, 600-900B per person including meals.

River Kwai Village Hotel: A 60-unit lodge composed of a dozen floating rafts and five longhouses subdivided into private chalets. All rooms are a/c with full amenities. Popular with group tours from Bangkok. Upper Kwai Noi River near Pak Sang Pier (70 km from Kanchanaburi), Bangkok tel. (02) 251-7552, 800-1000B per per-son including meals.

Restaurants

Kanchanaburi's best restaurants are the half-dozen floating cafes tied up at the south end of the fitness park. Most are marked in Thai script only, but all specialize in seafood and highly prized river carp favored for their fatty and suc-culent meat. Unfortunately, the giant *pla yi sok* (the Julien carp used for those terrific street signs) has been hunted nearly to extinction and other species now substitute.

Krua Thien Tong: Arrive for sunset and try deep-fried freshwater catfish or frog legs fried in garlic. Songkwai Road. Moderate.

Pae Karn: Another floating restaurant known for its *log tong* and country-style Thai dishes such as *tom yam pla* made with river carp. Songkwai Road. Moderate.

Foodstalls: Cheap meals are found at the outdoor foodstalls on Sangchuto Rd. near the bus terminal.

Punee Restaurant: The first *farang* bar in Kanchi is owned by Danny and his wife, Punee. Danny does local tours, sells sapphires, rents well-maintained motorcycles, gives fishing ad-vice ("don't bother"), operates a book exchange, and dabbles in real estate while running the bar. Ban Nuer Road. Inexpensive.

Services

The tourist office on Sangchuto Rd., one of the best TAT branches in Thailand, offers maps, information on river huts, plus tips on local transportation and conditions at the Burmese border. Post offices are located on Sangchuto Rd.and on Lak Muang Rd. near the city pillar. Visas can be extended at Thai Immigration, 286 Sangchuto Road. International phone service is available from the Telephone Center on U-Thong Road. An excellent map of the Kanchanaburi region is published by Prannok Vidhaya Publisher, though their town details fail to list most of the newer guesthouses.

Kanchanaburi Tracking Tours (tel. 034-514407) at 363 Mae Nam Kwai Road organizes raft trips on the Kwai Noi River, plus excursions to Three Pagodas Pass and Tung Yai National Park.

Getting There From Bangkok

Ordinary and a/c buses to Kanchanaburi leave every 15 minutes and take three hours from the Southern Bus Terminal in Thonburi. Trains for Kanchi leave twice daily at 0800 and 1350 from Thonburi Station.

Weekend Train Tours

Whirlwind tours sponsored by the State Railways are also possible. A special train leaves Bangkok's Hualampong Station weekends at 0635, stops at the *chedi* in Nakhon Pathom for 40 minutes (0735-0815), pauses for 30 minutes at the Kanchi bridge (0930-1000), and takes a three-hour lunch break at Nam Tok (1130-1430), enough time to visit the nearby waterfall or go down to the river for a quick look. On the return trip, it stops for 45 minutes at the war cemetery (1605-1650) before arriving back in Bangkok at 1930. Whew! Advanced bookings can be made by calling the State Railways Advance Booking Office at (02) 225-6964.

The State Railways sponsors other weekend tours of the Kanchanaburi region. The rafting program costs 280B and includes Nakhon Pathom, local sights, plus a short raft trip under the bridge. Another tour for 240B includes Nakhon Pathom, Kanchanaburi, and the Khmer ruins at Prasat Muang Sing. The final option at 280B includes Nakhon Pathom, Kanchanaburi, Sri Nakarin Dam, and Erawan Falls.

Getting Around

Bicycling is the perfect way to get around Kanchanaburi. Ratty old bikes can be rented for most guesthouses for about 20B per day. Motorcycles cost 150-250B per day from the Honda dealer and various guesthouses. Experienced cyclists will find this an excellent way to explore the countryside and visit remote temples and caves. Motorcycle prices and conditions vary widely, so it's best to shop around. Jeep rentals cost 700-800B per day.

Slow Train To Nowhere

A slow but romantic way to explore the historic railway is the funky third-class train which leaves Kanchanaburi daily at 0600 and 1030 and arrives in Nam Tok two hours later. The 1030 train allows you three hours to visit the river or a nearby waterfall before catching the 1520 train back to Kanchanaburi. Creaky, hair-raising, and historically poignant, many travelers consider the *Nam Tok Special* the most memorable train ride in Thailand.

Leaving Kanchanaburi

Kanchanaburi is connected by road and rail to Bangkok and other neighboring provinces. The chart below summarizes departing bus services.

Bangkok: Ordinary bus 81 for Bangkok and Nakhon Pathom departs from the main bus terminal. Air-conditioned buses leave every 15 minutes from the office on Sangchuto Road. Share taxis wait at the nearby intersection.

North: Travelers should go direct rather than backtracking to Bangkok. To Ayuthaya, take bus 419 from U-Thong Rd. to Suphanburi (two to three hours), then yellow bus 703 to Ayuthaya (one hour). To Sukothai, take bus 487 to Nakhon Sawan (four hours), then bus 99 to Sukothai (three hours).

South: For Petchburi, take bus 461 to Ratchaburi, then bus 73 to Petchburi. For Hua Hin, take bus 461 to Ratchaburi, then bus 71 to Hua Hin. Bus services are also available from Ratchaburi to Surat Thani and Phuket.

Floating Market: Public transportation is also available to the floating market at Damnern Saduak. An early start is essential to reach the market during prime time, 0700-0900. From the main bus terminal in Kanchanaburi, take yellow bus 461 to Bang Pae intersection, walk down the road, then take bus 78 or the minibus to Damnern Saduak. The market is one km south. Allow two hours for the journey. Alternatively, take bus 81 to Nakhon Pathom and then bus 78 to Damnern Saduak.

SOUTH OF KANCHANABURI

South of Kanchanaburi are several temples such as Wat Tam Mongkam (five km from Kanchanaburi), Wat Tam Sua (16 km), and Wat Pra Dong (40 km). None are major architectural triumphs, but rather curiosity pieces best appreciated for their sense of kitsch and unbridled commercialism.

Accommodations are unnecessary in this region since all temples can be visited on day-trips.

Transportation is somewhat difficult to these southern attractions. Wat Tam Mongkam and the Tha Muang temples are easy day journeys with public transportation, but the more distant Wat Pra Dong and the Don Chedi Memorial require private wheels. A few suggestions are given below. Motorcyclists can reach all three sites in a single day.

Wat Tam Mongkam
The Cave Temple of the Golden Dragon was chiefly known for a 75-year-old Thai nun who floated in a pool of water while meditating *and* whistling. Several years ago the old lady died and has been replaced with a younger nun who performs only for large crowds on weekends. This neat trick attracts a steady stream of devout Thais, but most Westerners find the commercialism and zoo-like atmosphere rather tawdry.

Aside from the floating meditation routine, the temple complex features a series of nondescript modern *wats* adjacent to the parking lot and a maze of limestone caves to the rear. The entrance is reached after a long climb up the stairs which stop near an old Chinese hermit who sits in quiet meditation. The illuminated walkway through the cave leads to viewpoints over Kanchanaburi and the surrounding countryside.

Wat Tam Mongkam is located across the river, some five km south of Kanchanaburi. Visitors with rented bicycles can pedal to the ferry crossing on Chaichumpol Rd., cross the river, then continue three km south to the temple. Motorcyclists can use the new bridge located farther

BUSES FROM KANCHANABURI

DESTINATION	BUS	HOURS
Bangkok	81	3
Nakhon Pathom	81	1½
Nam Tok	8203	1
Sai Yok Falls	8203	2
Sangklaburi	8203	4
Three Pagodas	8203	6
Ratchaburi	461	2
Suphanburi	411	2
Boploi	325	1½
Erawan Falls	8170	2
Tham Than Rot	325	3

south down Sangchuto Road. Public transportation may be available; inquire at the TAT office.

Temples Near Tha Muang
Two very impressive but half-completed temples are situated on a limestone hilltop near Tha Muang, 16 km south of Kanchanaburi. Wat Tam Sua, the Chinese-style pagoda to the left, is fronted by a fat, jolly Buddha surrounded by 18 superbly carved figures. To the right is Wat Tam Kao Noi which, in perhaps a show of religious competition, is separated from the adjacent temple by a concrete wall. This attractive Thai-style temple offers a worship hall with cool marble floors, mound-shaped tower, and a gigantic Buddha complete with automated treadmill to help expedite monetary donations! From the terrace you'll enjoy excellent views over the valley of Kanchanaburi.

To reach the temples, take bus 461 or 81 to the dam near Tha Muang. Motorcycle taxis charge 30-40B for the roundtrip excursion to the temples, located four km east on a limestone mountain.

Wat Pra Dong
This isolated temple, 40 km east of Kanchanaburi, is revered for its immense yellow-frocked stone where, according to Thai tradition, Buddha reclined before ascending to the heavens. A young monk will unlock the main *bot*. Another Buddha footprint surmounts the hill to the left.

KANCHANABURI REGION

© MOON PUBLICATIONS, INC.

NORTH OF KANCHANABURI— ROUTE 3199

The waterfalls, limestone mountains, caves, and other natural wonders north of Kanchanaburi comprise one of the loveliest regions in Thailand.

Attractions are mostly natural sites rather than historic or religious monuments. The region boasts three immense national parks, dozens of deep caves and plunging waterfalls, plus a wildlife conservation park at Khao Salakpra. Highlights include Bophloi (a gem-mining town 50 km from Kanchanaburi), Erawan Falls in Erawan National Park (65 km), Sri Nakarin Dam at the south end of Sri Nakarin Lake (70 km), Pratat Cave near Sri Nakarin Dam (75 km), Tham Lod Cave in Chalerm Ratanakosin National Park (100 km), plus Huay Khamin Falls in Sri Nakarin National Park (102 km). Erawan Falls is unquestionably the most popular sight because of its superb set of waterfalls and easy accessibility from Kanchanaburi.

Accommodations are plentiful throughout the region. Sri Nakarin Lake has several floating raft houses in all possible price ranges, including **Hadtong** and **Kwai Yai River Huts** near Si Sawat, **Dao Neu Island Resort** and **Feungfa Raft Resort** on the west side of the lake, and **Erawan Resort** near Khao Salak Pra Wildlife Conservation Park. The TAT in Kanchanaburi has a complete list and can make specific recommendations. Budget hotels are located in the towns of Si Sawat, Nong Prue, and Bophloi.

Transportation is rather straightforward. Popular destinations along Route 3199 such as Erawan Falls and Si Sawat can be reached with public bus 8170. Bus 325 reaches the gem mines at Bophloi and Tham Lod Cave west of Nong Prue. Inexpensive group tours to all these attractions can be arranged through most guest-houses and hotels.

Erawan Falls

The 300,000 *rai* of forested area around Erawan Falls was declared a national park in 1967, when its name was changed from Khao Salob to that of the divine elephant whose shape is found in a natural rock formation at the top of the falls. Erawan National Park consists of limestone mountains from which Erawan Falls crashes down through 10 levels before emptying into the Kwai Yai River. The lower falls and swimming pools are perpetually crowded with Thai tourists who rarely make the arduous climb to the far superior falls on the upper sections of the mountain. Keep climbing, and remember to bring along a swimsuit and sneakers for the hike. Unless you enjoy suffocating crowds, do not visit this park on weekends! As with all waterfalls in Southeast Asia, Erawan is best visited during the rainy season from July to November when water is most plentiful.

Accommodations are available in the park in a bamboo dormitory for 50B and in larger 10-man park chalets for 600B. Ten km south of the park entrance is the popular **Erawan Resort** (tel. 034-513001) where upscale bungalows cost 600-1000B.

Erawan National Park and falls are located 65 km from town. A full day is necessary to enjoy the falls. Bus 8170 to Erawan departs daily at 0800 from the bus terminal and takes almost two hours to reach the park turnoff, located about one km from the park entrance. Erawan Falls is another two km west of the park entrance. The last bus back to Kanchanaburi departs around 1600.

Sri Nakarin Lake

Sri Nakarin Lake is an immense freshwater lake formed by the Sri Nakarin Dam at the southern end. The lake offers fishing, luxurious raft hotels mentioned above, and weekend boat tours aboard the *J.R. Queen*. Prathat Cave is 10 km northwest of the dam on the west side of the lake.

Sri Nakarin National Park

The region's second most popular set of falls, Huay Khamin ("Tumeric Falls"), is located in Sri Nakarin National Park some 25 km northwest of Erawan National Park. Huay Khamin falls is actually larger and more powerful than the falls at Erawan, but the additional travel time minimizes the number of visitors.

Accommodations are available at the park headquarters and in several raft houses located on the lake. The Kanchanaburi TAT can help with recommendations and reservations.

The park can be reached by taking bus 8170 to Tha Kradan Pier on the east side of the lake about 24 km north of the dam, followed by a local ferry ride across the lake to the park entrance. Visitors with private transportation can drive directly to the park via the westside road.

Bophloi

Both blue and star sapphires are mined from open pits that pocket the farmland north and west of Bophloi. Many of the mines have been exhausted, but enough activity remains to make this a worthwhile stop for visitors interested in traditional mining activities. Gem prices are reasonably low from local shops, though many of the stones are either worthless or clever synthetics foisted off on unsuspecting tourists.

Chalerm Ratanakosin National Park

This 59-square-km national park, 100 km north of Kanchanaburi, is chiefly visited for its thick jungle, two immense caves of great interest to speleologists, and three waterfalls located within easy walking distance of the park headquarters. Tham Lod Yai, the largest of the caves with an estimated depth of over 500 meters, is filled with unusual limestone formations capped with miniature temples and images of the Buddha. The three waterfalls are Trai Trang, Than Ngun, and Than Thong.

The park has the usual choice of accommodations. Backpackers can pitch a tent near the headquarters for just 20B per night. Bungalows operated by the park service have dormitories for 100B and ten-man chalets from 600B. Reservations should be made in advance through the TAT office in Kanchanaburi.

Chalerm Ratanakosin National Park can be reached with bus 325 to the small town of Ban Nong Prue from where mini-trucks continue west to the park entrance. One-way travel consumes almost four hours, making this an overnight destination.

ROUTE 323 TO THE
BURMESE BORDER

Route 323, the road going northwest toward the Burmese border, is the most popular side trip from Kanchanaburi. Dozens of sights are located along the road, which parallels the Kwai Noi River. Cinema fans should note that many scenes in *The Deer Hunter* (jumping from helicopters into the river, and Russian roulette with the Viet Cong) were filmed near Sai Yok Yai Falls on the Kwai Noi River.

Attractions include the Ban Kao Museum (Neolithic remains located 38 km from Kanchanaburi), Wat Muang Sing Khmer Temple (43 km), Nam Tok (the railway terminus 60 km from Kanchanaburi), Hellfire Pass Memorial (78 km), Lawa Caves (75 km), Sai Yok Yai Falls (104 km), Hin Da Hot Springs (130 km), Tongpapum (153 km), Sangklaburi (235 km), and the border crossing at Three Pagodas Pass (241 km). No wonder people spend weeks around Kanchanaburi.

Accommodations on Route 323 and along the Upper Kwai Noi River are among the best in the Kanchanaburi region. An excellent way to relax and enjoy the area's great natural appeal is on an upriver raft house described above, or recommended by the Kanchanaburi TAT office. The TAT has a complete list of over 50 guesthouses and river houses situated outside Kanchanaburi. River-based accommodations are also available on Krung Kravia Lake near Tongpapum. Land-based hotels and guesthouses are found in Tongpapum, Sangklaburi, and Three Pagodas Pass. More details and specific recommendations are given below.

Transportation options include group tours, Nam Tok train, public buses, and motorcycle rentals. Inexpensive group tours are arranged by guesthouses, hotels, and travel agencies in Kanchanaburi. Prices vary sharply between low-end guesthouses and expensive travel agencies, making comparison shopping absolutely necessary. The Nam Tok train journey described above (see "Slow Train to Nowhere") is an excellent way to see the countryside and enjoy one of the best train journeys in Thailand. Most visitors take the 1030 train from the central station in Kanchanaburi and return on the 1530 train from Nam Tok.

Most attractions in the Kwai Noi Valley (except for remote spots such as Prasat Muang Sing and Ban Kao Museum) can be reached with bus 8203 departing from the main bus terminal in Kanchanaburi. Bus 8203 plies the highway between Kanchanaburi and Three Pagodas Pass from sunrise until sunset. Service is frequent and buses pass to pick up passengers every 15-30 minutes. Motorcyclists can reach most nearby sights in a single day before returning to Kanchanaburi. Alternatively, one can rent a motorcycle for several days and travel all the way up to the Burmese border at Three Pagodas Pass. Despite the danger and horrendous driving habits of most Thais, motorcycles provide an unparalleled degree of flexibility and allow you to quickly visit even the most remote destinations.

Chung Kai War Cemetery

Kanchanaburi has another war cemetery, almost identical to its counterpart in town, about three km away on the banks of the Kwai Noi River. Chung Kai contains some 1,750 inscribed tombstones set on the former site of the Chung Kai POW camp. The tombstones at Chung Kai and 6,982 at the Allied War Cemetery in Kanchanaburi account for only half the estimated 16,000 Allied prisoners who died during the railway construction. The missing prisoners were cremated and left unaccounted for by the Japanese.

The cemetery is best reached with rented bicycle or motorcycle taken across the ferry near the floating restaurants on Songkwai Road. Hikers might take the ferry and then attempt to hitch a ride to the cemetery. A long wait can be expected since traffic is very light.

Kao Poon Cave

Limestone caves near Kanchanaburi often serve as Buddhist temples filled with Buddhist and Saivite images illuminated with electric lights. Kao Poon Cave, six km from Kanchanaburi, is situated behind Wat Tham Kao Poon, where friendly monks have erected English-language signs and volunteer as guides through the caves. A small donation is appropriate after the tour.

Stone Gardens

Continue over the hill and turn right near the Thai Agricultural College, marked in Thai script only. Another left and then right leads to a curious collection of volcanic formations surrounded by poured concrete walkways. Motorcyclists can return to the main highway and continue northwest to Ban Kao Museum and the Khmer ruins at Prasat Muang Sing.

Ban Kao Neolithic Museum

Good news also came from the construction of the Death Railway. In 1943 a Dutch prisoner of war named Van Heekeren stumbled across some Neolithic artifacts while working on the railway near Nam Tok. In 1956 an American anthropologist, Heider, confirmed the importance of Van Heekeren's discoveries. Intrigued by these reports, Thai and Danish archaeologists undertook systematic excavations in 1961 and successfully uncovered evidence that the Kwai Noi Valley had been inhabited by early man for over 10,000 years. A new chapter in the prehistory of Southeast Asia had been opened.

A small museum housing a modest collection of pottery, ax heads, and jewelry made from animal bone has been constructed beside an open-air burial site. The displays will appeal most to amateur paleontologists since major artifacts have been transferred to the National Museum in Bangkok.

Ban Kao is located on a side road about 10 km off the main highway and is difficult to reach without private transportation. With the opening of Prasat Muang Sing, however, most guesthouses and hotels can now arrange daytours to Ban Kao, Muang Sing, and other nearby sights such as Sai Yok and Nam Tok. Independent travelers can take the train to Ban Kao (Tha Kilen) Station, and then walk or hitch the remaining two km west to Muang Sing and six km south to Ban Kao. Motorcyclists can easily visit Ban Kao and Muang Sing before continuing north to Sai Yok and Three Pagodas Pass.

Several popular raft houses are located on the Kwai Noi near the Ban Kao Museum. **River Kwai Farm** (Bangkok tel. 02-235-6433), four km south from Ban Kao Train Station, is a well-known raft lodge with rooms including meals from 600B.

Prasat Muang Sing

What were Cambodians doing so far west? This marvelous Khmer temple complex and military outpost, 45 km from Kanchanaburi, was constructed during the Lopburi Period, 1157-1207, as a Khmer trading post along the Kwai Noi River and to guard against Burmese invasion through Three Pagodas Pass. Now completely restored, Muang Sing ("City of Lions") marks the westernmost advance of Cambodian power and provides elegant testimony to their vast territorial claims. The 460-*rai* park was declared a national historic park under the administration of the Department of Fine Arts in 1987.

Muang Sing encompasses four groups of ruins composed of laterite bricks and surrounded by earthern walls arranged to suggest cosmological symbolism so favored by Angkorian rulers. Entrance is made through reconstructed gates which flank a dusty road that leads to the central compound. A small outdoor museum to the right of the main complex contains sculpture of Mahayana Buddhist deities and stuccowork removed from the interior shrines. Prasat Muang Sing, the principal shrine, faces east toward Angkor. Hemmed in by four laterite walls oriented toward each of the cardinal directions, the interior holds a sculpture of Avalokitesvara, which establishes the sanctuary as a Mahayana Buddhist center.

A pair of Neolithic skeletons are displayed *in situ* on the riverbanks to the south outside the earthern walls. Other Neolithic remains discovered near Muang Sing have been removed to the museums at Ban Kao and the National Museum in Bangkok.

Idyllic raft houses are plentiful near Prasat Muang Sing and Ban Kao to the south. Within sight of the burial site at Muang Sing are several raft houses where bamboo rooms with three meals cost from 600B per day. North of Muang Sing are the Yang Thone River Kwai and River Kwai Jungle House, two raft hotels with floating bamboo bungalows from 600B.

Prasat Muang Sing Historical Park is open daily 0800-1600 and entrance is 20B.

Nam Tok

Nam Tok, 60 km from Kanchanaburi, is a nondescript town located at the end of the railway line. Most visitors arrive on the 1030 train from Kanchanaburi and leave Nam Tok on the 1530 train. Public buses back to Kanchanaburi ply the highway until nightfall. A sign posted at the train station lists suggested prices for trips up the nearby Kwai Noi River: Lawa Cave 300B, Sai Yok Yai Falls 500B, Dawa Dung Cave 700B. Be prepared to bargain with the boatman.

The **Suvatana Hotel** in Nam Tok has basic rooms for 80-100B, while the **Sai Yok Noi Bungalows** located 300 meters north along the highway has better rooms for 200-500B.

Kwai Noi River Trip

Several good explorations start from Nam Tok. Visitors short on time might hire a *samlor* or walk three km north to Sai Yok Noi (Kao Phang) Waterfall, an unremarkable and perpetually crowded place surrounded by restaurants and tacky souvenir stalls.

A better option is to take a tricycle from the train station for 10B down to Pak Sang Pier. From here, eight-man longtail boats can be hired for upriver journeys. Boat prices are listed at the train station, but most journeys are prohibitively expensive except for larger groups. A recommended six-hour trip stops at Lawa Caves (biggest cave in the region) and Sai Yok Yai Falls, where the Russian roulette scenes from *The Deer Hunter* were filmed. This tour costs about 1000B per boatload—not bad for five or six people.

Excellent raft hotels are located around Pak Sang. The River Kwai Village Hotel and Jungle Rafts described above are two beautiful raft lodges which charge 600-800B for private room, boat ride from Pak Sang, and three meals. Travel agents in Bangkok and Kanchanaburi can make arrangements.

Hellfire Pass Memorial

A moving memorial to Allied prisoners and Asian conscripts who died while constructing the railway line near Hellfire Pass was erected several years ago by the Australian-Thai Chamber of Commerce. During three months of labor, over 1,000 Australian and British prisoners worked around the clock; only 300 survived the ordeal. The park consists of a series of trails which reach the Konyu Cutting where a memorial plaque has been fastened to the rock, and Hin Tok trestle bridge, which collapsed three times during its construction. The association hopes to restore some of the track and display trains used during the construction.

The memorial is located near Hellfire Pass, 80 km from Kanchanaburi and 18 km north of Nam Tok. English signs marking the turnoff are posted on Route 323. Bus travelers should alight at the Royal Thai Army Camp and then hike 500 meters to the trailhead which leads to the Konyu Cutting.

Sai Yok National Park

Tucked away inside 500-square-km Sai Yok National Park are the small but very pretty Sai Yok Yai Falls, which emerge from underground streams and tumble gracefully into the Kwai Noi River. The falls are widely celebrated in Thai poetry and song. Two large caves are located within the park boundaries but across the broad Kwai Noi River. Lawa Cave, the largest in the region, is a wonderland of dripping stalactites and stalagmites. Dawa Dung Cave is northwest of Sai Yok on the west bank of the Kwai Noi River. Other attractions inside the park include some Neolithic remains uncovered by Thai archaeologists, remains of a Japanese military camp, and a small bat cave known for its almost microscopic inhabitants.

The park entrance is about 38 km north of Nam Tok, but the falls and river are hidden three km off the main road. Bus travelers should get off at the national park sign and then flag down a passing car or face a long and dusty walk. Motorcycle taxis may be available.

Camping is permitted inside the park near the hanging bridge which vaguely resembles San Francisco's Golden Gate. The national park has several 10-man bungalows for 600-800B. Within sight of the curious bridge are several beautiful raft hotels where bamboo bungalows cost 450-600B.

Hin Da Hot Springs

Two small and very grubby swimming pools filled with warm water are located 500 meters off Route 323 about 130 km north of Kanchanaburi. Constructed by the Japanese in World War II, the two concrete tanks are now open to both male and female bathers. Not recommended.

TONGPAPUM

The first major town between Kanchanaburi and Three Pagodas Pass is Tongpapum, a cowboy village of twisted, rutted streets, ragged children, and hand-pump gasoline stations. Tongpapum lies at the southern edge of the vast Krung Kravia Lake created by the Khao Lam Dam, a major hydroelectric source for Bangkok and central Thailand. The town essentially serves as a petrol and rest stop en route to Sangklaburi and Three Pagodas Pass.

The paved road north from Tongpapum passes through rolling hills and limestone canyons which flank Krung Kravia Lake. Motorcyclists may stop at Krung Kravia Falls on the right and visit Khao Lam National Park at the midway point.

Accommodations

A few hotels are located on the main road which runs off the highway. **Som Chai Nuk Bungalows** has decent fan rooms with private bath from 100B and a/c from 200B. **Si Thong Pha Phum Bungalows** farther down the main road has 28 fan and a/c rooms in the same price range. **S. Bunyong Bungalows** at the end of the street is similar.

Several upscale raft hotels are located on nearby Krung Kravia Lake. **Kao Laem Raft Resort** (Bangkok tel. 02-277-0599) charges 400-600B, while **Thongphaphum Valley** and **Ban Rimdoi** (tel. 034-513218) charge 600-800B for floating bamboo bungalows.

SANGKLABURI

Sangklaburi is an old Mon town inhabited by an ethnic mix of Mon, Karen, Burmese, and Thai. The main attraction is an old Mon temple called Wat Wang Vivangkaram located three km southwest of town toward the reservoir. The complex consists of a *stupa* perhaps 300-400 years old and a newer *stupa*, Chedi Luang Paw Utama, modeled after the Mahabodhi shrine in Bodgaya, India. A smaller Buddhist temple is found within the city limits. Another good trip is to 36-tiered Takhian Thong Falls, and to Kroen Tho Falls just across the Burmese border. Sangklaburi also has a small market frequented on weekends by hilltribes and Karen smugglers down from Three Pagodas Pass.

Note that there are no banks in Sangklaburi; change enough money in Kanchanaburi.

Accommodations

P Guesthouse: Travelers usually stay at the P

Guesthouse, located 900 meters north of the bus stop on the edge of Songkalia Lake. Proprietor Darunee Yenjai can help arrange treks to nearby Mon villages, an underwater Thai town submerged by the dam, and the longest handmade wooden bridge in Thailand, which leads to an old Mon village. He also has motorbikes for rent. Rooms cost 60-150B.

Sri Daeng Hotel: The Sri Daeng Hotel near the bus stop has decent rooms. Sankla Rd., tel. (034) 512996, 100-120B.

Raft Hotels: Several raft hotels are located outside town. **Songkalia River Huts** (Bangkok reservations 02-427-1583) is two km north of town toward Wat Mon, where the Songkalia River empties into the lake. Large floating bungalows cost 300-500B. Another option is the **Runtee Palace** (Bangkok tel. 02-314-2656), 15 minutes by boat from Saphan Runtee Pier, where luxurious raft homes go from 1000B including boat ride and meals.

Transportation

Sangklaburi is 220 km from Kanchanaburi. Bus 8203 departs Kanchanaburi daily at 0645, 0900, 1045, 1315, and takes about five hours to reach Sangklaburi. Motorcyclists should allow a full day with stops at Ban Kao Museum, Muang Sing Khmer ruins, Nam Tok, and a brief swim at Sai Yok Yai Falls. Gasoline stations are located in Nam Tok, Tongpapum, and Sangklaburi.

THREE PAGODAS PASS

The border crossing into Burma at Three Pagodas Pass is named after a trio of historic cone-shaped *chedis* known as Pra Chedi Sam Ong. Centuries ago this was the spot from where marauding Burmese armies marched into Thailand on their traditional invasions. Today the small trading post at the pass is the scene of political struggles between the Burmese government, Mon National Liberation Army (MNLA), Karen National Union (KNU), and the All Burma Students Democratic Front (ABSDF), which has set up an opposition government to fight the regime of Ne Win.

Three Pagodas Pass remains in a constant state of flux. During the mid-1980s it thrived as a prosperous trading town dominated by the Karens, who collected a five percent tax on all goods smuggled across the border. Burmese products such as gems, jade, and *longyis* (sarongs) were exchanged for Thai batteries, roofing iron, and even television sets. After the political disruptions in 1988, the Burmese government renewed their military offensive against the Karens and Mons by attacking Three Pagodas Pass and burning the shantytown to the ground. The village has since revived itself but remains a staging ground for military and political struggle.

Attractions

Locals can point out the few sights around town: the three whitewashed pagodas, the site of the old station which marked the end of the Death Railway, and the track itself which, according to Thai archaeologists, dates back to the earliest human settlement in the region.

Westerners are occasionally allowed to cross the border and visit the adjacent Burmese village where handicrafts, cheroots, and silver jewelry are sold in the local market. A few travelers have reportedly ventured across the border to the Mon outpost of Kreng Thaw and continued by boat down to Kyain Seiggyi and Moulmein. Conditions change with the season and should be double-checked with travelers and the TAT office in Kanchanaburi.

Accommodations

Most travelers visit Three Pagodas Pass on a day-trip from Sangklaburi. **Three Pagodas Pass Resort** (tel. 034-511079, Bangkok reservations 02-412-4159) has large bungalows from 300B.

Transportation

Three Pagodas Pass is 241 km from Kanchanaburi and 22 km from Sangklaburi along a rough road passable only during the dry season from October to June. The road turns off Route 323 about four km before Sangklaburi. Mini-trucks to the border leave Sangklaburi each morning and return in the late afternoon.

SUPHANBURI

Suphanburi is an ancient city possibly connected with the mythical empire of Suwanaphum mentioned in early Buddhist chronicles. The present town was founded in the 15th century as a military outpost against Burmese incursions, although the discovery of Neolithic artifacts and terra-cotta figurines of U-Thong periods indicate that the region has been inhabited since prehistoric times.

Located 107 km northwest of Bangkok and 70 km from Kanchanaburi, modern Suphanburi is a prosperous town with little of interest aside from a handful of temples and Buddha images. The town is best visited as a short stop between Kanchanaburi and Ayuthaya. After arrival, hire a *tuk tuk* for 50B and make a two-hour tour of Wat Palalai, Wat Mahathat, the footprint at Wat Pra Rob, and Wat Suwanapum. Ask the driver to drop you at the appropriate bus terminal for onward connections.

Wat Palalai

Suphanburi's most impressive sight is the immense Buddha situated three km west of town on the road to Kanchanaburi. The whitewashed sanctuary features boat-shaped walls typical of the Ayuthaya Period and a pair of large bronze bells at the entrance. Surrounding the structure are humorous plaster images of an elephant, a monkey, and a camel in the rear courtyard.

The central image, Luang Por Toh ("Giant Buddha"), is one of the most impressive statues in Thailand, not only for its immense proportions but for its unusual, so-called European position. Cast during the early Ayuthaya Period, the figure sits with both hands on knees and right palm held skyward. The head features a stylized nose, upturned lips, oversized eyelids, and soaring top spires which almost pierce the roof. The ankles and three-meter feet have been almost completely covered with gold leaf. Flanking the massive figure are four seated Buddhas in Ayuthaya style.

Wat Chum Nun Song

On the opposite side of the road and slightly down from Wat Palalai is a restored red-brick *chedi* which dates from the early Ayuthaya Period.

Wat Mahathat

Situated on a side road off Highway 321 are the remains of a Khmer-style *prang* which dates from the first period of the Ayuthaya empire. The front courtyard has a modern *viharn* with Sukothai walking Buddhas mounted in the

SUPHANBURI

WAT MAHATHAT

TO ANG THONG

TO BANGKOK

TO KANCHANABURI

WAT CHAI NAWAT

KAT HOTEL

WAT CHUM NUN SONG

CITY PILLARS

PACHARA HOTEL

SUPHANBURI RIVER

PRA PHANWASA RD.

WAT PALALAI

WAT PRATU SAN

WAT SUWANAPHUM

POST OFFICE

OLD TOWN

SUKSUNT HOTEL

MARKET

WAT PRA ROB

BUS STATION

SULAK HOTEL

SRI SUPHAN HOTEL

VALENTIN HOTEL

BUSES FROM AYUTHAYA

MUN HAN RD.

0   100m

© MOON PUBLICATIONS, INC.

eaves, and an impressive wooden assembly hall with outstanding portico carvings. To the rear stands the ancient *prang* with a reconstructed concrete spire over corner guardians, *nagas,* and traces of original stucco. A steep staircase leads to the interior crypt which overlooks several small *salas* filled with seated Buddhas.

Wat Pra Rob

Wat Pra Rob features a large reclining Buddha in the right courtyard and a very rare wooden footprint of the Buddha stored inside the pavilion on the left. The footprint, perhaps the only example of its type in Thailand, is displayed vertically and protected in a case mounted on poles. Also note the back side carved with images of demons, long-haired maidens, and elephants. Resident monks can unlock the building for a modest donation.

Wat Suwanaphum

Situated on the main street in downtown Suphanburi, Wat Suwanaphum (Suwanaram) was established during the early Ayuthaya Period as Wat Klang. To the right of the central courtyard are several modern buildings, including a school

for the study of Pali, and a colorful *viharn* to the rear. The main attraction of Wat Suwanaphum is Luang Por Pleung Museum, at the back of the courtyard. Inside the museum is a rare collection of local antiques and religious artifacts collected by the late abbot of the temple. Tours are often provided by a local monk and English schoolteacher named Kaliang.

Accommodations

Suphanburi is a prosperous town dominated by Chinese who operate most of the hotels. Most of the hotels, restaurants, and nightclubs are located on Pra Phanwasa Rd. which parallels the Suphanburi River. The **KAT Hotel** (tel. 035-521639) at 533 Pra Phanwasa Rd. has fan rooms from 100B and a/c rooms from 220B. The hotel is located on the main road, two blocks north of the central intersection and just before Wat Chai Nawat. **King Pho Sai Hotel** (tel. 035-522412) at 678 Nen Kaew Rd. has 80 rooms in the same price range. Top-end choice is the **Kalpapreuk Hotel** which has a/c rooms with private bath from 350B. **The Valentin Hotel** adjacent to the main bus terminal is a clean midpriced hotel with fan rooms from 120B and a/c rooms from 250B.

Transportation

Suphanburi is best visited on a side trip between Kanchanaburi and Ayuthaya. Buses from Kanchanaburi pass the turnoff for Wat Pai Rong Rua, U-Thong National Museum, and Don Chedi Memorial before arriving two hours later in Suphanburi. Buses to Suphanburi leave from the central market in Ayuthaya. Suphanburi has several small bus terminals scattered around town and a main terminal several blocks from the river. *Tuk tuks* can be chartered for quick tours of the temples. Buses to Kanchanaburi and Ayuthaya also leave directly in front of Wat Suwanaphum on Pra Phanwasa Rd., a convenient place to continue your journey.

ATTRACTIONS
OUTSIDE SUPHANBURI

Don Chedi

Seven km west of Suphanburi is the turnoff to Don Chedi, site of a famous battle in 1582 during which King Naresuan of Ayuthaya defeated the prince of Burma and liberated Thailand from foreign domination. The site is marked by a ruined Sri Lankan-style *chedi* surmounted by a modern monument erected in the same style in 1951. A nearby bronze statue representing the victory of Naresuan is mounted by the king and a mahout who signals the troops with royal symbols.

Don Chedi sponsors a popular festival every January during which the historic battle is recreated with elephant battles and thousands of participants dressed in period costumes. Tours can be arranged through travel agents in Bangkok.

U-Thong

Excavations conducted by Thai and Western archaeologists indicate that U-Thong, 31 km west of Suphanburi, has been inhabited since Neolithic times and was one of the greatest cities of the Dvaravati Period. Relics from the Khmer occupation or the early Ayuthaya Period

have never been uncovered, though the town was apparently resettled in the 17th century as a provincial outpost of the Ayuthaya empire.

U-Thong is chiefly identified with a Thai school of art which thrived in Central Thailand from the early 13th to the mid-15th centuries. Confusion arises since the village of U-Thong was largely uninhabited from the 11th to 17th centuries; the school of art was most likely centered around Ayuthaya rather than U-Thong.

U-Thong art is generally divided into three groups which share a number of common characteristics. The A-style of the early 13th century shows Dvaravati influence in its heaviness and Mon facial features. The B-style of the 14th century was chiefly inspired by the Khmers. Sculptors of the U-Thong C-style in the 15th century attempted but largely failed to copy the styles of Sukothai and Ayuthayan artisans.

The principal attraction in U-Thong is the National Museum, which houses a rare collection of works from the Dvaravati, Srivijaya, Lopburi, Chaing Saen, and Ayuthaya periods. Among the highlights are a stone wheel discovered at a nearby *chedi*, beads of the Funan Period, terracotta busts from Ku Bua near Ratchaburi, and some Srivijaya bronzes.

Wat Pai Rong Wua

Buddha might not approve, but 40 km southwest of Suphanburi up a side road from Song Phi Nong, a local abbot has constructed a surrealistic Buddhist theme park more reminiscent of Disney on acid than Buddha in nirvana. Scattered amid the 200-acre park are countless concrete Buddhas, the largest bronze Buddha in Thailand, exotic Indian architecture such as a copy of the Mahabodhi in Bodgaya, and the Land of Hell where grotesquely shaped sinners are tortured for their sins. Buddhist novelty parks, such as Wat Pai Rong Wua and Wat Khaek near Nong Khai, reflect a strong love of the macabre kitsch among the rural Thai.

Ask the bus driver to drop you at Song Phi Nong, from where *songtaos* continue north up to Wat Pai Rong Rua.

NORTH OF BANGKOK

Nestled between Bangkok and Central Thailand are several small towns which have figured closely in Thai history. Bang Pa In is a riverside stop which once served as a summer retreat for Thai kings. Lopburi, 154 km north of Bangkok, offers both 12th-century Khmer ruins and a royal residence constructed in the 17th century by King Narai. Top draw is the town of Ayuthaya, which served as the second capital of Thailand for over four centuries.

The region owes its prosperity to the rich soil and network of canals and rivers which ensure a bountiful harvest of rice. The Thai people predominate, though large numbers of Thai-Chinese merchants reside in the larger towns. Smaller numbers of Mon and Khmer peoples live in remote villages. Climatic conditions are similar to Bangkok with a rainy season from July to October, a cool season until February, and the hot season until midsummer when the rains return.

Sightseeing Highlights

While most travelers go directly from Bangkok to Chiang Mai, a more leisurely and informative journey would include short visits to the historical sites of Ayuthaya and Lopburi just north of Bangkok, and the archaeological ruins in Central Thailand. Ayuthaya, a small town which once served as the capital of Thailand for over 400 years, is the most important destination in the region.

Bang Pa In: Some 60 km north of Bangkok is a small complex of royal shrines and pavilions which once served as a summer retreat for the kings of Thailand. Generally visited en route to Ayuthaya, Bang Pa In is rather unexceptional, though history and architecture buffs will find it a worthwhile stopover.

Ayuthaya: The city of Ayuthaya, 86 km north of Bangkok, reigned as the political, economic, and cultural center of the Thai peoples from 1350 until conquest by the Burmese in 1767. Set with hundreds of temples and palaces surrounded by rivers and canals, Ayuthaya was described by European traders as among the largest and most prosperous cities in the East. Though largely leveled by the Burmese in 1767,

large-scale restoration projects have made Ayuthaya one of the most important historical and cultural destinations in Thailand. The surviving monuments are widely scattered and a full day of exploration is necessary to appreciate the magnitude of Ayuthaya. Day-tours from Bangkok are not recommended.

Lopburi: One of Thailand's oldest cities, Lopburi served as a Khmer military outpost in the 13th century and as an alternative capital to Ayuthaya in the mid-17th century. Architectural attractions include a fine 12th-century Khmer temple and royal palace dating from the reign of King Narai. The town itself is small, sleepy, and rarely visited by Westerners, yet offers enough historic architecture to merit an overnight stop en route to Sukothai or the Northeast.

Pra Buddhabat: Thailand's most famous Buddha footprint is located at Pra Buddhabat, a religious sanctuary near Saraburi and about 20 km southeast of Lopburi.

Transportation

Attractions north of Bangkok can be easily visited en route to central or northern Thailand. One possible plan is to briefly visit Bang Pa In in the morning and continue up to Ayuthaya in the afternoon. A full day is necessary to properly explore Ayuthaya. Lopburi can be reached the following day on an early morning train. Allow about a half day to explore Lopburi, and perhaps make a side trip to Pra Buddhabat. Buses and trains continue north from Lopburi to Phitsanulok and Sukothai.

Ayuthaya and Lopburi—the two most important destinations north of Bangkok—are served by both bus or train. Buses to Bang Pa In and Ayuthaya depart every 15 minutes from Bangkok's Northern Bus Terminal.

Most trains go directly to Ayuthaya. Trains that stop in Bang Pa In depart Hualampong Train Station daily at 0827 and 0955 only. Trains to Ayuthaya depart daily at 0640, 0705, 0830, 1500, 1800, 1940, 2000, 2200. Whether ordinary, rapid, or express, all trains take about 90 minutes to reach Ayuthaya. Train travel, in general, is a relaxing and scenic way to travel around Thailand.

BANG PA IN

About 60 km north of Bangkok is a strange collection of palaces and pavilions in Thai, Italian, Victorian, and Chinese architectural styles which once served as summer retreat for Thai kings from the Ayuthaya Period up to the early part of the present century. The original palace was founded in the 17th century by King Prasat Thong (1630-1656) on an island in the middle of the Chao Praya. Successor kings vacationed here until the fall of Ayuthaya to Burmese invaders.

Early Chakri kings ignored Bang Pa In as too distant from Bangkok until King Mongkut reestablished the site in the latter half of the 19th century. King Chulalongkorn (1868-1910) erected a half-dozen buildings without any great concern for architectural unity and used the retreat as a reception site for distinguished visitors. Tragedy struck and the complex was abandoned after the king's wife drowned in the Menam River in 1880. At the time, royal law demanded death for any commoner who dared touch royalty; Queen Sunandakumariratna and her children died in full view of her royal entourage.

Bang Pa In is more odd than amazing, but it's an easy stopover between Bangkok and Ayuthaya or a quick side trip from Ayuthaya, 20 km north. Visitors with limited time should go direct to Ayuthaya and, time permitting, backtrack to Bang Pa In for an afternoon visit.

The outer grounds of the palace, which include most of the important buildings, are open daily 0900-1800. Interior palace buildings are closed on Mondays.

Attractions

Bang Pa In today no longer serves as a royal retreat but rather as a tourist site and occasional venue for state ceremonies. The original structures built by King Prasat Thong have disappeared and most of the remaining buildings are the legacy of King Chulalongkorn who was fascinated by European architecture.

Aisawan Thippaya Pavilion: The highlight of the small park is a delicate water pavilion erected by King Chulalongkorn to replace Prasat Thong's old palace in traditional style. Reconstructed by King Vajiravudh in reinforced concrete, the lovely building has been reproduced for several international expositions and is a favorite subject for photographers. Centerpiece is a life-size statue of King Chulalongkorn.

Peking Palace: Pra Thinnang Warophat Piman, nicknamed the Peking Palace, was a gift from Chinese Thais who modeled the palace after a Chinese imperial court. A magnificent collection of jade, Ming Period porcelains, Chulalongkorn's intricately carved bed, and lacquer tables are displayed inside the palace, constructed from materials imported from China.

Royal Residence: Warophat Piman Hall, north of the landing stage at the entrance to the palace, is a Western-style palace constructed by King Chulalongkorn to replace King Mongkut's original two-story wooden residence. The building is copied from the pavilion in the Grand Palace where royalty changed regalia before mounting a palanquin. Interior chambers and anterooms are decorated with oil paintings depicting events in Thai history and scenes from Thai literature. Most rooms are closed to the public and open only for state ceremonies.

Gothic Tower: All that remains of the Uthayan Phumi Sathiana Palace (Haw Pra), an old timber structure destroyed by fire in 1938, is a curious six-sided tower in a semi-Gothic style. The hexagonal tower was reconstructed in 1990 as a gingerbread green edifice that now resembles a wedding cake.

Queen's Monument: The white marble memorial across the small bridge honors Chulalongkorn's first queen, who tragically drowned in full view of her entourage. A marble obelisk and cenotaph commemorates the event with Thai and English eulogies composed by King Chulalongkorn.

Wat Nivet Dhammapravat: A fun cable car whizzes across the river to Thailand's only European-style Buddhist temple. Erected by King Chulalongkorn for monks of the Dhammayuttika sect, the incongruous temple features an important image cast by Pradit Varakarn, court sculptor during the reigns of Mongkut and Chulalongkorn.

Transportation

Buses leave from Bangkok's Northern Bus Terminal every 30 minutes and take about one hour to reach the small town of Bang Pa In. Minitrucks from the market in Ayuthaya take 45 minutes. *Samlors* from the town to the riverside palace cost 10B.

An interesting alternative is the Sunday morning boat trip organized by the Chao Praya Express Boat Company. The boat leaves at 0800 from Bangkok's Maharaj Pier, costs 160B, and includes stops at the Wat Pai Lom Stork Sanctuary and the Queen's Folk Arts and Handicraft Center in Bang Sai before returning to Bangkok around 1800.

AYUTHAYA

Ayuthaya, 85 km north of Bangkok, served as Thailand's second capital for over four centuries from 1350 to 1767. The city's scattered ruins, colossal Buddhas, decaying *chedis,* and multitude of soaring *wats* restored by the Fine Arts Department provide eloquent testimony to the splendor of this medieval metropolis. Recently declared a national historic park, Ayuthaya has been successfully developed into one of the country's major tourist attractions—a must-see for all visitors to Thailand.

Though Ayuthaya is often visited as a day-trip from Bangkok, it really takes a day or two of leisurely wandering to properly appreciate the sense of history evoked by the far-flung ruins. Travelers who enjoy romantic ruins and have a strong interest in Thai history should allow two full days in *both* Ayuthaya and Sukothai.

History

The first settlements near Ayuthaya were Khmer military and trading camps established in the 11th century as outposts for their far-flung empire. In 1350 a Thai prince named U-Thong (Ramatibodhi) transferred his capital from U-Thong to Ayuthaya to escape a smallpox plague and provide greater military security from Burmese invaders. The site was carefully chosen at the merger of the Lopburi, Prasak, and Chao Praya rivers where, with the creation of additional canals, the island fortress-city could be easily defended from outside attack. Ramatibodhi named his new city after the mythical kingdom of Ayodhya in the Hindu *Ramayana* epic and constructed a series of royal palaces and temples. Sri Lankan monks soon arrived to reinforce Theravada Buddhism and maintain religious purity in the new Thai kingdom.

Ayuthaya was ruled by a succession of 33 kings of various dynasties who embellished the island capital with magnificent temples and sumptuous palaces. Ayuthayan kings, however, were not the benevolent and understanding Buddhist monarchs of Sukothai, but rather paternalistic Khmer-influenced kings who hid themselves behind walls of ritual, taboo, and sorcery. As reincarnations of Shiva, they became focal points for political and religious cults which, in turn, sharply defined all levels of society.

Ayuthaya soon became the most powerful military empire in Southeast Asia. A policy of national military conscription gave Ayuthaya the strength to resist, expand, and then conquer the empires of the Burmese, Cambodians, and Muslims. In 1378, Sukothai was subjugated by King Boromaraja I, the successor of King Ramatibodhi, and in 1431 Angkor fell to Ayuthaya after a siege of seven months. By the end of the 15th century, Ayuthaya controlled Southeast Asia from Vientiane in the north to Malacca in south, and Angkor in the east to Pegu in the west.

A short period of decline in the mid-16th century marked the arrival of one of Ayuthaya's greatest rulers, King Naresuan the Great (1555-1605). As a young man, Naresuan demonstrated great military capabilities against Cambodia and subsequently liberated Ayuthaya from Burmese occupation in 1586. His rare combination of dynamic leadership, personal courage, and force of personality reunited the Thai peoples, who had suffered from more than a decade of defeat and humiliation at the hands of the Burmese and Cambodians. Naresuan formally became king of Ayuthaya in 1590 and, in 1592, fulfilled his legendary promise by defeating a Burmese crown prince in a sword duel atop war elephants. For the first time in 30 years, the tables of war turned in favor of the Thais. Naresuan had successfully unified Siam into an ethnic, cultural, and political framework that included the larger international order.

Under the rule of Naresuan and subsequent kings, Ayuthaya also became an important commercial center. First on the scene were the Portuguese, who traded guns and ammunition for rice and gems. Dazzled by the city's gilded opulence and sense of grandeur, emissaries dispatched in 1685 by Louis XIV and other astonished European visitors compared the riverine

AYUTHAYA

© MOON PUBLICATIONS, INC.

kingdom to Venice: Ayuthaya was reported as larger and more magnificent than contemporary London or Paris. Perhaps the most famous Western trader was Constantine Phaulkon, a colorful Greek adventurer who stirred up local resentment by preaching Christianity to a Buddhist monarch named King Narai. When word spread that a dying Narai was close to conversion, xenophobic Thai nobles seized the throne and executed the Greek merchant. Westerners were expelled and Ayuthaya entered into its own Golden Age of Arts—an amazing period of vibrant art, literature, and education.

After four centuries of rule, Ayuthaya went into an economic and military decline. In early 1763, an enormous Burmese army overran Chiang Mai and massed for a final assault on Ayuthaya. After two years of siege, the city capitulated and most of the citizens were either murdered or marched off to Burma as slave labor. Ayuthaya was burned to the ground—tremendous art treasures, museums, countless temples, priceless libraries, and historical archives all destroyed—an act of horror which still profoundly shocks the Thais.

Attractions

A European visitor reported in 1685 that the population of Ayuthaya exceeded one million and that the city boasted over 1,700 temples, 30,000 priests, and more than 4,000 images of Buddha, all of them gold or gilt. Contemporary Ayuthaya has three good museums with dozens of Buddhas and about 30 temples in various stages of reconstruction and renovation. Monuments are widely scattered and only the central temples near the modern town are within walking distance. A few suggestions on bicycle and *tuk tuk* rentals, and boat excursions are given below under "Getting Around."

Monuments near the city center and within walking distance of guesthouses and hotels include the Chandra Kasem Museum, Wat Rajaburana, Wat Mahathat, Rama Lake, Wat Pra Ram, Sam Praya Museum, Viharn Pra Mongkol Bopit, Wat Pra Sri Samphet, and Wat Na Praman. A full day of walking will cover all these sights which include the region's most important monuments.

A second set of monuments is located on the banks of the river which encircle the island of Ayuthaya. A convenient if somewhat expensive way to tour these temples and European churches is by rented boat leaving from the quay near the Chandra Kasem Museum. Alternatively, take a public *songtao* along U Thong Road and cross the river with public ferry.

Farther afield and located outside the city limits are a handful of temples such as the Golden Mount and the Elephant Kraal. A chartered *songtao* is necessary to reach these monuments.

Chandra Kasem Museum

King Thammaraja constructed this 17th-century palace for his son, who subsequently claimed the throne as King Naresuan. Partially destroyed by the Burmese, the palace was reconstructed by King Mongkut and later converted into one of the three museums in Ayuthaya. The Chantura Mukh Pavilion immediately on your left features an impressive standing Buddha flanked by a pair of wooden images, and a finely detailed royal bed. Behind this pavilion stands the Piman Rajaja Pavilion, filled with rare Thai shadow puppets and dozens of Ayuthaya and Sukothai images. Outside to the rear is the startling Pisai Salak Tower, constructed by Narai to study astronomy and follow the eclipses of the moon.

Chandra Kasem is open Wed.-Sun. 0900-1600. Exit the grounds and walk past the public riverside park and Hud Ra Market.

Wat Rajaburana

King Boromaraja II constructed this temple in 1424 to commemorate his two brothers who died on elephant-back fighting for the throne after the death of their father. Boromaraja wisely skipped the battle and, in accordance with royal custom, honored his two brothers with *stupas* erected at their cremation site.

A fascinating history lies behind Wat Rajaburana. The impressive *prang* was erected several years after King Boromaraja had captured Angkor Thom, the capital of Cambodia, and while Khmer influence was still strong in central Thailand. Inside the Khmer-style *prang,* a secret crypt was constructed to guard dozens of 15th-century murals, 200 Lopburi bronzes of Khmer-Bayon style, 300 rare U-Thong Buddhas, 100,000 votive tablets, and a fabulous treasure trove of priceless gold objects.

The crypt was sealed, covered with brick and plaster, and forgotten through the ensuing centuries. Thailand's equivalent of the Tutankhamen treasure lay untouched until 1957, when scavengers broke into the crypt and stumbled on the buried treasure. Much of the booty vanished into international art markets before the government stepped in, stopped the treasure hunters, and placed the remainder in the Ayuthaya National Museum. An unknown number of items vanished and many of the ordinary votives were sold to finance construction of the Ayuthaya National Museum, but enough relics remained to constitute one of Thailand's greatest archaeological discoveries.

Wat Rajaburana has, unfortunately, been badly restored by the Fine Arts Department with shiny concrete *garudas* and other artificial embellishments that detract from its original state.

Wat Rajaburana costs 5B for Thais and 20B for Westerners. As with all other monuments in Ayuthaya, visitors can wander in free after the guards leave around 1630. Almost everything of interest can be seen from the street.

Wat Mahathat

King Boromaraja constructed his "Temple of the Great Relic," across the street from Wat Rajaburana, in 1374 to honor his dream about a relic of the Buddha. Wat Mahathat architecturally fills the link between Lopburi's 10th-century Khmer *prangs* and the 15th-century-style *prangs* that characterized most monuments in Ayuthaya. The temple once contained murals of the life of the Buddha and a large stone image in the Dvaravati style (600-1000 A.D.) seated in the European manner, perhaps imported from Nakhon Pathom. The magnificent statue was transferred in 1835 to nearby Wat Na Praman. Valuable artifacts, including a tiny gold casket said to contain Boromaraja's holy relics, were discovered during a 1956 restoration project conducted by the Fine Arts Department. Except for the casket, now displayed in the Ayuthaya National Museum, most treasures have been moved to the National Museum in Bangkok.

Although the temple largely lies in ruins, the monumental floor plans and wildly directed pillars are impressive for what they suggest. One classic sight (in the southeast corner) is a dismembered Buddha head firmly grasped in the clutches of the banyan roots. Take a photo and return 10 years later—it will have grown to a higher level.

Admission is 20B; free after 1630.

Wat Pra Ram

Wat Pra Ram was constructed in 1369 by King Ramasuan as the burial spot for his father, King Ramatibodhi, the founder of Ayuthaya. The elegant Khmer-style *prang* was reconstructed in the 15th century by King Boromatrailokanat, the 8th king of Ayuthaya, and subsequently altered by the 31st ruler, King Boromakot.

The temple consists of symmetrical sanctuaries which flank a *prang* decorated with miniature chedis and stucco work interspersed with *garudas, nagas,* and walking Buddhas. Although less monumental than Wat Mahathat or Wat Rajaburana, Wat Pra Ram boasts a stunning location which casts a beautiful reflection in the placid lily ponds.

Ayuthaya National Museum

Chao Sam Praya, Thailand's second-largest museum, was constructed in 1959 from sale proceeds of votive tablets recovered from Wat Rajaburana, and named after Prince Sam Praya (King Boromaraja II), the founder of Wat Rajaburana. The museum consists of a central hall with two floors, and a second building opened in 1970. All major art styles are represented—Dvaravati (6th-11th century), Lopburi (7th-14th century), U-Thong (12th-15th century), Sukothai (13th-14th century), and, of course, Ayuthaya (14th-18th century). Ayuthayan kings were apparently avid collectors of early Thai art, though the best-represented styles are those of the Lopburi, U-Thong, and Ayuthaya periods.

The main floor of the central hall holds dozens of statues, votives, lacquer cabinets, decorated palm-leaf manuscripts, and priceless objects discovered inside the left shoulder of the Pra Mongkol Bopit Buddha. Displays are arranged in chronological order and a careful inspection will provide a good overview of the artistic legacy of

Thailand. Highlights on the main floor include a colossal bronze Buddha head with square face and broad features typical of the U-Thong Period, and a Dvaravati-style seated Buddha carved from white crystalline stone.

The second floor features a main room filled with lead and terra-cotta votive tablets, palm-leaf manuscript cabinets, and crystal objects found during the restoration of Wat Yai Chai Mongkol in 1980. Highlights of the upper floor are displayed in antechambers to the east and west. The small room on the east side contains

dazzling gold objects unearthed in 1956 from the central *prang* of Wat Rajaburana. The western room holds the previously described Buddha relic from Wat Mahathat. Look carefully: it's one-third the size of a rice grain and protected by five bronze stupas inserted one inside the other.

The modern addition to the rear offers a dusty and rather neglected collection of artifacts not native to Ayuthaya.

Chao Sam Praya Museum is open Wed.-Sun. 0900-1600.

THE ARTS OF AYUTHAYA

Ayuthaya from the 14th to 18th centuries was among the most powerful and wealthy kingdoms in Southeast Asia. During their four centuries of rule, a series of 33 kings constructed hundreds of glittering temples and supported the arts with lavish royal patronage. Ayuthayan rulers considered themselves heirs to the artistic and religious traditions of Sukothai, Cambodia, and Sri Lanka—a rich mixture manifested in the artistic achievements which survived the Burmese onslaught of 1767.

Some historians consider the art of Ayuthaya decadent when compared to earlier periods such as Sukothai and Chiang Saen. The fact is that Ayuthaya chiefly excelled in architecture and city planning rather than sculpture and painting. And yet, a great deal of sensitive work was created before the artistic decline toward the end of the Ayuthaya era.

The Ayuthaya National Museum provides a detailed look at Ayuthaya's art, plus a superb overview of the various epochs of Thai art. The following thumbnail sketches may help to distinguish the arts of Ayuthaya from other schools you will encounter during your travels.

Architecture

Ayuthaya's crowning artistic achievement was its architecture. At its height, Ayuthaya boasted over 600 major monuments and temples that impressed both Asiatic and European visitors with their sheer immensity and grandeur. The majority of these monuments were initiated during the reign of King Ramatibodhi, the founder of Ayuthaya, and completed during the first 150 years of the era. Another building frenzy occurred in the early 17th century during the reign of King Prasat Thong, a prolific monument builder who revived the popularity of Khmer-influenced architecture. Tradition demanded that only temples be constructed of stone and brick. Wooden

structures such as royal palaces and common residences have all been destroyed by fire by the conquering Burmese.

Ayuthayan architects borrowed the forms and traditions developed by other schools, but then modified them according to their own tastes. One of the most important influences was that of the Khmers, whose corncob-shaped *prang* slowly evolved in Ayuthaya from a squat and heavy form into a radically elongated and more elegant superstructure. The best examples are the magnificent *prangs* of Wat Mahathat, Wat Rajaburana, and Wat Pra Ram. Ayuthayan *prangs* were later incorporated into Bangkok religious architecture at Wat Pra Keo, Wat Arun, and Wat Po.

Ayuthayan architects were also influenced by the artistic traditions of Sri Lanka, as shown in the bell-shaped *chedis* adapted from Sri Lankan models. A new elegance emerged as local architects elongated the bulbous Sri Lankan-style *chedi* into soaring, slim spires that seem to defy gravity. Wat Sri Samphet and the memorial to Queen Suriyothai are prime examples.

Ayuthayan architecture evolved through four sub-periods until the city was destroyed in 1767. The Lopburi (Khmer-Thai fusion) and U-Thong styles of architecture dominated from the founding of Ayuthaya in 1350 to the end of King Boromatrailokanat's reign in 1488. Examples include Wat Pra Ram, Wat Mahathat, and Wat Rajaburana. Sukothai-influenced architecture and the Singhalese type of rounded *stupa* reached Ayuthaya in 1463 after King Boromatrailokanat left to rule the northern town of Phitsanulok. Wat Pra Sri Samphet and Wat Yai Chai Mongkol are the most famous examples. Khmer architecture regained popularity after the conquest of Cambodia by King Prasat Thong in the mid-17th century, as best demonstrated by the Khmer *prang* of Wat Chai Wattanaram.

(continued)

The final phase of Ayuthayan architecture was a period of restoration of older monasteries and temples which had fallen into disrepair, and the increased popularity of the redented *stupa* at Wat Pu Kao Tong. Late Ayuthayan architecture was also characterized by the use of curved foundations and roofs on *viharns*, column capitals in the form of lotus buds, and the increased use of brick and stone for domestic rather than strictly religious architecture. The surviving structures at Ayuthaya only hint at the magnificence of the former capital.

Ayuthaya Kings And Their Architecture

Ramatibodhi	1350-1369	Wat Buddhisawan, Wat Yai Chai Mongkol
Boromaraja I	1370-1388	Wat Mahathat
Ramasuan	1388-1395	Wat Pra Ram
Boromaraja II	1424-1448	Wat Rajaburana
Boromatrailokanat	1448-1488	Royal Palace, Wat Mahathat (Phitsanulok)
Ramatibodhi II	1492-1529	Wat Pra Sri Samphet
Chakrapet	1549-1565	Chedi Sri Suriyothai, City Walls
Naresuan	1590-1605	
Prasat Thong	1630-1656	Viharn Somdet, Wat Wattanaram
Narai	1657-1688	Narai Palace (Lopburi)
Pra Petraja	1688-1703	
Boromakot	1733-1758	Wat Pu Kao Tong

Sculpture

Ayuthaya is known for the quality of its architecture rather than its achievements in sculpture.

Ayuthayan sculpture is divided into several subperiods. Early sculpture continued the traditions of U-Thong, a school of art which predates the establishment of Ayuthaya and demonstrates an indebtedness to Mon and Khmer prototypes. The second period began in 1463 when King Boromatrailokanat went to rule Phitsanulok and local sculpture came under Sukothai influence. Some pieces produced during this period exhibit the sensitive and elegant traditions of Sukothai. But, as time progressed, the spirituality of Sukothai-influenced sculpture gave way to the more ritualistic and powerful images of the third period. These late-Ayuthayan images became increasingly cold and remote as Ayuthayan kings adopted the Khmer notion of *deva raja* (god-king) and hid themselves behind palace walls. The magnificence of the royal court—as reflected by Buddhas covered with princely attire and crowned with elaborate diadems—degenerated into a passion for decoration that obliterated all detail and reduced the images to formless masses of ornamentation. The end result was stereotyped abundance without the sensitivity of earlier eras: a triumph of style over spirituality.

Ayuthayan sculptors, however, were a remarkable creative force. Among their innovations was the depiction of Buddha in a wider variety of poses than earlier schools. Buddhas were seated with their feet on the ground in the "European fashion" once used by Dvaravati sculptors, and in the meditating *mudra* rather than the more common pose of touching-the-earth. Walking Buddhas were shown with alm bowls and with the weight centered on the right rather than left foot. Ayuthayan sculptors were also technical masters of large-scale bronze casting as demonstrated by the colossal seated Buddha in Viharn Pra Mongkol Bopit. Finally, Ayuthayan sculptors increased the size and magnificence of the pedestal (a tradition carried on during the Bangkok Period) and increased exterior ornamentation to reflect the glory of Ayuthayan kings who, like the Khmer *deva raja*, identified themselves as the Buddha King.

Painting

Ayuthaya's great murals were largely destroyed during the Burmese conquest of 1767, or have disappeared from shoddy painting techniques which left the frescoes vulnerable to the degenerative effects of rain and heat. Consequently, the best examples of Ayuthayan paintings are outside town in the *wats* of Petchburi, Uttaradit, and Nonthaburi.

The first period of Ayuthayan painting shows Khmer and Singhalese influences and the heavy use of blacks, whites, and reds with dashes of vermilion and gold leaf to ornament the costumes of deities. Crypt murals inside the main *prang* of Wat Rajaburana form the finest surviving example of early Ayuthayan painting. Illustrations from manuscripts and religious documents show the gradual development of Sukothai influence and the increased use of bright colors during the second period. Late Ayuthayan painting is typically Thai, with bright colors, representations of trees and wildlife, and the innovative use of zigzag lines to compartmentalize scenes. Ayuthaya's sole surviving example of late-period painting is in the pavilion at Wat Buddhaisawan, where interior frescoes relate important religious and secular works. Outstanding examples of late-Ayuthaya painting are found in Petchburi at Wat Yai Suwannaram and Wat Ko Keo Suttaram, in Uttaradit at Wat Pra Boromathat, and in Nonthaburi at Wat Po Bang Oh and Wat Prasat.

Ayuthaya Historical Study Center

Located on Rajana Rd. near the Provincial Teachers College is a modern museum designed to relate the history of Ayuthaya. Opened in August of 1990, the complex was constructed with a grant from the Japanese government on the site of an old Japanese settlement. Five exhibitions are included: Ayuthaya as the capital, port, seat of government, center of the Thai community, and center of international relations with the Western world. Top sights are a Chinese commercial ship, scale models of old Ayuthaya and the elephant *kraal,* and murals depicting merit-making ceremonies at Pra Buddha Pat in Saraburi, an annual event attended by the citizens of Ayuthaya. Other murals illustrate ordination ceremonies, the rice-planting season, an ancient theater, marriage ceremony, and Thai funeral.

The Ayuthaya Historical Center is open Wed.-Sun. 0900-1700. Admission is a reasonable 20B for Thais and a stiff 100B for Western tourists.

Lak Muang And Ayuthaya Model

Ayuthaya's modern city pillar features a scale model of the city which helps with local orientation.

Khum Khum House

Constructed in 1894 as the city jail and now used by the Fine Arts Department, Khum Khum House is an outstanding example of traditional domestic Thai architecture. The compound is surrounded by moats and elevated on teak piles that support a central *sala* roofed with dried palm leaves.

Viharn Pra Mongkol Bopit

One of the largest bronze Buddha images in Thailand is located inside a modern and very claustrophobic *viharn* immediately south of Wat Pra Sri Samphet. Originally erected during the Ayuthaya Period, the old *viharn* and brooding image were badly damaged in 1767 when the roof collapsed and broke off the statue's topknot and right arm. The image was repaired but allowed to remain outdoors until 1951 when the present shelter was erected to protect the enormous statue. Perhaps the Buddha, with its black coating and mysterious mother-of-pearl eyes, should have been left alone—an image of this size and power needs a great deal of *room.*

Today the statue is an object of great veneration to the Thai. The date of the image is uncertain, though it displays both U-Thong and Sukothai influences and may have been cast in the 15th century.

Adjacent to the *viharn* is a large parking lot and shopping complex which formerly served as royal cremation grounds. Several of the open-air shops and restaurants sell basketry, locally produced knives, imitation antiques, cold drinks, and spicy soups such as *tam yam kung.*

Wat Pra Sri Samphet

This famous trio of 15th-century Sri Lankan-style *chedis* is the most important temple complex within the former royal palace compound, similar in function to Wat Pra Keo in Bangkok. The temple was founded in the 15th century by King Boromatrailokanat and expanded by his successors. As with Wat Pra Keo, Wat Pra Sri Samphet served as the private chapel and ceremonial courtyard for the kings of Ayuthaya.

The temple is composed of three famous *chedis* which stand on a long terrace linked by stone *mondops.* In the manner of Khmer monuments at Angkor Wat, all served as royal tombs for Thai monarchs rather than as simple memorials to the Buddha. All once contained secret chambers adorned with frescoes and votive offerings for the dead and in conformity with classical rules were constructed on a circular ground plan with elongated cupolas flattened to accommodate a double-layered reliquary plinth. The east *chedi* was erected by King Ramatibodhi in 1492 to enshrine the ashes of his father, while the central shrine holds the remains of his elder brother, King Boromaraja III. The westernmost *chedi* was built in 1540 to contain the ashes of King Ramatibodhi II.

Their perfect symmetry has made them one of the most photographed scenes in Ayuthaya and the very essence of Middle Kingdom architecture. Unfortunately, insensitive restoration projects by the Fine Arts Department and repeated whitewashings have tragically obliterated all architectural detail.

Several famous Buddhas were discovered in the ruins after the destruction of Ayuthaya in 1767. The most famous image, Pra Sri Samphet, is a 16-meter bronze Buddha once covered with gold leaf from which the temple received its name. The image was stripped by the Burmese and subsequently brought by King Rama I to Wat Po in Bangkok. Pra Buddha Singh, another national treasure, now resides in Bangkok at Wat Buddhaisawan (the National Museum), while Pra Buddha Lokanat has been transferred to the west *viharn* of Wat Po.

Admission is 20B, but the *prangs* can be easily seen and photographed from the road.

Antique Shops

A cluster of small antique shops and restaurants is located just opposite Sri Samphet. Stonecarving is the local specialty. Excellent-quality Cambodian images, Ganeshas, and standing Ayuthayan Buddhas are sold at reasonable prices.

Royal Palace

North of Wat Pra Sri Samphet are some scattered foundations and modest ruins of the old royal palace. The site was chosen by King Boromatrailokanat, who began construction of the palace and Wat Pra Sri Samphet in 1448. The complex was later expanded by several kings, such as Narai, Prasat Thong, and Pra Petracha who erected reception halls, audience chambers, military review stands, and a royal palace covered with golden tiles.

The palace was burned and completely destroyed by the Burmese in 1767. The remaining brickwork, stucco molding, and Buddhas were removed to Bangkok by early Chakri kings to help rebuild the capital. All that remains today of the royal palace are narrow footpaths and brick foundations which distinguish the ground plans; a great deal of imagination is needed to re-create the palace's former magnificence and lost grandeur.

Wat Na Praman

This tremendous *bot,* located across the river from the old royal palace, is one of the most impressive temples in Ayuthaya—a must-see for all visitors. The foundation date is unknown, but documents record restoration projects during the reign of King Boromakot (1753-1759) and by the governor of Ayuthaya (1824-1851) in the Bangkok Period. Wat Na Praman (Wat Pra Meru) was one of the few temples which survived the Burmese destruction of 1767.

Wat Na Praman consists of a large recently rebuilt *bot* on the left and a small, but very important, *viharn* on the right. A long and rather convoluted history of the primary temple is given on the exterior noticeboard. The main *bot* is an elegant structure elevated on a stepped terrace and covered with varnished tiles over a four-tiered roof. Magnificent examples of classic Ayuthayan architecture are displayed in the monumental entrances, twin facades flanked by smaller porticoes, windows barred with stone colonnettes, and beautifully carved pediments over the southern entrance.

The interior is equally remarkable. The centerpiece altar displays a rare gold-leaf, six-meter Ayuthaya-style Buddha surrounded by 16 octagonal painted pillars, highly polished floors, and roofs carved with concentric lotus buds. Wat Na Praman is an excellent place to relax and meditate away from the more touristy temples in Ayuthaya.

To the right of the *bot* is a small chapel which guards a green stone Dvaravati Buddha (Pra Kantharat) seated in European fashion with splayed feet resting on a lotus flower and hands curiously placed on the knees. The broad Mon face and firm facial expression exude a meditative serenity rarely experienced in Thai sculpture. Although located in a modest and often neglected setting, this powerful image richly deserves its reputation as one of the masterpieces of Mon Buddhist art.

The combination of striking architecture, stunning sculpture, and pleasant surroundings makes Wat Na Praman one of the finest experiences in Ayuthaya: a refreshing change from the overrestored and dead monuments controlled by the Fine Arts Department.

Reclining Buddha

Wat Logya Suthat is known for its picturesque 20-meter statue of a reclining Buddha. The image features a very long face with a vertical arm supporting the head which rests on a lotus pillow, a pose characteristic of 16th-century Ayuthaya. The large wooden *viharn* which once covered the image has disappeared, leaving the Buddha alone to the elements and contented cows which occasionally graze in the nearby grasses. Cokes at the refreshment stand are expensive!

COSMIC SYMBOLOGY AND THE ARCHITECTURE OF AYUTHAYA

Thailand's architecture and the temples of Ayuthaya were designed to symbolize aspects of Theravada Buddhism and the powerful belief in Hindu cosmology. Most elements displayed today began as Hindu concepts which filtered through the Khmer empire and were finally reinterpreted with some degree of originality by Thai architects. A short summary may help to understand the motivations and design considerations of local architects.

As with Angkor Wat in Cambodia, Thai architecture embodies in stone the Hindu concept of the cosmology. Hinduism teaches that the world is composed of countless universes which, like their human counterparts, also experience endless cycles of destruction and rebirth. Each universe is dominated by a magical mountain, Mount Meru, the mythical home of the gods. This colossal mountain is surrounded by seven subordinate mountain ranges and seven seas, beyond which lie the four major continents, one in each cardinal direction. Below Mt. Meru are the four levels of hell inhabited by guardian demons with supernatural powers. The upper levels of Mt. Meru contain the world of angels, guardians of the four cardinal directions, and, at the summit, the city of gods where Indra reigns as king. Above Mt. Meru tower more levels of heaven, inhabited by abstract beings nearing nirvana.

Kings throughout most of Southeast Asia strived to recreate this cosmological order by modeling their royal palaces, temples, and general city plan after the Hindu universe. Ayuthaya, for example, was laid out as the cosmic center of the universe with four important cities in each cardinal direction: Sukothai to the north (the direction of death), Prapadang to the south (life), Nakhon Nayon to the east (birth), and Suphanburi to the west (dying). The city was constructed as a giant mandala with the royal palace at the center, surrounded by three circles of earthen ramparts and a series of circular moats to represent the great seas.

Hindu cosmology also dictates the shape and arrangement of individual temples. Centerpiece was a massive tower which represented Mt. Meru, the home of the gods. The tower was divided into 33 lesser tiers to symbolize the 33 levels of heavens. A row of demon guardian figures was often added just below the seventh tier. *Prangs* were surmounted by a *vajra* or thunderbolt, the heavenly symbol of Indra, while *chedis* were topped by a circular orb which represented the core of nirvana. To the west and east—the axis of purity—were the *bot* (ordination hall) and *viham* (meeting hall). Moats surrounding the temple complex represent the primordial oceans which separate the world of men from the abode of gods.

Thai architects reinterpreted Hindu forms in several ways. *Prangs* and *chedis* were subdivided into the familiar 33 tiers, but Thai love of curvature brought along redented corners which added vertical lines, and a bulbous parabolic shape which gave the monument a sense of soaring grace. Thai propensity for asymmetry inspired the use of trapezoidal doors and window frames, tapered columns capped with lotus bud finials, and overlapping roofs which added an effect of soft sensuality. The end result was Hindu cosmology mixed with Thai sensibilities: one of the great triumphs of Southeast Asian architecture.

Chedi Sri Suriyathai

The only remaining part of Wat Suan Luang Sopsawan is a rather inelegant and heavily restored *chedi* dedicated to Queen Suriyothai, the wife of King Maha Chakraphet. According to Thai chronicles, the queen sacrificed her life in 1563 by intervening during an elephant duel between King Chakraphet and a Burmese general. Wat Suan Luang Sopsawan was erected at the cremation site of the queen.

Wat Chai Wattanaram

One of the most intriguing monuments in Ayuthaya is located at the southwestern edge of town and across the Chao Praya River. Wat Chai Wattanaram was constructed in 1630 by King Prasat Thong on the site of his mother's palace, and modeled after the Khmer monument at Angkor Wat.

The temple can be approached by crossing the nearby bridge and following the narrow trail through the weeds to the deserted monument. The ruins are comprised of a Khmer *prang* surrounded by a square cloister interspersed with well-preserved *chedis* capped with wooden, coffered roofs. Stucco details include additional embellishments of Lanna Thai and Ayuthaya origins.

The overall effect—especially at sunset—is overwhelming: a magnificent and completely unrestored temple overgrown with weeds, headless Buddha torsos being swallowed by creeping vines, cows grazing next to the leaning

pre-restoration Wattanaram

radiating arches, large windows constructed without claustras, and the use of masonry on residential buildings. Windows constructed without claustras remained popular after the death of King Narai, though the other two innovations faded away.

Western capitalists were required to live outside the city limits, and could only enter Ayuthaya on official business. The Catholic community was served by this 17th-century church constructed by Monsignor de Beryte during the reign of King Narai. The modest church has been restored several times and still functions as an active house of worship.

A small ferry leaves from the dock at the end of a narrow dirt path.

prangs . . . everything you ever dreamed of in mysterious temples of the East.

Stop Press: Sources claim that the Fine Arts Department has "restored" Wat Chai Wattanaram. Heavy-handed projects invariably ruin historical monuments here in Thailand. Dear God, say it isn't so.

South Of Ayuthaya

The following sights are all situated along the south tributary of the Chao Praya River and in the southeast corner of Ayuthaya. U-Thong Rd. can be toured by bike or mini-trucks that circulate along the road and charge 10B for a ride of any distance. Temples situated across the river can be reached with local ferries.

St. Joseph's Cathedral

Western architecture in Ayuthaya is the legacy of a period of trade with European powers during the 17th and 18th centuries. European architectural themes introduced to Ayuthaya during the reign of King Narai (1656-1688) included

Wat Buddhasawan

Wat Buddhasawan, consecrated in 1353 by the prince of U-Thong (King Ramatibodhi), who lived on the site during construction of his new capital, features the most perfect reproduction of a Cambodian *prang* in Ayuthaya. The general layout is derived from Angkor Wat, with a large central *prang* which represents the Buddhist heaven of Mt. Meru, surrounded by six smaller *prangs* which signify the outer heavens. A long series of seated Buddhas fill the open gallery that surrounds the central *prang*. The niche in the northern wall contains a standing Buddha image cast during the reign of King Rama I to replace a statue removed to the Royal Pantheon at Wat Pra Keo in Bangkok.

Adjacent to the *prang* is a large, modern *wat* and public park which contains a statue of King Ramatibodhi flanked by two soldiers.

The small ferry which shuttles across the river charges 5-10B for the one-way journey.

Portuguese Settlement

During the reign of King Narai, foreign traders were encouraged to settle and set up residential centers south of Ayuthaya. The Portuguese arrived in 1511 after Viceroy Albuquerque sent a trading mission headed by Duarte Fernandez. Portuguese influence was tempered by the Dutch who enjoyed a monopoly on the hide trade with Japan, and the French who sent Jesuit missionaries to Ayuthaya in 1673. Western influence peaked in the reign of King Narai and then sharply declined under subsequent, more xenophobic rulers.

All of the Western residential enclaves constructed during the 17th and 18th centuries were destroyed in 1767 by the Burmese conquest of Ayuthaya. The former Portuguese community is marked with a memorial plaque.

Japanese Settlement

Soon after the Portuguese established trade agreements with Ayuthaya in 1516, Japanese entrepreneurs arrived to serve as merchants, soldiers, and diplomats. The most famous arrival was a Japanese chief named Nagamasa Yamada, who was later named viceroy of Nakhon Si Thammarat in South Thailand.

The site of the former Japanese community is marked with a stone inscription, memorial hall, and Japanese-style gate erected by the Thai-Japanese Society.

Wat Panam Chong

One of the oldest and largest temples in Ayuthaya lies on the Chao Praya River southeast of town. According to Thai chronicles, Wat Panam Chong was founded by the prince of U-Thong in 1324, 26 years before the formal establishment of Ayuthaya.

The temple was constructed to house a gigantic Buddha image donated by a Chinese emperor whose daughter had married a local Thai prince. Constructed of brick and stucco covered with gold leaf, Pra Chao Panam measures 19 meters in height and almost 14 meters in breadth—the largest single-cast bronze Buddha in Thailand. The image has been restored several times, but remains a source of great power and inspiration to Thai and Chinese pilgrims who divine their fortunes under the watchful gaze of the great Buddha.

The internal walls feature prayer flags, paper lanterns, and hundreds of small niches filled with votive statues of the Buddha—a rare element in Thai architecture.

Special note should be made of the Sukothai statues inside the small *viharn* to the left of the main *bot*. The 14th-century image on the left was discovered in 1956 when its heavy plaster covering cracked to reveal a statue estimated to be 60% pure gold.

Surrounding the exterior courtyard are dozens of stucco-covered Buddhas and grassy grounds kept neatly trimmed by a small army of Thai female devotees.

Wat Yai Chai Mongkol

Dominating the landscape southeast of town is the temple and *chedi* of Wat Yai Chai Mongkol. The monastery was established in 1360 by King Ramatibodhi as Wat Chao Praya Thai ("Temple of the Supreme Patriarch") for Thai monks who had returned from religious studies in Sri Lanka. The sect, known as Pa Kao, devoted itself to strict meditation, in contrast to other sects which emphasized the study of Buddhist scriptures. The temple now hosts a large community of *mae chi,* Buddhist nuns who maintain the buildings and keep the lawns in good condition.

The present *wat* derives its name from the towering Chedi Chai Mongkol, located within the fortified temple compound and elevated on a rectangular base bisected by smaller *chedis.* The whitewashed tower was constructed by King Naresuan to commemorate his single-handed slaying of a Burmese crown prince in 1592. The infamous battle was fought on elephant-back near Suphanburi and reestablished Thai control of the central Chao Praya plains.

Encircling the massive *chedi* are some 135 Buddhas which once sat in a rectangular cloister marked only by surviving columns. Also located within the perimeter wall is a huge reclining Buddha image of the Ayuthaya Period, still highly regarded by local Thais. To the rear is the spirit house of King Naresuan, patronized by Thais who seek counsel from the king's spirit with the aid of female mediums.

Wat Suwan Daram

This rarely visited temple is one of the most attractive and fascinating in Ayuthaya. Wat Suwan Daram was constructed by the grandfather of the first king of the Chakri Dynasty at the end of the Ayuthaya Period, and subsequently restored by King Rama II after his accession to the throne.

The curving, concave foundation of the boat-shaped *bot* illustrates mankind's voyage toward nirvana. Elaborate doors and pediments decorated with carved wood complete the exterior detail.

The highlights of the temple are the interior murals in the *bot,* which date from the period of Rama II and rank among the best in Thailand. Painted with great talent, these frescoes depict scenes from the Vessantara and Suvanasama *Jatakas* with an assembly of divinities in the upper registers. The wall opposite the altar relates the victory of the Buddha over Mara and the spirits of evil. A series of Ayuthaya-style Buddhas fills the central altar.

Also located on the temple grounds are a *kambarian* (sermon hall), *chedi*, and *viharn* completed during the reign of King Chulalongkorn, with modern murals depicting the life of King Naresuan the Great.

Unlike most temples in Ayuthaya, Wat Suwan Daram still serves as an active monastery where religious life continues in traditional fashion. The *bot* is kept locked, but young monks anxious to practice their English can open the building. A wonderful little gem.

North Of Ayuthaya
The following attractions can only be reached with hired *tuk tuk* or *samlor*.

Pu Kao Tong ("Golden Mount")
Situated in the open countryside almost five km from town is the gigantic silhouette of Pu Kao Tong, the Golden Mountain of Ayuthaya. The monastery was founded in 1387 by King Ramasuan, but the *chedi* was built by the Burmese to commemorate their conquest of Ayuthaya in 1569 and subsequently remodeled in Thai style by King Boromakot. The Ayuthaya-style *chedi* features four niches which rest on square-stepped platforms reached by monumental staircases.

To commemorate the 2,500th anniversary of Buddha's birthday, the towering *chedi* was capped in 1956 with a $2^1/_2$-kilogram solid-gold orb. Somebody immediately stole it, but views from the top of the 80-meter *chedi* remain outstanding, especially during the rainy season when the surrounding rice fields are flooded.

Elephant Kraal
One of the few surviving elephant *kraals* (stockades) in Thailand is located on Pu Kao Rd., some three km northwest of town. Inside the teak stockade, wild elephants were once herded and battle-trained under the watchful gaze of royalty and spectators. Hunters would gather up to 150 beasts before slowly leading them through the bottleneck opening into the kraal. The elephants were then lassoed with rattan cables and selected according to their size and color; white and reddish elephants were favored over gray or mixed-colored animals.

The present structure includes a royal pavilion, elephant gateway, stockade of teak posts, holy *sala* where hunters performed purification ceremonies before the chase, a central altar which once held an image of Ganesha, and an elephant statue near the spectators' arena. Old-fashioned elephant roundups were recreated here in 1891 for Czar Nicholas II and in 1962 for Danish royalty.

Accommodations—Guesthouses
Several new guesthouses have opened in recent years to provide cheap accommodations for backpackers.

Ayuthaya Guesthouse: Formerly known as B.J. Guesthouse, Ayuthaya's original homestay is located 50 meters up a small alley running north from Naresuan Road. Mr. Hong Singha Paisal has eight rooms in an old teak house with great atmosphere. Bicycles can be rented from their outdoor patio. 76/2 Chao Prom Rd., tel. (035) 251468, 50-80B.

B.J. Guesthouse: The most popular guesthouse in Ayuthaya has 20 rooms in a cinderblock building about 10 minutes west of the market. Banjong, the lady owner, is a good cook and can help with travel tips. 19/29 Naresuan Rd., tel. (035) 251512, 60-80B.

Ruandrum Ayuthaya Youth Hostel: Perhaps the most beautiful lodging in Ayuthaya is located in a series of teak houses overlooking the river. The central wing was built by an Ayuthayan aristocrat in the traditional *panya* style found in Central Thailand. The owner, Praphan Sukarechit (Kimjeng), has renovated the adjacent homes and refurbished all the rooms with antiques. Curiosities on the grounds include old rowing boats, a kitchen constructed on a floating barge, wooden door frames from the old elephant *kraal*, and other antiques from Kimjeng's antique shop. Rooms are somewhat expensive for a youth hostel, but Kimjeng also intends to open a budget dormitory for backpackers. 48 U-Thong Rd., tel. (035) 244509, 200-300B. The dormitory will cost around 100B per person.

Pai Tong Guesthouse: A floating hotel on a reconstructed barge. Rooms are small and the atmosphere is strange, but two good restaurants are located nearby. U-Thong Road, 60-100B.

Accommodations—Hotels

Ayuthaya has a very limited selection of hotels since most tourists visit the town on day-trips from Bangkok.

Sri Samai Hotel: Ayuthaya's central hotel was once a clean and comfortable place with a fairly decent restaurant. Standards, unfortunately, have dropped and the hotel can no longer be recommended aside from its convenient location near the marketplace. 12 Chao Prom Rd., tel. (035) 245228, 300-400B fan, 400-500B a/c.

Wang Fa Hotel: Although this hotel serves the short-time trade for locals, the clean and modern rooms make this the best budget hotel in Ayuthaya—better than the Sri Samai or U-Thong. All rooms have large beds with adequate furniture and private bath. Few Westerners stay here, but the managers seem friendly and helpful. 1/8 Rajana Rd., tel. (035) 241353, 150-200B fan, 250-300B a/c. Three-hour room rentals cost 100B.

> *The real meaning of travel, like that of a conversation by the fireside, is the discovery of oneself through contact with other people, and its condition is self-commitment in the dialogue.*
>
> —Paul Tournier,
> *The Meaning of Persons*

U-Thong Hotel: A rudimentary hotel for those who want traditional facilities at moderate cost. The U-Thong has rather dirty rooms with fan and common bath, and a few a/c rooms with private bath. Avoid rooms facing the street. The nearby Cathay Hotel is similar in quality and price. 86 U-Thong Rd., tel. (035) 251505, 120-300B.

U-Thong Inn: Located two km east of Ayuthaya and rather isolated from central Ayuthaya is the only semiluxurious hotel in town. 210 Mu 5, Rajana Rd., tel. (035) 242236, fax (035) 242235, 800-1200B a/c.

Restaurants

Most travelers dine in their guesthouse or at the market, though several good restaurants are located along the river and near the monuments on Chi Kun Road.

Night Market: The old night market has been relocated from downtown to a new location on the river across from the Chandra Kasem Museum. A small selection of foodstalls complement the hawkers' emporiums. A comfortable place to spend an evening.

Pakunkao Floating Restaurant: The better of Ayuthaya's two floating restaurants is hardly spectacular, but the atmosphere is relaxed and the food is tasty. U-Thong Road. Moderate.

Krung Kao Restaurant: A small, modern, and air-conditioned spot with Thai specialties and an English-language menu. Try the pepper steak or chicken sautéed with garlic. Located on Rajana Rd. near the bridge. Budget.

Youth Hostel: Kimjeng's wife operates a well-appointed restaurant furnished with antiques and knickknacks. The menu includes both Thai and Western dishes. 48 U-Thong Road. Moderate.

Tevaraj Restaurant: Riverside dining in a large bamboo hall with a small attached floating pavilion. Pictures of the cabaret singers are displayed at the front. A big place popular with Thais and tour groups. Railway Station Rd., just over the bridge. Moderate to expensive.

Binlar Restaurant: A large, open-air nightclub with rock music and Thai cabaret singers. Good food at reasonable prices, a popular hangout in the evenings. Naresuan Road. Budget to moderate.

Siam Restaurant: Located just opposite Wat Mahathat is a small a/c restaurant that offers a welcome escape from the heat. Chi Kun Road. Moderate.

Som Restaurant: One block north of the Binlar Restaurant is a modern cafe capped with gabled roofs. The restaurant is large and clean, but only marked with a sign in Thai script. Moderate.

Raja Restaurant: Dine outdoors surrounded by ponds filled with water lilies. Great atmosphere in a very quiet location. Rajana Road. Moderate.

Getting There

Ayuthaya is 86 km north of Bangkok and can be reached by bus or train.

Bus: Buses leave every half-hour from Bangkok's Northern Bus Terminal and take about two hours to reach Ayuthaya. Most buses terminate at the marketplace in the center of town. Stay on the bus until it arrives downtown; get off at the bridge and you are fed to mercenary taxi drivers. Some buses will drop you on the highway about five km east of town. *Tuk tuk* drivers will yell "no bus, no bus" but a public bus into town rolls by every 15 minutes. Walk to the intersection and wait at the corner.

Train: Trains leave Bangkok eight times daily at 0640, 0705, 0830, 1500, 1800, 1940, 2000, 2200 and take about two hours to reach Ayuthaya. From the station, stroll across the road and walk down to the river, where ferries continue across to town. Bicycles can be rented south of the train station past the Tevaraj Restaurant.

Boat: Public boats no longer operate between Ayuthaya and Bangkok or Bang Pa In. However, one-day luxury excursions to Ayuthaya and Bang Pa In are organized by the Oriental Hotel. These quickie trips leave daily at 0800 and cost 800B with lunch.

Getting Around

Most visitors attempt to see Ayuthaya on a single day-trip from Bangkok—a serious mistake. Ayuthaya is a sprawling place with dozens of great temples that deserve a day or two of exploration. Only the central temples can be reached on foot. A better idea is to rent either a bicycle, longtail boat, or mini-truck for a day-tour. Bicycles can be rented south of the train station past the Tevaraj Restaurant near the temple, and from Bai Thong Guesthouse. Motorcycles are no longer available in Ayuthaya.

Six-man longtail boats chartered from the landing stage opposite Chandra Kasem Museum cost 300-500B for the standard three-hour tour. During the dry season only the lower half of Ayuthaya can be reached due to low waters. Boats can also be hired to Bang Pa In: look for the "Boat Trid Bang Pa In" sign.

Mini-trucks cost 250-400B for an afternoon tour which should include the Golden Mount, Wat Chai Wattanaram, St. Joseph's Cathedral, and Wat Panam Chong. Central temples can be reached by foot. Temples on the southern riverbanks are served by small ferries for five *baht*.

Local *tuk tuks* and mini-trucks cost 10B for any distance. Ayuthaya, with over 1,100 registered three-wheelers, claims the title of *tuk tuk* capital of Thailand.

Leaving Ayuthaya

Minibuses to Bang Pa In leave from the market on Naresuan Road. To Kanchanaburi, take a yellow bus from the market to Suphanburi, from where buses continue to Kanchanaburi. Buses to Sukothai leave hourly from the market. Trains north to Phitsanulok and Chiang Mai depart eight times daily.

LOPBURI

Lying 150 km north of Bangkok is the pleasant and friendly little town of Lopburi, one of the oldest and most historic sites in Thailand. Lopburi is rarely visited by Westerners and initial impressions are hardly spectacular, though the town offers enough good architecture and historic background to merit an overnight stop.

Local people are friendly, hospitable, and often happy to show visitors around the major sites and point out the better restaurants and nightclubs. The study of English seems to be a major preoccupation with the population, who will gladly exchange guide services for a few hours of English conversation.

Lopburi is divided between the historic old town near the train station and the new town located three kilometers east. The old town has all the temples plus several good budget hotels near the train station. The only reasons to visit the new town are the main bus terminal at the first oversized traffic circle (Sakao Circle) and the nightclubs and swimming pool located along the main road towards the second circle. Minibuses shuttle between the old and new town until about 2000.

All major attractions are located in old town near the train station. Hurried visitors can visit the most important sites on the three-hour walking tour described below, and then continue north by train or bus. Note that the Fine Arts Department now collects a 20B admission fee for most monuments. Although the Royal Palace and Wat Mahathat are worth the cost, other monuments can be easily viewed and photographed from the street. Note: travelers can walk in free after the guards depart after 1630.

Lopburi's friendly population, pleasant pace of life, and small selection of historic attractions make it a fine place to break the northward journey.

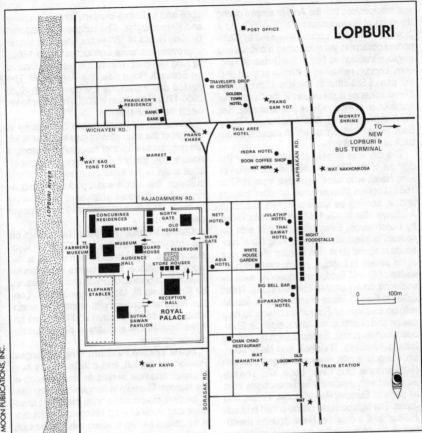

LOPBURI

- POST OFFICE
- TRAVELER'S DROP IN CENTER
- GOLDEN TOWN HOTEL
- ★ PRANG SAM YOT
- ★ PHAULKON'S RESIDENCE
- BANK
- BANK
- WICHAYEN RD.
- ★ PRANG KHAEK
- THAI AREE HOTEL
- ★ WAT SAO TONG TONG
- MARKET
- INDRA HOTEL
- BOON COFFEE SHOP
- WAT INDRA
- RAJADAMNERN RD.
- NETT HOTEL
- JULATHIP HOTEL
- THAI SAWAT HOTEL
- NIGHT FOODSTALLS
- CONCUBINES RESIDENCES
- MUSEUM
- NORTH GATE
- OLD HOUSE
- TI FARMERS MUSEUM
- MUSEUM
- GUARD HOUSE
- MAIN GATE
- RESERVOIR
- AUDIENCE HALL
- STORE HOUSES
- ASIA HOTEL
- WHITE HOUSE GARDEN
- BIG BELL BAR
- ELEPHANT STABLES
- RECEPTION HALL
- SUPARAPONG HOTEL
- SUTHA SAWAN PAVILION
- **ROYAL PALACE**
- ★ WAT KAVID
- CHAN CHAO RESTAURANT
- WAT MAHATHAT
- OLD LOCOMOTIVE
- TRAIN STATION
- SORASAK RD.
- WAT
- MONKEY SHRINE
- TO → NEW LOPBURI & BUS TERMINAL
- ★ WAT NAKHONKOSA
- NAPRAKAN RD.
- LOPBURI RIVER
- © MOON PUBLICATIONS, INC.
- 0   100m
- MOON

History

Lopburi has served as home to Neolithic settlers, an independent Dvaravati kingdom called Lavo (6th-10th centuries), Khmer military outpost (10th-13th centuries), and subcapital during the Ayuthaya Period (1350-1767). It was during the third period that Cambodian architectural and artistic patterns fused with traditional Mon styles to produce the famous Lopburi style—one of Thailand's most important and distinctive regional art movements.

The city has ridden the roller coaster of Thai history. Scholars believe the city (then called Lavo) was established some 1,400 years ago as the capital of a Mon (Dvaravati) kingdom which extended northward to the Mekong River.

According to tradition, Lopburi helped establish the northern Mon kingdom of Haripunchai (Lamphun) by sending up a number of holy men and providing national leadership under Cham Devi, the daughter of a Buddhist ruler who established the dynasty which lasted until the middle of the 11th century. All traces of Lavo have disappeared aside from some Dvaravati artifacts displayed in the Lopburi National Museum.

Lavo declined near the end of the 9th century as Angkor succeeded in replacing Dvaravati's hegemony over central Southeast Asia. In fact, sometime during the early 11th century, Lopburi was aided by the Khmers during a skirmish against an army from Haripunchai. Lopburi was incorporated into the Angkor empire during the reign of Suryavarman I (1007-1050). As a province of Angkor, Lopburi was ruled by Cambodian governors yet maintained a cultural and religious tradition as heir to the Dvaravati kingdom. Lopburi remained a Khmer outpost until the rise of Sukothai in the late 13th century. Khmer influence is still evident in the Cambodian architecture of Prang Khaek (Hindu shrine), San Pra Kan (Kala shrine), Wat Mahathat, and Prang Sam Yot, a Hindu shrine which appears on the back of the 500B note.

The city was largely abandoned after the demise of the Khmers until the ascension of King Narai, who ruled Ayuthaya from 1657 to 1688. Lopburi then entered its most brilliant phase, serving as the alternative capital to Ayuthaya after the Gulf of Siam was blockaded by Dutch ships. Even after the gulf was reopened to international trade, King Narai continued to spend up to nine months of each year at his palace in Lopburi, nicknamed the "Versailles of Siam." European influences were introduced on an unprecedented scale. Narai called in French Jesuit missionaries to discuss religion and invited French architects to help design and construct his new residence. European architects also helped design his military forts in Ayuthaya, Bangkok, and Nonthaburi, while exquisite gifts were exchanged between Narai and the "Sun King," Louis XIV. The city was filled with diplomats and merchants from all parts of Europe, Persia, India, China, and Japan. The high-powered phase ended in March 1688 after the death of Narai and the execution of his controversial advisor, Constantine Phaulkon.

Lopburi was abandoned in favor of Ayuthaya during the reign of King Petraja (1688-1703) and fell into a state of neglect and dilapidation over the next 150 years. A modest revival occurred in the mid-19th century when King Rama III reestablished Lopburi as an alternative capital to Bangkok and restored the Chantara Phisan Pavilion inside the royal complex. A residence was subsequently built by King Mongkut, who used Lopburi as a vacation resort from royal duties in Bangkok.

Royal Palace

Tours of Lopburi start inside the enormous complex constructed by King Narai between 1665 and 1677 in a combination of European and Khmer styles. The palace was restored by King Rama III 150 years later, and further improvements were conducted in the 1860s by King Mongkut. The main entrance is located on Sorasak Road near the Asia Hotel. The palace and museums are open Wed.-Sun. 0900-1700. Admission is 20B. This attraction is worth the admission fee.

A beautiful old house stands immediately to the right of the main eastern gateway. To the left are remnants of a water reservoir and storage houses while straight ahead, through the crenellated walls, is the inner courtyard and central buildings. The middle wall is pocketed with hundreds of small niches which once held glowing oil lamps, doubtless an impressive sight on royal celebrations.

Chantara Phisan Pavilion: The museum on the right was constructed in 1665 as the royal residence of King Narai. French architects designed the palace, which shows European influence in its pointed doorway arches. Restored by King Rama III, today it serves as the Lopburi National Museum with a small but worthwhile collection of Lopburi and Dvaravati images. Impressive statuary is placed on the palace grounds.

Sutha Vinchai Pavilion: Phiman Mongkut Pavilion, on the left, was constructed by King Mongkut and now serves as an extension of the National Museum in Bangkok. The top level of the three-story building holds the private apartment and study of King Mongkut. To the rear is a Farmer's Museum, which exhibits rare tools and farming artifacts, and eight bijou houses which once guarded the king's concubines.

Audience Hall: The Dusit Sawan Thanya Mahaprasat, an eerie hollow shell to the left of the museums, originally served as an audience hall for ambassadors and high-ranking foreign visitors. King Narai hosted guests from the court of King Louis XIV inside the hall once fitted with huge mirrors designed to imitate the Hall of Mirrors in Versailles.

Sutha Sawan Pavilion: Below the central courtyard is another audience hall which served as the final residence of King Narai until his death in 1688. Elephant kraals are found beyond the wide gates.

To truly understand the grandeur of the royal court, imagine it laid out with gardens, fountains, and statues surrounded by sumptuously dressed royalty, military leaders, and lovely concubines.

Wat Mahathat

Lopburi's finest architectural treasure and one of Thailand's best examples of Khmer provincial art is located just opposite the train station. The temple was constructed by the Khmers in the 12th century on the ruins of an earlier temple, but was heavily renovated by Siamese kings during the Ayuthaya and Sukothai periods. Centerpiece is the Khmer *prang* richly embellished with outstanding stucco lintels lacking the foliage ornamentation popular during the late 12th century. A beautiful and imposing sight, the *prang* architecturally marks the transition from pure Khmer to the Siamese style favored in Ayuthaya.

Also located on the grounds is a large brick *viharn* which dates from the reign of King Narai and shows European and Persian influences in its pointed arch window. *Chedis* nearby are later constructions dating from the Sukothai and Ayuthaya periods. Only traces of the square cloister which once surrounded the central *prang* remain visible.

Admission at the northern entrance is 20B. While some visitors are content to snap a few photos over the wall, this monument is worth the admission fee.

Located near the station is a locomotive manufactured in 1919 by North British Locomotive and a decrepit Khmer temple with odd European statues and racist posters illustrating the evolution of man.

Wat Nakhonkosa

Bangkok's Fine Arts Department has recently completed restoration on the ruins of this 12th-century Khmer *chedi, viharn,* and small *prang* originally dedicated to Hindu gods. Lopburi and U-Thong images uncovered from the lower *chedi* are now displayed in the Lopburi Museum.

Monkey Shrine

San Pra Khan—the so-called Kala Temple—consists of the ruins of a large 10th-century Khmer *prang* whose dimensions indicate its once considerable size, and a small later temple noted for its sandstone doorway graced with images of Vishnu and *naga*. To the rear stands a modern and rather nondescript temple erected in 1953 with statues of Hindu divinities highly revered by the Thai people. The temple is dedicated to, and dominated by, a gold-covered four-armed image of Kala, the Hindu god of time and death, incongruously capped with the head of Buddha. Behind is an elevated courtyard and giant banyan tree inhabited by aggressive monkeys who snatch purses and cameras from unsuspecting tourists. Hold on to your bags!

Prang Sam Yot

Prang Sam Yot—Temple of the Three Towers—is a fairly well-preserved example of Bayon-style Khmer architecture which, together with Wat Mahathat, once served as one of Lopburi's two principal Hindu temples. Archaeologists believe the structure was originally dedicated to Hindu gods and later converted into a Buddhist sanctuary as suggested by the modest interior collection of *nagas,* Hindu images, and life-size Buddhas in the Lopburi style.

Regarded as the primary landmark in Lopburi, the complex consists of a central corridor which links three laterite towers dedicated to Brahma, Shiva, and Vishnu. This finely balanced trio currently graces the back of Thailand's 500-*baht* currency note, though perfect symmetry has been marred by an east *viharn* erected during the reign of King Narai. The floor plan resembles a Greek cross with corbelled-roof porticoes on four sides.

Prang Khaek

The busiest intersection in Lopburi encircles a Hindu shrine erected in the 11th century by the Khmers, and restored in the 17th century by King Narai. The strange location intrigues more than the monument itself.

Wat Sao Tong Tong

Northwest of the Royal Palace stands another temple complex filled with an odd assortment of monuments. The *viharn* (Pra Viharn) to the right of the gaudily painted modern *wat* was originally constructed by King Narai to serve as a Christian chapel for Western diplomats. Though heavily restored in a pseudo-Western style, Pra Viharn shows typical Ayuthayan details such as tall and slightly concave foundations, superimposed roofs, and pilasters decorated with foliage capitals. The elegant structure

—now a Buddhist sanctuary—features an immense seated Buddha and recessed wall niches filled with a collection of small but remarkable Lopburi images.

Outside the temple is a modern *sala* which displays a carved wooden pulpit dating from the Ayuthaya Period, monastic buildings constructed by King Narai, and distinctive residences erected for visiting ambassadors and Christian missionaries.

Phaulkon's Residence

This complex displays a broad patchwork of architectural styles in which European predominates, but not to the exclusion of Thai influences. Chao Praya Wichayen was originally constructed by King Narai as a residence for a French ambassador sent from the court of King Louis XIV, but later became the final home to an infamous Greek adventurer named Constantine Phaulkon. Phaulkon's attempts to convert Narai to Christianity resulted in his beheading, the ouster of all Westerners from the royal courts in Lopburi and Ayuthaya, and the near-complete destruction of his residence and all ancillary buildings! Moral: don't mess with the king.

The narrow courtyard to the rear holds a Roman Catholic church, Jesuit residence, and remains of a bell-shaped tower. To the east are residences constructed for members of the 1685 French mission.

The complex has been completely restored, though there's less of interest here than at the Royal Palace and Wat Mahathat. Visitors with little interest might look from the street and pocket their 20 *baht*.

Accommodations

Hotels in Lopburi are geared toward Thai visitors rather than Western tourists. As elsewhere in Thailand, this situation means that facilities are basic but reasonably clean, proprietors are friendly, and prices are low—a great change from towns dominated by mass tourism.

Traveler's Drop In Center: Lopburi's small but popular travelers' center is actually an English-language school with two small communal bedrooms upstairs and two rooms for singles or doubles. Richard (Wichit Eungsuwanpanich), the friendly Thai citizen who runs the school, often invites Western visitors and Thai students out for dinner and conversation in local nightclubs. Richard is a great source for information on local music, vegetarian restaurants, the swimming pool located in New Lopburi, and the Nartasin School of Performing Arts, which attracts

IN THE SERVICE OF THE KING

No summary of the history of Lopburi would be complete without a mention of Constantine Phaulkon, one of the most daring and colorful Westerners in Thai history. The reign of King Narai—himself a dynamic leader—was a time of intrigue, scandal, and strong personalities as personified by the Greek merchant and adventurer.

Phaulkon (1647-1688) arrived in Siam in 1678 as a cabin boy with the English East India Company. With little education or diplomatic background, Phaulkon rose rapidly in the royal service by favoring private traders over the Dutch, English, and Persian companies which had previously dominated trade with the Siamese court. In a remarkably short time, this rambling seaman and ex-gunrunner dazzled the king with his remarkable linguistic skills (he spoke both ordinary and royal Thai), unwavering sense of loyalty, and legendary trading acumen. Accounts relate that Phaulkon earned Narai's royal treasury an enormous amount of revenue by outtrading even the Moors. In 1682 Phaulkon successfully directed the Cambodian defense against an invasion from Vietnam and later organized a military expedition against the rebellious Makassarese community in Ayuthaya.

Narai rewarded the Greek adventurer with the prime ministership and two magnificent residences in Ayuthaya and Lopburi where, according to legend, Phaulkon annually spent 14,000 crowns on wine alone. But Phaulkon failed in his delicate balancing act between the Thai court and French interests. When King Narai fell seriously ill in the spring of 1688, the stage was set for a revolution. The main target was Phaulkon, who had become the king's most powerful minister, married a Japanese Christian, and lived in European style surrounded by Jesuit priests and English merchants. Alarmed at Phaulkon's power and the conversion attempts of Catholic priests, palace ministers on the death of Narai seized the throne and imprisoned Phaulkon. The Greek adventurer was quickly convicted of treason and then tortured, gutted, and beheaded. A usurper seized the throne and ended the once-magnificent reign of Narai the Great.

students from all regions of Thailand. 34 Wichayen Rd. Soi 3, no phone, 40B dorm, 60-80B. Also on Wichayen is **Thai Aree**, with rooms 60-80B single, 100-120 double, tel. 411468.

Asia Hotel: Best bet for comfortable lodgings in the center of town is the basic hotel located just opposite the Royal Palace. 1 Sorasak, tel. (036) 411892, 100-250B.

Naprakoan Road Hotels: Several inexpensive hotels are strung along Naprakoan Rd. just opposite the train station. Rooms at the Suparapong, Thai Sawat, Julathip, and Indra start from 80B single and 120B double. Ask for the cheapest room rather than accepting the more expensive options offered by the manager.

Lopburi Inn: Located in New Lopburi on the main road between the two traffic circles, this is the only modern hotel in town with a/c rooms and modern facilities. 28/9 Narai Maharat Rd., tel. (036) 412300, fax (036) 411917, 250-500B.

Nett: Located at 17 Rajadamnern, singles go for 90-120B, doubles 120-200B; tel. 411738.

Restaurants

Lopburi is a sleepy place with a limited number of simple restaurants. Simple snacks are available from the **night market** on Naprakan (Na Kala) Rd. opposite the Julathip and Thai Sawat hotels. The Chinese restaurant in the **Asia Hotel** serves both Chinese and Thai dishes in fairly comfortable surroundings. An escape from the heat is provided in the two branches of the a/c **Foremost Restaurant** on Napraka Rd. and just north of the **Traveler's Drop In**. Other popular restaurants include the **White House Garden** in the center of town, the upscale **Chan Chao Restaurant** near Wat Mahathat, and **Boon Coffee Shop** near the Indra Hotel.

Nightclubs

Nightclubs and discos are located in New Lopburi near the first traffic circle. The most popular spot is **Chao Praya Nightclub**, where live music is offered during the week and disco on weekends. Back in the old town, **Big Bell Bar** adjacent to the Suparapong Hotel is a popular spot to spend an evening. As mentioned above, the proprietor of the Traveler's Drop In often takes visitors out to nightclubs for an evening of cabaret and meals plus conversation with English-language students.

Culture And Sports

Thai classical dance and music can be found at the Nartasin School of Art, where young students from nearby provinces train for professional careers in the performing arts. Mornings around 1000 are the best time to observe the students and take a tour of the facilities. Nartasin (Vithayalia Kalasilpa University) is in New Lopburi, about three km from old town. Richard from the Traveler's Drop In can arrange tours. Alternatively, take a blue *songtao* from Three Pagodas bus stop to the first traffic circle, walk 10 minutes south, then west along the canal to the Fine Arts College.

Lopburi's municipal swimming pool is on the right side of the road in New Lopburi, about one km beyond Sakao Circle. It's open daily 1000-2000 and charges a 25B admission fee.

Transportation

Lopburi, 150 km north of Bangkok and 75 km from Ayuthaya, can be visited as an overnight excursion or as an afternoon trip from Ayuthaya. Rushed travelers can leave their bags at the train station, conduct a three-hour walking tour, and continue by night train to either Phitsanulok or Chiang Mai.

Bus: Buses leave Bangkok's Northern Terminal every 30 minutes from 0600 to 1900 and take about three hours to reach Lopburi. Buses from the central market in Ayuthaya leave every 30 minutes. Lopburi can also be reached direct from Kanchanaburi, avoiding the nightmare of travel connections in Bangkok. From Kanchanaburi, take a bus to Suphanburi (two hours) where buses continue up to Singburi (three hours) and on to Lopburi (30 minutes). Travelers coming from Korat and the northeast should transfer to a connecting bus in Saraburi. The Lopburi bus station is located in the new town about two km east of the old town. Take any *songtao* going west.

Train: Trains from Bangkok's Hualampong Station depart every two hours from 0600 to 2000 and take about three hours to reach Lopburi. The train from Ayuthaya takes an hour and passes through lovely scenery of ricefields and idyllic villages. The express sleeper train from Bangkok to Chiang Mai passes through Lopburi at 2020. Reservations should be made on arrival in Lopburi. The Lopburi station is conveniently located within walking distance of all attractions and the budget hotels in the old town.

SARABURI AND PRA BUDDHABAT

Saraburi is a small provincial town 113 km from Bangkok on the highway to the northeastern town of Korat. Saraburi has little of interest aside from the shrine at Pra Buddhabat (Pra Buddhaphat) and the drug rehabilitation center at Wat Tham Krabok. Most travelers visit the two sites on side trips from Lopburi.

Pra Buddhabat, 29 km from Saraburi toward Lopburi, is regarded as one of the finest examples of classic architecture in Thailand and is the site of the country's most sacred festival. Along with temples in Doi Suthep, Nakhon Phanom, and Nakhon Si Thammarat, Pra Buddhabat constitutes one of the four most-sacred destinations in Thailand. The temple was originally constructed by the kings of Ayuthaya but destroyed by the Burmese in 1765. The present structure was erected by the early kings of Bangkok and improved upon by subsequent rulers.

Entrance is made up a long staircase flanked by a pair of impressive, undulating *nagas* which symbolically transport the visitor from the earthly realm to the heavenly home of the Buddha. The most significant building is an elegant *mondop* that enshrines a two-meter footprint which, according to Thai tradition, was discovered in 1606 by a hunter chasing a deer. Erected on a broad marble platform, the *mondop* features a highly ornate pyramidal roof decorated with a profusion of glass and gold mosaics. Inside the structure is the gold-leaf footprint filled with coins tossed by pilgrims. Also note the elaborate doors inlaid with mother-of-pearl, constructed during the reign of King Rama I.

Pra Buddhabat is considered a powerful place filled with divine magic. Thais believe they can improve their karma by tossing coins into the footprint, ringing the bells with bamboo sticks, and throwing fortune-telling sticks *(siem si)* which now compete with electronic counterparts. Other legends claim that you will live a full 93 years if you ring all 93 bells and count them correctly, and that three visits to Pra Buddhabat ensures admittance into heaven.

JUST SAY NO AT OPIUM PIPE MONASTERY

Can a radical therapy concocted of strange herbs and rigorous spiritual practice cure hard-core drug addiction? For over 30 years, a Thai monk named Pra Chamroon Parnchand has been saving addicts with an extraordinary 70% success rate. His unorthodox yet highly efficacious treatments won him the prestigious Ramon Magsaysay Award for Public Service in 1975, and his worldwide reputation ensures a steady stream of opium users, heroin addicts, cocaine freaks, and now the victims of the new scourge—crack cocaine.

Although all patients are ensured absolute privacy, visitors over the past two decades have included American lawyers, stockbrokers, corporate presidents, Asian politicians, Italian fashion designers, rock stars, senior Islamic religious authorities, disciples of the Dalai Lama, sons and daughters of the rich and famous, and an American black Vietnam veteran (Gordon Baltimore from Harlem) who now welcomes the nervous arrivals. All share the same quarters and conduct their therapy alongside prostitutes from Bangkok and mountain tribesmen hooked on poppies.

The 15-day rehabilitation course begins with a sacred vow never to use drugs again; the oath is written on rice paper and swallowed. The first five days include detoxifying vomit sessions in which patients drink a potion made from 100 wild plants that grow on the monastery grounds and "tastes like stale tobacco that burns like fire." Long gulps of holy water are followed by convulsions and violent spasms of vomiting which remove the toxic waste of years of addiction. Afternoons are spent in herbal saunas spiced with lemongrass to purify the blood and morning glory to restore the eyesight. The final 10 days involve working in the fields and helping the resident monks with construction projects. The treatment has been broadened with religious and psychological elements. To date, more than 100,000 drug addicts have taken the treatment, which is completely free aside from voluntary contributions.

Wat Tham Krabok ("Opium Pipe Monastery") is located in a hillside monastery some 125 km north of Bangkok and 25 km from Saraburi, midway between Lopburi and Saraburi. Anyone with a serious drug problem may want to seek out the extraordinary treatments offered by Pra Chamroon Parnchand, plus casual visitors are welcome.

The temple complex includes several other beautiful and significant buildings. Viharn Luang features a museum filled with religious paraphernalia and donations from pious visitors. Several small *chedis, bots,* and a temple dedicated to Kala are also located on the temple grounds.

The best time to visit Pra Buddhabat is during the religious festivals held twice yearly in the early spring and late fall. An estimated 800,000 pilgrims arrive to improve their karma and enjoy entertainment provided by Ferris wheels, magicians, beggars, swindlers, and folk shows of *likay* and *khon.* The first festival, held in the third lunar month, is popular with Chinese since it corresponds with the Chinese New Year. The second festival in the fourth lunar month is mainly attended by Thai pilgrims.

While still a popular event that celebrates the primordial concept of agricultural society, some of the significance has been lost to modernization, which downplays the importance of cyclical festivals.

Accommodations

Pra Buddhabat Hotels: The **Suk Sant** and the larger **Thanin Hotel** on the main road have fan-cooled rooms for 60-120B.

Saraburi Hotels: Saraburi has six hotels with both fan and a/c rooms. **Kiaw An** (Kaew Un) **Hotel** (tel. 036-211656) at 273 Phahonyothin Rd. has fan rooms for 100B and a/c from 220B. Other hotels in the same price range include the **Saen Suk** (tel. 036-211104) at 194 Phahonyothin Rd. and the **Sap Sin** (tel. 036-211047) at 471 Phahonyothin Road.

Transportation

Buses and *songtaos* to Pra Buddhabat leave from the bus terminal in New Lopburi. Keep your eyes open for the hillside monastery located on the right side of the road. Pra Buddhabat and Wat Tham Krabok are also served by buses and *songtaos* leaving from the Saraburi bus terminal on Banthat Rd. and from the bus halt near the Bank of Asia.

> *For my part, I travel not to go anywhere, but to go. I travel for travel's sake. The great affair is to move.*
> —Robert Louis Stevenson

CENTRAL THAILAND

Flanked by mountains to the north, west, and east, the vast plains of central Thailand form the heartland of the Thai nation, both past and present. The region is profiled by the provinces of Sukothai, Phitsanulok, Kamphang Phet, Tak, and Phetchabun. Watering the fertile region are several major rivers such as the mighty Chao Praya, which flows from the north through the historic heartland before emptying into the Gulf of Thailand. Together with other tributaries such as the Ping and Nan rivers, central Thailand has been carved into an incredibly complex network of waterways and canals which help produce the rice that sustains the country. Geography and nature have been generous to the region. Unlike the arid northeast and mountainous north, rainfall is abundant and the earth is fertile enough to provide a decent living for the people.

Central Thailand, outside the larger towns, has changed remarkably little over the centuries. Most of the population is of pure Thai decent without the mixtures of Chinese, Lao, Khmer, and Malay found throughout the border districts. Although large and modern towns are commonplace, most inhabitants continue to live and work in tiny hamlets where their lives revolve around family, farming, and faith. Rice cultivation remains the chief occupation.

Sightseeing Highlights

As with the rivers which flow through the region, Thai history has moved down through central Thailand and left behind remnants of the past. Most of the archaeological monuments date from the 13th and 14th centuries, when a Thai kingdom at Sukothai controlled central Thailand. Also of interest are several border towns where traditional architecture and simple life-styles still survive.

Phitsanulok: Located 380 km from Bangkok is the modern city of Phitsanulok, the hub of commerce and communication for central Thailand. Phitsanulok has few architectural blessings or great sights apart from the Jinaraj Buddha—widely considered the most beautiful image in Thailand—and nearby national parks and wildlife sanctuaries.

Sukhothai: An hour west of Phitsanulok is Sukhothai, a town which served in the 13th and 14th centuries as the first capital of a unified Thailand. Modern Sukhothai is rather nondescript, but nearby Sukhothai Historical Park offers the finest collection of historic ruins in the country. Budget guesthouses are plentiful and travel connections can easily be made in all possible directions. Sukhothai is the most important destination in Central Thailand.

Si Satchanalai: Some 55 km north of Sukhothai is Si Satchanalai, a small town which served as a provincial capital and viceroy seat during the Sukhothai Period. Although somewhat modest by Sukhothai standards, ruins inside the historical park have been well restored and provide a genuine sense of timelessness. Si Satchanalai can be visited on a day-trip from Sukhothai.

Kamphaeng Phet: Third part of the Sukhothai triumvirate was the garrison town of Kamphang Phet, 85 km southwest of Sukhothai. Visitors with a serious interest in Thai archaeology will enjoy the handful of partially restored

temples situated on the northern edge of town.

Tak: Located on Highway 1, which connects Bangkok and Chiang Mai, the modern town of Tak serves as the transportation hub for west-central Thailand. Tak lacks any great sights except for the finest collection of old wooden houses left in Thailand. Fans of traditional domestic architecture can spend a few hours exploring the charming neighborhoods before continuing on to Mae Sot or Chiang Mai.

Mae Sot: Mae Sot is an intriguing town situated on the Burmese border. While rarely visited by Westerners, it offers a few temples, a great morning market, and a diverse population of Thais, Chinese, Burmese, and hilltribe minorities. The completion of the road north from Mae Sot to Mae Sariang provides a unique approach to the region west of Chiang Mai.

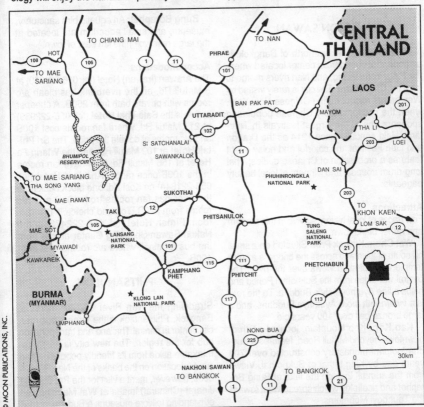

Transportation

Sukhothai is the main destination and tourist hub in central Thailand. Visitors short on time can briefly visit Sukhothai enroute to Chiang Mai. A more complete tour would include side trips to Si Satchanalai and Phitsanulok before heading west to Kamphang Phet, Tak, and Mae Sot on the Burmese border. Chiang Mai can be reached by bus from Mae Sot, or via Mae Sariang on a recently completed road which skirts the Burmese border.

Sukhothai is seven hours by private buses or public coaches leaving from Bangkok's Northern Bus Terminal. Ordinary buses are plentiful from Sukhothai to all other destinations.

Motorcycles can also be rented in Sukhothai.

The train line passes through Phitsanulok, from where buses continue west to Sukhothai. Trains from Bangkok to Phitsanulok depart seven times daily at 0640, 0705, 0830, 1500, 1800, 2000, and 2200. Ordinary trains from Bangkok take eight hours and rapid trains take six hours to reach Phitsanulok. The most convenient options are the 0640 rapid train which arrives in Phitsanulok at 1230, and the 1500 rapid train which arrives at 2115. As noted before, train travel is a very relaxing and scenic way to travel around Thailand.

Thai Airways flies twice daily from Bangkok to Phitsanulok and once daily to Tak.

HISTORIC HEARTLAND

NAKHON SAWAN

Nakhon Sawan, 240 km north of Bangkok, is an important commercial center located where the Ping, Yom, Wang, and Nan rivers merge to form the Chao Praya. The city is rarely visited by Westerners except during Chinese New Year, when the predominately Chinese population sponsors one of the largest festivals in Thailand. Held annually since 1914 as the Dragon and Lion Festival, the colorful and noisy event features a procession of Chinese deities, Thai long-drum troupes, and winners of local beauty pageants.

Attractions

Few traces of local history survive in this modern and rather bland town.

Wat Chom Kirinak Prot: Situated on a small hill south of town and across the bridge is a small temple with splendid views over the river. The central *wat* dates from the Sukhothai Period and holds a fine Ayuthaya-style Buddha. To the rear is a *viharn* with more Ayuthaya Buddhas, and a large bronze bell over 100 years old.

Kao Kob: Kob Mountain, located north of downtown beyond Matuli Road, features a Buddha footprint monastery constructed over 700 years ago by King Lithai of Sukhothai. Views from the summit include the lake at Bung Boraphet and ricefields which spread west toward the Taunggyi Mountains.

Bung Boraphet: An aquatic bird sanctuary, museum, and small aquarium are located at the large reservoir nine km east of town.

Accommodations

The **Arawan (Irawan) Hotel** (tel. 056-221889) at 5 Matuli Rd. on the riverbank has clean a/c rooms with private bath from 250B. A cheaper option is the **Sala Thai Hotel** (tel. 056-222938) at 217 Matuli Rd. where fan rooms cost 100B and a/c rooms at double the price. The **Sri Phitak Hotel** at 109 Matuli Rd. and the **Wiang Fa Hotel** at 156 Matuli Rd. both have fan rooms in the 100B price range. **Anodard Hotel** (tel. 056-221844) on Kosi Rd. one block back from the river has fan rooms from 100B and a/c rooms from 220B. Top-end choice is the 124-room **Piman Hotel** (tel. 056-222473) in the Nakon Sawan Shopping Center across from the bus terminal, where a/c rooms cost from 400B.

PHITSANULOK

Straddling the Nan River 380 km north of Bangkok, Phitsanulok is the largest commercial center in central Thailand and transportation hub for the region. The new city is hardly remarkable aside from its friendly population and superb location on the banks of the Nan River. It does, however, merit a visit for the Pra Buddha Jinaraj (Chinarat) image at Wat Mahathat, an outstanding folklore museum, a Buddha factory, and night markets and floating restaurants on the Nan River. Another important plus is the complete absence of tourists, making Phitsanulok a refreshing change from the more popular destinations in central and northern Thailand.

History

Phitsanulok is one of Thailand's oldest and most historic cities. The city originally served as a Khmer outpost called Song Kwae before the Kwai Noi River changed its course in the 11th century. Its chief prosperity was during the Sukhothai era, when it functioned as a military bastion, and after the decline of Sukhothai, when it served as the capital of Siam during the reign of King Trailokanat. In the 15th century Phitsanulok was the seat of the Ayuthaya viceroy, who ruled the province of Sukhothai.

Phitsanulok is highly regarded among the Thai people as the birthplace of King Naresuan the Great, who governed the province from 1569 to 1584. Then a vassal state of Pegu, Phitsanulok and central Thailand was subsequently liberated from foreign rule after Naresuan organized a Thai army which defeated the Burmese in the historic battle at Don Chedi. A memorial to King Naresuan is located on the north side of the river on the grounds of the former Chandahana Palace.

After a devastating fire in 1955, Phitsanulok was relocated five km from the old site and rebuilt in a modern shophouse style that offers few architectural blessings.

The following attractions follow a walking tour recommended by the local tourist office.

Wat Mahathat

Phitsanulok's major spectacle is the Jinaraj Buddha inside Wat Mahathat (Wat Yai), one of the few Ayuthaya Period temples to survive the catastrophic fire four decades ago.

The *wat* was erected in 1482 by King Boromatrailokanat of Ayuthaya as the symbol of his domination over Sukhothai and Phitsanulok. The *wat, prang,* and adjacent *viharn* were renovated by King Boromakot (1733-1758) and completely restored by the Fine Arts Department in 1991.

Entrance to the temple is made across a broad parking lot filled with souvenir shops selling gold-leaf offerings and reproductions of the famous image, palmists and blind fortune-tellers to the right rear, and a small pavilion where students occasionally perform the *khon.*

The *viharn* where the central image is stored is entered through beautifully carved wooden doors after which the splendid doors to Wat Pra Keo in Bangkok were modeled. Architecturally, the structure is a curious mixture of northern and southern styles with a three-leveled roof and low, sweeping eaves. The particularly fine interior is a stunning triumph of color and proportion. Black columns decorated with gold leaf support the rich red roof. Fine interior murals have been recently repainted with delightful scenes of a starving Buddha, courtesans, and hunters with their dogs. The lowness of the aisles and dramatic color scheme accentuate the nave and focus attention on the majestic image in the center.

The central Buddha, Pra Buddha Jinaraj ("Victorious King"), ranks as the great masterpiece of Sukhothai art. Regarded as the most beautiful and sacred image in Thailand, the highly polished bronze statue has been reproduced for the Marble Temple in Bangkok and a Thai temple at Bodgaya, India. Dramatic appeal is furthered by the black backdrop, narrow slit windows, and strong lighting which adds an almost surrealistic effect. The image is surrounded by pilgrims shaking fortune-telling sticks, four elephant tusks, and gold leaf bodhi trees in glass display cases.

The 36-meter *prang* in the center of the *wat* compound was constructed in Khmer style during the Ayuthaya Period. Surrounding the *prang* are long cloisters filled with an amazing array of Sukhothai, U-Thong, and Chiang Saen Buddhas. To the left is a small branch of the national museum with a fine collection of 19th-century wooden seals, mother-of-pearl monks' bowls, pottery, glassware, and figurines from Sawankalok and Si Satchanalai. Other buildings include a *bot* in the southwest corner and an immense *viharn* to the east.

Photographers are welcome but all visitors must be properly dressed; no shorts or immodest tops.

Wat Nang Phraya

Adjacent to Wat Yai is a small *viharn* where the famous Nang Phraya Buddha amulets were discovered in 1901.

PHITSANULOK

- #4 GUESTHOUSE
- TO CHIANG MAI
- KING NARESUAN SHRINE
- RIVERSIDE RESTAURANT
- WAT ARANYIK
- SINGAWAT RD.
- TO LOM SAK
- TO SUKOTHAI
- WAT MAHATHAT (WAT YAI)
- WAT NANG PHRAYA
- CROSSROADS NIGHTCLUB
- CITY GATE
- WAT RAJABURA
- BUS TERMINAL
- WANG CHAN RD.
- COUNTRY ROAD BAR
- FLOATING RESTAURANT
- PRA ONG DUM RD.
- CHANG PUAK HOTEL
- RAJAPRUK HOTEL
- PAILYN HOTEL
- CABLE CAR
- POST OFFICE SIAM HOTEL
- RAJAPRUK GUESTHOUSE
- MOTORCYCLES
- JUNGLE PUB
- POLICE
- MARKET
- NARESUAN RD.
- TOP LAND ARCADE
- PHIT HOTEL
- TRAIN STATION
- HERN FA RESTAURANTS
- SAIRUTHAI RD.
- AMARIN NAKHON HOTEL
- NIGHT FOODSTALLS
- BAKERY
- SOMBAT HOTEL
- CITY BUSES
- ASIA HOTEL
- RIVER
- CLOCK TOWER
- UNACHAK HOTEL
- HOH FA HOTEL
- TEHP NAKHON HOTEL
- WIN TOURS
- THAI AIRWAYS
- TOURIST OFFICE
- UNIVERSITY
- FOLKLORE MUSEUM
- BUDDHA FOUNDRY
- PUTTABUCHA RD.
- KHUN PHIREN RD.
- YOUTH HOSTEL
- BOROMATRAILOKANAT RD.
- NANCHAO HOTEL
- DAENG RESTAURANT
- TO NAKHON SAWAN
- TO WAT CHULAMANI 5 KM
- SLUPIE CLUB
- TO BANGKOK
- AIRPORT

0   300m

© MOON PUBLICATIONS, INC.

Wat Rajabura

Across the road and near the old city gate stands another temple which survived the fire of 1955. The partially reconstructed Ayuthayan Period chedi features a bot decorated with Ramayana frescoes painted during the reign of Rama III.

Nan River

A very pleasant walk can be made along the banks of the river which divides the city. Floating in the river are dozens of simple homes and restaurants, the only legal houseboats in Thailand since they predate municipal codes which banned such establishments. Opposite the General Post Office is a blue cable car which crosses the river and provides a glimpse of the houseboats and riverlife.

Clocktower And Central Phitsanulok

After walking past the Hern Fa Restaurant and riverside bazaar, turn left to the old clocktower on Phayalithai Rd. and continue through downtown to the railway station and central market. Top Land Arcade is a good place to shop and enjoy a meal in the restaurant on the top floor. The train station is fronted by a 10-wheel locomotive built in 1920 by the North British Locomotive Company. Farther east on Boromatrailokanat Road is the local tourist office.

Folklore Museum

With the finest collection of folkloric artifacts in Thailand, this small museum is a labor of love for Dr. Tawee, a retired major who has amassed an astounding assembly of agricultural and household instruments. Lower level of the front pavilion features Sawankalok ceramics, Thai instruments, and a creative assortment of coconut grinders sculpted in whimsical animal forms. Upstairs are traditional craftsmen's tools, Buddhas, fabrics, and bronzeware collected by the good doctor. To the rear is a lovely home filled with fish traps, old Victrolas, and elephant bells; the building itself is a remarkable structure.

Dr. Tawee's private museum is located on Visut Kasat Rd. two km south of the train station, and is extremely difficult to find. Entrance is made through an unmarked green gate adjacent to the Pan Ngarn Village sign. Admission is free but donations are accepted by volunteer guides.

Buddha Foundry

Opposite the folklore museum is a thriving Buddha factory, also owned by Dr. Tawee. Visitors are welcome to tour the foundry and watch the production of bronze Buddhas cast after prototypes from Sukhothai, Ayuthaya, and the Pra Jinaraj at Wat Yai. Explanation of the lost-wax method is provided by photo exhibits in the front room, while a small souvenir shop in the rear sells bronze images at reasonable cost. The foundry is a fascinating attraction and one of the few places in Thailand to watch the ancient tradition of bronze casting.

As with the nearby Folklore Museum, Dr. Tawee's foundry is difficult to find and marked only in Thai script. Entrance is through a green iron gate and door adjacent to a lamppost.

Wat Chulamani

Five km south of town are the ruins of Phitsanulok's oldest historical site, a Khmer-style *prang* constructed during the Sukhothai Period and restored by King Boromatrailokanat of Ayuthaya. The temple is chiefly noted for its ornate plaster

Chulamani master monk

designs and stucco friezes which decorate the lintels and exterior walls. Situated nearby is a modern monastery and ruined *viharn* constructed by King Narai to commemorate the Buddhist ordination of King Boromatrailokanat.

Wat Chulamani can be reached with public bus 5 heading south down Boromatrailokanat Road.

Phitsanulok—Lom Sak Road

Highway 12, which links Phitsanulok with Lom Sak, passes through several mountain ranges which separate the valleys of the Nan and Pasak rivers. The tourist office in Phitsanulok has a good map which shows the exact location of all waterfalls and national parks in the region. Tours can be arranged through local guesthouses and from travel agents located near the Phitsanulok tourist office.

Keangsopa Waterfalls: The falls at Kilometer 72 are recommended as the best in the region, especially during the rainy season and at the end of the monsoon season. The falls are signposted in English and located two km south of Highway 12.

Tung Saleng Luang National Park: Located 80 km west of Phitsanulok is a 1,200-square-km park covered with wooded mountains with a variety of flora and fauna. Accommodations in park bungalows can be booked in advance from the Forestry Office (tel. 02-579-0529) in Bangkok.

Phuhinrongkla National Park: From 1967 to 1982, Phuhinrongkla National Park served as the headquarters of the Communist Party of Thailand (CPT) and was the site of numerous battles between the Thai government and communist insurgents. After the surrender in 1982 of the People's Liberation Army of Thailand

(PLAT), the region was declared a national park and opened to the public. Today the park offers a cool climate, hiking trails, waterfalls, scenic views, and remnants of the communist occupation such as air-raid shelters and military headquarters. Reservations can be made from the Forestry Office in Bangkok. Large bungalows cost from 600B per night and camping costs 50B. The park is 125 km from Phitsanulok and can be reached by public bus going to the nearby village of Nakhon Thai.

Budget Accommodations

Phitsanulok has two good guesthouses that have opened in the last few years, and several low-end hotels located near the train station.

Youth Hostel: Phitsanulok's official youth hostel is somewhat isolated but otherwise an excellent place to stay. The owner, Sapachai Pitaksakorn, worked in Bangkok as a computer programmer before returning to his hometown and opening the hostel in 1990. The British-designed main house, over 40 years old, has three upstairs rooms with Burmese antique beds and a small dormitory. The new wing in the back has another dorm plus almost 20 rooms furnished with antique decorations, old boats and oxcart wheels, lanterns, and the remains of teak homes purchased by Sapachai in Tak.

The hostel is located two km south of the train station, one km from the airport, and four km from the bus terminal. A *samlor* should cost 10B from the train station or airport, and 25B from the bus terminal. Bus 3 goes from the bus terminal to the hostel. From the train station, take bus 4 south down Ekathotrot Rd., then left on Ramesaun Rd., then right on Sanambin Road. 38 Sanambin Rd., tel. (055) 242060, 50B dorm, 100-200B.

ADDITIONAL PHITSANULOK ACCOMMODATIONS

HOTEL	SINGLE	DOUBLE	ADDRESS	PHONE (055)
Nanchao	400-600B	500-800B	242 Boromotrailokanat	252510
Pailyn	600-800	700-900	38 Boromatrailokanat	252411
Thep Nakon	500-700	600-900	43 Srithamatraipidok	258507
Hoh Fa	100-200	100-200	73 Phyalathai	258484
Siam	100-140	120-160	4 Arthit Wong	258844
Unachak	80-100	80-120	66 Ekathotsarot	258837

Number 4 Guesthouse: Several years ago the schoolteachers from Sukhothai opened this small guesthouse in the north part of town. The lovely teakwood home has a courtyard patio which faces a street made rather noisy from the cars and nearby train line.

The guesthouse is located on the left side of Ekathrot Rd., about two km north of the big traffic circle. Bus 4 from the city bus terminal near the train station goes up Ekathrot Rd. and passes the poorly marked guesthouse. Bus travelers coming from Sukhothai should get off after the bridge but before the traffic circle and take a *songtao* going up Ekathrotrot Road. Rooms cost 60-120B.

Sombat Hotel: Inexpensive hotels in the 80-150B range are located near the train station on Sairuthai and Phayalithai roads. All are conveniently located in the center of town, but none are clean or very quiet. The Sombat Hotel is probably the best of a somewhat dismal lot. Overflow is handled by the nearby Unachak, Hoh Fa, and Asia hotels. 4 Sairuthai Rd., tel. (055) 258179, 70-160B.

Moderate Accommodations

Several hotels in Phitsanulok offer both inexpensive fan rooms and moderately priced a/c rooms.

Phitsanulok Hotel: Slightly better than the low-end hotels is this basic spot located on Naresuan Rd. just opposite the train station. Rooms are fairly clean but very spartan; ask for a quieter room facing the inner courtyard. The hotel is well-located in the center of town. 82 Naresuan Rd., tel. (055) 258425, 120-180B fan, 220-260B a/c.

Chang Puak Hotel: An older 70-room hotel with a restaurant and billiards hall. An okay place poorly located in the north part of town. 63 Pra Ong Dum Rd., tel. (055) 252822, 120-160B fan, 200-250B a/c.

Rajapruk Guesthouse: Located behind the upscale Rajapruk Hotel is a cheaper annex which calls itself a "guesthouse." While the name is just a marketing ploy, the annex has decent rooms for a fair price in an inconvenient location. 99 Pra Ong Dum Rd., tel. (055) 258788, 160-200B fan, 250-300B a/c.

Luxury Accommodations

Phitsanulok has several hotels which serve the businessman and upscale tourist market.

Rajapruk Hotel: Best luxury choice in town has 110 a/c rooms, a Thai-Chinese restaurant, nightclub, car rentals, and a swimming pool. The owner's wife is an American, and English is spoken by some of the staff. The main drawback is the poor location outside town center, across the train tracks.

Amarin Nakhon Hotel: While not as luxurious as the Rajapruk, this hotel compensates with a great location in the center of town just opposite the train station. Rooms are clean and the coffee shop is a popular spot for U.S. Army personnel from the nearby Thai military base. A very dark disco is located in the basement. 3 Chao Praya Rd., tel. (055) 258588, 320-600B a/c.

Restaurants

Phitsanulok has a wide selection of restaurants, from a/c dining in upscale hotels to alfresco meals down by the river.

Floating Restaurants: Several popular floating restaurants are tied up just south of the bridge. **Than Tip** has been recommended as the best, followed by **Yardfan Floating Restaurant** and then the **Songkwae Houseboat**. The boats wait for a full house, then serve meals as they slowly sail up and down the Nan River. A small charge is collected for the cruise and no minimum is enforced on food or drink orders. Puttabucha Road. Moderate.

Hern Fa Restaurants: Perhaps more fun than the floating restaurants are the hilarious food vendors who set up their portable shops each evening on the banks of the Nan River. A brilliant display of cooking and acrobatics is included with every order. First, the cook fires up the wok and sautées a mixture of vegetables and meats. A waiter then climbs to the top of a nearby truck and attempts to catch the mixture flung skyward by the chef. Misses are fairly common, but the best moment is when a drunken Westerner agrees to take the role of waiter and catch the flying morning glory. Look for the trucks mounted with ladders, wagons, and even small boats. **Pak Bung, Viroj Pochan**, and **Phakbung** ("The First in the World") are the most popular. Inexpensive.

Night Market: Over a dozen good foodstalls are located on the riverbanks just south of the Hern Fa restaurants. Inexpensive.

Top Land Arcade: A welcome relief from the daytime heat is provided in the a/c restaurant on the top floor of Phitsanulok's largest shopping center. Live music in the evening. A bowling alley is also located up on the sixth floor, while a small coffee shop sits in the basement. Boromatrailokanat Road. Inexpensive.

Other Spots: A great little **bakery** is located just across from the clocktower. Farther down the road and across from the Hoh Fa Hotel is the old-time **Poon Sri Restaurant**, which serves good Chinese and Thai dishes. Phayalithai Road. Inexpensive.

Nightlife

Phitsanulok is a big town with a fair amount of nightlife. Several of the better private clubs are located near the Pailyn Hotel. The **Jungle Pub** and **Country Road Bar** are Thai cowboy joints with both recorded and live music. The **Crossroads Nightclub** near the traffic flyover is similar. Disco devotees can check the late-night action in the **Pailyn Hotel** and the basement of the **Amarin Nakhon Hotel**. **Slupie Nightclub** just south of the youth hostel has live rock bands and cabaret shows. Phitsanulok is also a fairly pleasant place just to walk around in the evening.

Information

Tourist Office: Information on nearby attractions and national parks is available from the TAT office (tel. 055-252742) at 209 Boromatrailokanat Rd. near the clocktower. The Phitsanulok tourist office is managed by friendly and helpful people who are among the most competent in Thailand.

Tours: Travel agencies are located in upscale hotels and near the tourist office. Organized tours and rafting trips on the Yom River are available through the No. 4 Guesthouse and the youth hostel. The tour departs on Saturday mornings and includes a three-hour raft trip and overnight camping near Keng Luang Cave before returning Sunday evening.

Shopping: The local produce and fruit market is located under the covered shed near the train station. **Tup Tin Handicraft** shop, opposite the clocktower, has a small but high-quality selection of textiles and regional crafts.

Festivals: The Pra Buddha Jinaraj Fair is held on the sixth day in the third lunar month, generally in late February. The six-day fair includes folk performances and homage ceremonies to the Buddha image inside Wat Yai. Boat races are held on the Nan River during the first weekend of October. The Naresuan Festival in January honors the king who liberated Thailand from Burmese rule.

Motorcycles: Motorcycles can be rented from **Landi Motors** (tel. 055-242687) on Pra Ong Dum Rd. near the Rajapruk Hotel. Cars are available from most large hotels and tour companies on Sithamtraipidok Rd. near the TAT office.

Transportation

Phitsanulok serves as the transportation hub for central Thailand. The city is usually visited on a day-trip from Sukhothai or as an overnight stop between Ayuthaya and Sukhothai. Complete train and bus schedules are available from the TAT office.

Bus: Ordinary and a/c buses leave hourly from the Northern Bus Terminal in Bangkok and take five hours to reach Phitsanulok. Direct service from Bangkok is also provided by private bus companies such as **Yanyon Tours** (tel. 02-271-3110) and **Thawon Farm Tours** (tel. 02-271-3010).

BUSES FROM PHITSANULOK TO:

Bangkok	hourly 0700-23	five hours
Chiang Main	hourly until 1530	five hours
Sukhothai	hourly until 1800	one hour
Loei	six times daily	one hour
Khon Kaen	hourly 1000-1500	five hours

The Phitsanulok Bus Terminal (tel. 055-242430) is on Highway 12 about three km east of downtown. A *samlor* from the terminal to downtown hotels should cost 25-35B. Several city buses leave from the bus station. Bus 1 goes west to Wat Mahathat (Wat Yai), south along the river, east along Ramesuan Rd., and then returns to the bus station. Bus 7 does the same route in reverse. Bus 3 goes to the airport and Phitsanulok Youth Hostel.

Train: All trains from Bangkok, except the 1940 express service, stop in Phitsanulok. The 0640 and 1500 rapid trains from Bangkok arrive at 1233 and 2115. Phitsanulok can also be reached by trains from Ayuthaya and Lopburi, a pleasant alternative to the hot and rather boring bus journey.

The train station is conveniently located in the center of town near the Nan River, but about four km from the bus terminal. Travelers going direct to Sukhothai can hire a *samlor* from the train station to the bus terminal for about 25-35B. Alternatively, take bus 4 north to the big traffic circle and flag down any bus going west toward Sukhothai.

Air: Thai Airways flies from Bangkok to Phitsanulok twice daily at 0715 and 1550. Direct flights from Phitsanulok are available to Loei, Tak, and Phrae.

SUKHOTHAI

Thailand's original capital and birthplace of the Thai nation is one of the preeminent archaeological sites in Southeast Asia. Situated 450 km north of Bangkok where the northern mountains intersect the central plains, Sukhothai is to Thailand what Angkor is to Cambodia, Borobudur is to Indonesia, and Pagan is to Burma. Spread out over the 70-square-km national historic park are dozens of magnificently restored temples, palaces, Khmer *prangs,* gigantic Buddha images set with enigmatic smiles, and an outstanding museum which safeguards the grandeur of ancient Sukhothai.

The town also offers good guesthouses, friendly little cafes, and opportunities to become acquainted with the local Thais. Sukhothai is also a convenient base for exploring the nearby ruins of Si Satchanalai and Kamphang Phet. Sukhothai is the best stop between Bangkok and Chiang Mai—don't miss it.

History

Sukhothai was founded in 1238 by two rebellious Thai princes who liberated themselves from Khmer domination by establishing the first independent kingdom in Thailand. Although the city was but one of hundreds of small city-states in the region, it enjoyed a privileged location midway between the ancient empires of the Khmers to the east and Pagan to the west. Preaching a philosophy of political cooperation rather than military might, early kings of Sukhothai ("Dawn of Happiness") successfully united many of the small principalities between Laos and Malaysia to form the most brilliant empire in Thai history, and the only nation in Southeast Asia which has never fallen under foreign domination.

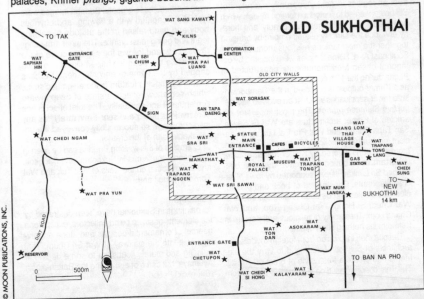

OLD SUKHOTHAI

Under the enlightened leadership of King Ramkamheng (1278-1318), Sukhothai enjoyed a golden age of political, cultural, and religious freedoms. Ramkamheng was a clever warrior and brilliant scholar who devised the modern Thai alphabet from Mon and South Indian scripts, introduced a free-trade economic sys-tem, promoted Theravada Buddhism as taught by Sri Lankan monks from Nakhon Si Tham-marat, and personally dispensed justice from his Manangasila Throne. According to Siamese traditions, citizens during his reign could ring a bell mounted outside his palace and ask for royal judgment.

THE ARTS OF SUKHOTHAI

Sukhothai during the reign of Ramkamheng blos-somed into a grand city of palaces, temples, monasteries, and wooden homes protected behind imposing earthen walls. Unlike Ayuthaya, which was destroyed by the Burmese, much of Sukhothai's great architecture and art still stands in good condi-tion. The only exceptions are the royal palaces, ad-ministrative buildings, and domestic homes which, according to religious protocol, were constructed entirely of wood and have completely disappeared.

Architecture

Sukhothai's superb range of religious and secular buildings—from Khmer *prangs* covered with terrify-ing *nagas* to Sinhalese *chedis* capped with distinctive lotus-bud towers—form the country's most complete ensemble of traditional Thai architecture and pro-vide a casebook study in the art styles of Southeast Asia.

Sukhothai architecture is a composite of styles from all regions in Asia. Apparently the rulers of Sukhothai wanted to reproduce foreign models which had a reputation for holiness and beauty, and there-by enhance the sanctity of their empire by bringing together the most famous religious monuments of Southeast Asia. Some temples were inspired by oc-tagonal-based Mon monuments constructed in Pagan during the 11th century. Sukhothai's heritage as a Khmer outpost is reflected in the Cambodian-style tower-sanctuaries which soon evolved into dis-tinctive Siamese *prangs*. The most important ex-amples of Khmer architecture are Wat Si Sawai, San Tapa Daeng, and Wat Pra Pai Luang, an an-cient sanctuary symbolically surrounded by the pri-mordial oceans favored by Khmer rulers. Another important contribution was made by large bell-shaped Sri Lankan *stupas* supported by rows of sa-cred elephants. Constructed of brick and plaster, elephant effigies can be seen ringing the bases of Wat Chedi Si Hong, Wat Chang Rob, and Wat Chang Lom. The variety of religious architecture in Sukhothai is nothing short of astounding.

Despite their inspiration from foreign models, the architects of Sukhothai managed to vary the ele-ments and create a fresh style of great originality. The Thai *chedi* is based on the massive *stupas* from Sri Lanka, but is smaller in size with more delicate proportions. Thai *prangs* may imitate Khmer tow-ers, but they have been altered with rounded corners, more numerous terraces, and construction from brick and laterite rather than cut stone. Sukhothai ar-chitects also added new elements such as lotus bud finials on the *chedis* and narrow slit windows in the *vi-harns* which provide an atmosphere of intimate solemnity.

Sculpture

Sukhothai's crowning artistic achievement wasn't architecture or painting, but stuccowork and sculpture considered by most art historians as the pinnacle of Thai artistic achievement. An astonishing inven-tion, Sukhothai sculpture is best represented by the sensual, almost otherworldly walking Buddha who moves with his right foot forward and left hand raised in the gesture of *vitaka mudra*.

Often cast of bronze using the *cire perdu* (lost-wax) method, these graceful Buddha images were typically elongated with a flowing, androgynous body and hand raised in the attitude of calming fears and giving reassurance. The other arm hangs rhythmically and follows the sensual curve of the torso while the head is shaped like a lotus bud capped by the flame of enlightenment. Perhaps the most intriguing feature is the enigmatic smile, which somehow reflects a state of deep inward contentment and spirituality. The total effect is one of marvelous power and sensitivity; rarely has any religious image so successfully conveyed the un-speakable faith of the creator.

Examples of this walking Buddha can be seen in the national museums in Sukhothai and Bangkok, and in Sukhothai on the walls of Wat Tuk and Wat Trapang Tong Lang.

Paintings

All paintings in Sukhothai have been destroyed by the elements or stolen by art collectors, except for a handful of ornamental designs and stone engrav-ings built into the stairway of Wat Sri Chum. Thai painting and murals flourished to some degree in Ayuthaya, but came of age during the Rattanakosin (Bangkok) Period.

Art and architecture reached their apogee in the mid-14th century under the reign of King Maha Lithai (King Mahatammaraja I). By the end of the 14th century, Sukhothai had become one of the largest Buddhist centers in the world. The city continued to prosper through a succession of six kings until losing a power struggle in 1378 with the rising kingdom of Ayuthaya. The last vestige of autonomy was lost in 1438 when the final king abdicated and Sukhothai came under the rule of an Ayuthayan prince.

The city lay abandoned until 1782 when a new line of kings, the Chakri Dynasty, came to power in Bangkok. Anxious to legitimize their rule by honoring the past, Rama I gathered together hundreds of Sukhothai statues to fill the newly built monasteries in Bangkok; Sukhothai's largest bronze Buddha was installed inside Wat Suthat. Interest in Sukhothai was further revived by Rama IV who, after a visit in 1833, returned with two stone tablets which established the mythology of Sukhothai.

In 1977 the Thai government, with assistance from UNESCO, began a restoration project that will culminate in the completion of the Sukhothai National Historical Park in 1993.

Orientation

Sukhothai is divided into two sections. The unattractive new town has the hotels, restaurants, and transportation facilities. Old Sukhothai with the museum and ruins is located 14 km west on the road to Tak. Minibuses to the old city leave across the bridge about 200 meters on the right side, just beyond the police station.

Ruins in old Sukhothai have been divided into five zones lettered A through E. Each zone now charges a 20B admission fee although the fee can sometimes be avoided by entering through the back roads.

Sukhothai's ruins are widely scattered and difficult to explore on foot except for the central monuments in Zone A. To visit the temples in a single day you must hire a *tuk tuk* at 30-50B per hour, a five-passenger taxi for 500B for a full day, or a bicycle for 20B from the stores just opposite the museum. Determined bicyclists who don't mind working up a sweat can reach all major monuments in a single day, including those to the far west and south. Ruins below are described with English-language signboards and are now safe to visit.

Please remember that all Buddhist images—no matter their age or condition—are considered sacred objects to the Thais. Visitors should be properly dressed and never touch or climb any image. This is no joke! Several years ago, a few Western missionaries—dressed only in shorts—posed for photographs on the shoulders of a Buddha. A national scandal erupted after the Bangkok photo lab turned the negatives over to a local newspaper, which then printed them on the front page. The Westerners were thrown in jail and deported from the country.

Central Sukhothai (Zone A)

Visitors with limited time should first see the monuments located in Zone A and Zone B to the north. Minibuses from the new town drop you at the entrance to the National Museum and admission gate into Zone A. Nearby restaurants provide the last chance for refreshment before reaching the foodstalls in the center of the park. Here in Sukhothai, *som tam* (spicy papaya salad) is prepared Thai-style with peanuts and dried shrimp, *bu* with pickled crab, *bla laa* with fermented fish and eggplant, *mangda* with smashed beetles, or in a vegetarian style called *jae*.

Bicycles can be rented from Vitoon Guesthouse at the park entrance.

Ramkamheng National Museum

Located inside the old city walls and just before the entrance gate to Zone A, Sukhothai's National Museum offers an outstanding introduction to the arts and crafts of Sukhothai and vassal cities of Si Satchanalai and Kamphang Phet. Inside the spacious building are Khmer statues, Sukhothai Buddhas, Sawankalok ceramics, and other archaeological artifacts gathered from central Thailand.

Facing the front entrance stands a bronze walking Buddha, considered the finest example of its kind in the country. Ground-floor highlights include a model of the ancient city (useful for orientation) and a replica of the four-sided pillar inscribed with Thailand's first written script. The original, now displayed in the Bangkok Museum, was reputedly discovered by King Rama IV while on pilgrimage during his monkhood.

Dozens of superb statues are exhibited upstairs. Buddha figures of the Sukhothai style are typically simple and unembellished images fashioned with slim torsos and serene expres-

A MYSTERY IN STONE

Carefully guarded inside the Sukhothai National Museum is a four-sided pillar of dark stone covered with ancient inscriptions traditionally attributed to King Ramkamheng. One section relates that "Sukhothai is good. There is fish in the water, rice in the fields, and the king does not levy tax on his subjects. Those who wish to trade are free to trade. The faces of the people shine bright." Identified as Stone Inscription Number 1, the stone also provides information on city planning, Buddhist law and philosophy, and the development of Thai script. Since its discovery in 1833 by King Mongkut during his monkhood, the stone has almost single-handedly created the mythology of Sukhothai and the foundation of the Thai nation.

But is it real? Since the early 1990s, Ramkamheng's reputation as the mastermind of Sukhothai's cultural development has come under increasing suspicion from both Thai and Western scholars. One skeptic is Dr. Piriya Krairiksh, a history professor from Thammasart University in Bangkok who claims the stone is a fake piece of historical writing created by King Mongkut sometime between 1851 and 1855. Understandably, Thais are very unhappy about the bombshell and reluctant to discuss the theory which has rocked the academic world.

Piriya, however, stands by his assertion based on textual analysis: the art and architecture mentioned are not supported by archaeological and historical evidence, the author freely lifted phrases verbatim from writings of later kings, and some inscription phrases are common to late-18th century Thai literature. On the other hand, Western archaeologists and historians such as Betty Gosling and David Wyatt still feel the puzzling aspects are not sufficient to disprove the authenticity of the inscription. While the controversy remains unresolved, the academic community continues to debate the famous stone on which rests the fundamental concepts of early Thai history.

sions. A small sample of Ayuthaya-style Buddhas are denoted by their regal attire and heavily bejeweled air of haughty arrogance.

Sculpture on the exterior grounds includes a rare phallic shrine of Khmer origins and stucco elephants removed from local shrines.

Sukhothai National Museum is open Wed.-Sun. 0900-1600.

Statue Of King Ramkamheng

Sukhothai's great ruler sits on a replica of the historic Manangasila throne, discovered in 1833 by King Rama IV and now protected in the Grand Palace Museum in Bangkok. The original throne was installed in the sugar palm grove of the royal palace, and was charged with such magic and mystical potency to make it an object of reverence to many Thais. Visitors can summon the ghost and ask for judgment from King Ramkamheng by ringing the bell on the right.

Wat Mahathat

Sukhothai's principal monastery and royal temple was constructed by Sukhothai's first king, Sri Indradita, but substantially remodeled in 1345 by Sukhothai's fourth ruler, King Lo Thai. The front sanctuary, with two rows of columns and a restored seated Buddha, dates from the Ayuthaya Period. Though largely in ruins, the complex once contained 185 *chedis* filled with funeral ashes of noblemen, a dozen *viharns* for public worship, and a central *bot* gilded with stucco surrounded by reflective moats. Most of the stone structures have collapsed and all of the wooden buildings have been destroyed by fire, but large Buddhas and fine stucco remain intact within the royal sanctuary. The monastery reflects both Khmer and Sri Lankan architectural influences, as evidenced by the presence of Hindu sculptures and Buddhist finials.

Towering over the minor *chedis* is a large central tower erected by King Lo Thai to house two important relics—a hair and neckbone from the Buddha—brought back from Sri Lanka by a monk named Sisatta. The monument is chiefly noted for its bulbous, lotus-bud *prang* derived from Singhalese prototypes but copied throughout Thailand as a symbol of Sukhothai's magical powers. The large bronze Buddha which once sat in the principal *viharn* to the rear was moved by King Rama I to Wat Suthat in Bangkok. Excellent views can be enjoyed from the summit of the central *chedi*.

The Fine Arts Department has extensively restored the monument and recast many of the better stucco friezes. The most important examples are the disciples walking in ritual procession around the base of the main *chedi*, and the demons, elephants, and lion-riding angels on the southern *chedi*.

Royal Palace

Across from Wat Mahathat lie the foundations of the old royal palace of King Ramkamheng. According to ancient principals, only temples and closely related monuments were built of stone, while royal palaces and domestic architecture were limited to wood which has disintegrated over the centuries. The controversial Stone Inscription 1 Pillar and Manangasila Throne were discovered here in 1833 by King Mongkut.

Wat Sri Sawai

Surrounded by two concentric enclosures and a deep moat, this well-preserved Khmer sanctuary was originally constructed by King Jayavarman VII (1181-1220) but left unfinished when the Khmer withdrew in the 13th century. As suggested by the exterior Hindu images, the temple first served as a Brahmanic sanctuary but was converted to a Buddhist monastery sometime in the 15th century.

The complex consists of a central nave and three brick *prangs* in a modified Angkor style embellished with both original and reconstructed *nagas* and *garudas*. Narrow, vertical windows pierce the walls. The central tower has been subjected to cement restoration that imparts a hybrid effect and compromises its sense of antiquity. The overall effect remains powerful, though many wish the ruins had been left untouched except for necessary support work.

Wat Trapang Ngoen

Wat Trapang Ngoen ("Silver Lake Monastery") features a *chedi* of exceptional elegance that copies the lotus-bud tower of Wat Mahathat, and the remains of an ancient *viharn* and *bot*. Located on a small island in the center of Silver Lake, this complex serves as the focal point for Sukhothai's annual Loy Kratong Festival.

Wat Sra Sri

Simplicity of design and elegance of location make this one of the most attractive temples in Sukhothai. The central tower, with its bell-shaped dome, square base, and tapering spire, is typical of the Sinhalese style adapted by local Theravadan architects. Overlooking the expanse of still water is a large Buddha image, well re-

---

RESTORATION OR RUIN?

When French archaeologist Lucien Fournerau visited the ruins of the abandoned city of Sukhothai in 1890, he was greeted after his one-month journey from Bangkok with little more than dense jungle and ancient monuments almost completely buried under the thick foliage. Today, the monuments visited by Fournerau have been restored by the Fine Arts Department and transformed into the Sukhothai Historical Park.

The project is not without controversy. With little regard for historical tradition or artistic heritage, Thai archaeologists from the Fine Arts Department departed from standard international practice and substantially reconstructed many of the major monuments. Roads and walkways were laid that did not follow the ancient pathways, and an immense concrete plaza complete with reflecting pool and statue of Ramkamheng was erected near the museum. Even more disturbing were stucco details and plaster moldings which have obliterated much of the historic detail on the surviving Khmer and Sukhothai monuments.

Intense criticism also surrounds the restoration of Buddha statues with little, if any, regard for their artistic content. Many of the extremely rare images now sport remodeled, brightly smiling heads—a practice which is anathema to art historians and archaeologists. The Fine Arts Department—guardian of Thailand's ancient monuments—tragically sacrificed historical accuracy for an idealized version of the past.

---

stored by the Fine Arts Department. Also located on the grounds is a small and very black Buddha in the walking style, an invention which epitomizes the ephemeral achievements of Sukhothai sculpture.

San Tapa Daeng

To the left of the road is a laterite temple characteristic of the Hindu type, with an elevated base and four porticoes which once held figures of the Lopburi school. Khmer statuary and Angkor Wat-style divinities uncovered inside the monument date from the reign of King Suryavarman II, in the first half of the 12th century.

Wat Sorasak

The Sri Lankan *chedi* of Wat Sorasak features a

square base surrounded by elephant buttresses. A stone inscription dates the *chedi* to 1412. Minor monuments such as Wat Sorasak may seem trivial to the casual visitor, but a careful comparison of *chedi* shapes will reveal an amazing variety of architectural compositions in Sukhothai.

North Of The City (Zone B)

Several of the finest monuments in Sukhothai are located in Zone B, just north of the old city walls. Entrance can be made through the gate near the new Information Center, or on the road which leads to Wat Sai Chum.

Information Center

Situated near Wat Pra Pai Luang is a complex of attractive buildings opened by the Fine Arts Department in 1990. The center includes replicas of images now displayed in the national museums of Bangkok and Sukhothai, a small bookstore, cafe, and an exhibition room with model displays of the old city.

young monks in Sukhothai

Wat Pra Pai Luang

This 12th-century "Temple of the Great Wind," about one km north of Wat Mahathat, was originally constructed by the Khmers as a Hindu sanctuary in the center of their military stronghold. A fragmented Buddha image in the Khmer style of the reign of King Jayavarman VII, builder of Angkor Thom, was discovered in the *viharn* and moved to the Ramkamheng National Museum. Subsequent excavations also brought to light a Shiva *lingam* dating from the original Hindu temple. Thai kings later converted the complex into a Buddhist monastery second in religious importance only to Wat Mahathat. The monument was tragically pillaged by looters in the 1950s for its valuable collection of Hindu and Buddhist images, but restored in 1988 with great sensitivity by the Fine Arts Department.

Entrance to the sanctuary passes over the foundations of a *viharn* and *chedi* once decorated with dozens of Buddha images fashioned in the preclassic style of the late 13th century. Most of the images have been vandalized or damaged beyond recognition, aside from the frontal walking image and standing Buddha on the northern wall. Behind the central *viharn* are the collapsed remains of two of the original three Khmer *prangs,* and a restored tower which displays corner *nagas* and a doorway lintel set with praying bodhisattvas and floral motifs.

Pottery Kilns

Archaeologists working near Sukhothai and Si Satchanalai have uncovered hundreds of massive kilns that once produced the most famous celadons in all of Southeast Asia. Traditionally it was believed the kilns were first used around 1300 by experienced Chinese potters brought to Sukhothai by King Ramkamheng after his second visit to China. However, recent research by a joint Thai-Australian team has uncovered the existence of an indigenous ceramic industry that predates the establishment of Sukhothai, making it doubtful that local pottery owes its origins to the Chinese.

Kilns were typically divided into three compartments—the fire area, baking oven, and flue—which produced a wide variety of ceramic goods such as terra-cotta tiles, balustrades, gables, dishes, and bottles fired with the bluish-green glazes that characterize Sawakhalok ceramics. An informative display on these enormous structures can be seen in the Sukhothai Museum. Several of the larger kilns in Si Satchanalai have been fully restored and opened to the public.

Wat Sri Chum

Sukhothai's most impressive Buddha, a monumental 15-meter image seated in the attitude of subduing Mara, dominates the rather dull square *mondop* in the northwest corner of old Sukhothai. The giant Buddha is believed to have been created in the late 14th century after Sukhothai came under the rule of the Ayuthaya kingdom. A must-see for all visitors, the monument provides a lively scene as Thai pilgrims arrive to pray, make offerings, and burn incense in front of the enormous, superbly modeled hand.

The monument is chiefly noted for the slate slabs engraved with *Jataka* scenes that line the narrow and claustrophobic passageway which leads to the roof. Illuminated only by small windows, these unusual carvings are of the highest artistic and literary value. Unfortunately, in December 1988 the passageway was sealed and closed to the public after a series of falls from the roof, and due to the Buddhist principle that no human should elevate himself above the position of the Buddha.

West Of The City (Zone C)

Few visitors make the effort to visit the monuments west of the city in Zone C. While most of the temples are rather modest by Sukhothai standards, the region still retains the timeless quality and sense of tranquillity lost from the renovated regions of Sukhothai. A bicycle ride along the dirt track that leads from Wat Trapang Ngoen to Wat Chedi Ngam is a wonderful experience in the early evening hours. Children wave and suddenly you feel light-

years away from the commercialism of historic Sukhothai. The entrance gate near Wat Saphan Hin can be avoided by backtracking on the dirt road.

Wat Chedi Ngam

The dirt road winds past several modest temples set among rice and sugarcane fields before turning right to Wat Chedi Ngam. Located on a plateau up a short dirt road, this round Sinhalese-style *chedi* has been vandalized by thieves who burrowed a deep hole in the back side.

A left turn at the dusty intersection leads to an ancient reservoir which once supplied water for the royal residence and kingdom of Sukhothai. The dam now supplies the modern city of Sukhothai and has been landscaped into a modern park with roving buffaloes and a few noodle stalls. To the right is a deserted modern *wat* and mountain spring reached by a stiff climb up 888 steps.

Wat Saphan Hin

Standing at the summit of Wat Saphan Hin ("Stone Causeway Monastery") is a 12-meter Buddha who overlooks and appears to bless the scattered ruins of ancient Sukhothai. The remote monastery once served as the seat of the Buddhist patriach and site of the annual Tod Kathin Festival during the reign of King Ramkamheng. Today the sanctuary consists of a restored *viharn* and colossal image whose raised right hand signifies the *mudra* of granting peace. The brick-paved floor of the adjoining *chedi* has been raided by temple robbers—a depressing but familiar sight at many of the remote and unprotected temples in Sukhothai.

Wat Saphan Hin is reached by an exhausting climb up a jumble of stone slabs which gave the temple its rather odd name. Determined hikers are rewarded with expansive views on clear days.

yaksha (demon)

KAREN WHITE

South Of The City (Zone D)

Monuments to the south of Sukhothai are the last to be fully restored by the Fine Arts Department. While none of the temples compare to those in the central and northern zones, several monuments boast rare and fine stuccoes from the Sukhothai Period. The region has been left unguarded by the Fine Arts Department and pillage of ancient monuments is a common occurrence.

Entrance to Zone D is through the admissions gate near Wat Chetupon.

Wat Chetupon

Wat Chetupon is chiefly known for its pair of surviving 10-meter stucco Buddhas which capture the sides of the ancient *mondop*. The *mondop* once displayed the holy quartet of Buddha poses—standing, walking, seated, and reclining—but only the walking and standing Buddhas remain intact. The plaster walking image is a masterpiece of Sukhothai sculpture and among the finest stucco creations in Thailand. Adjacent images have been renovated by the Fine Arts Department.

Wat Chedi Si Hong

Chedi Si Hong provides an example of the tragic destruction wrought by artifact collectors throughout Southeast Asia. When I visited the monument in 1987, it was under careful reconstruction and well protected by guards and walls. After being fully restored in 1990, the tomb robbers arrived to strip the *chedi* of its stucco elephants, divinity figures, and well-crafted *garudas*. During my most recent visit, the *chedi* lay abandoned, stripped of its artistic heritage, and largely forgotten: a monument to the destructive power of greed.

The dirt track continues past several small temples before intersecting the road north to the city.

East Of The City (Zone E)

Monuments east of the historical park are relatively unrestored and rarely visited by foreign tourists. All can be quickly reached by bicyclists.

Wat Trapang Tong

Surrounded by a symmetrical pool called the Golden Lake, the *chedi* of Wat Trapang Tong contains an important Buddha footprint honored each year during Loy Kratong Festival. The holy impression was taken from Wat Pra Bat Yai where, according to Buddhist chronicles, King Li Thai discovered the image in 1360. To the west is a modern *bot, mondop,* and ruined laterite *chedi* of Sinhalese type.

Wat Trapang Tong Lang

Hidden away among the rice and sugarcane fields is a monastery with four rows of laterite columns and square *mondop* renowned for its remarkable assemblage of stucco decorations. The southern panel shows the descent of Buddha to earth, surrounded by angels and bodhisattvas, to preach his doctrine after a three-month sojourn in the heavenly abodes. Superbly crafted with striking elegance and masterly serenity, the image has traditionally been considered among the crowning masterpieces of Sukhothai art.

Tragically, the stucco relief has deteriorated and lost its artistic appeal through pillage, neglect, and the ebbs of nature. A reproduction is displayed in the national museums of Sukhothai and Bangkok.

Wat Chang Lom

Supported by a ring of 36 sculpted and partially ruined elephants, Wat Chang Lom ("Elephant Temple") features an upper balustrade with 19 Buddha niches filled with miniature figurines. The circular Sinhalese-design *chedi* is accessed by walking through the grounds of the Thai Village House.

Wat Chedi Sung

Easily visible from Wat Trapang Tong Lang, Wat Chedi Sung has been called the finest *chedi* of the Sukhothai period. The bell-shaped superstructure and stepped platform cap a powerful base which together reflect the cultural minglings of Srivijayan and Sinhalese elements. An adjacent *viharn* is a later design of more classical style and harmonic proportions.

Other Attractions

Wat Rajathani: Located in new Sukhothai at the eastern bank of the river is a modern temple and secondary school for boys. Visitors are welcome to wander around and feed the soft-shelled tortoises and giant carp. A popular time to visit is on *wan pra,* Buddhist holy days when

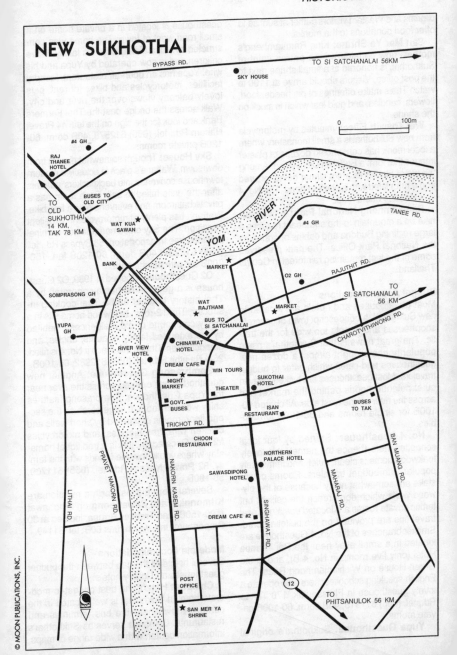

NEW SUKHOTHAI

BYPASS RD.

TO SI SATCHANALAI 56KM

SKY HOUSE

#4 GH

RAJ THANEE HOTEL

TO OLD SUKHOTHAI 14 KM, TAK 78 KM

BUSES TO OLD CITY

WAT KUA SAWAN

YOM RIVER

TANEE RD.

#4 GH

BANK

MARKET

O2 GH

RAJUTHIT RD.

TO SI SATCHANALAI 56 KM

SOMPRASONG GH

WAT RAJTHANI

MARKET

YUPA GH

BUS TO SI SATCHANALAI

CHAROTVITHIWONG RD.

RIVER VIEW HOTEL

CHINAWAT HOTEL

DREAM CAFE

WIN TOURS

SUKOTHAI HOTEL

NIGHT MARKET

THEATER

GOVT. BUSES

ISAN RESTAURANT

BUSES TO TAK

TRICHOT RD.

CHOON RESTAURANT

NORTHERN PALACE HOTEL

NAKORN KASEM RD.

PRAVET NAKORN RD.

LITHAI RD.

SAWASDIPONG HOTEL

DREAM CAFE #2

MAHARAJ RD.

BAN MUANG RD.

SINGHAWAT RD.

POST OFFICE

SAN MER YA SHRINE

12

TO PHITSANULOK 56 KM.

0   100m

© MOON PUBLICATIONS, INC.

pilgrims and Western visitors gather at sunrise to offer food donations to the monks.

San Mer Ya Shrine: King Ramkamheng's mother, now considered the patron saint of Sukhothai, is honored at a small shrine next to the post office. Visitors should arrive at 1100 to watch Thais make offerings of pig heads, food, flowers, candles, and gold leaf which is stuck on the shrine.

Wat Thawit: Fifteen minutes by motorcycle from new Sukhothai is a small monastery where a local monk has constructed dozens of plaster images that form a Buddhist Disneyland. Among the weird highlights are a sinner being tortured and a man fitted with a chicken head. The No. 4 Guesthouse has a map.

Ramkamheng National Park: A five-hour hike up a mountain to the southeast reaches a large reclining Buddha and cabins operated by the National Park Office. The park preserves some of the last remaining rainforest in Central Thailand.

Budget Accommodations

Most guesthouses and hotels are located in new Sukhothai, a nondescript town of concrete shophouses and streets too wide for the traffic. The great news is that Sukhothai's rising popularity has brought almost a dozen new guesthouses and cafes which cater to budget travelers. Most guesthouses are tucked away in quiet neighborhoods behind the market and across the river on the west side. All charge 60-100B for single rooms and 80-120B for doubles.

No. 4 Guesthouse: Started by four local schoolteachers (hence the name), this lovely teakwood home is clean, quiet, and immensely popular with budget travelers. Rooms downstairs are somewhat noisy because of the plywood walls which don't reach the ceiling, but terrific private rooms are located upstairs. Local travel tips are provided on the bulletin board. Smaller branches of the No. 4 Guesthouse are located in a small alley near the Raj Thanee Hotel (only five rooms in No. 4 B), and in the Green House on Wichianjamnong Road. The English-speaking schoolteachers also operate a lovely guesthouse in Phitsanulok. 170 Tanee Rd., tel. (055) 611315, 40B dorm, 60-100B private rooms.

Yupa Guesthouse: Sukhothai's original guesthouse is located in a private home on a small road west of town. The home was constructed by Yupa Mekapai for his family of five children and is now operated by Yupa and his wife. Yupa has an open-air restaurant, laundry facilities, motorcycles and bikes for rent, plus lovely balcony views over the river and city. Walk across the bridge past the Thai Farmers Bank and look for the sign on the left. 44 Pravet Nakorn Rd., tel. (055) 612578, 40B dorm, 60-120B private rooms.

Sky House: Though somewhat distant from downtown, Wattana's place is actually a modern townhouse converted into backpackers' quarters after the units failed to sell. Each room has a private bathroom and everyone gets a free bike. Wattana has plenty of motorcycles in excellent condition. The Sky office near the bus terminal provides free transportation. 58 Bypass Rd., tel. (055) 612237, 40B dorm, 60-120B fan, 150-200B a/c with private bath.

O2 Guesthouse: Opened in 1989, O2 Guesthouse is a genuine homestay operated by a Thai history teacher and a Thai cooking instructor. The 12-room teakwood home sits in a lovely compound of old residences inhabited by the extended family of aunts, uncles, and grandchildren. Check this place if No. 4 is filled. 26/4 Rajuthit Rd., tel. (055) 612982, 60-100B.

Somprasong Guesthouse: Another new guesthouse has opened across the river near the Yupa Guesthouse. Somprasong features shiny wooden floors, a large porch on the second floor, rooms separated by short walls and chicken wire, free bicycles, and motorcycles for hire. Once again, this is a traditional homestay where you'll become friends with the family. 32 Pravet Nakorn Rd., tel. (055) 611709, 50-100B.

Several more places worth a mention are **Kitmongkoi** and **Sawatipong** on Singhawat (100-150B) and **Trekker House**, located at 30 Praponbumrung, which runs 60B; tel. 61149.

Moderate Accommodations

Several hotels fill the gap between the budget guesthouses and luxury hotels.

Chinawat Hotel: The best budget-to-moderate hotel in Sukhothai is well located in the center of town near the bus terminals and restaurants. Chinawat serves as Sukhothai's information center, with a wide range of maps, brochures, and travel tips on buses and nearby attractions. The hotel has 40 rooms with private baths, a money-exchange service, overseas-calls facilities, laundry, organized tours, and a popular restaurant which serves both Thai and Chinese dishes at reasonable cost. 1 Nakorn Kasem Rd., tel. (055) 611385, 80-120B fan, 160-220B a/c.

River View: A somewhat luxurious hotel on the banks of the Yom River with clean rooms, private baths, a patio restaurant, and lobby with TV. Pricier than other moderate hotels, but a big improvement in comfort and cleanliness. All rooms come with a/c and private bath. 92 Nakorn Kasem Rd., tel. (055) 611656, fax (055) 613373, 250-350B.

Sukhothai Hotel: Once the travelers' favorite, now a noisy and dirty dump. 204 Singhawat Road, tel. 611133, 100-200B.

Luxury Accommodations
Northern Palace Hotel: The old Kit Mongkol has been completely renovated and renamed. New facilities include a swimming pool, snooker parlor, and coffee shop which doubles as a nightclub for evening entertainment. All rooms are a/c with private bath. 43 Singhawat Rd., tel. (055) 611193, 650-900B.

Raj Thanee: Also called the Ratchathani or Rajthanee, this once-great hotel has slipped in recent years though it still offers 86 a/c rooms with private bath and a comfortable coffee shop. 229 Charotvithiwong, tel. (055) 611031, 250-600B.

Accommodations Near Old Sukhothai
Most visitors stay in new Sukhothai though a few guesthouses and hotels have opened recently near the ruins in the historic quarter.

Vitoon Guesthouse: Just opposite the entrance to Sukhothai Historical Park are several rudimentary guesthouses with basic cubicles and bicycle rentals.

Thai Village House: Sukhothai's old cultural center operates souvenir shops and a small zoo with peacocks and black bears. Wooden bungalows decorated in traditional Thai style are equipped with fan or a/c rooms with private or common baths. Beautiful teakwood dorms are also available at low cost. Thai specialties are served and an entertainment revue is sponsored in their restaurant during the tourist sea-

Sukhothai beauty

son. Located one km before old Sukhothai on the right side of the road. 214 Charotvithiwong, tel. (055) 611049, 50B dorm, 350-600B private rooms.

Pailyn Sukhothai Hotel: Sukhothai entered the high-end market in early 1992 with the opening of the monstrous 238-room Pailyn Hotel located about four km before the entrance to the Sukhothai Historical Park. The Pailyn has several restaurants, a swimming pool, disco, fitness center, conference facilities, and shuttle services to the ruins and new Sukhothai. Charotvithiwong Rd., tel. (055) 612893, Bangkok reservations (02) 215-7110, 1200-2500B.

Restaurants
All of the hotels in Sukhothai have restaurants, but smaller cafes offer a more unique culinary and aesthetic experience.

Night Market: Cheap eats are plentiful at the market which sets up nightly in the alley near Win Tours and the Rainbow Cafe. Popular dishes include *pad thai, gawetio thai nam* (noodle soup with peanuts and greens), *yam nom tok* (spicy beef), and *kanom jinn* (Thai spaghetti). Other choices include mussel omelets, thick rice soups, ice *kachang*, and *won ton* dishes.

Take-away Foodstalls: Across the street from the night market are several foodcarts that serve food to go wrapped in plastic bags. Simply point to the more appealing dishes and say *ha baht*. A grand total of 25 *baht* will guarantee a delicious and filling meal which you consume back at your guesthouse. Take-away dishes are often more tasty and varied than stir-fried food from the night market.

Rainbow Cafe: Next to the bus station is a popular open-air restaurant with European fare, Thai noodles, and terrific ice cream. Rainbow is owned by the Chinawat Hotel and has an upstairs a/c dining room.

Dream Cafes: Sukhothai's most eclectic restaurants are the brainchildren of Ms. Chaba Suwatmaykin, who has outfitted her cafes with an amazing collection of memorabilia such as old telephone sets, bottles, and ancient gramophones. The small outlet across from Win Tours is an intimate coffee shop with a sign that reads "The best coffee is as black as devil, hot as hell, pure as a fairy, fragrant as love."

Dream Cafe 2 at 861 Singhawat Road has a menu with over 200 items. Try *kao tang naa tang* (fried rice with pork and rambutan), *muu kam wan kanaa sop* (grilled pork with honey and vegetables), or *laab* (spicy northeastern-style minced pork).

Nightlife

Nightlife in Sukhothai is a fairly calm affair limited to a pair of fan-cooled cinemas and folk entertainment in the Dream Cafe. Sukhothai has three swimming pools that charge a 20B admission fee. Thai Village House on the road to the ruins has a nightly cultural show during the tourist season which includes traditional dances and music put on by students from the local dramatic arts college. A more rewarding option is to volunteer to teach English to the wonderfully shy students at the International Friendship Center in Ampur, down the road toward Phitsanulok. The No. 4 Guesthouse has more information.

Shopping

Sukhothai is hardly a shopper's paradise, though the increasing number of Western visitors has

helped revive some of the traditional crafts.

Markets: A very picturesque and lively farmers' market operates daily in new Sukhothai near the river and behind the modern temple of Wat Rajathani. The nearby indoor market has a fish section, take-away foodstalls, and fruit vendors on the northern side. A bullock and buffalo market is held on Friday mornings near the Caltex station and Father Ceramics.

Other markets are located outside new Sukhothai. A large public market is held on Thursdays in the large wooden building near the Ramkamheng Museum in the old city. Markets are also held on Tuesdays in Ban Kwang, Sundays in Ban Gluay, and Mondays in Ban Suan.

Teak Carving: Several families in the village near the ruins continue to carve teakwood figures in styles dating back to the days of King Ramkamheng. Walk east from the National Museum and wander up the second street on the left. None of the houses have signs since taxes are collected from signposted businesses. A large collection of teak carvings is sold from the shop at the intersection to Wat Sri Chum.

Ceramics: The best ceramics in Sukhothai are sold at the house of Lung Fang inside the southern wall of the old city. Lung Fang has a small ceramics museum and new creations recognized by the royal family. The Kingdom of Father Ceramics in new Sukhothai is an expensive place patronized by group tours.

Transportation

Sukhothai is 447 km from Bangkok in the heart of Central Thailand.

Bus: Public buses from Bangkok to Sukhothai depart 10 times daily from the Northern Bus Terminal and take about seven hours. The most convenient departures are early in the morning before 0900, or overnight buses which leave between 2200 and 2300. Companies running a/c coaches include Win Tours (tel. 02-271-2984) and Phitsanulok Yanyon Tour (tel. 02-278-2063). Travel agents in Bangkok sell tickets which include pick-up from your hotel.

From Chiang Mai, buses leave hourly from the government bus terminal and take about five hours to reach Sukhothai. Private minibus companies from Chiang Mai often include a brief stop at a temple near Lampang and terminate at the Sky House in Sukhothai.

Train: The nearest train terminus is at Phitsanulok, 60 km east of Sukhothai. From the Phitsanulok train station, bus 1 reaches the main bus terminal from where buses depart hourly to Sukhothai. Buses can also be hailed in Phitsanulok at the Naresuan Bridge near Wat Mahathat.

Air: Thai Airways International operates three daily flights from Bangkok to Phitsanulok at 0710, 1010, and 1550. Bus 1 goes to the government bus terminal.

Leaving Sukhothai

Three bus companies are located in the center of Sukhothai. Ordinary buses operated by the government transportation company (Bor Kor Sor) leave 12 times daily for Bangkok and eight times daily for Chiang Mai. Eight of the 12 departures to Bangkok are between 2100 and 2350. Their small office is located in the alley near the night market. Bor Kor Sor buses are much cheaper and almost as fast as private bus companies.

Win Tours has three a/c buses daily for Bangkok and Chiang Mai. Win also sells tickets to Chiang Rai, Si Satchanalai, and Phitsanulok. Seats should be booked well in advance, especially for the overnight buses. Phitsanulok Yanyon Tour in the Chinawat Hotel has five buses daily to Bangkok.

Public buses to most destinations near Sukhothai leave from the government bus terminal. Buses to Si Satchanalai and Sawankalok leave hourly from the corner near Wat Rajathani, just down from the Chinawat Hotel. Buses to Tak leave on Ba Muang Rd., four blocks up the main street.

Buses to the ruins in old Sukhothai leave from the dirt yard on the right side of the road, 200 meters across the bridge. Don't get suckered into an expensive *tuk tuk* or taxi ride.

SI SATCHANALAI

The evocative ruins of old Si Satchanalai rest 56 km north of Sukhothai between Sawankalok and the new town of Si Satchanalai. Although less extensive than the ruins at Sukhothai, the superb setting and lonely sense of the past make Si Satchanalai a memorable place.

History

Si Satchanalai was established by the Khmers in the 12th century as a military outpost for their northeastern empire. In 1238, two local Thai chiefs joined forces to free the Thai people from Khmer domination. Although Sukhothai was the seat of Khmer strength, Si Satchanalai was liberated first to serve as the launching pad for an assault on Sukhothai.

Archaeological evidence suggests that many of the surviving temples were constructed by King Indradita, Sukhothai's first ruler, though the city was expanded over the span of many reigns. During the Sukhothai Period, Si Satchanalai served as the residence of the crown prince and enjoyed great importance, as demonstrated by the size of its monastery and other religious ruins.

Si Satchanalai declined in importance during the Ayuthaya Period and was abandoned in the 18th century as a result of the incessant wars with Burma.

Attractions

Si Satchanalai consists of three areas along the western bank of the Yom River. The central ruins are enclosed inside an irregular laterite wall that defines the original boundaries. Two km south is Chaliang, which served as the original seat of the Khmer administration. North of the central ruins are dozens of pottery kilns which once produced the famous Sawankalok ceramics.

The present renovation of the monuments was initiated in 1982 by the Fine Arts Department. Today the ruins are connected by a network of paved roads and described by signs which provide detailed histories of the individual monuments. Adjacent to the entrance is a small office with a relief model of the city. The central ruins can be easily seen on foot, though a rented bicycle or organized tour is necessary to reach Chaliang and the pottery kilns.

Wat Chang Lom

The most important religious sanctuary in Si Satchanalai is this Sinhalese-style *chedi* constructed in 1285 by King Ramkamheng and possibly modeled after Wat Mahathat at Nakhon Si Thammarat. The monument is enclosed by a beautiful laterite brick wall distinguished by terraced shoulders, ornamental pilasters, and niches penetrated by four gates. Approach is made up a paved laterite walkway which leads to a frontal *viharn* and *chedi* to the rear.

Supported by 36 crumbling stucco elephants which give the monument its name, Wat Chang Lom ("Elephant Temple") probably contains Buddha relics brought up from Chaliang by the first ruler of Sukhothai. Deterioration of the elephant images reveals construction techniques of a square brick tower and hollow core covered with stucco. Columns between the standing elephants once supported lanterns. Lining the upper terraces are 20 rare stucco Buddhas in the attitude of subduing Mara. Most of the images have been vandalized by robbers searching for buried treasure.

Wat Khao Phanom Pleung

In the northeastern area of the city is a steep 114-step staircase which leads to Satchanalai's hilltop "Temple of the Mountain of Fire." According to the *Northern Chronicles,* a hermit named Satchanalai ordered King Thammaraj of Sukhothai to reserve the hill as a spot for fire worship and the cremation of high dignitaries.

To the right of the landing are stucco-coated octagonal columns and a Buddha poorly restored in 1967. To the left is a collapsed *chedi* which shows Lanna influence and an extremely unusual brick *mondop* whose back wall shadows the Buddha image once housed in the structure. The *mondop* is known locally as Sala Chao Mae Laong Samli, or "Sacred House of the Goddess Laong Samli."

Views from the hill provide an overview of the architectural layout of Si Satchanalai.

Wat Khao Phanom Khiri

A narrow pathway leads to the well-proportioned Sinhalese-style *chedi* known as the "Temple of the Golden Mountain." Architecturally similar to Wat Chang Lom, the monument is situated in a strategic position from where Thai soldiers once surveyed the movements of enemy troops over the northern plains. A smaller *chedi,* remains of a *viharn,* and old lampposts are also located on the grounds.

Across the road to the west are several Buddhist edifices where monks of the *vipassana* sect once meditated in solitude. Wat Khao Kaew and Wat Khao Yai are enigmatic monuments, but difficult to reach through the thick underbrush.

Wat Chedi Chet Tao

South of Wat Chang Lom, and on the same axis, is the complex of over 30 *chedis* that provide a gold mine of architectural styles drawn from several regions in Southeast Asia. The main sanctuary, built in the 1340s and modeled after Wat Mahathat in Sukhothai, features an almost Laotian-style *chedi* capped with a distinctive lotus-bud finial. Adjacent to the *chedi* is a *viharn* to the south and a *bot* to the north between the two sets of walls.

To the east of the central monument are seven rows of *stupas* constructed as funerary monuments for members of the royal family. The *stupas* are of great importance because they replicate in stone various shrines once found throughout central Thailand. Some are in Sri Lankan style while others show the influence of Dvaravati and Lanna kingdoms. Another resembles a wooden *viharn* with a roof capped by a *prasat* and bell-shaped *chedi.* Also of note are the wide variety of doorways and Sukhothai-style walking Buddhas contained in the northern monuments.

From an architectural standpoint, Wat Chedi Chet Tao is the most significant monument in Si Satchanalai.

Wat Suan Kao Utayan Yai

This "Monastery of the Large Precious Garden" features a Sri Lankan-style *chedi* on a square pedestal surmounted by a laterite stairway. Surrounding the ruined *viharn* and restored *chedi* is a laterite wall which has beautifully collapsed into rhythmic shapes.

Wat Nang Phya

Wat Nang Phya, the "Queen's Monastery," is chiefly noted for the remains of a 15th-century *viharn* whose wall is adorned with stucco floral moldings that imitate Ayuthayan woodcarvings. Constructed during the early Ayuthaya Period and now protected by a sturdy roof, the solitary wall and its embossed motifs are penetrated by twin rows of six tall, very narrow slits in lieu of windows.

Also located on the grounds is a circular Sinhalese *chedi* whose interior can be accessed up the eastern staircase.

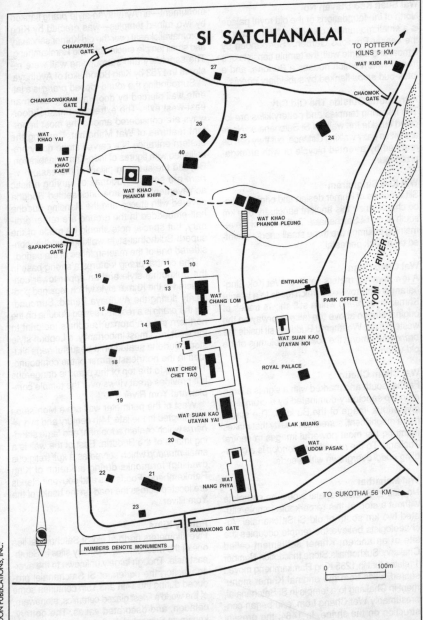

SI SATCHANALAI

TO POTTERY
KILNS 5 KM

WAT KUDI RAI

CHANAPRUK
GATE

27

CHAOMOK
GATE

CHANASONGKRAM
GATE

26

25

24

WAT
KHAO YAI

40

WAT
KHAO
KAEW

WAT KHAO
PHANOM KHIRI

WAT KHAO
PHANOM PLEUNG

YOM RIVER

SAPANCHONG
GATE

12   11

16   10

13

15

14

ENTRANCE

PARK OFFICE

WAT
CHANG LOM

17

WAT SUAN KAO
UTAYAN NOI

ROYAL PALACE

18

WAT CHEDI
CHET TAO

19

WAT SUAN KAO
UTAYAN YAI

LAK MUANG

20

WAT
UDOM PASAK

22   21

WAT
NANG PHYA

TO SUKOTHAI 56 KM

23

RAMNAKONG GATE

NUMBERS DENOTE MONUMENTS

0   100m

© MOON PUBLICATIONS, INC.

Wat Suan Kao Utayan Noi

North of the foundations of the old royal palace is a small monument called the "Monastery of the Lesser Precious Garden." Surrounded by a moat and laterite wall, the temple consists of a frontal *viharn* which houses a Buddha, and a lotus-bud *stupa* flanked by subsidiary *chedis*.

Attractions Outside The Old City

The following temples and pottery kilns are located outside the walls of Si Satchanalai. None are within easy walking distance, but they can be reached by a rented bicycle or with an organized tour.

Wat Kok Singharam

Slit windows of Khmer design and original stucco characterize this ancient sanctuary one km south of old Si Satchanalai. To the rear of the remaining columns are three small *chedis* elevated on a brick pedestal.

Wat Chao Chan

A few hundred meters south of Wat Kok Singharam is a narrow road which leads to a laterite Khmer-style *prang* which still shows traces of original stucco above the false doorway on the western side. Weathered Buddhas sit inside the *prang* and among the collapsed columns of the old *viharn*.

Wat Chom Cheun

Farther south and marked with a sign is a large *mondop* sanctuary dominated by a crumbling, mysterious image of the Buddha. The statue has a magnificent, surrealistic quality that makes it among the most powerful images in central Thailand. To the rear of the *mondop* is a crumbling *chedi* overgrown with weeds.

Wat Mahathat

No visit to Si Satchanalai would be complete without a stop at this remarkable temple situated two km south of old Si Satchanalai. Archaeologists believe the temple occupies the site of an ancient Khmer settlement called Chaliang. Sukhothai's Stone Inscription Number 1 relates that in 1285 King Ramkamheng moved sacred relics from the original Khmer monument in Chaliang to a temple in Si Satchanalai, presumably Wat Chang Lom, and began construction on the shrine. In 1464, the present monument—an Ayuthayan-style *prang* flanked by two ruined temples—was erected by King Boromatrailokanat over the old Khmer sanctuary and small temple erected by King Ramkamheng. The sanctuary and surrounding wall were restored in 1753 by King Boromakot of Ayuthaya.

Surrounding the round-topped *prang* is a laterite wall pierced by doorways aligned on an east-west axis. The extremely unusual doorways are considered among the most important features of Wat Mahathat. Capping the eastern entrance is a carved stone richly embellished with figures of Indo-Khmer inspiration. Beyond the standing pillars of the eastern *viharn* are several Buddhas of varying artistic achievement. The large brick seated Buddha covered with stucco and the standing Buddha half-embedded in the ground are rather ordinary, but special note should be made of the superb Sukhothai-style walking Buddha, considered one of the masterpieces of the period.

The central *prang* features a strong base in the Sukhothai style and an upper tower constructed in the Khmer style which regained popularity during the Ayuthaya Period. Surrounding the *prang* is a restored seated Buddha on the northern side, a bronze Buddha's footprint to the west, and most importantly, a Lopburi-style stone Buddha seated on a beautiful *naga* situated in the northeast corner of the compound. The climb to the top of the *prang* is dangerous but provides great views over the temple complex and Yom River.

West of the perimeter wall are a Mon *stupa* constructed in the late 14th century and two *viharns* which contain a footprint and large standing image of the Buddha. East of the wall is a small *mondop* which served as a *kuti* (religious dwelling) for monks during the reign of King Ramkamheng. Foodstalls and souvenir stands are located across the road on the banks of the Yom River.

Pottery Kilns

Five kilometers north of old Si Satchanalai lies one of the most extensive pottery sites in Southeast Asia. Though largely unknown to the average visitor, the potters of Si Satchanalai produced during the 14th and 15th centuries some of the world's finest glazed ceramics, stoneware, celadon, and decorated vases. The pottery, known as Sawankalok (Sawankhalok) after an early name for Si Satchanalai, played a major role in Southeast Asian trade and was exported to maritime sites throughout the Indonesian and Philippine islands.

Early scholars theorized that the industry was developed by Chinese potters brought to Thailand by King Ramkamheng, but recent research indicates that the technology was developed by Thai potters and craftsmen. A joint project funded by the Thai and Australian governments has systematically excavated many of the ancient kilns and opened them as public museums.

Sanghalok Kiln 61 Museum: Opened in 1987 by the Fine Arts Department and Siam Cement, this beautiful museum contains Kiln 61, surrounded by walkways, photographs and diagrams of the excavation, and examples of misfired ceramics uncovered from the site. Pottery shops with "old and new creations" are across the street. Kiln 61 Museum is 4½ km north of Si Satchanalai on the road through Chaomok Gate.

Kiln 42 and 123 Museum: Some 500 meters farther north is another excavated kiln with pottery displays of smiling elephants, horses, and celadon turtles.

Sawakhalok Museum

A small branch of the National Museum is 37 km north of Sukhothai in the town of Sawakhalok. The museum is open Wed.-Sun. 0900-1630.

Accommodations

Most visitors return to Sukhothai before nightfall, but simple hotels are found in Sawankalok, the new town of Si Satchanalai, and near the ruins.

Wang Yom Resort: About 300 meters south of the park entrance is an upscale development that features a beautiful restaurant, handicraft village, and comfortable bungalows set in landscaped lawns and tropical gardens. Wang Yom (tel. 055-642244) has 20 a/c cottages for 1200B and 15 simple country huts for 400B. The adjacent Kang Sak Restaurant caters to tour groups.

Sawakhalok: Simple hotels in Sawakhalok, 20 km south of the ruins, include the **Muang Inn** on Kasamrat Rd. and **Sri Sawan Hotel** on Thesaban Damri Road. Both have fan-cooled rooms from 130B and a/c rooms from 220B.

Si Satchanalai: The new town of Si Satchanalai is 12 km north of the ruins. **Kruchang Hotel**, 300 meters north of the Bangkok Bank, has rooms with bath from 120B.

Si Satchanalai is known for a locally woven silk embroidery called *tinchok* available from several shops such as Sathorn Silks at the far end of town. Another attraction is the famous Elephant Ordination Festival, held annually in early April during Buddhist Lent. Unlike other monk-initiation ceremonies in Thailand, novices wear special *nak* costumes and elaborate *chada* headdresses while being paraded around town on the backs of elephants.

Transportation

The ruins at old Si Satchanalai are 56 km north of Sukhothai between the towns of Sawankalok and new Si Satchanalai. Buses to the ruins leave from the temple opposite Sukhothai's Chinawat Hotel and take two hours to reach the turnoff. The historical park is a 30-minute walk from the highway. Bicycles can be rented from a small shop near the bus stop. The latest gimmick is elephant rides starting from Wat Chang Lom.

Win Tours in Sukhothai has public buses and organized tours to Si Satchanalai. Tours are a more efficient way to see the ruins than public transportation, which is often slow and sporadic. An excellent option is to rent a motorcycle in Sukhothai and enjoy a great ride through the Thai countryside. Motorcyclists can easily visit in a single day the central ruins, kilns to the north, and southern monuments near Chaliang.

KAMPHANG PHET

Kamphang Phet is an old garrison town on the left bank of the Ping River some 85 km southwest of Sukhothai. Established in 1347 by King Li Thai, the small town served as a regional capital and one of the three primary cities of the Sukhothai empire. The city later operated as a buffer state between Sukhothai and Ayuthaya until 1378, when the final sovereign of Sukhothai surrendered to King Boromaraja.

The modern town of Kamphang Phet is rather ordinary, but to the north are several intriguing *wats* in various states of repair and restoration, a worthwhile museum, and other *chedis* and sculpture of great historical significance. None of the monuments compare with those in Sukhothai or Si Satchanalai, but visitors with a strong interest in Thai history and archaeology will enjoy exploring the ruins.

Attractions

Kamphang Phet is a long and narrow town with three distinct sections. To the south and along the river is the new town with all the businesses, hotels, and restaurants. The old city with the museum and a few modest ruins is centrally located inside the trapezoid walls. To the north and outside the city walls are the most impressive monuments, constructed by Buddhist monks away from the city to ensure a meditative environment.

Some of the monasteries predate even Sukhothai, but most display post-classical Sukhothai style as Kamphang Phet served as a regional capital after the demise of Sukhothai and Si Satchanalai. Most of the monuments north of the old city walls were constructed by forest-dwelling monks in a Sinhalese style but were heavily restored during Ayuthayan occupation. Taken together with Sukhothai and Si Satchanalai, Kamphang Phet serves as the third

Giocometti Gautama

most important historical and archaeological site in Central Thailand.

A small tourist information office with handicraft displays, an aerial map of the region, and lacquerware for sale is on Thesa Rd. in the new town.

National Museum

Located in the old walled city behind Wat Pra Keo, Kamphang Phet National Museum provides a quick historical background and general orientation to the widely scattered monuments. The museum has a small but well-described assortment of artifacts from all periods of Thai art.

Ground Floor: The Khmer Shiva sculpture at the entrance is considered one of the masterpieces of bronzework in Thailand. The life-sized Bayon-style image was cast in 1510 during the reign of King Thammasokaraj, but tragically dismembered in 1886 by a German visitor who intended to give the severed head and hands to the Berlin Museum. Quick actions by King Rama V saved the image, which was skillfully restored and returned in 1971 for the opening of the museum.

Among the highlights on the ground floor are excellent descriptions of the three major U-Thong schools, Ayuthaya bronzes covered with fine patinas, and the superb U-Thong Buddha flanked by large busts at the right end of the hallway. Also note the five Chiang Saen images, two display windows of Lopburi Buddhas with authoritative explanations, Srivijayan votive tablets, Dvaravati stucco fragments, and a standing wooden Buddha from Ayuthaya.

Second Floor: Farm implements and handicrafts comprise most of the upper floor. The most significant items are the superb bronze torsos of Vishnu and Lakshmi discovered inside a local Shiva shrine.

The museum is open Wed.-Sun. 0900-1630.

Wat Pra Keo

Little remains of the old royal chapel except scattered foundations, a pair of rebuilt *chedis,* and cantilevered columns which once supported the religious structures. Behind the final northern *chedi* are several weathered Buddhas which have lost their skin and now resemble the abstract sculpture of Giacometti.

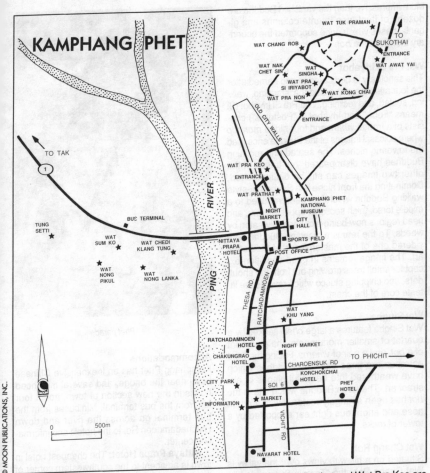

KAMPHANG PHET

WAT TUK PRAMAN

WAT CHANG ROB

TO SUKOTHAI
ENTRANCE

WAT NAK
CHET SIN

WAT
SINGHA

WAT AWAT YAI

WAT PRA
SI IRIYABOT

WAT PRA NON

WAT KONG CHAI

ENTRANCE

RIVER

TO TAK

1

WAT PRA KEO
ENTRANCE

WAT PRATHAT

KAMPHANG PHET
NATIONAL
MUSEUM

OLD CITY WALLS

NIGHT
MARKET

CITY
HALL

BUS TERMINAL

NITTAYA
PRAPA
HOTEL

SPORTS FIELD

TUNG
SETTI

WAT
SUM KO

WAT CHEDI
KLANG TUNG

POST OFFICE

THESA RD.

PING

WAT
NONG
PIKUL

WAT
NONG LANKA

RATCHADAMNOEN RD.

WAT
KHU YANG

RATCHADAMNOEN
HOTEL

NIGHT MARKET

CHAKUNGRAO
HOTEL

CHAROENSUK RD

TO PHICHIT

CITY PARK

KORCHOKCHAI
HOTEL

SOI 6

PHET
HOTEL

MARKET

INFORMATION

VICHIT RD.

NAVARAT HOTEL

0   500m

© MOON PUBLICATIONS, INC.

Admission to the monuments inside the city walls is 20 *baht*. The ticket also includes admission to the ruins to the north and provides a discount into the National Museum.

Wat Prathat

A few hundred meters south of Wat Pra Keo stands the circular *chedi* of Wat Prathat, surrounded by columns and flanked by symmetrical *stupas*. The axial alignment of Wat Prathat and Wat Pra Keo shows the same concern for city planning as practiced in Sukhothai and Si Satchanalai.

Encircling Wat Prathat and Wat Pra Keo are ancient moats and crenellated walls which form a trapezoidal shape that names the city: Kamphang ("wall") Phet ("diamond").

Wat Pra Non

The temple of the reclining Buddha consists of a large *bot* in the foreground, the *mondop* sanctuary of the reclining Buddha in the middle, and a well-preserved *chedi* to the rear. The reclining Buddha has completely disappeared, though small signs scattered in the courtyard indicate locations of the image's neck, head, and feet.

More impressive than the vanished Buddha are dozens of immense laterite columns and gigantic bases which once supported the boundary stones of the *bot.*

Wat Pra Si Iriyabot

This sanctuary is dedicated to and named after the four attitudes of the Buddha: standing, walking, seated, and reclining. Wat Pra Si Iriyabot (Si means "Four," and Iriyabot is "Postures") consists of a frontal *viharn* and four-sided *mondop* where colossal images of the Buddha once filled the towering niches. The seated and reclining Buddhas have disappeared, but traces of the other two images can still be distinguished. Dominating the front niche is a Sukhothai-style walking Buddha which has been reduced to a middle torso, thigh sections, upper left arm, and head regions now being picturesquely eaten by weeds. To the rear is a standing Buddha considered one of the masterpieces of Sukhothai art. The image remains in good condition except for small trees growing out from the shoulders, and chipping stucco which reveals the laterite core of the chest.

Wat Singha

Wat Singha features a large *chedi* flanked by a quartet of smaller monuments, the pediment of a *bot,* and a pair of *viharns.* Facing the front entrance are three standing Buddhas which have weathered into beautiful pieces of abstract art. The large Buddha which sits in the *bot* has been strangely restored with a crude nose and enormous right ear supported by a tower of rocks.

Wat Chang Rob

Situated on a hill with views over the valley is Wat Chang Rob, the "Temple Surrounded by Elephants." Beyond the remains of an old *bot* and *viharn* is one of the most impressive monuments in Kamphang Phet, an enormous *chedi* surrounded and supported by 68 elephants carved in the round. Flanking the elephantine buttresses are stucco figures of demons, divinities, and sacred bodhi trees. The quality and elegance of decoration makes Wat Chang Rob a rare example of Sukhothai-style craftsmanship and among the finest monuments in Central Thailand.

Phet parade

Accommodations

Kamphang Phet has an inexpensive Chinese hotel near the bridge, and several midpriced hotels in the new section of town, about four km from the bus terminal. Minibuses from the bus terminal go across the river and down Ratchadamnoen Rd. to the hotels and information center.

Nittaya Prapa Hotel: The cheapest hotel in town is adjacent to the southwestern corner of the roundabout near the bridge and old town. Nittaya Prapa lacks an English sign and can be difficult to find, but is conveniently located near the central ruins and national museum. Rooms inside the unmarked wooden hotel are basic cubicles with fan and bath. 49 Thesa 1 Rd., tel. (055) 711381, 60-100B.

Korchokchai: Another one in the budget category, rooms here run 100-200B single or double. Ratchadamnoen Soi 6, tel. 711531.

Ratchadamnoen Hotel: As with most other hotels in Kamphang Phet, the Ratchadamnoen is an older property with both fan and a/c rooms in a variety of price ranges. Hotel owners assume that all Western travelers are rich and want an expensive a/c room rather than a cheaper fan-cooled room. 114 Ratchadamnoen Rd., tel. (055) 711029, 100-150B fan, 220-280B a/c.

Navarat Hotel: A few blocks south of the new town is a clean and comfortable hotel with 80 a/c rooms. 2 Soi Prapan Thesa Rd., tel. (055) 711211, 250-500B.

Phet Hotel: The best hotel in town has 235 a/c rooms, a coffee shop, small swimming pool, and Princess nightclub. 99 Vichit Rd. Soi 3, tel. (055) 711283, Bangkok reservations (02) 215-2920, 350-600B.

Chakungrao: At 123 Thesa, rooms are 300-500B single, 350-600B double; tel. 711315.

Restaurants

Kamphang Phet has two night markets. The most convenient is on Vichit Rd. just north of

Charonsuk. Foodstalls are also found near the provincial hall and old city walls.

All of the hotels have coffee shops, but more memorable are the restaurants located on the Ping River near the bridge.

The local specialty is the small egg banana *(kluay khai)*, named after the fruit's short oval shape. A fruit festival held in September features food competitions, cultural performances, and a Miss Banana beauty pageant.

Transportation

Kamphang Phet is 85 km southwest of Sukhothai. Most visitors take a bus from Sukhothai and spend a single night before continuing northwest to Tak and Mae Sot. The bus terminal is inconveniently located three km from town on the west side of the river. Travelers coming from Sukhothai might get off the bus at the ruins and continue into town with a *samlor* or public minibuses.

> *I have always had a fanatic belief that travel enriched individual lives, increased the community's prosperity, raised a nation's living standards, opened political barriers, and most important, functioned as the most effective eye-opener between different cultures. We in the travel business are a lucky lot to be in such a useful, joyful, and peaceful endeavor.*
>
> —Eugene Fodor,
> *Condé Nast Traveler*

WESTERN BORDERLANDS

TAK

Tak is a provincial capital 423 km north of Bangkok on the east bank of the Ping River. The town is situated at the intersection of Highway 1, which connects Bangkok with Chiang Mai, and the Pan-Asian Hwy. which, in a more perfect world, would link Singapore with Istanbul.

Tak is laid out in grid pattern with the central business district wedged between Highway 1 and the Ping River. Business activity is centered along Jompol Road, an absurdly wide boulevard not unlike the oversized road through Mae Sai. Inexpensive hotels and cafes are located on the more cozy lanes of Taksin and Mahathai Bamroong.

Tak is rarely visited by Western tourists, though the town has some outstanding teakwood architecture and is known throughout Thailand as the birthplace of King Taksin. The town also serves as a useful base for excursions to the hilltribe center and waterfalls of Lansang National Park (19 km west), the traditional riverine settlement of Ban Tak (23 km north), and water sports at Bhumibol Dam (65 km north), the largest artificial lake in Southeast Asia.

Wooden Architecture

Tak is a western outpost located near the vast teak forests of Burma. For several centuries, the town has served as a major teak trade center and conduit for logs which were harvested and then floated down the Ping River to Bangkok. This abundance of teak has traditionally permitted residents to construct their homes and businesses from the valuable wood.

Today, Thais come to Tak to purchase these rare teak homes, dismantle them, and move them to other regions in the country. Despite the destruction and removal of many homes, Tak still boasts several streets and neighborhoods blessed with old teakwood structures carved and assembled with great skill. Both Mahathai Bamroong and Taksin roads have fine examples, especially in the northern stretches near Thai Air and Wat Bot Mani Sibunruang.

An amazing collection of teak homes is located in the small alleys just south of the town park.

Another location known for traditional teakwood homes is the small village of Ban Tak, 23 km north of Tak on the banks of the Ping River. Ban Tak also has several old *chedis* and monasteries constructed in the Sukhothai Period during the reign of King Ramkamheng.

Wat Sibunruang

Located in the north end of Tak is a gold-topped *chedi* and northern-style chapel which contains Pra Buddhamon, an early-Sukhothai image considered among the finest examples of its type.

King Taksin Shrine

Across the road from Wat Sibunruang is a small modern chapel dedicated to the early Chakri king who hailed from Tak. The greatly revered king sits with sword in hand and backed by a romantic painting of the king. A celebration in his honor is held in Tak each year in early January. Pilgrims often come here to burn incense and shake fortune-telling sticks.

Bhumibol Dam

The largest lake in Southeast Asia was created in the early 1960s with the construction of Bhumibol Dam, 65 km north of Tak. The resulting Mae Ping Lake reaches from the dam northward to Lamphun and Chiang Mai, submerging many villages, ancient temples, and tracts of forest which rise eerily from the ribbon of water. Visitors can cruise the waters with the Education Tour Center (Bangkok tel. 02-221-5183) or the *Far East Queen* (Bangkok tel. 02-511-1872), a 78-meter ship fitted with observation rooms, restaurant, and 46 a/c cabins. The cruise goes 140 km north from the dam to the self-help settlement at Dai Tao.

Accommodations

Hotels are situated on the three main roads which run parallel to the river.

Tak Hotel: A popular choice for budget travelers with 29 fan-cooled rooms. 18 Mahathai Bamroong Rd., tel. (055) 511234, 100-150B.

Mae Ping Hotel: Down the road is a slightly larger hotel with somewhat cheaper rooms. 231 Mahathai Bamroong Rd., tel. (055) 511807, 80-120B.

Sanguan Thai Hotel: Located near the central market and shopping district. 619 Taksin Rd., tel. (055) 511265, 100-180B.

Viang Tak 1 Hotel: Top-end choices are the two branches of the Viang Tak. The original branch has 100 a/c rooms in an older neighborhood. 25 Mahathai Bamroong Rd., tel. (055) 511910, 500-800B.

Viang Tak 2 Hotel: The best hotel in Tak is lo-cated on the main drag near the river. Facilities include a comfortable restaurant, small nightclub, and dining veranda overlooking the river. Chompol Rd., tel. (055) 512686, fax (02) 235-5138, Bangkok reservations (02) 233-2690, 500-800B.

Restaurants

Foodstalls are located in the central market and, in the evenings, across from the Mae Ping Hotel. **Far Far Fastfood**, across from the Viang Tak 2 Hotel, has great dishes in a clean environment. The restaurant inside the **Viang Tak 2** is expensive but the most elegant in town. Tour

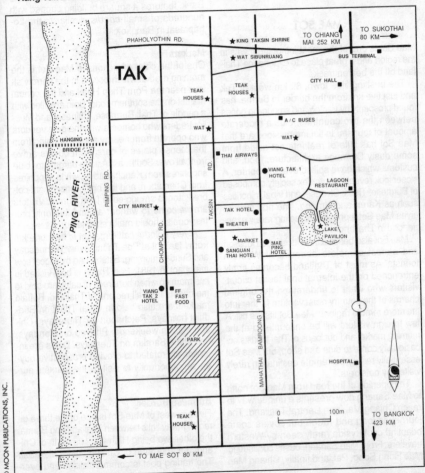

groups often stop at the **Lagoon Restaurant** surrounded by giant water lilies on Highway 1. Across the road is the lagoon with pavilions and gardens.

Transportation

Most visitors reach Tak by bus from Sukhothai or Kamphang Phet. The bus terminal is northeast of town across the ultrabroad Highway 1. *Song-taos* shuttle into town. Air-conditioned buses to Bangkok can be booked from the private bus office off Mahathai Bamroong Rd. just north of the Viang Tak 1 Hotel.

MAE SOT

Mae Sot is one of the most intriguing towns in the region and a great place to experience Thailand off the beaten track.

The bustling little town, 80 km west of Tak and just five km from the border to Burma, has found prosperity by trading and smuggling goods between the two countries, plus a moderate amount of tourism. Initial impressions are that Mae Sot has little of real interest aside from some dusty Burmese architecture, food, and customs which have spilled over the border. A closer look reveals a complex society composed of Burmese, Thais, Chinese, and tribal minorities such as Karen and Hmong. The rich mixture gives Mae Sot a poly-racial feeling rarely experienced in Thailand.

Mae Sot also benefits from its isolated location and almost complete absence of Western tourists. As most of Thailand becomes firmly entrenched on the international tourist circuit, visitors who want to understand the original charms of the country must venture farther into the more remote regions. Mae Sot fits the bill. A few foreign visitors will be encountered at the morning market and busloads of Thai tourists occasionally come to dine and shop, but Mae Sot essentially remains a remote destination rarely visited by outsiders.

The opening of the road from Mae Sot north to Mae Sariang now presents a unique way to reach Chiang Mai from Central Thailand. The journey is long and rough but covers some beautiful countryside rarely seen by Western travelers. From Mae Sariang, buses continue to Mae Hong Song, Pai, and finally, Chiang Mai.

Temples

Wats and monasteries in Mae Sot reflect Burmese influence brought across the nearby border. Wat Chumphon Khiri, the largest *chedi* in town and visible from the morning market, is covered by brass brickwork and surrounded by 20 smaller plaster *chedis*. Adjacent to Wat Mae Sot Luang is a small *chedi* and reclining Buddha completely covered with shiny brass plates. The accompanying monastery holds bronze Buddhas and three small alabaster images in display cases to the right. Unusual Wat Maune Pai Son, east of the Siam Commercial Bank, features a square building capped with hundreds of small *chedis*, similar to the Lohaprasat in Bangkok.

Markets

One of the chief attractions in Mae Sot is the morning market which occurs in the narrow alleys near the Porn Thep Hotel and the central market on the southern road. Both are filled with a gaggle of Thai, Burmese, Chinese, and Muslim traders who compete with the gem vendors who operate from nearby shops. Judging from the license plates of cars, gem buyers arrive from all over Southeast Asia to bargain for blue sapphires from Kanchanaburi, white sapphires from Chantaburi, and the highly prized light-colored stones smuggled in from Burma. Visitors are welcome to wander around, but only professionals should make sizable purchases.

A very colorful cattle market is held one km from Mae Sot at Poe Thong every Wednesday and Sunday morning. Established by a local cow merchant in 1981, Poe Thong is best visited in late morning when hundreds of cattle are sold to merchants from all regions of Thailand. Buffalo markets are also held in Uthai Thani on Buddhist holidays, Petchabun on Thursdays, Chiang Mai on weekends, Phayao on Mondays, and Maha Sarakm on Tuesdays. Dates are intentionally rotated to provide prospective buyers an opportunity to visit all the markets during the week.

Burmese Border

Five km west of Mae Sot is one of the three direct highway links between Thailand and Burma, the other two being Highway 106 north of Chiang Mai and north of Chiang Rai at Mae Sai. The trading post is commercialized and over-

MAE SOT

AIRPORT
TO BURMA 5 KM
MAE SOT GH
WAT ARANYAKET
TO BURMA 5 KM
PRASAT VITHI RD.
MAE SOT TRAVEL CENTER & MAE SOT HOUSE
BUSES TO MOI RIVER
WAT CHUMPHON KHIRI
CENTRAL MARKET
SIAM HOTEL
INDRAKIRI RD.
BUSES
BUSES SOUTH
MARKET
BANK
BUS TERMINAL NORTH
FIRST HOTEL
TO MAE SARIANG 230 KM
1085
PORN THEP HOTEL
BAKERY
CANTON RESTAURANT
PIM HUT RESTAURANT
CITY HALL
MOSQUE
MOTORCYCLES
GOVT. BUSES
POLICE
SP TOURS
WAT LUANG
MAE MOEY HOTEL
CHINESE HALL
RECLINING BUDDHA
ONE WAY
SUWANNAVIT HOTEL
MAE SOD HILL HOTEL
CINEMA
POST OFFICE
ONE WAY
SCHOOL
NEUNG NUT RESTAURANT
ARMY POST
WAT MAUNE PAI SON
ONE WAY
4 KM
ASIA HIGHWAY
0   100m
TO UMPHANG 150 KM
TO TAK 70 KM
1090

© MOON PUBLICATIONS, INC.

run with tourist shops, but visitors can gaze across the narrow Moi River to watch local merchants conduct the carefully regulated trade between Myawaddy and Rim Moi. At one time, taxes collected by rebel groups helped fund several resistance movements against the Burmese government, but today the border crossing is firmly controlled by Thai and Burmese officials.

Minibuses to the border crossing leave from Prasat Vithi Rd., one block west of the Siam Hotel. Visitors are occasionally allowed to cross into Burma for shopping or sightseeing.

Attractions Near Mae Sot

The following attractions are somewhat difficult to visit except on an organized tour or with a rented motorcycle. Street vendors on Prasat Vithi Rd. rent 100cc motorcycles for 150B daily.

Wat Wattanaram: A Burmese temple with a large alabaster Buddha is three km west of Mae Sot on the road to the border. The *wat* is marked with an English-language sign.

Wat Prathat Doi Din Kui: Twelve km northwest of town and on a small hill is a forest monastery with a hanging rock shrine similar to the monument in Kyaiktiyo, Burma. Motorcyclists should turn right at Ban Mae Tao, four km west of Mae Sot on the road to the border.

Pratat Hin Kiew: Twelve km east of Mae Sot on the road to Tak stands a small hillside shrine with panoramic views over Mae Sot valley.

Pravor Shrine: On the north side of the road and 18 km east of Mae Sot toward Tak is a small monument dedicated to local spirits whose powers are respectfully greeted by passing drivers.

Pra Hin Oon: North of Mae Sot, near the village of Mae Ramat, is Wat Don Keo with Pra Hin Oon, a small Buddha carved from a large block of marble.

Mawka Refugee Camp: About 30 km north of Mae Sot is an unofficial but very large refugee camp inhabited by Karen refugees from Burma. The subject of several BBC documentaries, Mawka is supported by donations from Hunger International and the Burmese Refugee Council in Chiang Mai. Visitors are encouraged to tour the village and learn about the political problems of the displaced Karens.

Tours
Travel agencies such as Maesot Travel Centre and SP Tours in the Siam Hotel now offer several multi-day excursions to nearby attractions. Northern tours visit the marble Buddha at Pra Hin Oon, U Su Cave, elephant rides, Mon Krating Resort, trekking and overnight stay at a Karen refugee camp, black-market shopping, and a raft trip down the Moi to the Salween River. Southern tours include a longtail journey down the Klong River, Pra Charoen and Tararak waterfalls, and trekking through some of Thailand's last remaining teak forests near Umphang. Trekking is popular from Mae Sot since nearby hilltribes are less exploited than those near Chiang Mai.

Maesot Travel Centre (tel. 055-531409) at 14/21 Asia Highway next to the radio station can help with tours and make reservations at resorts and guesthouses outside Mae Sot, such as Mon Krating Resort, Umphang Hill Resort, Umphang Guesthouse, Mae Salid Guesthouse, and Sob Moei House. They also run a small guesthouse.

Budget Accommodations
Mae Sot has a half-dozen hotels that cater to Thai merchants and a small number of Western visitors.

Mae Sot Guesthouse: Backpackers generally stay in this lovely teakwood house located west of town in a quiet residential neighborhood. The owners can help with free maps and information on trekking in nearby provinces. 736 Indrakiri Rd., 40B dorm, 60-90B.

Mae Sot House: Maesot Travel Centre operates a small guesthouse on the highway just outside town. 14/21 Asia Hwy., tel. (055) 531409, 40-60B.

Suwannavit Hotel: The Suwannavit and adjacent Mae Moey hotels bridge the gap between the Mae Sot Guesthouse and midpriced hotels. 1 Soi Wat Luang, tel. (055) 531162, 100-160B.

Moderate Accommodations
First Hotel: An old favorite located opposite the former bus terminal. Rooms are large and clean with private bath. Keys are provided on small piston rods. 444 Indrakiri Rd., tel. (055) 531233, 140-180B fan, 220-300B a/c.

Siam Hotel: The most popular midpriced hotel in Mae Sot has a shopping center, cafe, and outlet for SP Tours. 185 Prasat Vithi Rd., tel. (055) 531376, 120-180B fan, 220-350B a/c.

Luxury Accommodations
Mae Sod Hill Hotel: A luxury hotel complete with swimming pool, two tennis courts, coffee shop, and disco. Each a/c room includes TV, refrigerator, and telephone. 100 Asia Hwy., tel. (055) 532601, fax (055) 532608, Bangkok reservations (02) 541-1234, 900-1200B.

Restaurants
Street stalls are most plentiful near the Siam Hotel on Prasat Vithi Road. A great little **cafe** filled with local Muslims is located just opposite the town mosque. The place has good Indian curries and freshly baked breads. Nearby **Pim Hut** is a comfortable place with a large English-language menu just opposite a popular bakery. **Neung Nut Restaurant** has live music and is decorated with Christmas lights mounted on wagon wheels. Chinese food is best at **Canton Restaurant** on the back street behind the market.

Transportation
Mae Sot can be reached by bus from Sukhothai, Tak, Bangkok, or Chiang Mai. Thai Airway flies four times weekly from Chiang Mai and Phitsanulok.

Leaving Mae Sot is problematical since buses leave from several different locations. Tickets can be purchased and timetables checked at the Siam and First hotels. Government buses to Bangkok depart three times nightly between 2000 and 2100 from the office on Indrakiri Road. Sukhothai Tours opposite the First Hotel has buses to Tak every 30 minutes and service to Phitsanulok at 0930. Tranjit Tours in the First Hotel also goes to Bangkok. Tavorn Frame Tours in the Siam Hotel has buses to most destinations including Tak, Phitsanulok, and Bangkok.

Songtaos to nearby destinations such as Umphang and Tak leave from the central market, the halt near the First Hotel, and behind the Porn Thep Hotel. The Mae Sot Guesthouse can help with details.

SOUTH OF MAE SOT

Highway 1090 goes south from Mae Sot toward a series of border towns and natural attractions such as waterfalls and national parks. Transportation has recently improved with the completion of a new road from Pob Rab to Umphang via Ban Rom Klao. *Songtaos* to Umphang depart in the early morning behind the Porn Thep Hotel.

Waley
Some 25 km south of Mae Sot is the small town of Waley where Thais, Burmese, and Karens conduct smuggling operations between the Burmese town of Phalu and the Thai border. *Songtaos* to Waley depart from the mosque and behind the Porn Thep Hotel in Mae Sot.

Umphang
Some of the last remaining stands of teakwood forest are located in Umphang Forest, 150 km south of Mae Sot. Highway 1090 which reaches Umphang passes several natural attractions. Tararak Waterfalls, 27 km south of Mae Sot, and Pra Charoen Waterfalls, 37 km south, are lovely cascades best visited during the rainy season from June to December. Midway to Umphang is the village of Ban Rom Klao 4, whose population consists mostly of Hmong and Karen hilltribes. Thirty km before Umphang is the village of Mae Klong Kee, where accommodation is available with locals or at Border Patrol campsites on the Mae Klong. Just outside Umphang is Telawsu Falls, the largest falls in the country. Visitors can also camp on Khao Hoa Lan and enjoy the sunrise.

Umphang is surrounded by several national parks and wildlife sanctuaries such as the Klong Lan, Huay Kha Kaeng, and Thung Yai Naresuan Wildlife Park. Activities near Umphang include rafting down the Mae Klong and visits to nearby waterfalls and tribal villages. One of the most interesting destinations is the village of Le Tong Khu, where the Karens continue to follow spiritual customs derived from Hindu traditions.

Accommodations in Umphang include the **Um Phang Huts** for 200B and bungalows situated on the Mae Klong.

MAE SOT TO MAE SARIANG

One of the most adventurous journeys in Thailand is along the winding road which leads north from Mae Sot to Mae Sariang. This route provides a unique way to reach the far north since it avoids backtracking to Tak or Phitsanulok. The road skirts the banks of the Moi River, a geographical oddity which flows north through the Dawna Range until it intersects the Salween which, in turn, continues south though the Burmese Shan states. The spectacular scenery includes teakwood forests, waterfalls, and a series of villages inhabited by Thais, hilltribes, and refugee camps maintained by the Karen National Liberation Army and other freedom fighters.

A map of the region is available from the Mae Sot Guesthouse.

Accommodations
Several guesthouses and resorts have recently opened on the highway between Mae Sot and Mae Sariang.

Tan Song Yang: Simple bungalows are available in this rather prosperous village composed of teak and concrete houses located 83 km north of Mae Sot. *Songtaos* from Mae Sot usually terminate here or farther north at Mae Salit. U Su Cave is 15 km north of Tan Song Yang. The local mayor can help arrange boats down the Moi River to Ban Tan Song Yang and the village of Mae Sam Riep on the Salween River.

Mae Sam Riep can also be reached from Mae Sariang.

Chao Doi House: One of the most remote but memorable lodges in Central Thailand is located on a mountaintop some 15 km east of Mae Salit. Ask the bus or *songtao* driver to drop you at the police box near Mae Salit, then hitch a ride up the mountain. The bungalows are operated by Mr. Narong, who charges 160-200B for an all-inclusive package of rooms, meals, drinks, and escorted tours to Karen refugee camps and hill-tribe villages. Chao Doi House has been highly recommended by several travelers.

Mon Krating Resort: This upscale resort is located on a hilltop east of Mae Salit and 135 km north of Mae Sot. Most tours overnight here and continue the following day to hilltribe villages and the Moi River. 1421 Asia Hwy., tel. (055) 531409, fax (055) 532279, 650-750B per person including all meals.

Ban Tan Song Yang: Highway 1085 veers east from Ban Tan Song Yang and continues north up to Mae Sariang. Ban Tan Song Yang is 137 km north of Mae Sot and 89 km south of Mae Sariang.

Transportation

Highway 1085 is now fully paved, though direct bus service from Mae Sot to Mae Sariang is still under development. As of this writing, the journey can only be completed with a series of buses and *songtaos* which cover limited segments of the highway. *Songtaos* depart in the early morning from Mae Sot and terminate at the small village of Mae Salit, slightly north of Tha Song Yang. Travelers often spend the first night at Chao Doi House located up the mountainside from the nearby police box.

From Mae Salit to Ban Tha Song Yang (not to be confused with Tha Song Yang) a chartered *songtao* will probably be necessary and cost about 100B per person. Public buses and *songtaos* from Ban Tha Song Yang to Mae Sariang cost an additional 50B. Travelers have reportedly done the entire journey in a single day, but it's a long and very tough haul.

> *People generally think of travel in terms of displacement in space, but a long journey exists simultaneously in space, in time, and in the social hierarchy.... Travel can hardly ever fail to wreak a transformation of some sort, great or small, and for better or for worse, in the situation of the traveller.*
>
> —Claude Lévi-Strauss,
> *Tristes Tropiques*

NORTHERN THAILAND
INTRODUCTION

The cool mountainous landscapes, friendly people, unique arts and architecture, dazzling handicrafts, unsurpassed ethnological variety, and superb shopping make northern Thailand among the highlights for any visitor to the country. Until two decades ago, the north was unknown to all but the most adventurous of travelers. Now, with improved transportation, new hotels, and an unprecedented boom in tourism, millions of visitors are discovering the exotic charms and romantic appeal of the far north.

Northern Thailand embraces eight provinces bordered by Burma to the west and Laos and the Mekong River to the north. The political and geographic center of the region is Chiang Mai, the second-largest city in Thailand and home to over 200,000 citizens. Beyond the valley of Chiang Mai are five regions which can be easily toured by all visitors. To the west are the thick jungles and remote towns of Mae Sariang, Mae Hong Son, and Pai. South of Chiang Mai lie the historic and cultural centers of Lampang and Lamphun. The third region to the east emcompasses the rarely visited towns of Phayao,

Phrae, and Nan. North of Chiang Mai is a series of small towns which lead to Thaton on the banks of the Kok River. The fifth region is the so-called Golden Triangle long associated with the cultivation of opium and battles between warlords for control of the drug trade. Principal towns in the extreme north include Chiang Rai, Mae Sai on the Burmese border, and the historic site of Chiang Saen on the banks of the Mekong River.

Sightseeing Highlights

Most visitors to northern Thailand begin their explorations in the city of Chiang Mai and then make forays to the following destinations depending on their time and interests. The following thumbnail sketches are designed to help you avoid the overrated towns spoiled by tourism and discover the remote sites where the simple spirit of Thailand still survives.

Chiang Mai: Thailand's second-largest city serves as the hub for local tourism and provides a worthwhile introduction to the charms of the north. Chiang Mai has changed dramatically in

NORTHERN THAILAND

LAOS

BURMA
(MYANMAR)

CHIANG RAI

CHIANG MAI

LAMPANG

LAMPHUN

PHRAE

PHAYAO

NAN

UTTARADIT

MAE HONG SON

DOI CHIANG DAO

DOI INTHANON
NATIONAL PARK

MAE SAI

CHIANG KHONG

CHIANG SAEN

SOP RUAK

MAE CHAN

CHAE

PA TAN

PANG KHA

THOENG

CHIANG KHAM

PAN

NA RAI
LUANG

BAN PUA

NAM
POON

BAN KHOK

NA NAM

KHUN SATAN
RAM
PAT

SALI

NA NOI

RONG KWANG

BAN LUANG

CHIANG MUAN

THA WANG PHA

PONG

NGAO

DEN
CHAI

SOP HOK

SAN KAMPHANG

WANG
NUA

PHAN

MA SUAI

MAE KHAJAN

PHRAO

WIANG PA PAO

FANG

CHIANG DAO

HUAI SOM

SAMOENG

HANG DONG
SAN PA TONG

CHOM THONG

HOT

MAE CHAEM

PA
PONG

MAE SARIANG

MAE SAM
LAE

SOP MOEI

MAE SURIN

PAI

MAE AW

SOPPONG

THATON

MAE SALONG

HIN TAEK

30km

© MOON PUBLICATIONS, INC.

the last decade and now suffers from traffic gridlock and industrial pollution, but still offers dozens of superb temples, a great selection of guesthouses and restaurants, and the finest shopping in Thailand. Best of all, the people continue to exude the warmth and hospitality that first popularized the north.

Lamphun: Some 26 km south of Chiang Mai is a small town which served as the capital of an independent Mon kingdom until the 13th century. An easy day-trip, Lamphun offers a small museum, a royal monastery with almost a dozen buildings, and an intriguing *chedi* that ranks as the finest surviving example of Dvaravati architecture in Thailand.

Lampang: The busy commercial center of Lampang, 100 km southeast of Chiang Mai, has the best collection of Burmese-style temples in Thailand. Twenty km southwest of Lampang is Wat Prathat Lampang Luang, considered among the finest temple complexes in Thailand.

Mae Hong Son: Tucked away near the Burmese border is the remote village of Mae Hong Son, now being aggressively promoted by the tourist office as the next major tourist destination in the north. Much of the charm has been lost to uncontrolled development, though the region still offers beautiful landscapes, rivers, caves, and tribal villages still relatively untouched by mass tourism. Mae Hong Son has several expensive hotels and over a dozen budget guesthouses.

Pai: The finest town west of Chiang Mai isn't Mae Hong Son or Mae Sariang, but the lovely little village of Pai. Tucked away in a valley that resembles Chiang Mai of two decades ago, the town has a handful of comfortable guesthouses and is an excellent place for tribal trekking and visits to hot springs and remote villages.

Thaton and the Kok River: Four hours north of Chiang Mai is a small village where a steady stream of travelers spend the night before taking a longtail boat down the Kok River to Chiang Rai. En route to Thaton are the lovely valley of Mae Sa, a privately owned elephant camp, Chiang Dao Caves, and the dusty village of Fang.

Chiang Rai: Probably the most overrated destination in northern Thailand is the drab city of Chiang Rai. The town has a few mundane temples and is almost unavoidable for an overnight stay, but a better option is to breeze right through and proceed directly to other destinations or one of the mountain lodges described below.

Mae Sai: Situated on the Burmese border is a prosperous but completely nondescript town where Thai and Burmese citizens are allowed to cross and conduct a bit of shopping. Aside from the border crossing and views from the hillside temple, Mae Sai has little of great interest.

Golden Triangle: Thailand's notorious Golden Triangle is centered at the town of Sop Ruak, a disappointing collection of souvenir stalls, touristy restaurants, pushy merchants, and luxury hotels which have eliminated whatever atmosphere that town once possessed. Sop Ruak is more popular with tour groups than armed terrorists, so forget those fantasies about caravans of drug smugglers.

Chiang Saen: Beautifully situated on the banks of the Mekong is the sleepy little town of Chiang Saen, one of Thailand's oldest and most historic sites. The surviving temples are very modest when compared to Sukothai's or Ayuthaya's, but the relaxed atmosphere and lack of tourists make it one of the best untouched destinations in the north.

Chiang Khong: To escape the hordes of tourists in northern Thailand, you'll need to explore the more remote towns such as Chiang Khong and others described below. Chiang Khong has several guesthouses and simple restaurants perched on the edge of the Mekong River.

Phayao: Situated midway between Lampang and Chiang Rai and nestled on the edge of a beautiful lake, this completely untouched town has a pair of outstanding temples and a modern *viharn* with some of the finest modern murals in Thailand.

Phrae: Another good choice to escape the tourist crowds is the provincial capital of Phrae, known for its Burmese-style architecture and textile industry. As with all other towns in northern Thailand, Phrae has several decent Thai hotels with fan-cooled rooms from 100B per night.

Nan: Some 340 km west of Chiang Mai is a prosperous town that many travelers consider among the most attractive in the north. Nan has a half-dozen temples, a branch of the national museum, and a few guesthouses and hotels that cater to the small but steady trickle of international travelers. To the north and east are some of Thailand's most remote and untouched forests. As with Pai and Chiang Saen, Nan has the potential to become one of the leading travel destinations in the next decade.

Routes

Chiang Mai can be reached directly from Bangkok by air, train, or bus, but stopovers in Ayuthaya and Sukothai are highly recommended for visitors interested in history and archaeology. Travelers in Kanchanaburi can avoid backtracking to Bangkok by busing directly to Ayuthaya via Suphanburi. An intriguing alternative approach to Chiang Mai is by bus from Mae Sot up to Mae Sariang, and onward to Chiang Mai via Mae Hong Son and Pai. Several routes are possible from Chiang Mai.

Side Trips: Tribal trekking into the neighboring hills has become somewhat commercialized in recent years, but most travelers who undertake a five- to seven-day adventure still seem satisfied. Lampang and Lamphun are the two most popular side trips from Chiang Mai. Lamphun can easily be visited in a single day, but Lampang needs a day or two to visit the temples and markets. One option is to visit Lampang at the end of a loop through the northern towns of Chiang Rai, Nan, and Phrae.

Western Loop: Among the most popular journeys from Chiang Mai is the long and very rugged journey to Mae Sariang, Mae Hong Son, Soppong, and Pai, before returning to Chiang Mai. Bus service is frequent, though travelers with limited time can fly directly to Mae Hong Son and explore the nearby attractions with an organized tour or rented motorcycle.

Golden Triangle: The extreme north of Thailand can either be explored as a short four-day journey through the triangle region, or on a two-week excursion through the more remote towns of Nan and Phrae. The shorter version begins with a four-hour bus ride to Thaton, where longtail boats load up passengers and depart at 1300 for an exciting but deafening five-hour downriver trip to Chiang Rai. Before returning to Chiang Mai, a few days can be spent exploring the villages, hilltribes, and historic ruins in Chiang Saen.

The Grand Adventure: Visitors who want to escape the standard tourist trail can explore all the remote regions of the far north in about two

or three weeks. The journey begins in Chiang Mai and heads north to Thaton for the boat ride down the Kok River to Chiang Rai. The trail then goes north to Mae Salong and Mae Sai on the Burmese border. After a brief look at the commercialized town of Sop Ruak, a few days can be enjoyed relaxing in the village of Chiang Saen. Buses continue east to Chiang Khong and then south down to Nan via Chiang Kham. The last leg passes through Phrae and Lampang before returning to Chiang Mai.

Leaving the North: After exploring the north, most travelers head directly back to Bangkok and continue to the islands of Southern Thailand. An alternative route is by bus to Phitsanulok and then directly east to Lom Sak, Loei, and other towns in the northeast. Depending on the current political situation, an intriguing option is to visit Laos and run the Mekong River from Luang Prabang to Vientiane. Shades of 1968!

Motorcycle Touring

Transportation around northern Thailand is very simple. Public buses connect all the smaller towns and private bus companies provide direct connections to major destinations. The problem is getting off the beaten track to reach the isolated mountain lodges and small villages where authentic Thai life-styles remain unaffected by mass tourism.

The solution to the problem is touring northern Thailand with a rented motorcycle. While problems with rough roads and the irrational driving habits of the Thais may seem daunting, an amazing number of Western tourists are now touring Thailand by motorcycle.

An excellent little pocket guide to motorcycle touring is published by David Unkovich, owner of the Library at 21/1 Ratchamankha Soi 2, just off Moon Muang Rd. near the Bierstube and Oasis Nightclub in Chiang Mai. Tours are arranged by the northern Motorcycle Club upstairs from the Domino Bar in Chiang Mai. Before setting out, read the cautions in the "Introduction."

Almost a dozen shops on Moon Muang Rd. in Chiang Mai rent motorcycles at extremely competitive rates. Small 100cc scooters which cost 100-150B daily are perfectly adequate for local touring and visiting attractions near Chiang Mai. Larger bikes such as 125cc Honda trail bikes cost 150-180B daily and provide enough power to climb the steepest of roads in northern Thailand. Carefully inspect the bike for damage and make note of any problems such as dangling rearview mirrors and loose chains. You'll be required to leave your passport as deposit, so exchange enough money to finance your motorcycle tour. Motorcycles in the best condition are rented in the early morning, so shop early for vehicles with the lowest mileage. Oil levels should be checked daily and bikes should be locked inside the compound of your guesthouse each night.

During the research for this guidebook, I rented a motorcycle for almost two months and rode nearly all the roads in northern Thailand. The only time I felt in danger was riding through the larger towns such as Chiang Mai and Chiang Rai. Outside of the larger towns, the traffic was very light and roads were in excellent condition. Gasoline stations were relatively plentiful and bike mechanics could be found in almost every village. The Thai government has put up English-language signs throughout the country and, with a good map, it's almost impossible to get lost. The finest rides were the small roads which wind through the hills and parallel the borders of Burma and Laos.

Dozens of routes are possible from Chiang Mai, but most motorcyclists begin by riding north up to Thaton and spending a night in a local guesthouse on the banks of the Kok River. From Thaton, continue along the new dirt road through opium country to the village of Mae Salong where you can spend your second night. Continue down to Chiang Rai and then north to Mae Sai or one of the mountain lodges described below. Continue east from Mae Sai to Sop Ruak and spend a few days relaxing in Chiang Saen. Motorcyclists short on time can then return to Chiang Mai via Chiang Rai and Phayao. A longer and more fascinating journey is to continue east to Chiang Khong, Chiang Khan, Nan, Phrae, and Lampang before returning to Chiang Mai about a week later. Although the entire journey takes two or three weeks, it remains a world-class ride through some of the most beautiful regions in Thailand.

Mountain Lodges

Guesthouses and hotels are located in virtually every town in northern Thailand, but a wonderful alternative to urban dwelling is the handful of mountain lodges tucked away throughout the region. Travelers who wish to experience rural life at its finest are advised to spend a few nights in one of the following lodges. Unless otherwise noted, all have simple rooms for 60-100B.

The list is incomplete and subject to change since many of these mountain lodges change location or close down with the seasons. Gathering information on remote lodges is a difficult task for any travel writer, and only with the help of fellow travelers can this list be kept current. Please write to Moon Publications and let me know about any new discoveries. Be sure to include a business card of the lodge, plus a brief description of facilities, prices, and other amenities.

Pan House: Travelers going to Mae Hong Son via the southern route can stay with Mr. Werapan Tarasan (Mr. Pan) and use his guide services for trekking and elephant excursions. Pan House is located on Highway 108 at km 68, 158 km from Chiang Mai and 32 km east of Mae Sariang. Ask the bus driver to drop you at Ban Mae Wan and then hike five km south from the highway.

Cave Lodge: Several popular mountain lodges are located north of Soppong, between Mae Hong Son and Pai, in a district famous for caves and tribal villages. Cave Lodge is the original lodge, operated by an Australian writer, John Spies, and his Thai wife.

Mae Lana Guesthouse: Also located near Soppong is a bamboo guesthouse operated by a French lady and her Thai husband. The turnoff is marked by a small sign 56 km from Mae Hong Son and about 20 km west of Soppong. Mae Lana Guesthouse is known for its friendly management, good food, and family atmosphere. Activities include cave explorations, tribal trekking, and relaxing in the natural environment.

Trekker House: Defying all conventional wisdom, several young Thais have constructed a few guesthouses 63 km northeast of Chiang Mai and seven km south of Hwy 1019. Trekker House is beautifully situated in a forested area which remained completely untouched until Highway 1019 was opened as a faster alternative to Highway 1. The owners speak some English and conduct guided treks to nearby villages inhabited by Lahu, Lisu, Kuomintang, Meo, Yao, and Karen.

Ban Khum Bungalows: Though rarely visited, Ban Khum Bungalows provides decent accommodations on the slopes of Doi Angkhang. Located in the town of Ban Khum on Highway 1249, 137 km north of Chiang Mai and 15 km south of Fang.

Karen Coffeeshop: Probably the oldest mountain lodge in Thailand still operates north of Thaton near the Kok River and small village of Ban Mai. Trekking is popular throughout the region, though tribal villages are now accustomed to Westerners and fairly commercialized. Visitors should be *very* cautious about interfering with the local opium trade. This region—wedged between the Kok River and Burma to the north—is the authentic Golden Triangle through which passes most of the world's opium crop.

Laan Tong Lodge: Several outstanding mountain resorts are located in the foothills north of Chiang Rai and east of Mae Chan. The region is firmly controlled by the Thai government and visitors can safely do self-guided treks to tribal villages. The lodge consists of several bamboo cottages surrounded by landscaped gardens and fruit trees. Facilities are in good condition and the Thai owners specialize in vegetarian dishes and homebaked breads. Laan Tong Lodge is located on Highway 1089 near the Mae Chan River, 13 km west of the town of Mae Chan.

Mountain View Bungalows: Located on Highway 1207 just 14 km northwest of Chiang Rai is another lodge that arranges tribal trekking, river rafting, and elephant rides. Mountain View Bungalows is just outside the Karen village of Huai Khom and within hiking distance of Akha, Lahu, Lisu, and Meo tribal villages.

Akha Guesthouse: Another longtime favorite is the Akha Guesthouse, located on old Highway 1149, 44 km north of Chiang Rai and seven km west of the town of Ban Huai Krai. Views are spectacular from the guesthouses and trails which wind through nearby Akha villages. Motorcyclists can continue up Highway 1149 to a temple on Doi Tung and around the back of the mountain range to Mae Sai on the Burmese border.

Festivals In Northern Thailand

Visits to Thailand can be planned to coincide with festivals which are celebrated with particular zest in northern Thailand. Tourist events organized by the TAT and local governments often occur on fixed dates. Religious festivals are set according to the lunar calendar and therefore tend to float around the calendar. Exact schedules should be checked with the TAT and then reconfirmed by calling a local hotel.

Borsang Umbrella Fair: A colorful but modest festival which honors the craftsmen in a handicraft village east of Chiang Mai. Umbrella competitions and exhibitions are highlighted by the Miss Umbrella Beauty Contest. Borsang. Late January.

Chinese New Year: Chinese comprise a relatively small part of the population in Chiang Mai, and their celebration tends to be a private event shared between family members. However, this is an excellent time to go trekking among the hilltribes since most celebrate their new year according to the Chinese calendar. February.

Luang Wiang Lakhon: A beautiful and very impressive event organized by the Society for the Preservation of Lanna Culture. During the day, the five most important Buddha images in Lampang are paraded through the street. Nighttime events feature a sound-and-light presentation at Wat Prathat Lampang Luang, considered among the finest temples in northern Thailand. Lampang. Early February.

Flower Festival: An elaborate procession of floral floats, marching bands, and the pride of the north: the beautiful women of Chiang Mai. Hotel rooms are booked months in advance. Chiang Mai. Early February.

Maha Puja: To commemorate the spontaneous gathering of 1,200 disciples to hear a sermon of the Buddha, monks and pilgrims throughout Thailand gather at local *wats* to pray, burn incense, and follow a monk-led procession around the temple. *Farangs* are invited to attend. February.

Poy Sang Long: This very unusual ceremony honors young Shan men who don robes and are ritually initiated into the Buddhist monkhood. A photographer's dream. Mae Hong Son. Early April.

Songkran: Thailand's wet and wild water festival is celebrated with wild abandon throughout Chiang Mai, but most enthusiastically on the banks of the Ping River. Mid-April.

Visaka Puja: The holiest of all Buddhist holidays—the birth, death, and enlightenment of the Buddha are commemorated by Chiang Mai residents who make the long climb to the summit of Doi Suthep. Chiang Mai. Late May.

Lychee Fair: A three-day fair which features agricultural displays, handicraft demonstrations, and the selection of the sweetest Miss Lychee. Chiang Rai. Late May.

Intakin Festival: To invoke blessing for Chiang Mai and its inhabitants, a week-long festival is held at Wat Chedi Luang. Other animist rituals are held at Tapae Gate. Chiang Mai. Late May.

Asaha Puja: Buddha's first sermon to his disciples is celebrated with monk-led processions around temples in northern Thailand. July.

Longan Fair: Similar to the Lychee Fair in Chiang Rai except that the beauty contest crowns Miss Lamyai, the local variety of the longan fruit. Lamphun. August.

Nan Boat Races: *Kathin* season, a period when laymen present new robes to local monks, is kicked off with regatta competitions between distinctive boats painted with bright colors and decorated with traditional designs. Nan. October.

Loy Kratong: The most beautiful of all Thai festivals is celebrated with a monstrous parade followed by the launching of thousands of illuminated boats into the Ping River. Travelers disturbed by large crowds and explosive firecrackers might prefer the smaller and more pleasant ceremony in Sukothai. Chiang Mai. November.

Sunflower Fair: Mexican sunflowers bloom amid the hills west of Chiang Mai during the cooler winter months. While nothing spectacular to Western visitors, the Thais consider sunflowers absolutely delightful. The three-day festival features oxcarts decorated with the flowers, traditional folk shows, and, what else, the crowning of Miss Sunflower. Mae Hong Son. Late November.

Chiang Mai Winter Fair: Cultural shows, agricultural displays, and the Miss Chiang Mai Beauty Contest is held at the Municipal Stadium. Chiang Mai. Late December.

CHIANG MAI

Chiang Mai, principal city of the north, is the favorite destination for many travelers to Thailand. Situated on the banks of the River Ping and surrounded by green hills and lazing rivers, this thriving city is blessed with a rich history, friendly citizens, and a cool, dry climate—the perfect remedy to the sweltering cities of the south.

Chiang Mai is a world apart. With its unique forms of architecture, dance, music, food, and festivals, Chiang Mai has always been a region both physically and emotionally separated from the remainder of Thailand. The people not only consider themselves superior to their cousins in Bangkok, they also happily agree with national consensus that their fair-skinned ladies are the most beautiful in the country.

Chiang Mai, however, is also a city in transition. While the so-called Rose of the North still provides a refreshing change from the ordeals of Bangkok, travelers expecting a charming little village of wooden houses and rural lanes are in for a rude surprise. In many ways, the city represents the classic struggle between the national drive for industrialization and its desire to preserve the quality of traditional life.

Sadly, it appears that real estate developers and commercial speculators are winning. Massive projects are routinely approved without regard for land use or zoning considerations. Billboards near the airport and along the Superhighway plug the imminent appearance of golf courses, housing estates, mega-hotels, air-conditioned shopping centers, factories, and other monuments to modern commerce. Chiang Mai also suffers from air pollution, unending noise, and traffic jams in even the smallest of *sois*. In less than a decade, walking in Chiang Mai has gone from a pleasant escape to an ordeal not unlike a stroll in Bangkok.

Is Chiang Mai doomed? An economic report stated that the Board of Investment recently approved a record number of projects in Chiang Mai and Northern Thailand: 56 major construction sites worth over US$250 million, 320 factories, 15 new hotels with an additional 5,000 rooms, and construction space up 80% from the previous year. To satisfy local developers, government officials have authorized the construction of a 10,000-seat convention stadium, dozens of new condominium projects, and a twin city in San Kamphang district, 15 km east o

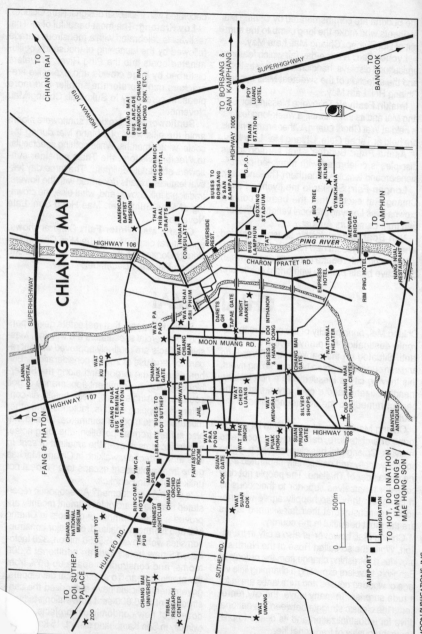

CHIANG MAI

SUPERHIGHWAY

TO CHIANG RAI

HIGHWAY 1019

TO BORSANG & SAN KAMPHANG

SUPERHIGHWAY

TO BANGKOK

POY LUANG HOTEL

CHIANG MAI BUS ARCADE (BANGKOK, CHIANG RAI, MAE HONG SON, ETC.)

TRAIN STATION

HIGHWAY 1006

McCORMICK HOSPITAL

G.P.O.

THAI TRIBAL CRAFTS

BUSES TO BORSANG & SAN KAMPANG

MENGRAI KILNS

BIG TREE

GYMKHANA CLUB

AMERICAN BAPTIST MISSION

INDIAN CONSULATE

RIVERSIDE REST.

BOXING STADIUM

TAT

BUS TO LAMPHUN

TO LAMPHUN

MENGRAI BRIDGE

HIGHWAY 106

PING RIVER

WAT CHAI SRI PHUM

CHARON PRATET RD.

EMPRESS HOTEL

RIM PING HOTEL

NANG NUAL RESTAURANT

WAT PA PAO

WAT KU TAO

DARETS GH

TAPAE GATE

NIGHT MARKET

BUSES TO DOI INTHANON & HANG DONG

NATIONAL THEATER

MOON MUANG RD.

CHIANG MAN

CHANG PUAK GATE

WAT CHEDI LUANG

CHIANG MAI GATE

OLD CHIANG MAI CULTURAL CENTER

LANNA HOSPITAL

HIGHWAY 107

THAI AIRWAYS

CHANG PUAK BUS TERMINAL (FANG, THATON)

BUSES TO DOI SUTHEP

JAIL

WAT MENGRAI

SILVER SHOPS

BANYEN ANTIQUES

TO FANG & THATON

LIBRARY

WAT PRA PONG

WAT PUAK HONG

SUAN PRUNG GATE

HIGHWAY 108

FANTASTIC ROOM

SUAN DOK GATE

WAT PRA SINGH

YMCA

RINCOME HOTEL

MARBLE PUB

CHIANG MAI ORCHID HOTEL

WAT SUAN DOK

HENNESSY NIGHTCLUB

CHIANG MAI NATIONAL MUSEUM

WAT CHET YOT

THE PUB

HUAI KEO RD.

IMMIGRATION

TO DOI SUTHEP, PALACE

ZOO

CHIANG MAI UNIVERSITY

TRIBAL RESEARCH CENTER

WAT UMONG

SUTHEP RD.

AIRPORT

TO HOT, DOI INATHON, HANG DONG & MAE HONG SON

500m

0

© MOON PUBLICATIONS, INC.

the city. Local students and environmental groups have sounded the alarm on uncontrolled development, but the future of Chiang Mai looks grim unless the economic relationship between developers and politicians can be changed.

And yet visitors continue to arrive in record-breaking numbers, and the vast majority leave satisfied with the wonders of Chiang Mai and northern Thailand. The unique ambience and warm welcome extended by the residents still give Chiang Mai an irresistible appeal.

History

Chiang Mai has long been separated from the mainstream of Thai history. Isolated by its mountainous terrain and vast jungles, the region developed independently under the influence of the Burmese and Tai peoples who migrated down from Southern China. Northern Thailand remained almost completely independent from lower Siam until the Northern Railway reached the Ping Valley in the early 20th century.

The region's original inhabitants were Paleolithic settlers who domesticated plants and animals quite independently of the Indians and Chinese. The second known residents were the Lawas, a primitive tribe later forced from the fertile valley by Mons who established a thriving empire at Haripunchai in present-day Lamphun. Other centers of civilization included the kingdom of Phayao, which traded with Pala rulers in India, and Khmer chieftains who operated military outposts ruled from the Cambodian empire at Angkor Wat.

Chiang Mai was formally founded in 1292 by King Mengrai, a Thai-Laotian prince from the Mekong River district who had previously founded Chiang Rai in 1261 and established himself as the paramount power in the north by conquering Haripunchai in 1281. After discovering that his military headquarters at Wiang Kung Kam was poorly sited and subject to floods, Mengrai began searching for a new capital for his powerful Lanna Thai empire, the "Land of a Million Ricefields."

According to legend, the present-day site was chosen after his entourage spotted three lucky omens: two white barking deer, two white sambar deers, and a white mouse. Mengrai immediately ordered the construction of a royal city, regal palace, and Buddhist temples protected by earthenwork walls and 10-meter

moats. Mengrai ruled for 21 years and successfully established a dynasty which dominated northern Thailand for over two centuries. Legends also claim that Mengrai dramatically died when struck by lightning at the intersection of Rajadamnern and Pra Poklao roads. The unlucky spot is now marked by a modest spirit temple dedicated to the ambitious king.

Some 20 Thai monarchs ruled the Lanna Thai kingdom of northern Thailand during the next 240 years. Chiang Mai enjoyed its own golden age during the 15th-century reign of King Tilokaraja, a beloved ruler who organized the Eighth Buddhist World Council in 1477 and constructed many of the present-day temples.

But warfare between Chiang Mai and the Burmese undermined the vitality of the kingdom. Northern Thailand fell to the Burmese in 1556, who ruled the region until 1774, when King Taksin took formal possession of Chiang Mai. After Taksin was declared insane and put to death in 1781, his successor, King Rama I, appointed a governor-prince who revived the hereditary line of rulers of Chiang Mai.

An American Presbyterian Mission was established in Chiang Mai in 1867 to improve the health and education of the people, rather than as an attempt at large-scale conversion to Christianity. Evidence of Western occupation can still be seen in the colonial-style mansions and enclosed compounds located on the east side of the Ping River. Northern Thailand remained a semiautonomous state until 1939, when the final prince of Chiang Mai fell from power and the Bangkok administration took full control of the region.

ATTRACTIONS ON TAPAE ROAD

Since the establishment of the city in the late 13th century, Chiang Mai has remained the principal religious center in northern Thailand and focal point for the construction of temples and monasteries. As a result, today there are 36 temples within the ancient city walls, 80 officially registered religious sites in the metropolitan area, and over 1,000 *wats* scattered throughout Northern Thailand.

Temples in Chiang Mai range stylistically from early Mon and Sukothai prototypes to Ayuthayan and Burmese-style monuments. Northern ar-

singha

BOB RACE

chitects characteristically favored large multi-layered roofs which swoop down lower than Bangkok temples and muted exterior colors that typically employ less of the brazen reds, yellows, and blues found on southern temples. Northern architecture is also noted for flamboyant decoration and woodcarving such as filigree umbrellas and long-necked lions which reflect its two centuries of Burmese occupation.

Some of the following temples stand in original condition, while others have been heavily restored in unrepresentative styles. Older temples have largely disappeared except for their crumbling *chedis* which often predate by several centuries the primary *bot* and *viharn*.

The following walking tour describes temples on Tapae Road, followed by those inside the old city walls. All can be reached on foot or by rented motorcycle or a chartered *tuk tuk* at about 50B per hour. Monuments outside the city walls are described below and can be reached with public transportation or rented motorcycle.

Chiang Mai has a staggering number of temples, but the best monuments for rushed visitors are Wat Pra Singh, Wat Chedi Luang, Wat Chiang Man, Wat Chet Yot, Wat Suan Dok, and the temple on Doi Suthep.

Wat Saen Fang

Four temples of varying architectural interest are located on Tapae Rd. between the shopping district and Tapae Gate. All provide a welcome respite from the heat, noise, and carbon monoxide fumes generated by the ceaseless traffic.

Wat Saen Fang is approached up an undulating *naga*-flanked lane that parallels new construction and the crumbling remains of an old city wall. As with all other temples in Chiang Mai, Wat Saen Fang is composed of several distinctive buildings designed for specific purposes. The Burmese-style *chedi* is decorated with four corner cannons, whitewashed *singha* lions, parasols, and golden tortoises on the second tier. To the rear is a Burmese-style building used as a monks' residence and a brightly painted *viharn* fronted by modernistic, abstract *nagas*. The interior ceiling has been embellished with carved leather animal figures and a swinging chandelier.

Wat Bupparam

Just opposite Wat Saen Fang is another temple compound with three *viharns* that illustrate the past, present, and future of Thai religious architecture.

To the left is a soaring, garish, and ostentatious monument to bad taste that displays every gimmick used in modern Thai architecture: gaudy colors, ferroconcrete instead of wood, slapdash workmanship on the window eaves and pillared supports, and strange mythological animals that resemble Disney worm-dragons rather than traditional Thai creatures. Outside the front entrance a sign aggressively solicits donations from Western visitors, who can then gaze at the interior cartoon murals which depict the life of the Buddha.

Two other buildings in the *wat* compound make a better impression. The large *viharn* in the rear is rather ordinary aside from the unusual carvings of hellish scenes to the right of the entrance.

The chief fame of Wat Bupparam is the tiny, three-centuries-old wooden *viharn* to the right. Exquisitely decorated with stucco on wood, and modeled with superb proportions, the ancient structure features unusual horizontal windows set with old wooden pegs and a mysterious interior filled with dozens of Buddha images.

Wat Mataram

Farther west toward Tapae Gate is a temple complex with both Burmese and Lanna Thai influences. The Burmese-style *viharn* is distinguished by an entrance doorway beautifully carved with the Buddha preaching to the animals, and small tinkling bells which dangle from roof *nagas*. Adjacent buildings include a Burmese-style *chedi* girded with monumental

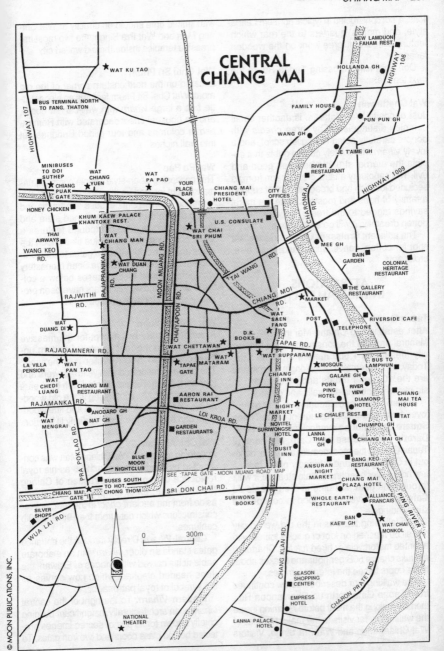

CENTRAL CHIANG MAI

WAT KU TAO

BUS TERMINAL NORTH TO FANG, THATON

HIGHWAY 107

HIGHWAY 106

NEW LAMDUON FAHAM REST.

HOLLANDA GH

FAMILY HOUSE

PUN PUN GH

WANG GH

JE T'AIME GH

RIVER RESTAURANT

MINIBUSES TO DOI SUTHEP

WAT CHIANG YUEN

WAT PA PAO

YOUR PLACE BAR

CHIANG MAI PRESIDENT HOTEL

CITY OFFICES

CHARONRAJ RD.

HIGHWAY 1009

CHIANG PUAK GATE

HONEY CHICKEN

KHUM KAEW PALACE KHANTOKE REST.

U.S. CONSULATE

MEE GH

BAIN GARDEN

COLONIAL HERITAGE RESTAURANT

THAI AIRWAYS

WAT CHAI SRI PHUM

WAT CHIANG MAN

WANG KEO RD.

MOON MUANG RD.

TAI WANG RD.

CHIANG MOI RD.

THE GALLERY RESTAURANT

WAT DUAN CHANG

RAJAPRANIKAI RD.

CHAIYAPOON RD.

MARKET

WAT SAEN FANG

POST

RIVERSIDE CAFE

RAJWITHI RD.

TELEPHONE

WAT DUANG DI

D.K. BOOKS

TAPAE RD.

BUS TO LAMPHUN

RAJADAMNERN RD.

WAT CHETTAWAN

WAT MATARAM

WAT BUPPARAM

MOSQUE

GALARE GH

LA VILLA PENSION

WAT PAN TAO

TAPAE GATE

CHIANG INN

PORN PING HOTEL

RIVER VIEW DIAMOND HOTEL

CHIANG MAI TEA HOUSE

WAT CHEDI LUANG

CHIANG MAI RESTAURANT

AARON RAI RESTAURANT

NIGHT MARKET

LE CHALET REST.

TAT

RAJAMANKA RD.

ANODARD GH

NAT GH

LOI KROA RD.

NOVITEL SURIWONGSE HOTEL

LANNA THAI GH

CHUMPOL GH

CHIANG MAI GH

WAT MENGRAI

PRA POKLAO RD.

GARDEN RESTAURANTS

DUSIT INN

BANG KEO RESTAURANT

BLUE MOON NIGHTCLUB

ANSURAN NIGHT MARKET

CHIANG MAI GATE

BUSES SOUTH TO HOT, CHONG THOM

SEE 'TAPAE GATE - MOON MUANG ROAD MAP'

SRI DON CHAI RD.

CHIANG MAI PLAZA HOTEL

SILVER SHOPS

SURIWONG BOOKS

WHOLE EARTH RESTAURANT

ALLIANCE FRANCAIS

WUA LAI RD.

BAN KAEW GH

WAT CHAI MONKOL

PING RIVER

0   300m

CHANG KLAN RD.

CHARON PRATET RD.

SEASON SHOPPING CENTER

NATIONAL THEATER

EMPRESS HOTEL

LANNA PALACE HOTEL

© MOON PUBLICATIONS, INC.

lions, a *bot* constructed in typical northern Lanna style, and monks' quarters to the rear which feature excellent filigree work on the wooden facade.

Don't get killed crossing Tapae Rd. to the next temple.

Wat Chettawan

Just opposite Wat Mataram is another small complex distinguished by three *chedis* with donors carefully noted in English script, and a lovely *viharn* with a finely carved gable that depicts the eternal struggle between good and evil. The sanctuary attains great charm from its secluded location and broad lawns that support a family of hens and roosters. Note the moral sayings tagged to the trees: "If everything is gotten dreamily, it will go away dreamily too."

The adjacent **Croissant Cafe** is an excellent spot for coffee, conversation, and, what else, croissants.

ATTRACTIONS IN THE WALLED CITY

Tapae Gate

After establishing Chiang Mai in 1292, King Mengrai ordered the construction of a fortified city measuring 1,500 meters on each side. Today, all that remains of the original enclosure are the 10-meter moats and modern reconstructions of the ancient walls and gates.

Superb views and decent grub can be enjoyed from the rooftop restaurant of the **Times Square Guesthouse** overlooking Tapae Gate. **Daret's Guesthouse and Cafe**, just north of Tapae Gate, is the most popular travelers' hangout in Chiang Mai and a friendly place to kill a few hours over beer and buffalo steaks. Or walk through the gate and dine in the upscale **JJ Cafe**, which serves great food in comfortable surroundings.

The following temples in the old walled city can all be reached on foot or quickly toured with a rented motorcycle or hired *tuk tuk*. Chartered *tuk tuks* charge 50B per hour and it takes about three hours to see the interior temples.

The walking tour described below continues from Tapae Gate north up Chaiyapoon Rd., then west along the moat before returning inside the walled city for visits to the major temples of Wat Chiang Man and Wat Pra Singh. Visitors with limited time should go directly to Wat Chiang Man and Wat Pra Singh, the two most impressive temples inside the old walled city.

Wat Chai Sri Phum

Located on the northeastern corner of the old moat, Wat Chai Sri Phum features an elegant little *bot*, a large *viharn* with well-carved doors, and an unusual *chedi* decorated with Romanesque columns and four gilded Buddhas set into wall niches.

Wat Pa Pao

This collapsing Shan-style temple complex, unmarked but located up the alley adjacent to the immense Toshiba sign, exudes a romantic and poetic charm due to its abandoned state and deserted silence. The compound features a small *chedi* with attractive blue tilework on the steps and teetering entrance gates to the north and east. To the left is a large Shan monastery with richly carved display cases below a coffered ceiling whose teak pillars have been profusely embedded with colored glass.

Wat Chiang Yuen

A rather ordinary *wat* except for the massive white *stupa* in the rear courtyard and an unusual octagonal Chinese pavilion near the street. The *stupa* is decorated with yellow flowers and four cartoon characters painted with blue ears and eyebrows. More intriguing is the old wooden pavilion whose triple roofline and fine woodwork can be seen through the dimly lit interior.

Wat Chiang Man

According to legend, Wat Chiang Man was constructed by King Mengrai in 1296 as his royal residence during the construction of Chiang Mai. However, all of the present structures, aside from the ancient *chedi* in the rear, are reconstructions which date from the 19th and 20th centuries.

Central *Viharn*: Directly through the entrance gates stands an older *viharn* with an elaborate gable richly carved with images of Erawan, the three-headed elephant which now serves as the symbol of royal patronage.

Modern *Viharn*: To the right of the central *viharn* is an architecturally insignificant building chiefly known for its pair of sacred images protected behind glass doors and two iron gates. To

Wat Chiang Man

the left is the Crystal Buddha, Pra Setang Kha-mani, an image miraculously endowed with rain-making powers and the centerpiece for the annual Songkran Festival. The Marble Buddha on the right, Pra Sila, is an Indian bas-relief image carved in the Pala style of the 8th century. Both are highly venerated and considered the most powerful images in northern Thailand. Interior murals are numbered and explained in English with a free guide wrapped in plastic.

Bot: To the left of the central *viharn* is a small modern chapel and an old *bot* surrounded by flowering plants and a brilliantly green lawn. The 19th-century Lanna-style *bot* contains a fine collection of Lanna and U-Thong bronzes, plus a stone slab carved in ancient hieroglyphics which remain undeciphered.

Library: Between the old *bot* and the rearside *chedi* stands an elevated *ho trai* (library), considered a masterpiece of woodcarving and lacquer decoration, despite a recent repainting in gaudy colors.

Chedi: Behind the modern *viharn* towers one of the more interesting buildings in the complex, a 15th-century square *chedi* supported on the backs of 15 life-size stucco elephants. The use of elephant buttresses reflects Sri Lankan influences filtered through the Thai empires at Sukothai and Kamphang Phet.

Wat Duang Di

Tucked away in a circular alley and only marked with a small sign is a minor temple chiefly noted for its fine wooden pediments on the east side of the central *viharn,* and elaborate plasterwork on the rear pavilion capped by four ascending roofs. The baroque pediments are regarded as the finest in Chiang Mai.

The old provincial office across the street is worth a quick look.

Monument To King Mengrai

The founder of Chiang Mai is honored with a small monument erected in 1975 to replace an older shrine, "not suitably located for the public."

Wat Pan Tao

Adjacent to Wat Chedi Luang and marked only in Thai script, Wat Pan Tao features a large *viharn* that ranks among the masterpieces of Lanna woodcarving. Note the traditional construction techniques of wooden columns which support the roof and freestanding walls made entirely of carved wooden panels.

Wat Chedi Luang

Named after the massive but ruined *chedi* behind the modern *viharn,* this famous monument was erected in 1401 by King Sam Feng Ken and raised to 90 meters by his son, King Tilokaraja. An earthquake in 1546 partially destroyed the *chedi* and reduced its size to 42 meters, though the well-preserved foundations still give a strong impression of its architectural magnitude. Restoration work has been underway for several years and re-creations of the elephant buttresses and *naga*-lined staircases will soon be in place.

Other nearby buildings are less significant, though the triple-roofed *viharn* once held the famous Emerald Buddha during its travels between Lamphun, Luang Prabang, and Bangkok. Today the sanctuary displays 32 *Jataka* panels and a bronze standing Buddha cast in 1441. Each diorama includes English-language captions which help visitors understand the history and teachings of the Buddha.

Also located in the courtyard is a remarkably large gum tree that shades the Lak Muang shrine of Chiang Mai.

Wat Mengrai

A small blue sign on Soi 6 marks the entrance to a minor chapel noted for its 4½-meter bronze Buddha which, some claim, is a life-size model of King Mengrai himself. More intriguing is the gilded ceremonial gate set with *devas, kinarees, nagas,* and other mythological creatures.

Wat Pra Singh

Wat Pra Singh ("Monastery of the Lion Lord") was founded in the 14th century to house the ashes of King Kham Fu and serve as the principal religious center of the Lanna kingdom. The complex is composed of several buildings of varying architectural and artistic merit that form the most famous *wat* in Chiang Mai.

Central *Viharn:* Directly facing the street is a modern yet stately *viharn* constructed in 1925 and restored several years ago. The Lanna-style structure features a balustrade with a *naga* grasping a *makara* in its mouth, and a starkly plain interior with an indifferent collection of Buddhas.

Library: A registered historical monument, the *ho trai* of Wat Pra Singh features outstanding stucco *devas* and scrollwork around the concrete foundation which supports the delicate wooden building. The divinities were inspired by those of Wat Chet Yot, while the upper structure of teak paneling has been lacquered in red with gilt trim. To the right is another modern *viharn* that serves the large community of monks at Wat Pra Singh.

Bot: Directly behind the central *viharn* stands a Lanna-style *bot* constructed entirely of wood with an impressive entrance of stucco and gold leaf. Strangely constructed with its axis perpendicular to the other *viharns*, the building is kept locked to guard the elaborate altar in the form of a *ku*.

Chedi: To the rear of the *bot* stands a circular *stupa* erected in the 14th century to house the ashes of King Kham Fu. According to architectural traditions borrowed from Sri Lanka, the bulbous reliquary is mounted on sacred elephants constructed from brick and plaster.

Viharn Laikam: The most famous and beautiful structure at Wat Pra Singh—and among the most elegant structures in all of northern Thailand—is the small chapel in the southwest corner of the *wat* compound. Viharn Laikam was built in 1811 in Lanna-style architecture before the influences of Bangkok began to dominate the north.

The exterior is a remarkable melange of fine proportions and delicate woodcarvings in the window frames and ancient doorways. Interior murals, though dimly lit, remain the best preserved in Chiang Mai and provide a glimpse of the religious and civil traditions of 19th-century Siam. Among the humorous vignettes are children riding water buffaloes, men gambling in a circle, and topless maidens collecting fruit.

More significant than the murals is the central Buddha image, the mysterious and ultra-powerful Pra Buddha Singh. Cast in northern Thailand during the late 15th century, exact copies of the highly venerated image are also enshrined in Wat Buddhaisawan in Bangkok and Wat Mahathat in Nakhon Si Thammarat.

Two good restaurants are located near Wat Pra Singh. Sri Phen on Rajadamnern Road is known for its varieties of *som tam*, while Ta Krite has decent Thai food in a comfortable old building.

Wat Pra Pong

Adjacent to Wat Pra Singh is a tiny temple with beautifully carved teakwood windows and doors, depicting strange themes such as sinking ships, charioteers, battle scenes, mythological serpents, and giant *yaksas* ripping apart their victims.

Wat Muang Yakon

South on Samlan Rd. is an old wooden Lanna edifice, badly restored several years ago. The once-significant *viharn* was ruined after the original wooden walls were covered with thick black paint and bright orange embellishments. Worse yet, the old wooden roof was ripped off and replaced with bright orange tiles that completely ruined whatever architectural integrity the temple once possessed.

Wat Puak Hong

Fortunately, the circular *chedi* at Wat Puak Hong has wisely been declared a national registered ruin and, therefore, protected against insensitive restoration efforts by local monks. Displaying an unusual Chinese influence, the 17th-century brick *chedi* features patches of original stucco on the upper nine terraces, and 10 Buddhas tucked away in elevated niches.

ATTRACTIONS
NEAR CHIANG MAI

The following temples, monasteries, and museums are just outside Chiang Mai and can be reached with public minitrucks, though a rented motorcycle or chartered *tuk tuk* will save a great deal of time.

Chiang Mai National Museum

Located on the Superhighway near Wat Chet Yot, the National Museum provides an overview of both Lanna and other art styles of Thailand.

Main Floor: Centerpiece on the main floor is a gigantic Chiang Saen-style Buddha head over three meters tall. Discovered at Wat Chedi Luang and still believed to possess magical powers, the complete image must have been among the largest bronzes ever cast in Thailand. Other schools of Thai art are represented on the ground floor by prehistoric pottery from Kanchanaburi, Srivijayan votives, Lopburi bronzes, an outstanding collection of Chiang Saen images, and Haripunchai terra-cotta figurines.

Upper Floor: Displays here are oriented more toward handicrafts and household goods than Buddha images. Among the better pieces are examples of northern Thai regalia, betel nut sets, giant drums mounted on carts, an extremely fine old rice cart, a royal bed complete with mosquito netting, 19th-century coffin covers, hilltribe displays, and a special room devoted to Burmese-Shan arts.

The Chiang Mai National Museum is open Wed.-Sun. 0900-1600.

Wat Chet Yot

From both historical and architectural standpoints, Wat Chet Yot ("Monastery of the Seven Spires") is considered the most important monument in Chiang Mai. The rather unique structure was constructed by King Tiloka in 1455 and vaguely modeled after the Mahabodhi Temple in Bodgaya, India, where the Buddha attained enlightenment. According to legendary chronicles, King Tiloka convened the Eighth Buddhist Council here in 1477 to commemorate the 2,000th anniversary of the Buddhist era. Wat Chet Yot continued to serve as a monastery and center of Lanna Thai Buddhism for several centuries. Subsequent kings covered the temple with a profusion of gold ornamentation, but this was tragically stripped by the Burmese in 1556.

The principal structure is a seven-spired *chedi*, which gives the temple its name, erected on a rectangular laterite base. Mounted on the walls are the chief glory of Wat Chet Yot: 12 stucco figures of seated divinities framed by standing celestial deities. Some have been defaced by vandals and art collectors, though as a unified ensemble the remaining images comprise the finest stuccoes in Thailand.

Wat Suan Dok

Established in 1383 to enshrine a relic of the Buddha, Wat Suan Dok ("Monastery of the Flowers") is now dominated by an extremely large *viharn* erected in 1932 by the same monk who built the road up Doi Suthep. The massive concrete and steel shed—the largest religious structure in Chiang Mai—is fashioned as an open-air *sala* and filled with painted columns, cool hardwood floors, and a large collection of Buddhas including the famous Pra Chao Kao Tue, a 500-year-old image considered among the largest and finest in all of Thailand.

In the courtyard to the west is a vast garden of white *chedis* and cenotaphs which contain the ashes of Chiang Mai nobles. A type of royal graveyard, the largest *chedi* contains a legendary relic which figured in the establishment of both Wat Suan Dok and Wat Doi Suthep. The forest of *chedis* is incredibly hot during the day, but a wonderful place for sunsets.

Wat Suan Dok is also known as a massage center where old women offer authentic Thai massage at bargain prices.

Wat Umong

Wat Umong, the oldest forest monastery in the region, was constructed around 1380 as a series of underground cells used by forest monks for silent meditation. Interior walls were painted with birds and flowers in styles similar to Chinese counterparts. A relic chamber and *chedi* were constructed above the caves in the early 15th century, but the present *chedi* dates from the early 16th century.

Wat Umong was abandoned until 1948 when local monks returned to clear out the caves and reestablish the old forest monastery. Today, a large community of both Thai and Western monks live in simple meditation huts located in the forests near the lake to the west. A large map at the entrance describes the general layout and somewhat bizarre highlights like the "Spiritual Mural Painting Hall" and "Herb's Garden." Equally amusing are the dog posters carefully labeled with religious admonitions, and trees thoughtfully tagged with amusing proverbs such as "Those with good eyes are inclined to fall into wells."

Wat Umong is five km west of Chiang Mai, at the end of a long and winding road, and only recommended to visitors with hired transportation.

Wat Ku Tao

Constructed during the 17th century to contain

MOTORCYCLE RIDES AROUND CHIANG MAI

Extended rides to Mae Hong Son or the Golden Triangle may seem daunting, but short rides around Chiang Mai are a great way to briefly explore the countryside. A small 100cc step-through motorcycle is adequate for the following journeys.

Doi Suthep: The most popular motorcycle ride near Chiang Mai is up to Doi Suthep to visit the temple, Phuping Royal Palace, and Doi Pui hilltribe village. Go in the early morning for best visibility, and allow about four hours for the roundtrip journey. On the return, visit the zoo, hilltribe center at Chiang Mai University, and the Pub Restaurant for drinks and grub in an old-English atmosphere.

East of the Ping River: Another popular ride begins across the Ping River near the American Baptist Mission in a neighborhood long populated with missionary groups, foreign medical associations, and Western expatriates; a beautiful enclave of narrow alleys, elaborate teakwood homes, and old commercial buildings surrounded by gardens and landscaped lawns.

Then ride south down Hwy. 106 (the old Chiang Mai-Lamphun Rd.) to the Gymkhana Club, Mengrai Kilns, and the big tree festooned with offering scarves and miniature shrines. Continue south another kilometer, cross the Mengrai Bridge, and ride north along Charoen Prathet Rd. past the Sacred Heart Cathedral and the former British Consulate back to town.

Umbrellas and Silk: Everyone with an interest in traditional Thai handicrafts should spend a full day exploring the shops and factories which line the highway between Chiang Mai and the village of San Kamphang, 16 km east of town. Bicyclists will find the road too busy, and group tours are shuttled through the shops too quickly. The perfect solution is a motorcycle shopping tour.

Mae Sa Valley Loop: Try this four-hour ride to see some backcountry almost completely untouched by tourism. Ride north 16 km up Hwy. 107 and turn left at the busy town of Mae Rim. Highway 1096 continues through lovely Mae Sa Valley until it finally encircles the entire mountain range and returns to Hang Dong, south of Chiang Mai. The road is in excellent condition and it's impossible to get lost, but keep your gas tank filled and watch for aggressive truck drivers. Views from the back side of the mountain range are simply spectacular.

Lamphun Loop: The following motorcycle tour involves several hours of riding on busy highways, and can only be recommended to experienced motorcyclists. Drive south down Hwy. 108 and stop briefly at the pottery village of Meang Koong, the basket shops at Hang Dong, and the woodcarvers' village of Ban Tawrai before turning left at San Patong and following Hwy. 1015 to the historic town of Lamphun. After lunch and a look at the temples, return to Chiang Mai via Hwy. 106. Get an early start to avoid the heat and traffic, which peaks around sunset.

Doi Inthanon Loop: This very long ride of 220 km passes through a national park and some of the last remaining rainforests near Chiang Mai. Leave Chiang Mai on Hwy. 108, visit the beautiful *chedi* in Chom Thong, and head up Hwy. 1009 through Doi Inthanon National Park. Continue down to Mae Chan and along the newly paved road back to the main highway at Ob Luang Gorge, extravagantly billed as "Thailand's Grand Canyon." Fill the gas tank in Hot and continue north some 90 km to Chiang Mai. Accommodations are available in Mae Chan and Hot.

the ashes of a Burmese ruler of Chiang Mai, the completely bizarre Chinese-style *chedi* of Wat Ku Tao resembles five hemispherical balls arranged in descending order of size. The strange, rather than elegant, structure has been variously described as piles of pumpkins, begging bowls, or onions.

One of the most unusual *chedis* in Thailand, Wat Ku Tao is located on Soi 6 off Chotana Rd., a few hundred meters north of White Elephant Gate.

Tribal Research Center

Chiang Mai University maintains a small museum and research library with information on local hilltribes. Various displays illustrate the costumes, cultures, and handicrafts of the major groups. Most of the research material in the library is in Thai, but a small selection of books in English is available for casual reading.

The Tribal Research Center is located in Building 15 at the far western edge of campus, and difficult to find and reach without private transportation. The center is open Mon.-Fri. 0830-1700.

Chiang Mai Zoo

Thailand's second-largest zoo, arboretum, and open-air bird sanctuary was founded by a Westerner who donated hundreds of endangered animals to the local government. A sketchy map is available from the entrance kiosk. The zoo has a large collection of monkeys, reptiles, barking deer, and an Asiatic elephant with a single tusk.

The Chiang Mai Zoo is located on the road up to Doi Suthep, and can be a convenient stop on the return journey. The zoo is open daily from 0800 to 1700.

ACCOMMODATIONS

Budget Accommodations

Chiang Mai's 100-plus guesthouses comprise one of the finest accommodation scenes in all of Asia. Guesthouses, ideally, are teak houses owned and operated by local families with fewer than a dozen rooms that face a courtyard filled with flowers, books, and lounge chairs. A perfect guesthouse is not only a wonderful experience but a source of trekking services, bike rentals, and advice on sightseeing, restaurants, and shopping. Genuine guesthouses—a marvelous experience for everyone no matter their age or wealth—have become so popular that many of Chiang Mai's conventional hotels are now calling themselves "guesthouses."

Guesthouses and hotels are located in four areas of town. Those on the east bank of the Ping River are comfortable and quiet, but a bicycle (often provided free) is necessary to get around. Between the Ping River and Moon Muang Rd. are mid-priced guesthouses and hotels ideally located within walking distance of the night market and shopping centers. Inside the old city walls is the largest concentration of guesthouses, especially in the northeast corner. West of town, in the direction of Doi Suthep, are the upscale hotels which are quiet and luxurious, but far removed from the temples and restaurants.

Guesthouse prices are fairly uniform throughout Chiang Mai. Low-end choices charge 60-100B for simple rooms with fan and common bath, or 100-180B with fan and private bath. The emerging trend appears to be better guesthouses with a/c rooms and private bathrooms in the 250-400B range, described below under "Moderate Accommodations." Standards of comfort and cleanliness are similar, but those guesthouses which appear to offer superior ambience have been briefly described below and designated on the map of Central Chiang Mai.

The question of which guesthouse to recommend is a difficult one: ask a dozen travelers and you'll get a dozen different selections. The best tactic is to take a minibus from the main bus terminal, or hire a tricycle from the train station, to the general neighborhood and make a walking inspection. Guesthouse touts at the bus and train stations are fairly reliable sources of information. Other travelers throughout Thailand are often happy to make personal recommendations, and these will often prove your best choice.

Daret's Guesthouse: The backpackers' center in Chiang Mai has a popular outdoor cafe with good food, and dozens of rooms with fan and private baths. Daret's also rents motorcycles and sells treks. 4 Chaiyapoon Rd., tel. (053) 235440, 80-150B fan.

Moon Muang Golden Court: A new three-story hotel with patio restaurant, travel services,

TAPAE GATE - MOON MUANG ROAD

WAT CHANG MAN

WAT DUAN CHANG

SOI 9
SOI 8
SOI 7
SOI 6
SOI 5

SOMPHET MARKET

THOR LOONG NIGHT MARKET

RAJAWITHI RD.

SOI 1
SOI 2
SOI 3

RUAMMIT RESTAURANT

RATCHAWONG RD.

SITHIWONG RD.

CHANG MAI RD.

CHAIYAPOON RD.

MOON MUANG RD.

THANOM RESTAURANT

CROISSANT RESTAURANT

WAT CHETTAWAN

WAT SAEN FANG

DK BOOKS

TAPAE GATE

USIS AUA

RAJADAMNERN RD.

DOMINO BAR

BIERSTUBE

TAPAE RD.

WAT MATARAM

WAT BUPPARAM

HARD ROCK

AROON RAI RESTAURANT

RUAM COME RESTAURANT

LIBRARY

THAI GERMAN DAIRY

RAJAPHANIKAI RD.

RAJAMANKA RD.

WAT CHIANG KHONG

MOO'S BLUES

KAITHONG RESTAURANT

GARDEN RESTAURANT

LOI KROA RD.

KOTCHASAN RD.

KAMPHANG DIN RD.

SOI 1
SOI 2
SOI 3
SOI 4
SOI 5

0   50m

© MOON PUBLICATIONS, INC.

and 30 rooms in various price ranges. Clean and well located near the center of town. 95

TAPAE GATE-
MOON MUANG ROAD

1. Peter Guesthouse
2. Nice Guesthouse
3. Racha Guesthouse
4. Supreme Guesthouse
5. SK Guesthouse
6. Moonshine House
7. Lamchang House
8. SP Guesthouse
9. Friendship Guesthouse
10. Eagle Guesthouse
11. Pata Guesthouse
12. Summit Guesthouse
13. Prince Hotel
14. New Asia Hotel
15. Lek Guesthouse
16. Rose Garden Guesthouse
17. Your House Guesthouse
18. Rama Guesthouse
19. Rendevous Guesthouse
20. Ampawan House
21. Golden Court Guesthouse
22. Montri Hotel
23. New Chiangmai Guesthouse
24. Villa Guesthouse
25. VK Guesthouse
26. Daret's Guesthouse
27. Gap's Antique House
28. Top North Guest House
29. Saithum Guesthouse
30. Times Square Guesthouse
31. Home Place Guesthouse
32. Living House Guesthouse
33. Midtown Guesthouse
34. Ratchada Guesthouse
35. Fang Guesthouse
36. Travel Lodge
37. Primpaw Guesthouse
38. Banpi Guesthouse
39. Yuttana Guesthouse
40. Thana Guesthouse
41. Inter Guesthouse
42. Rose Guesthouse
43. Julie Guesthouse
44. Pha Thai Guesthouse
45. DJ Guesthouse
46. Top North Guesthouse
47. Kent Guesthouse
48. Lai Thai Guesthouse
49. Montha Hotel
50. Mae Ping Hotel

Moon Muang Rd., tel. (053) 212779, 140-220B fan, 250-300B a/c.

Rendezvous Guesthouse: Another new hotel located on a quiet back street with large rooms, common hot showers, and giant TV in the garden courtyard. Rajadamnern Rd. Soi 5, tel. (053) 248737, 100-150B fan.

Ampawan House: Just across from the Rendezvous is another new place that is modern, clean, and very quiet due to its alley location. Rajadamnern Rd. Soi 5, tel. (053) 210584, 100-150B fan.

Pata Guesthouse: An old wooden house with rustic charm and tree-covered courtyard. Rooms are small and somewhat dark, but adequate. Moon Muang Rd. Soi 6, tel. (053) 213625, 60-100B fan.

Moonshine House: A modern hotel located just opposite Wat Chiang Man with clean rooms and tasty meals prepared by Duan, wife of the English owner. A very friendly place. 212 Rajaphanikai Rd., 80-150B fan.

Racha Guesthouse: Racha and the adjacent Supreme Guesthouse are modern, clean places with good-value rooms. Both are off the beaten track and popular with long-term visitors. Moon Muang Rd. Soi 9, tel. (053) 210625, 80-120B fan.

Times Square Guesthouse: An old place with mediocre rooms, but a great cafe on the top floor and convenient location near Tapae Gate. French manager Dominique can help with Thai boxing lessons at Jo's Gym. Tapae Rd. Soi 6, tel. (053) 282448, 80-120B common bath, 250-300B a/c.

Rose Guesthouse: Popular spot with beer garden decorated with hanging parasols, cane chairs, and other attempts at atmosphere. Services include motorcycle rentals, overseas phone calls, and trekking services. Good value. 87 Rajamanka Rd., tel. (053) 276574, 80-150B fan with common bath.

Pha Thai Guesthouse: Modern 15-room guesthouse with clean rooms and hot showers. 48 Rajaphanikai Rd., tel. (053) 213013, 120-150B low season, 150-200B high season from November to March.

Kent Guesthouse: A very quiet place with small garden and trekking services. English management. Recommended by many travelers. Rajamanka Rd. Soi 1, tel. (053) 278578, 100-140B fan.

Midtown Guesthouse: Small but modern hotel in a great location near Tapae Road. Nice restaurant. All rooms include private bath and hot showers. Tapae Rd. Soi 4, tel. (053) 273191, 150-200B fan.

Rama Guesthouse: Modern three-story hotel with a small cafe, but a large yard with swing set for the children. Moon Muang Rd. Soi 5, tel. (053) 216354, 150-200B fan.

Lamchang House: An old wooden house with swaying trees over the courtyard cafe. Somewhat funky, but more atmosphere than modern places. 24 Moon Muang Rd. Soi 7, tel. (053) 210586, 80-120B fan.

Moderate Accommodations

Most of the newer guesthouses which have recently opened in Chiang Mai are charging 150-250B for a clean room with fan and private bath, and 250-500B for an a/c room. While somewhat more expensive than the budget guesthouses listed above, the improved cleanliness and touch of luxury make these guesthouses an outstanding value.

Gap's Antique House: One of the finest guesthouses in Chiang Mai offers antique decor with modern amenities, plus a memorable cafe filled with artworks and teakwood carvings. Rajadamnern Rd. Soi 4, tel. (053) 213140, 250-500B a/c.

Fang Guesthouse: Beautiful four-story hotel with small garden, open-air dining room, and outstanding rooms with private bath. Highly recommended. 46 Kampangdin Rd. Soi 1, tel. (053) 282940, 200B fan, 300-400B a/c.

Top North Guest House: Not really a guesthouse, but a modern, clean, good-value hotel with reasonably priced a/c rooms and less expensive fan rooms. Located on a quiet back street in the old city. Top North even has a swimming pool! 15 Moon Muang Rd. Soi 2, tel. (053) 278900, fax (053) 278485, 150-250B fan, 300-500B a/c.

Baan Kaew Guesthouse: Tucked away in an alley just south of Alliance Française is this beautiful and quiet guesthouse with spacious gardens and a comfortable restaurant. A real escape from the hustle and bustle. 142 Charoen Prathet Rd., tel. (053) 271606, 300-350B fan, 400-500B a/c.

Pension La Villa: The somewhat isolated location is compensated by the lovely teakwood house and elevated dining room with some of the best Italian food in Chiang Mai. Italian management. 145 Rajadamnern Rd., tel. (053) 215403, 200-250B fan, 250-300B a/c.

Home Place Guesthouse: Back in town, Home Place lacks a coffee shop but is clean, modern, and in a good location near shops and restaurants. 9 Tapae Rd. Soi 6, tel. (053) 273493, 200-250B fan, 350-400B a/c.

Living House: Another modern and very clean guesthouse in a convenient location near Tapae Gate. Friendly manager and a small restaurant. Tapae Rd. Soi 5, tel. (053) 275370, 200-250B fan, 250-300B a/c.

Lai Thai Guesthouse: A very large 90-room guesthouse which faces the old city and ancient moat. Rooms are clean and the restaurant is a popular hangout for both backpackers and tourists. Highly recommended. 111 Kotchasan Rd., tel. (053) 271725, fax (053) 272724, 300-350B fan, 400-500B a/c.

YMCA: The Chiang Mai Y has a swimming pool, restaurant, convention facilities, and over 200 clean and comfortable rooms. Unfortunately, the location can be a problem since it's outside of city center and isolated from the shops and the night market. 11 Mengrai Rasmi Rd., tel. (053) 221819, fax (053) 215523, 80-200B a/c dorm, 300-600B a/c rooms with private bath.

Riverside Guesthouses

All of the guesthouses which hug the west bank of the Ping River offer either fan or a/c rooms with private baths, comfortable restaurants, and delightful views over the river. As with all other guesthouses and hotels in Chiang Mai, vacancies are scarce during the busy season from November to March and advance reservations are strongly recommended. Reservations by fax are much better than phone calls or relying on the Thai mail system.

River View Lodge: The River View Lodge is nicely decorated with Thai furnishings and traditional woodcarvings, and has a wonderful little restaurant. The helpful and courteous owner speaks flawless English. An excellent upscale addition to the Ping River guesthouses. 25 Charoen Prathet Rd., tel. (053) 271109, fax (053) 279019, 1000-1800B.

Galare Guesthouse: A modern Thai-style guesthouse with both fan and a/c rooms with private baths. None of the rooms offer river

CENTRAL CHIANG MAI ACCOMMODATIONS

HOTEL	SINGLE	DOUBLE	ADDRESS	PHONE (053)
Chiang Mai Plaza	1200-1800B	1200-1800B	92 Sri Donchai	252050
Chiang Mai President	1000-1400	1200-1600	226 Witchayanon	252050
Diamond	600-800	800-1200	33 Charoen Prathet	234155
Hollanda Montri	100-120	120-140	365 Charoenraj	242450
Je T'aime Guesthouse	60-100	80-160	247 Charoenraj	241912
Lek Guesthouse	80-160	100-180	22 Chaiyapoon	
Montri	300-600	300-600	2 Rajadamnern	211070
Porn Ping	1000-1200	1000-1200	46 Charoen Prathet	235099
Prince	600-800	800-1000	3 Taiwang	236744

views, but Galare remains a good choice in a great location. 7 Charoen Prathet Rd., tel. (053) 293885, 400-450B fan, 500-700B a/c.

Chumpol Guesthouse: Like many other guesthouses in the center of town, the Chumpol has lost much of its atmosphere to noise and traffic jams. Neither the Chumpol or the adjacent, and extremely dumpy, "New" Chiang Mai Guesthouse can be recommended. 89 Charoen Prathet Rd., tel. (053) 234526, 250-400B.

Riverfront Resort: A few kilometers south of Chiang Mai on the banks of the Ping River is a 21-room resort constructed in traditional Lanna style with teakwood bungalows and riverside restaurant. Tons of atmosphere. 43 Changklan Rd., tel. (053) 275235, 600-800B.

Chiang Mai Lakeside Ville: Also located a few kilometers south of town, and similar to the Riverfront Resort, the Lakeside Ville resembles a cluster of teakwood homes on the banks of the Ping River. Chiang Mai-Lamphun Rd. (Hwy. 106), tel. (053) 510-0258, fax (02) 255-7744, 500-1000B.

Luxury Accommodations

Upscale hotels in Chiang Mai are conveniently located downtown near the night market or away from town toward Doi Suthep. Rates quoted in the accompanying hotel chart are high-season prices in effect from November to March. Discounts of 30-50% are offered during the hot summer months from March to June, and during the rainy season from July to October. All hotels charge an additional 11% government tax and 10% service charge.

Novotel Suriwongse: Located in the center of town near the night market and restaurants are several luxurious hotels with all the standard amenities. The Suriwongse is co-managed by a French hotel chain and caters to group tours and business travelers. 110 Changklan Rd., tel. (053) 270051, Bangkok reservations tel. (053) 251-9883, fax (053) 270064, 1800-2500B.

Royal Princess: In the heart of town is this refurbished hotel with two restaurants, poolside bar, and popular nightclub. Formerly the Dusit Inn. 112 Changklan Rd., tel. (053) 281033, fax (053) 281044, 2800-3200B.

Chiang Inn: Another well-located hotel that caters to Western tour groups. The Chiang Inn is an older hotel; upper-floor rooms are large and quiet. 100 Changklan Rd., tel. (053) 270070, 1200-1800B.

Mae Ping Hotel: Downtown Chiang Mai is dominated by this immense 374-room hotel which opened in late 1989. Amenities include two restaurants, swimming pool, meeting rooms, and great views from the top floor. 153 Sri Donchai Rd., tel. (053) 270160, fax (053) 270181, 1600-2200B.

Chiang Mai Orchid: Chiang Mai's original four-star hotel has maintained a good reputation despite the opening of newer and more luxurious properties. The principal drawback is the location outside town. 100 Huay Kaeo Rd., tel. (053) 222099, Bangkok reservations (02) 233-8261, fax (053) 221625, 2800-3500B.

Empress Hotel: Chiang Mai's first luxury hotel with convention center opened in 1991 just south of city center. The 17-story landmark features various function rooms, restaurants, and the most exclusive disco in town. 199 Changklan Rd., tel. (053) 278000, fax (053) 272467, 1600-2800B.

RESTAURANTS

Chiang Mai offers a wide range of dining experiences from northern Thai dishes to European and Asian specialties. Prices are very low, and dining environments run the gamut from simple streetstalls to elaborate teakwood homes. Dining in Chiang Mai is also made pleasant by the relatively small size of the town and the presence of the Ping River, which provides for riverside cafes and nightclubs.

Daret's Restaurant: Chiang Mai's most popular travelers' hangout serves fairly good food, plus outstanding fruit shakes and smoothies in a friendly atmosphere. Daret's is also a great place to meet other travelers and swap information. Chaiyapoon Road. Inexpensive.

JJ Restaurant: A modern, clean, a/c cafe with bakery, espresso, ice cream, and Thai and American dishes. Great spot for breakfast and the *Bangkok Post.* Montri Hotel. Moon Muang Road. Inexpensive.

Croissant Cafe: Walking tours of Chiang Mai might start with breakfast at either JJ Restaurant, Times Square, or this small a/c cafe near the Tapae Rd. temples. Not much atmosphere but decent food and a good escape from the traffic and noise. 318 Tapae Road. Inexpensive.

Times Square Roof Garden: Great views and thick coffee can be enjoyed from the rooftop cafe near Tapae Gate. Enter through the dark lobby of the Times Square Guesthouse and climb the back steps to the roof. Best at breakfast. Tapae Rd. Soi 6. Inexpensive.

AUM Veggie Cafe: Among the excellent dishes are vegetarian spring rolls, tofu specialties, and meatless entrees drawn from the traditions of the north and northeast. Great food at rockbottom prices served by followers of the Indian guru, Satya Sai Baba. Moon Muang Rd. just south of Rajadamnern. Inexpensive.

Thai German Dairy: Excellent Western dishes such as muesli, homemade yogurt and breads, porridge, and pizza. Dairy products are fresh and safe to eat. Moon Muang Rd. Soi 2. Inexpensive.

Aaron Rai: Some of the city's best northern Thai dishes are served in this simple cafe located near Tapae Gate. An English-language menu is available. Specialties under the native dishes section include *gang hang ley* (pork curry), *nam prik* (spicy salsa), and *kao neow* (sticky rice). Be sure to try the unlisted regional favorite *laab,* a dish of diced pork mixed with chilies, basil, and sautéed onions. Other selections include *tabong* (fried bamboo shoots) and *sai owa* (sausage stuffed with pork and herbs). Brave souls can feast on *jing kung* (roasted crickets) and other exotic specialties. 45 Kotchasan Road. Inexpensive.

Lek Steakhouse: Charcoal-grilled buffalo steaks with baked potatoes and veggies are immensely popular dishes in Chiang Mai. Few prepare better steaks than Yves, the French chef who operates this popular cafe. Yves also serves strawberry crepes, homemade yogurts, and vegetarian specialties. 22 Chaiyapoon Road. Moderate.

Bierstube: Ask a local where to dine and the answer will often be this cozy restaurant located in the center of Chiang Mai. Though the German and American dishes are popular, Bierstube cooks some of the best Thai dishes in town. Friendly management and waitresses. 33 Moon Muang Road. Moderate.

Pension La Villa: The best Italian restaurant in Chiang Mai is known for its pastas, veal dishes, and pizzas cooked inside the wood-fired oven. Pension La Villa also rents a few rooms in the rear. Italian management. 145 Rajadamnern Road. Moderate.

Ta Krite Cafe: Located near Wat Pra Singh is a small joint known for Thai dishes and transvestite servers called *pai.* The nearby Sri Phen specializes in a wide variety of spicy *som tam* salads, though they aren't listed on their English menu. Near Wat Pra Singh. Inexpensive.

The Pub: Superb English and French meals served in a homey place considered one of the most genial gathering spots in town. The Pub is decorated in English decor with darts, old beer signs, a collection of cigarette packs, and a roaring fireplace in the winter months. Located outside town but worth the *tuk tuk* ride. Highly recommended. Huay Kaeo Rd. near the Rincome Hotel. Moderate.

Whole Earth Restaurant: Thai, vegetarian, and Pakistani dishes served in a beautiful Thai building surrounded by lovely gardens. Nightly entertainment at 1900 ranges from Indian sitar to Thai folk guitar. No shoes in this very elegant restaurant. 88 Sri Donchai Road. Moderate.

Kaithong: For a taste of the bizarre, try Kaithong for python steak, cobra, crocodile, and mountain frog. The place is unpretentious but expensive. 67 Kotchasan Road. Expensive.

Bankao Restaurant: Upscale and memorable, the teakwood "Old House" near the Ansuran night market is a romantic spot with loads of atmosphere. Sit upstairs for piano music, photographs of the royal family, and decent entrees priced from 70 to 100 *baht*. Bankao is touristy but not badly overpriced. Ansuran Road. Moderate to expensive.

Ban Rai Steakhouse: Once located on Moon Muang Rd., this old favorite moved several years ago to larger but less-pleasant surroundings near Wat Chiang Man. The steaks are still good, but the atmosphere has been ruined by tacky furnishings and a new apartment complex in the backyard. Wang Keo Road. Inexpensive.

Al Shiraz: A downtown cafe with Indian, Pakistani, and Arabic dishes. Fixed meals cost 60-100B in the best cafe of its type in Chiang Mai. 123 Chiang Klan Road. Moderate.

Chalet: French dishes served in a genuine old northern teak mansion. Chef John Evalet operates one of the most famous French restaurants in Asia on the banks of the Ping River. 71 Charoen Prathet Road. Expensive.

The Hill Restaurant: Somewhat reminiscent of a Tom Sawyer house, the Hill is a weird multilevel treehouse situated in a small forest. Food is only average but the atmosphere is unique and prices are low. 122 Suan San Sai Road. Inexpensive.

Buffets: Several of Chiang Mai's large hotels offer luncheon buffets with northern Thai specialties for about 150-200B. A welcome relief from steaming cafes and chaotic night markets. La Grillade Restaurant in the Chiang Inn and the Lanna Coffee Shop in the Rincome Hotel are recommended.

Markets

Chiang Mai has one major night market and several small spots popular with Thais and budget travelers.

Ansuran Night Market: Chiang Mai's most lively and authentic dining experience is the food market which operates nightly on Ansuran Rd. between Chang Klan and Charoen Prathet roads, just around the corner from the night bazaar. Dozens of stalls prepare a wide range of inexpensive dishes. Try rich mussel omelets from the sidewalk showman, steamed crabs large enough for two people, and grilled fish served with choice of sauces. Other possibilities include honey chicken roasted over an open fire, fried noodles with shrimp and bean sprouts, and the spectacle of "flying morning glory." English-language menus are often available, though the point-at-the-pot method of ordering is more direct. Ansuran Road. Inexpensive.

Thor Loong Market: Budget travelers staying in the guesthouses near Tapae Gate often frequent the streetstalls and cafes of Thor Loong. Chaiyapoon Road. Inexpensive.

Somphet Market: Actually in operation only during the day, Somphet is an open-air fruit market with a wide variety of fruits and fresh produce. Moon Muang Rd. Soi 7. Inexpensive.

Restaurants East Of The Ping River

Some of the best restaurants are located across the river in the old neighborhood once favored by foreign missionaries and diplomats.

Riverside Cafe: Probably the most popular *farang* hangout in Chiang Mai offers relaxed dining on their riverside terraces. Go for the Thai entrees, then stay for the live music which ranges from light folk to heavy rock. 9 Charoenraj Road. Moderate.

Gallery Restaurant: This outstanding place combines an art gallery with a beautiful garden in a renovated Chinese shophouse. Superb atmosphere with pleasant views across the river. Highly recommended. 25 Charoenraj Road. Moderate.

Bain Garden: Located in the compound of the old Bombay-Burma teak consortium is a simple cafe with low-priced meals. Not fancy but offers a refreshing garden atmosphere across from an imposing mansion owned by a Chinese jade merchant (not Khun Sa). 2 Wat Gate Rd. Soi 1. Inexpensive.

Colonial Heritage: An old mansion converted into an upscale restaurant with a spacious backyard dining area. A memorable place for northern Thai specialties. 8 Wat Gate Rd. Soi 1. Moderate.

New Lamduon Faham: A simple cafe famous for its curried noodle soup dish called *khao soi* served with either chicken, beef, or pork. Very rudimentary but popular with Thais and the occasional Westerner. 352 Charoenraj Rd. near the Rama IX Bridge. Inexpensive.

Nang Nual Seafood Restaurant: The largest and certainly the most ostentatious restaurant in Chiang Mai offers seafood dishes in a riverside environment five km south of town. 27 Koalklang Road. Moderate.

Dinner Dance Shows

Chiang Mai's classic dining experience is *khantoke,* a traditional northern buffet accompanied by a brief demonstration of Thai dance. It's completely touristy but also fun, reasonably priced, and presents one of the few opportunities in Thailand to see traditional dance. *Khantokes* cost 200-300B and reservations should be made in advance. Photographers can request a spot in the front row, center stage. A typical *khantoke* dinner includes:

Kao neo: Glutinous rice pinched into a bite-size pieces and dipped into a variety of sweet and spicy sauces.

Sai oua: Spicy Chiang Mai sausage roasted over a fire fueled with coconut husks.

Naem: Pickled pork sausage.

Nam prik ong: Minced pork cooked with chilies and shrimp paste.

Gang hang lay: Burmese curried pork mixed with tamarind or *kathorn.*

Larb: A northeastern dish of minced meat mixed with fresh mint leaves.

Old Chiang Mai Cultural Center: Since 1971, the complex south of downtown has been presenting meals and dance shows in their teakwood compound. After a very mild but unlimited meal, northern Thai dances are presented in the dining room, followed by hilltribe and folk dances in the adjacent amphitheater. Be sure to try a hand-rolled cigar filled with locally grown tobacco. 185 Wulai Road. 300B.

Khum Kaew Palace: A large teakwood residence near Thai Airways also presents *khantoke* meals and traditional dance. Rajaphanikai Road. 250B.

Diamond Hotel: The most convenient location for *khantoke* is the teakwood mansion located behind the Diamond Hotel and near the banks of the Ping River. Unlike the Old Chiang Mai Center, this is an intimate spot where everyone is guaranteed a close look at the dancers. Diamond Hotel. 350B.

NIGHTLIFE

Nightlife in Chiang Mai is a subdued affair limited to a few nightclubs and restaurants with live music.

Night Bazaar: Chiang Mai's best nightlife activity is wandering around the night bazaar on Changklan Road. Several small beer bars are located in the basement of the central emporium. More rewarding are the free dance shows given nightly from 2100 to 1200 in the rear of the Vieng Ping Market.

Riverside Cafe: The hippest spot in town offers entertainment from folk guitar to country and western and heavy rock. The Riverside is uncomfortably packed with *farangs,* but the best place to meet and mix with local expatriates. Music starts around 1900 and ends at 0200. Arrive early to secure a table on the veranda. Dutch management. 9 Charoenraj Road.

Chiang Mai Tea House: Also located on the east side of the Ping River, this cozy joint is the low-key alternative to the brash Riverside. Jazz and folk rock are popular here. 27 Chiang Mai-Lamphun Road.

Marble Bar: Cozy and high-class with intimate jazz combos in a refined atmosphere. Located just above a marble store. Popular with Thai students from Chiang Mai University. 100 Huay Kaeo Rd., just past the Chiang Mai Orchid Hotel.

The Pub: Second only to the Riverside in popularity, this English inn has a warm atmosphere plus jazz or folk musicians. Huay Kaeo Rd. near the Rincome Hotel.

Fantastic Room: Daeng Fantastic, the most famous jazz musician in Thailand, headlines in this small club along with visiting musicians and friends. Open from 1800 to 2400. Arrug Rd. below the Chiang Roy Hotel.

Hennesy Nightclub: An old-fashioned taxi dance hall patronized almost exclusively by Thai males who pay small sums to dance with young girls dressed in Thai cheerleader outfits. A very strange place that all visitors should experience for insight into Thai society. Photos outside provide clues. Muang Mai Hotel on Huay Kaeo Road.

Girlie Bars: Several sedate bars with girls are located on Kotchasan Rd. just south of Tapae Road. Unlike their cousins in Bangkok, girls are polite and uninterested in pushing drinks. Several other joints such as the Black Cat and Oasis are located across the canal on Moon Muang Road.

Traditional Massage: Thai curative techniques (without sex) are practiced and taught in various places in Chiang Mai. The Petngarm Hatwait behind the Diamond Hotel has traditional ("Ancient") massage from 200B per hour. Ancient massage is also given at the Blue Moon Nightclub on Moon Muang Road and at the Chiangmai Sauna Club on Chotana Road. The best deal is at the Rinkaew Complex (old Chiang Mai Hospital) across from the Old Cultural Center where an hour of professional massage from the talented instructors costs only 100B. The Northern Blind School near Suan Dok Gate also offers authentic but low-priced Thai massage from blind masseuses.

Classical Thai Dance: *Khon, lakhon,* Thai puppetry, and *likay* performances are occasionally given at the Chiang Mai National Theater (tel. 053-235966) in the Fine Arts College south of the city at Suriwongse Rd. Soi 5. The TAT has details.

SHOPPING

Chiang Mai is Thailand's center of traditional arts and crafts, a veritable bazaar of silverwork, ceramics, antiques, and hilltribe handicrafts—along with tons of tacky junk churned out for nondiscriminating tourists. Take your time and shop selectively. Bargaining is the rule except at leading shops, where prices are fixed.

Hilltribe Handicrafts: Ethnographic souvenirs such as imitation opium pipes, newly manufactured opium weights, weavings, and chunky jewelry are sold at the night bazaar and from dozens of shops along Tapae Rd. near the East Gate. Most has already been picked over by Bangkok dealers and the remainder is often shoddy and badly overpriced. Remember that what looks exotic here often becomes a dusty relic back home. Two shops for better-quality hilltribe handicrafts are Thai Tribal Crafts on Bumrungraj Rd. and Hilltribe Products Foundation on Suthep Rd. near Suan Dok.

Silverwork: Chiang Mai's most famous handicraft has traditionally been produced on Wulai Rd., where silversmiths sweat, smile, and pound away under extremely primitive conditions. Repousse rice containers and cigarette boxes ornamented with scenes from the *Ramakien* are especially attractive. Several woodcarving shops with salad bowls and life-sized elephants are located nearby. Wulai Rd. shops have suffered in recent years, and most of the craftsmen have relocated in better facilities on the road to San Kamphang.

Antiques: High-quality authentic antiques such as Karen frog drums and Kalong ceramics have become, in recent years, both rare and extremely expensive. One reliable source is Borisoothi Art Gallery on Chiang Mai—San Kamphang Rd., an honest shop which provides export licenses and guarantees of authenticity.

Instant Antiques: Casual shoppers should stick with newly manufactured antiques such as those sold at Banyen Antiques located south of Chiang Mai on Highway 108 near the airport. This amazing place, owned by Ms. Banyen Aksornsri, produces superb "instant" antiques with carefully guarded techniques. The original shop burned down in 1990, but Ms. Banyen has successfully recreated her original endeavor at her new location.

Shopping On
Chiang Mai-San Kamphang Road

Chiang Mai's most extensive collection of handicraft and arts shops is located along Hwy. 1006 between Chiang Mai and the silk weaving village of San Kamphang. At last count, over 50 stores and factories were selling silverwork, woodcarvings, lacquerware, leather products, dolls, gems, and Thai silk. Together they form the greatest concentration of handicraft industries in Southeast Asia, rivaled only by the artistic centers of Bali.

Perhaps the most fascinating reason to explore Hwy. 1006 are the handicraft demonstrations where visitors can watch the time-consuming production of silks, silvers, and woodworks. Rarely in Asia can you enjoy such a range of handicrafts and learn firsthand the enormous time and skill involved in their production. Whether you buy anything or not, visiting these factory workshops is an experience worth the trip. You'll never feel blasé about brassware again!

Shoppers are strongly advised to spend a full day exploring the showrooms on San Kamphang Road. Group tourists are frantically shuttled from store to store and allowed little time to watch the craftsmen and bargain for discounts. The best strategy is to rent a motorcycle or car and spend an entire day casually visiting the shops. Taxi drivers only charge about 50B per hour since they receive a commission on your purchases.

Selection is great and prices low for the unhurried traveler. On my last visit, I discovered that many shops will offer discounts of up to 50% to independent travelers not attached to a tour group. All shops can help arrange packing, shipping, and insurance. A few of the better shops, with distances from the Superhighway, are listed below.

Jolie Femme Silk (1 km): First stop might be the enormous silk factory located on the right side of the road. Behind the modern weaving facilities in the front is a display center where visitors can learn about silk production and watch weavers work the old-fashioned looms.

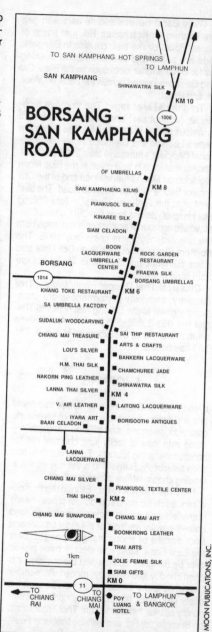

TO SAN KAMPHANG HOT SPRINGS
TO LAMPHUN
SAN KAMPHANG
SHINAWATRA SILK
KM 10

BORSANG - SAN KAMPHANG ROAD

1006

OF UMBRELLAS
SAN KAMPHAENG KILNS — KM 8
PIANKUSOL SILK
KINAREE SILK
SIAM CELADON
BOON LACQUERWARE UMBRELLA CENTER — ROCK GARDEN RESTAURANT

BORSANG
1014
PRAEWA SILK
BORSANG UMBRELLAS
KHANG TOKE RESTAURANT — KM 6
SA UMBRELLA FACTORY
SUDALUK WOODCARVING
CHIANG MAI TREASURE — SAI THIP RESTAURANT
LOU'S SILVER — ARTS & CRAFTS
BANKERN LACQUERWARE
H.M. THAI SILK — CHAMCHUREE JADE
NAKORN PING LEATHER — SHINAWATRA SILK
LANNA THAI SILVER — KM 4
V. AIR LEATHER — LAITONG LACQUERWARE
IYARA ART — BORISOOTHI ANTIQUES
BAAN CELADON

LANNA LACQUERWARE

CHIANG MAI SILVER — PIANKUSOL TEXTILE CENTER
THAI SHOP — KM 2
CHIANG MAI SUNAPORN — CHIANG MAI ART
BOONKRONG LEATHER
THAI ARTS
JOLIE FEMME SILK
SIAM GIFTS
KM 0

0   1km

11
TO CHIANG RAI — TO CHIANG MAI — POY LUANG HOTEL — TO LAMPHUN & BANGKOK

© MOON PUBLICATIONS, INC.

Thai Shop (2 km): On the left is a large showroom with a superb brassware factory in the rear. A careful inspection of the production techniques shows that brassware still remains a cottage industry little changed from generations ago.

Chiang Mai Silver (2.1 km): Most of the silversmiths once located on Wulai Rd. have reestablished their cooperatives in the enormous showrooms on Hwy. 1006. A very good tour and detailed explanation of silver production is given free of charge at Chiang Mai Silver.

Iyara Art (3.5 km): Inside this beautifully designed building is an outstanding collection of old Burmese furniture and other antiques imported from Burma. Iyara Art grants discounts of 35-40% for tourists, and 50% for wholesalers, Thais, and independent travelers.

Borisoothi Antiques (4 km): Chiang Mai's leading antique dealer relocated several years ago from central Chiang Mai to the new showroom on the right side of Hwy. 1006. Products range from Burmese Buddhas and Ming Dynasty porcelains to Kalong ceramics and newly manufactured teakwood furniture.

Shinawatra Thai Silk (4.4 km): Thailand's largest manufacturer of silk products operates a large factory in San Kamphang and a more convenient showroom 4.4 km from the Superhighway. Prices are somewhat high, but Shinawatra has the finest quality in the country.

Nakorn Ping Leather (4.4 km): Friendly young ladies are happy to show the differences in leather quality and explain how elephant hide can be simulated from buffalo leather. Visitors should remember that hides from endangered animals cannot be imported into most Western countries.

Chiang Mai Treasure (5.3 km): A woodcarving showroom where life-sized elephants and smaller souvenirs are sold to tourists. Since Buddhas cannot be exported from Thailand, most woodcarvers specialize in other images such as animals or cute children.

Arts and Crafts (5.3 km): This immense complex is where most tour buses stop for lunch in the cafe or nearby Sai Thip Restaurant. Arts and Crafts has a good demonstration area.

Borsang Village (6.3 km): Borsang is the center for Thailand's famous umbrellas, made from cotton or *sah* paper stretched over a bamboo frame. Visitors are welcome to wander around Boon Umbrella Center and have a simple drawing quickly painted on their bag or T-shirt.

San Kamphaeng Kilns (8 km): Pottery of all types is fashioned and fired in the large factory on the left side of the road.

Shinawatra Silk Factory (10.9 km): An immense modern factory lies in the town of San Kamphang. The tourist center and demonstration rooms on the left provide every possible detail on silk production.

PRACTICALITIES

Tourist Information

The tourist office (tel. 053-248604, fax 053-252812) moved several years ago from the convenient location in the middle of town to a remote location on the Chiang Mai-Lamphun Road. Free publications include maps, magazines, and lists of bus and train departures, hotels, guesthouses, and licensed trekking agencies. Information officers are friendly and speak English, but are uninformed about the more remote and intriguing destinations in Northern Thailand. The TAT is open daily from 0900 to 1630. The tourist police (tel. 053-232508) are downstairs. Another TAT information center is out at the airport.

Mail

Chiang Mai's main post office is on Charoen Muang Rd. near the train station. The GPO is open Mon.-Fri. 0900-1700 and Saturday until noon. The old Mae Ping postal branch on Soi Praisani has been converted into a postal museum. Independent postal branches such as the small outlet on Rajadamnern Ave. just west of the Montri Hotel are reliable, if somewhat more expensive than the GPO.

International Telephone:

Phone calls can be made from most hotels and guesthouses, the GPO and their branch on Praisani Rd., the airport, and until midnight from the international telephone service at 44 Sri Donchai Road.

Immigration

Visas can be extended at Thai Immigration (tel. 053-213510) at 97 Sanambin Rd., on the left side of the road some 300 meters before the airport. Thirty-day extensions to the standard tourist visa cost 300B and require two photos plus some paperwork. Hours are Mon.-Fri. 0830-1200 and 1300-1630. Travelers who wish to stay in Thailand beyond 90 days must leave the country to obtain a new visa.

Consulates
Consular posts are maintained by India (tel. 053-242491) at 113 Bumrungraj Rd., Japan (tel. 053-235473) at 12 Boonrungrit Rd. near Sri Tokyo Hotel, Sweden (tel. 053-210877) in the YMCA, and the U.S.A. (tel. 053-235566) at 387 Vichayanon Rd. across from the city municipal offices.

Bookstores
Chiang Mai's best bookstore is **Suriwong Books** on Sri Donchai Road. **DK Books** on Tapae Rd. and the small bookstore near Tapae Gate have a smaller selection of books and maps.

   Background Reading: The a/c reading room inside the **United States Information Service** (USIS) on Rajadamnern Rd. stocks current magazines and newspapers. **David's Traveler Library** near the Saithum Guesthouse off Moon Muang Rd. Soi 2 is a good information center on motorcycle touring and a convenient place to shop for used paperbacks.

Local Magazines
Welcome to Chiang Mai is a free monthly guide with good stories and useful maps.

Maps
Nancy Chandler's *Map of Chiang Mai* is absolutely indispensable for information on restaurants, local transportation, and important places —names in Thai script—*highly recommended*. Motorcyclists who intend to tour northern Thailand should purchase the *Map of Chiang Mai & Around* published by Prannok Witthaya, and the outstanding *Guide Map of Chiang Rai* published by Bangkok Guides. Both are indispensable for a successful tour.

Hospitals
Medical services are available from McCormick Hospital (tel. 053-241311) on Kaew Nawarat Rd., Lanna Hospital (tel. 053-211037) near the Superhighway, and Suan Dok Hospital (tel. 053-

221122) at the corner of Boonrungrit and Suthep roads. All hospitals have foreign-trained doctors who speak English and provide top-notch services at very low cost.

Sports
Runners can join the Hash House Harriers (tel. 053-278503) on their weekly runs from the Domino Bar on Moon Muang Road. **Swimming pools** open to the public include the Top North Guesthouse (50B) and at the Rincome Hotel (40B). Among the many **golf courses** near Chiang Mai are Chiang Mai Country Club (tel. 053-248321) on the Superhighway, the 18-hole Lanna Golf Course (tel. 053-221911) on Chotana Rd., the nine-hole Gymkhana Club (tel. 053-241035) south of town off the Chiang Mai-Lamphun Rd., and the nine-hole Mae Sa Golf Course (tel. 053-248180) north of town in Mae Sa Valley. Greens fees are 200-600B plus an additional 50B for the caddy.

Thai Language Instruction
The language center of the American University Alumni (A.U.A.) at 24 Rajadamnern Rd. (tel. 053-211407, fax 053-211377) offers both group and private lessons taught by native speakers. Private instruction costs 150B per hour, while 50 hours of group lessons over five weeks cost 2200B. Registration is ongoing and new courses start every five weeks. Classes are also given by FLC Language Center at 19 Singharaj Road.

Massage Instruction
Traditional Thai massage is taught at the Rinkaew Complex (tel. 053-235085) in the old Chiang Mai Hospital across from the Old Cultural Center on Wulai Road. Rigorous courses last 12 days and cost 2500B. This is a very professional school with long hours and tons of homework!

Meditation
Thai *vipassana* meditation is taught at Wat Ram Poeng (tel. 053-211620), also called Wat Tapotaram. One-month courses are led by a Thai monk with English interpretation provided by Westerners or bilingual Thais. Wat Ram Poeng is located south of Wat Umong on Canal Road. *Vipassana* meditation is also taught at Wat U Mong where a German monk gives *dharma* talks most Sunday afternoons from 1500 to 1700.

Environmental Groups

The **For Chiang Mai Group** (tel. 053-214171) at P.O. Box 123 Chiang Mai University 50002 has fought to preserve the forests and wildlife of northern Thailand since its victory in 1986 over the proposed cable car up Doi Suthep. **The Informal Northern Thai Group** sponsors discussions on both culture and the environment. Other activist groups include the **Project for Ecological Recovery** on the Superhighway near the Kaiwan Restaurant, and monks at **Wat Pala** on Doi Suthep Rd. en route to the Galae Restaurant. Further information on these groups and upcoming meetings is listed in the highly recommended monthly magazine, *About Chiang Mai.*

Warnings

Penalties for the use or possession of drugs are extremely severe in Thailand. Tricycle drivers sell the dope and turn you in for the reward. Guesthouses are periodically raided by the police, and those who can't immediately settle their fine go directly to jail. Chiang Mai is a town with heavy drug penalties.

Just as deadly are the bar girls in Chiang Mai. Recent surveys indicate that almost 70% of the prostitutes in northern Thailand are HIV-positive. While full-blown AIDS cases are still relatively rare, the writing is on the wall: Thailand will be devastated by AIDS in the 1990s.

TRANSPORTATION

Transportation To Chiang Mai

Chiang Mai is 700 km north of Bangkok and can be reached by air, train, or bus.

Air: Thai International has eight daily flights from Bangkok to Chiang Mai. The one-hour flight costs 1400B in coach and 1700B in first class. Thai Airways also flies to Chiang Mai from Phuket, Hat Yai, Surat Thani (Ko Samui), Korat, Taipei, and Hong Kong. Airport facilities include a TAT information counter, post office, and bank with favorable exchange rates.

The airport is about ten minutes from downtown Chiang Mai. Taxis to most hotels cost 50B, but minibuses with the Thai Airways logo are half the price. *Songtaos* in front of the airport charge 30-35B per person.

Thai International has offices at 240 Pra Poklao Rd. (tel. 053-211044) behind Wat Chang Man and at the airport (tel. 053-277782).

Train: Trains are the best way to reach Chiang Mai, especially an overnight second-class coach with sleeper. The only advantage of first class, at twice the price, is having two bunks per compartment instead of four. Express trains depart Bangkok's Hualampong Station nightly at 1800, 1940, and 0640. The journey takes 13 hours and costs 440B in second class with lower sleeping berth. Rapid trains depart at 1500 and 2200 and take 15 hours. As the train from Bangkok to Chiang Mai passes through a flat landscape of ricefields, the best trains to take are the overnight sleepers departing at 1500, 1800, and 1940. Ordinary trains leave throughout the day. Advance reservations are recommended, especially during festivals and the high season.

Tricycles from the station cost 20-30B to any guesthouse. Most will deliver you to a guesthouse that offers them a small kickback. Cheaper options include bus 3 to Tapae Gate for three *baht,* or a *songtao* for five *baht.* Buses and *songtaos* pass along the road in front of the train station.

Bus: Buses to Bangkok depart from the Northern Bus Terminal on Paholyothin Road. Air-conditioned buses leave three times daily from 0900 to 1000 and eight times daily from 2000 to 2145. Air-conditioned buses cost 250B and take 10 or 12 hours via Nakhon Sawan and Ayuthaya. Ordinary buses depart hourly and cost 150B. Tickets can be purchased directly at the bus terminal.

Private bus companies in Bangkok offer similar service at slightly higher prices. Surcharges are added for VIP and Super-VIP buses, which have fewer seats and hence more leg room. Meals, soft drinks, and, most importantly, hotel pick-up are included in the price. The bus journey from Bangkok to Chiang Mai is inexpensive and fast, but also cramped, cold, and hairraising. Trains are recommended over buses.

Buses terminate at the Arcade Bus Terminal in Chiang Mai, located in the northeast section of town near the Superhighway. Yellow minibuses 3 and 4 continue to hotels and guesthouses. *Tuk tuk* and *songtao* drivers provide inexpensive rides to guesthouses that give them a kickback.

Getting Around

Chiang Mai is a compact town and all sights in the central section are within walking distance.

Bicycles: To explore the more far-flung destinations, a rented bicycle or motorcycle is recommended. Bicycles cost only 20-25B per day, but the traffic conditions make bicycle touring a dangerous proposition.

Motorcycles: Motorcycles cost 100B daily for small 90cc Honda Dreams, which are perfectly adequate for local destinations, 150B for 125-175cc motorcycles that provide additional power to climb up Doi Suthep, and 180-250B for larger bikes for extended tours. Rental is for a 24-hour period and discounts are given for longer periods. Fuel is your responsibility but unlimited mileage is allowed. Passports must be surrendered for the duration of the rental, so change money first. Some of the shops are content with a photocopy of your passport together with a deposit of 2000B. Ask about the free use of a helmet, additional charges for insurance, and check the condition of the bike before leaving your passport. Minor problems such as broken mirrors and brake levers are best fixed at local repair shops.

Motorcycles in the best condition go early in the morning. Several rental shops are located on Moon Muang Rd. south of Tapae Gate. **Daisy** has 100cc bikes and Honda MTXs in good shape. Bikes from **Pop** are trashed but **65** has several well-maintained Honda Wings. Larger bikes in the 250-400cc range are available from **VIP** and **Hard Rock Cafe** on Kotchasan Road.

Three-wheelers: Pedal trishaws called *samlors* cost 5-10B for short trips. Motorized three-wheel taxis called *tuk tuks* charge according to the distance, starting at 10B for short journeys. Bargain before boarding. *Tuk tuks* around the old city should never cost more than 20B.

Minibuses: Local minibuses called *songtaos* or *seelors* (four wheels) are numbered 1-6 and described on Nancy Chandler's map. Chiang Mai has both yellow and red buses which charge two to five *baht* depending on the distance. Yellow bus 1 runs east and west from the Arcade Bus Terminal to the base of Doi Suthep, stopping at Tapae Gate near the budget guesthouses. Yellow bus 2 runs north and south from Chang Puak Bus Station to the western bank of the Ping River. Yellow bus 3 connects the railway station with guesthouses near Tapae Gate. Red bus 5 runs along the city wall. Red bus 6 circles the city along the Superhighway and connects the airport with the Arcade Bus Terminal.

Jeeps and Cars: Cars and jeeps can be rented at several locations. Rates begin at 1000B per day and mileage is unlimited. Ask

BUS SERVICE FROM CHIANG MAI

DESTINATION	TERMINAL	KM	HOURS	A/C	FARE	DEPARTURES
Bangkok	Arcade	696	10	150B	250-300B	0730-1030, 1800-2100
Chiang Rai	Arcade	180	3	50	70-90	0600-1700
Fang Chang	Puak	151	3	35	60	0530-1900
Khon Kaen	Arcade	720	12	160	220-280	0500-0900, 1700-2000
Lampang Chang	Puak	100	2	25	40-50	0700-1900
Lamphun Chang	Puak	26	½	10	20	0700-1900
Mae Hong Son	Arcade	355	10	100	180-200	0700-1000, 2000-2100
Mae Sai	Arcade	242	5	60	80-100	0700-1500
Mae Sariang	Arcade	191	5	50	70-80	0600-0800, 2000-2100
Nan	Arcade	318	8	70	120-140	0600-1000, 2200-2230
Pai	Arcade	135	4	50	70-80	0700-1400
Phrae	Arcade	225	5	60	80-100	0700-1600
Phetchabun	Arcade	580	8	140	140-180	0700-0900, 2000-2100
Phitsanulok	Arcade	265	5	80	120-150	0700-2300
Thaton Chang	Puak	179	4	40	70-80	0530-1900

rickshaw nap

for "First Class" insurance, which covers damage to you and other vehicles, minus a 2000B deductible. Leading rental agencies include **Avis** (tel. 053-222013) at 14 Huay Kaeo Rd. and branches at the Royal Princess and Chiang Inn, **Hertz** (tel. 053-279473) at 12 Loi Kroa Rd. and Novotel Suriwongse Hotel, **Suda Car Rent** (tel. 053-210030) at 18 Huay Kaeo Rd., and **Aod Car Rent** (tel. 053-279197) at 49 Chang Klan Rd. opposite the night bazaar.

Leaving Chiang Mai

Air: Thai International flies from Chiang Mai to most destinations in Thailand. Flights to the south usually include a stopover in Bangkok, except for direct flights to Phuket and Hat Yai. The most useful flight is the twice-daily 30-minute service to Mae Hong Son, which avoids a difficult full-day journey on the bus.

The Thai Airways office on Pra Poklao Rd. is open from 0730 to 1700. Tickets can be purchased directly at the airport after closing hours. Flights should be booked several days in advance. Thai Airways provides transportation from your hotel to the airport for an additional 20 *baht*.

Train: Four very comfortable overnight trains run daily from Chiang Mai to Bangkok. A rapid train departs at 1530 and arrives in Bangkok the next morning at 0530. The *Bangkok Express* leaves at 1715 and arrives at 0625. The *Nakorn Ping Special Express* departs at 1930 and arrives in Bangkok at 0825. A final rapid train departs at 2045 and arrives at Hualampong Station at 1040. Second class with a sleep-

ing berth is your best choice, but reservations should be made well in advance.

Bus: Buses to destinations *outside* Chiang Mai Province such as Chiang Rai, Mae Hong Son, Sukothai, and Bangkok leave from the Chiang Mai Arcade Bus Terminal northeast of town. Departures are hourly except for Mae Sai, Khon Kaen, and Korat buses, which leave only in the mornings and evenings. Choices include ordinary, a/c, and VIP buses which provide additional room for long-legged *farangs*. Air-conditioned fares listed below show the price range from standard a/c to VIP services.

Buses to most destinations *within* Chiang Mai Province such as Fang, Thaton, and Lampang leave from the Chang Puak Bus Terminal north of the city. Lamphun can also be reached by buses from Nawarat Bridge on a longer but more picturesque route that follows the old Chiang Mai-Lamphun Highway.

Buses and minibuses to points south but within Chiang Mai Province such as Chom Thong and Hot leave from the Chiang Mai Gate on the southern edge of the old walled city.

Minibuses to Doi Suthep leave every 15 minutes from the west side of Chang Puak Gate.

HILLTRIBE TREKKING

One of Thailand's most memorable experiences is visiting and living briefly among the semino-madic hilltribe people of northern Thailand. Most of these agriculturalists migrated here from Laos and southern China via Burma over the last century. Today, despite the inroads of Westernization and government programs to encourage their assimilation into mainstream Thai society, these groups have to a surprising degree maintained their distinct languages, animist customs, patterns of dress, and strong sense of ethno-consciousness.

Although these packaged adventures are called "treks," they more closely resemble long walks than some Nepalese marathon. Treks generally last three to seven days and involve several hours of daily hiking over foothills, wading across streams, and tramping under bamboo forests before spending the evening in a village. After a late-afternoon arrival at the village, visitors are welcome to politely wander around, watch the women weave or pound rice, play with the kids, and take a few discreet photos. Western comforts are rare: accommodations are limited to wooden floors in the headman's house, bathrooms are in the distant bushes, and bathing takes place in nearby streams. Dinner is often a simple meal of sticky rice, boiled vegetables, and hot tea. After the plates are cleared, dozens of villagers, children, curious teenagers, and shy young girls fill the lodge for an awkward but fascinating conversation conducted through your interpreter-guide. You can ask about their customs and beliefs, but be prepared to explain yours and perhaps sing a song! Opium is offered after the villagers wander back to their houses and all the children have been put to bed.

Where To Go

Golden Triangle: Hilltribe villages are scattered over most of northern Thailand but the first trekking, some 20 years ago, was in the Golden Triangle area north of the Kok River. Although the hill people continue to live and dress in traditional manner, some of the more accessible villages have been overtrekked and become sadly commercialized. This is, however, one of the only areas to visit Akhas and the easiest place to do some self-guided trekking. Pick up *The Mae Kok River* map from Suriwong Books in Chiang Mai and then take the bus up to Thaton. Self-guided treks can start here or halfway down the river. Another good spot to start is from Mae Salong, a small Kuomintang village northwest of Chiang Rai. Guesthouses in Chiang Dao, Fang,

Thaton, Chiang Rai, Chiang Saen, and Mae Salong can help with details.

North of Chiang Mai: The region around Chiang Dao and Wiang Papao, midway between Chiang Mai and Fang, was the next area opened to explorers. Treks typically begin with a three-hour jeep ride to a drop-off point on the Chiang Mai-Fang Hwy., then a half day of hiking to reach the first village. Trekking groups occasionally pass each other and the villagers are now quite accustomed to Westerners.

Mae Hong Son: The early '80s saw the focus shift west of Chiang Mai toward the isolated town of Mae Hong Son, the newest and least-commercialized trekking area in Thailand. Trekking agencies are located in Chiang Mai, Mae Hong Son, Pai, Soppong, and Mae Sariang.

Trekking Tips

Research: Paul and Elaine Lewis's *Peoples of the Golden Triangle* is the best of recently published books. Other useful books include the Time-Life publication of Frederic Grunfeld's *Wayfarers of the Thai Forest,* which details Akha life-styles, and *Highlanders of Thailand,* which provides a comprehensive collection of well-edited essays, including a chapter on the effects of tourism. These books are difficult to find in Chiang Mai and should be read in advance. *People of the Hills* by Preecha Chaturabhand is somewhat trashy (sex lives of the Akhas) but available locally and small enough to be carried on the trek. A few hours browsing in the Tribal Research Center at Chiang Mai University will also help.

When to Go: Winter months (late October to early February) are the ideal time to enjoy the cool nights and warm days without the threat of rain; also the best season to find poppies in full bloom. The rainy months (June to September) can be difficult if not impossible.

Group or Self-guided Tour?: Organized treks are best because of language difficulties, security problems, and the possibility of getting lost on the winding trails.

Selecting the Trekking Agency: Chiang Mai's 40 registered trekking agencies meet together monthly, make reports to the police department, set agreements on rates, and discuss problems. Neither the TAT nor Tribal Research Center makes specific recommendations on trekking agencies, but everyone agrees that the most important factor is the qualifications of the guide. Meet with him to determine his age, maturity, trekking experience, knowledge of tribal customs, local dialects spoken, and sensitivity to the hilltribes.

Trek Details: Make a firm agreement on all services the trekking company will provide. How many days will the trek last? Since it takes at least two days to reach the relatively untouched villages a trek of five to seven days will prove much more rewarding than shorter treks. How big will the group be? Groups of more than six people are large and unwieldy and should be avoided. What areas will be visited? Everybody promises the "newest untrekked area" but exactly how many other trekking groups will be in the region with yours? Crossing tracks with another group is to be expected but it should still be held to a minimum. What hilltribes will be visited? Ideally you should visit three or four distinct groups rather than just five Karen groups in five days.

What about the price? Rates set by the Chiang Mai Trekking Guide Association average 800-1000B for a five-day trek but special trips with elephant rides and river rafting are much higher. What else is included? Lodging, food, and transportation are normally included with the package price but check on exclusions. Rucksacks and sleeping bags for cooler winter months may also be provided.

Behavior: Experts emphasize the importance of remembering that hill people are human beings with customs, values, and emotions just as valid as those of the tourist. Visitors should act politely and observe local customs. Your guide can advise on local taboos such as avoiding villages marked with a bamboo cross or touching the fertility symbols which guard some villages. Modesty should always be observed. Revealing halter tops on the ladies and nude bathing in the local streams are definitely taboo. Before unpacking the camera, establish some kind of rapport with the villagers. Most tribespeople allow photos when taken discreetly, but it's best to ask permission. Rather than handing out sweets, cigarettes, cheap trinkets, or money for photos, offer food, Band-Aids, disinfectants, soap, toothpaste, and other necessities.

Warning: Should the trekking company or guesthouse offer to keep your valuables, both parties should prepare a complete list of valuables and issue an itemized receipt. Some travelers report that stored valuables, such as traveler's checks or camera equipment, have disappeared during their trek. Even worse, trekkers' credit cards have been surreptitiously used to purchase goods in Bangkok with the cooperation of agreeable shopkeepers—a theft undetected until your Visa bill arrives back home. To prevent this type of fraud (more common than robbery during the trek), make a detailed report and leave all valuables in a locked bag of which you have the only key.

A good holiday is one spent among people whose notions of time are vaguer than yours.

—J.B. Priestley

PEOPLES OF THE HILLS

Inhabiting the hills of northern Thailand are thousands of hilltribe peoples who struggle to maintain their traditional life-styles against poverty, overpopulation, and the pressures of encroaching civilization. Most of these seminomadic tribes are of Tibetan-Burmese or Tibetan-Chinese origin, having migrated across the border from southern China via Burma less than 100 years ago. Today they wander from camp to camp employing slash-and-burn (swidden) farming techniques to cultivate rice, vegetables, and their most famous crop, opium.

Swidden agriculture typically begins in January when secondary or tertiary forests are cut down and left to dry before being burned in March or April. Rice is planted in the fertilizing ash after the monsoon rains break in June. Rice stalks are cut four months later with small hand sickles, then threshed and winnowed to remove the chaff. Opium and maize are planted in October and harvested during an 8-week period from December through January. Although one of the world's oldest agricultural techniques, slash-and-burn farming is extremely destructive since it depletes the soil of important nutrients and leaves the fields abandoned to useless shrub such as *lalang*. It also perpetuates tribal migrations, making it impossible to divide the region into neatly defined ethnic districts.

Thailand's hilltribes are sometimes described as peaceful people living in idyllic harmony with nature—something of a forgotten Shangri-La—but nothing could be further from the truth. Most are extremely poor and live in dirty wooden shacks without running water, adequate sanitation, medical facilities, or educational opportunities for their children. Illiteracy, disease, opium addiction, and deforestation are other problems. Uncontrolled erosion and soil depletion have reduced crop yields while land, once plentiful and rich, has become scarce due to tribal overpopulation and the arrival of land-hungry lowlanders. Royal aid projects provide help and encourage alternative cash crops to opium, but tribal political power remains minimal since tribespeople are stateless wanderers, not Thai citizens.

The Thai government recognizes six major groups of hilltribes, divided into dozens of subtribes with distinct languages, religious beliefs, customs, costumes, and historical backgrounds. The following descriptions include those tribes most likely to be encountered by trekkers. The Western tribal designation is given first, followed by the local Thai terminology.

Akha (Ekaw)

Population: 27,000
Origins: Yunnan, China
Location: Golden Triangle

Considered among the poorest and least sophisticated of all hilltribes, the Akha are also among the most dazzling in costume. Women's dress typically includes a long-sleeved jacket and short skirt woven from homespun cotton dyed dark blue with indigo. The crowning glory is the Akha headdress, an elaborate pile of cloth stretched over a bamboo frame festooned with bird feathers, iridescent wings of beetles, silk tassels, dog fur, squirrel tails, and Indian silver rupees. Leggings are worn to protect against brambles and thorns.

The shy and retiring Akha construct their villages at high elevations to escape neighbors and provide privacy for opium cultivation. Primitive wooden figures flanking the village entrance gates are carved with prominent sex organs to ensure fertility and ward off evil spirits. Don't touch these talisman gates or the bamboo spirit houses scattered throughout the village. Most villages have giant swings used during festivals and a courting ground where young people meet to find mates. Homes are enormous structures divided into separate sleeping quarters for males and females. Like most tribespeoples,

Akha

Akhas are animists who believe that the spirits of nature, departed ancestors, and graveyard-dwelling malevolent ghosts must be appeased with frequent animal sacrifice.

Despite efforts to preserve their traditional lifestyle, Akhas face the challenges of poverty, political impoverishment, deforestation, overpopulation, and discrimination from other tribespeople, who consider them the bottom of the social order.

Hmong (Meo)
Population: 65,000
Origins: Laos
Locations: Chiang Mai, Laotian border

The Hmong, called Meo by the Thais, are a fiercely independent people who fled Chinese persecution over the last century for the relative peace of northern Thailand. Today the second-largest tribal group in Thailand, Hmong have become the country's leading opium producers by establishing their villages on mountaintops since higher elevations are considered best for opium cultivation. Thai Hmong are subdivided into White and Blue, color distinctions which refer to costume hues rather than linguistic or cultural differences.

Despite their isolation, Hmongs are not shy or rare; you will see them in Chiang Mai's night market selling exquisite needlework and chunky silver jewelry. Traditional female costume includes a short jacket of Chinese design, circular silver neck rings, and a thickly pleated dress handwoven from cannabis fiber. Their striking and voluminous hairstyle is made by collecting old hair and braiding it together into a bun. Young people enjoy sexual freedom and premarital sex is the rule rather than the exception. Courting begins during the New Year festivals, when teenagers meet and make arrangements to rendezvous again during rice-planting season. Early sexual sprees end when the prospective husband makes a monetary offering of five silver ingots to the girl's parents.

A useful introduction to the Hmong is provided in *The Hmong* by Robert Cooper, published by Artasia Press in Bangkok.

Karen (Yang, Kariang)
Population: 275,000
Origins: Burma
Location: Thai-Burmese border

Karen

Thailand's largest hilltribe is the only group not heavily engaged in opium cultivation. Settlements are so numerous that most trekking groups pass through at least one of several subdivisions. Karens are divided into the Sgaw, who live near Mae Hong Son, and the Pwo to the south of Mae Sariang. Smaller Burmese groups include the Kayahs (Karenni or Red Karens) in Kayah State (just across the border from Mae Hong Son) and the Pao who live in southern Shan State.

Karens are a peaceful, honest, and hardworking people who use sound methods of swidden agriculture to save topsoil and minimize cogon growth.

Hmong

(continued)

Their women are superb weavers whose multicolored skirts, blouses, and wedding garments have become prized collector's items. Female dress often denotes marital status: young girls wear white cotton shifts while married women wear colored sarongs and overblouses. Multiple strands of beads are popular but most women shun the heavy silver jewelry favored by other tribal groups. Males are often covered with elaborate tattoos that permanently satisfy ancestral spirits and so eliminate expensive spirit ceremonies. Religious beliefs run the gamut from animism and Buddhism to visionary millennial movements which prophesy a future, messianic king. Karen Christians call him the final Christ, Buddhists call him the fifth and final incarnation.

Lahu (Musser)
Population: 45,000
Origins: Southwestern China
Locations: Chiang Dao, Fang, Golden Triangle

Lahus are one of the most assimilated of all northern tribes. Most belong to the Black (Lahu Na) or Red (Lahu Nyi) linguistic groups while a minority speak two dialects of the Yellow (Lahu Leh and Shi). Older Lahus, who haven't yet adopted modern costume, dress in black robes richly embroidered with red zigzagged stitching and silver ornaments. Children often wear Chinese beanies sprouting red puff balls.

Like most tribals, Lahus are animists who believe their village priests can exorcise evil spirits with black magic and heal the sick with sacred amulets.

Lisu

And like the Karens, they anticipate a messianic movement lead by Guisha, the supreme Lahu god who created the heavens. Their most famous postwar messiah was Maw Naw, the gibbon god who failed in his attempts to restore true Lahu religion and lead his people back into Burma. Ceremonial life revolves around the lively New Year festival when, after dancing, top spinning, and other games, males court females by blowing a gourd signal and poking them with sticks through the slats of the bamboo floor. Special pavilions are available for marriage proposals and lovemaking.

Lisu (Lisa)
Population: 20,000
Origins: Burma
Locations: Chiang Dao, Fang, Mae Hong Son

Thailand's premier opium cultivators and the most culturally advanced of all hilltribes are an outgoing, friendly, and economically successful group of people. While most hilltribe villages are poor and dirty, Lisu villages are often clean and prosperous, loaded with sewing machines, radios, motorcycles, and perhaps a Datsun truck. Terrific salespeople, they enjoy setting up stalls and selling their handicrafts in Chiang Mai's night market.

Their enthusiasm and determination to outshine every other tribal group are reflected in their beautiful and extremely stylish clothing. Females typically wear a brilliant blue skirt topped with an electric red blouse and a rakish turban festooned with long

Lahu

strands of multicolored yarn. This dazzling costume is complemented by a cascade of silver buttons and long dangling ornaments which hang over the chest. Lisu religion revolves around the familiar animist spirits, but also weretigers and vampires which might take possession of a person. Lisus are also noted for their complicated marriage rituals and hedonistic New Year festival of endless dancing, drinking, and religious ritual.

Mien (Yao)
Population: 35,000
Origins: Southern China
Location: Chiang Rai Province

Mien are a hardworking and materially advanced people whose Chinese characteristics have made them the cultural sophisticates of Thai tribals. Called Yao by the Thai, the Mien originated in southern China as a non-Han group before migrating into Thailand via Laos between 1910 and 1950. Most have dutifully kept their Chinese cultural links such as Chinese script and Taoist religion. Sacred scrolls which function as portable icons (similar to Tibetan *tankas)* are their great artistic creation. When unrolled and hung up, these Taoist tapestries change ordinary rooms into temporary temples. Tragically,

Mien

most have been sold to Bangkok antique merchants by impoverished Mien.

Yao women wear large black turbans, distinctive red boas around their necks, and loose-fitting pants embroidered with a stunning pastiche of triangle, tie-dye, and snowflake designs.

VICINITY OF CHIANG MAI

WEST OF CHIANG MAI

The most popular excursion from Chiang Mai is west to the mountain of Doi Suthep, where fresh air and local culture can be enjoyed on a half-day outing. The following three attractions— Wat Doi Suthep, Phuping Royal Palace, and Doi Pui village—are all located some 20 km from Chiang Mai on the ridge of Doi Suthep.

Wat Prathat Doi Suthep

One of northern Thailand's top attractions is the temple and golden 16th-century *stupa* which overlooks Chiang Mai from the summit of Doi Suthep. The architecture is quite modest by Thai standards, but perched on a hilltop at 1,053 meters and nicely situated in a national park,

Wat Prathat Doi Suthep

the temple commands a panoramic view of the entire valley and offers a welcome escape from the congestion of Chiang Mai. The full title means temple *(wat)* of the relic *(prathat)* on Mount *(Doi)* Suthep—named after a legendary monk who founded Lamphun and then promptly withdrew into the solitude of the hills.

More importantly to Thai pilgrims, Wat Prathat Doi Suthep is considered among the nation's most sacred places by virtue of its possession of a sacred Buddha relic. According to tradition, the central *stupa* was erected in 1383 after a wandering white elephant carrying the holy relic stopped at the site of the temple, trumpeted three times, and promptly knelt in homage to the Buddha—an auspicious sign by Thai standards. In 1935, Lamphun abbot Sri Vinchai announced the construction of the winding road up to the remote summit and, with the help of thousands of volunteers, completed the project in just six months. Sri Vinchai is honored with a statue just up from the base of the hill.

Wat Prathat Doi Suthep is approached up a monumental, heart-pounding, 304-step staircase flanked by tremendous mythical *nagas* which symbolize man's progress from earth into nirvana. The present *wat* is composed of several buildings which have been expanded and restored by various rulers since the 16th century. Centerpiece is a golden *stupa* covered with gilded copper plating and flanked by enormous ornamental umbrellas at each corner. *Viharns* on either side feature carved doorways and gilded gables which outrank the interior murals and indifferent collection of Buddhas. The entire complex is almost completely overrun with camera-clicking tourists who snap away at the monks, views, and oddities such as chicken memorials and signs which warn "Don't push the bell." Go ahead, push the bell.

Wat Prathat Doi Suthep is located 20 km west of Chiang Mai. Minibuses leave every 20 minutes from Chang Puak Gate (North Gate) on Manee Noparat Rd., and from Tapae Rd. in front of the Bangkok Bank. The fare is 35B up and 25B down.

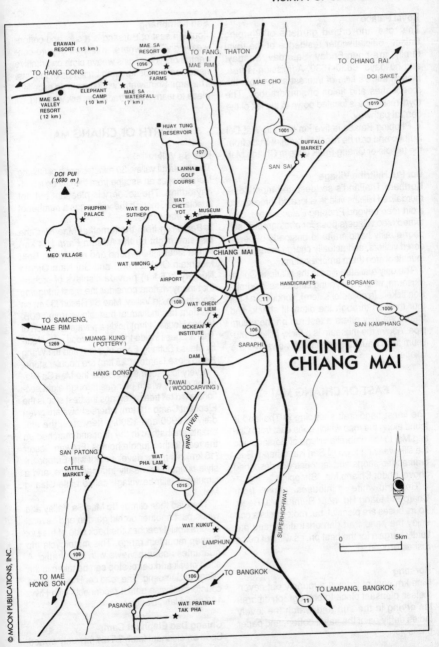

VICINITY OF
CHIANG MAI

TO HANG DONG

ERAWAN RESORT (15 km)

MAE SA VALLEY RESORT (12 km)

ELEPHANT CAMP (10 km)

MAE SA WATERFALL (7 km)

MAE SA RESORT

ORCHID FARMS

1096

MAE RIM

TO FANG, THATON

MAE CHO

MAE CHO

TO CHIANG RAI

DOI SAKET

1019

DOI PUI (1,690 m)

HUAY TUNG RESERVOIR

107

LANNA GOLF COURSE

1001

BUFFALO MARKET

SAN SAI

PHUPHIN PALACE

WAT DOI SUTHEP

WAT CHET YOT

MUSEUM

MEO VILLAGE

WAT UMONG

CHIANG MAI

AIRPORT

HANDICRAFTS

BORSANG

1006

11

TO SAMOENG, MAE RIM

1259

MUANG KUNG (POTTERY)

108

WAT CHEDI SI LIEM

SAN KAMPHANG

HANG DONG

MCKEAN INSTITUTE

106

SARAPHI

DAM

TAWAI (WOODCARVING)

PING RIVER

SAN PATONG

WAT PHA LAM

CATTLE MARKET

1015

WAT KUKUT

LAMPHUN

SUPERHIGHWAY

N

0   5km

TO MAE HONG SON

108

PASANG

WAT PRATHAT TAK PHA

106

TO BANGKOK

TO LAMPANG, BANGKOK

11

© MOON PUBLICATIONS, INC.

Royal Palace

The rose and orchid gardens of Phuping Palace, official winter residence of the royal family, are open Friday, Saturday, Sunday, and holidays 0830-1630. Admission is free, though there's little of interest aside from the rosebushes and fields of snapdragons. The royal residence is located down to the left of the central pathway.

Phuping Palace is five km beyond Wat Doi Suthep and can be reached by mini-truck from the temple or Chang Puak Gate in Chiang Mai.

Doi Pui Hilltribe Village

Northern Thailand's saddest and most commercialized hilltribe village is located three km up a dirt road beyond Phuping Palace. Here, costumed Meo villagers pose for photographs, sell poor-quality handicrafts to busloads of bewildered visitors, and actually charge money to let tourists *watch* them smoke opium.

The only real attraction is the hilarious Opium Museum, where the young curator sells admission tickets (a collector's item), conducts a brief tour through through the dimly lit shack, and then cheerfully offers a test run on the opium pipe. Above the museum is a tacky hilltribe museum and beautiful gardens with views over the village.

EAST OF CHIANG MAI

The finest handicraft shopping in Thailand is found along the road which goes east from Chiang Mai to the umbrella village of Borsang and the silk-weaving town of San Kamphang. Recommended shops and factories are described above, under Chiang Mai "Shopping."

Red-and-white minibuses leave from Charoen Muang Rd. near Bumrungraj Road. Tours buses are plentiful, but motorcyclists can enjoy the handicraft demonstrations and patiently bargain for the best prices without being rushed around.

Borsang

Nine km east of town is a touristy but nevertheless pleasant place to photograph umbrellas drying in the sun and watch the lovely ladies deftly paint the satin, cotton, and paper parasols.

San Kamphang

Four km east of Borsang is a silk- and cotton-weaving village where, in a show of pure concentration, young girls weave cloth on primitive handlooms while ignoring busloads of tourists. The large Shinawatra workshop is an excellent place to learn about traditional silk weaving.

NORTH OF CHIANG MAI

Mae Sa Valley

This beautiful valley, 30 minutes north of Chiang Mai, provides an escape from the city on a half-day outing. The scenery is pleasant but not spectacular, though the valley has a number of decent attractions.

Beginning from the turnoff at Mae Rim, the first stop might be the Adisara Farm (1.4 km) with a small fishing pond and restaurant. Both Mountain Orchid Farm and Sai Nam Orchid Nursery (2.5 km) provide displays of orchids that many visitors consider the most intriguing sight in Mae Sa Valley. Mae Sa Resort (3 km) on the right has individual bungalows from 600B. Maesa House (4 km) holds a private collection of Thai antiques inside the all-teakwood villa. Nearby Maesa Butterfly Farm (4.2 km) and the Wang Kulap Rose Garden (5.5 km) are popular stops.

Every tour seems to include the Mae Sa Waterfall (7 km) which plunges through eight sections amid tall trees. Perhaps the best stop is the Elephant Camp (10 km) where shows are given daily at 0900 and 1300. Afterwards, the elephants are bathed in the river and marched up the road to their jungle homes. Erawan Resort (15 km) is a major development with European-style bungalows, neatly trimmed lawns, and a simulated hilltribe village called Little Chiang Mai.

The road then climbs up Mae Sa Valley and winds past another orchid garden and several resorts until it reaches the back side of the Doi Suthep mountain range. This motorcycle trip guarantees superb views with light traffic. A short break and petrol stop can be taken in the village of Samoeng. The road continues circling counterclockwise until it reconnects with Hwy. 108 near Hang Dong.

Chiang Dao Elephant Camp

Seen an elephant lately? This privately owned

elephant camp on the Ping River sponsors daily shows at 0900 sharp for just 60 *baht*. The elephant show begins with a procession of animals up the Ping, followed by log-rolling exhibitions and demonstrations by the mahouts. Afterwards, elephant rides around the grounds cost 40B per person. Boatmen leaving from the open-air restaurant run bamboo rafts 4¹/₂ km down the Ping River to Tha Rua. The quoted price is about 500B but the fare drops quickly after the tour buses have departed. The whole experience is touristy but loads of fun.

The camp is located 56 km north of Chiang Mai, under a small patch of jungle on the right side of Hwy. 107. Public buses leave from the Chang Puak Bus Terminal and take about 90 minutes to reach the camp. To make the 0900 show, take the 0700 bus and watch the highway signs to help remind the bus driver.

SOUTHWEST OF CHIANG MAI

The following towns, temples, and natural features are best visited on an organized tour or with private transportation. Motorcyclists might enjoy the loop through Lamphun, though the traffic can be daunting to inexperienced cyclists. Public minibuses leave from the Chiang Mai Gate at the southern end of the old walled city.

Muang Kung

Muang Kung ("Meong Koong" on the sign) is a small but well-known pottery village which produces red pots from natural irons or castor oil, and black pots from charcoal. Locally known as Ban Nam Ton after the production of *nam ton* (water jugs), the entire village still produces both giant water jugs and handicraft vessels more admired for their aesthetic than utilitarian beauty. Visitors are welcome to wander around and watch potters shape their clay jars on primitive wheels tucked under elevated houses.

Muang Kung is 10 km south of Chiang Mai and one km west of the highway, where Hwy. 1269 continues west to Samoeng. Look for the sign marked "Samoeng."

Hang Dong

The village of Hang Dong, 13 km south of Chiang Mai, is chiefly known for its bamboo baskets and woodcarvings sold from several stalls

located two km before town. Better than these disappointing shops is an antique store called Ban Chang Come, 500 meters before Hang Dong on the west side of the road. This place has a great selection of old Thai and Burmese furniture, stored outside and exposed to the elements.

Ban Tawai

Ban Tawai ("Tawai Village") and nearby towns collectively form the largest woodcarving center in Thailand. Situated on both sides of the dusty road are dozens of small workshops and massive factories that produce most of the imitation antiques and immense wooden elephants sold throughout the country. Bargains are plentiful. The larger shops also provide packing and shipping services.

To reach Ban Tawai, turn left at the gas station in Hang Dong and drive 3¹/₂ km past dozens of instant-antique showrooms and shipping companies until you see the English-language sign. Turn right and continue along the dirt road past dozens of small shops and home industries that crank out thousands of Burmese Buddhas, Tibetan masks, and wooden horses. The road continues east to Saraphi Dam and back to Chiang Mai.

San Pa Tong

Two km south of San Pa Tong and located on the right side of the road are dozens of wooden pens which mark the largest cattle market in northern Thailand. Held every Saturday morning, the San Pa Tong cattle fair has recently expanded to include everything from Japanese electronics to used clothing.

Chom Thong

This small junction town is chiefly known for Wat Prathat Sri Chom Tong, a beautiful Lanna- and Burmese-style temple on the left side of the main road. Constructed between 1451 and 1516, this well-maintained temple features a central facade and gilded gables carved with remarkable skill.

Chom Thong is 58 km from Chiang Mai and one km beyond the turnoff to Doi Inthanon.

Doi Inthanon National Park

Doi Inthanon, Thailand's highest mountain at 2,590 meters, offers beautiful scenery, evergreen montane forests, dwarf rhododendron groves, rare birdlife, and impressive waterfalls. Mae Klang Falls, 10 km from the park turnoff, is the official entrance and the site of a tourist center. Beyond the entrance is Wachiratan Falls at km 20 and Sri Phum Falls at km 31. Other stops along the winding 47-km road include a Meo village and experimental farm where hilltribes raise alternative crops, several Karen villages, and the summit where the final king of Chiang Mai is buried. Bring warm clothing and rain gear.

Direct service from Chiang Mai to Mae Klang Falls is sporadic and most visitors must change buses in Chom Thong. Buses to Chom Thong leave regularly from inside Chiang Mai Gate at the southern moat in Chiang Mai. Mini-trucks from the temple in Chom Thong go up to the park entrance at Mae Klang Falls, where the park service operates bungalows and an information center. Chartered minitrucks from Chom Thong cost 500-600B per day. *Songtaos* from Mae Klang to the summit of Doi Inthanon leave hourly until late afternoon. Motorcyclists can continue west to Mae Chaem, where simple accommodations and restaurants are found on the main street.

CHIANG MAI TO LAMPHUN

The narrow and very busy road from Chiang Mai to Lamphun runs between twin rows of magnificent tung oil trees planted almost 100 years ago by the princess of Chiang Mai. Most of the trees have been meticulously fitted with wooden pegs which allow the trimmers to climb up and trim the leafy canopy.

While most visitors go directly to Lamphun, several attractions are worthing visiting for those with private transportation.

Wat Chedi Si Liem

Wiang Kum Kam is an ancient town established by King Mengrai six years before he moved his capital to the higher elevations of Chiang Mai. Previously buried under two meters of dirt, several of the remaining temples have recently been restored by the Fine Arts Department. The most important of these are Wat Chedi Si Liem, a stepped pyramid modeled after Wat Ku Kut in Lamphun which exemplifies the oldest *stupa* design in Thailand,

and Wat Chang Kham, which features a beautiful Lanna-style *chedi* and a reconstructed *viharn* adjacent to excavations conducted by the Fine Arts Department.

Wiang Kum Kam is 10 km south of Chiang Mai in a privately owned *lamyai* (longan) orchard just west of the Chiang Mai-Lamphun Highway. Motorcyclists should turn right at the sign marked "Ban Nong Hoi" and continue one km south.

McKean Leper Institute

Founded in 1908 by Presbyterian missionaries to treat sufferers of leprosy, this rehabilitation center has since become an internationally recognized model of a self-contained clinic. Visitors are welcome to tour the facilities, medical clinics, and church which serve the needs of over 200 patients who live in their own cottages on 160 secluded acres. A useful brochure is available from the administration office.

McKean Institute is four km off the main road on a small island in the middle of the Ping River, open Monday-Friday 0900-1700.

LAMPHUN

Lamphun, the old capital of the Haripunchai empire, lies 26 km south of Chiang Mai at the end of the lovely Chiang Mai-Lamphun Highway. In contrast to Chiang Mai, Lamphun remains a sleepy town unaffected by the commercialism and development of northern Thailand. Lamphun is generally visited for its handful of temples, which are of great artistic and historical interest.

History

Lamphun has a long and legendary history. According to the Siamese chronicles, Lamphun (then called Haripunchai) was founded in the 8th century by a wandering hermit named Suthep Reussi, from whom Doi Suthep gets its name. Seeking a resting place for a sacred Buddha relic, Suthep settled on this site and invited Chamdevi, a princess from Lopburi, to reign as the city's first queen. A moat and ramparts were constructed in a slightly deformed oval shape to suggest the conch pattern demanded by Buddhist traditions.

During the next six centuries, Lamphun was

LAMPHUN

1. temple museum
2. Suwana Chedi
3. Golden Chedi
4. gong
5. modern *viharn*
6. library
7. Chedi Mae Krua

TO CHIANG MAI (26 km)

YMCA

WAT CHANG SEE

TANANG RD.

ROB MUANG NAI RD.

KUANG RIVER

WAT SEEN BOONRUANG

WAT CHANG ROB

CITY HALL

TELEPHONE

TO WAT KUKUT (2 km), SAN PATONG (13 km)

WAT MAHAWAN

VANKAM RD.

ATTAROD RD.

MOAT

MUKDU RD.

WAT HARIPHUNCHAI NATIONAL MUSEUM

7
2 4
3 5
1 6

WAT PRAYUN

WAT CHAIMONGKOL

WAT SUPHANRANGSRI

LAMPHUN HOTEL

LAMPHUN ICE CAFE

MARKET

WANG WA RD.

INTHAYONG RD.

TO LAMPANG (72 km)

0   200m

WAT TONGSAJA

TO PASANG (12 km)

MOAT

WAT BAN LUAI

© MOON PUBLICATIONS, INC.

ruled by 49 kings and served as capital for an independent Mon kingdom that dominated most of northern Thailand until 1281, when the city fell to King Mengrai and his emerging Lanna Thai kingdom. Lamphun became an important religious center in 1369 when King Ku Na invited a Sukothai monk to establish the Sinhalese order of Theravada Buddhism. This is the religious form of Buddhism still favored by the modern-day Thais. Lamphun and the Haripunchai kingdom fell to the Burmese in 1556, but the city returned to Siamese control in 1775 under the rule of King Taksin.

Most of the present temples date from the early 16th century, except for Wat Kukut, which dates from the Dvaravati Period.

Lamphun National Museum

A perfect introduction to the arts of Haripunchai is a brief visit to the museum in the center of Lamphun. Inside the small but extremely well-organized museum is a collection of bronzes from Wat Prathat Haripunchai, as well as archaeological discoveries from the Haripunchai Period. Among the better pieces are stucco figurines with the fierce eyes and enigmatic smiles that characterize the early Haripunchai school (8th-10th centuries), and a howdah and gown from the final ruler of Lamphun.

The museum is open Wed.-Sun. 0900-1600.

Wat Pra That Haripunchai

The principal attraction in Lamphun was founded in 897 by a Mon king to enshrine a sacred relic of the Buddha, said to be either a fragment of the Buddha's skull or a hair from his head. The present compound was established in 1044 by King Athitayaraj of Haripunchai on the site of the former royal palace. The *wat* consists of almost a dozen buildings erected during the subsequent centuries which display Burmese rather than traditional Thai forms.

Golden Chedi: Dominating the central plaza is a towering 50-meter *chedi* covered with copper plates and surrounded by engraved plaques. The monument owes its present form to a 20th-century reconstruction project initiated when Burmese architecture was popular in northern Thailand. Capping the summit is a nine-tiered umbrella gilded with almost seven kilos of pure gold. The potbellied monk who brought the Buddha relics from India is commemorated with a statue in a nearby chamber. Legends claim the monk made himself obese to prevent youthful passion from interfering with his Buddhist meditations.

Temple Museum: Although most of the images have been moved to the nearby National Museum, a spectacular if somewhat dusty collection of rare Lanna-style Buddhas is displayed inside the museum near the entrance. The untouched images have acquired a splendid patina, normally lost when Buddhas are "restored" by resident monks.

Suwana Chedi: Tucked away in the northwest corner is an unusual pyramidal *chedi* with some stucco decoration and niches containing standing Buddhas. This fine brick Dvaravati-style *stupa* resembles Chedi Si Liem near Chiang Mai and the original prototype of nearby Wat Kukut.

Modern *Viharn:* Behind the golden *chedi* is the principal *viharn*, a fine example of contemporary religious architecture erected in 1925 but completely restored in 1960. Interior murals depict 13 scenes from the life of Buddha. Also note the large Chiang Saen-style bronze image, Pra Chao Thongtip, and the finely carved repositories to the left of the central Buddha.

Big Gong: Cast in 1860 and sheltered in an open pavilion, this immense bronze gong is among the largest in the world. The reddish building is decorated with images of serpents and gargoyles.

Library: Adjoining the modern *viharn* is a 19th-century Lanna-style *ho trai,* which, according to custom, stands on a high base to protect the manuscripts from termite attacks. Flanking the staircase are Chinese dog-lions and mythological *nagas.* The nearby bell tower shows clear Burmese influence, while the adjacent *bot* contains two bronze Buddha images. The *bot* is kept locked but local monks can provide a key.

Chedi Mae Krua: Situated north of the temple compound in an outside courtyard is a rare Chiang Saen-style *chedi* (Chedi Chang Yan) which shows influence of the Srivijayan school of architecture.

Wat Prayun

Located across the river and about one km from Lamphun, Wat Prayun was constructed in 1900 as a forest monastery for local monks. The square Burmese-style *chedi* is shaped like a terraced *mondop* with four standing Buddhas at the summit of each symmetrical stairway. Wat Prayun features a great deal of remaining stuccowork and an engraved stele which dates the original *mondop* to 1370. Note the mysterious cat figures at the top of the southern staircase.

Wat Kukut

Wat Kukut, Lamphun's most important monument, is considered by archaeologists the last surviving example of original Dvaravati architecture in Thailand. More properly known as Wat Chamdevi, after the legendary queen of Haripunchai, this intriguing *chedi* was constructed in 1218 and modeled after a similar reliquary located in Polonarawa, Sri Lanka. This Sinhalese monument, Samahal Prasat, also served as the model for Chedi Si Liem near Chiang Mai, the Suwana Chedi in Lamphun, Wat Praya in Nan, and a stepped *chedi* in Wat Mahathat in Sukothai. Another theory is that Wat Kukut is a miniature reproduction of the famous Mahabodhi Temple in Bodgaya, India. In any event, Wat Kukut means "Topless Chedi," a local nickname given to the monument after vandals stole the golden roof.

By constructing this pyramidal *chedi* (Suwan Chang Kot) with five diminishing tiers graced with 15 diminishing Buddhas, Mon architects created both a monument of great artistic merit and a clever optical illusion. To the left of the

statues at Wat Kukut

walkway is a smaller octagonal stone *chedi* (Ratana Chedi) with Hindu divinities, and a modern *viharn* insensitively constructed between the two historic monuments.

Wat Kukut is located two km up the small street next to the National Museum. The entrance is marked by a large blue "Bon Voyage" sign. Visitors can walk to the monument in about 45 minutes or hire a *samlor* from the museum.

Accommodations
Most visitors see Lamphun on a day-trip from Chiang Mai, though a few Thai hotels are scattered around town.

Lamphun Hotel: Simple rooms with common or private baths are available in the yellow building located four shops down from the corner. Also called the Notanon Hotel. 51 Inthayong Rd., tel. (053) 511176, 60-100B.

Tu's Guesthouse: Mr. Tu, a local character who hangs out near the bus stop, rents rooms in his home and offers tours to local silk factories and down the Ping River. Ask for him in the shops near the National Museum.

YMCA: The local branch of the YMCA doesn't have any rooms for rent, but American volunteers can sometimes help with accommodations. Visitors are invited to help teach English to the students.

Sawat Ari Hotel: Another hotel marked only with a Thai sign and located near Wat Kukut. Chamdevi Rd., 60-100B.

Suan Kaeo Bungalows: More luxurious digs

are located six km outside town on the road to Lampang. Highway 11 Km 6, 120-200B.

Restaurants
Several simple cafes are located along Inthayong Road and near the market in the southwest corner of town. Lamphun Ice Cafe on Mukdu Rd. is an a/c restaurant that guarantees a welcome relief from the blistering heat of Lamphun. Khum Ton Kaew, former residence of a local prince, has been converted into a combination handicraft center and open-air restaurant.

Transportation
Lamphun is 26 km south of Chiang Mai and can be reached with blue-and-white buses which leave every 30 minutes from Lamphun Rd., about 200 meters south of Nawarat Bridge near the TAT office.

PASANG

Pasang is a one-street town known for its cotton weaving, batik, lamyai fruit, and girls who are considered by many Thais the most beautiful in the country. Cotton production and weaving have left Pasang but survive in smaller villages such as Ban Nong Nguak some eight km southwest of Pasang. The tourist police has a map to the region.

Several stores in Pasang sell high-quality shirts and sarongs, but the best selection is at Nandakwang Laicum on the west side of the road. A batik shirt costs about 200-300B, while dresses run about 250-350B depending on the quality. Across the road, Suchada sells more traditional and less expensive clothing, plus bottles of local honey made from the aromatic *lamyai* blossom.

Pasang is 10 km south of Lamphun on Hwy. 106 and can be reached with *songtaos* from Lamphun and buses from Chiang Mai.

Wat Prathat Tak Pha
Some eight km south of Pasang is the turnoff for a famous Mahanikai *wat* dedicated to a famous northern monk named Luang Pu Phromma and erected on the site where several Buddha footprints were discovered. Wonderfully located on the side of a mountain, the temple is reached up a long tree-lined road that becomes steeper as it gains elevation. This popular pilgrimage spot has several footprint sanctuaries which have been painted with religious artwork and a steep staircase which leads to a golden *chedi* at the top of the mountain. Hikers are rewarded with magnificent views over the Ping River Valley.

LAMPANG

Lampang, 100 km southeast of Chiang Mai on the arterial highway between Bangkok and the north, was once a sleepy town known for its temples and nostalgic horse-drawn carriages. Today it's a busy commercial center of 50,000 residents and contains some of the finest Burmese-style temples in Thailand.

History
Lampang was founded in the 7th century by a son of Queen Chamdevi shortly after the rise of the Haripunchai kingdom in Lamphun. The town, originally called Kelang Nakorn and located on the east bank of the Wang River, was linked with several fortified settlements, of which only Wat Prathat Lampang Luang still survives.

The city joined the Lanna kingdom with the rise of King Mengrai, but fell to Burmese invaders in 1556. Two centuries of Burmese rule were reversed in the 18th century with the unification of Thailand under the Chakri Dynasty.

By the turn of the 20th century, Lampang had developed into a major teak center populated by Thai, Shan, and English traders who floated massive rafts of logs down the then-majestic

Wang River. The rich cosmospolitan mixture of merchants and vast stands of teak brought prosperity and a construction frenzy still reflected in the assortment of Thai, Burmese, and Chinese temples which have survived to the present day.

Old Architecture
Testimony to the long and rich history of Lampang is demonstrated by the well-preserved temples and domestic architecture hidden away in the smaller streets along the banks of the Wang River. Many of the old mansions and shophouses between the Riverside Cafe and the bridge reflect Western styles favored by Burmese architects during the reign of King Rama V. Most of the old architecture is located on the east banks of the Wang, since Lampang was centered here until several decades ago. Baan Sao Nok, the "House of Many Pillars," is an outstanding example of a teakwood house and rice granary elevated on 116 teak pillars.

Wat Pra Keo Don Tao
The main temple of Lampang is included on every tour of the city. Although located in the middle of a disorienting neighborhood and difficult to find, this Burmese shrine with its massive *chedi,* well-carved Burmese-style chapel, small museum, and Thai-style temple is worth seeking out.

The temple was an important religious center in the 15th century when it briefly housed the Emerald Buddha now enshrined in Bangkok at the Wat Pra Keo. The highlight of the complex is a Burmese-style *mondop* topped with an elaborate pinnacle and decorated with a profusion of ornamental detail. Details include pillars gilded with miniature Buddhas and a coffered ceiling which, reflecting Western influence, is carved with nine small cupids, below which rests a jeweled Buddha image in classic Mandalay style. Dating from the beginning of the 19th century, this chapel is considered one of the finest examples of Burmese architecture in Thailand.

Situated on the grounds are several other *viharns,* a reclining Buddha, and a fascinating museum filled with Lampang artifacts such as Lanna-style candlesticks and models of *viharns.* Adjacent Wat Suchada is kept locked but note the lintels carved with dragons and flowers.

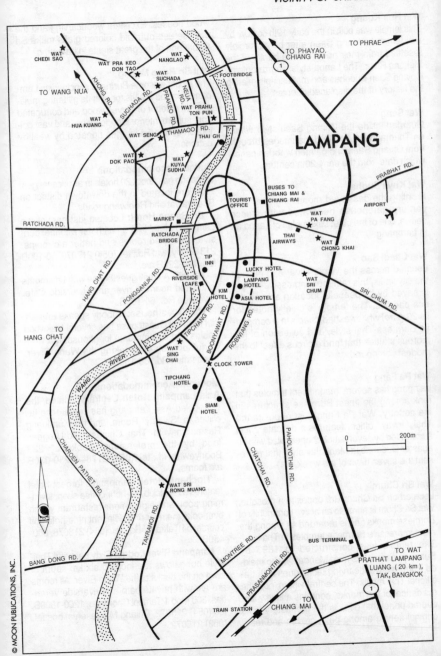

LAMPANG

TO PHRAE

TO PHAYAO, CHIANG RAI

WAT CHEDI SAO

WAT NANGLAO

WAT PRA KEO DON TAO

WAT SUCHADA

FOOTBRIDGE

KHONG RD.

SUCHADA RD.

PRAKEO RD.

NEUA RD.

WAT PRAHU TON PUN

TO WANG NUA

WAT HUA KUANG

WAT SENG

THAMAOO RD.

THAI GH

WAT DOK PAO

WAT KUYA SUDHA

PRABHAT RD.

RATCHADA RD.

TOURIST OFFICE

BUSES TO CHIANG MAI & CHIANG RAI

AIRPORT

WAT PA FANG

MARKET

THAI AIRWAYS

WAT CHONG KHAI

RATCHADA BRIDGE

TIP INN

LUCKY HOTEL

WAT SRI CHUM

HANG CHAT RD.

PONGSANUK RD.

RIVERSIDE CAFE

KIM HOTEL

LAMPANG HOTEL

ASIA HOTEL

SRI CHUM RD.

TO HANG CHAT

TIPCHANG RD.

BOONYAWAT RD.

ROBWIANG RD.

WAT SING CHAI

WANG RIVER

CLOCK TOWER

TIPCHANG HOTEL

SIAM HOTEL

0   200m

CHAROEN PATHET RD.

WAT SRI RONG MUANG

TAKRANOI RD.

CHATCHAI RD.

PAHOLYOTHIN RD.

BUS TERMINAL

MONTREE RD.

TO WAT PRATHAT LAMPANG LUANG (20 km), TAK, BANGKOK

BANG DONG RD.

PRASANMONTRI RD.

TRAIN STATION

TO CHIANG MAI

© MOON PUBLICATIONS, INC.

Wat Hua Kuang

This temple was built in the early 19th century by residents of Chiang Saen after being forcibly resettled from their home on the banks of the Mekong River. The Lanna-style *viharn* contains Chiang Saen Buddhas and manuscripts relating the history of the displaced peoples.

Wat Seng

Guarded inside the Chiang Saen-style *viharn* on Thamaoo Rd. are Buddha images brought from Chiang Saen and painted wooden panels which date from the early 20th century.

Wat Kuya Sudha

Fronting the destroyed monastery is a 15th-century gatehouse decorated with stucco deities, one of the oldest examples of Lanna art in Lampang.

Wat Chedi Sao

Located across the Wang River and outside the city limits, this rather unimpressive temple is saved by its peaceful location among the rice paddies. The temple is chiefly noted for its 20 *(sao)* whitewashed *chedis* in a composite Burmese-Thai style, and collection of humorous statues that lend a circus effect to the modest compound.

Wat Pa Fang

Lampang has several magnificent temples that rank among the finest Burmese structures in the country. Wat Pa Fang, just opposite the Thai Airways office, features a delicate *chedi* surrounded by seven small chapels filled with alabaster Buddhas in Mandalay style that represent the seven days of the week.

Wat Sri Chum

Located on Sri Chum Rd. opposite a mosque, Wat Sri Chum is home to an active community of Burmese monks and is regarded as among the most impressive Burmese temples in Thailand. The temple was constructed in 1893 by Burmese carpenters from Mandalay who melded Burmese woodcarving techniques with traditional Thai motifs. The central *viharn*, now the residence for the monks, contains a lovely lacquered panel that depicts the monastery in its original setting among palm groves and teak-wood houses. Excellent woodcarving and the profuse use of inlaid colored glass make Sri Chum one of the great sights in Lampang.

Wat Sri Rong Muang

The most awesome Burmese sanctuary in Lampang dazzles the visitor with its glittering multicolored exterior of carved wood and corrugated iron, superb interior woodcarving, and vast collection of sacred images donated by wealthy patrons.

Budget Accommodations

Lampang has about 20 hotels in all price ranges. Most are located in the downtown district on Boonyawat and Robiwang roads.

Sri Sanga Hotel: Located just east of the Lampang Hotel is a small hotel with inexpensive fan-cooled rooms and better a/c rooms. 213 Boonyawat Rd., tel. (054) 217070, 60-100B fan, 180-220B a/c.

Tip Inn: A small guesthouse with tiny rooms is located near the river and Riverside Cafe. Riverside Rd., 60-100B.

Thai Guesthouse: Nobody speaks English, but the Thai Guesthouse has several teakwood cabins and a communal longhouse in a wonderful location overlooking the Wang River. Pongsanuk Rd., 80-150B.

Moderate Accommodations

Asia Lampang Hotel: Centrally located, the remodeled Asia Lampang has conference facilities, a "Sweety" Room, and the Kumluang Restaurant with "Thai, Chinese and Uropean food by the professional cookers." 229 Boonyawat Rd., tel. (054) 217844, 250-330B a/c rooms.

Tipchang Hotel: Lampang's largest hotel features a nightclub, 24-hour coffee shop, swimming pool, and eighth-floor restaurant which overlooks the river and adjacent nine-hole golf course. 54 Takranoi Rd., tel. (054) 218078, 300-450B.

Lampang River Lodge: Sixty beautiful Thai-style bungalows are located six km south of town on the banks of the Wang River. All rooms are a/c with private bath and riverside verandas. 300 Moo 1 Tambol Chompoo, 1200-1800B, tel. (054) 215072, Chiang Mai reservations tel. (053) 215072.

Restaurants

Probably the best place to dine is in the Riverside Cafe, a teakwood restaurant operated by an Italian manager. The English-language menu offers both Thai and Western specialties. The Kumluang Restaurant inside the Asia Lampang Hotel has both an open-air dining room which overlooks the busy street and an a/c section in the rear. Lampang also has a dozen garden restaurants *(suan ahaan)* located along Takranoi, Chatchai, and Lampang-Chiang Mai roads.

Information

A small and rather useless tourist office is on Boonyawat Rd. in front of the provincial hall.

Transportation

Minibuses around town are plentiful, but many visitors prefer to hire a horse carriage for a leisurely ride in the early evening hours. Somehow the carriages reflect the confusing state of the local tourist industy, decorated in European style while the drivers are clad in cowboy outfits. Lampang is 100 km southeast of Chiang Mai and 602 km north of Bangkok. The town can be visited as a very long day-trip from Chiang Mai, or as an excellent stopover between Chiang Mai and points south.

Buses: Buses from the Arcade Bus Terminal in Chiang Mai take two hours along one of the best roads in northern Thailand. Direct bus service is also available from Phitsanulok, Sukothai, and Chiang Rai. Private bus companies in downtown Lampang sell tickets to most destinations. Another option is the ordinary buses to Chiang Mai and Chiang Rai which pass regularly on Paholyothin Rd. near the tourist office and central Lampang.

Trains: All trains between Bangkok and Chiang Mai stop in Lampang. Local minibuses go from the train station up Chatchai Rd. to the hotels on Boonyawat Road. Across from the train station is Thap Thim Thong Hotel, where simple rooms cost 60-100B.

Air: Thai Airways flies daily to Lampang from Bangkok via Phitsanulok. The Thai Airways office (tel. 054-217078) is at 314 Sanam Bin Rd. just opposite Wat Pa Fang.

ATTRACTIONS NEAR LAMPANG

Most tours to Lampang include the temples in town and a stop at Wat Prathat Lampang Luang, considered among the most impressive temples in Northern Thailand. Visitors with a motorcycle or car might also visit the nearby temples of Wat Pong Yang Kok and Wat Prathat Chomping.

Wat Pong Yang Kok

Though rarely visited by either Thais or Westerners, this exquisite little *viharn* typifies what is most natural and charming about Lanna-style architecture. The open-air *viharn* constructed of aging timbers contains an impressive interior profusely decorated with gold-leaf images of flowering plants, mandalas, golden geese, and famous bodhi tree frescoes behind the central altar. Supporting the brick-tiled roof—a feature rarely seen in modern Thailand—are teak pillars capped with studded crown pediments.

Wat Pong Yang Kok is five km south of Hang Chat on the road which connects Hang Chat with Wat Prathat Lampang Luang. The unmarked turnoff leads 50 meters to the temple, which is surrounded by a yellow wall and framed by a giant bodhi tree.

Wat Prathat Lampang Luang

Northern Thailand's finest monument is the 11th-century walled temple 20 km southwest of Lampang. Artistically, the wealth of its decorative arts and purity of architectural style make Wat Prathat Lampang Luang a singular highlight of Southeast Asian art.

The temple compound was once part of a fortified city founded in the 8th century by the legendary Princess Chamdevi of Lamphun but destroyed by Burmese invaders about 200 years ago. Today the monument is the site of several elaborate festivals such as Songkram and Loy

---

In traveling: a man must carry knowledge with him, if he would bring home knowledge.

—James Boswell,
Life of Samuel Johnson

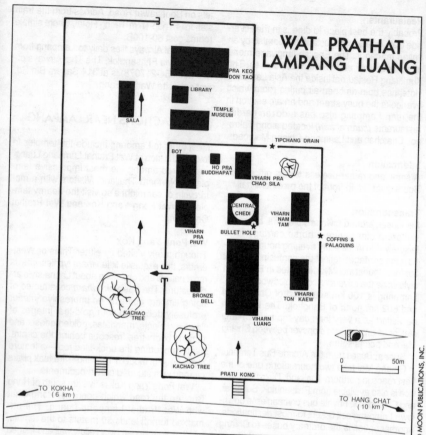

WAT PRATHAT LAMPANG LUANG

- PRA KEO DON TAO
- LIBRARY
- TEMPLE MUSEUM
- SALA
- BOT
- HO PRA BUDDHAPAT
- VIHARN PRA CHAO SILA
- ★ TIPCHANG DRAIN
- CENTRAL CHEDI
- ★ BULLET HOLE
- VIHARN NAM TAM
- VIHARN PRA PHUT
- ★ COFFINS & PALAQUINS
- BRONZE BELL
- VIHARN TON KAEW
- KACHAO TREE
- VIHARN LUANG
- KACHAO TREE
- PRATU KONG

0   50m

© MOON PUBLICATIONS, INC.

← TO KOKHA (6 km)

TO HANG CHAT (10 km)

Kratong, when thousands of pilgrims arrive to honor the jasper Buddha (Pra Keo Don Tao) and enjoy a light-and-sound show sponsored by a local preservation society.

Below the steps which lead up to the elevated compound are souvenir stalls and cafes which serve ice-cold drinks.

Main Gate: Entrance is made up of a flight of stairs guarded by mythological undulating *nagas,* and then through a magnificent 15th-century gateway. The monumental gatehouse has been decorated with delicate stuccowork and painted in brilliant shades of gold. Capping the doorway is a circular lintel, Pratu Kong, in the form of the Buddhist Wheel of the Law. A useful map is posted to the right of the central *viharn.*

Viharn Luang: First stop should be the massive *viharn* which dominates the central courtyard. Originally constructed in 1496 in the shape of an open *sala,* Viharn Luang features early 19th-century murals of the Lampang school, and a magnficent *ku* (altar) which enshrines a venerated Buddha image, Pra Chao Lan Thong, cast in 1563. Gracing the half-wall murals are images of big-nosed *farangs,* holy men, Chinese emissaries, scenes of palace life, and personages in Burmese costume.

Viharn Ton Kaew: To the right of Viharn Luang stands a small open-sided *viharn* tragically restored in 1967 with heavy concrete and whitewash which obliterated whatever artistic appeal it once possessed.

Viharn Nam Tam: Behind Viharn Ton Kaew is another small *viharn* which has blessedly been left unrestored by the local monks. The 16th-century building—possibly the oldest wooden structure in Thailand—houses a seated Buddha, four standing Buddhas, side murals etched in black and white, and a gold-leaf bodhi tree mural behind the images.

The surrounding compound gallery contains an interesting collection of ancient coffins and royal palanquins decorated with traditional Lanna motifs.

Viharn Pra Phut: To the left of Viharn Luang in the sandy courtyard is a large *kachao* tree, fine bronze bells in an open pavilion, and the so-called Buddha Viharn which dates from 1802. Ranked among the finest structures in northern Thailand, the carved wooden facade and two-tiered roof complement the harmonious proportions of the interior nave. Inside the architectural gem are several Chiang Saen Buddhas and restored murals of doves, *devas,* and gilded flowers.

Central *Chedi:* Directly behind Viharn Luang is an ungilded 45-meter *chedi* with extremely rare carved bronze plaques around the base and a gilded finial at the summit. A small bullet hole in the northwest corner is evidence of a local hero's (named Tipchang) efforts to liberate the town of Lampang. He shot and killed a Burmese general here.

Viharn Pra Chao Sila: Behind the central *chedi* is a *bot* constructed in 1476 but restored in 1924, an elevated sanctuary with a Buddha footprint, and Viharn Pra Chao Sila, possibly constructed by the father of Queen Chandevi. To the rear is a small drainage ditch where Tipchang surreptitiously entered the occupied compound to attack the Burmese general.

***Kachao* Tree:** Outside the interior compound is an immense bodhi tree supported by hundreds of sticks donated and signed by pilgrims. The pathway right leads to the following attractions.

Temple Museum: Opposite the resting pavilion is a rather dark museum containing a large bronze Buddha of the Lanna school, stone heads recovered from Phayao, and dozens of dusty manuscript cabinets.

Pra Keo Don Tao: Final stop is the unremarkable building filled with old photos of the royal family, stuffed blowfish, fake deer heads, amulets, fortune-telling sticks, and a highly revered crystal Buddha carefully protected behind two sets of iron gates. According to Buddhist legends, the image was carved from the same block of stone as the statue in Wat Pra Keo in Bangkok.

Transportation: Wat Prathat Lampang Luang is 20 km south of Lampang and six km west of the small town of Kokha. Minibuses to Kokha leave regularly from the intersection of Paholyothin and Prabhat roads in Lampang. Motorcycle taxis and *songtaos* continue from Kokha to the monument. Motorcyclists coming from Chiang Mai should turn right at Hang Chat, 10 km west of Lampang.

Elephant School

Thailand's official elephant-training camp recently moved from its old location, 54 km northeast of Lampang, to a new site between Lampang and Chiang Mai in the Tung Kwain Reforestation Center. Here in a beautiful wooded basin, mahouts train young pachyderms each morning, except on Buddhist holidays and during the hot season from March to June.

The elephant industry has changed dramatically in recent years. Once an authentic training camp for wild elephants, the ban on logging has forced local authorities to push the tourist potential of their elephant herds. The new elephant-preservation center has a small exhibit hall, museum, compound for the elephant show, and several bungalows.

The center is located well off the main road, making it essential to join an organized tour or have private transportation.

WEST OF CHIANG MAI

MAE SARIANG

This small town, midway between Chiang Mai and Mae Hong Son, serves as a good base for treks and river adventures down the Yuam and Salween rivers which separate Thailand from Burma. Progress has arrived slowly to the region, a blessing for the town, which has retained many of its fine old wooden buildings and simple temples constructed in Burmese-Shan style.

Attractions

A quick stroll around compact Mae Sariang turns up a few temples of fairly recent vintage. Wat Jong Sung (Wat Uttayarom), a modest temple which dates from 1896, fronts the more impressive Wat Sri Boonruang, which was constructed by Burmese craftsmen in 1930 in the typical architectural style of the borderlands. Wat Chong Kham down near the bridge is another example of Burmese monastic architecture with multitiered roofs, wooden latticework, and the inevitable corrugated tin roof. Overlooking Mae Sariang and strategically placed on a towering hillside is the concrete Buddha of Prathat Chom Mon, where motorcyclists can enjoy great views from the summit.

River Excursions

The main reason to visit Mae Sariang is to enjoy a boat ride down the Salween or Yuam rivers. Excursions can be organized at the Riverside Guesthouse and from Lek in the Sweet Pub. River journeys are best undertaken from December to March, just after the end of the rainy season.

Ban Mae Sam Lap: The Salween River journey begins with a jeep ride from Mae Sariang across the Danwa Range to Mae Sam Lap, a small village 46 km southwest of Mae Sariang on the banks of the Salween. Accommodations in the Riverside Huts chalets include verandas which overlook the Salween. A one-day roundtrip longtail boat journey north to Johta costs about 1500B, but this cost can be shared between eight passengers. Johta is the last town on the Thai border before the Salween veers west into Burma.

Boat trips are also possible south from Mae Sam Lap down to the junction of the Salween and Yuam rivers and the small village of Mae Leh Ta. The longtail boat races past rudimentary Burmese villages, waterfalls, and logging camps with working elephants.

Mae Kong Kha: Salween River journeys also originate from this Karen village directly west of Mae Sariang. Riverside Guesthouse has simple huts on the muddy banks.

Other Rivers: A third option is a river journey down the Yuam River, beginning from the town of Sop Moei on Highway 1085. Other tributaries of the Salween which can be rafted include the Ngao and Moei rivers.

Accommodations

Mae Sariang has a handful of simple guesthouses and hotels that cater to the steady trickle of Western tourists.

Riverside Guesthouse: Best choice in town is the lovely guesthouse overlooking the Yuam River. The breezy restaurant is a great place to relax after a long bus ride or to spend a few hours in the evening planning your river journey. Riverside has only 12 rooms, but an ambitious annex is planned across the river. 85/1 Lang Panit Rd., tel. (053) 681188, 60-350B.

Mae Sariang Guesthouse: The Mae Sariang and BR guesthouses near the bus depot are both dirty and depressing places, only suitable as an emergency crash pad when the Riverside is filled. Lang Panit Rd., 60-100B.

See View Hotel: A new place which betrays its name and offers concrete cubicles without views of the river or the "See." The modern and clean bungalows come with attached bath and quality furniture. Too bad they don't face the river. 100-150B.

Mitaree Hotel: Mae Sariang's original hotel has seen better days, though the rooms are large and kept fairly clean. Mitaree operates a so-called guesthouse next door in the old wooden wing. Mae Sariang Rd., tel. (053) 681110, 150-180B fan, 350B a/c.

WEST OF CHIANG MAI

BURMA
(MYANMAR)

DOI ANG KHANG ★

1178

MAE AW
NAPAPAK
PANG TONG
PALACE ★

KHA
HAN

BAN MAILUN

BAN MAI
MAE LANA
★ *THAM LOD CAVES*

BAN KAO

TO THATON

FISH
CAVE

NAM PLA
CHAT

BAN
JABO

BAN THAM

*CHIANG DAO
CAVES* ▲

TO
PHRAO

NA SOI

SOPPONG

SOP SOI

THAILAND

PAI

DOI CHIANG DAO
(2175 m) ▲

CHIANG
DAO

ELEPHANT
CAMP ★

MAE HONG SON

TAPAI

1265

1095

107

HOT SPRINGS ★

HOT SPRINGS ★

DOI MAE YA
(2005 m) ▲

BAN
PA PAE

MAE TAENG

108

WAT CHAN ★

TO PHRAO

KHUN
YUAM

BAN MAE
TALATA

1263

SAMOENG

MAE SA VALLEY ★

MAE RIM

TO CHIANG RAI

CHIANG MAI

HANG DONG

MAE WIN

SAN PATONG

LAMPHUN

BAN MAE
CHAN NOI

DOI
INTHANON
NATIONAL PARK ★

*VACHIRATAN
FALLS* ★

PARK
HEADQUARTERS ★

CAVE ★

PASANG

TO BANGKOK

MAE CHAEM

1192

MAE LA NOI

1088

*MAE KLANG
FALLS* ★

CHOM THONG

1184

1270

*OB LUANG
GORGE* ★

0   10km

BAN MAE
KHONG KHA

MAE TO

KONG LOI

108

HOT

BAN MAE
SAM LAP

MAE SARIANG

1085

TO MAE SOT

SOP MOEI

1099

1103

TO TAK

DOI TAO

1194

© MOON PUBLICATIONS, INC.

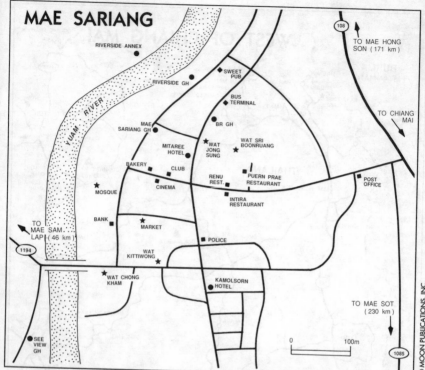

Kamolsorn Hotel: A new and modern three-story hotel with big fan-cooled rooms and private baths. Very clean and comfortable. A much better deal than the Mitaree. Wai Seuksa Rd., 200B.

Pan House: Travelers going to Mae Hong Son via the southern route can stay with Mr. Werapan Tarasan (Mr. Pan) and use his guide services for trekking and elephant excursions. Pan House is located on Hwy. 108 at Km 68, 158 km from Chiang Mai and 32 km east of Mae Sariang. Ask the bus driver to drop you at Ban Mae Wan and then hike five km south from the highway.

Restaurants

Mae Sariang is hardly a gourmet destination, though several passable Chinese and Thai restaurants are located along Wiang Mai Rd. in the center of town. The most popular seems to be **Intira Restaurant**, which serves chicken

with ginger, beef fried in oyster sauce, and fried fish with pepper and garlic. **Renu Restaurant** across the road is similar. Freshly baked goods are available from the shop adjacent to the curious **Black & White Cafe**.

A nice escape from the heat and noise can be made at the **Puern Prae Restaurant** near the entrance to Wat Sri Boonruang. This clean and quiet place serves Thai, Chinese, and "General Food" on teakwood tables across from their peaceful garden.

Transportation

Mae Sariang is 200 km southwest of Chiang Mai and 165 km from Mae Hong Son. Buses leave the Arcade Bus Terminal in Chiang Mai every two hours and take four or five hours to reach Mae Sariang. The same service is offered from the bus terminal in Mae Hong Son.

Buses from Mae Sariang to Chiang Mai depart every two hours between 0700 and 1700 from the dusty terminal on Mae Sariang Road. Service to Mae Hong Son runs from 0715 to 1530. An overnight express bus to Bangkok leaves at 1700 and arrives in Bangkok 13 hours later.

Songtaos and minitrucks from Mae Sariang to Mae Sam Lap on the Salween River and to Tak are sporadic and subject to delays. One songtao departs in the early morning for Mae Sam Lap. Another leaves for Tak down Hwy. 1085, but service usually terminates in the town of Sop Ngao or Tha Song Yang, 90 km south of Mae Sariang. The road is now fully paved, but government regulations still prevent direct service between Mae Sariang and Tak. This situation is expected to change and direct service will probably soon be available. More details on this scenic and exciting journey are given under "Mae Sot."

An airport about one km from town will be opened in early 1993.

MAE HONG SON

Tucked away close to the Burmese border and hemmed in by mountains which surround the Pai River Valley, Mae Hong Son has recently developed into one of the major destinations in northern Thailand. Before the torturous 369-km road from Chiang Mai was completed in 1965, the town served as a convenient dumping ground for disgraced bureaucrats, who graciously nicknamed it the "Siberia of Thailand."

Today, Mae Hong Son is aggressively marketed as Thailand's version of Shangri-La—complete with lost valleys, tribal trekking, caves, rivers, and waterfalls. While not the mystical vision described in tourist literature, the attractive scenery and sense of remoteness make it a welcome change from the more touristy destinations in Thailand.

Mae Hong Son also typifies the problems of rapid and unregulated development. Over the last five years, tourist arrivals have doubled annually to a present influx of over 200,000 visitors. During the high season from October through February, every flight and guesthouse is fully booked by legions of backpackers and tourists who arrive expecting to discover some quaint and forgotten destination. Mae Hong Son now has over 20 guesthouses, a post office with phone services, several banks which cash traveler's checks, trekking agencies, a handicraft center, and motorcycle rental shops. Several four-star hotels such as the Holiday Inn and Tara Mae Hong Son now cater to wealthy tourists surprised to discover traffic jams, noise, and commercialization competing with the bucolic charms of the once-neglected village.

Mae Hong Son still has a great deal of charisma, but the future is questionable unless local government authorities take strong measures to manage its growth and somehow preserve its unique heritage.

Chong Kham Lake

This natural lake was once an elephant bathing place where Chao Keun Muang, a Chiang Mai prince, set up a training camp for his newly captured herds in 1831. Several years ago, the municipality converted the area into a fitness park complete with an exercise par course and lush gardens.

More intriguing than the push-up bars are a handful of remaining wooden sangkasi houses covered with tongteung roofs and bamboo walls. A good example at 1 Singhanat Rd. still retains a tongteung-leaf roof which must be replaced every three years at a cost of over 2000 baht. Although tongteung is cooler and certainly more aesthetic, most of the old Tai Yai-style homes are now recovered with corrugated tin roofs for reasons of convenience and economics.

Wat Chong Klang

Picturesquely located on the banks of placid Jongkum Lake are two wats in typical Burmese style with tiered roofs and filigree woodwork along the eaves of the two monasteries. Fronting the grounds are a white-and-gold chedi and a small Burmese prasat that provide outstanding photographs in the misty morning hours.

Chief interest here is the famous collection of 35 wooden figures (tukatas) stored inside the small museum in the rear. Inspired by the Buddhist Vessantara Jataka, the images of starving monks and painted horses were brought from Burma in 1857. Equally famous but of less artistic appeal are the glass paintings which adorn the wall to the left of the central chamber. They also relate the story of the man who became the Buddha in his next reincarnation.

MAE HONG SON

TO PAI,
CHIANG MAI

1095

WAT DON CHEDI

THAI MASSAGE

SANG TONG HUTS

GOLDEN HUTS

BAN SUAN MAI GH

OM KHAO GH

JEAN GH

NIVAN GH

MAE HONG SON GH

SIAM HOTEL

IMMIGRATION

GARDEN GH

BUS STATION

KHUN TU GH

GALARE GH

CHENG DOI GH

PANG LO NIKITUM RD.

SASITHUN GH

PRACHA UTHIT RD.

WAT HUA WANG

MARKET

PANET WATTANA RD.

MAE TEE HOTEL

AIRPORT

SANGUAN HOTEL

NEYETPESAN RD.

CINEMA

BANK

SUNNY CAFE

FUJI FILM

SINHANAT RD.

TO AIRPORT

PEN PORN GH

TOURIST INFO

SANBANGA GH

THAI AIRWAYS

WAT KONG MU

UDOM CHOWNE RD.

CHAI MOK RESTAURANT

HOLIDAY GH

JUNGLE KING GH

WAT MOYTU

BAITONG GH

ROSE GH

CHEERS CAFE

DON'S GH

CHONG KHAM GH

BAIYOKE HOTEL

POST OFFICE

WAT PRA NAN

BLUE JEAN CAFE

CHONG KHAM LAKE

PIYA GH

RIM NONG GH

SPORTS FIELD

FERN RESTAURANT

WAT CHONG KLANG

WAT CHONG KAN

KHUNLUM PRATHAT RD.

TO MAE SARIANG (171 km)

108

0   100m

© MOON PUBLICATIONS, INC.

Wat Chong Kan

The large monastery on the left contains an elaborate gilded chair for the head monk, a strange collection of dusty typewriters, hanging Burmese gongs, and the bilingual story of sinners who descend to hell to be devoured by demons. Proper dress is required and shoes must be removed.

To the far left is a chipping building which houses the revered statue of Luang Pho To, a five-meter seated Buddha surrounded by a lovely tiled floor of blue swans and roses painted in art deco patterns.

Wat Kong Mu

The 424-meter peak at the north end of town offers great views and two *chedis* constructed in the mid-1800s by Governor Singnatraja, in the same year Mae Hong Son was declared an official Thai settlement. The *wat* also features a small monastery with an extremely beautiful Buddha carved from white alabaster and mounted on a gilded palanquin. Concrete steps lead to the summit, which is also accessible by car on a back road.

Wat Moytu

At the base of Doi Kong Mu are several temples worth exploring. The main sanctuary at Wat Moytu contains a fabulous bronze Mandalay-style Buddha mounted on an enormous palanquin. Note the benevolent yet somewhat sinister expression. To the rear and elevated on a raised platform are four unusual *chedis* embedded with hundreds of small chambers once filled with Buddhist amulets.

Wat Pra Nan

Wat Pra Nan was constructed over a century ago by a Shan ruler to enshrine a large 12-meter reclining Buddha, now swathed in a sheer orange robe. The image shows typical Burmese design with its carefully painted, realistic face that lacks the enigmatic countenance favored by Thai sculptors. To the left is a small museum with Mandalay Buddhas, Burmese laquerware, eight wall clocks, and, strangely enough, a bar of Lux soap. Behind the monastery stand a pair of stone Burmese lions which guard the old footpath up Doi Kong Mu.

Wat Pra Nan is an active pilgrimage spot that provides accommodations to Westerners for a modest donation; a good place to check when all the hotels and guesthouses are filled.

Wat Kum Ko

Visitors are also invited to spend a night in the monastery across the road from Wat Pra Nan. Constructed in 1890, Wat Kum Ko is a delightful wonderland of old religious objects including dozens of Buddhas in various styles, paintings, photographs, an elevated abbot's corner equipped with a telephone and refrigerator, and a carved 90-year-old peacock throne elevated on the central altar. This place really *feels* like Burma.

Wat Hua Wang

Several modest temples constructed in Burmese style with corrugated roofs arranged in diminishing tiers are located in the center of town. This particular temple, wedged between the morning market and the bus station, holds a highly venerated brass Mandalay-style Buddha cast in Burma and subsequently hauled over the mountains.

The adjacent market is occasionally visited by hilltribe ladies dressed in traditional garb. Fifty Burmese cheroots cost only 18 *baht*.

Trekking

Trekking in Mae Hong Son Province is a popular activity since the local population is 50% Shan (Thai Yai), 2% Thai, and 48% hilltribe people including Karens, Lawas, Lahus, Lisus, and Meos. *Farangs* are a common sight, but most villages are less deluged than those near Chiang Mai.

Popular stops near Mae Hong Son include the Shan village of Ban Mai, three km south of town, and opium fields several km to the southeast. Further treks can be arranged to the border town of Mae Aw and the small village near Na Soi where some Paduang long-necked women are held captive and shown to visitors. Crossing the Burmese border on the Pai River to visit Karenni army camps is also possible, but illegal and dangerous.

Treks cost 200-250B per day and can be arranged through guesthouses and trekking agencies such as **Don Enterprises** on the main road, **Mae Hong Son Travel** at 20 Singhanat Rd., and **Htanthong Travel** at 44 Singhanat Road. All offer short treks and longer five-day jaunts all the way to Chiang Mai. Morris at Don Enterprises and Henry at Htanthong Travel are recommended guides.

Budget Accommodations

Mae Hong Son's soaring popularity has brought dozens of guesthouses, several middle-priced hotels with a/c rooms, and five luxury hotels and countryside resorts. New facilities are being added each month. Simple rooms with fan, mattress, and common bath cost 40-60B s and 60-80B d, but the trend seems to be better rooms in the 100-200B price range.

Sang Tong Huts: Great views over ricefields and banana plantations make this somewhat remote guesthouse one of the best in Mae Hong Son. Sang Tong offers individual nipa huts plus a comfortable sitting room and small library. Rooms vary in price according to size, amenities, and how long you stay. Pracha Uthit Road, 100-200B.

Golden Huts: Adjacent to Sang Tong is a series of individual nipa huts clinging to the hillside amid trees, ferns, and winding walkways. Huts with hot showers cost extra. Traditional Thai massage and medicinal steam baths are available in the adjacent watchtower. Pracha Uthit Rd., 100-150B.

Mae Hong Son Guesthouse: Also located about 15 minutes from town is another popular guesthouse with small huts and nine wooden rooms. A good place to escape the crowds though a bicycle will be needed for local transportation. Pracha Uthit Rd., 50-100B.

Garden Guesthouse: Back in town is a quiet spot with solid, dark rooms covered with teak paneling and a great reception area. Khunlum Prathat Rd., 140-180B.

Sabanga Guesthouse: Centrally located and placed nicely back from the street, Sabanga has a small garden and elevated patio in front of the rooms with common baths. Udom Chowne Rd., 100-120B.

Jungle King Guesthouse: Offers five excellent teak rooms with mosquito nets and mattresses on the floor. Friendly management plus new bicycle rentals and trekking information. Pradit Jongkam Rd., 40-60B.

Chong Kham Lake Guesthouses: Several small places surround the wonderful lake and fitness park in the center of town. Baitong Guesthouse is a rudimentary collection of bamboo

huts on the verge of collapse, while Rose and Chong Kham guesthouses are somewhat better spots with views over the lake. Rim Nong Guesthouse is located on the southern edge. 50-100B.

Moderate Guesthouses

Piya Guesthouse: A relatively modern motel that faces a central garden. All rooms include fan and attached bathroom. Chong Kham Lake Rd., 200-250B.

Pen Porn Guesthouse: Clean and modern spot up the hill and away from the noise. All wood-decor rooms come with fan, private bath, and hot showers. Doi Kong Mu Rd., 150-200B low season, 200-250B high season.

Hotels

Baiyoke Chalet: Formerly called the Mitniyom, the Baiyoke is an older hotel with a popular a/c restaurant that converts into a disco in the evening. Nothing special, but all rooms are a/c and it's well-located in the center of town. 90 Khumlum Prathat Rd., tel. (053) 611486, 650-1000B.

Tara Mae Hong Son Hotel: Mae Hong Son came of age with the opening of this 104-room four-star hotel operated by the Imperial group of hotels. Facilities include a convention center, swimming pool, and several restaurants. Hwy. 108, Bangkok tel. (02) 254-0023, 2000-2500B.

Holiday Inn: The latest addition to the hotel scene is located south of town on the road to Mae Sariang. 114/5 Khumlun Prathat Rd., tel. (053) 612108, fax (053) 611524, Bangkok reservations (02) 254-2614, 2400-2800B.

Resorts

Several luxury resorts which cater to Thai weekenders and upscale Western travelers are found south of town.

Mae Hong Son Resort: Located six km south on the banks of the Pai River, Mae Hong Son Resort has 30 comfortable bungalows surrounded by manicured lawns, camping facilities, and a good restaurant. 24 Ban Huai Duea, tel. (053) 235344, Chiang Mai tel. (053) 236269, 1000-1200B fan, 1400-1800B a/c.

Rim Nam Glang Doi Resort: Four km south of town is another luxury resort with bungalows, campsites, and dormitory for budget travelers. Ban Huai Duea, tel. (053) 611298, 1000-1500B.

Restaurants

Night Market: A small but lively market sets up nightly in the center of Mae Hong Son near the police box and small tourist information center. Khunlum Prathat Road. Inexpensive.

Take-away: Excellent take-away dishes—some of the best food in Mae Hong Son—can be picked up from the shop near Fuji Photo. Just point to the best dishes and say *"ha baht, ha baht."* Singhanat Road. Inexpensive.

Fern Restaurant: An upscale cafe with cane furniture and backyard patio which overlooks palm trees and a small guesthouse. The gigantic menu features over 200 items. Khumlum Prathat Road. Moderate.

Blue Jean Cafe: Cozy cowboy-style joint decorated with buffalo skulls and rifles. A hangout for Thai hippies and musicians. Chong Kham Lake Road. Inexpensive.

Cheers Cafe: Inside the wild, elevated, semi-circular pub is a lakeside restaurant that serves Chinese and Thai dishes. Good views and friendly management. No, the owners have never heard of the American TV program "Cheers." Recommended. Udom Chowne Road. Moderate.

Practicalities

Tourist Information: A small information booth is located on Khunlum Prathat Rd. near the Sunny Cafe and the night market. The staff is friendly, helpful, and anxious to practice its English.

Police: Adjacent to the tourist office is a police booth which can help with emergencies.

Banks: Several banks which exchange traveler's checks at good rates are located along the main road.

Immigration: The immigration office just north of the Garden Guesthouse can extend tourist visas for an additional 30 days.

Motorcycle Rentals: Motorcycles can be rented from several agencies and guesthouses such as Khun Tu Guesthouse and a small shop near the bus station. Motorcycles cost 150-200B daily and are a great way to explore the countryside near Mae Hong Son.

Festivals: Several unique festivals are held each year in Mae Hong Son. The **Poy Sang Long** in March or April is a mass-ordination ceremony for young boys entering the Buddhist monkhood. Also called Buat Luk Kaew, this Shan festival features dozens of initiates ritualistically paraded through town on the shoulders of their relatives, one of the most visually exciting sights in Thailand.

Another unique celebration is **Chong Pala**, an October ceremony which welcomes the Lord Buddha as he returns from a visit to his heavenly mother. The week-long festival includes a candlelight procession, sword dancing, drum shows, and a parade of elaborately decorated Chong Pala floats.

Transportation

Mae Hong Son is located 368 km from Chiang Mai by the southern route through Mae Sariang on Rt. 108, or 270 km on the northern road through Pai on Rt. 1095.

Air: The most comfortable way to reach Mae Hong Son is on the three daily flights from Chiang Mai, which take 30 minutes and cost 380B one way. Tickets are heavily booked and should be reserved well in advance. It's best to purchase a roundtrip ticket and confirm return reservations immediately upon arrival in Mae Hong Son. A popular compromise is to fly to Mae Hong Son but return by bus via Soppong and Pai.

Thai Airways (tel. 053-611297) is at 71 Singhanat Rd. on the way to the terminal. Motorcycle taxis from the airport to downtown Mae Hong Son cost 10-15 *baht.*

Bus: Buses leave the Arcade Terminal in Chiang Mai every two hours from 0630 and 2100 and take 10-12 grueling hours to reach Mae Hong Son via the southern route. An overnight pause in Mae Sariang is a good way to break the ordeal. Public buses along the northern route through Pai are somewhat quicker and pass through better scenery. Pai is an excellent town to break the journey.

Buses from Mae Hong Son to Pai take four hours and depart every two hours from 0630 to 1400. Buses to Mae Sariang also take four hours and depart every two hours from 0600 to 2100.

MAE HONG SON TO SOPPONG

Excursions can be made from Mae Hong Son to several attractions north of town. Most are located off the main road and can only be reached with an escorted tour, rented motorcycle, or chartered mini-truck.

Na Soi

Twelve km north of Mae Hong Son is a left turn to the Shan village of Na Soi. The dirt road continues west to a border outpost where several long-necked women are held captive for Western tourists who must pay an additional 300B for photography privileges. An experience best avoided.

Pha Sua Waterfall

Turn left at Km 17 shortly before Huia Pha and continue past Mok Cham Pae and Huai Khan to these modest bathing falls, located 11 km off Hwy. 1095. Pha Sua Falls forms one stage of the Sa Nga River, which flows south from Burma. The falls are best visited during the rainy season, though the road is often impassable due to floods and landslides.

Mae Aw

North of Pha Sua Falls is a left turn to Pang Tong Royal Palace, where the king flies in by helicopter every year or two, and several villages inhabited by Shans and Karens.

The road continues up the mountain to Mae Aw, a desolate Hmong village controlled by renegade forces of the Kuomintang Army. Mae Aw lies directly opposite the military headquarters of opium warlord Khun Sa. Skirmishes occasionally break out between Sa and Thai battalions. For obvious reasons, this is a dangerous region best avoided during the opium season from January to May.

A public songtao to Mae Aw departs from the bus terminal in Mae Hong Son each morning around 0700 or 0800. Motorcyclists can reach Mae Aw in under two hours.

Fish Cave

Domesticated carp that measure up to one meter in length are fed papaya in Tham Pla, a rock pool 17 km north of Mae Hong Son. The fish are left unharmed since Buddhism teaches reverence for animal life. A one-km-long dry cave is situated across the road and 100 meters south. Just beyond is Huai Pha, the last town between Mae Hong Son and Soppong.

Nam Kong Wilderness Lodge

Ten km beyond Fish Cave and just past Mae Suya is a sign marking the turnoff to a wilderness lodge that offers trekking services and river excursions down the Nam Kong River. The lodge is operated by the owners of Cave Lodge near Soppong. The dirt road winds around and continues south to Mae Lana Guesthouse.

Mae Lana And Huay Hea

A Thai signpost, 56 km from Mae Hong Son and 10 km before Soppong, marks the road north to the Black Lahu village of Ban Jabo and Huay Hea, 16 km from the junction and just one km from the Burmese border. The Lahu Guesthouse in Huay Hea has simple rooms from 30B. The turnoff to Mae Lana and Huay Hea is also labeled in English with a small sign marked Mae Lana Guesthouse.

Mae Lana Guesthouse: Five km off Hwy. 1095 is the village of Mae Lana, where a French lady and her Thai husband operate the excellent Mae Lana Guesthouse. Facilities include a cheap dormitory and private rooms from 60B per night. The guesthouse is situated in beautiful countryside blessed with thick forests, cool streams, and limestone caves. Information from the guesthouse can help with treks to nearby Red and Black Lahu villages, and the trail over to the caves at Tham Lod. Mae Lana is a wonderful place to relax and escape the commercialism of northern Thailand.

SOPPONG

The small and sleepy village of Soppong chiefly serves as departure point for the nearby caves. Soppong is inhabited by Shans and Lisus who continue to wear their bright green and blue pantaloons. Several years ago the town was renamed Pang Mapha after the division of Mae Hong Son and Pai provinces.

Information on trekking is available from Jungle Trekking at the south end of town where a Burmese guide named Sunny claims to be a hilltribe multilinguist, master chef, expert masseuse, comedian, distiller of moonshine whiskey, and teacher of "Hokey Cokey" to local villagers.

Accommodations

Several guesthouses are located in Soppong. The **Central Guesthouse** behind the Islamic Restaurant is a rough but convenient spot for late-night arrivals. Better atmosphere is found at the **Jungle Guesthouse**, one km north of town and just opposite the Forestry office. Just beyond is the **Good View Lodge** where bamboo bungalows cost 50 *baht*.

Ten km beyond Soppong toward Pai, in the beautiful Lisu village of Ban Nam Rin, is the popular **Lisu Lodge**, operated by Mr. Tan, who speaks good English. A-frame chalets cost 40-70B.

Restaurants

The **Umpa Porchana Restaurant** near the bus stop has basic grub and a useful map posted on the wall which shows directions to Tham Lod and Cave Lodge. Similar meals are prepared at the **Islamic Restaurant** just across the road.

THAM LOD NATIONAL PARK

Most travelers continue from Soppong eight km north through the Lahu village of Ban Wana (Vanaluang) and the Shan village of Ban Tham to Tham Lod ("Through Cave") and a series of other limestone caves, each more than a kilometer long.

Guided cave explorations are conducted by all of the guesthouses in the region. Tham Lod National Park rangers also provide guides and lanterns to explore the vast interiors.

Tham Lod

The region's most famous cave is a huge river tunnel called Tham Lod (*tham* means cave in Thai), formed by the Nam Lang River and filled with stalactites, deep interior canyons, and prehistoric coffins carved from teak logs that resemble dugout canoes. Locals believe the immense coffins were built by unfriendly *phi* spirits that inhabit the caves, but most likely they were carved by Lawa tribesmen who lived in the northern hills long before the Thais arrived from the north. Rumor has it that another cave holds a vast amount of gold and archaeological treasures abandoned by the Japanese during their retreat from Burma.

Other Caves

Over a dozen other caves are located near Soppong. Twenty km from Tham Lod is Tham Nam Lang, an 8.3-km cave, reputedly one of the longest in Southeast Asia. Professional

spelunkers can also explore the Spirit Well—named after its shape and awesome dimensions, 100 meters across and almost 200 meters deep. Nearby Spirit Cave is where famed American archaeologist Charles Gorman conducted excavations in the mid-1960s and found evidence of human habitation dating back almost 14,000 years.

Accommodations

Situated in or near Tham Lod National Park are several bungalow operations that provide lodging, meals, guide services, and trekking advice.

Cave Lodge: Operated by Australian John Spies and his Thai wife, Cave Lodge was the first place to take advantage of the caves and surrounding topography. John has authored several articles about trekking and spelunking, and is an invaluable information source on the nearby caves. Bungalows cost 40-80B and Diu cooks tasty vegetarian meals and homemade brown bread.

Tum Lod Guesthouse: Slightly beyond Cave Lodge is another guesthouse with inexpensive bungalows and a good restaurant that serves communal meals.

National Park Bungalows: The national park also has cabins for rent.

Transportation

The road to Ban Tham and Tham Lod National Park leaves from the east end of Soppong. The hike takes about two hours or 100B by local minitruck. Treks from Ban Tham continue six km east to the Karen village of Ban Muang Paem, and 15 km west to Mae Lana. Maps are available from John at Cave Lodge.

PAI

Pai is one of the most beautiful destinations in Thailand. Situated in a broad valley surrounded by mountains and rivers, the idyllic landscape and easygoing pace of life remind you of Chiang Mai several decades ago. This is the kind of place where days lead into weeks and weeks into . . . you get the idea.

At first glance, Pai seems to be a rather nondescript town with little to offer the traveler. A closer inspection uncovers a great deal of superb attractions, from river rafting down the Pai to some of the best hilltribe trekking in northern Thailand. Added together with hot springs, mountains, and an immensely friendly population, Pai ranks as one of the last undiscovered paradises of the north.

Unlike Mae Hong Son, Pai has remained undisturbed because of its somewhat remote location midway between Chiang Mai and Mae Hong Son. Pai is blessedly free of Holiday Inns, fast-food restaurants, or an airport which could haul in planeloads of wealthy tourists. The tourist industry remains confined to simple guesthouses and small cafes that serve the needs of budget backpackers—a delightful town that will hopefully remain unspoiled well into the 1990s. Despite the growth in tourism, the standard greeting remains a lazy *"Bai nai?"* ("Where are you going?") to which you might respond *"Bai tai"* ("Just cruising") or *"Dun lin"* ("Taking a walk").

Most of the attractions in Pai are located outside town. Information on treks, river rafting, and hot springs can be obtained from all of the guesthouses. Bicycles will help you get around.

Wat Mae Yen
A 30-minute walk east of town past a Shan village is the "Temple on the Hill." Under the patronage of a community of vegetarian monks and situated at the top of a 350-step staircase, the modern temple complex offers great sunset views over Pai Valley and the surrounding mountains.

Waterfalls
Pai has several waterfalls best visited during or shortly after the monsoon season. The most popular is Morpang Falls, seven km west of town on the road past the hospital. En route to the falls are several villages inhabited by Shans, Lisus, and Kuomintang Chinese, plus the temples of Wat Houana and Wat Namhoo. Kim Guesthouse is just beyond the hospital, while Pai Mountain Lodge, with hot showers and campfire, is out near the falls.

Another small series of falls is east of town toward Wat Mae Yen.

Pong Rone Hot Springs
Eleven km southeast of town are several minor hot springs fed by bamboo pipes and located adjacent to a small stream. While hardly spectacular, Pong Rone provides a welcome soak after a long and dusty bike ride. Several of the guesthouses provide nighttime excursions to the baths.

Trekking
Pai is one of the most popular trekking areas in northern Thailand. Most treks head north and make overnight stops in Shan, Black Lahu, and Lisu villages before rafting down the Pai River. An elephant camp is also situated on the banks of the Pai River. Basic treks without elephant rides or river trips cost about 250B per day including guide services, accommodations, and all meals. Prices are fixed at the same levels in Chiang Mai. Treks can be arranged through most guesthouses and from independent agencies such as Thai Adventures.

The easiest way to avoid crowds is to skip any trek which includes a river trip or elephant ride. You have been warned.

River Trips
The Pai River and a tributary of the Ping near Doi Inthanon National Park are northern Thailand's most popular river-and-trekking destinations. Short day-trips down the Pai River begin north of town near the elephant camp. A longer multi-day journey to Mae Hong Son starts at Ban Muang Pang, 26 km south of Pai, and continues downstream to Pang Mu, eight km north of Mae Hong Son.

Arrangements can be made with **Thai Adventures** (tel 053-611077), a whitewater rafting company operated by a Frenchman from his office next to the Pai in the Sky restaurant on the main street. The three-day trip begins with a 70-km bus ride to the Nam Khong River, followed by lunch and a raft trip through canyons to an open-pavilion campsite. Day two includes waterfalls, caves, a series of Class 3 rapids, and an evening at a hot springs. Mae Hong Son is reached in the late afternoon of the third day. The rubber raft journey costs 800-1000B per person including food and all transportation from Pai.

Guesthouses
Over a dozen modest guesthouses are located in the dusty town of Pai. Most are located along the main road but the best places are found along the river and on the outskirts of town.

Charlie's Guesthouse: Conveniently located near the bus stop, Charlie's is a clean and

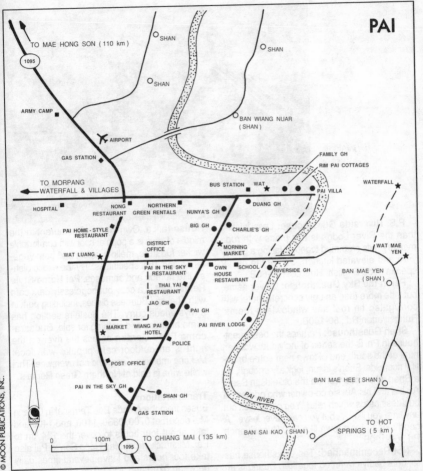

© MOON PUBLICATIONS, INC.

comfortable place with friendly management. Guide services are provided by a trilingual Shan-Karen named Seth. The owner can also direct you to Mr. Chan, a Burmese fellow who gives traditional massage and sauna smoked with special herbs. Rungsiyanon Road. Ordinary rooms cost 40-80B. Special rooms include Sweet Rooms II and III at 160B and the Sweet Room I for 200B.

Big Guesthouse: Also on the main road is another clean guesthouse with a small cafe over a pond. Rungsiyanon Road. Ordinary rooms cost 50-80B, but the larger rooms with private

bath for 100B are much better.

Nunya's Guesthouse: A two-story hotel with rooms tucked away in the back courtyard. Decent place but not as clean as Charlie's or Big Guesthouse. 84 Rungsiyanon Rd., 50-70B downstairs rooms with common bath, 100-140B upstairs rooms with private bath.

Pai River Lodge: River Lodge has a dozen bamboo huts arranged in a semicircle around the central dining area. The bungalows are fairly run-down, but the place is spacious and has a good location facing the Pai River. Huts cost 40-60B.

Pai paradise

P.S. Riverside Guesthouse: Less inviting than the River Lodge is this place with rudimentary huts crammed together facing a grassy yard and elevated kitchen. Samat the owner speaks good English. Huts cost 40-60B.

Pai in the Sky Guesthouse: Clever name, but little more than an ugly concrete motel with corrugated tin roof and windowless rooms. Rungsiyanon Rd., 60-100B.

Shan Guesthouse: Perhaps the best guesthouse in Pai is the series of individual wooden huts at the south end of town near some beautiful ricefields. Shan's is run, logically enough, by a Shan who once worked the oilfields in Saudi Arabia and his Aussie co-owner who printed up business cards which read "You can check out any time you like . . . but you can never leave." A good slogan for a town like Pai. Rungsiyanon Rd., 60-100B.

Not Recommended: Tao Guesthouse has six huts badly crammed together. Duang is an old and dusty two-story guesthouse across from the bus terminal. The road from the bus terminal to the river passes several disappointing places such as Family Guesthouse, badly overpriced Rim Pai Cottages, and the funky A-frames of Pai Villa. Back in town is the decrepit Jao Guesthouse and Wiang Pai Hotel, which should be condemned and used for firewood.

Restaurants

All of the guesthouses in Pai have simple cafes that serve Thai dishes and travelers' food. **Own House** (a.k.a. Own Home) Restaurant in the middle of town is a popular spot with comfortable wicker furniture, mellow tapes, and both vegetarian and Thai specialties. Try the exotic dishes like humus and samosas. **Pai Home-Style Restaurant** is a cozy but hopelessly dark cafe with Thai and Burmese dishes, including pork in a mysterious curry. The upstairs section has some antiques and clothing for sale. **Budsaracome Food Garden** across the river on the right is an outdoor cafe popular with local Mekong imbibers. Tasty and not oversweet Thai white wine is sold at Northern Green Rentals.

Transportation

Buses from the Arcade Bus Terminal in Chiang Mai depart at 0700, 0830, 1100, and 1400 and take about four hours to cover the 134 km to Pai. Minitrucks from Mae Hong Son to Pai also take four hours and leave several times daily between 0700 and 1300. The road from Mae Hong Son is incredibly rugged and winding, but has spectacular views over some of the most isolated regions of Thailand.

Buses from Pai to Chiang Mai depart hourly from 0630 to 1430. An a/c bus departs once daily around 1130. Passengers should arrive early and grab the first available seats. Minitrucks to Soppong and Mae Hong Son depart every two hours between 0700 and 1430.

Motorcycles can be rented from several guesthouses in Pai and from Northern Green Rentals just west of the bus station.

THE FAR NORTH AND GOLDEN TRIANGLE

Thailand's infamous Golden Triangle—properly located on the Mekong where Burma, Laos, and Thailand intersect—is the mysterious and untamed land where powerful opium warlords, remnants of Chiang Kai Shek's Kuomintang army, and communist insurgency groups once fought for control of Southeast Asia's immensely lucrative opium traffic. The Wild West image attracts large numbers of curious travelers who arrive searching for caravans of mules hauling tons of high-grade opium.

The reality is somewhat different. Smuggling continues to some degree, but visitors should also prepare themselves for modern towns, lines of tour buses, and a countryside completely in touch with the 20th century. Don't be discouraged by the commercialization—the varied scenery and sense of remoteness still make the Golden Triangle and the idyllic towns along the Mekong River an enjoyable destination.

Routes

Several different routes are possible through the far north depending on your time and interests. Visitors with only a few days should head directly for Chiang Rai and quickly see the border town of Mae Sai and the riverine towns of Sop Ruak (the actual Golden Triangle) and Chiang Saen, before returning to Chiang Mai.

Travelers with a week can explore the smaller towns and escape the tourist trail that now covers all the major spots in the north. The most popular route is an early morning bus up to Thaton (four hours north), and then the 1300 boat ride down the Kok River to Chiang Rai. After a night in Chiang Rai, head north to Mae Sai and then east to Sop Ruak and Chiang Saen. Several mountain lodges north of Chiang Rai provide great atmosphere and are excellent alternatives to city hotels. Hill villages such as Mae Salong are also worth visiting. Trekking north of the Kok River and river rafting are other popular activities.

Travelers with two or more weeks can continue exploring the very remote areas of the north, where a steady trickle of Westerners is now opening some of the last untouched regions in Thailand. Buses from Chiang Saen head east to Chiang Khong and then southeast down to Chiang Kham and Nan, an isolated town that receives rave reviews from most visitors. Heading back toward Chiang Mai, it's easy to visit the medium-sized towns of Phrae, Phayao, and Lampang.

Motorcycle touring—described at the beginning of the chapter on northern Thailand—is an excellent way to get off the beaten track and discover what is most attractive about the north.

CHIANG MAI TO CHIANG DAO CAVES

Most travelers take an early morning bus from Chiang Mai directly to Thaton and catch the 1300 longtail boat down to Chiang Rai—the most popular river journey in northern Thailand. Visitors with more time might stop at Mae Sa Valley (Km 12), Chiang Dao Elephant Camp (Km 56), and the Chiang Dao Caves (Km 69), before passing through the small town of Fang (Km 149) en route to Thaton (Km 175) on the banks of the Kok River.

Mae Sa Valley and the Chiang Dao Elephant Camp are described above under "North of Chiang Mai." An overnight stop in Thaton is highly recommended over the rushed journey taken by most travelers. Motorcyclists will pass the following towns and turnoffs en route to the caves at Chiang Dao.

Mae Malai (Km 33): Mae Malai is a small town which serves as the turnoff for Hwy.1095 to Pai and Mae Hong Son. The Mayura Restaurant on the east side of the road has cold drinks and an English-language menu.

Taeng River (Km 40): Forty km north of Chiang Mai is a left turn to several villages on the Taeng River used for river journeys by trekking agencies in Chiang Mai.

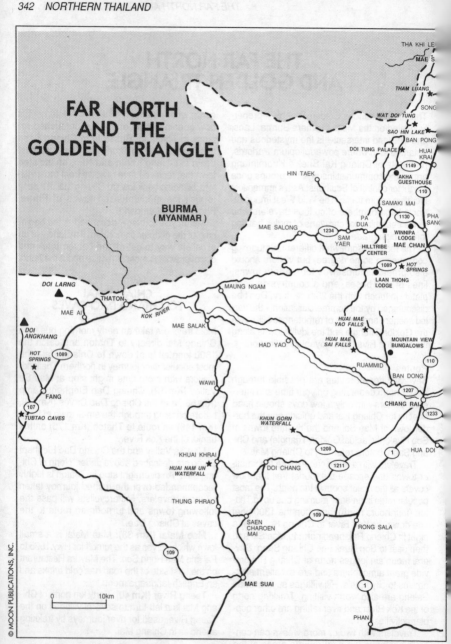

FAR NORTH
AND THE
GOLDEN TRIANGLE

BURMA
(MYANMAR)

THA KHI LE
MAE S
THAM LUANG
SONG
WAT DOI TUNG
SAO HIN LAKE
BAN PONG
DOI TUNG PALACE
HUAI
KRAI
1149
AKHA
GUESTHOUSE
HIN TAEK
110
SAMAKI MAI
1130
PHA
SANG
PA
DUA
MAE SALONG
1234
SAM
YAER
HILLTRIBE
CENTER
WINNIPA
LODGE
MAE CHAN
DOI LARNG
MAUNG NGAM
1089
HOT
SPRINGS
THATON
KOK RIVER
LAAN THONG
LODGE
MAE AI
MAE SALAK
HUAI MAE
YAO FALLS
DOI
ANGKHANG
HAD YAO
HUAI MAE
SAI FALLS
MOUNTAIN VIEW
BUNGALOWS
HOT
SPRINGS
1089
RUAMMID
110
1207
BAN DONG
FANG
WAWI
107
CHIANG RAI
TUBTAO CAVES
1233
KHUN GORN
WATERFALL
HUA DOI
KHUAI KHRAI
1208
HUAI NAM UN
WATERFALL
1211
DOI CHANG
THUNG PHRAO
109
SAEN
CHAROEN
MAI
RONG SALA
1
MAE SUAI
109
1
PHAN

0   10km

© MOON PUBLICATIONS, INC.

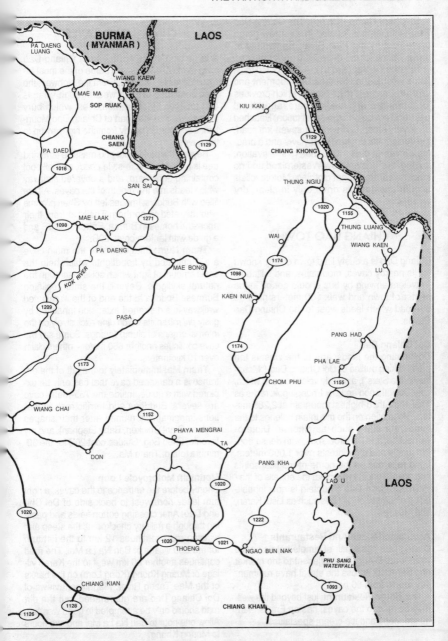

Elephant Camp (Km 56): The Chiang Dao Elephant Camp is located in a narrow gorge carved out by the Ping River. Remember to arrive in time for the daily 0930 performance.

Hilltribe Center (Km 61): A signposted track leads west to the Hilltribes Development and Welfare Center, a royal project which provides local hilltribes with medical care, agricultural help, and advice on crop substitution. Reached up a *very* steep and winding seven-km road, the center offers magnificent views and a bracing climate at over 1,000 meters in elevation, but the hilltribes are now Westernized and no longer wear traditional clothing. Motorcyclists should attempt this drive only in clear, dry weather.

CHIANG DAO TOWN

Chiang Dao is a dusty little town chiefly known for its nearby caves, mountains, and hilltribes. Travelers arriving by bus should get off in the center of town and walk 100 meters north to the road which leads west to the Chiang Dao Caves.

Doi Chiang Dao

Dominating the landscape to the west is the breathtaking outline of Doi Chiang Dao ("Mountain to the Stars"), a moody volcanic cone which, after Doi Inthanon and Doi Phahompok, ranks as Thailand's third-highest mountain at 2,285 meters. Vegetation on the mountain belongs to the temperate class such as Shorea, Dipterocarpaceae, and Dipterocarpus, with dense tropical jungle and pine forests over 1,000 meters. Long regarded as the home of magical spirits and animist ghosts which eat the entrails of their victims, Chiang Dao Mountain is now inhabited by a number of hilltribes such as Lisu, Karen, and Musers.

Accommodations And Restaurants

Chiang Dao has a pair of simple hotels on the main road. **Dieng Dao** adjacent to the market and **Santisuk** across the street have rudimentary rooms from 60 *baht*.

Our House Restaurant, just beyond the well-marked road to the caves, has an English-language menu and ice cream specialties.

CHIANG DAO CAVES

A large sign at the north end of Chiang Dao town marks the left turn to some of the most famous caves in Thailand. From the highway, the road continues five km west through villages and tobacco fields to the caves, which bury themselves into the heart of Chiang Dao Mountain. *Songtaos* go hourly from the highway up to the caves.

Beyond the parking lot and massive tamarind tree is an old Burmese-style *chedi*, a small pool containing tame carp, and a covered stairway which leads into the mouth of the caves. All are filled with Buddhist images left by Shan pilgrims who migrated to northern Thailand from their ancestral homes in Burma. Entrance is 5B and a guide with lantern costs 20B.

Tham Num: Images inside the main cave are illuminated by floodlights which help the small amount of light which spills in through the natural skylights. Beyond the small reclining Burmese Buddha at the end of the illuminated walkway is a darkened extension inhabited by grisly *phi rob* spirits which dine exclusively on the internal organs of plump *farangs*. Some say the cave continues another 660 meters, others claim over 10 kilometers.

Tham Ma: Immediately to the left of the entrance is a darkened cave that can only be explored with a guide. Inside the 735-meter cave are several Buddhas and terrific rock formations imaginatively named after their shapes such as Giant Chicken, Baby Elephant, and my favorite, Fried Egg. Guides cost 20B for the 30-minute tour of Tham Ma.

Mountain Motorcycle Loop

Shortly before the entrance to the caves, a right turn leads northwest to back side of Doi Chiang Dao. After crossing cotton fields and passing through a military checkpoint, the steep and winding road continues 12 km to the left turn for the Lisu village of Ban Na La Mai. The road continues another 20 km west to the Karen village of Muang Khong (Kong Lom) on the banks of the Mae Taeng River. Magnificent views of Doi Chiang Dao are guaranteed, but the dirt road should only be attempted in good weather. Allow one hour to Ban Na La Mai and two hours to Muang Khong.

Rather than turning left to Ban Na La Mai, you can continue north to Thung Khao Phuang and Muang Na near the Burmese border. Once again, this route should only be attempted in good weather and with a full tank of gas.

TUBTAO CAVES AND HOT SPRINGS

Three km west of Highway 107, and marked with a signpost at Km 117, are several caves which have served as pilgrimage centers for several centuries. Beyond the parking lot and small meditation huts are two staircases which lead to Tham Pha Kha ("Light Cave") on the right, and Tham Phan Jak ("Dark Cave") on the left. Light Cave guards a large seated Buddha and a 10-meter reclining image surrounded by statues of kneeling devotees. Guides with lanterns must be hired to explore the recesses of Dark Cave.

Eight km west of the caves is a town called Ban Mai Nong Por, established over a century ago by Chinese migrants from Yunnan Province. To a measurable degree, the town still retains the flavor, customs, and cultures of China, in a fashion similar to the Chinese village of Mae Salong north of Chiang Rai. Tucked away in the east end of town are several small hot springs that offer both communal and private baths.

Doi Angkhang

Motorcyclists might also enjoy the steep and winding 26-km road up to the summit of Doi Angkhang on Rt. 1248, which leaves Hwy. 107 at Km 134. One of the most spectacular motorcycle rides in northern Thailand, this dirt and gravel road offers great scenery and magnificent views over Fang River Valley. En route to the summit is a small Lahu hilltribe village where a government research station raises temperate fruits and sponsors reforestation projects.

FANG

Fang is a small and rarely visited town 151 km north of Chiang Mai. The region produces rice and a good-quality Virginia tobacco which is dried in striking brick kilns, easily visible from the highway. Top draws are trekking and the nearby hot springs.

History

Fang was founded in 1268 by King Mengrai as an important trading center for the Lanna kingdom. Destroyed by the Burmese in the early 18th century, Fang recently served as an important opium-smuggling center until the government allowed remnants of Chiang Kai Shek's Kuomintang Army to settle in the region and act as an independent border patrol. A Wild West atmosphere characterized the town until the mid-1970s, when opium warlord Khun Sa was finally driven from the region into the thick forests of Burma. Today, this modern town is firmly under the supervision of the Thai military and government officers.

Attractions

Fang today is occasionally visited by travelers who hire guides and conduct treks in the foothills to the west. The region is essentially free of opium pirates, though the security situation should be checked before setting out. Guides can be hired from most of the guesthouses. A Dutch guy near Mukda's Bar and the cinema can also help.

A signposted turnoff opposite the police station marks the road to the Fang Horticultural Station, where crop substitutes such as coffee

and apples are grown by local hilltribes. The road continues another 2.6 km to Ban Nam Rawn sulfur springs, where some of the boiling springs have been capped for geothermal energy. A small geyser on the right side of the road erupts every 30 minutes.

Motorcyclists can make a scenic diversion west from Mae Ai at Km 165, some 17 km north of Fang. The road goes 5.6 km west toward Doi Larng, once the home of Khun Sa, then turns north to a new road which backtracks to Thaton.

Accommodations

Fang is divided into the new town near the bus station in the south, and an older residential and business district in the north past the curve.

Crocodile Dundee Guesthouse: One km before the new town is a clean and popular guesthouse operated by Sayan Matayomehana, who worked on locally made films such as *Killing Fields, Year of the Dragon,* and *Rambo III.* His Thai ladyfriend named Amara (Taew) teaches massage and Thai cooking and leads treks to nearby Akha and Lahu villages plus visits to the hot springs at Ban Nam Rawn. 9 Moo Ta Vieng Rd., tel. (053) 451187, 50B per person.

New Wieng Kaew Guesthouse: The remainder of the guesthouses and hotels in Fang are located in the northern section where the road curves right and continues up to Thaton. Wieng Kaew has trekking information and several old bungalows for 80-140B.

Ueng Khum Hotel: Down the road from the Wieng Kaew is a better set of bungalows with clean rooms facing a pleasant courtyard. Rooms cost 80-150B.

Chok Thani Hotel: The only semiluxurious hotel in Fang is on the highway near the municipal administration building. Fan-cooled rooms cost 160B, while a/c rooms go for 220-280B.

THATON

This picturesque town on the banks of the Kok River chiefly serves as the launching point for downriver trips to Chiang Rai. Thaton is a very pleasant place to spend an evening and gather information for the river trip and hikes through the Golden Triangle region.

Wat Thaton

An imposing white Buddha, who seems to be contemplating the steady stream of Western travelers, dominates the town from the hillside to the west. Excellent views over the valley can be enjoyed by hiking the staircase from the main road or the pathway behind Thip's Travelers House.

Trekking

Self-guided treks to nearby villages are easy but less than pristine since this region has been trekked for over 20 years. Caution should be exercised since robberies remain a nagging problem despite the presence of the Thai police. Many of the villages can now be reached by public *songtaos* or hiked from stops along the Kok River.

A map of the Kok River published by Joseph S. several years ago is useful, but the single most important piece of information is the *Guide Map of Chiang Rai* published by Bangkok Guides and available from bookstores in Chiang Mai.

Accommodations

Several inexpensive guesthouses are located along the Kok River.

Thip's Guesthouse: Slightly upriver from the bridge is the best guesthouse in Thaton, operated by a talkative Thai woman named Thip who once worked with American GIs during the Vietnam War. Kok River Rd., tel. (053) 245538, simple bamboo bungalows cost 50B.

Thaton House: Across the river is a quiet guesthouse with 12 rooms facing a courtyard garden. All rooms include private bath and fan for 60-90B.

Apple Guesthouse: Directly opposite the boat launch is an old favorite with rudimentary rooms and a popular cafe.

Thaton Cottages: An upscale and clean operation with individual cottages and private baths. Located about 300 meters south of the main road. Bungalows cost 250-400B.

Mae Kok River Lodge: This amazing resort complex is wonderfully located on the banks of the river amid lychees and coconut palms, with Thai-style chalets and a great restaurant over the river. Amenities include a small swimming pool, animal sanctuary, and Track of the Tiger tour agency. Mae Kok River Lodge is owned

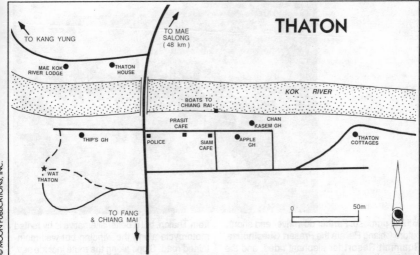

and operated by a pair of Irishmen named Tony and Shane. Budget travelers staying at Thip's often congregate here in the evenings for drinks and conversation. Ban Thaton, tel. (053) 211997, ext. 203, Chiang Mai reservations (053) 215366, 550-850B.

Transportation

Buses to Fang and Thaton depart from the Chang Puak Bus Terminal north of the White Elephant Gate in Chiang Mai at 0600, 0720, 0800, and 1130, but only the first three departures reach Thaton in time for the boat ride to Chiang Rai. Mini-trucks continue from Fang to Thaton.

KOK RIVER JOURNEYS

The main reason to visit Thaton is the river journey down to Chiang Rai. Longtail boats leave Thaton around 1230, cost 160B per person, and take four or five hours down the Mae Kok to Chiang Rai. Brief stops are made at Mae Salak for police registration and photos of the hanging bridge, and at the Highland Forestry Development Project for cold drinks. The trip is best undertaken during the high waters from October to January.

Early stages of the journey are relatively uncommercialized, but lower sections toward Chiang Rai are plagued with refreshment stalls, souvenir shops, TV antennas, and tacky signs announcing "Lahu Village." Longtail boat rides are exciting and provide a glimpse of the countryside, but not everyone is thrilled with the speed, noise, and cramped quarters.

Bamboo houseboats, constructed per order from Thip's Guesthouse in Thaton, are an excellent alternative to a frenzied longtail ride. Six-man bamboo rafts with cabin and primitive lavatories cost 2500B per boat and take three relaxing days to Chiang Mai . . . if they don't capsize on the rocks during the dry season from February to June. The boats are then resold to other travelers who continue downriver to Chiang Saen.

Guesthouses

Several guesthouses are located on or near the Kok River between Thaton and Chiang Rai. **Ban Mai Guesthouse**, on the north side of the river just opposite Mae Salak, has trekking information and simple bungalows from 40B. The oldest operation in the region is the infamous **Karen Coffee Shop** (also called Phanga's House) located between the river and the Chinese Kuomintang village of Ban Maung Ngam on the Thaton-Mae Salong road. Karen Coffee Shop is a freak center with information on treks, elephant rides, and ways to idle away weeks

without purpose. Farther downriver and shortly before Chiang Rai are the **Prasert Guesthouse**, **Ruammit Resort** for elephant rides, and the **Iam Sam Ang** on the south side of the river. All charge 40-60B.

Trekking From The Kok River

Treks starting from the Kok River are another alternative. Hikes can be made from a dozen different drop-off points such as Ban Mai and Mae Salak, but bring along food, appropriate clothes, small change, gifts, and a sense of caution. Robberies are still a problem, so leave your valuables in Chiang Mai.

The most popular trek begins from the Lahu village of Mae Salak, about one hour downriver from Thaton, and heads south to Wawi where more than 13 different tribes live in a large village on the Mae Nam Wawi. Pick-up service is available from Wawi to Fang, Mae Salak, and Mae Suai. The trek continues south from Wawi to the Lisu villages of Huai Khrai and Doi Chang, and through the enormous Akha village of Ban Saen Charoen Mai to Mae Suai on Highway 1019. The *Guide Map of Chiang Rai* by Bangkok Guides has an excellent detail map of the region.

THATON TO MAE SALONG

A great alternative to the Kok River journey is the new dirt road which connects Thaton with the Chinese village of Mae Salong, 48 km to the northeast. Mini-trucks leave in the early morning

from Thaton, but a better alternative is by rented motorcycle along the winding but well-maintained road. Stops along the route include several mountain lodges operated by various hilltribes, and the Chinese Kuomintang village of Hua Maung Ngam where a small shop has drinks and meals. Hilltribe touts with goods for sale and rooms for rent often wave frantically at passing motorcyclists.

The road is relatively flat until the final section, which climbs steeply through the mountains until it reaches the isolated village of Mae Salong, more properly called Ban Santikhiri.

Unlike Fang and the Golden Triangle town of Sop Ruak, this region remains under the control of opium cartels, which move tons of narcotics from Burma down to Chiang Mai and Bangkok. Although travelers who proceed directly through the region are rarely hassled, it's wise to avoid wandering around or acting curious about the heavily laden trucks. Keep your camera well hidden.

CHIANG RAI

Chiang Rai is a drab, medium-sized city without the hustle—or the great sights—of Chiang Mai. Despite the concrete monotony of the architecture and lack of major attractions, tourism is on a sharp rise, as indicated by the crowds and the amazing hotel developments being laid on the bewildered metropolis. Without charm or character, Chiang Rai is best considered a brief

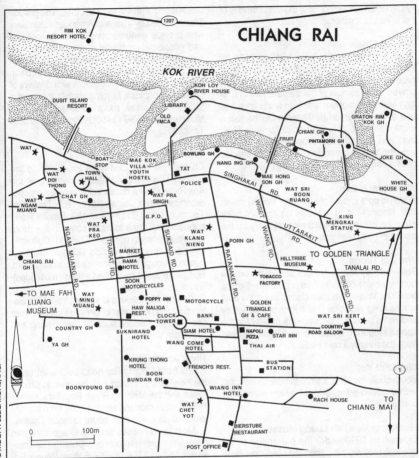

stop en route to the more idyllic towns farther to the north and east.

History

The city was founded in 1262 by King Mengrai as the nation's first independent kingdom, but the fickle king later moved his forces south to Lamphun and finally to Chiang Mai. Chiang Rai served as a trading center and focal point for struggles between Siam and Burma until 1786, when it was incorporated into the Thai kingdom.

Wat Pra Keo

Chiang Rai's monuments are modest structures which lack the architectural or historic interest of temples in Chiang Mai. This gaudily restored temple is chiefly noted for its recently reconstructed *chedi* where, according to legend, the Emerald Buddha was discovered in 1436 and later moved to Wat Pra Keo in Bangkok. In front of the *chedi* stands a wooden Lanna-style *bot* constructed in 1890 and now filled with several bronze images including an early Chiang-Saen statue, perhaps the largest example of its type in Thailand.

A replica of the famous Emerald Buddha was installed at Wat Pra Keo in late 1991. The image was carved in Beijing from a block of high-quality Canadian jade in honor of the 90th birthday of the princess mother.

Wat Pra Singh

Originally constructed from 1345 to 1400 by King Mahaproma, Wat Pra Singh contains a reproduction of the Pra Buddha Singh now displayed in the temple of the same name in Chiang Mai. The modern *wat* also features a fine pair of doors carved by Thawan Duchanee, a local artist who achieved great fame in Thailand and among international collectors. Also note the temple guardians with penises shaped after a serpent and an elephant's head.

Wat Ngam Muang

Situated up a short flight of *naga*-flanked stairs, Wat Ngam Muang features an ancient brick *chedi* constructed in 1318 as a reliquary for the ashes of King Mengrai.

Wat Doi Thong

This recently rebuilt temple atop a hill on the northwest side of town offers superb views of the Mae Kok Valley. Tradition claims this is the spot where King Mengrai first surveyed the valley and the site which became his capital for the Lanna kingdom. Better views can be enjoyed from the nearby Town Hall.

Wat Chet Yot

South of city center is a small temple constructed with a seven-pointed *chedi* which names the complex.

Hor Kham Mae Fah Luang Museum

Opened in 1990 under the patronage of the princess mother, this Lanna-style two-story teakwood museum contains a small but impressive collection of local handicrafts and religious artifacts. Chief draws are the wooden Buddha images, candelabras used in Lanna ceremonies, and carved wooden screens that represent the best of Lanna craftsmanship. The museum is on Rajyotha Rd. (the western extension of Tanalai Rd.) four km west of city center.

PDA Hilltribe Museum

Perhaps the most fascinating sight in Chiang Rai is this museum opened in 1990 by the Population and Community Development Association (PDA), a nongovernmental organization which works with the local hilltribes. The ground floor is staffed by Thai and American volunteers who provide genuine insight into the political and economic problems of the hilltribes. The second floor serves as a handicraft showroom and bookstore, while the third floor has been converted into a superb museum with displays of costumes, baskets, farming implements, and a slide show in an a/c room in the rear. The PDA Museum (tel. 053-713410) is located at 620/25 Tanalai Road.

Trekking

Chiang Rai is a good base for exploring the Golden Triangle and initiating journeys on the Kok River. Over a dozen trekking agencies offer organized tours. James Nelson with **Thai-Kiwi Tours** (tel. 053-711943) at 183 Tanalai Road sponsors trail-bike tours to some of the more remote regions in northern Thailand. Culturally sensitive tours to hilltribe villages are best booked through the PDA office described above. Budget treks can be booked through most guesthouses.

Self-guided trekking is easiest from Mae Salong, 67 km northwest of Chiang Rai, and from the mountain lodges such as Laan Thong and Mountain View.

River Journeys

Boats from Chiang Rai head both west up to the Kok River to Thaton and downriver to Chiang Saen and the Mekong River. Regular longtails depart each morning around 1000 from the city pier and take about six hours to reach Thaton.

Most guesthouses and travel agencies can help with downriver journeys. **Chiang Rai Travel** (tel. 053-713314) at 869/95 Pram Wipark Rd. across from the Wang Come Hotel organizes a four-day river journey down the Mae Kok River to Chiang Saen and the Mae Khong (Mekong) River. Prices vary dramatically, so shop around for the best deal and avoid the expensive agencies in the luxury hotels.

Guesthouses

Chiang Rai has exploded with dozens of new guesthouses in recent years. Older facilities are uniformly run-down and dirty, but many have refurbished themselves into better haunts. Operators are always on hand at the bus station and to greet boat arrivals from Thaton.

Chat Guesthouse: Several years ago the old Chat moved to a much nicer location in a small alley near the boat landing. Chat has a cozy cafe, laundry services, and information on trekking. Trairat Rd. Soi 1, tel. (053) 711481, 50-80B, 120B for luxurious doubles with hot showers. Recommended.

Koh Loy River House: A new place on the river behind the old YMCA, with spacious grounds and a pleasant restaurant overlooking a tributary of the Kok River. All rooms are large, clean, and include private bath with hot showers. 485 Tanam Rd., tel. (053) 715084, 120-140B rooms on the upper floors, 200B for individual A-frame chalets. Very good value.

Pintamorn Guesthouse: Operated by some Germans and a Hawaiian named Bob Watson, Pintamorn compensates for its isolated location with clean rooms, good food, and some of the best-condition motorcycles in Chiang Rai. 199/1 Mu 21 Soi Wat Sriboonruang, tel. (053) 714161, 60-120B with private bath.

Ya House: The old Lek Guesthouse is a funky, cramped, but popular place with communal rooms and five bamboo bungalows in the rear courtyard. The friendly owners conduct treks and provide free bicycles to their guests. 163/1 Banphaprakan Rd., tel. (053) 713368, 40-80B.

Fruit Guesthouse: Tucked away in a quiet residential neighborhood and overlooking a small creek, Fruit offers good vibes and a great escape from the hustle of Chiang Rai. Rustic but adequate facilities include rooms in the teakwood house, several individual bungalows, and a sign which reads "We Wish You Happiness . . . Take It Easy." A tricycle from the pier costs 10B. 91/2 Kohloy Rd., 60-100B.

Chian House: A modern hotel with solid walls, clean rooms with Western toilets and hot showers, and a small pool. The manager, Kiti Kumdee, is friendly and speaks good English. 172 Sriboonrong Rd., tel. (053) 713388, 80-120B small rooms, 100-150B large rooms.

Mae Kok Villa Youth Hostel: Like most other hostels in Thailand, the branch located in Chiang Rai is poorly run, poorly maintained, and best avoided. 445 Singhakai Rd., tel. (053) 771786, 140-220B.

Country Guesthouse: Country is a good example of the difficulties of writing travel guidebooks. When I researched Chiang Rai for my *Southeast Asia Handbook*, Country Guesthouse was a wonderful place with clean rooms at fair prices. When I returned to research *Thailand Handbook*, the guesthouse had been abandoned and replaced with an ugly concrete monstrosity without charm or character. Manager Elisa Tungboontina has recently constructed a large seven-story hotel called Sampho that overshadows the old residential guesthouse. All this happened in less than 18 months! 389 Banphaprakan Rd., tel. (053) 712994, 120-150B in the rear guesthouse.

Not Recommended: Pon House is an attractive teakwood house cursed with surly management. Graton Rim Kok is isolated and deserted, as is the similar Chiang Rai Guesthouse. Boonyoung Guesthouse is a collection of old A-frames crammed into a narrow alleyway. Bowling Guesthouse and Star Inn have small, grungy rooms. Joke Guesthouse is a terrible joke.

Moderate Accommodations

Chiang Rai has several midpriced hotels that bridge the gap between budget guesthouses and the luxury hotels.

Boon Bundan Guesthouse: The best deal in town has 36 new rooms centrally situated near the bus station and clock tower. All rooms are clean, modern, and include private bath with hot showers. Boon Bundan also has a fine restaurant, pool, trekking services, and rental motorcycles. 1005/13 Chet Yod Rd., tel. (053) 717040, fax (053) 712914, 150-250B fan, 350-400B a/c.

Rach House: A small but very clean hotel tucked away in a back alley away from the noise of Chiang Rai. All rooms are a/c with private bath and hot showers. Good value, and not a *farang* in sight. 90/2 Sanpanard Rd., tel. (053) 715969, 300-400B.

Golden Triangle Guesthouse: Right in the heart of Chiang Rai is this small hotel that blends modern amenities with traditional touches such as thatched walls, teakwood furniture, and Thai paintings. The owners, a Thai man and his American wife, also operate a terrace cafe and popular touring company. 590 Paholyothin Rd., tel. (053) 711339, fax (053) 713963, 700-900B.

Suknirand: Located at 424 Banprapakan, rooms run 200-360B singles and doubles; tel. 711055.

Luxury Accommodations

Wiang Inn: Top choice in the center of town is the three-star Wiang Inn Hotel with swimming pool, several restaurants, disco, and traditional massage parlor. Popular with tour groups and well located near the bus station and night market. 893 Paholyothin Rd., tel. (053) 711543, fax (053) 711877, 1400-1800B.

Wang Come Hotel: A big hotel with all the standard amenities including a circular pool, lively coffee shop, convention facilities, and "luxurious massage parlor with 50 pretty, fully qualified masseuses." Rooms are small but well appointed with Lanna-style furnishings. 896 Pemawiphata Rd., tel. (053) 711800, fax (053) 712973, 1500-2000B.

Rim Kok Resort: Although inconveniently located across the river, the Rim Kok offers great views, striking restaurants, and a wonderful pool shaped like a blue amoeba. The lack of customers has kept rates low and open to negotiation. 6 Moo 4 Tatorn Rd., tel. (053) 716445, fax (053) 715859, Bangkok reservations (02) 279-0102, 1800-2400B.

Dusit Island Resort: The splashiest addition to Chiang Rai's expanding tourist scene has been erected on a large delta island in the Mae Kok River. A taxi is necessary to shuttle between town and this enormous hotel. 1129 Kraisorasit Rd., tel. (053) 715777, fax (053) 715801, Bangkok reservations (02) 238-4790, 3200-3800B riverview rooms.

Restaurants

Most of the restaurants in town are located in the alleys near the Wang Come Hotel.

Night Market: Though it pales in comparison to the grand affair in Chiang Mai, a small but lively night market with foodstalls operates on Trairat and Tanari roads near the Wang Come Hotel. Nearby are several small go-go bars, Thai cafes, Turkish massage parlors, trekking agencies, and souvenir shops.

Haw Naliga Restaurant: Listed in every tourist guide is this Thai-Chinese garden restaurant located near the clock tower. Dishes recommended by Joe Cummings in his Lonely Planet guide have been carefully noted on the English-language menu. Way to go, Joe. 402 Banphaprakan Road. Moderate.

Cheap Cafe: The corner cafe just east of the clock tower has great dishes for just 20B, plus a friendly manager who cooks, serves, and collects the money. Clock Tower Circle. Inexpensive.

Bierstube: Karl Leinz from Mainz runs a small cafe that serves Thai dishes prepared by his wife, and German specialties from sauerkraut to weisswurst. A popular spot for local expatriates. Karl also runs a trekking agency and has motorcycles for rent. 897 Paholyothin Road. Moderate.

French's: Big buffalo steaks and cold beer are served in this cozy cafe located on restaurant row. Chet Yot Road. Moderate.

Baitong Cafe: Australians Ken Jones and Ray Sawyer operate the popular restaurant just opposite the Wang Come Hotel. 869 Pemawipat Road. Moderate.

Napoli Pizza: Best Italian dishes and pizzas in Chiang Rai are served in the expatriate favorite just up from the night market. 595 Paholyothin Road. Moderate.

Boat Stop Cafe: A riverside setting and decent Thai food make this funky cafe worth a visit at sunset. Kok River boat landing. Inexpensive.

Shopping

Shopping in Chiang Rai is disappointing when compared to the wonders of Chiang Mai, but the situation seems to improve with each passing year.

Chiang Rai Handicraft Center: The largest collection of hilltribe shops in Chiang Rai is located four km out of town on the highway to Mae Sai. The center also has ceramics, celadon, textiles, carved woodwork, jewelry, and an adjoining factory which produces much of the pottery and cotton goods.

Ego: Across from the Wang Come Hotel is an upscale shop with a fine collection of hilltribe handicrafts and designer silk clothing.

AIM Department Store: South of town and opposite the Little Duck Hotel is a shopping mall with several stores that specialize in northern Thai handicrafts.

Ban Du: *Sa* paper is still produced with traditional methods in the village of Ban Du, a few kilometers north of Chiang Rai at Km 834. A small sign points the way to the paper demonstration house.

Practicalities

Tourist Information: The TAT plans to open a tourist office in Chiang Rai, but only after such tourist hot spots as Nakhon Si Thammarat and Khon Kaen have branches. Talk about messed-up priorities! In the meantime, check with other travelers and guesthouse operators for the latest information on treks, river trips, and accommodations in other northern towns.

Motorcycle Rentals: Several shops and guesthouses rent motorcycles, but most bikes have been badly trashed and are unsafe for exploring the hills of Northern Thailand. Bikes in better condition are available from the Bierstube Restaurant and Pintamorn Guesthouse. Soon Motorcycles on Trairat Road is the largest rental agency in town. Daily rates are about 150-200B for a 100cc or 125cc motocross, or 250-300B for a large 250cc model.

Festivals: Each February the city sponsors a week of traditional northern culture during the colorful Wai Sa Mae Fah Luang Festival. Activities include the re-creation of an old northern market, an afternoon parade with participants from 73 provinces, Shan folkloric plays, and a theatrical sound-and-light show based on a legendary king who predates the founding of Chiang Rai.

A Lychee Festival is held in May.

Transportation

Chiang Rai is 844 km north of Bangkok and 180 km northeast of Chiang Mai.

Air: Thai Airways flies twice daily from Bangkok for 1800B and Chiang Mai for 400B. Thai Airways has offices in town at 870 Paholyothin Road (tel. 053-711179) and at the airport (tel. 053-711464), four km south of city center. The airport has a bank exchange and taxis which charge 50B to most hotels and guesthouses.

Bus: Buses leave every 30 minutes from 0600 to 1600 from the Arcade Bus Terminal in Chiang Mai. Note that buses follow two different routes. The direct route on Highway 1019 via Doi Saket and Wiang Papao takes about four hours, while the old route via Lampang and Phayao takes almost seven hours. Check carefully. Buses following the old route can also be picked up at the Nawarat Bridge.

Buses from Chiang Rai to Chiang Mai depart every 30 minutes from 0600 to 1600. Air-conditioned first-class buses leave at 0800, 1200, and 1645, and only take two hours to Chiang Mai. Ordinary buses to Bangkok leave

hourly from 1530 to 2000 and take 12 hours, while a/c buses depart at 1800, 1830, and 1900 and take 10 hours. Buses to Mae Sai, Chiang Saen, and Chiang Khong depart every 20 minutes from 0600 to 1800.

KOK RIVER REGION

Highway 110 leaves Chiang Rai and heads north up to Mae Sai and the Burmese border. Several mountain lodges and hilltribe treks are located between Chiang Rai and Mae Chan, along and just north of the Kok River. Excellent detail maps of the Kok River and Mae Chan district are provided on the *Guide Map of Chiang Rai* published by Bangkok Guides.

Highway 1207: About one km beyond the Kok River Bridge is the paved highway which leads west and skirts the Kok River. First stop on the south side of the highway is the enormous Rimkok Resort Hotel. A dirt path one km farther leads down to Bank & Boom's Guesthouse on the river, where bamboo bungalows cost 100-150B.

Highway 1207 continues five km west to Ban Dong, where a dirt track heads south down to a beach, a small cave called Tham Pra, and an old bamboo bridge which crosses the Kok River to Pattaya Noi Beach. The dirt road also continues west along the river to eventually reach the Ruam Mit Resort and Prasert Guesthouse, where bamboo bungalows cost 40-70B. Motorcyclists can continue on the dirt road all the way to Thaton.

From Ban Dong, Hwy. 1207, now a dirt track under construction, continues west to Huai Mae Sai Waterfall, where treks originate to nearby hilltribe villages. One popular trek heads 18 km north through several Lahu villages to the Laan Tong Lodge on Hwy. 1089. Elephant rides are possible from Suan Plan Forest Park near the falls.

Mountain View Bungalows: On Hwy. 1207 and just 14 km northwest of Chiang Rai is a popular lodge that arranges tribal trekking, river rafting, and elephant rides. Mountain View Bungalows is just outside the Karen village of Huai Khom and within hiking distance of Akha, Lahu, Lisu, and Meo tribal villages. Rooms cost 50-100B.

Pon Phat Bat Falls: Six km from the Kok River Bridge is a good asphalt road which leads eight km west to a small and disappointing set of falls.

MAE CHAN

Mae Chan is a dull market town from where minitrucks head west up Hwy. 1089 to Laan Thong Lodge and up Hwy. 1130 to Mae Salong.

Accommodations

A small guesthouse/brothel is located north of town where the road splits to Mae Sai and Chiang Saen.

Transportation

Songtaos leave from the center of town near the main temple and police station. Minitrucks to Laan Thong Lodge leave hourly from 0900 to 1700. To reach Mae Salong, take a short minitruck ride two km north to Pha Sang, from where *songtaos* up to Mae Salong cost 40B. Fares from Mae Chan to Mae Sai and Chiang Saen are 10B.

WEST OF MAE CHAN

Highway 1089 heads west from Mae Chan to several mountain lodges and tribal villages where visitors can safely trek without fear of bandits. Nine km west are some hot springs on the left side of the road near the Mae Chan River. Dear House Lodge near the hot springs has bamboo bungalows from 200B.

Laan Thong Lodge: One of the finest mountain lodges in northern Thailand, Laan Thong Lodge (tel. 053-713669, fax 053-771093) consists of several bamboo cottages surrounded by landscaped gardens and fruit trees. Facilities are in good condition and the Thai owners specialize in vegetarian dishes and homebaked breads. Bungalows cost 40-100B. The lodge is 13 km west of Mae Chan. Air-conditioned minitrucks return to Chiang Rai and Chiang Mai daily at 0900. Reservations at Mae Salong Tours (tel. 053-612515) near the Wiang Inn in Chiang Rai.

Treks: Treks from Laan Thong Lodge head either south to Chiang Rai, west to Karen Coffee Shop on the banks of the Kok, or north up to Mae Salong through Yao, Lahu, Lisu, and Akha villages. Self-guided treks are relatively easy, though guides can be hired at Laan Thong.

HIGHWAY 1130 TO MAE SALONG

Motorcyclists can stop at several spots en route to Mae Salong. The road is in excellent condition, with superb mountain views and hilltribe villages. Tragically, most of the forest cover has been stripped by hilltribes who used slash-and-burn cultivation to plant their opium poppies. The Royal Forestry Department is now providing cassia, bamboo, and pine saplings to help reforest the region.

Winnipa Lodge: Four km west of Pha Sang, on a hillside overlooking the road, is a mountain lodge with 16 individual bungalows priced from 100B.

Hilltribe Center: Twelve km from Highway 110 is a rudimentary village with handicraft shops and costumed kids who pose for photos. Donations can be deposited in the wooden box. The rough and challenging dirt road north from the Hilltribe Center continues through several Akha villages to the Akha Guesthouse and Doi Tung.

Pa Dua: Eighteen km from Highway 110 is a small Yao village visited by tour groups.

Hin Taek: Sam Yaek, an Akha village 24 km west of the main highway, is the turnoff for Hin Taek (now renamed Thoed Thai), where Khun Sa maintained his opium empire until 1982. The 13-km dirt route is steep, winding, and should only be attempted by groups of experienced motorcyclists.

MAE SALONG (SANTIKHIRI)

Mae Salong is a precariously sited Chinese village populated by descendants of the Kuomintang Nationalist Army (93rd Regiment) who fled China after their defeat and the Communist takeover in 1949. Initially welcomed by the Thai government as protective forces against Chinese and warlord aggression, they soon took up opium cultivation and smuggling. Drug warlord Khun Sa made his base in the region at Ban Hin Taek (now Ban Thoed Thai) until the early 1980s, when he was routed by the Thai

MAE SALONG (SANTIKHIRI)

MAE SALONG RESORT
WAT SANTIKHIRI
MAE SALONG GH
MOSQUE
SHIN SHANE GH
TO THATON (47 km)
1234
CHURCH
MARKET
SCHOOL
RAINBOW GH
MAUSOLEUM
TEA FACTORY
POLICE
MAE SALONG VILLA
1234
TO MAE CHAN & CHIANG RAI
0   100m
© MOON PUBLICATIONS, INC.

military. Soon afterward, the Thai government officially renamed the Kuomintang village to Santikhiri, a pleasant term which means Mountain of Peace.

Mae Salong has changed dramatically in recent years. The Chinese-language school—reputed for its high teaching standards and once popular with Sino-Thai families from Bangkok—has been closed and converted into a Thai school with a national curriculum. At the same time, financial and technical assistance from Taipei was ended. Roads now push into the more remote regions, as property speculators and farsighted Chinese purchase the fertile land from displaced hilltribes. The isolation and innocence of Mae Salong are quickly coming to an end.

Mae Salong today is a sleepy—and often cold—place where Mandarin is still spoken by the older residents and homes remain guarded by ancient protective talismans.

Attractions

Mausoleum: The most striking landmark in Mae Salong is the mausoleum of General Duan Xi Wen, the former chief of staff of China's 93rd who led 2,000 Chinese Kuomintang soldiers and their families from China into Thailand. The leader lies buried in a marble mansion on the south side of the mountain.

Around Town: Village architecture consists of modern structures and old wooden houses reminiscent of the Yunnan style. A small tea factory is down the road toward the police station.

Morning Market: A lively hilltribe market is held at the west end of town past the school in the mornings between 0500 and 0800. Hilltribe peoples are extremely reluctant to have their photographs snapped.

Road to Thaton: A wonderful dirt road winds past the school and morning market and continues 48 km down to Thaton on the banks of the Kok River. Great views and several hilltribe villages, but do not attempt this road in the rainy season.

Cherry Blossom Festival: A festival honoring the pink *sakura* flower is held in early January. Activities include a floral procession attended by contingents of local hilltribes, exhibits which illustrate the colorful history of Mae Salong, agricultural displays, and the crowning of Miss Cherry Blossom.

Trekking

Mae Salong is an excellent place to begin self-guided treks to nearby hilltribe villages. Rough but adequate maps of the region can be picked up from Rainbow and Mae Salong guesthouses. Shin Shane Guesthouse has a useful trekking map on their wall.

Shopping

Best buys in town include home-brewed medicinal wine, preserved fruits, Chinese herbs, Burmese cheroots, and locally grown Taiwanese tea called Mei Qing, Mei Long, and Qing Qing. Small shops also sell a smuggled Chinese whiskey called *senji* flavored with bizarre roots and centipedes.

Accommodations

Several guesthouses and medium-priced hotels are located in Mae Salong. All have cafes which serve Thai and Yunnanese specialties such as rice noodles topped with spicy chicken curry, steamed pork buns, and pickled vegetables.

Mae Salong Guesthouse: Up the hill and on the left is a small guesthouse (tel. 053-712962) with trekking information, a fading but useful map posted on the wall, and horseback tours to nearby villages. Rooms cost 80B with hot showers outside the compound.

Shin Shane Guesthouse: Another barebones guesthouse is located just off the main road in an old wooden Chinese home. The friendly owners run a small cafe and can help with trekking information. Rooms cost 50-80B. Hot showers run an additional 10B.

Rainbow Guesthouse: A rudimentary spot with views from the cafe and a solitary room with three beds. 40B.

Mae Salong Villa: Two km down the road is a medium-quality place with an elevated restaurant and comfortable rooms equipped with hot showers. Highway 1234, tel. (053) 713444, 400-600B.

Mae Salong Resort: The best hotel in town is wonderfully located up a steep road with views over the entire valley. The adjacent flower park and cherry blossom orchards are popular with visiting Chinese and Thais. Mae Chan, tel. (053) 713400, fax (053) 714047, 400B standard, 600B deluxe. Camping appears possible in the flower park.

Transportation

Mae Salong lies 36 km west of Pha Sang (Basang or Pasang) on top of Doi Mae Salong, 1,418 meters above sea level. From Chiang Rai, hire a motorcycle or take the green bus to Pha Sang, three km beyond Mae Chan, from where minibuses continue up the winding road to Mae Salong. Mini-trucks from Pha Sang run from 0800 to 1700 and cost 40B up, 30B down.

MAE CHAN TO MAE SAI

Between Mae Chan and Mae Sai are several lodges, temples, and natural attractions accessible by public minitrucks and rented motorcycles.

Ban Huai Krai: The small town of Huai Krai, 13 km north of Mae Chan and 19 km south of Mae Sai, marks the junction of Hwy. 1149, which leads west to the Akha Guesthouse and Wat Doi Tung. The turnoff is located before the town and signposted with directions to Akha Guesthouse. Mini-trucks leave from the intersection every 30 minutes.

Akha Guesthouse: Another longtime favorite is the Akha Guesthouse, located on old Hwy. 1149, 44 km north of Chiang Rai and seven km west of Ban Huai Krai. The lodge offers spectacular views and trails which wind through nearby tribal villages. Rooms cost 40-60B.

Motorcyclists should note that the guesthouse is on old Highway 1149, on a side road which veers left off the newer bypass at the village of Ban Paka. Watch carefully or you'll miss the turnoff.

Doi Tung Palace: Some 13 km from Ban Huai Krai is a Swiss chalet which serves as home to her majesty the queen mother, whose foundation (Mae Fa Luang) conducts reforestation projects and helps hilltribes grow crops such as macadamia trees and temperate vegetables. Her presence also accounts for the excellent roads and prosperous hilltribe communities.

Wat Doi Tung: Eighteen km from the highway and 2,000 meters above sea level, this 10th-century monastery is considered one of the most venerated shrines in northern Thailand. The complex features a pair of *chedis* which encase relics of the Buddha, and an impressive bronze image seated under a *naga*. All note the jolly fat Buddha with an immense navel!

Wat Doi Tung isn't very impressive, but the views are terrific on clear days. Motorcyclists can continue along a dirt road to the rear of Doi Tung and reach Mae Sai on the Burmese border. The unmarked dirt road heads left from the main road, several kilometers before Doi Tung. Very tricky to find.

A Lake and Four Caves: Highway 110 continues north from Ban Huai Krai past a strangely disfigured mountain called Khun Nam Nang Non ("Sleeping Lady"), named after the anatomically recognizable face but hopelessly contorted body. Several caves are located west of Ban Pong at Km 877, or 13 km south of Mae Sai. Sao Hin, Pla, and Kaeo caves are all sited around large Soa Hin Lake. A rather strange Khmer temple stands near the entrance of one flooded cave, which can be explored with flashlights.

Ban Tham, a village you must pass to reach the lake and caves, is inhabited by Muslim Chinese Haw from Yunnan Province in Southern China. They are responsible for the Chinese gardens, fishponds, and pavilions which surround the lake.

The road west from Km 878 leads to Tham Phum and the Akha village of Ban San Pasak.

Tham Luang: The Tham Luang ("Great Cave") of Mae Sai is west of Hwy. 110 at Km 884. Beyond the first cavern is a narrow passageway which leads into other chambers thick with dripping formations of fantastic shapes. A narrow path leads south from Tham Luang to Saitong Caves and the hot springs of Khun Nam Nang Non. The hot springs can also be reached by turning left at Ban Jong at Km 882, eight km south of Mae Sai.

MAE SAI

Mae Sai, 891 km from Bangkok, is the northernmost town in Thailand and the final stop before crossing the Mae Sai River into Burma. Along with the Golden Triangle, Mae Sai possesses a frontier reputation of opium smugglers and gangs of renegade soldiers. The reality is somewhat different since Mae Sai is hardly more than a nondescript town of concrete shophouses, video stores, souvenir shops, Chinese restaurants, and an enormous road that perhaps anticipates the opening of Burma to convoys of logging trucks.

Despite the romantic location, Mae Sai has little appeal except for the bridge and views from Wat Doi Wao.

The Bridge

The border crossing into Burma (the sign says "MAYANMA") is where Thai citizens arrive searching for Chinese goods, sweet orange wine, and Burmese cheroots, while Burmese from Tha Khi Lek and Kengtung (100 km north) cross the bridge for shaving blades, pens, and Western medicines.

The scene at the bridge is a strange collision of cultures—blond-haired Westerners stopped by grim guards, Burmese handicrafts such as

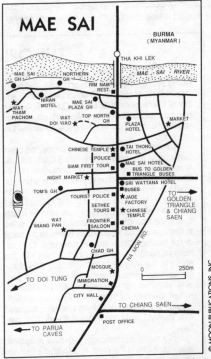

opium weights ("very old, very old") hawked by aggressive Indian hustlers, and cute Thai girls posing in tribal costumes. A lively market is held on the bridge during Buddhist holidays.

Thais and Burmese are allowed to cross the bridge, but foreigners are presently barred from all land crossings into Burma. To promote tourism in the far north, the Thai government recently requested permission to allow Westerners to visit the adjacent Burmese town of Tha Khi Lek.

Tha Khi Lek

The following attractions will be open to Westerners when permission is granted for land entry into Burma.

Wat Prathat Sai Muang: Thai Yai *samlor* drivers waiting in Burma at the far end of the bridge can quickly take you to the market and Wat Prathat Sai Muang, located two km north of the market. This Thai Yai temple was constructed about 25 years ago with a golden *chedi* lavishly decorated with pieces of glass. Displayed inside the *viharn* are ceramics, prayer beads, and rare Chiang Saen images of the Buddha.

THE OPIUM TRAIL

In Homer's *Odyssey*, Helen of Troy mixes an opium-laced potion "to quiet all pain and strife, and bring forgetfulness of every ill." Thomas De Quincey, author of *Confessions of an English Opium Eater,* tells how he experienced "music like perfume and ecstasies of divine enjoyment, living a hundred years in one night."

Papaver somniferum, the opium poppy, has been cultivated as a narcotic since the early Greek empire. Arab traders during the reign of Kublai Khan (1279-1294) introduced the drug to the Chinese, who later used it as a form of currency and method of taxation during the Han Dynasty. The so-called Black Mud later dominated British-Chinese trade after the British East India Company discovered that opium sales to Chinese addicts miraculously balanced the trade deficit between China and the Company. The Chinese responded by planting vast regions with the poppy to the extent that, by 1875, one-third of the farmland in Yunnan Province was covered with poppies. Hilltribes from the region, which traditionally raised the crop as their primary source of cash, brought their poppies with them when they migrated into Thailand and Laos during the early 20th century.

Opium, and its medicinal derivative morphine, was introduced to the West in 1815 after a German pharmacist isolated the principal alkaloid and named it for Morpheus, the Greek god of dreams. Public usage became commonplace in the early 20th century after Bayer, the pharmaceutical company, promoted diacetyl morphine (heroin) as a miracle cure and packaged the pills in small boxes marked with lions and globes. The Bayer trademark was later used by Laotian traffickers who sold their product under the Double-Globe brand.

Air America

Opium and its derivatives became popular drugs during the Vietnam War era, with a degree of help from the Central Intelligence Agency. The genesis was a CIA-controlled airline called Civil Air Transport (also known as Air America) which first helped supply Chiang Kai Shek's forces during World War II and later secured a French contract to airlift Catholic refugees from Tonkin to Southern Vietnam during the early days of the Indochina War. Air America later worked with Hmong guerillas, Khambas from Tibet, and remnants of the Kuomintang army to fight the communist insurgency from Hanoi. Despite denials by the American government, most observers agree that, in addition to humanitarian efforts, Air America purchased and transported opium to aid their rebel allies in Laos and Vietnam.

A good account of their smuggling operations is retold in Alfred McCoy's classic, *The Politics of Heroin in Southeast Asia.* International opium trafficking is also recounted in the more recent *Drugs, the U.S., and Khun Sa* by Francis Belanger, and *Burma's Golden Triangle* by Andre Bouchaud. The movie *Air America* also recounts the story of the most famous airline ever operated by the Central Intelligence Agency.

The Opium Trail

The Golden Triangle—the world's largest source of illicit opium—produces an estimated 2,000-2,500 tons annually from Burma, Laos, and, to a lesser degree, northern Thailand. The opium trail begins in the early spring as farmers scour the countryside looking for highly alkaline soils best suited for cultivation. Connoisseurs claim the sweeter taste of limestone soil can actually be recognized by the discriminating palate. Fields are cleared of standing trees with a spectacular burnoff, and planting begins in September after the tree ash has dissolved into natural fertilizers. The soil is chopped, turned, and strewn with select poppy seeds.

By January, bright red-and-white flowers appear, blossom, and then drop away to reveal an egg-shaped bulb filled with resinous opium. The bulb is scored—like a Vermont maple or Malay rubber tree—with a three-bladed knife, and the milky sap then rises to the surface before turning into brownish-black droplets. Tribeswomen return the following morning to scrape the bulb and deposit the residue into a cup hanging around their necks. The sticky gum is then packed into banana leaves, tied into bundles, and sold to Chinese middlemen who refine it to morphine or heroin and export it to Western countries.

The upward spiral of its value is amazing. One square km of poppy field produces almost 2,000 kilos of raw opium. One kilo of raw opium, worth only US$35 in Burma or US$4,000 as heroin in Chiang Mai, brings US$250,000 as Grade 4 heroin in America. And that's the price *before* being cut six times by street dealers. The final tally: one kilo of raw opium eventually brings US$2.5 million, and a single square km of land can yield heroin worth US$50-200 million. Small wonder the hilltribes refuse to grow peanuts.

Wat San Sai: Also in Tha Khi Lek is Wat San Sai, a picturesque temple surrounded by rice-fields. Inside the *viharn* stands a bizarre collection of bamboo poles under which pilgrims crawl and receive prayers for good luck. Burmese astrological symbols and Buddhas adorn the ceiling.

OPIUM WARLORD KHUN SA

The Golden Triangle—an isolated area of 75,000 square miles wedged between Burma, China, Laos, and Thailand—annually produces an estimated 2,000-2,500 tons of opium and over 70% of the world's illicit heroin supply. Current crop estimates are 2,500 tons from Burma, 500 tons from Laos, and under 30 tons from Northern Thailand. Most of the product is refined into heroin in sophisticated jungle laboratories located inside Burma, and then exported through Thailand to Hong Kong and the West. Western narcotics officers in Bangkok lament that less than one percent of the drug haul is now being intercepted before it reaches the addicts in the Western world.

The mastermind of the Triangle's opium industry is Khun Sa (a.k.a. Chang Chi Fu), a half-Chinese, half-Shan warlord widely regarded as one of the world's most prolific drug dealers, right up there with the Mafia and the Medellin cartel.

Khun Sa came to the attention of the world's press in 1967 when he launched his Opium Wars to wrestle control of the lucrative trade from the remnants of Chiang Kai Shek's Nationalist Chinese army. After being captured by Burmese forces and thrown in a Rangoon prison, his private army (the Shan States Army or SUA) kidnapped two Soviet doctors as hostages for Khun Sa. Khun Sa was released in 1978, and within a decade he controlled 70-80% of the region's opium trade.

Khun Sa first established his drug headquarters inside Thailand at Ban Hin Taek, north of Chiang Mai near Mae Salong, where his SUA troops worked closely with the Thai Border Patrol Police. This embarrassing situation ended in January 1982 when a major assault drove Khun Sa and his army across the border back into Burma. Khun Sa soon reestablished his new headquarters at Ho Mong, a jungle village in Shan State, just 16 km from the Thai border and almost within earshot of Mae Hong Son. Khun Sa has lived here without pressure from the Burmese or Thai governments for over a decade. Today, a road constructed by the Thai government, with financial aid provided by the Americans, connects Mae Hong Son with Ho Mong. Visitors report that opium, jade, and logging profits have transformed his once-drab military camp into a thriving boomtown, complete with nine schools that provide free education, a 100-bed hospital, Buddhist monastery, and hundreds of houses given free to his officers.

A recent split in the Burma Communist Party, Khun Sa's main rival in the drug world, has made life much easier for the warlord, who continues to raise several million dollars each month from his control of opium, jade, and teakwood exports. His biggest current rival for control of the drug industry is another opium warlord named Lo Hsing Han, who, when he isn't playing golf with the Burmese generals in Yangon (Rangoon), spends his time in the town of Lashio. Recent reports indicate that the Burmese government now supports Lo over Khun Sa as the next government-approved drug kingpin of Southeast Asia.

Capturing this outlaw has proven difficult. The U.S. government once offered US$25,000 for his head, but Khun Sa countered by offering payments for the murder of Americans in Chiang Mai. Dozens of concerned citizens were quickly evacuated from Thailand. Despite the 10-count federal drug indictment handed down by the American government in 1990, Khun Sa continues to operate with impunity from his military camp at Ho Mong. Apprehending the warlord remains problematical since he controls a well-armed military force of over 15,000 insurgents, and is believed to have reached a de facto peace pact with the Burmese military, which remains busy battling other separatist groups.

Khun Sa (a local title which means "Prince of Prosperity") is also something of a public-relations whiz, having repeatedly offered to sell all his opium to the U.S. government for US$500 million over a six-year period. So far no American president has taken him up on his bizarre proposal. In 1990, the drug king sent President Bush a video message that invited narcotics agents to visit his camp to see the widespread deforestation being conducted by Thai logging companies with cooperation from the Rangoon military regime.

Khun Sa is also a media manipulator who frequently meets with the press, including a 1989 visit by Tom Jarrell and the ABC crew for "20/20" magazine. In 1991 new rules for visiting journalists were initiated. Journalists must now pay 50,000B and electronic newsmen 250,000B to Khun Sa's representatives in Mae Hong Son before being escorted on good roads to his camp just inside Burma, only 20 km from the tourist center of Mae Hong Son.

Wat Pra Chao Ra Keng: Probably the wealthiest temple in Tha Khi Lek boasts a modern and very spacious *viharn* decorated with a Mandalay-style Buddha and five strange images of a faceless Buddha. Behind the temple is a small hill capped with a white Burmese *stupa* and Chinese shrine.

Wat Prathat Doi Wao

A long flight of over 200 steps and a *naga*-flanked balustrade lead up a small hill with views of white pagodas, a Chinese cemetery, and the tin roofs of Tha Khi Lek inside Burma. The *wat* and whitewashed *chedi* were constructed by King Ong Wao of Chiang Saen to enshrine hair of Lord Buddha, but all structures were completely rebuilt in 1953 by the local abbot.

Guesthouses

Most visitors spend a few hours at the bridge and perhaps climb the hill for views, then head east to Sop Ruak or the idyllic town of Chiang Saen. If you decide to stay, Mae Sai has several well-placed guesthouses down near the river and a handful of better hotels on the main road.

Mae Sai Guesthouse: The best place to escape the concrete drabness of Mae Sai and relax in a riverside setting is the series of bungalows located about one km west of the bridge. Facilities include a small restaurant, trekking information, and a sign posted on the front lawn which denotes the division between Thailand and Burma. Motorcycles can be safely stored inside the guesthouse compound. Bungalows cost 50-200B depending on the size and amenities. The guesthouse is isolated and a long, hot walk from the bridge. Nearby Ya Guesthouse (of Chiang Rai fame) is similar. A *samlor* costs about 15 *baht*. 688 Wiang Pakam Rd., tel. (053) 732021, 50-200B.

Mae Sai Plaza Guesthouse: A decent place much closer to town but with less atmosphere than the Mae Sai Guesthouse. Some 100 bungalows hang precariously from the cliff which rises sharply from the left side of the road. Best bet is a bowl of spicy Burmese-style *pad thai* from their large, elevated restaurant. 386 Sairomjoi Rd., tel. (053) 732230, 80-250B.

Northern Guesthouse: Another riverside option with funky rooms and good views across the river. 402 Tumphjom Rd., tel. (053) 731537, 60-80B common bath, 100-140B private bath.

Chad Guesthouse: The second-best place in Mae Sai is a favorite of motorcyclists, who can obtain good maps and helpful advice from the Thai-Shan family of owner Khun Chad. Located in a quiet neighborhood and well removed from the tourist hype near the bridge, Chad has motorcycles for rent and leads extended journeys around the more remote regions of Northern Thailand. Highly recommended. Soi Wangpan, 50-120B.

Hotels

Top North Hotel: A 32-room hotel just 100 meters from the bridge. Convenient to reach and popular with midlevel travelers. 306 Paholyothin Rd., tel. (053) 731955, 200-250B fan, 350-450B a/c.

Transportation

Buses to Mae Sai leave every 15 minutes from Chiang Rai and take about 90 minutes. Both buses and minitrucks reach Mae Sai from Chiang Saen and Sop Ruak.

Siam First Tours on the main road has nightly a/c buses direct to Bangkok.

SOP RUAK
(GOLDEN TRIANGLE)

Thailand's notorious Golden Triangle is centered at Sop Ruak, where Thailand, Laos, and Burma meet at the confluence of the Mekong and Ruak rivers. Sensationalized fiction and worldwide media attention have cursed the Triangle with a ruinous popularity. Although the mysterious scenery encourages fantasies about drug smugglers and opium warlords, you're more likely to find busloads of German tourists and Chinese gamblers than armed terrorists among the haphazard collection of guesthouses, luxury hotels, restaurants, and a nauseating string of souvenir stalls that hug the banks of the Mekong River. The appeal of this geopolitical oddity typifies what is worst about international mass tourism.

Recent developments have been extremely discouraging. Two separate resorts—one on a spit of sand in Burma and another on the Laotian side of the Mekong—are under construction, with well-heeled Thai, Chinese, and Japanese tourists expected to be the main targets. Businessmen are furiously converting the region into a playground for rich gamblers. The 400-room Golden Triangle Paradise Resort recently built inside Burma territory includes a casino, dog racing track, and golf course. Another golf course is planned for the Laotian project, while an international airport is being built midway between Chiang Rai and the Golden Triangle.

Attractions

Triangle Monument: The actual intersection of Thailand, Laos, and Burma is conveniently framed by a modern signpost—worth a photo for friends back home.

Opium Museum: 212 House of Opium down the road features an excellent collection of opium weights, pipes, headrests, photos of Khun Sa at his rainy camp, and a small hut with a very wasted addict.

Wat Pukao: A hillside temple, located up a winding dirt road to the rear, offers great views and a small *viharn* with an image that provides miracles to visiting pilgrims. Wishes are granted to anyone who can lift the image.

Wat Sam Mung Maung: On another hill to the rear is a reconstructed temple which once held a large outdoor Buddha before it mysteriously disappeared several years ago.

Boat Rides: Boats down to Chiang Saen and far shorter journeys around the principal island in the Mekong leave from the landing below the Golden Triangle Monument. Fares are steep unless you split the cost with several other travelers.

Guesthouses

Fifteen years ago, Sop Ruak was a deserted site with a few sets of rickety huts occupied by opium-smoking travelers. Most of the old bungalows have since given way to run-down but overpriced guesthouses, and several luxury hotels sadly misplaced in such a romantic setting.

Golden Hut Guesthouse: One of Sop Ruak's last guesthouses now charges an unreasonable 150B for rudimentary rooms and complimentary breakfast. Rooms are reserved across the road at the immense Golden Triangle Resort Hotel.

Golden Triangle Guesthouse: Old concrete rooms about to fall into the Mekong River cost 50-100B.

Bua Guesthouse: Across from the Opium Museum is another old joint similar in style and price to the Golden Triangle Guesthouse.

Phukam Guesthouse: To the left of the Opium Museum is another choice which appears somewhat cleaner and slightly more expensive than the other guesthouses in Sop Ruak.

Tham Chat Village Center: Six km northwest of Sop Ruak in the village of Wiang Kaew is a clean guesthouse within hiking distance of several Akha and Yao villages. 40-60B.

Hotels

Golden Triangle Resort Hotel: An immense white-elephant hotel wedged between the cliffs and the souvenir stalls on the riverside road. Facilities include an outdoor pool, two restaurants, tennis courts, and nightly classical Thai dances. Sop Ruak tel. (053) 714031, fax (053) 714805, Bangkok reservations (02) 532-0966, 2200-3000B.

Baan Boran Hotel: An amazing hotel, designed and managed by the same group that runs the Phuket Yacht Club, is located a few kilometers west of Sop Ruak on the banks of the Mekong. All 110 rooms overlook the casino which now mars the island inside the Golden Triangle. Sop Ruak tel. (053) 716678, fax (053) 716702, Bangkok tel. (02) 254-4262, fax (02) 254-5365, 3200-3600B.

Transportation

Sop Ruak is 28 km southeast of Mae Sai and 11 km west of Chiang Saen, where most travelers spend their nights. Buses and minitrucks to Sop Ruak leave periodically from the intersection just south of the Mai Sai Hotel. From Chiang Saen, it's best to rent a motorcycle or bicycle, though *songtaos* leave in the mornings from the Sala Thai Restaurant.

CHIANG SAEN

Chiang Saen is among the most interesting and attractive towns in the far north. Blessed with some minor ruins which attest to its historical legacy, the bucolic village provides a welcome relief from the tourist centers and frantic pace of life which has seized much of Thailand. Chiang Saen—a sleepy place wonderfully located in a dramatic setting—is highly recommended for its lethargic atmosphere and pastoral charm.

History

Scholars believe that Chiang Saen was founded in the 10th century by Thai chieftains as the first independent principality in northern Thailand. The town was later abandoned and perhaps destroyed by Khmer forces but reestablished in 1328 by King Saen Phu, a grandson of King Mengrai who brought with him a group of villagers from Haripunchai (Lamphun). Mengrai's grandson was a devout Buddhist who constructed many of the *stupas* and *chedis* which have survived to the present day. King Saen Phu died in 1334, and Chiang Saen was subsequently absorbed into the Lanna kingdom with the ascendancy of Chiang Mai.

The city and surrounding region were seized by the Burmese in 1558, who ruled until 1804 when King Rama I reconquered and razed the city to prevent foreign occupation. Chiang Saen lay abandoned until 1874 when Chao Inta, a prince of Lamphun, reconstructed the town and brought back descendants of the former population.

Chiang Saen today is a lovely place blessed with hundreds of trees which complement its idyllic location on the banks of the lazy Mekong River.

Attractions

Chiang Saen offers a great little museum and several restored temples that bear witness to the city's turbulent history. None compare with those in Sukothai or Ayuthaya, but they are worth a quick look to help pass the day. The widely scattered monuments can be quickly toured in a few hours on foot or with a rented bicycle.

Visitors uninterested in temples should spend a few days simply watching the pace of life from the riverside cafes or the veranda of their guesthouse.

Chiang Saen National Museum

The Chiang Saen National Museum, on the main road near the old west gate, provides an excellent introduction to the handicrafts, carvings, and splendid Buddhas of the Chiang Saen Period, considered among the most beautiful in Thailand.

Front Room: Displayed inside the front room are demon heads and *garudas* recovered from Wat Pasak and four large seated bronze Buddhas in Lanna style with distinctive topknots. Each is worth a careful inspection. Other artifacts include stone inscriptions which relate the arrival of Buddhism to Lamphun in 1498, and an elegant, mysterious, stone Buddha head carved in Lanna style, Payao school. The collection is small but of extremely high quality.

Back Rooms: To the rear are several rooms filled with gongs, bronze kettledrums, Buddhist banners, lacquerware, Burmese tobacco boxes, Akha rattanware, and Lanna-style swords.

Second Floor: Highlights include a useful map of the more important monuments in Chiang Saen, a huge terra-cotta pipe, an elegant bronze Buddha hand from Wat Ton Phung, and humorous divinity figurines discovered at Wat Chedi Luang.

The museum is open Wed.-Sun. 0900-1600.

CHIANG SAEN

WAT PRATHAT CHOM KITTI
WAT CHOM CHANG
TO GOLDEN TRIANGLE & GIN GH
ROBWIANG RD.
SAI 2 RD.
SAI 1 RD.
WAT SAEN MUANG MA
SOI 6
WAT SANG KA KAO
SIAM GH
WAT SAO KIEN
NONG MUT RD.
WAT PRA KHAO PAN
SUREE GH
WAT PRACHAO LANTHONG
CHIANG SAEN GH
WAT MAHATHAT
WAT MUNG MUANG
POST OFFICE
BANK
POLICE
SALA THAI REST.
WAT PASAK
TO CHIANG RAI
WAT CHEDI LUANG
WAT PRA BUAT
IMMIGRATION
POONSUK HOTEL
MOTORCYCLES
MEKONG RIVER (MAE NAM KHONG)
NATIONAL MUSEUM
WAT SAWASDI
WAT KU TAO
GAS
THAPMAN RD.
LANNA GH
SOI 1
SAI 2 RD.
SAI 1 RD.
TO CHIANG KHONG
OLD CITY WALLS
0   100m

© MOON PUBLICATIONS, INC.

Wat Chedi Luang

Behind the museum towers an immense 58-meter octagonal *chedi* (spelled Wat Jadeeloung on the sign) perhaps constructed in 1331 by King Saen Phu, but reconstructed in 1551 shortly before the Burmese seized Chiang Saen. The ancient *bot* adjacent to the *chedi* houses a highly venerated Buddha.

Wat Pasak

Beyond the reconstructed walls of ancient Chiang Saen lies the city's oldest surviving *chedi*, constructed in 1295 and modeled after the Mon prototype of Wat Chiang Yan in Lamphun. Erected before the formal foundation of the city in 1328, Wat Pasak testifies to the importance of the valley before the rise of Chiang Mai and the Lanna kingdom.

The restored, extremely rare stepped pyramid is adorned with niches which once held dozens of Buddha images. Standing Buddhas surrounding the basement have been poorly restored, but excellent stuccowork of *nagas, kalas,* floral motifs, and small elephants still graces the upper levels.

Wat Pasak ("Temple of the Teak Forest") is under the supervision of the Fine Arts Department, which charges *farangs* a 20B admission fee.

Wat Prathat Chom Kitti

Two km northwest of town and situated on a hill with good views over the Mekong River, Wat Chom Kitti and the small ruined *chedi* of Wat Chom Chang are old monuments which scholars believe also predate the founding of Chiang Saen by King Saen Phu. New copper paneling covers the top half of the central *chedi* and little of the original stuccowork remains on the monument, but note the beatific expressions and wonderful reddish patina of the four standing Buddhas.

Wat Pra Khao Pan

Situated behind a modern *viharn* stands an ancient *chedi* whose concrete stele inaccurately claims a construction date of 761. The monument features four restored Buddhas standing in hollowed niches, two in the classic walking style of Sukothai.

Other Monuments

The remainder of the temples of Chiang Saen are quite minor, though they provide an excuse to ride your bicycle through the peaceful neighborhoods.

Wat Pra Buat: The unusually shaped "Temple of the Holy Ordination," across from Wat Chedi Luang, sports a fine stucco torso of the Buddha on the entrance gate.

Wat Mung Muang: This small indented *chedi* dates from the reign of King Kum Phu, who abdicated rule of Chiang Mai in 1334 to rule Chiang Saen after the death of King Saen Phu.

Wat Prachao Lanthong: All that remains of the "Temple of a Million Golden Weights" is a large solid base which once supported the enormous *chedi.* Inside the nearby modern *viharn* sits a large bronze Buddha in the so-called Third Period of Chiang Saen art, as established by the famous Thai art historian Alexander Griswold.

Wat Sao Kien: Hidden away in a weedy yard are the foundations of an old temple and a solitary, seated, completely headless Buddha.

Tobacco Kilns

The rich soil and climatic conditions of Chiang Saen have long made the region a principal source of Virginia tobacco and temperate vegetables such as cabbages and tomatoes. One of the most interesting sights near Chiang Saen are the tobacco kilns located northwest of town on the road to the Golden Triangle. Visitors are welcome to wander through the yards and inspect the smoking kilns kept fired with prodigious amounts of coal. Note the ingenious mechanisms for elevating the leaves and pulley systems for controlling the amount of heat and smoke. Workers often sort and bundle piles of green leaves in the front yards.

Wat Prathat Pha Ngao

One of the most awesome and mysterious Buddha images in Thailand is displayed inside a temple located 4.2 km east of Chiang Saen on the road to Chiang Khong.

Fronting the complex are two wildly misspelled signs which attempt to relate Buddhist tales with the aid of garish statues. The modern *viharn* to the rear may be an awful portent of popular Thai architecture (precast images, lousy workmanship, trite themes), but inside the gaudy building is a gigantic Buddha torso whose powerful and dramatic shape suggests the ethereal nature of Buddhism with unbelievable clarity. An amazing image which has rarely been mentioned in travel literature on Thailand.

Outside the complex are some of the Disneyesque Buddhist statues so popular in modern Thai society, and a *chedi* constructed on a large rock, somewhat similar to the hanging rock of Kyaiktiyo in Burma.

Accommodations

Chiang Saen offers several basic but relaxing guesthouses on the banks of the Mekong River. Midlevel guesthouses are now appearing as the focus slowly shifts from budget to better quality digs.

Lanna Guesthouse: One of the most popular spots in Chiang Saen appears rudimentary at first glance, but the funky surroundings seem absolutely perfect in such a laid-back town. Lanna has an open-air restaurant in the middle of the weedy grounds, common hot showers that are quirky but eventually work, and a variety of wooden bungalows in all price ranges. A very friendly and fun place to idle away a few days. 39 Rimkhong Rd., 40-100B.

Chiang Saen Guesthouse: Not much atmosphere, though the rooms are fairly clean and manager Chan Chai is friendly. A good location in the center of town near the temples and river. 45 Rimkhong Rd., 40-60B common bath, 80-100B with private bath in new bungalows facing a concrete courtyard.

Siam Guesthouse: An old and run-down dive with three bungalows crammed together. 294 Rimkhong Rd., 60-80B.

Gin Guesthouse: Two km west of town is a wonderful place with A-frame chalets facing grassy lawns and an inner orchard filled with lychee and mango trees. Several years ago, the owners sold their riverside plot of land across the road and moved their operations to this new location. Gin's has a small circular cafe surrounded by wagon wheels and marked "Thai Garden Cowboy Restaurant is opened too you're welcome," and dependable rental bicycles for exploring the ruins and peddling out to the Golden Triangle. A nearby trail leads down to a sandy beach. Small bamboo rooms in the rear cost 60-100B, lovely A-frames with private bath cost 250-350B.

Suree Guesthouse: Inside the city perimeter and near the museum is another basic guesthouse that provides an alternative when the better places near the river are filled. Rooms cost 50-100B.

Restaurants

Most of the guesthouses provide meals, but travelers often spend their evening hours in the **Sala Thai Restaurant**, which serves mediocre meals but great river views. **Streetstalls** set up in the evenings near the Poonsuk Hotel. Several kilometers west of town toward the Golden Triangle is the open-air **Rim Khong Restaurant**, with Thai dishes and caged peacocks. Farther on is the upscale **Meakong Riverbanks Restaurant** with views into Laos. Several midpriced hotels have been constructed in the vicinity.

Yonok Restaurant, outside town near Chiang Saen Lake, is a popular garden restaurant which serves freshwater catfish and northern Thai specialties. Yonok also has several bungalows with private baths and hot showers from 500B.

Practicalities

Siam Commercial Bank near the post office is closed on weekends. Gin's Guesthouse has the best bicycles in town. Motorcycles can be rented in the mornings near the Sala Thai Restaurant and the decrepit La Mekong Guesthouse.

Transportation

Buses from Chiang Rai to Chiang Saen take about an hour and pass through countryside where villagers still harvest rice without the use of machinery. Chiang Saen can also be reached by mini-trucks from Mae Sai.

Songtao service to the Golden Triangle is sporadic and not as reliable as a rented motorcycle or bicycle. Minitrucks to Chiang Khong leave in the mornings from the market along the river.

CHIANG KHONG

Most travelers return to Chiang Rai from Chiang Saen, but motorcyclists and those intrigued with the more remote destinations in northern Thailand can continue east to the small town of Chiang Khong, located on the banks of the Mekong

River and directly opposite the Laotian town of Ban Houei Sai. Chiang Khong has little appeal aside from its tranquil atmosphere and splendid views of the Mekong and Laos.

Attractions

The chief interest in Chiang Khong is simply watching the river flow from a cafe or the lawn of the Mae Khong Resort.

Ban Houei Sai, on the opposite side of the river, was once a French trading post named Fort Carnot. Laotian officials still work in the ghostly ramparts of the old French citadel. Ferries to Ban Houei Sai leave from the small pier at the north end of Chiang Khong, though only Thais and Laotians are presently allowed to cross. Another possibility, depending on the political situation, is a boat journey down the Mekong River through narrow canyons and dangerous whirlpools. In an earlier day, Chiang Khong was the terminus for river journeys down from Luang Prabang, Vientiane, and Chiang Saen—the infamous Laotian loop.

Accommodations

A handful of very sleepy guesthouses and hotels cater to the steady trickle of Western and Thai visitors.

Ban Tam Mi La Guesthouse: Best choice in town is the small Thai-style guesthouse on the main road near Wat Kao. The owners can help with sightseeing excursions to nearby waterfalls, caves, tribal villages, and the historical sights at Doi Patang. They also organize boat trips down the Mekong and horse rides through the countryside. 8/4 Sai Klang Rd., 40-80B.

Mae Khong Resort: Great views and a comfortable cafe make this resort a popular, if somewhat expensive, alternative to the Ban Tam Mi La. The owners also organize boat trips down the Mekong, and can help with van and motorcycle rentals. Sai Klang Rd., 160-350B.

Hmong Guesthouse: Tribal life among the Hmongs can be enjoyed at this small guesthouse in the Meo village of Kiu Khan, located on Hwy. 1129 some 16 km west of Chiang Khong and 39 km from Chiang Saen. Owners John and Su have huts from 60B.

Transportation

Chiang Khong is about 75 km east of Chiang

MONSTERS OF THE MEKONG

Restaurants in Chiang Khong occasionally serve *pla buk*, a monstrous type of catfish considered the largest of its kind in the world. *Pla buk*—a term which means "Great and Powerful Fish"—can grow up to three meters in length and weigh over 300 kilograms, making it the undisputed monster of the Mekong. The fish is praised for its white, succulent meat, which tastes like milk-fed veal and guarantees long life to all who eat it. Gourmets also favor the lightly salted eggs, which are reddish in color and nicknamed Laotian caviar by the northern residents.

The process of catching *pla buk* begins when local priests invoke dockside prayers to summon the spirits of the legendary fish and bring good luck to the fishermen. Fishermen then set out in sleek pirogues on 24-hour fishing shifts, only returning after a successful catch. Some fishermen drag heavy nylon nets called *maung li* through the narrow channels while others throw stones to drive the *pla buk* into the net. Once snagged, the giant catfish are hauled into the boat and secured with ropes pushed through their mouths and out their gills. A successful expedition is celebrated with bottles of Mekong whiskey and all-night parties; a single catch can pay for a new boat or provide for the children's education.

Sadly, the *pla buk* is an endangered species. Earlier this century, *pla buk (Pangasianodon gigas)* were plentiful and could be captured from the Tonle Sap in Cambodia to Th Li Lake in Southern China. Overfishing, however, has severely reduced their numbers to the point where just a few dozen are now caught during the April-June spawning season. The Thai Fisheries Department has recently taken steps to save the fish by initiating a strict quota system and conducting an ambitious breeding program at nearby Ban Had Khrai.

Saen. Minitrucks leave in the morning from the riverside market in Chiang Saen. Motorcyclists can use two different routes. Highway 1129 is a dirt-and-gravel road which passes through the Meo villages of Kiu Khan and Huai Yen. A more scenic route is the road which skirts the Mekong River. The turnoff is 22 km east of Chiang Saen and marked with a signpost to Suan Dok.

MOTORCYCLE JOURNEY FROM CHIANG KHONG

Some of the most spectacular motorcycling in Thailand is found south of Chiang Khong, on the roads which lead down to Chiang Kham and Nan. Although in an extremely remote region of Thailand, the roads are well paved and kept in excellent condition by the Thai government. The curious reason for this happy state of affairs is an embarrassing defeat of the Thai army by the Laotians in the mid-1980s, after which all perimeter roads were completely repaved to provide an access zone against future border disputes. The result provides great rides for motorcyclists.

All motorcyclists should carry the *Guide Map of Chiang Rai,* published by Bangkok Guides, and a copy of David Unkovich's guide to motorcycle touring in northern Thailand.

The journey from Chiang Khong back to Chiang Mai necessitates overnight stops in Chiang Kham, Nan, and Phrae. A basic schedule is Chiang Khong to Chiang Kham (four hours), Chiang Kham to Nan (five hours), Nan to Phrae (three hours), Phrae to Lampang (two hours), and Lampang to Chiang Mai (two hours).

Hotels are located in all major towns and gasoline is plentiful.

Chiang Khong To Chiang Kham

From Chiang Khong, head south down Hwy. 1020 to the junction with Hwy. 1155. Highway 1020 continues south to Thoeng, but it's a straight and boring road through monotonous ricefields and dusty towns. A much better route is Hwy. 1155 along the Mekong River and then south on the winding, roller-coaster road. Great views, hilltribe villages, and Thai Lue towns with distinctive architecture and unique weavings are found along the way. Several side roads lead east toward Laos, but the best detour is east from Pang Kha to a road which skirts the border and continues south through Meo Lao U, Huak, Phu Sang Waterfalls, and down Hwy. 1093 to Chiang Kham. Pang Kha to Chiang Kham takes about three hours.

Chiang Kham: Stay at the **Chiang Kham Hotel** located between the Bangkok Bank and Thai Farmers Bank, opposite the market and police booth. Two blocks northwest is the **Bou**

Thong Restaurant, with an English-language menu. Sights around Chiang Kham include Wat Nantarm, some 500 meters from the Chiang Kham Hotel, and Wat Saen Muang Ma behind the Bou Thong Restaurant. Several Laotian refugee camps are nearby, but entry is limited to visitors with official permission.

Chiang Kham To Nan

Motorcyclists with limited time can head directly from Chiang Kham to Phayao and west to Chiang Mai in a single day. A much more leisurely and scenic route goes southeast on Hwy. 1148 to Tha Wang Pha, from where Hwy. 1080 continues south to Nan. The scenery and mountain views are extremely impressive near Sakoen and Pha Lak. Travel time is about five hours, but allow extra time to visit the hilltribe villages and explore the small roads which branch off toward the Laotian border. Possible side roads include the 26-km route up to the summit of Doi Tiu, and east from Tha Wang Phua to Ban Pua and Nam Poon where a road continues northeast to Luang Prabang. Now *that* would be a motorcycle ride!

Nan To Chiang Mai

Two basic routes are possible back to Chiang Mai. The slower route is down to Phrae on major Hwy. 101 with a possible side trip down Highway 1026 to Nan Noi and Khun Satan, the mountain home of a tribal group called "Spirits of the Yellow Leaves." Spend a night in Phrae and continue back to Chiang Mai the following day, with a few hours exploring the temples in Lampang.

A longer journey heads west on Hwy. 1091 to Ban Luang, followed by 90 km of gravel and asphalt roads to the small town of Ngao. This backroads option avoids the busy highway which connects Nan with Phrae and Lampang. Ngao to Chiang Mai takes another three or four hours.

PHAYAO

Phayao is a medium-sized town on Hwy. 1 midway between Lampang and Chiang Rai. Though rarely visited by Westerners, Phayao has several worthwhile temples and a magnificent location on the edge of Phayao Lake.

History
The region is of considerable interest to archaeologists, who believe that settlements have existed on the banks of Phayao Lake since the early Bronze Age. Phayao was abandoned by the Bronze Age settlers but reestablished in 1096 as the capital of a small kingdom allied with Chiang Saen, and later, the Lanna kingdom of King Mengrai. Burmese invasions forced another evacuation in the late 18th century, but the city was reoccupied in 1840 by emigrants from Lampang. Formerly a subdistrict of Chiang Rai Province, Phayao was granted provincial status in 1977, with the lakeside town as its new capital.

Phayao Lake
Phayao lies on the eastern edge of a large freshwater lake which measures four by six km and supports over 5,000 acres of fish farms. Across the quiet waters looms Doi Bussaracum, a 1,856-meter-high mountain which separates Phayao from the western Wang River Valley. The riverside promenade features several good seafood restaurants, a public park, and a boat launch which rents funny little paddleboats.

Wat Sikhom Kham
The principal temple in Phayao and among the most significant sanctuaries in Northern Thailand, Wat Sikhom Kham is highly regarded by scholars for its 400-year-old Buddha image housed inside the central *viharn.* Named Phra Chao Ton Luang and greatly venerated among the Thais, the gigantic 16-meter brick-and-stucco image impresses with its size despite the poor restoration conducted by local abbots. Note the variety of Buddha poses displayed on the right side of the *viharn,* and engraved steles which flank the interior perimeter.

Outside and on the grounds to the north is another of those bizarre collection of stucco statues so popular in modern Thailand. A sense of humor helps understand the leap from Lanna Art to Lanna Kitsch, but it's hard to resist the silly statues of E.T. (does Spielberg know about this?), dinosaurs, and evildoers being boiled in oil or dissected by devils. The sculptures are inspired by Hollywood films and Buddhist legends to serve as both moral guidelines and campy entertainment.

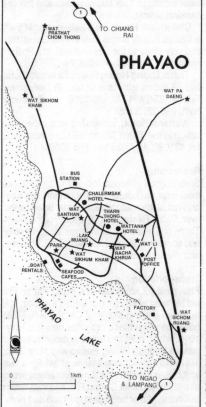

Much more impressive than garish statues or monster Buddhas are the exquisite murals which grace the modern *viharn* back by the lake. The *viharn* itself is a masterpiece of architectural design, blessed with great symmetry and wonderful location on the edge of the lake. Inside the dazzling *viharn* are some of the finest modern murals in all of Thailand, designed and painted under the supervision of an extremely talented artist named Angkarn Kalyanaponsga. Angkarn wisely used traditional Lanna motifs but added an almost surrealistic approach that suggests the ethereal nature of inspired Buddhism. Do not miss this temple.

Accommodations
Hotels in Phayao are limited to three places that

cater mostly to Thai businessmen and the occasional *farang*.

Chalermsak Hotel: The cheapest place in town is located directly across from the minibus station and very close to the bus terminal. 915 Phahonyothin Rd., tel. (054) 431063, 70-120B fan.

Tharn Thong Hotel: Phayao's largest hotel has 96 rooms with fans or a/c. 55 Donsanam Rd., tel. (054) 431772, 180-220B fan with private bath, 280-360B a/c.

Wattana Hotel: Somewhat less expensive option to the Tharn Thong. 69 Donsanam Rd., tel. 431086, 80-140B fan, 160-200B a/c.

Restaurants
Several good cafes are located in the center of town near the hotels. Sunset dinners are best enjoyed at the seafood restaurants down by the river. **Cabin Restaurant**, just south of the Tharn Thong and near the Lak Muang shrine, is a cozy and somewhat elegant spot with Thai, Chinese, and Western dishes.

Transportation
Phayao is 92 km south of Chiang Rai on the old highway which once provided the main link between Chiang Mai and Chiang Rai. Most buses between these two cities now use Hwy. 1019, which cuts through the mountains and passes through Wiang Papao and Mae Suai. Travelers from Chiang Mai must ask for a bus which uses the old route. An easier alternative is to visit Phayao after Chiang Rai, and then return to Chiang Mai or head east to Phrae and Nan.

Motorcyclists can enjoy a wonderful ride west from Phayao on Hwy. 1282, across the towering mountain range, and down to Wang Nua and Hwy. 1019, which returns to Chiang Mai.

PHRAE

Phrae is a modern, provincial capital made prosperous from coal mining and the logging industry. The city once served as a Burmese outpost during the Burmese occupation of Thailand, and later hosted a large number of Burmese and Laotian loggers involved in the teak trade. Today the town is known for its temples, which uniquely combine Burmese and Laotian styles, rattan furniture, and homespun blue farmers' shirts now worn all over Thailand.

Opinions differ sharply on the merits of Phrae. Some visitors cast negative votes on the modern drabness and uniformity of the architecture, while others regard Phrae as a lovely town with a great deal of charm and character.

Wat Chom Sawan
The Burmese heritage of Phrae is demonstrated by this Shan-style temple constructed some 80 years ago outside the old city walls. The sanctuary features Burmese-tiered roofs with fine coffered ceilings, and a monumental *chedi* gilded with a copper crown.

Wat Sra Bo Kaew
Another Burmese-style temple with a Shan *chedi* and richly decorated altars inside the modern *viharn*.

Wat Prabat Ming
Located near the center of town, Wat Prabat Ming Muang Vora Viharn features a modern *viharn* and an 18th-century *bot* constructed in the Laotian style with sloping columns and a slat-covered roof. Inside the *viharn* is the most significant Buddha image of the province, Pra Buddha Kosa Srichai Maha Sakayamuni.

Wat Luang
Chief interest here are the Burmese-style *chedi* and decorated wooden beams inside the central *viharn*. A small but worthy museum is also located here.

Wat Pong Sunan
Laotian influences predominate in the handsome *viharn* graced with carved wooden pediments and gilded reliefs.

Wat Pra Non
Another Laotian-style temple with a lovely *viharn* carved with fine wooden pediments, and an interior space mysteriously illuminated by narrow vertical slits. The chapel to the left contains a reclining Buddha which names the temple and dates from the 18th century.

Ban Prathup Teakwood House
Certainly the most curious sight in Phrae is the old teakwood home in Ban Prathup (also called Ban Sao Roi Tan), about one km west of town. Constructed from an almost unbelievable

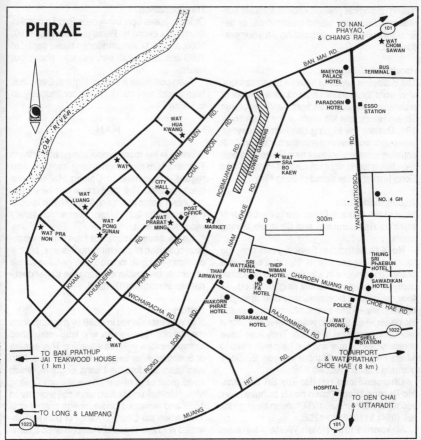

amount of precious wood, the opulent home and private museum is a testament to the breathtaking beauty of teakwood, and man's insatiable lust for the precious commodity. Never again will the world see such lavish use of teakwood.

Wat Prathat Choe Hae

Phrae's most famous temple is eight km west of town, about one km beyond the village of Padang, at the top of a teak-clad hill cut by two stairways flanked by Burmese lions and guardian *nagas*. The right-hand stairway leads to a small shrine which houses the highly revered Buddha image of Pra Chao Tan Chai,

widely believed to have the power to grant wishes and cure sterility. Crammed inside the small grounds of the *wat* stands a 33-meter *chedi* sheathed with gilded copper plates, and a modern *viharn* noted for its unusual cruciform pattern. Wat Prathat Choe Hae derives its name from a type of heavy satin fabric *(Choe Hae)* which pilgrims often wrap around the *chedi*.

Mini-trucks to the temple can be flagged down on Choe Hae Road.

Muang Phi (Ghost City)

Eighteen km from Phrae, off Hwy. 101 on a side road just before Km 143, is an eerie natural wonder created by soil and wind erosion. The resulting geological phenomenon resembles sur-realistic chimneys, magic mushrooms, or as-teroid dwellings . . . depending on your per-spective.

Handicraft Villages

The distinctive *seua ma hawn,* a bluish farmers' shirt worn throughout Thailand as a symbol of proletariat unity, originates from the village of Ban Thung Hong, four km north of Phrae on Hwy. 101. Despite the logging ban initiated several years ago, woodcarving remains a traditional oc-cupation in several villages near Phrae. The best selection is found eight km south of Phrae at Hua Dong Market in the district of Sung Men.

Accommodations

Most of the hotels in Phrae are in the center of town on Rajadamnern and Charoen Muang roads.

No. 4 Guesthouse: Several years ago, the four schoolteachers from Sukothai opened a branch guesthouse in a teakwood home tucked away in a quiet residential neighborhood. As their calling card proclaims, they offer "free gold drinking water, free tourist information, free toi-let paper"—all the essential ingredients for a wonderful vacation in Phrae. They also have motorcycles for rent and can help with visits to Mrabi ("Yellow Leaf") tribal villages. 22 Soi 1 Yantara Kitkosol Rd., 40-80B.

Charoen Road Hotels: The **Sri Wattana**, **Ho Fa**, and **Thep Wiman** hotels all have basic rooms at basic prices. 153 Charoen Muang Rd., tel. (054) 511047, 80-120B.

Nakhorn Phrae Hotel: Western travelers who need a better hotel with standard amenities stay at the Nakhorn Phrae just opposite Thai Airways. The hotel offers tourist information, maps, and guided tours from the *samlor* drivers who hang out at the front door. Their popular cafe has great food and some of the most amus-ing cabaret singers in Northern Thailand. 69 Rajadamnern Rd., tel. (054) 521901, 220-280B a/c rooms with private bath.

Maeyom Palace Hotel: Phrae's newest and most luxurious hotel is just west of the bus ter-minal. The six-story hotel has 100 rooms, a large swimming pool, several restaurants, and conference facilities. 181 Yantara Kikosol Rd., tel. (054) 522906, fax (054) 522904, 1100-1600B.

Transportation

Ordinary buses from the Arcade Bus Terminal in Chiang Mai depart for Phrae daily at 0800, 1100, 1500, and 1700. Air-conditioned buses depart at 1000 and 2200. Both services take about four hours.

Train commuters should alight at Den Chai, from where mini-trucks shuttle continuously up to Phrae.

NAN

Situated in the most remote region of Northern Thailand, Nan ranks high among travelers, who regard it as similar to Chiang Mai of three decades ago. The landscape combines the mountain vistas of Chiang Mai with the bucolic charms of the lazy, brown river which slowly winds to the east.

Nan is a fairly prosperous town with the stan-dard collection of concrete shophouses, but the old temples, idyllic location, and genuine sense of remoteness make it among the better desti-nations in northern Thailand.

History

Nan was established in 1368 by migrants from the Mekong River region, who later established formal relations with the emerging Thai empire at Sukothai. After the demise of Sukothai, Nan was absorbed into the Lanna kingdom, which ruled most of northern Thailand from Chiang Mai. Nan fell under Burmese sovereignty in 1558 and remained under foreign control until 1786 when the Chakri Dynasty of Bangkok lib-erated northern Thailand. Nan remained a semi-autonomous principality ruled by hereditary princes until 1931 when it came under the full control of Bangkok.

Nan achieved a modest degree of interna-tional acclaim in 1927 when the filmmaking team of Schoedsack and Cooper produced *Chang* in the forests outside town. Six years later the pair produced their most famous film, *King Kong,* modeled after their efforts in Nan. More recent-ly, *The Elephant Keeper* was filmed in 1990 near Phrae and Nan by a Thai writer-director named Chatri Yukol.

Nan National Museum

An excellent starting point for an exploration of Nan is the centrally located museum, recently

NAN

© MOON PUBLICATIONS, INC.

opened in a palace (Ho Kham) constructed in 1903 by Prince Phalida. Inside the small but outstanding museum are informative ethnographic displays, detailed explanations of the history of Thai art, and the highly revered black elephant tusk on the second floor, reputedly brought to Nan some 300 years ago by the king of Chiang Tung.

The museum is open Wed.-Sun. 0900-1630.

Wat Chang Kham Vora Viharn

Across from the museum stands a temple and *chedi* constructed in 1547 with elephant *(chang)* buttresses around the perimeter. One of the two rather unexceptional *viharns* in the *wat* compound contains a 145-cm walking Buddha made of pure gold, discovered by Alexander Griswold in 1955 after the plaster covering the image was broken. The monastery is still actively used to train young novices in the traditions of Buddhism.

Wat Phumin

The finest architectural piece in Nan dates from 1603 with extensive restorations in 1867 and 1991. Unlike most temples in Thailand, the central *viharn* was constructed in a curious cruciform pattern to showcase the four large Sukothai-style Buddhas which face the cardinal points. The superb arrangement of pillars and coffered ceilings make Wat Phumin an excellent example of northern Thai architecture. Also note the carved doors, comparable only to the famous doors of Wat Suthat in Bangkok.

The temple is chiefly noted for its outstanding murals, which provide historical study of local society some 100 years ago. Art historians believe the murals were painted by Thai Lue artists who possessed both a fine degree of humor and an amazing attention to detail. Based on the Buddhist Khatan *Kumman Jakatas,* the murals include a famous scene of a young man courting a thinly clad girl, and a fine portrait of a former governor of the province.

Wat Praya Phu

Enshrined in the undistinguished *bot* are two rare Sukothai-style Buddhas commissioned by a Nan prince named Ngua Phan Sum and cast in 1426. The walking images display slightly different positions with finely varied expressions of great power and sensitivity. Centering the display is an enormous seated Buddha.

Wat Suan Tan

Highlights at Wat Suan Tan include a 40-meter *prang* with a spire of Khmer design and a 15th-century *viharn* which enshrines an important Buddha image named Pra Chao Thong Tip. According to local chronicles, the four-meter bronze image was cast in 1449 by King Tilokarja of Chiang Mai after his conquest of Nan. The image shows both Sukothai and Chiang Saen influences.

Wat Prathat Chae Heng

Two km southeast of town on Hwy. 1168 lies another impressive temple, constructed six centuries ago on the original site of the city established by King Chao Khun Fong. Leading to the summit of Mount Phubhiang is a royal staircase guarded by two enormous *naga makara* figures. The elevated courtyard is dominated by a 55-meter golden *chedi* and a marvelous *viharn* capped with a five-level roof of Laotian inspiration.

Wat Prayawat

South of the city stands a strangely shaped *chedi* believed to be the oldest structure in the region. Placed inside the pyramidal *chedi* are niches containing standing Buddhas in the Sinhalese manner. The modern *viharn* contains an altar richly embellished in Laotian style.

Wat Prathat Khao Noi to the rear offers fine views and pair of Buddha statues in the late Chiang Saen style.

Wat Nongbua

Situated outside town in the district of Tha Wang Pha is a century-old temple constructed by Thai Lue artists that boasts the finest murals in the region. Unlike the murals of Wat Phumin, the frescoes remain in outstanding condition with bright shades and livelier colors. Perhaps painted by the same artists of Wat Phumin, the stories depict legends from the *Candgada Jataka,* which once served to encourage ethical behavior among young Thais.

Doi Phukha National Park

A popular day-ride for motorcyclists is 60 km

north to Doi Phukha, past waterfalls, caves, and hilltribe villages on one of the most scenic roads in northern Thailand. Take Hwy. 1169 to Santisuk and then Hwy. 1256 east from the town of Pua. The return loop can be completed via Pua and Tha Wang Pha down Hwy. 1080.

Mrabi Hill Tribe

Phrae and Nan both serve as launching points for excursions to the Mrabi tribes, called Phi Thong Luang by the Thais and nicknamed the Spirits of the Yellow Leaves from the color of their temporary leaf huts. The Mrabi are elusive nomadic hunters whose very existence remained mythical until their discovery by a jungle expedition several decades ago. Numbering fewer than 150 in the entire country, the Mrabi are now proselytized by American missionaries from Florida, and the subject of tours organized by international trekking agencies and guesthouses in Phrae and Nan.

Accommodations

Kiwi Guesthouse: Nan's first guesthouse is operated by a Kiwi named Peter who provides trekking information, bicycle and motorcycle rentals, and tips on nearby waterfalls and border excursions. Mahawong Rd., tel. (054) 710658, 40-80B.

Sukasem Hotel: A simple Thai hotel conveniently located near the bus terminal and across from the night market. Each room includes a fan and shower. 119 Anathat Wararicharad Rd., tel. (054) 710141, 100-160B.

Devaraj Hotel: The best hotel in Nan offers large, clean rooms with hot showers, a popular cafe with cabaret singers in the evening, and tourist information. 466 Sumon Devaraj Rd., tel. (054) 710094, 200-250B fan, 200-600B a/c.

Restaurants

Tip Top Cafe: The most popular travelers' spot in Nan is opposite the post office and Krung Thai Bank. Manager Ferrini Paolo and his wife prepare Thai and Italian dishes, not to mention his famous Caesar salad and cordon bleu.

Night Market: Food vendors serve noodle soups and fried dishes under the tin-roofed lot just across from the Sukasem Hotel.

Transportation

Nan is 668 km north of Bangkok and 318 km southeast of Chiang Mai.

Air: Thai Airways flies once daily from Chiang Mai (400B) and Phitsanulok (425B) via Phrae. Thai Airways (tel. 054-710377) is located at 34 Mahaprom Road.

Bus: Ordinary buses depart from Chiang Mai at 0800, 1100, 1500, and 1700, and take eight hours along the old route via Lampang and Phrae. Air-conditioned buses leave at 1000 and 2200. Buses from Chiang Rai depart at 0930 and take four hours to cover the 270 kilometers.

Overnight buses from Bangkok's Northern Bus Terminal depart hourly from 1800 to 2200.

Train: The nearest train terminus to Nan is at Den Chai, 20 km south of Phrae. Minitrucks and buses from the Den Chai train station head north to Phrae and Nan.

NORTHEASTERN THAILAND

Northeastern Thailand—referred to as the Issan (Ee-saan) by the Thais—is one of the most traditional and least visited regions in Thailand. In many ways, the Issan comprises the heartland of Thailand, where old Thai customs and lifestyles survive among the friendly and polite population. Few travelers visit the northeast, but promotional efforts of the TAT and the opening of Laos and Cambodia promise to increase the numbers of visitors to the last untouched region in the country.

Issan refers to an old Mon-Khmer kingdom named Isana which once flourished in the region. The term can be loosely translated into either "Vastness" or "Prosperity," though only the former seems appropriate.

The Issan spreads over a vast and arid limestone plateau bounded on the north by the Mekong River, which separates Thailand from Laos, to the south by the Dong Rek Mountains, which form the border with Cambodia, and on the west by Phang Hoei Mountains, which divide the Issan from Central Thailand. Comprising some 170,000 square km, this gigantic region sprawls across one-third of the total land acreage in Thailand. The sheer geographic immensity makes it a challenging destination for the visitor with limited time but also helps preserve the region against the onslaught of mass tourism. The Issan is a world apart, which quickly separates the tourist from the traveler.

> *For too long it has appeared that normal project cycle for many tourist resorts in developing countries is thus: Discovery of a pristine natural site ready for tourism development, development of the site in a hasty and unplanned fashion, success with tour operators, hordes of foreign tourists, internal migration of labour to meet demand in the resort, springing up of shanty towns to provide necessary work force, degradation of the environment, and decay of the resort as it loses favour with tours.*
>
> —Antonio Savignac, Secretary-General, World Tourism Organization

INTRODUCTION

The People

Issan inhabitants include Thais, Chinese, and large numbers of Laotians who migrated into the infertile region from their homeland across the Mekong River. Laotian culture and character is readily apparent in the traditional temple architecture near the Mekong, unique languages which mix standard Thai with Laotian loanwords, and the physiognomy of the people, who can often be recognized by their darker skins, burned by years of toil in the ricefields.

There are also many speakers of Khmer, especially in the Cambodian border districts of Sisaket, Buriram, and Surin provinces. Less well known are the earlier, pre-Khmer peoples such as the Suay who have traditionally worked as *mahouts* and hunters of wild elephants.

The Issan has the highest population density, unemployment levels, and rates of poverty in the nation. Consequently, large numbers of Issan people (Khon Issan) migrate to the Middle East where they work the oil fields or to southern Thailand where they take jobs on fishing boats. Most, however, go to Bangkok where they drive *tuk tuks,* operate portable foodstalls, fall into prostitution, or find employment as construction workers on Sukumvit Road.

Despite their poverty, the people of the Issan remain an independent lot who view life with a refreshing blend of fatalism and good humor.

Under The Surface

Nature, unfortunately, has not been kind to the region. Cursed with sandy soils which limit farmers to a single rice crop each year, erratic rainfall that brings famine and floods, a searing hot season, and the country's highest population density, northeastern Thailand ranks as the problem child of Thailand. The Issan is not only its poorest region, but also a land plagued by environmental degradation, peasant landlessness, malnutrition, desertion by the young to the cities, encroachment by farmers into protected forests, and an agriculture based almost exclusively on rice. Newspaper stories relate sad tales of landless farmers forced off their meager plots by well-connected businessmen, who develop the land into golf courses or industrial estates. Floods, heat waves, drought, and political fights over dams and reforestation programs are other Issan tragedies which fill the newspaper headlines.

Even the spelling of the region seems to be a problem. Over the last few years, tourist and government publications have spelled the territory as Issan, Isarn, I-San, Isan, Isaan, Esarn, E-sarn, Esan, and E-san!

Political and economic solutions have been attempted with varying results. The region now has a good system of highways, and electricity reaches most of the villages. Dozens of dams have successfully been constructed, though large-scale dam construction appears to have ended with the 1992 cancellation of the Pak Moon project near Ubon Rachathani. Other proposals, such as the ambitious Green Issan project which was announced with great fanfare several years ago, seem to appear and then disappear with the changing administrations in Bangkok. Despite the rhetoric, critics charge that the Issan remains largely ignored except during election campaigns, when politicians arrive to buy votes for 50 *baht* per household.

Certainly the most controversial project currently raging in the northeast is the Khor Chor Kor, a reforestation plan sponsored by the Thai army which intends to move some 1.25 million farmers from degraded forest reserves controlled by the Royal Forestry Department onto other lands already inhabited by other farmers. The evacuated land would then be replanted with forest cover such as nonnative eucalyptus gum trees which would, in turn, help expand wildlife habitat and rebuild watersheds. The plan appears well intended, but landless peasants believe it is a camouflage operation designed to convert their farms into corporate pulp and gum plantations for the benefit of privileged Thais.

Sightseeing Highlights

In recent years, the Thai government has mounted a concerted effort to sell the Issan as a major tourist destination. This is an uphill task. A relative lack of historical and cultural attractions makes the Issan less appealing than other regions, plus the landlocked plateau obviously

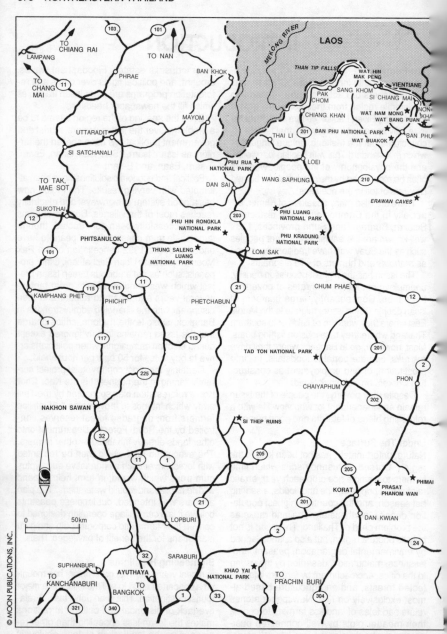

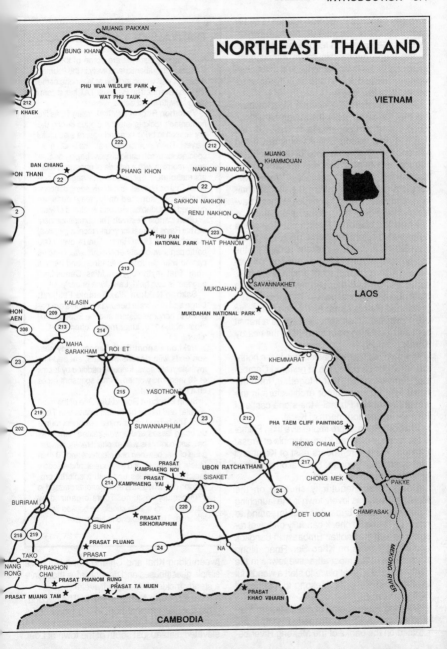

lacks any beaches or tropical islands. Equally discouraging are the vast distances between points of interest, which require frequent flights or long, tough, overland journeys. Although unquestionably the most authentic and untouched region in Thailand, tourist arrivals in the Issan remain at very low levels.

Should you visit the northeast? Most travelers feel that the Issan lacks the strong attractions found in northern and southern Thailand, and that first-time visitors should explore Chiang Mai and the southern islands before venturing into the remote northeast. On the other hand, Issan fans insist that the absence of Western visitors is a great change from the rest of Thailand, and recommend the region to those travelers who enjoy getting off the beaten track.

Khao Yai National Park: First stop in the northeast is a large national park four hours from Bangkok. A quick weekend escape for the asphyxiated citizens of Bangkok, Khao Yai provides a lush environment of jungle, waterfalls, some wildlife, and a dozen hiking trails. The most popular national park in Thailand.

Nakhon Ratchasima: Also called Korat, this busy town has little to offer except as a transit spot and launching point for visits to the nearby Khmer temples.

Phimai: Top historical attractions in the northeast are the rich collection of restored Cambodian temples which, taken together, form the finest spectrum of Khmer architecture in the world. Prasat Hin Phimai—the stone castle of Phimai—is one hour north of Korat.

Phanom Rung: More impressive than Phimai is the recently restored Khmer temple of Prasat Phanom Rung, three hours east of Korat and slightly south of Buriram. Several other Khmer temples are also near Korat.

Nong Khai: Beautifully situated on the Mekong River, this lovely town is the launching point for visits to Laos. Visitors intending to reach Laos should check carefully on travel restrictions with the Laotian Embassy in Bangkok and with travelers on Khao San Road. Nong Khai is one of the most attractive towns in the northeast, and a great place to start a wonderful journey west along the Mekong to a series of riverside villages.

Mekong River: Some of northeastern Thailand's most idyllic and unspoiled villages are situated on the banks of the Mekong River be-

FESTIVALS OF THE NORTHEAST

Northeast festivals are some of the most colorful, authentic, and lively in the country. A perfect visit would include at least one of the following events. The Bangkok TAT has a complete list with exact dates.

Yasothon Rocket Festival: Issan Thais fire homemade rockets into the clouds during the dry season to bring rain and ensure a bountiful harvest. The Yasothon Festival, Thailand's most spectacular pyrotechnic display, begins on Saturday morning with a parade of enormous rockets elaborately decorated with *nagas*, traditional Thai orchestras, and lovely *serng* dancers. Rockets are launched on Sunday; duds are dumped in mudholes. Second weekend of May.

Ubon Candle Festival: The commencement of Thai Rains Retreat for young monks *(phansa)* is celebrated in Ubon Ratchathani by over 4,000 participants who haul enormous wax candles carved with *garudas,* elephants, and heroes from Thai mythology. A Miss Candlelight pageant is also held. Late June or early July.

Sakhon Nakhon Wax Temple Festival: Large and elaborate beeswax temples are paraded to honor ancestors and the Buddha. Full moon of the 11th lunar month, often mid-October.

Nakhon Panom Boat Races: Rainy season ends with dozens of boats, shaped like mythological *nagas,* furiously paddled by teams of 40 men and women. Pimai sponsors races on a smaller scale.

Surin Elephant Round Up: One of the most popular and highly promoted festivals in Thailand. The big day starts with an elephant round-up using lassos and a well-trained female as bait, and continues with elephant races, dances, a tug-of-war between one elephant and 70 men (guess who wins), and hilarious elephant soccer matches. Festivities end with a colorful procession of pachyderms and *mahouts* dressed in 17th-century costume. Tours organized by Bangkok travel agents should be booked well in advance. Third weekend in November.

tween Nong Khai and Chiang Khan. All have simple guesthouses and decent cafes that serve a steady trickle of Western travelers.

Phu Kradung National Park: The second-most popular national park in the Issan offers spectacular views and thick vegetation on an elevated plateau just south of the town of Loei.

Nakhon Phanom: Few travelers venture beyond the Friendship Highway, which connects Nakhon Ratchasima with Nong Khai, but hardy travelers sometimes visit Nakhon Phanom to see the small, golden, Laotian-style *chedi* of That Phanom, a temple highly venerated by both the Thai and Laotian communities.

***Vipassana* Meditation:** Northeastern Thailand has long been the center of Buddhist *vipassana* meditation, as practiced in several famous *wats* near the Laotian border. This state of affairs seems to stem from the traditional piety of northeastern Thais and from the legacy of a famous Thammayut monk named Achaan Man (1870-1949) who hailed from Ubon Ratchathani. Three famous *wats* near Ubon Ratchathani include Wat Paa Nanachat ("International Forest Monastery") where most of the monks are English-speaking Westerners, a cave monastery named Wat Tham Saeng Phet also popular with foreign monks, and Wa Non Paa Phong where several American masters including Jack Kornfield once served their monkhood.

Routes

Several routes are possible depending on your interests and time.

Korat and Khmer Monuments: Visitors keen on Khmer architecture but with a limited schedule should use Korat as a base for short side trips to the nearby monuments. The finest Cambodian architecture is at Phimai, Phanom Wan, Phanom Rung, and Muang Tam. After a tour of the monuments, return to Bangkok with a stop at Khao Yai National Park. Travelers who need some sun and beach after all the dusty monuments should note that buses now directly connect Korat with Pattaya and other beach resorts on the east coast of Thailand. Allow three to five days for this brief look at the northeast.

Korat to Nong Khai: The most popular journey in the Issan starts with Korat and the Khmer temples described above. Trains and buses head north from Korat to Khon Kaen and Udon Thani, two ordinary towns with little of great interest. Chaiyaphum, however, is a somewhat attractive town that provides a worthwhile side trip between Korat and Khon Kaen.

The journey up the Friendship Hwy. terminates in the lovely town of Nong Khai, on the banks of the Mekong River. If border conditions permit, continue across to Laos to visit Vientiane and other towns. Otherwise, head west by bus or rented motorcycle to the fine little villages which hug the banks of the Mekong. Spend a few nights in either Sang Khom or Pak Chom before reaching Chiang Kham. The road then heads south to Loei and Phu Kradung National Park before returning to Udon Thani or Nong Khai. Alternatively, proceed west from Loei to Lom Sak and Phitsanulok in central Thailand.

This 10-day to two-week excursion covers the highlights of the northeast and avoids the long and exhausting bus ride to the more remote regions.

The Grand Tour: Travelers with over three weeks, and a great deal of patience, can circumnavigate the entire region through Korat, Khon Kaen, Udon Thani, Nong Khai, Nakhon Phanom, Ubon Ratchathani, and Surin before returning to Korat.

Countries, like people, are loved for their failings.

—F. Yeats Brown,
Bengal Lancer

EN ROUTE TO THE MONUMENTS

KHAO YAI NATIONAL PARK

Thailand's most popular national park, south of Pak Chom and 200 km northeast of Bangkok, is a world of rich and diverse flora from evergreen and rainforest to *lalang* and rolling hills of tropical grasslands. Established in 1972 as the first national park in Thailand, Khao Yai spreads across four provinces and a variety of ecological zones including marshlands, tropical forests, and the sandstone mountains which form the Dongrak Range.

A small visitors center a few kilometers north of the closed Khao Yai Motorlodge offers some haphazard but informative displays on local wildlife and hiking trails. Adjacent foodstalls provide the cheapest meals in the park. Maps and more details can be picked up from the visitors center.

Waterfalls And Caves

Hiking trails starting from the visitors center lead to several waterfalls and limestone caves. However, the great distances from headquarters to the falls often necessitates a private vehicle or tour organized by the park or a private tour company such as Jungle Adventures in Pak Chom.

Kong Kao Falls adjacent to the headquarters is small and rather unimpressive except during the rainy season from July to November. A narrow trail from the campsite east of the golf course heads to Pha Kluai Mai ("Orchid Falls"), Haew Suwat, Haew Sai, and Haew Pratun waterfalls. These falls can also be reached by walking along the asphalt road which passes through the abandoned golf course, or the eight-km trail which starts at Kong Kao Falls.

Roads west of the motor lodge lead to Manao Falls (7 km), Tatapu Falls (10 km), Tadtakong Falls (14 km), and Nan Rong Falls (20 km), the largest cascade of water in Khao Yai. Tours often include the bat-infested limestone cave at Khao Rub Chang, situated at the periphery of the park.

Hiking Trails

A guide distributed at the headquarters describes 12 hiking trails originally made by wild elephants. Trails near the visitors center are kept in fairly good condition and marked with color-coded trees set 20-30 meters apart. Trails located farther into the jungle are often buried under wild vegetation and difficult to follow. Guides can be hired at the lodge.

Trail 1, the most popular hike at Khao Yai, starts behind the visitors center and leads eight km to Haew Suwat Falls, from where a paved road leads back to the visitors center. Trail 2 leads six km north from Trail 1 to an elephant salt lick near the main road. Trail 5 from Haew Sawat Falls cuts through grasslands and emerges onto a spectacular view of Khao Laem Mountain. Trail 6 is a good beginner's trail that goes four km to Nong Phak Chi, a rebuilt wildlife observation tower northwest of the visitors center. Visitors are allowed to spend the night on the tower, but bring along all essentials including rain gear, warm clothes, sleeping bags, and flashlights. Trail 10 is a popular hike for visitors staying at the park lodge, while Trail 11 is an eight-km roundtrip hike that visits rivers, caves, and small waterfalls.

Wildlife

Wildlife inside the 2,168-square-km park includes wild elephants, a few remaining tigers, and birds such as hornbills and kingfishers. Larger animals such as leopards and Asiatic black bears are extremely shy and rarely seen, though the birdlife and fascinating sounds of a tropical rainforest are ample rewards for most visitors.

Although unchecked logging and illegal poaching have sharply reduced indigenous wildlife, elephants and wild deer rummaging through trash dumpsters could sometimes be spotted on "Night Shining" truck drives which were organized by the motor lodge. Aside from spending a night in a watchtower, night safaris provide the only chance to see wildlife.

Tours

The immensity of Khao Yai and the lack of organized transportation within the park boundaries make an organized tour a sensible idea.

KHAO YAI
NATIONAL PARK

TRAIL 12

ELEPHANT
SALT LICK ★

VIEWPOINT ★

TO PAK CHONG

PONG KAENG BIN
WILDLIFE TOWER

1 KM

TO KLONG KHAO
WILDLIFE TOWER

LAM TAKHONG RIVER

NONG PAK CHI
★ WILDLIFE TOWER

1 KM

TRAIL 2

4 KM

TRAIL 6   5 KM

TRAIL 1

4 KM

TRAIL 1   4 KM

HAEW PRATUN
FALLS ★

TRAIL 7   3 KM

KONG KAO FALLS

TRAIL 8

TRAIL 6   1.5 KM

VISITORS CENTER

TRAIL 9   1 KM

TRAIL 3   4 KM

HAEW SAI
FALLS ★

HAEW
SUWAT
FALLS ★

GOLF
COURSE

CAMPSITE ■

TRAIL 5

TRAIL 4

PHA KLUAI
MAI FALLS ★

TRAIL 10

GAS STATION
TAT OFFICE

TRAIL 11

TATAPHU
FALLS ★

VIEWPOINT ★

TO PRACHINBURI

0   1km

KRACHAI FALLS ★

★ HIN KLANG FALLS

★ PHATABAK FALLS

KHAO KEO
(1351 m) ★

© MOON PUBLICATIONS, INC.

Park Tours: Day-tours sponsored by park rangers to various waterfalls and viewpoints leave daily around 0900 and 1300 from the visitors center.

Jungle Adventures: As of this writing, only one private company organizes comprehensive tours for Westerners. Jungle Adventures (tel. 044-312877) at 752/11 Kongvaksin Rd. Soi 3 in Pak Chom sponsors 36-hour tours to various spots inside the park such as Buddhist caves, bat caves, three waterfalls, viewpoints, and a rainforest jungle, and offers a night safari. With a minimum of four hikers, tours leave at 1500 from the Jungle Adventures office on the main road in Pak Chom, a few hundred meters north of the train station and just opposite the a/c bus stop. Tours cost 700B including breakfast, guide services, and guesthouse accommodations in Pak Chom. Call first to verify if they are still in business.

Accommodations

Khao Yai Motorlodge: The rambling TAT-operated set of bungalows was closed in late 1992 to minimize the environmental impact at the park.

Juldis Khai Yai Resort: A private corporation operates an expensive set of luxurious chalets fixed with facilities such as tennis courts, swimming pool, and animal-spotting tours. Rooms can be booked in advance from their office in Bangkok or directly at the lodge. Advance reservations are imperative on weekends, when the park is flooded with Thai tourists from Bangkok. 54 Mu 4 Dhanarat Rd., Bangkok tel. (02) 255-4960, fax (02) 255-2460, 1500-2000B.

Jungle Adventures Guesthouse: The small private tour operator in Pak Chom operates a small guesthouse in an alley due south of the stoplight. 752/11 Kongvaksin Rd. Soi 3, Pak Chom, tel. (044) 312877, 60-150B.

Getting There

Khao Yai is 200 km northeast of Bangkok on the road to Nakhon Ratchasima.

Buses: Buses from Bangkok's Northern Bus Terminal to Pak Chom take three or four hours on the Friendship Hwy., constructed during the Vietnam War by the Americans. Attractions en route include an immense white Buddha and cave complex on the right called Wat Theppitak (Wat Teppitakpunaram), Lam Ta Klong Dam, souvenir stalls and experimental projects where Danish experts have established milk farms, a roadside Buddha surrounded by comical figurines, and several expensive hill resorts and golf courses which cater to wealthy Thais and Japanese tourists. Khao Yai region has gone from untamed wilderness to condo hell in just 10 years.

The turnoff to Khao Yai is five km before Pak Chom. Since only limited bus service is available from Pak Chom, independent travelers should ask the bus driver to stop at the small Khao Yai signpost on the right side of the road, and then wait for a mini-truck or hitchhike up to the park.

The TAT also organizes direct bus service from Bangkok to Khao Yai.

Pak Chom to Khao Yai: Orange trucks from Pak Chom to Khao Yai depart daily at 1700. Trucks go from the visitors center back to Pak Chom on weekdays at 0800, and weekends at 0800 and 1700. *Songtaos* from Pak Chom to Khao Yai are plentiful on weekends, but scarce during the week.

KORAT (NAKHON RATCHASIMA)

Korat, officially called Nakhon Ratchasima, is the region's largest city and gateway to the northeast. The modern town has little interest or charm but serves as a handy base from which to explore the nearby Khmer ruins and rest up after a long bus or train ride from Bangkok.

Korat was established during the reign of King Narai after he merged the twin cities of Sema and Khorapura. Evidence of the ancient city is limited to some reconstructed walls and an old moat.

The city enjoyed a brief heyday during the late 1960s and early 1970s when it served as a major base for U.S. forces assigned to the Vietnamese conflict. Legacies of this turbulent era include a handful of retired American veterans who gather for darts and cocktails in the VFW Cafe, massage parlors, nightclubs, and Turkish baths patronized almost exclusively by local Thais.

Suranari Statue

Modern Korat spreads around a statue honoring Thao Suranari, the national heroine who in 1826 convinced Korat ladies to seduce and then murder invading Laotian soldiers. A two-week festival held in March honors the patron saint of Korat. Her highly revered image—fashioned with a strange but once-chic haircut—is surrounded by stages for itinerant musicians and local dancers.

Korat National Museum

The small Maha Viriwong Museum, in the compound of Wat Suthachinda, offers a very small but somewhat informative display of religious artifacts and archaeological discoveries from northeastern Thailand. Unfortunately, few of the objects are labeled in English, lighting is poor, and most of the pottery is hidden inside dusty glass cases. Among the better pieces are a standing Dvaravati image from Nonthai, Lopburi-style figures, "Buddhas in Abgumentation," and rare statues recovered from Wat Phanom Wan.

The museum is open daily from 0900 to 1600.

Wat Sala Loi

A completely unusual modern temple designed in the shape of a Chinese junk is located in the far northeastern end of town along the Lam Tha Khong River. Deviating from the strict geometrical style of traditional temples, Wat Sala Loi has won several modern architectural awards, including a prize from the Thai Architects Guild.

Markets

A great little morning market operates in an alley one block west of the Thao Suranari statue. Less lively but worth visiting for cheap cassettes and foodstalls is the small night market on Manat Rd. just north of the Chomsurang Hotel.

Ban Dan Kwian

Unique pottery fashioned from iron-oxide-rich soil is produced in a small village 15 km south of Korat. Dan Kwian itself is nothing special except for the outstanding collection of antique carts displayed in the rear courtyard of the Village Museum owned by artist Viroj Srisuro, which deserve better treatment in a more accessible location than Dan Kwian.

Bus 1307 to Dan Kwian runs every 20 minutes from the ordinary bus terminal on Burin Lane, and from the south gate bus stop near the intersection of Chainarong and Kamheng Songkram roads, a few blocks east of the Chomsurang Hotel.

Pak Thong Chai

Several of the most famous silk manufacturers in Thailand operate factories in the Pak Thong Chai, 32 km south of Korat on Hwy. 304. Shops to visit on Sripolratana Rd. include Srithai Silk and Praneet Thai Silk, though prices are somewhat steep and many of the garments are now produced with varying blends of polyester. A silk museum and cultural center managed by the Silks Weavers Association of Korat opened in 1992.

Bus 1303 to Pak Thong Chai leaves from the ordinary bus terminal on Burin Lane and from the Friendship Hwy. just opposite the TAT office.

Budget Accommodations

Korat Doctor's Guesthouse: Dr. Sunan's hostel is Korat's first spot geared for backpackers rather than tourists. The good doctor of Bangkok and his sister Sue, who spent 17 years in Chicago as a nurse, operate one of the friendliest places in the northeast, providing information on tours to nearby Khmer monuments, motorcycle rentals, laundry service, and transportation schedules. Visitors are invited to use their kitchen and crash in either the main house or the teakwood home a few doors away.

Doctor's House is one block east of the TAT office and two km west of the train station, on the second lane on the right before the railway tracks. 78 Sueb Siri Rd. Soi 4, tel. (044) 255846, 50-120B.

Siri Hotel: Korat's most memorable hotel/pub is constantly filled with budget travelers, Vietnam vets, foreign-service employees, and American GIs doing temporary duty at the nearby Thai airbase. Large and clean rooms are furnished with private bath, horizontal mirrors, and notices warning "no lepers, prostitutes or mischievous persons allowed."

The downstairs VFW restaurant has great Western food, sizzling T-bone steaks, and ice-cold beer—the best place to hang out and throw darts in Korat. 167 Poklang, tel. (044) 242831, 80-250B.

Far Thai Hotel: Clean, cheap, and close to city center, but somewhat noisy from street traffic. 35 Poklang, tel. (044) 242534, 100-250B.

Damrong Rak: 120-180B single, 160-200B double. 120 Champong, tel 242504.

Thal Pokopong: 120-140B single, 140-160B double. 104 Astadang, tel. 242454

Tokyo: 100-150B single, 150-200B double. 256 Suranari, tel. 2427888.

Moderate Accommodations

Korat Hotel: Popular with group tours, this old hotel features a nightclub and massage parlor which roar on weekends. 191 Atsadang, tel. (044) 242260, 200-250B fan, 300-450B a/c.

Royal Plaza Hotel: A new megahotel equipped with generic rooms, convention halls, cafes and restaurants, and the Lasertheque, the most expensive and exclusive disco in Korat. 547 Chomsurang Rd., tel. (044) 254127, Bangkok fax (02) 234-9409, 600-1000B.

Chomsurang Hotel: Once the best in Korat, the Chomsurang has faded badly and no longer attracts Western visitors. 2701 Mahadthai Rd., tel. (044) 257088, 700-1000B.

Luxury Accommodations

Klang Plaza Hotel: Tourism came of age in Korat with the 1992 opening of several new deluxe hotels including the Klang Plaza, Sher-aton, and Dusit Inn. Klang Plaza has the best location of the three, being only a few blocks from city center. Chomsurang Rd., tel. (044) 254998, 1600-2400B.

Sima Thai Sheraton: The international hotel group recently opened their newest property on the outskirts of town adjacent to the tourist office. The inconvenient location matters little to their main clientele, business travelers and tour groups. Facilities inside the four-story hotel include a swimming pool, health club, business center, and three restaurants. Friendship Hwy., Bangkok tel. (02) 234-5599, fax (02) 236-8320, 2000-2800B.

Restaurants

Night Market: Foodstalls are plentiful in the night market on Manat Rd. just north of the Chomsurang Hotel, and in the day market just west of the Thao Suranari Statue. Try the fresh fruit shakes and point-and-order foodstalls.

VFW Cafe: Certainly the most curious restaurant in the northeast is the small, crowded cafe

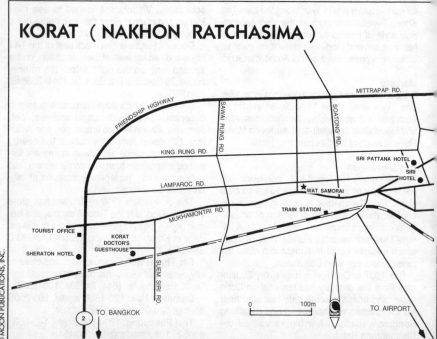

KORAT (NAKHON RATCHASIMA)

MITTRAPAP RD.

FRIENDSHIP HIGHWAY

SAWAI RUNG RD.

SOATONG RD.

KING RUNG RD.

SRI PATTANA HOTEL

SIRI HOTEL

LAMPAROC RD.

★ WAT SAMORAI

MUKHAMONTRI RD.

TRAIN STATION

TOURIST OFFICE

KORAT DOCTOR'S GUESTHOUSE

SHERATON HOTEL

SUEM SIRI RD.

0   100m

TO BANGKOK

2

TO AIRPORT

© MOON PUBLICATIONS, INC.

on the ground floor of the Siri Hotel. As the name implies, the cafe serves as headquarters for the Veterans of Foreign Wars (VFW) and is the gathering point for dozens of American veterans who served in the Vietnam conflict and then retired here in Korat. The a/c cafe resembles an American truck stop and serves good burgers, beer, and T-bone steaks in three sizes. Recommended for a flashback to the sixties. Inexpensive.

Downtown Cafes: Several small spots are located in the center of town near the Chompol and Nakon hotels. **Family Restaurant** is a clean and new cafe decorated with artwork and wicker furniture. Nearby **Spider Restaurant** features live music in cozy surroundings. **Dot Pub** near the night market is a dark cowboy bar with expensive drinks and blasting rock n' roll behind the rustic exterior.

Nightlife

Korat's most dubious attractions are the colossal nightclubs and massage parlors left over from the Vietnam War era. For a revealing insight into the world of prostitution, visit the enormous massage parlor adjacent to the Royal Plaza Hotel.

The Lasertheque inside the Royal Plaza Hotel is the best disco in Korat. Admission with two drinks is 80-120 *baht.*

Practicalities

Tourist Information: The TAT office (tel. 044-243751) is inconveniently located at 2102 Mittrapap Rd. at the extreme west end of town, three km west of the train station and adjacent to the Sheraton Hotel. Take any bus heading west.

Travel Agencies: The single biggest failure of tourism in Korat is the lack of organized tours to the nearby Khmer monuments. None of the travel agencies offer scheduled tours for solo travelers, unless you are prepared to charter a minibus for about 1500B per day. **United Eastern Tour** next to the TAT office on Mittrapap Rd., and **Korat Business** on Buarong Rd. cater

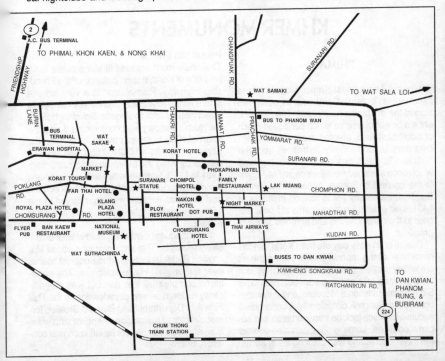

almost exclusively to group tours with advance reservations.

Motorcycle Rentals: Check with the Doctor's Guesthouse and **Virojyarnyon Motorcycles** at 554 Poklang Road. Bikes cost 150B for 80-100cc models and 200B for 125cc dirt bikes. Motorcycles are a great way to visit the handicraft villages and far-flung Khmer monuments.

Transportation

Korat is 256 km northeast of Bangkok.

Air: Thai Airway flies four times weekly from Bangkok for 650B. Thai Airways (tel. 044-257211) is at 14 Manat Road.

Bus: Ordinary and a/c buses from the Northern Bus Terminal in Bangkok leave every 15 minutes and take four hours to reach Korat.

Train: Thirteen trains a day depart from Hualampong Train Station in Bangkok. Most convenient are the rapid trains at 0615 and 0650, express at 0820, and ordinary diesels at 0910, 1105, 1145, and 2225. The train passes through lovely scenery including views of the golf courses near Khao Yai National Park and the eerie white Buddha at Wat Theppitak.

Leaving Korat

Bus: Korat has an ordinary bus terminal in Burin Lane near the First Hotel and Erawan Hospital, and an a/c bus terminal on the Friendship Hwy. (Mittrapap Rd.) about 500 meters north of town. The ordinary terminal has buses to nearby sights such as Ban Don Kwian and Phimai, plus major towns in the northeast such as Udon Thai and Nong Khai. Bus Terminal II on Friendship Highway serves all major towns in the northeast.

Train: Trains are the best way to travel around the northeast. A diesel train to Khon Kaen departs at 0807, while an express to Khon Kaen and Udon Thani leaves at 1226, 1515, and 0258. Seven trains a day leave for the eastern towns of Buriram, Surin, and Ubon Ratchathani. The most convenient departures are the 1130 rapid train, 1355 ordinary, and overnight services at 2350, 0155, 0402, and 0530.

KHMER MONUMENTS

PHIMAI

Southeast Asia's finest Khmer *prasats* (stone sanctuaries) outside Cambodia lie scattered across the dry plains near Korat. The Khmers, once a powerful empire which controlled much of Southeast Asia, erected dozens of magnificent temples and military fortresses from the 10th to 13th centuries along a royal highway which once stretched from their capital at Angkor to the borders of Burma. Although the Hindu-Buddhist monarchy fell to foreign invaders in 1431, their expansive monuments still bear witness to their artistic vision and primeval sense of grandeur.

Phimai is an easy day-trip from Korat, but the remainder of the monuments in the northeast are widely scattered and difficult to reach without an organized tour or hired transportation. The Siam Society, National Museum, and major tour operators in Bangkok occasionally sponsor group excursions which include transportation and accommodations. Large groups can also contact the travel agents and first-class hotels in Korat.

Prasat Hin Phimai

Thailand's most accessible stone castle is 60 km north of Korat, a short distance off the Friendship Highway. Phimai itself is a very old site where Neolithic artifacts and jewelry have been unearthed by archaeologists. Scholars believe the main sanctuary was constructed during the reign of King Surayavarman I, who ruled the Khmer empire from 1002 to 1050, with later additions by King Jayavarman, who ruled from 1181 to 1220. Contemporary with (and perhaps the model for) Angkor Wat, this vassal outpost and religious enclave was abandoned in the 15th century after the collapse of the Khmer empire.

In subsequent centuries, Phimai was extensively rebuilt by Thai architects who added Mahayana Buddhist imagery and Buddhist figures over the original Hindu sculpture. The sandstone complex fell into ruin but was magnificently restored several decades ago by the Thai Fine Arts Department and Bernard Groslier, former director of restoration at Angkor who wisely insisted that stuccowork be left in original condition. Bravo!

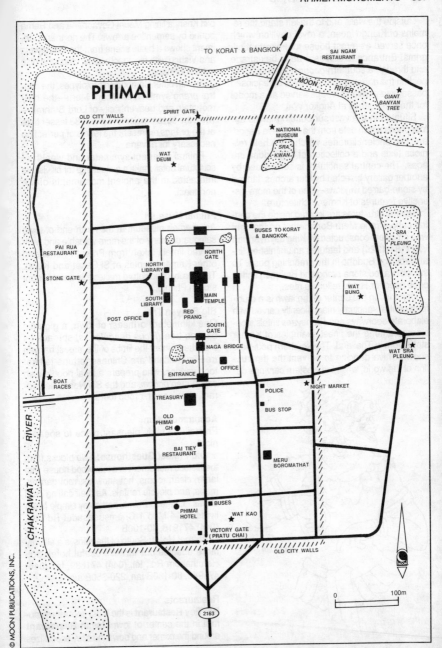

PHIMAI

TO KORAT & BANGKOK

SAI NGAM
RESTAURANT

MOON RIVER

GIANT
BANYAN
TREE

OLD CITY WALLS   SPIRIT GATE

NATIONAL
MUSEUM

SRA
KWAN

WAT
DEUM

BUSES TO KORAT
& BANGKOK

SRA
PLEUNG

PAI RUA
RESTAURANT

NORTH
GATE

STONE GATE

NORTH
LIBRARY

WAT
BUNG

SOUTH
LIBRARY

MAIN
TEMPLE

POST OFFICE

RED
PRANG

SOUTH
GATE

WAT SRA
PLEUNG

NAGA BRIDGE

POND

BOAT
RACES

OFFICE

ENTRANCE

TREASURY

POLICE

NIGHT MARKET

BUS STOP

OLD
PHIMAI
GH

BAI TIEY
RESTAURANT

MERU
BOROMATHAT

PHIMAI
HOTEL

BUSES

WAT KAO

VICTORY GATE
(PRATU CHAI)

OLD CITY WALLS

CHAKRAWAT

RIVER

0   100m

MOON

2163

© MOON PUBLICATIONS, INC.

Outside the walls and to the left stand the remains of Klang Ngoen, a royal pavilion which once served as a rest house for important pilgrims. Entrance is across a *naga* balustrade and through a southern *gopura* gateway. Connecting the gateway and gallery is an enclosed passageway which perhaps served as a model for the sanctuaries at Angkor Wat.

Situated in the vast surrounding lawns are four ponds which date from the Ayuthaya Period, and two ancient libraries which once held religious texts and a collection of 30 Buddha images. The central sanctuary is surrounded by another gallery bisected by four arches flanked by stone-barred windows—one of the more distinctive features of Khmer architecture.

Several structures are located inside the central patio. Prang Meru Boromathat on the right was probably constructed by King Jayavarman VII (1181-1220) and features an unfinished lintel depicting Buddha in the preaching pose. To the left is a red stone *prang* and Brahman shrine once used for Hindu religious rites.

Dominating the center of the lawn is a cruciform central sanctuary magnificently carved with elaborate doorways and *Ramayana* lintels, considered among the finest examples of Khmer stonework in Thailand. The southern pediment shows Shiva dancing to prevent the destruction of the world, while the western carvings depict Krishna lifting Mount Govadhana and Rama bound by serpentine arrows. The northern pediment shows a battle scene from the *Ramayana* and Vishnu with his conch, lotus, club, and disc in his four hands.

As with other Cambodian prototypes, the central *prang* symbolizes Mount Meru—the holy mountain and heavenly city of Lord Brahma—while the seven major levels and 33 lesser tiers of the *prangs* represent the levels of perfection necessary for nirvana.

Phimai's perfect symmetry and wealth of sculptural detail make it a must-see for all visitors interested in the ancient monuments of the northeast.

Phimai Museum
An open-air museum at the north end of town safeguards many of the more valuable and well-carved lintels taken from Prasat Phimai and other Khmer temples at Si Saket and Korat. The quality of sculpture makes this an important stop in Phimai.

Big Banyan Tree
One kilometer northeast of town, a gigantic banyan tree *(Ficus bengalensis)* spreads its branches. Under the limbs of the largest banyan tree in Thailand are Chinese fortune-tellers, food vendors who prepare a local noodle dish called *mee phimai,* and the Sai Ngam Restaurant, popular with group tours.

Accommodation
Phimai is a fairly pleasant place to spend a night.

Old Phimai Guesthouse: Two blocks from the historic monument is a teakwood house with large, clean rooms, hot showers, roof garden, maps, and bicycle rentals. As their calling card claims, "Come to Phimai and enjoy simple Issan living." 214 Moo 1 Chomsudasadet Rd., tel. (044) 471918, 40-100B.

Phimai Hotel: South of the ruins is a slightly more upscale but far less useful hotel. 305 Haruthairom Rd., tel. (044) 471689, fax (044) 471940, 80-180B fan, 220-350B a/c.

Restaurants
Bai Tiey Restaurant is the most popular restaurant in the center of town. **Issan Restaurant** around the corner and down the alley specializes

Hanuman

BOB RACE

in local dishes. Out-of-town favorites include the **Rim Moon Restaurant** on the banks of the Moon River, and **Sai Ngam Restaurant** near the giant banyan tree.

Practicalities
Tourist information is available from the Bai Tiey Restaurant just south of the temple entrance. Bicycles can be rented from Old Phimai Guesthouse and Phimai Bikes at the ruins and Bai Tiey Restaurant. The three banks in Phimai are open Mon.-Fri. 0830-1500. English-language volunteers are always welcome at Taoururanaree primary school some 200 meters from the main highway. A popular boat race and a cultural festival are held in late October or early November.

Transportation
Buses to Phimai from Korat leave hourly from the ordinary bus station on Burin Lane behind the Erawan Hospital. The last bus back to Korat departs at 1800.

PRASAT PHANOM WAN

This small but attractive Khmer temple, set in an evocative and tranquil setting 20 km north of Korat, can be visited in conjunction with Phimai. Originally built as a Hindu temple by King Suryavarman I, the 10th-century *phanom* ("hill") sanctuary follows the standard layout of a courtyard dominated by a central *prang* surrounded by four smaller towers. The temple has a number of Buddha statues still honored by a community of monks, and a finely carved lintel above the north entrance of the main sanctuary. The Fine Arts Department intends to dismantle and reconstruct the decaying complex in the near future.

Prasat Phanom Wan is somewhat difficult to reach, but worth a side trip for visitors seriously interested in Khmer architecture.

Transportation
Direct buses leave at 0700, 1000, and 1200 from Pratu Phonsean, a city gate near Wat Samakkhi in Korat. Alternatively, take a bus bound for Korat and ask the driver to let you off at Ban Long Thong, 11 km from Korat, from where you can walk or hitch a *songtao* ride the remaining six kilometers.

En route to Phanom Wan is the small village of Ban Makam, where craftsmen specialize in the production of handmade knives.

PRASAT PHANOM RUNG

The most spectacular Khmer monument in Thailand is Prasat Phanom Rung, 132 km east of Korat and 50 km south of Buriram.

Prasat Phanom Rung ("Temple of the Great Mountain") is splendidly sited on the southern ridge of an extinct volcano which dominates the surrounding countryside and provides views toward Angkor and the Dongrak Mountains which demarcate the present border between Thailand and Cambodia. Typical of most Khmer architecture and Hindu temple orientation, Phanom Rung faces the east, toward the dawn and the original capital at Angkor.

The political and military significance of Phanom Rung derives from its strategic location just above the Khmer highway which once connected Angkor with Phimai on the Korat

Prasat Phanom Rung

Plateau. More importantly, the Hindu traditions of ancient geomancy teach that mountains are ideal sites for religious monuments since they touch the heavens and symbolize Mount Meru, the highest mountain in Hindu cosmology.

History

Historians believe that the hill originally served as a retreat for a community of Hindu *rishis* until the 12th century when a local Khmer ruler named Prince Narendratitya began construction of the principal sanctuary. Narendratitya was a contemporary and relative of King Suryavarman II (1112-1150), the famous Khmer ruler who constructed the complex of Angkor Wat. Local inscriptions suggest that Narendratitya was ordained as a yogi after the birth of his son, Hiranya, who continued construction of the sanctuary and added the yogi figures now seen on the temple walls. The sanctuary was never completed, though additions continued into the reign of Jayavarman VII.

Khmer power waned in the 13th century and the empire finally collapsed in 1431 with the sack of Angkor by the Thai. Prasat Phanom Rung was abandoned and fell into ruin until 1972, when the Fine Arts Department initiated a massive reconstruction effort, finally completed on 21 May 1988. The restoration project employed the anastylosis method, in which every building was systematically dismantled and rebuilt on a ferroconcrete base and fashioned around a superstructure of ferroconcrete walls and beams. The massive and difficult project took almost 17 years but resulted in the most impressive singular monument in Thailand.

Prasat Phanom Rung

White Elephant Hall: Entrance to the complex begins 400 meters east of the central complex where a series of three earthen terraces leads up to a large cruciform platform. To the north stands a small, ruined, sandstone-and-laterite structure called the White Elephant Hall, once used for Hindu religious ceremonies.

Royal Promenade: Immediately ahead stretches one of the most remarkable design elements of Phanom Rung, a 160-meter promenade and monumental staircase flanked by ruined *nagas* which symbolically transport the visitor from the earthly realm to the world of the gods.

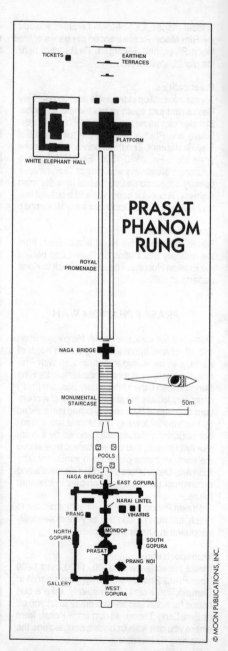

PRASAT PHANOM RUNG

TICKETS

EARTHEN TERRACES

PLATFORM

WHITE ELEPHANT HALL

ROYAL PROMENADE

NAGA BRIDGE

0   50m

MONUMENTAL STAIRCASE

POOLS

NAGA BRIDGE

EAST GOPURA

NARAI LINTEL

PRANG

VIHARNS

NORTH GOPURA

MONDOP

SOUTH GOPURA

PRASAT

PRANG NOI

GALLERY

WEST GOPURA

© MOON PUBLICATIONS, INC.

CONTROVERSY IN STONE

One of the most controversial events in the world of archaeology erupted several years ago over the Narai Lintel which now graces the top of the east *gopura* at Prasat Phanom Rung. According to local authorities, the sandstone slab was last seen at the temple complex in 1960, when a curator from the Fine Arts Department photographed the broken lintel where it had fallen at the base of the doorway. Art robbers subsequently hauled the lintel to Bangkok where it was sold on the open market in 1966 to an art collector from New York. In 1967, the 75- by 150-cm carving was purchased by the Chicago-based Alsadorf Foundation, which donated it to the Art Institute of Chicago. In 1976, Professor Diskul of Silpakorn University spotted the lintel in the Art Institute and reported his discovery to the Thai Ministry of Foreign Affairs.

The situation turned explosive in February of 1988 when the Thai government demanded the return of the lintel to its rightful place after 21 years of display at the Art Institute of Chicago. Backed by a broad array of politicians, journalists, and residents of Buriram Province, an unprecedented international effort was mounted to recover the stolen artifact. The Fine Arts Department erected a sign at Phanom Rung announcing that the stolen lintel was on display in Chicago. Bangkok newspapers published provocative advertisements which claimed the missing lintel was removed with the use of American military equipment and quickly spirited abroad because of special privileges enjoyed by the U.S. forces. Thai residents and American citizens demonstrated at the Art Institute of Chicago, while a socially conscious Thai rock group called Carabao recorded a popular song which demanded, "Take back Michael Jackson—Give us back the Pra Narai!" Never before had the government and citizens of Thailand appeared so united about preserving their artistic and cultural treasures.

The Art Institute of Chicago initially suggested an exchange of a comparable work of equal artistic merit to replace the Narai Lintel. After a series of discussions, a Chicago-based philanthropic group offered to donate comparable Thai artwork to help resolve the negotiations which had broken off in July of 1988. The campaign failed to restore the lintel in time for the official Phanom Rung opening in May of 1988, but served to raise the level of artistic consciousness among the Thai people. The Narai Lintel—the most controversial piece of stone in Thailand—was restored to its original home in 1989 and now surmounts the eastern entrance to Prasat Phanom Rung.

Naga Bridges: Bordered by 68 sandstone pillars carved in early Angkor style, the ceremonial avenue leads down to an extremely unusual *naga* bridge at the foot of the monumental staircase. The cruciform bridge is guarded by 16 five-headed *nagas* carved in Angkor style with Hindu Wheels of the Universe embedded on both sides.

Monumental Staircase: Beyond the *naga* bridge towers a staircase whose massive dimensions reflect the power and drama typical of Khmer design.

East *Gopura*: Situated at the top of the staircase are four rectangular pools arranged symmetrically in front of a second *naga* bridge, and the eastern *gopura* entrance whose perfect alignment characterizes the geometric precision of Angkor architecture. Particular attention should be given to the lintels and pediments elevated over the *gopuras* at the four cardinal points. Carved above the eastern *gopura* is an image of Shiva Mahayogi, patron of all ascetics, while other iconography related to both Shivaite and Vaishnavite deities can be seen on other *gopuras* and the curvilinear galleries which surround the complex. Art historians consider Phanom Rung sculpture and craftsmanship to represent the pinnacle of Khmer artistic achievement, comparable only to the murals and tableaux at Angkor Wat.

Narai Lintel: Immediately through the east *gopura* is a third *naga* bridge followed by the most famous piece of sculpture at Phanom Rung—and perhaps the most controversial work of art in Thailand. Elevated above the eastern portico to the central *mondop* is the infamous Narai Lintel, a stone slab which depicts a reclining Lord Narai (more commonly known as Vishnu) asleep on the Milky Sea of Eternity as represented by a *naga* snake. Narai is shown elaborately dressed with his right hand supporting his head, while his other hand embraces a baton, conch shell, and discus. Emerging from his navel is a lotus stem which blossoms into many stems, one of which depicts the newborn Brahma and the Hindu creation of the world.

Seated at his feet are his consort, Lakshmi, surrounded by Kala, the god of time and death, and other figures of *garudas, nagas,* parrots, elephants, and monkeys. The Narai Lintel establishes the importance of the Shivaite religion at Phanom Rung, and cosmically represents the Vaishnavite myth of creation.

Directly above the Narai Lintel is a sandstone depiction of Shiva Nataraja, lord of the dance, carved in late Baphuon or early Angkor style. The extremely sensual and smooth-limbed image beautifully illustrates the cosmic dance of Shiva which sustains but ultimately destroys the universe. The juxtaposition of these two creation myths—Shiva dancing and Vishnu sleeping on the cosmic ocean—is rarely encountered in the Hindu art of Southeast Asia.

Central *Prasat:* Dominating the center of the temple complex is a towering *prasat* festooned with ornately carved Shivas, charging elephants, shapely Khmer dancers, and images of Hindu *rishis.* Among the highlights are the pediment and lintel at the west portico, which illustrates the battle of Sri Lanka as described in the famous *Ramayana* epic, a triumphant procession of warriors and elephants on the north and south faces, and motifs of the five yogis on the lintels at the east and south entrances. Interior details include several Khmer statues and a Hindu *lingam* on which temple priests once poured holy waters and placed offerings of garlands and fruit.

Prang Noi: Situated in the southwest corner of the courtyard is a small square chapel dating from the reign of Suryavarman I and covered with remarkable decoration in the style of Angkor Wat.

Prasat Phanom Rung is open daily from 0900 to 1700.

PRASAT MUANG TAM

A fine contrast to Prasat Phanom Rung is provided by the Khmer temple at Muang Tam ("Lower City"), a 10th-century complex initiated by King Indravarman but completed by Jayavarman V, and therefore older than its more acclaimed neighbor. Although the setting in Ban Chorakae Mak ("Town of Many Crocodiles") is hardly picturesque, the bas-reliefs, intriguing architectural symbolism, and fine state of collapse make it a worthwhile visit for fans of Khmer architecture.

The monument is entered through a thick wall which, like most of the monument, has suffered from ground subsidence and achieved a bizarre state of dilapidation. Despite restoration efforts by the Fine Arts Department with help from German consultants, the perimeter wall has collapsed into a magnificent bulwark that resembles a huge and undulating serpent. Clusters of *nagas* ring the inner ponds, which symbolically represent the primordial oceans of Hindu-Buddhist cosmology. Cows and young monks often wander around the grounds, oblivious to the tour buses parked at the front entrance.

The central sanctuary features five reconstructed brick towers with exquisite sandstone carvings of Krishna killing a *naga* and Shiva mounted on the back of Nandi the bull. Window mullions and delicately carved lintels relate other themes from Hindu mythology. Another unique feature is the three materials used in construction: bricks for the central sanctuaries, sandstone for the sills, and laterite for the walls.

Restoration of Prasat Muang Tam will be completed by 1995.

Transportation

Prasat Muang Tam is 10 km southeast of Phanom Rung in the Khmer-speaking village of Chorakae Mak. Public transportation is unavailable to the monument, though motorcycle taxis and *songtaos* can be chartered from Ban Tako and Phanom Rung.

The site is open daily from 0900 to 1700.

OTHER KHMER MONUMENTS

Travelers intrigued with the Cambodian architecture of northeastern Thailand can continue east and visit a half-dozen additional monuments. The nearest sanctuary, Prasat Ta Muen, is just 22 km east of Muang Tam on the Thai-Cambodian border.

Khmer *prasats* near Surin include Prasat Pluang and Prasat Sikhoraphum. Farther east in the vicinity of Si Saket stand Prasat Kamphaeng Yai and Prasat Kamphaeng Noi. About 100 km south of Si Saket is Prasat Khao Viharn, considered among the most spectacular Khmer monuments in Southeast Asia.

Narai Lintel

Several towns can be used as a base for temple explorations, but the most centrally located is Surin, where Mr. Pirom at Pirom Guesthouse can help with organized tours to the widely scattered monuments.

A complete description of each sanctuary is listed below under "Surin."

KORAT TO THE MEKONG

KHON KAEN

Khon Kaen, 449 km from Bangkok and strategically located at the intersection of Friendship Highway and National Rd. 12, is an important crossroads and gateway for visitors arriving from Korat, Phitsanulok, and northern Thailand. Khon Kaen is a bustling city and site of several prestigious establishments, such as Khon Kaen University and Channel 5 Television, but it has little to recommend to the Western visitor except for the National Museum and a look at the locally produced silk.

Khon Kaen National Museum
The leading attraction in Khon Kaen offers a small but high-quality collection of arts, with special emphasis on the Dvaravati Period and Ban Chiang artifacts. Engraved steles in the Dvaravati style dating from the 8th and 9th centuries are arranged on the exterior lawns and on the ground floors. Exhibits on the right concentrate on prehistoric objects discovered at Ban Chiang, and *sema* boundary stones carved with bas-reliefs of Buddha's return to Kapilapasatu.

The second floor features archaeological discoveries from the northeast, such as Lopburi Period images discovered at Nakhon Champasi and a prized 11th-century lintel discovered at Ku Suan Tang in Buriram Province.

The museum is open Tues.-Sun. 0900-1700.

Khon Kaen Silk
The finest silk in Thailand is produced near Korat, Chaiyaphum, and in Chonnabot, a small *mut mee* silk-weaving village 56 km southwest of Khon Kaen.

Several shops in town offer silks and handicrafts, but the best selection is found at the Prathamakant Handicraft Center (tel. 043/224736, fax 043/224080) at 79 Ruenrom Rd., just one block east of the train station. Prathamakant stocks a wide selection of silks from all regions of the Issan, plus silver jewelry and tribal handicrafts from northern Thailand. The staff speaks English and accepts credit cards.

Bung Kaen Lake
This 241-acre freshwater lake provides a quick escape for the citizens of Khon Kaen. Recreational facilities include several seafood restau-

KHON KAEN

TO UDON THANI & NONG KHAI

TO AIRPORT & PHITSANULOK

THAI AIRWAYS

TO KORAT & BANGKOK

TO KALASIN →

Roads and locations:

NA MUANG RD.

KLANG MUANG RD.

LANG MUANG RD.

KASITKORN RD.

THEPARAK RD.

ROB MUANG RD.

SOON RACHAKAM RD.

NASOON RD.

PRACHASAMOSON RD.

PHIMPASUT RD.

AMMAT RD.

SRI CHAN RD.

SHETAKON RD.

CHUEN CHAUN RD.

LAO NADI RD.

NATIONAL MUSEUM

PROVINCIAL HALL

STUPA

PARK

STATUE

BUS TERMINAL

BUNG THUNG SANG

SUKSAWAD HOTEL

ROSE SUKHON HOTEL

CINEMA

PJ DISCO

KHON KAEN HOTEL

ROMA HOTEL

SANSUMRAN HOTEL

THIPAROT CAFE

VILLA HOTEL

KAEN INN

A/C BUSES

PHU INN

NIGHT MARKET

WHALE CAFE

PARROT RESTAURANT

KOSA RAMA HOTEL

SHOPPING

POST OFFICE

CHINESE TEMPLE

SWATDEE HOTEL

SILK SHOP

THANI BUNGALOWS

TRAIN STATION

HANDICRAFTS

MARKET

SEAFOOD RESTAURANTS

BUNG KAEN NAKHON

0   100m

© MOON PUBLICATIONS, INC.

rants, boat tours, and a fitness park. Situated on the lakeshore is an old *wat* constructed in typical Issan style with Thai and Laotian influences.

Budget Accommodations

Khon Kaen is a major transit and business center in the northeast, with a wide selection of hotels in all price ranges. All accommodations are within walking distance or short *songtao* ride from the bus station. Train passengers can take the yellow minitruck which shuttles into town.

Sansumran Hotel: Behind the funky green wooden exterior is a popular and conveniently located hotel with rooms arranged left and right off the central corridor. Manager Montree Saraboon is friendly, helpful, and speaks excellent English. 55-59 Klang Muang Rd., tel. (043) 239611, 80-120B.

Suksawad Hotel: Another old wooden place with rooms in various price ranges. Suksawad is well located in a quiet alley, and the managers seem friendly if somewhat disorganized. Try the large, clean rooms with private bath in the separate building. 2 Klang Muang Rd., no phone, 60-120B.

Thani Bungalows: Adjacent to the train station is a very decrepit joint with dismal, noisy upstairs rooms and dirty, overpriced bungalows in the rear. Skip the Thani and head into town. 222 Ruen Rom Rd., tel. (043) 224833, 50B rooms, 180B bungalows.

Moderate Accommodations

Roma Hotel: The old favorite has been renovated and improved with a new lobby, elevators, and reconditioned rooms. Good value for middle-priced travelers. 50 Klang Muang Rd., (043) 236276, 140-200B fan, 280-380B a/c.

Phu Inn: Tucked away in a small alley near the central market is a cozy, clean, and modern hotel with coffee shop, business services, and 98 a/c rooms. Big discounts are given on request and for longer stays. 26-34 Sathid Juthithum Rd., tel. (043) 243174, 500-750B.

Rose Sukon Hotel: *Farangs* on business often stay in this cozy hotel, which has good rooms and a very dark cocktail lounge but, curiously enough, lacks an English-language hotel sign out front. 1/11 Klang Muang Rd., tel. (043) 236899, fax (043) 238579, 550-700B.

Kosa Rama Hotel: Of the three big hotels in Khon Kaen—the Kosa Rama, Kaen Inn, and Khon Kaen—the Kosa is probably in the best shape with a decent coffee shop, popular disco, postage-stamp swimming pool, and acceptable furnishings in the a/c rooms. 250 Srichan Rd., tel. (043) 225014, 650-750B.

Restaurants

A lively night market operates in the alley behind the a/c bus terminal and near the Phu Inn Hotel. The Whale Cafe, across from the Phu Inn, is a spotlessly clean restaurant with Foremost desserts and tasty Thai dishes. The Parrot Restaurant opposite the Kosa Rama Hotel serves steaks, pizzas, and hamburgers. Farther left is the High Tech Disco.

Travelers often hang out at the cheap Thiparot Cafe, just a few meters south of the Roma Hotel, where Issan-style dishes are served from the English-language menu.

Local Thais prefer Bung Kaen Lake, where several excellent seafood restaurants face the water, and dinner cruises occur nightly on a Thai party boat.

Practicalities

A TAT office opened several years ago in the municipal offices in the north section of Khon Kaen. The December Silk and Friendship Festival features silk displays, cultural performances, and the crowning of Miss Silk.

Transportation

Khon Kaen is 449 km northeast of Bangkok, 190 km north of Korat, and 115 km south of Udon Thani. The city serves as an important junction for travelers entering the northeast from Phitsanulok in central Thailand.

Air: Thai Airways flies three times daily from Bangkok for 1300B and three times weekly from Chiang Mai for 1400B. Thai Airways (tel. 043/236523) is located en route to the airport at 183 Mailan Road.

Train: Trains are the most comfortable way to travel around the northeast. Five trains leave daily from Bangkok and take seven hours by express or eight hours on rapid train. Trains depart Korat at 0600, 0823, 1145, 1226, and 1515. Departure schedules should be confirmed with the Korat TAT.

Bus: Buses leave hourly from the ordinary bus terminal in Korat and take about three hours to reach Khon Kaen. Air-conditioned buses leave from the terminal on Friendship Highway in the north of Korat.

Buses from Phitsanulok leave hourly and take about five hours to reach Khon Kaen, passing through excellent scenery and several national parks.

CHAIYAPHUM

Chaiyaphum is a medium-sized town that, because of its location well off the main highway, has escaped mass tourism and maintained a relatively untouched atmosphere.

The town was established during the Ayuthaya era as a trading station between Ayuthaya and Vientiane, then a protectorate state of the Thai nation. Local folklore revolves around a citizen named Phya Lae who was executed by Laotian soldiers after he refused to join a rebel movement against authorities in Bangkok. A monument to the hero stands in front of the provincial hall.

Today the region is primarily known for its silk weaving, caves, migratory birdlife, and Chaiyaphum Elephant Festival held each year in late January or early February.

Attractions
Chaiyaphum itself has little of great interest, but tours to nearby attractions can be arranged through the Chaiyaphum and Yin's guesthouses.

Silk Weaving: Top draw are the famous silks which are reputedly woven from 100% silk and collected by the royal family. Several shops in town provide samples of the various designs, though prices are lowest directly at weaving villages such as Ban Kwiao. Silk bolts from the weavers start at 200B per meter, about half the cost of Bangkok or Chiang Mai.

Wat Prang Ku: Two km east of town in the old section of Chaiyaphum is a Khmer temple constructed on the royal highway which once connected Angkor with Prasat Phanom Rung and Phimai. The central laterite tower houses several images including a seated stone Buddha of the Dvaravati Period and an Ayuthaya-style standing Buddha on the western side.

Tad Ton National Park: A small national park with caves and multilayered waterfalls is located 21 km north of town on the road toward Kaset Sombun. Park bungalows cost from 250B.

Birdlife: Thousands of birds migrate and nest from November to April in freshwater Waeng Lake northeast of Chaiyaphum. Water birds can also be seen at Lake Laharn some 40 km south of town.

Elephant Festival: One of the most popular festivals in the northeast attracts thousands of visitors for the elephant procession, re-creation of ancient elephant duels, and an elephant tug-of-war between people and pachyderm. Hotel reservations should be made in advance.

Accommodations

Chaiyaphum has two backpackers' guesthouses and several midpriced Thai hotels.

Yin's Guesthouse: Five hundred meters north of the main bus station is Chaiyaphum's original guesthouse. Yin's can help arrange visits to silk-weaving towns and overnight stays in nearby villages. *Samlors* from the bus station cost 10 *baht*. 143 Niwetraj Rd., no phone, 40-80B.

Chaiyaphum Guesthouse: Chaiyaphum's second guesthouse opened in 1990 in the center of town near the Sirichai Hotel. The owners also help with tours to silk villages and national parks. Look for the big sign across from the office of Air Chaiyaphum. 477 Non Muang Rd., no phone, 40-80B.

Paibun Hotel: A older Chinese hotel with simple but clean and very inexpensive rooms. 227 Yititham Rd., tel. (044) 811021, 80-160B.

Lert Nimit Hotel: An upscale hotel with both inexpensive fan rooms and two-story a/c chalets. Located about 200 meters due north of the bus station. 447 Niwetraj Rd., tel. (044) 811522, 130-180B fan, 250-400B a/c.

Transportation

Chaiyaphum is 332 km from Bangkok, 118 km north of Korat, and approximately midway between Korat and Khon Kaen on Route 202.

Buses leave hourly from Bangkok's Northern Bus Terminal and from both bus terminals in Korat. Ordinary buses arrive at the main bus terminal on Anantakul Rd. near the central market. Air-conditioned buses usually stop at the Air Chaiyaphum office on Non Muang Rd., just opposite the Sirichai Hotel and Chaiyaphum Guesthouse, or at the Nakorn Chai Tour office a few blocks south.

Direct bus connections are also available from Phitsanulok, Nakhon Sawan, Chiang Mai, and Chiang Rai.

UDON THANI

This busy commercial center—usually called Udon or Udorn—chiefly serves as a base for visiting the archaeological site at Ban Chiang and the caves and national parks situated in the province.

The city was founded in 1893 by a Laotian general who moved his army from Nong Khai after a dispute with the occupying French forces. Together with Korat and Ubon Ratchathani, Udorn experienced a tremendous boom during the Vietnam conflict after the Americans established a huge military base just outside the city perimeter. The base was closed in 1975 and presented to the Thai government, but the legacy continues with a handful of Western advisers and diplomatic personnel who chose military retirement in Udon. Other reminders include a small American consulate near Nong Prajak Reservoir, the enormous air base that now serves both Thai military and civilian sectors, and a few restaurants where retired servicemen gather to throw darts and complain about their delayed benefits.

Attractions In Town

Udon's few sights are limited to a rather sad little zoo near the sports field, Ban Huay Market which runs best on weekends, and colorful cinema poster shops near the clock tower. The Chinese temple near Kannika Tours features a baroque facade of dragons and mythical birds, plus an unnerving photo collection of people killed in auto accidents on the interior walls. Also note the strange roofless *tuk tuks* constructed with wooden carriages, circular benches, custom wheels, and wild paint jobs.

The remainder of attractions in Udon are outside town and require the service of a tour operator, public transportation, or motorcycle rented from Kannika Tours.

Ban Chiang

The region's top draws are the new museum, archaeological excavations, and Bronze-Age artifacts discovered at Ban Chiang, a small hamlet 58 km east of Udon Thani on the Sakhon Nakhon Highway.

The story began in 1966 when a young American sociology student named Steve Young literally stumbled across some pottery shards which were carbon-dated to around 3600 B.C. News of the findings spread and the village became an overnight sensation. Excavations conducted in 1974 and 1975 by the Fine Arts Department of Silapkorn University and Chester Gorman of the University of Pennsylvania led to startling discoveries of ceramic vessels and human skeletons that date back over 5,000 years. Predating the earliest recognized bronze ages, these findings prompted scholars to rethink Southeast Asian history and challenge the traditional notion that civilization originated in the Middle East or China.

Today, Ban Chiang has reverted into a sleepy backwater that offers the infrequent visitor an older museum established in 1976 to house earlier excavations, and a much more impressive modern museum opened in 1986 and funded by the Kennedy Foundation. Installations were designed by the Smithsonian Institution for a worldwide exhibition which now permanently resides in the modern wing of the Ban Chiang Museum.

Somewhat unimpressive excavation sites are located five minutes away within the walls of Wat Pho Si Nai.

The Ban Chiang Museum is open Wednesday-Saturday.

To reach Ban Chiang, take a bus or minibus east toward Sakhon Nakhon from the bus stop near the Charoen Hotel. Be sure to get off at Km 50 in the tiny village of Ban Chiang, from where *tuk tuks* continue six km north to the museum and excavation sites.

West Of Udon Thani

Highway 210 leads west to Loei and Phu Kradung National Park, one of the most popular parks in Thailand. While most visitors travel north to Nong Khai and then west along the Mekong River to Chiang Khan and Loei, the route could easily be reversed to include the following stops. Motorcyclists will enjoy the flat and lightly trafficked highway.

Wat Tham Klong Phaen: A famous cave temple, once home to a renowned meditation master named Luang Phu Kaeo, is found 40 km west of Udon in the Phuphan Mountain Range.

Erawan Caves: The stalactite caves of Tham Erawan, 50 km west of Udon, are filled with Buddha images illuminated by electric lights. Views over the ricefields are possible after the long climb up 107 steps. Take a bus and look for the sign: THAM ERAWAN.

Budget Accommodations

Most hotels are clustered on Prachak Rd. and near the clock tower in the center of town.

Sri Sawat Hotel: Budget travelers usually stay in this small hotel located just up from the clock tower. The hotel is divided into an old and cheap wing on the left and a newer wing on the right. Rooms can get noisy from courtyard reverberation, but the manager is friendly and the rooms are kept fairly clean. 123 Prachak Rd., tel. (042) 221560, 60-120B.

Pracha Pakdee Hotel: Across the street is a clean and modern hotel with good-value rooms. 156 Prachak Rd., tel. (042) 221804, 140-160B fan, 240-260B a/c.

Queen Hotel: An older joint that gets the overflow from the Sri Sawat and Pracha Pakdee. 6 Udon Dusadi Rd., tel. (042) 221451, 100-140B fan, 200-220 a/c.

Moderate Accommodations

The best hotels in Udon Thani are geared to traveling Thai businessmen rather than Western tourists who expect first-class comforts at bargain rates.

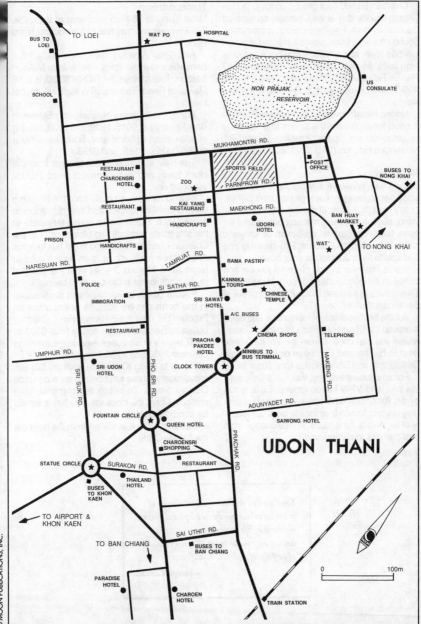

TO LOEI

BUS TO
LOEI

WAT PO

HOSPITAL

SCHOOL

NON PRAJAK
RESERVOIR

US
CONSULATE

MUKHAMONTRI RD.

RESTAURANT

CHAROENSRI
HOTEL

ZOO

SPORTS FIELD

PARNPROW RD.

POST
OFFICE

BUSES TO
NONG KHAI

RESTAURANT

KAI YANG
RESTAURANT

MAEKHONG RD.

HANDICRAFTS

UDORN
HOTEL

BAN HUAY
MARKET

PRISON

HANDICRAFTS

WAT

TO NONG KHAI

NARESUAN RD.

TAMRUAT RD.

RAMA PASTRY

POLICE

SI SATHA RD.

KANNIKA
TOURS

IMMIGRATION

SRI SAWAT
HOTEL

CHINESE
TEMPLE

A/C BUSES

RESTAURANT

CINEMA SHOPS

TELEPHONE

UMPHUR RD.

PRACHA
PAKDEE
HOTEL

MINIBUS TO
BUS TERMINAL

SRI UDON
HOTEL

CLOCK TOWER

ADUNYADET RD.

FOUNTAIN CIRCLE

QUEEN HOTEL

SAIWONG HOTEL

CHAROENSRI
SHOPPING

UDON THANI

STATUE CIRCLE

SURAKON RD.

RESTAURANT

BUSES TO KHON
KAEN

THAILAND
HOTEL

TO AIRPORT &
KHON KAEN

SAI UTHIT RD.

TO BAN CHIANG

BUSES TO
BAN CHIANG

0   100m

PARADISE
HOTEL

CHAROEN
HOTEL

TRAIN STATION

PHO SRI RD.

SRI SUK RD.

PRACHAK RD.

MAKENG RD.

© MOON PUBLICATIONS, INC.

Charoen Hotel: Tour groups en route to Ban Chiang usually stay at the Charoen, considered the best in town. Facilities include a swimming pool on the front lawn, rooms furnished in a garish '50s style, and a "yellow bird bar for man of high taste" as described by their brochure. 549 Pho Sri Rd., tel. (042) 221331, fax (042) 246126, 400-500B in the old wing, 650-750B in the new wing.

Udorn Hotel: An older, unrenovated hotel in a good location near the shops and *kai yang* restaurants on upper Prachak Road. 81 Maekhong Rd., tel. (042) 222166, 300-600B.

Restaurants

Udon Thani is known among the Thais for its spicy beef sausages, finely ground pork dishes, crispy fried pork legs, and most notably, for *kai yang,* succulent sweet chicken barbecued on open fires. The largest collection of *kai yang* cafes is located on Prachak Rd. near the zoo and sports field. Just follow your nose.

Rama Pastry is a good place for sweets and coffee in air-conditioned comfort. Inexpensive Thai dishes are served in the cafe just south of the immigration office.

But the best selection of restaurants and cafes is around the Charoensri Plaza Shopping Center, where you can choose from the Western-style Best Pub, Thai and European dishes at Jingjo Restaurant, and Donut House for a sugar fix.

For an unusual evening, visit T.J.'s Cafe near the lake and VFW headquarters. T.J.'s is run by an American who serves authentic hamburgers and french fries for the local community of expatriate Americans. A nice change from *pad thai* and *tom yam kung.*

Transportation

Udon Thani is 564 km northeast of Bangkok, 305 km north of Korat, and 51 km south of Nong Khai.

Air: Thai Airways flies once daily from Bangkok and three times weekly from Nakhon Sakhon. Thai Airways (tel. 042-2432220) is at 60 Makkang Road. The airport is eight km east of town.

Train: Trains leave Hualampong Station in Bangkok daily at 0615, 1900, and 2030, arriving in Udon about 10 hours later. Trains leave Korat at 0807, 1226, 1515, and 0258.

The train station is about two km from the clock tower and *samlor* drivers need 25B for the short ride.

Bus: Buses leave hourly from the Northern Bus Terminal in Bangkok and take nine hours to reach Udon Thani. Some buses terminate at the streetside terminal two blocks north of the Charoen Hotel, but others go to the bus terminal about three km north of town on the road to Nong Khai. Minibus 3 goes from the terminal to the clock tower in the center of town.

Private buses to Bangkok and destinations in the north can be ticketed at the office on Prachak Rd. near the Sri Sawat Hotel. Ordinary buses to Bangkok leave hourly from 0500 to 2300, while VIP a/c buses leave in the evenings between 2030 and 2130.

Buses to Nong Khai leave from the bus terminal located three km north of town on Udon Dutsadi Road. To reach the terminal, take minibus 3 from the clock tower or hire a *samlor* for about 20 *baht.*

Buses to Khon Kaen leave from the halt near the Statue Circle.

Some men go skimming over the years of existence to sink gently into a placid grave, ignorant of life to the last, without ever having been made to see all it may contain of perfidy, of violence, and of terror.

—Joseph Conrad

(top left) band leader, parade in Kamphaeng Phet; (top right) floating market onlooker, Damnern Saduak; (bottom left) young athlete, sports festival in Korat; (bottom right) costumed surprise, king's birthday celebration in Sukhothai (all photos by Carl Parkes)

(top) intricately painted Moslem fishing boat, Narathiwat;
(bottom) temple entrance, Chiang Mai (photos by Carl Parkes)

MEKONG RIVER REGION

NONG KHAI

Nong Khai rates as the most popular destination in the northeast. Superbly located at the terminus of the Friendship Highway on the banks of the Mekong River, the small and rather sleepy town is chiefly known as an important link with Laos and the national capital of Vientiane. A highly recommended journey west from Nong Khai to Chiang Khan passes through great landscapes, a culturally diverse environment, and charming towns almost completely unaffected by tourism.

Unlike most other towns in Thailand, Nong Khai is endowed with a degree of individuality. French-Laotian influence is reflected in some of the surviving hybrid architecture, and in the bakeries which still produce baguettes and loaves of fresh French bread. Shopping includes a range of goods from Laotian handicrafts to northeastern creations. Best of all, the people are friendly and anxious to help Western visitors enjoy their Issan vacation.

With the imminent completion of the new bridge to Laos and the arrival of several luxury hotels, Nong Khai has changed to some degree, and yet it retains the timeless atmosphere that has long made it a great destination. Visitors with limited time in the northeast should see the Khmer monuments near Korat and then head directly to Nong Khai.

Rimkhong Road And Mae Nam Khong

A new bridge planned for completion in 1995 with the help of the Australian and Lao governments will probably phase out the boat crossing in Nong Khai, but the riverbank trailhead will remain a popular spot at which to enjoy a meal from the cantilevered restaurants and gaze across the river to Laos. A humorous note is provided by the trilingual sign which describes aliens with hippie characteristics.

A short geographical sidebar should be made about the Mekong River, variously spelled as Mekong, Maekhong, or Mae Nam Khong depending on the source. Thais prefer Mae Nam Khong ("Mother Water Khong"), and not the somewhat redundant Mekong River used by *farangs*.

The upcoming US$31 million bridge to Laos will be located five km west of town in the subdistrict of Ban Chommani, across the river from the Laotian town of Tha Nan Laeng and 18 km from Vientiane.

Wat Po Chai

Tucked away in a back alley east of the bus terminal, Wat Po Chai houses a highly venerated solid-gold statue called Luang Pho Phra Sai, cast in Laos and brought here from Vientiane by General Chakri. Murals in the principal *viharn* relate the legendary casting of the image and miraculous recovery after it was lost in the Mekong River. Also note the well-carved doors, window panels, and outstanding murals of angels, fish, and jungle elephants behind the central altar.

Wat Khaek

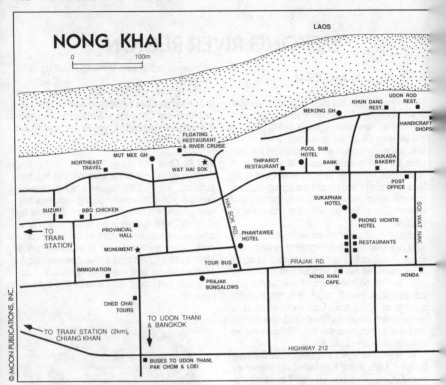

Wat Po Chai is the venue for several important festivals, such as the spectacular Rocket Festival held in April on the full moon, a Candle Festival, boat races on the Mekong, and Songkram.

Wat Prathat Nong Khai

A venerable temple which slid into the river over a century ago is located a few kilometers east of town.

Wat Khaek

Certainly the most bizarre and memorable temple in northeastern Thailand is the strange Hindu-Buddhist wonderland of Wat Khaek (also called Wat Phuttama Makasamakhom), located four km east of town at the end of a dusty side road.

Wat Khaek is the eccentric vision of Luang Pu Bunleuau Surirat, a refugee monk from war-torn Vietnam and Laos who settled in Nong Khai in 1978 to construct his Disneyland of psychedelic statues. Aided by a large community of local devotees, Luang Pu ("Venerable Grandfather") neatly combined his eclectic religious beliefs into a religious theme park that fuses elements of Buddhism, Hinduism, and Eastern shamanism.

Resembling something from the imagination of Hieronymus Bosch, temple ground sculptures feature familiar deities such as the elephant-headed Hindu god Ganesh, Vishnu, and Shiva, nestled alongside huge aquatic creatures, barking cement dogs, and Buddhas cast with Jimmy Durante noses. A rearside courtyard entered through a demon's mouth includes humorous depictions of model children, the perfect general, and lovers in the flesh and after death. Morality tales continue inside the hall, where followers of Luang Po have realistically cast images of Buddhas, Hindu deities, and other gods of indeterminate origins. The whole affair is mad, amusing, and wildly entertaining.

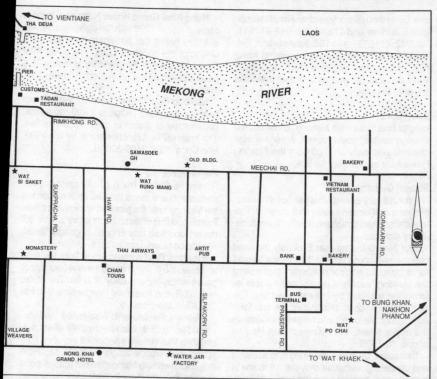

Goony-Golf Wat Khaek is four km east of town a few hundred meters beyond St. Paul School. Take a *songtao* east and look for the sign marked Sala Kaeoku, from where the dirt road continues 500 meters to the temple parking lot.

Across To Laos

Although crossings to Laos are permitted for Thai citizens at Nakhon Phanom, That Phanom, and Mukdahan, the only legal entranceway for Westerners is at Nong Khai. Visas should be obtained whenever possible in advance from the Laotian Embassy in Bangkok. Guesthouses and travel agencies in Nong Khai can sometimes help with border formalities, but entrance regulations change with the seasons. For example, Laos was open to independent travelers up to 1989 but suddenly closed in early 1990 after problems with theft and lost tourists.

The following guidelines were in effect in 1992. Visas from the Laotian Embassy in

Bangkok cost 500B, but they are granted only to businessmen and visitors with official sponsors in Laos. Independent travelers are required to join a group tour for about 2500B, which guarantees a visa and access to the capital city of Vientiane. Travel beyond Vientiane requires additional permits which cost up to 2500B for each supplemental destination. The restrictive travel policies of the Laotian government are intended to promote group tourism and discourage visits by budget travelers.

The best strategy is to first check with travel agencies and guesthouses in Bangkok, especially around Khao San Road. Visiting the Laotian Embassy in Bangkok is probably a waste of time, though a few travelers have reported success and miraculously obtained cheap visas.

Information in Nong Khai is somewhat sketchy and subject to haggling with uninformed agents and guest dee Guesthouse on Meechai Road. Northeast Business and Travel (tel. 042-412511, fax 042-411073) at 1105 Kaeworarut Rd. books trains to Bangkok, tours around Nong Khai, and provides accurate information about visits to Laos. Several other travel agencies are near the pier.

Boat Rides
Longtail boat trips on the Mekong can be booked through several guesthouses. A sunset river cruise leaves daily at 1700 from the Floating Restaurant behind Wat Hai Sok.

Budget Guesthouses
Nong Khai has several budget guesthouses, almost a half-dozen hotels that cater to Thai tourists, and two upscale hotels for international tour groups.

Mut Mee Guesthouse: Probably the most popular guesthouse in town, Mut Mee is favored for its beautiful outdoor restaurant overlooking the Mekong, excellent meals, and reliable information provided by the management. The somewhat run-down bungalows are subdivided into concrete lowers and better teak rooms on the upper floors. 1111 Kaeworawut Rd., no phone, 80-150B.

Sawasdee Guesthouse: Nong Khai's newest and cleanest guesthouse provides 16 rooms in a convenient location near the center of town. Heavy restoration has removed whatever charm the old building once possessed, but the place is popular with cleanliness freaks and midlevel travelers. Sawasdee has bicycles for rent, hot showers, laundry services, and tourist information from their English-speaking managers. 402 Meechai Rd., tel. (042) 412502, 80-120B fan, 250-350B a/c.

Mekong Guesthouse: A poorly run guesthouse with small and grubby rooms. Meechai Rd., tel. (042) 412320, 60-80B.

Hotels
Nong Khai has over 10 simple and low-priced Thai hotels, and two new luxury properties.

Phantawee Hotel: Probably the best of a fairly dismal lot, the Phantawee is divided into an older wing with fan-cooled rooms and a newer addition with 30 a/c rooms. 1241 Hai Sok Rd., tel. (042) 411568, 180-240B fan, 250-400B a/c.

Nong Khai Grand Hotel: Nong Khai tourism came of age in 1993 with the opening of several luxury hotels that anticipate the 1995 completion of the bridge to Laos. The Nong Khai Grand features all the standard amenities in a good location on the main road. Highway 212, 1600-2400B.

Mekong Royal Hotel: Located west of town near the proposed bridge is a 200-room hotel constructed at a cost of over US$12 million. The hotel will be fully operational by late 1993. Ban Chommani, 2400-3000B.

Restaurants
Riverside Cafes: Nong Khai's most popular restaurants are those located on the banks of the Mekong near the pier and immigration office. Tadan and Bifern restaurants serve simple but decent food from their English-language menus. Rimkhong Road. Inexpensive.

Floating Restaurant: Aside from the food and beer, the novelty here is the one-hour dinner cruise which departs daily at 1700. The cruise fee is 20B, and meals are inexpensive. Wat Hai Sok Alley. Inexpensive.

Vietnam Restaurant: Also called the Indochine Restaurant, this kitschy cafe offers outstanding Vietnamese specialties including pork spring rolls, wonderful gai yang (friend chicken), and steaming Mongolian hot pots. A good alternative to the bare-bones cafes located on the riverside. 189 Meechai Road. Inexpensive.

Dukada Bakery: The French influence from Laos has spilled across the border and blessed Nong Khai with several traditional bakeries where fresh breads and croissants are prepared each morning. Dukada also serves pastries, Thai dishes, Western breakfasts, and brewed local coffees. Meechai Road. Inexpensive.

Mut Mee Guesthouse: Nong Khai's best riverside restaurant is in the guesthouse west of town. Good food and pleasant service in a relaxing atmosphere. Bring a book to read. 1111 Kaeworawut Road. Inexpensive.

BBQ Chicken: A good escape from the tourist venues is provided by the crowded barbecue cafe located west of the provincial hall near the Suzuki dealership. Meechai Road. Inexpensive.

Restaurant Row: Almost a dozen small cafes with Thai and Chinese dishes are located just south of the Phong Vichitr and Sukaphan hotels.

Adjacent Nong Khai Cafe is slightly more upscale. Banthoenjit Road. Inexpensive.

Shopping
Best buys in Nong Khai include Laotian silverwork, locally produced baskets, and traditional cotton and silk weavings.

Rimkhong Road: Handicrafts shops along Rimkhong Rd. sell inexpensive Laotian silverwork such as bracelets, necklaces, boxes, and tightly woven rattan baskets from Udon Thani. Silverwork is sold by weight rather than quality; the going rate is 8-12B per gram.

Village Weavers Handicraft: The best-quality handicrafts in Nong Khai are found in the charitable foundation established in 1982 by the Good Shepherd Sisters to aid villagers toward self-sufficiency. Excellent quality indigo-dyed cotton ikats and *mut mees* are sold at very reasonable prices, as well as stylish clothes and household items featured in the annual Oxfam gift catalogue. 786 Prajak Rd. Soi Weva, tel. (042) 411236.

Practicalities
Tourist Information: Although the TAT strangely decided to establish a tourist office in Khon Kaen rather than Nong Khai, travel information is readily available from the Sawasdee, Mut Mee, and Niyana guesthouses. Tours and information on Laos can be obtained from Northeast Business and Travel and from the Nong Khai Grand Hotel.

Motorcycle Rentals: Motorcycles are an outstanding way to tour the region around Nong Khai and the Mekong River. However, the soaring popularity of motorcycle touring has created a serious shortage of bikes. Availability is best assured by checking the night before with a motorcycle agency. Motorcycles are available from the Honda dealership on Prajak Rd., Mekong Guesthouse, and the Suzuki dealership in the west end of town.

Transportation
Nong Khai is located 615 km northeast of Bangkok, 356 km north of Korat, 51 km north of Udon Thani, and 20 km southeast of Vientiane.

Air: The nearest airport is in Udon Thani. Reservations can be made at Thai Airways (tel. 042-411530) at 453 Prajak Road.

Train: Trains from Bangkok depart daily at 0615, 1900, and 2030, and take 10-12 hours. Sleepers are available on the 2030 service.

Trains from Nong Khai to Bangkok depart at 1740, 1900, and 0740. The 1900 express train has sleepers.

Bus: Ordinary and a/c buses depart hourly from 0530 to 0800 and 2000 to 2130 from the Northern Bus Terminal in Bangkok. Trains are much more comfortable than buses.

Government buses depart from the Bor Kor Sor terminal on Prajak Road. Private bus companies with a/c services to Bangkok, Chiang Mai, and other major destinations include Baramee Tours just opposite Prajak Bungalows, Chan Tours on Prajak Rd., and Ched Chai Tours on Friendship Highway.

Buses to nearby destinations such as Udon Thani, Pak Chom, and Loei leave from Friendship Hwy. just south of Hwy. 212.

ATTRACTIONS NEAR NONG KHAI

Several Laotian-style temples and geological oddities are located outside Nong Khai. Their isolated locations make them difficult to reach with public transportation, but they are great rides for motorcyclists.

Wat Bang Puan
Eighteen km southwest of Nong Khai is a modern Laotian-style *chedi* built by a ruler from Vientiane and reconstructed in 1978 by the Fine Arts Department. Considered among the most sacred sites in the northeast, Wat Ban Puan is somewhat unimpressive aside from several Buddhas displayed under open tin roofs and a small museum filled with wooden figurines, Dvaravati stone inscriptions, and odd statues of policemen and model *wats*. Photographs of the original *chedi* are posted on the interior walls.

Wat Bang Puan can be reached with a *songtao* to Ban Nong Hong Song and a second minitruck west to the compound.

Wat Prathat Buakok
Far more interesting than Wat Bang Puan is this Laotian *stupa* and historical park 55 km southwest of Nong Khai.

The principal *stu*

Phanom, which is in turn fashioned after the original structure of That Luang in Vientiane. Constructed from 1917 to 1927 to enshrine a footprint of the Buddha, Wat Buakok features exterior friezes of horses, elephants, buffaloes, and monkeys. A billboard points out nearby prehistoric wall paintings and abstract designs painted by former monks.

Ban Phu Historical Park

A dirt road shortly before Wat Buakok leads two km uphill to one of the most curious geological sights in Thailand. An information center at the park entrance shows hiking trails through the bizarre rock formations named after Buddhist legends and ancient folk tales. English-speaking guides are usually on hand.

First walk left to several rock formations (Tham Wua and Tham Khon) covered with crude paintings of Dvaravati Buddhas and Hindu gods from the Lopburi Period. The path then circles around an upper plateau covered with outlandishly shaped rocks which resemble giant toadstools carved by Martians. A side path leads back to a lookout point called Pha Sadej, and then returns to Wat Luk Koei ("Temple of the Son-in-Law"), recently reconstructed to support the collapsing overhanging rock. The complete hiking loop takes about 90 minutes.

The historical park is 13 km from the town of Ban Phu, which can be reached by *songtao* from either Nong Khai or Si Chiang Mai. A chartered *songtao* will be necessary from Ban Phu, or a chartered *samlor* from Ban Tu.

THA BO

One of the prettiest and least visited regions in Thailand is the northern perimeter of the Issan between Nong Khai and Chiang Khan. The towns seem to improve with distance from Nong Khai, with the best atmosphere at Pak Chom and Sang Khom, followed by Chiang Khan and Si Chiang Mai.

The road west from Nong Khai first passes through Tha Bo, a town located 25 km west of Nong Khai on the banks of the Mekong. Tha Bo lies in a fertile region which produces tomatoes, rice, tobacco, and noodles. The main industry is the production of spring-roll wrappers, as evidenced by the thousands of rice-paper

circles which dry on crosswork racks. Another unusual product is *kenaf*, which is lowered into shallow ponds to rot until the fiber can be worked into basketry.

Sights west of town include Wat Nam Mong, which contains a highly regarded solid-gold Buddha image (Pra Chao Ong Due) cast in the 17th century, and a public park with strangely sculpted topiary.

Accommodations

Accommodations in Tha Bo are limited to the Isan Orchid Guest Lodge (tel. 042-431665) on Gaowarawud Rd. where Mr. Thom and Don Beckerman run a very clean homestay with rooms for 500-850B. They can also help with tours to nearby temples and the rock formations at Buakok Historical Park.

Transportation

Yellow buses to Tha Bo and Si Chiang Mai leave from the street just west of the Suzuki dealership in Nong Khai. Motorcyclists can follow the road which skirts the Mekong, or take Highway 211 west of Nong Song Hong and visit Wat Bang Puan.

SI CHIANG MAI

Si Chiang Mai is a thriving commercial center located 58 km west of Nong Khai and just across the river from Vientiane. First impressions are discouraging since the town has replaced much of its original wooden architecture with concrete cubicles so typical of contemporary Thailand, but the town has a degree of charm and is a useful point for visits to nearby temples and beaches. Most of the population are Lao and Vietnamese citizens who fled here after the communist takeover of Laos, and today remain stateless peoples without passports or land ownership rights.

Attractions

Lao and Vietnamese refugees in Si Chiang Mai have established a roaring business in the production of spring-roll wrappers, exported to all corners of the planet. Visitors can watch the production of the rice-paper wrappers and visit the bakery on the riverfront road at Soi 30 which still produces fresh French breads daily at 1500.

Other sights include a small beach best visited at low tide, a large tomato-canning factory marked Chico-Thai, and Wat Aranyabanpot, about 10 km west of town. Saturday events include cockfights during the dry season and fish fighting during the rainy months.

Wat Hin Mak Peng: Temple fans may also want to visit Wat Hin Mak Peng, located west of Si Chiang Mai and 30 km before Sang Khom. This peaceful forest monastery is known for its rigorous precepts followed by a large community of monks and *mae chis*. Residents live in monastic *kutis* constructed among giant boulders elevated over the banks of the Mae Nam Khong.

Than Thong Falls: A small set of falls best visited during the rainy season is located past Wat Hin Mak Peng and 11 km east of Sang Khom.

Accommodations

Hotels: Kusonsuk Hotel at 14 Rimkhong Rd. and Sithisuwan Hotel at 35 Rimkhong Rd. have rooms from 80 to 100 *baht*.

Tim Guesthouse: Several years ago a Swiss citizen named Jean-Daniel Schranz opened a small guesthouse on the riverfront road between Sois 16 and 17. Jean-Daniel and his Thai wife can help with bicycles, motorcycles, boats, car rentals, and information on nearby attractions. Other services include international telephone calls, laundry, hot solar-powered showers, traditional massage, Western and Thai meals, fresh coffee, and home-baked breads, not to mention his collection of over 350 cassette tapes. Rimkhong Rd. Soi 16, tel. (042) 451072, 40-120B.

SANG KHOM

The atmosphere improves considerably in the small town of Sang Khom, 63 km west of Nong Khai. Populated by Thais rather than the Laos and Vietnamese, Sang Khom provides a useful base from which to visit the region's waterfalls, temples, and caves.

Attractions

The only sight in town is Wat Kang Sila, the so-called Leaning Tower of Sang Khom. Maps to attractions outside town can be picked up at the local guesthouses.

Wat Patak Sua: A small temple-monastery with great views is tucked away in the cliffs above Sang Khom. Start from the trailhead four km east of town, and hike one hour through the forest.

Caves: Hikers and bicyclists may also want to visit Padeng Cave and Wat Punakaba, 28 km southeast of town near Ban Dong Tong, and a pair of caves in the hills near Ban Nam Pu.

Than Tip Falls: The best waterfalls in the region are 15 km west of Sang Khom and two km off the main highway. Stop at the sign and hike through rice and tapioca farms to the five-level falls which eventually empty into the Mekong.

Accommodations

Five guesthouses are located on the riverbanks in Sang Khom. All have simple bungalows priced from 40 to 80 *baht*.

River Huts: First on the right is the deserted yet friendly Sunflower Guesthouse, followed closely by the River Huts, which offers boat trips down the Mekong, bicycle rentals, rough maps, and "lice removal—one *baht* each." River Huts has a small cafe perched over the river and 10 primitive bamboo bungalows, but only four face the river. Rimkhong Rd., 40-60B.

DD Guesthouse: Probably the best in town, DD features a useful wall map, herbal saunas for 25B, and expert Issan dinners prepared by Mr. Pong. Seven bungalows, but only two face the river. 190 Rimkhong Rd., tel. (042) 412415, 60-80B.

Bouy Guesthouse: Intense competition means that many of the guesthouses in Sang Khom can't support their owners, such as Mr. Boon who plans to find his fortune in New Zealand and not Issan. His wife may continue to operate the guesthouse. Rimkhong Rd., 40-80B.

TXK Guesthouse: Sang Khom's original guesthouse has the distinct advantage of being somewhat removed from the other places which are badly crammed together. TXK is widely known for its excellent communal meals prepared by Mr. Root. Rimkhong Rd., 40-80B.

Grandpa's Global Twin Village: A well-known American potter and "Global Coordinator" named Ernest Rolstone operates an ambitious resort and spa center 13 km south of Sang Khom near the village of Na Yung. An upscale escape that offers fishing, rafting, and handicrafts. 74 Ban Som Sowan Moo I, Nonthong, Ampur Ging Na Yung, Udon Thani Province. Bungalows with private baths cost 250-350B.

PAK CHOM

The Lao village of Pak Chom is the prettiest and most laid-back town between Nong Khai and Chiang Khan. Travelers seeking to discover what is most authentic and charming about rural Issan will enjoy a few days gazing at the river and wandering around the surrounding countryside. A wonderful, almost completely untouched destination.

The main activity is simply watching the river and perhaps taking a boat down the Mekong. Gold miners can sometimes be seen working the sandy islands and crumbling riverbanks. Ban Vinai Refugee Center closed in 1992, and the Hmong residents were relocated to a large camp near Chiang Kham in northern Thailand. The Cambodian residents were sent off to a camp near the Kampuchean border.

Accommodations

The sheer beauty of Pak Chom will probably bring more guesthouses, but for the present time the town offers only a few simple bungalows.

Maekhong Guesthouse: The best place in town has a dozen bamboo bungalows at the end of a dirt trail at the north end of Pak Chom. Started by Niyana from Nong Khai but now managed by a Swiss traveler, the locale and atmosphere of the Maekhong remind you of the Golden Triangle before the arrival of mass tourism. The grounds are surrounded by bamboo forests and a meditation wat with lagoon and beach chairs. Soi 1, no phone, twin bungalows with no electricity and common bath cost 40-80B. Walk west of town until you reach the small signpost on the right.

Chumpee Guesthouse: The only alternative to the Maekhong Guesthouse is the rather dismal collection of bamboo huts thoughtlessly crammed together near the river two blocks east of the main intersection. Chumpee (Champi) sponsors jungle tours at 450B for three people, and has a small cafe with good views over the river. Rooms cost 50-80B.

Restaurants

Pim's Cafe on the main street in the center of town is operated by a very friendly lady who speaks English and serves shots of rice whiskey in addition to Thai dishes listed on the chalkboard menu. A small Thai restaurant is located near the river just one block east of the Chumpee Guesthouse.

CHIANG KHAN

Chiang Khan is a fairly large town 50 km north of Loei on the banks of the Mekong River. Almost entirely constructed of teakwood homes now covered with a fine patina of red dust, Chiang Khan guarantees a refreshing change from other towns in Thailand created from concrete and cinder block. The town is also known for its cotton blankets and excellent bananas.

While it lacks the simplicity and rural charms of Pak Chom, Chiang Khan serves as a useful transit point on the Mekong journey and a good spot for boat cruises on the Mekong River.

Temples

Religious architecture in Chiang Khan somewhat reflects the cultural interaction of Thai and French-Lao influences, from the northern-style rooflines to the Lao glasswork and pseudo-French shutters. Examples of local wats include Wat Sri Khun Muang with its guardian demons and primitively painted murals, and Wat Pa Klang constructed after Chiang Khan was established by Laotian migrants several centuries ago.

Travelers with motorcycles may want to visit Wat Phu Pha Baen, a small temple and cave complex set with meditation platforms and excellent views, 10 km east of Chiang Khan and one-third the distance up the mountain. Closer temples include Wat Tha Khaek, two km east of town, and a forest temple called Wat Si Song Nong near Khaeng Khut Ku. Wat Si Song Nong serves as residence for a highly respected monk named Achaan Mahabun Nak.

Curiosity seekers might visit Ban Kok Lao, 25 km east, where childless women worship huge stone phalluses as fertility symbols.

River Journeys

Guesthouses in Chiang Khan arrange upriver boat trips through sublime scenery to Menam

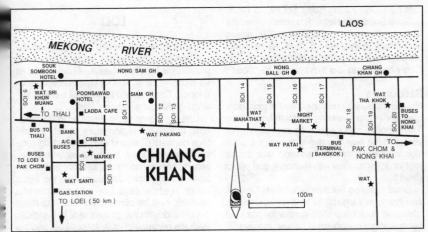

Heuang and the point where the Mekong turns north into Laos. The downriver journey reaches the rapids at Kaeng Khut Ku in about 30 minutes. Fares are 60-120B depending on distances and number of passengers. Most trips include cold drinks and stops for swimming.

Several small companies have announced plans to boat down the Mekong from Chiang Kham to Pak Chom, and perhaps farther east to Sang Khom and Si Chiang Mai. Problems with this exciting route include political disputes with Laotian authorities and dangerous rapids on the Mekong.

Festivals

Chiang Khan celebrations include the Miss Banana Beauty Contest in the fall and the Cotton Festival held in February. The end of the Buddhist retreat season in late October is celebrated with a week-long festival of boat races, performances of Issan musical comedy, and displays of wax model *prasats* at the local temples.

Kaeng Khut Ku

A large set of rapids and a scenic overlook are located five km east of Chiang Khan at the end of a very long side road. Kaeng Khut Ku is popular with Thai tourists who consume barbecued fish, prawn fritters, and *som tam* in bamboo observation decks elevated over the riverbanks. Accommodations are available at See View Bungalows for 200-250B, and Coot Cao Resort for 140-180B.

Kaeng Khut Ku can be reached from Chiang Khan by *songtao, tuk tuk,* rented bicycle, or boats chartered from local guesthouses.

Accommodations

Nong Sam Guesthouse: Previously called the Tamarind Guesthouse, the friendliest place in Chiang Khan is operated by a Brit named Rob, his Thai wife Noi, and their two children (Nong and Sam) who look Thai but have the frantic energy levels of Western kids. Rob, the primary information source for the region, distributes maps and helpful advice to his guests. Other services include boat trips on the Mekong, bicycle rentals, and popular breakfasts in his cozy cafe. Chai Khong Road. Soi 12, no phone, 60-100B.

Nong Ball Guesthouse: Previously called the Nong Sam Guesthouse, Nong Ball is a large and comfortable place that runs a close second to Nong Sam. As you can see, the guesthouse situation in Chiang Khan changes constantly as landlords reclaim popular guesthouses and attempt to milk the tourist boom, while forcing guesthouse owners to move their operations elsewhere. The Thai lady who runs Nong Ball is friendly though not as helpful or articulate as Rob. Chai Khong Road. Soi 16, no phone, 60-100B.

Chiang Khan Guesthouse: Previously called the Amnatsiri Hotel, but now called a guesthouse to cash in on the travelers' market. A fairly run-down place redeemed by a decent riverside cafe. Chai Khong Road. Soi 19, 60-100B.

Souk Somboon Hotel: Previously called the Suksambuh, this is the only hotel worth checking when the guesthouses are filled. All 16 rooms are fan-cooled with common baths down the hall. Chai Khong Road. Soi 9, no phone, 80-100B.

Restaurants

Nong Sam Guesthouse operates the most popular cafe in town, serving Western breakfasts, Thai dinners, and vegetarian specialties. Favorites in the riverview dining area at the Souk Somboon Hotel include *laab moo, laab gai, ya mut ya* (spicy noodles with sausage), and *pla tot* (fried fish).

Small cafes on Soi 9 include Ladda Cafe for *pad thai*, a *gai yang* stall for fried chicken, and an unnamed duck soup shop across the road. All serve prodigious amounts of Laotian *mao lao* (literally "drunk on liquor"), a grain-alcohol whiskey both cheaper and stronger than Thai Mekong. Shots are thrown down like tequila and washed with beer chasers.

The central market near the cinema and a/c bus terminal has a few foodstalls for morning servings of fried *pla tong goh* (donuts) and steaming cups of *nam ta hu* (sweetened soybean milk). Evening foodstalls are located at the night market near Soi 18.

Transportation

Chiang Khan is 50 km north of Loei and about 160 km west of Nong Khai. Buses from Nong Khai to Chiang Khan and all other towns on the Mekong leave from the street just beyond the Suzuki dealership. Direct service to Chiang Khan takes about five hours but is available only in the early morning. Late departers will need to patch together a series of *songtaos* between the various towns.

Buses and *songtaos* depart frequently from the main bus terminal in Loei.

Direct a/c buses to Bangkok leave at 0800 and 1830 in front of the pharmacy and opposite the central market. Orange bus 99 to Bangkok leaves across from the night market at 0730 and 1730.

Songtaos to Loei leave every 20 minutes from Loei Rd. opposite the Shell gas station. *Songtaos* to Tha Li occasionally leave from the west of town, depending on passenger demand and road conditions.

LOEI

Situated midway between the north and the northeast on the western edge of the Issan plateau, the provincial capital of Loei serves as an important transit spot for visitors arriving from northern Thailand, and as a useful base for visiting Phu Kradung National Park.

Loei is geographically classified in the northeast, though the region more closely resembles northern Thailand with its freezing temperatures and heavy fog in the winter months, searing heat during the hot season, and mountainous topography that surrounds the fertile valley. In earlier days, Loei was considered a hardship post for bureaucrats who had fallen out of favor with the government in Bangkok. Perhaps because of its isolation, Loei and the western valleys have retained some of the traditional flavor lost in the more developed regions of Thailand.

Attractions

The region's principal sights are the three national parks located outside town. However, a few hours can be enjoyed wandering around the municipal lake at the south end of town and exploring the small market near the bridge which crosses the narrow Loei River. Adjacent to the lake is a small Lak Muang and a Chinese shrine called Sanjao Por Kud Pong.

Hot-season visitors can cool off in the swimming pool at Loei Land, about three km north of town on the road to Chiang Khan.

Loei is situated in a rich valley which produces minerals and some of the finest cottons in Thailand. Shops on Charoenraj and Ruamchai roads sell warm cotton blankets and clothing, quite useful when temperatures plunge to zero Celsius during the winter months.

Accommodations

Muang Loei Guesthouse: Budget travelers usually stay in the guesthouse located two blocks east of the bus terminal. The place is run by a retired Thai military officer who once served as a liaison between Thai and American forces. Guesthouse walls are covered with all possible travel tips, including bus schedules and information on motorcycle touring. Other services include bicycle and motorcycle rentals, and organized

© MOON PUBLICATIONS, INC.

tours to the nearby national parks. A smaller and less popular branch of the guesthouse is located down Saeng Sawang Road. Ruamchai Rd., tel. (042) 812302, 50-90B.

Phu Luang Hotel: A good middle-quality hotel with big rooms, private baths, and acceptable cafe. 55 Charoenraj Rd., tel. (042) 811570, fax (042) 812558, 150-200B fan, 250-300B a/c.

Udom Thai Hotel: Loei's most popular hotel is similar to the Phu Luang and King hotels, but perhaps in the better location in the center of town. 112 Charoenraj Rd., tel. (042) 811763, 150-200B fan, 250-300B a/c.

Restaurants

Night Market: A small night market sets up around 1800 in the alley just off Charoenraj Road. Rather than sitting around, try the take-away option by pointing at each intriguing dish and saying *"ha baht, ha baht"* ("five *baht*, five *baht."*) Borrow a plate and silverware from your hotel to enjoy the best and cheapest meal in town. A larger night market takes place at the south end of the city lake.

Nong Ploy Beer House: Directly across from the Phu Luang Hotel is a decent restaurant with an English-language menu that lists everything from chicken *laab* to tasty potato soup. 66

Charoenraj Road. Moderate.

Savita Bakery: Breakfasts are best in this clean cafe that serves both Western and Thai specialties. Savita is also a popular place to hang out and eat ice cream late in the evening. Adjacent Chuan Lee is a traditional Chinese cafe with coffee and curries. 137 Charoenraj Road. Inexpensive.

Transportation

Loei is 520 km northeast of Bangkok, 344 km north of Korat, and 269 km east of Phitsanulok.

Air: Thai Airways flies four times weekly from Khon Kaen and three times weekly from Phitsanulok. Thai Airways (tel. 042-812344) is at 191 Charoenraj Road.

Bus: Buses leave eight times daily from the Northern Bus Terminal in Bangkok. Loei can also be reached by bus from Phitsanulok via Lom Sak. Buses and *songtaos* also connect Nan with Loei via Nam Pat and Dan Sai.

Buses from Loei to Chiang Mai via Phitsanulok leave five times daily and take four hours to Phitsanulok and nine hours to Chiang Mai. Government buses leave from both the main bus terminal on Ruamchai Rd. and directly in front of the Phu Luang Hotel. Private bus companies with a/c services include Chumprae Tours at the Udom Thai Hotel and Sir Kuarinter at the King Hotel.

PHU KRADUNG NATIONAL PARK

This outstanding park, located on a sloping plateau 82 km south of Loei, is a high-elevation retreat set with pine trees, tall grasses, six waterfalls, dozens of hiking trails, and fields of springtime azaleas and rhododendrons.

Phu Kradung ("Bell Mountain") National Park was established in 1967 to help preserve the unique temperate flora and indigenous mammals such as black bears, barking deer, and wild dogs. The park closes from July through October when monsoon rains reduce the trails to muddy quagmires. Rangers advise to visit the park on weekdays to avoid crowds, and, if possible, during the less popular but very lush months of May and June.

The trail begins at the base of the mountain at Ban Si Than, where the Park Service operates an information center with maps, restaurant, and bungalows. Bags can be stored and porters can be hired at the information center. The trail from Si Than climbs steeply for the first kilometer before easing off and finally starting the final ascent. Bamboo ladders and ropes help through the steeper sections. The trail ultimately emerges onto a sweeping plateau carpeted with grass and covered with wildflowers from February to May. The total distance of about nine kilometers takes four or five hours.

Park headquarters at the summit has a small shop with basic provisions, another restaurant with hot meals, bungalows, tent sites, and maps which describe the 50 kilometers of trails. Popular hikes include the trail to Liam Phan Nok Aen at the eastern edge of the plateau for views over the Petchabun Mountains, and a southern trail which runs 12 kilometers along the edge of the plateau.

Visitors should bring warm clothes, extra food, flashlight, candles, and insect repellent.

Accommodations

Accommodations include 16 10-man bungalows that cost 500 to 1500B. Tents cost 50B per night. Bedding and blankets can be hired. Reservations can be made in Bangkok with the National Park Division of the Forestry Department (tel. 02-271-3737), or with the Forestry Department in Loei (tel. 042-800776) on the main highway inside the provincial offices.

The Loei Provincial Office also arranges group tours for parties of 10 or more. The three-day, two-night tour costs 800B per person and includes transportation, food, drink, and accommodations in bungalows.

Transportation

Phu Kradung is 74 km south of Loei on Highway 201 and then eight km west on Highway 2019. Direct minibuses are available on weekends from the main bus terminal. Exact departure schedules can be checked at Muang Loei Guesthouse. Alternatively, take any bus heading south toward Khon Kaen and alight at the park turnoff. Hitchhike or wait for a *songtao*.

PHU LUANG NATIONAL PARK

Phu Luang is an 848-square-km wildlife reserve controlled by the Forestry Department to help protect the remaining wildlife, reputed to include wild tigers and elephants. Similar to Phu Kradung, Phu Luang is situated on a high plateau covered with tropical jungles, deciduous pine forests, and vast stretches of savannah. The park is also known for its variety of rare Paphiopedilum and Sukul orchids, which have been depleted by poachers to the verge of extinction. Trails established by the park rangers lead to Pa Chang Phan ("Elephant Cliff") for sunrises, the wild roses at Pa Somdej, and Pa Talien, where dwarf trees are collected and sold as potted bonsais. Thick jungle and wild orchids are best seen at Khok Prommajan, north of the Forest Reserve Camp, and in Black Forest, where white orchids cling to moss-covered trees.

Accommodations
Accommodations are similar to Phu Kradung's, with group bungalows from 500B and tents on site for 50B. Reservations can be made at the provincial offices in Loei. Bring food, drink, warm clothes, flashlight, and candles.

Transportation
Phu Luang is 26 km south of Loei down Highway 201 and then 15 km west from Wang Saphung. Although somewhat closer than Phu Kradung, Phu Luang is more difficult to visit because of its inaccessibility and lack of organized transportation. The easiest option is a tour arranged by the Forestry Department at the Loei Provincial Office. The three-day, two-night tour costs 800B per person and includes transportation, food, drink, and accommodations in park bungalows.

Mini-trucks from the bus terminal in Loei go halfway up the mountain, from where a tough trail reaches the summit and park headquarters. Allow three or four hours for the trek.

TOWNS NEAR LOEI

One of the most intriguing travel routes in Thailand is between Loei and northern Thailand, unquestionably one of the most beautiful yet least visited regions in Thailand. Tucked away in the mountains which divide Issan from central and northern Thailand are dozens of small towns and villages that probably receive only a few dozen Western visitors each year. Most towns have small and inexpensive hotels and can be reached by buses and mini-trucks.

The most common route is from Loei to Phitsanulok via Lom Sak, past the national parks at Phu Rua, Phu Hin Rongkla, and Thung Salang Luang. A more scenic route is from Loei to Dan Sai, from where the road splits to either Nakhon Thai and Phitsanulok, or north to Nan Pat and eventually Nan. Simple Thai hotels are available on the northern route in Dan Sai, Nam Pat, and Na Noi.

Tha Li
Another lovely town somewhat similar to Pak Chom is situated eight km south of the Heuang River in a remote valley about 50 km west of Chiang Khan and 45 km north of Loei.

Once under the control of local smugglers who exchanged Thai merchandise for Lao whiskey and other contraband, Tha Li today is firmly guarded by the Thai government to prevent another surprise border incursion by the Laotian army. Roads north of Tha Li head up to a military camp at Ban Pak Hua, the large town of Nong Peu, and the trading village of Ahi (Aharn). All three villages are situated on the Heuang River, a tributary of the Mekong. Longtail boats can be chartered to tour the river and visit some bathing beaches.

Tha Li can be reached by motorcycles and by songtaos from Loei and occasionally Chiang Khan. As of this writing, accommodations are unavailable except by donation at local temples.

Dan Sai
About 86 km west of Loei is the small town of Dan Sai, an important junction point chiefly known among the Thais for its strange ghostly procession called Pi Ta Khon ("Dance of the Ghosts"). The three-day Bun Luang Festival begins with a masked parade to honor the guardian spirits of a highly revered Buddha image and to kick off the annual rainmaking ceremonies in June. Local residents don bizarre Halloween masks made from coconut husks crowned with a hat formed from glutinous rice steamers. Each ghost carries a phallic-shaped sword in accordance with the fertility rites of Bun Bung Fai (Rocket Festival) and follows the sacred Buddha image from the Moon River to the gates of Wat Por Chai. The festival ends on the third day after the ghosts circumnavi-

gate the principal *bot* three times and fling their masks into the Moon River.

The principal sight in Dan Sai is Wat Prathat Sri Song Rak, located on a hill on the west bank of the Moon River, about one kilometer from the center of town. The 30-meter brick *stupa* was constructed in 1560 to commemorate a diplomatic treaty between King Chakrapet of Ayuthaya and King Chaichetha of Vientiane. Sri Song Rak is one of the few temples in Thailand without resident monks, being left to the guardian spirits of Chao Por Kuan and Chao Mae Nan Tiam. Visitors should bring white flowers and avoid wearing red clothing.

A small hotel in Dan Sai has rooms from 80B.

Lom Sak

Lom Sak is a small town situated in a fertile valley between the Phang Hoei Mountains to the east and the southern extension of the Luang Prabang Range to the west. Lom Sak is a major transit point for visitors traveling between Phitsanulok and Loei and Khon Kaen.

About 175 km south of Lom Sak are the ruins of Muang Si Thep, an important Khmer site which dominated the valley from the 9th to 11th centuries.

Accommodations are available at the Sawang Hotel on Samakichai Rd. and at the Pen Sin Hotel on Wachi Road.

THE FAR NORTHEAST

BUNG KHAN

Highway 212 leaves Nong Khai and continues 135 km east to the small town of Bung Khan, situated on the Mekong River just opposite the Laotian village of Muang Paksan. Bung Khan provides a useful pause or overnight stop for travelers heading down to Nakhon Phanom. Enjoying a drink from a local cafe and watching fishermen maneuver the rapids are the main interests of Bung Khan.

Phu Wua Wildlife Park

A small nature park located on Phu Wua Mountain, 45 km southeast of town, features several waterfalls, crumbling cliffs, and a small forest *wat*. Phu Wua can be combined with a visit to Wat Phu Tauk, or get there by taking a bus east on Highway 212 to Ban Chayphet, from where *songtaos* continue south down to Ban Noi near Dansanan Falls and Ban Donset near Chetsei Falls.

Wat Phu Tauk

Formally known as Wat Chedi Kiri Viharn, Wat Phu Tauk (or Phu Tok) is one of the most sacred forest temples in the northeast. It is also among the most spectacular in location, being situated on a sandstone mountain which soars vertically from the flat dry plains. The entire outcropping has been fashioned by resident monks into a bewildering maze of stairways and tunnels that dissect the mountain and provide sensational views over the vast expanses.

Wat Phu Tauk is climbed up a series of seven passageways which symbolically represent the seven heavens of the Buddhist universe, and pass dozens of monastic *kutis* inhabited by friendly monks and *mae chis*. A small headquarters features photographs of the present head monk, Achaan Jun, who studied under a legendary monk named Achaan Man. Issan Thais credit Achaan Man with almost single-handedly revolutionizing *vipassana* practices in northeastern Thailand.

Wat Phu Tauk is 47 km southeast of Bung Khan. Take a bus or mini-truck south from Bung Khan 25 km down to Ban Siwilai, from where *songtaos* continue 22 km east on the dirt road to the temple. Visitors can spend the night or continue to Phu Rua Wildlife Park and stay in park bungalows.

Accommodations

The Santisuk, Somanmit, and Neramit hotels on Prasatchai Rd. in Bung Khan have fan-cooled rooms from 60 to 100B.

SAKHON NAKHON

Sakhon Nakhon is a provincial center located 647 km from Bangkok, on the edge of 32-square-km Nong Han Lake, the largest natural lake in Thailand. Surrounded by lakes and rivers,

SAKHON NAKHON

Sakhon Nakhon Province provides a welcome relief from the dry monotony typical of the Issan.

Sakhon Nakhon was established as a Khmer outpost but was abandoned after a severe drought forced Khmer rulers to relocate to Khotraboon. Prior to the rise of Bangkok, Sakhon Nakhon was controlled by the kingdom of Lanchang. In the 19th century, King Rama III recaptured the city and returned it to Thai control.

Sakhon Nakhon landed firmly on the map of Buddhist pilgrimages several decades ago when a *vipassana* teacher named Achaan Man Bhuidato spent his life propagating insight meditation at Wat Pa Suthawat. After his mysteri-

ous disappearance in 1949, Achaan Man was succeeded by his student Achaan Fan Ajaro, who established a cave hermitage at Tham Kham in the Phu Phan Mountains. Pilgrims continue to visit local memorials dedicated to both monks.

A very curious sidelight to Sakhon Nakhon is provided by a gecko shop on Sukkasem Rd. where live geckos are purchased from villagers, dried, and exported to Taiwan and Hong Kong. Chinese consume the dried lizards with herbal medicines,to ensure good health and cure kidney diseases.

Festivals

Sakhon Nakhon sponsors a nationally famous Wax Festival in October, when enormous replicas of *prasat* are paraded through the streets.

Nong Han Lake

Thailand's largest natural lake is a popular place for early-morning joggers and older folks practicing tai chi. Boats can be hired to reach the interior islands.

Wat Chong Chum

Sakhon Nakhon's major religious monument features a modern whitewashed Laotian *chedi* which encases a 10th-century Khmer *prang*. The adjacent *viharn* contains a large seated Buddha and archaeological remains stored in a back room.

Wat Pa Suthawat

A small temple and modern museum opposite the provincial hall displays the paraphernalia and wax figure of Achaan Man, the fierce meditation master whose intensity is reflected in his lifelike image.

Wat Narai Cheng Weng

Six km northeast of town in the village of Ban Thai stands a Khmer *prang* reputedly constructed in the 10th century by a Khmer princess using only female labor. Also called Wat Prathat Naweng, the sandstone sanctuary features several excellent lintels carved with dancing Shivas and Krishna struggling with mythical lions.

Wat Pa Udom Somphon

Buddhist pilgrims visit this temple to honor and view the religious emblems of Achaan Fan, a *vipassana* master whose life-size wax image is displayed inside the central *viharn*. The temple is located three km outside of town.

Phu Phan National Park

Situated 17 km southwest of town on Highway 213, this 645-square-km nature preserve offers hiking trails, three waterfalls, and forest cover over a vast expanse of remote mountains once used by Thai resistance guerrillas in World War II and communist insurgents in the early 1970s. After peace was restored in the late 1970s, the royal family established a palace and research center to help promote the revival of ancient textile weaving.

Accommodations

All of the following hotels are located within a few blocks of the bus terminal on Raj Pattana Road. The Sirimit Hotel (tel. 042/711416) on Yuwa Pattana Rd., two blocks east of the bus terminal, has basic rooms from 60 to 100B. On the same road, the large Dusit Hotel (tel. 042/711198) at 1782 Yuwa Pattana Rd. has clean fan rooms with private bath from 120B and air-cons from 220B.

Several hotels are located in the center of town near the intersection of Kamchadphai and Premprida roads. The Araya Hotel (tel. 042/711224) at 1432 Kamchadphai Rd. has fan-cooled rooms from 100B and air-cons at double the price. Other choices on the same road include the Supom Pakdi Hotel (tel. 712161) with rooms from 80B and the Somkait Hotel (tel. 042/711044) with rooms from 60 to 120B.

The best hotel in Sakhon Nakhon is the 106-room Imperial Hotel (tel. 042/711119) at 1892 Sukkasem Rd. where air-cons with private bath cost 200 to 350B. The Imperial runs a popular nightclub.

Transportation

Sakhon Nakhon is 145 km southeast of Bung Khan, 117 km west of Nakhon Phanom, and 155 km east of Udon Thani. Direct buses are available from Ubon Ratchathani, Nakhon Phanom, That Phanom, Kalasin, Korat, and Bangkok. Travelers coming down from Bung Khan can take a direct bus or patch together a journey along the Mekong with a stop in Nakhon Phanom.

NAKHON PHANOM

Nakhon Phanom is set along the banks of the Mekong River, across from the small Laotian town of Muang Ta Kaek (Muang Khammouan). The town was once the site of a busy American airbase during the Vietnam conflict but has since returned to being a sleepy place populated by Issan farmers, Chinese merchants, Vietnamese refugees, and a modest number of Laotian traders.

Attractions

Attractions in town include the modern murals inside Wat Sri Thep, and simply gazing across

the river into Laos. Thai citizens are allowed to legally cross the river, but foreign visitors must travel west to Nong Khai or south down to the border checkpoint near Ubon Ratchathani. Access to Laos changes with the seasons. First check with the Laotian Embassy in Bangkok and other travelers on Khao San Road.

The large Laotian refugee camp at Ban Napho is closed to visitors.

Festivals
Festivals at the end of the rainy season in late October include the renowned Nakhon Phanom Boat Races and an illuminated boat procession augmented by cultural performances and handicraft fairs.

Accommodations
River Inn Hotel: Probably the best budget hotel in town and the only decent place on the river features a terrace restaurant with good food and views into Laos. 137 Sunthon Wichit Rd., tel. (042) 511305, 80-150B.

First Hotel: A good alternative to the River Inn is provided by the large hotel across from the clocktower and close to the river and immigration office. The staff is friendly and the rooms are clean. 370 Si Thep Rd., tel. (042) 511253, 80-120B fan, 220-250B a/c.

Nakhon Phanom Hotel: Top-end choice is the 58-room hotel located across from the market in the center of town. Facilities include a restaurant and nightclub, swimming pool, and snooker parlor. 403 Aphiban Bancha Rd. (Highway 212), tel. (042) 511074, 250-350B a/c with private bath.

Transportation

Nakhon Phanom is 740 km northeast of Bangkok, 252 km east of Udon Thani, 303 km southeast of Nong Khai, and 271 km north of Ubon Ratchathani.

Air: Thai Airways flies three times weekly from Bangkok via Udon Thani. Thai Airways (tel. 042-712259) is at 1446 Yupa Patana Road.

Bus: Buses reach Nakhon Phanom from the Northern Bus Terminal in Bangkok, but most travelers arrive by bus from Nong Khai, Sakhon Nakhon, or Ubon Ratchathani. Buses from Nong Khai depart hourly from 0700 to 1500 and take about seven hours via Sakhon Nakhon. Buses

also run hourly from both Ubon Ratchathani and Sakhon Nakhon.

THAT PHANOM

That Phanom, a small town on the banks of the Mekong River midway between Nakhon Phanom and Mukdahan, is a major pilgrimage site and home to the most sacred religious monument in the northeast.

A Lao market occurs near the river on Monday and Thursday mornings.

Wat Prathat That Phanom

Highly venerated by both Thai and Laotian citizens, the Laotian-style *chedi* of That Phanom forms the talismanic symbol of the Issan people

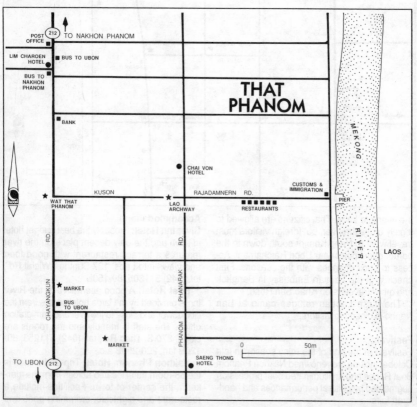

and a source of magical power for the residents of Laos.

The origins of the monument are unknown, though Buddhist legends claim that the original buildings were constructed about 2,500 years ago after a wandering monk name Maha Kasapa brought the breastbone of the Buddha to the region. Folklore relates that five local princes housed the relic in a new *chedi*, which was subsequently renovated in 1614 by the king of Laos and in 1692 by a famous Vientiane monk named Pra Kru Luang Phonsamek.

Disaster struck in 1975 when the principal tower collapsed after heavy rains. Horrified at the plight of the Issan icon, local authorities, aided by the Fine Arts Department, immediately began a reconstruction project which succeeded in erecting a new *chedi* in 1977.

The rebuilt structure features ancient Laotian ornaments and Khmer-style brick reliefs recovered from the original monument. Interior murals depict contemporary social problems such as drug addiction and the communist struggle in Laos.

The full moon of the third lunar month (February or March) is an excellent time to visit, when thousands of devout Buddhists gather for a popular festival.

Renu Phanom

Renu Phanom is a small village renowned for the weaving of cotton and silk fabrics. Several of the weaving homes also produce a rare version of Thai *ikat,* partially dyed before being painstakingly woven into ceremonial robes. A weekly handicraft market is held on Wednesdays near Wat Prathat Renu Nakhon, a diminutive copy of the more famous monument in That Phanom.

The turnoff to Renu Phanom is 12 km north of That Phanom and 44 km south of Nakhon Phanom. Direct *songtao* service is available from That Phanom, or take any bus to the turnoff and wait for a *songtao* heading seven km west to the weaving village.

Accommodations

That Phanom is a very small town with a new guesthouse and two hotels located east of the monument and just beyond the Laotian Arch.

Niyana Guesthouse: Lovely and vivacious Niyana operates a popular guesthouse with kitchen facilities, garden, and information on boat trips for travelers. Over the past decade, Niyana has established guesthouses in Pak Chom, Nong Khai, and now, That Phanom. 73 Weteshawrachon Rd., no phone, 50-100B.

Hotels: Chai Von Hotel at Phanom Phanarak Rd. has 20 fan-cooled rooms from 70 to 120B. Saeng Thong Hotel on the same street, but a right turn through the archway, has similar facilities at identical prices. Saeng Thong also has information on nearby attractions such as the ikat-weaving village of Renu Phanom. Similar rooms are found at the Lim Charoen Hotel (tel. 042-541019) on Chayangkun Rd., where fan-cooled rooms cost 90-140B.

Transportation

That Phanom is 52 km south of Nakhon Phanom and 225 km north of Ubon Ratchathani. Buses and *songtaos* from the intersection near the Nakhon Phanom Hotel in Nakhon Phanom take about 90 minutes to reach the *chedi* in That Phanom. Buses from the terminal in Ubon Ratchathani to Nakhon Pathom pass through That Phanom.

MUKDAHAN

Mukdahan is the provincial capital of the newest province in the northeast. Situated on the right banks of the wide and sluggish Mekong, Mukdahan has few important sights but offers a degree of atmosphere unique to remote destinations throughout the northeast.

The busy village is directly opposite the Laotian town of Savannakhet ("Golden Fields") and receives a small amount of trading between the two countries. A small riverside restaurant with views into Laos is located south of the customs office and two blocks east of the traffic circle.

Wat Sri Mongkol Thai, sited on the riverbanks a few blocks south of city center, was constructed in 1956 by Vietnamese refugees who melded Thai contours, Vietnamese script, and Chinese dragons into the eclectic result. Nearby Wat Jok Keo is worth a quick inspection.

Views over Mukdahan and the Mekong can be enjoyed from the summit of Phu Manoram, three km south of town, and from 353-meter Phu Muu ("Pig Hill"), named for the wild pigs that once lived in the region.

Mukdahan National Park

South of Mukdahan is a small national park known for its strange rock formations which resemble giant toadstools and homes of space aliens. The park straddles the geologic division between the northern half of the Issan and the southern half which stretches down to Cambodia. Also known as Phu Pha Thoep National Park, the 52-square-km enclave features dozens of geologic oddities, prehistoric cave paintings, and modest views from the summit of 420-meter Phu Si Chom and Phu Mano near the park entrance.

Mukdahan National Park is 16 km southeast of town on Highway 2034, which skirts the Mekong River.

Accommodations

Siam Hotel (tel. 042-611379) on Wiwit Surakan Rd. and opposite the bus terminal has fan-cooled rooms from 100B and a/c rooms from 220B. One block toward the river on Phitak Santirat Rd. is the Hong Kong Hotel (tel. 042-611123) with fan rooms from 80 to 120B.

Three adequate hotels are another block east toward the river on Samut Sakdarak Road. Hua Nam Hotel (tel. 042-611137) on the left has fan rooms from 80B and a/c rooms from 220B, while Bunthorn Kasem Hotel (tel. 042-611235) on the right has only fan-cooled rooms priced from 80B.

The top-end choice is the 55-room Mukdahan Hotel (tel. 042-611169) at 8 Samut Sakdarak Rd., where fan rooms cost 100-150B and a/c rooms with private bath start at 250B.

Transportation

Mukdahan is 70 km south of That Phanom and 163 km north of Ubon Ratchathani. Buses and songtaos from That Phanom stop on Wiwit Surakan Rd. near the public park. Buses to and from Ubon stop one block south near the Siam Hotel.

YASOTHON

Yasothon is the provincial capital of the province of the same name. The term Yasothon derives from the Sanskrit Yasodhara ("Preserver of Glory"), a son of Krishna as related in the Mahabharata. Isolated in the searing hot plains of lower Issan, Yasothon is rarely visited by Westerners except during the Rocket Festival described below.

Rocket Festival

Yasothon is home to the wildly popular Rocket Festival (Soeng Bung Fai) held in mid-May to celebrate the end of the dry season and ensure heavy rains throughout the region. While a fertility-rain festival is held in most Issan towns, Yasothon receives official support from the TAT and is considered to have the most extravagant production of any northeastern destination.

The festival centers on a procession of floats through the center of town to Wat Si Thai Phum, followed by the launching of enormous rockets from open fields outside the city limits. An enormous fireworks display occurs in the evening. Visitors should book rooms well in advance or join one of the many tours organized by travel agencies in Bangkok.

Accommodations

Yasothon has six small hotels in the center of town on Chang Sanit and Uthai Ramrit roads. Surawet Wattana Hotel (tel. 045-711690) at 128 Chang Sanit Rd. has 30 fan-cooled rooms that cost 80-120B. On the same street you'll find other hotels in the same price range, such as Suk Niran (tel. 045-711196), Serm Siri, and Phan Pricha.

Udom Phon Hotel (tel. 045-711564) at 82 Uthai Ramrit Rd. has acceptable fan-cooled rooms from 80B. Yot Nakhon Hotel (tel. 045-711122) at 141 Uthai Ramrit Rd. is the largest hotel in town, and the only place with a/c rooms. Fan rooms with private bath cost 100-140B, while a/c doubles with private bath cost 220-260B.

Transportation

Yasothon is 103 km northwest of Ubon Ratchathani, 196 km southeast of Khon Kaen, and 275 km northeast of Korat.

Yasothon is located in a very isolated region that remains well off the beaten track of tourism. One possible route to consider is to visit Yasothon, Roi Et, and Kalasin on a tour from Ubon Ratchathani to Khon Kaen. This shortcut skips Mekong River destinations such as That Phanom and Nakhon Phanom, but it's the most direct connection from Ubon to Nong Khai and the superb towns west along the Mekong.

UBON RATCHATHANI

Ubon Ratchathani—often called Ubon—is a major destination being positioned as the international gateway to Laos, Cambodia, and Vietnam. Ubon lies in the so-called Emerald Triangle due to its proximity to Laos and Cambodia, and firmly on the proposed Asian Highway, a network of road originally planned to link Istanbul with Saigon (Ho Chi Minh City) in Vietnam. Although the road remains a pipe dream, the completion of the proposed eastern extension will allow visitors to reach Angkor Wat and Saigon in less than a single day.

Ubon was established by the Khmers in the 10th century and came under Thai control after the rise of Ayuthaya in the 15th century. Tremendous growth occurred two decades ago when the Americans established an air base just outside Ubon to conduct bombing missions into Indochina. The Americans withdrew in 1975, leaving behind a legacy of deserted hotels, restaurants, and darkened nightclubs. The town quickly slipped back into its old ways, as if the Yanks had never existed.

Since the departure of the Americans, Ubon has grown into the major economic center of the Issan. Recent developments include an international airport designed to serve the expanding economic markets of Indochina, industrial estates with fertilizer and processed-food factories, a new university, and major hotels earmarked for both business and leisure visitors. On the planning boards is the world's first truly international golf course, an 18-hole project which would overlap Thailand, Laos, and Cambodia.

National Museum

A good overview of the historical development of the lower Issan and a broad selection of Khmer and Thai artifacts are displayed in the 19th-century building once used as the office of the provincial governor. The museum also offers an ethnographic section with Thai and Laotian handicrafts, costumes, and farm implements.

The museum is on Sri Narong Rd. and open Wed.-Sat. 0830-1630.

Wat Supatnaram

Financed by King Rama IV as the first Issan temple dedicated to the Thammayut sect of Buddhism, Wat Supatnaram on the Moon (Mun) River reflects the complex interaction of religious traditions in Southeast Asia. The temple was constructed in 1853 by Vietnamese craftsmen in a fusion of Thai, Western, and Khmer styles to house the highly venerated image of Phra Sapphanya Chao.

The chief wonder is a small open-air museum which houses an outstanding collection of rare artifacts. Among the masterpieces are Chinese-style Buddhas, Dvaravati stone boundary markers, 7th-century Khmer lintels, priceless frescoes, carved pillars in Angkor style, and Hindu images of the deity Ganesha. The National Museum in Bangkok has requested the collection be moved to a safer location, either the national museum in Bangkok or in Ubon.

Wat Tung Sri Muang

Constructed during the reign of King Rama III (1824-1851), this *wat* is renowned for its Tripitaka library elevated in the middle of a small pond, ancient *mondop* housing a Buddha footprint, and erotic wall murals inside the principal *viharn*.

kinnari

UBON RATCHATHANI

AIRPORT

WAT BA NA MUANG

TO YASOTHON

WAT NONG BUA

Pathumrat Hotel

THAI AIRWAYS

HONG FAH RESTAURANT

BUS TERMINAL

RACHA HOTEL

GOLF COURSE

CHAIYANGKUN RD.

APARISAN RD.

SURIYAT HOTEL

PHADENG RD.

NAKHON BAI RD.

THEPYOT RD.

POLPAN RD.

BURAPANI RD.

SURIYAT RD.

POST OFFICE

WAT CHANG

POLICE

HOSPITAL

SAMPASIT RD.

WAT PA YAI

PICHITRUNGSAN RD.

TOKYO HOTEL

UPPARAT RD.

CHARANOK CHANGSANIT RD.

VEGGIE CAFE

BODIN HOTEL

WAT PA NOI

CINEMA

PALORUNGRIT RD.

WAT SUTHASANARAM

WAT TUNG SRI MUANG

KRUNG THONG HOTEL

PARK

PROVINCIAL HALL

SRI NARONG RD.

NATIONAL MUSEUM

TOURIST OFFICE

POST OFFICE

WAT LIAP

KUANG THANI RD.

UBON HOTEL

RATCHATHANI HOTEL

WAT SUPATNARAM

PROMARAT RD.

WAT KLANG

MARKET

WAT LUANG

NEW ISSAN HOTEL

FLOATING RESTAURANT

WAT TAI ISLAND

MOON RIVER

0   100m

TRAIN STATION

WARIN CHAMRUN

TO SI SAKET & WAT PA NANACHAT

TO EMERALD TRIANGLE

TO CHONG MEK & LAOS

© MOON PUBLICATIONS, INC.

The *wat* is in the center of town just west of Sri Luang Road.

Wat Ba Na Muang
Four km northeast of town on the road past the airport, the latest addition to the *wat* scene is this exotic creation covered with dark red glazed tiles and fronted by a eccentric royal barge filled with dozens of red-tiled boatsmen.

Wat Nong Bua
An impressive copy of the Mahabodhi *chedi* from Bodgaya, India, is located on the outskirts of town on the road to Nakhon Phanom. Nong Bua features a pair of four-sided towers covered with *Jataka* reliefs and recessed images of Dvaravati Buddhas.

Wat Nong Pa Pong
The region near Ubon offers several *wats* that welcome Western students of *vipassana* (insight) meditation.

Wat Nong Pa Pong is the principal residence of a meditation master named Achaan Cha, a disciple of the famous Achaan Man (1870-1949) who is credited as the inspiration for over 40 forest monasteries located throughout the Issan. Achaan Cha furthered the work of Achaan Man by establishing new branches of the strict order, including one in Sussex, England.

A book by Jack Kornfield titled *A Still Forest Pool* provides a useful introduction to the meditation theories of Achaan Cha. Kornfield once studied at Wat Nong Pa Pong under the direction of the master, but now lives in San Rafael, California, where he conducts retreats at Spirit Rock Meditation Center (tel. 415-488-0164).

Wat Nong Pa Pong is 15 km southwest of Ubon and can be reached by a Si Saket-bound *songtao* or bus from Ubon. However, Achaan Cha is now quite old and unable to accept new students. Westerners generally have better luck at Wat Pa Nanachat.

Wat Pa Nanachat
Westerners interested in Buddhism and *vipassana* meditation are advised to visit the forest monastery located across the road from Wat Nong Pa Pong. Wat Pa Nanachat ("Temple of the International Forest") is a Western-oriented temple with a Canadian abbot, Japanese vice-abbot, and several dozen European and Amer-

ican monks who speak English. Laypeople are welcome to stay as guests and conduct a brief study of Buddhism and insight meditation. Discipline is strict and all residents are expected to follow the schedule which involves early-morning meditation and work details in the grounds or kitchen. Visitors should arrive in the early morning to avoid interfering with afternoon silent meditations and are expected to make commitments after a stay of three days. A small store at the *wat* distributes free English-language booklets on the teachings of Achaan Cha.

Wat Pa Nanachat is 15 km southwest of Ubon on Highway 2193, the road that connects Ubon with Si Saket. From the Ubon bus station, take a bus going south toward Si Saket and watch for the English-language sign on the right side of the road. A *tuk tuk* from Ubon to the temple costs around 60 *baht*.

Accommodations
Ubon has over 20 hotels that charge 80-150B for fan-cooled rooms and 220-350B for a/c rooms with private baths. Many of the hotels are signposted only in Thai script, and serve the brothel business.

Tokyo Hotel: A clean and popular hotel in the center of town two blocks north of the park. 178 Upparat Rd., tel. (045) 241739, 90-140B fan, 220-250B a/c.

Racha Hotel: Somewhat north of city center is a low-priced hotel with both fan and a/c rooms. 149 Chaiyangkun Rd., tel. (045) 254155, 80-140B fan, 220-250B a/c.

Ratchathani Hotel: A very large hotel nicely situated in the center of town across from the tourist office and National Museum. Probably the best midpriced place in Ubon. 229 Kuan Thani Rd., tel. (045) 254599, 150-200B fan with private bath, 260-340B a/c.

Pathumrat Hotel: The top hotel in Ubon is the choice of Thai and Western tour groups. Facilities in the seven-story highrise include a swimming pool, coffee shop, and tourist information from the front desk. The Pathumrat can help with organized tours to sights near the Mekong River. 173 Chaiyangkun Rd., tel. (045) 241501, 450-800B.

Restaurants
Night Markets: Ubon has two night markets for inexpensive dishes such as *laab pet* (minced

duck salad), *yam makheua yao* (fried eggplant), and *gai yang* (fried chicken). The central market is on Chaiyangkun Rd. near the hotels and a smaller market is near the river.

Mae Moon Restaurant: A popular place for sunset dinners is located on a floating pavilion in the Moon River. Moderate.

Hong Fah Restaurant: Opposite the Pathumrat Hotel is a Chinese restaurant that also operates a river cruise on its private boat. 200 Chaiyangkun Road. Moderate.

Practicalities

The TAT office (tel. 045-243770) at 264 Kuan Thani Rd. has maps and sponsors weekend tours to the sights near the Mekong River. Tourist information is also available from the Pathumrat Hotel.

Transportation

Ubon is 629 km northeast of Bangkok and 370 km east of Korat.

Air: Thai Airways flies once daily from Bangkok to Ubon. Thai Airways (tel. 045-254431) is at 364 Chaiyhangkun Road. The new international airport is located on the northern perimeter of town.

Train: Ubon is connected by rail with Bangkok via Korat, Buriram, and Surin. Seven trains leave Bangkok daily. An express train with sleepers departs at 2100 and arrives in Ubon the next morning at 0705. Rapid trains without sleepers leave at 0650, 1845, and 2245. Rapid trains leave Korat at 1136 and 2356.

An express train from Ubon departs at 1700 and takes 10 hours to Bangkok. Rapid trains leave Ubon at 0640, 1650, and 1745.

The train station is five km southwest of town in the suburb of Warin Chamrun. Take a taxi, *tuk tuk*, or bus.

Bus: Buses leave every 15 minutes from the Northern Bus Terminal in Bangkok and take 12 hours to reach Ubon. Air-conditioned buses leave Bangkok from 1900 to 2130. Buses leave seven times daily from Korat and take five hours to Ubon.

The Ubon Bus Terminal is on Chaiyangkun Rd. about four km north of city center. Take public bus 2 or a *songtao* for 20 *baht*. An a/c bus terminal is located on Palo Rungrit Rd., two blocks north of the TAT office.

THE MEKONG RIVER AND LAOTIAN BORDER

Pha Taem Cliff Paintings

Well-preserved cliff paintings, dating back 2,000-4,000 years, cover a 300-meter section of sandstone cliffs overlooking the Mekong River basin. Figures possibly related to the Neolithic inhabitants of Ban Chiang include human images, galloping buffalo, gigantic catfish *(pla muk)*, and abstract designs that eerily resemble patterns of the American Indians.

Pha Taem is 95 km east of Ubon and 15 km north of the confluence of the Mekong and Moon rivers. The cliffs are almost impossible to reach by public transportation. Tours arranged by the TAT office in Ubon leave on weekend mornings at 0800. The tour costs 60B and includes stops at other natural attractions such as Saphue Rapids, the waterfalls and cliffs at Kaeng Tana National Park, and the two-colored river confluence of the Mekong and Moon rivers. En route to the cliffs are some curious rock formations called Sao Chaliang.

Boat tours to Pha Taem and Kaeng Tana are also arranged at the Khong Chiam Hotel in Khong Chiam.

Khong Chiam

Khong Chiam, one of the most isolated yet scenic spots in northeast Thailand, is now attracting a few hardy travelers who discover one of the last untouched regions in Thailand. The town offers great views across the river into Laos and is well sited near the cliff paintings of Pha Taem, Kaeng Tana National Park, Tad Ton Falls, and the Laotian border crossing at Chong Mek. A ferry traverses the Moon River for quick access to the southern waterfalls and parks.

Khong Chiam has several small cafes including the Araya Restaurant, a lively market, and an emerging cluster of guesthouses that cater to backpackers. Mut Mee Guesthouse has decent rooms for 60-100B. Information on Mekong River boat tours can be picked up at the Khong Chiam Hotel (tel. 045-351074), where Mungkorn Ruamprom and his wife Boonkwang charge 100B for clean rooms. Khong Chiam Hotel also distributes a rough but useful map of the region.

Khong Chiam is 85 km east of Ubon at the confluence of the Moon and Mekong rivers. Direct buses leave from the terminal in Ubon. Attractions en route include modern Wat Phokhaokaew, Saphue Rapids just beyond Phiboon, and Tad Ton Falls near Kaeng Tana National Park.

Chong Mek

Only two official land crossings exist between Thailand and Laos. The Nong Khai crossing provides direct access to the capital of Vientiane and the cultural center of Luang Prabang. The crossing here at Chong Mek heads east to the large town of Pakse, an emerging tourist destination with several important temples and a hill resort up at Muang Pakxong.

Travelers who have obtained a Laotian visa in advance from the embassy in Bangkok can continue by mini-truck from Chong Mek to Pakse. Lao Air flies three times weekly from Pakse to Vientiane and Luang Prabang.

SI SAKET

Si Saket, 63 km west of Ubon Ratchathani, is a convenient starting point for visits to several excellent Khmer temples. The town is also known for its tasty kai yang and waterfalls at Huai Chan.

Accommodations

The Si Saket Hotel (tel. 045-611846) on Si Saket Rd. has 68 fan-cooled rooms priced from 80 to 140B. The only hotel with a/c rooms is the Phromphiman Hotel (tel. 045-611141) at 849 Lak Muang Rd., where fan rooms go from 100B and a/c rooms cost 250-350B.

Prasat Kamphaeng Noi

Eight km west of town on the road to Surin are the ruins of a Khmer sanctuary, constructed in the 13th century by King Jayavarman VII. The unrestored prang and crumbling laterite foundations are noted for fine carvings, especially the depiction of Hindu mythology on the decorative lintels.

The monument is now under the supervision of the Fine Arts Department, and open daily from 0830 to 1630 with an admission charge of 25 baht.

Prasat Wat Kamphaeng Yai

The largest Khmer sanctuary near Si Saket has been targeted for restoration by the Fine Arts Department, with an expected completion date of 1995. Kamphaeng Yai was constructed in the mid-11th century and dedicated to the Hindu deity Shiva, but, like many Hindu-Khmer temples in the Issan, it was converted into a Mahayana Buddhist complex by the Thais after the 13th century. Hindu-Khmer influences are still apparent on the northern lintel of Vishnu in slumber, and the southern lintel engraved with Shiva riding Nandi his bull.

The sanctuary is located on Route 2080, about 10 km west of Prasat Kamphaeng Noi.

Prasat Pra Viharn

One of the most spectacular but inaccessible jewels of Khmer architecture appears ready to welcome visitors after a span of over three decades.

Prasat Pra Viharn crowns a spur of the Dongrak Mountains which mark the frontier between Cambodia and Thailand. The main entrance is on Thai soil in Kantaralak District, Si Saket Province, but the main sanctuary is located several hundred meters south in Cambodian territory. The exact location was disputed by the Thai and Cambodian governments in the late 1950s. The territorial claims were submitted to the World Court, which ruled in 1962 that the prasat is in Cambodia but the entrance is in Thailand. Neglected and overgrown with weeds, the site was occupied by a handful of young Cambodian soldiers until 1991 when the Cambodian Peace Accord was signed in Paris and the temple finally cleared of landmines and wire fences.

Prasat Pra Viharn was constructed from the 11th to 13th centuries in a series of courts and gopuras connected on different levels by paved stone avenues and imposing stairways. Similar to Prasat Phanom Rung, the complex grows successively larger and more complex with each ascending level. Hindu myths are depicted in the rich craftsmanship on the stairways, lintels, and pediments sited on the three levels. Further information is noted in the Siam Society publication, The Lofty Sanctuary of Khao Phra Viharn.

Prasat Pra Viharn is 115 km south of Si Saket and very difficult to reach without private transportation. From Si Saket, buses and *songtaos* head south to Kantharalak and Phumsaron, 10 km north of the Cambodian border, from where *tuk tuks* can be hired to the ruins.

Permission to visit Prasat Pra Viharn must be obtained in advance from the Tourism Authority of Thailand in Bangkok, who will contact the military offices in Surin who control the entrance to the temple.

SURIN

Most visitors associate Surin with its famed Elephant Fair, held on the third weekend in November. Though the elephant festival is certainly the highlight, Surin is well located near several Khmer temples and serves as a base for visits to an elephant camp, basketry and silk-weaving villages, and with special permission, a Cambodian refugee camp.

Surin is probably the single best northeastern base from which to explore the Khmer monuments scattered along the Cambodian border.

Elephant Festival

Perhaps the most internationally famous festival in Thailand, Surin's annual week-long Elephant Fair is something like the Super Bowl but without the bowl, beer, or football. The madness starts with an elephant roundup and mass procession of over 200 elephants into the Surin Sports Park. Next is a Rocket Festival, followed by a two-hour spectacle of elephants at work, elephants dancing, elephants racing, elephant soccer, elephant war parade, and an elephant tug-of-war with 70 men. The elephant always wins. Afterward, the elephants wander around town and give rides to tourists.

Hotel reservations should be made months in advance. Tours with transportation and accommodations can be booked through the TAT and several tour operators in Bangkok.

Tha Klang Elephant Village

City ordinances prohibit Surin citizens from keeping elephants as house pets, so most elephants live outside town where they are trained for exciting careers in log rolling and entertaining wealthy tourists. Several dozen elephants reside in the town of Tha Klang, 58 km north of Surin, where they are trained by descendants of the Suay peoples, Cambodians who have traditionally been elephant hunters since the Ayuthaya empire.

Avoid visiting Tha Klang during the day, when most of the elephants are out working in the nearby fields and rivers. The only way to learn about the dying art of Thai elephant management is with an overnight homestay arranged by Mr. Pirom at Pirom Guesthouse in Surin.

Silk-weaving Villages

Two villages which specialize in traditional silk production and weaving are located within 20 km of Surin. Khawao Sinarin, north of Surin on Highway 214, and Ban Chanron, east of town on Highway 2077, both produce and sell handwoven silks.

Public transportation is available, or hire a car from Gopchai Rentals (tel. 045-511775) on Tesaban I Road. Rental cars without gas cost about 1000B daily.

Butom Basket Village

Located 12 km east of Surin, and slightly off Highway 226, Ban Butom is a small village where many of the residents weave tightly woven baskets adorned with intricate designs. People from Bangkok come to Butom for their baskets, which cost under 100B for even the most extravagant pieces.

Cambodian Refugee Camp

After two decades of struggle and warfare, Thailand's 350,000 Cambodian refugees were finally scheduled for repatriation in November 1991 after an agreement was reached between Thailand's foreign minister and the Cambodian Supreme National Coalition. Refugees are being repatriated at the rate of about 6,000 per month and the process will be completed around 1996.

Sites along the border are operated by a wide variety of organizations from the United Nations to political entities such as the Khmer Rouge and Khmer Peoples Liberation Party. Some camps, such as Khao I Dang, hold officially recognized refugees who may eventually return home or emigrate to a Western nation. Other camps, such as Site 2 near Surin, hold displaced Cambodians who are now being repatriated.

SURIN

TO BURIRAM, KORAT, & BANGKOK

TO ROI ET & THA KLANG

TRAIN STATION

TO UBON

★WAT

NEW HOTEL

A/C BUSES

PHETCHKASEM HOTEL

THETSABAN 1 RD.

BANK

BUS TERMINAL

UBOL HOTEL

BANK

SCHOOL

POST OFFICE

AMARIN HOTEL

PIROM GH

THANACHAI HOTEL

WAT ★

MARKET

SANG THONG HOTEL

KRUNG SRI HOTEL

BANK

HOSPITAL

KRUNG SRI RD.

MEMORIAL HOTEL

WAT ★

WAT BURAPARAM

WAT LAK MUANG ★

LAK MUANG RD.

POLICE

TARIN HOTEL

WAT ★

WAT ★

TO UBON & PRASAT SIKHORAPHUM

NATIONAL MUSEUM

WAT ★

0   100m

MARKET ★

TO KORAT & BANGKOK

STADIUM

TO AIRPORT

WAT ★

© MOON PUBLICATIONS, INC.

Site 2 is officially closed to Western visitors, though permission is occasionally granted on weekend market days. Mr. Pirom at his guesthouse in Surin can help with current details.

Prasat Sikhoraphum

Thirty km east of Surin near the town of Sikhoraphum is an 11th-century Khmer *prasat* recently restored by the Fine Arts Department. The sanctuary consists of five brick *prangs* surrounded by moats and studded with lintels carved with scenes from Hindu mythology. Of particular note is the Shiva lintel over the central *prang*.

Prasat Pluang

Twenty km south of Surin near the silk-weaving town of Ban Pluang is another restored *prasat*, constructed in the late 11th century during the reign of King Suriyavoraman I. Pond and rem-

nants of an old moat surround the sandstone-and-laterite Khmer *prang*, which features an east-facing lintel elegantly carved with Indra on his elephant Ganesh. As with other major Khmer monuments in the Issan, Prasat Pluang stands on the royal road which once connected Angkor with Phimai.

Prasat Ta Muen And Muen Tom

Two clusters of recently opened Khmer ruins are located exactly on the Thai-Cambodian border, some 55 km due south of Surin and quite close to the ruins at Muang Tam and Phanom Rung. The border region is still monitored by the Thai military, which operates several checkpoints near the towns of Ban Ta Miang and Ban Ampin. Both ruins are inaccessible by public transportation but can be reached with a private car hired in Surin or Buriram.

Prasat Phanom Rung And Muang Tam

Prasat Phanom Rung is widely considered the most impressive Khmer monument in Thailand. Muang Tam is about nine km southeast of Phanom Rung. Both monuments can be visited on day excursions from Surin or Buriram, and are described under "Korat."

Accommodations

Hotels in Surin are fully booked and charge a 50% premium during the Elephant Roundup in late November.

Pirom Guesthouse: The backpackers' hotel scene in Surin improved dramatically several years ago with the opening of this guesthouse, two blocks west of the market and 500 meters from the bus terminal and train station. Mr. Pirom has converted his six-room teakwood house into a very cozy place with the best travel information in the province. Pirom speaks excellent English and conducts daily excursions to the elephant village and Khmer ruins near the Cambodian border. 272 Krung Sri Rd., no phone, 60-100B.

Memorial Hotel: A clean and inexpensive hotel well located in the center of town near the temples and restaurants. 186 Lak Muang Rd., tel. (045) 511288, 160-240B fan, 260-340B a/c.

Tarin Hotel: Top hotel in town is the Tarin, a few blocks south of city center. Facilities include a swimming pool, 24-hour coffee shop and nightclub, snooker hall, and "cosmic atmosphere at Hi-Tech Discotheque, Surin's favorite disco for swingers." 60 Sirirat Rd., tel. (045) 514281, fax (045) 511580, 800-1200B.

Transportation

Surin is 457 km northeast of Bangkok and 198 km east of Korat.

Air: Bangkok Airways flies once daily from Bangkok. Their office (tel. 045-511274) is in the Phetchkasem Hotel at 104 Chao Bamrung Road.

Train: Surin is connected by rail with Bangkok via Korat and Buriram. Seven trains leave Bangkok daily. An express train with sleepers departs at 2100 and arrives eight hours later in Surin. Rapid trains without sleepers leave at 0650, 1845, and 2245 and take nine hours. Rapid trains leave Korat at 1136 and 2356.

Bus: Buses leave every 15 minutes from the Northern Bus Terminal in Bangkok and take 10 hours to reach Surin. Air-conditioned buses leave Bangkok from 1900 to 2130. Buses leave seven times daily from Korat and take three hours to Surin.

BURIRAM

Although Buriram lacks any great attractions within the city boundaries, the town can serve as a base for exploring the numerous Khmer monuments located south along the Cambodian border.

Attractions

Archaeologists have identified over 50 *prasats* in Buriram Province, of which almost a dozen have been restored by the Fine Arts Department. The Khmer sanctuaries are described above under "Surin" and "Korat."

The only problem with touring Khmer architecture in the northeast is transportation. The TAT has attempted for over a decade to encourage tourism in the Issan, but few Westerners are prepared to deal with the challenges of public transportation.

As elsewhere in the world, tourism begins when budget travelers arrive and lay the foundation for group tourism. Budget guesthouses in this section of the northeast are still in their infancy, but it's encouraging to find new guesthouses in a few spots such as the Pirom Guesthouse in Surin.

Unfortunately, the only options for visiting the widely scattered monuments in the lower Issan are with public transportation or with the odd tour company which pops up with grandiose plans and then typically disappears after a few short years.

With those cautions in mind, you might check with the Buriram Teachers College, which has established a tour organization called Phanom Rung Tours (tel. 044-612046, fax 044-612691) at 131 Buriram-Prakonchai Road. If this group survives, both one- and two-day tours to nearby monuments will be offered on a demand basis. Other contacts include the provincial tourist information office (tel. 044-611449) and Miss Vondi at the Buriram Tour Guides (tel. 044-611170).

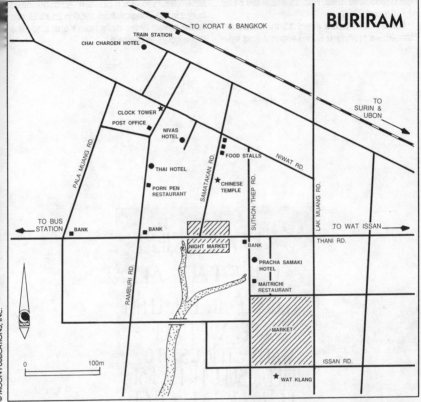

BURIRAM

TO KORAT & BANGKOK

TRAIN STATION

CHAI CHAROEN HOTEL

TO SURIN & UBON

CLOCK TOWER

POST OFFICE

NIVAS HOTEL

PALA MUANG RD.

SAMATAKAN RD.

FOOD STALLS

NIWAT RD.

THAI HOTEL

PORN PEN RESTAURANT

CHINESE TEMPLE

SUTHON THEP RD.

LAK MUANG RD.

TO BUS STATION

BANK

BANK

TO WAT ISSAN

THANI RD.

RAMBURI RD.

NIGHT MARKET

BANK

PRACHA SAMAKI HOTEL

MAITRICHI RESTAURANT

MARKET

ISSAN RD.

WAT KLANG

0   100m

© MOON PUBLICATIONS, INC.

A new cultural center and Issan Museum have recently been established at the Teachers College.

Accommodations

Several inexpensive hotels are located near the train station. Most of the hotels in Buriram are labeled in Thai script only.

Chai Charoen Hotel: Just opposite the train station is an acceptable spot for an overnight crash. 114 Niwat Rd., tel. (044) 611640, 80-150B.

Thai Hotel: Somewhat better rooms about three blocks from the train station. Facilities include a coffee shop just off the parking lot and both fan and a/c rooms. 38 Romburi Rd., tel. (044) 611112, 120-180B fan, 280-380B a/c.

Buriram Plaza Hotel: The latest and greatest hotel is located in the center of town on the highway connecting Buriram with Surin. Facilities include two restaurants, pool, and nightclub. Buriram-Surin Rd., tel. (044) 411123, 650-900B.

Transportation

Buriram is 410 km northeast of Bangkok and 151 km east of Korat.

Air: A new airport opened north of Buriram in 1992. Daily service from Bangkok is provided by Bangkok Airways.

Train: Buriram is connected by rail with Bangkok via Korat. Seven trains leave Bangkok daily. An express train with sleepers departs at 2100 and arrives in Buriram the next morning at 0335. Rapid trains without sleepers leave at

0650, 1845, and 2245. Rapid trains leave Korat at 1136 and 2356.

Bus: Buses leave every 15 minutes from Bangkok's Northern Bus Terminal and take seven hours to reach Buriram. Air-conditioned buses leave Bangkok from 1900 to 2130. Buses leave seven times daily from Korat and take three hours to Buriram.

SOUTHERN THAILAND
INTRODUCTION

Stretching 1,250 km from Bangkok to the border of Malaysia, the long and narrow peninsula of southern Thailand encompasses a world of thick jungles, rugged mountains, limestone pinnacles, emerald-blue bays, fishermen and sea gypsies, graceful temples and bulbous mosques, coral reefs, colorful marinelife, and some of the most spectacular beaches in Southeast Asia. The south is a fascinating region, not only for its famous beaches and island resorts, but for its ethnic diversity, geography, and long history. Landscapes, religions, languages, and even the people change as you travel deeper into the south: rice paddies give way to rubber plantations, Muslim mosques outnumber Buddhist temples, even the beaches seem to change . . . they get better!

Climate
The climate varies from the remainder of Thailand due to the effects of seasonal monsoons, which sweep across the west coast on the Andaman Sea from May to September and bring heavy rains to the east coast on the Gulf of Thailand from November to late February. Travelers deluged by heavy rains can usually improve their situation by simply moving across the peninsula.

History
The 14 provinces of southern Thailand once comprised the fabled lands of the Golden Chersonese, an ancient region that prior to the 9th century centered on independent city-states at Pahang, Trang, Nakhon Si Thammarat, Takua Pa, and Chaiya. The region was later consolidated into and influenced by the Indonesian culture, in particular the Buddhist Indo-Srivijayan civilization of the 8th-13th centuries.

Following the disintegration of the Srivijayan empire, Nakhon Si Thammarat became the center of an independent kingdom closely aligned

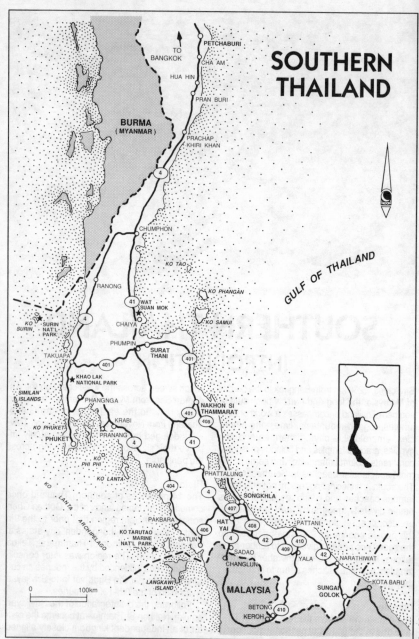

SOUTHERN THAILAND

© MOON PUBLICATIONS, INC.

(top) umbrella village;
(bottom) woodcarving, Chiang Mai (photos by Carl Parkes)

(top) floating market coconut vendor, Damnern Saduak;
(bottom) soccer players, Kamphaeng Phet (photos by Carl Parkes)

with the original Thai kingdom at Sukothai. The southern provinces were brought under the dominion of Ayuthaya in the mid-14th century, though Nakhon Si Thammarat remained the center of authority for the entire peninsula. With the fall of Ayuthaya in 1767, the southern provinces came under the control of the Bangkok administration, yet were left semi-independent under the rule of regional governors. Administrative reforms during the rule of King Chulalongkorn included consolidation of the provinces into several regions under the direct control of Bangkok, chiefly to counteract the dangers of Western colonial expansion in Southeast Asia. Nakhon Si Thammarat and Pattani joined the Thai nation in 1906.

Chinese and Muslim influence has long been strong, resulting in a vivacious, polyglot society with intermingled religious and ethnic traditions. Regional differences distinct from Central Thailand are still evident in the customs, dialects, cultural expressions, cuisine, entertainments, and sports of the *Thai pak tai,* the southern Thais.

Sightseeing Highlights

Petchburi: Southern Thailand is chiefly famous for its beaches, but culturally minded travelers may want to briefly tour Petchburi, a historic town with the best temples south of Bangkok.

Prachuap Khiri Khan: Although there is little of great interest in this small fishing village, the complete lack of tourists, friendly population, and stunning topography make this beach town an enjoyable destination.

Ko Samui: Ko Samui is a relatively simple and absolutely beautiful island on the east side of the peninsula. Though rapidly approaching saturation, the atmosphere remains much less frantic than on Phuket. Budget travelers, however, have largely abandoned Ko Samui for the less developed islands of Ko Phangan and Ko Tao.

Deserted beaches in Southern Thailand are now rather rare, but with nearly 2,000 km of coastline and hundreds of untouched islands, a few gems still await discovery.

Phuket: Southern Thailand's two most popular destinations are the tropical islands of Phuket and Ko Samui. Both have distinct personalities which appeal to different types of travelers. Phuket, the more developed of the two, offers a stunning combination of superb beaches, upscale hotels, outstanding seafood restaurants, sports activities from parasailing to scuba diving, and heady nightlife rivaled only by Bangkok and Pattaya. Most of the island is very expensive and highly commercialized, but a few beaches are still pristine . . . at least for the moment.

Krabi: This bustling fishing town serves as the gateway to several beach destinations such as Ko Phi Phi, Pranang, and Ko Lanta.

Hat Yai: The largest commercial and transportation center in the south provides excellent shopping, restaurants, and nightlife, though few travelers are impressed with the concrete drabness of the city center.

Songkhla: This pleasant and very mellow beach town, one hour outside Hat Yai, is a popular place to soak up local atmosphere without hordes of tourists.

Narathiwat: Visitors who want to experience the traditional side of the Muslim south will enjoy this lovely town almost completely off the standard tourist trail.

Routes

Most visitors head directly to Phuket or Samui from Bangkok, but travelers intrigued with Thai architecture and painting should visit Petchburi for a recommended four-hour walking tour described below. Those who prefer a more leisurely approach can also try the family-oriented beach resorts of Hua Hin or Cha Am. One possible route is an early-morning bus to Petchburi for the walking tour, then afternoon bus to Hua Hin. Prachuap Khiri Khan is a recommended stop prior to Ko Samui.

Ko Samui can be reached by train, bus, or air from Bangkok. Routes from Samui often proceed west over to Phuket or southwest down to Krabi, the access town for Pranang Beach and the islands of Ko Phi Phi and Ko Lanta. South of Krabi are Trang and Satun, near the remote and rarely visited islands near the Malaysian border.

From Hat Yai, the commercial center of the deep south, you can continue southwest to Penang or southeast through the Muslim fishing towns of Pattani and Narathiwat to Sungai Golok, the last stop before crossing to Kota Baru on the east coast of peninsular Malaysia.

Air

Visitors with limited time can reach Phuket and Ko Samui directly by air from Bangkok. Thai International connects Phuket and Hat Yai with Bangkok, Penang, and other international gateways. Bangkok Airways flies daily to Ko Samui and between Samui and Phuket.

Bus

Regular and a/c buses leave frequently from Bangkok's Southern Bus Terminal in Thonburi. Private a/c buses to major destinations such as Ko Samui and Phuket can be booked through most travel agents.

Buses are fast and departures are frequent, though you'll arrive in better condition on a train.

Train

Train travel is an excellent way to tour the south and see the countryside rather than just the concrete expressways used by bus services. Trains depart nine times daily 0900-2155 from Hualampong Station in Bangkok. Services include departures at 0900 (diesel), 1235 (rapid), 1400 (special express), 1515 (special express), 1600 (rapid), 1730 (rapid), 1830 (rapid), 1920

(express), and 2155 (diesel express). Sleepers are available on all trains except the 0900 (diesel) and 2155 (diesel express).

Advance reservations from Bangkok's Hualampong Station or a travel agent are *strongly* recommended on all trains going south, especially on weekends and holidays.

Second- and first-class fares from Bangkok are:

Petchburi	71/138B
Hua Hin	92/182B
Prachuap Khiri Khan	122/245B
Chumphon	172/356B
Surat Thani (Ko Samui). . .	224/470B
Trang	282/597B
Nakhon Si Thammarat . . .	279/590B
Phattalung.	288/611B
Hat Yai.	313/664B
Yala	346/748B
Sungai Golok	378/808B
Padang Besar.	326/694B
Butterworth (Malaysia) . . .	431/927B

To Malaysia

See "Departures for Malaysia" in "The Deep South" for details.

> *Travel can hardly ever fail to wreak a transformation of some sort, great or small, and for better or for worse, in the situation of the traveller.*
>
> —Claude Lévi-Strauss,
> *Tristes Tropiques*

BANGKOK TO SURAT THANI

PETCHBURI

Petchburi (also spelled Phetchburi, Petchaburi, Phetburi, and Petburi!), 126 km south of Bangkok, is a charming town with a long history and a half-dozen outstanding temples. All can be easily visited on the four-hour walking tour described below.

History

Much of the city's superb art and architecture reflects its long and rich history. Founded as a Mon city which traded with Europe during the Middle Ages, Petchburi remained in the orbit of the Dvaravati kingdom until the 12th century when it fell to the Khmers. At the end of the 13th century it was absorbed into the emerging Thai nation at Sukothai, and it formed part of the Ayuthaya empire from 1350.

The present township is a treasure house of historical artifacts from nearly all possible eras: Mon sculpture unearthed within the ancient city walls; a small but intriguing Khmer temple in a quiet neighborhood; monastery walls gilded with Thailand's finest Ayuthaya Period murals; Wat Mahathat's 19th-century *prang;* and a hilltop palace of neoclassical inspiration. It's difficult to understand why Petchburi isn't mentioned in most guides to Thailand and Southeast Asia.

Wat Yai Suwannaram

Petchburi's artistic fame is chiefly due to the murals in Wat Yai Suwannaram and Wat Ko

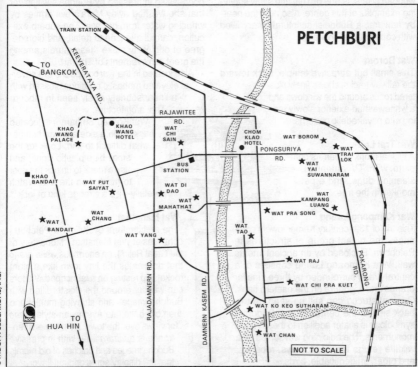

PETCHBURI

TRAIN STATION

TO BANGKOK

KEEVERATAYA RD.

RAJAWITEE RD.

KHAO WANG PALACE

KHAO WANG HOTEL

WAT CHI SAIN

CHOM KLAO HOTEL

WAT BOROM

PONGSURIYA RD.

WAT TRAI LOK

KHAO BANDAIT

BUS STATION

WAT YAI SUWANNARAM

WAT PUT SAIYAT

WAT DI DAO

WAT MAHATHAT

WAT KAMPANG LUANG

WAT BANDAIT

WAT CHANG

WAT PRA SONG

WAT YANG

WAT TAO

WAT RAJ

TO HUA HIN

RAJADAMNERN RD.

DAMNERN KASEM RD.

WAT CHI PRA KUET

POKARONG RD.

WAT KO KEO SUTHARAM

WAT CHAN

NOT TO SCALE

© MOON PUBLICATIONS, INC.

Keo Sutharam. Thai murals typically date from the fall of Ayuthaya in 1767 until royal patronage ended about 1910. Ayuthaya Period murals were almost completely destroyed by the Burmese after the destruction of the capital; only Petchburi murals survive to illustrate early Thai painting.

Among the best are in the small *bot* of Wat Yai Suwannaram. Gracing the interior of the lateral walls and separated by distinct red triangles are rows of 17th-century worshipping divinities that represent Indra, Brahma, and lesser divinities such as *devas* and *yaksas*. Those on the lower registers are chipping and desperately need attention, although the interior door murals are still in good condition. Despite the deterioration, these murals provide fascinating illustrations of naturalistic decorative art and insight into the flora and fauna of 17th-century Thailand.

The adjacent wooden *sala,* supported by wooden pillars, is one of Thailand's few surviving examples of this genre. Also note the nearby *haw trai,* a Buddhist scriptural library filled with copies of the Tripitaka.

Wat Borom

This small but attractive temple, back toward the railway tracks, shows finely plastered roses around the windows and a whitewashed exterior slowly fading into psychedelic patterns.

Wat Trai Lok

A typical monk's quarters complete with TV antennas, sleeping dogs, and a pet monkey in the tree.

spirit house

Wat Kampang Luang

This trio of 13th-century Khmer towers comprises the oldest group of structures in Petchburi. Enclosed by an ancient laterite wall, Wat Kampang Luang consists of a central *prang* surrounded by three smaller *prangs* and a *gopura* on the eastern flank. Original stucco can still be seen on the back side of the central *prang*. Buddhist symbology is a later addition to these Hindu monuments. The adjoining *wat* serves as a wildlife refuge for wild turkeys, roosters, and other, unidentifiable, birds.

Wat Pra Song

Two uniquely circular and rather strange bell-towers face the primary *bot*. Although in danger of falling down, the wonderful old monks' quarters to the right remain more appealing than the modern replacements to the rear of the courtyard.

Wat Ko Keo Sutharam

Petchburi's most famous temple is a must-see for all visitors. Inside the small *bot* are some of Thailand's finest, best-preserved, and oldest murals, dated by inscription to 1734. Side walls of dramatic triangles show scenes from the life of the Buddha and comical figures of Arab merchants, a Jesuit wearing the robes of a Buddhist monk, and other big-nosed *farangs*. Facing the Buddha is a wall of Buddhist cosmology—usually placed *behind* the Buddha image—while the posterior wall shows Buddha's victory over the temptations of Mara. Just below the central Buddha image is long-haired Torani, the earth goddess so impressed by Buddha's willpower that she washed away Mara's evil armies by wringing water from her hair. The superb execution, careful attention to detail, and high degree of originality make these murals among the great achievements of Thai art.

Also located in the *wat* compound are several elevated monastic buildings blessed with a linear sobriety rarely seen in modern Thai architecture.

Wat Ko Keo Sutharam is located back down a side alley and somewhat difficult to find. Look for the small blue plastic signs, and ask a monk to unlock the door to the *bot* on the left. Watch carefully—it's a strange kind of lock.

Wat Mahathat

The architectural evolution at Petchburi continues at Wat Mahathat ("Monastery of the Great Relic"), an enormous white *prang* that dominates the tiny town like a giant rocketship resting on a launchpad. Visitors can wander around the cloister filled with Buddha images and studying monks and then climb the late Ayuthayan-style *prang* for views over the town. Near the east entrance is a *viharn* filled with impressive Buddha images and patches of old murals that still display some original flavor.

KAREN WHITE

Khao Wang Palace

Towering over Petchburi and reached by cable car or tough hike up a steep path is Pra Nakhon Khiri ("Holy City Mountain"), a 19th-century neoclassical palace constructed in a delightful mixture of Siamese style and chinoiserie by King Mongkut. The palace comprises a group of *pra thi nang* (throne halls) constructed in different styles. Views are outstanding from several of the buildings, including the astronomical observation tower constructed in 1862 by King Rama IV.

The TAT and local authorities sponsor an annual sound-and-light show on the hill every year in early February. Pra Nakhon Khiri has been declared a national historic park; admission is 20 *baht*.

Wat Kao Bandait, another beautiful temple with historical significance, is three km west of town at Bandait hill.

Khao Luang Caves

The cave sanctuary of Khao Luang, five km north of town on Highway 3173, is the most famous of Petchburi's dozen caves. Inside the central chamber are dozens of Buddhas donated by pilgrims and King Mongkut, a magnificent array of stalactites, and miniature *chedis* illuminated by sunlight streaming through the roof. The Wagnerian effect is a favorite subject for photographers.

Kaeng Krachan National Park

Thailand's largest national park sits on the rugged Tanaosri mountain range, which separates Thailand from Burma, 115 km south of Bangkok and some 60 km from Petchburi off Hwy. 3175.

The immense 2,915-square-km park is known for its "Swiss Lake," wildlife, thick rainforest, savannah grasslands, impressive waterfalls, and treks starting from park headquarters at Kaeng Krachan Lake. One of the better hikes begins at Kilometer 30 and proceeds uphill to the summit of Mount Panernthung, some 1,207 meters above sea level. Guides can be hired at park headquarters, located three km beyond the dam at the end of the road. Rafting tours on the Petchburi River are also organized by park authorities.

Another highlight is the falls, best experienced during or shortly after the rainy season from July to November. Pala-U is an 11-tiered falls noted for the distinctive butterflies which claim different levels: blue-green butterflies on the first level, brown ones on the second, golden butterflies near the top falls. The 18-level Ha Thip Falls is five km from Panernthung Peak, while Nam Yod Clif is on the banks of the Petchburi River.

A Karen village is located 13 km from park headquarters.

Accommodations: Accommodations include campsites for 25-50B per night, large bungalows operated by the park service for 300-600B, and upscale floating bungalows called Kaeng Krachan Resorts (Bangkok reservation, tel. 02-513-3238).

Transportation: Kaeng Krachan National Park can be visited from either Petchburi or Hua Hin. The park is served by public mini-truck from Tha Yang, about 20 km south of Petchburi. Alternatively, take a minibus from Hua Hin to Ban Kang Krajaren from where motorcycle taxis continue another four km to park headquarters. Tours can also be arranged in Hua Hin and Cha Am.

Accommodations

Day-trippers can store their bags at the train station or in the small office at the bus station. Petchburi, however, is a pleasant place to learn something about local history, art, and contemporary Thai life.

Chom Klao Hotel: Situated on the east bank of the Petchburi River is a small Chinese hotel with adequate rooms. 1 Pongsuriya Rd., tel. (032) 425398, 80-150B.

Khao Wang Hotel: The best hotel in town has both fan and a/c rooms at the bottom of Khao Wang. 174 Rajawitee Rd., tel. (032) 425167, 100-150B fan, 180-220B a/c.

Restaurants

The cafe in the Khao Wang Hotel is probably the best spot in town for local seafood. Streetstalls are located along the main street near Wat Mahathat and opposite the clock tower.

Petchburi is known throughout Thailand for its excellent sweets made from local sugars. The primary showcase for specialties such as *khanom mor kang* (baked coconut custard) is a restaurant called Ban Khanom Thai ("House of Thai Sweets"), on Petchkasem Highway just outside the city limits. This collection of 13 Thai houses includes displays of sweets, a folkcraft museum, and a Thai restaurant with classical entertainment in the evenings.

Transportation

Petchburi is 126 km south of Bangkok.

Bus: Buses leave every 10 minutes from the Southern Bus Terminal in Thonburi, and terminate three hours later in central Petchburi.

Train: Trains from Hualampong Station in Bangkok leave nine times daily from 0900 to 2155. Departures and fares are listed above in the "Southern Thailand" Introduction.

Samlor drivers charge about 10B to city center.

CHA AM

A typical Thai beach resort 212 km south of Bangkok and 26 km north of Hua Hin, Cha Am features a narrow beach almost deserted during the week and a long strip of undistinguished bungalows popular on weekends with Thai families and teenagers on holiday. Although Cha Am lacks character, it's an easy escape from Bangkok, and the addition of deluxe hotels between Cha Am and Hua Hin has put the region firmly on the tourist map.

The TAT has recently opened a tourist office on the main highway about one km south of the intersection, an illogical location that makes it convenient only to visitors with private transportation.

Attractions

The main road skirts the beach and heads north five km to a small fishing village and Wat Neranchara Rama, one km past the bridge and narrow lagoon. The large Cambodian-style stone temple features a six-armed alabaster Buddha which local monks claim is the largest prototype in the world. Otherwise, relaxing on the sand and trying the local seafood are the main activities.

Accommodations

Most of the midpriced hotels in the 250-500B range are located on the beach road some two km east of the bus stop and highway intersection. Inexpensive bungalows under 200B are in short supply, though bargains are available midweek when Cha Am is almost completely deserted. A string of expensive hotels has recent-

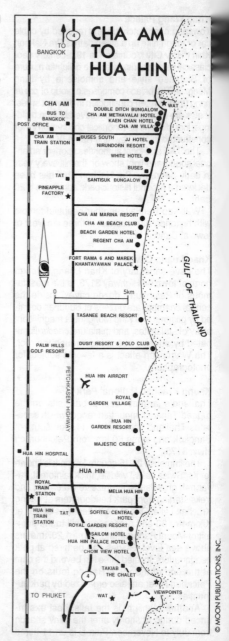

CHA AM TO HUA HIN

TO BANGKOK

CHA AM
BUS TO BANGKOK
POST OFFICE
CHA AM TRAIN STATION
TAT
PINEAPPLE FACTORY

DOUBLE DITCH BUNGALOW
CHA AM METHAVALAI HOTEL
KAEN CHAN HOTEL
CHA AM VILLA
WAT

BUSES SOUTH
JJ HOTEL
NIRUNDORN RESORT
WHITE HOTEL
BUSES

SANTISUK BUNGALOW

CHA AM MARINA RESORT
CHA AM BEACH CLUB
BEACH GARDEN HOTEL
REGENT CHA AM

FORT RAMA 6 AND MAREK KHANTAYAWAN PALACE

0   5km

TASANEE BEACH RESORT

PALM HILLS GOLF RESORT
DUSIT RESORT & POLO CLUB

HUA HIN AIRPORT

ROYAL GARDEN VILLAGE

HUA HIN GARDEN RESORT

MAJESTIC CREEK

HUA HIN HOSPITAL

HUA HIN

ROYAL TRAIN STATION

MELIA HUA HIN

HUA HIN TRAIN STATION
TAT
SOFITEL CENTRAL HOTEL
ROYAL GARDEN RESORT
SAILOM HOTEL
HUA HIN PALACE HOTEL
CHOM VIEW HOTEL

TAKIAB
THE CHALET

TO PHUKET   WAT   VIEWPOINTS

PETCHKASEM HIGHWAY

GULF OF THAILAND

© MOON PUBLICATIONS, INC.

y been constructed farther south, midway between Cha Am and Hua Hin. Prices on most
properties double on weekends, when thousands of Thais arrive with their guitars and
booming radios.

Cha Am Villa: Most of the older bungalows
on the beach offer fan rooms for 200-300B and
a/c rooms from 400B. Comparison shopping is
easy since dozens of bungalows are packed
together on both sides of the central intersection.
241 Ruamchit Rd., tel. (032) 471010, 200-300B
fan, 400-800B a/c.

Double Dutch: A modern, clean, German-run
hotel with a fine restaurant that serves both Thai
and European dishes. Located 2.2 km north of
the main intersection on a less crowded and
cleaner stretch of beach. All rooms are a/c with
mini-refrigerator. 223 Ruamchit Rd., tel. (032)
471513, fax 471072, 400-700B. Good value.

Cha Am Methavalai Hotel: A five-story terraced hotel with landscaped gardens, swimming pool, sports center, and 115 spacious
rooms. Located at the north end of the beach
near the terminus for the hydrofoil to Bangkok
and Pattaya. 220 Ruamchit Rd., tel. (032)
471028, fax 471590, 2400-2800B.

Dusit Resort and Polo Club: The name
says it all: one of the most prestigious and luxurious resorts in Thailand. Designed for the Thai
elite and wealthy tourists, the Dusit features all
possible amenities including five restaurants,
an enormous pool, mini-golf course, scuba diving, and a polo club. 1349 Petchkasem Rd., tel.
(032) 520008, fax 520010, 4000-25,000B.

Transportation

Buses from Petchburi and the Southern Bus
Terminal in Bangkok usually stop on the highway at the intersection toward the beach. Motorcycle taxis to most hotels cost 10B; mini-
trucks can be chartered for 20-30B. A small
bus station is also located at the south end of
the beach near the Viwanthana and Santisuk
bungalows.

HUA HIN

Hua Hin, 238 km south of Bangkok on the sunrise side of the gulf, is a middle-class beach resort favored by families and Western travelers
seeking an alternative to Pattaya.

History

The eastern shore of the Gulf of Thailand has
long been favored by the royalty of Siam. In
1868, King Mongkut constructed his "Town of
the Eclipse" to house hundreds of *farangs* whom
the king had invited to witness the August solar
eclipse. The next royal discovery took place in
1910 after a hunting party organized by Prince
Chakrabongse charged across the lovely beach
of Hua Hin. The prince was so impressed that he
built a huge summer villa which still stands in the
northern perimeter of town. In 1923, King Vajiravudh erected a long, teakwood palace called
Deer Park connected by wooden corridors to
the white-sand beach.

Hua Hin developed as Thailand's original
beach resort shortly after WW I with the construction of the Southern Railway and the new
summer palace of King Prajadhipok, called Klai
Kangwon, "Far From Worries." The final touch
was the completion of the nation's first international golf course and the famous Railway Hotel.
Initially favored by Thai royalty and the wealthy
elite, the Railway Hotel—an elegant Victorian
structure now renamed the Sofitel—later stood
in as Cambodia's leading hotel in the film *The
Killing Fields*. Among the Thais, Hua Hin still
plays an important role in royal history since
His Majesty, King Bhumibol, maintains a palace
and occasionally visits to sail his single- and
double-handed boats.

Recently, Hua Hin has witnessed explosive
growth that threatens to transform the once-
idyllic seaside resort into a mega-destination
that belies her nickname—Queen of Tranquility.
The beach is a messy affair of tacky souvenir
stalls, plastic bags, waterscooters, and other
curses of uncontrolled development. Massive
hotels loom over a rather intimate beach. Local
authorities are now working to implement some
much-needed zoning laws and sort out the other
problems that confront Hua Hin.

Hua Hin Beach

The beach at Hua Hin is unspectacular and the
modern town undistinguished, but for many visitors, the beautiful bay and picturesque backdrop of green hills make this a fine place to relax
for a few days. Early risers can watch fishermen set sail from the northern piers, then walk
six km south to a pair of limestone hills for excellent views over the arching bay. Khao Takiab

("Chopstick Hill") can also be reached by motorcycle. Below Khao Takiab is Wat Khao Lad, a Buddhist temple with a 20-meter alabaster Buddha image. Two km west of Khao Takiab lies Khao Krilas ("Spirit Mountain"), a mystical site festooned with over 200 spirit houses, holy relics, and miniature *chedis*.

During the day there's little to do but relax, read a book, wander around the beach, and perhaps visit the quaint burgundy-and-cream building next to the train station which once served as the private waiting room for Thai royalty.

Frustrated pilots might investigate the local flying school, which provides English-language training and awards pilot's licenses for about 75,000 *baht*.

More information on local attractions, tours, and transportation is available from the municipal tourist office.

Marek Khantayawan Palace
Fifteen km north of Hua Hin, on the grounds of the Rama IV Army Base, is a wooden palace constructed in 1924 as a royal retreat for King Rama VI. Entirely made of teak and fashioned in Thai-Victorian style, the Palace of Love and Hope has recently been renovated and opened to the public. Open daily 0800-1600.

Three Caves
To the west of Hua Hin rises a verdant backdrop of humpbacked mountains. Near the village

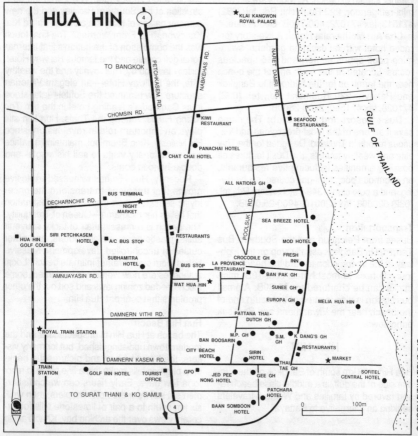

of Nong Phlab—home to the second-largest pineapple plantation in the world (Dole)—are three ancient caves named Dao, Lablae, and Kailon which show scalloped stalactites and twisting stalagmites. But which is which? Guides with gas lanterns are available to show you around, tell tall stories, and answer silly questions. Take an escorted tour from Hua Hin, or a local bus opposite Chatchai market. The caves are located behind the village police station: Dao Cave is 500 meters distant, Lablae Cave is 2 1/2 km, and Kailon Cave is 3 1/2 km.

Khao Sam Roi Yot National Park

The region's major attraction is the 98-square-km national park located in Prachuap Khiri Khan Province, 65 km south of Hua Hin. The park is a geological wonderland of limestone caves, secluded beaches, over 300 strangely disfigured mountains which resemble the angular humps of a sea dragon, countless prawn farms that scar the interior landscapes, and endangered wildlife such as serow mountain goats and crab-eating macaques. An incredible 885 species of birds have been identified here; they're best seen during the birdwatching season from November to February.

Despite the widespread disruption of unregulated prawn farms, Khao Sam Roi Yot ("Three Hundred Peaks") is one of the more spectacular parks in Thailand, worth the effort to visit.

The main attractions are the four caves of Tham Kaeo, Tham Sai, Tham Sam Praya, and Tham Praya Nakhon where an interior royal pavilion was constructed in 1896 to honor the visit of King Rama V. Sai and Keo caves are underwater time capsules filled with petrified waterfalls, monstrous limestone domes, and dangling stone tentacles resembling prehistoric jellyfish.

Accommodations: Accommodations inside the park include campsites at 35B per night and 10-man bungalows from 500B. Tents can also be pitched near the beach at Hat Laem Sala and Hat Sam Praya. Food supplies are available at Khao Dang Village and at Hat Laem Sala.

Transportation: All four caves are reachable by public transportation from Pranburi, and by boat from park headquarters followed by steep and tough hikes. Visitors can also cruise from Ban Bang Pu up Khao Daeng Canal past serrated pinnacles, exotic birds, crocodiles, rare tiger-striped catfish, and landwalking fish which crawled ashore to evolve into apes and, eventually, humans.

Tours are arranged through local travel agencies, or you can hire a motorcycle at 200B per day from the nearby shops. Alternatively, take a bus 25 km south to Pranburi, from where mini-trucks continue 30 km east to Ban Bang Pu (for Praya Nakhon Cave), and another 30 km to the park headquarters near Ban Khao Dang. The Hua Hin tourist office has a map.

Pranburi

Pranburi is a sleepy seaside resort located south of Hua Hin at the entrance to Khao Sam Roi Yot National Park. Several moderate-to-expensive resorts are located down at the beach, which attracts visitors discouraged by the commercialism of Hua Hin. **Borkaew Resort, Yom Doyee Cottages**, and **Pranburi Beach Resort** have rooms for 600-1500B.

An intriguing side trip can be made to Ban Khun Tanot, where a traditional Thai fishing village exists where nature refuses to survive. Ban Khun Tanot is a bizarre decomposed marsh of sculpted clay, eerie black birds, and thousands of charred trees which stand like forgotten skeletons in a lifeless land. The surrealistic scene will jog your memory: the Killing Fields in the Cambodian war movie.

Budget Accommodations

Hua Hin's dozen-plus guesthouses are tucked away in the alleys one block back from the beach. Rooms during the low season and midweek start from 100B, while weekend, holiday, and high-season rates October-March are 200-350B.

Beach Road Guesthouses: Sriosrapusin, Europa, and **Sunee** guesthouses have simple fan-cooled rooms for 150-250B. Cheaper rooms are found in the private homes down the alley at the **S.M., M.P.**, and **Pattana Thai-Dutch** guesthouses. M.P. Guesthouse features a useful noticeboard and cozy veranda.

One block north is another narrow alley with several inexpensive guesthouses such as **Crocodile, Phuen**, and **Ban Pak**; most charge 100-150B.

Thai Tae Guesthouse: A newer place in a quiet location slightly back from the street. 6 Damnern Kasem Rd., tel. (032) 511906, 150-250B fan, 350-450B a/c.

Gee Guesthouse: An older wooden place with a busy cafe and nightly videos. Damnern Kasem Rd., 150-250B.

All Nations Guesthouse: Aussie-run guesthouse with clean rooms and ice-cold beer. 10 Decharnchit Rd., 150-250B.

Subhamitra Hotel: An older six-story hotel with a small pool and clean, large rooms. Away from the action, but a good-value choice. Amnuayasin Rd., tel. (032) 511208, 200-300B fan, 400-500B a/c.

Chat Chai: Another reasonably priced guesthouse, Chat has rooms for 120-250B single and double. 59 Petchkasem, tel. (032) 511034

Moderate Accommodations

Jed Pee Nong Hotel: Very popular spot with small swimming pool and great outdoor cafe. 13/7 Damnern Kasem Rd., tel. (032) 512381, 450-550B.

Sirin Hotel: An attractive and spotlessly clean cantilevered hotel centrally located near the beach and restaurants. Very luxurious. Damnern Kasem Rd., tel. (032) 511150, 950-1200B.

Fresh Inn: Modern and comfortable hotel under Italian management; try their Lo Stivale Restaurant for pastas and pizzas. 132 Naret Damri Rd., tel. (032) 511389, 350B fan, 550-700B a/c.

Ban Somboon Hotel: An older but very friendly spot with a small garden; room rates include breakfast. Tucked away in a less hectic alley, tel. (032) 512079, 650-750B.

Ban Boosarin Hotel: Another cozy hotel with immaculate rooms for "tourists, executive and even the golf gang." All rooms are a/c with refrigerators and TV. Recommended. 8/8 Poolsuk Rd., tel. (032) 512076, 600-750B.

A few more worth a mention are **Golf Inn**, 600-800B, on Damnern Kasem, tel. (032) 512473, and **Suphamit**, 250-400B, 19 Petch Kasem, tel. (032) 511208.

Luxury Accommodations

Sofitel Central Hotel: Hua Hin's most famous hotel is the grand old dame constructed in 1921 by Prince Purachtra. Formerly known as the Railway Hotel, the European-style hotel has been completely renovated and redecorated by a French hotel firm. Features sports facilities, spacious gardens, and a beautiful swimming pool. Damnern Kasem Rd., tel. (032) 512021,

fax (032) 511014, Bangkok reservations (02) 233-0974, U.S. reservations (800) 221-4542, 3400-6500B.

Royal Garden Resort: Hua Hin's other luxury choice, located about two km south of town, is a stunning crescent-shaped, low-rise complex with pool, tennis courts, and sports center outfitted with catamarans, lasers, and windsurfers. Ideally suited for those who seek sports and a beach removed from the clutter of central Hua Hin. 107 Petchkasem Rd., tel. (032) 511881, fax (032) 512422, Bangkok reservations (02) 251-8659, 3200-5400B.

Restaurants

Despite ill-conceived development in recent years, Hua Hin remains a fairly sleepy place without the tawdriness and commercial excesses of other beach resorts like Pattaya and Phuket. Nightlife revolves around seafood dinners and drinks at simple open-air cafes down by the water, and restaurants located in the better hotels.

Night Market: A popular place to dine inexpensively while shopping for socks and cassettes. Streetside specialties include seafoods, Thai sweets, mussel omelets, and "pigs bowels."

Beach Road (Naret Damri) Cafes: Several small and inexpensive cafes are located on the beach road near the budget guesthouses.

Fishing Pier: Three basic but lively spots are located at the pier in the north of town. **Sang Thai** provides a good display of fresh seafood packed over ice and a useful photographic menu, but **Charoen Pochana** has a longer pier with better views and finer ambience. **Meekaruna Seafood** across the street features a snooker club and an upstairs a/c dining room with English-language menus. Good food, too.

European Restaurants: Restaurants rise and fall quickly in Hua Hin, but as of this writing the most popular choices are **La Villa Italian Restaurant** with an Italian chef, **Ban Lan Sao Restaurant** for a curious culinary combination called "Thai-Italian Cuisine," and the beautiful **La Provence Restaurant** situated in a back-alley courtyard graced with trees and flowers.

Transportation

Hua Hin is 170 km south of Bangkok on the shorter freeway that bypasses Nakhon Pathom and 238 on the older route through Nakhon Pathom.

Air: Bangkok Airways and Brom Airways, a small private outfit, fly several times weekly from Bangkok.

Train: Trains from Hualampong Station in Bangkok leave nine times daily from 0900 to 2155. Departures and fares are listed above in the "Southern Thailand" Introduction.

Two trains leave daily from Kanchanaburi; a better alternative than returning to Bangkok.

Advance reservations for train travel south can be made at local agencies, including Western Tours on Damnern Kasem Road. Travelers without reservations will probably need to stand for several hours until seats are vacated by departing passengers.

Bus: Buses from the Southern Bus Terminal in Bangkok leave every 30 minutes and take three or four hours depending on the route and traffic. Buses terminate in the center of town on the main highway or back one block on Sasong Road. Beachside bungalows are a 10-minute walk.

Travel agencies in Hua Hin can sometimes book direct a/c bus travel south to Ko Samui and Phuket. Ordinary buses can be picked up during the day on Sasong Rd. and in the evenings near the clock tower on Petchkasem Road.

PRACHUAP KHIRI KHAN

One of the more delightful and untouristy towns in the northern third of Southern Thailand is the unassuming village of Prachuap Khiri Khan, situated on a magnificently arched bay flanked by towering limestone peaks. Prachuap Khiri Khan ("Town Among Mountains") lacks historical monuments and the beach inside the city limits is disappointing, but the genuine Thai feel and nearby geological attractions make it an excellent stop for visitors with extra time.

Attractions

The limestone peaks and arching Prachuap Bay once inspired a travel writer to nickname the town the Rio of Southern Thailand. While something of an overstatement, it's hard to deny that Prachuap boasts one of the most attractive layouts in the region. A small tourist office behind the night market displays photos of the nearby

PRACHUAP KHIRI KHAN

TO AO NOI BEACH

TO HIGHWAY 4 & HUA HIN

KHAO CHONG KRACHOK (MIRROR MOUNTAIN)

WAT

CHURCH

PHITAK CHAT RD.

SARACHIP RD.

THETSABAN MIRROR MOUNTAIN BUNGALOWS

CITY HALL

SAI THONG RESTAURANT

CHIO OCHA RESTAURANT

INTHIRA HOTEL

BUSES

TOURIST OFFICE

NIGHT MARKET

SUSEUK RD.

PARK

CHAI THALE RD.

PIER

TRAIN STATION

YUTICHAI HOTEL

VIBUL SANTISUK HOTEL

KONG KIAT RD.

SEAFOOD STALLS

COFFEE SHOP

PAN POCHANA CAFE

SUKSANT HOTEL

BANK

MC RENTALS

HAD THONG HOTEL

POST OFFICE

GULF OF THAILAND

BANK

KING HOTEL

SCHOOL

MARKET

0   100m

TO AO MANAO

© MOON PUBLICATIONS, INC.

beaches and can help with transportation details.

Khao Chong Krachok: Looming over the northern end of the bay is a limestone buttress called Mirror Tunnel Mountain after an illuminated arch which appears to reflect the sky. Visitors can climb the stairway to enjoy the panoramic views over the bay and west toward the mountains of Burma, feed the hordes of wild monkeys, and visit Wat Thammikaram, established by King Rama VI. The small monastery is shaded by fragrant frangipani trees.

Ao Noi Beach: Fairly clean and white beaches are located both north and south of town. Ao Noi, six km north and reached by minitrucks heading up Chai Thale Rd., has several small spots such as Ao Noi Beach Bungalows, where a Thai-German couple rent rooms from 450B, serve both Thai and German meals, and operate a water sports center with windsurfers and sailboards.

Ao Khan Kradai Beach: Eight km north of Prachuap and within walking distance of Ao Noi is another deserted beach with excellent sand. A narrow trail to the rear leads up a limestone peak to a modest temple and then an impressive cave called Tham Khao Khan Kradai. The cave *wat* features excellent views and an immense 16-meter reclining Buddha image illuminated by spilling sunlight.

Manao Bay: South of Prachuap and beyond the limestone peak is an attractive bay and beach under the supervision of the Thai military. Manao was the scene of a battle between the Thai Army and Japanese forces in World War II, an event commemorated each year with a light-and-sound show in early December.

Accommodations
Prachuap has several budget places and one midpriced hotel down by the beach.

Yutichai Hotel: The first hotel near the train station has decent rooms in a convenient location. 35 Kong Kiat Rd., tel. (032) 611055, 80-140B.

Inthira Hotel: Directly across from the night market is a popular spot with inexpensive rooms. No English sign, but look for the car in the lobby and the small hotel desk on the right; avoid the noisy streetside rooms. Phitak Chat Rd., no phone, 60-100B.

Suksant Hotel: An older 80-room hotel painted green with 80 fairly clean rooms. 131 Suseuk Rd., tel. (032) 611145, 100-140B fan, 220-350B a/c.

Thetsaban Mirror Mountain Bungalows: Facing the bay in the north end of town is a collection of seaside bungalows owned and operated by the city. Suseuk Rd., tel. (032) 611150, 150B double rooms, 400B individual bungalows.

Had Thong Hotel: The newest hotel in Prachuap features a small swimming pool, comfortable cafe, and well-furnished a/c rooms. 7 Suseuk Rd., tel. (032) 611960, fax (032) 611003, 600-750B.

Restaurants
The small night market in the center of town offers the standard collection of quick-cook specialties. Seaside vendors, who set up stalls in the evenings along the waterfront just south of the pier, display fresh seafood which can be cooked to order in a variety of sauces. Sai Thong Restaurant just north of the park and the small Pan Pochana Cafe are more formal affairs with local specialties such as *haw mok haw* (fish curry and mussels) and *pla samli tae daw* (fried cottonfish with mango salad). Prachuap's most attractive restaurant is located inside the Had Thong Hotel.

Transportation
Prachuap Khiri Khan is 252 km south of Bangkok and 82 km south of Hua Hin.

Train: Trains from Hualampong Station in Bangkok leave nine times daily from 0900 to 2155. For train departures and fares, see "Southern Thailand" Introduction.

Bus: Buses leave regularly from the Southern Bus Terminal in Bangkok and from the bus station on Sasong Road in Hua Hin. Buses terminate and depart from the shed just opposite the Inthira Hotel.

PRACHUAP TO CHUMPHON

Thap Sakae
Thap Sakae is a small town with fairly decent beaches both north and south. Hotels in the city limits include the **Chan Ruan** with rooms from 120B, the **Chawalit** on the main highway with rooms from 100B, and the **Suk Kasem** on Sukhaphiban Rd. with rooms from 120B.

Better atmosphere is found at **Talay Inn** (tel. 671417), located on a small lake about one km back from the Thap Sakae train station. Proprietor Khun Yo can advise on visits to Huay Yang Waterfall and other recreational activities. Bamboo bungalows cost 50-80B.

Kee Ree Wong Beach
Several beach resorts patronized almost exclusively by Thais are located south of Thap Sakae. Seven km south at Km 372 is an upscale development called **Had Kaeo Beach Resort** (tel. 611035) with 30 bungalows in various price ranges starting at 200B.

Two km farther south is the small village of Ban Krut, and the turnoff to a long and attractive beach with several inexpensive bungalows such as those at **Tawee Resort** and **Kee Ree Wong Beach Resort**. The latter is operated by a Westerner and his Thai wife, who charge 70-100B for bungalows with private bath and shower. A motorcycle from the Ban Krut train station to Kee Ree Wong Beach costs 20B during the day and 30B at night. Note that only the ordinary diesel trains stop in Thap Sakae, Ban Krut, and Bang Saphan.

Bang Saphan Yai

Bang Saphan Yai, a fishing town 76 km south of Prachuap, also serves as a Thai resort known for its seafood, big-game fishing, and offshore islands such as Ko Thalu. Several beach hotels and bungalows are located in the small town and along the bay. **B.S. Guesthouse, Had Soom Boon Seaview Hotel, Bang Saphan Resort, Vanveena Bungalows**, and **Sarikar Villa** have fan rooms from 120B and a/c rooms at double the price. Fishing boats and tackle can be chartered at Sarikar Villa.

Travelers generally hire a motorcycle taxi for 20B and head six km south to a beautiful beach to stay at **Karol L's Bungalows**. Operated by a retired American and his Thai wife, Karol's is an idyllic place almost completely untouched by mass tourism. Karol can help with boat trips and overnight stays on nearby Thalu Island, plus fishing and skin-diving tips. Pick-up is arranged in Bang Saphan Yai by calling (032) 691058 and leaving your time and mode of arrival. Wooden bungalows cost 80-120B; Raisa does the cooking.

CHUMPHON

Almost 500 km south of Bangkok and situated on the Kra Isthmus, Chumphon is an extremely drab provincial capital located near several fine beaches on the eastern perimeter. Chumphon is considered the start of southern Thailand, and an important crossroads where the highway splits to Phuket on the Indian Ocean side and Ko Samui in the Gulf of Thailand. Chumphon offers little of interest to most visitors, aside from the nearby beaches and scuba diving—considered among the finest in Thailand. It also serves as a departure point for boats to Ko Tao, an option which saves heading down to Surat Thani. The following beaches can be reached with

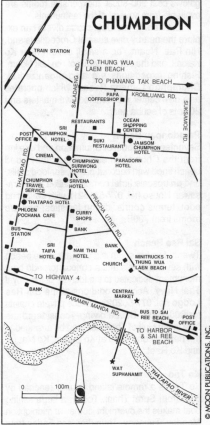

mini-trucks leaving opposite the bus terminal in Chumphon, and on Paramin Manda Rd. two blocks east of the market. The **Chumphon Travel Service** (tel. 077-501880) at 66 Thatapao Road can also help with transportation, hotel reservations, and boats to Ko Tao.

Thung Wua Laen Beach

Fifteen km north of Chumphon is the fine bay and clean but brownish sand of Thung Wua Laen. The beach is almost completely deserted except for small weekend crowds from Chumphon. Accommodations and scuba-diving facilities are provided at **Chumphon Cabana Resort** (tel. 077-501990, Bangkok reservations 02-224-1884) where individual beachside bungalows cost 300-800B. Inexpensive rooms are available from several of the restaurants.

From Feb. to late Oct., scuba divers can explore the nearby dive sites of Crocodile Island, Hin Pae, Ngam Yai, a small cavern near Ko Kaloak, and the colorful corals of Hin Lak Ngam. Fishing expeditions are also organized by **Chumphon Cabana Resort**, which operates as a dive center with certified dive masters and 20 sets of scuba gear.

Paradonpap Beach

Seventeen km south of Chumphon and one km from the Chumphon estuary is a fairly good beach lined with coconut palms, seafood stalls, and an upscale hotel complex called the Pornsawan House (tel. 077-521521), with swimming pool, tennis courts, diving facilities, and a/c rooms from 700B.

Sai Ree Beach

Twenty-two km south is a very attractive beach with several hotels and a curious torpedo boat monument dedicated to the founder of the Royal Thai Navy. Accommodations at the **Sai Ree Lodge** (tel. 077-502023) include private chalets for 600-900B. Scuba diving—considered the best in the Gulf of Thailand—can be arranged to the nearby coral reefs at Ko Samet, Ko Mattra, and Ko Raet.

Ko Tao

Ko Tao is a remote island usually reached by boat from Surat Thani. Today, a large fishing boat makes the overnight journey at midnight on Monday, Tuesday, Thursday, and Friday from Chumphon harbor. Tickets can be purchased from Chumphon Travel Service. One-way fare is about 200B.

Accommodations

Travelers generally head down to a beach, though Chumphon has plenty of hotels in all price ranges.

Sri Taifa Hotel: The travelers' favorite is a Chinese hotel with decent restaurant, balcony views, and 20 fan-cooled rooms. 74 Saladaeng Rd., tel. (077) 511063, 80-160B.

Srivena Hotel: Another budget choice in the center of town. Saladaeng Rd., no phone, 60-90B.

Chumphon Suriwong Hotel: A Chinese hotel whose lobby and hallway resemble the interior of a tiled bathroom. The adjoining restaurant has been decorated with aquariums and caged singing birds. 176 Saladaeng Rd., tel. (077)511776, 80-160B.

Thatapao Hotel: An acceptable mid-priced hotel just one block north of the bus station. 66 Thatapao Rd., tel. (077) 511479, 260-550B.

Paradorn Inn Hotel: A modern and fairly luxurious hotel with over 100 a/c rooms and a popular nightclub. 180/12 Paradorn Rd., tel. (077) 511500, 500-600B.

Jansom Chumphon Hotel: The best hotel in town opened in 1991 just down from the large Ocean Shopping Center. Facilities include a restaurant on the lobby floor, massage parlor, and Town Disco. 188/65 Saladaeng Rd., tel. (077) 502502, fax (077) 502503, 750-1000B.

Restaurants

For an escape from the heat and concrete monotony of Chumphon, try the a/c restaurants in the **Jansom Chumphon** and **Paradorn Inn**. **Phloen Pochana Cafe** just north of the bus terminal is good for a quick bite, as are the curry shops on Saladaeng Rd. in the center of town. Several good and inexpensive cafes are located on the narrow road which leads to the Jansom Chumphon Hotel and the Ocean Shopping Center. Try the **Suki Restaurant** and an unnamed cafe just opposite for point-and-choose dishes in clean surroundings. **Papa Coffeeshop** serves espresso in a somewhat trendy atmosphere behind the shopping center. Foodstalls and a night market are also located near Papa Coffeeshop.

Transportation

Chumphon is 485 km south of Bangkok and 193 km north of Surat Thani.

Air: An airport is planned for 1994, with service to be provided by Bangkok Airways.

Train: Trains from Hualampong Station in Bangkok leave nine times daily from 0900 to 2155. Train departures and fares are listed above at the beginning of the Southern Thailand chapter. Luggage can be stored at the train station for 10B per day. Motorcycle taxis into town cost 10B.

Bus: Buses from Bangkok and the deep south terminate at the small bus station on Thatapao Rd. near the cinema and taxi stand.

RANONG

Situated on the Kra Isthmus and facing the Andaman Sea, Ranong is the regional capital of the least populous but rainiest province in Thailand. The region is primarily visited for its incredibly lush rainforests, national parks, hot springs, and waterfalls, rather than the beaches, which tend to be muddy flats and mangrove swamps due to the heavy rains. Ranong is also the launching point for visits to the Surin Islands.

Hot Springs

Ranong is known among the Thais for its boiling hot springs located in the town park and about two km east of city center in the compound of Wat Tapotharam. The springs at the *wat* have been fashioned into organized ponds surrounded by manicured gardens and tropical forests. Visitors can soak in the public Jacuzzi for 50B and explore the organized trails which lead up to a small *wat*. Waters rising from the ground reach the surface at almost 70° centigrade—hot enough to cook eggs—but the mineral baths are cooled to a more modest 40-42 degrees.

The hot springs can also be enjoyed at the Jansom Thara Hotel, which pipes down the waters and charges 50B for a sexually segregated communal soak.

Nai Kai Rayong

The most important historical figure from Ranong is not a Thai, but a wealthy Fukien Chinese immigrant who served as regional tax collector during the reign of King Rama V. Koh Su Chiang is honored as the founder of Rayong at his former residence, Nai Kai Rayong, located on the northern edge of town near the post office and police station. One of the three original residences has been filled with mementos and ancestor figurines which bear the names of the deceased members of the Koh family.

Koh Su Chiang Mausoleum

Two km north of the Koh residence on Chao Rakathong Hill is the spacious graveyard for the Koh family, complete with eight 19th-century stone sculptures imported from China, which lead up to the primary mausoleum.

Victoria Point

Across the broad Pak Chan estuary lies the southern end of Burma at Victoria Point and dozens of islands that serve as trading posts for Thai-Burmese commerce. Foreigners are forbidden to cross, but Thai nationals are allowed to visit Victoria Point and several other Burmese islands on organized day-trips. A private boat operated by the Jansom Thara Hotel visits the pearl farms at Ko Phayam.

Accommodations

Most hotels in Ranong are located on Ruangrat Rd. between the main highway and the post office.

Asia Hotel: A large hotel with decent fan and a/c rooms. 39 Ruangrat Rd., tel. (077) 811113, 100-280B.

Sin Ranong Hotel: Better rooms are found in this somewhat newer hotel near the market and town park. 26 Ruangrat Rd., tel. (077) 811454, 120-300B.

Spa Inn: A popular option to the expensive Jansom Thara is strategically sited just off the main highway. Chonraua Rd., tel. (077) 811011, 400-600B.

Jansom Thara Hotel: The leading hotel in Ranong offers thermal pools to both residents and visitors, swimming pool, health club, and boat excursions to the Surin Islands on their luxury speedboat *Wanna 1* from January to April. 2 Petchkasem Hwy., tel. (077) 811511, fax (077) 821821, 1000-1400B.

Restaurants

Ranong is famous for its seafood, such as deep-fried soft-shell crabs, barbecued prawns, and steamed white snapper served in coconut sauce. **Sommboon Restaurant** on Ruangrat Rd. just opposite the Jansom Thara Hotel has local specialties described on their English-language menu. Another popular spot is **Khun Nunt** on Luvang Rd. on the north end of town down the hill from the governor's house. Both serve fried crabs and grilled venison during the hunting season from September to December.

Transportation

Ranong is 568 km south of Bangkok, 117 km south of Chumphon, and 412 km north of Phuket.

Bus: Direct bus service to Ranong is available from Bangkok, Chumphon, Surat Thani, and Phuket. The Ranong bus terminal is located on the highway near the Jansom Thara Hotel, though most buses also stop in the center of town on Ruangrat Road near the restaurants and budget hotels.

Direct minibus service to the Jansom Thara Hotel is provided from the Jansom Chumphon Hotel in Chumphon, Muang Thai Hotel in Surat Thani, and the Imperial Hotel in Phuket.

SURIN ISLANDS
NATIONAL PARK

Four hours from the west coast of Southern Thailand lie the five islands which comprise Ko Surin National Park. Blessed with shallow-sea corals, a hypnotizing undersea world, and pristine beaches, Ko Surin has recently opened to tourism—as shown by the estimated 20,000 visitors who reached the islands last year.

The Surin archipelago is home to some 3,000 sea nomads or Chao Lay ("People of the Sea") who prefer to call themselves *mokens*. According to French anthropologists, the *mokens* trace their origins back to the Riau Archipelago between Singapore and Indonesia, but moved north to these islands to resist the influx of Islam. Today, they are the last traditional sea gypsies in Thailand who remain animists and speak Malay rather than Thai. Despite the inroads of tourism, the *mokens* still conduct boat-floating ceremonies to honor ancestral sprits on the full moon of the fifth month in the lunar calendar.

Attractions

Surin National Park is comprised of two large islands—Ko Surin Nua and Ko Surin Tai—and several other islets inhabited by the Chao Lay. Scuba diving is said to be best in the coral reefs situated between the two large islands. Big-game fishing boats occasionally visit to test the waters to the west near the Burmese border.

Accommodations

The National Park Service operates several bungalows and campsites on the southwest side of Ko Surin Nua, the northern island which is home to a small community of Chao Lay. Six-man bungalows cost 600-1000B and two-man tents cost

60-100B. Reservations, included with all organized tours, can be made through the park office located 70 km south of Ranong in the town of Khuraburi. The park service also operates a small cafe and supply store on Ko Surin.

Transportation

The Surin Islands are located midway between Phuket and Ranong, about 60 km west of Khuraburi. Weekend boat tours from December to April are organized by the Jamsom Thara Hotel in Ranong and large tour operators in Phuket such as Songserm and Asia Voyages. Package tours cost 1000-1500B for day visits including transportation and meals, 2000-2500B for a two-day, one-night excursion, and 3000-3500B for three days and two nights.

Boats can also be chartered with the help of the park rangers at Surin headquarters in Khuraburi. Eight-man boats from Phae Pla Chumphon Pier at Ban Hin Lat cost about 2000B; the journey takes four hours and should only be undertaken between monsoons from December to April.

RANONG TO PHUKET

Laem Son National Park

Fifty km south of Ranong is a marine national park spanning three districts, two in Ranong and one in Phangnga Province. The park encompasses over 100 km of coastline on the Andaman Sea and over 20 islands inhabited by birds, monkeys, and crab-eating macaques.

Park headquarters is on Ban Ben Beach, from where several beautiful islands—Ko Kam Yai and Ko Kam Noi—can be seen and reached with hired longtails. Neaby Ko Phayam has a decent swimming beach near a small village populated by fishermen and cashew farmers. Ko Kam Tok also has a good beach, coral beds for divers, and public campsites. Hat Laem Son, four km north of park headquarters, is known for its birdwatching and strange geological formations.

Accommodations: Park headquarters on Ban Ben Beach has campsites for 25-50B and large bungalows for 300-600B. Camping is also permitted on all the offshore islands. Komain Villa just outside the park entrance has small bungalows for 100-220B.

Transportation: The road to Laem Son is 58 km south of Ranong. Trucks from the turnoff to Laem Son village often pick up hitchhikers. The rough road continues two km west to park headquarters.

Takua Pa

This small Thai town, 170 km south of Ranong, 130 km north of Phuket town, and 160 km east of Surat Thani on the west coast of southern Thailand, is a fairly easy stop when traveling between Ko Samui and Phuket.

The town itself has nothing of interest, but within 30-50 km are several national parks with thick rainforest, good beaches with moderately priced bungalows, and relatively inexpensive boat transportation to the Surin and Similan islands. The pier for boats to the islands is at Tap Lamu, 30 km south of Takua Pa.

Accommodations: Extra Hotel (tel. 076-421027) just off the highway has rooms for 120-180B. **Chok Thawi, Kiti Phong, Suak Suk,** and **Takola** hotels have rooms for 80-150B. Best in town is the **Amarin Hotel** (tel. 076-421534) with rooms for 200-380B.

Khao Lak National Park

Thirty km south of Takua Pa, and situated back from the national highway, is a tropical jungle with over a dozen inexpensive bungalows; an excellent place to escape the tourist crowds of Phuket. Measured from the north end of Phuket Island is Tap Lamu Pier (Km 54), Khao Lak Resort (Km 58), Poseidon Bungalows (Km 58), Puppa Bungalows (Km 58), Khao Lak Bungalows (Km 59), Nan Thong Resort (Km 60), Paradise Cabana (Km 76), Bang Sak Resort (Km 76), Sun Splendor Lodge (Km 77), and Takua Pa (Km 86).

Khao Lak Bungalows: Operated by a German named Gerhard and his Thai wife who can help with jungle trekking in Khao Lak National Park, cave explorations, and boat tours to the Similan Islands at far lower cost than tour operators in Phuket. Bus travelers can spot their hotel sign on the main highway at Km 59. Box 25, Phangnga, no phone, 120-450B.

Khao Lak Resort: Thirty-six km south of Takua Pa and 70 km north of the Phuket Airport at Km 58 is a comfortable and well-kept lodge near beautiful beaches and untouched jungle.

158 Sritakuap Rd., phone (076) 421061, fax (076) 211072, 120-600B.

Khao Sok National Park

Khao Sok is a 646-square-km park in the western section of Surat Thani Province. Park attractions include several waterfalls, the Klong Sok River which winds through thick jungle, huge limestone cliffs that resemble those of Guilin in China, the immense Chio Larn Reservoir, and wildlife from monkeys to wild boars.

Accommodations: Park headquarters has campsites for 25-50B and large bungalows for 300-600B.

Most visitors stay at Tree Tops Jungle Guesthouse, a popular place just outside the park entrance that offers an escape from the touristy destinations of Ko Samui and Phuket. Tree Tops is owned and operated by an American lady who champions wildlife preservation and sponsors activities such as jungle walks and caving in the national park, bamboo raft trips down the Klong Sok River, and excursions to nearby beaches and islands. Tree Tops can be reached by buses and shared taxis from Phuket, Surat Thani, and Takua Pa; look for the sign at Km 108. Box 13, Surat Thani, tel. (077) 273772, 250-600B per day including meals and tours.

Transportation: Khao Sok is 40 km east of Takua Pa, 120 km west of Surat Thani, and 180 km north of Phuket. All buses between Surat Thani and Phuket pass the park entrance at Km 108.

CHAIYA

Chaiya is a small but historic town located on the Gulf of Thailand, thirty minutes north of Surat Thani. Chaiya occupies the site of an ancient empire which archaeologists believe was connected with the mythical Indonesian empire of Srivijaya. While the exact location of the Srivijayan empire described in the 7th century by Chinese merchants remains a mystery, Chaiya has provided Thai archaeologists with a bounty of statuary and architectural remnants strongly influenced by Indonesian culture. Among the more important discoveries is the famous Avalokitesvara Bodhisattva, an acclaimed masterpiece of Buddhist art now displayed in the Bangkok National Museum.

Wat Boromothat

The most important Srivijayan monument is located south of Chaiya on the road between town and the national highway. Wat Boromothat is chiefly noted for its exposed bases and excavated altars which show Indonesian influence and closely resemble the *candis* of Central Java. Much of the remaining temple has been heavily restored in contemporary patterns. A small museum displays copies of statues discovered at Chaiya but now guarded inside the Bangkok National Museum.

Accommodations

Na Yai Park Guesthouse: Chaiya lacks hotels aside from a solitary guesthouse down at Phumriang Beach, about four km east of town. Phumriang, a Muslim community settled by fishermen from Pattani, is known for its exquisitely woven fabrics, which are popular among Thai tourists. Na Yai Park has simple huts and bungalows with private baths within walking distance of the beach, village, and old temples. 233 Moo 1 Phumriang, tel. (077) 431387, 80-180B.

Transportation

Chaiya is 54 km north of Surat Thani, and four km east of Highway 41 which connects Chumphon with Surat Thani. Train travelers coming from the north can get off at the small train station in Chaiya and continue to Suan Mok or Surat Thani by bus. Public buses also connect Surat Thani with Chaiya and Suan Mok.

WAT SUAN MOK

Wat Suan Mokkhablarama—the Garden of Liberation—is a forest monastery near Chaiya dedicated to the study of *dhamma* and *vipassana* meditation. Wat Suan Mok (also called Wat Suan Mokkh) was founded some five decades ago by a highly revered Thai monk named Achaan Buddhadasa, known for his back-to-basics approach which emphasizes discipline and rationality over ritual and superstition. Achaan Buddhadasa began his monastic career in 1927 in his home province of Ubon Ratchathani, and later studied Buddhism and Pali in Bangkok before establishing an Issan

forest monastery near his hometown in the northeast. After moving his headquarters to Chaiya in the 1940s, Buddhadasa was joined by other Buddhist disciples such as Phra Dusadee Methangkuro, Santikaro Bhikku, and Abbot Achaan Poh, who brought his successful meditation retreats from Ko Samui to Suan Mok in 1988. Today, Wat Suan Mok serves as the most popular temple in Thailand for Westerners to study Buddhism and traditional forms of Thai meditation.

Suan Mok is spread over 80 hectares of forested hillside with dormitories and huts for monks, library and bookstore with literature on Buddhism, a Spiritual Theater decorated with Buddhist murals, and the new International Dharma Heritage Center located two km distant near a small mountain and hot springs.

Both novice and experienced practitioners of *vipassana* are invited to join other Westerners during the 10-day meditation retreats held on the first day of each month. Instruction is provided in English. The daily program includes a 0400 wake-up and meditation session, vegetarian breakfast, morning lectures on Buddhism, chores around the international center, lunch, private study, afternoon tea, an evening lecture and soak in the mineral baths. Meditation focuses on *anapanasati,* which combines mindfulness with breathing, together with daily lectures which describe the principles of meditation and *dhamma.*

Accommodations

The basic fee of 600B includes dormitory accommodations, vegetarian meals, and all instruction. Visitors are expected to follow local guidelines such as modest dress and periods of silence. Space is limited and reservations should be made by arriving at Suan Mok a few days in advance.

Transportation

Wat Suan Mok is located on Highway 41, about 50 km north of Surat Thani and four km south of the junction to Chaiya. Buses from the main bus terminal in Surat Thani take about 50 minutes to reach the temple entrance. Taxis can be hired from the train station at Phun Phin. Buses and *songtaos* also connect central Chaiya with Suan Mok.

SURAT THANI

Located on the southeastern coast of Southern Thailand 644 km from Bangkok, the prosperous port of Surat Thani chiefly serves as a launching point for ferries to Ko Samui, Thailand's third-largest island and one of the leading tourist destinations in Southeast Asia. Surat Thani offers good shopping but otherwise has little of great interest aside from some natural attractions and the historical/religious draws in nearby Chaiya.

The Surat Thani TAT office (tel. 077-281828) is inconveniently located at 5 Talad Mai Rd. in the east end of town. An excellent resource for exploring Surat Thani Province and the nearby islands is the *Map of Koh Samui, Koh Tao & Koh Phangan* published by Prannock Witthaya Publications.

Tickets to Ko Samui can be purchased from the Songserm agents near the harbor and from Samui Tours on Talad Mai Road.

Budget Accommodations

Most visitors head directly to Ko Samui, but late arrivals by train or bus may need to overnight near the train station in Phun Phin or in downtown Surat Thani.

Lipa & Kasem 2 Guesthouses: Adjacent to

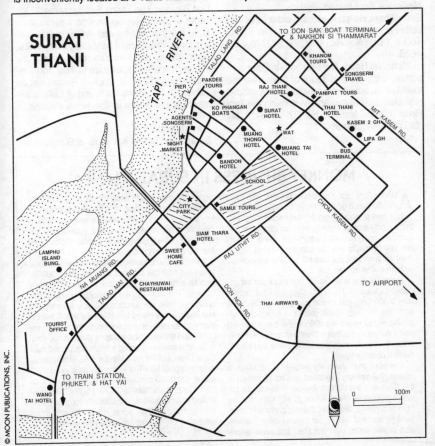

SURAT THANI

TAPI RIVER

TO DON SAK BOAT TERMINAL & NAKHON SI THAMMARAT

TALAD LANG RD.

KHANOM TOURS

SONGSERM TRAVEL

PAKDEE TOURS

PIER

RAJ THANI HOTEL

PANIPAT TOURS

KO PHANGAN BOATS

SURAT HOTEL

THAI THANI HOTEL

MIT KASEM RD.

AGENTS SONGSERM

WAT

KASEM 2 GH

NIGHT MARKET

MUANG THONG HOTEL

MUANG TAI HOTEL

LIPA GH

BANDON HOTEL

BUS TERMINAL

SCHOOL

CHOM KASEM RD.

CITY PARK

SAMUI TOURS

SIAM THARA HOTEL

LAMPHU ISLAND BUNG.

SWEET HOME CAFE

RAJ UTHIT RD.

NA MUANG RD.

TALAD MAI RD.

CHAYHUWAI RESTAURANT

DON NOK RD.

TO AIRPORT

THAI AIRWAYS

TOURIST OFFICE

TO TRAIN STATION, PHUKET, & HAT YAI

WANG TAI HOTEL

0   100m

© MOON PUBLICATIONS, INC.

the bus terminal are several small guesthouses acceptable for an overnight crash. Both have cafes and travel agencies with tickets to Ko Samui, Phuket, and Krabi. 80-140B.

Thai Thani Hotel: Also next to the bus terminal is this sprawling old hotel with amazing wooden furniture on the ground floor and reception facilities on the third floor. 442 Talad Mai Rd., tel. (077) 272977, 160-200B fan, 260-300B a/c.

Bandon Hotel: A very clean hotel entered through a Chinese coffee shop. Recommended. 168 Na Muang Rd., tel. (077) 272167, 100-180B.

Moderate Accommodations

Siam Thara Hotel: A popular, older hotel with coffee shop and nightclub located near Samui Tours. 1 Don Nok Rd., tel. (077) 273740, 320-460B.

Wang Tai Hotel: The best hotel in Surat is inconveniently located south of town near the tourist office, but offers a swimming pool, cabaret nightclub, and restaurant overlooking the Tapi River. 1 Talad Mai Rd., tel. (077) 273410, fax (077) 281007, 550-650B.

Accommodations In Phun Phin

The train station for Surat Thani is 14 km west in the town of Phun Phin. Except for the very late trains, all arrivals are met by buses which connect directly with the boats to Ko Samui. Late-night arrivals can take a taxi into Surat Thani, or stay at one of the guesthouses opposite the train station. Among the choices with rooms from 100B are the **Tai Fah, Sri Thani,** and **Kaew Fah**.

Restaurants

Surat Thani is famous throughout Thailand as home to delicious rambutans known as *ngoh rongrien* and giant tilam oysters grown in Ban Don Bay and Tha Thong Estuary some 30 km south of town. Restaurants here serve tasty *kung kuladam* shrimp and the succulent oysters for as little as eight *baht* each. **Chayhuwai, Soon Hieng,** and **Yim Yim** restaurants in the center of town all specialize in Thai and Chinese seafood dishes. Lucky's Restaurant on Talad Mai Rd. in the north end of town is another popular choice for inexpensive dishes.

Transportation

Surat Thani is 644 km south of Bangkok and

MONKEY BUSINESS IN SURAT THANI

At the age of four, Kai Nui earns more than most middle-grade government officials in Bangkok.

Nui isn't a working girl or real estate magnate, but a highly trained monkey who can pick up to 500 coconuts each day. At the standard rate of 50 *baht* per 100 coconuts, Kai Nui can earn almost 10,000 *baht* each month; not bad for a stubborn monkey with an evil temperament.

Surat Thani and Ko Samui provinces are the coconut capitals of Thailand, shipping each month over 3,000 tons—six *million* coconuts—to the copra factories and export merchants in Bangkok. Collecting all that copra is a difficult and dangerous job since palms in southern Thailand are particularly tall and . . . well, when was the last time you tried to climb a coconut tree?

The solution to this nutty problem is the *Macaca nemestrina* monkey (pig-tailed macaque), known to the Thais as a *ling kiang* or *ling gep maphrao*, the coconut-picking monkey. Although *ling kiang* can be bred in captivity, seasoned trainers prefer wild creatures because of their higher innate vitality. Trainers also prefer males over females, and avoid "short-sighted" monkeys with white brows, which are considered stubborn lazybones. A knowledge of a monkey's *ngow heng* (personality) is also drawn from the size of his hands, mouth, lips, thickness of fur, and detail of the fingerprints, which should closely resemble a human print.

Male *ling kiang* monkeys between one and three years old cost the coconut collector about 3000B, with an additional 1000B in training fees at monkey schools. The monkeys are first taught how to distinguish ripe from unripe coconuts, and then how to bite and spin the stems to release the fruit. Advance training includes placing poison on trees to kill rodents, and removing the master's shoes at naptime!

Several monkey-training schools are located near Surat Thani, but the most famous is 13 km southeast in the village of Ban Tha Thong. Established in 1985 with a 100,000B endowment from Princess Sirindhorn, Surat Thani Monkey Training School and trainer Somphorn Saekaew occasionally sponsor public demonstrations. The Surat Thani TAT office can advise on the next scheduled performance.

two hours by boat from Ko Samui.

Air: Thai Airways flies three times daily from Bangkok, once daily from Phuket, and twice daily from Chiang Mai. Thai Airways (tel. 077-272610) at 3/27 Karunraj Rd. provide minibus service to the airport.

Train: Trains depart nine times daily 0900-2155 from Hualampong Station in Bangkok. See the "Southern Thailand" introduction for more details.

The 1630 and 1920 overnight trains with sleepers are recommended, since they arrive in the early morning and allow plenty of time to catch a boat to Ko Samui. Advance reservations are strongly recommended.

The State Railways also sells combination tickets to Ko Samui which include all necessary train, bus, and boat connections.

Trains for Surat Thani terminate 14 km west in Phun Phin. Buses wait for passengers and then connect directly with Ko Samui. Advance reservations for trains departing from Phun Phin can be made at travel agencies on Ko Samui and in Surat Thani at Panipat Tours near the bus terminal. Travelers without reservations often need to stand for several hours until a seat is vacated.

Bus: Air-conditioned and ordinary buses depart from the Southern Bus Terminal in Thonburi daily 0700-0830 and 1900-2100, arriving in Surat Thani 11 hours later. Private bus companies in Bangkok offer VIP coaches with fewer seats and extra leg room. Most sell all-inclusive packages which include boat transportation to Ko Samui.

Direct bus and minibus service is also available from travel agents in Phuket, Krabi, Hat Yai, and Penang.

Boats To Ko Samui

Boat tickets to Ko Samui can be purchased at **Samui Tours** on Talad Mai Rd., and from **Songserm** agents near the waterfront on Na Muang Road. Samui Tours is slightly cheaper than Songserm. Boats depart daily 0730-1600 from either Don Sak Pier, 50 km east of Surat, or from Khanom, 60 km east. A slow, overnight boat departs at midnight from the pier in Surat Thani.

Tickets to Ko Phangan are sold at the office near the pier. The head office of Songserm Travel (tel. 077-272928) at 295 Talad Mai Rd. also sells tickets to Ko Samui and Ko Phangan.

KO SAMUI

Thailand's third-largest island (247 square km) lies in the warm seas of the gulf some 644 km south of Bangkok. With its long beaches of dazzling white sand, aquamarine waters, and sleepy lagoons fringed with palm trees, this tropical retreat has justifiably become one of Southeast Asia's premier beach resorts.

Ko Samui has, since the mid-18th century, been visited by Chinese merchants to trade for coconuts and cotton, the two traditional products of the Chao Samui, the local peoples. The island was opened to tourism in the late 1960s by shoestring travelers who found passage on coconut boats from Bangkok and trickled in to construct their simple thatched huts on deserted beaches. For over a decade, Samui remained an untouched paradise visited only by backpackers drifting up and down the overland trail between Bali and Kathmandu. This happy state of affairs ended in the early 1980s as the island's reputation attracted Thai and foreign developers who replaced the bamboo huts with middle-priced bungalows and luxury hotels geared strictly for well-heeled tourists.

Ko Samui today is a major tourist destination with some 500,000 annual visitors and over 240 hotels and bungalows lining the beaches. For better or for worse, since the opening of the airport in 1989 Samui has gone from backpacker's paradise to an upscale resort with all the glitz, glamour, and problems that plague other Thai beach destinations. Group tourists now vastly outnumber the backpackers, who have largely moved on to more remote destinations. Land prices on Samui are reputedly higher than on Australia's Gold Coast, and many of the simple, smiling coconut pickers have become slick millionaires more concerned with their pocketbook than traditional Chao Samui hospitality. The get-rich-quick mentality permeates the entire island: menus list cute dishes such as "fried prawn noodles sautéed in aromatic sauces—80 *baht*," which turns out to be *raht nah,* which sells for 15 *baht* elsewhere in Thailand.

KO SAMUI

© MOON PUBLICATIONS, INC.

0   3km

Despite all the changes, Ko Samui beaches remain absolutely spectacular, and the interior is still a tangled mess of jungle and coconut; a dazzling island that still ranks among the best of Southeast Asia.

Weather

Samui is best visited from January until the monsoons begin in September. Torrential rains often lash the island from October until late December; during these months try the islands on the west coast of southern Thailand.

NATHON

Nathon is Ko Samui's main commercial center and arrival point for express and night-boat passengers. The town has hotels, restaurants, travel agencies, souvenir shops, banks, dive shops, and other necessary services such as immigration and police.

Arrival

Boat arrivals at both Nathon and Thong Yang pier to the south are met by mini-truck drivers yelling "Chaweng, Chaweng, Chaweng!" or "Lamai, Lamai, Lamai!" Pick your beach and pay the fare; 20B to Chaweng, 15B to Lamai. Important: tell the driver which beach *and* bungalow you want to be dropped at, or expect to be dumped at an inconvenient location. Travelers unsure of their hotel should get off in the middle of the beach and then leave their bags at the closest restaurant before inspecting a few bungalows.

Travelers with minimal luggage might rent a motorcycle or jeep from one of the agencies in Nathon, and return the vehicle on departure.

Accommodations

Few travelers stay in Nathon except to catch an early morning boat back to Surat Thani.

Town Guesthouse: Two small and inexpensive guesthouses are located in the alley one block back from the pier. Both are usually deserted during the day. 140-180B.

Chao Ko Bungalows: North of town past the post office is a quiet operation with 20 comfortable if somewhat expensive bungalows. North Nathon, tel. (077) 421214, 300-600B.

Seaside Palace Hotel: The best place in town is overpriced but conveniently located near

the pier and restaurants. The unnamed hotel next door is a brothel. 152 Beach Rd., tel. (077) 421079, 300-350B fan, 400-600B a/c.

Services

Travelers staying on Ko Samui for an extended period will need to visit Nathon for services and official business.

Banks: Banks in Nathon are open daily 0800-1600, with outside exchange facilities open until 2200. Several banks also have branches at the more popular beaches. A useful message center is located at the Thai Farmers Bank on Beach Rd. near the pier.

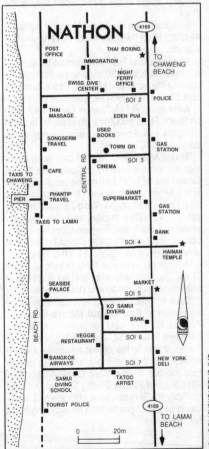

Mail: The Post and Telecommunications office (tel. 077-421013) at the northern end of the waterfront road handles mail, post restante, faxes, telegrams, and money transfers. The GPO is open Mon.-Fri. 0830-1630, and weekends 0830-1200.

Telephone: The Overseas Call Office upstairs from the post office is open Mon.-Fri. 0700-2200, and weekends 0830-1200. Phone calls can also be made from larger hotels throughout the island, and from metered phones in local markets and pharmacies. The cheapest place is the office in Nathon.

Police: The tourist police station (tel. 077-421281) south of the pier is open around the clock.

Hospital: The Ko Samui Hospital (tel. 077-421230) is on the main road, two km south of Nathon.

Immigration: Tourist visas can be extended for an additional 30 days at the immigration office in the north end of town. Visa extensions cost 500B and require two passport photos.

Airlines: Bangkok Airways (tel. 077-421196) on Beach Rd. distributes a timetable for flights to Bangkok (six times daily) and Phuket (once daily at 1230).

Travel Agencies: Over a dozen travel agencies are located in Nathon. **Songserm Travel Center** (tel. 077-421228) on the beachfront road is the largest outlet in town for boats to Surat Thani and Ko Phangan. **World Travel Service** (tel. 077-421475) is another major tour operator which can book transportation, confirm airline tickets, and book rooms at Samui hotels if you arrive without reservations. **Phantip Travel** (tel. 077-272230) sells car ferry tickets to Surat Thani. The night ferry office is in the north end of town near the highway and police station.

Dive Shops: Scuba divers can pick up information at **Koh Samui Divers** (tel. 077-421465, fax 077-421178) in the narrow alley between Beach Rd. and the highway. Koh Samui divers is the oldest and most experienced dive shop on the island. Other operators include **Swiss Dive Center** (tel. 077-421538) and **Samui Diving School**. All offer four-day PADI certification courses and multi-day dive packages to Ko Tao and Angthong National Park.

KO SAMUI ATTRACTIONS

Samui is about 70 km in circumference and can be easily toured in a single day. The following sights are described in counterclockwise order starting from Chaweng Beach. Samui's splendid scenery is best seen by rented car or motorcycle, but first, a word of caution. Motorcycle touring is deceptively dangerous. Far too many Westerners are killing or badly crippling themselves on the two-lane highway that circles the island. Please drive slowly, stay sober, and wear long pants, shoes, and a shirt to prevent sunburn and protect against minor scrapes.

Coconut Industry

Samui's claims to fame are the sandy beaches, clear waters, and thriving coconut industry which forms the traditional occupation of Samui's 35,000 residents. At times it seems the entire island is yanking down coconuts with long swaying sticks or burning huge piles of coconut shells. Watch for trained *ling gaeng* monkeys which deftly climb the palm trees, spin the coconut until it falls to the ground, and then return for their reward. Nearly every part of the coconut is used: flesh for eating, milk for cooking, and fiber for thatching and bed stuffing. Much of the fruit is converted into a sweet coconut oil, a process that requires scraping the meat from the shell, drying it for several weeks, and then pressing it with hydraulic machinery.

Almost every type of coconut tree grows on the island, including several two-headed mutants and one rare four-headed specimen near Mae Nam Beach; perhaps the only one in the world since it bears no nut.

Chong Mon Bay

Begin your tour with a motorcycle ride along the dirt road which hugs the coast to the arching bay at Chong Mon—a highly recommended route through fabulous scenery. A decade ago, the beach was lined with magnificent dry-docked fishing boats elegantly carved with gigantic rudders. Then—as it always seems to go in places like Samui—a hotel conglomerate purchased the boats and converted them into private chalets elevated on varnished supports. The bizarre effect detracts from the beach but certainly proves the creativity of Thai hoteliers.

Big Buddha Beach

Samui's famous 12-meter Big Buddha statue, surrounded by meditation huts elevated on stilts, is a few km west of Chong Mon and can be reached on the main road or along the dirt trails which skirt the coastline. Big Buddha Beach—more properly called Ao Bang Rak ("Bang Rak Bay")—is named after the image at Wat Hin Ngu which sits atop Ko Farn ("Barking Deer Island"), a tiny islet surrounded by polychrome Buddhas, the earth-goddess Torani, souvenir shops, and small cafes. Attached to the temple is a meditation center which offers instruction to Thais and *farangs*.

The road continues west past bungalows and hotels, boat service to Ko Phangan, and the turnoff to Ko Samui Airport and a meditation center tucked away under the mountains. Back on the highway, posterboards nailed to trees advertise upcoming buffalo fights, Thai kick boxing, and nightclubs with everything from reggae to world beat.

Bophut Beach

Bophut Beach has long been the backpacker's choice for its reasonably good sand, isolated location, and magic mushrooms which grew to mythical sizes and were served by local cafes in soups and omelets. Now, massive development has almost completely transformed the dusty wooden village into a continuous string of expensive bungalows and luxurious hotels that tower over the narrow beach. Asking for mushroom soup only brings quizzical looks and nostalgic stories about the good old days . . . pre-1987.

Bophut town is still worth a visit for its restaurants with French names, banking facilities, used bookstore, and boat connections to Ko Phangan. Beyond the dead-end road to the west are several bungalows still untouched by all this commercial activity.

Mae Nam Beach

Mae Nam Beach is 12 km from the ferry pier, midway between the principal town of Nathon and Chaweng Beach. The beach is long, narrow, somewhat coarse, and relatively untouched by mass tourism because of its isolation and because the main road essentially bypasses its beach. Visitors who want a look should drive up a dirt road to visit one of the bungalows. **Na-ture, Moon, Lolita, Mae Nam Resort,** and **Shangrila** are good places to stop for a meal and walk on the beach.

Ban Mae Nam, the commercial center, has several restaurants, hygienic bakery, laundries, medical clinic, gas station with fair prices, and a big monkey tied to the tree on the interior road.

Hin Lad Falls

The small set of waterfalls and bathing pools, two km south of Nathon, can be reached with a half-hour hike up a narrow pathway through thick jungle. Hin Lad is rather disappointing, but it provides the drinking water for Nathon.

Samui Highlands

Motorcyclists might *try* to follow the poorly maintained road just south of the Hin Lad turnoff to the top of the mountain where **Samui Highlands Bungalows** provides cold drinks, great views, and rooms with meals for 150B. The path climbs through a rubber plantation and fields of wildflowers to a park constructed by Khun Kosol, a man in his 60s who modeled his resort after Genting Highlands in Malaysia.

Emerald Cove

Phang Ka Bay, a very pretty and isolated cove at the southwest corner of Ko Samui, has several small bungalows in a magnificent setting of limestone peaks and swaying palms. **Pearl Bay** and **Seagull** bungalows provide a welcome escape from the commercialism of Samui.

The nearby beach at Tong Yang lacks the splendid sand of Chaweng and Lamai, but it does offer good corals and blazing sunsets over dragon-spired Angthong Marine National Park.

Thong Krut Beach

Longtail boats can be chartered from Thong Krut Beach to explore the nearby islands of Ko Katen ("Dog Island") and Ko Mat Sum. Both islands have coral beds on the eastern fringes. Snorkeling is best during low tides Aug.-April. A primitive set of bungalows is located on Ko Katen.

Wat Laem Sor

An unusual Indian-style *chedi* modeled after Bodgaya is situated on the isolated cape. The dirt road continues east past several modest bungalows to the Muslim fishing village of Ban Bang Kao.

Na Muang Falls

The best falls on Ko Samui are located past Ban Thurian, a village famous for its enormous durian trees which bear fruit in the hot summer months. Visited by several kings of the Chakri dynasty, the 30-meter falls are best experienced shortly after the rainy season ends in December or January.

Hua Thanon

Located about 200 meters from this small Chinese fishing village are several coral blocks carved in Buddha images. One km farther is Silangu, with a venerated pagoda reputed to enshrine a bone fragment of the Buddha. Traditional *vipassana* meditation courses geared to Western visitors are occasionally sponsored at Silangu.

Phallic Rocks

Hin Yai and Hin Ta ("Grandfather Rock" and "Grandmother Rock") are geological oddities located at the south end of Lamai Beach that closely resemble enormous sexual organs. A large and humorously mislabeled sign "Wonderfull Rock" shows the way to the curious formations.

Lamai Cultural Hall

Wat Lamai at the north end of Lamai Beach features a small cultural center dedicated to the arts and crafts of the Chao Samui, the local inhabitants who consider themselves different than their northern cousins. The wooden showroom is filled with old lanterns, gramophones, pottery recovered from shipwrecks, *nang talang* buffalo-hide puppets, and agricultural implements used in the coconut industry.

Angthong Marine National Park

The beautiful archipelago of Angthong ("Golden Basin") northwest of Ko Samui comprises 40 islands covering 250 square kilometers. Once an experimental training ground for the Royal Thai Navy, Angthong was declared a marine national park in 1980 to protect the coral beds and short-bodied mackerel which spawn in the surrounding waters from February to April. The park has dozens of pristine beaches, aquamarine bays, and islands named after whimsical forms such as Broken Stone, Rhinoceros, Camera Head, and Tree Sorrow Island.

Tours from Nathon include stops at various coral reefs for snorkeling before arriving at the main island, where visitors can climb to the top of a 240-meter hill for panoramic views of lakes and islands. The boat continues to a second island with a crystal-green saltwater lake connected to the sea with a subterranean tunnel.

Tour agencies in Nathon and other Samui beaches offer day-trips 0800-1730 to Angthong Park for 250-300B, including soft drinks and snorkeling equipment.

Accommodations are available on Ko Wua Ta Lap ("Sleeping Cow Island") at the National Park Headquarters. Two-man tents or dormitory space in 20-man bungalows cost 100-150B per night. Camping elsewhere is free, since the island is under the supervision of the National Park Service. A small restaurant and freshwater lake are also located on the main island.

KO SAMUI ACCOMMODATIONS

Ko Samui has a half-dozen beaches in various stages of development and with distinct personalities. Chaweng Beach and Lamai Beach on the east coast are the most popular beaches for good reasons: best sand, longest uninterrupted terrain, and ideal climate. North-coast beaches such as Bophut and Menam are quieter and less expensive, but the sand isn't as white or plentiful. Robinson Crusoe types might check the isolated bungalows on the west and south coasts.

Each beach appeals to different types of travelers, depending on their finances and desired ambience. One possible plan of action is to spend your first few days on Chaweng or Lamai, then move to a more isolated beach if you crave solitude and want to escape the beer gardens, discos, and pick-up bars.

Ko Samui beaches offer all ranges of accommodations, from cheap shacks under 100B to luxurious hotels with landscaped gardens and swimming pools. Basic wooden huts with electricity, mosquito net, and common bath charge 60-150B. Most of these original hippie huts have been torn down and replaced with better bungalows with tiled rooms, verandas, private baths, and comfortable mattresses. These cost 300-600B during the slow season, and generally double in the high summer months and Christmas holidays. Many of these middle-priced bungalows represent extraordinary value when you consider the comfort level and fabulous beach just a few steps away. Air-conditioned bungalows with fancy restaurants and manicured gardens cost 800-1500B, while luxury hotels over 2000B per night are now commonplace on most beaches.

Samui bungalows have evolved into a veritable patchwork of huts and chalets in various styles and prices. For example, Joy Bungalows—one of the first sets of huts on the island—offers old hippie huts at 200B, duplexes with fans at 500B, large family rooms for 700B, and a/c suites from 1000B. Another curious phenomenon is that low-end cheapies are often wedged between expensive hotels, such as K John Bungalows for 150B adjacent to Samui Villa Flora for 2200B.

Recommending a specific hotel is a difficult task, since room quality, price, and overall value vary widely at almost every property. A sensible compromise for budget travelers is to stay at the cheapest room in a moderate-priced hotel. High season can be an extremely difficult time to find a room; expect to take an expensive room until cheaper bungalows are vacated. Reservations are best made by fax rather than phone to avoid miscommunications with reception personnel.

All hotels listed below, except for inexpensive bungalows, add 11% tax and 10% service charge.

CHAWENG BEACH

Chaweng Beach—Ko Samui's longest and prettiest stretch of sand—is almost completely blanketed with bungalows, hotels, restaurants, dive shops, convenience stores, and nightclubs, and yet has somehow managed to keep a reasonably mellow atmosphere. During the day you can wander the beach without bumping into hordes of people, and nightlife remains limited to a few discos and open-air restaurants which screen the latest videos. Chaweng is now very middle class, but there's no denying

the beauty of the beach and brilliance of the water. Budget travelers can still find huts in the 60-150B range.

The six-km curving beach is divided into three sections: Chaweng Noi (Little Chaweng to the south), Chaweng Yai (Big Chaweng in the center), and North Chaweng Yai (Big Chaweng to the north).

South Chaweng Noi Beach

Chaweng Noi (Little Chaweng) is a small arching bay at the southern end of Chaweng Beach. Somewhat isolated and less crowded than the central region, Chaweng Noi has both cheap shacks and luxurious hotels, described below from south to north.

Tropicana Beach Resort: A moderately priced hotel elevated on a cliff above the south end of the beach. 4 Moo 3 Chaweng Noi Beach, tel. (077) 421137, 1000-1400B.

Thawee, Maeo, and Chaweng Noi Bungalows: Three sets of cheap bungalows are wedged at the southern end of the beach. All are friendly places popular with budget travelers for over a decade. 50-250B.

Imperial Samui: Ko Samui entered the big leagues with the construction of this enormous Mediterranean-style property in the mid-1980s. Operated by a Thai-owned hotel chain, the Imperial has several restaurants, swimming pools, and workers frantically adding sandbags to save the eroding beachwall. Ban Chaweng Noi, tel. (077) 421390, fax (077) 421378, Bangkok reservations (02) 254-0023, 2600-4000B.

Fair House: A very popular midlevel spot on squeaky-clean sand. As with most other bungalows at Chaweng, Fair House has older huts in the bargain category and more expensive chalets added in the last few years. The trend has been toward more expensive rooms, so expect the low-end choices to rapidly disappear. 4/3 Chaweng Beach, tel. (077) 421373, 450-1200B.

First Bungalows: Good location midway between the two beaches. The office and restaurant are on Chaweng Yai; the bungalows are across the bridge on Chaweng Noi. Tel. 421444, 500-1000B.

Central Chaweng Yai Beach

Central Chaweng Yai is a superb beach with great sand, clean water, sailboarding schools, dive shops, entertainment from video shows to

Thai classical dance, dozens of reasonably priced bungalows, and an increasing number of luxurious hotels. A handful of cheap huts in the 100-300B range are hanging on, but their lives are limited. The accompanying map and hotel chart shows the range of possibilities.

The mini-truck from Nathon takes the southern turnoff to the beach near First Bungalows and continues north up the beachside road until it terminates at Samui Cabana. Travelers should tell the driver which hotel to stop at or expect to be dropped at the northern end. Charlies is a centrally located guesthouse with over 100 low-priced rooms; a good place to start your bungalow search.

The following representative bungalows and hotels are described from south to north.

White House and the Village: The White House and two nearby properties—the Village and Princess Village—are owned and operated by a Swiss hotel manager and a female Thai architect who run the best midpriced places on Chaweng Beach. The White House and the Village are identically priced; the Village is a newer and better choice. Chaweng Beach, Box 25, tel. (077) 421382, 1200-1800B.

Munchies Resort: A longtime favorite whose name harks back to the days of mushroom omelets and magic brownies, no longer available in their cozy restaurant. 17 Chaweng Beach, tel. (077) 421374, 300-600 fan, 1000-1500B a/c chalets.

Joy Resort: All types of rooms including 30 comfortable chalets with private verandas. 28 Group 3 Chaweng Beach, tel. and fax (077) 421376, 200B old hippie bungalows, 500B fan duplex, 700-900B family rooms, 1000-1200B a/c suites.

Samui Pansea Resort: A stunning set of bungalows connected with wooden walkways and surrounded by tropical foliage. Tons of charm; a much better choice than the expensive hotels to the north. 38/2 Moo 3 Chaweng Beach, tel. (077) 421384, fax (077) 421385, 2200-3800B.

ADDITONAL CHAWENG BEACH ACCOMMODATIONS

North Chaweng Beach

Antara Hotel	2500-3500B
Era House	400-600B
Samui Villa Flora	1800-2600B
Venus	350-450B

Central Chaweng Yai Beach

Best Beach	200-300B
B.O.P.	300-500B
Central Bay Resort	600-1200B
Chaba	1600-2200B
Chaweng Cabana	1600-1800B
Chaweng Cove	1600-2000B
Chaweng Guesthouse	500-1200B
Chaweng Resort	1600-2400B
Chaweng Top Beach	500-800B
Chaweng Villa	300-1000B
Coconut Grove	200-500B
Coral Park	150-250B

Kings	600-800B
Long Beach	250-400B
Lotus	250-400B
Milky Way	100-150B
Montien	200-300B
Natural	80-100B
Samui Cabana	400-600B
Samui Coral Resort	250-350B
Samui Country Resort	400-1000B
Sang Tip	800-1500B
Seaside	300-400B
Silver Sand	100-800B
Sun East	300-400B
Thai	150-200B
Wisan	200-300B

South Chaweng Noi Beach

New Star	1500-1800B
Sunshine Resort	400-1000B
Victorian Resort	2500-3500B

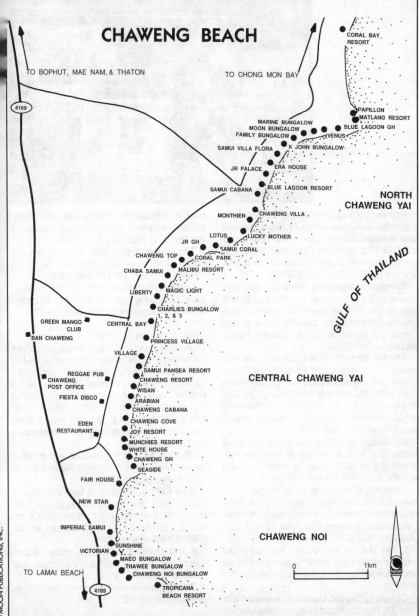

CHAWENG BEACH

TO BOPHUT, MAE NAM, & THATON

TO CHONG MON BAY

4169

CORAL BAY RESORT

PAPILLON
MATLANG RESORT
BLUE LAGOON GH

MARINE BUNGALOW
MOON BUNGALOW
FAMILY BUNGALOW
VENUS
SAMUI VILLA FLORA
K JOHN BUNGALOW

JR PALACE
ERA HOUSE

SAMUI CABANA
BLUE LAGOON RESORT

NORTH
CHAWENG YAI

MONTHIEN
CHAWENG VILLA

LOTUS
LUCKY MOTHER

JR GH
SAMUI CORAL

CHAWENG TOP
SAMUI PARK
CORAL PARK

CHABA SAMUI
MALIBU RESORT

LIBERTY
MAGIC LIGHT

CHARLIES BUNGALOW
1, 2, & 3

CENTRAL BAY

GREEN MANGO
CLUB
BAN CHAWENG

PRINCESS VILLAGE

VILLAGE

SAMUI PANSEA RESORT

REGGAE PUB
CHAWENG
POST OFFICE

CHAWENG RESORT
WISAN

CENTRAL CHAWENG YAI

FIESTA DISCO

ARABIAN
CHAWENG CABANA

EDEN
RESTAURANT

CHAWENG COVE
JOY RESORT
MUNCHIES RESORT
WHITE HOUSE
CHAWENG GH
SEASIDE

FAIR HOUSE

NEW STAR

IMPERIAL SAMUI

SUNSHINE

VICTORIAN

MAEO BUNGALOW
THAWEE BUNGALOW
CHAWENG NOI BUNGALOW

CHAWENG NOI

TO LAMAI BEACH

4169

TROPICANA
BEACH RESORT

GULF OF THAILAND

0   1km

© MOON PUBLICATIONS, INC.

Princess Village: A rare chance to sleep in traditional teak houses from Ayuthaya, restored and elevated over lily ponds. This unique creation of Thai architect Patcharee Smith has great character. Chaweng Beach Box 25, tel. and fax (077) 421382, 2400-3600B.

Charlies Bungalows: The largest travelers' center on Ko Samui now has three extremely popular branches with over 100 low-priced bungalows. Still owned and operated by the famous Teera, also known as Mama. Chaweng Beach, no phone, 100-250B.

Malibu Resort: Good upstairs bar with happy-hour prices, and home to Ko Samui Divers, with organized dives to Angthong Marine Park (1750B), one-day introductory (2500B), three days at Ko Tao (5000B), and three-day PADI certification (8500B). Chaweng Beach, tel. (077) 421386, 450-700B.

JR Bungalows: Beautiful shady courtyard, palms, and ferns make this an excellent low-priced choice. 90/1 Chaweng Beach, tel. (077) 421401, fax (077) 421402, 250-550B.

Chaweng Garden: Attractive bungalows arranged abstractly rather than in uniform lines, plus a decent restaurant and a few surfboards lying around. Chaweng Beach, tel. 421403, 350-500B fan, 900-1000B a/c.

Lucky Mother: Very popular and well-priced bungalows facing a beautiful sandy courtyard and swaying palms. Highly recommended. 80-300B.

Chaweng Regent: Luxurious new resort with over 70 Thai-style cottages, amoeba-shaped pool, and natural swimming area behind offshore rock barriers. 155/4 Chaweng Beach, tel. and fax (077) 286910, 2800-4500B.

The Island: High-quality rooms at very low prices. Recommended. Box 52, tel. (077) 421288, fax (077) 421178, 300-600B.

Louis Bungalows: Decrepit huts (no electricity, no running water, no furniture), but some of the wildest people on the island. 50-70B.

North Chaweng Yai Beach

Chaweng's finest and most intimate bungalows are tucked along the shallow bay north of the last cape, the most beautiful stretch of sand on Ko Samui. Conditions are ideal for wading in the shallow waters, sailboarding, swinging from a rope suspended from a leaning coconut tree, and just staring out to Matlang Island. Minitrucks continue by request to the following bungalows and hotels.

JR Palace: Wild architecture and creative interior decorations distinguish this well-priced set of bungalows. 300-600B.

Blue Lagoon Resort: A luxury hotel with beautiful pool, open-air restaurant, and 61 Thai-style bungalows and hotel complex. Also, a pet elephant. 99 Moo 2 Chaweng Beach, tel. and fax (077) 421401, 2800-6000B.

K John Bungalows: Unusual octagonal bungalows, pet monkey, and friendly management. Recommended. 150-250B.

Family Bungalows: Very good value for budget travelers. 50-150B.

Moon Bungalows: Well-named operation with a comfortable cafe. 150-300B.

Marine Bungalows: Another inexpensive place with decent bungalows. As with most other Chaweng spots, videos are shown nightly in their breezy restaurant. 150-300B.

Matlang Resort: Tucked away at the far northern corner of the beach are several spots well removed from the commercialism of central Chaweng. Matlang, Samui Island, and Papillon are welcome escapes at fair prices. 400-1200B.

LAMAI BEACH

Ko Samui's second most popular beach has been developed in a rather haphazard manner with little thought to traffic patterns or hotel aesthetics. The beach is long and beautiful, and a visit can be made to the fishing village at the north end, but bungalows in the central region are packed closely together and the nightlife is turning toward noisy discos and bar girls—a bad sign. And with all the tax dollars flowing into local coffers, government authorities can certainly afford to pave the dusty roads and hire a crew to pick up trash from the beach. The get-rich-quick and me-first mentality is quite evident at Lamai.

Dozens of bungalows crowd the center but those isolated on the hills to the east are quieter and more relaxing. Unlike Chaweng Beach, Lamai still has a good supply of inexpensive bungalows in the 80-150B range. Budget travelers should check the western end of the beach (Noi, White Sand, Samui Pearl) and just east of the central beach (Marine Park, My Friend, New Huts, Tapi).

Mini-trucks terminate in the center near the restaurants and bars. Lamai has all possible services, including money exchanges, supermarkets, bookstores, motorcycle and jeep rentals, and countless bars and discos that rage on until dawn. The following places are described from west to east.

Rocky Chalet: Just beyond Lamai is a popular and very private place run by two Germans, Linn and Erwin Werrena, on a private beach with scuba diving facilities. Nearby Rocky Bungalows is also recommended as a quiet escape from the noise of Lamai. 438 Lamai Beach, 400-900B.

Noi Bungalows: Many of the cheaper places are located at the south end of Lamai on narrow but very private beaches. Noi is owned by a Thai-Swiss couple who cater to singles and families. 80-300B.

White Sand Bungalows: Backpackers' favorite with cheap huts. 50-80B.

Samui Pearl: Another old favorite with original hippie huts and more expensive bungalows. Paradise and Buffalo Bill are similar. 60-250B.

Casanova Resort: Huge rooms elevated on a hillside, lovely restaurant, and stunning swimming pool make this a good choice in the middle price range. 124 Lamai Beach, tel. (077) 421425, 800-1000B.

Marina Villa 1: Nothing outstanding but conveniently located in the center of Lamai near the restaurants and nightclubs. 250-350B.

Lamai Inn 99: Central location, beautiful grassy grounds, and inexpensive huts without fans make this a good choice. Lamai Beach, tel. (077) 421427, 150-600B.

Coconut Villa: Over 50 big bungalows, all with private baths. 124/4 Lamai Beach, tel. (077) 421424, 200-250B.

ADDITIONAL LAMAI BEACH ACCOMMODATIONS

Swiss Chalet	400-900B	Golden Sand	300-800B	Samui Laguna	2000-2500B
Nice	80-250B	Miramare	200-300B	Sand and Sea	600-1200B
Palm	80-300B	Best	300-600B	Lamai Villa	150-250B
Paradise	60-200B	Animal House	400-700B	Sukasame	200-250B
Buffalo Bills	60-200B	Coconut	80-120B	Rose Garden	180-1000B
Phai Garden	100-150B	Weekender	150-800B	Comfort	200-400B
Aloha	300-1200B	Magic	200-500B	Tong Gaid	300-500B
		Royal Marina	400-500B		

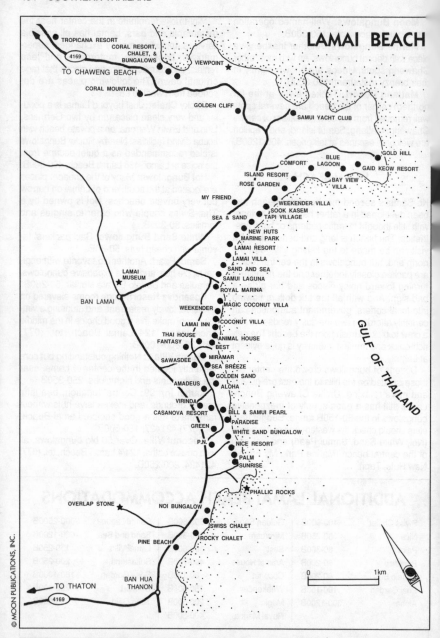

LAMAI BEACH

TROPICANA RESORT
CORAL RESORT, CHALET, & BUNGALOWS
VIEWPOINT
4169
TO CHAWENG BEACH
CORAL MOUNTAIN
GOLDEN CLIFF
SAMUI YACHT CLUB
GOLD HILL
COMFORT
BLUE LAGOON
GAID KEOW RESORT
ISLAND RESORT
BAY VIEW VILLA
ROSE GARDEN
MY FRIEND
WEEKENDER VILLA
SOOK KASEM
SEA & SAND
TAPI VILLAGE
NEW HUTS
MARINE PARK
LAMAI RESORT
LAMAI MUSEUM
LAMAI VILLA
SAND AND SEA
SAMUI LAGUNA
BAN LAMAI
ROYAL MARINA
MAGIC COCONUT VILLA
WEEKENDER
COCONUT VILLA
LAMAI INN
ANIMAL HOUSE
THAI HOUSE FANTASY
BEST
MIRAMAR
SAWASDEE
SEA BREEZE
GOLDEN SAND
AMADEUS
ALOHA
VIRINDA
BILL & SAMUI PEARL
CASANOVA RESORT
PARADISE
GREEN
WHITE SAND BUNGALOW
P.N.
NICE RESORT
PALM
SUNRISE
PHALLIC ROCKS

GULF OF THAILAND

OVERLAP STONE
NOI BUNGALOW
SWISS CHALET
PINE BEACH
ROCKY CHALET
BAN HUA THANON
TO THATON
4169

0   1km

© MOON PUBLICATIONS, INC.

Pavilion Resort: The most luxurious resort in central Lamai features large octagonal suites and a beautiful pool. Lamai Beach, tel. and fax (077) 421420, 1200-1800B.

Marine Park, New Huts, and Tapi Bungalows: Three places with aging A-frames, good music, and the feel of Lamai a decade ago. Nearby My Friend and No Name bungalows are also cheap and very popular. Recommended for budget travelers. 80-120B.

Weekender Villa: All bungalows face a beautiful inner courtyard lined with sandy walkways and palms. Very good value. Box 4 Lamai Beach, tel. (077) 421372, 200-250B.

Bay View Villa: Stunning restaurant and idyllic location make the Bay View one of the finest places away from central Lamai. Highly recommended. North Lamai Beach, tel. (077) 272222, 200-300B.

Blue Lagoon: Upscale hotel complex with inexpensive small bungalows, a/c suites, and an attractive pool. North Lamai Beach, tel. (077) 421178, 400-2400B.

Gaid Keow Resort: The final spot on north Lamai features a small pool on the wooden deck and bungalows overlooking a stony beach. Quiet and relaxing. 146 North Lamai Beach, tel. (077) 272222, 300-400B.

NORTH COAST BEACHES

Chong Mon Beach

Ko Samui's prettiest bay is a graceful crescent with excellent sand and offshore islands with deserted beaches. Chong Mon was considered well off the beaten track until the 1990 opening of the immense Imperial Chong Mon Resort, which creatively utilized the old fishing boats which once lined the bay. Chong Mon now has regular mini-truck service from Nathon and Chaweng Beach.

Sun Sand Resort: A superb arrangement of 33 individual bungalows, breezy restaurant, and stunning views over Chong Mon Bay have made this resort a popular choice with European group tours. Highly recommended. Chong Mon Beach, tel. (077) 421024, fax (077) 421322, 950-1200B.

P.S. Villa: The spotless bungalows, spacious lawns, and bamboo restaurant make this the best bargain on the beach. Chong Mon Beach, tel. (077) 286956, 200-400B.

Chat Kaeo Resort: Small but very pretty bungalows at reasonable cost. 59/4 Chong Mon Beach, no phone, 400-450B fan, 800-1000B a/c.

Choeng Mon Bungalows: Three classes of bungalows which increase in price the closer to the beach. Chong Mon Beach, no phone, 200-400B.

Imperial Tongsai Bay: A super-exclusive Mediterranean-style hotel with 24 hotel rooms and 48 individual a/c cottages overlooking a private beach just north of Chong Mon Bay. Facilities include a free-form saltwater pool, landscaping tended by an army of gardeners, several restaurants, and all possible water sports.

Lamai Beach

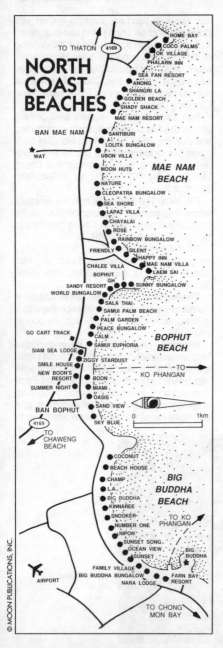

NORTH COAST BEACHES

TO THATON 4169
HOME BAY
COCO PALMS
OK VILLAGE
PHALARN INN
SEA FAN RESORT
ANONG
SHANGRI LA
GOLDEN BEACH
SHADY SHACK
MAE NAM RESORT
BAN MAE NAM
SANTIBURI
LOLITA BUNGALOW
WAT
UBON VILLA
MOON HUTS   MAE NAM BEACH
NATURE
CLEOPATRA BUNGALOW
SEA SHORE
LAPAZ VILLA
CHAYALAI
ROSE
RAINBOW BUNGALOW
FRIENDLY   SILENT
HAPPY INN
MAE NAM VILLA
CHALEE VILLA
BOPHUT   LAEM SAI
GH
SANDY RESORT   SUNNY BUNGALOW
WORLD BUNGALOW
SALA THAI
SAMUI PALM BEACH
PALM GARDEN
GO CART TRACK   PEACE BUNGALOW
CALM
SAMUI EUPHORIA   BOPHUT BEACH
SIAM SEA LODGE
ZIGGY STARDUST
SMILE HOUSE   TO
NEW BOON'S   BOON   KO PHANGAN
RESORT
MIAMI
SUMMER NIGHT
OASIS
SAND VIEW
BAN BOPHUT
4169   SKY BLUE
TO
CHAWENG
BEACH

0   1km

COCONUT
BEACH HOUSE
CHAMP
L.A.   BIG
BIG BUDDHA   BUDDHA
KINNAREE   BEACH
SNOOKER
NUMBER ONE   TO KO
NIPON   PHANGAN
SUNSET SONG
OCEAN VIEW
SUNSET   BIG
FAMILY VILLAGE   BUDDHA
BIG BUDDHA BUNGALOW   FARN BAY
AIRPORT   NARA LODGE   RESORT

TO CHONG
MON BAY

© MOON PUBLICATIONS, INC.

One of the most spectacular resorts in the world. Ban Plailaem, Bophut, tel. (077) 421451, fax (077) 421462, 4800-8000B.

Big Buddha Beach

Ao Bang Rak—more commonly called Big Buddha after the nearby image—offers almost a dozen inexpensive to moderate bungalows on an arching beach which is narrow and brownish but generally deserted. Bungalows are clean and comfortable, though beach conditions and noise from highway traffic here make Bophut and Mae Nam beaches more idyllic locations.

Dive facilities are available at the Champ Villa, where the **Swiss Dive Center** organizes one-day dives for 1500B.

Boats to Ko Phangan depart near the Buddha daily at 1530 and return from Had Rin on Ko Phangan at 0930.

Farn Bay Resort: An expensive hotel with Thai dance shows on weekends. But, as their brochure claims, "No more hustle-bustles, no more pollution, no more rat-race." Big Buddha Beach, tel. (077) 273920, 1000-1600B.

Nara Lodge: An American-operated hotel with renovated rooms, pool, and ambience popular with families. Box 9, tel. (077) 421364, 950-1500B.

Big Buddha Bungalows: Large new wooden bungalows and friendly management make this one of the best bargains on the beach. Recommended. Big Buddha Beach, no phone, 200-300B.

Sunset Song: Another inexpensive place with clean rooms, big porches, and comfortable cafe. Big Buddha Beach, tel. (077) 421363, 150-200B.

Number One: German management under Dim and Hans. Good value. Big Buddha Beach, no phone, 150-250B.

Kinnaree Bungalows: Large bungalows somewhat crammed together, but the cheapest spot on the beach. Big Buddha Beach, no phone, 80-120B.

Bophut Beach

Travelers who want to escape the congestion of Chaweng or Lamai will find Bophut an acceptable alternative. The narrow and coarse beach isn't as impressive as Chaweng or Lamai, but many visitors consider the friendly people and sense of isolation adequate compensation. Bophut also has wonderful sunsets.

ADDITIONAL NORTH COAST BEACHES ACCOMMODATIONS

Big Buddha Beach

Beach House	150-200B
Champ Villa	400-1000B
Como	60-100B
Family	100-500B
Fledgling	150-200B
L.A.	150-300B
Nipon	200-600B
Ocean View	600-800B
Snooker	150-250B

Bophut Beach

Boon Bungalows	60-100B
Bophut Guesthouse	150-300B
Calm	100-250B
New Boon's Resort	150-250B
Sala Thai	150-250B
Samui Euphoria	1800-2500B
Samui Palm Beach	1800-2500B

Sand View	100-150B
Sandy Resort	400-1000B
Siam Sea Lodge	550-800B
Sky Blue	60-80B

Mae Nam Beach

Anong Villa	80-300B
Chaya Lai	1000-1800B
Friendly	300-400B
Home Bay	80-300B
Nature	60-100B
New Lapaz Villa	60-200B
OK Village	100-200B
Phalarn Inn	100-200B
Silent	80-150B
Rose	40-60B
Sea Shore	100-300B
Santiburi	1500-2500B
Shady Shack	80-200B

Bophut town has a branch of Siam Commercial Bank, Reader Mate Bookstore, and several restaurants with Thai and European dishes. Cafes here once served the most potent magic mushroom soups on the island, but the banning of psychedelics in 1989 forced the trade over to Ko Phangan and Ko Tao.

Bophut is a convenient departure point for Ko Phangan. The *Hadrin Queen* departs daily at 0900 and 1300 for Had Rin Beach on the southeast corner of the island. The "Midnight Express" taxi service leaves Bophut nightly at 2200 and returns from the discos on Chaweng and Lamai beaches at around 0300-0400.

Basic bungalows and midlevel hotels are situated in the town, but bungalows farther down the beach are quieter and located on better sand. Bophut remains cheaper than Chaweng or Lamai, but bungalows have sharply raised rates in recent years and expensive hotels are arriving in rapid order.

Smile House: At the edge of town is a very clean place with small fan-cooled bungalows and pricier a/c chalets, plus a wonderful pool surrounded by palms. Bophut Beach, tel. (077) 421361, 350-1250B.

Ziggy Stardust: Beautiful Lanna-style bungalows, lovely garden, and popular restaurant make Ziggy's a great choice for midlevel travelers. Bophut Beach, no phone, 450-1250B.

Peace Bungalows: A longtime favorite located away from town on a quieter stretch of sand. Low-end bungalows are dismal, but those in the 250-400B range are clean and comfortable. Large restaurant and friendly management. Bophut Beach, tel. and fax (077) 421357, 150-600B.

World Bungalows: One of the most popular and reasonably priced places at Bophut features a small swimming pool, lush gardens, and a luxurious restaurant facing the deserted beach. A great place to escape the crowds. Bophut Beach, tel. and fax (077) 421355, 150-250B small bungalows, 550-650B large bungalows, 900-1000B a/c chalets.

Sunny Bungalows: Very popular for its adequate if rudimentary bungalows and isolated location at the end of the beach. Bophut Beach, tel. (077) 421486, 80-150B.

Mae Nam Beach
Mae Nam is an isolated and relatively undeveloped beach located midway between Nathon and Chaweng Beach. Over a dozen inexpensive to mid-level bungalows on this beach are signposted on the main highway. Well hidden behind scrub and jungle, most offer quiet rooms facing a deserted beach and a relaxed atmosphere ideal for reading and relaxation. Beaches are narrow, but the solitude and remote location are quite appealing.

The following spots are described from east to west.

Laem Sai and Mae Nam Villa: Both of these inexpensive and very popular guesthouses are located at the end of the cape which forms the extreme southern end of Ao Mae Nam (Mae Nam Bay). Both are difficult to reach without private transportation but well suited to determined escapists and families with children. Mae Nam Beach, no phones, 80-250B.

Rainbow: Good-value bungalows constructed with brick and wood. Bophut Beach, 60-200B.

Cleopatra: Friendly and inexpensive spot with older but adequate huts. Mae Nam Beach, 100-250B.

Moon Huts: Attractive bamboo bungalows, an elevated restaurant with views, and a brilliant stretch of sand make well-named Moon a good choice. Recommended. 67/2 Mae Nam Beach, no phone, 200-250B.

Lolita Bungalows: Lolita boasts an excellent beach with stunning palms, easy access to the town of Ban Mae Nam, and decent bungalows in all possible price ranges. Mae Nam Beach, no phone, 100-700B.

Mae Nam Resort: Beautiful bungalows, comfortable restaurant, and grassy landscapes make this the best midpriced resort at Mae Nam Beach. Highly recommended. Mae Nam Beach, tel. (077) 272222, 200-500B.

Shangrila: Inexpensive bungalows, new restaurant, and safe swimming make Shangrila popular with families. Mae Nam Beach, no phone, 80-200B.

Sea Fan Resort: A fully developed resort complex with luxurious cottages, pool, and sports activities on a remote and almost completely unspoiled beach; the best choice for upscale travelers. Mae Nam Beach, tel. and fax (077) 421350, 3000-3500B.

Coco Palms Village: Escape the crowds at the west end of the beach. Coco Palms is a friendly place with great meals prepared by a Western chef. Good value, plus dazzling aquamarine waters. Mae Nam Beach, no phone, 400-600B.

SOUTH COAST BEACHES

The south and west sides of Ko Samui are characterized by stony landscapes with minimal beaches, but they offer the last possible relief from the crowds which fill the more popular beaches on the west and north shores.

The following bungalows and hotels are described from west to east, starting with Emerald Bay and ending at the town of Ban Hua Thanon.

Sea Gull and Pearl Bay Bungalows: Emerald Bay (Pungka Beach) is a stunning destination tucked away at the southwest corner of Ko Samui. En route to the beach you'll pass the rather mundane Emerald Cove Bungalows and Gem's House. The road terminates at several wonderful spots on a sandy beach flanked by striking limestone mountains. Both hotels above have rooms for 80-300B.

Thong Krut Bungalows: Nisit and Nu run a decent place with fishing tours, snorkeling boats, and seaside bungalows for 150-300B.

Diamond Villa Bungalows: Small but new huts with volleyball net and snorkeling from April to August when the seas are calm and tides low. 80-120B.

River Garden Bungalows: A great place with friendly managers, good beach, and small river with wading fisherwomen. Recommended. Bang Kao Bay, 100-150B.

Laem Set Inn: Luxurious resort with elevated bungalows and surly management. International reviews seem to have gone to their heads. 100 Moo 2, Hua Thanon, Laem Set Beach, tel. (077) 281430, 2400-8500B.

Samui Orchid Resort: A fabulous resort hidden away on a 25-acre coconut plantation. Features two large swimming pools, luxurious restaurant, and small but well-appointed bungalows on a deserted beach. Reservations and transportation can be arranged at their Seaside Palace Hotel in Nathon. Ban Harn Beach, tel. (077) 421079, 650-1400B.

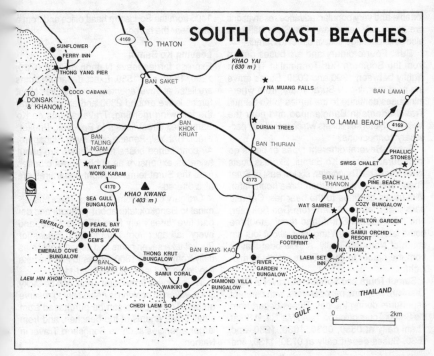

SOUTH COAST BEACHES

Cozy Bungalows: Inexpensive huts set on grassy grounds under swaying palms. Well located within walking distance of an interesting fishing village. Recommended. Ban Harn Beach, 150-250B.

Natta Guesthouse: A small guesthouse is in the colorful fishing village of Ban Hua Thanon, the only Muslim community on Ko Samui and a good place to experience traditional life rather than a tourist ghetto. 40-80B.

TRANSPORTATION

Getting There
Ko Samui is 644 km south of Bangkok and 84 km northeast of Surat Thani.

Ko Samui can be reached by air, train, bus, and boat. Travel agents in Bangkok sell package tickets which include all necessary transfers and boat connections. Although tours are the easiest way to reach Ko Samui, independent travelers will have few problems reaching the

island on their own. Ko Samui is a major tourist destination, and transportation touts are always there to greet you, take your hand, guide you to the appropriate connection, show you to your seat, collect your money, and deliver you to Samui. No need to worry about confusing place-names or variable schedules—someone is *always* there to point the way. Don't you just love Thailand?

Air: Bangkok Airways (tel. 02-255-8964 in Bangkok) at 144 Sukumvit Rd. flies from Bangkok to Ko Samui six times daily and once daily from Phuket. Thai Airways International flies from Bangkok to Surat Thani three times daily, once daily from Phuket, and twice weekly from Chiang Mai. Airport transfers to the Surat Thani pier are included in the price of the one-way ticket.

Train: The State Railway has rapid trains with sleepers from Bangkok to Surat Thani (Phun Phin Station) at 1730, 1830, and 1920. All arrive early enough to catch the 0730 boat to Ko Samui. Overnight trains with sleepers are comfortable and very popular; advance reservations are *absolutely* necessary. The State Railways also sells package tickets direct to Samui.

Bus: Four ordinary and a/c buses depart from the Southern Bus Terminal in Thonburi nightly between 1900 and 2030. Buses arrive the next morning in Surat Thani, from where minibuses continue to the ferries to Ko Samui. Travel agents in Banglampoo and near the Malaysia Hotel sell tickets which include all necessary connections.

Ferry: Several different types of boats go from Surat Thani to Ko Samui. Express boats leave from Tha Thong pier, six km east of Surat Thani, and arrive at Nathon three hours later. Mini-trucks continue to the beaches. Car and passenger ferries depart from Don Sak pier, one hour east of Surat, and terminate three hours later at Thong Yang jetty, about four km south of Nathon. Finally, a slow boat leaves from the harbor in Surat Thani nightly at midnight.

Samui Tours and **Songserm Travel** in Surat Thani are the principal operators, with different departures during the day. Buses depart from the Samui Tours office on Talad Mai Rd. in Surat Thani daily at 0650, 0830, 1030, 1230, and 1530. Buses depart daily at 0730, 1130, and 1400 from the Songserm head office and from a stop near the harbor.

Leaving Ko Samui

Express ferries leave Nathon daily at 0730, 1200, 1330, and 1530. Exact departure times are listed at travel agencies near the pier. Night ferries leave around 2300 and arrive in Surat the following morning. Travel agents on Ko Samui sell direct tickets to Bangkok, Phuket, Krabi, Hat Yai, Penang, and even Singapore. Air-conditioned buses from Nathon are about twice as expensive as public non-a/c buses from the Surat terminal. Night departures are also offered.

Ordinary buses from the Surat Thani bus terminal to Bangkok take about 10 hours and depart five times daily from 0700 to 1230, and every half hour from 1700 to 2100. Buses for Phuket take seven hours and depart eight times daily from 0530 to 1300. Buses to Hat Yai take five hours and leave at 0830 and 1130.

Train service from Surat Thani can be tricky since advance booking is necessary to reserve a seat. Train tickets can be purchased from small travel agents at the beaches, and from larger agencies such as Songserm Travel in Nathon.

> *Journeys, like artists, are born and not made. A thousand differing circumstances contribute to them, few of them willed or determined by the will—whatever we may think.*
>
> —Lawrence Durrell, *Bitter Lemons*

KO PHANGAN

Phangan Island, 20 km north of Ko Samui, is a wild and primitive place with isolated beaches, tropical jungles, and arching coves accessible only by long hikes or chartered boats. For those searching for the Samui of a decade ago, Ko Phangan seems a return to the mid-1970s with its colonies of gypsyish travelers bedecked with amulets and beads, more concerned with blazing sunsets and local herb than raucous nightclubs and a/c resorts. During the day there's little to do but relax on the beach and perhaps rent a motorcycle to visit some of the local waterfalls. Nightlife remains limited to a few video shows and meditation classes directed by Buddhist monks and Rajneesh devotees.

Destined for cataclysmic changes, Ko Phangan—like Ko Samui—also faces major challenges. Transportation hassles and the isolated beaches have long kept the island relatively undeveloped, but modern pressures have wrought great changes on the once-pristine island. Phangan now reels under a boom cycle fueled by entrepreneurs who anticipate a Ko Samui-style explosion. Over the last five years, hundreds of bungalows have been constructed with wild abandon and little thought to zoning codes or pollution controls. Without adequate compensation for hotel operators or funding from municipal authorities, trash piles up on beaches and sewage is dumped directly into the waters.

Ko Phangan still remains a backpackers' favorite, but to enjoy the better side, travelers should avoid the more developed beaches and head directly to the remote, off-the-beaten-track coves.

THONG SALA

Thong Sala is the main port and commercial center of Ko Phangan. No one stays in Thong Sala, but all necessary services are located near the pier and main street along the beach, including a bank which changes money at fair rates and several travel agencies which sell tickets to Surat Thani, Ko Samui, and Ko Tao. A post office and overseas phone office are just south of the pier on the first paved street.

Thong Sala is also the hub for the primitive road system which snakes around the island. Several shops rent motorcycles at 150-250B per day. Mini-trucks leave from the pier to all accessible beaches, and to a few spots where the driver drops you and tells you to walk! Longtail boats whose destinations are displayed on stubby masts leave from the pier to nearby beaches such as Ban Tai, Had Rin, and Nai Wong.

Transportation

Thong Sala and other beaches on Ko Phangan can be reached by boat from Surat Thani, Nathon, Bophut, and Big Buddha Beach.

From Surat Thani: Phangan Ferry Company (tel. 077-286461) boats depart from Surat Thani daily at 0720 and arrive at Thong Sala at 1100. Tickets are sold at their office at 10 Chon Kasem Rd. just across from the pier. Songserm Travel also serves Ko Phangan via Ko Samui.

A night ferry departs at 2300 and arrives at dawn at Thong Sala.

Boats return twice daily to Ko Samui from Thong Sala and Had Rin Beach.

From Nathon: Songserm Travel boats depart daily at 1000 and 1530 from Nathon, and arrive in Thong Sala about one hour later. Tickets can be purchased at the Songserm Travel office near the pier.

From Bophut Beach: The *Hadrin Queen* departs daily at 0930 and 1530 from the small pier in the town of Bophut and takes about 45 minutes to Had Rin Beach. This is the most convenient option for travelers staying at Chaweng and beaches on the north coast of Samui.

From Big Buddha Beach: A fishing boat to Had Rin Beach departs from the east end of Big Buddha Beach daily at 1530.

KO PHANGAN BEACHES

The best sand is found on the southern and eastern sides of Ko Phangan. Beaches to the north and west are narrow and spotted with mangrove swamps, but offer coral beds and the best sunsets on the island.

The following beaches are described in counterclockwise order starting from Thong Sala.

Thong Sala Beach

Also called Ao Bang Charu, Thong Sala Beach has mediocre sand but is a convenient place for early boats to Ko Tao or back to Ko Samui. As with all of Ko Phangan's beaches, Thong Sala has a continuous string of wooden bungalows in the 50-250B price range. **Charm Beach Resort** is a typical example, with primitive shacks from 50B and deluxe chalets with toi-

let, shower, and fan from 200B. **Chokana Resort** is similar.

Ban Tai Beach

The beach starts to improve about two km east of Thong Sala, near the small villages of Ban Tai and Ban Khai. Wat Khao Tham, located on a hill behind Ban Tai, occasionally sponsors 10-day meditation retreats geared to Western visitors. Boat service is available to Had Rin.

Just east of town are several inexpensive bungalows such as **Birdsville**, **SP Resort**, **Pink's**, **Triangle Lodge**, **Liberty**, and **Mac Bay**

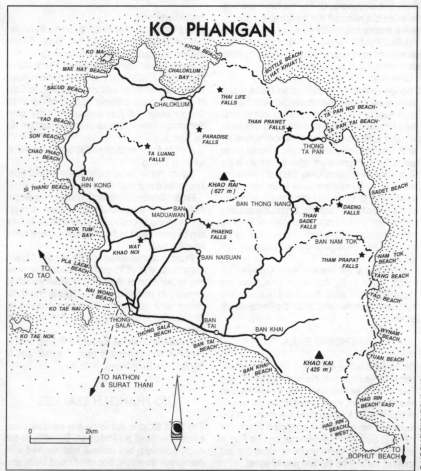

KO PHANGAN

KO MA
MAE HAT BEACH
SALUD BEACH
YAO BEACH
SON BEACH
CHAO PHAO BEACH
SI THANU BEACH
KO TAE NAI
KO TAE NOK

KHOM BEACH
CHALOKLUM BAY
BOTTLE BEACH (HAT KHUAT)
CHALOKLUM
THAI LIFE FALLS
TA PAN NOI BEACH
THAN PRAWET FALLS
TA PAN YAI BEACH
PARADISE FALLS
THONG TA PAN
TA LUANG FALLS
BAN HIN KONG
KHAO RAI (627 m)
BAN THONG NANG
SADET BEACH
DAENG FALLS
BAN MADUAWAN
THAN SADET FALLS
WOK TUM BAY
PHAENG FALLS
BAN NAM TOK
NAM TOK BEACH
PLA LAEM BEACH
WAT KHAO NOI
BAN NAISUAN
THAM PRAPAT FALLS
YANG BEACH
TO KO TAO
NAI WONG BEACH
YAO BEACH
THONG SALA
BAN TAI
BAN KHAI
WYNAM BEACH
THONG SALA BEACH
BAN TAI BEACH
YUAN BEACH
KHAO KAI (425 m)
TO NATHON & SURAT THANI
BAN KHAI BEACH
HAD RIN BEACH EAST
HAD RIN BEACH WEST
TO BOPHUT BEACH

0   2km

© MOON PUBLICATIONS, INC.

Resort with rooms for 50-150B. Travelers staying for a week should ask for and receive a sizable discount.

Ban Khai Beach

Ban Khai is the last town before the road ends at the rocky headlands. Beaches here are narrow but very quiet, clean, and dotted with impressive granite boulders. **Sabai, Baan Kai Bay Huts, Phangan Lodge, Lee Garden, Free Love, Copa, Pan Beach, Rainbow, Golden Beach,** and **Boom's** all have bungalows for 50-150B. Better chalets for 150-250B are available at **Lee Garden, Green Peace, Golden Beach, Sun Sea Resort,** and **Thong Yang.**

Longtails continue from Ban Khai east to Had Rin Beach, though it's a beautiful one-hour walk past narrow coves filled with crystal-clear waters.

Had Rin Beach West

Had Rin West and East were the first beaches to open up on Ko Phangan some 10 years ago. Both have excellent sand and aquamarine waters but suffer from overdevelopment and piles of trash which wash up on the shore. Bungalows at the end of the rocky coastline are now being torn down for more expensive places.

Star, Bird, Sun Beach, Sandy, Seaside, Rainbow, Coral, Palm Beach, Neptune's, Black and White, and **Friendly House** have huts for 50-150B. More expensive chalets with private bath and fan are found at **Blue Hill, Crystal Palace, Coral Bungalows, Sunset Bay, Black and White, Friendly, K Bungalows,** and the **Light House** down on the rocky promontory.

Had Rin Beach East

The eastern side of the craggy peninsula features white powder sand, arched in a curving cove flanked by rocky cliffs. Scuba diving is fairly good, and the surf gets high during the stormy months from October to February.

Over a dozen bungalows occupy virtually every square centimeter of the original and most popular beach on Ko Phangan. Bungalows from south to north include **Tai Chi Chuan, Paradise, Sea Garden, Haad Rin, Tommy's, Palita, Seaview, Mountain Sea,** and **Serenity Hill.** All have simple huts for 50-150B and several offer better cottages with private bath and fan for 150-250B. Restaurants at **Tommy's Resort**

and **Palita Lodge** are the current favorites for Thai soups, Mekong, and nightly videos.

Boats from Mae Nam and Big Buddha beaches on Ko Samui head directly to Had Rin East. The beach can also be reached with longtails from Thong Sala, Ban Tai, and Ban Khai.

Yang Beach

Six km north of Had Rin, and about midway up the east coast, is a lovely little cove with coconut palms and sparkling sand. A narrow trail heads north to Nam Tok Beach, Tham Prapat Falls, and a stone bearing the initials of King Rama V.

Sea Hill Hat Yang Bay Resort has several bungalows for 50-120B.

Sadet Beach

Had Sadet and nearby Had Thong Reng are now receiving some visitors who arrive by longtail from Had Rin or public mini-truck from Thong Sala. The road from Thong Sala ends a few kilometers beyond Ban Thong Nang, making the beach a long hike or treacherous motorcycle ride. Along the dirt track is a small river with several falls, for which Than Sadet, Sampan, and Daeng are worth visiting during the rainy season from November to February. Also located in the valley are stones incised with the initials of Kings Rama V, VII, and IX. Trails connect Sadet Beach with Ban Nam Tok to the south and Ban Thong Ta Pan to the north.

Bungalows on Sadet Beach include **Pra Thip, Ka Wao,** and several places aptly called **No Name Bungalows.**

Ta Pan Beach

Thong Ta Pan Bay is formed by two small bays, Ta Pan Noi to the north and Ta Pan Yai on the south. The beach is so impressive that it once was the favorite of King Rama V. Ban Thong Ta Pan can be reached by truck from Thong Sala.

Bungalows near the village on Ta Pan Yai Beach include **Pen's, Pingjun Resort,** and **Chanchit Dreamland.** Ta Pan Noi Beach has **Thong Ta Pan Resort** at the northern end and **Panviman Resort** (tel. 077-272570) on the south.

Bottle Beach (Khuat Beach)

The far northeastern corner of Ko Phangan offers an immaculate and isolated beach with squeaky white sands and excellent swimming in the protected cove. Bottle Beach—the perfect place to *really* escape civilization—can be reached by longtail boats from Chalok Lam or Had Rin beaches.

Sea Love, **Bottle Beach**, and **O.D.** bungalows at the northern end have wooden shacks for 50-100B.

Chaloklum Bay
The north-shore fishing village of Chaloklum (Chalok Lam) faces a curving bay ringed with emerald-green mountains. Chaloklum is a somewhat interesting destination for its large fleet of fishing craft and simple restaurants which serve local fish and shellfish specialties. Beaches near the town are brownish but improve sharply to the east, especially at Khom Beach. Trucks take about 90 minutes from Thong Sala.

Thai Life, **Fanta**, and **Chalok Lam Resort** near the town have acceptable bungalows for 50-80B. **Wattana Resort** at the west end of the bay has over a dozen huts in various price ranges. Better spots to the east include (yet another) **No Name**, **Buddy**, and **Coral Bay** bungalows near Khom Beach.

Mae Hat Beach
Similar to the situation on Ko Samui, beaches on the west coast tend to be brown and coarse, but compensate with coral beds and blazing sunsets. Mae Hat features nearby Wongsai Falls and the offshore island of Ko Ma with coral beds and deserted beaches. Mae Hat can be reached in about one hour with trucks from Thong Sala.

Mae Hat Bungalows and **Mae Hat Villa** are located on the beach path to the north. Both have huts for 50-100B. Better operations on the southern side include **Mae Hat Bay Resort** and **Island View Cabanas**. Both have older huts for 50-100B and newer chalets with private bath and fan for 150-250B. Rudimentary huts are also found on nearby Ko Ma.

Yao Beach
Bungalows on the small cove include **Sandy Bay**, **Ibiza**, **Had Yao**, **Blue Coral Beach**, **Phong Sak**, and **Dream Hill Bungalows**.

Chao Phao Beach
The beach at Chao Phao is somewhat brownish and dotted with mangrove trees, but coral beds and spectacular sunsets make this a popular

alternative to Had Rin Beach. Freshwater Lake Laemson is located back from the beach.

Bungalows for 50-100B include **Bovy Resort** in the south, **Seetanu**, **Sea Flower**, and **Great Bay Resort** at the northern end.

Si Thanu Beach
The circular cove of Si Thanu is situated near the small fishing town of Si Thanu. Coral beds lie offshore, though swimming can be dangerous during the rainy season.

Beachside bungalows include Loy Fah at the southern end of the cape, **Ladda Guesthouse** near the town, and **Sea View** and **Laemson** on the northern stretches. All are simple huts with common bath for 50-100B and chalets with private bath for 100-150B.

Wok Tum Bay
Beaches along the long and nondescript bay of Wok Tum are narrow and speckled with mangrove trees.

Bungalows at the southern end include the **O.K.**, **Kiat**, **Darin**, and **Tuk**. Mr. Ban at Kiat Bungalows can help with boats to Ko Samui and visits to Angthong Marine National Park. **Lipstick** and several other inexpensive bungalows are located at the northern end, also called Hin Kong Beach.

Pla Laem Beach
The four-km road north of Thong Sala passes some decent beaches almost continuously lined with inexpensive bungalows and better spots with private bath and fans.

A track behind the main road leads up to **Mountain View Resort** and **Bungtham Bungalows**. Beachside bungalows include **Beach**, **Cookies**, **Sea Scene**, and **Darin**.

Nai Wong Beach
The rocky beach just north of Thong Sala is a convenient location for travelers taking early-morning boats to Ko Samui and Ko Tao. A Thai boxing arena and cockfighting field are located north of the pier near Ban Nai Wong.

Phangan Bungalows has basic huts and more luxurious chalets with private baths. **Charn** and **Siriphun** are low-end favorites, while **Tranquil Resort** at the north end has a popular restaurant and bungalows in all price ranges. All bungalows are within walking distance of the Thong Sala pier.

KO TAO

Tiny Ko Tao is a turtle-shaped island 38 km north of Ko Phangan and 58 km from Ko Samui. Named after its peculiar shape, which resembles a kidney bean or abstract turtle shell, Ko Tao measures just seven km long and three km wide, for a grand total of 21 square km. The population of 750 is occupied with coconuts, fishing, and bungalow operations which attract a steady trickle of world travelers. The island is chiefly known for its outstanding coral beds off nearby Ko Hang Tao and Ko Nang Yuan, and a half-dozen beaches with fairly good sand and crystal-clear waters.

As the last island in the Samui archipelago to develop, Ko Tao skipped the traditional grass shack phase and went directly to better bungalows fixed with tin roofs and video bars. All of the beaches now offer bungalows which charge 40-80B for rooms with common baths, and more expensive operations with private bath and fans.

Beaches are narrow and lack the splendor of Chaweng and Lamai but compensate with small crowds and sense of isolation. Ko Tao should be avoided during the stormy fall season

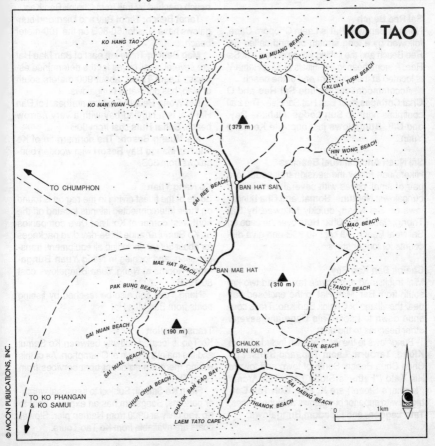

KO TAO

KO HANG TAO

KO NAN YUAN

MA MUANG BEACH

KLUAY TUEN BEACH

(379 m)

HIN WONG BEACH

TO CHUMPHON

SAI REE BEACH

BAN HAT SAI

MAO BEACH

MAE HAT BEACH

BAN MAE HAT

PAK BUNG BEACH

(310 m)

TANOT BEACH

SAI NUAN BEACH

(190 m)

LUK BEACH

CHALOK BAN KAO

SAI NUAL BEACH

CHALOK BAN KAO BAY

SAI DAENG BEACH

CHUN CHUA BEACH

THIANOK BEACH

LAEM TATO CAPE

TO KO PHANGAN & KO SAMUI

0   1km

© MOON PUBLICATIONS, INC.

when monsoons drench the island and muddy the normally clear waters.

Ban Mae Hat

Ban Mae Hat is the principal town and arrival point for all boats from Surat Thani, Ko Samui, Ko Phangan, and Chumphon. The town has several cafes, dive shops that organize trips to Nang Yuan Island, and travel agents who sell boat tickets to Chumphon and points south. Exchanging money on Ko Tao can be costly, so bring plenty of small bills.

Accommodations on the northern beach include **Nuan Nang**, **Dam**, and **Khao** bungalows. All have small huts for 40-60B and larger rooms for 80-120B.

Sai Ree Beach

North of Ban Mae Hat is Laem Choporo Cape, followed by a long stretch of sand called Sai Ree Beach and the fishing village of Ban Hat Sai Ree. A stone bearing the initials of King Rama V is located at the southern end of the beach.

Accommodations include **Sai Ree** and **O Chai Cottages** near Ban Hat Sai Ree. The trail continues north to **Sun Lodge**, **Mahana Bay**, and **C.F. Bungalows** just opposite Ko Nang Yuan.

Sai Nuan And Sai Nual Beaches

Hikers can follow the seaside trail south to a pair of small coves with several inexpensive bungalows: **Neptune**, **Somat**, and **Cha** bungalows on Sai Nuan, quickly followed by **Sai Thong**, **Sabai**, and **Char Huts** over the cape on Sai Nual Beach. All cost 40-80B and give discounts for longer stays.

Chalok Ban Kao Bay

Mini-trucks and motorcycle taxis head two km south from Ban Mae Hat to the enclosed bay near the village of Chalok Ban Kao. Trails continue down to Laem Tato Cape and several other beaches to the east.

Bungalows to the west of town include **Laem Klong**, **Tarporn**, **Laem Tap**, and **Sunset** on Chun Chua Beach. South of town and toward Hin Tato ("Father's Stone") and Hin Arame ("Mother's Stone") are **K. See**, **Koh Tao Cottages** with superior bungalows at higher prices, **Tato Lagoon**, and **Freedom Bungalows**.

Thianok And Sai Daeng Beaches

East of Chalok Ban Kao are several small coves with modest beaches. Snorkeling is said to be good at offshore corals and nearby Shark Island.

Thianok (Thien Ok) has **Niyom Huts** and **Rocky Resort**, while Sai Daeng has **Kiat** and **Bai Sai Daeng** bungalows. All cost 50-100B.

East Coast Beaches

All of the following beaches can only be reached on foot, or with longtails leaving from Ban Mae Hat and Chalok Ban Kao. Every possible cove now has simple bungalows which charge 50-80B, plus big discounts for travelers staying several weeks.

Luk Beach: Ao Luk Resort sits on a small beach reached by trail from Chalok Ban Kao.

Tanot Beach: Tanot Bay and **Diamond** bungalows have huts for 50-80B on the 100-meter beach.

Mao Beach: Three km east of Ban Mae Hat are several small coves for the determined escapist. **Laem Thian**, about 900 meters south of Mao, has one set of bungalows.

Hin Wong Beach: Four km northeast of Ban Hat Sai is a curving bay with a very narrow beach. **Sahat Huts** cost from 30B.

Ma Muang Beach: The northern tip of Ko Tao has **Mango Bay Resort** with wooden bungalows from 30B.

Ko Nang Yuan

Some of the finest diving in the region is found on three interconnected islands located off the northwest corner of Ko Tao. Dive companies on Ko Samui arrange three-day dive packages for about 5000B, including all equipment, transportation, and lodging in **Nang Yuan Bungalows**. Rooms at Nang Yuan Bungalows cost 80-100B.

Nang Yuan can also be reached by fishing boats from Ban Mae Hat.

Transportation

Ko Tao is located midway between Ko Samui and the mainland town of Chumphon. As of this writing there are no direct boat services from Surat Thani.

From Ko Samui: Subject to seasonal weather patterns, Songserm has an express boat to Ko Tao daily at 0900 from Nathon pier. Slower boats are available from Ko Tao Tours.

From Ko Phangan: Songserm Travel and Ko Tao Tours have boats to Ko Tao from Thong Sala. Services are subject to cancellation during the rainy season from October to January.

From Chumphon: Back-door services are available from Chumphon, an option which saves traveling down to Surat Thani or Ko Samui. Schedules change frequently and should be checked with **Chumphon Travel Service** (tel. 077-501880) at 66 Thatapao Rd. just north of the bus station and Thatapao Hotel. Fishing boats currently depart from Chumphon harbor at midnight on Monday, Tuesday, Thursday, and Friday.

SOUTH OF KO SAMUI

NAKHON SI THAMMARAT

One of Thailand's oldest and most historic sites, Nakhon Si Thammarat (Nakhon) is a prosperous city known for its bell-shaped *chedi* at Wat Mahathat and a large collection of Thai art in the National Museum. The rather undistinguished town is divided into three districts. To the south is the old city with Wat Mahathat, the museum, and a few other sights worth a brief visit. North of the old city walls is the hot and dusty new town with the train station, travel agencies, and all the hotels and restaurants. East of town on the highway to Thung Song is the bus terminal and a long string of monotonous concrete buildings that form the newer economic heart of the city.

History
Nakhon first served in the early Christian era as the Hindu capital of the Tambralinga empire at a city-state called Ligor. Sometime in the 8th century, Ligor fell under the suzerainty of the Srivijaya empire, which ruled the Malay archipelago from its lost capital in Sumatra. At the end of the 10th century, a Tambralinga king conquered the Mon kingdom of Lopburi (Lavo) and placed his son, Suryavarman I (1011-1050), on the Khmer throne at Angkor. Ligor became a vassal state of the Khmer kingdom until a brief spell of independence in 1250 and final incorporation in 1292 into the Sukothai kingdom.

By the early 13th century, Nakhon Si Thammarat (or Muang Nakhon) had become the leading economic power in the region and an important religious center which promoted the Sri Lankan school of Hinayana Buddhism. Subsequently embraced by the rulers of Sukothai, Hinayana (Theravada Buddhism) remains the official religion of Thailand.

Wat Mahathat
Wat Pra Mahathat Woramahaviharn—the most sanctified and architecturally significant monument in southern Thailand—was constructed over 800 years ago by King Sri Thammasokaraj in conjunction with his founding of Nakhon Si Thammarat. The religious significance of Wat Mahathat is attributed to its former possession of the Pra Buddha Singh, a historical image now kept in a small modern chapel wedged between two administrative buildings near the clock tower.

Chedi: Wat Mahathat (also called Wat Prathat Muang Khon) centers on a towering bell-shaped *chedi* of Sinhalese style crowned with a solid-gold spire that weighs over 200 kilograms. Over the centuries, the 77-meter *chedi* has been restored and enlarged by royalty of both the Ayuthaya and Rattanakosin periods, including a massive 1992 project sponsored by Princess Sirindorn.

Surrounding the reconstructed *chedi* is a vast cloister filled with Buddha images and elephant heads derived from Sinhalese inspiration. Two symmetrical chapels hidden deep inside the monument feature standing Sukothai-style Buddhas and a narrow stairway which leads to an inner sanctum.

Viharn Luang: South of the central *chedi* is Viharn Luang with a beautiful red ceiling held aloft by unadorned pillars angled like a trapezium, an architectural canon derived from Ayuthaya but rarely carried to such an extreme. The central image smiles, while 16 Buddhas in various styles are displayed in a rear room.

Temple Museum: North of the *chedi* is another chapel which serves as a museum and repository for donations from pilgrims. Aside from the bric-a-brac and silver trees called *bunga mas* in Malaysia, the museum features several worthwhile pieces including a standing stone

Buddha of the Dvaravati Period, and a seated Buddha in Srivijaya style.

Wat Mahathat is located two km south of the new town center, and about 300 meters south of the clock tower shown on the map. Take a *song-tao* or make the long hike past several minor temples and remains of the old city walls.

National Museum

One of the most comprehensive arrays of artifacts in the south is displayed in the six rooms of the Nakhon Si Thammarat National Museum. The collections are arranged in chronological order, with the finest pieces shown in the third room on the left.

Front Rooms: The first room is devoted to prehistoric artifacts such as the largest Dong Son kettledrum uncovered in Thailand, and a 5th-century stone Vishnu considered the oldest of its type in the country. Bronze Buddha images in the next room display typical traits of the Nakhon Si Thammarat school: exaggerated eyebrows, bulbous eyelids, distinctive neck folds, and long and narrow torsos.

Rear Room: Displayed in the back room are several extremely fine sculptures, including a centerpiece 9th-century Vishnu stone image in the Pallava style, and two Vishnu attendants and Ganesha images derived from Indian prototypes. Discovered near Takua Pa and once abandoned in a weedy grove, the curious history of the Takua Pa images is related with photographs mounted on the wall. Also note the rare silver standing Buddha and Shiva incarnated as Nataraja.

Second Floor: Upstairs rooms are devoted to ceramics from various Thai dynasties and folkcrafts such as shadow puppets, basketry, theater costume ornaments, textiles, and a fascinating display of children's games.

The museum is 2¹/₂ km south of the new town center and about 200 meters beyond Wat Mahathat. Mini-trucks travel frequently from the new town.

Wat Suana Puang

Several other temples are located on Rajadamnern Rd. between the downtown hotels and Wat Mahathat in the old city. Behind a peaceful garden sits an immense Buddha and a modern *chedi* constructed in classic Nakhon style, with tiny trees sprouting from the spire.

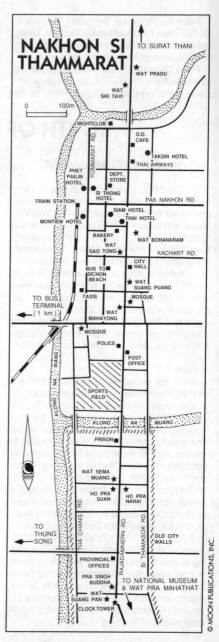

Mosque

Beautifully constructed with green cupolas, gray minarets, and elegant balustrades, the small mosque near Na Wong Canal is considered among the most attractive in southern Thailand.

City Walls

The ancient walls and moats which once surrounded the "City of Priests" are now being reconstructed to the original dimensions of 460 by 2,230 meters. Much of the old brickwork was used to construct the prison near Klong Na Muang.

Ho Pra Suan

Nakhon Si Thammarat originated as a Hindu community that supplied many of Thailand's first Brahman court astrologers who had considerable influence on contemporary Thai Buddhism. Even today, Brahmans from Nakhon participate in the annual Hindu ploughing ceremony held at Sanam Luang in Bangkok. The Hindu legacy is reflected in the dancing Shiva (Suan), stone lingam, and Ganesha image displayed in the modern shrine of Ho Pra Suan. Also note the miniature Giant Swing in the courtyard, formerly used to honor the Hindu gods.

Ho Pra Narai across the street is another modern Hindu shrine with a life-sized Vishnu identical to the original image displayed in the national museum.

Pra Singh Buddha

Although of little artistic merit, Pra Singh Buddha is among the most sacred and revered images in all of Thailand. The history of the image is a mystery. According to Buddhist tradition, the statue was cast in Ceylon and brought to Sukothai by the king of Ligor (ancient Nakhon) and, after various vicissitudes, moved to Chiang Mai in the 16th century. The most puzzling feature is the existence of three similar images—one in Nakhon Si Thammarat, a second at Wat Pra Singh in Chiang Mai, and a third in the National Museum in Bangkok. The bottom line is that the three images differ in size and style, lack Sinhalese influence, and are probably local works dating from the Srivijaya Period.

Much more intriguing are the adjacent complementary Buddhas fashioned from silver and copper.

INTO THE SHADOWS

Nakhon is also known for leather puppet plays called *nang talung*. Shadow puppets were introduced to Thailand during the Ayuthaya Period and gained great popularity in both Phattalung and Nakhon Si Thammarat. Several different styles developed over the centuries. *Nang yai* puppets were very large nonarticulated pieces brightly painted for daytime performances, or transparent versions used for night shows. Smaller *nang talung* images featured articulated arms, legs, and even genitals. Both versions were manipulated by highly talented puppet masters called *nai nang talung* who sang and spoke the dialogue in various voices and were accompanied by a small ensemble of gongs, drums, cymbals, wooden clappers, *chatri* drums, and a Javanese oboe. Performances began around 1800 and continued until around 0600 the next morning.

Today, *nang yai* puppetry is almost a lost art aside from troupes at Wat Khanom in Ratchaburi Province and Wat Sawang Armon in Singburi. *Nang talung* is almost singlehandedly promoted by an old master named Suchat Sapsin, who demonstrates the ancient art form daily in his house in Nakhon Si Thammarat. Performances are occasionally given at Wat Mahathat during temple festivals, and on the grounds of city hall under the patronage of the Southern Artists Association.

Accommodations

Modern-day Nakhon is built alongside a single road, which makes most temples, hotels, and transportation facilities easy to find. Visitors arriving by train disembark near the hotels, but the bus terminal is about one km west of town on Highway 4015. *Tuk tuks* and motorcycle taxis are plentiful.

Thai Hotel: The largest hotel in Nakhon is divided into an older and cheaper wing to the right of the main lobby and a more expensive section entered just opposite the small bakery. Rooms are large and clean but noisy from street traffic. Ask for a room facing the inner courtyard or on the upper floors, and check out the lounge lizards in their Thai Cafe. 1373 Rajadamnern Rd., tel. (075) 356505, fax (075) 344858, 120-150B old wing, 150-200B new wing, 250-400B a/c.

Siam Hotel: A somewhat cheaper hotel with adequate rooms. Similar prices and facilities are also found at the nearby **Si Thong, Laem Thong,** and **Phet Pailin** hotels. 1403 Charoenvithi Rd., tel. (075) 356090, 80-150B.

Montien Hotel: Adjacent to the train station is a 110-room hotel with comfortable rooms above the rather grim lobby. The sign says Mun Tien Hotel. 1509 Yommarat Rd., tel. (075) 341908, fax (075) 345560, 300-350B a/c.

Restaurants

The small bakeries on Pak Nakhon Rd. and across from the Thai Hotel are good spots for breakfast. **D.D. Cafe** caters to young Thais and the odd *farang* seeking out Western dishes. The cleanest spots for inexpensive Thai meals are the foodstalls on the third floor of the Sala Thai Department Store, just north of the Siam Hotel. A rather chaotic night market is located on Charoenvithi Rd. near the Siam.

Several travelers have raved about the **Yellow Curry House** on Yommarat Rd., just south of the train station and opposite the Montien Hotel. Kaeng Som ("yellow curry" in Thai) serves great food including vegetable plates and seafood dishes buried under—what else—yellow curry.

Transportation

Nakhon Si Thammarat is 780 km south of Bangkok, 125 km south of Surat Thani, and 122 km northeast of Trang.

Train: Nakhon Si Thammarat is connected by a trunk route from the interior town of Khao Chum Thong, 30 km west of Nakhon. Direct trains from Bangkok leave at 0835 and 1730. Otherwise, get off the train at Khao Chum Thong and continue to Nakhon by local bus.

Bus: Buses from Surat Thani, Trang, and Bangkok terminate at the bus station about one km west of the hotels. Motorcycle taxis head to the hotels. Departures are somewhat sporadic in the late afternoon and share taxis might be a better option.

Share Taxis: Taxis shared by three or four passengers are faster but about 50% more expensive than buses. The taxi stand is located on Yommarat Rd. just one block north of the mosque.

PHATTALUNG

Phattalung, better known as Muang Luang among southerners, is a small provincial town situated between verdant ricefields and towering limestone mountains pocked with cave temples and meditation grottoes. Although an uninspiring destination, Phattalung is renowned among Thais as the home of shadow plays, *norah* dance, waterfowl at nearby Thale Noi, and a geological landscape somewhat similar to Phangnga Bay. The morning market north of the Ho Fah Hotel is one of the best in the south, and a photographer's dream since produce merchants display their goods outside the covered enclosure.

Wat Kuhasawan

Located inside the limestone peak west of town and once used by Srivijayan monks, Wat Kuhasawan features a lower cave packed with old votive tablets dating from the 8th-11th centuries, and over 40 highly stylized statues of monks, gurus, and Buddhas. Dozens of monkeys roam the grounds and beg for peanuts near the burial sites carved in the steep terrain.

A hillside trail leads up to another cave filled with seated and reclining statues, and excellent views over Phattalung and nearby Khao Ok Talu.

Tham Malai

Wat Tham Malai, three km northeast of Phattalung, features illuminated grottoes filled with stalagmites, and endless views from the Chinese shrines at the peak.

The grotto is flanked by two limestone peaks. Khao Ok Talu ("Broken Chest Mountain") on the right and Khao Hua Taek ("Broken Head Mountain") on the left are named after a legendary struggle between two jealous women over their adulterous lover. Their resulting wounds—a broken chest and broken head—somewhat resemble the geological peculiarities of the limestone peaks.

Wat Wang

Wat Wang, seven km east of Phattalung on the road to Thale Luang, was constructed simultaneously with the establishment of Phattalung during the reign of King Rama III. The temple

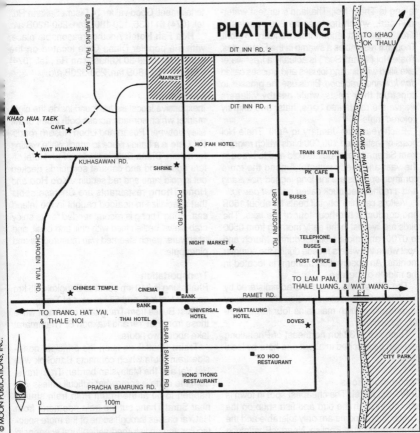

PHATTALUNG

DIT INN RD. 2

MARKET

DIT INN RD. 1

BUMRUNG RAJ RD.

KHAO HUA TAEK CAVE ▲

WAT KUHASAWAN ★

KUHASAWAN RD.

SHRINE ★

HO FAH HOTEL

TRAIN STATION

PK CAFE

BUSES

POSART RD.

NIGHT MARKET ★

UBON NUSORN RD.

TELEPHONE

BUSES

POST OFFICE

TO LAM PAM, THALE LUANG, & WAT WANG ➤

CHAROEN TUM RD.

CHINESE TEMPLE ★

CINEMA

BANK

RAMET RD.

BANK

THAI HOTEL

UNIVERSAL HOTEL

PHATTALUNG HOTEL

DISARA SAKARIN RD.

DOVES ★

TO TRANG, HAT YAI, & THALE NOI ◄

KO HOO RESTAURANT

HONG THONG RESTAURANT

PRACHA BAMRUNG RD.

0   100m

© MOON PUBLICATIONS, INC.

TO KHAO OK THALU

KLONG PHATTALUNG

CITY PARK

once served as the venue for an oath ceremony in which local officials drank consecrated water and pledged allegiance to the authorities in Bangkok.

The chief draw of the reconstructed chapel is the outstanding murals painted by Rattanakosin artists in the late 18th century. Considered as precious as those of Wat Pra Keo in Bangkok, the murals of Wat Wang complement the beautifully carved sermon seat donated by King Rama V and the array of gilded Buddhas on the central altar.

Lam Pam And Thale Luang
A small fishing village called Lam Pa hugs the banks of Thale Luang, a freshwater lagoon

that forms the northern end of Songkhla Lake. Vendors at nearby Hat Saen Suk Lumphum ("Lumpum Beach of Happiness") sell freshwater specialties and rent beach chairs for an afternoon of escape. Boats can be hired to visit the nearby islands of Ko Si and Ko Ha, where hundreds of swallows create the highly prized nests used in Chinese soups. Accommodations are available in bamboo bungalows at Lumpum Resort.

Lam Pam and Thale Luang, eight km east of Phattalung, can be reached by mini-trucks from the Phattalung canal.

Thale Noi Waterbird Sanctuary
Top draw among the natural wonders near Phat-

talung is Thale Noi, Thailand's largest water-fowl park, which hosts some 200 species of birds in the vast lagoon from January to April. Though it resembles a swamp in the Everglades, Thale Noi ("Small Sea") is actually a freshwater lake filled with floating lotuses and grasses called *don kok* and *krachood.* Birds use the grasses to construct their nests, while nearby villagers weave the reeds into bags, hats, and brightly colored mats.

Each year from January to April, Thale Noi hosts an estimated 100,000 birds which migrate from Siberia to escape the cold and to breed in the vast and reedy swamp. Among the more common species are the long-legged *nok ikang* and a redheaded duck called *nok pet daeng.*

Visitors can hire longtail boats for about 150B and conduct a two-hour tour of the lake. The birds are liveliest in the early morning from 0500 to 0700, and most plentiful during March and April when the waters recede during the summer months. An observation platform is located in the middle of the lake.

The 475-square-km park is administered by the Wildlife Conservation Division of the Forestry Department, which maintains four large shelters for visitors.

Thale Noi is 32 km northeast of Phattalung and can be reached in about one hour by local bus.

Accommodations

Universal Hotel: The cheapest spot in town is entered through the bird and fish shop on the ground floor. Rooms are only tolerable and the owner speaks little English. Nearby Phattalung Hotel is a dump. 61 Ramet Rd., tel. (074) 611078, 70-100B.

Thai Hotel: The best choice in Phattalung has large rooms with private bath, friendly managers, and a small coffee shop with nightly entertainment. Good value. 14 Disara Sakarin Rd., tel. (074) 611636, 120-180B fan, 250-320B a/c.

Hoa Fah Hotel: Another reasonable place, with the popular Diana Cafe located on the ground floor. 28-30 Kuhasawan Rd., tel. (074) 611645, 130-180B fan, 250-320B a/c.

Restaurants

Inexpensive foodstalls are found inside the night market which spreads across both sides of the alley between Posart and Ubon Nusorn roads. **PK Cafe** is a handy place to snack while waiting for a train. **Diana Cafe** in the Hoa Fah Hotel offers good food and cabaret songbirds decked out in gold lamé and red sequins. **Koo Hoo** and **Hong Thong** restaurants are Chinese spots that specialize in seafood caught in the inland sea. Hong Thong is recommended for its spicy crab claws, catfish fried with chili and basil, and freshwater perch steamed with mushrooms and pineapple.

Transportation

Phattalung is 840 km south of Bangkok, 95 km north of Hat Yai, and 57 km east of Trang.

Bus: Buses from Trang take one hour, while those from Hat Yai and Nakhon Si Thammarat take about two hours.

Train: Phattalung is on the principal northside train route which connects Bangkok with Hat Yai and the Malaysian border. Train travel from the north is somewhat difficult unless you happen to be at the Phum Phin train station near Surat Thani, but the train ride north from Hat Yai passes through some of the more spectacular and undisturbed agricultural scenery in southern Thailand. Trains depart Hat Yai four times between 1400 and 1650.

Train schedules are posted on the walls inside the Phattalung station.

Every man carries within himself a world made up of all that he has seen and loved; and it is to this world that he returns incessantly, though he may pass through, and seem to inhabit, a world quite foreign to it.

—Chateaubriand, *Voyage en Italie*

PHUKET

The island of Phuket—Thailand's most popular beach resort—is located in the sparkling green Andaman Sea, 885 km south of Bangkok.

Like all other successful beaches in Asia, Phuket was discovered by backpackers searching for an escapist holiday of simple huts, local food, and cheap grass. Facilities were limited or nonexistent; early arrivals slept on the sand or lived with locals. The scene was so idyllic that William Duncan wrote in his 1976 guide that "for a few years more, Phuket may be allowed to sleep undisturbed, for this island province is not yet ready to cater to the needs of foreign tourists. There are no first-class hotels or restaurants . . ."

But word of the tropical paradise spread among world travelers and soon a steady trickle of curious visitors tiptoed down to Phuket, hoping to beat the rush and inevitable commercialization. Entrepreneurs spotted the island's potential and quickly constructed massive resorts at Patong Beach, and then spread out to other tranquil bays and remote coves. In the remarkably short span of just one decade, the island transformed itself from hippie paradise to yuppie nirvana.

Present-day Phuket will disappoint travelers who dislike commercial development and delight those who find perverse pleasure in running down resorts once they become popular. And yet Phuket remains an outstanding holiday destination. First, few islands in the world can boast of so many excellent beaches in so small an area. Comparisons between Phuket and Ko Samui are almost inevitable, but I'd say that Phuket's beaches are just as beautiful—and certainly more plentiful—than the handful on Ko Samui. Secondly, Phuket's enormous size has allowed the beaches to absorb a great deal of development without being completely overwhelmed. Areas such as Patong have suffered badly from gargantuan hotels and seedy bars, but other regions on the island have generally been spared the tourist-ghetto fate of Pattaya and other Southeast Asian resorts.

Most of Phuket, the largest island in Thailand, remains unaffected by mass tourism. Tourists generally stay glued to the beach and rarely venture into the interior or up to remote coves, but a 10-minute motorcycle ride away from Patong and Kata-Karon beaches reveals the secret of Phuket: the remote corners of the island are pristine, unspoilt, and still fabulously beautiful.

In addition, Phuket offers far more geographic and historical diversity than Samui, as well as outstanding scuba diving, a national park with thick rainforest, several waterfalls, tin mines, pearl farms, Buddhist temples, villages of sea gypsies, and a handful of deserted beaches rarely seen by Western visitors. Don't dismiss Phuket for its yuppie tag—the people remain friendly, the weather is perfect, and enough scenic wonders and cultural highlights remain to keep even the most jaded of travelers happy for several weeks.

History

Phuket, surprisingly, actually has some history worth considering. Little is known about the early history of the island, though archaeologists suggest that the region was first inhabited by Mon-Khmers from Burma who lived in the northern regions, and Chao Lay or sea gypsies who constructed settlements along the southern coastlines. The Thais reached the island in the 13th century during the reign of King Ramkamheng of Sukothai, settling the region to mine the vast deposits of tin which could be easily extracted from veins near the surface of the earth.

Western explorers arrived in the 16th century to ride out storms in Phuket's calm bays and to avoid pirates who terrorized the Andaman coastline. The island later played an important role in Western imperialistic aspirations after Captain Francis Light, an explorer employed by the East India Company, settled in Phuket and married a local woman. Light later bowed to suzerainty demanded by the Thai royal court in Bangkok and moved his fledgling outpost down to Penang. Had Light remained, Phuket might well have been incorporated into the British empire, which eventually moved to Singapore.

PHUKET ISLAND

Phuket was invaded by the Burmese in 1785, a five-week insurgence which elevated two young sisters to the status of national heroines. After the death of the governor of the northern town of Thalang, his widow Chan and her sister Muk assumed responsibility for the defense of Phuket against the murderous Burmese. Disguised as male warriors to intimidate the Burmese, Chan and Muk successfully led the Thai forces and drove the Burmese from Phuket. In reward for their bravery, King Rama I conferred titles of nobility on Chan, who became Lady Tepsatri, and Mok, who was honored as Tao Srisuntorn. Statues honoring the two heroines now stand on the road in Thalang near the site of their brave deed.

Phuket since the early 20th century has been the story of tin, rubber, and tourism. In 1907 an Australian captain introduced the first tin dredger and opened dozens of fabulously lucrative mines. Foreign traders and Chinese laborers subsequently arrived to work the mines, grow wealthy, and construct the Malacca colonial houses which still grace the side streets of Penang town. The island was declared an official province in 1933.

Although tin and rubber are still major industries, tourism has dominated the local economy since the mid-1970s. The opening of an international airport and construction of a Club Med and the Phuket Yacht Club firmly placed Phuket on the tourist—not traveler's—trail. The importance of tourism was forcefully demonstrated in June of 1986 when demonstrators set fire to and virtually destroyed a newly built US$44 million tantalum plant on the northern outskirts of Phuket town. Environmentalists believed the plant would disturb the ecology and ruin tourism. Phuket today attracts over a million annual visitors—making it the most successful resort island in Southeast Asia.

Weather
Phuket lies near the equator and temperatures are fairly uniform throughout the year. The island is hot and dry from November to May, and affected by the annual monsoons from June to late October. Rains start slowly in early summer and worsen in September and October. Visitors can generally escape the heavy storms of late summer by moving over to Ko Samui on the east coast.

ATTRACTIONS

Visitors to Phuket generally spend the first few days relaxing on the beach and working on their tans, but to discover the beauty of the island you should rent a motorcycle or car and visit the more remote regions.

The following attractions are described in clockwise fashion starting from Patong Beach. A full day is necessary to explore the northern half of the island and the east coast. Tour Phuket town and the southern beaches on the second day.

North Of Patong Beach
Most tours start at Patong or Kata-Karon beaches, the two most popular spots on the island. Rather than heading inland to Phuket town, drive north past some outdoor restaurants and stop briefly to enjoy the views from Khao Phanthurat pass. The road descends *very* steeply down to Kamala Bay, where simple cafes are nestled at the northern end. To the rear are ricefields and a circular road that winds past residential neighborhoods and a small mosque.

The beachside road then climbs up past several small coves and cozy Laem Sing Beach, accessible down a narrow pathway. At Surin Beach, turn left at the golf course and head toward the Pansea and Amanpuri resorts, two of the most exclusive digs in Thailand. The narrow road cuts along the coast and reaches the broad, clean stretches of Bang Tao Beach. Sited on the rarely visited beach are dozens of fishermen's huts that face enormous tin barges moored in the shallow waters. Bang Tao is a great place to relax and experience the flavor of old Phuket.

After reconnecting with the main road, you might detour left and marvel at the enormous proportions of the Sheraton Grand Laguna Beach Resort. Back on the main highway, continue up to Ban Thalang and visit the following attractions.

Ban Thalang
Thalang town was the first settlement on Penang, and site of the famous battle between two Thai ladies and Burmese invaders. The following three attractions are all located near Ban Thalang.

Wat Pra Na Sang

About 50 meters south of the central intersection stands a 200-year-old *wat* on the right and its modern counterpart on the left. A walking Sukothai-style Buddha stands in the front courtyard. Exterior doors of the modern *bot* feature well-carved guardians on the right, and heroines Chan and Mok on the left; note their tiny feet but enormous eyes. Murals on the interior walls relate the fall of Ayuthaya, King Narusen's famous elephant fight, Chan and Mok defending Phuket against Burmese invaders portrayed as horrid creatures, and the four traditional industries of Phuket—tin, rubber, fishing, and pineapples. What happened to tourism?

To the right is an old, unrestored *bot* whose *bai sema* resemble giant pawns from a monstrous chess set. Although often closed, the *bot* is highly regarded for its ancient metal Dvaravati-style heads and unusual rear doors which indicate that the temple once served as a site for white magic rites. It is said that Wat Pra Na Sang monks still bless weapons and provide magical incantations to protect devotees against bullets and black forces. The *wat* reputedly contains the longest *lai tong* in the country, an accordion-like religious manuscript covered with maps of buried treasure.

Wat Pra Thong

One of the most bizarre Buddha images in Thailand lies half-buried in the middle of Wat Pra Thong, an otherwise ordinary temple located about one km north of Thalang. Once coated with plaster to thwart Burmese invaders, the unaesthetic but immense statue has since been gold-leafed by pilgrims into an unwieldy blob. Of more interest are the burial vaults embedded in the rear walls, dozens of small images perched near the ceiling, and eight auxiliary Buddhas dedicated to each day of the week, plus an additional Buddhist day called Palae-lai.

Khao Prapa Tao National Park

Four km east of Thalang is one of the most spectacular scenes on Phuket: an awesome park which provides a rare opportunity to experience the splendor of an endangered rainforest. Rainforests in Southeast Asia are uniformly difficult to visit, since most are well off the beaten track and impossible to reach without long bus rides or arduous treks. Located at the end of a rubber plantation, Prapa National Park might be your *only* chance to see a rainforest; don't miss it.

Khao Prapa Tao was created in 1978 to conserve indigenous vegetation such as the *Karedoxa dolphin*, a silver palm which survives only on Phuket. The park is also home to several species of birds such as the crimson sunbird, scops owl, and paradise flycatcher. At the park entrance is a ranger station, map to the nearby Ton Sai Waterfall, refreshment stalls, and bungalows rented from park headquarters. Overnighting in the park is highly recommended.

A road passable only with dirt bikes and four-wheel-drive vehicles continues across the park to the east coast. Escorted jeep tours are provided by several companies on Phuket.

Nai Ton Beach

Head north and then west down Highway 4031 to the turnoff for Nai Ton Beach. Suddenly, all the tourists are gone and Patong Beach seems like a distant nightmare. Nai Ton is a spectacularly sited stretch of sand with simple cafes, private homes which admit overnighters, and beach chairs for sun worshipers. The road continues south past a beautiful swimming cove before finally disintegrating into an impassable and dangerously rutted mess. Return to Highway 4031 and continue north to Nai Yang.

Nai Yang Beach

After driving through a beautiful stretch of rubber trees, turn left into Pearl Village and continue through their back lot to Nai Yang Beach, a narrow stretch of sand under the supervision of Nai Yang National Marine Park. Nai Yang offers seaside restaurants, windsurfing, jet skis, swaying casuarina trees, and elephant rides into the surf. Accommodations are available at the Nai Yang Visitors Center at the north end of the beach.

Continue north around the airport to the next beach.

Mai Khao Beach

Mai Khao is an absolutely deserted beach, eyed covetously in recent years by ambitious developers. The road which parallels the beach passes several Thai villages and fields of grapes which produce the sweet reds and unpretentious whites of Thailand. Highway 402 terminates at the Sarasin Bridge.

Northwest Passage And Pearls

Highway 4027 heads east from Muang Mai past some enormous old trees which have miraculously escaped the chainsaws and become holy symbols to local residents. A left turn brings you to Po Bay (Ao Po) and a small fishing village for cold drinks. Ao Po is the departure point for visits to Naga Island Pearl Farm on Naka Noi Island. Phuket travel agents can arrange tours to the farm which provide insight into the considerable skills of pearl cultivation. The highly successful operation once created the world's largest cultured pearl, a 30-gram monster now displayed in the Mikimoto Pearl Museum in Japan.

Heroines Monument And Thalang National Museum

Highway 4027 intersects Highway 402 at the monument dedicated to the two sisters who successfully defended Phuket against Burmese invaders. A fruit and vegetable market is held here on Mondays.

Thalang National Museum, 100 meters east of the monument, is a new attraction with displays on local history, industry, the environment, and a highly prized 9th-century Vishnu image discovered near Takua Pa. The museum is open Tues.-Sat. 0900-1630.

South of the intersection are a striking Islamic school, native handicraft center, Thai performance venue, and Phuket town.

Ko Siray

Ko Siray is an extremely disappointing fishing village populated by Malay-Burmese pearl divers who prefer to be called "New Thais" rather than sea gypsies. Ko Siray largely consists of dusty roads, rough tin huts, and kids yelling "ten baht, ten baht"—an experience best avoided.

Panwa Cape

Phuket's Marine Biology Research Center and Aquarium on the south coast contains displays of tropical sealife, fishing devices, and facilities to ensure the survival of endangered ridley sea turtles which once laid their eggs on Nai Yang Beach. Despite the turtle release each year during Songkram, egg hunters and turtle poach-

ers have pushed the ridley toward extinction. The aquarium is open daily 0900-1630.

On the grounds of the Cape Panwa Sheraton Resort stands a classic Sino-Portuguese mansion filled with a quality collection of antique furniture and art objects. The public is invited to tour Panwa House and enjoy high tea on the veranda.

Wat Chalong

Wat Chalong ("Celebration Temple") is the largest and most sacred temple of the 29 monasteries on Phuket. Enshrined in the modern viharn are the gilded statues of two monks and herbal doctors—Luang Po Chaem and Luang Po Chuang—who helped quell an 1876 rebellion by warring tin miners.

As with other Buddhist temples in Thailand, Wat Chalong is best visited on wan pran, the weekly holy day when monks chant Pali scriptures 0900-1200 before having their final meal at noontime. The date is determined by the lunar calendar but the tourist office and hotel owners can help with schedules.

Seashell Museum

An impressive collection of shells is exhibited in the modern, blue-tiled building on Hwy. 4021 just north of Rawai Beach. Shells sold at the shop include key scallops, variegated sundials, spiney venus murexes, and humpback cowries.

Rawai Beach And Tristan Jones

Situated behind a mediocre stretch of sand is a commercialized sea gypsy village often inundated with groups of tourists. Several lackluster cafes are located near the old pier.

A few hundred meters west is the small boat which crossed the Kra Isthmus in 1987 with a crew of disabled sailors, including a blind German and a one-legged Englishman named Tristan Jones. Jones later sailed the craft north up the Chao Praya to Chiang Rai and penned a book about his experiences.

Promtep Cape

Promtep Cape and the viewpoint at the south end of Kata Noi Beach are the best spots on Phuket for spectacular sunsets. Promthep is marked with a large parking lot filled with Thai tourists and an elevated shrine of a four-headed Brahma who calmly surveys the fingertipped peninsula. Note the signpost which lists approximate sunset times, which vary from 1804 in November to 1850 in July—only a 46-minute differential throughout the year. That's what happens when you live near the equator!

Nai Harn Bay

The road continues north past an experimental but inoperative windmill before dropping down to Nai Harn Bay and the luxurious Phuket Yacht Club. The entire valley is now under heavy development and hardly resembles the hippie retreat of the mid-1970s. Visitors can drive right through the parking lot of the Phuket Yacht Club and continue past cozy Ao Sane Beach to a wonderful little hideaway called Jungle Beach Resort. Stop for a drink.

Rather than returning on the beach road, head west past Nai Harn Beach Bungalows to Crazy Horse Ranch, where escorted rides tour the nearby ricefields and beaches. The beautiful backwoods road continues east to the highway and then north past a viewpoint to Kata and Karon beaches. A terrific ride for motorcyclists.

PHUKET TOWN

The capital of Thailand's only island province is worth visiting for its shopping, restaurants, and delightful examples of Indo-Portuguese mansions constructed by Chinese tin and rubber barons. Phuket town was originally settled about a century ago by Chinese from Malaysia who were lured by the lucrative mineral deposits. Tin and rubber fortunes created by the great rush formed the great Sino-Thai dynasties which still dominate the economies of southern Thailand.

Most visitors simply pass through town en route to a beach, but if you have some extra time, an informative walking tour can be made in about two hours. Start your tour in the middle of town at the tourist office.

Rasda Road

Rasda (Rajada) Rd. is the main tourist center, with all types of restaurants and travel services. Asia Voyages and Songserm Travel are located on the U-shaped road on the left. Kanda Bakery on the right is overpriced but a good place to relax for a few minutes. Continue west on Rasda

Rd. through the traffic circle to the central market on the left. A beautiful old colonial house is tucked away behind the nearby offices of Thai Airways. On the left is a pottery shop and bird emporium opposite a Thai temple.

Pu Jao Temple

Pu Jao (the sign says Kwanim Teng) is a Chinese Taoist temple dedicated to Kuan Yin, goddess of mercy. The central chamber contains both plastic and traditional bamboo sticks used to tell fortunes and diagnose illnesses. Visitors can shake the sticks, read the number, and select a matching fortune from the boxes in a room on the left. The red wooden blocks shaped like mangoes simply answer questions with a yes or no.

To the right is another room filled with dozens of small statues, including a monkey god wearing a mock leopard-skin robe. An oven used to burn hell notes is located in the alley to the next temple.

Jui Tui Temple

This much more impressive Chinese Taoist temple honors Kiu Won In, a vegetarian god who oversees frantic celebrations during the Vegetarian Festival. Inside the central hall are images of Chinese deities, including Laosia, and small spears with carved heads used in magical Taoist rites. The building also features a red-tile roof with green porcelain dragons and outstanding doors carved with fierce gods.

A smaller room on the right has six life-sized statues of Taoist gods and a small tiger also used in Taoist rites. Over 50 smaller images crowd the altar in the left room, including frightening black-faced gods guaranteed to scare small children. Also note the photographs which show the evolution of the temple from 1911 to the latest reconstruction in 1982.

Samjao Shrine

Constructed in 1853, Samjao is dedicated to Tien Sang Sung Moo, goddess of the sea and patron saint of Chinese sailors. Ceremonies are held here to bless new ships and ensure the safety of the crew. Note the five-level pagoda and brass Chinese dog with ball in mouth.

Sino-Portuguese Homes

Head north up Satool (Satun) Road. Though

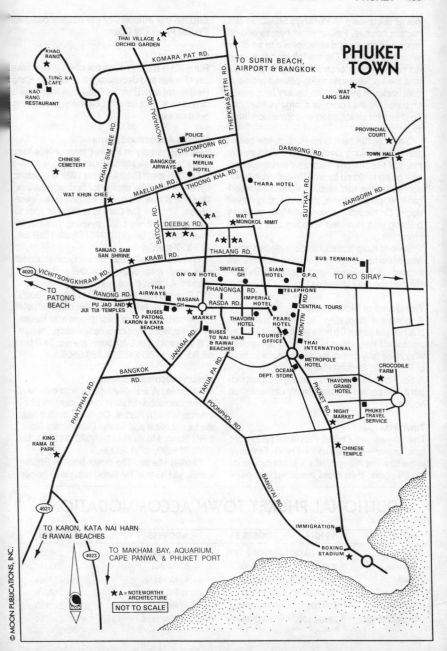

not as impressive as Penang's Malaccan-style terrace houses, Phuket's old homes and estates add charm and atmosphere to an otherwise ordinary city. On the left stands a lovely home behind an ornamental ironwork fence, and then a fabulous cream-colored residence constructed in the late 19th century by a wealthy tin baron. At the corner is a large yellow home destined for destruction or conversion into a tourist attraction.

Some of the best Sino-Portuguese homes are located along Deebuk Road. Fortunately, many of the ornately decorated residences are now being restored by wealthy individuals who appreciate the rare beauty of the floral wood-carvings, pastel tilework, and elaborately carved doors. On the left is a wonderful blue two-story building with louvered windows and graceful balconies.

Several more fine structures, including an ornate white home with gingerbread molding, are located up Yaowaraj Road. Return to Deebuk Rd. and the next attraction.

Wat Mongkol Nimit

A somewhat interesting Thai temple is on Deebuk Rd. just past a Chinese ancestral hall. Lucky visitors will be greeted by Mr. Tim Punyaputho, who cheerfully poses for photographs in front of the central Buddha image.

Soi Romanni returns to Thalang Rd. past old-fashioned barbershops and seedy Chinese shop houses.

Town Hall

The 70-year-old Phuket Provincial Hall might look familiar—it served as the French Embassy in the film *The Killing Fields*. Visitors can count the 99 doors, then cross the street and peek through the windows of the equally beautiful Phuket Provincial Court.

Khao Rang

Rang Hill is a tough climb but offers great views over Phuket and decent meals in the Kao Rang Restaurant and Tung Ka Cafe. The hill is now a fitness park, popular with Chinese yuppies airing out their lungs.

Budget Accommodations

Few visitors stay in Phuket town unless they arrive late or need to catch an early bus.

On On Hotel: Established in 1929, the historic On On is the best choice for budget travelers. Overflow is handled by the adjacent P.R. Guesthouse. The On On Cafe is a popular spot to hang out and wait for evening buses. 19 Phangnga Rd., tel. (076) 211154, 80-180B fan, 220-350B a/c.

Wasana Guesthouse: The only other budget spot worth mentioning is located just past the market. A clean place with friendly managers. 159 Ranong Rd., tel. (076) 211754, 200-300B.

Thavorn Hotel: A convenient midlevel hotel in the center of town near shops and restaurants. Facilities include a coffee shop, lounge, and swimming pool. All rooms are a/c. 74 Rasada Rd., tel. (076) 211333, 350-550B.

Luxury Accommodations

Metropole: A first-class hotel with over 400 rooms, convention facilities, and a massive lobby overloaded with marble. Centrally located near the tourist office and Ocean Department Store. 1 Soi Surin, Montri Rd., tel. (076) 215050, fax (076) 215990, 1800-2800B.

Phuket Merlin: The finest hotel in Phuket town is just north of the Sino-Portuguese homes

ADDITIONAL PHUKET TOWN ACCOMMODATIONS

HOTEL	SINGLE	DOUBLE	ADDRESS	TEL. (076)
City	1000-1600B	1200-2400B	Thepkrasatree	216997
Imperial	350-450	350-550	51 Phuket	212311
Pearl	1200-1600	1400-2400	42 Montri	211044
Siam	100-120	120-150	13 Phuket	212328
Sin Tawee	120-200	140-240	81 Phangnga	212153
Thavorn Grand	2200-2800	2600-3800	16 Tilok Uthit	211750

on Deebuk Road. Free shuttle service is provided four times daily to their sister hotel on Patong Beach. 158/1 Yaowaraj Rd., tel. (076) 212866, 1800-2800B.

Restaurants:

Phuket has plenty of restaurants in the center of town near the travel agencies and souvenir shops. All serve standard Thai fare, plus southern specialties such as:

khao yam	rice with fermented shrimp paste
khao mu daeng	roast pork over rice
khao mun gai	grilled chicken over rice
khao mok gai	Muslim chicken with saffron rice
pla yang	barbecued fish
phat phet satah	bitter lima beans with shrimp or pork
khanon chin	minced beef in a spicy red sauce
nam prik kung siap	grilled prawns with chili
mi sapam	thick seafood soup
gaeng tai pla	fermented curry sauce over noodles

Ocean Department Store: Over a dozen clean and inexpensive foodstalls are located on the top floor of the shopping center across from the Metropole Hotel. A good escape from the heat and crowds of downtown. Inexpensive.

Kanda Bakery: A popular cafe and coffee shop in the center of town. Familiar surroundings and tasty if somewhat pricey dishes. Rasda Road. Moderate.

Krua Thai: One of the best Thai cafes in Phuket serves barbecued fish, prawns topped with coconut sauce, and lemon chicken. 62/7 Rasda Center. Moderate.

Tung Ka Cafe: Authentic and very fiery dishes are served in the simple cafe atop Rang Hill. Specialties include seafood marinated in coconut sauce, mixed grill, and dried shrimp fried with peanuts. Excellent views. Rang Hill. Moderate.

Nightlife

Thai Boxing: Pugilists attempt to kill each other Fridays at 2000 inside the Phuket Boxing Stadium, south of Phuket town in the suburb of Saphan Hin. Tickets cost 40-100B.

Ram Wong **Clubs:** Nightlife revolves around restaurants, shopping, and Thai boxing, but for something different, visit one of the curious and slightly twisted *ram wong* clubs. Inside the seedy clubs—marked by red and yellow lightbulbs—young Thai girls dressed like girl scouts and innocent schoolgirls taxi dance for *baht* tickets. Nu Jah Club still gives a traditional *wai kru* introductory dance.

Massage: Body bubbles and Tora sandwiches are available from the 170 girls at Pearl Massage in the Pearl Hotel on Montri Rd. and from Grand Plaza Parlour on Tilok Uthit Road. Sauna, soap, and sex costs about 1000B. AIDS is rampant, so wear a condom.

Traditional massage (sans sex) is offered at Daeng Plaza Hotel on Phuket Road. 80B per hour, plus 60B for sauna.

Services

Tourist Information: The TAT has an office at the Phuket Airport and a center at 73-75 Phuket Rd. (tel. 076-212213) with maps, brochures, and hotel prices. Ask for a list of current *songtao* prices to the various beaches. The TAT is open daily 0800-1600.

Immigration: Visas can be extended at the Immigration Division (tel. 076-212108) on the eastern end of Phuket Rd. in an area called Saphan Hin. The office is open Mon.-Fri. 0830-1200 and 1300-1630. Thirty-day extensions require two passport-sized photos, a photocopy of your passport pages, and 500 *baht*. All applicants *must* be neatly dressed and well groomed.

Mail: The GPO (tel. 076-211020) at the corner of Montri and Thalang roads is open Mon.-Fri. 0830-1630 and weekends until noon.

International Telephone: Overseas calls can be made from countless small agencies, but the least expensive rates are at the Overseas Telephone Office (tel. 076-216875) on Phangnga Rd., open 24 hours a day.

Maps: Good maps of Phuket include *Phuket Island* from Prannok Witthaya and *Guide Map of Phuket* from Bangkok Guides.

Bookstores: Seng Ho Books at 29 Montri Rd. opposite the GPO has the best selection of books and maps in Phuket town.

Travel Agencies: Sea Tours (tel. 076-216979) at 95/6 Phuket Rd. next to the TAT is the recognized agent for American Express. **World Travel Service** (tel. 076-214020)—the largest travel agency in Thailand—is located in the Phuket Merlin Hotel. Other WTS offices are in eight beach hotels. **Songserm Travel** (tel. 076-214301) in the Rasada Shopping Center on Rasada Road is the leading operator of boats to Ko Phi Phi and Similan Islands. Other travel and dive agencies located in the Rasada Shopping Center include **Asia Voyages** and **Phuket Aquatic Safaris**.

TRANSPORTATION

Getting There

Phuket is 885 km south of Bangkok, 287 km southwest of Surat Thani, and 176 km by road northwest of Krabi.

Air: Thai Airways International offers nine daily flights from Bangkok to Phuket for about 2600B. Daily service is also provided by Thai International from Hat Yai, Surat Thani, Nakhon Si Thammarat, and Trang. Bangkok Airways flies daily from Ko Samui.

Phuket is also served by international charter flights from Europe and other Asian destinations. Both Thai International and Malaysian Airlines fly daily to Phuket from Penang Island in Malaysia, a quick and relatively inexpensive flight which avoids lengthy overland travel and time-consuming border formalities. Dragon Air flies from Hong Kong, and Tradewinds from Singapore.

Thai International (tel. 076-212400) is at 41/33 Montri Road. Domestic tickets are sold at their office (tel. 076-216678) at 78 Ranong Rd. near the central market. **Bangkok Airways** (tel. 076-212341)—for tickets to Ko Samui—is at 158/2 Yaowaraj Rd. near the Phuket Merlin Hotel. For direct flights to Singapore, contact **Tradewinds Airlines** (tel. 076-213891) at 95/20 Phuket Road. **Malaysian Airlines** (tel. 076-216675) is in the Merlin Hotel.

Phuket International Airport is 30 km north of Phuket town. Facilities include luggage storage, tourist information, travel agencies, car rentals, a hotel reservation office, and several banks. Minivans operated by Thai International from the airport to their office in Phuket town cost 50B. Limousines which hold four passengers to various beaches cost 250-500B.

Bus: Ordinary and a/c buses leave every 15 minutes 1800-2200 from Bangkok's Southern Bus Terminal in Thonburi. Buses are fast and inexpensive but tiring because of wild driving and winding roads. Direct a/c buses from Bangkok, Surat Thani, Ko Samui, Krabi, Hat Yai, and Penang can be arranged through travel agents.

Bus tickets from Phuket should be purchased *several* days in advance from a travel agent at the beach or directly at the bus terminal in Phuket town. Private bus service to Bangkok is provided by **Central Tours** on Montri Rd., and **Phuket Travel Service** just south of the Thavorn Grand Hotel.

Buses from Bangkok and other points terminate at the main bus stop in Phuket town, a few locks east of the tourist office. Minibus drivers head down to the beaches for about 50-100B per carload. Drivers generally collect commissions from hotels and guesthouses but are happy to drive around until they find you a room at your requested price; not a bad deal for larger groups.

A cheaper option is to walk into town, pick up some information from the tourist office, and take a public minibus from the stops shown on the map of Phuket town. Public service ends at 1800.

Fares from town are:

Patong	15B
Karon	15B
Kata	15B
Rawai	15B
Nai Harn	20B
Kamala	20B

Getting Around

Around Phuket Town: *Tuk tuks* and minibuses within Phuket town cost five *baht.*

Around the Island: Travelers not in a hurry can take open-air wooden buses from all beaches into Phuket town and then transfer for onward connections.

Car and Motorcycle Rentals: Cars and motorcycles can be rented in town and at most beaches—a great way to get around and avoid the hassles of public transportation. Car rates begin at 800B per day with unlimited mileage. A 30% discount is given during the low season from August to October.

Motorcycles cost 150-250B per day depending on the size. Shop around and check the condition of motorcycles before handing over your passport. Better-condition bikes are usually rented by hotel owners, not the shops on the beaches.

ACTIVITIES

Festivals

Three festivals are unique to Phuket.

Turtle Festival: Phuket's Mai Khao Beach and Nai Yang National Park once served as nesting grounds for thousands of giant ridley turtles which laid their eggs during the winter months from October to February. Over the last few decades, turtle poachers and egg hunters searching for the highly prized delicacies have pushed the ridley toward extinction. In an effort to save the giant turtles, an ambitious turtle-breeding project is now being conducted at the Phuket Marine Biological Center. The young turtles are released at Nai Yang Beach at Songkram, the Buddhist New Year on 13 April.

Loy Rua: A sea gypsy festival is held on the full moon of the sixth and eleventh lunar months—usually June and November—to celebrate the beginning and end of the monsoon season. Somewhat like Loy Kratong, Loy Rua involves the construction of small model boats filled with animist statues which are set adrift in the sea, symbolically carrying away black magic and bad luck.

Vegetarian Festival: Phuket's Vegetarian Festival honors the nine emperor gods with colorful processions and elaborate parades of Chinese deities. One of the most spectacular and bizarre events in Thailand, the festival has achieved great international fame for its masochistic demonstrations: devotees under magical trances run skewers and spears through their cheeks and tongues, climb ladders made of sharp knives, and run across pits of burning coals. Five Chinese temples in Phuket town co-organize the daily processions, which are staggered so that everyone can enjoy the performances. The festival runs from the first to ninth day of the ninth lunar month, usually in late September or early October.

Sports

Golf: Old tin mines that scoured the island have turned into gold mines for golf developers. The island's first golf course, **Phuket Country Club** (tel. 076-321038), opened in 1989 on an abandoned tin mine between Phuket town and Patong Beach. Greens fees are 1200B, lady caddies 200B, and rental clubs 350B.

The Phuket Country Club has recently been joined by the **Phuket Century Country Club**, an 18-hole championship course near the Dusit Laguna Resort Hotel, and 36-hole **Blue Canyon Country Club** (tel. 076-311176) near the airport. All charge 1200B greens fees, but 30-50% discounts are available from participating hotels and travel agencies.

Hash House Harriers: The running fraternity established by British soldiers in Malaysia sponsors weekly footraces followed by serious pub crawls. *Warning:* James Eckardt in his *Waylaid by the Bimbos* describes the Hashiers as a "wretched, loutish, bedraggled, nomadic tribe which can be found periodically gallumping half-naked through the jungle, blowing horns and whistles and screeching their barbaric war cries."

Visitors can join the Saturday mayhem through the Expat Bar on Patong Beach.

Horse Riding: Crazy Horse Stables, tucked away on a beautiful road back from Nai Harn Bay, offers horse rides with Western instructors through fabulous country. Several inexpensive guesthouses are located nearby. 300B per hour.

Cultural Shows

Phuket is hardly a cultural center, but a few companies sponsor traditional entertainment.

Thai Village: The one-hour show includes *nang talung* shadow puppets, *nora* classical dance from southern Thailand, *chak pra* religious procession, wedding ceremony, Thai boxing, drums, and the *ram wong:* Instant Thailand. Daily performances at 1100 and 1730; admission is 250B.

Gong Puppets: Mr. Bloomdidoo, a "dweller in the Land of Gongs," presents a 20-minute puppet show with marionettes from Burma, India, China, Bali, and Thailand. Sponsored by Alliance Francaise de Bangkok, Gong Puppet Theater is located in a small theater near Kathu Waterfall.

THE BEACHES

Phuket's best beaches are all located on the western coast of the island. Each differs from the others in natural setting and degree of development, but all offer superb sand, warm waters, and endless sports activities.

Hotels are available in all possible price ranges. Budget hotels charge 400-800B for clean, modern rooms, while superluxurious resorts with all possible amenities cost 1800-3000B.

Contrary to popular belief, simple bungalows under 300B are still available at all beaches—even the top-end world of Patong. The largest concentration of inexpensive bungalows is at the junction of Karon and Kata beaches, appropriately called Karon-Kata. An easy way to locate a budget hotel is to tell your mini-truck driver which beach you want, and what price range you can afford.

Phuket's hotels use a double-pricing system. Rates are highest during the high season (Nov.-May), when Europeans flood the island, but discounted 30-50% during the rainy season (May-Oct.), when tropical storms lash the west coast. Luxury hotels add 10% service charge, 11% government room tax, and 8.25% food and beverage tax.

Phuket's most popular beaches are Patong, Karon, and Kata. Patong is the commercialized and tawdry tourist center of Phuket, but the best place for nightlife and water sports. Karon and Kata beaches attract a more sedate crowd who want to avoid the excesses of Patong.

The following beaches are described in counterclockwise order starting from the north.

NAI YANG BEACH

Tucked away near the northwest corner of Phuket, Nai Yang National Park encompasses the beach area once known for its annual turtle nestings. The sand is fairly good, and the beach is deserted except on weekends, when Thai families flood the park.

National Park Bungalows: Accommodations from park headquarters (tel. 076-212901) include campsites from 60B, bungalows off the beach for 200-300B, and beachside chalets for 500-800B.

Pearl Village: Located on the edge of the national park, Pearl Village is probably the most isolated hotel on the west coast of Phuket. The hotel is quiet, friendly, and far removed from the nightlife action of Patong—both a plus and a minus. Nai Yang Beach Box 93, tel. (076) 311338, fax (076) 311304, 3000-3800B.

NAI TON BEACH

Looking for an immaculate yet absolutely deserted beach? Nai Ton fits the bill. Nai Ton lacks hotels, restaurants, beer bars, waterscooters, and parasailing—just a place to relax under a beach umbrella and stare into the dazzling waters.

The only drawback is the complete lack of formal accommodations. However, facing the

YACHT CHARTERS AND SPECIAL CRUISES

Several private companies charter yachts for snorkeling, scuba, or simply sailing around the islands. American operators such as Ocean Voyages are described in the "Introduction."

Asia Voyages Pansea

Private yachts for cruising, scuba diving, and big-game fishing, plus escorted tours to secluded beach resorts, can be arranged from Asia Voyages Pansea offices in Thailand, Southeast Asia, and Europe. Asia Voyages—the largest agency in Southeast Asia—conducts extended sails from Phuket November to April, and from Ko Samui July to October.

Asia Voyages operates several unique crafts. Their 20-man Chinese junk, *June Bahtra,* conducts one-day cruises around Phuket for 6000B per boat, two-day sails to Ko Raja for 4000B per person, and three-day junkets to Ko Phi Phi for 10,000B each. The *Macha Nou* is an ordinary cruise boat for sails and snorkeling in Phangnga Bay for 800-1000B per person. *Suwan Macha* is a 17-meter traditionally crafted wooden junk that departs Phuket on Saturdays for four-day cruises to Phangnga Bay and Ko Phi Phi; prices are 10,000-14,000B per person.

Contact Asia Voyages at Charn Issara Tower, 942 Rama IV Road, Bangkok 10500, tel. (02) 235-4100, fax (02) 236-8094. Other offices are located in Chiang Mai (tel. 053-235655), Hong Kong (tel. 521-1314), Singapore (tel. 65-732-7222), Bali (tel. 361-25850), Paris (tel. 1-43261035), Brussels (tel. 2-217-9898), and London (tel. 1-491-1547). Asia Voyages' Phuket headquarters (tel. 076/216137) is at 64/1 Rasada Center in Phuket town.

Southeast Asia Yacht Charter

Owner Dave Owens in Phuket manages five yachts, including the 45-foot *Tonga Queen,* 48-foot sloop *Buccabu,* French-skippered *Celestius,* Aussie-skippered *Wanderlust,* and American-sailed *Quilter II.* The 17-meter *Wanderlust* holds eight passengers comfortably and costs 18,000B per day. 89-71 Thaweewong Rd. (the Beach Rd.), Patong Beach, Phuket 83121, or Box 199, Patong Beach, Phuket, tel. (076) 321292.

Thai Yachting

Thai Yachting is a highly professional organization with three fully skippered yachts that sail to Phi Phi, Similan, and Surin islands from November to May. Weekly per-person fees run US$900-2500 depending on the number of passengers. Contact their Bangkok office (tel. 02-251-6755) at 95 Rajdamri Arcade 7th floor, or their Phuket office (tel. 076-321301) at 94 Thaveewong Rd. in the Patong Beach Hotel.

Sea Canoes

An excellent way to see the remarkable limestone formations and deserted beaches near Phuket is on board clean and quiet inflatable sea canoes. Trips cost US$50-100 per day and range from overnight excursions in Phangnga Bay to week-long expeditions from Phangnga to Krabi. These unique tours have been highly recommended by several travelers. Reservations can be made with Diethelm Travel on Wireless Rd. in Bangkok (tel. 02-255-9150, fax 02-256-0248), or at Sea Canoes offices (tel. 076-213934) in Phuket at the Pearl Village Hotel, and on Ko Samui at the Chaweng Beach Hotel.

---

long expanse of untouched beach is a line of private residences that rent rooms to visitors. Check at the cafe at the end of the beach, or with the owner of the blue-and-white cafe in the middle. Homestays in a/c rooms cost 300-500B depending on length of stay and your bargaining abilities.

BANG TAO BAY

Used for the filming of *The Killing Fields,* the 2¹/₂-km white beach has long been an untouched corner of Phuket, far removed from the commercialism of Patong. Despite some jarring changes in recent years, a small fishing village still sits on the beach and Western tourists are still regarded as the rare oddity. Bang Tao

has a fairly good beach, though ecological damage is evident from tin dredgers still moored in the bay.

The northern end of the bay is almost completely occupied by the massive 780-acre **Laguna Beach Resort**, a planned community which includes the 240-room Dusit Laguna Hotel, 250-room Pacific Islands Club, and 380-room Sheraton Grande Laguna. Inexpensive bungalows are located at the south end.

Bang Tao Lagoon Bungalows: Travelers wanting to escape the crowds but not break the bank are well served by this small operation near the fishing village at the south end of the bay. Facilities include a restaurant with Thai and European dishes, campsites, and 25 simple but clean bungalows with fan and private bath.

Recommended. 72/3 Moo 3 Tambon Cheang Talay, Amphur Talang, tel. (076) 391396, 350-650B.

Royal Park Travelodge Resort: A cozy but upscale resort somewhat removed from the gargantuan complexes to the north. First-class amenities. Moo 2 Tambon Cheong Talay, Amphur Talang, tel. (076) 311453, fax (076) 311409, 2600-3800B.

Dusit Laguna Resort: Thailand's leading hotel chain offers 240 luxurious rooms, two swimming pools, tennis courts, water sports, and other amenities such as matching private lagoons facing a deserted beach. 390 Srisoontorn Rd., Tambon Cheong Talay, Amphur Talang, tel. (076) 311320, fax (076) 311174, 4500-6800B.

SURIN BEACH

Also known as Pansea Bay, Surin is essentially a series of small coves and private beaches dominated by two super-exclusive resorts. Swimmers should be careful of dangerous undercurrents during the rainy season.

Pansea Hotel: An upscale property owned and operated by one of the most prestigious hotel chains in Thailand. Pansea Beach, tel. (076) 311249, fax (076) 311252, 4000-6000B.

Amanpuri Resort: Few resorts in Asia can compare with the almost legendary Amanpuri Resort—a place for the "Privileged Few" with prices to stop your heart: high-season rates *start* at 9000B! Pansea Beach, tel. (076) 311394, fax (076) 311100, 9000-18,000B.

KAMALA BEACH

This almost picture-perfect half-moon bay offers good sand, a friendly Thai fishing village, and few Western visitors.

Budget Bungalows: Several inexpensive bungalows and cafes are tucked away on the north end of the beach and down the path on Laem Sing Beach. Villagers in town also rent rooms at negotiable rates.

Phuket Kamala Resort: Situated on the central bay is a midpriced resort with swimming pool and dive facilities. 74/8 Moo 3 Kamala Beach, tel. (076) 212901, 1800-2400B.

Kamala Beach Estate: Private homes owned by top executives and Western investors are rented to visitors at Estates One and Two; an unusual opportunity for homestay rather than hotel accommodations. Fishermen's Tavern, under the supervision of a Michelin-rated chef, is considered one of the best on Phuket. Kamala Beach, tel. (076) 214803, 2600-3800B.

PATONG BEACH

This crowded yet beautiful four-km-long beach is the island's liveliest and most popular, the Pattaya of Phuket. Although it's fashionable to condemn Patong as overdeveloped, raunchy, polluted, expensive, and the worst example of unplanned madness (all true), the beach is outstanding and daytime activities run the gamut from sailboarding and snorkeling to parasailing and sunbathing. Nightlife revolves around countless bars, discos, massage parlors, and nightclubs which rage on until sunrise. Your impression will largely depend on what you expect from Phuket: Patong is a place for parties and good times, not solitude and contemplation!

Patong has all possible facilities: banks, police, post office, tourist police, international phones, travel agencies, car and motorcycle rentals, and scuba diving shops.

Water Sports

Patong Beach is the center for water sports on Phuket Island. Equipment rented from beach boys should be carefully inspected for signs of damage. Rates are variable and subject to negotiation. These are high season rates:

sailboarding	150-250B per hour
catamarans	300-500B per hour
Lasers	200-250B per hour
waterskiing	600-1000B per hour
parasailing	500B per sail
waterscooters	300-350B per hour
Jet Skis	600-800B per hour
deep-sea fishing	1500B per day

Budget Accommodations

Although budget travelers avoid Patong and generally head to Karon-Kata, over a dozen bungalows still survive with rooms for 250-400B. The best hunting ground is on Soi San Sabai,

he eastern extension of Bangla Rd. in the cen-
ral beach area. Soi San Sabai is a good location
since it's within walking distance of the beach
and Soi Bangla nightclubs, but somewhat removed from the general mayhem. Several other
acceptable spots with rooms under 400B are
located on North Rachautit Road. These are
quiet, but you'll need public transportation or
motorcycle to reach the beach and nightlife centers.

Patong has over 50 hotel and bungalow operations, so I'll just mention a few which appeared clean, quiet, and friendly.

Soi San Sabai: A half-dozen inexpensive
hotels are tucked away on the quiet extension of
Soi Bangla. **Summer Breeze Pension** (Bangkok tel. 02-723-0859) is a clean place with a/c
rooms from 500B. **Suksan Mansion** is a modern four-story hotel with fan rooms from 300B
and a/c rooms from 400B. Well-named **Duck
Tonight** and **Charlies Tonight** cost 250-350B
for fan-cooled rooms. German-managed **Jagerstube** (tel. 076-321202) has a popular restaurant
with award-winning breads and large a/c rooms
from 700B.

Bangla Road: Soi Bangla is the heart of the
beast—a nonstop string of honky-tonk bars,
wild nightclubs, pick-up joints, raging discos,
and low-life restaurants. Hence, bungalows are
noisy, but easy to find after consuming a case of
Singha. **Swiss Garden**, **Jeep 1** (tel. 076-
321264), **Valentine** (tel. 076-321260), and
Nordic Bungalows cost 250-350B fan and double for a/c.

Rachautit Road: Several inexpensive hotels are located north of Bangla Road. **Expat
Hotel** (tel. 076-321300) is quiet but has somewhat overpriced a/c rooms from 800B facing a
small pool. **P.S.** and **C & N** bungalows cost 300-
400B. Farther north are **Jeep 2** (tel. 076-
321100), **Star** (tel. 076-321517), Scandinavian-
run **Odin's Guesthouse**, and the spotless
Ladda Apartments with rooms from 350B.

Moderate Accommodations

Midpriced hotels in the 800-1500B range sport
a/c rooms, private baths, TVs, restaurants, and
perhaps a small swimming pool. Reservations
should be made in advance during the high season from November to March.

Lower Thavewong Road: A half-dozen
small, inexpensive hotels are tucked away at

ADDITIONAL PATONG BEACH ACCOMMODATIONS

HOTEL	RATES	TEL. (076)
A.A. Villa	1000-1500B	321499
Banthai	1600-2200	321329
Casuarina Lodge	900-1400	321123
Coconut Villa	600-900	321160
Coconut Village	1500-2200	321160
Club Andaman	1400-2400	321102
Diamond Cliff	3500-6000	321501
Duang Chit	2000-3200	321069
Holiday Inn	2600-4800	321020
Holiday Resort	800-1800	321119
Le Meridien	4500-8000	321480
Nordic	250-350	321284
Panorama	800-1400	321451
Paradise	500-650	321172
Patong Inn	800-1200	321126
Patong Lodge	1800-2600	321286
Patong Merlin	2800-5000	321070
Patong Palace	500-700	321359
Patong Resort	1200-1600	321333
Patong Villa	600-800	321132
Phuket Cabana	2000-3200	321138
Safari Beach	1400-1800	321230
Seaview	600-1200	321103
Sunset Mansion	300-900	321516
Sunshine	800-1400	321314
Thara Patong	1200-2200	321135
Tropica	1200-1800	321204

the south end of the beach road, variously
spelled Thavewong, Thawiwong, Taweewong,
and Taveewong! **Swiss Hotel** (tel. 076-321008)
costs 1500-1800B, **Bay View House** 1000-
1200B, **Patong Bed & Breakfast** 800-1000B,
and **K.V. House** (tel. 076-212236) 800-1000B.
Seagull Cottages (tel. 076-321328) is a good-
value complex with inexpensive fan-cooled bungalows for 700-900B and superior seaview
chalets for 1200-1500B.

Soi Post Office: Situated in the narrow alley
adjacent to the post office are several hotels
and restaurants such as Shalimar (Indian), Fuji
(Japanese), Cowboy (Western), Roma (Italian),

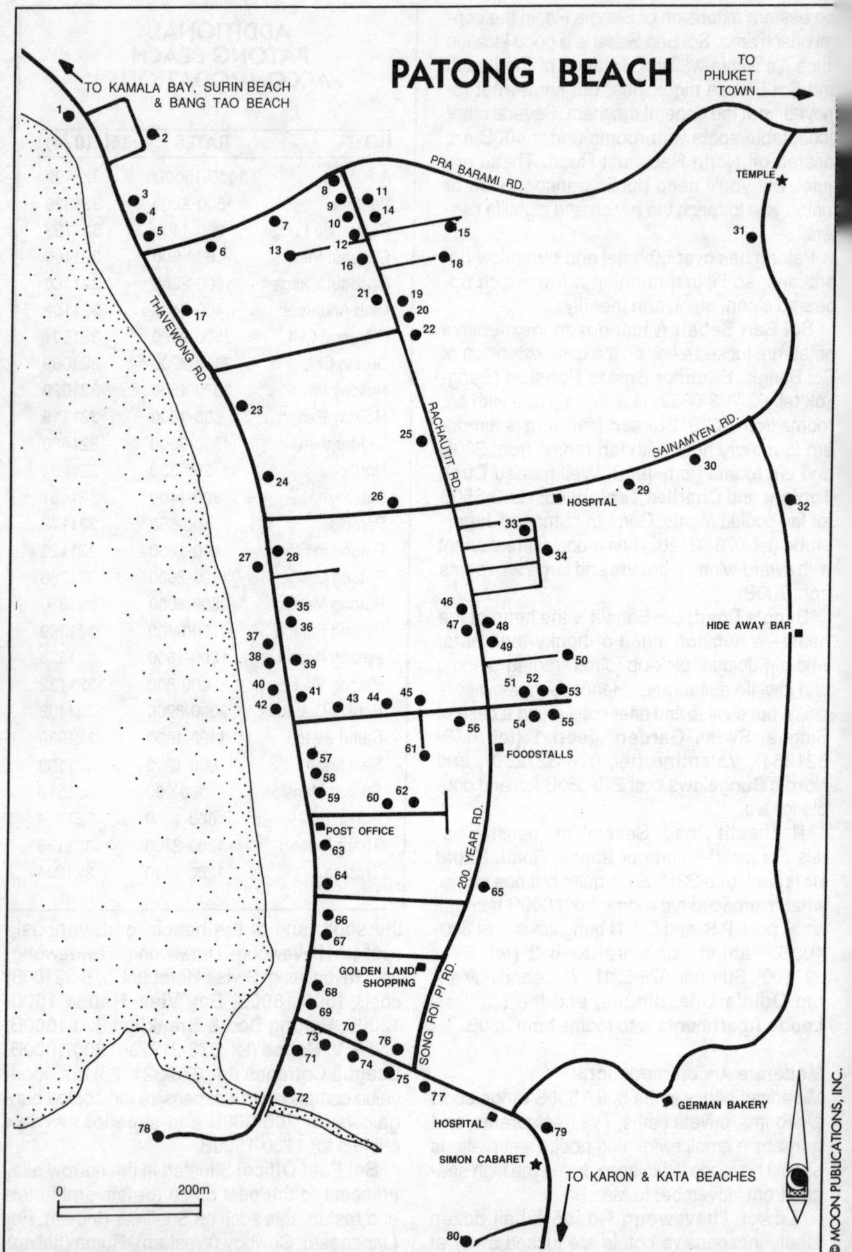

PATONG BEACH

TO KAMALA BAY, SURIN BEACH & BANG TAO BEACH

TO PHUKET TOWN

PRA BARAMI RD.

TEMPLE ★

THAVEWONG RD.

RACHUTIT RD.

SAINAMYEN RD.

HOSPITAL

HIDE AWAY BAR

FOODSTALLS

POST OFFICE

200 YEAR RD.

GOLDEN LAND SHOPPING

SONG ROI PI RD.

GERMAN BAKERY

HOSPITAL

SIMON CABARET ★

TO KARON & KATA BEACHES

0   200m

© MOON PUBLICATIONS, INC.

and My Way (gay). Bungalow choices include **Palace Inn**, **Patong Ko**, and **Cowboy Inn** with a/c rooms for 700-1000B.

Middle Thavewong Road: Paradise Hotel (tel. 076-321172) is a fine place with fan-cooled bungalows from 500B facing a lovely garden. Nearby **Club Oasis** (tel. 076-321258) has older but acceptable rooms in a quiet garden with singing birds.

On the Beach: Several midpriced hotels are located right on the beach. **Sandy House** (tel. 076-321458) lacks beach views but has cheap a/c rooms for 700-900B. **Islet Mansion** (tel. 076-321404) has rooms without views from 700B, and seaside vistas for 1000-1200B. Patong Beach Bungalows are old and not recommended.

Patong Beach Hotel: Gorgeous pool, outstanding views from the top floors, and spacious rooms make this deluxe hotel one of the better bargains at Patong. Bananas Disco is also recommended. 94 Patong Beach, tel. (076) 321301, fax (076) 321541, 1500-2400B.

K Hotel: Beautiful gardens, small pool, and efficient German management make this another good choice; popular with European group tours. Rachautit Rd., tel. (076) 321124, 800-1400B.

Neptuna Hotel: A lovely French-owned hotel with sculpted gardens, intimate French cafe, and a small but acceptable pool. Recommended. 82/49 Rachautit Rd., tel. and fax (076) 321188, 1400-1800B.

Sunset Mansion: Good-value rooms at the far north end of Rachautit Road. A.A. Villa is another modern, clean place. 73/24 Rachautit Rd. tel. (076) 321516, 300-400B fan, 600-800B a/c.

Luxury Accommodations
Top-end hotels over 2500B typically include a swimming pool, fitness center, tennis courts, and whatever else the marketing director has dreamed up. All can be booked through Bangkok travel agents.

Coral Beach: Removed from the clutter of central Patong, Coral Beach is an all-inclusive resort with swimming pool, squash, tennis courts, and fitness club. 104 Moo 4 Patong

PATONG BEACH

1. Thavorn Bay
2. Nerntong Resort
3. Patong Lodge
4. Diamond Cliff
5. Panorama Beach
6. Best GH
7. Similan
8. A.A. Villa
9. Sunset Mansion
10. Eden
11. P.S. 2
12. Patong Penthouse
13. Swiss Mansion
14. Shamrock
15. Berliner GH
16. Beau Rivage
17. Patong Seaview
18. Patong Grand Condotel
19. Odin's GH
20. Star
21. Ladda Apts.
22. Patong Bayshore
23. Club Andaman
24. Casuarina
25. Jeep 2
26. William Swiss
27. Phuket Cabana

28. Thara Patong
29. Nipha
30. Vises
31. New Tum
32. Royal Crown
33. Asia Guesthouse
34. Royal Paradise Hotel
35. K.S.R.
36. Patong Bay
37. Patong Beach Bungalow
38. Patong Bay Garden
39. Patong Villa
40. Islet Mansion
41. Safari Beach
42. Sandy House
43. Swiss Garden
44. Jeep 1
45. Valentine & Nordic
46. Neptuna
47. K
48. C & N
49. P.S.
50. Expat
51. Suksan
52. Super Mansion
53. Jagerstube
54. Summer Breeze

55. Duck Tonight
56. Ban Sukothai
57. Tropica
58. Patong Inn
59. Patong Beach
60. Palace
61. Patong Resort
62. Patong Ko
63. Banthai Beach
64. Club Oasis
65. Happy Home
66. Paradise Hotel
67. Holiday Inn
68. Patong Merlin
69. Holiday Resort
70. Thamdee
71. Seagull Cottages
72. Swiss, Bay View, Patong, & K.V.
73. Coconut Village
74. Holiday
75. Duang Chit
76. Coconut Cottages
77. Coconut Village
78. Coral Beach
79. Patong Hill
80. Le Meridian

Beach, tel. (076) 321106, fax (076) 321114, 3000-4500B.

Patong Bay Garden: The best hotel directly on the beach features a pool, roof garden terrace, and fine restaurant. 61/13 Thavewong Rd., tel. (076) 321297, fax (076) 321331, 3000-4500B.

Ban Sukothai: Ban Sukothai is something different: an attempt at traditional Thai archi-

tecture with pavilions and cottages in a landscaped tropical garden. A welcome change from the concrete cubicle. 95 Rachautit Road, tel (076) 321195, fax (076) 321507, 1800-3000B.

Royal Paradise Hotel: It's impossible to ignore the controversial architecture of the tallest hotel on Patong Beach. All rooms have panoramic views and the pool is spectacular, but the hotel is a long walk from the beach. 70

SCUBA DIVING NEAR PHUKET

Thailand's finest scuba and skin diving is centered on the islands and coral atolls near Phuket. Dive season is during the dry season from November to June, while waters during the rainy season get so murky you can't see your flippers.

Nearby Islands

Similan and Surin islands are considered the two finest dive sites, but beginners might enjoy the closer dives off the south and west coasts of Phuket.

Ko Pu and west coast islands are suitable for both scuba and skin divers who want a quick look at underwater Phuket. Coral Island and the Rajah (Raja or Racha) Islands, six and 15 km south of Rawai, offer fairly colorful coral beds and limited sealife. Shark Point and Ko Dak Mai, off Cape Panwa, feature submarine caves and a 30-meter wall dive with moray eels and (perhaps) leopard sharks. Anemone Reef includes striking rock formations, harmless gummie sharks, and blazing corals. Maiton Island is popular with divers, especially Japanese yuppies residing at Maiton Island Resort.

Distant Islands

Dive sites away from Phuket are superior, undisturbed by two decades of tourism and almost a century of tin dredging.

Similan Island National Park: Famous for its crystal-clear waters, tremendous marinelife, big-game fishing, and unsurpassed corals, this archipelago of nine wondrous islands reputedly offers the finest diving in Thailand. Island 8 is popular with divers; Island 4 offers simple bungalows and restaurant. Camping is permitted by the National Parks Department, but bring some extra water, food, and suntan lotion.

Similan, 70 km northwest of Phuket, is recommended for both scuba and skin divers since coral reefs lie just a few meters underwater. Dive expeditions are organized by all major dive shops, but the most experienced operators are Fantasea, Songserm, and Magnum. Five-day dives with transportation, accommodations, meals, drinks, all equip-

ment, and unlimited dives cost US$100-125 per day. Less expensive but very rushed day-trips are sponsored by Songserm Travel. Boats can also be hired from Ta Muang, north of Phuket; more information below.

Ko Phi Phi: The curiously named set of islands about two hours from Phuket are surrounded by sheer cliffs and crystal-clear waters rarely explored by Western divers. Dive groups are usually taken to the idyllic islands on the northwest and the isolated coves to the south. Many of the ordinary boats to Ko Phi Phi now stop for a two-hour dive near the birds' nest caves; everybody gets a free mask and dives overboard.

Dive Shops

Dive junkets can be arranged through dive shops in Patong, Karon, and Kata beaches. All rent equipment, fill tanks, and offer PADI certification courses. Fantasea, the first self-contained dive shop on Phuket, is represented in most of Phuket's major hotels, but their main office (tel. 076-321309) is on the beach road at Patong adjacent to the Paradise Hotel. Other reputable dive operators include Marina Divers (tel. 076-381625) at Kata-Karon Beach near Marina Cottages, and Andaman Sea Diving (tel. 076-381834) at Chalong Bay.

Prices

Prices and itineraries are fairly uniform from all shops. Equipment rentals cost 600-750B per day. Sample prices:

single dive	600-800B
two dives	1000-1200B
introductory course	1500-2000B
five-day course	6500B
PADI certification	8000-10,000B
divemaster certification	15,000B
Rajah Islands	1000-1200B
Phi Phi Islands	1400-2000B
Similan Islands	2500B per day

Paradise Complex, tel. (076) 321566, fax (076) 321565, 1500-6000B.

KARON BEACH

Phuket's second most popular beach remains beautiful, despite the rising tide of hotel construction and the creeping presence of nightclubs and so-called Bar Beers. Along with Kata Beach to the south, Karon seems much less crowded than Patong, and the hotel employees seem a little more willing to smile rather than stretch out their hands. There's little to do at Karon but sailboard, eat Phuket lobster, laze on the beach, and act nutty with the working girls. Surprisingly, an idyllic lagoon lies in the north end, and fishermen still pull in baskets of fish from the ocean.

Karon and Kata are far superior beaches to Patong.

Budget Accommodations
Karon is probably 80% upmarket hotels, but a handful of inexpensive bungalows under 300B are located at the south end, on a hill usually called Karon-Kata (or Kata-Karon) Beach. None are great value, but they're cheap enough to allow you to check out Phuket without wrecking your budget.

Kata-Karon Hill: The largest bungalow operation on Phuket is a sprawling complex of over 100 huts called **Kata Tropicana** (tel. 076-381408), located up a dirt road opposite Ruamthep Inn. The place has a limited number of bungalows for 150-300B, but most cost 300-600B. Facilities include a backpackers' restaurant and an enormous pig that wanders around and poses for pictures.

Up the hill and in a small valley with palms is **Happy Huts**, where old but acceptable bungalows cost 150-300B. **Kata Villa** on the main road costs 180-200B, but the huts are quickly falling down. **Kampong Kata** has six beautiful elevated bungalows with porches and flowers for 350-450B, plus a stunning restaurant decorated with Burmese antiques.

Su's Pool Hall has, logically enough, a pool hall on the main floor and 10 rooms upstairs which cost 250-300B with fan and 450-550B a/c. **Fantasy Hill** only costs 200-250B, but most of the rooms are in an ugly concrete longhouse.

On the Beach: A handful of other inexpensive bungalows still exist on Karon Beach. **Krayoon Bungalows,** just north of Kata-Karon Hill, is a clean place with small huts from 150B and larger chalets with private bath from 300B. **Dream Huts** in the north is friendly, cheap, and well removed from the crowds of central Karon. Original hippie huts here cost 180-280B.

Several inexpensive places are located in central Karon near the raging Club 44 Disco, including **Robin House** (tel. 076-381496), **Sandy Inn, Brazil**, and **Jor Guesthouse**. All cost 250-600B.

Karon Sea View is nicely isolated between open grounds and the beach, with okay bungalows for 300-400B.

Karon Hotel: A modern, clean hotel located in the new shopping development at the north end of Karon Beach. Manager Eric Conger runs one of the better value places. Recommended. 33/76 Patak Road, 300-400B.

Karon Guesthouse: Spotless rooms and friendly management make this another good-value place in north Karon. Rooms with fan and private bath cost 250-350B depending on length of stay. I stayed a week, but forgot to pick up their business card!

Crystal Beach Hotel: A large, modern hotel with restaurant, travel facilities,

ADDITIONAL KARON BEACH ACCOMMODATIONS

HOTEL	RATES	TEL. (076)
Golden Sand Inn	1200-1800B	381493
Kampong Karon	800-1000	212901
Karon Beach Resort	2600-3400	381521
Karon Royal Wing	3600-9000	381139
Karon Viewpoint	2600-3400	214440
Karon Villa	2600-3800	381139
Much My Friend	120-300	
Phuket Arcadia	3000-4800	381433
Phuket Island View	1600-2000	381633
Phuket Ocean	1400-1800	381599
Sand Resort	1400-1600	212901

and well-priced rooms. 36-10 Patak Rd., tel. (076) 381580, 350-700B.

Moderate Accommodations

Garden Resort: The former Kata Guesthouse is a Thai-style resort with both inexpensive fan rooms and pricier a/c chalets. Conveniently located on Kata-Karon Hill near the restaurants, nightclubs, and scuba diving shops. 121/1 Kata Beach, tel. (076) 381627, fax (076) 381466, 900-1500B.

Ruam Thep Inn: An older property in a wonderful location at the south end of Karon Beach. Other nearby midpriced hotels include the **Karon Beach Hotel** and popular **Marina Cottages**. 120/4 Moo 4 Pratak Rd., 600-800B fan, 1200-1500B a/c.

Green Valley Bungalows: Visitors with private transportation will enjoy this idyllic spot hidden away in a lush valley behind Hwy. 4028. Features a small pool, landscaped gardens, and plenty of coconut trees. 66/3 Patak Rd., tel. and fax (076) 381468, 900-1400B.

Luxury Accommodations

South Sea Resort: Not quite luxurious, but a good alternative to the very expensive hotels that dominate most of the beach. As with all other luxury hotels on Phuket, room rates are subject to 10% service charge, 11% government tax, and peak-season surcharges of 550-700B. 36/12 Moo 1 Karon Rd., tel. (076) 381611, fax (076) 381618, 2800-3400B.

Thavorn Palm Beach Hotel: Four swimming pools, five restaurants, luxurious rooms, and enormous grounds (just try to find the reception desk!) make this the best upscale choice on Karon Beach. 128/10 Moo 3 Karon Beach, tel. (076) 381034, fax (076) 381555, 3400-6000B.

KATA BEACH

Kata's two beaches—Kata Yai in the north and Kata Noi to the south—once served as Phuket's main hippie area until Club Med opened its facilities in 1978. Now, both have been largely blanketed with upscale hotels and expensive restaurants. Kata Yai is almost completely dominated by Club Med, though public access is provided by a beachside road. Kata Noi is a cozy cove with good sand and plenty of inexpensive bungalows.

KARON AND KATA BEACHES

1. Karon On Sea
2. Kampong Karon
3. Karon Viewpoint
4. Lume & Yai
5. Phuket Ocean Resort
6. Coco Cabana
7. Dream Huts
8. Phuket Golden Sand
9. Karon Hotel
10. Karon Guesthouse
11. Crystal Beach Hotel
12. Karon Bungalow
13. Much My Friend Guesthouse
14. South Sea Resort
15. Karon Villa
16. Royal Wing
17. Sand Resort
18. Karon Sea View
19. Phuket Arcadia
20. Thavorn Palm Beach Hotel
21. Karon Inn
22. Karon Village
23. Green Valley Bungalows

24. Holiday Village
25. Sandy Inn
26. Brazil
27. Jor Guesthouse
28. Phuket Island View
29. Krayoon Bungalow
30. Ruam Thep Inn
31. Karon Beach Hotel
32. Marina Cottages
33. Kata Villa
34. Kata Tropicana
35. Garden Resort
36. Happy Huts
37. Fantasy Hill
38. Kampong Kata
39. Hallo Guesthouse
40. Kata On Sea
41. Peach Hill Hotel
42. Lam Sai Village
43. Rose Inn
44. Dome
45. Inter House
46. Kock Chang
47. Bourgainvillea

48. Club Med
49. Sawasdee Guesthouse
50. Kata Sanuk Village
51. Kata Beach Resort
52. Kata Plaza
53. Sea Bees
54. Bell Guesthouse
55. P&T Katat House
56. Hayashi
57. Friendship Guesthouse
58. Sea Wind
59. Chao Kheun
60. Boat House
61. Cool Breeze Bungalow
62. Kata Delight
63. Pop Cottages
64. Chin's, Sweet Home Bungalows, Mr. At
65. Kata Thani
66. Island Bungalow
67. Kata Noi Riviera
68. Mansion
69. Kata Noi Club
70. Chew Bungalow

KARON AND KATA
BEACHES

TO PATONG BEACH

KARON BEACH

HOSPITAL

KARON - KATA

BAR BEER

CLUB 44

EASY
RIDER
BAR

POST OFFICE

TO PHUKET TOWN

KATA YAI BEACH

KATA NOI BEACH

TO NAI HARN BEACH
& PROMTHEP CAFE

0   500m

© MOON PUBLICATIONS, INC.

Budget Accommodations

Contrary to popular folklore, over a dozen bungalows and small hotels on Kata Beach have rooms for 300-500B. Most are located on Kata Noi Beach near the expensive hotels, or at the south end of Kata Yai near Kata Plaza.

North Kata Yai Beach: Several small spots near the clubs and Easy Rider Bar have acceptable if sometimes noisy rooms. **Hallo Guesthouse** (tel. 076-381631) is a modern high rise with clean fan and a/c rooms for 350-700B. Good value. Nearby **Rose Inn, Dome Bungalows, Kata On Sea,** and **Inter House** are nothing special but have cheap rooms from 300B. **Sawasdee Guesthouse** (tel. 076-381905) is a another choice with clean and modern well-priced a/c rooms for 350-600B.

South Kata Yai Beach: Several inexpensive places are located near Kata Plaza. Best choice is **Kata Sanuk Village** (tel. 076-381476) with small pool, comfortable restaurant decorated with European porcelains, and decent bungalows for 300-700B. **Friendship, Sea Bees,** and **Bell Guesthouse** have rooms for 300-600B. Longtime favorite Bell offers older nipa huts for just 150-200B.

Kata Noi Beach: Hippiedom survives in several bungalows wedged back from the big hotels that dominate the beach. **Cool Breeze** on the hill behind Kata Inn has four bungalows for 100B, three at 200B, and eight for 500B. **Chin's** above the Western Inn Restaurant and nearby **Sweet Home Bungalows** costs 200-300B. **Mr. At**—if you can find him—rents pleasant nipa bungalows under the trees for just 100-150B.

Island Bungalows directly on the beach is probably doomed for destruction, but until then offers breezy bungalows for just 200-500B; a rare opportunity to stay directly on the beach. **Chew Bungalows** are run down but situated on a great stretch of beach far removed from the hordes of tourists. Rooms cost just 200-300B.

Moderate Accommodations

Peach Hill Hotel: A clean and modern hotel with Chinese restaurant, snooker hall, and 40 a/c rooms. Centrally located on Kata-Karon Beach. 113/16 Patak Road, tel. (076) 381603, fax (076) 212807, 600-800B including breakfast.

Kata Noi Riviera: Several good-value hotels are located at the south end of Kata Noi, including the Riviera just opposite the desert-

ADDITIONAL KATA BEACH ACCOMMODATIONS

HOTEL	RATES	TEL. (076)
Boathouse	3400-6000B	381557
Bougainvillea	1400-1800	381463
Chao Kheun	600-1400	381403
Hayashi	1800-2400	381710
Kata Plaza Apts	1800-2400	381511
Kok Chang	400-500	381575
Mansion	1000-1400	381565
P&T Kata House	300-500	
Sea Wind	1200-1800	381564
Su's Bar	300-450	381443

ed beach. 3/21 Moo 2 Karon Beach, tel. (076) 381726, 300-700B.

Kata Noi Club: Attractive duplex bungalows make this another popular choice for midlevel travelers. Karon Beach, tel. (076) 215832, 400-700B.

Luxury Accommodations

Club Med: Club Med commands an enormous and highly coveted section of beachfront property on Kata Yai Beach. The aging resort offers all the standard amenities such as swimming pool, health club, tennis courts, water sports, and minicamp for the kids. An article in *Condé Nast Traveler* informed readers that last-minute discounts of 33-50% can be obtained by calling the Club Med Bangkok sales office at (02) 253-0108. Kata Yai Beach, tel. (076) 212901, 2800-4600B.

Kata Beach Resort: An enormous and very luxurious property which opened in 1990. Facilities include two swimming pools, water sports, and a soaring marble lobby that marks the most deluxe hotel on the beach. Kata Beach, tel. (076) 381530, fax (076) 381534, 3000-4500B.

NAI HARN BEACH

Phuket's most picturesque lagoon is backed by sweeping hills studded with coconut palms and exotic scrub. Once the haunt of hippies and backpackers, Nai Harn hit the big times with the 1985 opening of the extravagant Phuket Yacht Club. The entire valley is now under massive development and most of the natural lagoons have been converted into condo complexes with private waterways. Despite the drastic changes, swimming remains excellent except during the dangerous monsoon season, and the sunsets are still spectacular at nearby Promthep Cape.

Budget Accommodations

Most of the cheap huts have disappeared, except for a small collection of rudimentary bungalows just below the Phuket Yacht Club. **Grandpa's** and **Coconut Huts** cost 150-250B. **Ao San Bungalows**, located through the driveway of the Phuket Yacht Club, is a fine place tucked away on a private cove with old huts for 200-450B.

The last remaining choice is **Sunset Bungalows**, set on a hillside with excellent views over Nai Harn Bay. Sunset has over 25 cheap nipa bungalows and more expensive concrete cubicles. Rooms cost 200-500B, but it's often difficult to find the owners.

Moderate Accommodations

Jungle Beach Resort: The best-value place at Nai Harn is about one km beyond the Phuket Yacht Club, at the end of a dirt path surrounded by thick foliage. Facilities include a beautiful little pool, comfortable if somewhat funky restaurant, and 40 cantilevered bungalows in various price ranges. Ao San Beach, tel. (076) 214291, fax (076) 381108, 550-800B fan, 1500-2000B a/c. Phone ahead for transportation from the airport or Phuket town.

Luxury Accommodations

Phuket Yacht Club: One of the most exclusive hotels on Phuket Island dominates the northern end of Nai Harn Bay. Facilities include a small swimming pool, fitness club, and five dining venues under Swiss supervision. The prestigious Phuket King's Cup Regatta is held here each December. Nai Harn Beach, tel. (076) 381156, fax (076) 381164, 5000-9000B.

RAWAI BEACH

Beaches south and east were the original destinations for international tourists. Unfortunately, the region has suffered from past offshore tin mining, and the once-pristine beaches now tend to be muddy, unappealing, and lacking the nat-

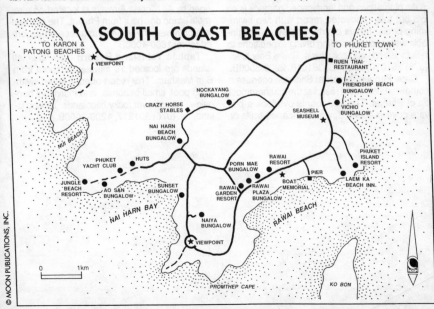

SOUTH COAST BEACHES

ural splendor of Patong and Karon beaches. However, if you prefer solitude over sand, then Rawai and Chalong beaches might be ideal. Both remain popular with scuba divers and have good restaurants facing tropical lagoons.

Budget Accommodations

Rawai Garden Resort has several large and lovely bungalows overlooking ponds and surrounded by coconut trees. Room rates vary on the season—and how wealthy you appear—but probably run 250-350B. **Rawai Plaza Bungalows** (tel. 076-381346) opened in 1990 with new, but unimpressive, bungalows for 300-500B. **Porn Mae Bungalows** (tel. 076-381300) has six decrepit nipa huts from 100B, and newer concrete rooms for 250-500B. **Rawai Resort** (tel. 076-381302) appears deserted, but the grounds are spacious and the bamboo bungalows are a good value at just 150-300B.

A few kilometers northeast and situated down narrow dirt tracks are **Vichio** and **Friendship Beach** bungalows with cottages on a narrow beach for 300-800B.

Luxury Accommodations

Phuket Island Resort: Nestled amid 65 acres of palm plantations and landscaped gardens is an old but fully renovated resort with two swimming pools, tennis courts, and every imaginable water sport including diving expeditions to nearby islands and coral beds. Rawai Beach, tel. (076) 381010, fax (076) 381018, 2200-3500B.

Cape Panwa Sheraton: Sheraton operates a somewhat neglected resort at the southernmost tip of Phuket. The 160 rooms overlook a private cove reached down landscaped trails or an electric tram. Dinners are served in the faux-colonial Panwa House and in the English-style grill of the Lighthouse. 27 Moo 8 Sakdidej Rd., tel. (076) 391123, fax (076) 391177, 3000-5800B.

OTHER ISLANDS

Located off the southeast coast of Phuket are a half-dozen islands developed with midlevel resorts. Boat service leaves from Rawai Beach, the pier on Chalong Bay, and the town of Ban Makham. Reservations and transportation can be arranged through agents in Phuket town.

Coral Island Resort: Thirty minutes by boat from Chalong is beautiful Ko Hay ("Coral Island") with dazzling beaches, isolated coves, and a resort with 40 bungalows and diving facilities. Contact their office in Phuket town at 53 Phuket Rd., tel. (076) 216381, 1000-1500B.

Lone Pavilion: Somewhat closer to Chalong is Lone Island, with a small fishing village, deserted beaches, and a 30-room resort on the northern side. 47/5 Chalong Bay, Phuket town office at 25 Bangkok Rd., tel. (076) 381374, 900-1400B.

Maiton Island: An expensive resort developed by All Nippon Airways is located on a remote island one hour from Phuket. The clientele is mostly wealthy young Japanese on escorted tours. 1800-4000B.

Taphao Yai Island Resort: Several small islands are located 10 minutes offshore from Ban Makham. This resort offers a tiered swimming pool, small beaches, and individual bungalows spread over rocky headlands. Taphao Island, tel. (076) 391217, 1200-2000B.

VICINITY OF PHUKET

PHANGNGA BAY

The surrealistic and unforgettable limestone mountains in Phangnga Bay—one of the great natural wonders in Southeast Asia—costarred with James Bond (if you consider Roger Moore the *real* James Bond) in the 1973 classic, *The Man with the Golden Gun*. Created by glacial flow some 10 millennia ago, Phangnga (pronounced pang GA) resembles Neolithic skyscapers not unlike the ethereal Chinese landscapes of Guilin; a world not to be missed.

Escorted Tours

Typical excursions glide through mangrove swamps thick with mudskippers, countless limestone outcroppings on the verge of collapse, caves festooned with prehistoric rock paintings, and stop briefly at Ko Panyi, a highly commercialized Muslim sea gypsy village constructed entirely on stilts. Nearby Khao Ping Gan (Ko Tapu or Leaning Mountain) is James's famous cliff.

Boat tours last four to six hours, cost 350-500B per person from Phuket agents, and leave mornings 0800-1000 from Tha Don Pier, 10 km south of Phangnga town. Transportation from Phuket beaches is included in the tariff.

An alternative tour along a less-traveled route leaves from Ao Po on Phuket Island, the departure point for Naga Island Pearl Farm. Asia Voyages conducts tours on their *Macha Nou*.

Independent Tours

Phangnga Bay is a wildly popular destination that sometimes resembles the Jungle Cruise in Disneyland. Independent travelers can cut costs, and escape the tourist hordes, by joining an organized party directly at the launching point. First, take an early-morning bus from Phuket town to Phangnga (93 km), then minibus to the boat dock at Tha Don. Bus arrivals between 0600 and 0800 are often met by Sayan Tamtopol, who has been leading tours for over a decade, or Mr. Kean, who operates from the Rattanapong Hotel in Phangnga town. The 150-200B price includes boat tour, seafood dinner, and a memorable night in a Muslim fishing village.

An early start from Phuket is essential, or spend a night in Phangnga and hook up with an independent boatman the following morning. Ten-man longtail boats chartered directly at the pier cost 300-400B.

Attractions

The whole of Phangnga Province is riddled with limestone caves now converted into Buddhist monasteries. Somdet Nakharin Park, three km south of Phangnga town, is known for Russi Cave, guarded by an image of a holy hermit. Suwan Khuna Cave, 13 km east of Phangnga, serves as a pilgrimage spot with dozens of reclining and seated Buddhas illuminated by shafts of sunlight.

Phangnga town itself offers Sonjao Mae Majabo Temple, a 150-year-old Chinese shrine in Penang style famous for its rare ink drawings which depict scenes from Chinese legends.

Accommodations

Phangnga town has several small and inexpensive hotels on the main street, and more expensive resorts down at the pier.

Ratanapong Hotel: A small and friendly hotel on the main road near the market. 111 Petchkasem Rd., tel. (076) 411067, 100-180B.

Ruk Phang Nga Hotel: Another choice near the market with inexpensive rooms. 100 Petchkasem Rd., tel. (076) 411090, 100-160B.

Lak Muang 2 Hotel: The best midpriced hotel is located slightly out of town near the tourist information center. Features the Mala Cafe, friendly management, and a/c rooms. 540 Petchkasem Rd., tel. (076) 411500, 300-750B.

Phangnga Bay Resort: An upscale hotel with swimming pool, restaurant, and private boat tours. Located down near Tha Don Pier. 20 Tha Don Road, tel. (076) 411247, 700-2000B.

SIMILAN ISLANDS

The nine islands of the Similan archipelago are widely regarded by underwater experts as among the finest dive destinations in Southeast Asia. Reaching the Similans and exploring the stunning corals and beaches is time-consuming and expensive, but worth the effort for serious divers and determined beach enthusiasts. The Similans—also called Ko Kao or Nine Islands—were declared a national park in the mid-1980s.

The Similans are 95 km northwest of Phuket and 65 km east of the closest mainland town of Thap Lamu. Their remoteness keeps them undisturbed, though increasing numbers of Thai and Western visitors now arrive to dive and perhaps spend a few days camping at the national park headquarters. Dangerous typhoons lash the islands, which can only be visited during the dry season from November to April.

Similan derives from *sembilan,* a Malay word which means "nine" to indicate the number of islands. Boats from Phuket and Thap Lamu first stop at Ko Miang (Island 4), where bungalows can be rented from the National Park Service. The western shores are pocketed with giant boulders on sparkling beaches, while the best diving is on the eastern coast where coral reefs extend toward Islands 3 and 5. Sealife includes giant groupas, poisonous lionfish, stonefish, and several species of harmless sharks such as hammerheads, blacktips, and bulls.

Visitors can overnight on Ko Miang, or continue north to Similan Island (Island 8) or Bhangu (Island 9) for about three hours of diving before returning to the mainland.

Accommodations

Bungalows on Ko Miang cost 450-1000B depending on the size of cabin and number of people. Independent travelers are allowed to share the cabins on a space-available basis. The park service also maintains 40 two-man tents which cost 150B per night. Campsites are also located on Similan and Bhangu islands. Reservations can be made by writing to National Parks Division, Lodging Service, Bang Khen, Bangkok 10900, or by calling their Bangkok office at (02) 579-0529. Arrangements can also be made on arrival, a risky proposition during the busy months of December and January.

Transportation From Phuket

The Similans can be reached from either Phuket or Thap Lamu. Dozens of tour operators on Phuket Island organize both day-trips and five-day excursions. **Songserm Travel** (tel. 076-

214472, fax 076-214301) charges about US$100 for a one-day tour which leaves Phuket hotels at 0630 and returns at 2000. The one-day quickie includes bus transfers to Thap Lamu, speedboat to the Similans, lunch, snorkeling equipment, and return to Phuket. Dive stops include 90 minutes on Miang Island and 2 1/2 hours at Similan Island.

Five-day tours with transfers, accommodations, and meals cost US$600-700 with an additional US$20 daily charge for scuba equipment. Contact Songserm, Seatran, Andaman Divers, or Phuket Aquatic Safaris in the Rasada Shopping Center in Phuket town. Other options include **Southeast Asia Tours** (tel. 076-321292), which operates a live-aboard dive boat, and **Fantasea** (tel. 076-321309) on Patong Beach, which cruises its 16-meter ketch, the *Andaman Explorer.* Departures are usually on Mondays and Fridays.

Transportation From Thap Lamu

Cheaper options are fishing boats and private charters departing from Thap Lamu, about 40 km south of Takua Pa or 109 km north of Phuket. The Similans are 40 km from Thap Lamu and take about three hours by fishing boat. Travelers have reportedly been able to hook up with Songserm speedboats at lower cost, but only on a space-available basis.

The best way to obtain information and organize a group party is to contact the bungalows north of Thap Lamu near Khao Lak National Park. Try Khao Lak Resort, Khao Sok Bungalows, or Poseidon Bungalows, described above under "Khao Lak National Park." All can be reached from Phuket by bus to Thap Lamu, then motorcycle taxi. As of this writing, three-day tours to the Similans with all amenities cost 1500-2500B.

KO PHI PHI

Phi Phi's almost indescribable combination of powdery white sands, brilliant blue waters, soaring limestone cliffs, and colorful corals makes it one of the most beautiful islands in all of Asia.

Phi Phi (pronounced Pee Pee to the amusement of visitors) was discovered in the early 1970s by backpackers who hitched rides with fishermen from Krabi and stayed with villagers in the port of Tonsai. It was a marvelous time.

The following decade witnessed an incredible amount of change as developers replaced the grass shacks with expensive resorts, and cheap cafes with pricey restaurants. Local authorities did little to control the sprawl which quickly spread up the mountains and off to the most isolated coves.

Ko Phi Phi (spelled Pee Pee and Pi Pi in other guidebooks) is now deluged with over a quarter-million annual visitors who completely pack every square centimeter of land and sand. Tonsai is a rather ugly village that has sold its soul to tourism, while piles of trash lie uncollected on even the most remote of beaches. In the space of less than a decade, Ko Phi Phi transformed itself from travelers' paradise to an environmental horror show.

Although this description will certainly infuriate local bungalow operators—and eliminate any warm welcome once extended to this travel writer—visitors to Ko Phi Phi should arrive fully informed about both the positive and negative aspects of the island.

And despite the damage, many visitors still regard the island as a wonderful place to laze in the sun, snorkel around the coral beds, and perhaps enjoy spectacular views from the limestone peak behind the small village.

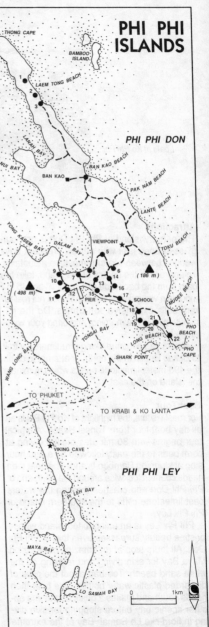

PHI PHI ISLANDS

1. P.P. International Resort
2. P.P. Coral Resort
3. Phi Phi Palm Beach
4. Pee Pee Island Village
5. P.P. Hill
6. P.P. Viewpoint
7. Krabi Pee Pee Resort
8. Charlie's
9. Gift Bungalow
10. Chang Khao
11. Tonsai Village
12. Pee Pee Island Cabanas
13. Ruen Thai
14. Rimna Villa
15. Phi Phi Don Resort
16. Gipsy Village
17. Pee Pee Andaman
18. Phi Phi Bayview Resort
19. Funnyland
20. Viking Village
21. P.P. Paradise Pearl
22. Long Beach Bungalow

boats at Ko Phi Phi

Attractions

The primary island of Phi Phi Don is an hour-glass-shaped islet with narrow crescent bays wedged between soaring limestone mountains. To appreciate the beauty of the island, take the path from the back side of Tonsai village to the mountain viewpoint where a thatched hut restaurant sells expensive soft drinks. Do the 45-minute hike in the morning, and bring your wide-angle lens.

Hikers can continue along a rudimentary trail to Bakao Beach in the north, or attempt to climb the 498-meter limestone peaks which dominate the island on the east.

Boat Tour

For most visitors, the highlight of Ko Phi Phi is an all-day boat tour from Tonsai Beach. A typical tour begins with 30 minutes of skin diving at coral beds to the east, followed by a one-hour stop at stunning Bamboo Island. The boat then heads counterclockwise around the north end of Phi Phi Don and crashes through the waters past limestone cliffs to the southern island of Phi Phi Ley.

Phi Phi Ley is an uninhabited island whose pristine beauty surpasses even that of Phi Phi Don. All tours stop at an amazing cove called Maya Bay for skin diving and relaxing on the white-sand beach. Too bad about the piles of discarded plastic water bottles. The boat then heads south and makes a quick detour into another scenic bay before stopping for skin diving in fiord-like Lo Samah Bay at the extreme

southern end. Pi Leh is another amazing bay, though most boat operators skip this cove in favor of Viking Cave; insist on a 15-minute cruise or you'll miss one of the wonders of Phi Phi.

The day cruise ends with an hour-long visit to famous Viking Cave, an immense cathedral named after cave pictographs which vaguely resemble ancient viking ships. Viking Cave is overrun with tourists but intriguing for its bamboo scaffolding used by bird-nest collectors and rickety gateway strung with a bizarre assortment of cables and cords.

Budget Accommodations

Phi Phi Don is a fully developed resort with dozens of bungalows and hotels in all price ranges. The least expensive places are located back from the pier on the west end of Lo Dalam Bay and east of Tonsai on narrow but uncrowded beaches. Most are rapidly being replaced by more expensive resorts. Prices have escalated sharply. Bamboo bungalows which cost 50-80B in the mid-1980s now cost 200-500B for the same decrepit shacks: Ko Phi Phi is *not* good value.

Accommodations are fully booked during the high season from November to May, and during the summer holiday months of July and August. Travelers can escape the tourist hordes by visiting Ko Phi Phi in October or June. Rooms can be located by walking along the beach, or with hotel touts who greet arrivals at the pier.

Lo Dalam Bay: Gift Bungalows has rudimentary huts for 100-150B, though the place is usually full and the owners are impossible to find. Nearby **Chong Khao** has similar digs for 150-200B.

Interior Bungalows: **Ruen Thai** across from the **Rock Bar**, and **Blue Moon, Thara Inn**, and **Twin Palm** are cheap, but located in noisy tourist ghettos that will depress you.

Tonsai Beach: Phi Phi Don Resort has small bamboo bungalows back from the water for 150-200B, and large concrete cubicles facing the water for 350-500B. The place is primitive and bisected by the beachside trail, but conveniently located near the restaurants and pier.

Pee Pee Andaman Resort (tel. 01-213-0691) is a large operation with over 100 huts in all price ranges. Their primeval shacks cost 100-150B, good-value huts with private bath are 200-250B, and better beachside chalets with private bath cost 400-500B. Ask for beachside huts numbered 26-45.

Long Beach: Farther east on Had Yao (Long Beach) is **Funnyland, Viking Village,** and **Long Beach Bungalows** with bamboo huts and wooden A-frames for 200-450B, plus newer rooms at twice the price. Had Yao offers a touch of tranquility, plus excellent skin diving over the nearby coral beds. Longtail boats shuttle passengers from Tonsai pier to Had Yao.

Moderate Accommodations

Ko Phi Phi lacks direct phone service, but most of the midlevel bungalows can be reserved by calling their agents in Krabi (area code 075), Phuket (076), or Bangkok (02)—a good idea in the high season and during July and August.

Lo Dalam Bay: Charlie's Resort (tel. 02-224-2786) is a low-priced, acceptable-quality complex with rooms for 400-800B. The overflow is handled by adjacent **Krabi Pee Pee Resort** (tel. 075-611484), with 60 rooms for 300-600B.

Interior Bungalows: Probably the best mid-level place is a cantilevered hillside complex called **P.P. Viewpoint Resort** (tel. 075-612193), where individual bungalows connected by rickety wooden walkways cost 650-900B. The beach is a 10-minute walk. Highly recommended.

P.P. Hill (tel. 076-723-0865) to the rear is fairly luxurious but lacks vegetation and gets very hot from March to June. Another excellent choice is **Rimna Villa** (tel. 076-212901) with well-spaced clean bungalows for 500-800B overlooking a small valley. Very quiet and secluded.

Nearby **Gipsy Village** (radio tel. 01-723-0674) has 30 new bungalows lined up in perfectly straight lines. The arrangement is unimaginative, but rooms are good value at 250-400B.

Tonsai Beach: Several midpriced resorts are located east of the pier on Tonsai Beach and over the rocky headlands on Long Beach. **Pee Pee Andaman** has some good-value bungalows for 400-600B.

Long Beach: Had Yao, probably the best beach in the region, can be reached on foot in 45 minutes or with longtail boat from Tonsai pier. **P.P. Paradise Pearl** is an old favorite with over 100 bungalows priced 350-800B. **Long Beach Bungalows** at the end of the beach has cheap huts under 200B, and better chalets from 350B. A trail continues over the headlands to a small cove and the fishing village of Lo Mudee.

Luxury Accommodations

Almost a half-dozen resorts are now located on Ko Phi Phi at Tonsai Beach, Bakao Beach, and Laem Tong Beach.

Tonsai Beach: Left of the pier you'll find **Pee Pee Island Cabanas** (tel. 02-255-7600, 075-611496), where a/c chalets are badly overpriced at 1800-2200B. **Tonsai Village** is another overpriced resort which dates from the early 1980s. Both have expensive restaurants and crowded beaches frequented only by group tours booked by uninformed travel agents.

Ba Koa Beach: The upscale situation improves considerably once you escape Tonsai Beach. **Pee Pee Island Village** (tel.02-277-0038, 076-215014) offers elevated native-style bungalows on a private beach for 1000-2000B. The beach is beautiful and the atmosphere laid back, but the huts should cost half the price.

Laem Tong Beach: Once home to a large colony of sea gypsies, Tong Beach Cape is where all the new development has occurred in the last decade. A 60-meter concrete pier has recently been completed, and the sea gypsies have fled to quieter coves.

P.P. Coral Resort (tel. 02-251-1909, 076-211348) has over 30 individual bungalows connected by wooden walkways over pure white sand. **P.P. International Resort** (tel. 02-250-0768, 076-214297) is a very luxurious destination with over 120 a/c rooms for 2000-3500B. Facilities include a glass-bottom boat for coral spotting, water sport rentals, and a restaurant with Thai, European, and Chinese seafood specialties.

Phi Phi Palm Beach Resort (tel. 076-213654, fax 076-215090) is the latest addition, with the widest range of facilities: the only freshwater pool on the island, tennis, windsurfing, sauna, two restaurants, and private cottages for 3000-4500B. Highly recommended for upmarket visitors.

Transportation

Ko Phi Phi is 40 km southeast of Phuket and 42 km southwest of Krabi. The island is served by an amazing variety of boats from both Phuket and Krabi. Daily boat service runs during the dry season from October to June, with limited crossings during the monsoons from July to October.

From Phuket: Songserm has 10 boats ranging from 40-man fishing vessels to the enormous 600-passenger *King Cruiser* catamaran which is actually an automobile ferry, a curious contradiction since there are no roads and no cars on Ko Phi Phi. Songserm express boats cost 200-250B each way, take two hours, and depart several times daily from Phuket harbor at Ao Makham.

Other services from Phuket are offered by over 20 companies including Andaman Queen, Aloha Tours, CBC Ventures, Pee Pee Hydrocraft, Seatran, Silver Queen, and Diamond Travel. All travel agents on Phuket sell tickets which include transportation from your hotel to Phuket pier.

From Krabi: Transportation from Krabi includes over a dozen daily departures on anything from fishing boats to sleek cruisers. Krabi guesthouses sell tickets, or wander down to the pier and take the next available boat.

PHUKET TO HAT YAI

KRABI

Krabi Province comprises one of the most geologically interesting and scenically stunning landscapes in Thailand. Situated within a few hours of the provincial capital of Krabi lies an oceanic wonderland of magnificent limestone outcroppings surrounding white-sand beaches and primeval islands.

Krabi town is a pleasant place, but has little to offer except for a good selection of guesthouses and transportation connections to nearby destinations such as Ko Phi Phi, Pranang Cape, and Ko Lanta. Visitors should be forewarned that Krabi—once the idyllic counterpart to Phuket and Ko Samui—is now completely overrun with travelers and tourists. Last year, an estimated 300,000 visitors passed through town, mostly Europeans on holiday in search of an untouched paradise.

Although the original Thai character has disappeared, the friendly people and well-developed infrastructure make Krabi an acceptable stop en route to nearby beaches.

Wat Tham Sua

Krabi is known for its beaches and islands, though a few cultural sidelights are located near the provincial capital.

Tiger Cave Monastery, seven km east of Krabi, is a decade-old retreat set in a natural amphitheater of caves and gigantic trees. Named after a rock formation which resembles a tiger paw, southwestern Thailand's most important forest *wat* was established by Achaan Jumnean Silasetho, a venerable monk from Nakhon Si Thammarat who uses grisly pictures of internal organs to emphasize the transitory nature of life. Each day, an estimated 200 monks and nuns gather before dawn to collect alms in Krabi, then return to the monastery to study Theravada Buddhism and listen to sermons broadcast over loudspeakers mounted in the banyan trees. Afternoons are spent in meditation, or perhaps chatting with the infrequent Western visitor.

Meditation practices at Tiger Cave Monastery emphasize *vipassana,* a yogic system which translates to "insight meditation," and the Buddhist precept of *mehta* (loving kindness). Visitors are welcome to climb up the long staircase at the end of the parking lot and politely wander past the cave sanctuaries and *kuti* huts to a pair of absolutely huge banyan trees with soaring buttresses that would dwarf an elephant. The jungle path continues through some thick foliage before returning to the stairway. Be sure to visit the meditation hall and museum with Buddhist images and photos of Achaan Jumnean. Tiger Cave Monastery is highly recommended for anyone interested in Buddhism or *vipassana* meditation.

Wat Tham Sua can be reached from Krabi by mini-truck to Krabi junction at Talat Kao, then any bus heading south to the turnoff to the monastery. The monastery is two km up the road. Motorcycle taxis from Krabi junction to the monastery cost five *baht.*

North Of Krabi

Several worthwhile caves and waterfalls are situated north of Krabi in the direction of Ao Leuk Nua, a small town 42 km up Highway 4. Mini-trucks and buses head to Ao Leuk Nua, but most of the attractions are well off the main highway and difficult to reach without private transportation.

The best option is a rental motorcycle. Traffic is light and most of the sights are marked with English-language signs. An extremely scenic tour can be done in a single day with an early start, but bring along the *Guide Map of Krabi* published by V. Hongsombud—an absolute necessity!

Reclining Buddha: A colorful concrete Buddha lies serenely under a pair of limestone peaks on Hwy. 4034. The road continues southeast down to the shell cemetery and Ao Nang Beach.

Shell Cemetery Beach: Su San Noi is a famous shoreline collection of fossilized seashells at Laem Pho, 19 km west of Krabi. The site is composed of limestone slabs flecked with thousands of oyster shells that date back some 75 million years. Although a rare geological phe-

KRABI

TO MAIN HIGHWAY,
KRABI JUNCTION,
PHUKET, & TRANG

SNOOKER
HALL

SANONG RD.

GAS
STATION

UTTARADIT RD.

KRABI
RIVER

HEMATANON RD.

LANTA VILLA
OFFICE

2

BOXING
STADIUM

SUKHON RD.

TO
AO NANG BEACH

BANK

3

MARKET

CHAN PHEN
TOURS

SRISAWAT RD.

5

4

BANK

6

REAN PARE
RESTAURANT

PATANA RD.

SUZUKI
BIKES

KRABI
RESORT

CINEMA

PRACHA CHUEN RD.

MINIBUS TO
MAIN HIGHWAY

15

7

16

8   9   10   11

12

CHAO FA
PIER

RUEN RUDEE RD.

14

WAT KORAVARAM

13

ISARA RD.

BOOKS

NIGHT MARKET

TO
KO
LANTA

17

18

21

19

SOI RUAM CHIT

20

POST OFFICE

22

25

ISARA RD.

WANAPUK RD.

23

SAMUSAN RD.

CITY HALL

26

24

SOI RUAM CHAI

27

CHAO FA RD.

IMMIGRATION

KRABI RD.

CHAMAI RD.

VICHIT RD.

PROVINCIAL
HALL

TELEPHONE

POLICE

0   100m

© MOON PUBLICATIONS, INC.

TO KO
PHI PHI

...omenon, Su San Noi actually resembles a slab of parking lot that fell into the ocean; unimpressive and hardly worth the effort unless you arrive at low tide in the early-morning hours.

Ao Nang Beach: Ao Nang is described below. Have a cold drink and then continue north. Beyond the coconut tree near Ban Khao Klom, the deserted road passes limestone mountains, rubber plantations, and sheets of latex drying in the sun. Take a photo and the kids laugh at you.

Khao Phanom Benja National Park: Ten km north of Krabi is the turnoff to the 50-square-km national park known for Tham Khao Phung Cave and the three-tiered falls of Huay To. Campsites are located at park headquarters.

Diamond Cave: A right turn 40 km north of Krabi and two km south of Ao Leuk Nua leads to Tham Phet, one of the largest and most beautiful caves in the region.

Ao Leuk Nua: This small town is the junction point for stops to nearby caves and falls. **Ao Luk Bungalows,** about 200 meters west on Hwy. 4039, has private bungalows from 200B.

Tham Bokarani National Park: A small national park with limited trails and some minor falls is located two km west of Ao Leuk Nua. The trail to the left leads to greenish bathing pools which drain through the mixed forests. Nearby **Waterfall Inn** has rooms from 200B fan and 300B a/c.

Dirt roads farther east lead to Than Khao Pra (past the golf course!) and the boat dock for Tham Hua Kra Lok, a riverside cave with ancient pictographs.

Budget Accommodations

Krabi has exploded in recent years after a massive renovation project replaced most of the old wooden shacks with modern shop houses, since converted into guesthouses, cafes, and travel agencies. The best guesthouses are located on the new street of Ruen Rudee, or outside town in quieter locales.

Walker Pub & Guesthouse: A "Place for all Nations" is a clean and modern joint with authentic beds (not mattresses on the floor) and a popular cafe with Western food and country and western music. 34-36 Ruen Rudee Rd., tel. (075) 612756, 100-150B.

Seaside Guesthouse: A new, clean, and quiet spot with both fan and a/c rooms. 105/5 Maharaj Rd., tel. (075) 612351, 100-150B fan, 250-300B a/c.

K.L. Guesthouse: Another good choice with 43 rooms tucked between their a/c cafe and liquor store. 28 Ruen Rudee Rd., tel. (075) 612511, 100-250B.

K.R. Mansion: Slightly outside town is a very comfortable guesthouse with fully furnished rooms, spotless bathrooms, and popular cafe. A recommended escape from downtown Krabi. 52/1 Chao Fah Rd., tel. (075) 612545, fax (075) 612762, 120-200B.

Rong's Guesthouse: Krabi's most peaceful guesthouse has great views and comfortable restaurant about one km northwest of town. Another idyllic alternative to Krabi town. 17 Maharaj Rd., no phone, 100-150B.

Other Guesthouses: Inexpensive crash pads are springing up on a near-weekly basis. Most charge 50-80B for mattresses spread on floors and common bath, or 100-150B for furnished rooms with private bath. Current favorites include **Mark & May** on Ruen Rudee Rd., **Suzuki Guesthouse** above the Suzuki dealership, overpriced **Chao Fa Valley Resort** on Chao Fa Rd., and several near the pier such as **Songserm, Sea Tours, Kanaab Nam, Cha, L.R.K.,** and **Thammachat** guesthouses.

KRABI

1. Rong's Guesthouse
2. Ban Sib Guesthouse
3. Vieng Thong Hotel
4. Jungle Guesthouse
5. B&B Guesthouse
6. New Hotel
7. K.P.B. Guesthouse
8. Coconut Guesthouse
9. Walker Guesthouse
10. K.L. Guesthouse
11. Mark & May Guesthouse
12. Pine Guesthouse
13. Seaside Guesthouse
14. Krabi Thai Hotel
15. L.R.K. Guesthouse
16. Thammachat Guesthouse
17. Songserm
18. Sea Tours Guesthouse
19. Kanaab Maw Guesthouse
20. Cha Guesthouse
21. Ruamjid Guesthouse
22. Lek Guesthouse
23. New Best Guesthouse
24. Sunshine Guesthouse
25. Friendly Guesthouse
26. Chao Fa Valley Resort
27. K.R. Mansion

Moderate Accommodations

Krabi has two midpriced hotels which cater to group tours, and several luxury hotels under construction.

Vieng Thong Hotel: A recently renovated hotel with clean and large, but badly overpriced rooms. 155 Uttaradit Rd., tel. (075) 611188, 350-450B fan, 650-800B a/c.

Krabi Thai Hotel: Krabi's best has less expensive rooms in the old building and more luxurious choices in the newer wing. 7 Isara Rd., tel. (075) 611122, fax (075) 612556, 250-350B fan, 500-800B a/c.

Transportation

Krabi is 815 km south of Bangkok, 176 km east of Phuket, 211 km southwest of Surat Thani and 282 km north of Hat Yai.

Air: Bangkok Airways will fly from Bangkok, and possibly Phuket, after the Krabi airport is completed in the next few years. At present, the nearest airport is on Phuket.

Boat: By far the most interesting approach to Krabi is by sea from Phuket via Ko Phi Phi. Boats depart 0700-1100 from Phuket and take about three hours to Ko Phi Phi. Boats continue from Ko Phi Phi to Krabi at 0900 and 1300. A better option is direct boat from Ko Phi Phi to Ao Pranang ("Pranang Cape"), the premier beach destination near Krabi.

Ko Lanta, a relatively untouched island two hours south of Krabi, can be reached by direct

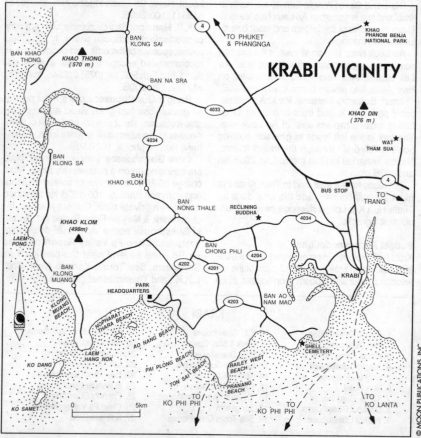

KRABI VICINITY

© MOON PUBLICATIONS, INC.

boat service at 0930, 1100, and 1430. Buses to Ko Lanta leave from Patana Rd. just opposite the bank.

Probably the ultimate adventure is to hire longtail boats from Krabi south to Tarutao National Park, with overnight stops at the islands of Pu, Lanta, Ngai, Muk, Libong, and Sukorn.

Bus: Most buses from Bangkok, Phuket, Surat Thani, Ko Samui, Trang, and Hat Yai drop passengers in Talat Kao (Krabi junction), a small town five km north of Krabi. Mini-trucks continue south to town for five *baht*. Arrivals are often greeted by touts who help with direct connections to the major beach destinations near Krabi, such as Pranang Cape and Ko Phi Phi.

Bus tickets from Krabi can be purchased from dozens of agents, including the **Songserm** agency (tel. 075-611741) across from the customs house, and helpful Miss Lee at **Chan Phen Tours** (tel. 075-612004) on Uttaradit Road. **Leebi Travel** (tel. 075-611150) on Isara Rd. organizes direct bus/boat connections to Tarutao National Park and Langkawi Island in Malaysia. Sample schedules:

Destination	Depart	Hours
Phuket	hourly	3
Surat Thani	hourly	3
Hat Yai	0700, 1100	4
Ko Tarutao	1030	6
Ko Samui	hourly	6
Langkawi	1030	8
Penang	0700	10
Bangkok	1600, 1700	14
Kuala Lumpur	0700	16
Singapore	0700	24

AO NANG BEACH

Geographical terminology is somewhat confusing around Krabi. Ao Nang Beach, 17 km northwest of Krabi, is a disappointing stretch of sand that caters mostly to group tourists shuttled here by uninformed travel agents. Hat Nopharat Thara is a somewhat better beach to the north. Pranang Cape—also called Ao Phra Nang (Pranang Beach) or Laem Phra Nang (Pranang Cape)—is one of the most stunning destinations in Thailand and the focal point for informed visitors.

Ao Nang, however, is cursed with mediocre sand and murky waters, but offers decent accommodations in a dramatic juxtaposition of beach and mountains. Longtail boats to Pranang Beach leave on demand from the waiting shed in the middle of the beach. **Marine Sports Center** adjacent to Sea Breeze Bungalows runs inexpensive snorkeling tours to nearby Pada and Chicken islands—probably the best reason to stay on Ao Nang. **Last Cafe** at the south end of the beach serves homemade brown bread, cakes, and yogurts; the most pleasant spot on the beach.

Ao Nang is best considered an overnight stop en route to Pranang Beach.

Accommodations
Bungalows are springing up weekly to serve the ever-increasing crowds. Minitrucks from Krabi pause at the Bank of Siam and the boat launch to Pranang Beach, then continue west past the bungalows facing the beach.

The best spots appear to be **P.S. Cottages** (directly on the beach), **Coconut Garden** with simple huts arranged around a landscaped courtyard, and semiluxurious **Krabi Resort** for upscale visitors.

Sample prices from south to north:

Dum Guesthouse	60-100B
Jungle Hut	80-150B
Krabi Seaview	350-800B
Green Park	150-200B
B.B. Bungalows	150-200B
Princess Garden	150-300B
Phra Nang Inn	1000-1200B
Ao Nang Villa	300-900B
Peace Bungalows	600-1000B
Gifts	150-250B
Coconut Garden	150-250B
Sea Breeze	150-250B
Ao Nang Bungalows	150-250B
P.S. Cottages	200-500B
Ao Nang Ban Lae	250-400B
Krabi Resort	1200-2000B
Ao Nang Thara	300-600B

Transportation
Ao Nang can be reached from Krabi in 40 minutes with mini-trucks leaving from Uttaradit Road near Chan Phen Tours.

NOPHARAT THARA BEACH

One km north of Ao Nang, and 18 km from Krabi, is a broad and clean beach supervised by Phi Phi Islands National Marine Park. The road from Ao Nang terminates at the parking lot adjacent to park headquarters and several small cafes. Just beyond is a broad estuary which can be waded across, except during and immediately after the monsoon season. The sand is very fine and known for the quality of its seashells, best uncovered at low tide. Nopharat Thara is usually deserted and a fine place to wander around for some solitude.

Accommodations

Bungalows and campsites can be arranged at the park headquarters just behind the parking lot. The remainder of the privately owned bungalows are across the estuary.

Emerald Bungalows: Pleasant restaurant, nightly videos, and bungalows for 120-500B make this a popular spot. For transportation details, contact Emerald Tours (tel. 075-612258) at 2/1 Kongka Rd., just up from the Krabi pier.

Krabi Andaman Inn: Another remote place with dozens of bungalows set amid pine trees. Small huts cost 60-100B, while private bungalows cost 250-350B. Krabi office (tel. 075-611932) is at 6/1 Patana Road.

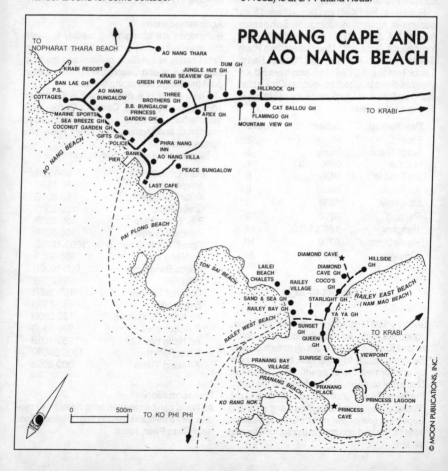

PRANANG CAPE AND AO NANG BEACH

Pranang Beach

Pine Bungalows: Located about six km west of Nopharat Thara Beach and around the cape on Ao Siam Beach. Dives can be arranged to nearby Ko Dang and Ko Bileh, and to coral beds just offshore. Pine has small huts for 60-100B and larger bungalows with attached bath for 120-250B. Contact Pine Tours (tel. 075-612192) on Prasak Uthit Rd. near the Thai Krabi Hotel.

Transportation

Mini-trucks from Uttaradit Rd. in Krabi leave frequently for park headquarters. Bungalows across the estuary on Nopharat Thara Beach are served by longtail boats from the parking lot, or with free transportation arranged from travel agents and guesthouse representatives in Krabi.

PRANANG CAPE

Pranang Cape is only comparable to the wonders of Ko Phi Phi: an amazing landscape of soaring limestone mountains, aquamarine waters, and squeaky white sand in an outlying corner of paradise. The special grandeur of Pranang comes from the limestone cliffs encrusted with vegetation that resembles an instant designer garden, and pinnacles leeched by rains into phantasmagoric shapes not unlike embryonic dollops of dripped wax. Pranang Beach is composed of silken sand so white it almost hurts your eyes. Few places in Thailand offer such a stunning combination of water, sand, and land.

Pranang was first discovered in the early-1970s by travelers who whispered to fellow trippers the almost unbelievable beauty of the remote cape. As it goes with such places, Pranang was subsequently developed by wealthy speculators into a major tourist destination with all the benefits and drawbacks of famous resorts.

Compared to Phuket or Ko Samui, Pranang is still somewhat off the beaten track, but the pace of change has accelerated in recent years, and it seems inevitable that serious damage will be done unless government officials stem the uncontrolled development. Bungalows are now packed together and occupy almost every square centimeter of available land, while discos blast away until dawn. Pranang—like Ko Phi Phi—is a very small place that has quickly become overwhelmed without any signs of government intervention.

The worst news is that upscale resorts are planned by Thai hotel consortiums. Several years ago, Siam Lodge tried to purchase a nearby cove called Pai Pong and construct Paradise Cove Hotel, an exclusive resort connected to the main road through a 400-meter tunnel. Plans have been temporarily shelved, but it's only a matter of time before Pranang changes from a simple paradise to another developed resort. Stay tuned.

Attractions

Lazing on the beach and volleyball at sunset are the main activities, but hikers and divers will also enjoy the natural wonders.

Princess Cave: A large cave at the south end of Pranang Beach derives its name from a mythical sea goddess who gave birth to her earthly lover. Fishermen now place wooden phalli inside to ensure successful fishing and protect against seasonal monsoons.

Princess Lagoon: Spectacular views and unforgettable photographs are possible by climbing the steep trail up the limestone peak behind Princess Cave. Ropes help with the treacherous trail which winds left to the viewpoint and then descends down to a gigantic lagoon of seawater. Rock climbers can continue up the mountain for views over the entire cape and the islands of Ko Poda and Ko Hua Kwan.

Diamond Cave: Up the hill behind Diamond Cave Bungalows is a large cave with a short walkway and dripping stalactites. Borrow a flashlight from the caretaker and slide between the iron bars. Local folklore claims this the grand palace of the mythical sea princess, while Princess Cave is her summer palace.

Ton Sai Beach: The secluded beach just north of Railey Beach can be reached at low tide, but first check the tide charts at Sunset Bungalows or risk a long swim back to Pranang.

Ko Poda and Chicken Island: Islands east of Pranang Beach provide excellent diving and simple accommodations on deserted beaches. Ko Rang Nok ("Bird Nest Island") is a closer alternative known for its birds' nests, undersea cave, and sunken boat for skin divers. Day-trips and overnight stays can be arranged through most bungalows. Multi-day kayak trips are organized from a small shop on Pranang Beach.

Accommodations

Pranang Cape is divided into three beaches with distinct price classes. Pranang Beach at the south end has the most expensive digs, Railey West is midpriced, while Railey East is the last refuge of cheap bungalows under 100B. Bungalows are filled to capacity during the high season from November to March, when visitors must sometimes camp out under the coconut trees while waiting for a vacancy. Bungalow reps in Krabi can help with reservations.

Railey Beach East: Also called Nam Mao Beach, Railey East is hardly more than a long mudflat overgrown with mangrove trees.

Sunrise Bungalows at the west end has semiluxurious chalets for 300-500B. Queen Bungalows has decent if somewhat overpriced huts for 150-250B. Ya Ya Bungalows, and the aptly named Swamp Shack Disco, are somewhat cheaper but suffer from loud music that might drive you crazy. Coco's is a small place with just six huts. Diamond Cave Bungalows has a small basketball court, the lively Blue Bar tucked away under the limestone mountain, and bungalows for 60-120B. Hillside Bungalows at the far eastern end offers good views from the restaurant and distinctively painted huts for 50-100B.

Pranang Beach: The south end of the cape offers the finest sand, best swimming, yachts bobbing in the blue lagoon, and a pair of mid-priced resorts.

Pranang Bay Village (Krabi tel. 075-611944) is a slightly upscale place with decent bungalows for 250-500B, but select a room away from the noisy Bamboo Pub. Nearby La Cave Bar offers live saxophone music and "drinks at normal prices." Phra Nang Place (Krabi tel. 075-612172) is where the yachties hang out and sip exotic drinks in the attractive restaurant. Elevated bungalows with private bath cost 300-650B. The information center at the reception desk has tidal charts and notes on boat rentals and yacht owners searching for crew.

Railey Beach West (Lailei Beach): The longest and most popular beach, with a half-dozen bungalow operations and private homes at the northern edge. Flanked by a pair of towering limestone mountains, Lailei Beach is the place to start your room search.

Sunset Bungalows at the western end is a very pretty place with 45 bungalows elevated on wooden platforms, rather than the ugly concrete bases used elsewhere. Rooms here cost 350-600B. Railey Bay and and Starlight Bungalows to the rear offer ordinary, overpriced bungalows for 200-350B. Sand & Sea has the most popular restaurant on the beach, volleyball games at sunset, and average bungalows for 150-300B. Railey Village at the eastern end is a better choice, with bungalows for 150-250B facing a grassy courtyard and rows of palms.

The final word in luxury is provided by Lailei Beach Chalets (Bangkok tel. 02-278-2676, Krabi tel. 075-611944), a private American development. Luxurious chalets rented from expat homeowners cost 600-1200B. This property will soon become a major hotel.

Transportation

Pranang Cape is 15 km northwest of Krabi and can only be reached by longtail boat from Krabi or Ao Nang Beach. Don't confuse Ao Nang with Pranang; if you are on a beach with a road, you haven't reached the latter.

Boats from Krabi cost 30B and take about 45 minutes. Ask to be dropped on Railey Beach West, not the first stop at Pranang Beach. High-tide arrivals are sometimes dropped on Railey East.

Boats from Ao Nang cost 20B and take about 15 minutes, passing Pai Pong Cave and Ton Sai Beach.

KO LANTA

The search for an undiscovered paradise is quickly pushing travelers south from Krabi toward the Malaysian border and dozens of islands located near Trang and Satun. Several years ago, Ko Lanta was an offbeat destination inhabited only by Muslim fishermen who couldn't understand why anyone would visit their hot and remote island. Ko Lanta today has over a dozen bungalows stretched along the west coast, from the northern village of Ban Sala Dan down to Ban Sangka U at the southern tip.

Ko Lanta archipelago consists of over 50 islands, but only Ko Lanta Yai (Big Ko Lanta) and a few small islets have formal accommodations. Ko Lanta offers some fairly good beaches almost completely untouched by mass tourism, and a bit of skin diving over offshore coral beds. Another sidelight is the near-complete dominance of Islam on the island; a world where Muslim mosques vastly outnumber Buddhist *wats*.

Ko Lanta has a few drawbacks. The isolated location demands at least two full days of travel from Bangkok or Phuket, though direct boat service is now offered from Krabi and Ko Phi Phi. Secondly, the sand ranges from fairly good crystal to rough volcanic rock depending on the beach. Weather can also be a problem: the island is murderously hot in the dry season from March to June, and like other islands on the west coast of southern Thailand, monsoons bring heavy downpours from June to October. Getting around is difficult since transportation along the west coast is sporadic; visitors often find themselves limited to a single beach. Finally, most of the bungalows are senselessly crammed together to the point of absurdity and constructed from concrete and tin rather than natural materials. What Lanta desperately needs are enlightened bungalow operators who understand that Western visitors want clean bamboo huts, restaurants without concrete, and enough space to swing a cat.

Although the island has drawbacks—and lacks the stunning topography and pristine beaches of Ko Phi Phi and Pranang Cape—visitors searching to escape the crowds and willing to endure some transportation hassles will probably enjoy their discovery.

Ban Sala Dan

The largest village on Ko Lanta is where most boats from Krabi and Ko Phi Phi terminate. Ban Sala Dan is a typical Thai fishing village, with several cafes overlooking the bay and Ko Lanta Noi, new spots like La Creperie which serves French crepes and sells boat tours, and motorcycle rentals from Petchpalin Restaurant. Money-exchange services will probably arrive by the time you visit.

Sahamit Tours at the central intersection sells bus tickets to Bangkok and boat tickets to Krabi and Ko Phi Phi. Seaside Restaurant down the dusty street is a good place for a cold drink.

Kor Kwang Beach

A few bungalows are located west of town on the rocky promontory called Laem Kor Kwang. The beach itself (Kaw Kwang) is nicely curved, absolutely deserted, and has aquamarine waters with a few fishing boats.

Deer Neck Cabanas at the northern edge of the cape, and Kar Kwang Beach Bungalows to the south, have decent huts for 100-150B.

Klong Dao Beach

Nearly all the bungalows on northwestern Ko Lanta are situated on a two-km stretch of sand called Klong Dao. The perfectly straight beach with rocky outposts at both ends is shaded by casuarina trees rather than much-preferred palms. Almost a dozen bungalows are sited here.

Golden Bay Cottages (radio phone 01-723-0879) at the north end is a major operation with small huts for 40-80B, and larger digs with private bath for 150-200B. Formerly called Club

TO KRABI

4206

TO KRABI

HUA HIN

KO RAPULE

KLONG MAK

KO PHI

TO KO PHI PHI

KO LANTA

KO LANTA NOI

KO DAENG

KOR KWANG BEACH

DEER NECK CABANAS

BAN SALA DAN

GOLDEN BAY COTTAGES

LANTA VILLA

KLONG DAO BEACH

LANTA SEA HOUSE

LANTA GARDEN BUNGALOW

PALM BEACH BUNGALOW

PALM BEACH

LANTA BUNGALOWS

LANTA CHARLIE BUNGALOW

▲ (287 m)

KO TALABENG

TO KO BO MUANG

BAN THUNG SAN

BAN PRA AE

BAN KLONG KHONG

MARINA HUTS

KO LANTA YAI

KLONG KHONG BEACH

BAN JALEE

KO KAM

BAN KLONG NIN

LANTA ANDAMAN

KLONG NIN BEACH

LANTA PARADISE

BAN KLONG NAM JUD

BAN KO LANTA

KO PO

▲ (488 m)

SUN SEA BUNGALOW

BAN KAN TIANG

KAN TIANG BEACH

BAN KLONG CHAK

BAN SANGKA U

KO KLANG

KLONG CHAK BEACH

AO MAE PAI BAY   LAEM TANOT

0   3km

© MOON PUBLICATIONS, INC.

...anta, the place has friendly managers, but cafe service is so slow you might starve to death.

Lanta Villa features a large and popular restaurant, money-exchange facilities, fishing trips, longtail rentals, and dozens of huts senselessly crammed together and priced 50-150B. They also sell tickets to Bangkok. Nearby **Lanta Bungalows** is trashy.

Lanta Charlie Bungalows' 40-plus deluxe chalets are packed together like canned sardines. Rooms cost 200-500B. The whole affair goes downhill with an ugly concrete-and-tin restaurant that makes you want to return to Ko Samui.

Sea House's decrepit old huts and newer bungalows that need porch railings cost 50-150B. The place appears popular with middle-aged tourists who would probably appreciate some landscaping and trash collection. Just okay.

Lanta Garden Bungalows, the original hippie huts on Ko Lanta, is a better choice with 10 huts priced 40-150B.

Palm Beach

South of Klong Dao is a beautiful four-km beach with excellent pure white sand and small surf in the winter months.

Mr. Bat at **Lanta Palm Beach Bungalows** rents simple but decent bamboo huts for 50-150B.

Ban Pra Ae, a fishing village at the southern end of Palm Beach, has some abandoned huts under groves of palms trees and new bungalows up on the hill.

Palm Beach seems destined to be the next major beach on Ko Lanta. Let's hope the hotel owners are blessed with some sense of aesthetics.

Klong Khong Beach

Nine km south of Ban Sala Dan is a small beach with limited sand but plenty of offshore corals for diving and an excellent grove of swaying palms.

Marina Huts, just south of the small village of Ban Klong Khong, is a beautifully situated guesthouse with about 30 A-frame bamboo huts for 50-120B, plus a tent campsite on grassy lawns. Kerosene lamps substitute for electricity—a welcome touch which hopefully won't change with the arrival of mass tourism.

Klong Nin Beach

The road splits at Ban Klong Nin, forking south to Laem Tanot and other beach bungalows, and east across the hilly spine to Ban Ko Lanta, from where boats depart to the mainland.

Klong Nin is a five-km-long, perfectly straight, and absolutely deserted beach with a handful of fishing boats pulled up over tons of white sand. Great potential here.

Lanta Andaman Bungalows is an ugly dive without views of the beach.

Lanta Paradise Island (mobile tel. 01-723-0528) offers about 40 bungalows priced 80-250B at the south end of a very fine beach. Huts, unfortunately, are unimaginatively packed together in rows four deep, and the restaurant is nothing short of tacky. Tours and dives can be arranged to the nearby islands of Ko Son, Jam, Bubu, Talabeng, Hai, Bok, and even Phi Phi. Other services include windsurfing, gamefishing, and motorbike rentals. Lanta Paradise is aggressively marketed and appears popular with families, kids, and German tour groups.

Kan Tiang Beach

Eighteen km south of Ban Sala Dan is the final series of coves and deserted beaches. Sun Sea Bungalows on Had Kan Tiang offers bamboo huts for 50-120B.

The dirt road continues south to Klong Chak Beach and Ao Mai Phai Beach near the cape of Laem Tanot. The road ends at the cape, but a narrow path continues east around the rocky headlands to the Thai Muslim fishing village of Ban Sangka U.

Transportation

Ko Lanta Yai is 100 km southeast of Krabi, 77 km northwest of Trang, and 12 km from the mainland pier at Ban Bo Muang.

Boat: The most convenient way to reach Lanta is by direct boat from Krabi or Ko Phi Phi. Travel agents sell tickets and can advise on the latest schedules.

Most boats terminate in the town of Ban Sala Dan at the north end of Ko Lanta Yai. Minitrucks and motorcycle-taxis continue south down to the beaches. Bungalow owners are often on hand with photos, personalized recommendations, and private transportation. Motorcycles can also be rented in Ban Sala Dan.

Land: Ko Lanta can also be reached with public transportation and by hired motorcycle. Two routes are possible. From the Talat Kao junction (Krabi junction) near Krabi, take a mini-truck or bus south to Ban Hua Hin and continue by public ferry to Ko Lanta Noi and finally Ban Sala Dan on Ko Lanta Yai. The entire 100-km journey takes a half day with public transportation, but only three hours with rented motorcycle.

Alternatively, take public transportation to Ban Ba Muang (Bo Muang), at the end of Highway 4042 and about 88 km south of Krabi. Ban Ba Muang is the primary ferry port for Ko Lanta; large 80-passenger ferries depart for Ko Lanta several times daily, take about one hour, and stop at Ban Ko Lanta on the east side of the island. Mini-trucks and motorcycle-taxis meet the ferry and then head over the mountains to the west-coast beaches.

ISLETS NEAR KO LANTA

Several of the small islets near Ko Lanta Yai have been developed into private hideaways. Most of the bungalows have representatives in Krabi who can show you photos of the property and advise on transportation.

The string of islands continues south to Ko Hai, Ko Muk, and Ko Kradan, before reaching the mainland town of Trang. All islands now have bungalows; islands to the south are described below under "Islands and Beaches Near Trang." Adventurous travelers can hire longtail boats on Ko Lanta, motor south, and visit each island before stopping at Trang or Ko Tarutao National Park.

Bubu Island
Bubu Bungalows is a typical operation with just 13 huts priced 200-500B per night.

To reach Ko Bubu, take a mini-truck from Krabi to Bo Muang pier on the mainland, followed by a private or chartered boat across to the small island. Transportation can also be arranged in Krabi from Thammachart Tours (tel. 075-612536) at 13 Kongka Rd. near the Chaofa pier.

Ko Si Boya
Ko Si Boya is a small island north of Ko Lanta with a solitary set of bungalows called Islander Huts. Ko Si Boya is deserted except for a few fishermen, and the beach is fairly clean despite murky waters.

Reservations and transportation clues in Krabi are available from Siboya Tours (tel. 075-611108) at 246 Uttaradit Road.

Ko Jum
North of Ko Lanta Yai is another small islet where Jum Island Resort offers basic bamboo huts for 100-150B, and more luxurious chalets for 250-600B. Up the beach is Joy Bungalows and Mama Bungalows with simple huts for 50-150B.

Transportation can be arranged in Krabi from the Jum Island Resort office, and from the New Krabi Hotel (tel. 075-611541) at 9/11 Patana Road.

TRANG

Trang is the gateway to one of the newest tourist regions in Thailand. The town itself is reasonably clean and attractive and within a day's journey are more than 20 waterfalls located within national parks, several large limestone caves filled with Buddhist images, and wildlife sanctuaries. The highlights of Trang, however, are the broad and deserted beaches on the western coastline, and a half-dozen small islands with pure-white beaches and outstanding diving.

Like Phuket, Trang owes its original prosperity to the Fukien Chinese who settled here in the late 19th and early 20th centuries. Originally located in Kantang at the mouth of the Trang River, the town was moved to its present location (the former Taptieng) by King Mongkut to avoid annual floods and protect against naval invasion. Trang now derives most of its wealth from hundreds of rubber and palm-oil plantations located in the outlying countryside.

Attractions In Town
Trang itself has little of great interest aside from a few historic monuments and its pleasant layout over a series of small hills or *khuans*. The central clock tower—constructed in an unusual shape with a narrow base and wide top—is a good spot to try local specialties such as roast pork braised in honey from local street vendors. East of the clock tower is the historic governor's house, city hall, and courthouse on a small

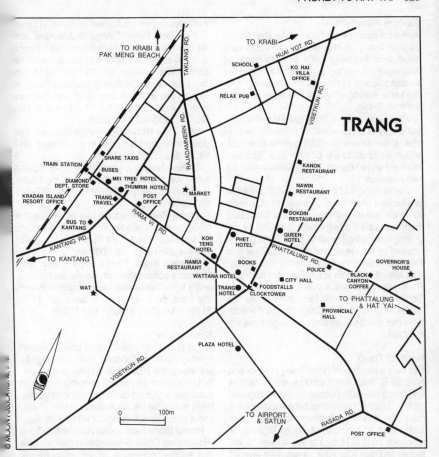

TRANG

TO KRABI &
PAK MENG BEACH

TO KRABI

TAKLANG RD.

HUAI YOT RD.

SCHOOL

KO HAI
VILLA
OFFICE

RELAX PUB

RAJADAMNERN RD.

VISETKUN RD.

TRAIN STATION

SHARE TAXIS

BUSES

DIAMOND
DEPT. STORE

MEI TREE HOTEL

THUMRIN HOTEL

KRADAN ISLAND
RESORT OFFICE

TRANG
TRAVEL

POST
OFFICE

MARKET

KANOK
RESTAURANT

NAWIN
RESTAURANT

DOKDIN
RESTAURANT

QUEEN
HOTEL

BUS TO
KANTANG

RAMA VI RD.

KANTANG RD.

TO KANTANG

KOH
TENG
HOTEL

PHET
HOTEL

PHATTALUNG RD.

POLICE

GOVERNOR'S
HOUSE

NAMUI
RESTAURANT

BOOKS

WATTANA HOTEL

CITY HALL

BLACK
CANYON
COFFEE

WAT

TRANG
HOTEL

FOODSTALLS

CLOCKTOWER

TO PHATTALUNG
& HAT YAI

PROVINCIAL
HALL

VISETKUN RD.

PLAZA HOTEL

0   100m

TO AIRPORT
& SATUN

RASADA RD.

POST OFFICE

© MOON PUBLICATIONS, INC.

---

khuan which provides views toward Khao Nong Yuan, where a small temple enshrines a footprint of the Buddha.

Trang often wins the "Cleanest City in Thailand" award, which makes a visit to its municipal market and wholesale Taklang Market a fairly pleasant experience. One km south of the clocktower is Praya Rusadanupradit Park, which honors the civic leader who introduced rubber to the province, and Kapang Surin Park, where a pleasant pond has been covered with acres of flowers and lotus blossoms.

Since a majority of local residents are of Chinese descent, Trang features over 20 Chinese temples or joss houses rather than the typical collection of Buddhist *wats*. The largest and most famous of these Chinese temples are Kew Ong Eia and the century-old Chao Por Muen Ram. Both serve as venues for the famous 10-day Vegetarian Festival celebrated in late October to honor the nine major deities of the Chinese pantheon.

Trang is also known for its bullfights which pit bull against bull, and wickerwork baskets woven from pandanus leaves that serve as bridal gifts and household decorations. Shadow puppet plays are occasionally given at the municipal hall.

Eastern Waterfalls

Almost a dozen waterfalls are located 20 km east of Trang on Highway 4125, which runs south from Highway 4. En route to Kachong National Park, visitors might enjoy a stop at the weaving village of Namunsri on Highway 4, or the knife-making village of Pranapor some 10 km from Trang.

Kachong National Park has limited wildlife but plenty of birds, a wildlife museum, beds in shared bungalows for 100B, and the Blue Trail, which leads up to the primary falls. The falls are best visited during or immediately after the rainy season.

The remainder of the falls and wildlife refuges are located south down Highway 4125. Similar to Thale Noi near Songkhla, Lam Chan Bird Park resembles a large swamp visited by migrating fowl during the fall months. Sairung Falls, created by the meeting of the Palian River and Banthat Mountains, is signposted and located four km off the main road. Four km farther is Praisawan Falls, with a series of cold plunges. Tonteh is a 320-meter falls, considered the largest and finest near Trang. Nearby Tonetok Falls can now be accessed up a rough three-km dirt road.

North of Trang

Highway 4 heads north from Trang to Krabi and Nakhon Si Thammarat, past several waterfalls and caves filled with Buddha images. A large reclining Buddha is protected behind railings in a cave called Wat So Rachapradit (Wat Tham Iso), about 20 km north of Trang. Highway 4 proceeds west at Huay Yot and arrives 15 km farther at Tham Kao Pina, where a six-leveled limestone cave offers the Bantom Image and views from the top of the staircase. Wat Kao Pra, 15 km north of Huay Yot, has been studied by anthropologists for its mysterious red symbols carved into the walls, and the mummified body of an abbot which shows few signs of decay. Seventeen km east of Klongpang is Wat Tham Pra Buddha, with a reclining Buddha perhaps dating from the Ayuthaya Period.

Accommodations

Trang remains well off the tourist trail and most of the hotels cater to Thai visitors rather than *farangs*. Nearly all the hotels are in the center of town within a few blocks of the bus terminal, train station, and clock tower on Rama VI Road.

Koh Teng Hotel: Trang's backpackers' center offers a very useful bulletin board with maps and bus schedules, photos of nearby beach resorts, and a notebook with firsthand tips on current travel conditions throughout Trang Province. Rooms are spacious and clean, and the manager is extremely helpful. 77-9 Rama VI Rd., tel. (075) 218622, 120-180B.

Mei Tree Hotel: Somewhat cheaper digs down near the train station. 4-8 Sathani Rd., tel. (075) 218103, 80-120B.

Queen Hotel: A good-value hotel located near several decent restaurants and nightclubs. Visetkun Rd., tel. (075) 218119, 160-180B fan, 160-300B a/c.

Trang Hotel: A refurbished hotel near the clock tower that often grants 30-50% discounts by request. 134/2 Visetkun Rd., tel. (075) 218944, 300B fan, 700-800B a/c.

Thumrin Hotel: Trang's only luxurious hotel features a comfortable cafe, convention facilities, and a limited amount of tourist information from the front desk. Thumrin Square, tel. (075) 211011, fax (075) 218057, 600-1200B.

Restaurants

Trang specialties include roast pork marinated overnight in honey, coconut-filled dumplings for breakfast, and *khanom jin*, a Chinese-style curried noodle dish served with condiments such as cucumbers, pickled cabbage, and mint leaves. Night stalls near the clock tower are fast, cheap, and a good place to hang out with the locals.

Namui Restaurant across from the Koh Teng Hotel serves Chinese seafoods in their a/c cafe and garden enclosure to the rear. Kanok Restaurant on Visetkun Rd. is a popular modern place that, unfortunately, overlooks a badly polluted canal. Probably the most comfortable, clean, and reasonably priced stop is the a/c Hoa Coffeeshop in the Diamond Department Store down near the train station.

Transportation

Trang is 870 km south of Bangkok, 136 km south of Krabi, and 163 km northwest of Hat Yai.

Air: Thai Airways International flies once daily at 1625 from Phuket. Thai Airways office (tel. 075-218066) is at 199 Visetkun Road.

Train: Rapid train No. 41 departs from

ualampong Station in Bangkok at 1830 and kes 16 hours to Trang. The train back to angkok departs at 1400.

Bus: Air-conditioned buses from the Southern us Terminal in Bangkok take about 14 hours to rang. Direct bus service is also available from Krabi, Satun, and Hat Yai.

Getting Around: Nearby waterfalls, national parks, and beaches can be reached with public buses and mini-trucks leaving from the informal terminals near the train station. Buses to Kantang leave from Kantang Rd., just off Rama VI Road. Share taxis to Krabi, Satun, and Hat Yai can be found on Rama VI Rd. near the train station.

Motorcycles are a handy way to quickly tour the region. Bikes can be rented from the Koh Teng Hotel, free-lance operators who hang out in the market, and from a fellow named Prechai at the Pak Meng bus stop.

Services
Most of the islands near Trang have representatives in town who can help with transportation and reservations. Trang Travel on Rama VI Rd. conducts one-day island tours with snorkeling on weekends only. Kradan Island Resort office is on the new road adjacent to Diamond Department Store. Ko Hai Villa office is on Visetkun Rd. past the cafes and nightclubs.

Scuba divers can contact Arrien Cornils at Rainbow Divers (tel. 075-218820) at 63/6 Soi 2 Visutkun Road. Arrien and his German partner operate a dive boat fitted with new equipment, and plan to establish a dive resort in the next few years.

ISLANDS AND BEACHES NEAR TRANG

The star attractions of Trang are the nearby beaches and islands which are rarely visited by Western tourists. Most are administered by the National Park Service, which grants permits to private bungalow owners and dive operators headquartered in Trang.

Bungalows are now located on Ko Kradan, Ko Sukorn, Ko Muk, Ko Hai, and Ko Libong. Without direct competition, most are somewhat expensive, but as tourism increases this situation will probably improve. The latest information can be picked up at the Koh Teng Hotel in Trang.

Tour operators in Trang can help with transportation and escorted tours to the islands. Boats to Ko Hai and Ko Kradan leave in the mornings from the small village of Pak Meng, though service is sporadic and subject to cancellation during the monsoon season. Ko Kradan and Ko Muk can be reached by longtails from Sinchai Bungalows on Hat Yao Beach. Ko Libong is served by boats from Kantang, the primary port town for Trang Province. Ko Sukorn is reached by ferry from Palian.

Pak Meng Beach
Pak Meng is a small fishing village 38 km from Trang. The modest beach has a few small cafes, an offshore limestone peak called Ko Meng, and the fishing pier from where boats depart in the mornings for Ko Hai and Ko Kradan. Simple accommodations are available with Kit in the first foodstall, and with Joi in the last bungalow on the left. Nong Dam Guesthouse, about three km south of the intersection, has rooms for 100-150B and a very friendly lady manager.

Pak Meng can be reached with a mini-truck from Trang toward Sikao, with a change at the intersection.

Chang Lang Beach
Hat Chao Mai National Park headquarters is located on a long and deserted stretch of sand called Chang Lang, 47 km from Trang. The visitor center has a hand-painted map which describes the park boundaries, topographic and oceanic maps, bathrooms, large bungalows from 600B, and tent sites on the front lawn.

The side road continues south to another campsite situated under casuarina trees near an impressive limestone outcropping with a small cave on the right.

Kuan Tunggu is a small fishing village with an intriguing charcoal factory and chartered longtails across to nearby Ko Muk.

Yong Ling Beach
A dirt track leads west to a narrow but clean beach flanked by a limestone mountain and usually deserted except for some partying Thais. Visitors can hike north along the coast and crawl through a series of interconnected caves.

Chao Mai Beach
Hat Chao Mai (Hat Yao) is probably the most at-

tractive and popular mainland beach near Trang. The five-km beach stretches from the fishing village of Chao Mai around a pair of limestone buttresses north to Yao and Yong Ling beaches. Beneath the limestone peak is a 30-meter cave with dripping stalactites over a sandy walkway. Backed by casuarina trees and with magnificent views across to Ko Libong, Chao Mai provides an idyllic counterpart to the more populated beaches near Krabi and on Ko Lanta.

Several Thai entrepreneurs have recently opened simple bungalows on Chai Mai. North of the limestone buttress is Mr. Wong's, with good food and bungalows from 100B, though it's not clear who runs the place: Mr. Wong, his wife, or the ducks? Bungalows are also available at Sinchai's Chao Mai Resort, owned and operated by a friendly guy who once served in Vietnam with the Thai army before being stationed in Florida. Sinchai has picnic tables under the trees, two longhouses with rooms from 100B, and full-day boat trips to the nearby islands of Ko Muk, Kradan, and Libong.

Chao Mai can be reached by shared taxi from Bangkok Bank in Trang to the port town of Kantang, followed by a ferry ride across the inlet, from where mini-trucks leave around 1100. Late arrivals can check on additional trucks or hire a motorcycle taxi for about 60B. Holding on to your bags for the long and dusty ride is an ordeal.

Ko Hai

Technically included with Krabi Province to the north, Hai Island (Ko Ngai) features sandy beaches, crystal-clear waters, and some excellent diving on the west coast. Divers can also explore the seven-colored coral gardens and watery caves at nearby Ko Chuak—ranked one of the best dive sites in the region—and a cathedral-shaped cavern filled with sharks and barracudas at Ko Wan.

Ko Hai now has three sets of bungalows on the east shore. Koh Hai Village (tel. 075-218674) at the north end has 28 bungalows for 250-1000B. Koh Hai Villa (tel. 075-218923) in the middle costs 150-300B, while Koh Ngai Resort (tel. 075-210317) at the south-end pier costs 400B in the longhouse and 900-1400B for private a/c chalets. The first two resorts rent two-man tents for 150B. Reservations and transportation can be arranged by their travel representatives in Trang.

Ko Muk

Ko Muk ("Pig Island"), the second-largest island in Chao Mai National Park, is considered the premier dive site of the archipelago. The leading excursion is a low-tide boat entrance into 60-meter Tham Morakot ("Emerald Cave") at the southwest corner. After passing through 80 meters of darkness, the boat emerges into an illuminated cavern filled with an emerald-green lagoon surrounded by circular limestone walls. Passengers must escape the lagoon before high tide or risk being stranded inside the watery cathedral.

Phangka Cove and the fishing village of Hua Laem are situated on the east side of the island.

Accommodations are provided at Koh Mook Resort, where modern individual bungalows cost 150-200B with common bath and 200-300B with private facilities.

Ko Kradan

Kradan, a teardrop-shaped formation south of Ko Muk and Ko Hai, is another lovely island administered by the Parks Department with limited land set aside for the private cultivation of rubber and coconuts. Aside from the sparkling beaches, Ko Kradan ("Plank Wood Island") features a magnificent coral reef on the east side with a diversity of sealife such as moray eels, leopard sharks, and barracudas. Due south lies a 60-meter Japanese freighter sunk in the 1940s which once supplied troops stationed on Phuket. The wreck is largely untouched, though it lies in over 60 meters of water.

Ko Kradan Resort (tel. 075-211367) has tents for 150B, old bungalows from 500B, and newer chalets from 800B. Reservations and transportation are arranged from their Trang office near the Diamond Department Store.

Ko Libong

Trang's largest island has three Islamic fishing villages accessed by regular ferries from Kantang. Wide beaches are found near the villages, while divers can visit the bird sanctuary island on the north. Tung Yakha Beach on the west side is clean and deserted, but the most popular spot is Tonke Bay on the north, where swimmers can rinse off under Thung Yaka Falls. Ko Libong is also known for its delicious *hoi chakten* oysters harvested from October to March.

Ko Libong (Talibong) accommodations include homestays and Shosin Guesthouse in the middle fishing village, though the villagers are fundamentalist believers who often charge unreasonable prices. The Forest Conservation Office maintains inexpensive shelters and campsites at Tonke Bay, while camping is permitted on Tung Yakha Beach. Bungalows and campsites operated by the Botanical Department are located at Juhoi Cape Wildlife Sanctuary at the eastern tip.

Regular ferry service is provided from Kantang, but most visitors take a longtail from Sinchai on Chao Mai Beach. Sinchai can also help with the latest word on bungalows and campsites.

Ko Sukorn

Ko Sukorn is the final island near Trang, located south of Samran Beach and east of Palian, about 60 km from Trang. Ko Sukorn (also Ko Mu) is known for its fine light-yellow powder, coral beds, and sweet watermelons harvested from March to May.

The island is populated by Muslim fishermen who share the wedge-shaped formation with several bungalow operators. Accommodations at Black Pearl Bay Resort (Bangkok tel. 02-279-8317) cost 150-500B. Photos and further information can be picked up at the Koh Teng Hotel in Trang.

Ko Sukorn can be reached by share taxi from Trang to Palian, followed by a 30-minute ferry ride past Yong Sata Cape.

KO TARUTAO NATIONAL PARK

The 61-island archipelago of Tarutao comprises one of the final frontiers in Thailand untouched by mass tourism. Once the haunt of sea pirates and later a penal colony for political dissidents, Tarutao was declared Thailand's first marine park in 1974 to help protect the fragile environment and its luscious combination of deserted beaches, thick jungle, and blazing coral beds. The remote location at the extreme southwestern corner of Thailand—only five km from the Malaysian island of Langkawi—has served to maintain the pristine nature of Tarutao, which remains a wild and relatively untouched destination blessed with stunning beaches, tranquil bays, and a seemingly endless number of deserted islands.

Tourism is on the increase, and foresty officials are now considering private hotel development. Go now, and avoid the rush.

Ko Bulon Lae

Bulon Lae and the two adjacent islands of Bulon Don and Bulon Yai comprise the Petra Island Marine National Park, established in 1982. Although not included in Tarutao National Park, this small island is also reached from Pakbara. Ko Bulon Lae features excellent beaches with shallow waters ideal for snorkeling, a bat cave on the southern coast, and a small town and pier on the northeastern corner. Sea gypsies living on the island were recently granted legal permission to reside inside the government park.

Pansand Resort on the beach facing the mainland offers campsites and private bungalows for 150-600B. Reservations can be made in Trang at Andaman Travel (tel. 075-219513) just opposite Queen's Hotel.

Ko Khai

Ko Khai—a small speck of land midway between Pakbara and Ko Tarutao—is a popular stop to enjoy some diving, a cave called Khao Kai, and fine white sandy beaches that end at a magnificent natural stone arch.

Tarutao Island

Ko Tarutao is the largest and closest island to the mainland port of Pakbara. Originally inhabited by sea gypsies, Tarutao received its first load of visitors in 1939 when political detainees were dropped here and ordered to construct their own prisons. The remains of their settlements at Tala Udang Bay on the southern tip, and Tala Wao Bay on the east coast, are now being restored by park authorities.

Pante Bay: Boats from Pakbara land at Pante Malacca Bay on the north coast, where park rangers rent bungalows and tents, maintain a visitor center with displays on local ecology, and raise endangered hawksbill and ridley turtles in nursing ponds. From park headquarters, visitors can climb up 114-meter Tapu Hill for views over the island and explore Crocodile Cave (Tham Choraka) at the mouth of Klong Pante. Jareki and Dong caves are located on Rusi Bay to the northeast, while excellent corals are found near Papillon Cliffs at the northern tip.

San Bay: Trails maintained by park rangers head south past mangrove swamps to a series of sandy beaches blessed with an amazing amount of shells and marinelife. Visitors can hire longtails or walk south at low tide to Ao San, eight km south of Pante, where campsites are located near a small fishing settlement.

Tala Wao Bay: Another rough trail heads southeast down to Tala Wao Bay, where an old concentration camp stands with concrete tanks for fish fermentation, charcoal furnaces, and remains of graveyards. Tham Nak That Falls is back from the beach. Visitors can camp on the beach, or stay in primitive longhouses for about 50B. Tala Wao is a four-hour hike from Pante Bay.

Tala Udang Bay: Reached along a narrow 12-km path originally constructed by political prisoners, Tala Udang Bay at the southern end also served as a settlement for exiled detainees from 1939 to 1947. Birds' nests highly prized by the Chinese are collected on the offshore island of Ko Letang.

Ko Adang

Adang Island, 43 km west of Tarutao and about 80 km from Pakbara, is the third-largest island in the archipelago and a destination for visitors who really want to escape civilization. The 30-square-km island is covered with jungle and freshwater streams which once provided drinking water for the local population of sea gypsies. Most of the Chao Lay now live on nearby Ko Lipe.

Laem Son at the south end of Ko Adang has a national park office with bungalows for 600B and campsites from 60B.

Longtails from Pante Bay on Ko Tarutao make a short stop on Ko Kai before reaching Laem Son about three hours later. Boat service is sporadic and subject to sudden cancellation depending on the weather and size of the waves.

Ko Lipe

South of Ko Adang lies a four-square-km islet, the only populated island in the archipelago

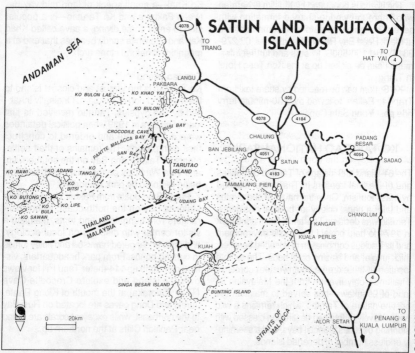

SATUN AND TARUTAO ISLANDS

side from Tarutao. Ko Lipe is inhabited by Chao Lay who fled Ko Adang for more abundant and dependable water sources. Today, the 500 residents continue to fish, grow coconuts, hawk seashells, operate a small cafe or visitors, and, to some extent, follow traditional culture such as language, dance, and styles of architecture.

Ko Lipe is relatively flat and somewhat resembles a tropical frying pan floating in blue waters, but offers several deserted beaches and coral beds off the southern coastline.

Visitors can camp at the park office or rent a bungalow from the local sea gypsies. The island can be reached by longtail from Ko Adang.

Ko Rawi

The second-largest island in the Tarutao archipelago measures almost 10 km across with a total landmass of over 31 square kilometers. Ko Rawi is uninhabited, aside from visiting fishermen, and covered with thick jungle surrounded by mangrove swamps. Diving is said to be excellent off the south coast and at the nearby islands of Ko Krai, Ko Bula, Ko Salai.

Ko Hin Ngam, southeast of Rawi, features deserted beaches composed almost entirely of shiny round stones made of granite and polished marble.

Accommodations

The National Park Service operates bungalows and campsites on several islands. Four-man concrete bungalows cost 600B, deluxe 10-man bungalows cost 800B, and campsites cost 60B. Bungalows and campsites are located at Pante Malacca Bay on the north side of Tarutao Island, at Laem Son at the south end of Ko Adang, and on the east side of Ko Lipe. Backpackers can camp at almost any beach. Reservations can be made at national park headquarters in Bangkok (tel. 02-579-4842) or at the Pakbara office (tel. 074-711383) near the pier.

Private accommodations are limited to homestays with the sea gypsies on Ko Lipe, and a few rustic bungalows on Ko Tarutao.

Transportation

Tarutao Island is 28 km from Pakbara, a mainland port 65 km north of Satun and 100 km south of Trang. Buses south from Trang take two hours to Langu (La Ngu), from where minitrucks and motorcycle taxis continue west to Pakbara. Langu has a bank, shops for supplies, and a branch of the National Park Service adjacent to the pier. Change enough money and, unless you want to be at the mercy of park officials, bring along extra food and drink.

Direct connections from Krabi are provided by Leebi Travel on Isara Road. Pakbara can also be reached via Langu with public transportation from Satun and Hat Yai. A special bus from Hat Yai direct to Pakbara departs at 0745 from the Plaza Market. Travel agents in Hat Yai arrange escorted tours on weekends which include transportation and accommodations. Alternatively, take a bus from Hat Yai toward Satun but get off in the dusty village of Chalung, from where songtaos continue north to Langu.

Boats to Tarutao depart daily from Pakbara at 1030 and 1400, but only during the tourist season from November to May. Tarutao National Park is closed during the monsoon season from May to November.

The Thai and Malaysian governments have discussed direct boat connections between Langkawi and Tarutao, a route which would avoid a great deal of backtracking and time wasted with tedious overland travel.

SATUN

Satun is a small town which chiefly serves as a departure point for sea travel south to Langkawi and Kuala Perlis in Malaysia. The town itself has little to offer aside from a muddy estuary, services such as banks and immigration office, and Bambang Mosque in the center of town. A pair of limestone peaks—Khao To and Khao Yong—are situated north of city center, on the banks of Klong Bambang.

Unlike most of Buddhist Thailand, Satun Province is populated chiefly by Muslims who worship in the 100-plus mosques scattered across the province. Chinese influence is also evident in the shops and restaurants.

Travelers heading from Hat Yai to Tarutao National Park need not stop in Satun but can change buses in Chalung, an intersection town about 20 km north of Satun.

Accommodations

Visitors arriving in the early evening may need to overnight before heading south to Malaysia or north to Tarutao. Otherwise, buses leave until around 1630 from the bus stop across from the police station.

Satun Thani Hotel: While not the cheapest spot in town, this small hotel has a cozy a/c cafe, friendly management, and very clean rooms with private baths. No English sign, and their business card says "Satool Thani." 90 Satun Thani Rd., tel. (074) 711010, 120-180B fan, 220-260B a/c.

Oasis Guesthouse: Rudimentary digs with mattresses on the floor. Run by an ex-accoun-

tant who speaks decent English. Riverside Rd no phone, 50-80B.

Rain Thong Hotel: Three doors before the end of the street is a narrow hotel with old but acceptable rooms. 4-6 Samanta Prasit Rd., tel (074) 711036, 100-150B.

Wang Mai Hotel: Satun's only luxurious hotel has a coffee shop, disco, and 108 a/c rooms. 43 Satun Thani Rd., tel. (074) 711607, 600-900B.

Restaurants

Downtown choices include Bakers Restaurant for ice cream and baked goods, Ajjara Restaurant for outside dining and live music, and a few foodstalls in the market near the river.

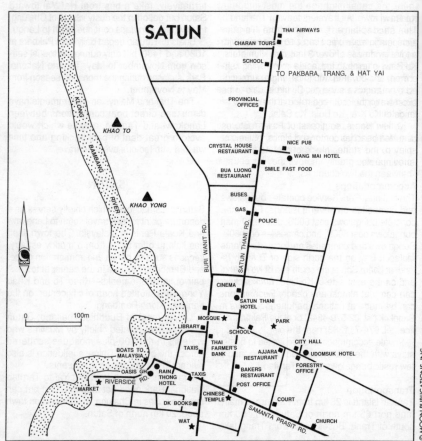

SATUN

TO PAKBARA, TRANG, & HAT YAI

© MOON PUBLICATIONS, INC.

North of town near the upscale Wang Mai Hotel is Smile Fastfood for ice cream and coffees, an outdoor emporium called Bua Luong, and the clean and comfortable Crystal House Restaurant across from the hotel. Nice Pub is an alternative to the hotel disco.

Services

Thai Farmers Bank provides exchange services, while the D.K. Bookstore sells topographic maps of Satun Province and Tarutao Islands. Thai Airways is north of town adjacent to Charan Tours. Satun has two cinemas and a small municipal park.

The Thai Immigration Office on Buriwanit Rd. near the canal might be the most important place in town. All travelers leaving Thailand by sea *must* obtain an exit stamp from this office. The immigration office can also help with quickie Malaysia visas. On my last visit, immigration officials offered to arrange a motorcycle to the border (80 km, 120B roundtrip) where I could obtain a Thai visa in the middle of beautiful Thale Ban National Park, and return to Satun before nightfall.

A new road is being constructed from Satun to the Malaysian border town of Perlis. When completed, this route will increase tourism in the province and greatly improve the flow of traffic between the two countries.

Transportation

Satun is 123 km southwest of Hat Yai, 152 km south of Trang, and 12 km north of Malaysia.

Bus and Share Taxi: Buses from Hat Yai leave from the bus terminal on the outskirts of town. An easier but somewhat more expensive option are share taxis which depart opposite the post office near the railway station.

Buses to Hat Yai and Langu (the junction for Pakbara and Tarutao) leave from the bus stop 150 meters up from the Satun Thani Hotel.

Train: The nearest train station to Satun is at Padang Besar near the Malaysian border. Train reservations can be made at the Thai Airways office on Satun Thani Road.

Boat: Boats to Kuala Perlis in Malaysia take about 90 minutes and leave from two locations. Longtails depart several times daily from the city pier on Klong Bambang near the Rain Thong Hotel. Larger boats leave from Tammalang Pier in the estuary about 15 km south of Satun. Tammalang Pier can be reached by *tuk tuk* or motorcycle taxi.

More useful than boat to Kuala Perlis is direct service to Langkawi Island, a well-developed Malaysian resort destination just 90 minutes south of Satun. Boats to Langkawi depart daily at 1600 from Tammalang Pier and return from Langkawi daily at 1300. Tickets cost 150B and can be purchased on the ship, or from Charan Tours near the Thai Airways office.

> *The glamour of the East had cast its spell upon him; the mystery of lands in which no white man had set foot since the beginning of things had fired his imagination; the itch of travel was upon him, goading him to restlessness.*
> —Hugh Clifford,
> *The Story of Exploration*

THE DEEP SOUTH

HAT YAI

Hat Yai—the dynamic commercial center and transportation hub of Southern Thailand—receives wildly divergent reviews from visitors. Many feel the city is monotonous, oversized, and lacks any compelling reason to stay more than a few hours. Others enjoy the outstanding shopping, lively street markets, heady nightlife, and don't mind that Hat Yai is a clean and well-ordered city rather than some romantic fishing village.

Named after a long beach once located on the city river, Hat Yai mainly serves as a transit point for departures and arrivals to Malaysia, and as the gateway to Songkhla and other seaside towns in Southern Thailand. Most visitors are Malaysians who shop for duty-free goods in the department stores and consider Hat Yai a pleasurable escape from the conservative strictures of their fundamentalist nation. Although the town has a rather wild and seedy reputation, the sex trade is kept well hidden and most visitors appear to be middle-class families rather than bachelors on weekend flings. Hat Yai is also one of the safest cities in Thailand.

Travelers from Malaysia who have little interest in Hat Yai can proceed directly to Songkhla, Krabi, Phuket, or Ko Samui by changing buses, taking the next train, or waiting for a share taxi near the train station. Schedules can be quickly checked at the score of travel agents located near the Cathay Hotel, three blocks east of the train station.

Wat Hat Yai

Hat Yai is known for its shopping and nightlife, not its historical or religious monuments. The only temple of note features a 35-meter reclining Buddha inside a *viharn* on Petchkasem Rd., four km southwest of the airport. Visitors are often greeted by friendly monks who conduct tours of their subterranean souvenir shop and encourage the pious to throw coins into a wooden carousel of miniature monks.

Songtaos to the temple leave from the intersection of Niphat Uthit 1 and Petchkasem roads.

Southern Thai Culture Village

This artificial but worthwhile attraction sponsors cultural shows from 1600 to 1730 Wed.-Sun., and weekend dinner shows from 1900 to 2030. The village is located in the Hat Yai Municipal Park, three km northeast of city center. Tickets from travel agencies include roundtrip transportation from your hotel.

Bullfights

Thai-style bullfighting matches, which pit bull against bull in a dramatic shoving match, are held on the first Saturday of each month at the Hat Yai Bullfighting Arena, on Hwy. 4 near the airport. Several weeks prior to the match, the

---

HAT YAI

1. Singapore Hotel
2. Inter Hotel
3. Asian Hotel
4. Regency Hotel
5. L.K. Hotel
6. Mandarin Hotel
7. Yong Dee Hotels
8. Park Hotel
9. Savoy Hotel
10. Central Sukontha Hotel
11. Grand Plaza Hotel
12. Tong Nam Hotel
13. Metro Hotel
14. Laem Thong Hotel
15. Indra Hotel
16. Prince Hotel
17. Nora Hotel
18. Rajthanes Hotel
19. Lada Guesthouse
20. Louise Hotel
21. Cathay Guesthouse
22. Montien Hotel
23. King's Hotel
24. Sakol Hotel
25. Kim Hua Hotel
26. Oriental Hotel
27. Rado Hotel
28. Pacific Hotel
29. New World Hotel
30. B.P. Grand Tower Hotel
31. Central Hotel
32. Sakura Hotel
33. Emperor Hotel
34. Scala Hotel
35. Kosit Hotel
36. Lee Gardens Hotel
37. Amarin Hotel
38. Florida Hotel

HAT YAI

TO BANGKOK

BUSES TO SONGKHLA

PETCHKASEM RD.

TO SONGKHLA

NIGHT FOODSTALLS

TO SONGKHLA

SUPHANSAN RANGSAN RD.

FUENG FAH RESTAURANT

TO IMMIGRATION, WAT NAI YAI, AIRPORT, & PHUKET

PETCHKASEM RD.

SOPHIA FABRICS

DUANG CHAN RD.

1

TAXIS

2

3

OCEAN DEPT. STORE

BIRD'S NEST RESTAURANT

5

POST OFFICE

PRACHA THIPAT RD.

4

10

D.K. BOOKS

6

ZODIAC DISCO

NIPHAT UTHIT 2 RD.

7

11

SAENG CHAN RD.

NASATANI RD.

8

9

12

HOLLYWOOD DISCO

15

16

NIPHAT UTHIT 1 RD.

14

13

17

TRAIN STATION

THAMNOEN VITHI RD.

RATAKAN RD.

CAFE

21

MAE TIP RESTAURANT

24

DIM SUM CAFE

19

20

O CHA RESTAURANT

25

FOODSTALLS

D.K. BOOKS

22

26

27

FOODSTALLS

18

HAAD YAI DEPT. STORE

23

OSMAN RESTAURANT MOTORCYCLES

SANEHANUSORN RD.

KIMPRADET RD.

MANASRUDE RD.

BANK

28

HILLMAN RESTAURANT

29

CHINESE TEMPLE

30

KLONG TOEY

PREDAROM RD.

THAI AIR

TECK NGEE RESTAURANT

31

NAKORN NAI CAFE

SEAFOOD GARDEN

NIYOMRAT RD.

RELAX PUB

MUSLIM CAFES

32

MAE TIP RESTAURANT

NIPHAT UTHIT 3 RD.

33

ANIRATANAKORN RD.

PADUNG PAKDEE RD.

35

SOI 2

34

BIRD SHOP

GAS

BEST CAFE

CAKE HOUSE

TOURIST OFFICE

THAI NIGHTCLUBS

36

37

SRIPOONAVART RD.

38

TO BUS TERMINAL & MALAYSIA

0   100m

© MOON PUBLICATIONS, INC.

bulls are displayed by their owners and bets are placed. The bulls are later brought to the stadium for a bath, massage, and inspection by the audience. The fight ends when one of the bulls is knocked down or simply runs away from his opponent.

Kick Boxing
Boxing fans can enjoy the mayhem on Saturday mornings from 1100 to 1330 in Channel 10's television station.

Budget Accommodations
Most of Hat Yai's 60-plus hotels are located in the center of town along the three Niphat Uthit roads, also called Sai Nueng (Road 1), Sai Song (Road 2), and Sai Sam (Road 3). Train arrivals are within easy walking distance of most hotels. Buses from the Malaysia border usually stop at the main bus terminal outside town, from where minitrucks continue to city center. Bus arrivals from Songkhla can walk or take any *songtao* heading south.

Cathay Guesthouse: Hat Yai's traveler center is a friendly and clean place with a popular cafe and a self-help soda machine. The bulletin board and travelers' logs are gold mines of information on upcoming beaches, new guesthouses, and travel tips on visas and shopping. Their downstairs travel agency can help with onward transportation and hotel bookings. The Cathay needs some paint, and the loud TV needs a quick death, but overall this is the best value spot in Hat Yai. Arrive early to find a room 93/1 Niphat Uthit 2 Rd., tel. (074) 243815, 60B dorm, 120-180B common bath, 180-220B private bath.

King's Hotel: An older hotel centrally located near the train station and popular Washington Nightclub. 126 Niphat Uthit 1 Rd., tel. (074) 243966, 180-250B fan, 250-340B a/c.

Tong Nam Hotel: Small and clean, the Tong Nam has a good fast-food cafe on the first floor, "Ancient Massage" in the lobby, and some of the cheapest a/c rooms in Hat Yai. 118-120 Niphat Uthit 3 Rd., tel. (074) 244023, 120-180B fan, 220-280B a/c.

Pacific Hotel: A fairly clean hotel with a pool hall on the ground floor. 149/1 Niphat Uthit 2 Rd., tel. (074) 245202, 150-180B fan, 320-360B a/c.

Louise Hotel: Tucked away in an alley near the train station is a new place with small but spotless a/c rooms. Nearby Laem Thong Hotel is unfriendly and overpriced. 13-15 Thamnoen Vithi Road, tel. (074) 243770, 320-380B.

Moderate Accommodations
Hat Yai's better hotels in the 350-600B range are popular with traveling businessmen, Malaysians on holiday, and Western visitors who want a/c comfort without breaking the bank.

ADDITIONAL HAT YAI ACCOMMODATIONS

HOTEL	SINGLE	DOUBLE	ADDRESS	TEL. (074)
Asian	500-650B	500-650B	55 Niphat Uthit 3	245455
Florida	550-700	600-900	8 Sripoonavart	234555
Indra	500-600	600-800	94 Thamnoen Vithi	245886
International	500-700	500-800	42 Niphat Uthit 3	231022
Kosit	750-850	750-950	199 Niphat Uthit 2	234366
Lada Guesthouse	300-340	320-380	13 Thamnoen Vithi	243770
Laem Thong	200-380	220-400	46 Thamnoen Vithi	244433
Lee Gardens	600-800	750-900	1 Lee Pattana	234422
New World	600-700	700-800	144 Niphat Uthit 2	246993
Nora	600-750	650-900	216 Thamnoen Vithi	244944
Park	400-550	400-650	81 Niphat Uthit 2	233351
President	800-900	800-1000	420 Petchkasem	244477
Rado	160-280	160-300	59 Sanehanusorn	243858
Yong Dee	360-420	380-500	99 Niphat Uthit 3	234350

COOING IN CHANA

This lovely and unique experience takes place in the town of Chana, 40 km southeast of Hat Yai. Zebra doves raised primarily by Muslims have long been fashionable throughout southern Thailand, but Chana is the acknowledged cooing capital of the region. Singing competitions are held in open fields on which hundreds of cages are hung from eight-meter metallic poles. The feathered competitors are judged on pitch, melody, volume, and length of tone, plus a special category in which all the tones are judged as a unified emsemble. Bird species include zebra doves and Java mountain doves, which cost 5000B at birth but bring over 600,000B after capturing grand prizes. Only the males sing, while the females serve for breeding.

Competitions are held in Chana on most weekends, with a grand finale in late December or early January.

Montien Hotel: Adjacent to the King's is a high-rise hotel with sparsely furnished but large and comfortable a/c rooms. Check the back of their hotel brochure to see what is really sold by most Hat Yai hotels. 120 Niphat Uthit 1 Rd., tel. (074) 234386, fax (074) 230043, 340-600B.

Central Sukontha Hotel: A small swimming pool, Zodiac disco, and brightly decorated rooms make the Sukhontha a popular choice. All rooms include TV, telephone, and refrigerator. Sanehanusorn Rd., tel. (074) 243999, fax (074) 243991, 500-650B.

Grand Plaza Hotel: Hat Yai's "only generous and gentle hotel" features a small pool, coffee shop, and 211 a/c rooms equipped with TV, refrigerator, and international direct dial phones. 24/1 Sanehanusorn Road, tel. (074) 234340, fax (074) 230050, 575-700B.

Luxury Accommodations

Hat Yai Central Hotel: The newest luxury hotel in Hat Yai features several restaurants, karaoke lounge, snooker club, and citywide views from the 12-story complex. 180 Niphat Uthit 3 Rd., tel. (074) 230000, fax (074) 230990, 800-1200B.

Regency Hotel: Teakwood lobbies, restaurant-cum-cabaret, and very large rooms make the Regency one of the best in town. The management also appear generous since their brochure claims "It's our policy to allow others to have a slide of the cake," whatever that means. 23 Pracha Thipat Rd., tel. (074) 234400, fax (074) 234515, 1000-1600B.

Restaurants

Most of Hat Yai's restaurants are on Niphat Uthit 1 and 2 roads and within easy walking distance of the hotels.

Foodstalls: A small but lively market sets up nightly in the northeast corner of central Hat Yai. Other foodstalls are located on Sheuthit Rd., opposite the Oriental Hotel. Suphansan Ransan Road. Inexpensive.

Fueng Fah Restaurant: A small, clean a/c cafe with buffalo steaks and other Western specialties. Suphansan Rangsan Road. Moderate.

Bird's Nest Restaurant: Unassuming cafe with sharks' fin soup (200-1800B!) and versions of bird's nest listed under the dessert section. Pracha Thipat Road. Moderate.

Osman's Restaurant: Small Malay cafe with regional specialties such as *soup daging, udang goreng, nasi etek,* and *telor bungkus.* A pleasant change from Thai fare. Niphat Uthit 2 Road. Inexpensive.

Nakorn Nai Cafe: Clean and modern, this stylish cafe serves rice dishes, salads, and lasagnes. To the south is a curious little shop which sells fresh honey. Niphat Uthit 2 Road. Inexpensive.

Muslim Cafes: Tasty Muslim and Indian dishes are prepared at three simple cafes at the south side of central Hat Yai. Aberdeen, Sharefa (Ruby's), and Mustafa 2 have English menus listing vegetable *korma,* mutton curry, and fish *marsala* served with fresh chapatis. An even *better* change from Thai fare. Niyomrat Road. Inexpensive.

PATA Food Center: Inside the Kosit Hotel is a large food emporium with live music in the evenings. 199 Niphat Uthit 2 Road. Moderate.

Nightlife

Hat Yai's action is centered on hotels, rather than bars or nightclubs as in Bangkok and Pattaya. The variety is amazing: sultry torch singers in cocktail lounges dimmed nearly to the point of absolute darkness, massage parlors packed with wealthy Muslims, live rock n' roll clubs, hotels that employ more prostitutes than maids, and Thai cinemas complete with special English-language sound booths.

A typical example of the local sex industry is found in the **Pink Lady Complex**, where over 200 ladies work the barbershop, cafe, and give traditional, body, and special tora-tora massages in the Turkish bath. The **Diana Club** in the Lee Gardens Hotel and the **Aladdin Club** in the Kosit Hotel are more conventional cabarets for dinner accompanied by warbling songbirds. Live bands play nightly at the **Hollywood Disco**, **Zodiac Disco**, and in the **Washington Nightclub** adjacent to King's Hotel. Drinks cost about 100B, but there's little pressure to keep drinking or pay for the services of a hostess. Thai nightclubs rarely visited by *farangs* are on Anratanakorn Rd. near the Scala Hotel.

Shopping

Prices are low and selection unlimited in the shops and streetstalls on Niphat Uthit 1, 2, and 3 roads. Among the larger department stores are **Ocean**, **Diana**, and Expo on Niphat Uthit 3 Rd., and **World**, **Odean**, and **Diana 2** on Sanehanusorn Road. High-quality and reasonably priced Indonesian batiks, shirts, and scarves are sold at **Pekalongan** and **Shah Panich** on the north end of Niphat Uthit 2 Road. **D.K. Books** sells topographic maps and travel guides from their well-stocked outlets near the train station and opposite the Zodiac Disco.

Services

The TAT office (tel. 074-243747) on Soi 2 Niphat Uthit 3 Rd.has maps and transportation schedules. Thai Immigration is on Nasatani Rd. near the Utapao Bridge. The Malaysian consulate is in Songkhla.

Transportation

Hat Yai—an important travel junction used by almost every traveler heading between Malaysia and Thailand—is 1,013 km south of Bangkok, 350 km south of Surat Thani, 60 km north of the Malaysian border at Padang Besar, and 260 km northwest of Kota Baru in Malaysia.

Motorcycles can be rented and purchased at the shop just south of Osman Restaurant.

Air from Thailand: Thai Airways International flies twice daily from Bangkok via Phuket, and weekly from Pattani and Narathiwat. Thai Airways (tel. 074-245851) is at 166/4 Niphat

Uthit 2 Road. Malaysian Air (tel. 074-243729) in the Nora Hotel on Thamnoen Vithi Road.

Air from Malaysia: Thai and Malaysian Air fl once daily from Phuket and Kuala Lumpur. Th Hat Yai airport, 12 km west of town, is served b inexpensive mini-trucks and private limousines

Train from Bangkok: Trains from Hualam pong Station in Bangkok to Hat Yai depart a 1235 (rapid), 1400 (special express), 1515 (spe cial express), and 1600 (rapid). The 1515 and 1600 departures are recommended since they arrive at 0704 and 0850. Sleepers are available on all trains.

Advance reservations from the Bangkok station or travel agent are *strongly* recommended on all trains going south, especially on weekends and holidays.

Train from Malaysia: The *International Express* leaves Butterworth (the train terminus for Penang) daily at 1340, crosses the Thai border, and arrives in Hat Yai three hours later. The *IE* is limited to first and second class and somewhat expensive because of supplemental charges for a/c and superior classes. Reservations can be made from Penang travel agents.

Ordinary trains no longer connect Butterworth with Hat Yai but rather terminate at the Malaysian border town of Padang Besar. Walk across the border, have your passport stamped, and catch a bus to Hat Yai.

Train from Hat Yai: Trains going north to Phattalung, Surat Thani, and Bangkok depart at 1534, 1617, 1814, and 1849. Sleepers are available on all trains. Trains going south to Sungai Golok on the Malaysian border near Kota Baru depart at 0452, 0605, 0810, 1035, and 1322. Trains to Padang Besar and Penang depart once daily at 0704.

Taxi from Malaysia: Share taxis are an important travel component in southern Thailand since they are fast, comfortable, and relatively inexpensive—about the same price as an a/c bus.

Share taxis leave 0600-1000 from the Butterworth station just across the channel from Penang. Share taxis from Kota Baru terminate at the border, from where you have your passport stamped and continue to Sungai Golok by rickshaw or *tuk tuk.*

Taxi from Hat Yai: Hat Yai has several share-taxi stands that specialize in specific destinations. Taxis to Phattalung, Nakhon Si Thammarat, Trang, Narathiwat, and Sungai Golok depart from Suphansan Ransan Rd. near the night market. Taxis to Surat Thani, Phuket, and Krabi leave one block south on Duang Chan Road. Taxis to Songkhla leave from Petch-kasem Rd., three blocks south of the President Hotel and within walking distance of the downtown hotels.

Travel agents near the Cathay Hotel organize share taxis to most destinations in Thailand and Malaysia. Taxis to Penang, Kota Baru, Krabi, Phuket, and Ko Samui depart from 0900 to 1200.

Bus from Malaysia: Bus 29 from Kota Baru terminates in the Malaysian border town of Rantau Panjang, from where you have your passport stamped and continue to the Sungai Golok train or bus station by *tuk tuk* or trishaw.

Bus from Hat Yai: The public bus terminal (tel. 074-232789) is located in a remote spot in the southeast corner of Hat Yai. An easier if somewhat more expensive option is private service arranged through travel agents near the Cathay Hotel. Sample fares:

Destination	Hours	*Baht*
Satun	2	40
Narathiwat	3	50
Trang	3	50
Krabi	4	150
Surat Thani	4	160
Penang	5	220
Ko Samui	6	220
Phuket	7	220
Kuala Lumpur	12	220-280
Bangkok	14	350-450
Singapore	18	300-450

SONGKHLA

Songkhla is a deceptively sleepy beach resort picturesquely sited between the Gulf of Thailand and a saltwater sea called Thale Sap ("Inland Sea") or Songkhla Lake. Somewhat off the beaten track and overshadowed by the economic powerhouse of Hat Yai, Songkhla has largely escaped commercialism and blessedly remained a pleasant and charming town of Sino-Portuguese buildings, bobbing fishing boats, and beaches filled with Thai families rather than Western tourists.

Songkhla National Museum

The regional history of Songkhla and the deep south can be traced in this 19th-century Sino-Portuguese mansion, constructed as a private residence for a wealthy Chinese merchant who later served as governor of Songkhla Province. Inside the elegant teak-beamed two-story estate is a fabulous collection of Thai and Chinese art treasures gathered primarily from the seven provinces of southern Thailand.

Ground Floor: Immediately to the left of the entrance is a useful topographic map and aerial photos of Songkhla Province. Arranged throughout the rear courtyard are artistic treasures such as a wooden gable from Wat Machimawat and curiosities such as giant tortoise shells, old Raleigh bikes dating from WW II, and coconut grinders fashioned like wooden dogs.

Second Floor: Highlights on the upper floor are a pair of leather *nang yai* puppets, beautifully cracked and peeling Ayuthaya-Period Buddhas, Thai furnishings including a teapot made from an ostrich egg, and the bed of King Mongkut—apparently a very small man.

The museum is open Wed.-Sun. 0900-1600.

Old Town

Songkhla was established over 300 years ago, though most of the present Sino-Portuguese architecture dates from the early 20th century when the town served as an important trading port for Thai and Chinese merchants. A fairly interesting walk through the old town can be made in about an hour, starting at the museum and walking south along the waterfront. First, quickly visit the modern fishing boats which unload their catch on private piers accessed through warehouses on Nakhon Nak Road. The road continues south for views from the rooftop of Lake Inn, then past a mosque before returning north past Wat Machimawat.

Several distinct styles of architecture survive on Saiburi and Nang Ngam roads: Peranakan homes with well-carved shutters, Chinese homes capped with long red-tiled roofs that dramatically slope toward the ground, and wooden Thai shop houses that will probably disappear in the next few years.

Watch out for the open sewers—Songkhla has more than any other town in Thailand.

CHOLCHARON RD.

LAEM SON ON RD.

SAMILA BEACH

GULF OF THAILAND

TO CAPE & SEAFOOD RESTAURANTS

LANG PRARAM RD.

LAEM SAI RD.

RAJADAMNERN RD.

MERMAID STATUE

SAMILA BEACH HOTEL

MALAYSIAN CONSULATE

CAFES

KHOA DANG KUA

KHAO NOI

VIEWPOINT

WAT LAMSAI

CHAI KAO RD.

VICHANCHOM RD.

SUKUM RD.

SONGKHLA

GOLF COURSE

NARAI HOTEL

WAT SIAM

SONGKHLA LAKE (INLAND SEA)

SADAO RD.

U.S. CONSULATE

CHOKDEE HOTEL

SAIBURI RD.

WAT CHANG

SRI SUDA RD.

CHAI NAM RD.

CHAIYA RD.

SONGKHLA HOTEL

RONG MUANG RD.

SUKSOMBOON 2 HOTEL

HOLLAND HOUSE

NASAN RD.

TAX CLEARANCE OFFICE

SONGKHLA NATIONAL MUSEUM

JANA RD.

QUEEN HOTEL

MARKET

CLOCKTOWER

PAVILON HOTEL

STADIUM

POST OFFICE

FERRY TO KO YOH

WAT DONRAK

BUSES TO HAT YAI

PHETCHKIRI RD.

SAN SABI HOTEL

PRATUA RD.

BANK

SUKSOMBOON 1 HOTEL

TAXIS

TRAIN STATION

SAKET RD.

FISHING BOATS

NAK RD.

NAKHON NAI RD.

RAAN AHAN TAE CAFE

RAMVITHI RD.

OLD TOWN

NANG NGAM RD.

WAT DONYE

NAM DHOY RESTAURANT

WAT CHAI MONGKOL

CHAI MONGKOL RD.

NAKHON

SAIBURI RD.

RAMAN RD.

0   100m

CINEMA

WAT MACHIMAWAT

PHATTALUNG RD.

PETCH MONGKOL RD.

MOSQUE

TO HAT YAI

LAKE INN

NARATHIWAT RD.

RAJADAMNERN RD.

TALAY LUANG RD.

TO KHAO SENG

CHAIYA TAI RD.

© MOON PUBLICATIONS, INC.

Vat Machimawat

Vat Machimawat (Wat Klang)—the oldest and most important temple in Songkhla—was established during the reigns of Kings Rama III and V when the maritime port served as a provincial outpost of the Bangkok administration.

Central Bot: Modeled after Wat Pra Keo in Bangkok, the principal sanctuary of Wat Klang features beautiful murals of 19th-century life in Songkhla and episodes from the Jatakas, and a highly venerated marble Buddha commissioned by King Rama III. The outer verandas are adorned with stone bas-reliefs imported from China which illustrate a Chinese epic called the Romance of the Three Kingdoms. The bot is kept locked to protect the treasures, though the abbot can provide a key.

Museum: The small museum north of the bot has a minor collection of jasper Buddhas, votive tablets, unlabeled bencharong ceramics, and the standard assortment of mechanical oddities.

South Viharn: Adjacent to the Buddhist monastery is an unusual viharn that incorporates both Chinese and Peranakan architectural styles, with European touches such as Dutch and English hanging lanterns.

Samila Beach

The focal point of Songkhla is the eight-km stretch of sand dotted with seafood restaurants, a municipally owned hotel, and hardly any tourists since Thais leave sunbathing to mad dogs and unenlightened backpackers. Sitting on a rocky promontory is the incongruous symbol of Songkhla: a bronze statue imitative of the fairytale mermaid of Danish writer Hans Christian Andersen. The road continues north from the mermaid to several popular cafes such as Seven Sisters, Nongnuch, and Mark's, but where, Mr. Eckardt, is Boontong's? The offshore humpbacked islands of Ko Maeo ("Cat") and Ko Nu ("Rat") are named after their respective shapes.

Excellent views over Songkhla are guaranteed from the deserted park at the top of Khao Noi.

South of the mermaid is a long and perfectly straight beach lined with swaying casuarina pines beneath cobbled promenades. A Thai naval base, three km south, rents sailboards and sailboats and operates a fairly good cafe with cheap beer. The road continues one more

km south to the Muslim fishing village of Khao Seng, known for its roadside market, seafood restaurants, and brightly painted kolae boats.

Ko Yoh

Yoh Island is known for its seafood restaurants, traditional weavings, and Institute of Southern Thai Studies. The thickly wooded island is 12 km from Songkhla and can be reached by bus from the clock tower. Ordinary boats from the pier near the post office cost just five baht. Do it Thai style: don't ask the price, just leave five baht on the bench when you get off the boat. Chartered longtails are extremely expensive, potentially dangerous, and unnecessary after the opening of the Tinsulanonda Bridge.

Institute of Southern Thai Studies: The newly opened Folklore Museum features a comprehensive collection of southern artifacts displayed in 17 traditional Thai houses capped with distinctive roof styles—balano, panya, and chua. Also located on the grounds is a cultural park, audiovisual center, and outdoor performance stage, considered the largest in Thailand. The museum is open daily from 0830 to 1630, and situated near Ban Ao Sai at the north end of the island. Maps and brochures are available at the roadside information center.

Weavings: Cotton weavers on the island produce both traditional cotton fabrics from home looms and spectacularly gaudy fashionware covered with flamingos, palm trees, and riotous tropical sunsets. Roadside stalls are concentrated in the center of the island.

Restaurants: One of the most popular choices is **Porntip II**, where visitors can select giant bass from the nearby fish pen or try a seafood combination called ai klang talay hut . . . passionate sea in sexual heat! Porntip is just across the 700-meter Tinsulanonda Bridge, which connects the southern extension of Songkhla with Ko Yoh.

Suan Kaeo Restaurant at the north end of the island is another popular choice.

Khu Khut Bird Sanctuary

A large 520-square-km wildlife refuge, similar to Thale Noi near Phattalung, is 50 km north of Songkhla near the town of Sathing Phra. Birds are most plentiful in the mornings and late afternoons from January to April. Accommodations and boat tours of the inland lake are available at park headquarters. Buses heading north across Ko Yoh and up the coastline stop at Sathing Phra, from where motorcycles continue three km to park headquarters.

Sathing Phra is also noted for its numerous Srivijaya-era monuments such as Wat Sathing Phra, with a pure Srivijaya *chedi*, and Pra Chedi Phratan, known for its reclining Buddha and preserved frescoes.

Accommodations
Songkhla is a compact town with most hotels within walking distance of the bus stop near the clock tower.

Holland House: Not much Dutch flavor, but a cozy cafe, motorcycle rentals, and a friendly Thai manager who runs the place in the absence of her Dutch husband. 28/20 Ramvithi Rd., tel. (074) 322738, 130-200B.

Narai Hotel: Run by a wonderful lady named Tip, the backpackers' favorite is somewhat isolated but compensates with travel tips, bicycle rentals, and decent rooms in the yellow building with a red-tiled roof. Recommended. 14 Chai Khao Rd., tel. (074) 311078, 90-150B.

Suksomboon 1 Hotel: Acceptable rooms in a small place near the clock tower. 40 Phetchkiri Rd., tel. (074) 311049, 140-220B fan, 280-320B a/c

Pavilon Hotel: Modern semiluxurious hotel with snooker hall, a/c restaurant, and large pool in the rear. Good value. 27 Pratua Rd., tel. (074) 311355, 420-550B.

Samila Beach Hotel: Top-end choice with water sports rentals, small pool, golf course, and seaside rooms facing the bronze mermaid. 1 Rajadamnern Rd., tel. (074) 311310, fax (074) 322448, 800-1200B.

Restaurants
A small night market is located on Saiburi Rd. near the old city walls and behind the new shopping complex. Several of the stalls offer an amazing array of local fruits and take-away specialties. East of the clocktower near the train station are open-air cafes with Thai and Chinese dishes at low prices. Local fare is also served at the rudimentary but popular **Raan Ahan Tae Cafe** and **Nam Dhoy Restaurant** in the old town. **Terrace Cafe** in the Pavilon Hotel serves excellent meals in a comfortable environment.

Songkhla, unfortunately, lacks any decent cafes facing Thale Sap except for the breezy but overpriced **Laguna Terrace** on the top floor of Lake Inn. Rudimentary cafes behind the Samila Beach Hotel include **Bour Keow Seafood** and **Boonriam Seafood**.

Services
Songkhla facilities include a post office, several banks, a Malaysian Consulate (tel. 074-311104) at 4 Sukum Rd., and a tax-clearance office near the golf course. The American Consulate closed in 1992.

Transportation
Songkhla is 1,001 km south of Bangkok and 28 km northeast of Hat Yai.

Songkhla can be reached from Hat Yai in 30 minutes by green buses which depart on Petchkasem Rd. near the Hat Yai Plaza Theater. Share taxis leave from the President Hotel. Buses stop at the clock tower and then continue to a halt on Saiburi Road near Wat Chang. The train station has been closed for several years.

Thai Transportation Company in the Chok Dee Hotel sells a/c bus tickets to Bangkok.

PATTANI

Thailand changes dramatically south of Hat Yai. Suddenly, Islamic mosques outnumber Buddhist *wats,* Yawi (a Malay dialect influenced by Arabic) doubles with Thai as the *lingua franca,* and old men sport Muslim *haji* caps rather than Buddhist robes. The style of domestic architecture changes from Thai to Malay, while women living outside the urban areas wear lace veils or brightly colored clothing typical of Muslim housewives.

Farangs are extremely rare in the deep south, aside from a handful of travelers heading from Hat Yai down to Kota Baru in Malaysia. Visitors who need to overnight or have a strong interest in Thai-Malay culture will discover the most pleasant interlude to be the idyllic fishing village of Narathiwat. Pattani, Yala, and Sungai Golok are modern concrete towns with little of great interest except for their political backgrounds, mosques, and women dressed in traditional Muslim garb.

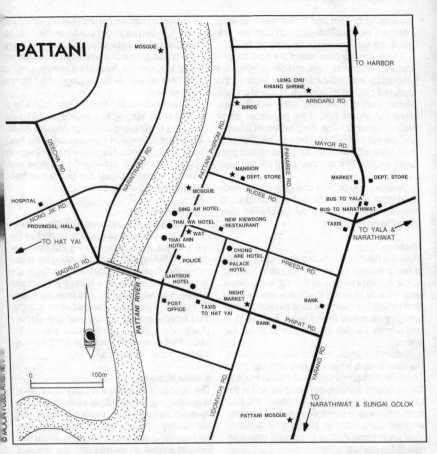

PATTANI

MOSQUE

TO HARBOR

LENG CHU
KHIANG SHRINE

ARNOARU RD.

BIRDS

MAYOR RD.

HOSPITAL

NONG JIK RD.

PROVINCIAL HALL

TO HAT YAI

DEECHA RD.

NARINTRARAJ RD.

PATTANI PHIROM RD.

PANAREE RD.

MANSION
DEPT. STORE

MOSQUE

RUDEE RD.

MARKET   DEPT. STORE

BUS TO YALA

BUS TO NARATHIWAT

SING AH HOTEL

THAI WA HOTEL

NEW KIEWDONG
RESTAURANT

WAT

THAI ANN
HOTEL

POLICE

CHONG
ARE HOTEL

PALACE
HOTEL

PREEDA RD.

TAXIS

TO YALA &
NARATHIWAT

MAGRUD RD.

SANTISUK
HOTEL

NIGHT
MARKET

BANK

PATTANI RIVER

POST
OFFICE

TAXIS
TO HAT YAI

BANK

PHIPAT RD.

0   100m

UDOMWITHI RD.

YARANG RD.

TO
NARATHIWAT & SUNGAI GOLOK

PATTANI MOSQUE

History

Archaeologists believe that Pattani and nearby Yarang originally served as as the mythical Buddhist empire called Langsigia by the Chinese and Langasuka by the Indians. Recent diggings conducted by Thai students from the Fine Arts Department have uncovered a number of miniature *chedis,* stone Buddha images inscribed in Pali, and Persian pottery destined for Chinese collectors.

Present-day Pattani takes its name from a powerful Malay sultanate under the influence of Malacca which rose to prominence in the 14th century. In 1516 the Portuguese established a post at Pattani, while the Dutch arrived toward the end of the 16th century. By the 17th century, Pattani served as the center of Islamic studies for all of Southeast Asia, and as the leading entrepot for trade between China and Southeast Asia. Western merchants left records of the wealth and power of its Islamic rulers, and of the marriage alliances which cemented relationships between Pattani and southern Malay empires.

Pattani flourished as an independent state until the late 19th century, when it was subjected to an intense and systematic program of national incorporation. That the deep south now belongs to Thailand is actually a historical accident created early this century by the political gerrymandering of Thai and British governments, which left the Thai Malays cut off from their religious and racial cousins below the border.

Today, the four provinces of the deep south—Pattani, Narathiwat, Yala, and Satun—form the ideological and political boundary between the Buddhist cultures of northern Thailand and the Muslim world of lower Southeast Asia. Surveys show that almost 75% of the population are of Malay stock and follow the precepts of Islam, a statistic not lost on the rulers in Bangkok who must cope with demands for greater ethnic privileges such as Islamic schools and *shariah* court systems.

Despite some political changes—and a modest degree of self-government—the deep south remains more devoted to the call of Islam than the culture of Bangkok.

Walking Tour

Pattani is hardly a fascinating destination, though a few pleasant hours can be spent walking through what remains of the old town. Begin your walk by crossing the bridge and heading north along the riverbank past dozens of large and gaily decorated fishing boats. Several small and brightly painted *kolae* boats sit under the bridge.

Return to city center and walk north along the river past a small mosque and city park. Traces of traditional architecture are still found at the impressive mansion on Rudee Rd. and in the Chinese shop houses with their sloped and tiled roofs, scrollwork in the roof eaves, and louvered windows surrounded by glazed tilework. Continue north along Pattani Phirom Rd. and turn right to the next attraction.

Leng Chu Khiang Shrine

The legends, history, and traditions of Pattani are preserved at this shrine and at Kreuze Mosque, seven km east of town. Leng Chu Khiang is dedicated to a Chinese goddess named Chao Mae Lim Ko Neo who possesses magical powers and is highly revered throughout Pattani and the deep south.

The legend begins in the mid-16th century after an immigrant Chinese merchant named Lim To Khiang marries a Pattani Muslim and converts to Islam. Distressed relatives in China send his sister Lim Ko Neo to Pattani to convince Mr. Lim to abandon Islam and return to his homeland. To prove the depth of his newfound faith, Lim begins construction of the Kreuze Mosque, but his sister puts a curse on the monument that dooms its completion. In a final attempt to reform her recalcitrant brother, Lim Ko Neo commits suicide by hanging herself from a cashew tree.

A shrine dedicated to the feisty lady, and a replica of the hanging tree, are displayed inside the Leng Chu Khiang Shrine on Arnoaru Road. An annual fair, held on the full moon of the third lunar month, honors Ms. Lim with a procession of Chinese dragons and religious devotees who walk across red-hot coals and pierce their bodies with swords and spears.

Pattani Mosque

Architectural variety is provided by the Matsayit Klang, a classic mosque constructed in the early 1960s which ranks among the most elegant and striking in Thailand. Flanking the broad sidewalk which approaches the sanctuary are twin minarets from where Islamic prayer calls are electronically broadcast five times each day. The primary hall is characterized by an orange-tiled facade, arched windows set with stained glass, and bulbous domes inlaid with green stone. Well-dressed visitors can watch the Friday afternoon prayer services.

Kreuze Mosque

The legendary companion to Leng Chu Khiang is another highly revered yet exceedingly controversial monument. As described above, the rudimentary shell stands half completed after the magical curse cast from Ms. Lim on her turncoat brother. In recent years, the mosque has been the scene of a political struggle by Sunni and Shiite groups which have demanded that the Thai government abrogate the mosque's historical status so that construction can be completed and religious services resumed. Political rallies at the mosque have criticized the government for alleged mistreatment of Muslims, urged the removal of a nearby Chinese shrine, and demanded the establishment of an Islamic State in Pattani Province.

In an effort to appease local Muslims who felt their mosque had been eclipsed by the adjacent Lim Ko Neo Chinese shrine, Kreuze Mosque was recently renovated by the Fine Arts Department. The monument is seven km

...outheast of town on Highway 42 and plainly ...isible from buses heading down to Narathiwat.

Accommodations
About a half-dozen small hotels are located in central Pattani, plus a midlevel choice about one km from city center.

Riverside Hotels: Three wooden Chinese hotels are located across from the police station and just down from the bridge. **Thai Ann Hotel** is entered through an old cafe, while **Thai Wa** is back behind a fairly modern restaurant. **Sing Ah Hotel** features a small cafe overlooking the river. All three are rough but survivable and have fan-cooled rooms for 80-120B.

Palace Hotel: This five-story hotel, the best deal in central Pattani, is set back in a quiet alley away from noisy Phipat Road. Fairly good meals are served in their Chongar Restaurant. 38 Soi Preeda, tel. (073) 349171, 120-180B fan, 200-250B a/c.

Chong Are Hotel: Another decent choice with rooms with either common or private bath. The reception is located inside the darkened restaurant and nightclub. 190 Preeda Rd., tel. (073) 349039, 120-180B.

My Gardens Hotel: The only luxury hotel in Pattani has large rooms and a narrow nightclub popular with Thai and Chinese residents. The hotel is two km from the bridge, down Magrud Road. 8/23 Charoen Prathet Rd., tel. (073) 348993, 450-600B.

Transportation
Pattani is 124 km southeast of Hat Yai, 40 km north of Yala, and 96 km northwest of Narathiwat.

Share taxis from Yala leave from various stops near the train station and take about 30 minutes. Buses from Narathiwat leave from the waiting shed near the clock tower and pass some of the lushest scenery in Thailand.

YALA

Yala Province and its Betong district on the Malaysian border comprise the southernmost region of Thailand. Yala itself is a modern and clean commercial center fashioned around a gridiron layout of roads with city parks and lakes in the perimeter. Most of the inhabitants are Chinese who dominate the rubber and rice in-

dustries, while the surrounding countryside is populated by Thai-Malays who follow the call of Islam and work the fields in the only land-locked province of southern Thailand.

Attractions
Aside from local festivals and cave temples outside town, Yala has little of interest for most visitors. Yala has won several awards for the cleanest town in Thailand, though the central market in the northeast corner is hardly an example of pristine beauty. Wat Phutapoom features a large walking Buddha elevated on a concrete pedestal and covered with small golden tiles. South of town at the terminus of Pipat Pakdee Rd. is Kwan Muang Park, with its city pillar shrine in the nearby traffic circle, and immense artificial lake fixed with small cafes and boat rentals.

Yala town is also known for its ASEAN Bird Singing Contest held in March in Kwan Muang Park, and Southern Thai Culture Week with parades and beauty pageants held in early August. The Lak Muang Fair occurs in late May.

Wat Kuha Phimok
The chief historical and architectural attraction of Yala is six km west of town on the road toward Hat Yai. Believed to date from the Srivijaya era, the cave complex at Wat Kuha Phimok (also called Wat Na Tham) features a highly venerated reclining Buddha image considered by southern Thais equal in religious stature to Wat Boromothat in Nakhon Si Thammarat and Wat Chaiya in Surat Thani Province.

Wat Tham Silpa, a cave grotto two km west of Wat Kuha Phimok, offers some fading patches of 13th-century cave art, perhaps the only surviving examples of Srivijaya paintings in Thailand.

Both caves can be reached by buses leaving from Sirirot Road. Ask the driver to stop at the English-language sign, and follow the path to the limestone sanctuary.

Sakai Village
Ban Sakai is home to some of Thailand's last remaining Sakai tribe peoples, dark-skinned and frizzy-haired descendants of the Proto-Malay race who once populated the entire Malay Peninsula. Most have now integrated into Thai society and found work in local rubber plantations, though about 20 families continue to live in a relatively traditional village 80 km south of Yala.

YALA

BUS TO PATTANI

TO PATTANI

ROTEFARI RD.

MARKET

SHOPPING CENTER

TRAIN STATION

PRACHIN RD.

TAXI TO BETONG

YUAN TONG HOTEL

AUN AUN HOTEL

BUS COMPANY

YALA RAMA HOTEL

THEP VIMARN HOTEL

TAXI TO HAT YAI

SRI BUMRUNG RD.

KOK TAI HOTEL

PHANGNGA RD.

YALA RD.

BANK

HAWAII HOTEL

RANONG RD.

SATELLITE RESTAURANT

SIRIROT RD.

TAXIS

NANAKORN RD.

CHALARUS RD.

SAMUKKI RD.

CAFE

CINEMA

THAI AIRWAYS

BUS TO HAT YAI

SRI YALA HOTEL

METRO HOTEL

GRAND PALACE CLUB

THANA VITHI RD.

PHUTAPOOM VITHI RD.

TAXIS

CAFES

CHINESE TEMPLE

MERRY HOTEL

WAT PHUTAPOOM

HUA ANN HOTEL

PHAN FAR HOTEL

ANALAO RESTAURANT

KOTCHASENI 2 RD.

KOTCHASENI 3 RD.

PIPAT PAKDEE RD.

KOTCHASENI 4 RD.

KOTCHASENI 1 RD.

COLA HOTEL

RUAMIT RD.

TO WAT KUHA PHIMOK, BETONG, & HAT YAI

POST OFFICE

0   50m

© MOON PUBLICATIONS, INC.

Visitors interested in anthropological matters should take a bus south on the road toward Betong and ask to be dropped in Thanto District near the village of Ban Rae. A laterite road continues four km to Ban Sakai, also called Village No. 3.

Betong

Betong is the southernmost district in Thailand, about 140 km south of Yala on the Malaysian border. Betong is popular with Malaysians, who are allowed to cross the border and conduct trade, but rarely visited by Westerners, who prefer the more convenient land crossings at Sadao (the Hat Yai-Penang route) and Sungai Golok (the Hat Yai-Kota Baru route). Betong valley is cool, mountainous, elevated at over 500 meters, and often foggy—a dubious charm which has earned Betong the nickname of "Misty City."

Betong has over a dozen hotels in the 120-250B price range, including the **Cathay, Fortuna, Kongka, Thai, Kings, Venus, First, Betong, Rama,** and **My House Hotel.** Thai immigration closes at 1800, so you might need to overnight before continuing south to Penang or Kuala Lumpur.

Accommodations

Budget Hotels: Several inexpensive Chinese hotels are located near the train station and taxi stops. The **Yuan Tong Hotel** in the yellow-and-white wooden building, **Aun Aun Hotel** in the five-story gray concrete tower, and **Kok Tai Hotel** with green shutters have acceptable if somewhat dreary rooms for 80-140B.

Thep Vimarn Hotel: Slightly more expensive but a big leap in comfort are the clean rooms in the deserted hotel just beyond the imposing Yala Rama Hotel. 31-37 Sri Bumrung Rd., tel. (073) 212400, 100-150B fan, 250-300B a/c.

Yala Rama: Facilities at Yala's top-end choice include the Rama Cafe, nightclub with live music, and 126 rooms in various price ranges. 21 Sri Bumrung Rd., tel. (073) 212563, fax (073) 214532, 220-260B fan, 450-600B a/c.

Transportation

Yala is 130 km southeast of Hat Yai and 100 km north of the Malaysian border at Sungai Golok.

Bus: Buses to Yala leave from the main bus terminal in Hat Yai, and from the bus halt in the south end of Sungai Golok. Buses from Yala to Hat Yai leave from a small office on Sirirot Rd. a few blocks south of the central market. The main bus terminal is on Sirirot Rd., several blocks south of the post office. A private bus company across from the train station can help with a/c coaches to Phuket, Ko Samui, and Bangkok.

Taxi: Share taxis to Yala leave from the Cathay Hotel in Hat Yai and from the train station in Sungai Golok. Taxis from Yala to various destinations leave from several spots near the train station. Exact locations change frequently, but approximate venues are shown on the map.

Train: Trains to Yala leave Hat Yai daily at 0625, 0810, 1035, and 1322.

NARATHIWAT

This small and sleepy fishing village is the most pleasant stop between Hat Yai and Sungai Golok. The town itself lacks any great monuments or historical sites, but the undisturbed wooden architecture, deserted beaches, and laid-back atmosphere make it a wonderful spot to escape the more congested and touristy towns of southern Thailand.

An excellent time to visit is in September, when Narathiwat celebrates the temporary residence of the king with parades, displays of local handicrafts, zebra dove cooing contests, and flotillas of handsomely painted *kolae* boats, the traditional craft of Malay fishermen.

Walking Tour

A very agreeable three-hour walking tour can be made starting from the clock tower and heading north along the riverfront road toward the Muslim fishing village and cafes at Narathiwat Beach. Several bird shops on the left display highly prized zebra doves cooing in lovely wicker baskets. A pair of brightly painted *kolae* fishing boats is docked at the north end of Pupa Pakdee Rd., followed by the large and modern but rather sterile Narathiwat Mosque. Across the bridge lies a typical Muslim fishing village where kids yell "hello good morning," and several cafes with English-language menus and beach parasols emblazoned with Coca-Cola logos.

Walking south down Pichit Bamrung Rd. you'll pass a large Muslim cemetery with distinctive gravestones before arriving back at the clock tower.

Wat Khao Kong

Six km south of Narathiwat is a small hill called Khao Kong on which local Buddhists have constructed the largest seated Buddha in Thailand. Known as Pra Buddha Taksin Ming Mongkol (Taksin Buddha), the 25-meter bronze image incongruously dominates a rural setting almost entirely populated by Muslims.

The image is plainly visible from the road and can be reached with any bus or mini-truck heading south down Hwy. 42 toward Sungai Golok.

Taksin Palace And Manao Bay

Sited on a lemon-shaped bay some 12 km south of Narathiwat is a summer palace visited by the royal family each year from August to October. Closed during the royal visit, which coincides with the Narathiwat *kolae* festival, the modern palace and landscaped gardens are otherwise open to the public daily from 0900 to 1600.

Manao Bay is the first of a series of almost completely deserted white-sand beaches which stretch south from Narathiwat to the Malaysian border.

Wadin Husen Mosque

One of the oldest and most intriguing mosques in Thailand is located in the village of Lubosawo in Bacho District, some 15 km north of Narathiwat and a few kilometers off Hwy. 42. The finely carved and heavily weathered wooden mosque was constructed in 1769 with both Thai and Muslim architectural styles.

Wat Chonthara Singhe

A temple which changed the course of Thai history is located in the small seaside town of Tak Bai, 34 km south of Narathiwat and 28 km north of Sungai Golok.

Wat Chonthara Singhe was constructed in 1873 by a young monk on land donated by the governor of Kelantan. Embodying a mixture of southern Thai and Chinese influences, the temple became well known for its beauty and idyllic location on the banks of the Tak Bai River. Toward the turn of the century, British colonialists in Malaysia attempted to expand their

domain by claiming the four northern Malay states under Thai suzerainty. King Rama V was forced in 1909 to disgorge the provinces of Trengganu, Kelantan, Kedah, and Perlis, but he argued that the surrender of Wat Chonthara Singhe would represent an irreplaceable cultural and religious loss for Thailand. The British agreed and today the present boundaries of Thailand and Malaysia are due to the existence of Wat Chonthara Singhe and the clever diplomacy of King Rama V.

Accommodations

Most of the hotels are located near the river on Pupa Pakdee Rd., or a block back on Pichit Bamrung Road.

Narathiwat Hotel: The cheapest spot in town is the yellow wooden hotel marked with a small English sign. Rooms fronting the street are noisy and badly need paint and new mattresses, but rooms facing the Bang Nara River are good value and worth requesting. 341 Phupa Pakdee Rd., tel. (073) 511063, 80-120B.

Bang Nara Hotel: Another budget spot similar to the Narathiwat but without the riverview rooms. Hok Huay Lai and Cathay hotels are in the same price range. 174 Phupa Pakdee Rd., tel. (073) 511148, 80-120B.

Rex Hotel: A small step up in quality. 6/1 Chamroen Nara Rd., tel. (073) 511134, fax (073) 511190, 130-180B fan, 220-260B a/c.

Yaowaraj Hotel: Narathiwat's second-largest hotel offers clean rooms with private bath at reasonable prices. 131 Pichit Bamrung Rd., tel. (073) 511148, fax (073) 511320, 120-180B fan, 220-280B a/c.

Tan Yong Hotel: Narathiwat's finest hotel features a snooker hall, Ladybird ancient massage, and a popular restaurant with live cabaret with young girls dressed as cheerleaders—a surprisingly luxurious hotel for such a small town. 16/1 Sopa Prisai Rd., tel. (073) 511477, fax (073) 511834, 650-800B.

Restaurants

The night market opposite the cinema is small and disappointing. Better atmosphere is found at the funky **Choem Chin Cafe** on the corner, and the row of informal restaurants just north of the clock tower. **Can Bakery** is a clean and comfortable spot popular with young Thais.

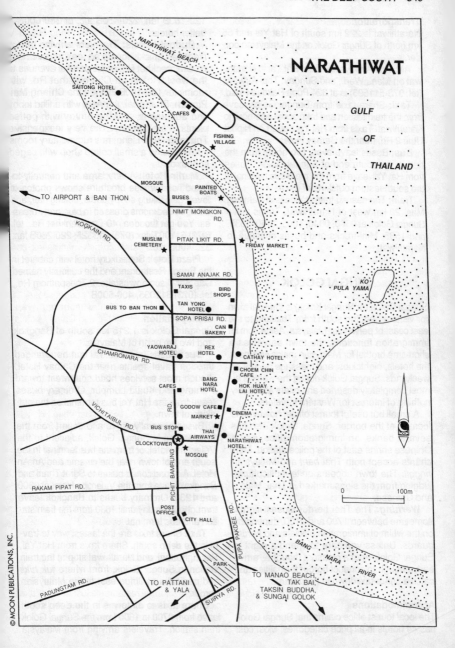

Transportation

Narathiwat is 222 km south of Hat Yai and 55 km north of Sungai Golok on the Malaysian border.

Air: Thai Airways flies from Hat Yai to Narathiwat on Mon., Wed., and Sunday. Thai Airways (tel. 073-511595) is at 324 Pupa Pakdee Road.

Taxi: Share taxis from Sungai Golok leave from the train station and take about one hour to Narathiwat. Taxis from Hat Yai depart on Niphat Uthit 2 Rd. near the Cathay Hotel.

Bus: Buses leave every two hours from the halt in the south end of Sungai Golok. Buses from Hat Yai leave from the main bus terminal in the southeastern outskirts of town.

Train: The nearest train station is at Tanyong Mas, 20 km west of Narathiwat. Trains leave Sungai Golok at 0600, 0840, 1005, 1150, 1335, and 1535. Mini-trucks and buses continue to Narathiwat.

SUNGAI GOLOK

Sungai Golok (or Sungai Kolok) is the final town for visitors heading south from Thailand to the east coast of peninsular Malaysia. Aside from its immigration functions, the town serves as a short-time brothel for Malaysian males who pack the hotels, nightclubs, and massage parlors on weekends. Sungai Golok during the week is almost completely deserted and offers absolutely nothing of interest for Western travelers.

A small but useful tourist office, however, is located at the border. Sungai Golok also has several banks, an immigration office, and a Chinese shrine east of the police station. Merchants accept both Thai *baht* and Malaysian *ringgit.* The town appears quite multicultural, judging from the signs marked in Thai, Malay, and Chinese.

Warning: The Thai border closes nightly sometime between 1700 and 2100, depending on the whim of immigration officials and border guards. Unless you care to spend a night in Sungai Golok—not a pleasant thought—arrive early enough to conduct border formalities and catch a share taxi down to Kota Baru.

Accommodations

The local tourist office claims that Sungai Golok has 44 hotels in all price categories. Most cost 120-160B fan, 220-450B a/c, or 350-600B i better hotels.

Budget Hotels: Travelers arriving late a night can quickly locate an inexpensive hote on Charoenkhet Rd. or the parallel avenues tc the west. Hotels on Charoenkhet Rd. witl rooms for 100-150B include the **Chiang Mai Pimarn, Shanghai,** the **Asia** with a tiled lobby and aquariums, and the **Savoy** with potted plants in the balcony. The very inexpensive **Thaliang** (Thai Lieng) has rudimentary rooms from 80B and a small coffee shop with caged songbirds.

Merlin Hotel: A very large and centrally located hotel whose brochure shows photos of lovely girls taking soapy baths, cutting hair, and sitting in bedrooms dressed in blue party dresses. You get the idea. 40 Charoenkhet Rd., tel. (073) 611003, fax (073) 613325, 220-260B fan, 320-400B a/c.

Plaza Hotel: Semiluxury hotel with cabaret in the Bunga Restaurant and the curiously named Cae Sar Disco downstairs. 2 Thespathom Rd., tel. (073) 611035, 400-500B.

Transportation

Sungai Golok is 1,215 km south of Bangkok and two km north of Malaysia.

Bus: Buses from Hat Yai can be arranged through travel agents near the Cathay Hotel, though most services head southwest toward Penang and Kuala Lumpur. Ordinary buses leave from the Hat Yai bus terminal on the outskirts of town.

Buses generally arrive and depart from the train station in Sungai Golok, adjacent to the Valentine Hotel, or from the bus terminal in the south end of town near the cinema and An An Hotel. Air-conditioned buses to Surat Thani and Bangkok leave from the Valentine Hotel at 0800 and 1230. Ordinary buses to Bangkok leave throughout the day until 1630 from the train station and bus terminal.

Taxi: Share taxis are the fastest way to travel in the deep south. Share taxis from Hat Yai, Satun, Pattani, and Narathiwat stop at the train station in Sungai Golok, from where *tuk tuks* and pedicabs continue east to the Malaysian border.

Share taxis to all towns in the deep south leave from 0700 to 1600 from the Sungai Golok train station. Travelers arriving from Malaysia

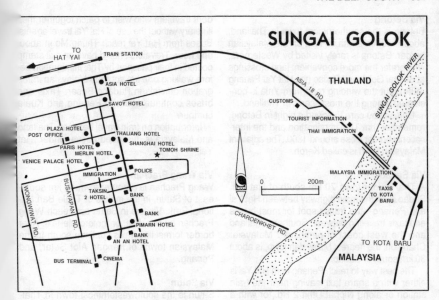

SUNGAI GOLOK

THAILAND

MALAYSIA

TO HAT YAI

TRAIN STATION

ASIA HOTEL

SAVOY HOTEL

PLAZA HOTEL
POST OFFICE

THALIANG HOTEL

PARIS HOTEL
MERLIN HOTEL

SHANGHAI HOTEL
TOMOH SHRINE

VENICE PALACE HOTEL

IMMIGRATION

POLICE

TAKSIN
2 HOTEL

BANK

BANK

PIMARN HOTEL

BANK

AN AN HOTEL

BUS TERMINAL

CINEMA

BUSAYAPAN RD.

WONGWIWAT RD.

SUNGAI GOLOK RIVER

ASIA 18 RD.

CUSTOMS

TOURIST INFORMATION

THAI IMMIGRATION

MALAYSIA IMMIGRATION

TAXIS
TO KOTA
BARU

CHAROENKHET RD.

TO KOTA BARU

0   200m

should proceed directly to the train station and find the next available taxi.

Train: Trains in the deep south are slow and limited to destinations shown below, but compensate with landscapes removed from dusty towns and concrete expressways. Train arrivals in Sungai Golok are greeted by trishaw drivers who continue to the border. There is no direct train service between Sungai Golok and Kota Baru.

Trains from Sungai Golok:

0600	to Surat Thani
0840	to Nakhon Si Thammarat
1005	rapid to Bangkok
1055	express to Bangkok
1150	to Phattalung
1335	to Hat Yai
1535	to Yala

DEPARTURE TO MALAYSIA

Via Sungai Golok

The border is about two km from the train station in Sungai Golok. Thai immigration will check your visa expiration date and charge 100B per

day for overstays beyond the allotted period.

Malaysian authorities across the Sungai Golok River grant free entry permits to most Western visitors on arrival. You then walk into the small Malaysian border town of Rantau Panjang. To the right is a small cafe where you can dine and wait for the next available share taxi to Kota Baru. The cafe manager and taxi drivers accept Thai *baht* at fair exchange rates.

Malaysia comes as a wondrous shock. Suddenly, signs are marked in English and not some indecipherable script, communication is easy with shopkeepers and taxi drivers, vegetation appears more trimmed and controlled, and the standard of living jumps dramatically. And wait until you try the food in the Kota Baru night market!

Via Tak Bai

Tak Bai is a small coastal village described above. Buses from Narathiwat take about an hour to reach Tak Bai. Ferries to the Malaysian border town of Pengkalan Kulor depart 0800-1700 from Tak Bai and Ban Taba, another small coastal town about five km south of Tak Bai. Bus 27 continues from Pengkalan Kulor to Kota Baru.

Via Betong

Betong is the southernmost town in Thailand, about 140 km south of Yala on the Malaysian border. Betong is rarely visited by Westerners, who prefer the more convenient land crossings at Sungai Golok and Sadao (the Hat Yai-Penang route), but the winding road from Yala is considered among the most scenic in Thailand.

Unless you care to spend a night in Betong, remember that Thai immigration and the international border close around 1800. The adjacent Malaysian town is called Keroh.

Via Sadao

A Thai border town 70 km south of Hat Yai, Sadao is on the main highway between Hat Yai and Penang—the transit spot for most buses and taxis traveling between Southern Thailand and the west coast of peninsular Malaysia. Changlun, the nearest Malaysian town, is about 30 km south of Sadao.

The best way to reach Penang from Hat Yai is either with a share taxi leaving near the train station or along Niphat Uthit 2 Rd., or with a bus organized from a travel agency near the Cathay Hotel.

More detail on bus and train departures from Hat Yai to Malaysia can be found above, under "Hat Yai Transportation."

Sadao can also be reached by public bus from Hat Yai, though transportation is sporadic and sometimes nonexistent to Changlun. A better option for Southeast-Asia-on-a-shoestring travelers is a bus or train from Hat Yai to Padang Besar, from where you walk across the border and continue to Penang with public transportation or private taxi.

Via Padang Besar

Padang Besar is a Malaysian border town 60 km south of Hat Yai and two km south of the Thai town of Thung Mo. Padang Besar and Thung Mo are on the main train line between Hat Yai and Penang, and most visitors take the train between the two countries.

Highway 4—the main highway between Hat Yai and Penang—is the primary route for buses and share taxis, but Thung Mo and Padang Besar are useful crossing points for indepen-

dent travelers who wish to patch together their itinerary without the use of Hat Yai travel agents. Buses from Hat Yai reach Thung Mo in about one hour. Travelers should have an exit stamp posted in their passport by Thai immigration before walking one km south to Malaysian immigration officials in Padang Besar. Taxis and buses continue south to Penang and Kuala Lumpur.

Information on train travel between Thailand and Malaysia is described above, under "Hat Yai."

Via Wang Prachan

Wang Prachan is a border town 40 km southeast of Satun, in the middle of Thale Ban National Park. Visitors in Satun can reach Wang Prachan by bus, taxi, or motorcycle-taxi. After border formalities, taxis continue south to the Malaysian towns of Kangar, Alor Setar, and Penang.

Via Satun

Satun is the southwesternmost town in Thailand, and a useful spot from which to reach Malaysia after a visit to nearby Tarutao National Park.

The land route to Malaysia involves a car or motorcycle-taxi to the Thai border town at Wang Prachan, followed by a bus south to Kangar and Penang.

A more intriguing and adventurous option is a boat from Satun to Kuala Perlis in Malaysia. Boats take about 90 minutes and leave from two locations. Longtails depart several times daily from the city pier on Klong Bambang near the Rain Tong Hotel. Larger boats leave from Tammalang Pier in the estuary about 15 km south of Satun. Tammalang Pier can be reached by *tuk tuk* or motorcycle-taxi.

More sensible than boat to Kuala Perlis is direct service to Langkawi Island, a well-developed Malaysian resort destination just 90 minutes south of Satun. Boats to Langkawi depart daily at 1600 from Tammalang Pier and return from Langkawi daily at 1300. Tickets cost 150B and can be purchased on the ship, or from Charan Tours near the Thai Airways office.

RESPONSIBLE TOURISM

Tourism, some say, broadens the mind, enriches our lives, spreads prosperity, dissolves political barriers, and promotes international peace. While concurring with most of these sentiments, others feel that mass tourism often destroys what it seeks to discover; it disrupts the economy by funneling dollars into international travel consortiums rather than local enterprise, exploits the people who find themselves ever more dependent on the tourist dollar, and reinforces cultural stereotypes rather than encouraging authentic dialogue between peoples. Responsible tourism is a movement that attempts to address both the virtues and vices of mass tourism by making each traveler more sensitive to these issues. The fundamental tenet is that travel should benefit *both* the traveler and the host country, and that travelers should travel softly and thoughtfully, with great awareness of their impact on the people and the environment.

Spearheading this movement is the Center for Responsible Tourism (P.O. Box 827, San Anselmo, CA 94979; tel. 415-258-6594, fax 415-454-2493), an interfaith group which holds annual conferences on the impact of mass tourism, publishes a thought-provoking newsletter, and offers workshops on how to lead a responsible tour. Visitors are encouraged to seek out low-impact and locally based travel experiences by patronizing cafes, guesthouses, and pensions owned by indigenous people. Their guidelines:

1. Travel in a spirit of humility, with a genuine desire to meet and talk with the local people.

2. Sensitize yourself to the feelings of your hosts.

3. Cultivate the habit of listening and observing, rather than merely hearing and seeing.

4. Realize that other people's concepts of time and thought patterns may be dramatically different than—not inferior to—your own.

5. Seek out the richness of foreign cultures, not just the escapist lures of tourist posters.

6. Respect and understand local customs.

7. Ask questions and keep a sense of humor.

8. Understand your role as a guest in the country; do not expect special privileges.

9. Spend wisely and bargain with compassion.

10. Fulfill any obligations or promises you make to local people.

11. Reflect on your daily experiences; seek to deepen your understanding of the people, the culture, and the environment.

SUGGESTED READINGS

GENERAL TRAVEL LITERATURE

The following books will help orient you to Southeast Asia, discuss the impact of mass tourism on third-world destinations, and fire up your imagination.

Bloodworth, Dennis. *An Eye for the Dragon.* New York: Farrar, Straus and Giroux, 1970. The former Far East correspondent of *The Observer* incisively examines the comedies and tragedies of Asia, from the fanatic wranglings of Sukarno to racial tensions in Malaysia. Bloodworth makes history and politics—often dry and dull subjects—fascinating and memorable.

Culture Shock. Singapore: Times Books. A series of practical guides to the rules of Asian etiquette, customs, and recommended behavior for every visitor to Asia. Lightweight and well distributed; excellent books to purchase and read while on the road. Highly recommended.

Fenton, James. *All the Wrong Places.* New York: Atlantic Monthly Press, 1988. James Fenton, journalist, poet, and critic, is one of the new breed of travel writers: jaundiced, self-indulgent, hard-hitting, and more concerned with personal impressions than scholarly dissertation. The result is a mesmerizing book full of great perceptions.

Insight Guides. Singapore: APA Publications. Superb photography and a lush text make this the best set of background guides to Southeast Asia. Read before traveling.

Iyer, Pico. *Video Night in Kathmandu.* New York: Vintage, 1988. Iyer's incongruous collection of essays uncovers the Coca-colonization of the Far East in a refreshingly humorous and perceptive style. His heartbreaking accounts of decay in the Philippines, brothels in Bangkok, and cultural collisions in Bali form the finest travel writing in the last decade. Very highly recommended; do not miss this book.

Nelson, Theodora, and Andrea Gross. *Good Books for the Curious Traveler—Asia and the South Pacific.* Boulder: Johnson Publishing, 1989. Outstanding in-depth reviews of over 350 books including almost 50 titles on Southeast Asia. Written with sensitivity and great insight. The authors also run a service which matches books with a traveler's itinerary. Write to Travel Source, 20103 La Roda Court, Cupertino, CA 95014, tel. (408) 446-0600.

Reimer, Jo, Ronald Krannich, and Caryl Krannich. *Shopping in Exotic Places.* Manassas, VA: Impact Publications, 1987. Step-by-step guide to the secrets of shopping in Southeast Asia. Detailed descriptions of shopping centers, arcades, factory outlets, and exclusive boutiques in Hong Kong, Singapore, Thailand, and Indonesia.

Richter, Linda. *The Politics of Tourism in Asia.* Honolulu: University of Hawaii Press, 1989. A scholarly study of the complex political problems which confront the tourist industries in Thailand, the Philippines, and other Asian destinations. Filled with surprising conclusions about the impact of multinational firms and the importance of targeting grass-roots travelers rather than upscale tourists.

Schwartz, Brian. *A World of Villages.* New York: Crown Publishers, 1986. A superbly written journal of a six-year journey to the most remote villages in the world. Filled with tales of unforgettable people and lands of infinite variety and beauty.

Shales, Melissa, ed. *The Traveler's Handbook.* Chester, CT: Globe Pequot Press, 1988. Fifth edition of the award-winning guide that puts together the contributions of over 80 experienced travelers, all authorities in their particular fields. Practical suggestions on climate, maps, airfares, internal transportation, backpacking, visas, money, health, and theft.

Simon, Ted. *Jupiter's Travels*. New York: Doubleday, 1980. Fascinating account of a 63,000-km motorcycle journey (500cc Triumph Tiger) from Europe, down the continent of Africa, across South America, Australia, and India. And what does Ted do now? Raises organic produce in northern California!

Theroux, Paul. *The Great Railway Bazaar*. New York: Houghton Mifflin, 1975. One of the world's best travel writers journeys from London to Tokyo and back on a hilarious railway odyssey. Rather than a dry discourse on sights, this masterpiece of observation keeps you riveted with personal encounters of first order. Highly recommended for everyone!

BOOKS ON THAILAND

Description And Travel
Blofel, John. *Bangkok: The Great Cities*. New York: Time-Life, 1973. Good local insight into both the upside and downside of this vibrant metropolis.

Clarac, Achille. *Guide to Thailand*. Malaysia: Oxford University Press, 1981. Published over a decade ago, but still the most comprehensive guide to the architecture of Thailand. Rudimentary travel information; highly recommended for historical background and temple descriptions.

Davis, Bonnie. *Postcards of Old Siam*. Singapore: Times Editions, 1987. A fascinating pictorial record of the Siamese kingdom from 1883 to World War II. Good reproduction of hand-tinted black-and-white postcards.

Tettoni, Luca Invernizzi. *Guide to Chiang Mai and Northern Thailand*. Bangkok: Asia Books, 1989. Detailed information and excellent photography by Khun Tettoni on the attractions of northern Thailand.

Veran, Geo. *50 Trips through Siam's Canals*. Bangkok: Duang Kamol, 1979. A fascinating but outdated guide to the confusing labyrinth of rivers and canals that stretch across southern Thailand. Included are over 30 maps, Thai prices, and brief descriptions of the temples.

Humor And Personal Tales
Eckardt, James. *Waylaid by the Bimbos*. Bangkok: Post Publishing, 1991. James Eckardt—writer-in-residence and dominant guru in Songkhla—finally received worldwide acclaim with his deranged ramblings that resemble a Thai-style Fear and Loathing in the Land of Smiles. Weird and *very* funny stuff recommended for twisted readers.

Hollinger, Carol. *Mai Pen Rai*. Boston: Houghton Mifflin, 1965. The story of an American housewife's humorous introduction to life in Bangkok. One of the warmest books you will ever read. Highly recommended.

Culture And Peoples
Fieg, John Paul. *A Common Core: Thais and Americans*. New York: Intercultural Press, 1989. A fine book which explains with great insight the key similarities and differences between Western and Thai cultures. Highly recommended for any visitor who intends to live or work in Thailand.

Lewis, Paul, and Elaine Lewis. *Peoples of the Golden Triangle*. London: Thames and Hudson, 1984. Paul and Elaine have worked as missionaries among the tribals of northern Thailand since 1947. This lavishly illustrated book is the best available guide to these intriguing peoples.

Segaller, Denis. *Thai Ways*. Bangkok: Allied Newspapers, 1984. A collection of short essays on Thai ceremonies, festivals, customs, and beliefs. This and his sequel *More Thai Ways* are great books to read while traveling in the country.

Arts And Architecture
Boisselier, Jean. *The Heritage of Thai Sculpture*. Bangkok: Asia Books, 1987.

Written by one of the world's leading authorities on the art of Southeast Asia, the original 1974 edition has been reprinted and is now available from Asia Books in Bangkok.

Van Beek, Steve, and Luca Invernizzi Tettoni. *Arts of Thailand*. New York: Thames and Hudson, 1991. The best introductory guidebook to Thai arts in print. Rich text and great photos.

Warren, William, and Luca Invernizzi Tettoni. *Legendary Thailand*. Hong Kong: Travel Publishing Asia Limited, 1986. Outstanding photographs and clean text; a good introduction to the land and people.

Warren, William, and Luca Invernizzi Tettoni. *Thai Style*. Bangkok: Asia Books, 1988. Thai interior design ranks with Japanese as among the most elegant and highly refined in the world. Bill and Luca will convince you of the sensitive creativity of the Thai peoples.

Current Events

McCoy, Alfred. *The Politics of Heroin: CIA Complicity in the Global Drug Trade*. New York: Lawrence Hill, 1991. Wisconsin University history professor updates his 1972 classic with new information on CIA collaboration with Thai heroin smugglers, Panama's Noriega, Afghan *mujahedeen*, and the Pakistani military. Still the classic story of drugs in the Golden Triangle.

Wright, Joseph. *The Balancing Act: A History of Modern Thailand*. Bangkok: Asia Books, 1991. Solid analytical framework and a careful attention to detail make this the best guide to modern Thai politics. The controversial final chapter on the 1991 coup forced the front-page disclaimer.

GLOSSARY

Geographic Terminology

amphoe	district
amphoe muang	provincial capital
ao	bay
ban	village
bang	village along a waterway
ba nam ran	hot springs
bung	lake or swamp
buri	town
changwat	province
chiang	town or city
doi	mountain
hat	beach, also *had*
hin	stone
Issan	northeastern Thailand
kaeng	rapids
kamphang	wall
khao	hill or mountain
klong	canal
ko	island, also *koh*
laem	cape or point
mae nam	river
muang	town or city
nakhon	town or city, also *nakorn*
nam tok	waterfall
nong	lake or swamp
paknam	estuary
phanom	hill or mountain
phu	hill or mountain
rai	1,600 square meters
sanam	open grounds
saphan	bridge
soi	lane
sra	pond
suan	garden
talat	market
tambon	precinct
tha	pier
thale	sea
tham	cave
thanon	road
thung	savannah

Religious Terminology

achaan	religious teacher
apsara	female celestial being
bo	tree under which the Buddha became enlightened; *bodhi*
bodhisattva	saint in Mahayana Buddhism; the future Buddha in previous incarnations in Theravada Buddhism; an enlightened being who has returned to help mankind
Brahma	four-faced creator in Hindu mythology
dharma	law and teachings of the Buddha
dhammachakha	Buddhist Wheel of Law; circular motif used in Dvaravati sculpture
deva	angel or divine being
Erawan	mythical three-headed white elephant; mount of Indra
Ganesha	elephant-headed Hindu god of literature and success
garuda	mythical animal with bird head and human torso; the mount of Vishnu; half-brother and enemy of the *naga*
Hanuman	mythical monkey warrior who leads the monkey army in the Ramakien epic
Indra	chief Hindu god of heaven; resides at the top of Mt. Meru
Jatakas	previous life stories of the Buddha

kinnari . . . . . mythical animal with bird and female elements

mae chi . . . . Buddhist nuns

Mahayana. . . One of the two principal Buddhist sects; Zen and Nichiren traditions; uncommon in Thailand

Mara. . . . . . evil goddess who tempted the Buddha during his meditations

metta . . . . . loving kindness

Mt. Meru. . . . mythical mountain abode of the gods; symbolized by the *prang* and *chedi* in Thai and Khmer architecture

mudra . . . . . symbolic hand gesture of the Buddha

naga . . . . . . mythical animal; the snake that protected the Buddha against rain; Khmer origins

nirvana . . . . a state of enlightenment

Pali . . . . . . scriptural language derived from Sanskrit; language of Thai Theravada texts

pra phum . . . earth spirits

Ramakien . . . Thai version of the Ramayana epic; recounts the adventures of Rama and Sita and their battles with Totsakan, king of the demons

Shiva . . . . . Hindu god of death, destruction, and regeneration

thep . . . . . . angel or divine being

Theravada . . one of the two principal Buddhist sects; the main form of Buddhism in Thailand; also called Hinayana or the Lesser Vehicle

thu thong . . . monks who have taken ascetic vows

Tripitaka. . . . Theravada Buddhist scriptures

vajra . . . . . thunderbolt of Vishnu

vipassana . . . Buddhist insight meditation

Architectural Terminology

bot . . . . temple building for sermons and services; surrounded by foundation stones

chedi . . . . . decorative spire containing amulets or religious icons

chofa . . . . . slender, curved temple decoration adorning the end of roofline ridges; symbolizes the *garuda*

gopura . . . . . Khmer ornamental covered gateway

ho trai . . . . . temple library

kan tuei . . . . carved wood supporting roof eaves

keo . . . . . . gem, precious stone, honorific title

kuti . . . . small huts used as monk residences

lak muang . . . city pillar; home to animist spirits

luang . . . . . royal

mahathat . . . honorific term for very sacred temples which contain Buddha relics

mondop . . . . temple building erected over a sacred relic, often a footprint of the Buddha

pra . . . . honorific title given to important Buddhas and temples; also spelled *phra*

prang . . . . . solid spire-shaped temple building containing religious icons; Khmer origins

prasat . . . . . royal religious edifice with distinctive rooflines; Khmer origins

pratu . . . . . . decorated door

sala . . . . . . open-air building used for resting

sema	sacred boundary stones placed at corners and axes of the *bot*
stupa	synonymous with *chedi*
that	northeast religious shrine; reliquary for religious objects
ubosot.	another term for *bot*
viharn	major temple building similar to but less important than the *bot*
wang	royal palace
wat	temple complex, not a single building

General Thai Terminology

aahan	food
achaan	religious leader; teacher
bhikku.	Buddhist monk
chao nam . . .	sea gypsies
farang	foreigner of European descent
gatoei	transvestite
hang yao . . .	longtailed boat
Jiin.	Chinese
kaw lae	traditional fishing boats of southern Thailand
khaen	reed instrument common to northeastern Thailand
khon.	masked dance-drama based on Ramakien stories
klawng.	Thai drums
kuay haeng . .	Chinese-style work shirt
lakhon.	Thai classical dance-drama
lao khao. . . .	white liquor popular in the northeast

likay	Thai folk dance
longyi	Burmese sarong
mai ku	pan pipe played at Thai kick boxing
maw hawn . .	Thai work shirt
maw kwan. . .	triangular-shaped pillow
muay Thai. . .	Thai kick boxing
mut mee. . . .	tie-dyed silk
nam	water
nang.	Thai shadow play
ngop.	traditional Khmer rice farmer's hat
Pak Thai. . . .	people of southern Thailand
pa tai	batik
phi pat.	Thai classical orchestra
pong lang . . .	musical instrument made of resonant logs
ram muay . . .	Thai boxing dance
ram wong . . .	traditional Thai dance
reua duan . . .	river express boat
reua kam fak .	cross-river boat
rot thammada.	ordinary bus
rot thua	tour bus
sala klang . . .	provincial offices
samlor.	three-wheeled pedicab
somtam	green papaya salad
songkran . . .	Thai new year
songtao	small pickup truck used for public transportation
susaan	cemetery
talaat nam. . .	floating market
tuk tuk	three-wheeled motorized transportation
wai.	Thai greeting with palms pressed together

INDEX

Page numbers in **boldface** indicate the primary reference. *Italicized* page numbers indicate information in callouts, charts, illustrations, or maps.

ABOUT THE AUTHOR

Carl Parkes, author of *Southeast Asia Handbook,* was born into an American Air Force family and spent his childhood in California, Nebraska, Alabama, and Japan, where his love of Asia first began. After graduating from the University of California at Santa Barbara, Carl traveled throughout Europe and later returned to work in Hawaii, Lake Tahoe, Aspen, Salt Lake City, and finally, San Francisco. But childhood memories of Asia continued to pull him eastward. After a 12-month journey across Asia, Carl returned to San Francisco to work as a stockbroker and plan his escape from the nine-to-five world. A chance encounter in Singapore with Bill Dalton offered a more intriguing option: research and write a travel guidebook to Southeast Asia. Carl followed the release of his highly acclaimed *Southeast Asia Handbook* two years later with publication of his 550-page *Thailand Handbook.*

Carl fervently believes that travel is an immensely rewarding undertaking that affirms the basic truths of life. "Travel is much more than just monuments and ruins. It's an opportunity to reach out and discover what's best about the world. Travel enriches our lives, spreads prosperity, dissolves political barriers, promotes international peace, and brings excitement and change to our lives."

Besides travel writing, Carl enjoys straight-ahead jazz, photography, Anchor Steam beer, opera, art openings, poetry readings, and samba nightclubs in his favorite city of San Francisco. Future plans include a summer of motorcycling around Europe and more books on his favorite destinations.

ABOUT THE ILLUSTRATOR

Terra Muzick is one of America's premier illustrators of children's books, calendars, and toys. Her career began with Hallmark Cards soon after graduation from art school in Ohio. In 1980, she moved to San Francisco where she drew Snoopys before going freelance the following year. Since then, Terra has rafted in Thailand, enjoyed a massage on Kuta Beach, and kept busy with gallery openings, Cacophony capers, and the Art Deco Society.

READER PROFILE

Knowing a bit about you and your travel experiences will help me improve this book. I'll collect the results—including your picks for Thailand's Top 10 lists—and report my findings in the next edition. Include suggestions on guesthouses, restaurants, and transportation secrets that might help the next traveler. Remember to send along corrected copies of photocopied maps from this book and business cards collected from your favorite hotels and restaurants. All contributors will be acknowledged in the next edition of this book and *Southeast Asia Handbook*.

Please send the following survey, plus your comments and recommendations, to:

Carl Parkes/Reader Survey
Moon Publications
722 Wall Street
Chico, CA 95928 U.S.A.

1. Gender: ☐ male ☐ female
2. Age: ☐ under 25 ☐ 25-30 ☐ 31-35 ☐ 36-40 ☐ 41-50 ☐ 51+
3. Status: ☐ single ☐ married
4. Income: ☐ 20K ☐ 21-30K ☐ 31-40K ☐ 41-50K ☐ 50K +
5. Occupation_____
6. Education: ☐ high school ☐ some college ☐ college grad ☐ post grad
7. Travel style: ☐ budget ☐ moderate ☐ luxury
8. Vacations: ☐ once yearly ☐ twice yearly ☐ 3 + yearly
9. Why do you travel?_____
_____
10 What's best about travel? _____
_____
11. What's worst about travel?_____
_____
12. This journey:
  Length of time: _____
  Countries visited: _____
_____
  Expenses:
  a. Total: _____
  b. Average daily expenses _____
  c. Average hotel price_____
  d. Average meal price _____
  e. Total airfare _____
  f. Shopping expenses_____

3. Favorites (also include a list of your *least* favorites):
  a. Best countries (in order of preference) _____

  _____

  b. Favorite hotels and guesthouses (address, price, description): _____

  _____

  c. Favorite restaurants (address, price range, favorite dishes): _____

  _____

  d. Airline: _____

  e. Cuisine: _____

  _____

  f. Night spots: _____

  _____

  g. Cultural events: _____

  _____

  h. Outdoor adventures: _____

  _____

  i. Temple or historical sites: _____

  _____

  j. Beaches: _____

  _____

  k. People: _____

  _____

  l. Travel moments: _____

  _____

14. This Book:
  Strongest points: _____

  _____

  Weakest points: _____

  _____

  How accurate did you find the information? _____

  _____

  Favorite introduction section (history, government, etc., none) _____

  _____

  Did you use the hotel charts? _____

  Suggestions for improvements: _____

  _____

  _____

15. Name and Address_____

  _____

  _____

  _____

Thanks for your help!

THE METRIC SYSTEM

1 inch = 2.54 centimeters (cm)
1 foot = .304 meters (m)
1 mile = 1.6093 kilometers (km)
1 km = .6214 miles
1 fathom = 1.8288 m
1 chain = 20.1168 m
1 furlong = 201.168 m
1 acre = .4047 hectares (ha)
1 sq km = 100 ha
1 sq mile = 2.59 sq km
1 ounce = 28.35 grams
1 pound = .4536 kilograms (kg)
1 short ton = .90718 metric ton
1 short ton = 2000 pounds
1 long ton = 1.016 metric tons
1 long ton = 2240 pounds
1 metric ton = 1000 kg
1 quart = .94635 liters
1 US gallon = 3.7854 liters
1 Imperial gallon = 4.5459 liters
1 nautical mile = 1.852 km

To compute centigrade temperatures, subtract 32 from Fahrenheit and divide by 1.8. To go the other way, multiply centigrade by 1.8 and add 32.

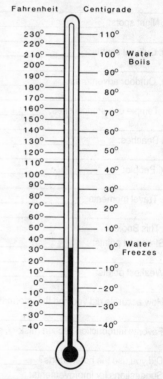

Moon Handbooks—The Ideal Traveling Companions

Open a Moon Handbook and you're opening your eyes and heart to the world. Thoughtful, sensitive, and provocative, Moon Handbooks encourage an intimate understanding of a region, from its culture and history to essential practicalities. Fun to read and packed with valuable information on accommodations, dining, recreation, plus indispensable travel tips, detailed maps, charts, illustrations, photos, glossaries, and indexes, Moon Handbooks are ideal traveling companions: informative, entertaining, and highly practical.

To locate the bookstore nearest you that carries Moon Travel Handbooks or to order directly from Moon Publications, call: (800) 345-5473, Monday-Friday, 9 a.m.-5 p.m. PST

The Pacific/Asia Series

BALI HANDBOOK by Bill Dalton
Detailed travel information on the most famous island in the world. 12 color pages, 29 b/w photos, 68 illustrations, 42 maps, 7 charts, glossary, booklist, index. 428 pages. **$12.95**

BANGKOK HANDBOOK by Michael Buckley
Your tour guide through this exotic and dynamic city reveals the affordable and accessible possibilities. Thai phrasebook, 16 color pages, 55 b/w photos, 30 maps, 19 illustrations, 9 charts, booklist, index. 214 pages. **$10.95**

BLUEPRINT FOR PARADISE: How to Live on a Tropic Island by Ross Norgrove
This one-of-a-kind guide has everything you need to know about moving to and living comfortably on a tropical island. 8 color pages, 40 b/w photos, 3 maps, 14 charts, appendices, index. 212 pages. **$14.95**

FIJI ISLANDS HANDBOOK by David Stanley
The first and still the best source of information on travel around this 322-island archipelago
8 color pages, 35 b/w photos, 78 illustrations, 26 maps, 3 charts, Fijian glossary, booklist,
index. 198 pages.   **$8.95**

INDONESIA HANDBOOK by Bill Dalton
This one-volume encyclopedia explores island by island the many facets of this sprawling
kaleidoscopic island nation. 30 b/w photos, 143 illustrations, 250 maps, 17 charts, booklist,
extensive Indonesian vocabulary, index. 1,000 pages.   **$19.95**

MICRONESIA HANDBOOK:
Guide to the Caroline, Gilbert, Mariana, and Marshall Islands by David Stanley
Micronesia Handbook guides you on a real Pacific adventure all your own. 8 color pages, 77
b/w photos, 68 illustrations, 69 maps, 18 tables and charts, index. 300 pages.   **$11.95**

NEW ZEALAND HANDBOOK by Jane King
Introduces you to the people, places, history, and culture of this extraordinary land. 8 color
pages, 99 b/w photos, 146 illustrations, 82 maps, booklist, index. 546 pages.   **$14.95**

OUTBACK AUSTRALIA HANDBOOK by Marael Johnson
Australia is an endlessly fascinating, vast land, and *Outback Australia Handbook* explores the
cities and towns, sheep stations, and wilderness areas of the Northern Territory, Western, and
South Australia. Full of travel tips and cultural information for adventuring, relaxing, or just
getting away from it all. 8 color pages, 39 b/w photos, 63 illustrations, 51 maps, booklist, index.
355 pages.   **$15.95**

PHILIPPINES HANDBOOK by Peter Harper and Evelyn Peplow
Crammed with detailed information, *Philippines Handbook* equips the escapist, hedonist, or
business traveler with thorough coverage of the Philippines's colorful history, landscapes, and
culture. 8 color pages, 2 b/w photos, 60 illustrations, 93 maps, 30 charts, index. 587 pages.
$12.95

SOUTHEAST ASIA HANDBOOK by Carl Parkes
Helps the enlightened traveler discover the real Southeast Asia. 16 color pages, 75 b/w photos,
11 illustrations, 169 maps, 140 charts, vocabulary and suggested reading, index. 873 pages.
$16.95

SOUTH KOREA HANDBOOK by Robert Nilsen
Whether you're visiting on business or searching for adventure, *South Korea Handbook* is an
invaluable companion. 8 color pages, 78 b/w photos, 93 illustrations, 109 maps, 10 charts,
Korean glossary with useful notes on speaking and reading the language, booklist, index. 548
pages.   **$14.95**

SOUTH PACIFIC HANDBOOK by David Stanley
The original comprehensive guide to the 16 territories in the South Pacific. 20 color pages,
195 b/w photos, 121 illustrations, 35 charts, 138 maps, booklist, glossary, index. 740 pages.
$15.95

TAHITI-POLYNESIA HANDBOOK by David Stanley
All five French-Polynesian archipelagoes are covered in this comprehensive guide by Oce-
ania's best-known travel writer. 12 color pages, 45 b/w photos, 64 illustrations, 33 maps, 7
charts, booklist, glossary, index. 235 pages.   **$11.95**